ITALY

Where to Stay and Eat
for All Budgets

Must-See Sights
and Local Secrets

Ratings You Can Trust

Fodor's Travel Publications   New York, Toronto, London, Sydney, Auckland
www.fodors.com

FODOR'S ITALY 2004

Editor: Matthew Lombardi

Editorial Production: David Downing

Editorial Contributors: Peter Blackman, Ryan Bradley, Linda Cabasin, Giovanna Dunmall, Elaine Eliah, Robin S. Goldstein, David Graham, Valerie Hamilton, Christina Knight, Patricia Rucidlo, Mark Walters, Megan Williams

Maps: David Lindroth *cartographer;* Bob Blake and Rebecca Baer, *map editors*

Design: Fabrizio La Rocca, *creative director;* Guido Caroti, *art director;* Melanie Marin, *senior picture editor*

Production/Manufacturing: Colleen Ziemba

Cover Photo (Umbria): Bullaty/Lomeo/The Image Bank

ISBN 1-4000-1262-7

ISSN 0361-977X

SPECIAL SALES

Fodor's Travel Publications are available at special discounts for bulk purchases for sales promotions or premiums. Special editions, including personalized covers, excerpts of existing guides, and corporate imprints, can be created in large quantities for special needs. For more information, contact your local bookseller or write to Special Markets, Fodor's Travel Publications, 1745 Broadway, New York, New York 10019. Inquiries from Canada should be directed to your local Canadian bookseller or sent to Random House of Canada, Ltd., Marketing Department, 2775 Matheson Boulevard East, Mississauga, Ontario L4W 4P7. Inquiries from the United Kingdom should be sent to Fodor's Travel Publications, 20 Vauxhall Bridge Road, London SW1V 2SA, England.

AN IMPORTANT TIP & AN INVITATION

Although all prices, opening times, and other details in this book are based on information supplied to us at press time, changes occur all the time in the travel world, and Fodor's cannot accept responsibility for facts that become outdated or for inadvertent errors or omissions. So **always confirm information when it matters,** especially if you're making a detour to visit a specific place. Your experiences—positive and negative—matter to us. If we have missed or misstated something, **please write to us.** We follow up on all suggestions. Contact the Italy editor at editors@fodors.com or c/o Fodor's at 1745 Broadway, New York, New York 10019.

PRINTED IN THE UNITED STATES OF AMERICA

10 9 8 7 6 5 4 3 2 1

DESTINATION ITALY

No less an observer of life than Goethe once recorded in the now-famous diaries he kept of his 18th-century journey through Italy, "I can honestly say I've never been as happy in my life as now." The great German poet was neither the first nor the last visitor to fall blissfully under the spell of this fabled land, with its stunning landscapes, stupendous contributions to Western civilization, and unabashed enthusiasm for life's pleasures. You may be enchanted by the impossible brushstrokes forming Michelangelo's Adam on the ceiling of the Sistine Chapel, or by the afternoon light cascading across the blazing red rooftops of Florence, viewed from Brunelleschi's dome. You may be taken in by the melodious frenzy amid the mountains of sardines and cured olives in Palermo's Vucciria market, or bewitched by a gondola gliding along a Venetian canal, its passage silently watched by Gothic palaces with delicately arched eyebrows. Be prepared to be swept away. Buon viaggio!

Karen Cure, Editorial Director

CONTENTS

Maps

CloseUps

A trip takes you out of yourself. Concerns of life at home disappear, driven away by more immediate thoughts—about, say, what marvels will beguile the next day, or where you'll have dinner. That's where Fodor's comes in. We make sure that you know all your options, so that you don't miss something that's just around the next bend. Because the best memories of your trip might well have nothing to do with what you came to Italy to see, we guide you to sights large and small all over the country. You might set out to immerse yourself in Florence's Renaissance treasures, but back at home you find yourself unable to forget a perfect afternoon spent strolling in an Umbrian hill town. With Fodor's at your side, serendipitous discoveries are never far away.

Our success in showing you every corner of Italy is a credit to our extraordinary writers. Although there's no substitute for travel advice from a good friend who knows your style, our contributors are the next best thing—the kind of people you would poll for travel advice if you knew them.

After completing his master's degree in art history, Peter Blackman settled permanently to Italy in 1986. Since then he's worked as a biking and walking tour guide, managing to see more of Italy than most of his Italian friends. When he's not leading a trip, you'll find Peter at his home in Chianti, listening to opera and planning his next journey.

Disinclined to stray far from superb wine and spectacular skiing, travel writer Ryan Bradley divides his time between northern Italy and northern California. Although his professional wine training and habitual alpinism have drawn him to the Dolomites, he never feels quite prepared for the existential challenge of a face-to-face encounter with Bolzano's iceman.

Giovanna Dunmall was born in Milan to an Italian mother and English father. After taking degrees in literature and journalism in Great Britain, she returned to Italy as an intern, and later an associate editor, for *Colors* magazine in Treviso. She transplanted to Rome in 2000, where she is a travel writer and stringer for magazines abroad.

From African war zones to Asian mountaintops, writer and journalist Elaine Eliah has captured pieces of the world in words. Since settling in Venice in 1999, she's rowed nearly every canal and sailed many of the Venetian Republic's Adriatic trade routes. She currently writes, teaches English, and helps travelers discover the magic of her adopted home.

While Robin Goldstein is trained in philosophy at Harvard and law at Yale, his heart has always been in his travel writing. His credits include not only his home base of Italy but also Spain, Mexico, Ecuador, and the Galapagos Islands. Once a resident of Genoa, he now spends most of his time in the *mezzogiorno* and along the Sicilian coast.

David Graham was a tour guide in Europe, Southeast Asia, and the Middle East before moving to Vicenza in the 1980s. During his years in the Venetian Arc region he's been particularly inspired by the hand-tended vineyards, the spectacular mountains, and Trieste's sparkling coastline. David now lives in Venice, where he is a translator specializing in art and architecture.

In 1996 Valerie Hamilton transplanted from San Francisco to Rome, where she works as a journalist, TV producer, and freelance bon vivant. She holds a degree in art history and archaeology, but travel is her first love.

Florence resident Patricia Rucidlo holds master's degrees in Italian Renaissance history and art history. When she's not extolling the virtues of a Pontormo masterpiece or angrily defending the Medici, she's leading wine tours in Chianti, catering private dinner parties, or working on a cookbook.

An editor, travel writer, and naturalist, British-born Mark Walters first settled in Naples as a British Council lecturer in the 1980s. He completed his graduate studies in classics and now, when not hiking or playing field hockey, he leads study tours around the Mediterranean.

Megan Williams has lived throughout North America, Europe, and Africa, but can't think of a place she'd rather be than her current home of Rome. A graduate of McGill University and Columbia journalism school, Megan covers politics, arts, business, and social trends for CBC, the *Canadian Globe and Mail,* and American public radio.

ABOUT THIS BOOK

There's no doubt that the best source for travel advice is a like-minded friend who's just been where you're headed. But with or without that friend, you'll have a better trip with a Fodor's guide in hand. Once you've learned to find your way around its pages, you'll be in great shape to find your way around your destination.

SELECTION

Our goal is to cover the best properties, sights, and activities in their category, as well as the most interesting communities to visit. We make a point of including local food-lovers' hot spots as well as neighborhood options, and we avoid all that's touristy unless it's really worth your time. You can go on the assumption that everything you read about in this book is recommended wholeheartedly by our writers and editors. Flip to On the Road with Fodor's to learn more about who they are. It goes without saying that no property mentioned in the book has paid to be included.

RATINGS

Orange stars ★ denote sights and properties that our editors and writers consider the very best in the area covered by the entire book. These, the best of the best, are listed in the Fodor's Choice section in the front of the book. Black stars ★ highlight the sights and properties we deem Highly Recommended, the don't-miss sights within any region. Fodor's Choice and Highly Recommended options in each region are usually listed on the title page of the chapter covering that region. Use the index to find complete descriptions. In cities, sights pinpointed with numbered map bullets ❶ in the margins tend to be more important than those without bullets.

SPECIAL SPOTS

Pleasures & Pastimes focuses on types of experiences that reveal the spirit of the destination. Watch for Off the Beaten Path sights. Some are out of the way, some are quirky, and all are worth your while. If the munchies hit while you're exploring, look for Need a Break? suggestions.

TIME IT RIGHT

Wondering when to go? Check On the Calendar up front and chapters' Timing sections for weather and crowd overviews and best days and times to visit.

SEE IT ALL

Use Fodor's exclusive Great Itineraries as a model for your trip. (For a good overview of the entire destination, follow those that begin the book, or mix regional itineraries from several chapters.) In cities, Good Walks guide you to important sights in each neighborhood; ☞ indicates the starting points of walks and itineraries in the text and on the map.

BUDGET WELL

Hotel and restaurant price categories from ¢ to $$$$ are defined in the opening pages of each chapter—expect to find a balanced selection for every budget. For attractions, we always give standard adult admission fees; reductions are sometimes available for children, students, and senior citizens.

BASIC INFO

Smart Travel Tips lists travel essentials for the entire area covered by the book; city- and region-specific basics end each chapter. To find the best way to get around, see the transportation section; see individual modes of travel ("By Car," "By Train") for details. We assume you'll check Web sites or call for particulars.

ON THE MAPS	Maps throughout the book show you what's where and help you find your way around. Black and orange numbered bullets ❶ ❶ in the text correlate to bullets on maps.
BACKGROUND	In general, we give background information within the chapters in the course of explaining sights as well as in CloseUp boxes and in Understanding Italy at the end of the book. To get in the mood, review the suggestions in Books & Movies.
FIND IT FAST	Within the book, chapters are arranged in a roughly north-to-south direction starting with Venice. Chapters are divided into smaller regions, within which towns are covered in logical geographical order; attractive routes and interesting places between towns are flagged as En Route. Heads at the top of each page help you find what you need within a chapter.
DON'T FORGET	Restaurants are open for lunch and dinner daily unless we state otherwise; we mention dress only when there's a specific requirement and reservations only when they're essential or not accepted— it's always best to book ahead. Hotels have private baths, phones, TVs, and air-conditioning and operate on the Continental Plan (with Continental breakfast included) unless otherwise indicated. We always list facilities but not whether you'll be charged extra to use them, so when pricing accommodations, find out what's included.
SYMBOLS	

Many Listings

★ Fodor's Choice
★ Highly recommended
⊠ Physical address
✛ Directions
🕮 Mailing address
☎ Telephone
🖷 Fax
🌐 On the Web
✉ E-mail
💵 Admission fee
🕓 Open/closed times
▻ Start of walk/itinerary
Ⓜ Metro stations
🖃 Credit cards

Outdoors

🏌 Golf
⛺ Camping

Hotels & Restaurants

🏨 Hotel
🛏 Number of rooms
⛄ Facilities
🍴 Meal plans
✗ Restaurant
🍸 Reservations
👔 Dress code
🚬 Smoking
🍷 BYOB
✗🏨 Hotel with restaurant that warrants a visit

Other

☺ Family-friendly
🛈 Contact information
⇨ See also
⊠ Branch address
☞ Take note

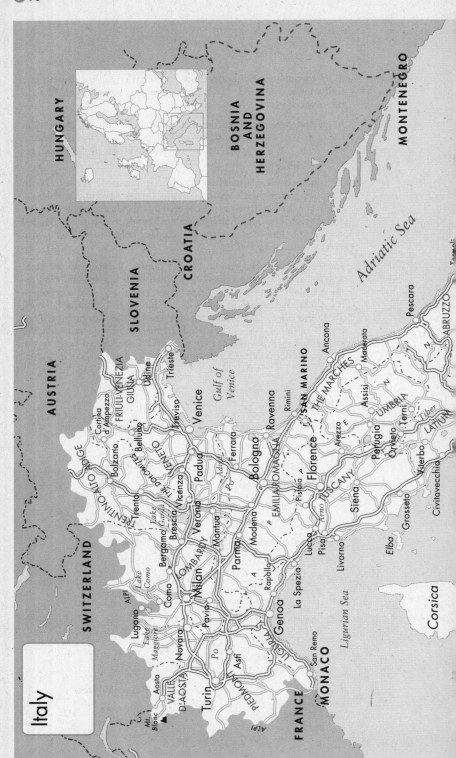

Italy

HUNGARY

BOSNIA AND HERZEGOVINA

MONTENEGRO

CROATIA

SLOVENIA

AUSTRIA

Adriatic Sea

Tremiti

FRIULI-VENEZIA GIULIA

Udine

Trieste

Cortina d'Ampezzo

THE DOLOMITES

Belluno

VENETO

Treviso

Venice

Gulf of Venice

Bolzano

Trento

Vicenza

Padua

Ferrara

Bologna

Ravenna

Rimini

SAN MARINO

THE MARCHES

Ancona

Pescara

ABRUZZO

Maderata

Assisi

Arezzo

UMBRIA

Perugia

Orvieto

Terni

LATIUM

Viterbo

Tiber

Florence

TUSCANY

Arno

Siena

Pistoia

Civitavecchia

Grosseto

Elba

Lucca

Pisa

Livorno

Ligurian Sea

Corsica

TRENTINO-ALTO ADIGE

Lake Garda

Brescia

Bergamo

Verona

Mantua

Modena

Parma

EMILIA-ROMAGNA

Po

ALPI

Como

Lake Como

LOMBARDY

Milan

Pavia

Rapallo

La Spezia

Genoa

LIGURIA

San Remo

MONACO

Asti

Po

PIEDMONT

Turin

Novara

Aosta

VALLE D'AOSTA

Mt. Blanc

ALPI

FRANCE

SWITZERLAND

Lugano

Lake Maggiore

AUSTRIA

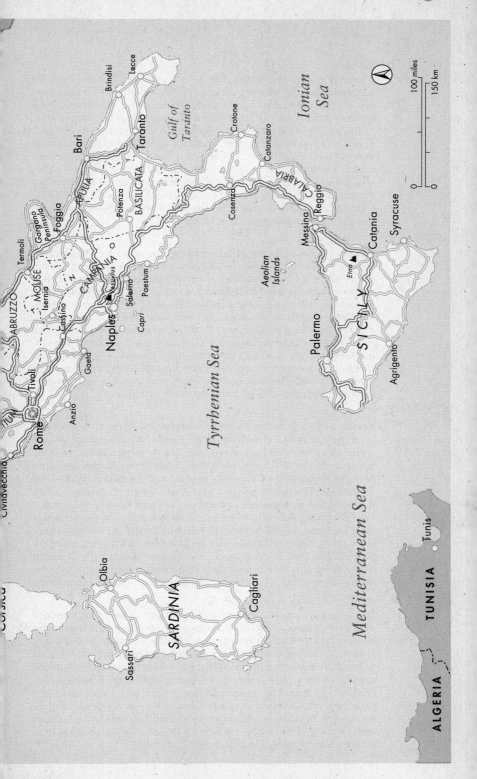

Brindisi

Lecce

*Ionian
Sea*

100 miles

150 km

Taranto

*Gulf of
Taranto*

Bari

Crotone

Catanzaro

PUGLIA

Catanzaro

C A L A B R I A

BASILICATA

Potenza

Foggia

Cosenza

Gargano
Peninsula

Messina

Reggio

Termoli

MOLISE

CAMPANIA

Aeolian
Islands

Catania

Syracuse

Isernia

Etna

Cassino

Vesuvius

S I C I L Y

Naples

Salerno

Paestum

Palermo

Capri

Agrigento

ABRUZZO

Gaeta

Tyrrhenian Sea

Tivoli

Anzio

Rome

Civitavecchia

Mediterranean Sea

Olbia

Tunis

Sassari

SARDINIA

Cagliari

TUNISIA

ALGERIA

1 Venice

A maze of waterways, bridges, alleys, and tiny squares, Venice is a magical place apart. In this city of Marco Polo, Titian, and Vivaldi, a vaporetto ride down the Grand Canal—Venice's own 5th Avenue—is a fairy-tale journey past the city's shimmering, sometimes decaying palaces. "Venice is like eating an entire box of chocolate liqueurs in one go," Truman Capote once remarked, and the city will indeed stuff you with the most spectacular Bellini, Veronese, and Tiepolo paintings, not to mention its distinctive, primarily fish-based cuisine. During February's Carnivale, you'll find even the pigeons are pressed for space in Piazza San Marco, the city's heart. The best time to catch Venice is during the Historic Regatta (the first week of September), when the 18th-century canvases of Canaletto seem to come to life.

2 The Venetian Arc

The green plains of the mainland stretching beyond Venice's lagoon hold some of Italy's smaller art cities. Elegant Vicenza, which bears the signature of the great 16th-century architect Andrea Palladio, blends rustic beauty with a jigger of 18th-century Venetian chic. Farther west, Verona is famed for the tombs of the Della Scala lords, the romantic settings associated with Shakespeare's *Romeo and Juliet,* and an ancient Roman arena, still packing in the crowds for everything from opera to rock and roll. Art lovers head for Padua for Giotto's Scrovegni Chapel and Donatello's powerful statue of the *condottiere* (mercenary general) Gattamelata. Farther east, the region of Friuli-Venezia Giulia has for centuries been coveted and conquered by warring powers; you can sense their influence in the cafés of Trieste and the castle of Miramare.

3 The Dolomites

Northern Italy's Dolomite Mountains—nature's skyscrapers—are known for stupefying cliffs and curiously shaped peaks, charming meadows and crystal-clear lakes, and splintered crags whose resplendent hues range from pale rose at dawn to purple at dusk. It's little wonder that Leonardo da Vinci depicted the Dolomites in the haunting background of his *Mona Lisa.* The region is Italy's year-round sports playground—with the seeing just as important as the skiing in jet-set Cortina d'Ampezzo. Take the Strada del Vino (Wine Route) from Bolzano to Trento, where there is a famous cathedral and the moated Castello del Buonconsiglio; enjoy the "grape cure" at Merano; zip along the 48 hairpin turns of the Stelvio Pass; absorb the vistas of the Grande Strada delle Dolomiti (Great Dolomites Road); and top it all off with a skydiving stop at the town of Bressanone, where Gothic and baroque art blend harmoniously.

4 Milan, Lombardy & the Lakes

Poets, royals, Roman emperors, and mere mortals have long swooned over Lakes Como, Garda, and Maggiore, where deep blue waters and hillsides clad with voluptuous gardens offer respite for the world-weary at Europe's toniest resorts. Other sophisticated pleasures are found in Milan, Italy's urbane commercial capital, where next season's fashions can be had for a price in the city's uniquely chic shops. Ringing Milan on the Po plain are the walled outposts of Cremona, Pavia, and Mantua, where renaissance dukes and counts built towering palaces and intricate churches. Majestic landscapes surround Riva del Garda, huddled under soaring cliffs on the northern tip of Lake Garda, and Bergamo, whose walls rise over a breathtaking Alpine vista.

5 Piedmont/Valle d'Aosta

Intimately linked to the House of Savoy, one of Europe's ancient aristocratic families, Piedmont has always felt the influence of nearby France. Don't be surprised if Paris comes to mind while you stroll down Turin's broad, tree-lined boulevards or sample the region's food, more elaborately and richly prepared than anywhere else in the country. But this is also Alpine territory, and the rigors that nature has imposed have created a hard-working and fiercely independent spirit that perfectly balances the cultured sophistication of the city. Tucked away in their own corner of northwestern Italy, Piedmont and the Valle d'Aosta are often neglected by international tourists, which makes a visit here all the more rewarding.

6 The Italian Riviera

In no other region of Italy are you reminded of the presence of the sea so often as in Liguria, site of the Italian Riviera. Hemmed in by the Alps on one side and the Ligurian Sea on the other, the towns in this swathe of northwestern Italy are either fishing villages, tiny harbors, seaside resorts, or major ports—most notable of the latter being Genoa. The history of the region is intimately linked to the sea, both as friend and as foe, an aspect of Ligurian reality picturesquely symbolized by the typical rows of buildings, called *palazzate,* that face the sea in practically every coastal town. Painted in earthy ochre, yellow, red, or brown, they attach together in rows as though to form a defensive wall, but with windows looking out toward the open sea. It's not surprising to learn that Christopher Columbus was a Ligurian.

7 Emilia-Romagna

Emilia-Romagna owes its beginnings to the Romans, who built the Via Aemilia in 187 BC; today the road spans the flat, foggy region, traversing a landscape of medieval castles and crumbling farmhouses from Piacenza to the murky Adriatic beaches and summer nightlife of Rimini. Mosaics in nearby Ravenna are glittering treasures left from Byzantine rule. Bologna is the region's principal city and intellectual center, with its rows of arcaded streets winding through grandiose towers and statues and concealing some of the best restaurants Italy has on offer; Emilia-Romagna is the pasta heartland of Italy, and its formidable gastronomic inventions include tortellini, the balsamic vinegar of Modena, buttery prosciutto, and the complex Parmigiano Reggiano cheese from the Parma area, now sprinkled all over the country, and the world.

8 Florence

Florence, the "Athens of Italy" and the key to the Renaissance, hugs the banks of the Arno River, where it lies folded among the emerald cypress-studded hills of north-central Tuscany. Elegant and somewhat aloof, as if set apart by its past greatness, this historic center of European civilization still shares with Rome the honor of first place among Italian cities for the magnitude of its artistic works, among them Botticelli's *Birth of Venus* and Michelangelo's powerful *David.* Down every street and *vicolo* (alley) and in every piazza you'll make new discoveries of Romanesque, Gothic, or Renaissance architecture; sheltered within these churches, cloisters, and towers are masterful painting and sculpture of the Quattrocento and Cinquecento periods. Equally as splendid are the magnificent chapels and palaces of the Medici—whose patronage rocketed Florence to the forefront of the Renaissance—which stand unabashed amid the city's vibrant modern pulse.

9 Tuscany

Nature outdid herself in Tuscany, the region on the Ligurian and Tyrrhenian seas that has Florence as its principal city. Punctuated by thickly wooded hills, snowcapped peaks, sun-warmed vineyards, olive groves, and dramatic hill towns, Tuscany's milk-and-honey vistas have changed little since Renaissance artists first beheld them. Not surprisingly, you'll find some of Italy's greatest art treasures here, including the 13th-century Leaning Tower of Pisa and Piero della Francesca's *Legend of the True Cross* frescoes in Arezzo. The time traveler will be entranced by medieval Siena, while the Chianti region has seduced many an expatriate who couldn't summon the will to return home. There are also miles of sandy and rocky beaches, and a couple of gorgeous islands, Elba being the largest.

10 Umbria & the Marches

Umbria, dubbed "Italy's green heart," has a rich artistic inheritance that includes the frescoes of Assisi's Basilica di San Francesco, the brooding Palazzo dei Consoli in Gubbio, and the Gothic glory of Orvieto's cathedral. Umbria bears the stamp of its Roman past close to the surface; most of the region's important towns lie either along the ancient Via Flaminia (opened in 219 BC to connect Rome to the Adriatic coast) or close to one of its many branch roads—so expect to see Roman villas, aqueducts, theaters, walls, and temples. Eastward, in the region of the Marches on the Adriatic, is Urbino, where the Renaissance first came to full flower. Its Ducal Palace reveals more about the wealth and artistic energy of the Renaissance than a shelf of history books.

11 Rome

It's hard to imagine another city in the world that offers so much pleasure for the senses. Rome's moderate weather may frustrate Italians dying to display their furs, but for travelers from less clement lands, the warm breeze with just a whiff of the sea is a delight. So, too, are the endless visual surprises: round any corner and be greeted by a dazzling fountain, a quiet Renaissance carving, or the green spray of a palm tree or maritime pine. Food is to the palette what the city's vistas are to the eye; luscious and ubiquitous. Climb almost any one of Rome's famous seven hills or take a walk in one of the huge, majestic parks and you're likely to find striking tranquility in the midst of the urban bustle.

12 Lazio, Abruzzo & Molise

Although you may be inclined to head for Rome and stay put, there are plenty of worthwhile, generally undervisited sights within a two-hour radius of the city. Lazio has an abundance of papal palaces, landscaped gardens, medieval hill towns, and antiquities both Etruscan and Roman. Trips farther afield in the mainly mountainous regions of Abruzzo and Molise will give you a chance to appreciate fine archaeological sites, the unadulterated culture of age-old hill towns, and the natural beauty of Italy's finest national park, Parco Nazionale d'Abruzzo.

13 Naples & Campania

A happy combination of spectacular geology, rich cultural heritage, and excellent standards of hospitality, Campania is the Italy many travelers dream about. At Pompeii, you can see how Romans once defined the good life, before heading to the pint-size island of Capri for a present-day dose of sybaritic pleasures. Among the almost clichéd list of names—Amalfi, Positano, Vesuvius, Ravello—the crowds seemingly dissipate and you can still "discover" pockets of undiluted beauty. In pole position, emerging from decades of decline and urban neglect, is the vibrant, heritage-rich Naples, the most operatic of cities.

14 Puglia

En route to Brindisi and Greece-bound ferries, many travelers speed through the 402 km (250 mi) of rocky coast and fertile farmland that make up Italy's heel. Linger awhile, though, and you'll discover that the sun-baked landscape yields more than olives and grapes. Greeks, Romans, Holy Roman Emperors, and other conquerors stayed long enough to leave their mark on places such as Gallipoli, a Casbah-like fishing port, and Lecce, where baroque palaces dominate a youthful nerve center remarkably unknown to tourists. Even more exotic are the eye-catching *trulli,* mysterious, conical-roofed dwellings built from blocks of local limestone; there are more than 1,000 of them in the inland town of Alberobello. Although Bari and Brindisi do lively business in shipping, one of the greatest appeals of the region is what still isn't here—large-scale development along the seductive coastline, at its most alluring on the cove-studded Gargano Promontory.

15 Basilicata & Calabria

The southernmost regions of the peninsula are known informally as the *mezzogiorno*—literally "midday" for the blazing sun that presides over white villages, shimmering seas, and barren landscapes. The pleasure of traveling here is stumbling upon largely undiscovered places far off the beaten path—the simple *sassi,* dwellings partially hewn from caves, in the Basilicata village of Matera, perhaps, or the churches perched upon rocky promontories all along the Tyrrhenian coast of Calabria. Some of the major treasures of the mezzogiorno are only now being unearthed. At Reggio di Calabria's national museum, some of the finest examples of Greek art command pride of place in the dazzling collection of antiquities, and the Calabrian provincial capital of Cosenza, a network of alleyways tossed across a hillside and presided over by a castle, is an urban landscape unfettered by time.

16 Sicily

The architecture of magical Sicily reflects the island's centuries of changing dominion under the Greeks, Byzantines, Arabs, Normans, and Spaniards. Baroque church–hopping could be a sport in the cacophonous streets of Palermo and seafaring Siracusa, where trademark bulbous wrought-iron balconies deck out the palaces of Sicily's former noble families. The breezes are sultry and everyday life is without pretense, as witnessed in the workaday stalls of the fish markets all along the ports of the Tyrrhenian and Ionian coasts, from Trapani to Siracusa, bursting with the island's ubiquitous tuna, swordfish, and sardines. Greek ruins stand sentinel in Agrigento's Valley of the Temples, blanketed in almond, oleander, and juniper blossoms. All over the island, the ins and outs of life are celebrated each day as they have been for centuries—over a morning coffee, at the family lunch table, and in the magical evening passeggiata.

17 Sardinia

Too distant from imperial and papal Rome to be influenced by the character of the mainland, Sardinia is as unique as its weather-worn landscape. Although the indigenous culture is one of Italy's most interesting, many travelers opt to explore the high-profile Costa Smeralda, the chic resort developed by the Aga Khan, who discovered its charms when his yacht took shelter from a storm. Intrepid travelers head for the *nuraghi,* cyclopean stones that are among prehistory's enigmas. Severely beautiful Sardinia is a prime destination if you're looking for a vacation getaway—of either the chic or the rugged variety.

GREAT ITINERARIES

Italian Gardens
7 to 9 days

Using the living materials and elements of nature to achieve studied aesthetic effects, Italians are masters at creating gardens, and have been from the Renaissance and baroque ages until well into the 19th century. Usually framing country villas or grand city palaces, the most spectacular gardens are laid out with an artist's eye for perspective and color; many are studded with statuary and fanciful fountains. A tour of some of Italy's most beautiful gardens begins in Milan, gateway to the Lake District—ideally in spring, when azaleas and rhododendrons are in glorious bloom. Note that some gardens are not open in winter or in inclement weather; always call ahead.

STRESA

3 days. Spend the better part of one day on an excursion from the stately Lake Maggiore resort town of Stresa, exploring the Borromean Islands, from the decorative baroque palace and terraced gardens on Isola Bella to the Renaissance-style villa on Isola Madre, surrounded by a lush park where peacocks strut amid banks of azaleas, rhododendrons, and camellias. To plant the elaborately tiered gardens of Isola Bella and Isola Madre, a 16th-century count had laborers haul soil to the islands in boats. The next day hop on a ferry to Verbania and get off at the embarcadero of the Villa Taranto. Adorned with terraces, cascades, and fountains, its vast garden was laid out in the 20th century and remains one of Europe's finest. Some 20,000 plant species—many rare and exotic—grow here. (⇨ Chapter 4, Lake Maggiore and Lake Orta.)

BELLAGIO

2 or 3 days. Settle into this beauty spot on Lake Como surrounded by romantic vistas. At Villa Melzi, which some regard as the most serendipitous site in the entire Lake District, a fabulous staircase blooms with azaleas in spring and is topped by a neoclassic palace. Just across the lake in Tremezzo, one stop away on the ferry, is Villa Carlotta, a wedding present to Charlotte of Russia in 1843. The luxuriant gardens and park are known for their spectacular rhododendrons and azaleas. From Tremezzo, take the ferry to Sala Comacina, where, during visiting hours, there is regular ferry service to Villa Balbaniello, one of the most romantic sites of all. Check opening times with the Bellagio or Tremezzo tourist offices. Afterward, if you have time, take the leisurely ferry trip around the Maggiore or Como lakes to get glimpses of many more villa gardens from the boat. (⇨ Chapter 4, Lake Como.)

FLORENCE

2 or 3 days. Make Florence your base for a series of visits to the gardens of the Medici villas on the city's outskirts. These gardens feel somewhat austere, their beauty lying in the artful arrangements of evergreens. Roam through the Giardini Boboli, behind Palazzo Pitti, laid out for Eleanor of Toledo, wife of Medici Grand Duke Cosimo I, noting how the plan was ingeniously adapted to a very irregular site. Then, together with some city sightseeing to help you focus on the Medici influence in Florence, continue your villa touring in half-day excursions. Villa Gamberaia, a legacy of the wealthy Capponi family, is an elegant Italian garden set in olive groves in the hills of Settignano. North of Florence, toward Sesto Fiorentino, the vast Medici gardens of Villa di Castello are festooned with more than 500 lemon trees. At the Medici Villa La Petraia, sculptures by Renaissance masters adorn the 16th-century Italian garden, and a park is landscaped in 19th-century style.(⇨ Chapter 8, Side Trips from Florence.)

By Public Transportation

Trains make frequent runs between Milan and Stresa (about 60 minutes), Como (30 minutes), and Lecco (30 minutes). The good lake ferry service makes it easy to explore villages on the Maggiore and Como lakes (ferry trips are no more than 30 minutes). Travel by bus from Como to Bellagio and between Lecco and Bellagio (both trips about 75 minutes, depending on traffic). By train it takes about 3½ hours to travel between Milan and Florence. To reach Villa Gamberaia from Florence, take Bus 10, marked Settignano. To reach Villa La Petraia take Bus 28; Villa di Castello is within walking distance.

Turin

Asti

60 km
(37 mi)

30 km
(18 mi)

Alba

San Remo

MAP KEY
Italian Gardens
A Food Lover's Tour

A Food Lover's Tour

10 to 14 days

Sampling Italy's best food and wines in the very places they are produced will enrich your understanding of the country and its people. On this itinerary through a country where good eating and drinking is the rule, you'll take in the birthplace of some wonderful wines, a gracious city renowned for exquisite chocolates and its grand fin de siècle cafés, truffle country, and, last but not least, Emilia-Romagna's Parma, which is as rich in history and art as in its culinary delights. In northern Italy, near the Dolomites, you'll see how irresistible cooking mixes Italian and Austrian accents.

TURIN

1 or 2 days. Dine on as many as 30 antipasti followed by a creamy risotto, and top off your meal with a delectable dessert. Then head for one of the city's historic cafés to savor the wonderful pastries along with your espresso. And don't forget to pick up some of the city's celebrated hazelnut chocolates, called gianduiotti. Southeast of Turin in the Monferrato and Langhe districts, rolling hills are blanketed with the vineyards that produce Barolo, "king of the wines and wine of kings," in addition to Barbaresco and others. (⇨ Chapter 5, Turin and Fortified Cities of the Po Plain.)

ASTI, ALBA & PARMA

2 days. Spend a day exploring the wineries in the area. Asti has lent its name to Spumante, a sparkling white that brings bubbles of gaiety to every kind of celebration in Italy. Some like it sweet, especially as a dessert wine, but many choose the brut version, much like champagne and made by the same method. Spend another day in Alba, stopping at the Castello di Barolo to sample the wine and visit the wine museum. While in the area, let the aroma of white truffles tickle your senses, and treat your taste buds to a range of culinary specialties that exalt this regal tuber. Alba is the capital of the Langhe wine country; its October wine and truffle fair features a rousing medieval-style tournament. En route to Verona, make a detour to Parma for a quintessential Italian meal. (⇨ Chapter 5, Fortified Cities of the Po Plain and Chapter 7, Emilia.)

VERONA

1 or 2 days. This could be your base for an excursion north to Trento, where some of Italy's best Spumanti are produced. Verona's ancient Roman Arena, medieval buildings, and characteristic restaurants deserve some attention, too. (⇨ Chapter 2, Padua, Verona, Vicenza and Chapter 3, Western Trentino.)

BOLZANO

1 or 2 days. If you spend the night here, you'll have time to enjoy the area's distinctive Austrian-Italian cuisine and to follow the Strada del Vino (Wine Road) that starts at Cal-

LIGURIAN SEA

daro, 15 km (9 mi) south of Bolzano. (⇨ Chapter 3, Alto Adige and Cortina and Heart of the Dolomites.)

TREVISO

2 days. Medieval buildings, canals, mill wheels, and an abundance of inns where you can savor local dishes and wines make this a good base for exploring the area. Spend a day on an excursion to Udine, or follow the Strada del Vino Rosso (Red Wine Road) through cabernet and merlot country along the Piave River from Conegliano, where sparkling, fruity Prosecco is made. A bowl of pasta e fagioli—the hearty bean-and-pasta soup, a specialty of the Veneto region—will sustain you. (⇨ Chapter 2, Treviso and the Hillside Towns and Friuli-Venezia Giulia.)

UDINE

1 day. Another optional overnight stop, this attractive city was ruled by Venice and shows it, with stone Venetian lions rampant on graceful buildings and columns in pretty piazzas. The Collio wine district nearby is known for its amazing and utterly distinctive local cheeses. (⇨ Chapter 2, Friuli-Venezia Giulia.)

CHIANTI

2 or 3 days. Spend at least two days roaming through the Chianti district between Florence and Siena, where you can delve into the subtle differences in vintages and perhaps swerve out of the district's official confines into the realm of Brunello di Montalcino. Here, it seems that even the tiniest village harbors a precious artwork or two by Tuscan masters. Many wineries offer guided tours of their cellars, often part of historic estates belonging to families that can trace their origins back to the Middle Ages or the Renaissance. (⇨ Chapter 9, Chianti and Southern Tuscany.)

By Public Transportation
Local trains and buses make the 45-minute run from Turin to Asti and Alba. Parma is on the Milan line; switch at Piacenza (30 minutes). Return to Turin to get a train on the main east–west line to Verona (3 hours from Turin). In Verona you'll find frequent service on another main line to Trento (1 hour) and Bolzano (a 2-hour trip). Return to Verona for a train to Padua, 60 minutes away. Treviso can be reached by train (60 minutes) or bus (70 minutes) from Padua. Udine is on a main line that passes through Padua; journey time is 2½ hours. There is fast service on the same line to Florence (2¾ hours from Venice), where you can get a local train or bus to make the 90-minute trip to Siena. Local buses serve the Chianti district.

Classical Highlights
8 to 12 days

Well colonized by the ancient Greeks, then epicenter of the Roman Empire, Italy has a wealth of classical sites, many of them in an excellent state of preservation. Rome was, of course, the capital of the Roman Empire, and a number of ancient sites remain here today, seemingly plunked down in the middle of the modern metropolis. Campania, too, is full of important classical landmarks, from both the Roman and the Greek eras, and Pompeii is not the only vestige of the eruption of nearby Mt. Vesuvius. If you have more time and a more intense interest in ancient history, you'll want to travel all the way to Sicily, the large island just off the toe of Italy's boot. Settled by the Greeks, it was a center of trade and culture in the Hellenic world, and it still is richly endowed with remarkable sites.

ROME
2 or 3 days. Spend at least a day exploring Ancient Rome—the Capitoline Hill, the Roman Forum, the Circus Maximus, the Colosseum, the Pantheon—and on subsequent days, venture out to the Via Appia and the Catacombs, or study classical sculptures in the Vatican Museums and antiquities in the Museo Nazionale Romano in Palazzo Altemps. It is quite an experience to turn a corner and see a famous building, such as the Colosseum, across the street, with traffic whizzing blithely past its crumbling arches. (⇨ Chapter 11, Exploring Rome.)

NAPLES AND CAMPANIA
2 or 3 days. After arriving in Naples from Rome, spend the afternoon at the Museo Archeologico Nazionale. Herculaneum and Pompeii can be visited in one day from Naples, but it would be a very full day, and it is best to break it into two separate excursions. The relics being unearthed from the lava at Herculaneum are even better preserved than the once-buried ruins at Pompeii. On another day, enjoy an excursion down the Amalfi Coast or take the A3 to Paestum, with its still-intact Greek temples. Take an optional day to tour the area just west of Naples—the Roman amphitheater at Pozzuoli, spooky Lake Avernus, the Roman resort town at Baia, with its excavated baths, and the Sibyl's Cave at Cumae, perhaps the oldest Greek colony in Italy. (⇨ Chapter 13, Naples; the Phlegrean Fields; Herculaneum, Vesuvius, Pompeii; and the Amalfi Coast.)

Pisa
Livorno
Florence
Siena
TUSCA

MAP KEY

Classical Highlights

A D R I A T I C   S E A

PALERMO, SICILY

1 day. Visit the Museo Archeologico Regionale and nearby Segesta, with its fine Doric Greek temple. (⇨ Chapter 16, Palermo and Western Coast to Agrigento.)

AGRIGENTO

1 or 2 days. Explore the Valley of the Temples, an extensive Greek site, and if you have time, make your way up the coast to see the spectacular Greek temple complex at Selinunte. (⇨ Chapter 16, Western Coast to Agrigento.)

SIRACUSA

1 or 2 days. Visit the Parco Archeologico in town, the splendid Museo Archeologico, and, if there's time, take an excursion to see the mosaics at the Imperial Roman Villa at Casale, just south of Piazza Armerina. (⇨ Chapter 16, Siracusa and Eastern Sicily.)

TAORMINA

1 day. Get a fine view of Mt. Etna and see the town's Greek theater, its backdrop the shimmering Mediterranean; the theater is still used for a summer arts festival. (⇨ Chapter 16, Eastern Sicily.)

By Public Transportation

Train service between Rome and Naples is fast and frequent, taking less than two hours on express trains. The Circumvesuviana train line can take you conveniently from Naples to Pompeii (a 35-minute trip) and Herculaneum (about 20 minutes' travel time). There's a train station right in Paestum (1½ hours from Naples). A ferry operates from Naples to Palermo,

Sicily (it's a four- to nine-hour trip), and a main train line makes the five-hour run between Palermo and Siracusa, which is also reached from Messina (a three-hour trip) and Catania (1½ hours). Taormina is a one-hour train ride from Messina. Other sites on Sicily—such as Agrigento (two hours from Palermo)— are better reached by bus than by the unreliable local train service.

WHEN TO GO

The main tourist season runs from April to mid-October. The so-called low season from fall to early spring may be cooler and inevitably rainier, but it has its rewards: less time waiting in line and more time to enjoy closer-up, unhurried views of what you want to see.

Tourists crowd the major art cities at Easter, when Italians flock to resorts and to the country. From March through May, busloads of schoolchildren on excursions take cities of artistic and historical interest by storm.

You don't want to be on an Italian beach in August if you can help it—unless it's a private beach—because of the crowds. June and September are best; July can be crowded in places such as Elba, Portofino, and Sicily.

Climate

Weather-wise, the best months for sightseeing are April, May, June, September, and October—generally pleasant and not too hot. The hottest months are July and August, when humidity can make things unpleasant. Winters are relatively mild in most places on the main tourist circuit but always include some rainy spells. In general, the northern half of the peninsula and the entire Adriatic Coast, with the exception of Puglia, are rainier than the rest of Italy.

Except for a few year-round resorts, such as Taormina and some towns on the Italian Riviera, coastal resorts usually close up tight from October or November until they reopen at Easter; they're at their best in June and September, when everything is open but less crowded.

☎ Forecasts **Weather Channel Connection** ☎ 900/932-8437, 95¢ per minute from a Touch-Tone phone 🌐 www.weather.com.

ROME

Jan.	52F	11C	May	74F	23C	Sept.	79F	26C
	40	5		56	13		62	17
Feb.	55F	13C	June	82F	28C	Oct.	71F	22C
	42	6		63	17		55	13
Mar.	59F	15C	July	87F	30C	Nov.	61F	16C
	45	7		67	20		49	10
Apr.	66F	19C	Aug.	86F	30C	Dec.	55F	13C
	50	10		67	20		44	6

FLORENCE

Jan.	48F	9C	May	73F	23C	Sept.	79F	26C
	36	2		54	12		59	15
Feb.	52F	11C	June	81F	27C	Oct.	68F	20C
	37	3		59	15		52	11
Mar.	57F	14C	July	86F	30C	Nov.	57F	14C
	41	5		64	18		45	7
Apr.	66F	19C	Aug.	86F	30C	Dec.	52F	11C
	46	8		63	17		39	10

VENICE

Jan.	42F	6C	May	70F	21C	Sept.	75F	24C
	33	1		56	13		61	16
Feb.	46F	8C	June	76F	25C	Oct.	65F	19C
	35	2		63	17		53	12
Mar.	53F	12C	July	81F	27C	Nov.	53F	12C
	41	5		66	19		44	7
Apr.	62F	17C	Aug.	80F	27C	Dec.	46F	8C
	49	10		65	19		37	3

ON THE CALENDAR

Italy's top seasonal events are listed below, and any one of them could provide the stuff of lasting memories. It is revealing that the Italian "festa" can be translated either as "festival" or "holiday" or "feast"—food is usually fundamental to Italian celebrations. Contact the **Italian Government Travel Office** (⇨ Visitor Information) for exact dates and further information.

ONGOING

Dec.–June	The Stagione Operistica (Opera Season) is in full swing in Milan and elsewhere, notably in Turin, Florence, Rome, Naples, Parma, Venice, and Genoa.

WINTER

Early Dec.	The Festa di Sant'Ambrogio (Feast of St. Ambrose) in Milan officially opens La Scala's opera season. The building itself is closed for a restoration estimated to take a few years; operas are temporarily happening at the Teatro degli Arcimboldi.
Dec. 31	Rome stages a rousing Capo D'Anno (New Year's Eve) celebration, dubbed the Festa di San Silvestro, with fireworks in Piazza del Popolo.
Jan. 5–6	Roman Catholic Epifania (Epiphany Celebrations) and decorations are evident throughout Italy. Notable is the Epiphany Fair at Piazza Navona in Rome.
Early Feb.	The Festa del Fiore di Mandorlo (Almond Blossom Festival) in Agrigento is a week of folk music and dancing, with groups from many countries, in the Valley of the Temples.
Feb. 14–24	A big do in the 18th century and revived in the latter part of the 20th century, Carnevale in Venice includes concerts, plays, masked balls, fireworks, and indoor and outdoor happenings of every sort. It is probably Italy's most famous festival, bringing in hundreds of thousands. During Carnivale di Viareggio, in the Tuscan beach town Viareggio, masked pageants, fireworks, a flower show, and parades are among the festivities. The Carnivale d'Ivrea, near Turin, includes three days of folklore, costumes, parades, and cooking in the streets. The party culminates with the Battle of the Oranges, which features real fruit flying through the air.

SPRING

Apr. 4–11	Settimana Santa (Holy Week) features parades and outdoor events in every major city and most small towns in Italy, but Rome, Naples, Assisi, and Florence have particularly notable festivities.
Apr. 9	In Rome, a torchlight nighttime Venerdì Santo (Good Friday Procession) led by the pope winds from the Colosseum past the Roman Forum and up the Palatine Hill.
Apr. 11	The Easter Sunday Scoppio del Carro (Explosion of the Cart) in Florence is the eruption of a cartful of fireworks in the Piazza del Duomo, set off by a mechanical dove released from the altar during High Mass. Needless to say, Messa di Pasqua al Vaticana (Easter

	Mass at the Vatican) in Rome is long, intense, and packed, with many people attending in elaborate holiday costumes.
Late Apr.–Early July	Maggio Musicale Fiorentino (Florence May Music Festival) is the oldest and most prestigious Italian festival of the performing arts.
May 1	The Festa di Sant'Efisio in Cagliari sees a procession of marchers and others in splendid Sardinian costume.
May 9	The Sagra del Pesce (Feast of the Fish), in Camogli on the Italian Riviera, is a high-spirited—and free—community-wide fish fry.
Mid-May	During the Corsa dei Ceri (Race of the Candles) in Gubbio, a procession to the top of Mt. Ingino features young men in local costume carrying huge wooden pillars.
May 23	The Cavalcata Sarda (Sardinian Cavalcade) is a traditional procession of more than 3,000 people in Sardinian costume winding through Sassari.
Late May–Early June	The Regata delle Quattro Repubbliche Marinare (Regatta of the Great Maritime Republics) sees keen competition among the four former maritime republics—Amalfi, Genoa, Pisa, and Venice.
May 30	The Palio della Balestra (Palio of the Archers) is a medieval crossbow contest in Gubbio, dating back to 1461.
SUMMER	
June	On three consecutive days in June, usually on the third week of the month, the Infiorata (Flower Festival), in Genzano (Rome), is a religious procession along streets carpeted with flowers in splendid designs.
June 2	The Festa della Republic, formerly the royal national holiday, is celebrated with a flurry of Italian flags.
June 24	Calcio Storico (Soccer Games in 16th-Century Costume), in Florence, commemorate a match played in 1530. Festivities include fireworks displays.
June 24	Florence grinds to a halt to celebrate the Festa di San Giovanni (Feast of St. John the Baptist) in honor of its patron saint. Many shops and bars close, and at night a fireworks display along the Arno attracts thousands.
June 27	The Gioco del Ponte (Battle of the Bridge) in Pisa, is a medieval parade and contest.
Late June–Mid-July	The Festival dei Due Mondi (Festival of Two Worlds), in Spoleto, is perhaps Italy's most famous performing arts festival, bringing in a worldwide audience for concerts, operas, ballets, film screenings, and crafts fairs. Plan well in advance.
June–Early Aug.	The Festival Internazionale dell'Operetta (Summer Operetta Festival) is held in Trieste.
July 2 & Aug. 16	The world-famous Palio in Siena is a bareback horse race with ancient Sienese factions showing their colors and participants competing for a prized *palio* (banner).

Early July– Late Aug.	The L'Arena di Verona Stagione Lirica (Arena of Verona Outdoor Opera Season) heralds spectacular productions in the 22,000-seat Roman amphitheater of Verona.
July	The Umbria Jazz Festival, in Perugia, brings in many of the biggest names in jazz each summer.
July 17	The Festa del Redentore (Feast of the Redeemer) is a procession of gondolas and other craft commemorating the end of the plague of 1575 in Venice. The fireworks over the lagoon are spectacular.
Late July– Mid-Sept.	Settimane Musicali di Stresa (Stresa Musical Weeks) comprise a series of concerts and recitals in Stresa.
Late Aug.– Early Sept.	The Festival di Venezia (Venice Film Festival), the oldest of the international film festivals, takes place mostly on the Lido.

FALL

Sept. 5	The Regata Storica (Historic Regatta) includes a traditional competition between two-oar gondolas in Venice. The Giostra del Saracino (Joust of the Saracen) is a tilting contest with knights in 13th-century armor in Arezzo.
Sept. 16	The Giostra della Quintana (Joust of the Quintana) is a 17th-century-style joust and historical procession in the Umbrian town of Foligno.
Oct. 3	Alba's Giostra delle Cento Torri (100 Towers Tournament) features costumes and races and is held a week before the opening of the Fiera del Tartufo (Truffle Fair), a food fair centered on the white truffle.
Oct. 4	The Festa di San Francesco (Feast of St. Francis) is celebrated in Assisi, his birthplace.

The Art of Enjoying Art

Travel veterans will tell you that the endless series of masterpieces in Italy's churches, palaces, and museums can cause first-time visitors—eyes glazed over from a heavy downpour of images, dates, and names—to lean, Pisa-like, on their companions for support. After a surfeit of Botticellis and Bronzinos and the 14th Raphael, even the miracle of the High Renaissance may begin to pall. The secret, of course, is to act like a turtle—not a hare—and take your sweet time. Instead of trotting after briskly efficient tour guides, allow the splendors of the age to unfold—slowly. Get out and explore the actual settings—medieval chapels, Rococo palaces, and Romanesque town squares—for which these marvelous examples of Italy's art and sculpture were conceived centuries ago and where many of them may still be seen in situ.

Museums are only the most obvious places to view art; there are always the trompe l'oeil renderings of Assumptions that float across baroque church ceilings and piazza scenes that might be Renaissance paintings brought to life. Instead of studying a Gothic statue in Florence's Bargello, spend an hour in the medieval cloisters of the nearby convent of San Marco; by all means, take in Michelangelo's *David* in Florence's Accademia, but then meander down the 15th-century street, a short bus ride away, where he was born. You'll find that after three days of trotting through museums, a walk through a quiet neighborhood will help restore your sense of perspective.

Of course, there may be many art treasures that will not quicken your pulse, but one morning you may see a Caravaggio so perfect, so beautiful, that your knees will buckle.

The Great Outdoors

The artistic beauty found in Italy is a logical complement to the gorgeous terrain from which it was born. Here you can climb and ski in the Dolomites and the Alps, lounge on beaches from Venice's Lido to Sicily's Aeolian Islands, and walk the sun-washed coastlines of the Riviera and Amalfi. The best thing about Italy's natural beauty may be that so much of it is so accessible: from the seat of your car or bicycle you have the privilege of watching the lakes of Lombardy or the hills of Tuscany pass before you. The landscape throughout the country achieves a remarkable harmony between man and nature. Architectural masterpieces sprout from hilltops and cliffs, while vineyards and olive groves add perfect Italian accents to the countryside.

Il Caffè

The Italian day begins and ends with coffee, and more cups of coffee punctuate the time in between. To live like the Italians do, drink as they drink, standing at the counter or sitting at outdoor tables of the corner bar. (In Italy, the term *bar* always means coffee bar—establishments serving primarily alcoholic beverages are called *pubs* or *American bars*.) A primer: *Caffè* means coffee, and Italian standard issue is what Americans call espresso—short, strong, and usually taken very sweet. *Cappuccino* is a foamy half-and-half of espresso and steamed milk; cocoa powder (*cacao*) on top is acceptable, cinnamon not. If you're thinking of having a cappuccino for dessert, think again—Italians drink only caffè or *caffè macchiato* (with a spot of steamed milk) after lunchtime. Confused? Homesick? Order *caffè americano* for a reasonable facsimile of good old filtered joe.

The Italian Table

You'll find the merits of Italian cooking sung throughout this book, from the "On the Menu" boxes at the beginning of each chapter to the often-glowing restaurant reviews to the "Portraits" in the back. Believe what you read. Each region of Italy has its own distinct, time-tested cuisine that's a source of pride equally felt in family kitchens, modest trattorias, and sophisticated restaurants. What Italians of all regions hold in common is a respect for the pleasures of the table. They take the utmost care in creating staples—bread, wine, cheese, and olive oil are just the beginning of the list—and build their cuisine from there. Another shared characteristic of Italian food is a tendency to revere the most humble ingredients; chefs will devote the same attention to day-old bread that they do to priceless truffles. There's often a hint of the exotic on the menu, but the more unusual an item seems to you, the more likely it is to be distinctly local in origin. When confronted with cuttlefish in Venice or tripe in Tuscany, remember that a brave diner is most often a happy diner.

La Passeggiata

A favorite Italian pastime is the *passeggiata,* literally, the promenade. In the late afternoon and early evening, especially on weekends, couples, families, and packs of teenagers stroll the main streets and piazzas of Italy's towns. It's a ritual of exchanged news and gossip, window-shopping, flirting, and gelato eating that adds up to a uniquely Italian experience. To join in, simply hit the streets for a bit of wandering. You may feel more like an observer than a participant, until you realize that observing is what la passeggiata is all about.

Shopping

"Made in Italy" has become synonymous with style, quality, and craftsmanship, whether it refers to high fashion or Maserati automobiles. The best buys are leather goods of all kinds—from gloves to bags to jackets—silk goods, knitwear, gold jewelry, ceramics, and local handicrafts. The most important thing to keep in mind when shopping in Italy is that every region has its specialties. Venice is known for glassware, lace, and velvet; Milan and Como for silk; the Dolomites and the mountainous regions of Calabria and Sicily for hand-carved wooden objects; Florence for straw goods, gold jewelry, leather, and paper products; Naples for coral and cameos; Assisi for embroidery; and Deruta, Gubbio, Vietri, and many towns in Puglia and Sicily for ceramics.

FODOR'S CHOICE

The sights, restaurants, hotels, and other travel experiences on these pages are our editors' top picks—our Fodor's Choices. They're the best of their type in Italy—not to be missed and always worth your time. In the destination chapters that follow, you will find all the details.

LODGING

$$$$ Cocumella, Sorrento, Campania. This cliff-top hotel has a centuries-old reputation for fine hospitality.

$$$$ De la Poste, Cortina D'Ampezzo, Dolomites. The owners make you feel like old friends at this chalet in the heart of one of Italy's poshest ski resorts.

$$$$ San Domenico Palace, Taormina, Sicily. A former convent is now a pleasure palace, with ultramodern facilities and timeless views.

$$$$ Villa d'Este, Cernobbio, Lombardy. The choice of Napoléon and the Duchess of Windsor is as grand as ever.

$$$–$$$$ Hotel Ripagrande, Ferrara, Emilia-Romagna. Everything feels just right in this immaculate 15th-century palazzo.

$$$ Britannia, Rome. A central location and an attentive staff are just part of what makes this small hotel a find.

$$$ Castello di Petrata, Assisi, Umbria. Peace and tranquility reign in this splendidly converted fortress; the view from the pool will take your breath away.

$$$ Villa Novecento, Courmayeur, Valle d'Aosta. Recuperate at this charming, cozy retreat after a day of hiking or skiing on the slopes of Monte Bianco.

$$–$$$ Beacci Tornabuoni, Florence. The definitive Florentine *pensione*, in the midst of the city's swankest shopping area.

$$–$$$ Pensione Accademia Villa Maravege, Venice. A garden with a view of the Grand Canal is just one of the pleasures at this Venetian villa.

$$ Calcione Country and Castle, Arezzo, Tuscany. Country living doesn't get much better than at this *agriturismo* convenient to Siena, San Gimignano, and Cortona.

$$ Grotta Palazzese, Polignano a Mare, Puglia. Here's your chance to stay in a cavelike nook literally carved into an Adriatic cliff.

$$ La Riserva, Ventimiglia, Italian Riviera. Tucked in the hills near the Franco-Italian border, this is frontier living at its very best and a great place for a romantic getaway.

$$ Villa Pisani, Padua, Venetian Arc. Experience sixteenth-century villa living, with frescoed rooms and formal gardens.

BUDGET LODGING

$ Locanda di Mirandolina, Tuscania, Lazio. The rooms are small but immaculate at this courteously run guest house; the restaurant is also top-flight.

$ **Villa Eva,** Capri, Campania. Every room has its own little cottage set amid a garden on the magical island of Capri.

¢   **B & B Belvedere,** Siracusa, Sicily. If you're a backpacker, or traveling on a backpacker's budget, you'll appreciate the spacious rooms and reasonable rates here.

¢   **La Pallotta,** Assisi, Umbria. Ask for a room with a view at this family-run Assisi bargain with a fine restaurant.

¢   **Residenza Johanna I,** Florence. Simple but appealing rooms in a good location make for this the savvy budget traveler's residence of choice in Florence.

RESTAURANTS

$$$$ **Cibrèo,** Florence. Chef/owner Fabio Pichi creates terrific Tuscan food with flair.

$$$$ **Gener Neuv,** Asti, Piedmont. Watch the River Tanaro drift by as you sip Asti Spumante and dine on first-rate local *cucina*.

$$$$ **La Pergola,** Rome. The most celebrated restaurant in Rome is one of the few places in the ancient city that understands modern cuisine.

$$$$ **San Domenico,** Imola, Emilia-Romagna. In the Italian region most dedicated to food worship, this is a gourmet's temple.

$$–$$$ **Su Gologone,** Nuoro, Sardinia. Sample recipes that date back hundreds of years at this country inn set among the olive groves. You can also spend the night here in supremely relaxing rustic comfort.

$$–$$$ **Taverna del Lupo,** Gubbio, Umbria. A great place to taste traditional Umbrian cooking at its earthy, hearty best.

$$ **Bucadisantantonio,** Lucca, Tuscany. The Tuscan cuisine here is handled with grace and aplomb.

$$ **Il Mulinazzo,** Palermo, Sicily. Palermo food-lovers happily take the 45-minute drive outside of town to indulge in chef Nino Graziano's sophisticated Sicilian cuisine. For what may be the island's finest restaurant, the prices are strikingly reasonable.

$$ **La Stanza del Gusto,** Naples. This relatively new addition to the Naples dining scene is a successful mix of elegance and authenticity.

$$ **Taverna Kerkira,** Bagnara Calabra, Calabria. This friendly, unpretentious eatery serves inspired creations with a distinctly Greek air.

BUDGET RESTAURANTS

$ **Al Donizetti,** Bergamo, Lombardy. Choose among the region's best hams and cheeses or order a full meal to complement this wine bar's selection of over 800 bottles.

$ **Antipastoteca di Mare,** Trieste, Venetian Arc. Order up a smorgasbord of sublime seafood in this cozy *osteria*.

$	**Bancogiro,** Venice. This *bacaro* with contemporary flair takes full advantage of its location next to the Rialto markets.
$	**Ditirambo,** Rome. You're in the hub of Campo de' Fiori street life as you dine here on surprising variations on traditional Mediterranean cuisine.
$	**Trattoria Casareccia,** Lecce, Puglia. Don't expect a menu—just wonderful southern Italian food.
¢–$	**Candidollo,** Imperia, Italian Riviera. A small country restaurant is the natural spot for the best in Ligurian cooking.
¢–$	**Cantina Palazzo dei Mercanti,** Viterbo, Lazio. This casual spot shares a kitchen with one of Lazio's most sophisticated restaurants. The result is great food for pocket change.

ANTIQUITIES

Imperial Roman Villa, Piazza Armerina, Sicily. Some of the best mosaics of the Roman world cover more than 12,000 square ft at what's thought to have been a hunting lodge of the emperor Maximianus Heraclius.

Mausoleo di Galla Placidia, Ravenna, Emilia-Romagna. Some of the most dazzling Byzantine mosaics in the Western world are hidden inside a humble brick tomb.

Ostia Antica, Lazio. Ancient Rome's port city is now a remarkably well-preserved archeological site in a pretty, parklike setting.

Pantheon, Rome. Sit in a café in the car-free piazza that overlooks this Roman architectural masterpiece and take pleasure in watching today's elegant Romans stroll by.

Pompeii, Campania. When Mt. Vesuvius erupted in AD 79, covering Pompeii in volcanic ash and mud, it created a museum of daily life in the ancient world.

Sassi, Matera, Basilicata. This spooky network of ancient cave dwellings is one of the most striking sights in all Italy.

Su Nuraxi, Sardinia. Dating back to the 16th century BC, the nuraghe—the stone fortresses of prehistoric civilizations—are Sardinia's most mysterious archeological feature, and this one is the island's most impressive.

Valle dei Templi, Agrigento, Sicily. These are some of the world's best preserved remains of classical Greece.

CHURCHES

Basilica di San Francesco, Arezzo, Tuscany. Piero della Francesca's *Legend of the True Cross,* executed on three walls of the choir in this 14th-century church, have been said to exhibit "the most perfect morning light in all Renaissance painting."

Basilica di San Francesco, Assisi, Umbria. The fresco cycle here illustrating the life of St. Francis is counted among the masterpieces of the Renaissance, and the soaring double basilica, still recovering from damage sustained in a 1997 earthquake, makes them a majestic home.

Cappella degli Scrovegni, Padua, Venetian Arc. Brilliant frescoes by Giotto, impeccably restored and preserved, decorate Italy's second-most famous chapel.

Duomo, Siracusa, Sicily. One of Italy's great monuments to the passing of time: a baroque cathedral built on top of still-visible Greek columns from the 6th century BC.

Santa Croce, Florence. The resting place of Michelangelo, Galileo, and Machiavelli also contains the most important art of any church in Florence.

Santa Maria Gloriosa dei Frari, Venice. The blazing colors of two of Titian's most spectacular altarpieces illuminate this monumental Venetian Gothic church.

Santo Stefano, Bologna. This splendid basilica stands on what's been the site of numerous churches through the ages.

MUSEUMS

Galleria degli Uffizi, Florence. Simply one of the world's great art collections.

Museo Archeologico dell'Alto Adige, Bolzano, Dolomites. The impossibly well-preserved body of the star attraction here, the Bolzano iceman, was unearthed in 1991 after 5,300 very cold years.

Museo e Galleria Borghese, Rome. With the setting as exquisite as the art, this small, supremely elegant museum showcases some of the best baroque and Renaissance art in the Italy.

Museo Egizio, Turin, Piedmont. A surprising treasure: one of the world's richest collections of Egyptian art outside Cairo.

Museo Nazionale della Magna Grecia, Reggio di Calabria. One of southern Italy's best museums, this complex showcases myriad treasures from Magna Graecia.

Musei Vaticani, Rome. The sheer size of the Vatican Museums is daunting, but the Sistine Chapel, the Raphael Rooms, and scores of masterpieces reward your effort.

ONLY IN ITALY

Colle Palatino, Rome. Wander through the ages of Rome, from imperial palaces to a peaceful Renaissance garden.

Festa di Sant'Efisio, Cagliari, Sardinia. Tradition isn't a cliché in Sardinia's tourist-trade lexicon, and of the island's time-honored festivals, none has greater exuberance than Cagliari's annual binge.

Gondola Ride, Venice. In sunshine or moonlight, it's magical plying these surreal waterways, where fairytale palazzi waltz by, veiled in silvery mist.

A Night at the Opera, Arena di Verona, Venetian Arc. Sit under the stars in this "second Colosseum" and enjoy world-class opera on a stage big enough for teams of horses.

Piazza del Campo, Siena, Tuscany. Perhaps it's the unique shell-shaped design that makes this one of Italy's most pleasing piazzas. Have a coffee or a gelato, then climb the Torre del Mangia for unparalleled views of Siena's red roofs and the surrounding countryside.

Piazza del Duomo, Parma, Emilia-Romagna. The medieval meets the baroque at this tranquil square in the heart of Parma.

Passeggiata Tappeiner, Merano, Dolomites. An amble along these promenades and you'll understand the year-round appeal of the spa town of Merano.

Sagra del Pesce, Camogli, Italian Riviera. Every year on the second Sunday in May, the normally quiet town of Camogli springs to life for what is certainly one of the world's most fun and festive (and free) outdoor fish fries—the feast day of San Fortunato.

PALACES

Palazzo Ducale, Urbino, the Marches. If the Renaissance was, in ideal form, a celebration of the nobility of man and his works, of the light and purity of the soul, then in no other palace in Italy are its tenets better illustrated.

Palazzo Reale, Genoa, Italian Riviera. The vast wealth of Genoa's 17th-century merchant princes are on impressive display at this magnificent palace.

Villa La Rotonda, Vicenza, Venetian Arc. A kind of Renaissance update of the Pantheon in Rome, Palladio's most famous villa was the inspiration for Thomas Jefferson's Monticello, as well as numerous capitol buildings.

TOWNS

Bellagio, Lombardy. Once called "Italy's prettiest town," it still seems to be more of an operetta set than a resort.

Cortina d'Ampezzo, Dolomites. For the classic Italian skiing experience, come to this old-school resort.

Lecce, Puglia. Extravagant baroque churches—a flowering of golden stone—are the showpieces of this town in Italy's deep south, stomping ground of the ancient Greeks, bold Crusaders, and a landed aristocracy. All left their marks.

Ravello, Campania. This town on the Amalfi coast has two spectacular villas that compete for the title of most beautiful spot in southern Italy.

SMART TRAVEL TIPS

*Finding out about your destination before
you leave home means you won't squan-
der time organizing everyday minutiae
once you've arrived. You'll be more street-
wise when you hit the ground as well, better prepared to explore the aspects of Italy
that drew you here in the first place. The
organizations in this section can provide
information to supplement this guide; contact them for up-to-the-minute details, and
consult the A to Z sections that end each
chapter for facts on the various topics as
they relate to Italy's many regions. Happy
landings!*

ADDRESSES

Addresses in Italy are fairly straightforward: the street is followed by the street
number. However, you might see an address with a number plus "bis" or "A";
for instance, "Via Verdi 3/bis" or "Via
Mazzini 8/A." This indicates that 3/bis
and 8/A are the next door down from Via
Verdi 3 and Via Mazzini 8, respectively. In
Rome, street numbers flow down one side
of a street and back up the other. In central Florence, the letter "r" following an
address (e.g., Via Santo Spirito 35/r) refers
to "rosso" (red), the color of the number
painted on the wall. Red addresses are
commercial; blue or black numbers are
residential.

In Venice addresses are made up of the
name of one the city's six neighborhoods
and a number. The hitch is that the numbers don't go in any sequential order, so
San Marco 3672 and 3673 might well be
several narrow winding streets away from
each other. When helpful, the Venetian addresses in this book include the nearest
campo, bridge, or calle.

In rural areas, some addresses give only the
route name or the distance in kilometers
along a major road (e.g., Via Fabbri, km
4.3), or sometimes only the name of the
small village in which the site is located.

AIR TRAVEL

The price of flying within Italy is often
comparable to the cost of train travel, although be sure to factor in the expense of
getting to and from the airport. When flying out of Italian airports, always check
with the airport or tourist agency about
upcoming strikes, which are frequent in
Italy and often affect air travel.

BOOKING

When you book **look for nonstop flights** and **remember that "direct" flights stop at least once.** Try to avoid connecting flights, which require a change of plane and increase the chance of misplaced luggage. Two airlines may operate a connecting flight jointly, so ask if your airline operates every segment of the trip; you may find that the carrier you prefer flies you only part of the way. To find more booking tips and to check prices and make on-line flight reservations, log on to www.fodors.com.

CARRIERS

When flying internationally, you must usually choose between a domestic carrier, the national flag carrier of the country you are visiting (Alitalia for Italy), and a foreign carrier from a third country. National flag carriers have the greatest number of non-stops. Domestic carriers may have better connections to your hometown and serve a greater number of gateway cities. Third-party carriers may have a price advantage.

On international flights, Alitalia serves Rome, Milan, and Venice. The major international hubs in Italy are Milan and Rome, served by Continental Airlines and Delta Air Lines. American Airlines, United Airlines, and Northwest Airlines fly into Milan. US Airways serves Rome.

Direct service from Heathrow and Gatwick is provided by Alitalia and British Airways (BA). From Manchester, there are two direct BA flights daily to Milan, and daily flights to Rome. Smaller, no-frills airlines also provide service between Great Britain and Italy. Go Fly connects London with Bologna, Virgin Express London and Rome (via Brussels), British Midland London and Milan, and Ryanair, departing from London Stansted, has daily flights to a number of cities in Italy. Privately run Meridiana has two or three direct flights between London and Olbia on Sardinia weekly in summer, and three direct flights daily to Florence throughout the year. Meridiana also connects London with Catania.

Alitalia and Air Canada have the most flights connecting Canada and Italy. Qantas flies from various cities in Australia via Bangkok, arriving in Rome. Alitalia and New Zealand Air fly from Auckland to Rome with a stop in London. Other options to consider if you're coming from either Australia or New Zealand are Thai Airlines (with a stop in Bangkok, landing in Rome), Malayasian Air (with a stop in Kuala Lumpur, landing in Rome), and Singapore Air (via Singapore).

Alitalia—in addition to other major European airlines and smaller, privately run companies such as Meridiana and Air One—offers an extensive network of flights within Italy. Ask your domestic or Italian travel agent about discounts.

Tickets for intra-Italy flights cost less when purchased from agents within Italy. Sales are frequent, so check the cost of flights, even one-way, as an alternative to train travel.

Major Airlines **Air Canada** ☎ 888/247-2262 in U.S. and Canada; 08705/247-226 in U.K.; 06/6557117 in Rome; 800/919091 elsewhere in Italy ⊕ www.aircanada.com. **Air New Zealand** ⊕ www.airnz.com. **Alitalia** ☎ 800/223-5730 in U.S.; 0870/544-8259 in U.K.; 61/292-44-2222 in Australia; 06/65641 in Rome; 848/865641 elsewhere in Italy ⊕ www.alitalia.it. **American Airlines** ☎ 800/433-7300 in U.S.; 02/679141 in Milan ⊕ www.aa.com. **British Airways** ☎ 800/AIRWAYS in U.S. and Canada; 0845/77-333-77 in U.K.; 02/8904-8800 in Australia; 09/356-8690 in New Zealand; 199/712266 toll-free in Italy ⊕ www.britishairways.com. **Continental Airlines** ☎ 800/231-0856 in U.S.; 02/69633256 in Milan, 800/296230 elsewhere in Italy ⊕ www.flycontinental.com. **Delta Air Lines** ☎ 800/241-4141 in U.S.; 06/65954406 in Italy ⊕ www.deltaairlines.com. **Lufthansa** ☎ 0516477730 ⊕ www.lufthansa.com. **Northwest Airlines** ☎ 800/225-2525 in U.S. and Canada; 08705/074-074 in U.K.; 1300/303-744 in Australia; 02/218981 in Italy ⊕ www.nwa.com. **Malaysia Air** ☎ 888/359-8655 in U.S.; 618/453-2113 in Canada, the U.K., Australia, and New Zealand ⊕ www.malaysiaair.com. **Qantas,** ☎ 06/52482725 in Rome ⊕ www.qantas.com. **Thai Airlines** ⊕ www.thaiair.com. **United Airlines** ☎ 800/241-6522 in U.S.; 02/69633707 in Milan ⊕ www.ual.com. **US Airways** ☎ 800/428-4322 in U.S.; 848/813177 in Italy ⊕ www.usairways.com.

Smaller Airlines **Air One** ☎ 06/488800 in Rome; 800/900966 elsewhere in Italy; 06/48880066 from cell phones ⊕ www.flyairone.it. **Go Fly** ☎ 0870/6076543 in U.K. ⊕ www.go-fly.com. **Meridiana** ☎ 199/111333 in Italy ⊕ www.meridiana.it. **Ryanair** ☎ 08701/569569 in U.K.; 199/114114 in Italy ⊕ www.ryanair.com. **Virgin Express** ☎ 0207/744-0004 in U.K.; 02/48296000 in Milan; 800/097097 in the rest of Italy: 32/70353637 in U.S., Canada, Australia, and New Zealand.

CHECK-IN & BOARDING

To avoid delays at airport-security check-points, try not to wear any metal. Jewelry, belt and other buckles, steel-toe shoes, barrettes, and underwire bras are among the items that can set off detectors.

Always **ask your carrier about its check-in policy.** Plan to arrive at the airport 2½ to 3 hours before international flights. When flying within Italy, allow at least two hours before scheduled departure time.

Assuming that not everyone with a ticket will show up, airlines routinely overbook planes. When everyone does, airlines ask for volunteers to give up their seats. In return, these volunteers usually get a several-hundred-dollar flight voucher, which can be used toward the purchase of another ticket, and are rebooked on the next flight out. If there are not enough volunteers, the airline must choose who will be denied boarding. The first to get bumped are passengers who checked in late and those flying on discounted tickets, so **get to the gate and check in as early as possible,** especially during peak periods.

Always **bring a government-issued photo I.D. to the airport;** even when it's not required, a passport is best.

CUTTING COSTS

The least expensive airfares to Italy are priced for round-trip travel and must usually be purchased in advance. Airlines generally allow you to change your return date for a fee; most low-fare tickets, however, are nonrefundable. It's smart to **call a number of airlines and check the Internet;** when you are quoted a good price, **book it on the spot**—the same fare may not be available the next day, or even the next hour. Always **check different routings** and look into using alternate airports. Also, price off-peak flights, which may be significantly less expensive than others. Travel agents, especially low-fare specialists (⇨ Discounts and Deals), are helpful.

Consolidators are another good source. They buy tickets for scheduled flights at reduced rates from the airlines, then sell them at prices that beat the best fare available directly from the airlines. Sometimes you can even get your money back if you need to return the ticket. Carefully read the fine print detailing penalties for changes and cancellations, purchase the ticket with a credit card, and **confirm your consolidator reservation with the airline.**

When you **fly as a courier,** you trade your checked-luggage space for a ticket deeply subsidized by a courier service. There are restrictions on when you can book and how long you can stay. Some courier companies list with membership organizations, such as the Air Courier Association and the International Association of Air Travel Couriers; these require you to become a member before you can book a flight.

Many airlines, singly or in collaboration, offer discount air passes that allow foreigners to travel economically in a particular country or region. These visitor passes usually must be reserved and purchased before you leave home. Information about passes often can be found on most airlines' international Web pages, which tend to be aimed at travelers from outside the carrier's home country. Also, try typing the name of the pass into a search engine, or search for "pass" within the carrier's Web site.

Consolidators AirlineConsolidator.com ☎ 888/468-5385 ⊕ www.airlineconsolidator.com; for international tickets. Best Fares ☎ 800/576-8255 or 800/576-1600 ⊕ www.bestfares.com; $59.90 annual membership. Cheap Tickets ☎ 800/377-1000 or 888/922-8849 ⊕ www.cheaptickets.com. Expedia ☎ 800/397-3342 or 404/728-8787 ⊕ www.expedia.com. Hotwire ☎ 866/468-9473 or 920/330-9418 ⊕ www.hotwire.com. Now Voyager Travel ✉ 45 W. 21st St., New York, NY 10010 ☎ 212/459-1616 🖷 212/243-2711 ⊕ www.nowvoyagertravel.com. Onetravel.com ⊕ www.onetravel.com. Orbitz ☎ 888/656-4546 ⊕ www.orbitz.com. Priceline.com ⊕ www.priceline.com. Travelocity ☎ 888/709-5983; 877/282-2925 in Canada; 0870/876-3876 in U.K. ⊕ www.travelocity.com.

Courier Resources Air Courier Association/Cheaptrips.com ☎ 800/282-1202 ⊕ www.aircourier.org or www.cheaptrips.com. International Association of Air Travel Couriers ☎ 308/632-3273 ⊕ www.courier.org.

Discount Passes Boomerang Pass, Qantas. ☎ 800/227-4500; 0845/774-7767 in U.K.; 131-313 in Australia; 0800/808-767 in New Zealand ⊕ www.qantas.com. FlightPass, EuropebyAir. ☎ 888/387-2479 ⊕ www.europebyair.com.

ENJOYING THE FLIGHT

All flights within Italy are smoke free. However, smoking is allowed on a limited number of international flights; **contact your carrier about its smoking policy. State your seat preference** when purchasing your ticket, and then repeat it when you confirm and when you check in. For more legroom, you can request one of the few emergency-aisle seats at check-in, if you are capable of lifting at least 50 pounds— a Federal Aviation Administration requirement of passengers in these seats. Seats behind a bulkhead also offer more legroom, but they don't have under-seat storage. Don't sit in the row in front of the emergency aisle or in front of a bulkhead, where seats may not recline.

Ask the airline whether a snack or meal is served on the flight. If you have dietary concerns, **request special meals when booking.** These can be vegetarian, low-cholesterol, or kosher, for example. It's a good idea to pack some healthful snacks and a small (plastic) bottle of water in your carry-on bag. On long flights, try to maintain a normal routine, to help fight jet lag. At night, **get some sleep.** By day, **eat light meals, drink water** (not alcohol), and **move around the cabin** to stretch your legs. For additional jet-lag tips consult *Fodor's FYI: Travel Fit & Healthy* (available at bookstores everywhere).

FLYING TIMES

Flying time to Milan and Rome is approximately 8½ hours from New York, 10–11 hours from Chicago, 11½ hours from Dallas (via New York), 11½ hours from Los Angeles, 2 hours from London (to Milan), and 23½ hours from Sydney.

HOW TO COMPLAIN

If your baggage goes astray or your flight goes awry, complain right away. Most carriers require that you **file a claim immediately.** The Aviation Consumer Protection Division of the Department of Transportation publishes *Fly-Rights,* which discusses airlines and consumer issues and is available on-line.

🔲 Airline Complaints **Aviation Consumer Protection Division** ✉ U.S. Department of Transportation, C-75, Room 4107, 400 7th St. NW, Washington, DC 20590 ☎ 202/366-2220 ⊕ www.dot.gov/airconsumer. **Federal Aviation Administration Consumer Hotline** ✉ For inquiries: FAA, 800 Independence Ave. SW, Room 810, Washington, DC 20591 ☎ 800/322-7873 ⊕ www.faa.gov.

RECONFIRMING

Check the status of your flight before you leave for the airport. You can do this on your carrier's Web site, by linking to a flight-status checker (many Web booking services offer these), or by calling your carrier or travel agent. Always confirm international flights at least 72 hours ahead of the scheduled departure time. Confirm flights within Italy the day before travel.

AIRPORTS

The major gateways to Italy include Rome's **Aeroporto Leonardo da Vinci,** better known as **Fiumicino** (FCO), and Milan's **Aeroporto Malpensa 2000** (MXP). There are direct connections from both airports to Florence. For information about regional airports, *see* the A to Z sections at the end of each chapter.
🔲 Airport Information **Aeroporto Leonardo da Vinci,** known as Fiumicino ✉ 35 km [20 mi] southeast of Rome ☎ 06/5951 ⊕ www.adr.it. **Aeroporto Malpensa** ✉ 45 km [28 mi] north of Milan ☎ 02/7485-2200 ⊕ www.sea-aeroportimilano.it.

DUTY-FREE SHOPPING

Duty-free shopping in airports has been eliminated in Italy (and other EC countries) when you are traveling within member nations; when flying out of Italy, however, duty-free shopping is still an option.

BEACHES

With 7,420 km (4,610 mi) of coastline facing three seas—the Adriatic to the northeast, the Ionian to the southeast, and the Tyrrhenean to the west—Italy offers every type of beach scene. Italy has several world-famous beaches, like those along the Costa Esmeralda in Sardinia and the town of Portofino in Liguria, and great stretches of deserted and untouched coastline, many found in eastern Calabria, Sardinia, and the islands around Sicily. In Emilia-Romagna, Riccione and Rimini are famous for their nightlife and seaside fitness programs ("spinning" classes to weight lifting, water gymnastics to Latin dance classes). The Tremiti Islands (off the Adriatic coast, between Molise and Puglia), the Gargano Peninsula (in Puglia), Tropea (in Calabria), Taormina (in Sicily), the islands of Capri and Ischia (in the Gulf of Naples), the Amalfi Coast (in Campania), Ponza (off the coast of Lazio), and the island of Elba (off the coast of Livorno in Tuscany) bring together a natural beauty with a low-key worldliness that includes discos and stylish restaurants.

Note the difference between the private and public beaches. Public ones are free but offer no services. Although on the most popular ones it's sometimes possible to buy sandwiches and soft drinks from kiosks or roaming vendors, don't depend on them, nor upon the presence of pay telephones, toilets, or showers. Private beaches charge admission and range from downright spartan (cold showers and portable toilets) to luxurious (with gardens, stylish bars, fish restaurants, and private guest huts). Admission policies and prices vary accordingly. Most establishments offer a chaise longue, chair, and umbrella for between €15 and €40 a day, with extra longues rented out for an additional fee. Some of the most exclusive places cater only to patrons who pay by the week or month. Inquire at local tourist offices for details.

Don't underestimate the scorching power of the Italian sun. The "tanning season" begins in early May, and beach life starts in earnest in early June, with the opening of beach concessionaires, called *stabilimenti*. During weekends and holidays and in August, most sea resorts and beaches tend to be very crowded, some posting "no-vacancy" (*completo*) signs by 10 AM, so an early start is essential. In northern and central Italy, sunbathing topless is common practice in the south, it could lead to undesired attention from local men. Nowhere in Italy, except at the rare nudist beach, is it common practice to walk around topless, and beach attire (bare chests and thighs) worn in town is frowned upon. The summer season ends in early September.

BIKE TRAVEL

Italians are great bicycling enthusiasts, and biking in Italy is a terrific way to see the country, particularly in places such as Tuscany, where two-lane roads wind through startlingly beautiful countryside. The best times to bike are in spring and fall; July and August are unbearably hot in most places. Rentals are easily obtained in most cities. Given the generally hilly terrain, it's essential to have a good map with eleva-

tions, distances, and the various types of roads clearly marked. An excellent map choice is the green regional series issued by the Italian Touring Club, available at major bookstores. Road conditions are generally good throughout Italy, but, as you move along, it's always a good idea to ask local tourist information offices about bike-friendly routes. Especially in smaller towns and villages, cyclists do not go unnoticed, and if you speak a little Italian you'll be likely to meet sympathetic native cyclists eager to give valuable tips about the region. Always park (and lock) your bike inside your hotel for the night. And an important related note: laundry facilities are rare in Italy and can be found only in the bigger cities.

The Federazione Italiana Amici della Bicicletta (FIAB) will help you plan your itinerary. The Web site www.cycling.it, under Itinerari Italiani, contains an interesting selection of articles (in Italian) from the publication *La Bicicletta*, with detailed descriptions of itineraries across national parks and areas of natural beauty.
Local Resources FIAB ⊠ Viale Col Moschin 1, 30170 Mestre, Veneto ☎ 041/921515 ⊕ www.fiab-onlus.it.
Rentals Happy Rent ⊠ Via Farini 3, Rome ☎ 06/481-8185. **I Bike Italy** ⊠ Viale Galoppatoio 33, Rome ☎ 06/3225240.
Bike Tours Backroads ⊠ 801 Cedar St., Berkeley, CA 94710 ☎ 510/527-1555 or 800/462-2848 ☎ 510/527-1444 ⊕ www.backroads.com. **Bike Riders** ☎ Box 130254, Boston, MA 02113 ☎ 617/723-2354 or 800/473-7040 ☎ 617/723-2355 ⊕ www.bikeriderstours.com. **Butterfield & Robinson** ⊠ 70 Bond St., Suite 300, Toronto, Ontario, Canada M5B 1X3 ☎ 416/864-1354 or 800/678-1147 ☎ 416/864-0541 ⊕ www.butterfield.com. **Ciclismo Classico** ⊠ 30 Marathon St., Arlington, MA 02474 ☎ 781/646-3377 or 800/866-7314 ☎ 781/641-1512 ⊕ ciclismoclassico.com. **Euro-Bike Tours** ☎ Box 990, De Kalb, IL 60115 ☎ 800/321-6060 ☎ 815/758-8851 ⊕ www.eurobike.com. **Europeds** ⊠ 761 Lighthouse Ave., Monterey, CA 93940 ☎ 831/646-4920 ☎ 831/655-4501. **Himalayan Travel** ⊠ 8 Berkshire Pl., Danbury, CT 06801 ☎ 203/743-2349 or 800/225-2380 ☎ 203/797-8077 ⊕ www.himalayantravel.com. **Naturequest** ⊠ 30872 South Coast Hwy., Suite 185, Laguna Beach, CA 92651 ☎ 949/499-9561 or 800/369-3033 ☎ 949/499-0812 ⊕ www.naturequesttours.com. **Uniquely Europe/Europe Express** ⊠ 19805 North Creek Pkwy., Suite 100, Bothell, WA 98011 ☎ 425/487-6711 or 800/927-3876 ☎ 425/487-3750 or 800/270-0509 ⊕ www.europeexpress.com.

BIKES IN FLIGHT

Most airlines accommodate bikes as luggage, provided they are dismantled and boxed; check with individual airlines about packing requirements. Some airlines sell bike boxes, which are often free at bike shops, for about $15 (bike bags can be considerably more expensive). International travelers often can substitute a bike for a piece of checked luggage at no charge; otherwise, the cost is about $100. U.S. and Canadian airlines charge $40–$80 each way.

BOAT & FERRY TRAVEL

Ferries connect the mainland with all major islands. To many destinations there is also hydrofoil (*aliscafo*) service, which is generally twice as fast as ferries and double the price. Service is considerably more frequent in summer. Car ferries go to Sicily and Sardinia and many islands, including Elba, Ponza, Capri, Ischia, and the Lido near Venice. A ferry to Capri from Naples will cost about €6 one-way; to the Aliscafo, €12. If you are traveling in July–August, try to make reservations at least a month ahead for Sicily or Sardinia. (Same-day ticket purchase is available for shorter trips.)

Tirrenia operates ferries to Liguria, Tuscany, Naples, Sicily, Sardinia, and Tunisia. SNAV operates high-speed ferries between Naples and Palermo (only from April to early October), hydrofoils between Naples and Capri, and ferries to Greece. Lauro has hydrofoils and car ferries between Naples and Ischia and that links Ischia and Capri to the Amalfi coast in summer. Capri is reached by Caremar. Adriatica connects Italy with Greece. Trenitalia ferries sail from Civitavecchia to Golfo Aranci, near Olbia. Moby Lines and Toremar serve Elba from Piombino. For the Lake District contact Navigazione Laghi.

FARES & SCHEDULES

You can pick up schedules and buy tickets from any local Italian travel agent, most of whom speak English. Major credit cards are generally accepted, but cash is always the preferred form of payment. Costs vary depending on car size and the type of accommodation on the ferry. Travel between Naples and Palermo, for instance, costs from €106 for a small-size car and no sleeping quarters to €212 for a large car and a sleeping cabin for two.

Adriatic Coast Ferries Adriatica ⊠ Via San Nicola da Tolentino 27, Rome ☎ 06/4818341 ⊕ www.adriatica.it.

Mediterranean Ferries Caremar ⊠ Molo Beverello, Napoli ☎ 081/5513882. **Lauro** ⊠ Molo Beverello, Napoli, ☎ 081/7611004 ⊕ www.lauro.it. **Moby Lines** ⊠ Piazzale Premuda, Piombino ☎ 0565/221212 ⊕ www.mobylines.com. **SNAV** ⊠ Via Giordano Bruno 84, Napoli ☎ 081/7612348 ⊕ www.snavali.com. **Tirrenia** ⊠ Rione Sirignano 2, Napoli ☎ 199/123199 within Italy; 081/3172999 from abroad and on cell phones ⊕ www.tirrenia.it. **Trenitalia** ☎ 892021. **Toremar** ⊠ Piazzale Premuda 13/14, Piombino ☎ 0565/31100 ⊕ www.toremar.it. **Navigazione Laghi** ⊠ Via Ludovico Ariosto 21, Milan ☎ 02/4676101; 800/551801 within Italy ⊕ www.navlaghi.it.

Northern Lakes Ferries Navigazione Laghi ⊠ Via Ludovico Ariosto 21, Milan ☎ 02/4676101; 800/551801 within Italy ⊕ www.navlaghi.it.

BUSINESS HOURS

Religious and civic holidays are frequent in Italy. Depending on their local importance, businesses may close for the day (businesses do not close on a Friday or Monday if the holiday falls on the weekend).

BANKS & POST OFFICES

Banks are open weekdays 8:30 to 1:30 and 2:45 to 3:45. Post offices are open Monday–Saturday 9–2; central and main district post offices stay open until 6:30 PM weekdays, 9–2 on Saturday. On the last day of the month all post offices close at midday.

MUSEUMS & SIGHTS

Most churches are open from early morning until noon or 12:30, when they close for three hours or more; they open again in the afternoon, closing about 6 PM. A few major churches, such as St. Peter's in Rome and San Marco in Venice, are open all day. Note that sightseeing in churches during religious rites is discouraged. Museum hours vary and often change with the seasons. Many museums are closed one day a week, often on Monday. During low season, hours are often abbreviated; during high season, many places stay open until late at night. Always check locally.

PHARMACIES

Pharmacies are generally open weekdays from 8:30 to 1 and from 4 to 8, and Saturday mornings 9 to 1. Local pharmacies cover the off-hours in shifts: on the door of every pharmacy is a list of which pharmacies in the vicinity will be open on Saturday afternoon, Sunday, or 24 hours.

SHOPS

Most shops are open from 9 to 1 and from 3:30 or 4 to 7:30, Monday–Saturday. Clothing shops are generally closed on Monday mornings. Barbers and hairdressers, with some exceptions, are closed Sunday and Monday. Some bookstores and fashion and tourist-oriented shops in places such as Rome and Venice are open all day, as well as Sunday. Chain supermarkets such as Standa have continuous hours and are open on Sunday; smaller *alimentari* (delicatessens) and other food shops are usually closed one evening during the week (it varies according to the town) and almost always on Sunday.

BUS TRAVEL

Italy's bus network is extensive, although buses are not as attractive an option as in other European countries, partly because of the comparative low cost and convenience of train travel. However, in some areas buses can be faster and more direct than local trains, so it's a good idea to **compare bus and train schedules.** To reach some smaller towns, the bus is likely to be your only option. Bus service outside cities is organized on a regional level and often operated by private companies.

If you're traveling by bus from the United Kingdom, **have some euros on hand to spend en route.** And be sure to consider the train, as bus fares are quite high, especially when you take the long and tiring overnight journey into account. Eurolines runs a weekly bus service to Rome that increases to three times a week between June and September.

CUTTING COSTS

Because there's no national bus line in Italy, all bus service is run by regional companies, some of which provide day excursions from their base of operations. Generally, children under 2 ride for free, and children ages 2–8 travel at half price. Contact the local tourist office for infor-

mation. If you need a car seat for your child, it's best to bring your own; bassinets are not provided.

TICKETS & SCHEDULES

Unlike city buses, for which you must buy your ticket from a machine, newsstand, or tobacconist and stamp it after you board, private bus lines usually have a ticket office in town or allow you to pay when you board. **Bus Information** Eurolines ⊠ 52 Grosvenor Gardens, London SW1W 0AU ☎ 020/7730-8235 or 020/7730-3499 ⊕ www.eurolines.it.

CAMERAS & PHOTOGRAPHY

Be on the lookout for signs indicating that photographs are not allowed; some museums and other institutions retain the sole right to photograph their works. Do not use flash when in museums or when photographing paintings or sculptures. The *Kodak Guide to Shooting Great Travel Pictures* (available at bookstores everywhere) is loaded with tips. **Photo Help** Kodak Information Center ☎ 800/242-2424 ⊕ www.kodak.com.

EQUIPMENT PRECAUTIONS

Don't pack film and equipment in checked luggage, where it is much more susceptible to damage. X-ray machines used to view checked luggage are extremely powerful and therefore are likely to ruin your film. Try to **ask for hand inspection of film,** which becomes clouded after repeated exposure to airport X-ray machines, and **keep videotapes and computer disks away from metal detectors.** Always **keep film, tape, and computer disks out of the sun.** Carry an extra supply of batteries, and **be prepared to turn on your camera, camcorder, or laptop** to prove to airport security personnel that the device is real.

FILM & DEVELOPING

In Rome and most major cities you'll see scores of photo developing shops, many with service in one hour (or less). In smaller cities look for a shop with a Kodak sign outside its door. Developing film in Italy costs around €12 per 36-exposure roll, and film is about €9 for a color 36-exposure roll. Because costs are higher in Italy, it's a good idea to **stock up on film before you leave.**

VIDEOS

While VHS videotapes and players are common, be forewarned that Italy, like other countries in Europe, uses a different video system than the one used in the North America. This means that you won't be able to play the videotapes that you bring from home on Italian equipment, and tapes purchased in Italy won't work in an American VCR.

CAR RENTAL

Renting a car in Italy is essential for exploring the countryside, but not if you plan to stick to city travel. Signage on country roads is usually good, but be prepared for fast and impatient fellow drivers.

Hiring a car with a driver can come in handy, particularly if you plan to do some wine tasting or drive along the Amalfi Coast. Ask at your hotel for recommended drivers, or inquire at the local tourist information office. Typically, drivers are paid by the day, and are usually rewarded with a tip of about 15% on completion of the journey.

Fiats in a variety of sizes are the most typical rental cars. Remember that most Italian cars have standard transmissions. If you want to rent an automatic, you must specify so when you reserve the car. Higher rates will apply.

⏻ Major Agencies Alamo ☎ 800/522-9696 ⊕ www.alamo.com. **Avis** ☎ 800/331-1084; 800/ 879-2847 in Canada; 0870/606-0100 in U.K.; 02/ 9353-9000 in Australia; 09/526-2847 in New Zealand ⊕ www.avis.com. **Budget** ☎ 800/527-0700; 0870/156-5656 in U.K. ⊕ www.budget.com. **Dollar** ☎ 800/800-6000; 0124/622-0111 in U.K., where it's affiliated with Sixt; 02/9223-1444 in Australia ⊕ www.dollar.com. **Hertz** ☎ 800/654-3001; 800/263-0600 in Canada; 0870/844-8844 in U.K.; 02/9669-2444 in Australia; 09/256-8690 in New Zealand ⊕ www.hertz.com. **National Car Rental** ☎ 800/227-7368; 0870/600-6666 in U.K. ⊕ www. nationalcar.com.

CUTTING COSTS

Most major American car-rental companies have offices or affiliates in Italy, but the rates are generally better if you make a reservation from abroad rather than from within Italy. The price of rentals is uniform for each company throughout the country: you will not save money, for example, if you pick up a vehicle at a city rental office rather than at an airport. For a good deal, **book through a travel agent who will shop around.** Weekend rates with limited mileage are usually good deals.

Do **look into wholesalers,** companies that do not own fleets but rent in bulk from those that do and often offer better rates than traditional car-rental operations. Prices are best during off-peak periods. Rentals booked through wholesalers often must be paid for before you leave home.

⏻ Local Agencies ⏻ Wholesalers Auto Europe ☎ 207/842-2000 or 800/223-5555; 800/223-5555-5 in Italy 🖷 207/842-2222 ⊕ www. autoeurope.com. **Europe by Car** ☎ 212/581-3040 or 800/223-1516 🖷 212/246-1458 ⊕ www.europebycar.com. **Destination Europe Resources (DER)** ✉ 9501 W. Devon Ave., Rosemont, IL 60018 ☎ 800/782-2424 ⊕ www.der.com. **Kemwel** ☎ 800/678-0678 🖷 207/842-2124 ⊕ www.kemwel.com.

INSURANCE

When driving a rented car you are generally responsible for any damage to or loss of the vehicle. Collision policies that car-rental companies sell for European rentals typically don't cover stolen vehicles. Indeed, all car-rental agencies operating in Italy require that you buy a theft-protection policy. Before you rent—and purchase collision coverage—see what coverage you already have under the terms of your personal auto-insurance policy and credit cards. All car-rental agencies operating in Italy require that you buy theft-protection policies.

REQUIREMENTS & RESTRICTIONS

In Italy your own country's driver's license is acceptable. An International Driver's Permit is nonetheless not a bad idea; it's available from the American or Canadian Automobile Association and, in the United Kingdom, from the Automobile Association or Royal Automobile Club. These international permits are universally recognized, and having one in your wallet may save you a problem with the local authorities. In Italy you must be 21 years of age to rent an economy or subcompact car, and most companies require customers under the age of 23 to pay by credit card. Upon rental, all companies require credit cards as a warranty; to rent bigger cars (2,000 cc or more), you must often show two credit cards. Call local agents for details. There are no special restrictions on senior-citizen drivers.

Car seats are required for children under three and must be booked in advance. The cost ranges from €26 to €40 for the duration of the rental.

SURCHARGES

Before you pick up a car in one city and leave it in another, **ask about drop-off charges or one-way service fees,** which can be substantial. Note, too, that some rental agencies charge extra if you return the car before the time specified in your contract. To avoid a hefty refueling fee, **fill the tank just before you turn in the car,** but be aware that gas stations near the rental outlet may overcharge. It's almost never a deal to buy the tank of gas that's in the car when you rent it; the understanding is that you'll return it empty, but some fuel usually remains. The cost for an additional driver is about €5 per day.

CAR TRAVEL

There is an extensive network of *autostrade* (toll highways), complemented by equally well-maintained but free *superstrade* (expressways). The ticket you are issued upon entering an autostrada must be returned when you exit and pay the toll; on some shorter autostrade, mainly connecting highways, the toll is paid upon entering. Viacard cards, on sale at many autostrada locations, or any major credit card make paying tolls easier and faster. *Uscita* means exit. A *raccordo* is a ring road surrounding a city. *Strade statali* (state highways, denoted by *S* or *SS* numbers) may be single-lane roads, as are all secondary roads; directions and turnoffs are not always clearly marked.

EMERGENCY SERVICES

Automobil Club Italiano (ACI) offers 24-hour road service. Dial 803/116 from any phone, 24 hours a day, to reach the ACI dispatch operator. Also, your rental car company may have an emergency tow service that can be reached with a toll-free call. Check your paperwork or ask when renting.

When you're on the road, always carry a good road map, a flashlight, and, if possible, a cellular phone so that in case of a breakdown you can call for help. When speaking to ACI, ask and you will be transferred to an English-speaking operator. Be prepared to tell the operator which road you're on, the direction you're going, e.g., "*verso* (in the direction of) Pizzo," and the *targa* (license plate number) of your car.

ACI Emergency Service ☎ 803/116.

GASOLINE

Gas stations are generally open Monday–Saturday 7–7 with a break at lunchtime. Many stations have automatic self-service pumps that accept only bills of 5, 10, 20, and 50 euros; some, but not all, also take credit cards. Gas stations on autostrade are open 24 hours. Gas costs about €1.05 per liter.

PARKING

Parking space is at a premium in most towns, especially in the *centri storici* (historic centers), which are filled with narrow streets and restricted circulation zones. Fines for parking violations are high, and rules are strictly enforced. Towing is common, and often the places where the cars are towed are difficult to get to, so it's simply not worth a risk. It is often a good idea (if not the only option) to park your car in a designated (preferably attended) lot. Parking in an area signposted ZONA DISCO (disk zone) is allowed for limited periods (from 30 minutes to two hours or more—the limit is posted); if you don't have the cardboard disk (inquire at the local tourist office or car rental agency) to show what time you parked, you can use a piece of paper. The *parcometro*, the Italian version of metered parking in which you put coins into a machine for a stamped ticket that you leave on the dashboard, has been introduced in some cities. It's advisable to **leave your car only in guarded parking areas.**

ROAD CONDITIONS

Autostrade are well maintained, well marked, and easy to follow, as are most interregional highways. The condition of provincial (county) roads varies, but road maintenance at this level is generally good in Italy.

ROAD MAPS

Street and road signs are often challenging—a good map and patience are essential. Local road maps can be obtained at the point of rental pickup. Alternatively, most bookstores such as Feltrinelli sell them as do most highway gas stations. In major cities, look for the Touring Club Italiano's shop. They sell maps (road, bicycle, hiking, among others). Probably the best road maps are those produced by Michelin.

RULES OF THE ROAD

Driving is on the right. Regulations are largely as in Britain and the United States, except that the police have the power to levy on-the-spot fines. Handheld mobile phones are illegal while driving; fines can exceed €100. In most Italian towns the use of the horn is forbidden in certain, if not all, areas; a large sign, ZONA DI SILENZIO, indicates where. Speed limits are 130 kph (80 mph) on autostrade and 110 kph (70 mph) on state and provincial roads, unless otherwise marked.

The blood-alcohol content limit for driving is 0.5 gr/ with fines up to €5,000 for surpassing the limit and the possibility of six months' imprisonment. Though enforcement of laws varies depending on region, fines for speeding are uniformly stiff: 10 kph over the speed limit can warrant a fine of up to €500; over 10 kph, and your license could be taken away from you.

Nonetheless, Italians drive fast and are impatient with those who don't. Tailgating is the norm here—the only way to avoid it is to get out of the way. Drivers also honk a lot, often to alert other drivers of their moves. Right turns on red lights are forbidden. Headlights are not compulsory when it rains or snows, but it's a good idea to turn them on. Both seat belts and children's car seats are compulsory.

CHILDREN IN ITALY

Although Italians love children and are generally very tolerant and patient with them, they provide few amenities for them. Some discounts do exist. Always ask about a *sconto bambino* (child's discount) before purchasing tickets. Children under a certain height ride free on municipal buses and trams. Children under 18 who are EU citizens are admitted free to state-run museums and galleries, and there are similar privileges in many municipal or private museums. *Fodor's Around Rome with Kids* (available in bookstores everywhere) can help you plan your days together.

If you are renting a car, don't forget to **arrange for a car seat** when you reserve.

For general advice about traveling with children, consult *Fodor's FYI: Travel with Your Baby* (available in bookstores everywhere).

FLYING

If your children are two or older, **ask about children's airfares.** As a general rule, infants under two not occupying a seat fly at greatly reduced fares or even for free. But if you want to guarantee a seat for an infant, you have to pay full fare. Consider flying during off-peak days and times; most airlines will grant an infant a seat without a ticket if there are available seats. When booking, **confirm carry-on allowances** if you're traveling with infants. In general, for babies charged 10% to 50% of the adult fare you are allowed one carry-on bag and a collapsible stroller; if the flight is full, the stroller may have to be checked or you may be limited to less.

Experts agree that it's a good idea to use safety seats aloft for children weighing less than 40 pounds. Airlines set their own policies: If you use a safety seat, U.S. carriers usually require that the child be ticketed, even if he or she is young enough to ride free, because the seats must be strapped into regular seats. And even if you pay the full adult fare for the seat, it may be worth it, especially on longer trips. Do **check your airline's policy about using safety seats during takeoff and landing.** Safety seats are not allowed everywhere in the plane, so get your seat assignments as early as possible.

When reserving, **request children's meals or a freestanding bassinet** (not available at all airlines) if you need them. But note that bulkhead seats, where you must sit to use the bassinet, may lack an overhead bin or storage space on the floor.

FOOD

In restaurants and trattorias you may find a high chair or a cushion for the child to sit on, but rarely do they offer a children's menu. **Order a *mezza porzione*** (half portion) of any dish, or **ask the waiter for a *porzione da bambino*** (child's portion) or ***pasta in bianca*** (pasta with butter), Italian children's favorite. Though spaghetti and meatballs are not found on menus, approximations to it, such as spaghetti *al pomodoro* (spaghetti with tomato sauce) are suitable substitutions. Italian children are fond of spaghetti with Parmesan, and even if it's not on the menu, most chefs will be happy to prepare it. Pizza, either in a pizzeria or at stand-up shops, offers a familiar treat for children. Generally, children are best taken to casual establishments such as trattorias. Only exceptionally well-behaved children should go to higher-end restaurants; indeed, it's rare to see Italian children in them.

LODGING

Most hotels will provide cots or cribs with prior arrangement; four- and five-star hotels normally have these on hand. The same holds true with baby-sitting; budget hotels will most likely be unable to provide the service. Some five-star hotels and *agriturismi* do not allow children, so inquire beforehand. Pools in city hotels are a rarity, and video games virtually unheard of. If you're staying at a hotel with satellite TV, you will have access to some English-language news programs, but little more. Even *The Simpsons* is dubbed into Italian.

Most hotels in Italy allow children under a certain age to stay in their parents' room at no extra charge, but others charge for them as extra adults; be sure to **find out the cutoff age for children's discounts.** The Luxury Collection of Sheraton Hotels has 15 properties in Italy, all of which welcome families. Club Med has a "Mini Club" (for ages 4–10) and a "Kids Club" at its ski village in Sestriere. There are also kids' programs at summer resort villages in Metaponto (Basilicata) and on the islands of Sicily and Sardinia, marketed mainly to Europeans. Some of the Valtur vacation villages also have special facilities and activities for children.
🄵 Best Choices **Club Med** ✉ 7001 N. Scottsdale Rd., Suite 1010, Scottsdale, AZ 85253 ☎ 800/258–2633 or 888/WEBCLUB ⊕ www.clubmed.com. **Sheraton Hotels** ✉ 1111 Westchester Ave., White Plains, NY 10604 ☎ 800/221-2340 ⊕ www.starwood.com. **Valtur** ✉ Piazza della Repubblica 59, Rome 00185 ☎ 06/471061 🖷 06/4706321 ⊕ www.valtur.it.

PRECAUTIONS

Italian tap water is heavily chlorinated, which is one reason why most Italians drink bottled water. Apple juice (*succo di mele*) is readily available in most bars and supermarkets, as are other fruit juices and popular soft drinks.

Mosquitoes can be pesky once the weather warms. Travel with your usual brand of children's insect repellant. There are several Italian brands—Autun, for instance—that also do the trick. They are available in pharmacies and supermarkets.

SIGHTS & ATTRACTIONS

Places that are especially appealing to children are indicated by a rubber-duckie icon (🐤) in the margin.

SUPPLIES & EQUIPMENT

The cost of diapers in Italy is similar to that in other places, though American brands such as Pampers and Huggies are slightly higher than in the United States. COOP is a reliable brand; you'll pay about €10 for 50 diapers.

Italian formula (both in premixed and powder forms) generally contains more vitamins than its American counterparts; Plasmon is a good brand. Italian bottles are identical to American ones, but it is difficult to find no-spill glasses for toddlers; it's best to bring a couple along with you.

COMPUTERS ON THE ROAD

Getting on-line in Italian cities isn't difficult: public Internet stations and Internet cafés, some open 24 hours a day, are becoming more and more common. Prices differ from place to place, so **spend some time to find the best deal.** This isn't always readily apparent: a place might have higher rates, but because it belongs to a chain you won't be charged an initial flat fee again when you move to a different city that has the same chain. Some hotels have in-room modem lines, but, as with phones, using the hotel's line is relatively expensive. Always check modem rates before plugging in, and set your computer to ignore the dial tone. You may need an adapter for your computer for the European-style plugs. As always, if you are traveling with a laptop, carry a spare battery and an adapter. Never plug in your computer into any socket before asking about surge protection. IBM sells a pea-size modem tester that plugs into a telephone jack to check whether the line is safe to use.

CONSUMER PROTECTION

Most stores in Italy do not allow customers to return or exchange merchandise, even if a minor flaw in the product exists. Clothing stores are particularly inflexibe and will often not permit shoppers to try on shirts or blouses. Whether you're shopping for gifts or purchasing travel services, **pay with a major credit card** whenever possible, so you can cancel payment or get reimbursed if there's a problem (and you can provide documentation). If you're doing business with a particular company for the first time, **contact your local Better Business Bureau and the attorney general's offices** in your state and (for U.S. businesses) the company's home state as well. Have any complaints been filed? Finally, if you're buying a package or tour, always **consider travel insurance** that includes default coverage (⇨ Insurance).

🖪 BBBs **Council of Better Business Bureaus** ✉ 4200 Wilson Blvd., Suite 800, Arlington, VA 22203 ☎ 703/276-0100 🖷 703/525-8277 ⊕ www.bbb.org.

CRUISE TRAVEL

Several major cruise lines offer Mediterranean cruises that feature stops in Italy as well as Italy-only cruises. Cunard cruises in the Mediterranean with ports of call in Genoa, Livorno, Rome, and Lipari. Festival Cruises has a "Carnevale" cruise that sails from Venice to Malta, Tunisia, Sicily, and Croatia, returning to Venice in time for the Carnevale celebration. Mediterranean Shipping Cruises (MSC) sails in Sicily, Tunisia, the Balearic Islands, Spain, and France. Royal Olympic Cruises has multiple departures leaving from Venice with ports of call in Dubrovnik, Istanbul, Corfu, Mykonos, and Santorini.

To learn how to plan, choose, and book a cruise-ship voyage, consult *Fodor's FYI: Plan & Enjoy Your Cruise* (available in bookstores everywhere).

🖪 Cruise Lines **Cunard** ✉ 6100 Blue Lagoon Dr., Miami, FL 33126 ☎ 800/728-6275 in U.S. and Canada; 0800/0523840 in U.K.; 612/92506666 in Australia and New Zealand ⊕ www.cunardline.com. **Festival Cruises** ✉ Medov, via XX Settembre 29/7, 16121 Genoa ☎ 010/549810 ⊕ www.festivalcruises.com. **Mediterranean Shipping Cruises** ✉ Via A. Depretis 31, 80133 Naples ☎ 081/7942400 in Italy; 081/794211 elsewhere ⊕ www.msccruises.com. **Royal Olympic Cruises** ✉ 805 3rd Ave., New York, NY 10022-7513 ☎ 800/872-6400 in U.S. and Canada 🖷 888/662-6237 ⊕ www.royalolympiccruises.com.

CUSTOMS & DUTIES

When shopping abroad, **keep receipts** for all purchases. Upon reentering the country, **be ready to show customs officials what you've bought.** Pack purchases together in an easily accessible place. If you think a duty is incorrect, appeal the assessment. If you object to the way your clearance was handled, note the inspector's badge number. In either case, first ask to see a supervisor. If the problem isn't resolved, write to the appropriate authorities, beginning with the port director at your point of entry.

IN AUSTRALIA

Australian residents who are 18 or older may bring home A$400 worth of souvenirs and gifts (including jewelry), 250 cigarettes or 250 grams of cigars or other tobacco products, and 1,125 ml of alcohol (including wine, beer, and spirits). Residents under 18 may bring back A$200 worth of goods. Members of the same family traveling together may pool their allowances. Prohibited items include meat products. Seeds, plants, and fruits need to be declared upon arrival.

🖪 **Australian Customs Service** 🖭 Regional Director, Box 8, Sydney, NSW 2001 ☎ 02/9213-2000 or 1300/363263; 02/9364-7222 or 1800/803-006 quarantine-inquiry line 🖷 02/9213-4043 ⊕ www.customs.gov.au.

IN CANADA

Canadian residents who have been out of Canada for at least seven days may bring in C$750 worth of goods duty-free. If you've been away fewer than seven days but more than 48 hours, the duty-free allowance drops to C$200. If your trip lasts 24 to 48 hours, the allowance is C$50. You may not pool allowances with family members. Goods claimed under the C$750 exemption may follow you by mail; those claimed under the lesser exemptions must accompany you. Alcohol and tobacco products may be included in the seven-day and 48-hour exemptions but not in the 24-hour exemption. If you meet the age requirements of the province or territory through which you reenter Canada, you may bring in, duty-free, 1.5 liters of wine *or* 1.14 liters (40 imperial ounces) of liquor *or* 24 12-ounce cans or bottles of beer or ale. Also, if you meet the local age requirement for tobacco products, you may bring in, duty-free, 200 cigarettes and

50 cigars. Check ahead of time with the Canada Customs and Revenue Agency or the Department of Agriculture for policies regarding meat products, seeds, plants, and fruits.

You may send an unlimited number of gifts (only one gift per recipient, however) worth up to C$60 each duty-free to Canada. Label the package UNSOLICITED GIFT—VALUE UNDER $60. Alcohol and tobacco are excluded.

🇫 **Canada Customs and Revenue Agency** ✉ 2265 St. Laurent Blvd., Ottawa, Ontario K1G 4K3 ☎ 800/461-9999, 204/983-3500, or 506/636-5064 ⊕ www.ccra.gc.ca.

IN ITALY

Of goods obtained anywhere outside the EU, the allowances are (1) 200 cigarettes or 100 cigarillos (under 3 grams) or 50 cigars or 250 grams of tobacco; (2) 2 liters of still table wine or 1 liter of spirits over 22% volume; and (3) 50 milliliters of perfume and 250 milliliters of toilet water.

Of goods obtained (duty and tax paid) within another EU country, the allowances are (1) 800 cigarettes or 400 cigarillos (under 3 grams) or 200 cigars or 1 kilogram of tobacco; (2) 90 liters of still table wine or 10 liters of spirits over 22% volume or 20 liters of spirits under 22% volume or 110 liters of beer.

There is no quarantine period in Italy, so if you want to travel with Fido or Tiger, it's possible. Contact your nearest Italian consulate to find out what paperwork is needed for entry into Italy; generally, it is a certificate noting that the animal is healthy and up-do-date on its vaccinations. Keep in mind, however, that the United States has some stringent laws about reentry: pets must be free of all disease, especially those communicable to humans, and they must be vaccinated against rabies at least 30 days before returning. This means that if you are in Italy for a short-term stay, you must find a veterinarian or have your pet vaccinated before departure. (This law does not apply to puppies less than three months old.) Pets should arrive at the point of entry with a statement, in English, attesting to this fact.

🇮 **Ministero delle Finanze, Direzione Centrale dei Servizi Doganali, Divisione I** ✉ Via Carucci 71, 00143 Rome, Italy ☎ 06/50242117. **Dogana Sezione Viaggiatori** ✉ Customs, Aeroporto Leonardo da Vinci, Fiumicino 00054 Rome ☎ 06/65954343.

IN NEW ZEALAND

All homeward-bound residents may bring back NZ$700 worth of souvenirs and gifts; passengers may not pool their allowances, and children can claim only the concession on goods intended for their own use. For those 17 or older, the duty-free allowance also includes 4.5 liters of wine or beer; one 1,125-ml bottle of spirits; and either 200 cigarettes, 250 grams of tobacco, 50 cigars, *or* a combination of the three up to 250 grams. Meat products, seeds, plants, and fruits must be declared upon arrival to the Agricultural Services Department.

🇳 **New Zealand Customs** ✉ Head office: The Customhouse, 17–21 Whitmore St., Box 2218, Wellington ☎ 09/300-5399 or 0800/428-786 ⊕ www.customs.govt.nz.

IN THE U.K.

If you are a U.K. resident and your journey was wholly within the European Union, you probably won't have to pass through customs when you return to the United Kingdom. If you plan to bring back large quantities of alcohol or tobacco, check EU limits beforehand. In most cases, if you bring back more than 200 cigars, 3,200 cigarettes, 10 liters of spirits, 110 liters of beer, and/or 90 liters of wine, you have to declare the goods upon return.

🇭 **HM Customs and Excise** ✉ Portcullis House, 21 Cowbridge Rd. E, Cardiff CF11 9SS ☎ 0845/010-9000 or 0208/929-0152; 0208/929-6731 or 0208/910-3602 complaints ⊕ www.hmce.gov.uk.

IN THE U.S.

U.S. residents who have been out of the country for at least 48 hours may bring home, for personal use, $800 worth of foreign goods duty-free, as long as they haven't used the $800 allowance or any part of it in the past 30 days. This exemption may include 1 liter of alcohol (for travelers 21 and older), 200 cigarettes, and 100 non-Cuban cigars. Family members from the same household who are traveling together may pool their $800 personal exemptions. For fewer than 48 hours, the duty-free allowance drops to $200, which may include 50 cigarettes, 10 non-Cuban cigars, and 150 ml of alcohol (or 150 ml of perfume containing alcohol). The $200 allowance cannot be combined with other individuals' exemptions, and if you exceed it, the full value of all the goods will be taxed. Antiques, which the U.S. Bureau of Customs and Border Protection defines as objects more than 100 years old, enter duty-free, as do original works of art done entirely by hand, including paintings, drawings, and sculptures. This doesn't apply to folk art or handicrafts, which are in general dutiable.

You may also send packages home duty-free, with a limit of one parcel per addressee per day (except alcohol or tobacco products or perfume worth more than $5). You can mail up to $200 worth of goods for personal use; label the package PERSONAL USE and attach a list of its contents and their retail value. If the package contains your used personal belongings, mark it AMERICAN GOODS RETURNED to avoid paying duties. You may send up to $100 worth of goods as a gift; mark the package UNSOLICITED GIFT. Mailed items do not affect your duty-free allowance on your return.

To avoid paying duty on foreign-made high-ticket items you already own and will take on your trip, register them with Customs before you leave the country. Consider filing a Certificate of Registration for laptops, cameras, watches, and other digital devices identified with serial numbers or other permanent markings; you can keep the certificate for other trips. Otherwise, bring a sales receipt or insurance form to show that you owned the item before you left the United States.

U.S. Bureau of Customs and Border Protection ⊠ For inquiries and equipment registration, 1300 Pennsylvania Ave. NW, Washington, DC 20229 ⊕ www.customs.gov ☎ 202/354-1000 ⊠ For complaints, Customer Satisfaction Unit, 1300 Pennsylvania Ave. NW, Room 5.5D, Washington, DC 20229.

DISABILITIES & ACCESSIBILITY

Italy has only recently begun to provide facilities such as ramps, telephones, and rest rooms for people with disabilities; such things are still the exception, not the rule. Travelers' wheelchairs must be transported free of charge, according to Italian law, but the logistics of getting a wheelchair on and off trains and buses can make this requirement irrelevant. Seats are reserved for people with disabilities on public transportation, but few buses have lifts for wheelchairs. High, narrow steps for boarding trains create additional problems. At many monuments and museums, and even in some hotels and restaurants, architec-

tural barriers make access difficult. Wheelchair access to bathrooms in restaurants is nearly nonexistent. Capdarco or Roma per Tutti can provide information about events and services for disabled people.

Contact the nearest Italian consulate about bringing a guide dog into Italy. This requires an import license, a current certificate detailing the dog's inoculations, and a letter from your veterinarian certifying the dog's health.

Local Resources Capodarco ⌀ C/o Co.In Cooperative Integrate, Via Enrico Giglioli 54/a, Rome, 00169 ☎ 06/71290123 🖷 06/71290125. **Roma per Tutti** ⊠ Via di Torricola 87, 00178 Rome ☎ 06/71623919 🖷 06/71290125 ⊕ www.romapertutti.it.

LODGING

The Italian Government Travel Office (ENIT: ⇨ Visitor Information) can give you a list of hotels that provide access and addresses of Italian associations for travelers with disabilities.

Because Italian lodgings are often in buildings that are several hundred years old, many are not equipped with elevators. Many of them have steps up, or down, at the entrance. When booking a hotel, inquire about entranceways: ramps are still rare.

In Rome, the five-star Hotel de Russie has four rooms available for people who use wheelchairs. The Locarno, also near Piazza del Popolo, has one accessible room. A budget option is the Alimandi, near the Vatican.

The Hotel Excelsior in Florence is wheelchair accessible.

In Venice, the San Zulian and the luxurious Danieli both have two rooms that are wheelchair accessible.

In Milan, the Grand Hotel Duomo has a junior suite available for people who use wheelchairs. The equally luxurious and modern Westin Palace has two wheelchair-friendly rooms.

RESERVATIONS

When discussing accessibility with an operator or reservations agent, **ask hard questions.** Are there any stairs, inside *or* out? Are there grab bars next to the toilet *and* in the shower/tub? How wide is the doorway to the room? To the bathroom? For the most extensive facilities meeting the latest legal specifications, **opt for newer accommodations.** If you reserve through a toll-free number, consider also calling the hotel's local number to confirm the information from the central reservations office. Get confirmation in writing when you can.

SIGHTS & ATTRACTIONS

Getting around in Italy with a wheelchair is difficult but not impossible. In Rome, for example, the Museo Vaticani and the Museo Nazionale di Castel Sant'Angelo are accessible (but the Colosseum and Forum are not). In Florence, the Uffizi, Palazzo Pitti, Duomo, Baptistery, and the Accademia are all accessible. Local tourist offices provide maps and lists, rated on degrees of ease and difficulty, of banks, supermarkets, sites, hotels, and restaurants.

TRANSPORTATION

Most buses in Italy cannot accommodate wheelchairs; only a few have special ramps. A handful of subway stops in the Rome subway system are accessible to people who use wheelchairs. Local tourist offices are sometimes helpful with information about mass transit.

Getting around in Venice on the vaporetti is relatively easy; however, when *acqua alta* (high water) happens, as it does sporadically between October and April, movement for people who use wheelchairs becomes virtually impossible.

More than 150 railroad stations throughout the country have a reception service for people who use wheelchairs; this service must be booked 24 hours in advance. To do this, consult a travel agency or go to www.trenitalia.com, select the Italian-language version, and click on "servizi per i disabili." The ferry line Tirrenia has two wheelchair-accessible cabins on their routes to Sardinia.

🚩 Complaints **Aviation Consumer Protection Division** (⇨ Air Travel) or airline-related problems. **Departmental Office of Civil Rights** ✉ For general inquiries, U.S. Department of Transportation, S-30, 400 7th St. SW, Room 10215, Washington, DC 20590 ☎ 202/366-4648 🖷 202/366-9371 ⊕ www.dot. gov/ost/docr/index.htm. **Disability Rights Section** ✉ NYAV, U.S. Department of Justice, Civil Rights Division, 950 Pennsylvania Ave. NW, Washington, DC 20530 ☎ ADA information line 202/514-0301; 800/ 514-0301; 202/514-0383 TTY; 800/514-0383 TTY ⊕ www.ada.gov. **U.S. Department of Transporta-**

tion Hotline ☎ For disability-related air-travel problems, 800/778-4838 or 800/455-9880 TTY.

TRAVEL AGENCIES

In the United States, the Americans with Disabilities Act requires that travel firms serve the needs of all travelers. Some agencies specialize in working with people with disabilities.

🚩 Travelers with Mobility Problems **Access Adventures** ✉ 206 Chestnut Ridge Rd., Scottsville, NY 14624 ☎ 585/889-9096 ✉ dltravel@prodigy.net, run by a former physical-rehabilitation counselor. **CareVacations** ✉ No. 5, 5110-50 Ave., Leduc, Alberta, Canada, T9E 6V4 ☎ 780/986-6404 or 877/ 478-7827 🖷 780/986-8332 ⊕ www.carevacations. com, for group tours and cruise vacations. **Flying Wheels Travel** ✉ 143 W. Bridge St., Box 382, Owatonna, MN 55060 ☎ 507/451-5005 🖷 507/451-1685 ⊕ www.flyingwheelstravel.com.

DISCOUNTS & DEALS

Be a smart shopper and **compare all your options** before making decisions. A plane ticket bought with a promotional coupon from travel clubs, coupon books, and direct-mail offers or purchased on the Internet may not be cheaper than the least expensive fare from a discount ticket agency. And always keep in mind that what you get is just as important as what you save.

DISCOUNT RESERVATIONS

To save money, **look into discount reservations services** with Web sites and toll-free numbers, which use their buying power to get a better price on hotels, airline tickets (⇨ Air Travel), even car rentals. When booking a room, always **call the hotel's local toll-free number** (if one is available) rather than the central reservations number—you'll often get a better price. Always ask about special packages or corporate rates.

When shopping for the best deal on hotels and car rentals, **look for guaranteed exchange rates,** which protect you against a falling dollar. With your rate locked in, you won't pay more, even if the price goes up in the local currency.

🚩 Airline Tickets **Air 4 Less** ☎ 800/AIR4LESS, low-fare specialist.

🚩 Hotel Rooms **Accommodations Express** ☎ 800/444-7666 or 800/277-1064 ⊕ www. accommodationsexpress.com. **Hotels.com** ☎ 214/ 369-1246 or 800/246-8357 ⊕ www.hotels.com. International Marketing & Travel Concepts ☎ 800/790-4682 ⊕ www.imtc-travel.com. **Steigenberger Reservation Service** ☎ 800/223-5652 ⊕ www.srsworldhotels.com. **Travel Interlink** ☎ 800/888-5898 ⊕ www.travelinterlink.com. **Turbotrip.com** ☎ 800/473-7829 ⊕ www.turbotrip.com.

PACKAGE DEALS

Don't confuse packages and guided tours. When you buy a package, you travel on your own, just as though you had planned the trip yourself. Fly/drive packages, which combine airfare and car rental, are often a good deal. In cities, ask the local visitor's bureau about hotel packages that include tickets to major museum exhibits or other special events. If you **buy a rail/drive pass,** you may save on train tickets and car rentals. All Eurailpass holders get a discount on Eurostar fares through the Channel Tunnel and often receive reduced rates for buses, hotels, ferries, and car rentals.

EATING & DRINKING

The restaurants we list are the cream of the crop in each price category. Properties indicated by an ✕🏠 are lodging establishments whose restaurant warrants a special trip.

CATEGORY	COST
$$$$	over €22
$$$	€17–€22
$$	€12–€17
$	€7–€12
¢	under €7

Prices are for a second course (secondo piatto) and are given in euros.

A few pointers on Italian dining etiquette: menus are posted outside most restaurants (in English in tourist areas); if not, you might step inside and ask to take a look at the menu, but don't ask for a table unless you intend to stay. Italians take their food as it is listed on the menu, seldom making special requests such as "dressing on the side" or "hold the olive oil." If you have special dietary needs, though, make them known, and they can usually be accommodated. Although mineral water makes its way to almost every table, you can always order a carafe of tap water (acqua di rubinetto or acqua semplice) instead, but keep in mind that such water is highly chlorinated.

Spaghetti should be eaten with a fork rolled against the side of the dish, although a little help from a spoon will not horrify the locals

the way cutting spaghetti into little pieces might. Wiping your bowl clean with a (small) piece of bread is fine in less formal eateries. Order your espresso (Italians almost never drink a cappuccino after breakfast) after dessert, not with it. When you are ready for it, ask for the check (il conto): unless it's well past closing time, no waiter will put a bill on your table without your having asked first. Don't ask for a doggy bag.

MEALS & SPECIALTIES

What's the difference between a ristorante and a trattoria? Can you order food at an enoteca? Can you go to a restaurant just for a snack, or order just a salad at a pizzeria? The following definitions should help.

Not too long ago, restaurants tended to be more elegant and expensive than trattorie and osterie, which served more traditional, home-style fare in an atmosphere to match. But the distinction has blurred considerably, and an osteria in the center of town might be far fancier (and pricier) than a ristorante across the street. In all these types of places, you are generally expected to order at least a two-course meal, such as: a *primo* (first course) and a *secondo* (main course) or a *contorno* (vegetable side dish); an antipasto (starter) followed by either primo or secondo; or a secondo and a *dolce* (dessert).

In an *enoteca* (wine bar) or pizzeria, it's common to order just one dish. An enoteca menu is often limited to a selection of cheese, cured meats, salads, and desserts, but if there's a kitchen, you'll also find vegetable soups, pasta, meat, and fish. Most pizzerias don't offer just pizza, and although the other dishes on the menu are supposed to be starters, there's no harm in skipping the pizza. The typical pizzeria fare includes *affettati misti* (selection of cured pork), simple salads, various kinds of bruschetta and *crostino* (similar to bruschetta, sometimes topped with cheese and broiled) and, in Rome, *fritti* (deep-fried finger food) such as *olive ascolane* (green olives with a meat stuffing) and *suppli* (rice balls stuffed with mozzarella). All pizzerias serve fresh fruit, ice cream, and simple desserts.

Throughout the country, the handiest and least expensive places for a quick snack between sights are probably bars, cafés, and pizza *al taglio* (by the slice) spots. Bars in Italy are primarily places to get a coffee and a bite to eat, rather than drinking establishments. Most have a selection of *panini* (sandwiches, often warmed up on the griddle—*piastra*) and *tramezzini* (sandwiches served on untoasted white bread triangles). In larger cities, bars also serve prepared salads, fruit salads, cold pasta dishes, and yogurt around lunchtime. Most bars offer beer and a variety of alcohol as well as wines by the glass (sometimes good but more often mediocre). A café (*caffè* in Italian) is like a bar but usually with more tables to sit down at. Pizza at a café is to be avoided—it's usually frozen and reheated in a microwave. If you place your order at the counter, ask if you can sit down: some places charge considerably more for table service, others do not. In self-service bars and cafés, it's good manners to clean up your table before you leave. Note that in some places you have to pay a cashier, then place your order and leave your *scontrino* (receipt) on the counter. Pizza al taglio shops sell pizza by weight: just point out which kind you want and how much. Very few pizza al taglio shops have seating.

Italian cuisine is still largely regional. Ask what the local specialties are: by all means, have spaghetti *alla carbonara* (spaghetti with bacon and eggs) in Rome, pizza in Rome or Naples, *crespelle* (savory crepes) in Florence and in Tuscany, truffles in the Piedmont, and risotto *alla milanese* in Milan.

MEALTIMES

Breakfast (*la colazione*) is usually served from 7 to 10:30, lunch (*il pranzo*) from 12:30 to 2:30, dinner (*la cena*) from 7:30 to 10. Peak times are usually 1:30 for lunch and 9 for dinner. Enoteche and bacari (wine bars) are open also in the morning and late afternoon for a snack at the counter. Most pizzerias open at 8 PM and close around midnight–1 AM, or later in summer and on weekends. Most bars and cafés are open from 7 AM until 8–9 PM; a few stay open until midnight or so.

Unless otherwise noted, the restaurants listed in this guide are open daily for lunch and dinner.

PAYING

Prices for goods and services in Italy include tax. Restaurant menu prices usually include service (*servizio*) unless indicated on the menu (in which case it is added on to the prices listed on the menu). It is cus-tomary to leave a small tip (one euro to 10%) in appreciation of good service. Tips are always given in cash. Most restaurants charge a separate "cover" charge per person, usually listed on the menu as *"pane e coperto."* It should be a modest charge (€1–€2.50 per person), except at the most expensive restaurants. Some restaurants instead charge for bread, which should be brought to you (and paid for) only if you order it. Whenever in doubt, ask about the servizio, pane, and coperto policy upon ordering to avoid unpleasant discussions about payment later. The price of fish dishes is often given by weight (before cooking), so the price you see on the menu is for 100 grams of fish, not for the whole dish. An average fish portion is about 350 grams. Tuscan *bistecca fiorentina* (florentine steak) is also often priced by weight.

Major credit cards are widely accepted in Italian eating establishments, though cash is usually the preferred, and sometimes the only, means of payment. More restaurants take Visa and MasterCard than American Express. Remember that there's no line to write a tip on the receipt; you will be presented with a slip that includes only the cost of the meal. Tips are made in cash.

RESERVATIONS & DRESS

Reservations are always a good idea in restaurants and trattorie, especially over weekends and holidays. We mention them only when they are essential or not accepted. Book as far ahead as you can, and reconfirm as soon as you arrive in town. Large parties should always call ahead to check the reservations policy.) Pizzerias and enoteche usually accept reservations only for large groups. We mention dress only when men are required to wear a jacket or a jacket and tie. But unless they are at a sea resort eating outdoors and perfectly tanned, Italian men never wear shorts or running shoes in a restaurant—no matter how humble—or in an enoteca. The same "rules" apply to ladies' casual shorts, running shoes, and plastic sandals. Shorts are acceptable in pizzerias and cafés.

WINE, BEER & SPIRITS

The grape has been cultivated in Italy since the time of the Etruscans, and Italians justifiably take pride in their local product. Though almost every region produces good-quality wine, the two most renowned areas are Piedmont and Tuscany.

If you're in a restaurant or trattoria, ask your waiter about the house wine; sometimes it's very good indeed, sometimes it isn't. Wine in Italy is considerably less expensive than almost anywhere else. Beer, oddly, is more expensive than a glass of wine, and though Italy does produce beer, it's not nearly as notable as its wine.

Beer, wine, and spirits can be purchased in any bar, grocery store, or enoteca, any day of the week. There's no minimum drinking age in Italy. Italian children begin drinking wine mixed with water at mealtimes when they are teens or even younger.

Many bars have their own *aperitivo della casa* (house aperitif). Italians are most imaginative with their mixed drinks—always shaken, never blended.

ELECTRICITY

To use electric-powered equipment purchased in the United States or Canada, **bring a converter and adapter.** The electrical current in Italy is 220 volts, 50 cycles alternating current (AC); wall outlets take Continental-type plugs, with two or three round prongs.

If your appliances are dual-voltage, you'll need only an adapter. Don't use 110-volt outlets marked FOR SHAVERS ONLY for high-wattage appliances such as blow-dryers. Most laptops operate equally well on 110 and 220 volts and so require only an adapter.

EMBASSIES

∄ Australia **Australian Embassy** ✉ Via Alessandria 215, 00198 Rome ☎ 06/852721 ⊕ www.australian-embassy.it.
∄ Canada **Canadian Embassy** ✉ Via G.B. de Rossi 27, 00161 Rome ☎ 06/445981 ⊕ www.dfait-maeci.gc.ca/canadaeuropa/italy.
∄ New Zealand **New Zealand Embassy** ✉ Via Zara 28, 00198 Rome ☎ 06/4417171.
∄ United Kingdom **British Embassy** ✉ Via XX Settembre 80A, 00187 Rome ☎ 06/42200001 ⊕ www.britain.it.
∄ United States **U.S. Embassy** ✉ Via Veneto 121 00187 Rome ☎ 06/46741 ⊕ www.usembassy.it.

EMERGENCIES

No matter where you are in Italy, **dial 113 for all emergencies,** including the police, or find somebody (your concierge, a passerby) who will call for you, as not all 113 operators speak English; the Italian word to use to draw people's attention in an emergency is *"Aiuto!"* (Help!, pronounced "ah-YOU-toh"). *"Pronto soccorso"* means "first aid" and when said to an operator will get you an *ambulanza* (ambulance). If you just need a doctor, you should ask for *"un medico"*; most hotels will be able to refer you to a local doctor. Don't forget to ask the doctor for *una ricevuta* (an invoice) to show to your insurance company in order to get a reimbursement. Other useful Italian words to use in an emergency are *"Al fuoco!"* (Fire!, pronounced "ahl fuh-WOE-co"), and *"Al ladro!"* (Follow the thief!, pronounced "ahl LAH-droh").

Italy has a national police force *(carabinieri)* as well as local police *(polizia).* Both are armed and have the power to arrest and investigate crimes. **Always report the loss of your passport to either the carabinieri or the police,** as well as to your embassy. Local traffic officers are known as *vigili* (though their official name is *polizia municipale*)—they are responsible for, among other things, giving out parking tickets and clamping cars. They wear white (in summer) or black uniforms and many are women. Should you find yourself involved in a minor car accident in town, you should contact the vigili. A country-wide toll-free number is used to call the carabinieri in case of emergency.
∄ Carabinieri ☎ 112. Emergencies ☎ 113.

ENGLISH-LANGUAGE MEDIA

BOOKS

Most major cities have bookstores that cater to an English-reading clientele. The nationwide chain Feltrinelli International, for example, has a large selection of English-language books (pricier than at home since they are all imported). Rome has several independent, English-language bookstores, as do several other cities such as Florence.

NEWSPAPERS & MAGAZINES

The best source for news in English is the *International Herald Tribune,* which is sold at most news agents in the major cities and major tourist towns. *USA Today,* and most of the London newspapers are also available. You can find the Sunday *New York Times* in some places, but be prepared to pay €12 for it. Various national versions of *Vogue* are obtainable, as are *Time, Newsweek, Elle, The Economist, InStyle, The New Yorker, Vanity Fair, The Tatler,* and *People,* among others. But they don't come cheap: *Vanity Fair,* for example, costs more than €8.

Rome's English-language bimonthly, *Wanted in Rome* lists events.

RADIO & TELEVISION

Radio broadcasts are almost completely in Italian. Unless you have satellite TV (with access to CNN or SkyNews), or unless you speak Italian, Italian television is completely inaccessible, as everything is either spoken in Italian or dubbed into Italian. MTV is sometimes broadcast in English with Italian subtitles—but that's the exception, not the rule. Vatican Radio broadcasts world news in English three times a day throughout Italy, with Vatican news included.

ETIQUETTE & BEHAVIOR

Italy is a country teeming with churches, and many of them have significant works of art in them. Because they are places of worship, care should be taken with appropriate dress. Shorts, spaghetti straps, sleeveless garments: these are taboo at St. Peter's in Rome, and in many other churches throughout Italy. So, too, are short shorts anywhere. When touring churches—especially in the summer when it's hot and no sleeves are desirable—it's wise to carry a sweater, or scarf, to wrap around your shoulders before entering the church. **Do not enter a church with food,** and do not drink from your water bottle while inside. **Do not go in if a service is in progress.** And if you have a cellular phone, **turn it off before entering.**

Italians who are friends greet each other with a kiss, usually first on the right cheek, and then on the left. When you meet a new person, shake hands.

BUSINESS ETIQUETTE

Showing up on time for business appointments is expected in Italy, especially in Milan. Business is done more over lunch than dinner. Business cards are used throughout Italy, and business suits are the norm for both men and women.

GAY & LESBIAN TRAVEL

Same-sex couples traveling in major cities and beach resorts should meet with no raised eyebrows on the part of the locals. However, overt displays of affection in public are rare. Gay bars, mostly catering to men (and some of which ban women), can be found in all major cities. Some mainstream bars and nightclubs have a gay night during the week; inquire at the local tourist office.

Gay- & Lesbian-Friendly Travel Agencies Different Roads Travel ⊠ 8383 Wilshire Blvd., Suite 520, Beverly Hills, CA 90211 ☎ 323/651-5557 or 800/429-8747 (Ext. 14 for both) ⊟ 323/651-3678 ✉ lgernert@tzell.com. **Kennedy Travel** ⊠ 130 W. 42nd St., Suite 401, New York, NY 10036 ☎ 212/840-8659 or 800/237-7433 ⊟ 212/730-2269 ⊕ www.kennedytravel.com. **Now, Voyager** ⊠ 4406 18th St., San Francisco, CA 94114 ☎ 415/626-1169 or 800/255-6951 ⊟ 415/626-8626 ⊕ www.nowvoyager.com. **Skylink Travel and Tour** ⊠ 1455 N. Dutton Ave., Suite A, Santa Rosa, CA 95401 ☎ 707/546-9888 or 800/225-5759 ⊟ 707/636-0951, serving lesbian travelers.

Local Contacts & Community Centers Azione Gay e Lesbica ⟳ C/o Andrea del Sarto, Via Manara 12, Florence ☎ 055/671298 ⊕ www.azionegayelesbica.it. **Circolo di Cultura Omosessuale Mario Mieli** ⊠ Via Corinto 5, Rome ☎ 06/59604622 ⊕ www.mariomieli.org.

GUIDEBOOKS

Plan well and you won't be sorry. Guidebooks are excellent tools—and you can take them with you. You may want to check out Fodor's regional gold guides: *Fodor's Rome; Fodor's Florence, Tuscany and Umbria; Fodor's Naples and the Amalfi Coast;* and *Fodor's Venice and the Veneto.* Or study color-photo-illustrated guides such as *Fodor's Exploring Italy, Exploring Rome, Exploring Venice,* and *Exploring Tuscany,* thorough on culture and history; *Escape to the Amalfi Coast, Escape to the Riviera,* and *Escape to Tuscany,* highlighting unique experiences; or pocket-size *Citypack Florence, Citypack Rome,* and *Citypack Venice,* which include supersize city maps. *Fodor's Holy Rome,* also with color photos, explores the city's Christian heritage. All are available at online retailers and bookstores everywhere.

HEALTH

The Centers for Disease Control and Prevention (CDC) in Atlanta caution that most of Southern Europe is in the "inter-mediate" range for risk of contracting traveler's diarrhea. Part of this risk may be attributed to an increased consumption of olive oil and wine, which can have a laxa-tive effect on stomachs used to a different diet. The CDC also advises all interna-tional travelers to swim only in chlori-nated swimming pools, unless they are absolutely certain the local beaches and freshwater lakes are not contaminated. Italy's private beaches are very clean, the public ones, less so.

The Italian desire for beef has not abated, and it is eaten with gusto. Due to concern about mad cow disease, traditional dishes such as *osso buco* (braised veal shank), oxtail, offal specialties, and *bistecca alla fiorentina* have been banned by the EU. By June, 2003, however, the EU is expected to lift the ban. (In Italy, over 90 cases of mad cow have been detected in cows; one case in a person.) *Vitello* (veal), *vitellone* (young beef), and *manzo* (beef) are consid-ered safe to eat by both the Italian govern-ment and the European Union (these are cuts that don't come in touch with spinal marrow).

OVER-THE-COUNTER REMEDIES

It's always best to **travel with your own tried and true medicines.** The regulations regarding what medicines require a pre-scription are not likely to be the exactly the same in Italy and in your home coun-try—all the more reason to bring what you need with you. Aspirin (*l'aspirina*) can be purchased at any pharmacy, but Tylenol and Advil are unavailable.

HIKING & WALKING

Italy has many good places to hike and an extensive network of long trails. The Sen-tiero Italia is a national trail running from Reggio Calabria on the toe of the Italy's boot to the central section of the Apennine mountains. There are plans to lengthen it farther north and to the western Alps, and from there to the Dolomites and Udine in the Friuli region. For detailed information on the Sentiero Italia contact the CAI (Club Alpino Italiano) headquarters or local offices. Local tourist information of-fices can also be helpful.

🚶 Hiking Organizations **CAI** ✉ Via Petrella 19, 20124 Milan ☎ 02/2057231 🖷 02/205723201.

🚶 Hiking & Walking Tours **Abercrombie & Kent** (⇨ Group Tours, Super-Deluxe). **Above the Clouds Trekking** 🖃 Box 388, Hinesburg, VT 15461 ☎ 802/482-4848 or 800/233-4499 🖷 802/482-5011. **Back-roads** (⇨ Bike Travel). **Butterfield & Robinson** (⇨ Bike Travel). **Ciclismo Classico** (⇨ Bike Travel). **Country Walkers** 🖃 Box 180, Waterbury, VT 05676-0180 ☎ 802/464-9255 or 800/464-9255 🖷 802/244-5661 ⊕ www.counrywalkers.com. **Euro-Bike Tours** (⇨ Bike Travel). **Italian Connection, Walking & Culinary Tours** ✉ 11 Fairway Dr., Suite 210, Ed-monton, Alberta, Canada ☎ 800/462-7911 ⊕ www.italian-connection.com. **Mountain Travel-Sobek** ✉ 6420 Fairmount Ave., El Cerrito, CA, 94530 ☎ 510/527-8100 or 888/687-6235 🖷 510/525-7710 ⊕ www.mtsobek.com. **Uniquely Europe/Europe Express** (⇨ Bike Travel). **Wilderness Travel** ✉ 1102 9th St., Berkeley, CA 94710 ☎ 510/558-2488 or 800/368-2794 🖷 510/558-2489 ⊕ www.wildernesstravel.com.

HOLIDAYS

If you can avoid it, don't travel at all in Italy in August, when much of the popula-tion is on the move, especially around Fer-ragosto, the August 15 national holiday, when cities such as Rome and Milan are deserted and many restaurants and shops are closed. (Of course, with residents away on vacation, this makes crowds less of a bother for tourists.)

National holidays include January 1 (New Year's Day); January 6 (Epiphany); April 20 and April 21 (Easter Sun. and Mon.); April 25 (Liberation Day); May 1 (Labor Day or May Day); June 2 (Festival of the Republic), August 15 (Assumption of Mary, better known as Ferragosto); November 1 (All Saints' Day); December 8 (Immaculate Conception); December 25 and 26 (Christmas Day and Boxing Day).

The feast days of patron saints are ob-served locally. Many businesses and shops may be closed in Florence, Genoa, and Turin on June 24 (St. John the Baptist); in Rome on June 29 (Sts. Peter and Paul); in Palermo on July 15 (St. Rosalia); in Naples on September 19 (San Gennaro); in Bologna on October 4 (San Petronio); in Trieste on November 3 (San Giusto); and in Milan on December 7 (St. Ambrose). Venice's feast of St. Mark is April 25, the same as Liberation Day, so the Madonna della Salute on November 21 makes up for the lost holiday. (*Also see* Festivals and Seasonal Events *under* When to Go.)

INSURANCE

The most useful travel-insurance plan is a comprehensive policy that includes coverage for trip cancellation and interruption, default, trip delay, and medical expenses (with a waiver for preexisting conditions).

Without insurance you'll lose all or most of your money if you cancel your trip, regardless of the reason. Default insurance covers you if your tour operator, airline, or cruise line goes out of business. Trip-delay covers expenses that arise because of bad weather or mechanical delays. Study the fine print when comparing policies.

If you're traveling internationally, a key component of travel insurance is coverage for medical bills incurred if you get sick on the road. Such expenses aren't generally covered by Medicare or private policies. U.K. residents can buy a travel-insurance policy valid for most vacations taken during the year in which it's purchased (but check preexisting-condition coverage). British and Australian citizens need extra medical coverage when traveling overseas.

Always **buy travel policies directly from the insurance company**; if you buy them from a cruise line, airline, or tour operator that goes out of business you probably won't be covered for the agency or operator's default, a major risk. Before making any purchase, **review your existing health and home-owner's policies** to find what they cover away from home.

Travel Insurers In the U.S.: **Access America** ⊠ 6600 W. Broad St., Richmond, VA 23230 ☎ 800/284-8300 🖶 804/673-1491 or 800/346-9265 ⊕ www.accessamerica.com. **Travel Guard International** ⊠ 1145 Clark St., Stevens Point, WI 54481 ☎ 715/345-0505 or 800/826-1300 🖶 800/955-8785 ⊕ www.travelguard.com.

Insurance Information In the U.K.: **Association of British Insurers** ⊠ 51 Gresham St., London EC2V 7HQ ☎ 020/7600-3333 🖶 020/7696-8999 ⊕ www.abi.org.uk. In Canada: **RBC Insurance** ⊠ 6880 Financial Dr., Mississauga, Ontario L5N 7Y5 ☎ 800/565-3129 🖶 905/813-4704 ⊕ www.rbcinsurance.com. In Australia: **Insurance Council of Australia** ⊠ Insurance Enquiries and Complaints, Level 3, 56 Pitt St., Sydney, NSW 2000 ☎ 1300/363683 or 02/9251-4456 🖶 02/9251-4453 ⊕ www.iecltd.com.au. In New Zealand: **Insurance Council of New Zealand** ⊠ Level 7, 111-115 Customhouse Quay, Box 474, Wellington ☎ 04/472-5230 🖶 04/473-3011 ⊕ www.icnz.org.nz.

LANGUAGE

In the main tourist cities, the language barrier is not a big problem. Most hotels have English speakers at their reception desks, and you can always find someone who speaks at least a little English otherwise. Remember that the Italian language is pronounced as it is written (many Italians try to speak English by enunciating every syllable, with disconcerting results). You may run into a language barrier in the countryside, but a phrase book and close attention to the Italians' astonishing use of pantomime and expressive gestures will go a long way. Try to **master a few phrases for daily use;** see the back of this book for a list of rudimentary terms.

LANGUAGES FOR TRAVELERS

A phrase book and language-tape set can help get you started. *Fodor's Italian for Travelers* (available at bookstores everywhere) is excellent.

LODGING

The lodgings we list are the cream of the crop in each price category. We always list the facilities that are available, but we don't specify whether they cost extra; when pricing accommodations, always ask what's included and what costs extra. Properties are assigned price categories based on the range between their least and most expensive standard double room at high season (excluding holidays) to the most expensive. Properties marked ✕⌂ are lodging establishments whose restaurants warrant a special trip. Assume that hotels operate on the **European Plan** (EP, with no meals) unless we specify that they use the **Continental Plan** (CP, with a Continental breakfast), **Modified American Plan** (MAP, with breakfast and dinner), or the **Full American Plan** (FAP, with all meals).

CATEGORY	MAIN CITIES	ELSEWHERE
$$$$	over € 300	over €210
$$$	€225-€300	€160-€210
$$	€150-€225	€110-€160
$	€75-€150	€60-€110
¢	under €75	under €60

Prices are for two people in a standard double room in high season, including tax and service, and are given in euros. "Main cities" are Florence, Milan, Rome, and Venice.

APARTMENT & VILLA [OR HOUSE] RENTALS

If you want a home base that's roomy enough for a family and comes with cooking facilities, **consider a furnished rental.** These can save you money, especially if you're traveling with a group. Home-exchange directories sometimes list rentals as well as exchanges.

Local Agents Homes International ✉ Via Bissolati 20, 00187 Rome ☎ 06/4881800 🖷 06/4881808 ✍ homesint@tin.it. **Property International** ✉ Viale Aventino 79, 00153 Rome ☎ 06/5743170 🖷 06/5743182 ✍ Property.rm@flashnet.it.

International Agents At Home Abroad ✉ 405 E. 56th St., Suite 6H, New York, NY 10022 ☎ 212/421-9165 🖷 212/752-1591 🌐 www.athomeabroadinc.com. **Drawbridge to Europe** ✉ 98 Granite St., Ashland, OR 97520 ☎ 541/482-7778 or 888/268-1148 🖷 541/482-7779 🌐 www.drawbridgetoeurope.com. **Hideaways International** ✉ 767 Islington St., Portsmouth, NH 03802 ☎ 603/430-4433 or 800/843-4433 🖷 603/430-4444 🌐 www.hideaways.com, membership $129. **Hometours International** ✉ 1108 Scottie La., Knoxville, TN 37919 ☎ 865/690-8484 or 866/367-4668 🌐 http://thor.he.net/~hometour/. **Interhome** ✉ 1990 N.E. 163rd St., Suite 110, North Miami Beach, FL 33162 ☎ 305/940-2299 or 800/882-6864 🖷 305/940-2911 🌐 www.interhome.us. **Solemar** ✉ 1990 N.E. 163rd St., Suite 110, North Miami Beach, FL 33162 ☎ 305/940-2299 or 800/882-6864 🖷 305/940-2911 🌐 www.visit-toscana.com. **Vacation Home Rentals Worldwide** ✉ 235 Kensington Ave., Norwood, NJ 07648 ☎ 201/767-9393 or 800/633-3284 🖷 201/767-5510 🌐 www.vhrww.com. **Villanet** ✉ 1251 N.W. 116th St., Seattle, WA 98177 ☎ 206/417-3444 or 800/964-1891 🖷 206/417-1832 🌐 www.rentavilla.com. **Villas and Apartments Abroad** ✉ 370 Lexington Ave., Suite 1401, New York, NY 10017 ☎ 212/897-5045 or 800/433-3020 🖷 212/897-5039 🌐 www.ideal-villas.com. **Villas International** ✉ 4340 Redwood Hwy., Suite D309, San Rafael, CA 94903 ☎ 415/499-9490 or 800/221-2260 🖷 415/499-9491 🌐 www.villasintl.com.

Local Agents Cuendet USA ✉ 165 Chestnut St., Allendale, NJ 07041 ☎ 201/327-2333. **Rentvillas. com** ✉ 700 E. Main St., Ventura, CA 93001 ☎ 800/726-6702 🖷 805/641-1630 🌐 www.rentvillas.com. **Vacanze in Italia** ✉ 22 Railroad St., Great Barrington, MA 01230 ☎ 413/528-6610 🌐 www.homeabroad.com.

Rental Listings *Wanted in Rome* is a bi-monthly magazine with extensive listings for short-term rentals in Italy. Another good source for rentals is *EYP*, the English yellow pages for Italy, available at English bookstores.

In Rome *Wanted in Rome* ✉ Via dei Delfini 17, 00186 Rome Italy ☎ 06/6790190 🖷 06/6783798 🌐 www.wantedinrome.com. *EYP* 🌐 www.intoitaly.it. **In the U.K. CV Travel** ✉ 43 Cadogan St., London SW3 2PR, England ☎ 020/7581-0851. **Magic of Italy** ✉ 227 Shepherds Bush Rd., London W6 7AS, England ☎ 020/8748-7575.

CAMPING

Camping is particularly prevalent in beach towns (and Italy has many of them) and in the mountains. Campgrounds are generally crowded in summer and vary in amenities depending on the place: some have showers, toilets, sinks, bars, restaurants, pools, and shade trees.

Sleeping on the beach is illegal in Italy, as is camping in farmers' fields or in the woods, which is not to say that people don't do it. Sicily and its satellite islands have excellent summer camping facilities. The two best are El Bahira, in San Vito Lo Capo, and Bazia, in Furnari Marina, west of Milazzo.

FARM HOLIDAYS & AGRITOURISM

Rural accommodations in the *agriturismo* (agritourism) are working farms or vineyards, often with stone farmhouses that accommodate a number of guests. Contact local APT tourist offices, or you can buy *Agriturism*, compiled by Agriturist, which includes more than 1,600 farms in Italy. Although it's available in Italian only from major bookstores, pictures and the use of international symbols describing facilities make the guide a good tool to use.

Agencies Italy Farm Holidays ✉ 547 Martling Ave., Tarrytown, NY 10591 ☎ 914/631-7880 🖷 914/631-8831 🌐 www.italyfarmholidays.com.

HOME EXCHANGES

If you would like to exchange your home for someone else's, **join a home-exchange organization,** which will send you its updated listings of available exchanges for a year and will include your own listing in at least one of them. It's up to you to make specific arrangements.

Exchange Clubs HomeLink International ✉ Box 47747, Tampa, FL 33647 ☎ 813/975-9825 or 800/638-3841 🖷 813/910-8144 🌐 www.homelink.org; $110 yearly for a listing, on-line access, and catalog; $40 without catalog. **Intervac U.S.** ✉ 30 Corte San Fernando, Tiburon, CA 94920 ☎ 800/756-4663 🖷 415/435-7440 🌐 www.intervacus.com;

$105 yearly for a listing, on-line access, and a catalog; $50 without catalog.

HOSTELS

Hostels in Italy are found both in remote towns and large cities, the latter offering dozens. While usually very clean, they range from the barebones (no linen) to near bed and breakfasts. Many offer rooms for couples or families. When booking, inquire about lights-out time and the noise level—some hostels with a young clientele are lax in enforcing evening quiet hours.

No matter what your age, you can **save on lodging costs by staying at hostels.** In some 4,500 locations in more than 70 countries around the world, Hostelling International (HI), the umbrella group for a number of national youth-hostel associations, offers single-sex, dorm-style beds and, at many hostels, rooms for couples and family accommodations. Membership in any HI national hostel association, open to travelers of all ages, allows you to stay in HI-affiliated hostels at member rates; one-year membership is about $28 for adults (C$35 for a two-year minimum membership in Canada, £13.50 in the United Kingdom, A$52 in Australia, and NZ$40 in New Zealand); hostels charge about $10–$30 per night. Members have priority if the hostel is full; they're also eligible for discounts around the world, even on rail and bus travel in some countries.
Organizations Hostelling International–USA ✉ 8401 Colesville Rd., Suite 600, Silver Spring, MD 20910 ☎ 301/495-1240 🖷 301/495-6697 ⊕ www. hiayh.org. **Hostelling International–Canada** ✉ 400–205 Catherine St., Ottawa, Ontario K2P 1C3 ☎ 613/237-7884 or 800/663-5777 🖷 613/237-7868 ⊕ www.hihostels.ca. **YHA England and Wales** ✉ Trevelyan House, Dimple Rd., Matlock, Derbyshire DE4 3YH, U.K. ☎ 0870/870-8808 🖷 0870/770-6127 ⊕ www.yha.org.uk. **YHA Australia** ✉ 422 Kent St., Sydney, NSW 2001 ☎ 02/9261-1111 🖷 02/9261-1969 ⊕ www.yha.com.au. **YHA New Zealand** ✉ Level 3, 193 Cashel St., Box 436, Christchurch ☎ 03/379-9970 or 0800/278-299 🖷 03/365-4476 ⊕ www.yha.org.nz.

HOTELS

All Italian hotels are graded on a star scale, from five stars for the most deluxe hotels to one star for the most modest. This system has no relation to the stars you'll find in this book denoting highly recommended properties; itís administered by local boards on the basis of a compli-

cated evaluation of facilities and services, and it can be misleading—it reflects the facilities available, but not necessarily how well they are maintained. No matter the hotel, **ask for one of the better rooms,** since less desirable rooms—and there usually are some—don't give you what you're paying for. Except in five-star and some four-star hotels, rooms may be very small by U.S standards.

In all hotels there's a rate card inside the door of your room or inside the closet door; it tells you exactly what you will pay for that particular room (rates in the same hotel may vary according to the location and type of room). On this card, breakfast and any other optionals must be listed separately. Any discrepancy between the basic room rate and that charged on your bill is cause for complaint to the manager and to the police.

By law, breakfast is supposed to be optional, but most hotels quote room rates including breakfast. When you book a room, **ask whether the rate includes breakfast** (*colazione*). You are under no obligation to take breakfast at your hotel, but in practice most hotels expect you to do so. The trick is to "offer" guests "complimentary" breakfast and have its cost built into the rate. However, it's encouraging to note that many of the hotels we recommend provide generous buffet breakfasts instead of simple, even skimpy "Continental breakfasts." Remember, if the latter is the case, you can eat for less at the nearest coffee bar.

The quality of rooms in older hotels may be very uneven; if you don't like the room you're given, request another. A front room may be larger or have a view, but it also may have a lot of street noise. If you're a light sleeper, **request a quiet room when making reservations.**

Rooms in lodgings listed in this guide have a shower and/or bath, unless noted otherwise. (Hotels with three or more stars always have private bathrooms). Remember to **specify if you prefer to have a bathtub or shower,** though rooms in the three-star category and under often have only showers.

Sheraton/The Luxury Collection has 15 Italian properties, almost all five-star deluxe. **Jolly** has 32 four-star hotels in Italy. **Atahotels** has 20 mostly four- and five-star hotels. **Starhotels** has 14 mainly four-star hotels.

Space Hotels has 80 independently owned four- and three-star hotels. **Prima Hotels** has about 20 independently owned four- and five-star hotels. **AGIP Motels** is a chain of about 50, mostly four-star motels on main highways; the motels are commercial, functional accommodations for business travelers and tourists needing 40 winks, but they—and the Jolly hotels—can be the best choice in many out-of-the-way places.

Best Western, an international association of independently owned hotels, has some 75 mainly three- and four-star hotels in Italy; call to request the *Europe and Middle East Atlas* that lists them. The **Sun Rays Pool** comprises four- and five-star hotels, as well as several *agriturismi* with horseback riding.

RESERVING A ROOM

High season in Italy generally runs from Easter through the beginning of November, and then for two weeks at Christmas time. During low season and whenever a hotel is not full, it's often possible to negotiate a discounted rate. Major cities, such as Rome and Milan, have no official off-season as far as hotel rates go, though some hotels do offer substantial discounts during the slower parts of the year and on weekends. Always **inquire about special rates.** Major cities have hotel-reservation service booths in train stations.

Useful terms to know when booking a room are *aria condizionata* (air-conditioning), *bagno in stanza* (private bath), *letto matrimoniale* (double bed), *letti singoli* (twin beds), *letti singoli uniti* (twin beds pushed together). Italy does not really have queen- or king-sized beds, though some beds, particularly in four- and five-star accommodations, can be larger than standard. Phrases that could come in handy include:

Vi prego di fornire informazioni riguardo il vostro albergo/pensione. Vorrei una camera doppia/camera matrimoniale con bagno in camera. (Please supply me with information regarding your hotel/pensione. I would like a room with two single beds/a double bed with private bath.)

Una camera su un piano alto e con vista. (A room on a high floor with a view.)

Una camera a un piano basso. (A room on a low floor.)

Una camera silenziosa. (A quiet room.)

It's always a good idea to have your reservation, dates, and rate confirmed by fax or e-mail. If you need to cancel your reservation, be sure to do so by fax or e-mail and keep a record of the transmission, particularly if dealing directly with an Italian hotel.

⊡ Toll-Free Numbers in Italy ATA Hotel ☎ 800/017086 in Italy ⊕ www.atahotels.it. **Prima Hotels** ☎ 800/822-005 ⊕ www.lhw.com

⊡ Toll-Free Numbers Best Western ☎ 800/528-1234 ⊕ www.bestwestern.com. **Choice** ☎ 800/424-6423 ⊕ www.choicehotels.com. **Clarion** ☎ 800/424-6423 ⊕ www.choicehotels.com. **Comfort Inn** ☎ 800/424-6423 ⊕ www.choicehotels.com. **Four Seasons** ☎ 800/332-3442 ⊕ www.fourseasons.com. **Hilton** ☎ 800/445-8667 ⊕ www.hilton.com. **Holiday Inn** ☎ 800/465-4329 ⊕ www.sixcontinentshotels.com. **Hyatt Hotels & Resorts** ☎ 800/233-1234 ⊕ www.hyatt.com. **Inter-Continental** ☎ 800/327-0200 ⊕ www.intercontinental.com. **Marriott** ☎ 800/228-9290 ⊕ www.marriott.com. **Le Meridien** ☎ 800/543-4300 ⊕ www.lemeridien-hotels.com. **Quality Inn** ☎ 800/424-6423 ⊕ www.choicehotels.com. **Radisson** ☎ 800/333-3333 ⊕ www.radisson.com. **Ramada** ☎ 800/228-2828; 800/854-7854 international reservations ⊕ www.ramada.com or www.ramadahotels.com. **Sheraton** ☎ 800/325-3535 ⊕ www.starwood.com/sheraton. **Space Hotels** ☎ 800/813-013 toll-free in Italy. **Starhotels** ☎ 800/860200 toll-free in Italy, 800/313132 in U.K. ⊡ 055/36924. **Supranational** ☎ 416/927-1133 or 800/843-3311. **Westin Hotels & Resorts** ☎ 800/228-3000 ⊕ www.starwood.com/westin.

MAIL & SHIPPING

The Italian mail system is notoriously slow. Allow up to 15 days for mail to and from the United States, Canada, Australia, and New Zealand. It takes about a week to and from the United Kingdom and within Italy.

OVERNIGHT SERVICES

Overnight mail is generally available in all major cities and at resort hotels. Pickups are daily, excluding Saturday and Sunday. Service is reliable; a Federal Express letter to the United States costs about €30, to the United Kingdom, €51, and to Australia and New Zealand €33. Overnight delivery usually means 24–36 hours.

If your hotel can't assist you, try an Internet shop, many of which offer overnight mail services as well at reasonable rates using major carriers.

⊡ Major Services DHL ☎ 199-199-345, 24 hrs a day. **Federal Express** ☎ 800/123800, weekdays 8–7.

SDA ☎ 800/016027, weekdays 8:30–7:30, Sat. 8:30–1:30.

POSTAL RATES

Airmail letters and postcards (lightweight stationery) to the United States, Canada, Australia, and New Zealand cost €0.52 for the first 20 grams; for heavier stationery you should go to the post office. Always stick the blue airmail tag on your mail, or write "Airmail" in big, clear characters to the side of the address. Postcards and letters (for the first 20 grams) to the United Kingdom, as well as to any other EU country, including Italy, cost €0.41.

Posta Prioritaria (stationery and small packages up to 2 kilograms) and the more expensive Postacelere (up to 20 kilograms) are special delivery services from the post office that guarantee delivery within 24 hours in Italy and three to five days abroad. Lightweight stationery sent as Posta Prioritaria to the United States and Canada costs €0.77 (for the first 20 grams, double that for parcels up to 100 grams); to the United Kingdom, Italy, and all other EU countries it costs €0.62. As regular stamps are not valid for this service, make sure you buy the special golden Posta Prioritaria stamps. Postacelere rates to the United States and Canada are between €23.76 (€15.49 to the United Kingdom and Europe) for parcels up to 500 grams (a little over a pound) and €184.90 (€76.44 to the United Kingdom and Europe) for packages weighing 20 kilos.

You can buy stamps at tobacconists and post offices.

🔲 Postal Information **Informazioni Poste Italiane** ☎ 803-160 for information in Italian or English about rates and local post offices' opening hours, as well as about Postacelere ⊕ www.poste.it.

RECEIVING MAIL

Correspondence can be addressed to you in care of the Italian post office. Letters should be addressed to your name, "c/o Ufficio Postale Centrale," followed by "Fermo Posta" on the next line, and the name of the city (preceded by its postal code) on the next. You can **collect it at the central post office** by showing your passport or photo-bearing I.D. and paying a small fee. American Express also has a general-delivery service. There's no charge for cardholders, holders of American

Express Traveler's checks, or anyone who booked a vacation with American Express.

SHIPPING PARCELS

You can ship parcels via air or surface. Air takes about two weeks, and surface anywhere up to three months. If you have purchased antiques, ceramics, or other objects, **inquire to see if the vendor will do the shipping** for you; in most cases, this is a possibility.

MONEY MATTERS

Prices vary from region to region and are substantially lower in the countryside than in touristy cities. Good value for the money can be had in the scenic Trentino–Alto Adige region and the Dolomites and in Umbria and the Marches. With a few exceptions, southern Italy, Sicily, and Sardinia also offer good values, but hotels are not always up to par. Of Italy's major cities, Venice and Milan are the most expensive. Resorts such as the Costa Smeralda, Portofino, and Cortina d'Ampezzo cater to the rich and famous and charge top prices.

Admission to the Vatican Museums is €9.30; to the Galleria degli Uffizi, €9.30. The cheapest seat at Rome's Teatro dell'-Opera runs €16.55. Getting into a Milan nightclub will set you back about €20. A daily English-language newspaper is €2. A Rome taxi ride (1⅓ km [1 mi]) costs €5.15. An inexpensive hotel room for two, including breakfast, in Rome is about €100; an inexpensive Rome dinner is €25, and a ½-liter carafe of house wine, €3.50. A simple pasta item runs about €8, a cup of coffee €0.70–0.80, and a rosticceria lunch, about €8.50. A Coca-Cola (taken standing at a café counter) is €1.40–2, and a pint of beer is €3.70. Prices are slightly higher in major cities and ski and beach resorts.

Prices throughout this guide are given for adults. Substantially reduced fees are sometimes available for children, students, and senior citizens from the EU; citizens of non-EU countries rarely get discounts. For information on taxes, *see* Taxes.

ATMS

Fairly common in cities and towns as well as in airports and train stations, ATMs are the easiest way to get euros in Italy. Don't, however, count on finding ATMs in small towns and rural areas. Italian ATMs are commonly attached to a bank—you won't find one, for example, in a supermarket—although are at times out of service. Do **check with your bank** to confirm you have an international PIN number, to find out your maximum daily withdrawal allowance, and to learn what the bank fee is for withdrawing money. The word for ATM in Italian is *bancomat,* for PIN, *codice segreto.* Five is the required number of digits for a PIN number in Italy; keypads have only numbers, no letters.

CREDIT CARDS

While increasingly common, credit cards aren't accepted at all establishments, and some require a minimum expenditure. If you want to pay with a card in a small hotel, store, or restaurant, it's a good idea to ask before conducting your business. Visa and MasterCard are preferred to American Express, but in tourist areas American Express is usually accepted. Acceptance of Diner's Club is rare.

Throughout this guide, the following abbreviations are used: **AE,** American Express; **DC,** Diners Club; **MC,** MasterCard; and **V,** Visa.

Reporting Lost Cards **American Express** ☎ 336/668-5110 international collect. **Diners Club** ☎ 702/797-5532 collect. **MasterCard** ☎ 800/870866 toll-free within Italy. **Visa** ☎ 800/877232 toll-free within Italy.

CURRENCY

The euro is the main unit of currency in Italy, as well as in 11 other European countries. Under the euro system, there are eight coins: 1, 2, 5, 10, 20, and 50 *centesimi* (at 100 centesimi to the euro), and 1 and 2 euros. There are seven notes: 5, 10, 20, 50, 100, 200, and 500 euros.

CURRENCY EXCHANGE

For the most favorable rates, **change money through banks.** Although ATM transaction fees may be higher abroad than at home, ATM rates are excellent because they're based on wholesale rates offered only by major banks. You won't do as well at exchange booths in airports or rail and bus stations, in hotels, in restaurants, or in stores. To avoid lines at airport exchange booths, **get a bit of local currency before you leave home.**

At this writing, the exchange rate was about 0.94 euros to the U.S. dollar; 0.61 euros to the Canadian dollar; 1.52 euros to the pound sterling; 0.55 euros to the Australian dollar; and 0.51 euros to the New Zealand dollar.

Exchange Services **International Currency Express** ✉ 427 N. Camden Dr., Suite F, Beverly Hills, CA 90210 ☎ 888/278-6628 orders 🖶 310/278-6410 ⊕ www.foreignmoney.com. **Thomas Cook Currency Services** ☎ 800/287-7362 orders and retail locations ⊕ www.us.thomascook.com.

TRAVELER'S CHECKS

Do you need traveler's checks? It depends on where you're headed. If you're going to rural areas and small towns, go with cash; traveler's checks are best used in cities. Lost or stolen checks can usually be replaced within 24 hours. To ensure a speedy refund, buy your own traveler's checks—don't let someone else pay for them: irregularities like this can cause delays. The person who bought the checks should make the call to request a refund.

PACKING

The weather is considerably milder, in the winter at least, in Italy than in the north and central United States or Great Britain. In summer, stick with very light clothing, as it can get steamy at the height of summer; a sweater may be necessary for cool evenings, especially in the mountains and on islands even during the summer months. Sunglasses, a hat, and sunblock are essential. Brief summer afternoon thunderstorms are common in Rome and inland cities, so an umbrella will come in handy. In winter bring a medium-weight coat and a raincoat for Rome and farther south. Northern Italy calls for heavier clothes, gloves, hats, scarves, and boots. Even in Rome and other milder areas, central heating may not be up to your standards, and interiors can be cold and damp; take wool or flannel rather than sheer fabrics. Bring sturdy shoes for winter and comfortable walking shoes in any season.

Italians dress exceptionally well. They do not usually wear shorts. Men aren't required to wear ties or jackets anywhere, except in some of the grander hotel dining rooms and top-level restaurants, but are expected to look reasonably sharp—and they do. Formal wear is the exception rather than the rule at the opera nowadays, though people in expensive seats usually do get dressed up.

A certain modesty of dress (no bare shoulders or knees) is expected in churches, and strictly enforced in many, especially in Rome at St. Peter's and the Vatican Museums and at the Basilica di San Marco in Venice.

For sightseeing, **pack a pair of binoculars;** they will help you get a good look at painted ceilings and domes. If you stay in budget hotels, **take your own soap and towel.** Many such hotels do not provide soap or they give guests only one tiny bar per room, and towels often look like what you'd use to dry dishes.

In your carry-on luggage, **pack an extra pair of eyeglasses or contact lenses and enough of any medication** you take to last a few days longer than the entire trip. You may also ask your doctor to write a spare prescription using the drug's generic name, as brand names may vary from country to country. In luggage to be checked, **never pack prescription drugs, valuables, or undeveloped film.** And don't forget to carry with you the addresses of offices that handle refunds of lost traveler's checks. Check *Fodor's How to Pack* (available at on-line retailers and bookstores everywhere) for more tips.

To avoid customs and security delays, carry medications in their original packaging. Don't pack any sharp objects in your carry-on luggage, including knives of any size or material, scissors, and corkscrews, or anything else that might arouse suspicion.

To avoid having your checked luggage chosen for hand inspection, don't cram bags full. The U.S. Transportation Security Administration suggests packing shoes on top and placing personal items you don't want touched in clear plastic bags.

CHECKING LUGGAGE

You're allowed to carry aboard one bag and one personal article, such as a purse or a laptop computer. Make sure what you carry on fits under your seat or in the overhead bin. Get to the gate early, so you can board as soon as possible, before the overhead bins fill up.

Baggage allowances vary by carrier, destination, and ticket class. On international flights, you're usually allowed to check two bags weighing up to 70 pounds (32 kilograms) each, although a few airlines allow checked bags of up to 88 pounds (40 kilograms) in first class. Some international carriers don't allow more than 66 pounds (30 kilograms) per bag in business class and 44 pounds (20 kilograms) in economy. On domestic flights, the limit may be 50 pounds (23 kilograms) per bag. Most airlines won't accept bags that weigh more than 100 pounds (45 kilograms) on domestic or international flights. Check baggage restrictions with your carrier before you pack.

Airline liability for baggage is limited to $2,500 per person on flights within the United States. On international flights it amounts to $9.07 per pound or $20 per kilogram for checked baggage (roughly $640 per 70-pound bag) and $400 per passenger for unchecked baggage. You can buy additional coverage at check-in for about $10 per $1,000 of coverage, but it often excludes a rather extensive list of items, shown on your airline ticket.

Before departure, **itemize your bags' contents** and their worth, and label the bags with your name, address, and phone number. (If you use your home address, cover it so potential thieves can't see it readily.) Include a label inside each bag and **pack a copy of your itinerary.** At check-in, **make sure each bag is correctly tagged** with the destination airport's three-letter code. Because some checked bags will be opened for hand inspection, the U.S. Transportation Security Administration recommends that you leave luggage unlocked or use the plastic locks offered at check-in. TSA screeners place an inspection notice inside searched bags, which are re-sealed with a special lock.

If your bag has been searched and contents are missing or damaged, file a claim with the TSA Consumer Response Center as soon as possible. If your bags arrive damaged or fail to arrive at all, file a written report with the airline before leaving the airport.

🔲 Complaints **U.S. Transportation Security Administration Consumer Response Center** ☎ 866/289-9673 ⊕ www.tsa.gov.

PASSPORTS & VISAS

When traveling internationally, **carry your passport** even if you don't need one (it's always the best form of I.D.) and **make two photocopies of the data page** (one for someone at home and another for you, carried separately from your passport). If you lose your passport, promptly call the nearest embassy or consulate and the local police.

U.S. passport applications for children under age 14 require consent from both parents or legal guardians; both parents must appear together to sign the application. If only one parent appears, he or she must submit a written statement from the other parent authorizing passport issuance for the child. A parent with sole authority must present evidence of it when applying; acceptable documentation includes the child's certified birth certificate listing only the applying parent, a court order specifically permitting this parent's travel with the child, or a death certificate for the non-applying parent. Application forms and instructions are available on the Web site of the U.S. State Department's Bureau of Consular Affairs (⊕ www.travel.state.gov).

ENTERING ITALY

Citizens of Australia, Canada, New Zealand, and the United States need only a valid passport to enter Italy for stays of up to 90 days. Citizens of the United Kingdom need only a valid passport to enter Italy for an unlimited stay.

PASSPORT OFFICES

The best time to apply for a passport or to renew is in fall and winter. Before any trip, check your passport's expiration date, and, if necessary, renew it as soon as possible.

🇦 Australian Citizens **Passports Australia** ☎ 131-232 ⊕ www.passports.gov.au.

🇨 Canadian Citizens **Passport Office** ✉ To mail in applications: 200 Promenade du Portage, Hull, Québec J8X 4B7 ☎ 819/994-3500 or 800/567-6868 ⊕ www.ppt.gc.ca.

🇳 New Zealand Citizens **New Zealand Passports Office** ☎ 0800/22-5050 or 04/474-8100 ⊕ www. passports.govt.nz.

🇬 U.K. Citizens **U.K. Passport Service** ☎ 0870/ 521-0410 ⊕ www.passport.gov.uk.

🇺 U.S. Citizens **National Passport Information Center** ☎ 900/225-5674; 900/225-7778 TTY (calls are 55¢ per minute for automated service or $1.50 per minute for operator service); 888/362-8668 or 888/498-3648 TTY (calls are $5.50 each) ⊕ www. travel.state.gov.

REST ROOMS

Public rest rooms are rather rare in Italy; the locals seem to make do with well-timed pit stops and rely on local bars. Although private businesses can refuse to make their toilets available to the passing public, some bars will allow you to use the rest room if you ask politely. Alternatively, it is not uncommon to pay for a little something—a few cents for a mineral water or coffee—to get access to the facilities. Standards of cleanliness and comfort vary greatly. In cities, restaurants, hotel lobbies, department stores such as La Rinascente and Coin, and McDonald's restaurants tend to have the cleanest rest rooms. Pubs and bars rank among the worst. In general, it's in your interest to carry some toilet paper with you. There are bathrooms in all airports and train stations (in major train stations you'll also find well-kept pay toilets for €0.25–0.50) and in most museums. There are also bathrooms at highway rest stops and gas stations: a small tip (€.25–€.50) to the attendant is always appreciated. There are no bathrooms in churches, post offices, public beaches, or subway stations. Aside from in Venice, pay toilets in the city center of Italian towns are the exception, not the rule. In Venice, pay toilets are well posted and strategically located along the main drags that link Piazzale Roma and the train station with the city center; the cost is €0.50.

SAFETY

The best way to protect yourself against purse snatchers and pickpockets is to **wear a concealed money belt or a pouch** on a string around your neck. **Don't wear an exterior money belt or a waist pack,** both of which peg you as a tourist. If you carry a bag or camera, be absolutely sure it has straps; you should sling it across your body bandolier-style, adjusting the height to hip level or higher. Don't hold your bag on the street-side of your body. Always be aware of pickpockets, especially when in city buses and subways, when making your way through train corridors, and in busy piazzas or tourist spots.

If you carry a purse or wallet, store only enough money there to cover casual spending. Distribute the rest of your cash and any valuables (including credit cards and your passport) between a deep front pocket, an inside jacket or vest pocket, and a hidden money pouch. Do not reach for the money pouch while in public.

LOCAL SCAMS

A word of caution: "gypsy" children are rife in Rome and other major cities, and are adept pickpockets. One tactic is to approach a tourist and proffer a piece of cardboard with writing on it. While you attempt to read the message *on* it, the children's hands are busy *under* it, trying to make off with purses or valuables. If you see such a group, avoid them—they are quick and know more tricks than you do. If traveling via rental car, it's a good idea when making stops at rest areas and auto-grills (a chain of highway cafeterias) to have someone remain near the car, as such cars are easily recognizable to professional thieves. Purse-snatching is not uncommon, and thieves operate on *motorini* (mopeds) as well as on foot.

WOMEN IN ITALY

The difficulties encountered by women traveling alone in Italy are often over-stated. Younger women have to put up with much male attention, but it is rarely dangerous or hostile. Ignoring whistling and questions is the best way to get rid of unwanted attention.

SENIOR-CITIZEN TRAVEL

To qualify for age-related discounts, **mention your senior-citizen status up front** when booking hotel reservations (not when checking out) and, if you are EU citizens over 65, before buying museum tickets. When renting a car, ask about promotional car-rental discounts, which can be cheaper than senior-citizen rates.
Educational Programs Elderhostel ⊠ 11 Ave. de Lafayette, Boston, MA 02111-1746 ☎ 877/426-8056; 978/323-4141 international callers; 877/426-2167 TTY 🖶 877/426-2166 ⊕ www.elderhostel.org. **Interhostel** ⊠ University of New Hampshire, 6 Garrison Ave., Durham, NH 03824 ☎ 603/862-1147 or 800/733-9753 🖶 603/862-1113 ⊕ www.learn.unh.edu.

SHOPPING

Italy produces fine wines, clothes, leather, and jewelry, among other things. The no-tice PREZZI FISSI (fixed prices) means just that—it's a waste of time to bargain unless you're buying a sizable quantity of goods or a particularly costly object. Always try to bargain, however, at outdoor markets (except food markets) and when buying from street vendors. For information on V.A.T. refunds, *see* Taxes.

KEY DESTINATIONS

Perhaps the best shopping of all can be had in Rome, which is teeming with stores to suit all tastes. Savvy shoppers should visit during the *saldi* (sales), which happen just after the New Year and run as late as March, and then again in July through early September. Serious bargains in shoes and clothing are on offer.

Factory outlets have only recently begun to appear in Italy. Prada has an outlet in Montevarchi, Fendi has one in Rignano sull'Arno, and there's a mall featuring Armani and Gucci in Leccio—all between Florence and Arezzo. The McArthur Glen designer outlet near Asti has bargains on Italian and international labels.

SMART SOUVENIRS

From the holy to the kitzch, Rome has no shortage of keepsakes. For rosary beads made of anything from glow-in-the-dark plastic to semi-precious stones, head for the shops that line Borgo Pio, near St. Peter's. The least expensive will cost about €5; the more expensive, several hundred. For center-piece fruit made of painted marble, look in shops near the Trevi fountain. Pieces costs about €15. The Porta Portese market has plenty of souvenirs. Aprons emblazoned with naked Davids (€5) and other figures are sold widely, along with historic prints of Rome, which can cost up to €50.

WATCH OUT

If you have purchased any work of art (painting, sculpture, miniature, cameo, etc.), make sure that the piece is certified as being less than 50 years old. Any art deemed older than that must receive clearance from the Italian government to leave the country.

If you have purchased an antique, the dealer will provide you with a certificate attesting to the integrity of the piece and the price paid. Some dealers will ship the object for you; others leave it to you to arrange shipping.

SIGHTSEEING GUIDES

Every province in Italy has licensed tour guides who are allowed by Italian law to take groups and individuals to selected sites. Some of them are eminently qualified in relevant fields such as history and art history; others have simply managed to pass the test. Inquire at any tourist office for a licensed, English-speaking guide. When you speak to the guide, ask about his or her qualifications and specialties. Also check to make sure that the guide's English is understandable. The rates are fixed; find out what they are before hiring the guide. It is illegal for the guide to charge you more than the fixed fee. Tipping is appreciated but not obligatory.

Some places, such as the Duomo in Florence, offer free guided tours in English by a volunteer staff. Such guides may be longer on enthusiasm than knowledge.

SMOKING

In 2002, laws were enacted banning smoking in many public places, including bars and restaurants, but Italians are unrepentant smokers and compliance is arbitrary. If you ask someone to smoke elsewhere or not to smoke in no-smoking areas, don't expect them to respond or respect your request. Smokers should check to see if there's a "Vietato Fumare" (No Smoking) sign before lighting up. For a smoke-free environment as possible, stick to large establishments and, weather permitting, eat outside. All FS trains have no-smoking cars: always specify when you make reservations.

STUDENTS IN ITALY

In the major art cities there are plenty of sources of information and lodging geared to students' needs. Students from member nations in the EU possessing valid I.D. cards may sometimes receive discounts at museums, galleries, exhibitions, and entertainment venues, and on some transportation. Students who aren't EU citizens generally pay the usual entrance fees.

LOCAL RESOURCES

The Centro Turistico Studentesco (CTS) is a student and youth travel agency with offices in major Italian cities. CTS helps its clients find low-cost accommodations and bargain fares for travel in Italy and elsewhere. CTS is also the Rome representative for EuroTrain International.

TRAVEL AGENCIES

To save money, **look into deals available through student-oriented travel agencies.** To qualify you'll need a student I.D. card. Members of international student groups are also eligible.

7 I.D.s & Services Centro Turistico Studentesco (CTS) ⊠ Corso Vittorio Emanuele II 297, Rome, 00186 ☎ 06/6872672 🕾 06/6872562 ⊕ www.cts.it. **STA Travel** ⊠ 10 Downing St., New York, NY 10014 ☎ 212/627-3111 or 800/777-0112 🕾 212/627-3387 ⊕ www.sta.com. **Travel Cuts** ⊠ 187 College St., Toronto, Ontario M5T 1P7, Canada ☎ 416/979-2406 or 800/592-2887; 866/246-9762 in Canada 🕾 416/979-8167 ⊕ www.travelcuts.com.

TAXES

HOTELS

The service charge and the 9% IVA, or V.A.T. tax, are included in the rate except in five-star deluxe hotels, where the IVA (12% on luxury hotels) may be a separate item added to the bill upon departure.

RESTAURANTS

There is no tax added to restaurant bills. You will, however, sometimes find a service charge of approximately 15% added to your check; in some cases the menu may say that the service charge is already included in the menu prices.

VALUE-ADDED TAX

Value-added tax (IVA, or V.A.T.) is 20% on clothing, wine, and luxury goods. On consumer goods, it's already included in the amount shown on the price tag, whereas on services it may not be. If a store you shop in has a "Euro Tax Free" sign outside and you make a purchase above €155, present your passport and request a "Tax Free Shopping Check" when paying.

Have the form stamped like any customs form by customs officials when you leave Italy or, if you're visiting several European Union countries, when you leave the EU. Be ready to show customs officials what you've bought (pack purchases together, in your carry-on luggage); budget extra time for this. After you're through passport control, take the form to a refund-service counter for an on-the-spot refund, or mail it back to the store or a refund service after you arrive home.

A refund service can save you some hassle, for a fee. Global Refund is a Europe-wide service with 190,000 affiliated stores and more than 700 refund counters—located at every major airport and border crossing. Its refund form is called a Tax Free Check. The service issues refunds in the form of cash, check, or credit-card adjustment, minus a processing fee. If you don't have time to wait at the refund counter, you can mail in the form instead.

🔳 **V.A.T. Refunds** **Global Refund** ✉ 99 Main St., Suite 307, Nyack, NY 10960 ☎ 800/566-9828 🖷 845/348-1549 🌐 www.globalrefund.com.

TELEPHONES

AREA & COUNTRY CODES

The country code for Italy is 39. When dialing an Italian number from abroad, **do not drop the initial 0** from the local area code (as was formerly the procedure). Here are area codes for major cities: Bologna, 051; Brindisi, 0831; Florence, 055; Genoa, 010; Milan, 02; Naples, 081; Palermo, 091; Perugia, 075; Pisa, 050; Rome, 06; Siena, 0577; Turin, 011; Venice, 041; Verona, 045. For example, a call from the United States to Rome would be dialed as 011 + 39 + 06 + phone number.

The country code is 1 for the United States and Canada, 61 for Australia, 64 for New Zealand, and 44 for the United Kingdom.

DIRECTORY & OPERATOR ASSISTANCE

For general information in English, dial 176. To place international telephone calls via operator-assisted service, dial 170 or long-distance access numbers (⇨ International Calls).

INTERNATIONAL CALLS

Since hotels tend to overcharge for long-distance and international calls, it's best to make such calls from public phones, using telephone cards.

You can **make collect calls from any phone by dialing 172,** which will get you an English-speaking operator. Rates to the United States are lowest on Sunday around the clock and 10 PM–8 AM (Italian time) on weekdays and Saturday.

You can place a direct call to the United States by reversing the charges or using your calling card. When calling from pay telephones, insert a coin, which will be returned upon completion of your call. You automatically reach an operator in the country of destination and thereby avoid all language difficulties.

LOCAL & LONG-DISTANCE CALLS

For all calls within Italy—local and long distance—you must dial the regional area code (*prefisso*), which begins with a 0, such as 06 for Rome, 041 for Venice. If you are calling from a public phone you must deposit a coin or use a calling card to get a dial tone. Rates are different at various times during the day; it's cheaper to call within Italy during nonworking hours (before 9 AM and after 7 or 8 PM), and it's cheaper to dial internationally at these times.

LONG-DISTANCE SERVICES

AT&T, MCI, and Sprint access codes make calling long distance relatively convenient, but you may find the access number blocked in many hotel rooms. First ask the hotel operator to connect you. If the hotel operator balks, ask for an international operator, or dial the international operator yourself.

🔳 **Access Codes** **AT&T Direct** ☎ 800/172-444. **MCI WorldPhone** ☎ 800/172-401/404. **Sprint International Access** ☎ 800/172-405. From cell phones call 892-176.

PHONE CARDS

Prepaid *carte telefoniche* (calling cards) are prevalent throughout Italy and more convenient than coins. Cards (values vary) are sold at post offices, tobacconists, most news stalls, and bars and may be used in almost every public pay phone. Tear off the corner of the card and insert it in the slot. When you dial, its value appears in the window. After you hang up, the card is returned. The best card for calling North America or Europe is the €5 or €10 Europa card, which gives you a local number to dial and roughly 180 minutes and 360 minutes, respectively, of calling time.

PUBLIC PHONES

Public pay phones are scarce, though they can be found at train and subway stations, post offices, in hotel lobbies, and in some bars. In rural areas, town squares usually have a pay phone. Some pay phones accept only euro coins, others only *carte telefoniche,* so it's smart have both ready (⇨ Phone Cards).

TIME

Italy is six hours ahead of Eastern Standard time, one hour ahead of Great Britain, 10 hours behind Sydney, and 12 hours behind Auckland. Like the rest of Europe, Italy uses the 24-hour (or "military") clock, which means that after 12 noon you continue counting forward: 13:00 is 1 PM, 23:30 is 11:30 PM.

TIPPING

The following guidelines apply in major cities, but Italians tip smaller amounts in smaller cities and towns. In restaurants a service charge of about 10% sometimes appears as a separate item on your check. Some restaurants say on the menu that cover and service charge are included. Either way, it's customary to leave an additional 5%–10% tip for the waiter, depending on the service. Tip checkroom attendants €1 per person and rest-room attendants €0.50 (more in expensive hotels and restaurants). Depending on where you are (Rome, for example) tip €0.05 for whatever you drink standing up at a coffee bar, €0.25 or more for table service in cafés. At a hotel bar, tip €1 and up for a round or two of cocktails.

Italians rarely tip taxi drivers, which is not to say that you shouldn't do it. A euro or two, depending on the length of the journey, is appreciated—particularly if the driver helps with luggage. Railway and airport porters charge a fixed rate per bag. Tip an additional €0.25 per person, and more if the porter is helpful. Give a barber €1–€1.50 and a hairdresser's assistant €1.50–€4.15 for a shampoo or cut, depending on the type of establishment.

On sightseeing tours, tip guides about €1.50 per person for a half-day group tour, more if they are very good. In monasteries and other sights where admission is free, a contribution (€0.50–€1) is expected. Service station attendants are tipped only for special services, for example, €1 for checking your tires.

In hotels, give the *portiere* (concierge) about 15% of his bill for services, or €2.50–€5 if he has been generally helpful with dinner reservations and such. For two

people in a double room, leave the chambermaid about €0.75 per day, or about €4.50–€5 a week, in a moderately priced hotel; tip a minimum of €1 for valet or room service. Double amounts in an expensive hotel. In expensive hotels, tip doormen €0.50 for calling a cab and €1.50 for carrying bags to the check-in desk, bellhops €1.50–€2.50 for carrying your bags to the room, and €2–€2.50 for room service.

TOURS & PACKAGES

Because everything is prearranged on a prepackaged tour or independent vacation, you spend less time planning—and often get it all at a good price.

BOOKING WITH AN AGENT

Travel agents are excellent resources. But it's a good idea to collect brochures from several agencies, as some agents' suggestions may be influenced by relationships with tour and package firms that reward them for volume sales. If you have a special interest, **find an agent with expertise in that area**; the American Society of Travel Agents (ASTA; ⇨ Travel Agencies) has a database of specialists worldwide.

Make sure your travel agent knows the accommodations and other services of the place being recommended. Ask about the hotel's location, room size, beds, and whether it has a pool, room service, or programs for children, if you care about these. Has your agent been there in person or sent others whom you can contact?

Do some homework on your own, too: local tourism boards can provide information about lesser-known and small-niche operators, some of which may sell only direct.

BUYER BEWARE

Each year consumers are stranded or lose their money when tour operators—even large ones with excellent reputations—go out of business. So **check out the operator.** Ask several travel agents about its reputation, and try to **book with a company that has a consumer-protection program.** (Look for information in the company's brochure.) In the United States, members of the National Tour Association and the United States Tour Operators Association are required to set aside funds to cover payments and travel arrangements in the event that the company defaults. It's also a good idea to choose a company that participates in the American Society of Travel Agents' Tour Operator Program; ASTA will act as mediator in any disputes between you and your tour operator.

Remember that the more your package or tour includes, the better you can predict the ultimate cost of your vacation. Make sure you know exactly what is covered, and **beware of hidden costs.** Are taxes, tips, and transfers included? Entertainment and excursions? These can add up.

Tour-Operator Recommendations American Society of Travel Agents (⇨ Travel Agencies). **National Tour Association (NTA)** ✉ 546 E. Main St., Lexington, KY 40508 ☎ 859/226-4444 or 800/682-8886 🖷 859/226-4404 ⊕ www.ntaonline.com. **United States Tour Operators Association (USTOA)** ✉ 275 Madison Ave., Suite 2014, New York, NY 10016 ☎ 212/599-6599 or 800/468-7862 🖷 212/599-6744 ⊕ www.ustoa.com.

TRAIN TRAVEL

The fastest trains on the Trenitalia, the Italian State Railways, are the *Eurostar* trains, operating on several main lines, including Rome–Milan via Florence and Bologna. Supplement is included in the fare; seat reservations are mandatory at all times. There are smoking and no-smoking cars on all trains. Nonsmokers should ask for seats located away from the smoking car, as the poorly designed partitions are not smoke-proof. Some Eurostar trains (the ETR 460 trains) have little aisle and luggage space (though there is a space near the door where you can put large bags). To avoid having to squeeze through narrow aisles, board only at your car (look for the number on the reservation ticket). Car numbers are displayed on their exterior. Next-fastest trains are the *Intercity* (IC) trains, for which you pay a supplement and for which seat reservations may be required and are always advisable. *Diretto* and *Interregionale* trains usually make more stops and are a little slower. *Regionale* and *locale* trains are the slowest; many serve commuters.

Note that in some Italian cities—Milan, Turin, Genoa, Naples, and Rome included—there are two or more main-line stations, although one is usually the principal terminal or through-station. Be sure of the name of the station where your train will arrive or depart.

There is refreshment service on all long-distance trains, with mobile carts and a cafeteria or dining car. Tap water on trains is not drinkable.

Traveling by night is inexpensive, but never leave your belongings unattended (even for a minute!) and make sure the door of your compartment is locked. More comfortable trains run on the longer routes (Sicily–Rome, Sicily–Milan, Sicily–Venice, Rome–Turin, Lecce–Milan); ask for the good value T3, Intercity Notte, and Carrozza Comfort. The Vagone Letto Excelsior has private bathrooms, coffee machines, microwave ovens, refrigerators, and a suite with a double bed and a VCR.

Train service between Milan, Florence, Rome, and Naples is frequent throughout the day. For the most part, trains stick to schedule, although during peak tourist season delays may occur. Train strikes of various kinds are also frequent, so it's a good idea to make sure the train you want to take is in fact running.

Train Information Trentalia ☎ 848/888088 in Italy ⊕ www.trenitalia.it.

From the U.K. British Rail ☎ 020/7834-2345 ⊕ www.rail.co.uk. **French Railways** ☎ 0891/515-477 ⊕ www.sncf.com.

CLASSES

All Italian trains have first and second classes. On local trains the first-class fare gets you little more than a clean doily on the headrest of your seat, but on long-distance trains you get wider seats, more legroom, and better ventilation and lighting. At peak travel times, first-class train travel is worth the difference. Remember **always to make seat reservations in advance,** for either class. One advantage of traveling first class is that the cars are almost always not crowded—or, at the very least, less crowded than the second-class compartments. A first-class ticket, in Italian, is *prima classe*; second is *seconda classe*.

CUTTING COSTS

To save money, **look into rail passes.** But be aware that if you don't plan to cover many miles, you may come out ahead by buying individual tickets. If Italy is your only destination in Europe, **consider purchasing an Italian Flexi Rail Card Saver** (sold only outside Italy), which allows a limited number of travel days within one month: for four days of travel ($239 first class, $191 second class) and eight days of travel ($261 first class, $210 second class). These tickets are cheaper if you travel in two or more or are under 26.

The Italian Kilometric Ticket (*biglietto chilometrico*) is valid for two months and can be used by as many as five people to travel a maximum of 20 journeys covering an overall distance of 3,000 km (1,800 mi). The price is €180.76 for first class and €116.72 for second class.

Once in Italy, **inquire about the Cartaverde (Green Card)** if you're under 26 (€25.82 for one year), which entitles the holder to a 30% discount on first-class travel and a 20% discount on second-class tickets. Those under 26 should also inquire about discount travel fares under the Billet International Jeune (BIJ) and Euro Domino Junior schemes. Also in Italy, you can **purchase the Carta d'Argento (Silver Card)** if you're over 60 (€25.82 for one year), which allows a 40% discount on first-class rail travel and a 30% discount on second-class travel. **Biglietti per mini-gruppi** entitle parties of three to five people traveling together to a 30% discount on all tickets except during Easter holidays, July–August, October 27–November 5, and December–January 14. For further information, check out the Trenitalia Web site (⊕ www.trenitalia.it).

Italy is one of 17 countries in which you can **use Eurailpasses,** which provide unlimited first-class travel in all of the participating countries. If you plan to rack up the miles, get a standard pass. Train travel is available for 15 days ($588), 21 days ($762), one month ($946), two months ($1,338), and three months ($1,654). You can also receive free or discounted fares on some ferry lines.

If your plans call for only limited train travel, **look into the Europass,** which costs less than a Eurailpass and allows train travel in France, Germany, Italy, Spain, and Switzerland within a two-month period ($360 for 5 days of travel; $400 for 6 days; $474 for 8 days; $544 for 10 days; and $710 for 15 days). Rail travel to Austria, Hungary, Portugal, Greece, and Benelux can be added for additional fees ($62 one country; $102 two countries). You can receive discounts for two or more

people. Please note that these fares are subject to change.

In addition to standard Eurailpasses, **ask about special rail-pass plans.** Among these are the Eurail Youthpass (for those under age 26), Eurail Saverpass and Eurail Saver Flexipass (which give a discount for two or more people traveling together), Eurail Flexipass (which allows a certain number of travel days within a set period), and the EurailDrive Pass (which combines travel by train and rental car).

Whichever pass you choose, remember that you must **purchase your Eurailpass or Europass before you leave** for Europe. You can get further information and order tickets at the Rail Europe Web site (⊕ www.raileurope.com).

Many travelers assume that rail passes guarantee them seats on the trains they wish to ride. Not so. You need to **book seats ahead even if you are using a rail pass.** Seat reservations are required on some European trains, particularly high-speed trains, and are a good idea on trains that may be crowded—particularly in summer on popular routes. You will also need a reservation if you purchase sleeping accommodations.

🚃 Information & Passes **CIT Rail** ✉ 15 W. 44th St., New York, NY 10036 ☎ 800/248-7245. **DER Tours** 🚗 Box 1606, Des Plaines, IL 60017 ☎ 800/782-2424 🖨 800/282-7474. **Rail Europe** ✉ 44 S. Broadway, White Plains, NY 10601 ☎ 914/682-5172 or 877/257-2887 ⊕ www.raileurope.com ✉ 2087 Dundas E., Suite 105, Mississauga, Ontario L4X 1M2 ☎ 800/361-7245.

PAYING

You can pay for your train tickets in cash or with any major credit card such as American Express, Diner's Club, MasterCard, and Visa.

TICKETS, SCHEDULES & RESERVATIONS

Trains can be very crowded; it's always a good idea to make a reservation. To avoid long lines at station windows, **buy tickets and make seat reservations up to two months in advance** at travel agencies displaying the FS emblem. Tickets can be purchased at the last minute, but seat reservations can be made at agencies (or the train station) up until about three hours before the train departs from its city of origin. For trains that require a reservation (all Eurostar and some Intercity), you may be able to get a seat assignment just before boarding the train; look for the conductor on the platform.

Tickets are good for two months after the date of issue, but right before departure you **must validate tickets in the yellow machines located in the departure area.** Once stamped, tickets are valid for 6 hours on distances of less than 200 km (124 mi) or for 24 hours on distances of 200 km or more. If you wish to stop along the way and your final destination is more than 200 km away, you can stamp the ticket a second time before it expires so as to extend its validity to a maximum of 48 hours from the time it was first stamped. If you forget to stamp your ticket in the machine, or you didn't make it to the station in time to buy the ticket, you must seek out a conductor and pay a €5.15 fine. Don't wait for the conductor to find out that you are without a valid ticket (unless the train is overcrowded and walking becomes impossible), as he might charge you a much heavier fine. You can buy train tickets for nearby destinations (within a 200-km [124-mi] range) at tobacconists and at ticket machines in stations.

RESERVATIONS

Though reservations are not mandatory (except on Eurostar trains), it's wise to reserve in advance through a travel agent or at a station sales office. It costs only an additional euro or so, and you are guaranteed a seat. Simply possessing a train ticket does not guarantee a seat on any Eurostar, intercity, or regional train. In summer, it's fairly common to stand for a good part of the journey, as trains are crowded.

TRANSPORTATION AROUND ITALY

Italy has an extensive network of train connections, though with the exception of the rapid Eurostar trains, don't expect efficient service: delays due to technical problems and frequent strikes will put you behind schedule. Buses may offer a more direct alternative for destinations reached by several train transfers. Always check the cost of flying between cities; plane tickets can cost less than train fare. If you

plan on venturing into the countryside, renting a car is the best option.

TRAVEL AGENCIES

A good travel agent puts your needs first. Look for an agency that has been in business at least five years, emphasizes customer service, and has someone on staff who specializes in your destination. In addition, **make sure the agency belongs to a professional trade organization.** The American Society of Travel Agents (ASTA)—the largest and most influential in the field with more than 20,000 members in some 140 countries—maintains and enforces a strict code of ethics and will step in to help mediate any agent-client disputes involving ASTA members if necessary. ASTA (whose motto is "Without a travel agent, you're on your own") also maintains a Web site that includes a directory of agents. (If a travel agency is also acting as your tour operator, *see* Buyer Beware *in* Tours and Packages.)
Local Agent Referrals **American Society of Travel Agents (ASTA)** ⊠ 1101 King St., Suite 200, Alexandria, VA 22314 ☎ 703/739-2782; 800/965-2782 24-hr hot line 🖷 703/739-3268 ⊕ www.astanet.com. **Association of British Travel Agents** ⊠ 68-71 Newman St., London W1T 3AH ☎ 020/7637-2444 🖷 020/7637-0713 ⊕ www.abtanet.com. **Association of Canadian Travel Agents** ⊠ 130 Albert St., Suite 1705, Ottawa, Ontario K1P 5G4 ☎ 613/237-3657 🖷 613/237-7052 ⊕ www.acta.ca. **Australian Federation of Travel Agents** ⊠ Level 3, 309 Pitt St., Sydney, NSW 2000 ☎ 02/9264-3299 🖷 02/9264-1085 ⊕ www.afta.com.au. **Travel Agents' Association of New Zealand** ⊠ Level 5, Tourism and Travel House, 79 Boulcott St., Box 1888, Wellington 6001 ☎ 04/499-0104 🖷 04/499-0786 ⊕ www.taanz.org.nz.

VISITOR INFORMATION

Learn more about foreign destinations by checking government-issued travel advisories and country information. For a broader picture, consider information from more than one country.
Tourist Information **Italian Government Tourist Board (ENIT)** ⊠ 630 5th Ave., Suite 1565, New York, NY 10111 ☎ 212/245-4822 🖷 212/586-9249 ⊠ 401 N. Michigan Ave., Chicago, IL 60611 ☎ 312/644-0996 🖷 312/644-3019 ⊠ 12400 Wilshire Blvd., Suite 550, Los Angeles, CA 90025 ☎ 310/820-1898 🖷 310/820-6357 ⊠ 175 Bloor St. E, Suite 907, South Tower, Toronto, Ontario M4W 3R8 ☎ 416/925-4882 🖷 416/925-4799 ⊠ 1 Princes St., London

W1R 8AY ☎ 020/7408-1254 🖷 020/7493-6695 ⊕ www.italiantourism.com. 🔳 Regional Offices **Florence** ✉ Via Cavour 1/r, next to Palazzo Medici-Riccardi, 50129 ☎ 055/290832 ⊕ www.firenze.turismo.toscana.it. **Milan** ✉ Via Marconi 1, 20121 ☎ 02/72524301 ⊕ www.mimu.it. **Naples** ✉ Piazza dei Martiri 58, 80121 ☎ 081/405311 ⊕ www.ept.napoli.it. **Palermo** ✉ Piazza Castelnuovo 35, 90141 ☎ 091/583847 ⊕ www.palermoturismo.it. **Rome** ✉ Via Parigi 5, 00185 ☎ 06/36004399 ⊕ www.romaturismo.it. **Venice** ✉ Castello Quattromille 4421, 30124 ☎ 041/5298711 ⊕ www.turismovenezia.it.

🔳 Government Advisories **U.S. Department of State** ✉ Overseas Citizens Services Office, Room 4811, 2201 C St. NW, Washington, DC 20520 ☎ 202/647-5225 interactive hot line; 888/407-4747 ⊕ www.travel.state.gov; enclose a cover letter with your request and a business-size SASE. **Consular Affairs Bureau of Canada** ☎ 800/267-6788 or 613/944-6788 ⊕ www.voyage.gc.ca. **U.K. Foreign and Commonwealth Office** ✉ Travel Advice Unit, Consular Division, Old Admiralty Building, London SW1A 2PA ☎ 020/7008-0232 or 020/7008-0233 ⊕ www.fco.gov.uk/travel. **Australian Department of Foreign Affairs and Trade** ☎ 02/6261-1299 Consular Travel Advice Faxback Service ⊕ www.dfat.gov.au. **New Zealand Ministry of Foreign Affairs and Trade** ☎ 04/439-8000 ⊕ www.mft.govt.nz.

WEB SITES

Do check out the World Wide Web when planning your trip. You'll find everything from weather forecasts to virtual tours of famous cities. Be sure to **visit Fodors.com** (⊕ www.fodors.com), a complete travel-planning site. You can research prices and book plane tickets, hotel rooms, rental cars, vacation packages, and more. In addition, you can post your pressing questions in the Travel Talk section. Other planning tools include a currency converter and weather reports, and there are loads of links to travel resources.

VENICE

FODOR'S CHOICE
Bancogiro, restaurant, Santa Croce
Gondola ride, Grand Canal
Pensione Accademia Villa Maravege, hotel, Dorsoduro
Santa Maria Gloriosa dei Frari, San Polo

HIGHLY RECOMMENDED

RESTAURANTS
Ai 4 Feri, Dorsoduro
Ai Gondolieri, Dorsoduro
Alle Testiere, Castello
L'Incontro, Dorsoduro
Osteria da Fiore, San Polo
Vini da Gigio, Cannaregio

HOTELS
Il Palazzo at the Bauer, San Marco
La Calcina, Dorsoduro
Metropole, Castello
Monaco & Grand Canal, San Marco
Quattro Fontane, Lido
San Zulian, San Marco

SIGHTS
Basilica di San Marco, Piazza San Marco
Burano
Ca' d'Oro, Cannaregio
Ca' Rezzonico, Dorsoduro
Gallerie dell'Accademia, Dorsoduro
Palazzo Ducale, Piazza San Marco
Ponte di Rialto
Santa Maria dei Miracoli, Cannaregio
Santi Giovanni e Paolo, Castello
Torcello

Updated by
Elaine Eliah
and Patricia
Rucidlo

IT IS CALLED LA SERENISSIMA, or "the most serene," a reference to the monstrous power, majesty, and wisdom of this city that was for centuries the unrivaled mistress of trade between Europe and the Orient and the staunch bulwark of Christendom against the tides of Turkish expansion. "The most serene" also refers to the way in which those visiting have looked upon Venice, a miraculous city imperturbably floating on its calm blue lagoon.

Built entirely on water by men who dared defy the sea, Venice is unlike any other town. No matter how many times you have seen it in movies or TV commercials, the real thing is more surreal and dreamlike than you could ever imagine. Its landmarks, the Basilica di San Marco and the Palazzo Ducale, seem hardly Italian: delightfully idiosyncratic, they are exotic mélanges of Byzantine, Gothic, and Renaissance styles. Sunlight shimmers and silvery mist softens every perspective here, and you understand how the city became renowned in the Renaissance for its artists' rendering of color. It's full of secrets, inexpressibly romantic, and at times given over entirely to pleasure.

Founded in the 5th century by refugee Veneti, mainlanders escaping barbarian invasion, Venice rose from the marshes to dominate the Adriatic and hold the gorgeous East in fee. Early in its history the city called in Byzantine artists to decorate its churches with brilliant mosaics, still glittering today. In the 13th through 15th centuries, the influence of Gothic architecture produced the characteristic type of palace in the Florid Gothic style, with the finely wrought facades for which the town is famous. The Renaissance arrived in Venice relatively late, at a time when the city had reached its peak in power and prosperity. In its early phase the style is referred to as Lombardesque, after the Lombardo family, who elaborated a specific kind of colored marble decoration made of intertwined discs, roundels, and crosses. Early Renaissance artists—Carpaccio, Giorgione, and the Bellini brothers, Giovanni and Gentile—were active in Venice between the late 15th and early 16th centuries. Along with the stars of the next generation—Veronese, Titian, and Tintoretto—they played a decisive role in the development of Western art, and their work still covers walls and ceilings all over the city.

Venice's height of political and economic importance came in the 15th and 16th centuries, when it extended its domain inland to include all of what is now known as the Veneto region and part of Lombardy. For 400 years the great maritime city-republic had been growing in power, but after the 16th century the tide changed. The Ottoman Empire blocked Venice's Mediterranean trade routes, and newly emerging sea powers such as Britain and the Netherlands broke Venice's monopoly by opening oceanic trading routes. Like its steadily dwindling fortunes, Venice's art and culture began a prolonged decline, leaving only the splendid monuments to recall a fabled past, with the 18th-century paintings of Canaletto and frescoes of Giambattista Tiepolo striking a glorious swan song.

You must walk everywhere in Venice (Venezia in Italian), and where you can't walk, you must go by water. Occasionally you're walking *in* water, when normally higher winter tides are exacerbated by falling barometers and southeasterly winds. The result is *acqua alta*—flooding in the lowest parts of town, especially Piazza San Marco, which lasts a few hours, until the tide recedes. Work has begun on the Moses Project, a plan that would close off the lagoon when high tides threaten, but it's 7a much-debated response to an emotionally charged problem. Protecting Venice and its lagoon from high tides, high use, and the damaging wave action caused by powerboats is among the city's most contested issues.

You could easily spend 10 days touring monuments, wandering in less-central neighborhoods, visiting lagoon islands, shopping, and eating great fish. But Venice is also a popular weekend destination, and it fills two days to the brim with sights, walks, and wonder.

If you have 2 days

Greet Venice with a morning cruise along the Grand Canal from Ferrovia to San Zaccaria. You'll treasure seeing Piazza San Marco for the first time from the water, as centuries of travelers have done before you. Visit the Basilica, Palazzo Ducale, and Museo Correr, and allow time to enjoy the view from atop the Campanile. Meander out Salizada San Moisè, shopping and lunching along the way. Take the traghetto in Campo Santa Maria del Giglio or cross the Grand Canal via Accademia Bridge. Bear left to reach Santa Maria della Salute, with over a dozen Titian paintings, and Punta della Dogana, one of the best panoramas in town. Top off your afternoon with Peggy Guggenheim's 20th-century collection, or let centuries of Venetian art at Gallerie dell'Accademia show you how this city has changed through the ages. Stretch your legs at sunset with a walk along the Zattere, accompanied by a gelato. After dinner, splurge on a romantic gondola ride. On day two, start early to beat the crowds at the Rialto Bridge and market. Don't miss the lively pescheria, where fish have been sold for more than 1,000 years. Follow the main drag to Campo San Polo and Basilica dei Frari, with two important works by Titian, then see more than 60 Tintoretto works at Scuola Grande di San Rocco. After lunch, choose between 18th-century art at Ca' Rezzonico and modern art at Ca' Pesaro. After dinner, if you're not yet out of money and energy, head to the Casinò, where composer Richard Wagner once lived.

If you have 4 days

Follow the itinerary above for days 1 and 2. Choose one of your remaining days—let the weather be your guide—to cruise the lagoon islands: Murano with its glassworks; Burano with its lace-making; romantic Torcello, one of the first islands settled by the Venetians; and San Michele, with what must be the best views of any cemetery in the world. Lunch at one of several island restaurants or carry along a picnic. On your other morning, let the Naval Museum and Arsenale show you the source of this maritime republic's power. Visit the Scuola di San Giorgio degli Schiavoni for the city's finest selection of Vittore Carpaccio's works. Wind your way to Campo Santa Maria Formosa and Querini-Stampalia gallery of Venetian art. Don't miss nearby Santa Maria dei Miracoli, a tiny jewel box of a church, and massive Santi Giovanni e Paolo, the final resting place of several doges. Wind your way through Cannaregio, visiting Ca' d'Oro, a building as beautiful as the art collection it houses. End your day in the rooftops synagogues of the Jewish Ghetto, and learn how that name, from Venetian dialect, became known worldwide.

If you have 7 days

If you're fortunate enough to have a full week in Venice, you'll be able to not only see the sights, but to relax and really enjoy the life, the pace, and the subtle charms of the great city. Rather than running out of time before you've run out of sights along the jam-packed itineraries listed above, you can cut any of the day's tours in half, leaving time in your sightseeing for more lingering in cafés and losing yourself along the canals less traveled. If you need a break from the sights, rent a bicycle for a trip along the beaches of Lido and Pellestrina.

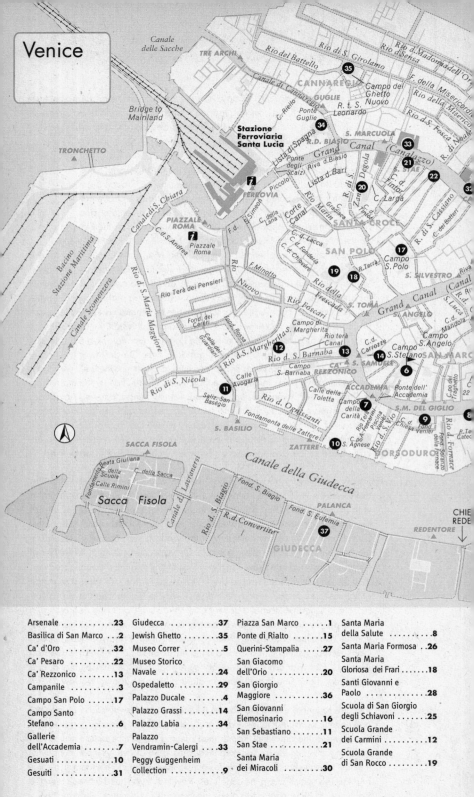

Venice

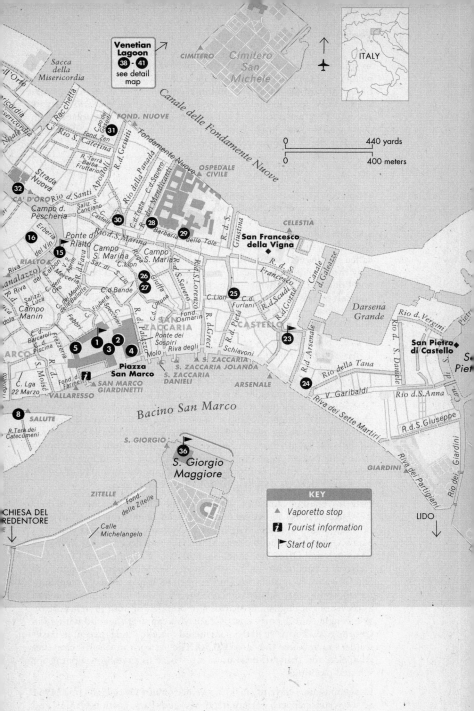

Venetian
Lagoon
38 - 41
see detail
map

CIMITERO

Cimitero
San
Michele

ITALY

Sacca
della
Misericordia

l'Orto

icordia

isericordia

Nedle

C. Racchetta

FOND. NUOVE

Canale delle Fondamente Nuove

0   440 yards
0   400 meters

C.po dei Greatti

31

Rio S. Caterina

Fond. Zen

Fondamente Nuove

OSPEDALE
CIVILE

R. Terrà
Barba
Fruttariol

R.d. Gesuiti

Strada
Nuova

32

CA' D'ORO

Rio d. Santi

Rio d. Santi Apostoli

C.d.Testa

Rio della Panada

C.d.Saveria

C.po delli Mendicanti

Campo d.
Pescheria

Saliz. S.
Canciano

Saliz. S.
Castelli

30

C.d. Marina

CELESTIA

Erberia

16

del Vin

Ponte di
Rialto

Rio d. S. Marina

28

Barbaria

29

delle Tole

Giustina

San Francesco
della Vigna

RIALTO

15

Campo
S. Marina

Campo
S. Maria

R.d. S.
Francesco

R. d. S.

analazzo

Riva del Carbon

C. dell' Ovo

Mercerie

Salz. di S. Lio

R.d.Fava

Rio di
S. Lorenzo

Campo
S. Maria

26

Giuffa

27

S. Saverio

25

C.d.
Furlani

R.d.Scudi

R.d.Crotte

Darsena
Grande

Rio d. Vergini

San Pietro
di Castello

S.
Pie

Campo
Manin

C.d.
Barcaroli

Fabbri

C. dei Monti
delle Ballotte

C. Fiubera

SAN
ZACCARIA

C.d. Bande

C.d. Cotona

Fond.
Osmarin

R.d.Greci

C.Lion

R. d. Pietà

CASTELLO

23

R.d. Arsenale

ARCO

Saliz.
S. Luca

Piscina

Frezzeria

C. dei
Speechier

Ponte dei
Sospiri

Riva degli

Schiavoni

Rio della Tana

R.d. Danièle

C. Lga
22 Marzo

Fond. di
Farine

1

5   1
3   2
4

Piazza
San Marco

Molo

S. ZACCARIA

S. ZACCARIA JOLANDA

24

V. Garibaldi

Rio d.S.Anna

VALLARESSO

SAN MARCO
GIARDINETTI

S. ZACCARIA
DANIELI

ARSENALE

Riva dei Sette Martiri

R.d.S.Giuseppe

8

SALUTE

R.Tera dei
Catecumeni

Bacino San Marco

S. GIORGIO

36

S. Giorgio
Maggiore

GIARDINI

Riva dei Partigiani

LIDO

Rio dei
Giardini

CHIESA DEL
REDENTORE

ZITELLE

Fond.
delle Zitelle

Calle
Michelangelo

KEY

▲ Vaporetto stop

🛈 Tourist information

▶ Start of tour

In spite of these drawbacks, Venetians have mastered the art of living well. You'll see them going about their daily affairs in *vaporetti* (water buses), aboard the *traghetti* (traditional gondola ferries) that ferry across the Grand Canal, in the *campi* (squares), and along the *calli* (narrow streets). They are nothing if not skilled—and remarkably tolerant—in dealing with the veritable armies of tourists from all over the world that inundate the city almost year-round.

EXPLORING VENICE

Updated by
Elaine Eliah

Piazza San Marco is unquestionably the heart of Venice. The city is made up of six *sestieri*, or neighborhoods: San Marco, west of Piazza San Marco; Castello, east of San Marco; Cannaregio, to the northwest; Santa Croce and San Polo, roughly between the station and the Grand Canal; and Dorsoduro, diagonally across the Grand Canal from San Marco. Canals, called *rii* (singular *rio*), have frequent bridges, but the Grand Canal has only three—Ponte degli Scalzi (near the train station), Ponte di Rialto, and Ponte dell'Accademia—which can complicate matters. If you find yourself on the wrong bank with no bridge in sight, look for signs that say *traghetto* (gondola ferry) and hop across in style, saving your legs and your mood.

A street is called a *calle*, unless it runs along a canal, in which case it's a *riva* or a *fondamenta*. Only San Marco is called a *piazza*; any other Venetian square is a *campo*. Winding backstreets can confuse anyone's sense of direction, and spotting reference points (such as bell towers) above rooftops is difficult. Even streets that seem familiar can be deceptive, and shops that were your landmarks can suddenly close their shutters for the night. Taking a vaporetto along the Grand Canal is a wonderful way to get an overview, but the city should really be explored on foot; sestieri are best savored by strolling from a Renaissance church to a chatty *bacaro* (wine shop), stopping on the way to admire the boats moored along a canal, or sitting at a café for cappuccino and pastry while you watch Venice's dolce vita unfold before your eyes.

Fifteen Venetian churches, known as the **Chorus churches,** (☎ 041/2750462 ⊕ www.chorus-ve.org) have been singled out for their artistic merit; Santa Maria del Giglio, Santo Stefano, Santa Maria Formosa, Santa Maria dei Miracoli, Santa Maria Gloriosa dei Frari, San Polo, San Giacomo dell'Orio, San Stae, Sant'Alvise, Madonna dell'Orto, San Pietro di Castello, Santissimo Redentore, San Sebastiano, Gesuati, and San Giovanni Elemosinario. They're open to visitors all day except Sunday morning, and usually someone there can provide information and a free leaflet in English. Postcards and booklets about the sights are on sale. Single church entry costs €2, or you can visit them all with a €8 Chorus pass. The price of the pass includes audio guides except in Basilica dei Frari, where they cost €0.50. The artwork in Chorus churches is labeled and the staff can show you where to switch on lighting for selected paintings.

Eleven museums currently make up Venice's **Musei Civici** (☎ 041/5224951 ⊕ www.museiciviciveneziani.it). A Museum Pass, costing €15.50 and valid for three months, lets you make one visit to each museum. A Museum Card, good only at the Piazza San Marco museums—Palazzo Ducale, Museo Correr, Museo Archeologico, and Biblioteca Nazionale Marciana—costs €11.

Note that Gallerie dell'Accademia and other Venetian museums have no cafés inside and don't permit you to bring in food or drink. The staff might allow you to run to the nearest bar and return without paying a

Carnevale

". . . All the world repaire to Venice to see the folly and madnesse of the Carnevall . . .'tis impossible to recount the universal madnesses of this place during this time of licence." So commented traveler John Evelyn in 1646, and indeed, Carnevale (Carnival) was once an excuse for all manner of carnal indulgence. In its 18th-century heyday, festivities began on December 26 and lasted two months; the festival has since traded some of its more outlandish flavor for vast commercialization and lasts only for the 10 days preceding Ash Wednesday.

1

Getting Lost

There's no escaping the fact that Venice is a difficult place to navigate. Narrow, winding streets, meaningless address numbers, and a shortage of easily visible landmarks to orient yourself by all add to the confusion. Fortunately, getting lost in Venice can be a pleasure. You may not find the Titian masterpiece you'd set out to see, but instead you might come across an ageless bacaro or a charming shop that makes your afternoon; opportunities for such serendipity abound. And the city is nothing if not self-contained—sooner or later, perhaps with the help of a patient native, you can rest assured that you'll regain your bearings.

Shopping

Alluring shops abound in Venice. You'll find countless vendors of trademark Venetian wares such as glass and lace; the authenticity of some goods can be suspect, but they're often pleasing to the eye regardless of their heritage. For more sophisticated tastes (and deeper pockets), there are jewelers, antiques dealers, and high-fashion boutiques, on a par with those in Italy's larger cities but often maintaining a uniquely Venetian flair.

---

second admission, but this is left to their discretion. There are, however, refreshments available in Palazzo Ducale, Museo Correr, Ca' Rezzonico, Querini-Stampalia, and the Peggy Guggenheim Collection.

Numbers in the text correspond to numbers in the margin and on the Venice and Venetian Lagoon maps.

Piazza San Marco

One of the world's most evocative squares, Piazza San Marco is the heart of Venice, a vast open space bordered by an orderly procession of arcades marching toward the fairy-tale cupolas and marble lacework of the Basilica di San Marco. Perpetually packed by day with people and fluttering pigeons, it can be magical at night, especially in winter, when mists swirl around the lampposts and bell tower.

a good walk

Start your tour of **Piazza San Marco** ① ⌐ at the **Basilica di San Marco** ②, with its Pala d'Oro and Museo Marciano. Next, get a bird's-eye view of the piazza and city from the **Campanile** ③. Move on to the Piazzetta San Marco to visit the glorious **Palazzo Ducale** ④ and its Ponte dei Sospiri. Return to Piazza San Marco and cross to the side opposite the Basilica, where you'll find the **Museo Correr** ⑤ in the Ala Napoleonica—so named because Napoléon built this wing enclosing the square.

TIMING

It takes a full day to really see everything, so if time is limited, you'll have to prioritize. Plan on 1½ hours for the Basilica and its Pala d'Oro,

Galleria, and Museo Marciano. You'll want at least two hours to appreciate Palazzo Ducale. Do take time to enjoy the piazza itself from a café table, or on a clear day, from atop the Campanile.

What to See

★ ❷ **Basilica di San Marco.** An opulent synthesis of Byzantine and Romanesque styles, Venice's gem is laid out in a Greek-cross floor plan and topped with five plump domes. It didn't become the cathedral of Venice until 1807, but its role as the Chiesa Ducale (doge's private chapel) gave it immense power and wealth. The original church was built in 828 to house the body of St. Mark the Evangelist. His remains, filched from Alexandria by the doge's agents, were supposedly hidden in a barrel under layers of pickled pork to sneak them past Muslim guards. The escapade is depicted in the 13th-century mosaic above the door farthest left of the front entrance, one of the earliest mosaics on the heavily decorated facade; look closely to see the church as it appeared at that time.

A 976 fire destroyed most of the original church. It was rebuilt and reopened in 1094, and for centuries it would serve as a symbol of Venetian wealth and power, endowed with all the riches admirals and merchants could carry off from the Orient, to the point where it earned the nickname Chiesa d'Oro (Golden Church). The four bronze horses that prance and snort over the doorway are copies of sculptures that victorious Venetians took from Constantinople in 1204 (the originals are in the Museo Marciano). Look for a medallion of red porphyry in the floor of the porch, inside the main door. It marks the spot where, in 1177, Doge Sebastiano Ziani orchestrated the reconciliation between Barbarossa—the Holy Roman Emperor—and Pope Alexander III. Dim lighting, galleries high above the naves—they served as the *matroneum,* (women's gallery)—the *iconostasis,* (altar screen), and the single massive Byzantine chandelier all seem to wed Christianity with the Orient, giving San Marco its exotic blend of majesty and mystery.

The basilica is famous for its 43,055 square ft of stunning mosaics, which run from floor to ceiling thanks to an innovative roof of brick vaulting. Many of the original windows were filled in to make room for even more artwork. At midday, when the interior is fully illuminated, the mosaics truly come alive, the shimmer of their tiny gold tiles becoming nothing short of magical. The earliest mosaics are from the 11th and 12th centuries, and the last were added in the early 1700s. One of the most recent is the *Last Judgment,* believed to be designed by Tintoretto (1518–94), on the arch between the porch and the nave. Inside the main entrance, turn right on the porch to see the Book of Genesis depicted on the ceiling. Ahead through a glass door, 13th-century mosaics depict St. Mark's life in the **Cappella Zen** (Zen Chapel). The **Cappella della Madonna di Nicopeia,** in the left transept, holds the altar icon that many consider Venice's most powerful protector. In nearby **Cappella della Madonna dei Mascoli,** the life of the Virgin Mary is depicted in fine 15th-century mosaics, believed to be based on drawings by Jacopo Bellini and Andrea Mantegna.

In the **Santuario** (Sanctuary), the main altar is built over the tomb of St. Mark, its green marble canopy lifted high on carved alabaster columns. Perhaps even more impressive is the **Pala d'Oro,** a dazzling gilded silver screen encrusted with 1,927 precious gems and 255 enameled panels. Originally commissioned in Constantinople by Doge Orseolo I (976–978), it was enlarged and embellished over four centuries by master craftsmen and wealthy merchants. The bronze door leading from the sanctuary into the sacristy is by Sansovino. In the top left corner the artist included a self-portrait and, above that, he pictured friend and fellow artist Titian. The **Tesoro** (Treasury), entered from the right transept, contains many treasures carried home from conquests abroad.

Climb the steep stairway to the **Galleria** and the **Museo Marciano** for the best overview of the basilica's interior. From here you can step outdoors for a sweeping panorama of Piazza San Marco and the Piazzetta dei Leoncini. The highlight of the museum is a close-up view of the original gilded bronze horses that were once on the outer gallery. The four were most probably cast in Rome and taken to Constantinople. Venetians claimed them after sacking that city; when Napoléon (1769–1821) sacked Venice in 1797, he took them to Paris. They were returned after the fall of the French Empire, but came home "blind"—their big ruby eyes had been sold.

Be warned: guards at the door turn away anyone with bare shoulders or knees; no shorts, short skirts, tank tops are allowed. If you want a free guided tour in English during summer months (less certain in winter, as the guides are volunteers), look for groups forming on the porch inside the main door. You may also arrange tours by appointment. ☒ *Piazza San Marco* ☎ *041/5225205 Basilica; 041/5225697 tours* ✉ *Basilica free, Tesoro €2; Santuario and Pala d'Oro €1.50, Galleria and Museo Marciano €2* ☉ *May–Oct., Mon.–Sat. 9:45–5, Sun. 2–5; Nov.–Apr., Mon.–Sat. 9:45–4, Sun. 2–4; last entry ½ hr before closing* Ⓥ *Vallaresso/San Zaccaria.*

☝ ❸ **Campanile.** Venice's famous brick bell tower (325 ft tall, plus the angel) had been standing nearly 1,000 years when in 1902, practically without warning, it collapsed, taking with it Jacopo Sansovino's 16th-century marble loggia at the base. The crushed loggia was promptly restored and the new tower, rebuilt to the old plan, reopened in 1912. In the 15th century, clerics found guilty of immoral behavior were suspended in wooden cages from the tower. Some were forced to subsist on bread and water for as long as a year, while others were left to starve. The stunning view from the tower on a clear day includes the Lido, the lagoon, and the mainland as far as the Alps but, strangely enough, none of the myriad canals that snake through the city. ☒ *Piazza San Marco* ☎ *041/5224064* ✉ *€6* ☉ *June–Sept., 9 AM–sunset but not later than 9 PM; Oct.–May, 9–4; last entry ½ hr before closing* ☉ *Closed 2–3 wks in Jan.* Ⓥ *Vallaresso/San Zaccaria.*

❺ **Museo Correr.** Exhibits in this museum of Venetian art and history range from the absurdly high-soled shoes worn by 16th-century Venetian ladies (who walked with the aid of a servant) to the huge *Grande Pianta Prospettica* by Jacopo de' Barbari (circa 1440–1515), which details in carved wood every nook and cranny of 16th-century Venice. It includes the old Rialto Bridge and an entire neighborhood that Napoléon demolished to create the Giardini della Biennale. Correr has a room devoted entirely to antique games, and its second-floor **Quadreria** (Picture Gallery) has works by Venetian, Greek, and Flemish painters. Through Correr, visitors can reach the **Museo Archeologico** and the **Stanza del Sansovino,** the only part of **Biblioteca Marciana** open to visitors. ☒ *Piazza San Marco, Ala Napoleonica* ☎ *041/5225625* ✉ *€11 Piazza San Marco museums, €15.50 Musei Civici pass* ☉ *Apr.–Oct., daily 9–7; Nov.–Mar., daily 9–5; last tickets sold 1½ hrs before closing* Ⓥ *Vallaresso/San Zaccaria.*

★ ❹ **Palazzo Ducale** (Doge's Palace). Rising above the Piazzetta San Marco, this Gothic-Renaissance fantasia of pink-and-white marble is a majestic expression of the prosperity and power attained during Venice's most glorious period. Some architectural purists find the building top-heavy, its dense upper floors resting awkwardly upon the graceful ground-floor colonnade, but one can hardly imagine the palace with any other design. Always much more than a residence, it was White House, Senate, torture chamber, and prison rolled into one. Venice's participatory democracy began around 700 with an elected doge, ruling for life. In practice he was little more than a figurehead; real power rested with the Great Council, which once had more than 2,000 members. Although originally an elected body, in the 13th century it became an aristocratic stronghold, members inheriting seats from noble ancestors. The Senate, a group of 200 elected from the Great Council, passed laws, but executive powers belonged to the College, a committee of 25. In the 14th century, the Council of Ten was formed to protect state security and soon became the most powerful and most feared branch of government.

Though a fortress for the doge existed here in the early 9th century, the building you see today was begun in the 12th century, and like the basilica next door, was continually remodeled over the centuries. Near the basilica you'll see the ornately Gothic **Porta della Carta** (Gate of the Paper), where official decrees were traditionally posted, but visitors enter under the portico facing the water. You'll find yourself in an immense courtyard with the **Scala dei Giganti** (Stairway of the Giants) directly ahead, guarded by Sansovino's huge statues of Mars and Neptune. Though ordinary mortals must use the central interior staircase, its upper flight is the lavishly gilded **Scala d'Oro** (Golden Staircase), also by Sansovino. It may seem odd that you have to climb so many steps to reach the government's main council rooms and reception halls, but imagine how this extraordinary climb must have overwhelmed, even intimidated, foreign emissaries.

The palace's sumptuous chambers are awe-inspiring in themselves, their walls and ceilings covered with works by Venice's greatest artists. Visit the **Anticollegio**, a waiting room outside the Collegio's chamber, where you'll see *Rape of Europa* by Veronese (1528–88) and Tintoretto's *Bacchus and Ariadne Crowned by Venus*. Veronese also painted the ceiling of the adjacent **Sala del Collegio**. The ceiling of the **Sala del Senato** (Senate Chamber) features *Triumph of Venice* by Tintoretto, magnificent surely, but dwarfed by his masterpiece *Paradise* in the **Sala del Maggiore Consiglio** (Great Council Hall). A vast work commissioned for a vast hall, this dark, dynamic piece is the world's largest oil painting (23 by 75 ft). The room's carved, gilded ceiling is breathtaking, especially with Veronese's majestic *Apotheosis of Venice* filling one of the center panels. Around the upper walls, study the portraits of the first 76 doges, and you'll notice one picture is missing near the left corner of the wall opposite *Paradise*. A black painted curtain, rather than a portrait, marks Doge Marin Falier's fall from grace; he was beheaded for treason in 1355, which the Latin inscription bluntly explains.

A narrow canal separates the Palace's east side from the cramped, gloomy cell blocks of the so-called **Prigioni Nuove** (New Prisons). High above the water arches the enclosed marble **Ponte dei Sospiri** (Bridge of Sighs), which earned its name from the sighs of those being led to execution. Look out its windows to see the last earthly view these prisoners had.

The palazzo's secret itinerary tour takes you to the doge's private apartments, through hidden passageways to the torture (interrogation) chambers, and into the rooftop *piombo* prison, named for its leaded roofing. Venetian-born writer and libertine Giacomo Casanova (1725–98), along with an accomplice, managed to escape piombo in 1756, the only men

CRUISING THE GRAND CANAL

VENETIANS CALL IT CANALAZZO, but to the rest of the world, it's the Grand Canal. Here 200 opulent palazzi, born of a culture obsessed with luxury and fantasy, appear by day in all their architectural splendor—and by night like something from a dream. The shallow ribbon of water (average depth 9 ft) winds like an inverted letter S, 4 km (2½ mi.) from the Ferrovia (train station) to Piazza San Marco. Though the canal may be more romantic viewed by gondola, sightseeing is more flexible (you can get on and off the boat at any stop) and less expensive by vaporetto, the Venetian water bus. If you board Line 1 at Ferrovia and take it straight through to San Marco, here are some of the sights to look for. (Try to grab one of the seats in the prow, where you'll have an unobstructed view.)

To your left as you leave the Ferrovia is Santa Maria di Nazareth, whose barefoot friars earned it the nickname Scalzi (shoeless) Church. Pass beneath Ponte di Scalzi, the first of three bridges, and where Canal di Cannaregio branches, a corner of **Palazzo Labia** towers behind the church. Opposite the San Marcuola stop is Fondaco dei Turchi, Venice's (closed) natural history museum. **Palazzo Vendramin-Calergi**, the city's casino, stands just past the dock. Next stop on the right is at the richly decorated **San Stae** church; leaving it, you'll pass Longhena's **Ca' Pesaro**, now a modern art museum, and the equally classical Ca' Corner della Regina. The vaporetto recrosses to stop at lovely, pink-and-white **Ca' d'Oro**; opposite, you'll see the market where Venetians have bartered for fish since the 1300s. With bridge number two, **Ponte di Rialto**, looming ahead, Fondaco dei Tedeschi (today the main post office) lies to the left, and opposite is Ca' dei Camerlenghi, 16th-century home of the State Treasury, and of unlucky tax evaders.

The vaporetto stops in front of Ca' Loredan and Ca' Farsetti, 12th- and 13th-century buildings that make up Venice's city hall. Ahead is Palazzo Grimani, Michele Sanmichele's Renaissance masterpiece, now an appeals court. At the San Angelo stop is another massive Renaissance piece, Ca' Corner Spinelli, this the work of Mauro Codussi. Opposite is large, salmon-colored Palazzo Pisani Moretta, faithfully restored down to candlelit chandeliers. The boat stops at San Tomà and—straight ahead, marking a sharp bend—is Ca' Foscari, once a doge's home and now site of the city's largest university. Veering left the boat pulls up beside Longhena's baroque **Ca' Rezzonico**, whose gilded salons hold the Museum of 18th-Century Venice. Directly opposite is **Palazzo Grassi**, one of the canal's newest properties, which today showcases art and historic exhibits. Approaching the canal's final bridge, you stop at a former church and monastery complex that houses the world-renowned **Gallerie dell'Accademia.**

Under Accademia Bridge the boat seems to move more quickly as you enter the home stretch, but it's hard to miss the patch of green ahead. A garden cradles Casetta Rossa (small red house), which has sheltered painters, poets, and princes. Today the house seems lost in a wake of boatloads of tourists whizzing by and the shadow of Palazzo Corner Ca' Grande next door. Opposite is Palazzo Venier dei Leoni, which once belonged to Peggy Guggenheim and continues to hold the **Peggy Guggenheim Collection** of contemporary art. The boat again stops on the left near the Gritti Palace Hotel; now you can see the canal beginning to widen out. One last stop on the right and you're at **Santa Maria della Salute**, Longhena's 17th-century creation thanking the Virgin for saving Venice from a plague. At the tip of Punta della Dogana (a former customs house), muscle men shoulder the world, while the golden goddess of fortune stands atop, pointing her way into the wind. At the Vallaresso stop, you've officially left the Grand Canal, but don't disembark before cruising past Piazza San Marco.

ever to do so. ⊠ *Piazzetta San Marco* ☎ *041/5224951* 🖅 *€11 Piazza San Marco museums, €15.50 Musei Civici pass* ☉ *Apr.–Oct., daily 9–7; Nov.–Mar., daily 9–5; last tickets sold 1½ hrs before closing* 🖅 *English guided tours* 🖅 *€6* ☉ *Tues.–Thurs., Sat. 11:30 "Secret Itinerary" tour* 🖅 *€12.50* ☉ *English tours daily 10 and 11:30; reservations advisable* Ⓥ *Vallaresso/San Zaccaria.*

▶ ❶ **Piazza San Marco** (St. Mark's Square). If you face the basilica from in front of the Correr Museum, you'll notice that rather than being a strict rectangle, this square opens wider at the basilica end, creating the illusion that its even larger than it is. On your left, the long, arcaded building is the **Procuratie Vecchie,** built in the early 16th century as offices and residences for the powerful procurators (magistrates) of San Marco. On your right is the **Procuratie Nuove,** built half a century later in a more grandiose classical style. It was originally planned by Venice's great Renaissance architect, Sansovino, to carry on the look of his **Libreria Sansoviniana** (Sansovinian Library), but he died before construction on the Nuove had begun. Vincenzo Scamozzi (circa 1552–1616), a neo-classicist pupil of Andrea Palladio (1508–80), completed design and construction. Still later, the Procuratie Nuove were modified by architect Baldassare Longhena (1598–1682), one of Venice's baroque masters.

When Napoléon (1769–1821) entered Venice with his troops in 1797, he called Piazza San Marco "the world's most beautiful drawing room"— and promptly gave orders to redecorate it. His architects demolished a 16th-century church with a Sansovino facade in order to build the **Ala Napoleonica** (Napoleonic Wing), or Fabbrica Nuova (New Building), which linked the two 16th-century procuratie, and effectively enclosed the piazza.

need a break?

Since **Caffè Florian** (☎ 041/5205641), located in the Procuratie Nuove, brewed its first cup of coffee, it has served the likes of Casanova, Dickens, and Proust. It's Venice's oldest café, continuously open since 1720 (though you'll find it closed on winter Wednesdays). Counter seating is less expensive than taking a table, especially when there's live music. In the Procuratie Vecchie, **Caffè Quadri** (☎ 041/5289299), exudes almost as much history as Florian across the way and is similarly pricey. It was shunned by 19th-century Venetians when the occupying Austrians made it their gathering place. During slow season, it closes Mondays. If you'd like to happy hour with the ghosts of Hemingway, Onassis, and Orson Welles, head to **Harry's Bar** (☎ 041/5285777). Walk out Piazza San Marco near the Correr Museum and turn left at Calle Vallaresso; you'll find the legendary hangout right at the vaporetto landing. Harry's still boasts Venice's driest martinis and freshest Bellinis (white peach juice and sparkling Prosecco wine).

Piazzetta San Marco. This "little square" leads from Piazza San Marco to the waters of Bacino San Marco (St. Mark's Basin). The *molo* (landing), once the grand entrance to the Republic, has two columns towering above the waterfront. One is topped by the winged lion, a traditional emblem of St. Mark that became the symbol of Venice itself; the other supports St. Theodore, the city's first patron, along with his dragon. Between these columns the Republic traditionally executed convicts.

Torre dell'Orologio. Five hundred years ago when this enameled clock was built, twin Moors would strike the hour, and three wise men with an angel would walk out and bow to the Virgin Mary during Epiphany (January 6) and Ascension Week (40 days after Easter). An inscription on the tower reads HORAS NON NUMERO NISI SERENAS ("I only count happy hours"); if that's true, perhaps happy hours will return to Venice when they finally fix the clock. It's been under restoration for years, but you can visit the three wise men in Palazzo Ducale where they and other clock parts are on display. ⊠ *North side of Piazza San Marco.*

Dorsoduro

If churches, rambling along dreamy canals, and great Venetian master-pieces by Titian and Tintoretto capture your interest, leave San Marco behind to explore the sestiere on the other side of the Grand Canal.

a good walk

Start out across the Grand Canal from Dorsoduro in **Campo Santo Stefano** ⑥ ☞ and visit its 14th-century church. Then take Ponte dell'Accademia over the canal to sestiere Dorsoduro (named for its "hard back" solid clay foundation) and **Gallerie dell'Accademia** ⑦, where you'll see an unparalleled collection of Venetian painting. Head toward the eastern point of the peninsula, Punta della Dogana, for one of the best views in town. **Santa Maria della Salute** ⑧ certainly deserves attention inside and out before you backtrack to the 20th-century **Peggy Guggenheim Collection** ⑨. Next stop, the Zattere, where on sunny days you'll swear half the city is out for a *passeggiata,* or stroll. Visit the church of the **Gesuati** ⑩ if only to peek at the Tiepolo ceiling, and don't miss the *bocca di leoni* (lion's mouth) between this church and its older sibling, Santa Maria della Visitazione.

Past the lion's mouth, take a right to see the Squero di San Trovaso, where wooden boats have been built and repaired for centuries. This architectural style arrived with the skilled woodworkers Venice imported from the mountains. Returning to Zattere, continue to the San Basilio vaporetto stop. Ahead lies Stazione Marittima, where summer cruise ships line the dock, but instead of crossing that bridge, turn right on Calle del Vento alongside the canal. Opposite the next bridge is the church of **San Sebastiano** ⑪, filled with Veronese's paintings and his grave. Calle del Vento angles right and opens into the small campo of Chiesa dei Carmini. Around the corner is the beautiful **Scuola Grande dei Carmini** ⑫, and just beyond is lively Campo Santa Margarita, packed with markets and kids, students and tourists. Stop here for a well-deserved coffee or glass of wine.

Leave the campo at Rio San Barnaba to see the most photographed vegetable vendor in town. You'll cross Ponte dei Pugni (Bridge of Fists), former battleground of the Nicolotti (westsiders) and Castellani (easterners), Venice's Hatfields and McCoys. The calle alongside San Barnaba church leads to **Ca' Rezzonico** ⑬ and the Museo del Settecento Veneziano. If you've had your fill of history, and **Palazzo Grassi** ⑭ has a show that catches your eye, hop across on a traghetto.

TIMING This walk takes about two hours without stops, but it's a full day, or more, if you want to see all the sights. The Gallerie dell'Accademia demand a few hours by themselves, but if time is short, an audio guide can help you cover the highlights in about an hour. Give yourself at least 1½ hours for the Guggenheim Collection. The churches and Scuola dei Carmini are not large, and unless something grabs your attention, a half hour should be enough for each one. Ca' Rezzonico deserves a couple of hours.

What to See

★ ⑬ **Ca' Rezzonico.** Designed by Baldassare Longhena in the 17th century, this palace was completed nearly 100 years later by Giorgio Massari and became the last home of English poet Robert Browning (1812–89). Elizabeth Taylor and Richard Burton danced in the baroque ballroom in the 1960s. Today, Ca' Rezzonico is the home of the **Museo del Settecento** (Museum of Venice in the 1700s). Its main floor is packed with period furniture and tapestries in gilded salons (note the four Tiepolo ceiling frescoes) and actually feels like an old Venetian palazzo. Upper floors contain hundreds of paintings, most from Venetian schools of artists. There's even a restored apothecary, complete with powders and potions. ⊠ *Fondamenta Rezzonico, Dorsoduro 3136* ☎ *041/2410100* ⏰ *€6.50, €15.50 Musei Civici pass* ◷ *Apr.–Oct., Wed.–Mon. 10–6; Nov.–Mar., Wed.–Mon. 10–5; last entry 1 hr before closing* Ⓥ *Ca' Rezzonico.*

▶ ❻ **Campo Santo Stefano.** In Venice's most prestigious residential neighborhood, you'll find one of the city's busiest crossroads; it's hard to believe this square once hosted bullfights, with bulls (or oxen) tied to a stake and baited by dogs. For centuries the campo was grass except for a stone avenue called the *liston*. It was so popular for strolling that in Venetian dialect *"andare al liston"* still means, "go for a walk." A sunny meeting spot popular with Venetians and visitors alike, the campo also hosts outdoor fairs during Christmas and Carnevale seasons. Check out the 14th-century **Chiesa di Santo Stefano** and its ship's-keel roof, created by shipbuilders. You'll see works by Tintoretto and the tipsiest bell tower in town—best appreciated from nearby Campo San Angelo. ⊠ *Campo Santo Stefano, San Marco* ☎ *041/2750462 Chorus* ⏰ *€2, €8 Chorus pass* ◷ *Mon.–Sat. 10–5, Sun. 1–5* Ⓥ *Accademia.*

★ ❼ **Gallerie dell'Accademia.** Napoléon founded these galleries in 1807 on the site of a religious complex he'd suppressed, and what he initiated amounts to the world's most extraordinary collection of Venetian art. Jacopo Bellini (1400–71) is considered the father of the Venetian Renaissance, and in Room 2 you can compare his *Madonna and Child with Saints* with such later works as *Madonna of the Orange Tree* by Cima da Conegliano (circa 1459–1517) and *Ten Thousand Martyrs of Mt. Ararat* by Vittore Carpaccio (1450–1526). Jacopo's son Giovanni (circa 1430–1516) draws your eye not with his subjects but with his rich color. Rooms 4 and 5 are full of his Madonnas; note the contrast between the young Madonna and child and the neighboring older Madonna after the crucifixion—you'll see the colors of dawn and dusk in Venice. Room 5 contains *Tempest* by Giorgione (1477–1510), a work that was revolutionary in its time and has continued to intrigue viewers and critics over the centuries. It depicts a storm approaching as a nude woman nurses her child and a soldier looks on. The overall atmosphere that Giorgione creates is as important as any of his figures.

In Room 10, *Feast in the House of Levi,* commissioned as a Last Supper, got Veronese dragged before the Inquisition over its depiction of dogs, jesters, and German (therefore Protestant) soldiers. The artist saved his neck by simply changing the title, so that the painting represented a different biblical feast. Titian's *Presentation of the Virgin* (Room 24) is the collection's only work originally created for the building in which it hangs. Don't miss Rooms 20 and 21, with views of 15th- and 16th-century Venice by Carpaccio and Gentile Bellini (1429–1507), Giovanni's brother—you'll see how little the city has changed.

Booking tickets in advance isn't essential but helps during busy seasons and costs only an additional €1. Booking is necessary to see the **Quadreria,** where additional works cover every inch of a wide hallway. A free map names art and artists, and the bookshop sells a more informative English-language booklet. In the main galleries, a €4 audio guide saves reading but adds little to each room's excellent annotation; audio/video guides (€6) are more exhaustive and also ease navigating. ⊠ *Campo della Carità, Dorsoduro 1050* ☎ *041/5222247; 041/5200345* *reservations.* ⊕ *www.gallerieaccademia.org* ✉ €6.50, €11 *also includes Ca' d'Oro and Museo Orientale* ☉ *Tues.–Sun. 8:15–7:15, Mon. 8:15–2* Ⓥ *Accademia.*

⑩ Gesuati. When the Dominicans took over the church of Santa Maria della Visitazione from the suppressed order of Gesuati laymen in 1668, Giorgio Massari was commissioned to build this church. It has a score of works by Giambattista Tiepolo (1696–1770), Giambiattista Piazzetta (1683–1754), and Sebastiano Ricci (1659–1734). ✉ *Zattere Dorsoduro* ☎ *041/2750462 Chorus* ✉ €2, €8 *Chorus pass* ☉ *Mon.–Sat. 10–5, Sun. 1–5* Ⓥ *Zattere.*

> **need a break?** If ice cream is the food of gods, then heaven's as close as the Zattere, where generations of Venetians have chosen **Gelateria Nico** (✉ Dorsoduro 922 ☎ 041/5225293). Grab a chocolaty *gianduiotto*, their famous nutty slab of chocolate ice cream floating on a cloud of whipped cream, and relax on the biggest, most welcoming deck in town.

⑭ Palazzo Grassi. The Grassi family from Bologna bought their way into aristocracy in 1718, then bought into the Grand Canal 30 years later, when Giorgio Massari designed their neoclassical palace; it was to become the canal's last grand addition. Fiat acquired the property in 1985 and turned it into a venue for art and history exhibitions. ✉ *Campo San Samuele, San Marco 3231* ☎ *041/5231680* ⊕ *www.palazzograssi.it* Ⓥ *San Samuele.*

⑨ Peggy Guggenheim Collection. Visit and delight in this small but choice gallery of 20th-century painting and sculpture, in the heiress Guggenheim's former Grand Canal home. Through wealth and social connections, Guggenheim (1898–1979) became a serious art patron, and her collection here in Palazzo Venier dei Leoni includes works by Picasso, Kandinsky, Pollock, Motherwell, and Ernst (at one time her husband). The museum serves up beverages, snacks, and light meals in its refreshingly shady, artistically sophisticated garden. ✉ *Calle San Cristoforo, Dorsoduro 701* ☎ *041/2405411* ⊕ *www.guggenheim-venice.it* ✉ €8 ☉ *Wed.–Mon. 10–6; Apr.–Oct., Sat. open until 10 PM; last entry 15 mins before closing* Ⓥ *Accademia.*

⑪ San Sebastiano. Paolo Veronese (1528–88) established his reputation while still in his twenties with these frescoes. Beginning with Old Testament scenes on the ceiling, he spent decades embellishing this, his parish church, with amazing trompe-l'oeil scenes. Don't miss his altarpiece *Madonna in Glory with Saints.* Veronese is buried beneath his bust near the organ. ✉ *Campo San Sebastiano, Dorsoduro* ☎ *041/2750462 Chorus* ✉ €2, €8 *Chorus pass* ☉ *Mon.–Sat. 10–5, Sun. 1–5* Ⓥ *San Basilio.*

⑧ Santa Maria della Salute. The view of La Salute from the Riva degli Schiavoni at sunset or from the Accademia Bridge by moonlight is unforgettable. Baldassare Longhena was 32 years old when he won a competition to design a shrine honoring the Virgin Mary for saving Venice from a plague that killed 47,000 residents. Outside, this simple white octagon is adorned with a colossal cupola lined with snail-like buttresses and a Palladian-style facade; inside are a polychrome marble floor and six chapels. The Byzantine icon above the main altar has been venerated as the Madonna della Salute (of health) since 1670, when Francesco Morosini brought it here from Crete. Above it is a sculpture showing Venice (left) on her knees while the plague (right) is driven from the city. The **Sacrestia Maggiore** contains a dozen works by Titian, including his *San Marco Enthroned with Saints* altarpiece. You'll also see Tintoretto's

The Wedding at Canaan, and on special occasions the altar displays a 15th-century tapestry depicting the Pentecost. For the Festa della Salute, November 21st, Venetians make a pilgrimage and light candles in thanksgiving for another year's health. ⊠ *Punta della Dogana, Dorsoduro* ☎ *041/5225558* ⊡ *Church free, sacristy €1.50* ✆ *June–Sept., daily 9–noon and 3–6; Oct.–May, daily 9–noon and 3–5:30* Ⓥ *Salute.*

⑫ Scuola Grande dei Carmini. Venice's institution of the *scuola* (plural *scuole*) were not schools as the word today translates. These secular institutions were established by different social groups—foreigners, tradesmen, followers of a particular saint—and concentrated on supporting their own members or helping society's neediest citizens. The tradesmen's or servants' scuole formed social security nets for their elderly and disabled members. Wealthier scuole assisted orphans and provided dowries so poor girls could marry.

When the order of Santa Maria del Carmelo commissioned Longhena to build Scuola Grande dei Carmini in the late 1600s, their brotherhood of 75,000 members was the largest in Venice and one of the wealthiest. Little expense was spared in the decorating of stuccoed ceilings and carved ebony paneling, and the artwork was choice, even before 1739 when Tiepolo painted the **Sala Capitolare.** In what many consider his best work, Tiepolo's nine great canvases vividly transform some rather unpromising religious themes into flamboyant displays of color and movement. ⊠ *Campo dei Carmini, Dorsoduro 2617* ☎ *041/5289420* ⊡ *€5* ✆ *Nov.–Mar., daily 9–4; Apr.–Oct., Mon.–Sat. 9–6, Sun. 9–4* Ⓥ *Ca' Rezzonico.*

need a break? Filled with cafés and restaurants, **Campo Santa Margarita** also has produce vendors, pizza by the slice, and benches where you can sit and eat. For more than a portable munch, bask in the sunshine at popular **il Caffè** (Caffé Rossa; ☎ 041/5287998). Open past midnight, Rossa offers drinks and light refreshment every day except Sunday.

San Polo & Santa Croce

The smallest of Venice's six sestieri, San Polo and Santa Croce were named after their main churches, though the Chiesa di Santa Croce was demolished in 1810. This walk includes some big attractions, such as Santa Maria Gloriosa dei Frari and the Scuola Grande San Rocco, as well as some worthwhile but lesser-known churches.

a good walk Begin your tour where the city of Venice itself began; *Rivo Alto* Rialto. **Ponte di Rialto** ⑮ ▶ bridges sestiere San Marco (west) with San Polo (east). Chiesa di San Giacometto, where you see the first fruit vendors, was probably built in the 11th and 12th centuries, the same time as the market. Public announcements were traditionally read in its campo; its 24-hour clock, though lovely, has rarely worked. While shops on the San Marco side of the bridge sell everything that's hip, this side sells everything edible. Come early to beat the crowds and bear in mind that "metà kilo" is about a pound and an "etto" is a few ounces.

Heading south away from Rialto on Ruga Vechia San Giovanni, look for a gate on your left. It marks the entrance to **San Giovanni Elemosinario** ⑯ , which is completely devoid of facade, because it always leased the outdoor space to vendors. This street continues to **Campo San Polo** ⑰ and **Santa Maria Gloriosa dei Frari** ⑱ ; you can save your feet by hopping a vaporetto from San Silvestro to San Tomà, where a short walk brings you to Frari. Two of Titian's finest hang there, and nearby **Scuola Grande di San Rocco** ⑲ is a treasury of works by Tintoretto.

Cross the bridge in front of Frari and turn left. After another bridge you'll enter Campo San Stin and take a right. Cross one more bridge and turn left to reach **San Giacomo dell'Orio** ⑳ campo and church, a peaceful place for a drink, a rest, and a chance to glimpse daily life. In the campo's northeast corner, cross over the right-angle canal and continue along Calle del Tentor until you reach Salizada San Stae. A left here brings you to the Grand Canal at the whimsically baroque **San Stae** ㉑. From here signs direct you over a bridge and down a narrow alley to **Ca' Pesaro** ㉒, the site of both the Museum of Modern Art and the Oriental Museum.

TIMING The walk itself takes only about an hour, but there's a lot to see. If you do any shopping, or even pop in at a few churches along the way, you'll easily stretch it into a half day. You'll want at least two hours to see both collections at Ca' Pesaro.

What to See

㉒ **Ca' Pesaro.** Longhena's grand baroque palace is the beautifully restored home of two impressive collections. The **Galleria Internazionale d'Arte Moderna** has works by 19th and 20th-century artists such as Klimt, Kandinsky, Matisse, and Miró. The **Museo Orientale** has a small but striking collection of oriental porcelains, musical instruments, arms, and armor. ✉ *San Stae, Santa Croce 2076* ☎ *041/5240695 Galleria; 041/5241173 Museo Orientale* ☽ *Apr.–Oct., Tues.–Sun. 10–6; Nov.–Mar., Tues.–Sun. 10–5* 🖭 *€5.50 includes both museums, €15.50 Musei Civici pass, €11 includes only Museo Orientale, Ca' d'Oro, Accademia* Ⓥ *San Stae.*

⑰ **Campo San Polo.** Only Piazza San Marco is larger than this square, where not even the pigeons manage to look cozy, and the echo of children's voices bouncing off the surrounding palaces makes the space seem even more cavernous. Not long ago Campo San Polo hosted bull races, fairs, military parades, and packed markets, but now it only really comes alive on summer nights, when it hosts the city's outdoor cinema. **Chiesa di San Polo** has been restored so many times that little remains of the original 9th-century Church of St. Paul, and sadly, 19th-century alterations were so costly that the friars sold off many great paintings to pay bills. Though Giambattista Tiepolo is represented here, his work is outdone by 16 paintings of his son Giandomenico (1727–1804), including the *Stations of the Cross* in the oratory to the left of the entrance. The younger Tiepolo also created a series of expressive and theatrical renderings of the saints. Look for altarpieces by Tintoretto and Veronese that managed to escape auction. San Polo's bell tower remained unchanged through the centuries—don't miss the two lions guarding it, playing with a detached human head and a serpent. ✉ *Campo San Polo* ☎ *041/2750462 Chorus* 🖭 *€2, €8 Chorus pass* ☽ *Mon.–Sat. 10–5, Sun. 1–5* Ⓥ *San Tomà.*

★ ▶ ⑮ **Ponte di Rialto** (Rialto Bridge). The competition to design a stone bridge across the Grand Canal (replacing earlier wooden versions) attracted the late 1500s' best architects, including Michelangelo, Palladio, and Sansovino, but the job went to the less famous but appropriately named Antonio da Ponte. His pragmatic design featured shop space and was high enough for galleys to pass beneath; it kept decoration and cost to a minimum at a time when the republic's coffers were low due to continual wars against the Turks and the opening of oceanic trade routes. Along the railing you'll enjoy one of the city's most famous views: the Grand Canal vibrant with boat traffic. Ⓥ *Rialto.*

⓴ San Giacomo dell'Orio. It was named after a laurel tree *(orio)*, and today trees give character to **Campo San Giacomo dell'Orio**. Add benches and a fountain (with drinking bowl for dogs), and this pleasantly odd-shaped campo becomes a welcoming place for friends, picnics, and neighborhood kids at play. Legend has it the **Chiesa di San Giacomo dell'Orio** was founded in the 9th century on an island still populated by wolves. The current church dates to 1225; its short unmatched Byzantine columns survived renovation during the Renaissance, and the church never lost the feel of an ancient temple sheltering beneath its 15th-century ship's-keel roof. In the sanctuary, large marble crosses are surrounded by a bevy of small medieval Madonnas. The altarpiece is *Madonna with Child and Saints* (1546), by Lorenzo Lotto (1480–1556), and the sacristies contain works by Palma il Giovane (circa 1544–1628). ⊠ *Campo San Giacomo dell'Orio, Santa Croce* ☎ *041/2750462 Chorus* 🖃 *€2, €8 Chorus pass* ⊘ *Mon.–Sat. 10–5, Sun. 1–5* Ⓥ *San Stae.*

⓰ San Giovanni Elemosinario. Storefronts make up the facade, and the altars were built by market guilds—poulterers, messengers, and fodder merchants—at this church intimately bound to Rialto Market. It's as rich inside as it is simple outside. During San Giovanni Elemosinario's restoration, workers stumbled upon a Pordenone-frescoed cupola that had been painted over centuries earlier. Don't miss Titian's *St. John the Almsgiver* and Pordenone's *Sts. Catherine, Sebastian, and Roch,* which in 2002 were returned after 30 years by Gallerie dell'Accademia, a rarity for Italian museums. ⊠ *Rialto Ruga Vechia S. Giovanni* ☎ *041/2750462 Chorus* 🖃 *€2, €8 Chorus pass* ⊘ *Mon.–Sat. 10–5, Sun. 1–5* Ⓥ *San Silvestro or Rialto.*

⓴① San Stae. The most renowned Venetian painters and sculptors of the early 18th-century—known as the Moderns—decorated this church with the legacy left by Doge Alvise Mocenigo II, who's buried in the center aisle. A broad sampling of these masters includes works by Tiepolo, Ricci, Piazzetta, and Lazzarini. ⊠ *Campo San Stae, Santa Croce* ☎ *041/2750462 Chorus* 🖃 *€2, €8 Chorus pass* ⊘ *Mon.–Sat. 9–5, Sun. 1–5* Ⓥ *San Stae.*

⓲ Santa Maria Gloriosa dei Frari. This immense Gothic church of russet-color brick, completed in the 1400s after over a century of work, is deliberately austere, befitting the Franciscan Brothers' tenets of spirituality and poverty. However, *I Frari* (as it's known locally) contains some of the most brilliant paintings in any Venetian church. Visit the sacristy first, to see Giovanni Bellini's 1488 triptych *Madonna and Child with Saints* in all its mellow luminosity, painted for precisely this spot. You'll appreciate the rapid development of Venetian Renaissance painting by contrasting Bellini with the heroic energy of Titian's *Assumption,* over the main altar, painted some 30 years later. Unveiled in 1518, this work was immediately acclaimed for its winning combination of Venetian color—especially the glowing reds—and classical Roman figure style.

Fodor'sChoice
★

Titian's beautiful *Madonna di Ca' Pesaro* (left nave) was modeled after his wife, who died in childbirth. The painting took almost 10 years to complete, and in it Titian totally disregarded the conventions of his time by moving the Virgin out of center frame and making the saints active participants. On the same side of the church, look at the spooky, pyramid-shape monument to the sculptor Antonio Canova (1757–1822). Across the nave is a neoclassical 19th-century monument to Titian, executed by two of Canova's pupils. ⊠ *Campo dei Frari, San Polo* ☎ *041/2728618; 041/2750462 Chorus* 🖃 *€2, €8 Chorus pass* ⊘ *Mon.–Sat. 9–6, Sun. 1–6* Ⓥ *San Tomà.*

need a break?

On a narrow passage between Frari and San Rocco, **Gelateria Millevoglie** (a Thousand Desires; ☎ 041/5244667) has pizza slices, calzones, and gelato so popular it backs up traffic. It's closed in December and January, but the rest of the year it's open 10 AM to midnight, seven days a week.

19 **Scuola Grande di San Rocco.** St. Rocco's popularity stemmed from his miraculous recovery from the plague and his care for fellow sufferers. Throughout the plague-filled Middle Ages, followers and donations abounded, and this elegant example of Venetian Renaissance architecture was the result. Bold and dramatic outside, its contents are even more stunning—a series of more than 60 paintings by Tintoretto. Born Jacopo Robusti, in 1564 Tintoretto edged out competition for a commission to decorate a ceiling by submitting not a sketch, but a finished work, which he moreover offered free of charge. *Moses Striking Water from the Rock, The Brazen Serpent,* and *The Fall of Manna* represent three bodily sufferings—thirst, disease, and hunger—that San Rocco and later his brotherhood strived to counteract. ⊠ *Campo San Rocco, San Polo 3052* ☎ *041/ 5234864* ⤢ *€5.50* ⊘ *Mar. 28–Nov. 2, daily 9–5:30; Nov. 3–Mar. 27, daily 10–4; last entrance ½ hr before closing* Ⓥ *San Tomà.*

need a break?

The music may get loud at **Café Noir** (⊠ Calle Crosera, Dorsoduro 3805 ☎ 041/710925), but the sandwiches are good, and buying food gives you discounts on Web-surfing. It's open until 2 AM but is closed Sunday. **Pasticceria Tonolo** (⊠ Dorsoduro 3764 ☎ 041/5237209), has been fattening Venetians since 1886. During Carnevale, it's still the best place in town for *fritelle,* fried doughnuts (traditional raisin or cream-filled); during acqua alta, the staff dons rubber boots and keeps working. The place is closed on Monday, and there's no seating anytime.

Castello & Cannaregio

Twice the size of tiny San Polo and Santa Croce, Castello and Cannaregio combined spread east to west from one end of Venice to the other. From working-class shipbuilding neighborhoods to the world's first ghetto, you'll see a cross section of city life that's always existed beyond the palace walls. Churches that could make a Renaissance pope jealous await you, as does one of the Grand Canal's prettiest palaces, Ca' d'Oro, but here, you'll also find detour options for leaving the crowds behind.

a good walk

Wake up with the lions, the ones guarding the awesome gates of **Arsenale** ㉓ ▶, and see where the Republic forged its mighty sea power. The **Museo Storico Navale** ㉔ just a bridge away, has ships and models from Venice and around the world. See some of Carpaccio's best paintings at **Scuola di San Giorgio degli Schiavoni** ㉕ before navigating the maze that leads to the square of **Santa Maria Formosa** ㉖. It has a fountain, vegetable market, church, and canal—all the prerequisites for a perfect Venetian campo—and has **Querini-Stampalia** ㉗, a library and art collection housed in an elegantly restored palace. Signs direct you north toward **Santi Giovanni e Paolo** ㉘ campo and church. With all its entombed VIPs, it's Venice's answer to Westminster Abbey.

If you're here in the afternoon, stop by a former foundling home at **Ospedaletto** ㉙, a short walk down Babaria de le Tole. Otherwise head west from Santi Giovanni e Paolo's main door, where three bridges lead to **Santa Maria dei Miracoli** ㉚, a stop you won't want to miss. Around the back of the church recross the bridge to Campo Santa Maria Nova and walk ahead to Campo San Canzian, where another bridge leads to Calle

Muazzo. If you take a right turn here, after two bridges and five minutes you'll arrive at the church of the **Gesuiti** ㉛, a baroque masterpiece of inlaid marble. A left turn at Calle Muazzo leads through Campo Santi Apostoli and then to Strada Nova, the main thoroughfare to the train station. Following the bold yellow signs toward the station, you'll see a small calle leading left to the Ca' d'Oro vaporetto landing, where you can visit the beautiful marble palace of **Ca' d'Oro** ㉜. Farther along the road to the station, signs leading to the San Marcuola vaporetto landing will put you near Venice's casino in **Palazzo Vendramin-Calergi** ㉝, where, if you've reserved ahead, you can see the ballroom of **Palazzo Labia** ㉞. Last stop on this tour is the **Jewish Ghetto** ㉟, for centuries the heart of Jewish culture in Venice.

TIMING   This tour requires time and energy: it involves a couple of hours walking, even if you never enter a building, and offers little chance to hop a boat and save your legs. Some sights have restricted hours, making it virtually impossible to see everything even in a full day. Your best bet is to choose a few sights to make your priorities, time your tour around their open hours, and then drop in at whatever others happen to be open as you're passing by. If you're touring on Friday, keep in mind that synagogues close at sunset.

What to See

㉓ **Arsenale.** The Venetian Republic never could have thrived without Arsenale shipyard, which is said to have been founded in 1104 on twin islands. The immense facility that evolved was given the old Venetian dialect name *arzanà,* borrowed from the Arabic *darsina'a,* meaning workshop. At times it employed as many as 16,000 "Arsenalotti," workers who were among the most respected shipbuilders in the world. (Dante immortalized these sweating men, armed with pitch and boiling tar, in his *Inferno.*) Their diligence was confirmed time and again—whether building 100 ships in 60 days to battle the Turks in Cyprus (1597) or completing one perfectly armed warship—start to finish—while King Henry III of France attended a banquet. Arsenale's impressive Renaissance **gateway** (1460) is guarded by four lions, war booty of Francesco Morosini, who took the Peloponnese from the Turks in 1687. The 10-ft-tall lion on the left stood sentinel more than 2,000 years ago near Athens, and experts say its mysterious inscription is runic "graffiti" left by Viking mercenaries hired to suppress 11th-century revolts in Piraeus. If you look at the winged lion above the doorway, you'll notice that the Gospel at his paws is open but lacks the customary *Pax* inscription; praying for peace perhaps seemed inappropriate above a factory that manufactured weapons. The zone belongs to the Italian Navy and isn't regularly open to the public, but it's open for the Biennale and for Venice's festival of traditional boats, held every May if you're here during those times, don't miss the chance for a look inside. ✉ *Campo dell'Arsenale, Castello* Ⓥ *Arsenale.*

★ ㉜ **Ca' d'Oro.** This lovely Venetian Gothic palace is adorned with marble traceries and ornaments, which were once embellished with pure gold. Today it houses the **Galleria Franchetti,** a fine collection of tapestries, sculptures, and paintings. ✉ *Calle Ca' d'Oro, Cannaregio 3933* ☎ *041/ 5222349* 🎟 *€5, €11 also includes Gallerie dell'Accademia and Museo Orientale* ⊙ *Tues.–Sun. 8:15–7:15, Mon. 8;15–2; last entry ½ hr before closing* Ⓥ *Ca' d'Oro.*

㉛ **Gesuiti.** Extravagantly baroque, this 18th-century church completely abandons classical Renaissance straight lines in favor of flowing, twisting forms. Its interior walls resemble brocade drapery, and only touching will convince skeptics that rather than paint, the green-and-white walls are inlaid marble. Over the first altar on the left, the *Martyrdom of St.*

Lawrence is a dramatic example of Titian's feeling for light and movement. ⊠ *Campo dei Gesuiti, Cannaregio* ☎ *041/5286579* ☉ *Daily 10–noon and 3–5* Ⓥ *Fondamente Nuove.*.

㉟ **Jewish Ghetto.** The neighborhood that gave the world the word *ghetto* is today a quiet warren of back streets that is still home to Jewish institutions, a kosher restaurant, a rabbinical school, and five synagogues. Though Jews may have arrived earlier, the first synagogues weren't built and a cemetery wasn't founded until the Askenazim, or Eastern European Jews, came in the late 1300s. Dwindling coffers may have prompted the Republic to sell temporary visas to Jews, but over the centuries they were alternately tolerated and expelled. The Rialto commercial district, as vividly recounted in Shakespeare's *The Merchant of Venice,* depended on Jewish merchants and moneylenders for trade, and to help cover ever-increasing war expenses.

Relentless local opposition forced the Senate in 1516 to confine Jews to an island in Cannaregio, named for its *geto* (foundry), which produced cannon. Gates at the entrance were locked at night, and boats patrolled the surrounding canals. The German accents of early residents changed "geto" into "ghetto." Jews were allowed only to lend money at low interest, operate pawnshops controlled by the government, trade in textiles, or practice medicine. Jewish doctors were highly respected and could leave the ghetto at any hour when on duty. Though ostracized, Jews were nonetheless safe in Venice, and in the 16th century the community grew considerably, with refugees from the Near East, southern and central Italy, Spain, and Portugal. The ghetto was allowed to expand twice, but it still had the city's densest population and consequently ended up with the city's tallest buildings (nine stories); notice the slanting apartment blocks on Campo del Ghetto Nuovo. Although the gates were pulled down after Napoléon's 1797 arrival, the Jews realized full freedom only in the late 19th century with the founding of the Italian state. On the eve of World War II there were about 1,500 Jews left in the ghetto: 247 were deported by the Nazis; eight returned.

The area has Europe's highest density of Renaissance-era synagogues, and visiting them is a unique cross-cultural experience. Though each is marked by the tastes of its individual builders, Venetian influence is evident throughout. Women's galleries resemble those of theaters from the same era, and some synagogues were decorated by artisans who were simultaneously active in local churches. Small but well-arranged **Museo Ebraico** (⊠ Campo del Ghetto Nuovo, Cannaregio 2902/b ☎ 041/ 715359 🖃 www.museoebraico.it 🖃 €3 museum, €8 museum and synagogues ☉ June–Sept., Sun.–Fri. 10–6:45; last tour 5:30; Oct.–May, Sun.–Fri. 10–5:45; last tour 4:30 Ⓥ San Marcuola or Guglie) highlights centuries of Jewish culture with splendid silver Hanukkah lamps and torahs, and handwritten, beautifully decorated wedding contracts in Hebrew. Tours of the ghetto in Italian and English leave hourly from the museum. You might complete your circuit of Jewish Venice with a visit to the **Antico Cimitero Ebraico** (Ancient Jewish Cemetery; ⊠ Via Cipro, Lido ☎ 041/715359 🖃 €8 ☉ Tours Fri. 10:30, Sun. 2:30; call for arrangements Ⓥ Lido–S.M.E.) on the Lido, full of fascinating old tombstones half-hidden by ivy and grass. The earliest grave dates to 1389; the cemetery remained in use until the late 18th century.

㉔ **Museo Storico Navale** (Museum of Naval History). The boat collection here includes scale models such as the doges' ceremonial *Bucintoro,* and full-size boats such as Peggy Guggenheim's private gondola, complete with its romantic cabin, or *felze.* There's a range of old galley and military pieces, and also a large collection of seashells. ⊠ *Campo San Bi-*

agio, Castello 2148 ☎ *041/5200276* ⬚ *€1.55* ⊙ *Weekdays 8:45–1:30, Sat. 8:45–1* Ⓥ *Arsenale.*

㉙ **Ospedaletto.** This 16th-century "little hospital" was one of four church foundling homes that each had an orchestra and choir of orphans. Entering through **Santa Maria dei Derelitti** (St. Mary of the Destitute) you'll see a large gallery built for the young musicians. The orphanage is now a home for the elderly; its beautiful 18th-century **Sala della Musica** (Music Room) is the only one of its kind to survive. On the far wall, the fresco by Jacopo Guarana (1720–1808) depicts Apollo, god of music, surrounded by the orphan musicians and their maestro, Pasquale Anfossi. ⊠ *Calle Barbaria delle Tole, Castello 6691* ☎ *041/2702464* ⬚ *€2* ⊙ *Thurs.–Sat. 3:30–6:30* Ⓥ *Fondamente Nuove or Rialto.*

㉞ **Palazzo Labia.** Once the home of 18th-century Venice's showiest family, this palace is now the Venetian headquarters of Italian media giant RAI—modern broadcasting goes baroque. In the **Tiepolo Room,** Labia's gorgeous ballroom, the final flowering of Venetian painting is seen in Giambattista Tiepolo's playful frescoes of Antony and Cleopatra set among dwarfs and Barbary pirates. You must call ahead here to arrange a visit; hours are limited. ⊠ *Campo San Geremia, Cannaregio 275* ☎ *041/781277* ⬚ *Free* ⊙ *Wed.–Fri. 3–4* Ⓥ *Ferrovia.*

㉝ **Palazzo Vendramin-Calergi.** This Renaissance classic, with an imposing carved frieze, is the work of Mauro Codussi (1440–1504). You can see some of its interior by dropping by the **Casinò di Venezia.** Fans of Richard Wagner (1813–83) might enjoy visiting the **Sala di Wagner,** the room (separate from the casino) in which the composer died. Though rather plain, it's loaded with music memorabilia. ⊠ *Cannaregio 2040* ☎ *041/5297111; call 041/2760407 or 041/5232544 Fri. AM to reserve Wagner Room tours* ⬚ *€5, free to gamblers, Sala di Wagner free* ⊙ *Slots 10 AM–3 AM, tables 3 PM–3 AM; Wagner Room Sat. AM by appointment* Ⓥ *San Marcuola.*

㉗ **Querini-Stampalia.** The art collection at this Renaissance palace includes Giovanni Bellini's *Presentation in the Temple* and Sebastiano Ricci's triptych *Dawn, Afternoon, and Evening.* Portraits of newlywed Francesco Querini and Paola Priuli were left unfinished by the death of Giacomo Palma il Vecchio (1480–1528); note the groom's hand and the bride's dress. Original 18th-century furniture and stuccoworks are fitting background for Pietro Longhi's portraits. Nearly 70 works by Gabriele Bella (1730–99) capture scenes of Venetian street life. Admission Friday and Saturday includes concerts with antique instruments at 5 and 8:30. ⊠ *Campo Santa Maria Formosa, Castello 5252* ☎ *041/2711411* ⊕ *www.querinistampalia.it* ⬚ *€6* ⊙ *Tues.–Thurs. and Sun. 10–6, Fri. and Sat. 10–10* Ⓥ *San Zaccaria.*

> **need a break?**
>
> **Florian Art e Caffé** (☎ 041/5206675), inside Querini-Stampalia, is an offshoot of the famed San Marco café and offers a way to enjoy Florian hospitality without paying uptown prices. Drinks, specialty pastries, and even full lunches are available daily except Monday.

㉖ **Santa Maria Formosa.** Guided by his vision of a beautiful Madonna, 7th-century St. Magno followed a small white cloud and built a church where it settled. Gracefully white, the marble building you see today dates from 1492, built by Mauro Codussi on an older foundation. The interior is a blend of Renaissance decoration, a Byzantine cupola, barrel vaults, and narrow-columned screens. Of interest are two fine paintings; *Our Lady of Mercy* by Bartolomeo Vivarini (1415–84) and *Santa Barbara* by Palma il Vecchio. The surrounding square bustles with sidewalk cafés and a produce market on weekday mornings. ⊠ *Campo Santa Maria Formosa, Castello* ☎ *041/5234645; 041/2750462 Chorus.* ⊠ *€2, €8 Chorus pass* ☉ *Mon.–Sat. 10–5, Sun. 1–5* Ⓥ *Rialto.*

★ ㉚ **Santa Maria dei Miracoli.** Tiny yet perfectly proportioned, this early Renaissance gem is sheathed in marble and decorated inside with exquisite marble reliefs. Architect Pietro Lombardo (circa 1435–1515) miraculously compressed the building into its confined space, then created the illusion of greater size by varying the color of the exterior, adding extra pilasters on the building's canal side, and offsetting the arcade windows to make the arches appear deeper. The church was built in the 1480s to house *I Miracoli,* an image of the Virgin Mary that is said to perform miracles—look for it on the high altar. ⊠ *Campo Santa Maria Nova, Cannaregio* ☎ *041/2750462 Chorus* ⊠ *€2, €8 Chorus pass* ☉ *Mon.–Sat. 10–5, Sun. 1–5* Ⓥ *Rialto.*

★ ㉘ **Santi Giovanni e Paolo.** This massive Dominican church, commonly called San Zanipolo, contains a wealth of art. The 15th-century stained glass window near the side entrance is breathtaking for its brilliant colors and beautiful figures, made from drawings by Bartolomeo Vivarini and Gerolamo Mocetto. The second official church of the Republic after San Marco, San Zanipolo is the Venetian equivalent of London's Westminster Abbey, with a great number of important people, including 25 doges, buried here. Artistic highlights include an outstanding polyptych by Giovanni Bellini (right nave, second altar); Alvise Vivarini's *Christ Carrying the Cross* (sacrestia); and Lorenzo Lotto's *Charity of St. Antonino* (right transept). Don't miss the *Cappella del Rosario* (Rosary Chapel), off the left transept, built in the 16th century to commemorate the 1571 victory of Lepanto, western Greece, when Venice led a combined European fleet to defeat the Turkish navy. The chapel was devastated by a fire in 1867 and restored in the early years of the 20th century with works from other churches, among them the sumptuous Veronese ceiling paintings. However quick your visit, don't miss the tomb Pietro Mocenigo, to the right of the main entrance, a monument built by the ubiquitous Pietro Lombardo and his sons. ⊠ *Campo dei Santi Giovanni e Paolo, Castello* ☎ *041/5235913* ⊠ *Free* ☉ *Mon.–Sat. 7:30–12:30 and 3:30–6, Sun. 3–6* Ⓥ *Fondamente Nuove or Rialto.*

㉕ **Scuola di San Giorgio degli Schiavoni.** Founded in 1451 by the Dalmatian community, this small scuola was, and still is, a social and cultural center for migrants from what is now Croatia. It's dominated by one of Italy's most beautiful rooms, lavishly yet harmoniously decorated with the *teleri* (large canvases) of Vittore Carpaccio (circa 1465–1525). A lifelong Venice resident, Carpaccio painted legendary and religious figures against backgrounds of Venetian architecture. Here he focused on saints especially venerated in Dalmatia: St. George, St. Tryphone, and St. Jerome. He combined observation with fantasy, a sense of warm color with a sense of humor (don't miss the priests fleeing St. Jerome's lion, or the body parts in the dragon's lair). ⊠ *Calle dei Furlani, Castello 3259/a* ☎ *041/5228828* ⊠ *€3* ☉ *Apr.–Oct., Tues.–Sat. 9:30–12:30 and 3:30–6:30, Sun. 9:30–12:30; Nov.–Mar., Tues.–Sat. 10–12:30 and 3–6, Sun. 10–12:30* Ⓥ *San Zaccaria.*

need a break?

Baking and catering since 1879 the **Rosa Salva** family today has several outposts scattered around Venice. Visit their bar in Campo SS. Giovanni e Paolo (☎ 041/5227949) for pastries and coffee or for some of their homemade gelato. Grab an outdoor table at **Bar ai Miracoli** (☎ 041/5231515) and gaze across the canal at Maria dei Miracoli, Lombardo's miracle in marble.

off the beaten path

SAN FRANCESCO DELLA VIGNA (St. Francis of the Vineyard) – Legend says this is where an angel awakened St. Mark the Evangelist with the famous words, "Pax tibi Marce Evangelista meus" (Peace to you Mark, my Evangelist), which became the motto of the Venetian Republic. The land was given in 1253 to the Franciscans, who kept the vineyard but replaced the ancient church. Bring some €.20 coins to light up the Antonio Vivarini (circa 1415–84) triptych of Sts. Girolamo, Bernardino da Siena, and Ludovico, which hangs to your right as you enter the main door, and Giovanni Bellini's *Madonna with Saints,* inside the Cappella Santa. Antonio da Negroponte's glittering gold *Madonna Adoring the Child,* near the side door, is an inspiring work of the late-15th century. Here you'll see the transition from Gothic period's formal rigidity to the Renaissance's naturalistic composition and detailed decoration. Two cloisters open out from the left nave, paved entirely with VIP tombstones. ⊠ *Campo San Francesco della Vigna, Castello* ☎ *041/5206102* ☜ *Free* ☉ *Daily 8:30–12:30 and 3–7* Ⓥ *Celestia.*

SAN PIETRO DI CASTELLO – Its stark campanile, the first in Venice built from marblelike Istrian stone, stands out against the picturesque, workaday slips along the Canale di San Pietro and the Renaissance cloister, which for years was a squatters colony. The Veneti settled here years before Venice was officially founded, but today the island is a sleepy, almost forgotten place, with little to suggest that for 1,000 years this church was Venice's cathedral—until the Basilica di San Marco superseded it in 1807. The interior has some minor 17th-century art and San Pietro's ancient *Cattedra* (throne). ⊠ *Campo San Pietro, Castello* ☎ *041/2750462 Chorus* ☜ *€2, €8 Chorus pass* ☉ *Mon.–Sat. 10–5, Sun. 1–5* Ⓥ *San Pietro di Castello or Giardini.*

San Giorgio Maggiore & the Giudecca

Beckoning travelers across St. Mark's Basin, sparkling white through the mist, is the island of San Giorgio Maggiore, separated by a small channel from the Giudecca. A tall brick campanile on that distant bank perfectly complements the Campanile of San Marco. Beneath it looms the stately dome of one of Venice's greatest churches, San Giorgio Maggiore. Giudecca's history may be shrouded in mystery, but today the island is about as down to earth as you can get and one of the city's few remaining neighborhoods that feels truly Venetian.

a good boat trip

Take vaporetto Line 82 from San Zaccaria across St. Mark's Basin to the island of San Giorgio to visit Palladio's church of **San Giorgio Maggiore** ㊱ ▶. In the adjacent monastery, Fondazione Cini operates a music institute and a school of art restoration. It's only open to the public for exhibitions, conferences, and performances at its lovely outdoor amphitheater, Teatro Verde. The next three vaporetto stops are on the **Giudecca** ㊲.

TIMING A half day should be plenty of time to enjoy the sights. Allow at least an hour to see each of the churches, and another hour or two to visit the Giudecca neighborhood.

What to See

㊲ **Giudecca.** The island's name is something of a mystery. It may have come from a possible 14th-century Jewish settlement, or because 9th-century nobles condemned to exile, *giudicato,* were sent here. It became a pleasure garden for wealthy Venetians during the Republic's long and luxurious decline, but today, like Cannaregio, it's largely working-class. Giudecca provides spectacular views of Venice and is becoming increasingly gentrified. While here visit the **Santissimo Redentore** church, designed by Palladio and built to commemorate a plague. The third weekend in July, it's the site of Venetians' favorite festival, Redentore, featuring boats, fireworks, and outdoor feasting. Thanks to several bridges, you can walk the entire length of Giudecca's promenade, relaxing at one of several restaurants or just taking in the lively atmosphere. Accommodations run the gamut, from youth hostels to the city's most exclusive hotel, Cipriani. ⊠ *Fondamenta San Giacomo, Giudecca* ☎ *041/5231415; 041/2750462 Chorus* ⬚ *€2, €8 Chorus pass* ☉ *Mon.–Sat. 10–5, Sun. 1–5* Ⓥ *Redentore.*

▶ ㊱ **San Giorgio Maggiore.** There's been a church on this island since the 8th century, with a Benedictine monastery added in the 10th century (closed to the public). Today's refreshingly airy and simply decorated church of brick and white marble was begun in 1566 by Palladio and displays his architectural hallmarks of mathematical harmony and classical influence. *The Last Supper* and the *Gathering of Manna,* two of Tintoretto's later works, line the chancel. Right of the entrance hangs *Adoration of the Shepherds* by Jacopo Bassano (1517–92); his foothills home, Bassano del Grappa, is evident in the natural subjects, country life, and terrafirma colors he chooses. The monks are happy to show Carpaccio's *George and Dragon,* hanging in a private room, if they have time. The campanile is so tall that it was struck by lightning in 1993. Take the elevator to the top for some of the finest views in town. ⊠ *Isola di San Giorgio Maggiore* ☎ *041/5227827* ⬚ *Church free, campanile €3* ☉ *June–Sept., daily 9:30–12:30 and 2–7; Oct.–May, daily 9:30–12:30 and 2–5.* Ⓥ *San Giorgio.*

Islands of the Lagoon

The perfect vacation from your Venetian vacation is an escape to Murano, Burano, and Torcello, the islands of the northern lagoon. Torcello offers greenery, breathing space, and picnic opportunities (remember to pack lunch). Burano is a toy town of houses painted in a riot of colors—blue, yellow, pink, ocher, and dark red. Visitors still love to shop here for "Venetian" lace, even though the vast majority of it is machine-made in Taiwan. Murano is renowned for its glass but also notorious for the high-pressure sales on its factory tours, even those organized by top hotels. Vaporetto connections to Murano aren't difficult, and for the price of a boat ticket you'll buy your freedom and more time to explore. The Murano "guides" herding new arrivals follow a rotation so that factories take turns giving tours, but you can avoid the hustle by just walking away.

a good boat trip

Line 41 leaves San Zaccaria (front of Jolanda hotel) every 20 minutes, circling the east end of Venice and stopping at Fondamente Nuova before making the five-minute hop to **San Michele** ㊳ ▶ island cemetery, with its church of San Michele in Isola. Another five minutes and you're on **Murano** ㊴. To see glassblowing, get off at Colonna; the Museo stop will put you near the Museo Vetrario, with a fascinating display of glass dating from 1st century AD to the 19th century. A bit farther down Fondamenta Giustinian you'll see Basilica di Santi Maria e Donato, with its mosaic floor complete with Murano glass. Make your way to the island's Faro, a lighthouse that still guides boats into the lagoon. From Faro stop, Line 12 runs to **Burano** ㊵, where you can see traditional lacemaking at the Scuola di Merletto di Burano. Line 12 continues to the sleepy island of **Torcello** ㊶, only five minutes away. A paved lane from the landing follows the canal across the island. You'll pass elegantly reclusive Locanda Cipriani before reaching a grassy square and beautifully eerie cathedral of Santa Maria Assunta.

TIMING In summer, San Zaccaria is connected to Murano by express vaporetto Line 5; the trip takes 25 minutes. In the winter the local Line 41 takes about 45 minutes. From Fondamenta Nuove, boats leave every 10 minutes. Line 12 goes from Fondamenta Nuove direct to Murano, Burano, and Torcello every 30 minutes, and the full trip takes 45 minutes each way. Hitting all the sights on all the islands takes a full day. If you limit yourself to Murano and San Michele, a half day will suffice.

What to See

★ ㊵ **Burano.** Cheerfully painted houses line the canals of this quiet village where centuries ago, lace-making rescued a faltering fishing economy. As you walk the 100 yds from the dock to Piazza Galuppi, the main square, you pass stall after stall of lace vendors. These good-natured ladies won't press you with a hard sell, but don't expect precise product information or great bargains—real handmade Burano lace costs $1,000 to $2,000 for a 10-inch doily.

The **Museo del Merletto** (Lace Museum) lets you marvel at the intricacies of Burano's lace-making. It's also a skills center—more sewing circle than school—where on weekdays you'll usually find women carrying on the tradition. They sometimes have authentic pieces for sale privately. ⊠ *Piazza Galuppi 187* ☎ *041/730034* 💶 *€4, €6 with Museo Vetrario, €15.50 Musei Civici pass* ☉ *Apr.–Oct., Wed.–Mon. 10–5; Nov.–Mar., Wed.–Mon. 10–4* Ⓥ *Burano.*

㊴ **Murano.** As in Venice, bridges here link a number of small islands, dotted with houses that once were workmen's cottages. The republic, concerned about fire hazard in the 13th century, moved its glassworks to Murano, and today you can visit the factories and watch glass being made. Many of them line the Fondamenta dei Vetrai, the canal-side walkway leading from the Colonna vaporetto landing. Before you reach Murano's Grand Canal (250 yds from the landing) you'll pass the **Chiesa di San Pietro Martire**. Reconstructed in the 16th century, it houses Giovanni Bellini's *Madonna and Child* and Veronese's *St. Jerome.* ⊠ *Fondamenta dei Vetrai* ☎ *041/739704* ☉ *Mon.–Sat. 9–12:30 and 2–5* Ⓥ *Colonna.*

The collection at **Museo Vetrario** (Glass Museum) ranges from priceless antiques to only slightly less expensive modern pieces. You'll see authentic Venetian styles and patterns, including the famous Barovier wedding cup (1470–80). ⊠ *Fondamenta Giustinian 8* ☎ *041/739586* 💶 *€4, €6 with Museo del Merletto, €15.50 entry to all Musei Civici, including Palazzo Ducale.* ☉ *Apr.–Oct., Thurs.–Tues. 10–5; Nov.–Mar., Thurs.–Tues. 10–4; last tickets sold ½ hr before closing.* Ⓥ *Museo.*

Basilica dei Santi Maria e Donato, just past the glass museum, is among the first churches founded by the lagoon's original inhabitants. The elaborate mosaic pavement includes the date 1140; its ship's keel roof and Veneto-Byzantine columns add to the air of an ancient temple. ⊠ *Fondamenta Giustinian* ☎ *041/739056* 💶 *Free* ☉ *Daily 8–noon and 4–7* Ⓥ *Museo.*

㊳ **San Michele.** This cypress-lined island is home to the pretty Renaissance church of **San Michele in Isola**—and to some of Venice's most illustrious deceased. The church was designed by Codussi; the graves include poet Ezra Pound (1885–1972), impresario and art critic Sergey Diaghilev (1872–1929), and composer Igor Stravinsky (1882–1971). Surrounded

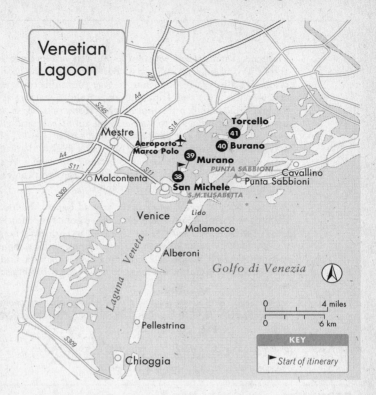

by the living sounds of Venice lagoon, this would seem the perfect final resting place. However, these days newcomers are exhumed after 10 years and transferred to a less grandiose location. ☎ 041/2730111 ✉ *Free* ⊙ *Apr.–Sept., daily 7:30–6; Oct.–Mar., daily 7:30–4* Ⓥ *San Michele.*

★ ㊶ **Torcello.** In their flight from barbarians 1,500 years ago, the first Venetians landed here, prospering even after many left to found the city of Venice. As malaria took its toll and the island's wool-manufacturing was priced out of the market, Torcello became a ghost town. In the 16th century there were 10 churches and 20,000 inhabitants; today you'll be lucky to see one of the island's 16 permanent residents.

Santa Maria Assunta was built in the 11th century, and Torcello's wealth at the time is evident in the church's high-quality Byzantine mosaics. The massive *Last Judgment* shows sinners writhing in pain, while opposite, above the altar, the Madonna looks calmly down from her field of gold. Ask to see the inscription dated 639 and a sample of mosaic pavement from the original church. The adjacent **Santa Fosca** church, added when the body of the saint arrived in 1011, is still used for religious services. It's worth making the climb up the adjacent **Campanile** for an incomparable view of the lagoon wetlands. ✉ *Torcello* ☎ 041/ 730119 ✉ *Santa Maria Assunta €3; Campanile €2* ⊙ *Apr.–Oct., daily 10:30–6; Nov.–Mar., daily 10–5* Ⓥ *Torcello.*

need a break?

Locanda Cipriani (☎ 041/730150), closed Tuesday and January and February, is famous for good food and Ernest Hemingway, who often came to Torcello seeking solitude. Today the restaurant (not to be confused with Giudecca's Cipriani hotel) is busy, with well-heeled customers speeding in for lunch (dinner also on weekends). Dining is pricey, but you can relax in the garden with just a glass of Prosecco.

WHERE TO EAT

Updated by
Patricia Rucidlo

The general standard of Venetian restaurants suffers from the effects of mass tourism, but it is still possible to eat well in Venice at moderate prices. It's always a good idea to reserve your table or have your hotel concierge do it for you. Dining hours are short, starting at 12:30 or 1 for lunch and ending at 2:30 or 3, when restaurants close for the afternoon, opening up again to start serving about 7:30 and closing again at 11 or midnight on weekend nights and earlier (10–11) on weekdays and in the low season. Most close one day a week and are also likely to close without notice for vacation or renovation. Few have signs on the outside, so when the metal blinds are shut tight you can't tell a closed restaurant from a closed TV-repair shop.

A great Venetian tradition revolves around *bacari,* the local name for the little watering holes where locals have gone for centuries to have a glass of wine, *cicheti* (little savory snacks), and a chat. Venetian fish specialties include *sarde in saor* (fried sardines, onions, pine nuts, and raisins), *baccalà mantecato* (cod creamed with milk and olive oil), *moeche* (soft-shell crabs), and *seppie in umido* (cuttlefish braised in tomato sauce).

WHAT IT COSTS In euros				
$$$$	**$$$**	**$$**	**$**	**¢**
AT DINNER over €22	€17–€22	€12–€17	€7–€12	under €7

Prices are for a second course (secondo piatto).

Cannaregio

$$$ ✕**Il Sole sulla Vecia Cavana.** Owner Stefano Monti opened this spot in 2001, and it immediately became a star of the Venice dining scene. The young talented kitchen staff create winning Italian and Venetian dishes such as *filetti di pesce a cottura differenziata* (fish fillet, cooked on one side and seared on the other), tender baby cuttlefish, and, among desserts, *gelato al basilico* (basil ice cream). The 18th-century *cavana* (boathouse) maintains its original low columns, arches, and brick walls, but has been decorated with contemporary flair. ⊠ *Rio Terà SS. Apostoli, Cannaregio 4624* ☎ *041/5287106* ▤ *AE, DC, MC, V* ☺ *Closed Mon., 2 wks in Jan., and in Aug.*

$$ ✕**Osteria del Bomba.** It's a bacaro and a trattoria; take a table if you can, as it's more pleasurable to enjoy the food while sitting down. Locals (mostly middle-age men) flock here to have a glass of wine and a plate of pasta while bantering with genial proprietors Marco and Giacomo. Here they do saor three ways, and the *gamberetti* (small shrimp) in saor might even be better than the classic version with sardines. The grilled vegetables provide a fine counterpoint to delicacies from the sea. ⊠ *Calle dell'Oca, off Campo Santa Sofia Cannaregio* ☎ *041/241146* ▤ *MC, V* ☺ *Closed Mon. No lunch Sat.*

★ **$$** ✕**Vini da Gigio.** A quaint, friendly, family-run trattoria on the quay side of a canal just off the Strada Nuova, da Gigio is very popular with Venetians and other visiting Italians, who appreciate the affable service; the well-prepared homemade pasta, fish, and meat dishes; the imaginative and varied cellar; and the high-quality draft wine. It's good for a simple lunch at tables in the barroom. ⊠ *Fondamenta de la Chiesa, Cannaregio 3628/a* ☎ *041/5285140* ▤ *AE, DC, MC, V* ☺ *Closed Mon., 3 wks Jan. and Feb., 1 wk in June, and 3 wks Aug. and Sept.*

ON THE MENU

VENETIAN CUISINE IS BASED ON SEAFOOD—granseola (crab), moeche (small, soft-shelled crab), and seppie or seppioline (cuttlefish) all are prominently featured. It's usually priced by the etto (100 grams, or about ¼ pound) and can be quite expensive. Antipasti may take the form of a seafood salad, prosciutto di San Daniele (of the Friuli region), or pickled vegetables. As a first course, Venetians favor risotto, the creamy rice dish, prepared here with vegetables or shellfish. Pasta, too, is paired with seafood sauces—Venice is not the place to order spaghetti with tomato sauce. Pasticcio di pesce is pasta baked with fish, usually baccalà (salt cod). A classic first course here and elsewhere in the Veneto is pasta e fagioli (thick bean soup with pasta). Bigoli is strictly a local pasta shaped like short, thick spaghetti, usually served with nero di seppia (squid-ink sauce). Polenta (creamy cornmeal) is another pillar of regional cooking. It's often served with fegato alla veneziana (calves' liver with onions).

Though it originated on the mainland, tiramisu is Venice's favorite dessert, a heavenly concoction of mascarpone (a rich, soft double-cream cheese), espresso, chocolate, and savoiardi (ladyfingers). Local wines are the dry white Tocai and Pinot from the Friuli region and bubbly-white Prosecco, a naturally fermented sparkling wine that is a shade less dry. Some of the best Prosecco comes from Valdobbiadene, rivaled only by the slightly more expensive Cartizze. Popular red wines include merlot, cabernet, Raboso, and Refosco. You can sample all of these in Venice's bacari (local watering holes), where wine is served by the glass (known as an ombra in Venetian dialect) and accompanied by cicheti (traditional Venetian appetizers such as marinated fish, deep-fried vegetables, and meatballs), often substantial enough for a light meal.

$ ✗ **Trattoria Ca' d'Oro.** Known commonly as La Vedova (the Widow), this warm osteria not far from the Ca' d'Oro was opened as a low-key bacaro by the owner's great-grandparents. A rough Venetian floor, old marble counter, and long tables invite conviviality. Cicheti include tender *seppie roste* (grilled cuttlefish), *polpette* (meatballs), and baccalà mantecato. The house winter pasta is the *pastisso de radicio rosso* (lasagna with sausage, radicchio, and béchamel sauce). In spring, the chef switches to pastisso *de asparagi* (with asparagus). ⊠ *Calle del Pistor, Cannaregio 3912* ☎ *041/5285324* ⊟ *No credit cards* ☾ *Closed Thurs. No lunch Sun.*

¢ ✗ **Tiziano.** They serve inexpensive salad plates and daily pasta specials at this tavola calda, but concentrate instead on the staggering array of *tramezzini* (sandwiches) that line the display cases. It's a handy place for a quick detour and snack at very modest prices. Vegetarians will delight in Tiziano's version of the classic Italian toast which, in this case, is a grilled cheese sandwich with eggplant slices and roasted zucchini. ⊠ *Salizzada San Giovanni Crisostomo, Cannaregio 5747* ☎ *041/5235544* ⊟ *No credit cards.*

Castello

$$$$ ✗ **Al Covo.** This small charming osteria changes its menu according to the day's bounty—mostly local seafood caught just hours before and specialties from other European waters. Cesare Benelli and his American wife, Diane, insist on only the freshest ingredients. Try the *zuppa di pesce* (fish soup) followed by the fish of the day (grilled, baked, or steamed). Desserts are homemade, and the wine list is extensive. At lunch, only a fixed-price menu (€33, with several options) is served; dinner is

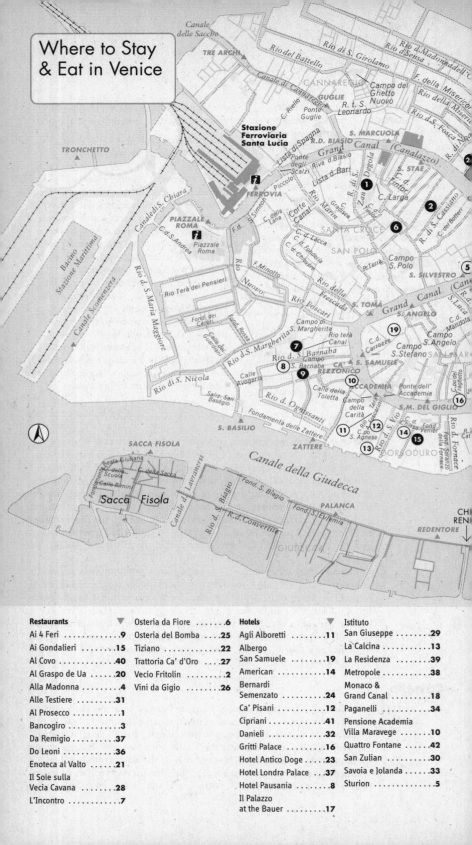

Where to Stay & Eat in Venice

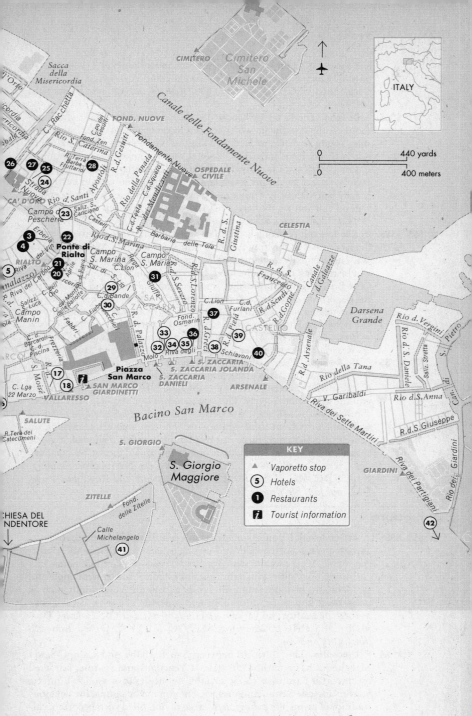

CIMITERO
Cimitero San Michele

ITALY

Sacca della Misericordia
d'Orio
cordia
C. Racchetta
FOND. NUOVE
Canale delle Fondamente Nuove
Rio S. Caterina
Fond. Zen
Fond. Gesuiti
OSPEDALE CIVILE
CELESTIA
26   27   95
28
Apostoli
R. della Panada
Fondamente Nuove
C.d.Squero
R. dei Mendicanti
24
Strada Nuova
Rio d. Santi
CA' D'ORO
Saliz. S. Canciano
C.d.Testa
R. d. S. Giustina
23
Campo d. Pescheria
Castelli
Barbaria   delle Tole
R. d. S.
Canale d. Galeazze
3
Erberia
22
Rio d. S. Marina
Campo S. Marina
Ruga
Campo S. Maria
R. d. S. Francesco
R.d.S.
4
Ponte di Rialto
andalzzo
5
RIALTO
21
20
Riva del Carbon
C. d. Fava
C. dell'Aseo
Calle degli Avvocati
29
Campo S.Giuffa
R. S. Lorenzo
R. S. Severo
Darsena Grande
Rio d. Vergini
31
C.d.Bande
C. Lion
C.d. Furlani
R. d. Scudi
R. d. Greci
R.d.Gorne
Rio d. S. Daniele
Saliz. Stretta
S. Pietro
Campo Manin
C. de Fuseri
30
ZACCARIA
37
39
CASTELLO
Fond. Osmarin
R. d. Pietà
R. d. Arsenale
Rio d. S. Anna
Frezzeria
Barcaroli
C. d. Piscina
33
34   35
36
38
Schiavoni
40
Rio della Tana
32
Riva degli
Molo
S. ZACCARIA JOLANDA
V. Garibaldi
17
Piazza San Marco
S. ZACCARIA DANIELI
ARSENALE
18
SAN MARCO GIARDINETTI
Riva dei Sette Martiri
R.d.S.Giuseppe
VALLARESSO
C. Lga 22 Marzo
SALUTE
R.Terra dei Catecumeni
Bacino San Marco
S. GIORGIO
GIARDINI
Riva dei Partigiani
Rio dei Giardini
S. Giorgio Maggiore

KEY
▲ Vaporetto stop
⑤ Hotels
❶ Restaurants
𝑖 Tourist information

ZITELLE
Fond. delle Zitelle
CHIESA DEL REDENTORE
Calle Michelangelo
41
42

0 _____ 440 yards
0 _____ 400 meters

à la carte. Given the steep prices here, it's more than a pity that it's cash only. ⊠ *Campiello della Pescaria, Castello 3968* ☎ *041/5223812* 🚫 *No credit cards* 🕐 *Closed Wed. and Thurs., 1 wk in Aug., and 4 wks Dec. and Jan.*

$$$$ ✕ **Do Leoni.** The Two Lions, located in the Hotel Londra Palace, is a sumptuous candlelit setting in which to sample Venetian and other Italian cuisine. Young Sicilian chef Stefano Mazzone is a veteran of stints in luxury hotels throughout Italy; his seasonal menu is inventive and indulges in savory flights of fantasy. He elevates such earthy soups as zuppa di fagioli to new levels; his seven-course tasting menu utilizes such non-Italian ingredients as vanilla and ginger. The summer terrace occupies a good portion of the Riva. ⊠ *Riva degli Schiavoni, Castello 4171* ☎ *041/5200533* 🍴 *Reservations essential* 🚫 *AE, DC, MC, V.*

★ **$$$–$$$$** ✕ **Alle Testiere.** A strong local following can make it tough to get one of the five tables at this tiny trattoria near Campo Santa Maria Formosa. With its decidedly unglamorous ceiling fans, the place feels as informal as a bistro (or a saloon); the food, however, is much more sophisticated. Chef Bruno Gavagnin's dishes stand out for lightness and balance: try the *gnocchetti con moscardini* (little gnocchi with tender baby octopus) or the linguine with *coda di rospo* (monkfish), or inquire about the carpaccio of the day. The well-assembled wine list is particularly strong on local whites. ⊠ *Calle del Mondo Novo, Castello 5801* ☎ *041/5227220* 🍴 *Reservations essential* 🚫 *MC, V* 🕐 *Closed Sun. and Mon.*

$$ ✕ **Da Remigio.** They may seat the foreigners in the first room and the later-arriving Venetians in the second, but that's a minor complaint, and it's clear why Venetians come here: the food is good, the service prompt, and the atmosphere lively. The *canocchio bollite* (boiled, then chilled, shredded mantis shrimp) is a perfect starter, particularly when paired with an effervescent local white wine. Though seconds are strong on fish, Da Remigio also turns out respectable nonfish dishes such as the spaghetti *con porcini* (with mushrooms) and grilled meats. ⊠ *Salizzada dei Greci, Castello 3416* ☎ *041/5230089* 🍴 *Reservations essential* 🚫 *AE, DC, MC, V* 🕐 *Closed Tues., 2 wks July and Aug., and 4 wks Dec. and Jan. No dinner Mon.*

Dorsoduro

★ **$$$–$$$$** ✕ **Ai Gondolieri.** If you're somewhat sick of fish, this is the place to come, as meat and food of the mainland are menu mainstays. Despite the tourist-trap name, it's a favorite with Venetians. Feast on *filetto di maiale con castraure* (pork fillet with baby artichokes), duck breast with apple and sweet onion, or more traditional dishes from the Veneto hills such as horse meat and game, gnocchim, and polenta. The wine list is above average in quality and variety. ⊠ *Fondamenta dell'Ospedaletto, Dorsoduro 366* ☎ *041/5286396* 🚫 *AE, DC, MC, V* 🕐 *Closed Tues. No lunch July and Aug.*

★ **$$** ✕ **L'Incontro.** This trattoria between San Barnaba and Campo Santa Margherita has a faithful clientele of Venetians and visitors, attracted by flavorful Sardinian food, sociable service, and reasonable prices. Starters include Sardinian sausages, but you might sample the delicious traditional primi like *culingiones* (large ravioli filled with pecorino, saffron, and orange peel). The selection of secondi is heavy on herb-crusted meat dishes such as *coniglio al mirto* (rabbit baked on a bed of myrtle sprigs) and the *costine d'agnello con rosmarino e mentuccia* (baby lamb ribs with rosemary and wild mint). ⊠ *Rio Terrà Canal, Dorsoduro 3062/a* ☎ *041/5222404* 🚫 *AE, DC, MC, V* 🕐 *Closed Mon., Jan., and 2 wks in Aug. No lunch Tues.*

★ $ ✕**Ai 4 Feri.** The paper tablecloths and cozy, laid-back ambience are all part of this small restaurant's charm. The menu varies according to what's fresh that day; imaginative combinations of ingredients in the primi—herring and sweet peppers, salmon and radicchio, giant shrimp and broccoli (with pumpkin gnocchi)—are the norm. A meal here followed by after-dinner drinks at Campo Santa Margherita, a five-minute walk away, makes for a lovely evening. The kitchen closes early on weekdays. ⊠ *Calle l Lunga San Barnaba, Dorsoduro 2754/a* ☎ *041/5206978* ▭ *No credit cards* ☾ *Closed Sun. and June.*

San Marco

$$$$ ✕**Al Graspo de Ua.** Opened in the 19th century as a small osteria, the "Bunch of Grapes" became the meeting place of artists and movie stars back in the 1960s. Today, it serves a faithful clientele of wealthy Italians. The decor is a miscellanea of plants, sculpture, candlelight, and paintings set against brick and white-stucco walls. The owner, Lucio Zanon, speaks fluent English and will introduce you to a wide-ranging menu of fresh pasta, seasonal risotto, and meat and seafood. A treat in late spring is the thick white asparagus from Bassano, which, with a couple of fried eggs, is eaten as a main course. Desserts are all homemade. ⊠ *Calle dei Bombaseri, San Marco 5094* ☎ *041/5223647* ▭ *AE, DC, MC, V* ☾ *Closed Mon. and 1 wk in Jan.*

¢ ✕**Enoteca al Volto.** Just steps away from the Rialto Bridge, this bar has been around since 1936; the fine cicheti and primi have a lot to do with its staying power. Two small, dark rooms with wooden tables and chairs provide the backdrop to enjoy simple fare. The place prides itself on its considerable wine list of both Italian and foreign wines; if you stick to the panini and a cicheto or two, you'll eat very well for very little. If you opt for one of the primi of the day, the price category goes up a notch. ⊠ *Calle Cavalli, San Marco 4081* ☎ *041/5228945* ▭ *No credit cards* ☾ *Closed Sun.*

San Polo

★ $$$$ ✕**Osteria da Fiore.** Tucked away on a little calle off the top of Campo San Polo, Da Fiore is a favorite among high-end diners for its superbly prepared Venetian cuisine and refined yet relaxed atmosphere. A superlative seafood lunch or dinner here might include delicate hors d'oeuvres of moeche, scallops, and tiny octopus, followed by a succulent risotto or tagliolini *con scampi e radicchio* (with shrimp and radicchio), and a perfectly cooked main course of *rombo* (turbot) or *tagliata di tonno* (tuna steak). ⊠ *Calle del Scaleter, San Polo 2202* ☎ *041/721308* ⌂ *Reservations essential* ▭ *AE, DC, MC, V* ☾ *Closed Sun. and Mon., Aug., and Dec. 24–Jan. 15.*

$ ✕**Alla Madonna.** It's true that many hotels in town send their guests here, and that sometimes there are more foreigners present than locals, but for quality and price, this osteria is hard to beat. In short, it's a rare Venetian bargain. Ubiquitous copper pots line the ceilings, walls are covered with paintings and prints, and bow-tied waiters in white jackets rush among tables delivering plates filled with hefty portions. The *granseola* (crab) is particularly winning here; make sure to ask for some extra-virgin olive oil. If possible, try to save room for the tiramisu. ⊠ *Calle della Madonna, San Polo 594* ☎ *041/5223824* ▭ *AE, MC, V* ☾ *Closed Wed. and part of Aug.*

Santa Croce

$$–$$$ ✕ **Vecio Fritolin.** Until not so long ago, fish was fried and sold "to go" throughout Venice just as in London, except that it was paired with polenta rather than chips. An old sign advertising fish to go still hangs outside the "Old Fry Shop," but nowadays you can only dine in. A second sign, announcing cicheti available to go, still holds true. At this neat bacaro con cucina you can have a traditional meal featuring such dishes as bigoli in salsa, baked fish with herbs, and non-Venetian lamb chops. ⊠ *Calle della Regina, Santa Croce 2262* ☎ *041/5222881* ⊟ *AE, DC, MC, V* ⊘ *Closed Mon., 2 wks in Jan., and 2 wks in Aug. No lunch Tues.*

$ ✕ **Bancogiro.** Come to this casual spot for a change from standard Vene-
Fodor'sChoice tian food. Yes, fish is on the menu, but offerings such as *mousse di gam-*
★ *beroni con salsa di avocado* (shrimp mousse with an avocado sauce) and Sicilian-style *sarde incinte* (stuffed, or "pregnant," sardines) are far from typical fare. The wine list and the cheese plate are both divine. The location is in the heart of the Rialto market in a 15th-century loggia, with tables upstairs in a carefully restored no-smoking room with a partial view of the Grand Canal; when it's warm, you can sit outdoors and get the full canal view. ⊠ *Campo San Giacometto, Santa Croce 122 (under the porch)* ☎ *041/5232061* ⊟ *No credit cards* ⊘ *Closed Mon. No dinner Sun.*

¢–$ ✕ **Al Prosecco.** Locals stream into this place, order the "spritzer bitter" (a combination of white wine, Campari, and seltzer water), and continue on their way; contemplating trying the drink while chewing on one of the fine panini, such as the *porchetta romane verdure* (roasted pig, Roman style, with greens). Proprietors Davide and Stefano preside over a young and friendly staff who reel off the day's specials with ease. When the weather's warm, you can eat outside on a beautiful campo. ⊠ *Campo S. Giacomo da l'Orlo, Santa Croce 1503* ☎ *041/5240222* ⊟ *No credit cards* ⊘ *Closed Sun.*

WHERE TO STAY

Updated by
Patti Rucidlo

Most of Venice's hotels are in renovated palaces, but space is at a premium—and comes for a price—with all Venice lodging. The most exclusive hotels are indeed palatial, although even they may have some small, dowdy rooms. In lower price categories, rooms may be cramped, and not all hotels have lounging areas. Because of preservation laws, some hotels are not allowed to have elevators. Air-conditioning can be essential if you suffer in summer heat; some hotels charge a supplement for it. Although the city has no cars, it does have boats plying the canals and pedestrians chattering in the streets, even late at night, so ask for a quiet room if noise bothers you. In summer, don't leave your room lights on at night *and* your window wide open: mosquitoes can descend en masse. If you find that these creatures are a problem, ask at your hotel's desk for a Vape, a plug-in antimosquito device.

It is *essential* to know how to get to your hotel when you arrive, as transport can range from arriving in a very expensive water taxi or gondola to wandering alleys and side streets—luggage in hand—with relapses of déjà vu. Many hotels accept reservations on-line; the handy Web site ⊕ www.veniceinfo.it offers free information (with photographs) about most hotels in town. It's advisable to book well in advance. If you don't have reservations, try **Venezia Sì** (☎ 800/843006 toll-free in Italy,

Mon.–Sat. 9–7 0039/0415222264 from abroad 🖷 0039/0415221242 from abroad), which offers a free reservation service over the phone. It's the public relations arm of **AVA** (Venetian Hoteliers Association; ☎041/5228004 for administration) and has booths where you can make same-day reservations at Piazzale Roma (☎ 041/5231397 ☽ Open daily 9 AM–10 PM), Santa Lucia train station (☎ 041/715288 or 041/715016 ☽ Open daily 8 AM–9 PM), and Marco Polo Airport (☎ 041/5415133 ☽ Daily 9 AM–10 PM).

Prices

Venetian hotels cater to all tastes and price ranges. Rates are about 20% higher than in Rome and Milan, but you can save off-season (November–March, excluding Christmas and Carnevale, and also to some degree in August).

WHAT IT COSTS In euros				
	$$$$	$$$	$$	$	¢
FOR 2 PEOPLE	over € 300	€225–€300	€150–€225	€75–€150	under €75

Prices are for two people in a standard double room in high season.

Cannaregio

$$ ▦ **Hotel Antico Doge.** If you're looking for a small, intimate hotel in a quiet yet central location, look no further. This delightful palazzo was once home to Doge Marino Falier; since then, it's been modernized with lovely results. Some rooms have *baldacchini* (canopied beds); all have fabric walls and hardwood floors. Located on a small canal, and only minutes away from San Marco and the Rialto Bridge, this is an oasis of tranquillity. An ample buffet breakfast is served in a room with a frescoed ceiling and Murano chandelier. ✉ *Campo SS. Apostoli, Cannaregio 5643, 30131* ☎ *041/2411570* 🖷 *041/2443660* ⊕ *www.anticodoge. com* ⇆ *13 rooms, 2 suites* ⚷ *In-room safes, minibars, cable TV, bar, Internet* ▭ *AE, DC, MC, V.*

$ ▦ **Bernardi Semenzato.** This is a particularly inviting little place just off Strada Nova and near the gondola ferry to the Rialto market. Rooms are well maintained, with exposed ceiling beams, matching headboard-bedspread sets, and tiled bathrooms. The nearby *dipendenza* (annex) has more the feeling of a private apartment, with large rooms featuring inlaid wooden floors, Murano chandeliers, and several 19th-century antiques. ✉ *Calle dell'Oca, Cannaregio 4366, 30121* ☎ *041/5211052* 🖷 *041/5222424* ⊕ *www.hotelbernardi.com* ⇆ *24 rooms, 14 with bath* ⚷ *Cable TV, some pets allowed, no-smoking rooms* ▭ *AE, MC, V* ☽ *Closed Dec. 8–Dec. 20.*

Castello

$$$$ ▦ **Danieli.** You'll feel like a doge in Venice's largest luxury hotel, a complex of newer buildings and a 14th-century palazzo. Sumptuous Venetian decor prevails from the moment you set foot in the soaring atrium, with its sweeping staircase. Long favored by world leaders and movie stars, it's predictably chic and expensive. The rooftop terrace restaurant has a heavenly view but unexceptional food. May through October, guests have access to the pool, tennis courts, and beach of the Hotel Excelsior on the Lido via a private (free) launch running on the hour. ✉ *Riva degli Schiavoni, Castello 4196, 30122* ☎ *041/5226480; 041/2961222 reservations in English* 🖷 *041/5200208* ⊕ *www.luxurycollection.com/danieli* ⇆ *221 rooms, 12 suites* ⚷ *Restaurant, room service, in-room data ports,*

in-room safes, minibars, cable TV, bar, baby-sitting, dry cleaning, laundry service, concierge, Internet, business services, meeting rooms, some pets allowed, no-smoking rooms ☐ AE, DC, MC, V.

$$$$ ⊡ **Hotel Londra Palace.** A hundred windows overlooking the lagoon and the island of San Giorgio impart a hearty dash of sunlight to many of the finely decorated rooms of this luxury hotel. The view must have been pleasing to Tchaikovsky, who wrote his 4th Symphony here in 1877. Neoclassical public rooms, with splashes of blue and green glass suggesting the sea, play nicely off guest rooms, which have fine fabric, damask drapes, Biedermeier furniture, and Venetian glass. A change in management in 2003 has brought a breath of fresh air to the place; the staff is top-notch, as are the restaurant and bar. ⊠ *Riva degli Schiavoni, Castello 4171, 30122* ☎ *041/5200533* 🖷 *041/5225032* ⊕ *www.hotelondra.it* ⇔ *36 rooms, 17 suites* ↳ *Restaurant, room service, in-room data ports, in-room fax, in-room safes, minibars, cable TV, wine bar, piano bar, baby-sitting, dry cleaning, laundry service, concierge, Internet, business services, meeting room* ☐ *AE, DC, MC, V.*

★ $$$$ ⊡ **Metropole.** Eccentrics, eclectics, and fans of Antonio Vivaldi (who taught music here) love the Metropole, the most intimate and affordable of the high-end hotels stretching along the Riva degli Schiavoni. The owner, a lifelong collector of odd objects, displays his collection of oil paintings and enough antiques to fill a dealer's shop—some of which make their way into the beautifully appointed rooms. Honeymooners should consider a stay in the just-this-side-of-kitsch Room of the Angels. ⊠ *Riva degli Schiavoni, Castello 4149, 30122* ☎ *041/5205044* 🖷 *041/5223679* ⊕ *www.hotelmetropole.com* ⇔ *43 rooms, 26 suites* ↳ *Restaurant, room service, in-room data ports, in-room safes, minibars, cable TV, bar, baby-sitting, dry cleaning, laundry service, meeting room, concierge, some pets allowed* ☐ *AE, DC, MC, V.*

$$$–$$$$ ⊡ **Savoia e Jolanda.** The location and views are the best features of this hotel, facing San Giorgio Maggiore on one side, the church of San Zaccaria on the other. All guest rooms are decorated with sumptuous tapestries and Murano glass chandeliers; all have high ceilings—some are coffered—and many get a great deal of light. There's a copious buffet breakfast. ⊠ *Riva degli Schiavoni, Castello 4187, 30122* ☎ *041/ 5206644* 🖷 *041/5207494* ⊕ *www.hotelsavoiajolanda.com* ⇔ *36 rooms, 15 suites* ↳ *Restaurant, room service, in-room data ports, in-room safes, some in-room hot tubs, minibars, cable TV, bar, baby-sitting, dry cleaning, laundry service, concierge, Internet, some pets allowed, no-smoking rooms* ☐ *AE, DC, MC, V.*

$$ ⊡ **La Residenza.** The word *residenza* in Italian suggests a good deal of aristocratic elegance, and this hotel, with more the feeling of a private noble house than a hotel, does not disappoint. The hall occupies the whole *portego* (entryway) of the patrician apartment of Palazzo dei Badoari-Partecipazi già Gritti and looks almost disproportionately opulent for this quiet hotel. Well-preserved 18th-century stuccowork adorns the ceilings and walls, along with precious oil paintings. Oriental carpets partially hide the beautiful Venetian floor. ⊠ *Campo Bandiera Re Moro, Castello 3608, 30122* ☎ *041/5285315* 🖷 *041/5238859* ⇔ *14 rooms* ↳ *In-room safes, minibars* ☐ *MC, V.*

$$ ⊡ **Paganelli.** The lagoon views here so impressed Henry James that he wrote the Paganelli up in the preface to his *Portrait of a Lady*. This enchanting small hotel on the waterfront near Piazza San Marco is tastefully decorated in the Venetian style. The quieter annex in Campo San Zaccaria is a former convent, and some rooms preserve the original coffered ceilings. ⊠ *Riva degli Schiavoni, Castello 4687, 30122* ☎ *041/ 5224324* 🖷 *041/5239267* ↳ *Cable TV, bar, baby-sitting* ☐ *AE, MC, V.*

¢ 🏠 **Istituto San Giuseppe.** This religious institution, in an excellent location north of Piazza San Marco, is one of several lodgings in Venice run by nuns. Rooms are spartan in decor but spotless and very quiet, overlooking the inner cloister. Book well ahead, as the unbeatable prices draw crowds, mostly Italians in the know. Curfew is at 11 (10:30 in the winter), and no breakfast is served. Couples must be prepared to prove that they are married, and patience should be observed if making reservations over the phone; language barriers aside, this convent is a remarkable deal. ⊠ *Castello 5402, 30122* ☎ *041/5225352* 🖷 *041/5224891* ➥ *12 rooms* ⚴ *No a/c, no room phones, no room TVs* 🖃 *No credit cards.*

Dorsoduro

$$$$ 🏠 **Ca' Pisani.** Here's a breath of fresh air: a Venetian hotel with no brocades and chandeliers to be found. Instead there's a tasteful mix of modern design and well-chosen antique pieces. The entrance hall has marble floors and an interesting play of colors and lights; the rooms contain original art deco pieces from the '30s and '40s (every bed is different). The no-smoking wine bar La Rivista serves light meals all day, and upstairs are a Turkish bath and a wooden rooftop terrace where you can take the sun. ⊠ *Rio Terà Antonio Foscarini, Dorsoduro 979/a, 30123* ☎ *041/2401411* 🖷 *041/2771061* ⊕ *www.capisanihotel.it* ➥ *25 rooms, 4 suites* ⚴ *Restaurant, room service, in-room data ports, in-room safes, minibars, cable TV with movies, Turkish bath, wine bar, concierge, dry cleaning, laundry service, Internet, some pets allowed, no-smoking floor* 🖃 *AE, DC, MC, V.*

$$$ 🏠 **American.** At first sight, it's hard to pick out this quiet, family-run hotel from the houses along the fondamenta: there are no lights, flags, or big signs on the hotel's yellow stucco facade. A hall decorated with reproduction antiques, Oriental rugs, and contemporary images of Venice on the walls leads to a breakfast room reminiscent of a theater foyer, with red velvet chairs and gilded wall lamps. A 2002 overhaul has given the place some zip, with new carpets and updated bathrooms. Rooms vary in size and shape, but sage green and delicate pink fabrics and lacquered Venetian-style furniture are found throughout. ⊠ *San Vio, Dorsoduro 628, 30123* ☎ *041/5204733* 🖷 *041/5204048* ⊕ *www. hotelamerican.com* ➥ *28 rooms, 2 suites* ⚴ *In-room data ports, in-room safes, minibars, cable TV, baby-sitting, Internet, no-smoking rooms* 🖃 *AE, DC, MC, V.*

$$$ 🏠 **Hotel Pausania.** From the moment you ascend the grand staircase rising above the fountain of this 14th-century palazzo, you sense the combination of good taste and modern comforts that characterizes Hotel Pausania. Light-colored rooms are spacious, with comfortable furniture and carpets with rugs thrown over them. Some rooms face the small canal (which can become a bit noisy early in the morning) in front of the hotel, while others look out over the large garden courtyard. The hotel has a convenient car service (€40) to and from the airport. ⊠ *Fondamenta Gherardini, Dorsoduro 2824, 30123* ☎ *041/5222083* 🖷 *041/5222989* ⊕ *www.hotelpausania.it* ➥ *26 rooms* ⚴ *Minibars, cable TV, bar, baby-sitting, dry cleaning, laundry service, concierge, airport shuttle, some pets allowed* 🖃 *AE, MC, V.*

$$–$$$ 🏠 **Pensione Accademia Villa Maravege.** A secret garden awaits just beyond an iron gate, complete with a mini Palladian-style villa, flower beds, stone cupids, and verdant trees—all rarities in Venice. Aptly nicknamed "Villa of the Wonders," this patrician retreat once served as the Russian embassy and was the residence of Katharine Hepburn in the movie *Summertime.* Conservative rooms are outfitted with Victorian-era an-

tiques and fine tapestry. The location is on a promontory where two side canals converge with the Grand Canal, which can be seen from the garden. Book well in advance. ⊠ *Fondamenta Bollani, Dorsoduro 1058, 30123* ☎ *041/5210188* 🖷 *041/5239152* ⊕ *www.pensioneaccademia. it* ⮐ *27 rooms* ☖ *In-room safes, minibars, cable TV, bar, baby-sitting, dry cleaning, laundry service* ⊟ *AE, DC, MC, V.*

$–$$ 🏨 **Agli Alboretti.** The Alboretti is one of the many hotels clustered at the foot of the Ponte dell'Accademia. Its unpretentious, rather small rooms are blessed with plenty of light. Their nautical decor, with original pieces taken from old ships' cabins, goes well with the cries of seagulls living along the nearby Giudecca Canal. Some steep climbing might be part of your stay, as there are four floors and no elevator. In warm weather, breakfast is served in an inner courtyard under a rose bower; a small terrace with potted plants is open during the warmer months. ⊠ *Rio Terrà Foscarini, Dorsoduro 884, 30123* ☎ *041/5230058* 🖷 *041/ 5210158* ⊕ *www.aglialboretti.com* ⮐ *20 rooms* ☖ *Restaurant, in-room data ports, cable TV, bar, dry cleaning, laundry service, concierge, some pets allowed, no-smoking rooms* ⊟ *AE, DC, MC, V.*

★ $–$$ 🏨 **La Calcina.** The Calcina sits in an enviable position along the sunny Zattere, with views across the wide Giudecca Canal. You can sunbathe on the *altana* (wooden terrace) or enjoy an afternoon tea in one of the reading corners of the shadowy, intimate hall with flickering candlelight and barely perceptible classical music. A stone staircase (no elevator) leads to the rooms upstairs, with shiny wooden floors, original Art Deco furniture and lamps, and firm beds. Some rooms suffer from a lack of storage space. A few of the single rooms have a shared bath. ⊠ *Zattere, Dorsoduro 780, 30123* ☎ *041/5206466* 🖷 *041/5227045* ⊕ *www. lacalcina.com* ⮐ *29 rooms, 26 with bath, 5 suites* ☖ *Restaurant, in-room safes, cable TV* ⊟ *AE, DC, MC, V.*

Giudecca

$$$$ 🏨 **Cipriani.** It's impossible to feel stressed in this oasis of stunning rooms and suites, some with garden patios. The hotel launch whisks you to Giudecca from San Marco and back at any hour; those dining at the exceptional Ristorante Harry Cipriani can use it as well. The restored 17th-century-style Palazzo Vendramin is preferable to the main hotel and the Palazzetto, a modern annex facing the Canale della Giudecca. Prices are high even by Venetian standards, but this is the only place in town with such extensive facilities and services, from an Olympic-size pool and tennis courts to cooking courses and fitness programs. ⊠ *Giudecca 10, 30133* ☎ *041/5207744* 🖷 *041/5207745* ⊕ *www.hotelcipriani.it* ⮐ *54 rooms, 50 suites* ☖ *2 restaurants, room service, in-room safes, minibars, cable TV, tennis court, saltwater pool, health club, massage, sauna, spa, bar, baby-sitting, concierge, dry cleaning, laundry service, Internet, meeting room, no-smoking rooms* ⊟ *AE, DC, MC, V* ☾ *Closed Dec.–Apr.; Palazzo Vendramin closed 2nd wk Nov.–early Mar.*

Lido

★ $$–$$$$ 🏨 **Quattro Fontane.** This fine hotel in a well-maintained mansion run by Danish sisters Bente and Pia Bevilacqua offers the serenity of the Lido, in a location that's a 15-minute walk and a 20-minute boat ride from Piazza San Marco. Well-decorated rooms, with period furniture and tasteful tapestries, overlook the surrounding garden. Common areas contain an odd collection of mason's aprons, pipes, ex-votos, masks from Jakarta, Roman seals, and seashells. A huge fireplace adds warmth and character in the colder months. After a full day you can relax in the library, stocked with books in many languages. ⊠ *Via delle Quattro*

Fontane 16, Lido, 30126 ☎ *041/5260227* 🖷 *041/5260726* ⊕ *www.
quattrofontane.com* 🛏 *54 rooms, 4 suites* 🍴 *Restaurant, in-room safes,
minibars, cable TV, bar, library, baby-sitting, dry cleaning, laundry service, meeting room; no a/c in some rooms* ▭ *AE, DC, MC, V* ☉ *Closed
Nov.–Mar.*

San Marco

★ $$$$ 🏨 **Il Palazzo at the Bauer.** A $38 million restoration has turned il Palazzo,
under the same management as the larger Bauer Hotel, into the ultimate
word in luxury. Bevilacqua and Rubelli fabrics cover the walls, and no
two rooms are decorated the same. What they have in common, however, are high ceilings, many with sweeping views, Murano glass, marbled bathrooms, and damask drapes. Breakfast is served on Venice's
highest terrace, appropriately named il Settimo Cielo (Seventh Heaven).
The outdoor hot tub, also on the seventh floor, offers views that won't
quit of La Serennissima. ✉ *Campo San Moisè, San Marco 1459, 30124*
☎ *041/5207022* 🖷 *041/5207557* ⊕ *www.bauervenezia.it* 🛏 *35 rooms,
40 suites* 🍴 *Restaurant, room service, in-room data ports, in-room fax,
in-room safes, some in-room hot tubs, minibars, cable TV with movies,
golf privileges, health club, outdoor hot tub, massage, sauna, Turkish
bath, dock, bar, baby-sitting, dry cleaning, laundry service, concierge,
Internet, some pets allowed, no-smoking rooms* ▭ *AE, DC, MC, V.*

$$$$ 🏨 **Gritti Palace.** Queen Elizabeth, Greta Garbo, and Winston Churchill
made this their Venetian address. The feeling of being in an aristocratic
private home pervades this legendary hotel, replete with fresh flowers,
fine antiques, sumptuous appointments, and old-fashioned service. The
dining terrace on the Grand Canal is best enjoyed in the evening when
the boat traffic dies down. Guests have access to pool and tennis courts.
✉ *Campo Santa Maria del Giglio, San Marco 2467, 30124* ☎ *041/
794611* 🖷 *041/5200942* ⊕ *www.luxurycollection.com* 🛏 *87 rooms,
6 suites* 🍴 *Restaurant, room service, cable TV with movies, in-room data
ports, in-room safes, minibars, bar, baby-sitting, dry cleaning, laundry
service, concierge, Internet, business services, meeting rooms, some pets
allowed, no-smoking rooms* ▭ *AE, DC, MC, V.*

★ $$$$ 🏨 **Monaco & Grand Canal.** Between the view onto the Bacino di San
Marco and the touches of elegance and comfort found at this luxurious
hotel, you may find little motivation to leave. The common rooms on the
ground floor are flooded with the shimmering light coming off the lagoon,
and the piano bar, with velvety light-sage couches, comes alive every night.
Rooms are spacious but warm and intimate, with carpeted floors, satin-
lined walls, handsome antique-style furniture, and ample terra-cotta bathrooms. The half-board option, with meals à la carte in the worthwhile Grand
Canal restaurant, is a good choice. ✉ *Calle Vallaresso, San Marco 1325,
30124* ☎ *041/5200211* 🖷 *041/5200501* 🛏 *64 rooms, 7 suites* 🍴 *Restaurant, room service, in-room data ports, in-room safes, some in-room hot
tubs, minibars, cable TV, dock, bar, piano bar, baby-sitting, concierge, dry
cleaning, laundry service, some pets allowed* ▭ *AE, DC, MC, V.*

★ $$$ 🏨 **San Zulian.** A minimalist entrance hall leads to rooms that are a re-
fined variation on the Venetian theme, with lacquered 18th-century-style
furniture and parquet floors. Room 304 is on two levels and has its own
delightful covered veranda. Two ground-floor rooms have bathrooms
equipped for people with disabilities. The handy location near San
Marco and the Rialto and the top-notch staff make a stay here eminently
worthwhile. ✉ *Campo della Guerra, San Marco 534/535, 30124* ☎ *041/
5225872 or 041/5226598* 🖷 *041/5232265* ⊕ *www.hotelsanzulian.
com* 🛏 *25 rooms* 🍴 *In-room safes, minibars, some pets allowed* ▭ *AE,
DC, MC, V.*

$ ⊡ **Albergo San Samuele.** Near the Grand Canal and Palazzo Grassi, this friendly hotel has clean, sunny rooms in surprisingly good shape for the price. Five of the bathrooms, with white and gray-blue tiles, are relatively new, and the walls are painted in crisp, pleasant shades of pale pink or blue. Curtains and bedspreads are made from antique-looking fabrics, and although the furniture is of the boxy modern kind, the owners are gradually adding more interesting-looking pieces. ⊠ *Salizzada San Samuele, San Marco 3358, 30124* ☎☎ *041/5228045* ➮ *10 rooms, 7 with bath* ⚐ *Fans, some pets allowed, no-smoking rooms; no a/c* ▭ *No credit cards.*

San Polo

$$–$$$ ⊡ **Sturion.** At the end of the 13th century this building housed foreign merchants selling their wares at the Rialto, and Carpaccio depicted it in his 1494 *Mircale of the Cross* (on view at the Accademia). Now it's decorated in 18th-century Venetian style and run with great care by a Venetian family. Rooms are done in red and gold brocade (two with views of the Grand Canal); there's also a small but inviting breakfast room. Two of the rooms comfortably sleep four and are perfect for families. Be warned that the stairs are steep here, and there's no elevator. ⊠ *Calle del Sturion, San Polo 679, 30125* ☎ *041/5236243* 🖨 *041/5228378* ⊕ *www.locandasturion.com* ➮ *11 rooms* ⚐ *Restaurant, in-room safes, minibars, library, Internet, some pets allowed, no-smoking rooms* ▭ *AE, MC, V.*

NIGHTLIFE & THE ARTS

The Arts

Updated by
Elaine Eliah

A Guest in Venice, a monthly bilingual booklet free at most hotels, is your most accessible, up-to-date guide to Venice happenings. It also includes information about pharmacies, vaporetto and bus lines, and the main trains and flights. You can visit their Web site, ⊕ www.aguestinvenice. com, for a preview of musical, artistic, and sporting events. *Venezia News,* available at newsstands, has similar information but also includes in-depth articles about noteworthy events. The tourist office publishes *Leo* and *Bussola,* bimonthly brochures in Italian and English listing events and updated museum hours. *Venezia da Vivere* is a seasonal guide listing nightspots and live music. Several Venice Web sites allow you to scan the cultural horizon before you arrive; try ⊕ www.ombra.net, ⊕ www.veniceonline.it, and ⊕ www.venicebanana.com.

The **Biennale** cultural institution organizes events year-round, including the film festival, which begins the last week of August. The Biennale international exhibition of contemporary art is held in odd-numbered years, usually from mid-June to early November, at the Giardini della Biennale, and in the impressive Arsenale. Visit ⊕ www.labiennale.org for information. Last but not least, don't ignore the posters you see everywhere in the streets. They're often the most up-to-date information you can find.

Festivals

Carnevale takes place on the 10 (or more) days leading up to Ash Wednesday; if you're not planning on joining in the revelry, you're wise to choose another time to visit, as prices skyrocket and sightseeing becomes almost impossible. For information about the various costume balls and parties, try one of the related Web sites (⊕ www.aguestinvenice. com, www.meetingeurope.com) or call the **Venice tourist office** (☎ 041/

5298711). The third weekend of July, the **Festa del Redentore** (Feast of the Redeemer) commemorates the end of a 16th-century plague that killed about 47,000 city residents. Just like doges have done annually for centuries, you, too, can make a pilgrimage across the temporary bridge connecting Zattere to the Giudecca. Venetians take to the water to watch fireworks at midnight, but if you can't find a boat, Giudecca is the best place to be. Young folks traditionally greet sunrise on the Lido beach while their elders attend church.

Music

Although there are occasional jazz and Italian pop concerts in clubs around town, the vast majority of music you'll hear is classical, with Venice's famed Vivaldi the composer frequently featured. A number of churches and palazzi regularly host concerts, as do Ca' Rezzonico and Querini Stampalia museums. You'll find these events listed in publications such as *A Guest in Venice*; also try asking the tourist information office or your concierge. The **Vela Call Center** (☎ 899/909090 ☉ daily 8 AM–8 PM) has information about musical events, and you can buy tickets at Vela sales offices in Piazzale Roma, Ferrovia, and Calle dei Fuseri (a 10-minute walk from San Marco). The travel agency **Kele & Teo** (✉ Ponte dei Bareteri, San Marco 4930 ☎ 041/5208722) has tickets for a number of venues and is conveniently located midway between Rialto and San Marco.

Opera & Ballet

Teatro La Fenice (✉ Campo San Fantin, San Marco), one of Italy's oldest opera houses, has witnessed many memorable premieres, including the 1853 first-night flop of Verdi's *La Traviata*. It's also had its share of disasters, the most recent being a terrible fire, deliberately set in January 1996. It's been closed since but is scheduled to reopen sometime in 2004.

Until Fenice reopens, symphony, opera, and ballet performances are staged in the **Teatro Malibran** (✉ Campo S. Giovanni Crisostomo, Cannaregio 5873), and in the tentlike structure known as the **Palafenice** (✉ Tronchetto parking area). Visit the Fenice Web site (⊕ www.teatrolafenice.it) for a schedule of performances and to buy tickets for both venues. Tickets are available at both theaters one hour before performances. Information is available at **Vela Call Center** (☎ 899/909090 ☉ 8–8), and you can buy tickets at Vela sales offices in Piazzale Roma, Ferrovia, and Calle dei Fuseri.

Nightlife

Piazza San Marco is a popular meeting place in nice weather, when the cafés stay open late and all seem to be competing to offer the best live music. The younger crowd of Venetians and visitors tends to gravitate toward Rialto Bridge, with Campi San Bartolomeo and San Luca on one side and Campo Rialto Nuovo on the other. Especially popular with university students are Cannaregio's Fondamenta della Misericordia and the area around Campo Santa Margarita and San Pantalon.

Bars

L'Olandese Volante (✉ Campo San Lio, near Rialto ☎ 041/5289349) is a popular hangout for many young Venetians. Nothing special by day, **Bar Torino** (✉ Campo San Luca ☎ 041/5223914) is one of Venice's liveliest nightspots, open late and spilling out onto the campo in summer. **Bácaro Jazz** (✉ Across from Rialto Post Office ☎ 041/5285249) has music and meals until 2 AM, and its gregarious staff is unlikely to let you feel lonely.

The **Martini Scala Club** (⊠ Campo San Fantin, San Marco 1983 ☎ 041/ 5224121), Antico Martini restaurant's elegant bar, has live music from 10 to 3:30. Full meals are served until 2.

One of the original late-night Venetian nightspots, **Paradiso Perduto** (⊠ Fondamenta della Misericordia, Cannaregio 2540 ☎ 041/720581) serves up inexpensive fish dishes and sometimes has live music on week-ends; it's closed on Tuesday and Wednesday. Campo Santa Margarita is a student hangout all day and late into the night. Try **Margaret Duchamp** (⊠ Campo Santa Margarita, Dorsoduro 3019 ☎ 041/5286255) for reasonably priced snacks and drinks. The bohemian **Il Caffè** (⊠ Campo Santa Margarita, Dorsoduro 2963 ☎ 041/5287998), also known as Caffè Rosso for its red exterior, is especially popular in nice weather.

Casinos

The city-run gambling casino in splendid **Palazzo Vendramin-Calergi** is a classic scene of well-dressed high-rollers playing French roulette, Caribbean poker, chemin de fer, 30–40, and slots. You must be 18 to enter, and men must wear jackets. ⊠ *Cannaregio 2040* ☎ *041/5297111* 🎫 *€10 entry includes €10 in chips* ☉ *Slots 2:45 PM–3 AM; tables 3:30 PM–3 AM* Ⓥ *San Marcuola.*

Mestre's **Ca' Noghera** casino, near the airport, has slots, blackjack, craps, poker, and roulette. Minimum age is 18. ⊠ *Via Triestina 222, Tessera, Mestre* ☎ *041/5297111* 🎫 *€10 entry includes €10 in chips* ☉ *Slots 11 AM–5 AM; tables begin 3:30 PM–5 AM.*

Nightclubs

Just a vaporetto hop from Venice is **Discoteca Acropolis** (⊠ Lungomare Guglielmo Marconi 22, Lido ☎ 041/5260466). It's a trendy, summer spot, open March–October, with disco, live performances, and a terrace bar.

An artistic blend of iron beams with silver candlesticks, old brick with white tablecloths, has transformed a vintage refrigerated warehouse into casually sophisticated **Frigo** (⊠ Viale Ancona, 18 Mestre ☎ 041/ 5319293). Flashback to the old supper-club days, when diners got up and danced any time during their meal, as Frigo's DJ varies the music with the night's clientele. (The well-designed sound system means danc-ing and dinner conversation aren't mutually exclusive.) A menu from pizza to pepper steak is available from 7:30 to 1:30 AM and though it's a five-minute taxi ride from Piazzale Roma (or buses 80 and N2 drop you within a 10-minute walk), your dining dollars go lots farther in Mestre.

For dancing in Venice, tiny **Piccolo Mondo** (⊠ Dorsoduro 1056/a ☎ 041/ 5200371), near the Accademia Gallery, charges no cover and has disco until 4 AM.

SPORTS

Golf

Updated by Elaine Eliah

The 18-hole **Golf Club Lido di Venezia** (⊠ Strada Vecchia 1, Alberoni, Lido ☎ 041/731333), closed Monday, isn't exceptional, but it fulfills the basic needs of golf addicts.

Horseback Riding

Circolo Ippico Veneziano (⊠ Ca' Bianca, Lido ☎ 041/5265162 ☎☎ 041/ 5268091), closed Sunday afternoon and Monday, rents horses for rid-ing trails on the premises and can refer you to terra firma clubs around the Veneto.

Running

The most scenic running route (6–7 km [4–4½ mi] long) heads east from Piazza San Marco, and skirts the lagoon along the Riva degli Schiavoni to the pine wood of Sant'Elena. You can return through the picturesque neighborhood of Castello and the island of San Pietro di Castello. This route can get packed with pedestrians from spring through fall, so unless you're adept at (and don't mind) running a slalom course, try Lido Beach or the area around Zattere.

Swimming

Venice's two public pools are open some hours for *nuoto libero* (free swim). Both close in July and August and charge €4.50 per visit. Though neither has lockers, receptionists will usually keep valuables for you. Venice's larger pool is the eight-lane, 26-meter **Piscina Comunale** (⊠ Island of Sacca Fisola, Giudecca ☎ 041/5285430 Ⓥ Sacca Fisola line 82). Four-lane, 25-meter **Piscina di Sant'Alvise** (⊠ Cannaregio 3161 ☎ 041/713567 Ⓥ Sant'Alvise) is in a building that was once the community laundry. Those looking for a cooling break in summer should head for the **Lido** (Ⓥ S.M Elizabetta). Large sections of the long, narrow beach are private, renting chairs and umbrellas, and offering toilets, showers and restaurants. If your hotel has no beach rights, you can pay for entry. The free beach areas, with no facilities, are generally crowded unless you head south by bus toward Malamocca and Alberoni.

Tennis

The **Lido Tennis Club** (⊠ Via Sandro Gallo 163, Lido ☎ 041/5260954) offers court time to nonmembers year-round. **Club Ca' del Moro** (⊠ Via F. Parri 6, Alberoni, Lido ☎ 041/770965) has courts available for non-members. The **Hotel des Bains** (⊠ Lungomare Guglielmo Marconi 17, Lido ☎ 041/5265921) rents tennis courts to nonguests from March through November. One private club near the **Hotel Excelsior** (⊠ Lungomare Guglielmo Marconi 41, Lido ☎ 041/5260335) offers court space March through November to guests of select Venice hotels.

SHOPPING

Updated by
Patricia Rucidlo

You'll find plenty of pleasant shops and boutiques as you explore Venice. It's always a good idea to mark the location of a shop that interests you on your map; otherwise you may not be able to find it again in the maze of tiny streets. Regular store hours are usually 9–12:30 and 3:30 or 4–7:30; some stores are closed on Saturday afternoon or Monday morning. Food shops are open 8–1 and 5–7:30, and are closed Wednesday afternoon and all day Sunday. Many tourist-oriented shops are open all day, every day. Some shops close for both a summer and a winter vacation.

Food Markets

The morning open-air fruit and vegetable market at **Rialto** offers animated local color and commerce. On Tuesday through Saturday mornings, the **fish market** (adjacent to the Rialto produce market) provides an impressive lesson in ichthyology, with species you've probably never seen before. In the Castello district you'll find a lively food market weekday mornings on **Via Garibaldi.**

Shopping Districts

The **San Marco** area is full of shops and couture boutiques such as Armani, Missoni, Valentino, Fendi, and Versace. **Le Mercerie,** along with the Frezzeria and Calle dei Fabbri, leading from Piazza San Marco, are some of Venice's busiest shopping streets. Other good shopping areas surround Calle del Teatro and Campi San Salvador, Manin, San Fantin, and San Bartolomeo. Less-expensive shops are between the Rialto Bridge and San Polo.

Specialty Stores

Glassware

Glass, most of it made in Murano, is Venice's number one product, and you'll be confronted by mind-boggling displays of traditional and contemporary glassware, much of it kitsch. Take your time and be selective. You will probably find that prices in Venice's shops and the showrooms of Murano's factories are pretty much the same. However, because of competition, shops in Venice with wares from various glassworks may charge slightly less.

Domus (⊠ Fondamenta dei Vetrai, Murano 82 ☎ 041/739215) has a selection of smaller objects and jewelry from the best glassworks. **Galleria San Nicolò** (⊠ Calle della Fenice, San Marco 1920 ☎ 041/5221535) is owned by American glass expert Louise Berndt. It shows the best of contemporary glass, including superb work by Micheluzzi, Michael Groot, and Maria Brandolini. For chic, contemporary glassware, Carlo Moretti is a good choice; his designs are on display at **L'Isola** (⊠ Campo San Moisè, San Marco 1468 ☎ 041/5231973).

Marina Barovier (⊠ Calle delle Botteghe, off Campo Santo Stefano, San Marco 3216 ☎ 041/5236748) has an excellent selection of collectors' contemporary glass. Go to Michel Paciello's **Paropàmiso** (⊠ Frezzeria, San Marco 1701 ☎ 041/5227120) for stunning Venetian glass beads and traditional jewelry from all over the world. **Pauly** (⊠ Piazza San Marco 73, 77, and 316; Ponte dei Consorzi ☎ 041/5209899) has four centrally located shops with an impressive selection of glassware at better prices than on Murano.

Lace & Fabrics

Much of the lace and embroidered linen sold in Venice and on Burano is really made in China or Taiwan. However, at **Il Merletto** (⊠ Sotoportego del Cavalletto, under the Procuratie Vecchie, Piazza San Marco 95 ☎ 041/5208406), you can ask for the authentic, handmade lace kept in the drawers behind the counter. This is the only place in Venice connected with the students of the Scuola del Merletto in Burano, who, officially, do not sell to the public. A top address for linen is **Jesurum** (⊠ Procuratie Nuove, San Marco 60–61 ☎ 041/5229864 ⊠ Merceria del Capitello, San Marco 4857 ☎ 041/5206177). Go to **Lorenzo Rubelli** (⊠ Campo San Gallo, San Marco 1089 ☎ 041/2584411) for the same brocades, damasks, and cut velvets used by the world's most prestigious decorators. At **Norelene** (⊠ Calle della Chiesa, Dorsoduro 727 ☎ 041/5237605) you'll find wonderful hand-printed fabrics. **Venetia Studium** (⊠ Calle Larga XXII Marzo, San Marco 2403 ☎ 041/5229281 ⊠ Merceria San Zulian, San Marco 723 ☎ 041/5229859) sells silk scarves, bags, and cushion covers, as well as the famous Fortuny lamps.

Masks

Giorgio Clanetti, credited with starting the revival in mask making, operates out of **Laboratorio Artigiano Maschere** (⊠ Calle Barbaria delle Tole, Castello 6657, near Campo dei Santi Giovanni e Paolo ☎ 041/5223110). **Mondonovo** (⊠ Rio Terà Canal, Dorsoduro 3063 ☎ 041/5287344) is a cut above most other mask stores.

VENETIAN MASKS UNVEILED

VENETIAN MASK-MAKING has experienced a rebirth. In the time of the Republic, the mask trade was vibrant—Venetians used masks all year long to go about town incognito—but it was suppressed by Napoléon, a by-product of his effort to end Carnival and other Venetian holidays. When Carnival was revived in the late 1970s, mask-making returned as well. Though many workshops stick to centuries-old techniques, none has been in business for more than 30 years.

A landmark date in the history of Venetian masks is 1436, when the mascareri (mask makers) founded their own guild. By then the techniques that are replicated today were well established: a mask is first modeled in clay, then a chalk cast is made from it and lined with layers of papier-mâché, glue, gauze, and wax. (You can buy a molded mask at this stage of production and paint it yourself.)

But masks were popular well before the mascareri's guild was established. Local laws regulating their use appeared as early as 1268, often intended to prevent people from carrying weapons when masked or in a vain attempt to prohibit the then-common practice of masked men disguised as women entering convents to seduce nuns. Even on religious holidays—when masks were theoretically prohibited—they were commonly used by Venetians going to the theater or attempting to avoid identification at the city's numerous brothels and gaming tables.

In the 18th century masks started being used by actors playing the traditional roles of the commedia dell'arte. Arlecchino, Pantalone, Pulcinella, and company would wear leather masks designed to amplify or change their voices. Inexpensive papier-mâché versions of these traditional, all-black masks can be found everywhere. Arlecchino has the round face and surprised expression, Pantalone is the one with the curved nose and long moustache, and Pulcinella has the protruding nose.

The least expensive mask is the white Bauta, smooth and plain with a short, pointed nose. It's also reproduced in ceramic and brass. Invented in the 18th century as a disguise, a properly made Bauta will also alter the tone of the wearer's voice. It was particularly popular for women going to the theater, and whether worn by a man or woman, it was always accompanied by a black three-cornered hat and an ample black cloak.

The pretty Gnaga, which resembles a cat's face, was used by gay men to "meow" compliments and proposals to good-looking boys. The basic Moretta is just a black oval with eyeholes. The most interesting-looking of the traditional masks is perhaps the Medico della Peste (the Plague's Doctor), with an enormous nose shaped like a bird's beak and surmounted by a pair of glasses. During the terrible plague of 1630 and 1631, doctors took some protective measures against infection: as well as wearing masks, they examined patients with a rod to avoid touching contagious bodies and wore waxed coats that didn't "absorb" the disease. Inside the nose of the mask they put medical herbs and fragrances thought to filter and clean the infected air, while the glasses protected the eyes.

Following the boom of mask shops, numerous costume rental stores opened in the 1990s and are still going strong now. Here you'll find an assortment of masks and simplified versions of 18th-century costumes (for men both civil and military) that are warm enough to be worn outdoors and at the same time suitable for dances and parties. They can be rented for one or more days (with reduced rates for longer periods), and most models are also for sale. If you plan to rent a costume during Carnival, it's a good idea to make a reservation several months in advance.

—Carla Lionello

VENICE A TO Z

To research prices, get advice from other travelers, and book travel arrangements, visit www.fodors.com.

AIRPORTS & TRANSFERS

Venice's Aeroporto Marco Polo is served by domestic and international flights, including connections from 21 European cities, plus direct flights from Moscow and New York's JFK. In addition, Treviso Airport, some 20 mi (32 km) north of Venice, receives daily arrivals from London's Stansted Airport.

A shuttle bus or 10-minute walk takes you from Marco Polo's terminal to a dock where public and private boats are available direct to Venice's historic center. For €10 per person, including bags, Alilaguna operates regularly scheduled service from predawn until nearly midnight. It takes about an hour to reach the landing near Piazza San Marco, stopping at the Lido on the way. A *motoscafo* (water taxi) carries up to four people and four bags to city center in a the sleek, modern powerboat. The base cost is €78 and the trip takes about 25 minutes. Each additional person, bag, or stop costs extra, so it's essential to agree on a fare before boarding.

Blue ATVO buses take 20 minutes to make the nonstop trip from airport to Piazzale Roma; from here you can get a vaporetto to the landing nearest your hotel. The ATVO fare is €2.70 and tickets are available on the bus when the airport ticket booth (open 9–7:30) is closed. Yellow ACTV local buses (Line 5) leave for Venice at 10 and 40 minutes past every hour (hourly service after 11:10 PM) and take 30 minutes; before boarding, you must buy a €0.77 ticket at the airport tobacconist-newsstand, open 6:30 AM–9 PM, or from ATVO/ACTV booths. During rush hour, luggage can be a hassle on the local bus. A land taxi from the airport to Piazzale Roma costs about €30.

🛈 Airport Information **Aeroporto Marco Polo** ✉ Tessera, 10 km [6 mi] north of the city on the mainland ☎ 041/2609260 ⊕ www.veniceairport.it.
🛈 Taxis & Shuttles **Alilaguna** ☎ 041/5235775. **ATVO** ☎ 041/929500. **Motoscafo** ☎ 041/5415084 airport transfers. **Radio Taxi** ☎ 041/936222.

BOAT & FERRY TRAVEL

BY GONDOLA It's hard to believe Venice could get any more beautiful, but as your gondola glides away from the fondamenta, a magical transformation takes place—you've left the huddled masses behind to marvel at the city as visitors have for centuries before you. To some it feels like a Disney ride, and some complain about flotsam, jetsam, or less than pleasant odors, but if you insist your gondolier take you winding through the tiny side canals, you'll get out of the city's main salon and into her intimate chambers, where only private boats can go. San Marco is loaded with gondola stations, but to get off the circuit, and maybe even have a canal to yourself, try the San Tomà or Santa Sofia (near Ca' d'Oro) stations. The price of a 50-minute ride is supposed to be fixed at €62 for up to six passengers, rising to €77.50 between 8 PM and 8 AM, but these are minimums and you may have difficulty finding a gondolier who will work for that unless the city is empty. Bargaining can help, but in any case, come to terms on cost and duration before you start and make it clear that you want to see more than just the Grand Canal.

BY MOTOSCAFO Water taxis aren't cheap; you'll spend about €48 for a short trip in town, €60 to the Lido, and €75 per hour to visit the outer islands. The fare system is convoluted, with luggage handling, waiting time, early or late hours, and even ordering a taxi from your hotel, adding expense. Always agree on the price first.

BY TRAGHETTO Few tourists know about the two-man gondola ferries that cross the Grand Canal at various fixed points. At €.40, they're the cheapest and shortest gondola ride in Venice, and they can save a lot of walking. Look for TRAGHETTO signs and hand your fare to the gondolier when you board.

BY VAPORETTO ACTV water buses serve several routes daily and after 11PM provide limited service through the night. Some routes cover the length of the Grand Canal while others circle the city and connect Venice with the lagoon islands. Landing stages are clearly marked with name and line number, but check before boarding to make sure the boat is going in your direction.

Line 1 is the Grand Canal local, calling at every stop and continuing via San Marco to the Lido. The trip takes about 35 minutes from Ferrovia to Vallaresso, San Marco. Circular Line 41 (the odd number indicates it goes counterclockwise) will take you from San Zaccaria to Murano, while Line 42 (clockwise) makes the return trip. Likewise, take Line 42 from San Zaccaria to Giudecca's Redentore, but Line 41 to return. Line 51 (counterclockwise) runs from the station to San Zaccaria via Piazzale Roma, then continues to the Lido. From the Lido, Line 52 circles clockwise, stopping at San Zaccaria, Zattere, Piazzale Roma, the station, Fondamente Nuove (connect to northern lagoon islands), San Pietro di Castello, and back to the Lido. From San Zaccaria, Line 82 (same number both directions) loops past Giudecca and Zattere, then stops at Tronchetto (parking garage) on the way to Piazzale Roma and the station. From the station, Line 82 becomes the Grand Canal express to Rialto, with some boats continuing to Vallaresso (San Marco) and in summer going all the way to the Lido beaches. Line N runs from roughly midnight to 6 AM, stopping at the Lido, Vallaresso, Accademia, Rialto, the train station, Piazzale Roma, Giudecca, and San Zaccaria, then returning in the opposite direction.

FARES & SCHEDULES An ACTV water bus ticket good for 90 minutes costs €3.50 excluding the Grand Canal, €5 including the Grand Canal. (Children under four ride free.) Another option is Travel Cards: €10.50 buys 24 hours and €22 buys 72 hours of unlimited travel on ACTV boats and buses, including Line 5 to the airport. A shuttle ticket allows you to cross a canal, one stop only, for €1.80

Line information is posted at each landing, and complete timetables for all lines are available for €.50 at ACTV/Vela ticket booths, located at most major stops. Buy tickets before getting on the boat and remember to validate them in the yellow time-stamp machines. Tickets are also sold on the boat; you must ask to buy one immediately upon boarding, which can be a hassle. When inspectors come aboard, ticketless riders are fined, as are those who didn't validate tickets. Ignorance will not spare you; the fine is €23, and getting fined can be embarrassing. The law says you must also buy tickets for dogs, baby strollers left unfolded, and bags over 28 inches long (there's no charge for your bag if you have a Travel Card). Though enforcement has been minimal, ACTV has been operating in the red for some time and is expected to intensify collection efforts.

Boat & Ferry Information **ACTV** ☎ 041/5287886 🌐 www.actv.it. **Vela** ☎ 041/2714747 or 899/909090 (€.40/min) 🌐 www.velaspa.com. **Motoscafo** ☎ 041/5224281 or 041/5222303.

BUS TRAVEL TO & FROM VENICE
From Venice's Piazzale Roma terminal, buses connect with Mestre, the Brenta Riviera, Padua, Treviso, Cortina d'Ampezzo, and other regional destinations as well as many major European cities.

ACTV buses to Mestre (€.77) are frequent, and there's night service; ACTV buses to Padua (€3.30) leave at 25 and 55 minutes past each hour and stop along the Brenta River. ATVO has daily buses to Cortina (€10.20) June–September and throughout the Christmas–New Year holidays. Buses leave Venice at 7:50 AM and depart Cortina 3:15 PM. September–May service is only available on weekends.

🚌 Bus Information **ACTV** ☎ 041/5287886. **ATVO** ☎ 041/5205530, ⊕ www.atvo.it. **Bus Terminal** ✉ Piazzale Roma, across the Grand Canal from the train station, Santa Croce.

CAR RENTAL

🚗 Local Agencies **Avis** ✉ Piazzale Roma, Santa Croce ☎ 041/5225825 ✉ Aeroporto Marco Polo ☎041/5415030 ⊕www.avis.com. **Hertz** ✉Piazzale Roma, Santa Croce ☎041/5284091 ✉ Aeroporto Marco Polo ☎ 041/5416075 ⊕ www.hertz.com. **Sixt Rent-a-Car** ✉ Aeroporto Marco Polo ☎ 041/5415032 ⊕ www.sixt.com.

CAR TRAVEL

Venice is on the east–west A4 autostrada, which connects with Padua, Verona, Brescia, Milan, and Turin. If you bring a car to Venice, you will have to pay for a garage or parking space. Warning: don't be waylaid by illegal touts, often wearing fake uniforms, who may try to flag you down and offer to arrange parking and hotels; drive directly to one of the parking garages and do not leave valuables in the car. There's a luggage-check office, open daily 6 AM–9 PM, next to the Pullman Bar on the ground floor of the municipal garage at Piazzale Roma. You can take your car to the Lido; the car ferry (Line 17) makes the half-hour trip every 50 minutes from a landing at Tronchetto, but in summer there can be long lines. It costs €8.78–18.08, depending on the size of the car.

Parking at Autorimessa Comunale costs €18.59 for 24 hours. The private Garage San Marco costs €19 for up to 12 hours, and €26 for 12–24 hours plus a €1 supplement Sunday, nights, and holidays. You can reserve a space in advance at either of these garages; you'll come upon both immediately after crossing the bridge from the mainland. Another alternative is Tronchetto parking (€18 for 1–24 hours); watch for signs for it coming over the bridge—you'll have to turn right before you get to Piazzale Roma. Many hotels have negotiated guest discounts with San Marco or Tronchetto garages; get a voucher when you check in your hotel and present it when you pay the garage. Line 82 connects Tronchetto with Piazzale Roma and Piazza San Marco and also goes to the Lido in summer. When there's thick fog or extreme tides, a bus runs to Piazzale Roma instead. Avoid private boats—they're a rip-off. Garage San Marco and Autorimessa Comunale accept reservations.

🅿️**Autorimessa Comunale** ✉Piazzale Roma, Santa Croce end of S11 road ☎041/2727301, ⊕ www.asmvenezia.it. **Garage San Marco** ✉ Piazzale Roma 467/f, Santa Croce turn right into bus park ☎ 041/5232213 ⊕ www.garagesanmarco.it. **Tronchetto** ☎ 041/5207555.

DISABILITIES & ACCESSIBILITY

In Venice, bridges, historic buildings that cannot be modernized, and traveling by boat complicate matters for people with mobility concerns. Don't rely on tourist maps that indicate lifts on certain bridges around town; these rarely if ever work. ACTV Bus 5 from the airport is ramped and vaporetto Lines 1 and 82 have the most deck space, but boarding water taxis can sometimes be hazardous. Kiosks in the airport, train station, and parking areas that book hotels can only dispense information member hotels provide; there are no set criteria for designating a hotel as accessible. InformaHandicap's Web site has helpful information for chair users, and questions e-mailed in English are answered. Palazzo

Ducale, Museo Correr, the Campanile di San Marco, Ca' Rezzonico, Palazzo Grassi, Ca' d'Oro, and the Scuola di San Rocco have either lifts or ramps. Most churches, including the Basilica di San Marco, have one or two low steps to overcome.

InformaHandicap ⊠ Viale Giuseppe Garibaldi 155, 30174 Mestre ☎ 041/5341700 🖷 041/5342257 ⊕ www.comune.venezia.it/handicap.

EMBASSIES & CONSULATES

There is no U.S. or Canadian consular service.

United Kingdom **U.K. Consulate** ⊠ Campo della Carità (near Gallerie dell'Accademia), Dorsoduro 1051 ☎ 041/5227207.

EMERGENCIES

The U.K. Consulate can recommend doctors and dentists, as can your hotel or any pharmacy. The nearest pharmacy is never far, and they take turns staying open nights, Saturday afternoons, and Sundays; the list of after-hours pharmacies is posted on the front of every pharmacy and appears in daily newspapers.

Emergency Services **General Emergencies** ☎ 113. **Ambulance** ☎ 118. **Carabinieri** ☎ 112.

ENGLISH-LANGUAGE MEDIA

BOOKS Cafoscarina, close to Università Ca' Foscari, has a large selection of English literature, mainly classics. Emiliana and Studium stock books about Venice and Italian food with a few fiction paperbacks. The Venice Pavilion, off Piazza San Marco near the Giardini Reali, has a good selection of books and novels featuring the city. For books about Venice's maritime culture, lagoon, and environment, try Maredicarta.

NEWSPAPERS & You can find English-language newspapers at a stall beside the San
MAGAZINES Marco post office (behind Museo Correr) and in Campo SS. Apostoli, between Rialto and Ca' d'Oro.

Cafoscarina ⊠ Campiello Squellini, Dorsoduro 3259 ☎ 041/5229602. **Emiliana** ⊠ Calle Goldoni, San Marco 4487, between Piazza San Marco and Campo San Luca ☎ 041/5220793. **Maredicarta** ⊠ Fondamenta dei Tolentini, Santa Croce 222, across from train station ☎ 041/716304. **Studium** ⊠ Calle de la Canonica, San Marco 337/c, off Piazzetta dei Leoncini ☎ 041/5222382. **Venice Pavilion** ⊠ San Marco 2 ☎ 041/5225150.

MAIL & SHIPPING

Venice's main post office (⊙ Monday–Saturday 8–6) is housed in the Fondaco dei Tedeschi, near the Rialto bridge. You'll find a Federal Express office just outside Piazza San Marco, opposite Hotel Luna.

TOURS

BOAT TOURS Boat tours to the islands of Murano, Burano, and Torcello, organized by Serenissima Motoscafi and Consorzio San Marco, leave various docks around Piazza San Marco daily. These 3–3½-hour trips cost €15–17 and can be annoyingly commercial, often emphasizing glass-factory showrooms and pressuring you to buy at prices even higher than normal. April–October trips depart at 9:30 and 2:30 and November–March at 2.

More than a dozen major travel agents in Venice have grouped together to provide frequent, good-quality tours of the city. Serenaded gondola trips, with or without dinner (€68/31), can be purchased at any of their offices or at American Express. Nightly tours leave at 7:30 and 8:30 May–September, at 7:30 only in April and October, and at 3:30 November–March.

American Express ⊠ Salizada San Moisè, San Marco 1471 ☎ 041/5200844 🖷 041/5229937. **Serenissima Motoscafi** ☎ 041/5224281. **Consorzio San Marco** ☎ 041/2406712.

PRIVATE GUIDES

Cooperativa Guide Turistiche Autorizzate has a list of more than a hundred licensed guides. Tours lasting about two hours with an English-speaking guide start at €113 for up to 30 people. Agree on a total price before you begin, as there can be some hidden extras. Guides are of variable quality.

Cooperativa Guide Turistiche Autorizzate ✉ San Marco 750, near San Zulian ☎ 041/5209038 📠 041/5210762.

TOURS OF THE SURROUNDING REGION

American Express and other agencies also offer several excursions in the Veneto region. A boat trip to Padua along the Brenta River makes stops at three Palladian villas, and you return to Venice by bus. The tours run three times a week (Tuesday, Thursday, and Saturday) from March to October and cost €62 per person (€86 with lunch); bookings need to be made a few days in advance.

The Palladio Villa Tour (by minibus, maximum eight people), includes villas plus a walking tour of Vicenza (Wednesdays; €108 per person, optional lunch €13).

The Hills of the Veneto tour (by minibus, maximum eight people) visits the picturesque hill towns of Marostica, Bassano del Grappa, and Asolo, with stops at Villa Barbaro at Maser and at a vineyard along Strada del Prosecco for Prosecco wine tasting (Tuesday, Thursday, and weekends; €104 per person, optional lunch €13).

For a break from the heat, consider the Dolomite Tour (by minibus, maximum eight people) through the stupendous scenery in the Dolomite mountains; stops include Titian's birthplace Pieve di Cadore, Lakes Santa Caterina and Misurina, the famous Cime di Lavaredo peaks, and Cortina d'Ampezzo (Monday and Friday, €113 per person, including a packed lunch). For these last three tours it is essential to make reservations at least a week in advance in high season.

Fees & Schedules American Express ✉ Salizada San Moisè, San Marco 1471, ☎ 041/5200844 📠 041/5229937.

WALKING TOURS

More than a dozen major travel agents offer a two-hour walking tour of the San Marco area (€24), which ends with a glassblowing demonstration daily (no Sunday tour in winter). From April to October, there's also an afternoon walking tour that ends with a gondola ride (€29). Venicescapes, an Italo-American cultural association, offers several themed itineraries focusing on history and culture as well as tourist sights. Their three- to seven-hour tours are private and groups are small (generally six to eight people). Reservations are recommended during busy seasons and prices start at €200 for two people. Walks inside Venice also does several themed tours for small groups starting at €57 per hour and lasting up to three hours.

Fees & Schedules Alba Travel ✉ Calle dei Fabbri, San Marco 4538 ☎ 041/5210123 📠 041/5200781. **Oltrex Viaggi** ✉ Castello 4192 ☎ 041/5242840 📠 041/5221986. **Venicescapes** ✉ Campo San Provolo, Castello 4954 ☎☎ 041/5206361 🌐 www.venicescapes.org. **Walks inside Venice** ☎☎ 041/5241706 or 041/5202434 🌐 www.walksinsidevenice.com.

TRAIN TRAVEL

Venice has rail connections with every major city in Italy and Europe. Some continental trains do not enter historic Venice but stop only at the mainland Mestre station. All trains traveling to and from Venice Santa Lucia stop at Mestre, and it's just a 10-minute hop on the next passing train. Remember if you swap a regional train for an Intercity or Eurostar, you'll need to upgrade with a *supplemento* (extra charge) or be liable for a hefty fine. You'll also be fined if before boarding you forget to purchase and validate train tickets in the yellow machines found on or near platforms.

🚆 Train Information **Stazione Ferroviaria Santa Lucia** ✉ Grand Canal, northwest corner of the city, Cannaregio 🕾 848/888088 Trenitalia train info
🌐 www.trenitalia.com. **Stazione Ferroviaria Venezia-Mestre** ✉ Mestre, 12
km [7 mi] northwest of Venice 🕾 848/888088 Trenitalia train info
🌐 www.trenitalia.com.

TRANSPORTATION AROUND VENICE

Getting around Venice presents some unusual problems: the city's layout has few straight lines; house-numbering seems nonsensical; and the
sestieri (six districts) of San Marco, Cannaregio, Castello, Dorsoduro,
Santa Croce, and San Polo all duplicate each other's street names. Traveling by vaporetto can be bewildering, and too often you're forced to
walk. Yellow signs, posted on many busy corners, point toward the major
landmarks—San Marco, Rialto, Accademia, etc.—but don't count on
finding these once you're deep into residential neighborhoods. Even buying a good map at a newsstand—the kind showing all street names and
vaporetto routes—won't necessarily keep you from getting lost. However, getting lost in Venice may mean you've also lost most of the other
tourists; patience with yourself and the Venetians you ask for help can
go a long way toward making the experience part of the adventure.

TRAVEL AGENCIES

🚆 Local Agent Referrals **Gran Canal** ✉ Ponte del Ovo, near Rialto Bridge, San Marco
4759 🕾 041/2712111 🖶 041/5223380. **Kele & Teo** ✉ Ponte dei Bareteri, San Marco 4930
between San Marco and Rialto 🕾 041/5208722 🖶 041/5208913.

VISITOR INFORMATION

The train station branch of the Venice Tourist Office is open daily
8–6:30; other branches generally open at 9:30.

The "Rolling Venice" Pass, costing €2.58 and valid throughout a calendar year, buys visitors ages 14–29 discounts on vaporetto passes, lots
of museums, and assorted hotels, restaurants, and shops. Just show your
passport or I.D. at Vela ticket offices (major vaporetto stops), at the Assessorato alla Gioventù (weekdays 9:30–1, plus Tuesday and Thursday
afternoons 3–5), or at the Associazione Italiana Alberghi per la Gioventù
(Monday through Saturday 8–2). A Venice Card allows visitors of all
ages to avoid lines at city museums and prepays for vaporetti and municipal toilets. Order on-line or by phone and pay cash when you pick
up the card. Price depends on how many days you're staying; though
convenient, it's not a significant discount.

🚆 **Assessorato alla Gioventù** ✉ Corte Contarina, San Marco 1529, behind Piazza San
Marco post office 🕾 041/2747651. **Associazione Italiana Alberghi per la Gioventù**
✉ Calle Castelforte, San Polo 3101, near San Rocco 🕾 041/5204414. **Rolling Venice** 🕾 041/
2714747 🌐 www.comune.venezia.it.

Venice Tourist Offices 🌐 www.turismovenezia.it ✉ Train Station Cannaregio, 🕾 041/
5298727 ✉ Procuratie Nuove San Marco 71/f, near Museo Correr 🕾 041/5298740
✉ Venice Pavilion San Marco near Giardini Reali 🕾 041/5225150 ✉ Garage Comunale, Piazzale Roma 🕾 041/2411499 ✉ S. Maria Elisabetta 6/a, Lido ☉ Summer only
🕾 041/5265721.

THE VENETIAN ARC

PADUA, VERONA, VICENZA, UDINE, TRIESTE

2

FODOR'S CHOICE

Antipastoieca di Mare, restaurant, Trieste

Arena di Verona

Cappella degli Scrovegni, Padua

Villa la Rotonda, near Vicenza

Villa Pisani, hotel, near Padua

HIGHLY RECOMMENDED

RESTAURANTS   Arquade, Verona

Da Bastian, near Villa Barbaro

Osteria Terraglio, Bassano del Grappa

Toni del Spin, Treviso

Trattoria Dominissini, Cividale

HOTELS   Duchi d'Aosta, Trieste

Due Mori, Marostica

Gabbia d'Oro, Verona

Riviera and Maximilian's, Trieste

Villa del Quar, near Verona

SIGHTS   Castello di Miramare

San Zeno Maggiore, Verona

Teatro Olimpico, Vicenza

Villa Barbaro

Updated by
David Graham

AS ROME PRESIDES OVER LAZIO, the arc around Venice—encompass-ing the Veneto and Friuli-Venezia Giulia regions and stretching from Verona east to Trieste—falls under the historical and spiritual influence of its namesake city. No lagoons, perhaps, but the architecture, paint-ings, and way of life all reflect the splendor of La Serenissima.

Whether in the cities or the small towns, the winged lion of St. Mark, the emblem of Venice (irreverently referred to as "the cat"), is very much in evidence, either emblazoned on palazzi or atop a lofty column. Long before its arrival, however, Ezzelino III da Romano (1194–1259), the larger-than-life scourge who was excommunicated by Pope Innocent IV and even had a crusade launched against him, laid claim to as much land as he could, seizing the cities of Verona, Padua, Este, Montagnana, and Monselice and their surrounding territory. After he was finally ousted, powerful families such as the Carrara in Padua and the della Scala (Scaligeri) from Verona vied with each other during the 14th century to annex these towns.

When not destroying each other, the noble families of the region bestowed on their progeny a rich legacy of architectural and artistic jewels, in-fusing an opulence into the area that is today the hallmark of Padua, Vicenza, and Verona. This trio of cities, though sharing the Venetian pat-rimony, has a diverse and multifaceted appeal, their individual charac-ters well defined long before Venice arrived on the scene. In the hinterland, redbrick castles and fortifications with fishtail or square crenellations bear testimony to the struggles of the medieval warring families. Once Venice had established its presence in the region, a time of relative peace ensued, exquisitely marked by the blooming of Venetian palazzi and the works of masters: The three Ts—Titian, Tintoretto, and Tiepolo—have all contributed to the impressive heritage of the zone.

When Venetians took vacations, they made sure they did it in style, their retreats designed by the best architects and decorated by the best painters of the day. Needless to say, Palladio was first choice for the job, and his work is nobly illustrated by the superlative Villa La Rotonda near Vi-cenza, and Villa Foscari near Venice.

Exploring the Venetian Arc

The Venetian Arc encompasses the coastal crescent and the inland plain that stretches from the mouths of the Po and Adige rivers south-west of Venice to Trieste and the Slovenian border east of Venice. It bridges two Italian regions—the Veneto and Friuli–Venezia Giulia—and is mainly flat green farmland spotted with low hills that swell and rise steeply inland in a succession of plateaus and high meadows to the snow-tipped Alps.

Much of the pleasure of exploring this area comes from discovering the individual variations on the overall Venetian theme that confer spe-cial charm on each of the towns. Some, such as Verona, Treviso, and Udine, have a solid medieval look; Asolo, the Town of a Hundred Hori-zons, has an idyllic setting; Bassano combines a bit of both. Padua is ennobled by Giotto's frescos, Vicenza by the villas of Palladio. Udine, home to the first important frescoes by Giambattista Tiepolo, is one of Italy's least-known towns: small and pleasantly bourgeois, it's a good base from which to explore the rest of the Friuli region. In Trieste, after a climb to the hill of San Giusto with its cathedral and castle, the aroma of freshly roasted coffee that fills the city center is hard to re-sist: a cappuccino (here called *caffelatte*) and a piece of Austro-Hun-garian pastry are de rigueur. Most of all, you'll find artistic jewels everywhere, from the great Venetian masters in Verona to Veronese's lighthearted frescoes in Villa Barbaro at Maser.

About the Restaurants & Hotels

Eating out in the Veneto and Friuli-Venezia Giulia is a major social event, especially for lunch on Sunday, when restaurants are often noisy and tables are at a premium. (Conversely, you'll encounter little traffic on country roads from midmorning to midafternoon on Sunday, making it a pleasant time to tour.) Throughout the week, restaurants stick to fairly rigid dining hours—you'll be lucky to find much more than a bar snack from 2:30 until 7 in the evening. The best restaurants change their menus regularly—even daily—so it's not uncommon to get a spoken list of offerings rather than a printed menu. Don't be daunted if your Italian doesn't go beyond *sì* and *no:* waiters and waitresses can usually offer passable translations.

The area around Venice has been playing host to visitors for centuries, and as a result there is a range of comfortable accommodations at every price. Common sense should tell you that smaller, slightly out-of-the-way places will cost you less than their counterparts in a posh Adriatic resort. Many of the hotels in the area have been renovated and stylishly redecorated. This often results in higher prices, but good low-cost options can still be found in the larger city centers, especially Trieste and Padua. Many hotels in Trieste offer substantial discounts on weekends. Expect to pay more as you approach Venice, since many of the mainland towns absorb the overflow during the times when Venice becomes most crowded, such as Carnevale (Carnival, held two weeks preceding Lent), and from mid-spring to early autumn.

WHAT IT COSTS In euros				
	$$$$	**$$$**	**$$**	**$**	**¢**
RESTAURANTS	over €22	€17–€22	€12–€17	€7–€12	under €7
HOTELS	over €210	€160–€210	€110–€160	€60–€110	under €60

Restaurant prices are for a second course (secondo piatto). Hotel prices are for two people in a standard double room in high season, including tax and service.

Timing

There is no particular good or bad time to see the sights around the Venetian Arc. But if you want to get the most out of your stay, come in late spring and early summer (May, June, early July) or in September. Winter is a good time to avoid travel to the region; foggy conditions and wet, bone-chilling cold are not unusual from November through March. Opera and theater buffs should come in spring and summer, when outdoor performances are held.

THE ROAD TO PADUA & VICENZA

Foremost among the treasures of the Veneto region are the beautiful villas of Andrea Palladio (1508–80) built to render *la vita* all the more *dolce* for 16th-century aristocrats. Other important sights include Giotto's 14th-century frescoes in Padua's Cappella degli Scrovegni and many of Donatello's greatest sculptures.

Villa Pisani

❁ ▶ ❶ *10 km (6 mi) southeast of Padua.*

Extensive grounds with rare trees, ornamental fountains, and garden follies surround this extraordinary 18th-century palace in Stra. It was one

2

Hard as it may seem to leave the unique beauty of Venice behind, the Venetian Arc is a perfect complement to a Venetian stay. The towns are beautiful, mixing grandiose architecture and medieval aristocracy flawlessly. One of these towns, Verona, also unknowingly produced the most tragic of all *storie d'amore* (love stories)—*Romeo and Juliet*. The sorrow that this tale inspires can be drowned in the delights of some of the best-known Italian wines.

Many towns can be seen on one- or two-day excursions from Venice itself. A three-day itinerary will exclude Trieste and restrict you to the other principal sights. A five-day exploration will give you plenty to remember and savor, but you will have to discipline yourself to keep up a swift pace. A seven-day trip will give you the time to fully experience the architecture, history, and culture of this beautiful region.

Numbers in the text correspond to numbers in the margin and on the Venetian Arc and Verona maps.

If you have 3 days

Begin your drive at **Villa Pisani** ① ▶, a spectacular palace on splendid grounds. Move on to **Padua** ②, taking in the Cappella degli Scrovegni. Continue toward ▣ **Verona** ④ – ⑱, the city of *Romeo and Juliet*. The following day, see some of Palladio's works in **Vicenza** ③ and head for **Marostica** ⑲, ▣ **Bassano del Grappa** ⑳, and **Asolo** ㉑. Save the last day for **Treviso** ㉓ and **Conegliano** ㉔, and stop for a tour of **Udine** ㉕. Return to Venice along the A4.

If you have 5 days

Follow the three-day itinerary until Asolo, but at a slower pace. Stop in ▣ **Verona** ④ – ⑱ for the first two nights; then, after visiting **Bassano del Grappa** ⑳ on the third day, instead of moving on directly to Treviso, travel toward **Villa Barbaro** ㉒, in Maser, and then on to **Treviso** ㉓ and ▣ **Conegliano** ㉔, where you can overnight. On the fourth day, head for **Udine** ㉕ and **Cividale** ㉖; then go down to ▣ **Trieste** ㉘. Spend the evening and most of the following day in this border city, then move on to **Castello di Miramare** ㉗ before taking the A4 back to Venice.

If you have 7 days

Follow the itinerary described above; in **Bassano del Grappa** ⑳ take the time to visit the famous Nardini distillery on the edge of town. ▣ **Treviso** ㉓, where you can spend the third and fourth nights, makes a good base for exploring the Marca Trevigiana and its various Strade del Vino (wine roads). On the fifth day, visit **Conegliano** ㉔, **Udine** ㉕, and **Cividale** ㉖; then head for ▣ **Trieste** ㉘. Spend two nights and a full day there; then move on to **Castello di Miramare** ㉗ before taking the A4 back to Venice.

of the last of many stately residences constructed along the Brenta River from the 16th to 18th centuries by wealthy Venetians for their *villeggiatura*—vacation and escape from the mid-summer humidity. The trompe l'oeil frescoes by Giambattista Tiepolo (1696–1770) on the ceiling of the ballroom alone are worth the visit. If you have youngsters in tow surfeited with old masters, explore the gorgeous **park** and **maze** (open April–September). ✉ *Stra* ☎ *049/502074* 🌐 *Villa, maze, and grounds*

€5, *maze and grounds* €2.50 ☉ *Apr.–Sept., Tues.–Sun. 9–7; Oct.–Mar., Tues.–Sun. 9–4; last entry 1 hr before closing.*

Padua

2 *37 km (23 mi) west of Venice, 92 km (57 mi) east of Verona.*

Bustling Padua (Padova, in Italian) has long been one of the major cultural centers in northern Italy. It's home to the peninsula's second-oldest university, founded in 1222, which attracted the likes of Dante (1265–1321), Petrarch (1304–74), and Galileo Galilei (1564–1642). Three great artists—Giotto (circa 1266/67–1337), Donatello (circa 1386–1466), and Mantegna (1431–1506)—left great works here. If you plan on visiting many of the local sights, get the **Padova Card** (€14), valid for 48 hours, or an entire weekend from Friday to Sunday evening, allowing you use of the Padua public transport system, entrance to many of the principal museums (including the Cappella degli Scrovegni, the Museo Civico, and the Palazzo della Ragione), and discounts for many of the other local tourist attractions, including the boats that go down the Brenta river. Buy the card at the tourist information office (☎ 049/8767927) at Padova railway station or in the central Galleria Pedrocchi.

FodorśChoice
★

The **Cappella degli Scrovegni** (Scrovegni Chapel) was erected in 1303 by a wealthy Paduan, Enrico Scrovegni, in atonement for his father's sins. Giotto was immediately commissioned to decorate its interior, a task that occupied the great artist and his helpers until 1305–6. They created a magnificent fresco cycle illustrating the lives of Mary and Christ; in typical medieval comic-strip fashion, the 38 panels are arranged in tightly knit tiers to be read from left to right. On the wall to the right of today's entrance is a powerful *Last Judgment.* The realism in these frescoes—which include the first blue skies in Western painting—at the time was revolutionary. Entrance is only by reservation, which must be made at least two days prior to the day of your visit. Entrances are scheduled every 20 minutes, and punctuality is mandatory. In any season it's a good idea to bring along a sweater, as the frescoes are preserved at a rather cold temperature. Visits last 30 minutes, including a 15-minute acclimatization period before entering. ⊠ *Piazza Eremitani 8* ☎ *049/ 8204551; 049/2010020 reservations* ⊕ *www.cappelladegliscrovegni.it* 🖾 €11 *or Padova Card* ☉ *Daily 9–7.*

The 13th-century **Chiesa degli Eremitani** contains some fragments of frescoes (most were destroyed by the Allied bombing of 1944) by Andrea Mantegna, the brilliant, locally born artist, some of whose masterpieces are in nearby Mantua. The **Museo Civico di Padova** (Civic Museum of Padua), housed in what used to be the monastery of the church, has its quota of works by Venetian masters, as well as a fine collection of ancient relics. ⊠ *Piazza Eremitani 8* ☎ 049/8204551 🖾 *Church free, museum* €9 *or Padova Card* ☉ *Feb.–Oct., daily 9–7; Nov.–Jan., daily 9–6; museum closed Mon.*

The 16th-century **Palazzo del Bo'** houses the **Università di Padova,** founded in 1222. The building, which now features an 18th-century facade, is named after the Osteria del Bo' (*bo'* means ox), an inn that once stood on the site. This is worth a visit to see the exquisite and perfectly proportioned anatomy theater and a hall with a lectern used by Galileo. You can enter only as part of a guided tour. Most guides speak English, but it is worth checking ahead by phone. ⊠ *Via VIII Febbraio* ☎ 049/ 8273047 🖾 €3 ☉ *Guided tours only. Apr.–Oct., Mon., Wed., and Fri. at 3, 4, and 5, Tues., Thurs., and Sat. at 9, 10, and 11; Nov.–Mar., Mon., Wed., and Fri. at 3 and 4, Tues., Thurs., and Sat. at 10 and 11.*

2

Concerts & Opera

Verona and Vicenza offer some of Italy's most spectacular opportunities for indulging in the passions of open-air operas and concerts. You can take your place in Verona's ancient Roman amphitheater and watch the grand spectacle of *Aida* or just take in a free jazz or folk concert on a warm summer evening. Alternatively, sit back like a true-born aristocrat and listen to a concert in the regal setting of a Vicentine villa. You can also treat yourself to an unforgettable performance in Palladio's Teatro Olimpico. You'll find that the smaller towns run concert seasons, too.

Shopping

Many of the goods associated with Venice are actually produced in the surrounding areas of the Venetian Arc—which means that with a bit of diligence or luck you can pick up a bargain from the source. Mountain towns and villages such as Bassano del Grappa and Asolo have the strongest handicraft tradition. Itinerant antiques markets are customarily held throughout the region, usually on Sunday, and many cities are filled with stores selling antique furniture and jewelry, Trieste and Verona being the most noteworthy examples. This region is also particularly strong on fashion, with the area around Treviso being home to both the Benetton and Replay clothing empires, and Diesel located not far from Vicenza. Finally, food shops, wine shops, and open-air produce markets are some of Italy's best.

Villas & Palazzi

The countless villas and palaces sprinkled throughout the Venetian hinterland and the Palladio villas along the Brenta River should not be missed. These gracious country homes give insight into the way wealthy Venetians used to—and still do—spend leisure time. Many of the villas are privately owned but are open to the public at certain times or by special request. Local tourist offices can be helpful in providing information on visiting these jewels.

Palazzo della Ragione, also called Il Salone, was built in the Middle Ages as the seat of Padua's parliament. Today its street-level arcades shelter shops and cafés. In the frescoed **Salone** (Hall) on the upper level is an enormous wooden horse, a 15th-century replica of the bronze steed in Donatello's statue of Gattamelata. At this writing the palazzo was being restored, but entrance to the Salone was still possible and temporarily free of charge; call the Padua tourist office to ask about the current status. ✉ *Piazza della Ragione* ☎ *049/8767911 Padua tourist office.*

The huge **Basilica di Sant'Antonio** is a cluster of Byzantine domes and slender, minaretlike towers that gives the church an Asian-inspired style reminiscent of San Marco in Venice. The interior is sumptuous, too, with marble reliefs by Tullio Lombardo (circa 1455–1532), the greatest in a talented family of marble carvers who decorated many churches in the area, among them Santa Maria dei Miracoli in Venice. The artistic highlights here, however, all bear Donatello's name: the 15th-century Florentine master did the remarkable series of bronze reliefs illustrating the life of St. Anthony—whose feast day, Festa di Sant'Antonio on June 13, draws pilgrims from all over Europe—as well as the bronze statues of the Madonna and saints on the high altar. Standing in front of the church is Donatello's powerful statue of the *condottiere* (mercenary general)

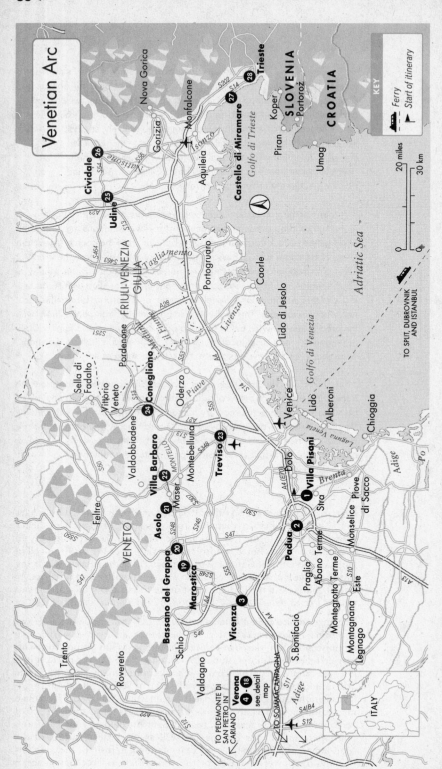

Venetian Arc

ON THE MENU

Seafood is the specialty along the coast, of course, and inland the cuisine varies from the delicate risotto of the Veneto to the more decisively flavored cooking of the Trieste area, heavily influenced by Austria and Slovenia. San Daniele del Friuli, near Udine, is famous for its delicious prosciutto of the same name. Polenta, made of cornmeal, is a staple throughout the area; it is served with thick, rich sauces or grilled as an accompaniment to meat or fish dishes. In the Veneto, a bowl of thick pasta e fagioli (pasta and bean soup), here typically prepared with the addition of wide pieces of fresh pasta, is perfect for a cold winter's night.

If you are a confirmed or fledgling oenophile, you'll enjoy tasting local wines within view of the vineyards that produce some of the most well-known Italian vintages, including Soave, Tocai, Prosecco, Bardolino, and Valpolicella.

Erasmo da Narni, known by the general's nickname, Gattamelata. It was cast in bronze—a monumental technical achievement—in 1453 and had an enormous influence on the development of Italian Renaissance sculpture. ⊠ *Piazza del Santo* ☏ *049/8242811* ⊕ *www.santantonio.org* ⊘ *Weekdays 6:30 AM–7 PM, weekends 6:30 AM–7:45 PM.*

The 12th-century **Battistero del Duomo** (Cathedral Baptistery) is an often-overlooked gem whose rich frescoes vie with those of Giotto at Cappella degli Scrovegni in terms of detail and pictorial complexity. In this, his greatest work, Giusto de' Menabuoi further developed Giotto's style of depicting the human figure naturally, using perspective and realistic lighting. The baptistry is a refreshingly cool retreat from the city where you can feast your eyes on these wonderfully restored mid-1370s frescoes depicting scenes from the Book of Genesis. ⊠ *Piazza Duomo* ☏ *049/656914* ▨ *€2.50, or €1.50 with Padova Card* ⊘ *Apr.-Oct., daily 10-7; Nov.–Mar., daily 10–6.*

The **Orto Botanico** (Botanic Garden) was founded in 1545 by order of the Venetian Republic to supply the university with medicinal plants and is one of the few Renaissance gardens to have kept its original layout. The so-called Palm of St. Peter, planted in 1585, still stands, protected in its private little greenhouse. You can wander through interesting hothouses, beds of plants that were first introduced to Italy in this garden, and the arboretum. ⊠ *Via Orto Botanico 15* ☏ *049/8272119* ▨ *€2.58* ⊘ *Apr.–Oct., daily 9–1 and 3–6; Nov.–Mar., Mon.–Sat. 9–1.*

Piazza dei Signori has some fine examples of 15th- and 16th-century buildings. On the west side, the **Palazzo del Capitanio** has an impressive **Torre dell'Orologio,** with an astronomical clock dating from 1344. The **Duomo** is just a few steps away.

The abbey of **Santa Giustina,** at the southwest end of the Prato della Valle, has finely inlaid choir stalls and a colossal altarpiece, the *Martyrdom of St. Justine,* by Veronese (1528–88). ⊠ *Prato della Valle* ☏ *049/8751628* ⊘ *Daily 8:30–noon and 3–7.*

| off the beaten path | **ABANO TERME AND MONTEGROTTO TERME –** These two spas, about 12 km (7 mi) south of Padua, lie at the foot of the Euganean Hills, whose rustic villages and hand-tilled vineyards are also well worth a visit. For a thermal swim, visit the **Columbus Center.** ⊠ *Via Martiri D'Ungheria 22* ☏ *049/86015* ▨ *€8 Mon.–Sat., € 8.50 Sun.* |

◷ *June–mid-Sept., daily 9* AM*–11* PM*; mid-Sept.–May, weekdays 12:30–11, weekends 9* AM*–11* PM.

PRAGLIA – You can tour the evocative 15th-century halls and cloisters of this Benedictine monastery hidden in the hills. Wine and honey produced by the monks are for sale. Head 12 km (7 mi) southwest of Padua, following signs for Abano Terme on the south side of the city. The monastery closes to the public on special occasions such as funerals, as well as on holy days, so it's advisable to call ahead before making a visit. Note that the monks who show you around speak Italian only. ☎ *049/9900010* ⊟ *Free, donations welcome* ◷ *Tours Apr.–Oct., Tues.–Sun. 3:30, 4:10, 4:50, and 5:30; Nov.–Mar., Tues.–Sun. 2:30, 3:10, 3:50, and 4:30.*

MONTAGNANA – The surrounding walls of this medieval city 50 km (30 mi) southwest of Padua are remarkably well preserved, enclosing a market square, a 500-year-old cathedral, and several tempting restaurants. Its former rivals, Este and Monselice, are only 20 km (12 mi) east on the same road.

Where to Stay & Eat

$$$$ ✕ **Antico Brolo.** Housed in a 16th-century building not far from central Piazza dei Signori, charming Antico Brolo is one of the best restaurants in town. Seasonal specialties are prepared with flair and might include starters such as tiny flans with wild mushrooms and herbs or fresh pasta with zucchini flowers. ⊠ *Corso Milano 22* ☎ *049/664555* ⊟ *AE, MC, V* ◷ *Closed Mon. and 1 wk in mid-Aug. No lunch Tues.*

$$$ ✕ **La Vecchia Enoteca.** The ceiling is mirrored, the shelves are filled with books and wine, the silverware once belonged to a cruise line, and the flower displays are extravagant. It's a luxurious setting for enjoying *branzino in crosta di patate* (sea bass with a potato crust) or beef with rosemary and balsamic vinegar, followed by a homemade dessert such as *crema catalana* (creme caramel). ⊠ *Via Santi Martino e Solferino 32* ☎ *049/8752856* ⊟ *MC, V* ◷ *Closed Sun., last wk in July, 1st 3 wks in Aug. No lunch Mon.*

$ ✕ **Vecchia Padova.** Locals flock here at lunchtime for the low-priced but hearty meals, taken amid beamed ceilings hung with copper cauldrons and antique-covered walls. The self-service menu offers three types of pasta, a range of grilled and roast meats and fish, and an extensive salad bar. In the evening it becomes a fairly standard restaurant and pizzeria with waiter service. ⊠ *Via Zabarella 41* ☎ *049/8759680* ⊟ *AE, DC, MC, V* ◷ *Closed Mon.*

¢ ✕ **Brek.** Fast-food Italian style: serve yourself from the hot and cold buffet islands, then dine comfortably at table. This is one of a chain of individually decorated and efficiently operated self-service restaurants that have become the preferred lunchtime option for many city workers in northern Italy. Watch the pasta sauces of olives and tuna or ricotta and tomato being expertly created before your eyes over hot bricks; wait a few minutes while your steak grills, then choose from peppers, zucchini, and roast potatoes to accompany your meal. Brek is a satisfying choice for an easy and very cheap lunch or dinner. You'll find other Brek locations in Vicenza (⊠ Corso Palladio 10–12), Verona (⊠ Piazza Brà 20), Treviso (⊠ Corso del Popolo 25), and Trieste (⊠ Via S. Francesco 10) ⊠ *Piazza Cavour 54* ☎ *049/8753788* ⊟ *AE, DC, MC, V.*

$$$ ▥ **Majestic Toscanelli.** The elegant entrance, with potted evergreens flanking the steps, sets the tone in this stylish, central hotel close to the Piazza della Frutta. Plants figure strongly in the breakfast room as well, and the charming bedrooms are furnished in different styles, from 19th-century mahogany and brass to French Empire. ✉ *Via dell'Arco 2, 35122* ☎ *049/663244* ᗑ *049/8760025* ⊕ *www.toscanelli.com* ⇦ *28 rooms, 6 suites* ᗑ *In-room data ports, minibars, cable TV, bar, meeting room, parking (fee), some pets allowed, no-smoking floor* ▤ *AE, DC, MC, V.*

$$$ ▨ **Plaza.** A modern luxury hotel in the city center just a few minutes from the train station, the Plaza has the elegant furnishings and deft service that leave no doubt you're in a quality hotel. The guest rooms are spacious and completely sound-proofed, while the genteel public lounges and cool bar are a haven after a hot day's sightseeing. ✉ *Corso Milano 40, 35139* ☎ *04/9656822* ᗑ *049/661117* ⊕ *www.plazapadova.it* ⇦ *142 rooms* ᗑ *Restaurant, in-room safes, minibars, cable TV, gym, bar, meeting room, parking (fee), some pets allowed* ▤ *AC, DC, MC, V.*

$$ ▨ **Villa Pisani.** The spacious high-ceilinged rooms in this enormous 16th-century villa are furnished entirely with period pieces—some units even have fully frescoed walls. All rooms look out over stunning formal gardens and beyond to a 15-acre park with rare trees, a chapel, a theater, and a concealed swimming pool. You'll also have access to three big *sale* (lounges), where you can chat with the few other lucky guests and Signora Scalabrin, who shares her patrician living areas, music, and books. With breakfast served on silver platters, this is a B&B that outstrips almost all the hotel competition. ✉ *Via Roma 19, 35040 Vescovana, 30 km (19 mi) south of Padua* ☎☎ *0425/920016* ⊕ *www.villapisani.com* ⇦ *8 rooms, 1 suite* ᗑ *Pool, bar, meeting room, some pets allowed; no a/c* ▤ *AE, DC, MC, V.*

FodorsChoice ★

$ ▨ **Al Fagiano.** Close to the Basilica di Sant'Antonio and the river, this modest hostelry has basic facilities (some with shower only), an amiable staff, and a calm atmosphere. Some rooms have views of the basilica's spires and cupolas. ✉ *Via Locatelli 45, 35100* ☎ *049/8750073* ᗑ *049/8753396* ⊕ *www.alfagiano.it* ⇦ *30 rooms* ᗑ *Bar* ▤ *AE, DC, MC, V.*

¢–$ ▨ **Casa del Pellegrino.** Facing onto the Basilica di Sant'Antonio, this rather austere hotel has something of a monastic air, with simple, fairly spartan rooms arranged hospital-fashion off long, polished corridors. Rooms in the newer annex, 100 yards behind the main hotel, are more luxurious, offering all the usual modern hotel amenities, including air-conditioning, and absolute silence. A cavernous restaurant downstairs serves cheap, simple fare. Breakfast is not included in the price. ✉ *Via Cesarotti 21, 35123* ☎ *049/8239711* ᗑ *049/8239780* ⇦ *162 rooms, 115 with bath* ᗑ *Restaurant, bar, parking (fee); no a/c in some rooms* ▤ *AE, MC, V* ☾ *Closed last wk Dec.–late Jan.* ⦿❘ *EP.*

Nightlife & the Arts

CAFÉS The ever-popular **Caffè Pedrocchi** (✉ Piazzetta Pedrocchi ☎ 049/8781231) serves excellent cappuccino in a 19th-century neoclassical coffeehouse that looks like a cross between a museum and a stage set. The upstairs rooms, with frescoed ceilings, often house **art shows** (☎ 049/8205007). The café downstairs is open daily from 9 AM to 9 PM, and until midnight Thursday–Saturday. Admission to upstairs shows, open Tuesday–Sunday 9:30–12:30 and 3:30–6, is €3.

NIGHTCLUBS & **Victoria** (✉ Via Savonarola 149 ☎ 049/8721530) is a *birreria* (a bar that
BARS serves primarily beer) that occasionally has live music; it's closed on Monday. **Limbo** (✉ Via San Fermo 44 ☎ 049/656882), closed on Monday and Tuesday, is a restaurant-pizzeria open late, with live music and a disco downstairs.

Shopping

You could be forgiven for spending more time on the ground floor of Padua's **Palazzo della Ragione** (✉ Piazza della Ragione) than in the gallery upstairs: it is the city's mouthwatering permanent food market, with shops offering choice salami and cured meats, local cheeses such as fresh Parmesan, wines, coffee, and even tea. With the fruit and vegetable market in the piazza outside, you can pick up all the makings for a fine picnic.

Padua's Saturday market in **Prato della Valle** has a wide range of goods, from garments and shoes to fabric, kitchenware, and handmade baskets. The large, formal open space was laid out in 1775 and features a central oval park surrounded by a canal overlooked by 78 statues of local worthies. An antiques market is held here the third Sunday of every month.

Vicenza

❸ *60 km (37 mi) east of Verona, 32 km (19 mi) west of Padua.*

Vicenza bears the distinctive signature of the 16th-century architect Andrea Palladio, whose name is the root of the "Palladian" style of architecture. He gracefully incorporated elements of classical architecture—columns, porticoes, and domes—into a style that reflected the Renaissance celebration of order and harmony. His elegant villas and palaces were influential in propagating classical architecture in Europe, especially Britain, and later in America—most notably at Thomas Jefferson's Monticello.

In the mid-16th century, Palladio was given the opportunity to rebuild much of Vicenza, which had suffered great damage during the bloody wars waged against Venice by the League of Cambrai, an alliance consisting of the papacy, France, the Holy Roman Empire, and several neighboring city-states. Palladio made his name with the basilica, begun in 1549 in the very heart of Vicenza, then embarked on a series of lordly buildings, all of which proclaim the same rigorous classicism. The **Corso Palladio** is lined with imposing palaces and churches that run the gamut from Venetian Gothic to baroque, including many designed by Palladio.

Vicenza's church of **Santa Corona** has an exceptionally fine *Baptism of Christ* (1500) by Giovanni Bellini (1430–1516) over the altar on the left, just in front of the transept. ⊠ *Contrà S. Corona* ☎ *0444/542168* ⊙ *Sept.–Jun., Tues.–Sun. 9–5; Jul.–Aug., Tues.–Sun. 9–7.*

The exquisite and unmistakably Palladian **Palazzo Chiericati** houses the Vicenza municipal art gallery and holds a representative collection of Venetian paintings. ⊠ *Piazza Matteotti* ☎ *0444/321348* ⊠ *€8 includes admission to Teatro Olimpico and Museo Naturalistico e Archeologico* ⊙ *Sept.–June, Tues.–Sun. 9–5; July–Aug., Tues.–Sun. 9–7.*

★ The **Teatro Olimpico** is Palladio's last, and perhaps most exciting, work. Based closely on the model of an ancient Roman theater, it represents an important development in theater and stage design and is noteworthy for its acoustics and the cunning use of perspective in the permanent backdrop. The anterooms are frescoed with images of important figures in Venetian history. ⊠ *Piazza Matteoti* ☎ *0444/222800* ⊠ *€8 includes admission to Palazzo Chiericati and Museo Naturalistico e Archeologico* ⊙ *Sept.–June, Tues.–Sun. 9–5; July–Aug., Tues.–Sun. 9–7.*

At the heart of Vicenza is **Piazza dei Signori,** the site of **Palazzo della Ragione,** commonly known as Palladio's basilica, though it's not a church at all, but originally was a courthouse and public meeting hall. Palladio made his name by successfully modernizing the medieval building, grafting a graceful two-story exterior loggia onto the existing Gothic structure. Take a look also at the **Loggia del Capitaniato,** opposite, which

Palladio designed but never completed. Note that the palazzo and its loggia are open to the public only when there's an exhibition. ✉ *Piazza dei Signori* ☎ *0444/32368.*

Fodor'sChoice Palladio's most famous villa, **Villa la Rotonda,** is a 20- to 30-minute walk
★ from the center of Vicenza. In truth, it can hardly be called a villa, since the architect was inspired by ancient Roman temples. Take the time to admire it from all sides, and you'll see that it was in turn inspiration not just for Monticello but for nearly every state capitol in the United States. The interior is typical of Palladio's grand style, with a distinctive use of negative space. The walk to the villa is along a pleasant route well away from the busy traffic. Go through the Palladio triumphal arch where Viale Margherita meets Viale Risorgimento and climb the steps. Turn left into Via Bastian which becomes Via dei Nani and leads to the Villa ai Nani. A pedestrian path (Via Valmarana) then winds down to Villa La Rotonda. Alternatively take Bus 8 from Viale Roma and ask the driver to let you off at La Rotonda. Note that the interior is open only on Wednesday, from April through October. ✉ *Via della Rotonda 29* ☎ *0444/321793* 🎫 *€6, grounds €3* ☉ *Grounds Apr.–Oct., Tues.–Sun. 10–noon and 3–6; villa Apr.–Oct., Wed. 10–noon and 3–6.*

Villa Valmarana ai Nani, an 18th-century country house, is decorated with a series of frescoes by Giambattista Tiepolo depicting fantastic visions of a mythological world, including one of his most stunning works, the *Sacrifice of Iphigenia.* The neighboring Foresteria, or guest house, holds more frescoes, showing 18th-century Veneto life at its most charming, by Tiepolo's son, Giandomenico (1727–1804). You can reach the villa on foot by following the same path that leads to Palladio's Villa la Rotonda. ✉ *Via dei Nani 2/8* ☎ *0444/54386; 0444/321803 Foresteria* 🎫 *€6* ☉ *Mar.–Oct., Wed., Thurs., and weekends 10–noon; also Tues.–Sun. 2:30–5:30.*

Where to Stay & Eat

$$ ✕ **Antico Ristorante agli Schioppi.** Gli Schioppi is an attractive, family-run restaurant established in 1897. The low-key decor in the Veneto country style matches the simple yet imaginative cuisine. Begin with the Parma ham served with aubergine mousse and Parmesan. The *baccalà* (salt cod) is a must, as are the *petto d'anitra all'uva moscata e indivia* (duck breast with muscat grapes and endive) and *coniglio alle olive nere* (rabbit with black olives). Desserts include ever-so-light fruit mousse and a pear cake with red wine sauce. ✉ *Contra' del Castello 26* ☎ *0444/ 543701* 🖹 *AE, DC, MC, V* ☉ *Closed Sun., last wk of July–mid-Aug., and Jan. 1–6. No dinner Sat.*

$ ✕ **Il Cursore.** The front section of this cozy, 19th-century osteria is given over mainly to bar service, offering local wines and typical savory snacks like *cotechino* (boiled sausage) and *soppressa* (premium salami). There are some cramped tables against the wall, but the back rooms are better for a sit-down meal of local classics like *bigoli* (thick, egg-enriched spaghetti) with duck, spaghetti with baccalà and, in spring, *risi e bisi* (rice with peas). Desserts include fruit tarts and the ubiquitous tiramisu. ✉ *Stradella Pozzetto 10* ☎ *0444/323504* 🖹 *V* ☉ *Closed Tues. and late July–mid-Aug.*

¢ ✕ **Righetti.** Simple, local cuisine is what keeps the locals coming back to this traditional self-service restaurant, especially for lunch: *orzo e fagioli* (bean and barley soup); pasta and risotto with asparagus, red radicchio, or *all'Amatriciana* (tomato and bacon); *stinco* (roast shin of pork); baccalà; and grilled vegetables or salads. The routine here is to find your table first and stake it out with paper place-mats and cutlery, then line up at the food counters. Help yourself to bread from the bread bin, wine and water on tap, then, after you've dined, tell the cashier what you've had so he can total up your (very reasonable) bill. ⊠ *Piazza Duomo 3* ☎ *0444/543135* ⊟ *No credit cards* ⊗ *Closed weekends.*

$$$–$$$$ 🏨 **Campo Marzio.** This elegant hotel sits right in front of the city walls and is a five-minute walk from the railway station. Some of the more expensive rooms are furnished in different styles; choose from Oriental, neoclassical, and floral themes. Many bathrooms have whirlpool baths. A special perk is the availability of bicycles free of charge. ⊠ *Viale Roma 27, 36100* ☎ *0444/545700* 🖷 *0444/320495* ⊕ *www.hotelcampomarzio. com* ➩ *35 rooms* ⚷ *Restaurant, bicycles, bar, free parking, some pets allowed* ⊟ *AE, DC, MC, V.*

$$ 🏨 **Giardini.** You're in good company here: the other sides of this central piazza are flanked by Palladio's Teatro Olimpico and Palazzo Chiericati, while the town center itself is just a few steps away. The hotel is tastefully furnished in modern Italian style. ⊠ *Viale Giruioli 10, 36100* ☎ *0444/326458* 🖷 *0444/326458* ⊕ *www.hotelgiardini.com* ➩ *18 rooms* ⚷ *In-room safes, minibars, cable TV, bar, meeting room, free parking* ⊟ *AE, DC, MC, V* ⊗ *Closed Dec. 23–Jan. 2.*

$ 🏨 **Due Mori.** In the heart of Vicenza off Piazza dei Signori, this is allegedly the first hotel in town, dating from 1883, and is a favorite with regular visitors. It's light and airy, yet at the same time cozy. The rooms are individually furnished with antiques and wood detail in the bathrooms. Breakfast is not included in the price. ⊠ *Contrà Do Rode 26, 36100* ☎ *0444/321886* 🖷 *0444/326127* ➩ *29 rooms* ⚷ *Some pets allowed; no a/c, no room TVs* ⊟ *AE, MC, V* ⊗ *Closed last 2 wks of July* ⊙ *EP.*

Nightlife & the Arts

MUSIC & **Teatro Olimpico** (⊠ Piazza Matteotti ☎ 0444/222801 ⊕ www.comune.
THEATER vicenza.it) hosts a jazz festival in May, classical concerts in June, and classical drama performances in September. Even if your Italian is dismal, it's thrilling to see a performance in Palladio's magnificent theater.

VERONA

On the banks of the fast-flowing Adige River, enchanting Verona lays claim to classical and medieval monuments, a picturesque town center where bright geraniums bloom in window boxes, and a romantic reputation, thanks to its being the setting of Shakespeare's *Romeo and Juliet*. It is one of Italy's most alluring cities, despite extensive industrialization and urban development in its newer sections. Inevitably, with its lively Venetian air, proximity to Lake Garda, and renowned summer opera season, it attracts hordes of tourists, especially vacationing Germans and Austrians, who arrive via the Brenner Pass to the north. In early April Verona hosts Vinitaly, one of the world's most important wine expos, where for five days you can sample wines from more than 3,500 wineries in 26 countries.

Verona grew to power and prosperity within the Roman Empire as a result of its key commercial and military position in northern Italy. After the fall of the Empire, the city continued to flourish under the guidance of Barbarian kings such as Theodoric, Alboin, Pepin, and Berenger I, reaching its cultural and artistic peak in the 13th and 14th centuries under the della Scala dynasty. (You'll see the *scala*, or ladder, emblem all over town.) In 1404, however, Verona traded its independence for security and placed itself under the control of Venice. (The other recurring architectural motif is the lion of St. Mark, symbol of Venetian rule.) Verona remained under Venetian protection until 1797, when Napoléon invaded. In 1814 the entire Veneto region was won by the Austrians, and it was finally united with the rest of Italy in 1866.

Exploring Verona

Note that the Duomo and churches in Verona enforce a strict dress code: no tanks, sleeveless shirts, shorts, or short skirts. You might want to consider buying the €5 combined ticket that includes admission to Verona's five major churches, including the Duomo, San Zeno, and Sant'Anastasia. For more information about these churches contact **Associazione Chiese Vive** (☎ 045/592813 ⊕ www.veronatuttintorno.it/chiesevive) Alternatively, you can buy a Verona Card ticket for €8 or €12 (valid for one or three days), which gains you admission to most of the city's major museums and churches. Public transport is also included in the ticket.

a good walk

Start at the **Arena di Verona** ④ ⏵ in Piazza Brà, the vast and airy square at the center of the city. Built by the Romans in the 1st century AD, the arena is one of the largest and best-preserved Roman amphitheaters anywhere. Take Via Mazzini, the main shopping street in town, to **Piazza delle Erbe** ⑤, a busy square with an open-air market. The **Casa di Giulietta** ⑥, with the most famous balcony in Italy, is a block down Via del Cappello. Return and take a few moments to stroll around **Piazza dei Signori** ⑦, and admire the **Palazzo della Ragione** ⑧, **Loggia del Consiglio** ⑨, and **Palazzo degli Scaligeri** ⑩. It's a short walk through Piazza Indipendenza to Ponte Nuova and across the river toward the church of **Santa Maria in Organo** ⑪ and the **Giardino Giusti** ⑫. Follow Via Santa Maria in Organo up to the Teatro Romano and **Museo Archeologico** ⑬. The Romanesque **Duomo** ⑭ is just over Ponte Pietra. From here either walk down Via Duomo and Corso Sant'Anastasia to **Sant'Anastasia** ⑮, and Via Forti to the **Galleria d'Arte Moderna** ⑯, or turn toward the riverbank and stroll (or alternately take Bus 76) down to the 14th-century **Castelvecchio** ⑰, which looks like a fairy-tale castle guarding the bridge reaching over the Adige. The stunning Romanesque **San Zeno Maggiore** ⑱ church is another few minutes' walk downriver.

TIMING It takes about 40 minutes to walk the route and three hours to see all the sights.

What to See

⏵ ④
Fodor's Choice
★

Arena di Verona. Only four arches remain of the outer rings of the arena, but the main structure is so complete that it takes little imagination to picture it as the site of the cruel deaths of countless gladiators, wild beasts, and Christians. Today it hosts Verona's summer opera, famous for spectacular productions before audiences of up to 16,000. The best operas to see here are the big, splashy ones that demand huge choruses, Cinerama sets, lots of color and movement, and, if possible, camels, horses, or elephants. The music can be excellent, and the acoustics are fine, too. If you book a place on the cheaper terraces, be sure to take or rent a cushion—four hours on 2000-year-old marble can be an ordeal. ⊠ *Piazza Brà 5* ☎ *045/8003204* 🎫 *€3.10 or Verona Card, €1 1st Sun. of month* ⊗ *Mon. 1:45–7:30, Tues.–Sun. 8:30–7:30, on performance days 8:30–3; last entry 45 mins before closing.*

⑥ **Casa di Giulietta** (Juliet's House). The balcony in the small courtyard will help bring Shakespeare's play to life, even if it was built in the 20th century. Historians now believe that the couple had no real-life counterparts, but this hasn't discouraged anyone from imagining that they did. ⊠ *Via Cappello 23* ☎ *045/8034303* 🎫 *€3.10 or Verona Card* ⊗ *Mon. 1:30–7:30, Tues.–Sun. 8:30–7:30; last entry 45 mins before closing.*

⑰ **Castelvecchio** (Old Castle). This crenellated, russet brick building with massive walls, towers, turrets, and a vast courtyard was built for Can-

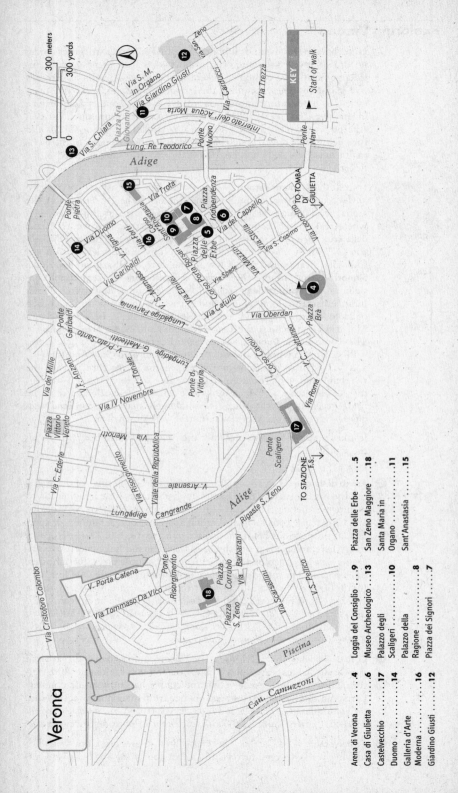

Verona

grande II della Scala in 1354. It presides over a street lined with attractive old buildings and palaces of the nobility. Inside, the **Museo di Castelvecchio** gives you a good look at the castle's vaulted halls and the treasures of Venetian painting and sculpture that they contain. ✉ *Corso Castelvecchio 2* ☎ *045/594734* 🎫 *€3.10 or Verona Card, free 1st Sun. of month* ⊗ *Mon. 1:45–7:30, Tues.–Sun. 8:30–7:30; last entry 45 mins before closing.*

⑭ Duomo. The ornate Romanesque Duomo has not only architectural characteristics typical of the Venetian style but also some Byzantine attributes. ✉ *Via Duomo* ☎ *045/8008813* 🎫 *€2, € 5 for combined churches ticket, or Verona Card* ⊗ *Nov.–Mar., Tues.–Sat. 10–1 and 1:30–4, Sun. 1–5; Apr.–Oct., Mon.–Sat. 10–5:30, Sun. 1:30–5:30.*

⑯ Galleria d'Arte Moderna. The handsome Palazzo Forti, where Napoléon once stayed, frequently hosts contemporary painting exhibitions of well-known artists; past shows have included the works of Marcel Duchamp (1887–1968) and Andy Warhol (1928–87). ✉ *Via Forti 1, entrance vicolo Volto Due Mori 4* ☎ *045/8001903* ⊕ *www.palazzoforti. it* 🎫 *Varies depending on exhibition* ⊗ *Varies depending on exhibition.*

⑫ Giardino Giusti. The formal Giusti Gardens, laid out on several levels around a 16th-century villa, are a symbol of things long past. There's a fine view of the city from the terrace, where the German poet and dramatist Johann Wolfgang von Goethe (1749–1832) recorded his impressions. ✉ *Via Giardino Giusti 2* ☎ *045/8034029* 🎫 *€4.50* ⊗ *Apr.–Sept., daily 9–8; Oct.–Mar., daily 9–5.*

⑨ Loggia del Consiglio. The graceful structure was built in the 12th century to house city council meetings and still serves as the seat of the provincial government. ✉ *Piazza dei Signori* ⊗ *Closed to the public.*

⑬ Museo Archeologico. The museum is housed in an old monastery above the **Teatro Romano,** which was built in the same era as the Arena di Verona. The Roman Theater is sometimes used for dramatic productions. From here there are good views over the entire city. ✉ *Rigaste del Redentore 2* ☎ *045/8000360* 🎫 *€2.60 or Verona Card, free 1st Sun. of month* ⊗ *Mon. 1:30–7:30, Tues.–Sun. 8:30–7:30; last entry 45 mins before closing.*

⑩ Palazzo degli Scaligeri. This was the medieval stronghold from which the della Scalas ruled Verona with an iron fist. ✉ *Piazza dei Signori* ⊗ *Closed to the public.*

⑧ Palazzo della Ragione. The 12th-century palace has a somber courtyard, Gothic staircase, and medieval tower overlooking the piazza. ✉ *Piazza dei Signori* ⊗ *Closed to the public.*

⑦ Piazza dei Signori. Verona's great piazza has been at the center of things for more than a thousand years, but the impressive facades and arched entrances surrounding it date from the early Renaissance.

⑤ Piazza delle Erbe (Vegetable Market Square). This square is the site of the ancient Roman forum and today hosts a colorful morning market, with huge rectangular umbrellas raised for shading neat ranks of produce.

★ **⑱ San Zeno Maggiore.** Possibly the finest example of a Romanesque church in Italy, with a 13th-century rose window and a magnificent 12th-century portal, San Zeno is set between two medieval bell towers. The light-gray and white-brick color scheme—typical of Italy's Romanesque churches—is especially impressive here. Inside, look for Mantegna's *Madonna* over the main altar; a peaceful cloister is off the nave to the left. Have a good look at the portal doors, which are covered in bronze plaques depicting scenes from the Bible and miracles accomplished by San Zeno. They were executed by local artisans and date from as early as 1100. ✉ *Piazza San Zeno* ☎ *045/8006120* 🎫 *€2, €5 for combined churches ticket, or Verona Card* ⏰ *Nov.–Feb., Tues.–Sat. 10–1 and 1:30–4, Sun. 1–5; Mar.–Oct., Mon.–Sat. 8:30–6, Sun. 1–5.*

⑪ **Santa Maria in Organo.** The choir and sacristy of this medieval church are decorated with inlaid-wood masterpieces by the 15th-century monk Fra Giovanni. A series of panels depicts varied scenes—local buildings, an idealized Renaissance town, wildlife, and fruit—that radiate a love of life and reveal the artist's eye for detail. ✉ *Piazzetta Santa Maria in Organo 1* ☎ *045/591440* ⏰ *Daily 7:30–noon and 2:30–6:30.*

⑮ **Sant'Anastasia.** Not far from the Duomo, Sant'Anastasia is Verona's largest church. In stark contrast to the simple, vaguely Romanesque facade, the impressive Gothic doorway is surrounded by elaborate carvings illustrating scenes from the New Testament, and down the steps you'll meet the famous *Gobbi,* two sculptures of crouching hunchbacks supporting the holy-water stoups. The highlight, on display inside the sacristy and sadly damaged, is a detached fresco painted in blue and gray pastel shades by Pisanello (1377–1455), called *St. George and the Princess.* ✉ *Vicolo Sotto Riva 4* ☎ *045/8004325* 🎫 *€2, €5 for combined churches ticket, or Verona Card* ⏰ *Nov.–Feb., Tues.–Sat. 10–1 and 1:30–4, Sun. 1–5; Mar.–Oct., Mon.–Sat. 9–6, Sun. 1–6.*

off the
beaten
path

TOMBA DI GIULIETTA – Romantic souls may want to see the pretty spot claimed to be Juliet's Tomb. Authentic or not, it's still popular with lovesick Italian teenagers, who leave notes for the tragic lover. The location is near the river, just a few minutes' walk south from the Arena di Verona. ✉ *Via del Pontiere 35* ☎ *045/8000361* 🎫 *€2.60 or Verona Card, free 1st Sun. of month* ⏰ *Mon. 1:45–7:30, Tues.–Sun. 8:30–7:30; last entry 45 mins before closing.*

GIARDINI DI VILLA ARVEDI – The 17th-century Villa Arvedi is surrounded by historic gardens that have preserved their original layout, with well-kept alleys, a spectacular fountain, and a frescoed church. Parts of the villa are open to the public, and the garden tour includes a visit to the Salone dei Titani (Salon of the Titans), with frescoes by L. Dorigny (1654–1742) depicting mythological scenes, and to the Salone dei Cesari, named after the portraits of Roman emperors derived from the more famous Titian originals at the Palazzo Te in Mantua. There are also luxury apartments for rent 1 km (½ mi) away from the gardens in a 19th-century villa overlooking a scenic green valley. See the Villa Arvedi Web site for more details. ✉ *Statale per Grezzana, 8 km (5 mi) northeast of town,* ☎ *045/907045* 📠 *045/908766* 🌐 *www.villarvedi.it* 🎫 *€5.20* ⏰ *By appointment only, minimum 8–10 people.*

Where to Stay & Eat

★ **$$$$** ✕ **Arquade.** Master chef Bruno Barbieri and his team of professionals present nouveau Italian cuisine that is a delight to both eye and palate in this highly acclaimed restaurant at the Villa del Quar hotel. The creative menu may include such delicacies as baked scallops with sautéed Treviso radicchio, crunchy speck, and egg and vinegar custard, or suckling pig stuffed with lamb medallions, accompanied by new potatoes, confit of shallots, and fried quails' eggs. The sommelier will then complement your choices with treasures from his wine cellar. ✉ *Via Quar 12, 37020 Pedemonte di San Pietro in Cariano, 5 km (3 mi) northwest* *of Verona* ☎ *045/6800681* 🖶 *045/6800604* ⌦ *Reservations essential* 🖃 *AE, DC, MC, V* ⊘ *Closed Jan.–mid-Mar. and Mon. Mar–Apr.*

$$$$ ✕ **Dodici Apostoli.** Vaulted ceilings, frescoed walls, and a medieval ambience make this an exceptional place to enjoy classic regional dishes. Near Piazza delle Erbe, it stands on the foundations of a Roman temple. Specialties include gnocchi *di zucca e ricotta* (with squash and ricotta cheese) and *vitello alla Lessinia* (veal with mushrooms, cheese, and truffles). ✉ *Vicolo Corticella San Marco 3* ☎ *045/596999* 🖃 *AE, DC, MC, V* ⊘ *Closed Mon., Jan. 1–6, and mid-June–early July. No dinner Sun.*

$$$ ✕ **La Greppia.** The classic decor with vaulted ceilings sets the tone in this bustling restaurant off Via Mazzini between the Arena and Piazza delle Erbe. The kitchen produces fine versions of local and regional dishes, especially *tortelli di zucca* (pasta filled with squash) and *bolliti* (assorted boiled meats served with a choice of sauces). Service is courteous and efficient. ✉ *Vicolo Samaritana 3* ☎ *045/8004577* 🖃 *AE, DC, MC, V* ⊘ *Closed Mon., and last 2 wks of Jan. and June.*

$ ✕ **La Stueta.** This friendly trattoria located between the Teatro Romano and the Giardino Giusti. Try the gnocchi *con la pastisada* (with a horsemeat sauce), baccalà *mantecato con polenta* (cooked in milk and served with polenta), or *maiale all'amarone* (pork shin in a red wine sauce with seasonal vegetables). Finish up with a homemade tart or mousse. ✉ *Via del Redentore 4/b* ☎ *045/8032462* 🖃 *AE, DC, MC, V* ⊘ *Closed Mon. and 2 wks in July. No lunch Tues.*

★ $$$$ 🏨 **Gabbia d'Oro.** Set in a historic building off Piazza delle Erbe in the ancient heart of Verona, this hotel is a tasteful fantasia of romantic ornamentation, lavish trimmings, exquisite fabrics, and gorgeous period pieces. Rooms—each one different and more attractive than the last— have frescoes, beamed ceilings, pretty wallpaper, antique prints and furnishings, and canopy beds, some festooned with rosy-cheeked cherubs. You can relax outdoors in the medieval courtyard, in the comfortable orangerie, or on the roof terrace. The breakfast spread (not included in the price during the summer opera season) is to die for. ✉ *Corso Porta Borsari 4/a, 37121* ☎ *045/8003060* 🖶 *045/590293* ⊕ *www. hotelgabbiadoro.it* ⇶ *19 suites, 8 rooms* ⌂ *In-room safes, minibars, cable TV, bar, parking (fee), some pets allowed* 🖃 *AE, DC, MC, V.*

★ $$$$ 🏨 **Villa del Quar.** This tranquil 16th-century villa is surrounded by gardens and vineyards in the Valpolicella country, only 10 minutes by car from the city center. Architect Leopoldo Montresor and his wife, Evelina, who live here with their children, converted part of the villa into a sophisticated luxury hotel. No expense has been spared: all rooms have marble bathrooms (some with whirlpool baths) and European antiques. ✉ *Via Quar 12, 37020 Pedemonte di San Pietro in Cariano, 5 km (3 mi) northwest of Verona* ☎ *045/6800681* 🖶 *045/6800604* ⊕ *www. relaischateaux.com/de/delquar* ⇶ *19 rooms, 2 suites* ⌂ *Restaurant, pool, gym, massage, sauna, bar, Internet, meeting room, some pets allowed* 🖃 *AE, DC, MC, V* ⊘ *Closed Jan.–mid-Mar.*

$ 🏨 **Armando.** In a largely residential area a few hundred yards southeast of the Arena, this bright, contemporary family hotel is a welcome respite from the busy city center just a few minutes' walk away. (Parking is easier here, too.) The rooms are decorated with light, modern furniture, and there are family rooms sleeping up to five. In the airy breakfast room downstairs, Signora Diana serves a hearty breakfast (not included in the price) of yogurt, fresh fruit, cheese, rolls and coffee, with melon and prosciutto in summer. ✉ *Via Dietro Pallone 1, 37120* ☎ *045/8000206 or 8036015* 🖶 *045/8036015* ⇶ *19 rooms* 🖃 *MC, V* ⊘ *Closed late Dec.*

$ 🏨 **Torcolo.** The warm welcome extended by the owners (Signoras Diana and Silvia), the pleasant rooms unfussily decorated, and the central location on a peaceful street close to Piazza Brà and the Arena make the Torcolo a good value. Breakfast, which costs an extra €7–€10, is served outside on the terrace in front of the hotel in summer. ⊠ *Vicolo Listone 3, 37121* ☎ *045/8007512* 🖷 *045/8004058* ✆ *hoteltorcolo@virgilio.it* ↝ *19 rooms* ♿ *Some pets allowed* ⊟ *AE, DC, MC, V.*

Nightlife & the Arts

Nightclubs
Alter Ego (⊠ Via Torricelle 9 ☎ 045/915130) packs in a hip twentysomething crowd. It's open Friday and Saturday nights from 9 to 4. **Berfi's** (⊠ Via Lussemburgo 1 ☎ 045/508024) is a popular and expensive nightspot with a restaurant and piano bar, open from 8:30 PM to 4 AM, Friday to Sunday. You'll need to take a taxi, as it's in the *zona industriale* (industrial area) of Verona.

Opera
FodorsChoice Of all the venues for enjoying opera in the region, pride of place must
★ go to the **Arena di Verona.** Its summer opera season runs from July through August, and the audience of as many as 16,000 sits on the original stone terraces, dating from the time when gladiators fought to the death, or in the modern cushioned stalls. The opera stage is huge and best suited to grand productions such as *Aida*, but the experience is memorable no matter what is being performed. Sometimes you can hear the performance from the cafés at **Piazza Brà.** Tickets can be ordered by phone or on-line. ⊠ *Fondazione Arena di Verona: Piazza Brà 28, Verona, 37121* ⊠ *Box office* ⊠ *Via Dietro Anfiteatro 6/b* ☎ *045/8005151* ⊕ *www.arena.it.*

Shopping

Antiques & Housewares
The area around the Gothic church of **Sant'Anastasia** is full of antiques shops, most catering to serious collectors. You can picnic on the Piazza dei Signori in the cool breeze after a strenuous day of antiques hunting. The perfect place to splurge on a modern gift or imaginative decorative piece is **Alternative** (⊠ Vicolo San Marco in Foro 2, ☎ 045/8010910), with trendy glass artworks and design objects.

Markets
Verona's two markets, on **Piazza delle Erbe** and on **Piazza Cittadella,** both open Monday–Saturday 8–1 and 3:30–sundown, have a selection of food, wine, clothing, antiques, and even pets.

Wine
Vinitaly (☎ 045/8298170 ⊕ www.vinitaly.com), the famous international wine show, takes place for five days in early April each year at the Fiera di Verona on Viale del Lavoro 8. It claims to make Verona the "world capital of quality wines" for the week, attracting more than 3,000 exhibitors from 25-odd countries. The show runs 9–7 daily and is open to the public (€30 per person).

TREVISO & THE HILLSIDE TOWNS

In this area directly north of Venice, market towns cling to the steep foothills of the Alps and the Dolomites alongside streams raging down from the mountains. Villa Barbaro, one of Palladio's most graceful country villas, is here, as are the arcaded streets of Treviso and the graceful Venetian Gothic structures of smaller hill towns.

Marostica

19 *7 km (4½ mi) west of Bassano del Grappa, 26 km (16 mi) northeast of Vicenza.*

The first and most evident feature of Marostica is the ancient stone wall snaking up to enclose the Castello Superiore with its commanding view over the surrounding countryside. But the most famous sight in town is Piazza Castello, the main square, paved in checkerboard fashion.

Where to Stay

★ **$$** 🏨 **Due Mori.** Modern, stylish rooms with wooden floors and soft-beige marble bathrooms offer classy Italian elegance in the heart of this medieval town center. Some rooms have magical views of the olive-studded terraces behind the town, the upper castle, and ancient city wall. There's a chic, minimalist restaurant downstairs. Due Mori makes an excellent base for visiting the surrounding hills and towns of the northern Veneto. ⊠ *Corso Mazzini 73, 36063* ☎ *0424/471777* 🖷 *0424/476920* ⊕ *www.duemori.it* ⤶ *10 rooms* ⚫ *Restaurant, minibars, cable TV, free parking* 🖃 *AE, DC, MC, V* ⊗ *Closed 1st wk Jan., 1 wk mid-Aug.*

Sports & the Outdoors

A game of **human-scale chess** is acted out in Piazza Castello by players in medieval costume on the second weekend in September in even-numbered years. The game lasts three evenings. Tickets go on sale in April; for information and bookings, contact Marostica's **tourist office** (☎ 0424/72127 ⊕ www.marosticascacchi.it).

Bassano del Grappa

20 *7 km (4½ mi) east of Marostica, 37 km (23 mi) north of Venice.*

Beautifully positioned directly above the swift-flowing waters of the Brenta River and at the foot of the Mt. Grappa massif (5,880 ft), Bassano has old streets lined with low-slung buildings adorned with wooden balconies and pretty flowerpots. Bright ceramic wares produced here and in nearby Nove are displayed in shops along byways that curve uphill toward a centuries-old square and, even higher, to a belvedere with a good view of Mt. Grappa and the beginning of the Val Sugana.

Bassano's most famous landmark is the **covered bridge** that has spanned the Brenta since the 13th century. Rebuilt countless times (floods are frequent), the present bridge is a postwar reconstruction using Andrea Palladio's 16th-century design. The great architect astutely chose to use wood as his medium, knowing that it could be replaced quickly and cheaply.

Bassano is home to the famous **Nardini** distillery, where the grappa liqueur has been distilled for more than a century. Stop in for a sniff or a snifter at any of the local cafés or at their very own *bottega* on the Ponte degli Alpini.

Where to Stay & Eat

★ **$-$$** ✕ **Osteria Terraglio.** The creative, modern menu here focuses on absolute freshness, from the wonderful array of savory snacks to the big, crisp *insalatone* (main-course salads with tuna or various cheeses) to the steak fillet, cut to order. Special tasting sessions of local delicacies such as asparagus, cold-pressed olive oil, and fine wines are a regular feature. There's live jazz on Tuesday evenings. ⊠ *Piazza Terraglio 28* ☎ *0424/521064* 🖃 *AE, DC, MC, V* ⊗ *Closed Mon.*

$-$$ ✕ **Ristorante Birreria Ottone.** Excellent cuisine and an old, central European, beer-hall atmosphere keep the locals coming back. The proprietors are the friendly Wipflinger family, headed by Otto, whose Austrian forebear founded the restaurant as a beer hall a century ago. Equally good for a simple lunch or more elaborate dinner, Ottone offers specialties such as a delicious goulash cooked with cumin. ⊠ *Via Matteotti 48/50* ☎ *0424/522206* ⊟ *AE, D, MC, V* ⊗ *Closed Tues. and first 3 wks in Aug. No dinner Mon.*

$$ 🏨 Bonotto Belvedere. This historic hotel has richly decorated public rooms with period furnishings and Oriental rugs; the lounge has an open fireplace and a piano. Guest rooms are decorated in traditional Venetian or contemporary style. There are two rooms with facilities for people with disabilities. The elegant, separately managed Belvedere restaurant offers classic Italian cuisine, focusing equally on seafood and meat dishes. ⊠ *Piazzale G. Giardino 14, 36061* ☎ *0424/529845* ⊟ *0424/529849* ⊕ *www.bonotto.it* ⇆ *83 rooms, 4 suites* ⚒ *Restaurant, bar, Internet, meeting rooms, some pets allowed (fee)* ⊟ *AE, DC, MC, V.*

$–$$ 🏨 Villa Palma. This gracefully refurbished 18th-century country villa, only a short drive from Asolo (10 km [6 mi]) and Bassano (5 km [3 mi]), combines modern comforts and conveniences with rural calm and old-fashioned style and charm—wooden beams, vaulted brick ceilings, and tasteful furnishings. Four rooms have whirlpool baths, one a Turkish bath. In summer, meals are served on the terrace overlooking the splendid garden. ⊠ *Via Chemin Palma 30, 36065 Mussolente* ☎ *0424/577407* ⊟ *0424/87687* ⊕ *www.villapalma.it* ⇆ *20 rooms, 1 suite* ⚒ *Restaurant, bar, meeting rooms* ⊟ *AE, DC, MC, V.*

$ 🏨 Al Castello. In a restored town house at the foot of the medieval Torre Civica, the Cattapan family's Castello is a reasonably priced, attractive choice. The simply furnished rooms all differ in shape and size. The best ones, at the front, have a small balcony offering a wonderful view of the charming square below. ⊠ *Piazza Terraglio 20, 36061* ☎☎ *0424/228665* ⇆ *11 rooms* ⚒ *Café* ⊟ *AE, MC, V.*

Shopping

Bassano del Grappa and nearby Nove are famous for ceramics. A large number of shops in town also feature wrought-iron and copper utensils, many of them made on the premises. At **L'arte della Ceramica** (⊠ Via Angarano 21 ☎ 0424/503901) you'll find some of the best handmade ceramics from Bassano: plates, bowls, jugs, and apothecary jars are decorated in traditional flowery and fruity patterns.

Asolo

㉑ *11 km (7 mi) east of Bassano del Grappa, 33 km (20½ mi) northwest of Treviso.*

The romantic charming hillside hamlet of Asolo was the consolation prize of an exiled queen. At the end of the 15th century, Venetian-born Caterina Cornaro was sent here by Venice's doge to keep her from interfering with Venetian administration of her former kingdom of Cyprus, which she had inherited from her husband. To soothe the pain of exile, she established a lively and brilliant court in Asolo. Over the centuries, Venetian aristocrats continued to build gracious villas on the hillside, and in the 19th century Asolo once again became the idyllic haunt of musicians, poets, and painters. From the outside, you can explore villas once inhabited by Robert Browning and the actress Eleonora Duse. Be warned that the town's charm vaporizes on holiday weekends when the crowds pour in. At the center of Asolo is **Piazza Maggiore**, with Renaissance palaces and fin-de-siècle cafés. The empty **Rocca** (☎ €1.50 ⊗ 10–12:30 and 3–7), uphill from the Piazza Maggiore and past Caterina's ruined castle, is a medieval fortress from which you get a view of Asolo's hundred horizons. It closes when the weather turns bad.

Where to Stay

$$$$ 🏨 **Villa Cipriani.** This historic villa is set in a romantic garden on the hillside and surrounded by other gracious country homes. Its 19th-century antiques are complemented by modern creature comforts and attentive service. The superb restaurant has a terrace overlooking the garden. The Asolo Golf Club is close by. ✉ *Via Canova 298, 31011* ☎ *0423/523411* 🖷 *0423/952095* ⊕ *www.starwood.com/italy* ⇆ *31 rooms* ♨ *Restaurant, bar, Internet, meeting room, some pets allowed (fee), no-smoking floor* ▭ *AE, DC, MC, V.*

Shopping

Asolo center hosts a two-day antiques market on the second weekend of every month except July and August.

Villa Barbaro

★ ㉒ *7 km (4½ mi) northeast of Asolo, 33 km (20½ mi) northwest of Treviso.*

Villa Barbaro is one of Palladio's most gracious creations. The fully furnished villa just outside the town of Maser is still inhabited by its owners, who make you slip heavy felt scuffs over your shoes to protect the highly polished floors. The elaborate stuccowork and opulent frescoes by Paolo Veronese bring the 16th century to life. After La Rotonda, this is Palladio's greatest villa and is definitely worth going out of your way to see. (Before making the trip, note the limited hours. Groups of more than 20 can visit at other times by appointment.) ✉ *Via Cornuda 7* ☎ *0423/923004* 🎫 *€5* ☾ *Mar.–Oct., Tues. and weekends 3–6; Nov.–Feb., weekends 2:30–5* ☾ *Closed Dec. 24–Jan. 6.*

Where to Eat

$–$$ ✕ **Agnoletti.** In the town of Giavera del Montello, about 25 km (16 mi) east of Maser, Agnoletti is an 18th-century inn of a bygone era with a lovely summer garden. From May to October the kitchen can produce an all-mushroom menu; if that's too much of a good thing, at least try the mushroom soup or *tortina ai funghi* (mushroom tart). ✉ *Via della Vittoria 190, Giavera del Montello* ☎ *0422/776009* ▭ *AE, DC, MC, V* ☾ *Closed Tues., 1 wk in Jan., and 2 wks in July.*

★ **$** ✕ **Da Bastian.** A good place to stop for lunch in Maser before visiting the Villa Barbaro (a five-minute walk away), this excellent restaurant has a pleasant garden for outdoor dining. Everything on the menu is seasonal; autumn and winter offerings include grilled mushrooms, homemade pumpkin tortelli, and, for second courses, baccalà, snails, and *trippa alla Veneta* (tripe cooked in a tomato and white wine sauce). The dessert trolley is laden with mouthwatering homemade cakes and fruit tarts. ✉ *Via Cornuda, follow signs* ☎ *0423/565400* ▭ *No credit cards* ☾ *Closed Thurs. and Aug. No dinner Wed.*

Treviso

㉓ *35 km (22 mi) southeast of Maser, 30 km (19 mi) north of Venice.*

Treviso is a busy commercial center, with fashionable shops and boutiques at every turn. "Little Venice" is a somewhat inflated claim for the town, though it does have canals and a Venetian air; "the painted city" is a less extravagant title, and an apt one: you'll come across frescoes practically everywhere you look. The most important church in Treviso is **San Nicolò**, an impressive Gothic structure with an ornate vaulted ceiling. San Nicolò has frescoes of the saints by 14th-century artist Tommaso da Modena on the columns. But the highlight is the remarkable series of 40 portraits of Dominican friars by the same artist in the seminary next door. They are astoundingly realistic, considering that some were painted as early as 1352, and include one of the earliest-known portraits of a subject wearing glasses. ⊠ *Seminario Vescovile, Via San Nicolò* ☎ *0422/3247* ⊙ *Mon.–Sat. 8:15–noon and 3–5, Sun. 3–5.*

Inside Treviso's **Duomo,** on the altar of one of the chapels to the right, is an *Annunciation* by Titian (circa 1488–1576). ⊠ *Piazza del Duomo* ⊙ *Daily 8:15–noon and 3–6; during Mass visits are not allowed.*

Piazza dei Signori is the heart of medieval Treviso and still the town's social center, with outdoor cafés and some impressive public buildings. One of these, the Palazzo dei Trecento, has a small alley behind it. Follow the alley for about 200 yards to the *pescheria* (fish market), on an island in one of the small rivers that flow through town. Shops in Treviso feature wrought-iron and copper utensils.

Where to Stay & Eat

★ **$–$$** ✕**Toni del Spin.** Wood-paneled with '30s decor, this place oozes delightful, old-fashioned character. Locals love the friendly and bustling feel as well as the wholesome food. The menu changes twice a week and is chalked on a hanging wooden board: try the filling *zuppa d'orzo e fagioli* (barley and bean soup) or the pasta e fagioli, delivered with panache and care. You shouldn't leave without quaffing a glass or two of Prosecco. ⊠ *Via Inferiore 7* ☎ *0422/543829* ⚐ *Reservations essential* ▭ *AE, MC, V* ⊙ *Closed Sun. and Aug. No lunch Mon.*

¢–$ ✕**Osteria Muscoli's.** The bar is always busy with locals popping in for an *ombra* (glass of wine), but there are rustic wooden tables out back where you can sit and enjoy the offerings of this traditional osteria. The young efficient staff will prepare a generous platter of savory delights, possibly with chunks of ham off the bone, a wedge of potato-and-porcini pie, pepper cheese, stuffed pickled tomatoes, and *crostini* (grilled bread) with *sfilacci* (shredded, cured horse meat). The menu, posted on a blackboard, changes daily. ⊠ *Via Pescheria 23* ☎ *0422/583390* ▭ *No credit cards* ⊙ *Closed Sun. and 3 wks in Sept.*

$$ ✕▯ **La Colonna.** Everything in this small hotel, set in a creeper-covered, 15th-century courtyard, is crisp and white. Flower-frescoed ceilings and old-fashioned washstands in the bathrooms add to the charm. It's essential to book one of the six rooms well ahead. You can feel the history seeping through the walls in the associated restaurant of the same name ($$$), where you can dine among the pillars, beamed ceiling, and low arches of the main room or on the mezzanine floor. The chef favors fish, and beef with rosemary is a perfumey delight. The wine bar next door is also worth a visit. ⊠ *Via Campana 27, 31100* ☎ *0422/ 544804* 🖷 *0422/419177* ⇋ *6 rooms* ♿ *Restaurant, bar, some pets allowed* ▭ *AE, DC, MC, V* ⊙ *Restaurant closed Mon. and 2 wks in mid-Aug. No dinner Sun.*

$$–$$$ ▯ **Cà del Galletto.** This modern, functional hotel on the outskirts of town offers plenty of personal and public space while being just five minutes by car or bus from the center. Facilities include a pool (summer only), gym, sauna, and elegant restaurant. Free use of bikes means you can park the car here and visit the historic center at a leisurely pace. ⊠ *Via Santa Bona Vecchia 30* ☎ *0422/432550* 🖷 *0422/432510* ⊕ *www. hoteldelgalletto* ⇋ *37 rooms* ♿ *Restaurant, in-room data ports, tennis court, pool, gym, sauna, bicycles, bar* ▭ *AE, DC, MC, V.*

¢ ▯ **Il Cascinale.** A five-minute urban bus ride will get you here, but this *agriturismo*, or farmstay, is in the open country. Don't expect time-worn rustic charm though: this is a modern block of bright, spacious rooms above the owners' equally modern residence. Rooms are smartly furnished to hotel standards, and a hearty, country breakfast (not included in the room rate) is on offer downstairs. The restaurant is open for other meals on weekends only. A big front lawn provides plenty of play space for children. ⊠ *Via Torre d'Orlando 6/B, 31100* ☎☎ *0422/402203* ⊕ *www.agriturismoilcascinale.it* ⇨ *8 rooms* ♿ *Restaurant, minibars, playground, meeting room, free parking; no a/c* ⊟ *No credit cards.*

Conegliano

㉔ *23 km (14 mi) north of Treviso, 60 km (37 mi) north of Venice.*

Conegliano is in the heart of wine-producing country. The town itself is attractive, with Venetian-style villas and frescoed houses, but the real draw is the wine, particularly the effervescent Prosecco di Conegliano.

Where to Stay

$-$$ 🏨 **Canon d'Oro.** The town's oldest inn, the Canon d'Oro is in an arcaded and frescoed 16th-century building in a central location within walking distance of the train station. The antique furniture, lovely bed linen, and terraced garden all add to its charm. ⊠ *Via XX Settembre 129, 31015* ☎ *0438/34246* 🖷 *0438/34246* ⊕ *www.hotelcanondoro.it* ⇨ *51 rooms* ♿ *Restaurant, in-room data ports, in-room safes, minibars, cable TV, bar, free parking, some pets allowed* ⊟ *AE, DC, MC, V.*

en route   Leading southeast from Conegliano, the well-marked **Strada dei Vini del Piave** wends its way through cabernet and merlot country along the Piave River. There are dozens of places to stop, sample, and buy the red—and sometimes rosé—wines. The road ends at Oderzo.

FRIULI-VENEZIA GIULIA

The peripheral location of the Friuli-Venezia Giulia region in Italy's northeastern corner makes it easy to overlook, but this ethnically mixed cocktail of Italian, Slavic, and central European cultures is a fascinating area. The old Austrian port of Trieste—a symbol of Italian nationalist aspirations for so long—and the medieval city of Udine are perfect bases for local excursions.

Udine

㉕ *71 km (44 mi) east of Conegliano, 127 km (79 mi) northeast of Venice.*

The city of Udine commands a view of the surrounding plain and the Alpine foothills; according to legend, it stands on a mound erected by Attila the Hun so he could watch the burning of the important Roman center of Aquileia to the south. Udine flourished in the Middle Ages, thanks to its location, favorable to trade, and the rights it gained from the local patriarch to hold regular markets. There is a distinctly Venetian feel to the city, noticeable in the architecture of Piazza della Libertà, under the stern gaze of the lion of St. Mark, symbol of Venetian power.

The **Galleria d'Arte Antica** has a wide-ranging collection of local and Italian art, including canvases by the prolific Neapolitan Luca Giordano (1632–1705), the Venetians Vittore Carpaccio (circa 1460–1525) and Tiepolo, and a painting of St. Francis receiving the stigmata attributed to Caravaggio (circa 1571–1610). ⊠ *Castello di Udine* ☎ *0432/502872* 🎫 *€2.60, free Sun.* ☉ *Tues.–Sat. 9:30–12:30 and 3–6, Sun. 9:30–12:30.*

Where to Stay & Eat

$$$ ✗ **Vitello d'Oro.** Udine's elegant, landmark restaurant is popular among locals for special occasions. The menu features both meat and fish in classic regional dishes as well as more *nouveau* creations. You can start with an antipasto of *scaloppa di fegato d'oca con mele al marsala* (goose liver with apples in Marsala wine) and follow up with *carrè di cinghiale al forno con suo sugo e patate schiacciate* (roast saddle of wild boar in its cooking juices with crushed potatoes)—though you'll also want to leave room for the range of rich sweets. There's a large terrace in front for dining al fresco in summer. ⊠ *Via Valvason 4* ☎ *0432/508982* ⚑ *Reservations essential* ▭ *AE, DC, MC, V* ☯ *Closed Sun. July–Sept. and Wed. Oct.–June.*

$ ✕ **Al Vecchio Stallo.** Hidden away in a narrow alley, this popular osteria offers a great selection of wine by the glass and a few well-prepared traditional soups and meat dishes, including *zuppa d'orzo* (barley soup) and *cinghiale in umido* (stewed wild boar). Seasonal vegetables, *frittate* (thick omelets), and fish on Friday round out the menu. ⊠ *Via Viola 7* ☎ *0432/21296* ▭ *No credit cards* ☯ *Closed Sun.*

¢ ✕ **Ai Provinciali.** Line up with the locals at this popular self-service osteria in the city center. Local cuisine is evident in pasta choices such as gnocchi with cream and speck, and *orecchiette* (small ear-shaped pasta) with sausage. Main courses include roast chicken leg, boiled meats, and seasonal vegetables. ⊠ *Via Prefettura 3* ☎ *0432/297816* ▭ *No credit cards* ☯ *Closed Sun.*

$$$ ▦ **Astoria Hotel Italia.** The facade of this elegant, arcaded building in the heart of the old city dominates the big piazza in front, and there are interesting city views from many of the rooms. The spacious public areas and lounges offer contemporary elegance, while the guest rooms are individually furnished in traditional style. ⊠ *Piazza XX Settembre 24, 33100* ☎ *0432/505091* ▦ *0432/509070* ⊕ *www.hotelastoria.udine.it* ⇖ *73 rooms, 2 suites* ⚐ *Restaurant, bar, Internet, meeting rooms, some pets allowed* ▭ *AE, DC, MC, V.*

Cividale

❷❻ *17 km (11 mi) east of Udine, 144 km (89 mi) northeast of Venice.*

Cividale dates from the time of Julius Caesar. It is popularly supposed (particularly by locals) that it was built by Caesar when he was commander of Roman legions in the area. The city straddles the Natisone River and contains many examples of Venetian Gothic buildings, particularly the **Palazzo Comunale.** Cividale's Renaissance **Duomo** has a striking silver-gilt altar. ⊠ *Piazza Duomo* ☎ *0432/731144* ☯ *Apr.–Oct., Mon.–Sat. 9:30–noon and 3–7, Sun. 3–7; Nov.–Mar., Mon.–Sat. 9:30–noon and 3–6, Sun. 3–6.*

The **Museo Archeologico** is the best place to trace the history of the area and the importance of Cividale and Udine in the formative period following the collapse of the Roman Empire. A large collection of Lombard artifacts includes weapons, jewelry, and domestic wares from this warrior race, which swept into what is now Italy in the 6th century. ⊠ *Piazza Duomo 13* ☎ *0432/700700* ▣ *€2* ☯ *Mon. 9–2; Tues.–Sun. 8:30–7:30.*

Where to Eat

★ **¢–$** ✕ **Trattoria Dominissini.** The rustic wood furnishings and simple decor here are perfectly in keeping with Cividale's old-world charm. The menu features typical dishes of game and cheese. Try the wonderful *frico di patate,* a mixture of potato and local Montasio cheese cooked in the pan like an omelette; game dishes might include *cinghiale in umido con polenta*(stewed wild boar with polenta). There's also a healthy selection of vegetables, along with mixed salads, tempting desserts, and excellent

Friuli wines. ⊠ *Via Jacopo Stellini 18* ☎ *0432/733763* ▤ *AE, DC, MC, V* ☺ *Closed Mon. No dinner Sun.*

> **en route** From Cividale, head south to Monfalcone, and then take the scenic S14 road eastward along the coast, under the shadow of the huge geological formation called the Carso, a barren expanse of limestone that forms a giant ledge, most of which is across the border in Slovenia. Italian territory goes only a few kilometers inland in this strip, and Italy's small Slovenian minority ekes out an agricultural existence in the region, which has changed hands countless times since the final days of imperial Rome.

Castello di Miramare

★ ㉗ *78 km (48 mi) south of Cividale, 7 km (4½ mi) north of Trieste.*

This seafront castle in Miramare is a 19th-century extravaganza in white stone, built for the Archduke Maximilian of Habsburg (brother of Emperor Franz Josef). Maximilian spent a brief, happy time here until Napoléon III of France took Trieste from the Habsburgs and sent the archduke packing. He was given the title of Emperor of Mexico in 1864 as a compensation but met his death before a Mexican firing squad in 1867. You can visit the lush grounds and admire the memorable views over the Adriatic. Reservations are required for a guided tour of the castle. ⊠ *Miramare* ☎ *040/224143* ☞ *Castle €4, optional guided tour €3, grounds free* ☺ *Castle and grounds daily 9–7; last entry 30 mins before closing.*

Trieste

㉘ *64 km (40 mi) southeast of Udine, 163 km (101 mi) east of Venice.*

Surrounded by rugged countryside and beautiful coastline, Trieste is built on a hillside above what was once the chief port of the Austro-Hungarian Empire. Typical of Trieste are its belle-époque cafés. Like Vienna's coffeehouses, these are social and cultural centers and much-beloved refuges from the prevailing northeast wind, the chilling *bora*.

The sidewalk cafés on the vast seaside **Piazza dell'Unità d'Italia** are popular meeting places in the summer months. The square is similar to Piazzetta San Marco in Venice; both are focal points of architectural interest and command fine views of the sea. Behind the **Palazzo Comunale** (Town Hall; ⊠ At the end of Piazza dell'Unità d'Italia), going away from the sea, steps lead uphill, following the city's pattern of upward expansion from its roots as a coastal fishing port in Roman times.

The **Civico Museo Revoltella e Galleria d'Arte Moderna** (Revoltella Museum and Gallery of Modern Art) was founded in 1872 when the Venetian baron Pasquale Revoltella left the city his palazzo, library, and collection of Triestine paintings. Next door, in a building redesigned by the architect Carlo Scarpa, is a gallery containing one of the most important collections of 19th- and 20th-century art in Italy, with Italian artists particularly well represented. It also hosts high-profile temporary exhibitions. ⊠ *Via Armando Diaz 27* ☎ *040/311361* ☞ *€5* ☺ *Tues–Sun. 10–1 and 3–7.*

The solidly Romanesque church of **San Silvestro** (⊠ Piazza San Silvestro 1 ☎ 040/632770), dating from the 11th century, is open Monday to Saturday 9:30–12:30 and Sunday for mass. The baroque extravagance of **Santa Maria Maggiore**, just beyond San Silvestro, backs onto a network of alleys closed to traffic.

TRIESTE'S CAFFÈ CULTURE

TRIESTE IS JUSTLY FAMOUS for its coffee, and so it is perhaps no coincidence that a former mayor is Riccardo Illy, patriarch of the famous über-roaster, Illycaffè, which can be credited with supplying caffeine fixes to most Italians and much of the free world. The elegant civility of Trieste plays out beautifully in a caffè culture rivaling that of Vienna. Know that in Trieste your cappuccino will come in an espresso cup, with only half as much frothy milk as you'll find elsewhere and a dollop of whipped cream. Many cafés are part of a torrefazione (roasting shop), so you can sample the beans before you buy. Few cafés in Trieste, in Italy, or in the world, can rival **Antico Caffè San Marco** (⊠ Via Cesare Battisti 18 ☎ 040/363538) for its glimmering art deco style and old-world atmosphere. On Friday and Saturday there's live music. **Cremcaffè** (⊠ Piazza

Carlo Goldoni 10, ☎ 040/636555) may not be the place to sit down and read the paper, but it's nonetheless one of the most frequented cafés in town, with 20 different blends to choose from. One of the city's finest roasting shops, **Caffè La Colombiana** (⊠ Via Giosuè Carducci 12, ☎ 040/370855), has been in the same location since the 1940s. There is no better locale in town than at **Caffè Piazza Grande** (⊠ Piazza dell'Unità d'Italia 5/c ☎ 040/369878), with a great view of the great piazza. **Gran Bar Malabar** (⊠ Piazza San Giovanni 6, ☎ 040/636226) is a wonderful stop for a coffee or an aperitif, with an excellent wine list and tastings every Friday after 6:30 PM.

The 14th-century **Cattedrale di San Giusto** incorporates two much older churches, one dating from as far back as the 5th century. The exterior adds even more to the jumble of styles involved by using fragments of Roman tombs and temples: you can see these most clearly on the pillars of the main doorway. The highlights of the interior are the 13th-century mosaics and frescoes. ⊠ Piazza Cattedrale 2 ☎ 040/309666 ⊙ Apr.–Sept., daily 8–7:30; Oct.–Mar., daily 8–6:30.

From the hilltop **Castello di San Giusto** you can take in some of the best views of the area. In the 15th century, this castle was built by the Venetians, who always had an eye for the best vantage point in the cities they conquered or controlled. The Habsburgs, subsequent rulers of Trieste, enlarged it to its present size. Some of the best exhibits in the **Museo Civico del Castello di San Giusto** are the displays of weaponry and armor. ⊠ Piazza Cattedrale 3 ☎ 040/309362 castle; 040/313636 museum ☜ Castle €1.03, museum and castle €1.55 ⊙ Museum Tues.–Sun. 9–1; castle Apr.–Sept., daily 9–7; Oct.–Mar., daily 9–5.

The **Piazza della Borsa** contains Trieste's original stock exchange, the **Borsa Vecchia**, a neoclassical building now serving as the chamber of commerce. A statue of Leopold I is at one end of the square.

off the beaten path

GROTTA GIGANTE – More than 300 ft high, 900 ft long, and 200 ft wide, this gigantic cave is dripping with spectacular stalactites and stalagmites. Allow 50 minutes for the tour (which is required). It's not far from Trieste, about 10 km (6 mi) north of the city (take Bus 42 from Piazza Oberdan). It's cool inside year-round, so bring a sweater, and be prepared for a 500-step climb. ☎ 040/327312 ☜ €7.50 ⊙ Apr.–June and Sept., Tues.–Sun.10–6; July–Aug., daily

*10–6; Mar. and Oct., Tues.–Sun. 10–4; Nov.–Feb., Tues.–Sun.
10–noon and 2–4. Apr.–Sept. tours leave every 30 mins; other
months, every hr.*

Where to Stay & Eat

$$$ ✕**Hostaria alle Bandierette.** Try to keep from bumping into the tank of
crayfish, then squeeze past the beds of flatfish and shellfish on crushed
ice . . . yes, you're in seafood territory. In fact, this restaurant serves nothing
but. It's small, hectic, and full of serious eaters admiring the cooks in
full view. Fish risottos, squid spaghetti, and lobster with capers all hit
the spot. You can dine on an outdoor patio in summer. ⊠ *Riva Nazario
Sauro 2* ☎ *040/300686* ⌖ *Reservations essential* ⊟ *AE, DC, MC, V*
⊘ *Closed Mon. and first 2 wks Jan.*

$$ ✕**Suban.** Although in the hills on the edge of town, this historic trattoria is worth the taxi ride. The rustic decor is rich in dark wood, stone,
and wrought iron, and you'll find typical regional fare with imaginative variations. Among the specialties are *jota carsolina* (typical local
minestrone made of cabbage, potatoes, and beans) and duck breast in
Tokay sauce. Finish with the Hungarian-influenced *rigo janci* (a mous-
selike chocolate pudding). ⊠ *Via Emilio Comici 2/d,* ☎ *040/54368*
⊟ *AE, DC, MC, V* ⊘ *Closed Tues., 3 wks in Aug., and 1 wk in early
Jan. No lunch Mon.*

$ ✕**Antipastoteca di Mare.** Hidden away halfway up the hill to the Castello
Fodor'sChoice di San Giusto, Roberto Surian's homely little restaurant is well worth
★ seeking out during the day and booking for the evening. You'll find here
some of the tastiest of hot and cold seafood combinations, from calamari and barley salad to scallops, mussels, and sardines with basil. The
extraordinary fish soup of sardines, mackerel, and tuna, sprinkled with
lightly fried, diced garlic bread and polenta, won Roberto first prize in
Trieste's prestigious Sarde Day competition. Fish is everything here, accompanied only by a simple salad, potatoes, polenta, and house wine.
⊠ *Via della fornace 1* ☎ *040/309606* ⊟ No *credit cards* ⊘ *Closed Mon.
No dinner Sun.*

★ **$$$$** ▥ **Duchi d'Aosta.** On the spacious Piazza dell'Unità d'Italia, this hotel,
beautifully furnished in Venetian-Renaissance style, has come a long way
since its original incarnation as a 19th-century dockers' café. Rooms have
dark-wood antiques, rich carpets, and drapes. On the ground floor is
Harry's Grill, one of the city's most elegant restaurants. ⊠ *Piazza del-
l'Unità d'Italia 2, 34121* ☎ *040/7600011* 🖷 *040/366092* ⊕ *www.
grandhotelduchidaosta.com* ⇌ *53 rooms, 2 suites* ⌂ *Restaurant, minibars, cable TV, hot tubs, Turkish bath, bar, meeting rooms, parking (fee),
some pets allowed* ⊟ *AE, DC, MC, V.*

★ **$$–$$$** ▥ **Riviera and Maximilian's.** Seven kilometers (4 mi) north of Trieste, this
lovely hotel with private access to the beach below commands stunning
views across the Golfo di Trieste to Castello di Miramare. Rooms are
beautifully furnished in modern style, some with balconies. ⊠ *Strada
Costiera 22, 34010* ☎ *040/224551* 🖷 *040/224300* ⊕ *www.
hotelrivieraemaximilian.com* ⇌ *57 rooms, 1 suite* ⌂ *Restaurant, minibars, cable TV, beach, bar, Internet, meeting rooms, free parking, some
pets allowed; no a/c in some rooms* ⊟ *AE, DC, MC, V.*

$$ ▥ **Alla Posta.** The reading lounge, with its high-back armchairs, parquet
floor, and potted plants—plus a roaring fire in winter—entice you into
this elegant, central hotel. Upstairs, stylishly decorated guest rooms are
outfitted with high-tech controls for heating, air-conditioning, and
wake-up calls, and the spacious bathrooms are done in Italian marble.
⊠ *Piazza Oberdan 1* ☎ *040/365208* 🖷 *040/633720* ⇌ *47 rooms*
⌂ *In-room data ports, in-room safes, minibars, cable TV with movies*
⊟ *AE, DC, MC, V.*

$ 🖼 **Alabarda.** The bright, spacious rooms in this restored, family-operated hotel are the best low-price offer in central Trieste, only 10 minutes' walk from the train station. You can check your e-mail at the Internet point in the lobby and catch an English news broadcast on the satellite TV in your room. Breakfast is included and the friendly staff will offer assistance with local services, maps, and city bus tickets. Some front rooms can be noisy. ⊠ *Via Valdirivo 22,* ☎ *040/630269* 🖷 *040/639284* ⊕ *www.hotelalabarda.it* 🛏 *18 rooms, 9 with bath* ⚲ *Internet; no a/c* ⊟ *AE, DC, MC, V.*

Nightlife & the Arts

The **opera** season in Trieste runs from October through May, with a brief operetta festival in July and August. Contact the **tourist information office** (⊠ Riva III Novembre 9 ☎ 040/3478312) or the **opera house** (⊠ Piazza Verdi 1 ☎ 040/6722111 ⊕ www.teatroverdi-trieste.com) for further details on events.

Shopping

Trieste's busy shopping street, **Corso Italia,** is reached from Piazza della Borsa. There are antiques markets on the streets of the city's old center on the third Sunday of each month. Trieste has some 60 antiques dealers, jewelers, and secondhand shops, and a large antiques fair is held in the city at the end of October.

VENETIAN ARC A TO Z

To research prices, get advice from other travelers, and book travel arrangements, visit www.fodors.com.

AIRPORTS

The main airport serving the Venetian Arc is Aeroporto Marco Polo, 10 km (6 mi) north of Venice, which handles international and domestic flights to the region. A few European airlines schedule flights to Aeroporto Valerio Catullo, southwest of Verona; it's also served by a number of charter flights. A regular bus service connects the airport with Verona's Porta Nuova railway station.

Treviso's Aeroporto San Giuseppe, 5 km (3 mi) southeast of Treviso, 32 km (19 mi) north of Venice, is also served by charter flights (check www.ryanair.com for flights to and from London's Stansted airport). Flights to Treviso sometimes include transportation from the airport to Venice or other destinations; otherwise there is an ACTT local bus service to Treviso every 30 minutes during the day (until 9 PM), or a taxi will come to the airport to pick you up from Treviso, only 6 km (4 mi) away. There are domestic and some European flights (including a daily Ryanair London service) to Aeroporto Ronchi dei Legionari, 35 km (22 mi) northwest of Trieste, linked with the Piazza della Libertà bus station (right by Trieste's central railway station) by regular APT bus service, or you can take the more convenient *servizio navetta* (shuttle).

🔲 Airport Information **Aeroporto Marco Polo** ☎ 041/2609260 or 041/2609240 ⊕ www.veniceairport.it. **Aeroporto Valerio Catullo di Verona Villafranca** ⊠ 11 km [7 mi] southwest of Verona ☎ 045/8095666 ⊕ www.aeroportoverona.it. **Aeroporto Ronchi dei Legionari** ☎ 0481/773224 ⊕ www.aeroporto.fvg.it. **Aeroporto San Giuseppe** ☎ 0422/315111.

🔲 Taxis & Shuttles **APT** ☎ 0481/593511 ⊕ www.aptgorizia.it. **Servizio Navetta** ☎ 348/4135865 ⊕ www.aeroporto.fvg.it. **Taxi** ☎ 0422/431515 automated system in Italian.

BUS TRAVEL

There are interurban and interregional connections throughout the Veneto and Friuli. Local tourist offices may be able to provide details of timetables and routes; otherwise contact the local bus station or, in some cases, the individual bus companies operating from the station, listed below.

🚍 Bus Information **ACTT buses** ✉ Piazzale Duca D'Aosta 25, Treviso ☎ 0422/327253. **ACTV buses** ✉ Piazzale Roma, Venice ☎ 041/5287886 buses to Brenta Riviera ⊕ www. actv.it. **APTV buses** ✉ Autostazione di Verona Porta Nuova, Piazzale XXV Aprile, Verona ☎ 045/8057911 ⊕ www.aptv.it. **ATVO buses** ✉ Piazzale Roma, Venice ☎ 041/ 5205530 ⊕ www.atvo.it. **FTV buses** ✉ Piazzale della Stazione near Campo Marzio, Vicenza ☎ 0444/223115 ⊕ www.ftv.vi.it. **SITA buses** ✉ Piazzale Boschetti, Padua ☎ 049/8206844 ⊕ www.sita-on-line.it. **TT buses** ✉ Piazza della Libertà, Trieste ☎ 800/016675 ⊕ www.triestetrasporti.it.

CAR RENTAL

🚗 Local Agencies **Avis** ✉ Piazza Stazione 1 Padua ☎ 049/664198 ✉ Piazzale Duca D'Aosta 1, Treviso ☎ 0422/542287 ✉ Stazione Marittima, Molo dei Bersaglieri 3, Trieste ☎ 040/300820 ✉ Aeroporto Ronchi dei Legionari, Trieste ☎ 0481/777085 ✉ Viale Giacomo Leopardi 5/a, Udine ☎ 0432/501149 ✉ Stazione Ferroviaria Verona Porta Nuova, Verona ☎ 045/8006636 ✉ Viale Milano 88, Vicenza ☎ 0444/321622 **Europcar** ✉ Piazzale della Stazione 6, Padua ☎ 049/657877. **Hertz** ✉ Molo dei Bersaglieri 3, Trieste ☎ 040/3220098 ✉ Aeroporto Ronchi dei Legionari, Trieste ☎ 0481/777025 ✉ Via Francesco Crispi 17, Udine ☎ 0432/511211 ✉ Piazzale della Stazione 1-VI Padua ☎ 049/8752202 ✉ Stazione Ferroviaria Verona Porta Nuova, Verona ☎ 045/8000832 ✉ Stazione Ferroviaria Vicenza, Vicenza ☎ 0444/231728

CAR TRAVEL

The main access roads to the Venetian Arc from southern Italy are both linked to the A1 (Autostrada del Sole), which connects Bologna, Florence, and Rome. They are the A13, which culminates in Padua, and the A22, which passes through Verona running north–south. The road linking the region from east to west is the A4, the primary route from Milan to as far as Trieste, skirting Verona, Padua, and Venice along the way. The distance from Verona, in the west, to Trieste is 263 km (163 mi). Branches link the A4 with Treviso (A27), Pordenone (A28), and Udine (A23).

EMERGENCY
SERVICES ACI Emergency Service offers 24-hour roadside assistance.
🚗 **ACI dispatchers** ☎ 803/116.

EMERGENCIES

For first aid, dial the general emergency number (113) and ask for *pronto soccorso*. Be prepared to give your address. (If you can find a concierge or some other Italian-speaker to call on your behalf, do so, as not all 113 operators speak English.) All pharmacies post signs on the door with addresses of pharmacies that stay open at night, on Saturday afternoon, and on Sunday.
🚓 **Police, Ambulance, Fire** ☎ 113.

TOURS

Many of the best tours begin and end in Venice, because so much of the region is accessible from there. The Burchiello excursion boat makes an all-day villa tour along the Brenta River Canal; contact American Express for information. For those who prefer to go it alone, the most practical way is to hire a car for the day. Local tourist offices will be able to put you in contact with the Tourist Guides Association or provide you with a list of authorized guides, for whom there is an official tariff rate.
🚩 **American Express** ✉ Salizada San Moisè 1471, San Marco, Venice ☎ 041/5200844 🖨 041/5229937. **Association of Trieste Authorized Guides** ☎ 040/365248.

TRAIN TRAVEL

Trains on the main routes from the south stop almost hourly in Verona, Padua, and Venice. From northern Italy and the rest of Europe, trains usually enter via Milan or through Porta Nuova station in Verona. To the west of Venice, on the main line running across the north of Italy, are Padua (30 minutes from Venice), Vicenza (1 hour), and Verona (1½ hours); to the east is Trieste (2 hours). Local trains link Venice to Bassano del Grappa (1 hour), Padua to Bassano del Grappa (1 hour), Vicenza to Treviso (1 hour), and Udine to Trieste (1 hour). Treviso and Udine both lie on the main line from Venice to Tarvisio, on which Eurocity trains continue to Vienna and Prague. Call Trenitalia for information, or check out their Web site.

🚆 Train Information **Trenitalia** ☎ 892021 ⊕ www.trenitalia.com.

TRAVEL AGENCIES

🚆 Local Agent Referrals **American Express** ✉ Fabretto Viaggi/American Express, Via Risorgìmento 20, Padua ☎ 049/666133 ✉ Uvet American Express, Via Francia 5, Verona ☎ 045/505200

VISITOR INFORMATION

🚆 Tourist Information **Asolo** ✉ Piazza Gabriele D'Annunzio 2, 31011 ☎ 0423/529046. **Marostica** ✉ Piazza Castello 1, 36063 ☎ 0424/72127 ⊕ www.marosticaonline.it. **Padua** ✉ Stazione Ferroviaria Padova Centrale, 35100 ☎ 049/8767911 ⊕ www.apt.padova.it. **Treviso** ✉ Piazza Monte di Pietà 8, 31100 ☎ 0422/547632. **Trieste** ✉ Riva III Novembre 9, 34100 ☎ 040/3478312 ⊕ www.triestetourism.it. **Udine** ✉ Piazza I Maggio 6/7, 33100 ☎ 0432/295972. **Verona** ✉ Piazza Brà, 37100 ☎ 045/8068680 ✉ Stazione Ferroviaria Verona Porta Nuova, ☎ 045/8000861 ⊕ www.tourism.verona.it. **Vicenza** ✉ Piazza Giacomo Matteotti 12, 36100 ☎ 0444/320854 ⊕ www.ascom.vi.it/aptvicenza.

THE DOLOMITES: TRENTINO- ALTO ADIGE

3

FODOR'S CHOICE

Cortina d'Ampezzo
De la Poste, hotel, Cortina d'Ampezzo
Museo Archeologico dell'Alto Adige, Bolzano
Passeggiata Tappeiner, Merano

HIGHLY RECOMMENDED

RESTAURANTS   Hopfen & Co. (Bozner Bier), Bolzano
Le Due Spade, Trento
Sissi, Merano
Zür Kaiserkron, Bolzano

HOTELS   Accademia, Trento
Adler, Ortisei
Alpenhotel Ratsberg, Dobbiaco
Elephant, Bressanone
Grand Hotel Palace, Merano
Hotel Greif, Bolzano
Schloss Korb, Bolzano
Turm, Fiè allo Sciliar

SIGHTS   Brunico
Castello del Buonconsiglio, Trento
Madonna di Campiglio
Merano
Passo dello Stelvio
Palazzo Pretorio, Trento

Updated by
Ryan Bradley

THE VAST, MOUNTAINOUS DOMAIN of northeastern Italy, unlike other famous Alpine ranges, has remained relatively undeveloped. The virginal landscape is a playground for outdoor sports: ski fanatics travel across the world to take on the steep slopes that have tested Olympic champions, and mountaineers scale the sheer rock faces. Subtler thrills can be enjoyed from a distance at dusk, when the last rays of sun create a pink hue that blends into purple: the *enrosadira*(the use of this word is, fittingly, reserved for the Dolomites). In the lowland valleys you'll find secluded villages, picture-book castles, and rustic bridges spanning rivers.

The Dolomites, sprawling over the Trentino-Alto Adige region and into parts of Lombardy by the Swiss border and the Veneto along the Austrian border, became known to Americans as a winter sports center after Cortina d'Ampezzo gained fame as host of the 1956 Winter Olympics. Today, scores of funiculars and chairlifts provide access to 1,200 km (750 mi) of ski runs, as well as ski jumps and bobsled runs.

Less accessible are the strange, rocky pinnacles themselves—which jut straight up like chimneys and look in places more like Utah's Monument Valley than any European ranges—looming over scattered, isolated mountain lakes. From plateaus atop the highest mountains, in the "untouchable zones" reached only after arduous hours of climbing beyond the lifts' end, you can see Italy on one side and Austria or Switzerland on the other. It's perhaps not surprising that Reinhold Messner, the first man to climb Everest without oxygen, lives in the Dolomites.

Called "the most beautiful work of architecture ever seen" by Le Corbusier, this expansive land of rocks and valleys is marked by a profusion of brilliant colors, as well as a variety of man-made architectural styles and several languages. A walk through the valleys can become a botanical escapade, with rare plant species abounding; high above you on the cliffs, ancient castles share the terrain with bears, deer, mountain goats, and birds of prey.

Straddling the Brenner Pass—the main access point between Italy and central Europe—the Dolomites play host to a mixture of cultures. Too often overlooked by travelers through the Brenner Pass are the picturesque and prosperous Alpine towns of Trento, Bolzano, and Merano. All three are marked by a departure in architectural style, with surrounding mountains serving as a backdrop for onion-bulb roofs and jutting spires uncharacteristic of the rest of Italy. The people of Alto Adige are predominantly German-speaking, and their crafts and food have an Austrian accent (until World War I, the area was Austria's South Tirol); in Bolzano and Merano you will get a chance to practice your German. (The region of Trentino, on the other hand, is largely Italian-speaking.) Pastry shops; dark, lively beer halls; frigid winter temperatures; a hearty meat-and-dumpling cuisine; and an earlier daily schedule round out the Austro-German influence.

Reflecting the diversity of this part of Italy, the area since 1848 has enjoyed special status as the Autonomous Region of Trentino-Alto Adige, made up of the independent provinces of Trento and Bolzano. And there is still another language to be heard in the area: Ladin, an offshoot of Latin still spoken by a small community primarily in the Val Gardena. The language can credit centuries of isolation in mountain strongholds for its survival. Signs throughout much of the Dolomites are bilingual. Place-names are given in Italian with German equivalents, where useful, in parentheses below.

Mountain roads are generally of excellent quality and well maintained, but in winter are often covered in snow and buffeted by high winds. Closures can begin as early as November and continue until May, in particular on the high mountain passes such as Passo di Gavia and Passo dello Stelvio.

Numbers in the text correspond to numbers in the margin and on the Dolomites: Trentino-Alto Adige and Bolzano maps.

If you have 3 days

Book two nights in ▦ **Bolzano** ⓻–⓬ �; explore the town on your first day, and on your second, start off early to **Trento** ❶. After a short tour continue south to **Rovereto** ❷ and **Riva del Garda** on the tip of Lake Garda, then on to the quaint towns of **Pinzolo** ❸ and **Madonna di Campiglio** ❹ for a bird's-eye view of the Dolomites. You'll have a scenic drive back via Dimaro to Bolzano. On your last day, make for the historic resort of ▦ **Cortina d'Ampezzo** ⓴. Choose to get there via the Great Dolomites Road or the quicker route arching through **Bressanone** ⓱ and **Brunico** ⓲.

If you have 5 days

Start with the three-day itinerary, but after **Madonna di Campiglio** ❹, swing west and head for the dizzyingly high Passo di Gavia and then down to the small town of ▦ **Bormio** ❺. The third day proceed to the breathtaking **Passo dello Stelvio** ❻ and on down to **Naturno** ⓭ before stopping in one of the pearls of the Alto Adige region, **Merano** ⓮. Spend your third night again in ▦ **Bolzano** ⓻–⓬. The next day head for **Cornedo** ⓯, **Chiusa** ⓰, and **Bressanone** ⓱. Move on to the resort ▦ **Cortina d'Ampezzo** ⓴. The next day head to **Canazei** ㉑ via the beautiful Passo di Sella and on to **Ortisei** ㉒, in the heart of the Val Gardena. Return to Bolzano via **Fiè allo Sciliar** ㉓.

If you have 8 days

Follow the five-day itinerary as far as ▦ **Bressanone** ⓱. The following day stroll through **Brunico** ⓲ and **Dobbiaco** ⓳ before moving on to ▦ **Cortina d'Ampezzo** ⓴ for the night. From here follow the Grande Strada delle Dolomiti through the Passo di Falzarego and slightly north through the Passo di Sella and into the Val Gardena and ▦ **Ortisei** ㉒. On the last day, drive to **Fiè allo Sciliar** ㉓ and south on the A22. Just south of Cornedo, turn left onto the S241 to get to **Lago di Carezza** ㉕. Continue along the road until you reach Vigo di Fassa, veering south onto the S48, passing through the small towns of Predazzo, Cavalese, and Ora, until you rejoin the A22 and continue south back to Trento.

Exploring the Dolomites

The only way to get around in this mountainous region is by following the river valleys as they carve their courses through the Dolomite massifs. Two of the most important are formed by the Isarco and Adige rivers: the Isarco begins at the Brenner Pass and runs due south to Bolzano, where it joins the Adige (which originates near the Swiss border and passes Verona on its way to the Adriatic Sea). Italy's main road and rail connections to central Europe follow these rivers northward en route to the Brenner Pass. Note that it's difficult to reach the ski areas—or any town outside of Rovereto, Trento, Bolzano, and Merano—without a car.

The Dolomites:
Trentino-
Alto Adige

AUSTRIA

SWITZ.

LOMBARDY

TRENTINO

VENETO

FRIULI-
VENEZIA
GIULIA

TO INNSBRUCK

Brenner
Pass

Vipiteno

Tirolo

Merano **14**

Naturno **13**

Lana

Gargazzone

Silandro

Spondigna

Glorenza

VAL VENOSTA

PARCO
NAZIONALE
DELLO STELVIO

Passo dello
Stelvio **6**

Bormio **5**

Passo di Gavia

S300

Dimaro

Madonna
di Campiglio **4**

Pinzolo **3**

ALTO ADIGE

Bressanone **17**

Chiusa **16**

Fiè allo
Sciliar

Ortisei **22**

Santa
Maddalena

VAL GARDENA

Cornedo **23**

Fiè allo Sciliar **15**

Col Rodella

Lago di
Carezza **25**

Campitello
di Fassa

Vigo di
Fassa

Predazzo

San Martino

Cavalese

Ora

Missiano

Caldaro **24**

Bolzano
7 - **12**
see detail
map

Talvera

Adige

PUSTERIA

Brunico **18**

Dobbiaco **19**

Sesto

Misurina

L. Misurina

Cortina
d'Ampezzo **20**

Pieve di
Cadore

Bellu...

Passo di
Falzarego

Corvara

Arabba

Passo di
Sella

Canazei **21**

S49

S49

S44

S44

S38

S38

S40

S42

S42

S48

S48

S48

S48

S51

S51

S50

S203

S242

S12

S12

S241

S244

S49

A22

A22

A22

S43

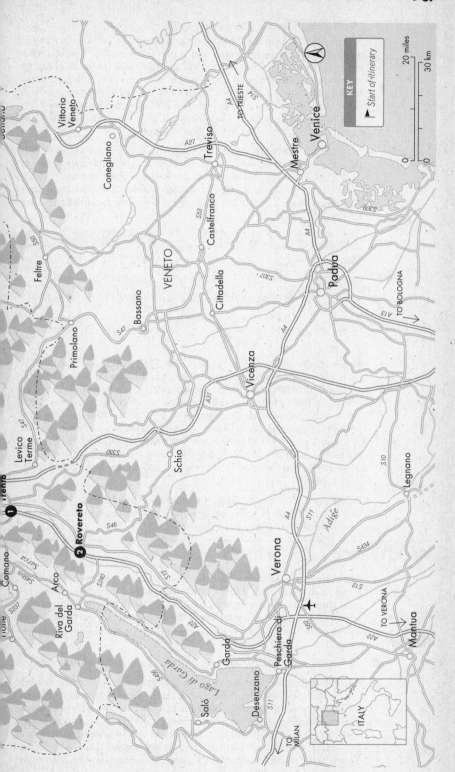

KEY
▲ *Start of itinerary*

20 miles
30 km

ITALY

Venice
Mestre
Treviso
A27
Conegliano
Vittorio Veneto
Feltre
S50
Primolano
S47
Bassano
VENETO
Castelfranco
S53
Cittadella
S307
Padua
A4
TO BOLOGNA
A13
Vicenza
A31
Schio
S350
Levico Terme
S47
Trento ①
Rovereto ②
S46
S240
S12
Arco
S45bis
S421ca
Comano
S237
Riva del Garda
S45
Salò
Lago di Garda
Garda
Desenzano
S11
Peschiera di Garda
S65
TO MILAN
S11
Verona
Adige
S11
A4
S10
Legnano
S434
S12
TO VERONA
Mantua
A22

About the Hotels & Restaurants

Accommodations in the Dolomites range from restored castles to spic-and-span chalet guest houses, from stately 19th-century hotels to chic modern ski resorts. Even a small village may have scores of places to stay, many of them very inexpensive. Hotel information offices at train stations and tourist offices can help you sidestep the language problem if you arrive without reservations. The Bolzano train station has a 24-hour hotel service, and tourist offices will give you a list of all the hotels in the area, arranged by location and price.

Many hotels in ski resorts cater primarily to longer stays at full or half board: it's wise to book ski vacations as packages in advance. Outside of the ski season, accommodations are easier to find, but reservations are still recommended. Nearly all rural accommodations close from early November to mid- or late December, as well as for a month or two after Easter.

	$$$$	$$$	$$	$	¢
WHAT IT COSTS In euros					
RESTAURANTS	over €22	€17–€22	€12–€17	€7–€12	under €7
HOTELS	over €210	€160–€210	€110–€160	€60–€110	under €60

Restaurant prices are for a second course (secondo piatto). Hotel prices are for two people in a standard double room in high season, including tax and service.

Timing

Skiers should plan their trip between mid-December and April, when most resorts are open. But powder hounds, beware: snowfall in early winter is unreliable; scrutinize snow reports if it's before mid- to late February. The Dolomites do not receive as much consistent snow as the Alps, and some years there is little snow all season. With the exception of the main bargain period known as *settimane bianche* (white weeks) in January and February, the slopes are relatively crowd-free. Booking well in advance of your ski holiday is highly recommended, as lack of snow in the early part of the season can sometimes cause overcrowding later on.

When autumn colors beautify the mountains and valleys, it's a tradition in South Tirol to make a tour of the cozy wine taverns to drink the new wine and eat hot roasted chestnuts.

WESTERN TRENTINO

The areas east and west of Trento are collectively known as Trentino, a region shaped roughly like a butterfly. Some of the passes in this region close during the winter months, so if you're traveling during this period you will not be able to follow the entire itinerary outlined above.

Trento

❶ *51 km (32 mi) south of Bolzano, 24 km (15 mi) north of Rovereto.*

Capital of the autonomous Trentino province, Trento is a fashionable university town that retains an architectural charm befitting its historical importance. Its stunning Piazza del Duomo is splendidly preserved, and its enormous medieval palazzo dominates the city landscape in virtually original form. It was here, from 1545 to 1563, that the structure of the Catholic Church was redefined at the famous Council of Trent. This was the starting point of the Counter-Reformation, which brought

3

Cross-Country Skiing

The Dolomites are an ideal place to learn or improve your *sci di fondo* (cross-country skiing). The major Alpine resorts, and even many out-of-the-way villages, have trails (usually loops marked off by kilometers) for differing ability levels. Two of the best are at Ortisei and Dobbiaco. You can usually get permission to blaze trails across virgin snowfields by asking at the nearest farmhouse or inquiring at local tourist offices.

Downhill Skiing

The craggy peaks of the Dolomites offer some of the best—and arguably the most beautiful—downhill skiing in Europe, with the facilities to match. The season generally runs from late November to April, by which time some people prefer to ski in shirtsleeves. The early season often suffers from light snowfall, and the best conditions often aren't seen until late February. The most comprehensive centers are Cortina d'Ampezzo, in the heart of the Dolomites to the east of Bolzano, and Madonna di Campiglio, west of Trento. These resorts are unabashedly upscale with the extras you expect from world-class centers: miles of interconnecting runs linked by cable cars and lifts, plus skating rinks, heated indoor pools, and lively après-ski. Less-expensive, family-oriented adventures can be had at Val Gardena (northeast of Bolzano) and Alta Badia (south from Brunico).

Folk Festivals

Chief among the Dolomite's rich selection of folk festivals, harvest fairs, and religious celebrations is Trento's weeklong festival of San Vigilio held the last week of June, when marching bands and costumed choirs perform in the streets. Other major towns have similar festivals, but equally enjoyable are the more informal and low-key celebrations in the villages of the many valleys, sometimes amounting to nothing more than excuses for hardworking mountain farmers to get together for some wine and song.

Hiking & Climbing

The Dolomites have a well-maintained network of trails for hiking and rock climbing, with *rifugi* (huts) in both hiking terrain and near the most difficult ascents. At these spartan accommodations you can just refuel with a meal or stay overnight in a dormitory-style room. Routes are designated by grades of difficulty (T, tourist path; H, hiking path; EE for expert hikers; EEA, for equipped expert hikers). It's important to follow safety procedures, have the necessary equipment, and obtain the latest information on trails and conditions. Summer is the best time for hiking.

Shopping

Shopping is an event in the Dolomites, where larger towns such as Bolzano, Bressanone, and Brunico have stores clustered in arcaded streets that keep shoppers dry on rainy or snowy days. The ethnic mix, with its strong Tirolean influence, makes for local products and crafts that are quite different from those elsewhere in Italy. Tirolean clothing—loden goods, lederhosen, dirndls, and linen suits with horn buttons—is a good buy, costing less than in neighboring Austria. Local crafts, such as embroidered goods, wood carvings, figures for nativity scenes, pottery, and handcrafted copper and iron objects, make good gifts. And of course, Trento, Bolzano, and Merano in particular have no shortage of boutiques supplying the under-35 Italian dress code: jet-black and icy-gray designer clothes and accessories.

half of Europe back to Catholicism. You'll see the word *consiglio* (council) everywhere in Trento—in hotel, restaurant, and street names, and even on wine labels.

Free guided tours of Trento are given on Saturday by the local **tourist office** (✉ Via Manci 2 ☎ 0461/983880). Tours leave at 10 AM for a trip to the Castello del Buonconsiglio and at 3 PM for a tour of the city center.

The massive, low, Romanesque **Duomo,** also known as the Cathedral of San Virgilio, forms the southern edge of the Piazza del Duomo. Locals refer to this piazza as the city's *salotto,* or sitting room, as in fine weather it's always filled with students and residents drinking coffee, enjoying an aperitif, or reading the newspaper. A baroque **Fontana del Nettuno** presides over it all. When skies are clear, pause here to savor the view of the mountaintops enveloping the city.

Within the Duomo, unusual arcaded stone stairways border the austere nave. Ahead is the *baldacchino* (altar canopy), a clear copy of Bernini's masterpiece in St. Peter's in Rome. In the small *Cappella del Crocifisso* to the right is a mournful 15th-century crucifixion, with the Virgin Mary and John the Apostle. This crucifix, built by German artist Sixtus Frei, was a focal point of the Council of Trent: each decree agreed on during the two decades of deliberations was solemnly read out in front of it. Outside, walk around to the back of the cathedral to see an exquisite display of 14th-century stonemasons' art, from the small porch to the intriguing knotted columns on the graceful apse.

★ The crenellated **Palazzo Pretorio,** which is situated so as to seem like a wing of the Duomo, was built in the 13th century as the fortified residence of the prince-bishops, who enjoyed considerable power and autonomy within the medieval hierarchy. The remarkable Palazzo has lost none of its original splendor. The crenellations are not merely decorative: the square pattern represents ancient allegiance to the Guelphs (the triangular crenellations seen elsewhere in town represent Ghibelline loyalty). The Palazzo houses the **Museo Diocesano Tridentino,** where you can see paintings showing the seating plan of the prelates during the Council of Trent; early 16th-century tapestries by Pieter van Aelst, the Belgian artist who carried out Raphael's 15th-century designs for the Vatican tapestries; carved wood altars and statues; and an 11th-century sacramentary, or book of services. These and other precious objects all come from the cathedral's treasury. Within the Duomo grounds, and accessible through the museum, is an **archaeological area,** displaying ancient ruins of a 6th-century Christian basilica and a gate dating from the 9th century. ✉ *Piazza del Duomo 18* ☎ *0461/234419* 🖾 *€3, includes archaeological area* 🕐 *Mon.–Sat. 9:30–12:30 and 2:30–6.*

Many sessions of the Council of Trent met at the Renaissance church **Santa Maria Maggiore.** Limited light enters through the simple rose window over the main door, so you'll have to strain to see the magnificent ceiling, an intricate combination of stucco and frescoes. The church is off the northwest side of the Piazza del Duomo, about 650 ft down Via Cavour. ✉ *Via Cavour* 🕐 *Daily 8:30–noon and 2:30–8.*

Locals refer to **Via Belenzani** as Trento's outdoor gallery because of the frescoed facades of the hallmark Renaissance palazzi. It's an easy 50-yd walk up the lane behind the church of Santa Maria Maggiore.

★ **Castello del Buonconsiglio** (Castle of Good Counsel) was once the stronghold of the prince-bishops; its position and size made it easier to defend than the Palazzo Pretorio. As you face it, you can see the evolution of architectural styles, starting with the medieval fortifications

ON THE MENU

The Dolomite region combines Italian cuisine with local Tirolean specialties, which are much like the dishes of Austria and central Europe. Alimentari (food shops) stock a bounty of regional cheeses, pickles, salami, and smoked meats—perfect for picnics—and bakeries turn out a wide selection of crusty dark rolls and caraway-studded rye breads. The best of the cheeses are the mild asiago and fontal and the more pungent puzzone di Moena (literally, "stinkpot").

Local dishes vary from one isolated mountain valley to the next. Don't miss speck (smoked ham). Other specialties include canederli, or knoedel, a type of dumpling with many variations, served either in broth or with a sauce; würstel and sauerkraut; ravioli made from rye flour, stuffed with spinach, and fried; and apple or pear strudel. The local wine vintages (and fruit brandies) are delicious.

of the Castelvecchio section on the far left, down to the more decorative Renaissance **Magno Palazzo,** built three centuries later in 1530. The Castello now houses the **Museo Provinciale d'Arte** (Provincial Art Museum), where permanent and visiting exhibits of art and archaeology are displayed in frescoed medieval halls or under Renaissance coffered ceilings. The 13th-century **Torre dell'Aquila** (Eagle's Tower) holds the highlight of the museum, a 15th-century *Ciclo dei Mesi* (Cycle of the Months). This four-walled fresco is full of charming and detailed scenes of medieval life in both court and countryside. An escorted walk through the castle walls is required to visit the tower; you'll need to follow the signs and ask someone in the small office to take you up. ⊠ *Via Bernardo Clesio 5* ☎ *0461/233770* ⊕ *www.buonconsiglio.it* ☎ *€5* ⊙ *Tues.–Sun. 9–noon and 2–5* ☞ *Admission and hrs vary when exhibitions are held.*

The emphasis of the **Museo Storico in Trento** (Trento Historical Museum), housed in the former joiner's shop inside the castle walls, is on modern Trentino history, with dioramas and displays about the region from the unification of Italy in 1861 up to and including World War II. ⊠ *Via Bernardo Clesio 3* ☎ *0461/230482* ☎ *Free with admission to the castle* ⊙ *Tues.–Sun. 9–noon and 2–5.*

The **Torre Verde** (Green Tower; ⊠ Piazza Raffaello Sanzio, near the castle), is part of Trento's 13th-century fortifications, standing alongside other fragments of the city walls. The **Torre Vanga** (⊠ Via Torre Vanga, near the river) dates from the 13th century and guards the medieval bridge Ponte San Lorenzo, which crosses the Adige River. A cable car (€2 round-trip) leaves from the bridge to the lookout point **Belvedere di Sardagna,** 1,200 ft above Trento.

The collections of the **Museo d'Arte Moderna e Contemporanea di Trento** are installed in a Renaissance villa next to the Adige River. Works date from the 19th and 20th centuries; rotating exhibitions display the work of contemporary artists. ⊠ *Palazzo delle Albere, Via Ruggero da Sanseverino 45* ☎ *0461/234860* ⊕ *www.mart.tn.it* ☎ *€4* ⊙ *Tues.–Sun. 10–6.*

off the beaten path

LEVICO TERME – About 20 km (13 mi) southeast of Trento and just east of the summer resorts of Lago di Caldonazzo is the Levico Terme, a medieval *terme* (thermal bath) town in the Val Sugana. This valley enclave was inhabited by the Celts and then conquered by the Romans; the Latin-derived Ladin is still spoken today. Settle into a hotel for summer sports and relaxation.

Where to Stay & Eat

$$ ✕ **Chiesa.** Near the castle, a 15th-century building conceals a bright, modern restaurant that attracts romancing couples and power lunchers alike. Ubiquitous apple imagery and excellent risotto *alle mele* (with apples) celebrate the local produce—there's even a set meal featuring apples in every course. Otherwise, the food is traditional: specialties are *maccheroncini con salsiccia e verze* (short, narrow pasta tubes with sausage and cabbage) and *tonco de Pontesel* (a stew of mixed meat made according to a 15th-century recipe). Reservations are recommended. ✉ *Via San Marco 64* ☎ *0461/238766* ▭ *AE, DC, MC, V* ⊘ *Closed Sun.*

★ $$–$$$ ✕ **Le Due Spade.** This Tirolean tavern near the Duomo offers superb, locally inspired food, able service, and the warmth of wood paneling and an antique stove. You can sample traditional *gnocchetti di ricotta* (ricotta cheese dumplings) and such savory *secondi*as *tagliata di Angus alla griglia* (grilled slivers of beef) served with an aromatic herb sauce. Given its deserved popularity with locals and limited seating, reservations are a must. ✉ *Via Rizzi 11* ☎ *0461/234343* ⚐ *Reservations essential* ▭ *AE, DC, MC, V* ⊘ *Closed Sun. No lunch Mon.*

¢ ✕ **Pizzeria Laste.** Owner Guido Rizzi invented pizza Calabrese, a white pizza with garlic, mozzarella, and hot red-pepper flakes. He's a deserving national pizza-making champion; each of his 35 pies—including the *sedano* (mozzarella, celery root, *grana* cheese, oregano)—is delectable. Save room for dessert: pizza *dolce,* with bananas, strawberries, kiwi, and caramel. The pizzeria is housed in a pleasant villa in the hills above the city center. ✉ *Via alle Laste 39, Cognola* ☎ *0461/231570* ▭ *MC, V* ⊘ *Closed Tues.*

$$ ✕▥ **Castel Pergine.** This hilltop 13th-century castle, appropriated by Trento's prince-bishops in the 16th-century, and now skillfully managed by the Austrian-Swiss Schneider-Neffs, is 12 km (7½ mi) east of Trento. Amid the labyrinth of stone and brick chambers, prisons, and chapels you'll find sparse, rustic rooms with carved-wood trim, lace curtains, and heavy wooden beds, some canopied. The grounds often have brightly colored modern-art installations. The popular candlelit restaurant serves ages-old seasonal recipes from Trento in lighter guises. ✉ *38057 Pergine Val Sugana* ☎ *0461/531158* 🖷 *0461/531329* ⊕ *www.castelpergine.it* ⌔ *21 rooms, 14 with bath* ⚒ *Restaurant, horseback riding, bar, library* ▭ *AE, DC, MC, V* ⊘ *Closed Nov.–Mar. No lunch Mon.*

$$$ ▥ **Boscolo Grand Hotel Trento.** Its contemporary rounded facade amid ancient palaces makes this hotel on Piazza Dante an anomaly. Inside, it has lush modern appointments, from the marble and woodwork in the lobby and lounges to the Clesio restaurant's rich drapery. Rooms are ample, with thick carpets and clubby, wood-trim furniture. ✉ *Via Alfieri 1, 38100* ☎ *0461/271000* 🖷 *0461/271001* ⊕ *www.grandtrento. boscolohotels.com* ⌔ *121 rooms, 15 suites* ⚒ *Restaurant, minibars, cable TV, sauna, bar, meeting rooms, laundry service, parking (fee)* ▭ *AE, DC, MC, V.*

$$$ ▥ **Imperial Grand Hotel Terme.** For spa treatment and modern comforts, choose this graciously restored estate—formerly home to Austrian nobility—in the nearby spa town of Levico Terme (20 km [12 mi] east of Trento). It has a beautiful indoor pool, a garden, and a fine Tuscan restaurant. ✉ *Via Silva Domini 1, 38056 Levico Terme* ☎ *0461/706104* 🖷 *0461/706350* ⊕ *www.imperialhotel.it* ⌔ *81 rooms* ⚒ *Restaurant, cable TV, 2 pools (1 indoor), gym, sauna, meeting rooms, free parking* ▭ *AE, DC, MC, V* ⊘ *Closed Nov.–Mar.*

★ $$ ▥ **Accademia.** This friendly character-filled hotel occupies an ancient house in the historic center of Trento, close to Piazza del Duomo. Framed by

a beautiful arched entryway, the public rooms retain the ancient vaulting, but the bedrooms are modern and comfortably equipped. There's
a courtyard garden. ☒ *Vicolo Colico 4/6, 38100* ☎ *0461/233600*
🖷 *0461/230174* ⊕ *www.accademiahotel.it* ☞ *41 rooms, 2 suites*
⌂ *Restaurant, minibars, meeting rooms* ⊟ *AE, DC, MC, V* ⊘ *Closed
Dec. 24–Jan. 6.*

$$ ▦ **Buonconsiglio.** Near the train station, this elegant hotel offers well-
kept, sizable rooms and efficient service, perfect for the business trav-
eler. The public spaces are decorated with modern art. ☒ *Via Romagnosi
18, 38100* ☎*0461/272888* 🖷*0461/272889* ⊕*www.hotelbuonconsiglio.
it* ☞ *46 rooms, 2 suites* ⌂ *Restaurant, in-room safes, minibars, cable
TV, bar, meeting rooms, parking (fee)* ⊟ *AE, DC, MC, V* ⊘ *Closed 2
wks mid-Aug.*

$ ▦ **Aquila d'Oro.** This small hotel offers comfort, efficiency, and a prime
location steps from Piazza del Duomo. Most rooms have nondescript
contemporary furniture in somber colors. The friendly owner can offer
good suggestions for what to see, do, and eat while in town. ☒ *Via Be-
lenzani 76, 38100* ☎☎ *0461/986282* ⊕ *www.aquiladoro.it* ☞ *20
rooms* ⌂ *Bar* ⊟ *AE, DC, MC, V* ⊘ *Closed Dec. 23–Jan. 7.*

Nightlife & the Arts

FESTIVALS From late June to late September, a regional **Superfestival** highlights his-
toric castles as venues for performances and evocations of fact and leg-
end. The festival includes music, costumes, banquets, and train excursions
to the castles. The **Festivale di Musica Sacra** (Sacred Music Festival;
☎ 0462/983880)—a monthlong series of concerts held in Trentino's
churches—takes place in May and June.

A summer bonus is the weeklong **Festive Vigiliane,** a spectacular pageant
in the Piazza del Duomo, culminating on June 26, when townspeople
don medieval clothing in honor of their patron saint. Since 1936 the June
wine festival **Mostra dei Vini** (☎ 0461/983880) has attracted every Bac-
chus, from farmers of surrounding hillside towns to sommeliers from
all over Italy. The weeklong festival includes tastings, tours, and prizes.
In July and August, wine buffs can take part in the **Vinum Bonum** (☎ 0461/
822820) program offering music and wine tastings for €8 at different
cellars in Trentino each Tuesday, Thursday, and Friday from 4:30 to 7.

I Suoni delle Dolomiti, held in June and July, offer the idyllic experience
of chamber music played in grassy meadows, echoing through the
mountain air. This series of free concerts is held at refuges high in the
hills of Trentino. For more information, contact the Trento APT (☎ 0461/
983880).

Shopping

MARKETS The **Enoteca di Corso** (☒ Corso 3 Novembre 54) is an extraordinary shop
laden with local products, including cheese, salami, and wine. The small
morning **Mercato di Piazza Lodron** is held in Piazza Allessandro Vittoria,
where you can pick up meats, cheeses, produce, local truffles, and
porcini mushrooms. A number of pleasant souvenir shops and glassware
outlets line **Via Manci,** near the church of Santa Maria Maggiore. A flea
market is held in **Piazza Garzetti** on the second Sunday of every month,
except in January and August.

WOODEN CRAFTS **Il Pozzo** (☒ Piazza Pasi 14/l) sells excellent handcrafted wooden objects.
& CERAMICS **Il Laboratorio** (☒ Via Roma 12) specializes in terra-cotta pieces molded
by local artists. **Galleria Trentino Art** (☒ Via Belenzani, 43/45) offers tra-
ditional Trentino handicrafts.

Rovereto

② *24 km (15 mi) south of Trento, 75 km (47 mi) south of Bolzano.*

A 15th-century castle looks down on this medieval town in the main north–south valley of the Adige. Some of the fiercest fighting of World War I took place in the wooded hills around Rovereto, with Italian and Austrian troops bogged down in prolonged and costly conflict. Every evening at nightfall you're reminded of the thousands who fell by the ringing of the *Campana dei Caduti* (Bell of the Fallen). Today, Rovereto is a noble, peaceful city filled with young families. Crumbling pastel-color medieval villas inhabit long-shadowed piazzas and winding streets.

need a break? Weathered wine barrels are used as tables at **Bacchus** (⊠ Via Garibaldi 29 ☎ No phone), where you can enjoy an excellent selection of local wines by the glass. Better yet, find a spot at the bar and ask for a bitter *negroni sbagliato* to be ladled out of the largest wine glass you've ever laid eyes upon (in addition to the usual Campari, gin, and vermouth, this "mistaken" negroni also includes vodka, oranges, and other undisclosed ingredients).

The **Museo Storico Italiano Della Guerra** (Italian Historical War Museum) was founded after World War I to commemorate the conflict—and to warn against repeating its atrocities. It remains an authoritative exhibition of artifacts from the Great War; a highlight is the artillery collection housed in a former air-raid shelter. ⊠ *Via Castelbarco 7* ☎ *0464/438100* ⊠ *€5.20* ☉ *Mar.–June and Oct.–Nov., Tues.–Sun. 8:30–12:30 and 2–6; July–Sept., Tues.–Fri. 10–6, weekends 9:30–6:30.*

The paintings of native son Fortunato Depero (1892–1960), a prominent futurist, are found throughout town. There's a good selection of his work at the **Archivio del '900**, where you'll also find works by Severini and Mazzoni as well as rotating exhibits. ⊠ *Corso Rosmini 58* ☎ *0464/438887* ⊕ *www.mart.tn.it* ⊠ *€4* ☉ *Tues.–Sun. 9–12:30 and 2:30–6.*

Where to Stay & Eat

$$$–$$$$ ✕ **Ristorante Al Borgo.** Renowned throughout Italy for its creative cuisine, Al Borgo has a modernist take on classics, even on the simple *tagliolini ai frutti di mare* (long ribbons of pasta with shellfish). Trentino specialties on the menu might include *strangola preti* (literally "priest-chokers," a heavy pasta dish). In fall, you might find *polentina* with a fondue of Trentino cheeses and truffle. The restaurant's interior is elegant and calm, with attractive art adorning the walls. ⊠ *Via Garibaldi 13* ☎ *0464/436300* ⚘ *Reservations essential* ⊟ *AE, DC, MC, V* ☉ *Closed Mon., 1 wk in mid-Jan., 3 wks in July, closed Sun. in Aug. No dinner Sun.*

$–$$ ✕⌑ **Hotel Rovereto.** This modern, central hotel capably hosts international travelers and its airy, candlelit Ristorante Novecento ($–$$$) is one of the city's most appealing restaurants. Marco and Fausto Zani preside over the hotel's welcoming public spaces and warm-color rooms and their mother Wanda cooks. Luscious dishes, paired with local wines, include *tortelli con fonduta di formaggi* (pasta squares with spinach and ricotta in a butter sauce) and *quaglia con finferli e polenta* (quail with wild mushrooms and polenta). ⊠ *Corso Rosmini 82/d, 38068* ☎ *0464/435222* 🖷 *0464/439644* ⊕ *www.hotelrovereto.it* ⌑ *49 rooms* ⚬ *Restaurant, in-room safes, minibars, meeting rooms, parking (fee)* ⊟ *AE, DC, MC, V* ☉ *Closed mid-Jan.–Feb. Restaurant closed Sun. and Aug.*

Nightlife & the Arts

The **Rovereto Oriente Occidente Festival** (☎ 0464/452159) in early September offers modern dance and art exhibitions. Late September brings the **Festival Internazionale W. A. Mozart** (☎ 0464/439988), with classical performances at the exquisite **Teatro Zandonai** (⊠ Corso Bettini 82 ☎ 0464/452159).

en route | Traveling south from Rovereto, head west on S240, passing the lovely town of Riva del Garda, and then north on S45 bis to Comano, a small, locally renowned spa. The road continues to Tione, a small farming community. From here, head north on S239 to reach Pinzolo.

Pinzolo

❸ *75 km (47 mi) northwest of Rovereto, 59 km (37 mi) northwest of Trento.*

Just north of the small mountain village of Pinzolo (on S239), stop at the church of **San Virgilio** to see the remarkable 16th-century fresco on the exterior south wall. Painted in 1539 by the artist Simone Baschenis, the painting describes the Dance of Death: a macabre parade of 40 sinners from all walks of life (in roughly descending order of worldly importance), each guided to his end by a ghoulish escort. Unfortunately, the church's interior is closed to the public.

Madonna di Campiglio

★ ❹ *14 km (9 mi) north of Pinzolo, 88 km (55 mi) southwest of Bolzano.*

The chichi winter resort of Madonna di Campiglio has surpassed Cortina d'Ampezzo as the most fashionable place to ski and be seen in the Dolomites. Madonna's popularity is well deserved, with more than 130 km (80 mi) well-groomed ski runs served by 39 lifts. The resort itself is at 5,000 ft altitude, and some of the ski runs, summer hiking paths, and mountain-biking routes venture onto the surrounding peaks, including Pietra Grande, more than 9,700 ft up. An excursion to the Punta Spinale (Spinale Peak) on the year-round cable car affords magnificent views of the Brenta Dolomites.

Where to Stay

$$$$ ⊞ **Golf Hotel.** You'll need to make your way up to Campo Carlo Magno, the famous pass north of town, to reach this grand hotel, the former summer residence of Habsburg emperor Franz Josef. A modern wing has been added, but old-world charm persists: rooms 114 and 214 still exhibit the lavish imperial style. The rest of the resort is replete with verandas, Persian rugs, and bay windows. In summer the golf course attracts a tony crowd. Note that the hotel offers only half- or full-board packages. ⊠ *Via Cima Tosa 3, 38084* ☎ *0465/441003* 🖷 *0465/440294* ⊕ *www.golfhotelcampiglio.it* 🖙 *107 rooms, 8 suites* ⚭ *Restaurant, minibars, cable TV, 9-hole golf course, bar, convention center, free parking* 🗟 *AE, DC, MC, V* ☉ *Closed May–mid-June and mid-Sept.–Nov.* ⑩l *FAP, MAP.*

$$$$ ⊞ **Savoia Palace.** This central hotel is one of the more traditional at the resort, full of carved-wood and mountain-style furnishings. Two fireplaces blaze away in the bar, where you can relax as you recall the day's exploits on the ski slopes. The elegant restaurant serves a mixture of local specialties and rich dishes drawing on Italian and Austrian influences. Full or half board is required. ⊠ *Viale Dolomiti di Brenta 18, 38084* ☎ *0465/441004* 🖷 *0465/440549* ⊕ *www.savoiapalace.com*

↻ *55 rooms* ♿ *Restaurant, in-room safes, minibars, cable TV, bar* 🖃 *AE, DC, MC, V* ⊘ *Closed Apr.–June and mid-Sept.–mid-Dec.* ⦿| *FAP, MAP.*

$$$ 🏨 **Grifone.** A comfortable Alpine lodge that catches the sun, the Grifone has a distinctive wood facade, flower-decorated balconies, and rooms with views of the forested slopes. The restaurant serves home cooking as well as international dishes. The hotel is south of the lake, a bit out of town, but the Spinale cable car is nearby. Half or full board is required. ⊠ *Via Vallesinella 7, 38084* ☎ *0465/442002* 🖷 *0465/440540* ⊕ *www.hotelgrifone.it* ↻ *40 rooms* ♿ *Restaurant, in-room safes, cable TV, bar, free parking* 🖃 *AE, DC, MC, V* ⊘ *Closed May and June and Sept.–Nov.* ⦿| *FAP, MAP.*

Sports & the Outdoors

GOLF On **Campo Carlo Magno** (☎ 0465/441003) is a 9-hole course, set in the mountains near Madonna di Campiglio, open from July through mid-September.

HIKING The local **tourist office** (⊠ Via Pradalago 4 ☎ 0465/442000) supplies maps of a dozen treks leading to waterfalls, lakes, and stupefying views.

SKIING **Madonna di Campiglio** offers some of the best skiing in the Dolomites, with kilometers of interconnecting runs linked by cable cars and lifts, a quite respectable vertical drop, and plenty of off-piste opportunities. Advanced skiers will delight in the extremely difficult terrain found on certain mountain faces accessible from town, and there are also many intermediate and beginner runs. Madonna's cachet as the ski resort of choice among young Italians is evident in its increasingly well-organized lodging, skiing, and trekking facilities. Ski passes (€32) can be purchased at the *funivia* (cable car) in town. ☎ *0465/447744* ⊕ *www.campiglio.to.*

en route Just a couple of miles north of Madonna di Campiglio is one of the highest points in the Dolomites, the **Campo Carlo Magno** pass. This is where Charlemagne is said to have stopped in AD 800 on his way to Rome to be crowned emperor. Stop here to glance over the whole of northern Italy. Resume your descent with caution (in the space of a mile or so, you will descend more than 2,000 ft via hairpin turns and switchbacks). Turn left at Dimaro and continue 37 km (23 mi) east to Ponte di Legno through another high pass, **Passo del Tonale** (5,600 ft). Here turn right on S300 and, passing the so-called Black Lake on your left, head for Bormio, the famous Lombard skiing center, through the **Passo di Gavia,** which also must be approached carefully.

Bormio

❺ *20 km (12 mi) south of Passo dello Stelvio, 100 km (60 mi) southwest of Merano.*

At the foot of the Stelvio Pass, in the Valtellina, Bormio is one of the most famous ski resorts on the western side of the Dolomites, with 38 km (24 mi) of long pistes and a 5,000-ft-plus vertical drop. With an altitude of close to 4,000 ft Bormio has clean, fresh air that in summer draws Italians escaping the humidity of the cities. There are plenty of shops, restaurants, and hotels throughout the town. Bormio has been known for the therapeutic qualities of its waters since the Roman era, so you'll also find numerous spas.

Though it has multiple entrances, Bormio is a good place to enter the Alps' biggest national park, the **Parco Nazionale dello Stelvio,** spread over 1,350 square km (520 square mi) and four provinces. Opened in 1935 with the express intent to preserve flora and protect fauna, today it thrives, with more than 1,200 types of plants—not to mention 600 different mushrooms—and more than 160 species of animals, including the chamois, ibex, and roe deer. ⊠ *S38* ☎ *0342/910100* ⊕ *www.parks.it/parco. nazionale.stelvio* 🎟 *Free.*

Where to Stay

$$$ 🏨 **Posta.** Ostelli della Posta hotels, stagecoach inns of days gone by, are a time-honored tradition in northern Italy. The reception and atmosphere of this town-center hotel, with its warm wood detail in the low-vaulted areas, help to temper the cold. Rooms are cozy and comfortable, with heavy drapery and bed linens. Perks include a small health club with a pool, sauna, gym, and Turkish bath—and a shuttle bus to the slopes. ⊠ *Via Roma 66, 23032* ☎ *0342/904753* 🖶 *0342/904484* ⊕ *www. hotelposta.bormio.it* 🛏 *50 rooms* ⌕ *Restaurant, in-room safes, indoor pool, health club, sauna, Turkish bath, pub* ⊟ *AE, DC, MC, V* ⊙ *Closed May and June and Sept.–Nov.*

$$ 🏨 **Nazionale.** Bordering the Stelvio National Park, this central hotel caters to the winter and summer crowd. Behind the wooden exterior, rooms are small but well-equipped, with balconies on all floors except the top. The hotel operates a shuttle bus to the cable cars. ⊠ *Via al Forte 28, 23032* ☎ *0342/903361* 🖶 *0342/905294* ⊕ *www.hotelnazionale.info* 🛏 *48 rooms* ⌕ *2 restaurants, in-room safes, minibars, sauna, bar, recreation room, shops* ⊟ *AE, DC, MC, V* ⊙ *Closed Oct.–Dec.*

Sports

SKIING The main mountain above the town is **Vallecetta,** and the secondary ski area is called San Colombano. The base funivia (☎ 0342/901451) is in the center of Bormio and connects you to a network of lifts above. You can buy a ski pass (€31) and pick up a lift map at the base. From there, the funivia takes you to the Bormio 2000 station, from where you can either ski down easy trails, or (better) get another funivia up to the Cima Bianca station. Bormio is a typical Italian ski resort in that, first, you can ski from the top of the mountain all the way down to the valley, and second, trails are not as well marked or easily discernible as their American counterparts. Terrain is mostly intermediate. The most reliable time to ski at Bormio is late February or after, as early season snowfall is variable.

Passo dello Stelvio

★ ❻ *20 km (12 mi) north of Bormio, 80 km (48 mi) west of Merano.*

At just over 9,000 ft, the Passo dello Stelvio is the second-highest pass in Europe, connecting the Val Venosta with the Valtellina in neighboring Lombardy. The view from the top is worth the drive; just to the north, as you enter the pass, is Switzerland. Stelvio is a year-round skiing center, with many of its runs open in summer.

> en route Between the Stelvio Pass and Spondigna are 30 km (19 mi) of picturesque, winding road, with 48 hairpin turns. This section of road can be a bit hair-raising if you don't like mountain driving. In Spondigna keep to the right for the road to Naturno.

BOLZANO (BOZEN)

▶ *32 km (19 mi) south of Merano, 50 km (31 mi) north of Trento.*

Bolzano (Bozen), the capital of the autonomous province of Alto Adige, is tucked in among craggy peaks in a Dolomite valley just 77 km

(48 mi) from the Brenner Pass to Austria. It's protected by the mountains to the north and the east and is on the main north–south artery between northern Europe and Italy (plied by the A22 *autostrada* and the well-traveled rail route to Innsbruck and Munich). Tirolean culture dominates Bolzano's language, food, architecture, and people. It may be hard to remember that you're in Italy when walking along the city's colorful, cobblestone streets and visiting its lantern-lit cafés, where you may enjoy sauerkraut and a *Weissbier* among a lively crowd of blue-eyed German-speakers. However, fine Italian espresso, fashionable boutiques, and reasonable prices will help remind you where you are. With castles and steeples topping the landscape, this quiet city at the confluence of the Isarco (Eisack) and Talvera rivers has retained a provincial appeal. Proximity to fabulous skiing and mountain climbing and pleasant coffee shops and bars make it a worthwhile, if little-known, tourist stop. And its streets are immaculate: with the highest per capita earnings of any city in Italy, Bolzano's residents enjoy a standard of living that is second to none.

Exploring Bolzano

Begin in **Piazza Walther** ⑦ ▶, Bolzano's geographical and cultural center, and head to the striking **Duomo** ⑧. Exit the cathedral to the west, heading away from Piazza Walther, and continue to the **Chiesa dei Domenicani** ⑨ and connected Cappella di San Giovanni, where you can see Bolzano's best collection of frescoes. Cross Piazza Domenicani (to the northeast), and head up Via Goethe to the market square, **Piazza delle Erbe** ⑩. Next, turn east onto Via dei Portici, Bolzano's most important shopping street. After making your way to Casa della Pesa (on the right), the seat of public weighings until 1780, turn south into Piazza del Grano, Bolzano's medieval center and grain market. Exit onto Via Argentieri, another *vicolo* (ancient street), to the west. When you return to Piazza delle Erbe, head west on Via Museo, which will take you to the **Museo Civico** ⑪ and **Museo Archeologico** ⑫, with its 5,300-year-old iceman. Spend the rest of your day at these two museums.

TIMING   Allow at least half a day for this walk.

What to See

Castel Mareccio (Schloss Maretsch). The castle dates from the 13th century and is situated below mountains and surrounded by vineyards. It's now a well-equipped conference center with a restaurant and bar, all open to the public. ✉ *Lungotalvera Promenade, head north along the river* ☎ *0471/976615* ⊘ *Closed Tues.*

Castel Roncolo (Schloss Runkelstein). This red-roof, meticulously kept castle sits among green hills and farmhouses north of town. It was built in 1237, destroyed half a century later, and then rebuilt soon thereafter. A beautifully preserved cycle of medieval chivalrous frescoes can be viewed inside. A **tavern** (☎ 0471/324073) in the courtyard serves excellent local food and wines. ✉ *Via San Antonio, from Piazza delle Erbe, head north along Via Francescani and continue through Piazza Madonna, connecting to Via Castel Roncolo* ☎ *0471/329808* ⊕ *www.comune.bolzano. it/roncolo/ie* ☞ *€8* ⊘ *Tues.–Sun. 10–6.*

⑨ **Chiesa dei Domenicani** (Dominican Church). This 13th-century church in Piazza dei Domenicani is renowned as Bolzano's main repository for paintings, especially frescoes. In the adjoining **Cappella di San Giovanni** you can see works from the Giotto school, one of which is a *Triumph of Death* (circa 1340). Despite its macabre title, this fresco shows the

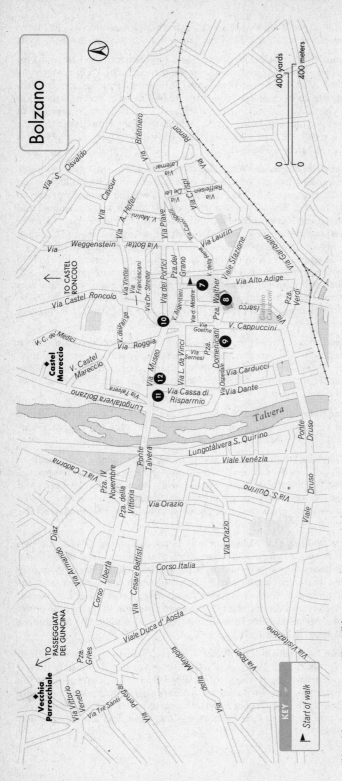

Bolzano

400 yards
400 meters
0 | 0

TO CASTEL
RONCOLO

Castel
Mareccio

Vecchia
Parrocchiale

TO
PASSEGGIATA
DEL GUNCINA

birth of a pre-Renaissance sense of depth and individuality. ⊠ *Piazza Domenicani* ☎ *0471/973133* ⊙ *Church and chapel Mon.–Sat. 9:30–5:30.*

⑧ Duomo. The city's Gothic cathedral was built between the 12th and 14th centuries; its lacy spire looks down on the mosaiclike tiles covering its pitched roof. Inside are 14th- and 15th-century frescoes and an intricately carved stone pulpit dating from 1514. Outside, don't miss the **Porta del Vino** (Wine Gate) on the northeast side; decorative carvings of grapes and harvest workers attest to the longstanding importance of wine to this region. ⊠ *Piazza Walther* ☎ *0471/978676* ⊙ *Weekdays 9:45–noon and 2–5, Sat. 9:45–noon.*

⑫ Museo Archeologico dell'Alto Adige (South Tirol Museum of Archeology).

This museum has gained international fame for Ötzi, its 5,300-year-old iceman, discovered in 1991 and the world's oldest naturally preserved body. In 1998 Italy acquired it from Austria after it was determined that the body lay 100 yds inside Italy. The iceman's leathery remains are displayed in a freezer, preserved along with his longbow, ax, and clothing. The rest of the museum relies on models and artifacts from nearby archaeological sites (with the help of an eloquent acoustic guide) to lead visitors not only through Ötzi's Copper Age, but also into the preceding Paleolithic and Neolithic eras, and the Bronze and Iron Middle ages that followed. An audio guide costs €2 ⊠ *Via Museo 43* ☎ *0471/982098* ⊕ *www.iceman.it* ☞ *€8* ⊙ *Tues. and Wed. and Fri.–Sun.10–6, Thurs. 10–8; last admission 1 hr before closing.*

⑪ Museo Civico (Civic Museum). You'll find a rich collection of traditional costumes, wood carvings, and archaeological exhibits here. The mixture of styles reflects the region's cultural cross-fertilization. ⊠ *Via Cassa di Risparmio 14* ☎ *0471/974625* ☞ *€5* ⊙ *Tues. 10–6, Wed. 10–8, Thurs.–Sun. 10–6.*

Passeggiata del Guncina. An 8-km (5-mi) botanical promenade dating from 1892 ends with a panoramic view of Bolzano. ✣ *Entrance near Vecchia Parrocchiale, in Gries, across the river and up Corso Libertà.*

⑩ Piazza delle Erbe. A bronze statue of Neptune, which dates back to 1745, presides over a bountiful fruit and vegetable market in this square. The stalls spill over with colorful displays of local produce; bakeries and grocery stores showcase hot breads, pastries, cheeses, and delicatessen meats—a complete range of picnic supplies. Try the speck and the Tirolean-style apple strudel.

▶ **⑦ Piazza Walther.** This pedestrian-only square is Bolzano's heart; it serves as an open-air living room where locals and tourists alike can be found at all hours sipping a drink (perhaps a glass of chilled Riesling) at café tables. This lively square is named after the 12th-century German wandering minstrel Walther von der Vogelweide, whose songs lampooned the papacy and praised the Holy Roman Emperor. In the middle of the plaza is Heinrich Natter's white marble, neo-Romanesque **Monument to Walther,** built in 1889.

Vecchia Parrocchiale (Old Parish Church). Said to have been built in 1141, this church is worth a visit, if only for the elaborately carved 15th-century wooden altar of Michael Pacher, a masterpiece of the Gothic style. The 11th-century Romanesque crucifix was probably brought here from France. ⊠ *Via Martin Knoller, in Gries, across the river and up Corso Libertà* ⊙ *Apr.–Oct., weekdays 10:30–noon and 2:30–4.*

> **off the beaten path**
>
> **RENON (RITTEN) PLATEAU** – The Earth Pyramids of Renon Plateau make up a bizarre geological formation where erosion has left a forest of tall, thin, needlelike spires of rock, each topped with a boulder. The Soprabolzano funicular leaves from Via Renon, about 300 yds left of the Bolzano train station. At the top, an electric train (⌨ €7 round-trip) takes you to the site, which is at Collalbo, just above Bolzano.

Where to Stay & Eat

★ $$–$$$ ✕ **Zür Kaiserkron.** Traditional Tirolean opulence and attentive service set the stage for some of the best food in town. Appetizers might include potato blini with salmon caviar, and marinated artichokes with butter (not to be missed if available). Main dishes, such as veal with black truffle–and–spinach *canederli* (dumplings) make use of ingredients from the local valleys. You're likely to find that many of your fellow diners are dignified local businesspeople. ✉ *Piazzetta Mostra* ☎ *0471/970770* ▤ *AE, DC, MC, V* ☉ *Closed Sun. No dinner Sat.*

$ ✕ **Alexander.** Typical Tirolean dishes are served up in a convivial atmosphere at this city-center restaurant. The venison ham and the lamb cutlets *al timo con salsa all'aglio* (with thyme and garlic sauce) are particularly good, but make sure to leave room for the rich chocolate cake. ✉ *Via Aosta 37* ☎ *0471/918608* ▤ *MC, V* ☉ *Closed Sat.*

$ ✕ **Batzenhausl.** A medieval building in the center of town houses this smart, modern take on the traditional *stübe* (drinking hall). It's a popular meeting place for locals, who hold animated conversations over glasses of local wine and tasty South Tirolean specialties, such as *speck tirolese* (smoked ham, thinly sliced) and *mezzelune casarecce ripiene* (house-made stuffed half moons of pasta). Ask for a table on the second floor, near the handsome stained-glass windows. ✉ *Via Andreas Hofer 30* ☎ *0471/050950* ▤ *MC, V* ☉ *Closed Tues. No lunch.*

$ ✕ **Cavallino Bianco.** Ask a local for a restaurant recommendation in Bolzano, and you're likely to be pointed toward this dependable favorite near Via dei Portici. A wide selection of Italian and German dishes are served in a spacious, comfortable dining room; you'll see lots of extended families enjoying a meal together. ✉ *Via Bottai 6* ☎ *0471/973267* ▤ *No credit cards* ☉ *Closed Sun. No dinner Sat.*

★ $ ✕ **Hopfen & Co. (Bozner Bier).** Authentic, tasty Tirolean specialties such as fried white würstel, sauerkraut, and grilled ribs complement the excellent home-brewed Austrian-style pilsner and wheat beer at this lively pub-restaurant. On some nights there's live music. ✉ *Piazza delle Erbe 17* ☎ *0471/300788* ▤ *MC, V* ☉ *Closed Sun. in June–Aug.*

★ $$$–$$$$ ▥ **Hotel Greif.** Even in a hospitable region, the Greif is a rare gem. This small central hotel has been a Bolzano landmark for centuries, and a beautiful renovation has set a standard for modern amenities in Alto Adige. In-room workstations with ISDN Internet connections and private whirlpool baths are just a few of the perks. Public spaces are light, airy, and immaculate, and each unique room was designed by a different local artist. ✉ *Piazza Walther 1, 39100* ☎ *0471/318000* 🖷 *0471/318148* ⊕ *www.greif.it* ⇥ *33 rooms* ♨ *In-room data ports, in-room safes, minibars, cable TV, hot tubs, Internet, parking (fee)* ▤ *AE, DC, MC, V.*

$$$–$$$$ ▥ **Park Hotel Laurin.** An exercise in art nouveau opulence, this hotel presides over a large park in the middle of town. Its history is speckled with visits from Europe's grand nobility, including the archduke Franz Ferdinand (whose murder in Sarajevo sparked World War I), King Leopold of Belgium, and Field Marshall Montgomery. Today, it's considered the

finest hotel in all of Alto Adige, offering art-filled modern guest rooms and handsome public spaces (one area with a fresco telling the legend of the Dwarf King Laurin). The popular Restaurant Laurin prides itself on its use of fresh seasonal ingredients. ⊠ *Via Laurin 4, 39100* ☎ *0471/311000* 🖷 *0471/311148* ⊕ *www.laurin.it* ↩ *88 rooms, 8 suites* ⚭ *Restaurant, in-room safes, minibars, cable TV, pool, bar, convention center, parking (fee), no-smoking rooms* ▤ *AE, DC, MC, V.*

$$ 🏨 **Luna-Mondschein.** This central yet secluded hotel in a tranquil garden dates from 1798. The comfortable rooms have wood paneling throughout; those overlooking the garden have balconies, others offer good views of the mountains. First-rate dining is available in both the cozy, convivial Tirolean Weinstube and the art nouveau Ristorante Van Gogh, one of the city's best. ⊠ *Via Piave 15, 39100* ☎ *0471/975642* 🖷 *0471/975577* ⊕ *www.hotel-luna.it* ↩ *85 rooms* ⚭ *Restaurant, Weinstube, meeting rooms, parking (fee)* ▤ *AE, DC, MC, V.*

★ **$–$$** 🏨 **Schloss Korb.** It's worth the 5-km (3-mi) drive west from Bolzano to reach this romantic 13th-century castle with crenellations and a massive tower, perched in a park amid vine-covered hills. Much of the ancient decor is preserved, and the public rooms are filled with antiques, elaborate wood carvings, paintings, and attractive plants. The rooms are comfortably furnished, and some in the tower have striking Romanesque arched windows. ⊠ *Missiano, Via Castel d'Appiano 5, 39050* ☎ *0471/636000* 🖷 *0471/636033* ⊕ *www.highlight-hotels.com/korb* ↩ *57 rooms, 5 suites* ⚭ *Restaurant, 2 tennis courts, 2 pools (1 indoor), sauna, bar* ▤ *No credit cards* ⊙ *Closed Nov.–Easter.*

Nightlife & the Arts

Fairs

Spring is heralded each May with large **flower markets** as well as other events, including concerts and folklore and art exhibits. On August 24 the **Bartolomeo Horse Fair** takes place on Renon Mountain northeast of the town. Hundreds of farmers converge for a day of serious trading and merriment.

Music

There's a lively music scene in town. Information is available at the tourist office. For opera information and schedules, call **Friends of Opera** (☎ 0471/913223). Orchestra concerts are often held at **Haus der Kultur** (⊠ Via Sciliar 1 ☎ 0471/977520). The **Park Hotel Laurin Bar** (⊠ Via Laurin 4 ☎ 0471/311000) hosts jazz combos on Fridays and a jazz pianist every other night.

Theater

Theater is popular in Bolzano—contact the tourist office for a weekly schedule. A frequently used venue is the imposing **Nuovo Teatro Comunale** (⊠ Piazza Verdi ☎ 0471/304112 ⊕ www.ntbz.net). **Cortile Theater im Hof** (⊠ Piazza delle Erbe 37 ☎ 0471/980756) specializes in children's theater. Note that performances may be in German.

Sports & the Outdoors

Biking

If you're in decent shape, a great way to see some of the surrounding castles, lakes, and forested valleys of the Dolomites is by bike. **Alp Bike** (☎ 0471/272024 ⊕ www.alpbike.it) offers guided excursions leaving from Piazzale dello Stadio Druso. Different trips are offered almost every day, at all levels, but you must reserve a week or more ahead for the more ambitious trips.

Hiking

Club Alpino Italiano (✉ Piazza delle Erbe 46 ☎ 0471/981391 ⊕ www.
cai.it) provides helpful information for hiking and rock climbing. It's
important to follow safety procedures and to have all the latest information on trails and conditions.

Shopping

Local Crafts

The long, narrow arcades of **Via dei Portici** house shops that specialize
in Tirolean crafts and clothing—lederhosen, loden goods, linen suits,
and dirndls. The best store for locally made handcrafted goods is **Arti-
giani Atesini** (✉ Via Portici 39 ☎ 0471/978590).

Markets

From the end of November to Christmas Eve there's a traditional
Christkindlmarkt in Piazza Walther, with stalls selling all kinds of Christmas decorations and local handcrafted goods. An outdoor fruit and vegetable market takes over the central **Piazza delle Erbe** Monday through
Saturday from 8 to 1. A weekly flea market takes place Saturday morning in **Piazza della Vittoria**.

ALTO ADIGE & CORTINA

Alto Adige (Südtirol), the northern half of the region and for centuries
part of the Austro-Hungarian Empire, was ceded to Italy at the end of
World War I. As a result, everything here has more than a tinge of the
Teutonic, which is nowhere more apparent than in the fact that the majority of the inhabitants speak German. Ethnic differences have led to
inevitable tensions, though a large measure of autonomy has, for the
most part, kept the lid on nationalist ambitions.

Naturno (Naturns)

⑬ *61 km (38 mi) east of Passo dello Stelvio, 44 km (27 mi) northwest of
Bolzano.*

Colorful houses with painted murals on their walls line the streets of
Naturno (Naturns), a major horticultural center. Art lovers will appreciate the church of **San Procolo,** which is frescoed inside and out and has
wall paintings that are the oldest in the German-speaking world, dating from the 8th century. It's northeast of the town center, just off S38.
✉ *Via San Procolo* ⊙ *Tues.–Sun. 9:30–noon and 2:30–5:30.*

A five-minute drive west of Naturno, in the hills above the hamlet of
Stava, is the 13th-century **Castel Juval,** since 1983 the home of the South
Tirolese climber and polar adventurer Reinhold Messner—the first man
to conquer Everest solo and the first to scale all 14 of the world's highest peaks without oxygen. Part of the castle has been turned into a museum, showing Messner's collection of Tibetan art, mountaineering
illustrations, and masks from around the world. ✉ *Viale Europa 2*
☎ *348/4433871, 0473/221852* ⊡ €6 ⊙ *Palm Sunday–June, Sept. and
Oct., Thurs.–Tues. 10–4.*

Where to Eat

$$ ✕**Juval Inn.** Just below Castel Juval, Reinhold Messner's Juval Inn is
an old-style hostelry in a restored farmhouse, serving traditional local
dishes and wines provisioned from his own farm. ✉ *Schlosswirt-Juval*
☎ *0473/668238* ⊟ *No credit cards* ⊙ *Closed Wed., July and Aug., and
Nov.–Palm Sunday.*

en route   The source of the full-flavored beer served throughout the region is the striking **Forst Brewery** (✉ Via Venosta 8, Lagundo ☎ 0473/260270), on the road connecting Naturno and Merano. Tours are offered in the summer, 2–4, but you'll need to call ahead for reservations. You can turn up anytime to sample the product line; in summer, cross the covered, flower-lined bridge to reach a delightful beer garden.

Merano (Meran)

★ ⑭ *24 km (15 mi) north of Bolzano, 100 km (62 mi) northeast of Bormio.*

The second-largest town in the Alto Adige, Merano (Meran) was once the capital of the Austrian region of Tirol; when the town and surrounding area were ceded to Italy as part of the 1919 Treaty of Versailles, Innsbruck became the capital. Merano, however, continued to be known as a spa town, attracting European nobility for its therapeutic waters and its peculiar grape cure, which consists simply of eating the grapes grown on the surrounding hillsides. Sheltered by mountains, Merano has an unusually mild climate, with summer temperatures rarely exceeding 80°F and winters that usually stay above freezing, despite the skiing that is within easy reach. Chairlifts and cable cars connect Merano with the high Alpine slopes of Avelengo and San Vigilio. Along the narrow streets of Merano's old town, houses have little towers and huge wooden doors, and the pointed arches of the Gothic cathedral sit next to neoclassical and art nouveau buildings. Merano serves as a good respite from mountain adventures, or from the bustle of nearby Trento and Bolzano.

The 14th-century Gothic **Duomo**, with a crenellated facade and an ornate campanile, sits in the heart of the old town. The Capella di Santa Barbara, just behind the cathedral, is an octagonal church containing a 15th-century Pietà. ✉ *Piazza del Duomo* ☉ *Easter–Sept., daily 8–noon and 2:30–8; Oct.–Easter, daily 8–noon and 2:30–7.*

The **Terme di Merano** (thermal baths) are a huge complex of spa facilities; although some hotels have their own, these separate *terme* are unique. Technicians are trained to treat you with mud packs, massages, and inhalation and sauna routines, or just with the thermal waters, which are said to be especially good for coronary and circulatory problems. Other cures include the famous grape cure at harvesttime in fall, when a two-week diet of fresh grapes has, since Roman times, been reputed to tone up digestive, liver, and urinary tract functions. ✉ *Via Piave 9* ☎ *0473/237724* 🎟 *€8 for baths, other treatments extra* ☉ *Tues.–Fri. 8–noon and 3–10; Mon. and Sat., 8–noon and 3–7.*

Overlooking the town atop Mt. Tappeinerweg is a castle that was the home of poet Ezra Pound from 1958 to 1964. Still in the Pound family, the castle now houses the **Brunnenburg Agricultural Museum**, devoted to Tirolean country life. Among its exhibits are a blacksmith's shop and, not surprisingly, a room with Pound memorabilia. To get there, take Bus 3, which departs every hour on the hour, from Merano to Dorf Tirol. ✉ *Ezra Pound Weg 6* ☎ *0473/923533* 🎟 *€2.50* ☉ *Apr.–Nov., Wed.–Mon. 10–5.*

Fodor'sChoice   **Passeggiata Tappeiner,** a 3-km (2-mi) botanical promenade that offers
★   panoramic views from the hills north of the Duomo, is a favorite stroll for locals. **Passeggiata d'Estate** (Summer Promenade) runs along the shaded south bank of the Passirio River, and the **Passeggiata d'Inverno** (Winter Promenade) on the exposed north bank provides more warmth, and even a covered sun trap.

Where to Stay & Eat

★ $$$ ✕ **Sissi.** In this relaxed leafy restaurant just off Via dei Portici, rustic regional dishes are prepared with the precision of haute Italian cooking. Menu choices may include risotto *alle erbe* (with herbs) and *filetto di vitello con salsa di alloro* (veal fillet with bay-leaf sauce); a set menu (about €50) provides a complete five-course dinner. ☒ *Via Galilei 44* ☎ *0473/231062* ⌕ *Reservations essential* ▭ *MC, V* ⊗ *Closed Mon. and Jan.*

$–$$ ✕ **Haisrainer.** This rustic stübe in Merano's old town is a favorite with locals and tourists alike. The menu focuses on Tirolean specialties: try the *zuppa al vino bianco* (stew with white wine) and the seasonal risottos, (with asparagus in spring, or Barolo in chillier months). ☒ *Via dei Portici 100* ☎ *0473/237944* ▭ *MC, V* ⊗ *Closed Sun.*

$–$$ ✕ **Seiben.** Centrally located in the town's arcade, this modern bistro has attentive service and a progressive menu. Young Meraners crowd the hip bar downstairs; upstairs is a more relaxed, jazz-themed dining room. Don't miss the Blues Brothers, poised over the staircase. ☒ *Via dei Portici 232* ☎ *0473/210636* ▭ *MC, V* ⊗ *Closed Tues. No lunch Sun.*

★ $$$$ ▥ **Grand Hotel Palace.** Merano's finest hotel is an old-world institution set in an extensive garden. The public spaces are attractive and comfortable, with art nouveau touches, Tiffany glass, marble pillars, and high ceilings; the guest rooms are spacious. The renowned spa—offering baths, massages, mud treatments, and other cures—attracts fatigued soccer stars and others in search of renewal. Rooftop suites have balconies with stunning views of Merano's steeples and the surrounding mountains. ☒ *Via Cavour 2, 39012* ☎ *0473/271000* ᵬ *0473/271100* ⊕ *www.palace.it* ᗌ *136 rooms* ⌕ *2 restaurants, minibars, cable TV, pool, spa, bar, wine shop, meeting rooms, free parking* ▭ *AE, DC, MC, V.*

$$–$$$ ▥ **Castello Labers.** On a hilltop amid forested slopes about 3 km (2 mi) northeast of Merano's center, this castle hotel with red-tile gables, towers, and turrets is unmistakably Tirolean in style. Ceiling beams, painted fresco decorations, and crossed halberds on the walls complete the look. The hospitable Stapf-Neubert family owns the hotel and takes an active part in its management. ☒ *Via Labers 25, 39012* ☎ *0473/234484* ᵬ *0473/234146* ⊕ *www.castellolabers.it* ᗌ *32 rooms* ⌕ *Restaurant, tennis court, pool* ▭ *AE, DC, MC, V* ⊗ *Closed mid-Nov.–Mar.*

$ ▥ **Conte di Merano.** If you don't feel like paying for one of Merano's resort hotels, this simple central hotel is a good alternative. Steps away from Via dei Portici and open year-round, it's an efficient base for exploring the town. Rooms are spartan, but clean, comfortable, and well-equipped. ☒ *Via delle Corse 78, 39012* ☎ *0473/232181* ᵬ *0473/211874* ᗌ *23 rooms* ⌕ *Restaurant, cable TV, bar, free parking* ▭ *AE, DC, MC, V.*

Nightlife & the Arts

There are plenty of nighttime options in and around Merano. Among them, **Bar Piccolo** (Corso Libertà 5) is a lively local drinking spot. Mellow cafés line the **Passerpromenade** along the river. **Dancing Club Exclusif** (☎ 0471/561711), 10 km (6 mi) east in the village of Lana, draws primarily twenty- and thirtysomethings.

The **Grape Festival** on the third Sunday of October has parades and wine tastings in Piazza del Duomo. Farmers test indigenous Haflinger horses in the highly charged **horse race** on Easter Monday.

Shopping

Merano's main shopping street, the narrow arcaded **Via dei Portici** (Laubengasse), runs west from the cathedral. You'll find regional products—wood carvings, Tirolean-style clothing, embroidery, cheeses, salami, and fruit schnapps—along with more standard clothing-boutique shopping. From the end of November until Christmas Eve, Merano holds a traditional **Christkindlmarkt** (Christmas market) in the main square.

Cornedo

⑮ *6 km (4 mi) east of Bolzano.*

At the mouth of the Ega Valley (Eggental), Cornedo is a place to savor the view of the Catinaccio Mountains. Craggy peaks seem to be props for a lighting display, as pink and purple reflections dance over huge rocks. Their origin is the subject of a local legend that tells of Laurin, King of the Dwarfs, who lived in a vast palace on the Catinaccio, at a time when the mountain was covered with roses. King Laurin became infatuated with Similde, the daughter of a neighboring king, and kidnapped her using a magic hood that made him invisible. But Similde's rose garden betrayed his whereabouts, and he was de-hooded and imprisoned. When he finally managed to escape and return home, he cast a spell turning the betraying roses into rocks, so that they could be seen neither by day nor by night. But Laurin forgot about dusk, which is why the spectacular pinkish-red display is at its best just before twilight.

Chiusa (Klausen)

⑯ *24 km (15 mi) north of Cornedo, 30 km (19 mi) northeast of Bolzano.*

Beautiful narrow streets are lined with houses built in the 15th and 16th centuries in Chiusa (Klausen), the main town in the Val Isarco. Geraniums and begonias fill window boxes beneath the carved wooden shutters. From here you can catch a bus east to Val di Funes, where the church **Santa Maddalena** is spectacularly hemmed in by the Geisler Peaks and offers good walking terrain and hotels.

Above the town of Chiusa is the Benedictine monastery of **Saviona** (Saeben), built as a castle in the 10th century but occupying a site that was fortified in Roman times. The monastery buildings date from the late Middle Ages and are a mixture of Romanesque and Gothic architecture, surrounded by walls and turrets. Guided visits are organized by the Tourist Association in Chiusa; contact the local **tourist office** (⊠ Piazza Tinne 6 ☎ 0472/847424).

Bressanone (Brixen)

⑰ *14 km (9 mi) north of Chiusa, 40 km (25 mi) northeast of Bolzano.*

Bressanone (Brixen) is an important artistic center of the Alto Adige and was the seat of prince-bishops for centuries. Like their counterparts in Trento, these medieval administrators had the delicate task of serving two opposing masters—the pope (the ultimate spiritual supervisor) and the Holy Roman Emperor (the civil and military leader). Since the papacy and the Holy Roman Empire were virtually at war throughout the Middle Ages, Bressanone's prince-bishops became experts at tact and diplomacy. The imposing **Duomo** was built in the 13th century but acquired a baroque facade 500 years later; its 14th-century cloister is decorated with medieval frescoes. ⊠ *Piazza Duomo* ☉ *Daily 8–noon and 3–6.*

The Bishop's Palace, which now houses the **Museo Diocesano** (Diocesan Museum), holds an abundance of local medieval art, particularly Gothic wood carving. The wooden statues and liturgical objects were all collected from the cathedral treasury. During the Christmas season, the curators highlight displays of the museum's large collection of antique nativity scenes; look for the shepherds wearing Tirolean hats. ✉ *Palazzo Vescovile* ☎ *0472/830505* ⊕ *www.dioezesanmuseum.bz.it* ✐ *€5, nativity scenes €3.50* ☉ *Mar. 15–Oct., Tues.–Sun. 10–5; nativity scenes Dec.–Jan., daily 2–5.*

Where to Stay & Eat

$$–$$$ ✕ **Fink.** This restaurant under the arcades in the pedestrian-only town center has a friendly staff and offers an affordable daily set menu. It has a rustic upstairs dining room, with lots of wood paneling, and serves international as well as hearty Tirolean specialties. Try the *carré di maiale gratinato* (pork roasted with cheese and served with cabbage and potatoes) or the *castrato alla paesana* (a lamb stew). ✉ *Via Portici Minori 4* ☎ *0472/834883* ☰ *MC, V* ☉ *Closed Wed., July 1–14, and Feb. 1–14. No dinner Tues.*

★ $$$ 🏨 **Elephant.** This cozy inn, one of the region's best, takes its name from an incident in 1550, when King John III of Portugal stopped here for a few days while leading an elephant over the Alps as a present for Austria's Emperor Ferdinand. Each room is unique, many with antiques and paintings. Housed on the park property is the separate Villa Marzari, with 14 rooms. Some of the best food in town is served in the hotel restaurant, a rustic three-room stübe. ✉ *Via Rio Bianco 4, 39042* ☎ *0472/832750* 🖷 *0472/836579* ⊕ *www.acs.it/elephant* ☎ *45 rooms* ⚭ *Restaurant, minibars, cable TV, 2 tennis courts, pool, sauna, gym, free parking* ☰ *DC, MC, V* ☉ *Closed early Jan.–Mar. and Nov.*

$ 🏨 **Croce d'Oro** (Goldenes Kreuz). A five-century-old tradition of hospitality is still practiced by the Reiserer family at this centrally placed hotel. Shops line the ground floor of the pink building, with styles inside ranging from the more modern reception area to the tavern-style bar. The rooms are spacious with sturdy wood appointments. ✉ *Bastioni Minori 8, 30042* ☎ *0472/836155* 🖷 *0472/834255* ☎ *70 rooms* ⚭ *Restaurant, bar* ☰ *No credit cards.*

Shopping

From the end of November until January 6 there is a traditional **Christkindlmarkt** (Christmas market) in Piazza Duomo, with stalls selling all kinds of Christmas decorations and local handcrafted goods.

Brunico (Bruneck)

★ ⑱ *33 km (20 mi) east of Bressanone, 65 km (40 mi) northwest of Cortina d'Ampezzo.*

With its medieval quarter nestling below the 13th-century bishop's castle, Brunico (Bruneck) is in the heart of the Val Pusteria. This quiet, picturesque town is divided by the Rienza River, with the old quarter on one side and the modern quarter on the other.

The **Museo Etnografico dell'Alto Adige** (Alto Adige Ethnographic Museum) re-creates a Middle Ages farming village, built around a more modern 300-year-old mansion. The wood-carving displays are the most interesting. It's in the district of Teodone, just outside the town. ✉ *Via Duca Diet 24, Teodone* ☎ *0474/552087* ⊕ *www.provincia.bz.it/volkskundemuseen* ✐ *€3.60* ☉ *Mid-Apr.–Oct., Tues.–Sat. 9:30–5:30, Sun. 2–6.*

Where to Stay

$ 🏨 **Andreas Hofer.** There's a Tirolean feel to this bright comfortable hotel set in a large garden outside the center of town. Rooms are modern, with chalet-style balconies overlooking the Val Pusteria. ✉ *Via Campo Tures*

1, 39031 ☎ *0474/551469* 🖷 *0474/551283* ⊕ *www.andreashofer.it*
⌇ *54 rooms* ⚥ *Restaurant, sauna, pool, bar, Weinstube* ⊟ *MC, V.*

$ 🖭 **Post.** This traditional, homey, yellow-and-blue hotel is distinguished
by its friendly rates and restaurant, café, and pastry shop. It has its own
parking, an unusual perk in the pedestrian-only town center. ⊠ *Via Bas-*
tioni 9, 39031 ☎ *0474/555127* 🖷 *0474/551603* ⊕ *www.hotelpost-*
bruneck.com ⌇ *54 rooms, 45 with bath* ⚥ *Restaurant, café, Weinstube,*
free parking ⊟ *AE, MC, V* ⊙ *Closed 1st 2 wks Nov.*

Sports

The **Alta Badia ski area** can be reached by heading south on S244 from
Brunico (⊕ www.altabadia.org). It's less expensive—and more Austrian—than other, more famous ski destinations in this region.

Dobbiaco (Toblach)

❶❾ *25 km (16 mi) east of Brunico, 34 km (21 mi) north of Cortina d'Am-*
pezzo.

In Dobbiaco (Toblach), Italian is spoken grudgingly, and the atmosphere is more Austrian than you can easily find in Austria. It's not surprising that Gustav Mahler (1860–1911), the great Austrian composer,
came here often for inspiration.

Where to Stay

$$$ 🖭 **Cristallo.** Wood beams and paneling lend an Old Tirolean patina to
this small hotel in a garden outside town. The architecture and furnishings
reflect the local preference for combining traditional chalet design with
functional, comfortable modern furniture. You can relax in the cozy and
informal stübe. ⊠ *Viale S. Giovanni 37, 39034* ☎ *0474/972138* 🖷 *0474/*
972755 ⊕ *www.hotelcristallo.com* ⌇ *30 rooms* ⚥ *Restaurant, in-*
room safes, cable TV, indoor pool, bar, free parking ⊟ *AE, MC, V*
⊙ *Closed Apr.–May and mid-Oct.–mid-Dec.*

★ $$ 🖭 **Alpenhotel Ratsberg.** To reach this hotel, you can take the 10-minute
cable-car ride to Monte Rota or drive up by car. It's in traditional style,
with the timeless look of local chalets. Front rooms have stunning
mountain views from balconies, and those in the back look out over the
dense mountain forest. You needn't take the cable car back down for
sustenance: the hotel has a good restaurant, a bar, and a Tirolean-style
stübe. ⊠ *Monte Rota 10, 39034* ☎ *0474/972913* 🖷 *0474/972216*
⊕ *www.alpenhotel-ratsberg.com* ⌇ *30 rooms* ⚥ *Restaurant, cable TV,*
tennis court, pool, sauna, bar, free parking ⊟ *No credit cards* ⊙ *Closed*
May and mid-Oct.–mid-Dec.

Sports

SKIING Groomed trails for **cross-country skiing** (usually loops marked off by the
kilometer) accommodate differing degrees of ability. Inquire at the local
tourist office. Downhill skiing can be found at **Monte Rota**, accessible
from Dobbiaco.

Cortina d'Ampezzo

❷⓪ *30 km (19 mi) south of Dobbiaco.*

Fodor'sChoice
★

Cortina d'Ampezzo has been the mountain resort of choice for the Italian elite for more than 100 years and hosted the Winter Olympics in
1956. While its glamorous appeal for younger Italians may have since
been eclipsed by steeper, sleeker Madonna di Campiglio, Cortina remains,
for many, Italy's most idyllic incarnation of the Alpine ski town.

Encircled by mountains and dense forests, the "The Pearl of the Dolomites" is in a lush meadow 4,000 ft above sea level. The town hugs the slopes beside a fast-moving stream; a public park extends along one bank. Higher in the valley, luxury hotels and the villas of the rich are identifiable by their attempts to hide behind stands of firs and spruces. The bustling center of Cortina d'Ampezzo has little nostalgia for old-time atmosphere, despite its Alpine appearance. The tone is set by smart shops and cafés as chic as their well-dressed patrons, whose corduroy knickerbockers may well have been tailored by Armani. Cortina is the place to go for a whiff of the heady aroma of wealth and sophistication and retains a more Italian feel than most of its Alto Adige neighbors; if you want authentic Tirolean gemütlichkeit, pass through Cortina and stop at one of the more low-key resorts.

On Via Cantore, a winding road heading up out of town to the northeast (becoming S48), you can stop and see the **Pista Olimpica di Bob** (Olympic Bobsled Course), a leftover from the 1956 Winter Games. The course is open for bobsledding at unpredictable times.

Where to Stay & Eat

$$ ✕ **Tavernetta.** Near the Olympic ice-skating rink, this popular restaurant has Tirolean-style, wood-paneled dining rooms and a local clientele. Here you can try Cortina specialties such as *zuppa di porcini* (porcini mushroom soup), ravioli *di cervo* (stuffed with venison), and game. ✉ *Via dello Stadio 27/a* ☎ *0436/867494* ▭ *AE, DC, MC, V* ☾ *Closed Wed., mid-June–mid-July, and Nov.*

$$$$
FodorsChoice
★
✕▥ **De la Poste.** Skiers who want to see and be seen return year after year to this lively hotel; its main terrace bar is one of Cortina's social centers. The hotel has been under the careful management of the Manaigo family since 1936. Each unique room has antiques in characteristic Dolomite style; almost all have wooden balconies. A refined main dining room—with high ceilings and large chandeliers—serves nouvelle cuisine and superb soufflés; there's also a more informal grill room with wood paneling and the family pewter collection. ✉ *Piazza Roma 14, 32043* ☎ *0436/4271* 🖷 *0436/868435* ⊕ *www.delaposte.it* ⇗ *83 rooms* ⌂ *2 restaurants, minibars, cable TV, bar, free parking* ▭ *AE, DC, MC, V* ☾ *Closed Apr.–mid-June and Oct.–mid-Dec.* ¶◎¶ *MAP, FAP.*

$$$$ ▦ **Miramonti Majestic.** This imposing and luxe hotel, more than a century old, has a magnificent mountain-valley position about 1 km (½ mi) south of town. A touch of formality comes through in the imperial Austrian design, and the interior reflects the period style throughout. There's always a roaring fire in the splendid bar, and the hotel's recreation rooms are framed by windows overlooking mountain vistas. The history of Cortina is intricately tied into the Miramonti, and you'll feel a part of it all here. ✉ *Località Peziè 103, 32043* ☎ *0436/4201* 🖷 *0436/ 867019* ⊕ *cortina.dolomiti.org/hmiramonti* ⇗ *105 rooms* ⌂ *Restaurant, minibars, cable TV, 9-hole golf course, 2 tennis courts, indoor pool, gym, sauna, bar, meeting rooms, free parking* ▭ *AE, DC, MC, V* ☾ *Closed Apr.–June and Sept.–mid-Dec.* ¶◎¶ *MAP, FAP.*

$$$$ ▦ **Corona.** This cozy Alpine lodge is run by Luciano Rimoldi, a noted ski instructor who has coached such luminaries as Alberto Tomba. Modern art adorns small but comfortable pine-paneled rooms; the convivial bar is a pleasant place to relax. The hotel is a five-minute walk—across the river—from the center of town, and a 10-minute ride to the lifts (a ski bus stops out front). ✉ *Via Val di Sotto 12, 32040* ☎ *0436/ 3251* 🖷 *0436/867339* ⊕ *www.sunrise.it/cortina/link/hcorona.html* ⇗ *44 rooms* ⌂ *Restaurant, bar, cable TV, free parking* ▭ *AE, DC, MC, V* ☾ *Closed Apr.–June and Sept.–Nov.* ¶◎¶ *MAP.*

Nightlife & the Arts

At the **Europa** hotel (⊠ Corso Italia 207 ☎ 0436/3221) you can expect to mingle with the couture set at the VIP disco; nonguests are welcome, but don't expect to spend less than €30.

Sports

SKIING Cortina's long and picturesque ski runs will delight intermediates, although advanced skiers might lust for steeper terrain, which can be found only off-piste. The most impressive views (and steepest slopes) are on **Monte Cristallo,** based at **Misurina.** The **Faloria** gondola runs from the center of town. From its top, you can get up to most of the other central mountains. Farther out of town, don't miss the **Cinque Torri** and **Passo Falzarego** runs. All runs are covered by the **Dolomiti Superski** pass (☎ 0471/795397 ⚐ €35 ⊕ www.dolomitisuperski.com), good for the entire region.

en route   As you enter the Crepa Tunnel along the S48 from Cortina d'Ampezzo, the ascent for the Passo di Falzarego begins. The **Passo Pordoi** will lead to the so-called Heart of the Dolomites. The roads around this region of the Sella mountains are among the most spectacular in Europe. A fork in the road farther ahead will lead left to Canazei and right into Val Gardena.

HEART OF THE DOLOMITES

The area between Bolzano east to the mountain resort Cortina d'Ampezzo is dominated by two major valleys, Val di Fassa and Val Gardena. Both share the spectacular panorama of the Sella mountain range, known as the Heart of the Dolomites. Val di Fassa cradles the Grande Strada delle Dolomiti (Great Dolomiti Road—S48 and S241), which runs from Bolzano as far as Cortina d'Ampezzo. The route, opened in 1909, comprises 110 km (68 mi) of easy grades and smooth driving between the two cities.

With some of the best views of the Dolomites, Val Gardena is famous as a ski resort, freckled with well-equipped, picturesque towns overlooked by the oblong Sasso Lungo (Long Rock), which is more than 10,000 ft above sea level. It's also home of the Ladins, descendants of soldiers sent by the Roman emperor Tiberius to conquer the Celtic population of the area in the 1st century AD. Forgotten in the narrow cul-de-sacs of isolated mountain valleys, the Ladins have developed their own folk traditions and speak an ancient dialect that is derived from Latin and is similar to the Romansch spoken in some high valleys in Switzerland. Like Alto Adige, this area is very Germanic as well.

Canazei

② *60 km (37 mi) west of Cortina d'Ampezzo, 52 km (32 mi) east of Bolzano.*

Of the towns in the Val di Fassa, Canazei is the most popular ski resort as well as a summer haven. The mountains around this small town are threaded with hiking trails and ski slopes, surrounded by large clutches of conifers. Four kilometers (2½ mi) west of Canazei, an excursion from Campitello di Fassa to the vantage point at **Col Rodella** is a must. A cable car rises some 3,000 ft to this most panoramic of vistas. From the balcony at the top you can see full circle around the region, including the Sasso Lungo and the rest of the Sella range.

Where to Stay

$$$ 🏨**Alla Rosa.** The view of the imposing Dolomites is the real attraction at this central hotel; ask for a room with a balcony. The reception area is spacious and welcoming, and guest rooms pleasantly blend rustic and modern elements. There's a modest restaurant, serving local and international cuisine, and a cozy bar. Half board is required. ⊠ *Via del Faure 18, 38032* 🕾 *0462/601107* 🖷 *0462/601481* ⊕ *www.hotelallarosa. com* ⤡ *49 rooms* ♿ *Restaurant, minibars, cable TV, bar, recreation room, free parking* 🖃 *MC, V* ⊙ *Closed Oct.* ⟦◯⟧ *FAP, MAP.*

> en route
>
> **Passo di Sella** is one of the most famous mountain passes in the Dolomites. It can be approached from the S48 and continues into Val Gardena through the most panoramic mountain scenery in Europe. The road descends to Ortisei, passing the small ski resorts of Selva Gardina and Santa Cristina.

Ortisei (St. Ulrich)

㉒   *28 km (17 mi) north of Canazei, 35 km (22 mi) northeast of Bolzano.*

Ortisei (St. Ulrich), the jewel in the crown of Val Gardena's ski resorts, is a hub of activity in summer as well as winter. There are hundreds of miles of hiking trails and accessible ski slopes, including the Siusi slopes to the south. Hotels are everywhere and facilities are excellent, with swimming pools, ice rinks, health spas, tennis courts, and bowling. Most impressive of all is the location, a valley surrounded by formidable views in all directions. The Val Gardena comes alive with a parade of horse-drawn sleighs on January 1.

For centuries Ortisei has also been famous for the expertise of its wood-carvers, and there are still numerous workshops. Apart from making religious sculptures—particularly the wayside Calvaries you come upon everywhere in the Dolomites—Ortisei's carvers were long known for producing wooden dolls, horses, and other toys. As itinerant peddlers, they traveled every spring on foot with their loaded packs as far as Paris, London, and St. Petersburg. Fine historic and contemporary examples of all kinds of locally carved wooden sculptures and artifacts can be seen at the **Museo della Val Gardena** (Val Gardena Local Heritage Museum) ⊠ *Via Rezia 83, Ortisei* 🕾 *0471/797554* ⊕ *www.val-gardena.com* 🎟 *€3* ⊙ *Feb.–mid-Mar., Tues.–Fri. 2:30–5:30; June and Sept.–mid-Oct., Tues.–Fri. 2–6; July–Aug., Tues.–Sat. 10–noon and 2–6, Sun. 2–6.*

Where to Stay

★ $$$$ 🏨**Adler.** This hotel, arguably the best in the valley, has been under the same family management since 1810. The original building has been enlarged several times, yielding spacious guest rooms and an expansive spa complex, but retaining much of the old turreted-castle appeal. Most guests stay for a full week, picking up the busy schedule of activities (such as guided ski tours and snowshoe walks) when they arrive on Saturday evening. Half board is required. ⊠ *Via Rezia 7, 39046* 🕾 *0471/775000* 🖷 *0471/775555* ⊕ *www.hotel-adler.com* ⤡ *123 rooms* ♿ *Restaurant, in-room safes, minibars, cable TV, pool, hair salon, health club, sauna, bar, free parking* 🖃 *MC, V* ⊙ *Closed mid-Apr.–mid-May and mid-Oct.–early Dec.* ⟦◯⟧ *MAP.*

$$$$ 🏨**Cavallino Bianco.** In the town center and only a five-minute walk from the main ski facilities, this hotel looks like a gigantic dollhouse, with delicate wooden balconies and an eye-catching wooden gable. Beyond this facade lies a sprawling, all-inclusive modern resort, but the cozy bar—with its large, handcrafted fireplace—retains some of the charm of the

old postal hotel. ⊠ *Via Rezia 22, 39046* ☎*0471/783333* 🖷*0471/797517*
⊕ *www.cavallino-bianco.com* 🛏 *184 rooms* ⚗ *Restaurant, coffee
shop, minibars, cable TV, pool, sauna, spa, bar, dance club, free parking* ⊟ *AE, DC, MC, V* ⊙ *Closed mid-Apr.–mid-May and mid-Oct.–mid-
Dec.* ⦿ *MAP.*

Sports

With almost 600 km (370 mi) of accessible downhill slopes, Ortisei is
one of the most popular ski resorts in the Dolomites. Prices are good
and facilities are among the most modern. An immensely popular route,
the **Sella Ronda** relies on well-placed chairlifts to connect 26 km[16 mi]
of downhill skiing around the colossal Sella massif, passing through several towns along the way. You can ski the loop, which requires inter-
mediate ability and a full day's effort, either clockwise or counterclockwise.
Going with a guide is highly advised; consult the tourist office in **Selva
Gardena** (☎ 0471/795122) or **Ortisei** (☎ 0471/796328) for more information.

There are more than 90 km (56 mi) of cross-country skiing trails. The
Val Gardena Ski cooperative (☎ 0471/792092 ⊕ www.val-gardena.com)
has snow reports and information on seasonal events.

Fiè allo Sciliar (Völs am Schlern)

㉓ *26 km (16 mi) southwest of Ortisei, 18 km (11 mi) east of Bolzano.*

Fiè (Völs) is in a valley with the Renon mountains on one side and the
Siusi on the other. The town is surrounded by acres of green coniferous
forests. In the town is the parish church of **Santa Maria Assunta,** built in
the 16th century in the late Gothic style.

Where to Stay

★ $$$ 🏨 **Turm.** The *turm* (tower) that houses this welcoming hotel on the edge
of Sciliar National Park dates from the 13th century and has been used
as a courthouse, dungeon, and tavern. Now owned and run by the Pram-
strahler family, it's furnished with their charming collection of paint-
ings and antiques. The picturesque onion-domed hostelry also has an
excellent restaurant. ⊠ *Piazza della Chiesa 9, 39050* ☎ *0471/725014*
🖷 *0471/725474* 🛏 *35 rooms* ⚗ *Restaurant, 2 pools (1 indoor), spa,
free parking* ⊟ *MC, V* ⊙ *Closed 2 wks mid-Jan. and mid-Nov.–mid-
Dec.*

Sports

The **Oswald von Wolkenstein Cavalcade,** named after the medieval South
Tirolese knight and troubadour, is held every year over the first or sec-
ond weekend of June. After a colorful procession, teams of local horse-
back riders compete in fast-paced events.

Caldaro (Kaltern)

㉔ *22 km (14 mi) south of Fiè allo Sciliar, 15 km (9 mi) south of Bolzano.*

Caldaro (Kaltern) is a vineyard village with clear views of castles high
up on the surrounding mountains, a backdrop that reflects the centuries
of division that forged the unique character of the area. Caldaro archi-
tecture is famous for the way it blends Italian Renaissance elements of
balance and harmony with the soaring windows and peaked arches of
the local Gothic tradition. The church of **Santa Caterina,** on the main
square, is a good example.

Close to Caldaro's main square is the **Museo Provinciale del Vino** (South
Tirolean Museum of Wine), with exhibits on how local wine has his-

torically been made, stored, served, and worshiped. ✉ *Via dell'Oro 1* ☎ *0471/963168* ⊕ *www.provinz.bz.it/volkskundemuseen* 🎫 *€2* ⊘ *Easter–Oct., Tues.–Sat. 9:30–noon and 2–6, Sun. 10–noon.*

Lago di Carezza

㉕ *35 km (22 mi) east of Caldaro, 29 km (18 mi) east of Bolzano.*

Glacial Lake Carezza is some 5,000 ft above sea level. The azure blue of the waters can at times change to magical greens and purples, reflections of the dense surrounding forest and rosy peaks of the Dolomites. You can hike down to this most quintessential of mountain lakes from the nearby village of the same name; there's a fountain with two marmots in the center of town.

THE DOLOMITES:
TRENTINO-ALTO ADIGE A TO Z

To research prices, get advice from other travelers, and book travel arrangements, visit www.fodors.com.

AIRPORTS
The nearest airport, but the least well connected, is the Aeroporto Bolzano Dolomiti (BZO), with frequent flights to Rome and irregular service to Frankfurt, Innsbruck, and Vienna. A bit farther to the south, Verona's Aeroporto Villafranca (VRN) is well connected by road and rail with the Dolomite area. Direct intercontinental flights are available into Milan's Malpensa Airport (MXP) to the southwest or Munich's International Airport (MUC) to the north, both about a four-hour drive from Bolzano.

🛈 Airport Information **Aeroporto Bolzano Dolomiti** ☎ 0471/254070. **Aeroporto Villafranca** ✉ 11 km [7 mi] southwest of Verona ☎ 045/8095666 ⊕ www.aeroportoverona. it. **Aeroporto Milan Malpensa** ✉ 50 km (30 mi) northwest of Milan ☎ 02/74852200 ⊕ www.sea-aeroportimilano.it. **Munich International Airport** ☎ 049/ 8997500 ⊕ www.munich-airport.de.

BUS TRAVEL
Only a handful of buses link Bolzano with Milan and Venice; the service between these cities and Trento is more frequent (for instance, there's hourly bus service between Riva del Garda and Trento), but if you want to get to Merano or Cortina d'Ampezzo you will have to change in either Trento or Bolzano. For information, call SASA.

Local buses connect the train stations at Trento, Bolzano, and Merano with the mountain resorts. The service is fairly frequent between most main towns during the day. Though some parts of the region remain out of the reach of public transportation, it's possible to visit even the remotest villages without a car if you are equipped with the local bus timetables, available from regional and local tourist offices, and lots of time. Still, most towns are designed for people with cars, and getting between your hotel, ski lifts, and après-ski locales without a vehicle can be very tricky.

🛈 Bus Information SASA (Società Autobus Servizi d'Area) ☎ 0471/974292.

CAR RENTAL
🛈 Local Agencies **Avis** ✉ Piazza Verdi 18, Bolzano ☎ 0471/971467 ⊕ www.avis.com. **Hertz** ✉ Piazza Verdi 22, Bolzano ☎ 0471/981411 ⊕ www.hertz.com.

CAR TRAVEL

The most important route in the region, A22, is the main north–south autostrada linking Italy with northern Europe by way of the Brenner Pass. It connects Bressanone, Bolzano, Trento, and Rovereto, and near Verona joins the A4, running east–west across northern Italy from Trieste to Turin.

A car is highly recommended for exploring this region. Roads in the broad mountain valleys are usually wide two-lane routes, but the roads up into the highest passes can be narrow, winding, and, especially in winter, subject to sudden closure. (Some are closed to traffic entirely in winter.) Call Autostrada Weather Information Service in Bolzano for information on weather-related closures. Whatever the weather, expect to enjoy the scenery on mountain roads at a speed of about 48 kph (30 mph).

EMERGENCY
SERVICES

ACI Emergency Service offers 24-hour roadside assistance.
🄵 **ACI dispatchers** ☎ 803/116. **Autostrada Weather Information Service** ☎ 0471/413810.

EMERGENCIES

For first aid, ask for *pronto soccorso,* and be prepared to give your address. Pharmacies take turns staying open late and on Sunday; for the latest information, consult the current list posted on the front door of each pharmacy or ask at the local tourist office.
🄵 **Ambulance** ☎ 118. **Carabinieri** ☎ Military police, 112. **Police** ☎ 113.

LANGUAGE

Alto Adige is the only region in Italy with two official languages: Italian and German. In Bolzano, Merano, and environs, street signs, menus, city names, and street chatter are completely bilingual, and depending on your features you may be spoken to in a local dialect of German rather than Italian when you're at a shop or café. Meanwhile, all of Trentino and the ski resorts of Madonna di Campiglio and Cortina d'Ampezzo are strictly Italian-speaking, but the regional accent—most noticeable in the "r," which is guttural rather than rolled—is still quite distinctive.

MAIL & SHIPPING

Post offices are open on weekdays 8–6:30 and Saturday 8–12:30.
🄵 Post Offices **Bolzano** ✉ Piazza Parrocchia, 15. **Cortina d'Ampezzo** ✉ Largo Poste 18/a. **Rovereto** ✉ Via Vittorio Veneto 1. **Trento** ✉ Piazza a. Vittoria 20.

SPORTS & THE OUTDOORS

HIKING &
CLIMBING

Local tourist offices can provide information on less-demanding trails.
🄵 Hiking & Climbing **Associazione Rifugi del Trentino** ✉ Piazza Centa 13/7, 38100 Trento ☎☎ 0461/826066. **Club Alpino Italiano** ✉ Piazza delle Erbe 46, Bolzano ☎ 0471/981391 ✉ Corso della Libertà 188, Merano ☎ 0473/448944 ✉ Via Manci 57, Trento ☎ 0461/981871 🌐 www.cai.it. **Società degli Alpinisti Tridentini** ✉ Via Manci 57, 38100 Trento ☎ 0461/981871.

TOURS

If you are without a car or if you don't care to drive over mountain roads, guided tours from Bolzano or Trento can show you the Dolomites the easy way. However, the sudden and frequent snowfalls mean that tours are offered in summer only.

BUS TOURS

In Bolzano, city sightseeing and local excursions are organized by the SAD bus company, near the train station. In Trento, city sightseeing can be arranged through the city tourist office.
🄵 Fees & Schedules **SAD** ✉ Via Conciapelli 60 ☎ 167/846047.

SINGLE-DAY
TOURS

In July and August, the SAD bus company's full-day mountain tours include a "Great Dolomites Tour" from Bolzano to Cortina and a tour of the Val Venosta that climbs over the Stelvio Pass into Switzerland. A tour of the Val Gardena and the Siusi Alps is available from April to October.

From June through September, the Calderari e Moggioli travel agency offers a full-day guided bus tour of the Brenta Dolomites and its own "Great Dolomites Tour," a full-day drive over the Pordoi and Falzarego passes to Cortina d'Ampezzo and Lake Misurina. The Trentino tourist office also organizes guided tours and excursions by train to castles in the region.

🔳 Fees & Schedules **Calderari e Moggioli** ✉ Via Manci 46 ☎ 0461/980275.

TRAIN TRAVEL

The express train line that links the towns of Bolzano, Trento, and Rovereto connects with other main lines at Verona, just south of the region. Eurocity trains on the Dortmund–Venice and Munich–Innsbruck–Rome routes also stop at these stations. An express train line follows the course of the Adige Valley from Munich and Innsbruck to the Brenner Pass southward past Bolzano, Trento, and Rovereto. Branch lines from Trento and Bolzano go to some of the smaller valleys, but most of the mountain attractions are beyond the reach of trains. Contact Ferrovie dello Stato, the national train operator, for more information.

🔳 Train Information **FS–Trenitalia** ☎ 848/888088 🌐 www.trenitalia.com.

VISITOR INFORMATION

🔳 Tourist Information **Alto Adige Tourism** ☎ 0471/999999 🖷 0471/999900 🌐 www.hallo.com. **Bolzano** ✉ Piazza Walther 8 ☎ 0471/307000. **Bormio** ✉ Via Roma 131/b ☎ 0342/903300 🖷 0342/904696 🌐 www.valtellinaonline.com. **Bressanone** ✉ Viale Stazione 9 ☎ 0472/836401 🖷 0472/836067. **Brunico** ✉ Via Europa 26 ☎ 0474/555722 🖷 0474/555544. **Caldaro** ✉ Piazza Mercato 8 ☎ 0471/963169 🖷 0471/963469. **Canazei** ✉ Piazza Marconi ☎ 0462/601113 🖷 0462/602502. **Chiusa** ✉ Piazza Tinne 6 ☎ 0472/847424 🖷 0472/847244. **Cortina d'Ampezzo** ✉ Piazzetta San Francesco 8 ☎ 0436/3231 🖷 0436/3235 🌐 www.sunrise.it/cortina. **Dobbiaco** ✉ Via Dolomiti 3 ☎ 0474/972132 🖷 0474/972730. **Fiè allo Sciliar** ✉ Via Bolzano 4 ☎ 0471/725047 🖷 0471/725488. **Madonna di Campiglio** ✉ Via Pradalago 4 ☎ 0465/442000 🖷 0465/440404. **Merano** ✉ Corso della Libertà 45 ☎ 0473/27200 🖷 0473/235524. **Naturno** ✉ Piazza Municipio 1 ☎ 0473/666077 🖷 0473/666369. **Ortisei** ✉ Via Rezia 1 ☎ 0471/796328 🖷 0471/796749. **Rovereto** ✉ Corso Rosmini 6 ☎ 0464/430363 🖷 0464/435528. **Santa Cristina** ✉ Via Chemun 9 ☎ 0471/793046 🖷 0471/793198. **Selva Gardena** ✉ Via Mëisules 213 ☎ 0471/795122 🖷 0471/794245. **Trentino Tourism** ☎ 0461/839000 🖷 0461/260245 🌐 www.trentino.to. **Trento** ✉ Via Manci 2 ☎ 0461/983880 🖷 0461/984508.

MILAN, LOMBARDY & THE LAKES

4

FODOR'S CHOICE

Bellagio
Al Donizetti, restaurant, Bergamo
Villa d'Este, hotel, Cernobbio

HIGHLY RECOMMENDED

RESTAURANTS
Al Bersagliere, Goito
Ambasciata, Quistello
Centrale, Cremona
Da Abele, Milan
Don Carlos, Milan
Gualtiero Marchesi, Erbusco
L'Antica Osteria del Ponte, Cassinetta di Lugagnano
Taverna Colleoni dell'Angelo, Bergamo
Vecchia Lugana, Lugana di Sirmione
Villa Fiordaliso, Gardone Riviera

HOTELS
Grand Hotel Villa Serbelloni, Bellagio
London, Milan
Principe di Savoia, Milan
Terminus, Como
Villa Cortine, Sirmione
Villa del Sogno, Gardone Riviera

SIGHTS
Duomo, Milan
Galleria Vittorio Emanuele, Milan
Pinacoteca di Brera, Milan
Santa Maria delle Grazie, Milan
Sirmione
Villa Serbelloni, Bellagio

Updated by
Ryan Bradley

ONE IS TEMPTED TO DESCRIBE LOMBARDY as a place with something for everyone—Milan, capital of all that is new in Italy; the great Renaissance cities of the Po plain, Pavia, Cremona, and Mantua, where even the height of summer can be comparatively peaceful; and the lakes, where glacial waters framed by the Alps have been praised as the closest thing to paradise by writers as varied as Virgil, Tennyson, and Hemingway.

"Nothing in the world," wrote Stendhal in 1817, "can be compared to the fascination of those burning summer days passed on the Milanese lakes, in the middle of those chestnut groves so green that they immerse their branches in the waves." Millions of travelers have since agreed that, for sheer beauty, the lakes of northern Italy—Como, Maggiore, Garda, and Orta—have few equals. Adding to their unspoiled beauty are the Alpine foothills, 18th- and 19th-century villas and exotic formal gardens, toy villages, and dozens of resorts that were once Europe's most fashionable. Still, one cannot imagine Catullus returning to his "jewel" Sirmione, on Lago di Garda, without being a little daunted by its development as a resort town. Milan can be disappointingly modern—rather too much like the place you have come here to escape—but its historic buildings and art collections rival those of Florence and Rome.

More than 3,000 years ago, explorers from the highly civilized realm of Etruria in central Italy wandered northward beyond the River Po. The Etruscans extended their dominance into this region for hundreds of years but left little of their culture. They were succeeded by the Cenomani Gauls, who were conquered in turn by the legions of Rome in the latter days of the Republic. The region became known as Cisalpine Gaul ("Gaul across the Alps"). Under the rule of Augustus it became a Roman province and its warlike, independent people citizens of Rome. Virgil, Catullus, and both Plinys were born in the region during the relatively tranquil era known to its victors as the Pax Romana.

The decline of the Roman Empire was followed by invasion by Attila of the Huns and Theodoric of the Goths. These conquerors, in turn, gave way to the Lombards, who then ceded to Charlemagne their iron crown, which became the emblem of his vast but unstable empire. Even before the fragile bonds that held this empire together had begun to snap, the cities of Lombardy were erecting walls in defense against the Hungarians and against each other. These city-states formed the Lombard League, which, in the 12th century, finally defeated the German Frederick Barbarossa.

Once the northern invaders had been defeated, new and even bloodier strife began. In each city the Guelphs (bourgeois supporters of the popes) and the Ghibellines (noblemen loyal to the so-called emperors) clashed with each other. The city-states declined, and each fell under the yoke of powerful local rulers. The Republic of Venice dominated Brescia and Bergamo. Mantua was ruled by the Gonzaga, and the Visconti and Sforza families took over Como, Cremona, Milan, and Pavia.

The Battle of Pavia in 1525, where the generals of Holy Roman Emperor Charles V (1500–58) defeated the French, brought on 200 years of Spanish occupation. It was then that the routed Francis I famously declaimed, "All is lost, save honor." The Spaniards were, on the whole, less cruel than the local tyrants and were hardly resisted by the Lombards. The War of the Spanish Succession, in the early years of the 18th century, threw out the Spaniards and brought in the Austrians instead, whose dominion was "neither liked nor loathed" during the nearly 100 years of its existence.

Napoléon and his generals defeated the Austrians at the turn of the 19th century. The Treaty of Campoformio resulted in the proclamation of the

Cisalpine Republic, which quickly became the Republic of Italy and, just as rapidly, the Kingdom of Italy, which in turn lasted only until Napoléon's defeat brought back the Austrians. But Milan, as the capital of Napoléon's Republic, had enjoyed a taste of glory, and the city's independent citizens, along with those of the other Lombard cities, were not slow to resent the loss of new national identity. From 1820 on, the Lombards joined the Piedmontese and the house of Savoy in a long struggle against the Habsburgs and, in 1859, finally defeated Austria and brought about the re-creation of the Kingdom of Italy two years later.

Milan and other cities of Lombardy have not lost their independence and their hatred of domination. Nowhere in Italy was the eventual partisan insurrection against Mussolini—to whom they had first given power—and the German regime better organized or more successful. It was in the city's Piazza Loreto that the dead bodies of Mussolini and his lover, Claretta Petacci, were put on display, in the same spot where a group of partisans had been shot a few weeks before. Milan was liberated from the Germans by its own partisan organization before the entrance of Allied troops; escaping Allied prisoners could find sanctuary there when fighting was still going on to the south. In recent years, the independent Milanesi spirit has been demonstrated in the right-wing political movement known as the Lega Nord (Northern League). Although the Lega's accusations that revenue from the prosperous north is squandered on ill-fated projects in the poorer south continue to strike a chord, other party positions—including, in the 1990s, a call for secession—have been less widely supported by the ever-sensible Milanese.

Exploring Milan, Lombardy & the Lakes

Lombardy's greatest merit may be its diversity. Jagged Alpine vistas and deep glacial lakes stretch from the Swiss border down to Milan's outskirts, where they meet the flat, fertile plain that extends from banks of the Po River. The A4 autostrada connects Milan to Italy's industrial belt, which extends west to Turin and east through Brescia, Lombardy's second-biggest city. Scattered across the plains below are the Renaissance city-states of Pavia, Cremona, and Mantua.

Most international travelers arrive at Malpensa airport, some 50 km (31 mi) northwest of Milan. As the airport is closer to Lakes Como and Maggiore than to Milan itself, you can skip the city and head straight for the hills if you like; Lake Garda is a two-hour drive east of Milan. The best way to see the lake country is to rent a car in fall or spring and thread a leisurely path along the small mountain roads that link the lakes' least-spoiled northern tips. This is splendid mountain-driving country, with some of the most beautiful and challenging roads in the world. Without a car, however, it's still possible to see many of the region's sights, thanks to extensive bus routes and the many *vaporetti* (water taxis) that thread across the lakes. The throngs that descend upon the lakes in July and August, on weekends particularly, make reservations absolutely necessary—especially at Lake Como, the quintessential Italian lake resort.

About the Restaurants & Hotels

Milan is becoming increasingly cosmopolitan; Chinese restaurants abound, and it's also possible to dine on Japanese, Mexican, and Middle Eastern dishes, among other diverse offerings. The Lake District is only in full swing from late Spring through early fall; many restaurants and hotels close down for the winter.

The hotels in Italy's richest region generally cater to a clientele willing to pay for extra comfort. Many are converted from handsome old vil-

4

A week is enough to see the area thoroughly; five days will give you time to see all the sights, but you'll have to keep on the move. Three days will give you a taste of the major sights in the area, but time will be precious and morning starts will have to be early.

Numbers in the text correspond to numbers in the margin and on the Milan and Lombardy and the Lakes maps.

If you have 3 days

Spend the first day walking around ⊠ **Milan** ① –⑯ ►. The next morning, head east on the A4 autostrada and stop in the Alpine, medieval town of **Bergamo** ㉙ before continuing on to ⊠ **Sirmione** ㉗ on Lake Garda. If you arrive early enough, you may wish to drive around the lake a bit before bedding down for the night. On Day 3, take the A4 west past Bergamo, switch to the S432, and drive around the southern shore of Lake Como, stopping in **Bellagio** ㉚ for lunch, and spending the night in ⊠ **Como** ㉞.

If you have 5 days

Follow the three-day itinerary but after Bergamo, continue east and take the A22 south to ⊠ **Mantua** ⑳, where you can enjoy Mantegna's masterpieces. On Day 3 drive around Lake Garda, stopping at any gorgeous lakeside spot that catches your fancy, and spend the night in⊠ **Riva del Garda** ㉔ on the north side of the lake, or ⊠ **Sirmione** ㉗ on the south. The next morning, take the A4 back west to Lake Como, visiting Madonna del Ghisallo and **Bellagio** ㉚ and taking ferries to the lake towns of **Varenna** ㉛ and **Tremezzo** ㉜, where you'll find the magnificent Villa Carlotta. On the final day, head west to **Orta San Giulio** ㉟ on Lake Orta. It's only a short hop from there to Lake Maggiore, which you can explore by steamer.

If you have 7 days

Spend two days in ⊠ **Milan** ① –⑯ ►, and then start south along the A7 to **Pavia** ⑰ and **Cremona** ⑱, before continuing on to ⊠ **Mantua** ⑳. From there, follow the five-day plan above; make sure to stop in **Gargnano** ㉕ and **Gardone Riviera** ㉖ on Lake Garda, where you should visit Gabriele d'Annunzio's former home, Il Vittoriale.

las and have well-landscaped grounds—try to visit one or two, even if you don't stay the night. Most of the famous lake resorts are expensive; more reasonably priced accommodations can be found in the smaller towns and villages.

WHAT IT COSTS In euros				
$$$$	$$$	$$	$	¢
RESTAURANTS				
over €22	€17–€22	€12–€17	€7–€12	under €7
HOTELS				
IN MILAN	over €300	€225–€300	€150–€225	€75–€150	under €75
ELSEWHERE	over €210	€160–€210	€110–€160	€60–€110	under €60

Restaurant prices are for a second course (secondo piatto). Hotel prices are for two people in a standard double room in high season, including tax and service.

ON THE MENU

Unlike most other Italian regions, Lombardy traditionally exhibits a northern European preference for butter rather than oil as its cooking medium, which imparts a rich and distinctive flavor to the cuisine. Alla milanese—Milanese-style cooking—usually means the food is dipped in egg and bread crumbs mixed with grated Parmesan, then sautéed in butter. One of the most popular specialties here, osso buco, is almost always paired with risotto, which the alla milanese preparation enriches with chicken broth and saffron.

The lakes are a good source of fish, particularly trout and pike. Gorgonzola— a strong, creamy, veined cheese—and panettone—a sweet yeast bread with raisins, citron, and anise—both hail from the Milan area and can be found throughout Lombardy. The most rewarding wines of the region, worth searching wine lists for, are red Grumello and Sangue di Giuda (Blood of Judas) and the delicious light sparkling whites from the Franciacorta area.

Timing

Lake roads can become congested in July and August, especially on evenings and weekends. Fewer people visit in spring and fall, and in winter the lakeside towns are positively deserted. Note that many of the ferry services stop running in October and recommence in May. Early summer and early fall are the best times to see the area, though October can be chilly for swimming.

MILAN

Italy's business hub and crucible of chic is the country's most populous and prosperous city, serving as the capital of commerce, finance, fashion, and media. It's also Italy's transport hub, with the biggest international airport, most rail connections, and best subway system. Da Vinci's *Last Supper* and other great works of art are here, as well as a spectacular baroque Duomo, the finest of its kind. Milan even reigns supreme where it really counts (in the minds of many Italians), routinely trouncing the rest of the nation with its two premier soccer teams.

And yet, Milan hasn't won the battle of hearts and minds. Most tourists prefer Tuscany's hills and Venice's canals to Milan's hectic efficiency and wealthy indifference, and it's no surprise that in a country of medieval hilltop villages and skilled artisans, a city of grand boulevards and global corporations leaves visitors asking the real Italy to please stand up. They're right, of course. Milan is more European than Italian, a new buckle on an old boot, and although its old city can stand cobblestone for cobblestone against the best of them, seekers of Roman ruins and fairy-tale towns may pass. But Milan's new faces are hidden behind splendid beaux-arts facades and in luxurious 19th-century palazzos, and those lured by its world-class shopping and European sophistication enjoy the city's lively, cosmopolitan feel.

For their part, most Italians consider the Milanese an affront to their ideal of *la dolce vita,* and they, too, are right. The Milanese don't conform to the Italian stereotypes. Whereas Florentines boast about its past and politicians in Rome bicker about its present, the Milanese are too busy building Italy's future to live the slow, sensual lifestyle preferred by their countrymen. This is part choice and part necessity. Milan never had it easy. To turn their landlocked outpost into a regional power, they had to dig an extensive network of deep canals, eventually linking the

Auto Racing

Lombardy Formula I fans are passionate, living and dying with the fortunes of their beloved team Ferrari. All converge on the second Sundy in September for the Italian Grand Prix, held 15 km (9 mi) northeast of Milan in Monza. The track was built in 1922 in the Parco di Monza, where there are also a hippodrome, a golf course, and other facilities.

Golf

The success of Italy's most famous professional golfer, Bergamo resident Costantino Rocca, has added to the sport's popularity among Italians in the region. Facilities have improved dramatically over the last decade, resulting in a proliferation of courses groomed into northern Italy's landscape. Several courses are convenient to Milan and to Lake Como.

Water Sports

Schools for sailing, scuba diving, waterskiing, and windsurfing are in Riva del Garda, on the northern tip of Lake Garda. Torbole, 5 km (3 mi) east of Riva del Garda on S240, is a prime spot for windsurfing. Lake Como also has well-equipped sailing and windsurfing schools as well as waterskiing.

---

city to the Po, Ticino, and Adda rivers. Lacking natural defenses, they built strong walls to keep the marauding hordes at bay. For income, local merchants took advantage of nearby Alpine trade routes to build a great trading center. Even talent was imported when needed; from St. Ambrose and Leonardo da Vinci to the waves of migrants who fueled its growth in the second half of the 20th century, outsiders have been drawn to Milan for its open, freewheeling commercial culture and acceptance of new ideas. The result has been an ever-expanding power, and a juicy target for conquest.

Virtually every invader in European history—Gaul, Roman, Goth, Longobard, and Frank—as well as a long series of rulers from France, Spain, and Austria, took a turn at ruling the city. After being completely sacked by the Goths in AD 539 and the Holy Roman Empire under Frederick Barbarossa in 1157, Milan became one of the first independent city-states of the Renaissance. Its heyday of self-rule proved comparatively brief. From 1277 until 1500, it was ruled by the Visconti and subsequently the Sforza dynasties. These families were known, justly or not, for a peculiarly aristocratic mixture of refinement, classical learning, and cruelty, and much of the surviving grandeur of Gothic and Renaissance art and architecture is their doing. Be on the lookout in your wanderings for the Visconti family emblem—a viper, its jaws straining wide, devouring a child.

Exploring Milan

The city center is compact and walkable, although it's faster to use the efficient Metropolitana (subway) to reach locations farther afield. Navigating the streets of Milan is difficult at best, and parking can be downright miserable, so leave the car behind.

Milan's main sites and arteries radiate out from the massive baroque Duomo. Corso Vittorio Emanuele leads northeast into the *quadrilatero* (fashion district), lined with elegant window displays from Milan's cel-

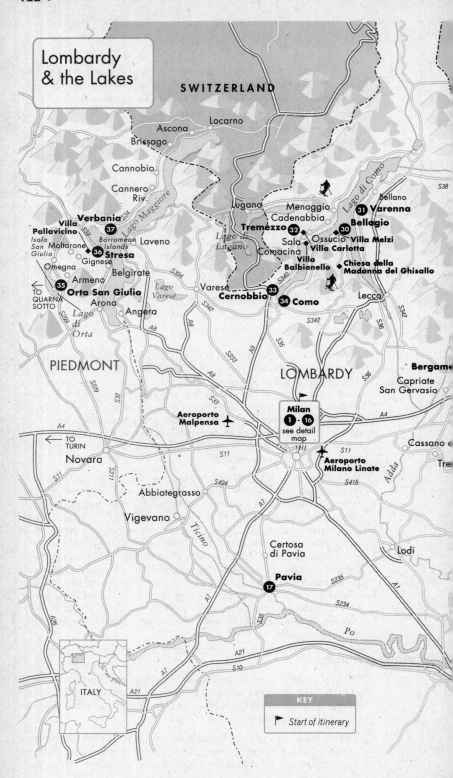

Lombardy & the Lakes

SWITZERLAND

Locarno

Ascona

Brissago

Cannobio

Cannero Riv.

Verbania 37

Villa Pallavicino

Isola San Giulio

Moltarone

Gignese

36 **Stresa**

Omegna

Armeno

35 **Orta San Giulio**

← TO QUARNA SOTTO

Arona

Angera

Lago di Orta

Laveno

Belgirate

Lago Maggiore

Lago Varese

Varese

Lugano

Lago di Lugano

Menaggio

Cadenabbia

Tremezzo 32

Sala Comacina

Villa Balbianello

Cernobbio 33

Bellano

31 **Varenna**

Lago di Como

Bellagio

30 Ossucio **Villa Melzi**

Villa Carlotta

● **Chiesa della Madonna del Ghisallo**

34 **Como**

Lecco

S38

S342

S36

S342

PIEDMONT

LOMBARDY

Bergam

Capriate San Gervasio

Novara

← TO TURIN

Aeroporto Malpensa ✈

Milan 1 - 16 see detail map ►

✈ **Aeroporto Milano Linate**

Cassano

Tre

Adda

Abbiategrasso

Vigevano

Ticino

Certosa di Pavia

Pavia 17

Lodi

Po

ITALY

KEY
► *Start of itinerary*

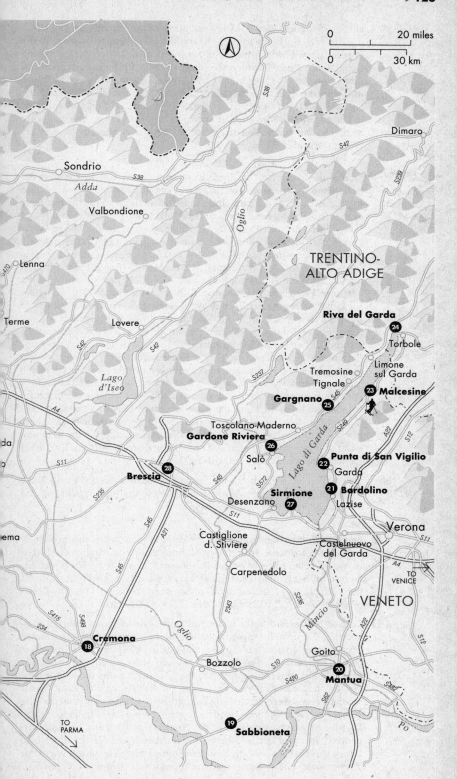

0   20 miles

0   30 km

Dimaro

Sondrio

Adda

Valbondione

TRENTINO-
ALTO ADIGE

Lenna

Terme

Lovere

Riva del Garda

24

Torbole

*Lago
d'Iseo*

Tremosine

Tignale

Limone
sul Garda

23 **Malcesine**

Gargnano

25

Toscolano-Maderno

Gardone Riviera

26

Salò

Lago di Garda

22 **Punta di San Vigilio**

Garda

Brescia

28

21 **Bardolino**

Lazise

Sirmione

Desenzano

27

Verona

Castiglione
d. Stiviere

Castelnuovo
del Garda

A4

TO
VENICE

Carpenedolo

VENETO

Oglio

Mincio

Cremona

18

Bozzolo

Goito

20 **Mantua**

Po

TO
PARMA

19 **Sabbioneta**

ebrated designers. Beyond La Scala, north of the Duomo, are the winding streets of the Brera section, the traditional bohemian quarter. To the northwest, past Milan's most exclusive residential district, is the imposing Renaissance Castello Sforzesco. Banks cluster in the ancient financial district just west of the Duomo, and bookshops and cafés can be found in the university quarter to the southeast. The **tourist office** (⊠ Via Marconi 1 ☎ 031/303440 ⊙ Mon.–Sat. 8:45–1 and 2–6, Sun. 9–1 and 2–5) in Piazza Duomo is an excellent place to begin your visit. Free maps are available, but the pocket-size MiniCity® version may be the best €3 you can spend in Milan.

North & East of the Duomo

a good walk

Start at the **Duomo** ❶ ▶ and visit its roof, museum, and the **Battistero Paleocristiano** ❷. Then move on to **Galleria Vittorio Emanuele** ❸, just beyond the northern tip of the cathedral's facade. Continue across the transepts of the Galleria and head north to **Teatro alla Scala** ❹, where Verdi found fame. Head northeast on Via Manzoni, stopping in the **Museo Poldi-Pezzoli** ❺ to view its collection of Renaissance paintings. Continue on Via Manzoni, then turn right on Via Monte Napoleone, plunging into the *quadrilatero d'oro* (golden quadrangle), Milan's high-fashion district. Turn left on Via Sant'Andrea, then left again on Via della Spiga to return to Via Manzoni. From here, you can make a detour to the Giardini Pubblici (great for kids) and the **Museo Civico di Storia Naturale** ❻ on the eastern side of the park. Backtrack south on Via Manzoni and return to the Montenapoleone metro station; take a right onto the short Via Croce Rosa, then an immediate left onto Via Monte di Pietà. At Via di Brera, turn right into the bohemian district anchored by the **Pinacoteca di Brera** ❼. After exploring the gallery (and the outdoor cafés), head west on Via Fiori Chiari, which tapers to a tiny *vicolo* (alleyway) before hitting busy Via Mercato. Turn left, then right on Via Arco and cross a small piazza with intersecting tram tracks. You'll see the imposing stone towers of **Castello Sforzesco** ❽ rising straight ahead—make your way to the entrance in the central, square tower. After viewing the castle's collections, walk back past the fountain, past the statute of Garibaldi, and onto the pedestrian-only boulevard Via Dante, which leads back toward the Duomo.

TIMING   The walk itself will take about two hours; allow a full day to roam the museums, shop for gifts, and sip caffè. Note that most museums and some churches are closed Monday.

What to See

❷ **Battistero Paleocristiano.** Beneath the Duomo's piazza lies this baptistery ruin dating from the 4th century. Although opinion remains divided, it is widely believed to be where Ambrose, Milan's first bishop and patron saint, baptized Augustine. Tickets are available at the kiosk inside the cathedral. ⊠ *Piazza del Duomo, enter through Duomo* ☎ 02/86463456 🖹 €1.50 ⊙ *Daily 9:30–5:15* Ⓜ *Duomo.*

❽ **Castello Sforzesco.** For the serious student of Renaissance military engineering, the Castello must be something of a travesty, so often has it been remodeled or rebuilt since it was begun in 1450 by the *condottiere* (hired mercenary) who founded the city's second dynastic family, Francesco Sforza, fourth duke of Milan. Though today the word "mercenary" has a pejorative ring, during the Renaissance all Italy's great soldier-heroes were professionals hired by the cities and principalities that they served. Of them—and there were thousands—Francesco Sforza (1401–66) is considered one of the greatest, most honest, and most organized. It is said he could remember the names not only of all his men but of their horses as well. His rule signaled the enlightened age of the Renaissance, but preceded the next foreign rule by a scant 50 years.

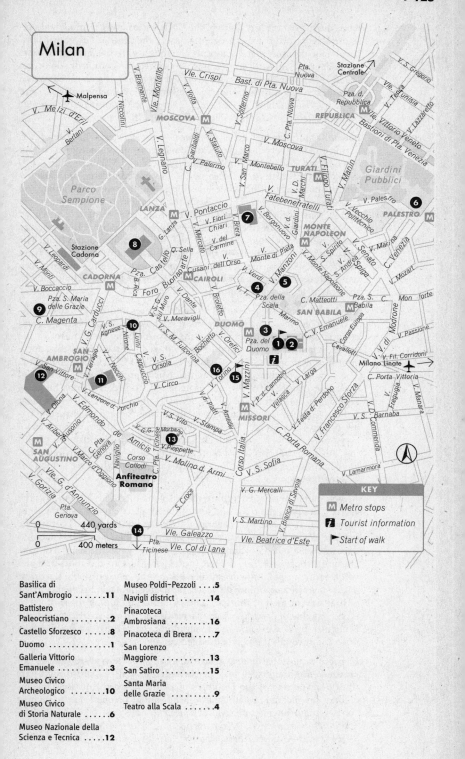

Milan

✈ Malpensa

Parco Sempione

KEY

Ⓜ Metro stops

ℹ Tourist information

▶ Start of walk

0 ____ 440 yards

0 ____ 400 meters

Since the turn of the last century, the Castello has housed municipal museums devoted variously to Egyptian and other antiquities, musical instruments, paintings, and sculpture. Highlights are the **Salle delle Asse,** a frescoed room still sometimes attributed to Leonardo da Vinci (1452–1519). Michelangelo's unfinished *Rondanini Pietà,* is believed to be his last work—an astounding achievement for a man nearly 90, and a moving coda of his life. ⊠ *Piazza Castello* ☎ *02/86461404* ⊕ *www.milanocastello.it* ≊ *Free* ◷ *Tues.–Sun. 9–5:30* Ⓜ *Cairoli.*

★ ▶ ❶ **Duomo.** This intricate Gothic structure—Italy's largest—has been fascinating and exasperating visitors and conquerors alike since it was begun by Galeazzo Visconti III (1351–1402), first duke of Milan, in 1386. Consecrated in the 15th or 16th century, it was not completed until just before the coronation of Napoléon as king of Italy in 1809. Whether you concur with travel writer H. V. Morton, writing in 1964, that the cathedral is "one of the mightiest Gothic buildings ever created," or regard it as a spiny pastiche of centuries, there is no denying that for sheer size and complexity it is unrivaled; its look is more Gotham than Milan. The capacity is reckoned to be 40,000. Usually it is empty, a sanctuary from the frenetic pace of life outside and the perfect place for solitary contemplation. The poet Percy Bysshe Shelley swore by it—claiming it was the only place to read Dante.

The building is adorned with 135 marble spires and 2,245 marble statues. The oldest part is the **apse.** Its three colossal bays of curving and counter-curved tracery, especially the bay adorning the exterior of the stained-glass windows, should not be missed. At the end of the southern transept down the right aisle lies the **tomb of Gian Giacomo Medici.** The tomb owes some of its design to Michelangelo but was executed by Leone Leoni (1509–90) and is generally considered to be his masterpiece; it dates from the 1560s. Directly ahead is the Duomo's most famous sculpture, the rather gruesome but anatomically instructive figure of **San Bartolomeo** (St. Bartholomew), whose glorious martyrdom consisted of being flayed alive. It is usually said the saint stands "holding" his skin, but this is not quite accurate. It would appear more that he is luxuriating in it, much as a 1950s matron might have shown off a new fur stole.

As you enter the apse to admire those splendid windows, glance at the **sacristy doors** to the right and left of the altar. The lunette on the right dates from 1393 and was decorated by Hans von Fernach. That on the left also dates from the 14th century and is ascribed jointly to Giacomo da Campione and Giovanni dei Grassi. Don't miss the view from the Duomo's **roof**; walk out the left (north) transept to the stairs and elevator. Sadly, air pollution drastically reduces the view on all but the rarest days. As you stand among the forest of marble pinnacles, remember that virtually every inch of this gargantuan edifice, including the roof itself, is decorated with precious white marble dragged from quarries near Lake Maggiore by Duke Visconti's team along road laid fresh for the purpose and through the newly dredged canals.

Inspection and possible repair of 12 of the northern spires means the facade facing the Piazza may be shrouded in scaffolding through part of 2004. The rest of the Duomo's intricate masonry and statuary, including the gleaming, emblematic **Madonnina** perched on the highest spire, remain unencumbered. ⊠ *Piazza del Duomo* ☎ *02/86463456* ≊ *Stairs to roof €3.50, elevator €5* ◷ *Mid-Feb.–mid-Nov., daily 9–5:45; mid-Nov.–mid-Feb., daily 9–4:15* Ⓜ *Duomo.*

Exhibits at the **Museo del Duomo** shed light on the cathedral's history and include some of the treasures removed for safety from the exterior. ⊠ *Piazza del Duomo 14* ☎ *02/860358* 🎫 *€6, €7 with ticket for the Duomo's elevator* ⊘ *Daily 10–1:15 and 3–6.*

★ ❸ **Galleria Vittorio Emanuele.** This spectacularly extravagant, late-19th-century glass-topped, barrel-vaulted tunnel is essentially one of the planet's earliest and most select shopping malls. It's rivaled perhaps only by GUM, off Red Square in Moscow, for sheer belle epoque splendor. Its architect, Giuseppe Mengoni, is the only mall designer known to have died for his cause—he lost his footing on the roof and tumbled to his death on the floor below just days before the Galleria's opening in 1877.

Like its suburban American cousins, the Galleria fulfills numerous social functions vastly more important than its ostensible commercial purpose. This is the city's heart, midway between the cathedral and La Scala, and it is sometimes called *Il Salotto* (the Living Room). It teems with life, inviting people-watching from the tables that spill from the Galleria's bars and restaurants, where you can enjoy a ridiculously overpriced coffee. Books, records, clothing, food, wine, pens, jewelry, and myriad other goods are all for sale in the Galleria, and you'll also find here Savini, one of Milan's classic restaurants.

Like the cathedral, the Galleria is cruciform in shape. Even in poor weather, the great glass dome above the octagonal center is a splendid sight. And the floor mosaics, usually unnoticed, are a vastly underrated source of pleasure, even if they are not to be taken too seriously. They represent Europe, Asia, Africa, and the United States; those at the entrance arch are devoted to science, industry, art, and agriculture. ⊠ *Piazza del Duomo* ⊘ *Most shops daily 9:30–1 and 3:30–7, others later or all day* Ⓜ *Duomo.*

🐾 ❻ **Museo Civico di Storia Naturale** (Municipal Natural History Museum). Exhibits here appeal to animal and nature lovers, and anyone else who can appreciate stilted arrangements of narwhals, elephant seals, and bug-besieged hippopotami. It's on the eastern edge of the **Giardini Pubblici** (Public Gardens), an outlet for active young children. ⊠ *Corso Venezia 55, Porta Venezia* ☎ *02/88463289* 🎫 *Free* ⊘ *Tues.–Fri. 9–6, weekends 8–6:30 last entry 30 mins before closing* Ⓜ *Palestro.*

❺ **Museo Poldi–Pezzoli.** This exceptional museum, opened in 1881, was once a private residence and collection, and contains not only pedigreed paintings but also porcelain, textiles, and a cabinet with scenes of Dante's life. The gem is undoubtedly the *Portrait of a Lady* by Antonio Pollaiolo (1431–98), one of the city's most prized treasures and the source of the museum's logo. The collection also includes masterpieces by Botticelli (1445–1510), Andrea Mantegna (1431–1506), Giovanni Bellini (1430–1516), and Fra Filippo Lippi (1406–69), whose uncomplicated, heartrending style won him the favor and patronage of Florence's Piero de' Medici, son of Cosimo and father of Lorenzo il Magnifico (1449–92). ⊠ *Via Manzoni 12, Scala* ☎ *02/794889* ⊕ *www.museopoldipezzoli.it* 🎫 *€6* ⊘ *Tues.–Sun. 10–6* Ⓜ *Duomo.*

★ ❼ **Pinacoteca di Brera** (Brera Gallery). The collection here is star-studded, even by Italian standards. The entrance hall (Room I) displays 20th-century sculpture and painting, including Carlo Carrà's (1881–1966) confident, stylish response to the schools of cubism and surrealism. After that, the museum's 38 other rooms are arranged in chronological order—pace yourself.

The somber, moving *Cristo Morto* (Dead Christ) by Mantegna (1430–1506) dominates Room VI, with its sparse palette of umber and its original perspective. Mantegna's shocking, almost surgical precision—in the rendering of Christ's wounds, the face propped up on a pillow, the day's growth of beard—tells of an all-too-human agony. It is one of Renaissance painting's most quietly wondrous achievements, finding an unsuspected middle ground between the excesses of conventional gore and beauty in representing the Passion's saddest moment.

Room XXIV offers two additional highlights of the gallery. Raphael's (1483–1520) *Sposalizio della Vergine,* with its mathematical composition and precise, alternating colors, portrays the betrothal of Mary and Joseph (who, though older than the other men gathered, wins her hand when the rod he is holding miraculously blossoms). *La Vergine con il Bambino e Santi* (Madonna with Child and Saints), by Piero della Francesca (1420–92), is an altarpiece commissioned by Federico da Montefeltro (shown kneeling, in full armor, before the Virgin); it was intended for a church to house the Duke's tomb. The ostrich egg hanging from the apse, depending on whom you ask, either commemorates the miracle of his fertility—Federico's wife died months after giving birth to a long-awaited male heir—or alludes to his appeal for posthumous mercy, with the egg symbolizing the saving power of grace. ⊠ *Via Brera 28, Brera* ☏ *02/722631* ⊕ *www.brera.beniculturali.it* 🎫 *€5* ⊙ *Tues.–Sun. 8:30–7:15; last admission 45 mins before closing* Ⓜ *Cairoli, Lanza, or Montenapoleone.*

off the beaten path

LATIN QUARTER – Take time to wander around the lively quarter surrounding the Pinacoteca di Brera. The narrow streets, lined with boutiques, crafts shops, cafés, restaurants, and music clubs, make up what's often referred to as Milan's Greenwich Village. A longtime haunt of artists and musicians, it has a number of clubs and cafés presenting live music late into the night.

❹ **Teatro alla Scala.** You need know nothing of opera to sense that, like Carnegie Hall, La Scala is closer to a cathedral than an auditorium. Here Verdi established his reputation and Maria Callas sang her way into opera lore. It looms as a symbol—both for the performer who dreams of singing here and for the opera buff who knows every note of *Rigoletto* by heart. Audiences are notoriously fickle and have been known to jeer performers who do not do appropriate justice to their beloved *opera lirica.* The opera house was closed after destruction by Allied bombs in 1943, reopened at a performance led by Arturo Toscanini in 1946, and closed again in 2002 for long-overdue renovations, scheduled to last three seasons (reopening night planned for December 7, 2004).

In the meantime, performances are held at the Teatro Arcimboldi on the outskirts of Milan. Outside La Scala itself, signboards provide an extensive history of the theater, as well as explanation of the renovation work. ⊠ *Piazza della Scala, Scala* ☏ *02/860775 box office* ⊕ *www. teatroallascala.org* Ⓜ *Duomo.*

South & West of the Duomo

a good walk

From the Duomo, head southwest on Via Torino, pausing to admire Bramante's Renaissance masterpiece, the Church of **San Satiro** ⓯ ▶. Backtrack a bit toward the Duomo, turning left on Via Spadari, then left again on Via Cantù to reach Piazza Pio XI—and the beautiful **Pinacoteca Ambrosiana** ⓰ gallery and attached library. Find your way south to Via Fulcorina, then turn right, walking northwest until you hit Corso Magenta. Turn left, visiting the city's **Museo Civico Archeologico** ⑩ before continuing on to visit Milan's most precious painting: the *Last Supper,* in the monastery of **Santa Maria delle Grazie** ❾. Across the street is the temporary home of the Museo Teatrale alla Scala, exhibiting treasures from

Milan's proud operatic tradition. Backtrack on Corso Magenta, turning right onto Via Carducci. At the intersection of Via Carducci and Via San Vittore you will find the medieval **Basilica di Sant'Ambrogio** ⑪; walking a block west on Via San Vittore will take you to the **Museo Nazionale della Scienza e Tecnica** ⑫. When finished in the Sant'Ambrogio neighborhood, head east on Via de Amicis, then (after about a 5-minute) turn left on Corso Porta Ticinese to reach the church of **San Lorenzo Maggiore** ⑬. South on Corso Porta Ticinese, just outside the limits of the old city, is the bustling **Navigli district** ⑭. You can hike back toward the Duomo, or hop on the subway to return to the city center.

TIMING   Allow a full day for this walk. Note that most museums and some churches are closed Monday. Your itinerary should be adapted to accommodate the time of your reservation to view the *Last Supper*.

What to See

⑪ **Basilica di Sant'Ambrogio** (Basilica of St. Ambrose). Noted for its medieval architecture, the church was consecrated by St. Ambrose in AD 387, and is the model for all Lombard Romanesque churches. ⊠ *Piazza Sant'Ambrogio 15, Sant'Ambrogio* ☎ *02/86450895* ☉ *Mon.–Sat. 7–noon and 2:30–7, Sun. 7–1 and 3–8* Ⓜ *Sant'Ambrogio.*

⑩ **Museo Civico Archeologico** (Municipal Archaeological Museum). Housed in a former monastery, this museum has some enlightening relics from Milan's Roman past—from everyday utensils and jewelry to several fine examples of mosaic pavement. ⊠ *Corso Magenta 15, Sant'Ambrogio* ☎ *02/86450011* ⊠ *Free* ☉ *Tues.–Sun. 9–5:30* Ⓜ *Cadorna.*

need a break?   A bit overcrowded at night, the **Bar Magenta** (⊠ Via Carducci 13, at Corso Magenta, Sant'Ambrogio ☎ 02/8053808) can be a good stop en route during the day. Beyond lunch, beer, or coffee, the real attraction is its casual but civilized, quintessentially Milanese ambience.

⑫ **Museo Nazionale della Scienza e Tecnica** (National Museum of Science and Technology). This museum houses an extensive, eccentric collection of engineering achievements, from metal-processing equipment to full-size locomotives. But the highlights are undoubtedly the exhibits based on the inventive technical drawings of Leonardo da Vinci. On the second floor, a collection of models based on these sketches are artfully displayed, with Leonardo's paintings offering striking counterpoint overhead. Explanations are not offered in English, leaving you to ponder possible purposes for the contraptions. On the ground level—in the hallway between the courtyards—is a "workshop" featuring interactive, moving models of the famous *vite aerea* (aerial screw) and *ala battente* (beating wing), thought to be forerunners of the modern helicopter and airplane, respectively. ⊠ *Via San Vittore 21, Sant'Ambrogio* ☎ *02/485551* ⊕ *www.museoscienza.org* ⊠ *€6.20* ☉ *Tues.–Fri. 9:30–4:50, weekends 9:30–6:20* Ⓜ *Sant'Ambrogio.*

Museo Teatrale alla Scala. While the La Scala opera house undergoes renovations, its museum makes its temporary home at Palazzo Busca—directly across from Santa Maria delle Grazie. You can admire librettos, posters, costumes, instruments, and design sketches for the theater, curtains and viewing box decorations. A highlight is the collection of antique gramophones and phonographs. ⊠ *Corso Magenta 71* ⊕ *www. teatroallascala.org* ☎ *02/4691249* ⊠ *€5* ☉ *Daily 9–6; last admission at 5:15* Ⓜ *Duomo or Cordusio.*

⑭ **Navigli district.** In medieval times a network of navigable canals, called *navigli,* crisscrossed Milan. Almost all have been covered over, but in this romantic, bohemian neighborhood two long canals—Naviglio Grande and Naviglio Pavese—and part of a third—Darsena—survive. They're lined with quaint shops, art galleries, cafés, restaurants, and clubs. ✉ *South of Corso Porta Ticinese, Porta Genova* Ⓜ *Porta Genova.*

❶❻ Pinacoteca Ambrosiana. This museum, founded in the 17th century by Cardinal Federico Borromeo, is one of the city's treasures. Here you can contemplate works of art such as Caravaggio's *Basket of Fruit,* prescient in its realism, and Raphael's awesome preparatory drawing for *The School of Athens* in the Vatican, as well as paintings by Leonardo, Botticelli, Luini, Titian, and Brueghel. The adjoining library, the Biblioteca Ambrosiana, also sometimes hosts exhibits and is considered to be the oldest Italian public library, dating from 1609. ✉ *Piazza Pio XI 2, Duomo* ☎ *02/806921* ⊕ *www.ambrosiana.it* ✍ *€6.20* ⊘ *Museum Tues.–Sun. 10–5:30. Library Mon.–Sat. 9:30–5.*

❶❸ San Lorenzo Maggiore. Sixteen ancient Roman columns line the front of this sanctuary; 4th-century paleo-Christian mosaics survive in the Cappella di Sant'Aquilino (Chapel of St. Aquilinus). ✉ *Corso di Porta Ticinese 39, Ticinese* ☎ *02/89404129* ✍ *Mosaics €2* ⊘ *Church daily 7:30–12:30 and 2–6:45. Mosaics daily 9:30–12:30 and 2–6:30.*

▶ ❶❺ San Satiro. First built in 876, this architectural gem was later perfected by Bramante (1444–1514), demonstrating his command of proportion and perspective, keynotes of Renaissance architecture. Bramante tricks the eye with a famous optical illusion that makes a small interior seem extraordinarily spacious and airy, while accommodating a beloved 13th-century fresco. ✉ *Via Torino 9, Duomo* ⊘ *Weekdays 7:30–11:30 and 3:30–6:30, weekends 9–noon and 3:30–7.*

★ ❾ Santa Maria delle Grazie. *The Last Supper,* housed in the church and former Dominican monastery of Santa Maria delle Grazie, has had an almost unbelievable history of bad luck and neglect—its near destruction in an American bombing raid in August 1943 was only the latest chapter in a series of misadventures, including, if one 19th-century source is to be believed, being whitewashed over by monks. Yet da Vinci chose to work slowly and patiently in oil pigments—which demand dry plaster—instead of proceeding hastily on wet plaster according to the conventional fresco technique. Well-meant but disastrous attempts at restoration have done little to rectify the problem of the work's placement: it was executed on a wall unusually vulnerable to climatic dampness. Novelist Aldous Huxley (1894–1963) called it "the saddest work of art in the world." After years of restorers' patiently shifting from one square centimeter to another, Leonardo's famous masterpiece is free of the shroud of scaffolding—and centuries of retouching, grime, and dust. Astonishing clarity and luminosity have been regained. *Reservations are required* to view the work; call several days ahead for weekday visits and several *weeks* in advance for a weekend visit. The reservations office is open 9 AM–6 PM weekdays and 9 AM–2 PM on Saturday. Viewings are in 15-minute slots.

Despite Leonardo's carefully preserved preparatory sketches in which the apostles are clearly labeled by name, there still remains some small debate about a few identities in the final arrangement. But there can be no mistaking Judas, small and dark, his hand calmly reaching forward to the bread, isolated from the terrible confusion that has taken the hearts of the others. One critic, Frederick Hartt, offers an elegantly terse explanation for why the composition works: it combines "dramatic confusion" with "mathematical order." Certainly, the amazingly skillful and unobtrusive repetition of threes—in the windows, in the grouping of the figures, and in their placement—adds a mystical aspect to what at first seems simply the perfect observation of spontaneous human gesture.

The painting was executed in what was the order's refectory, now called the **Cenacolo Vinciano.**Take a moment to visit Santa Maria delle Grazie itself. It's a handsome church, with a fine dome, which Bramante added along with a cloister about the time that Leonardo was commissioned to paint *The Last Supper.* If you're wondering how two such giants came to be employed decorating and remodeling the refectory and church of a comparatively modest religious order, and not, say, the Duomo, the answer lies in the ambitious but largely unrealized plan to turn Santa Maria delle Grazie into a magnificent Sforza family mausoleum. Though Ludovico il Moro Sforza (1452–1508), seventh duke of Milan, was but one generation away from the founding of the Sforza dynasty, he was its last ruler. Two years after Leonardo finished *The Last Supper,* Ludovico was defeated and imprisoned in a French dungeon for the remaining eight years of his life. ⊠ *Piazza Santa Maria delle Grazie 2, off Corso Magenta, Sant'Ambrogio* ☎ *02/89421146* ⊠ *€6.50 plus €1.50 reservation fee* ⊙ *Tues.–Sun. 8-7* Ⓜ *Cadorna.*

off the beaten path

LEONARDO'S HORSE – In 1482, Leonardo da Vinci proposed and undertook a daunting project: building the largest equestrian statue in the world, to honor the father of Ludovico Sforza. To da Vinci's great regret, he never got further than a full-scale (at 24 ft high) clay model—with the French army threatening Milan, bronze became too scarce. The project lost momentum for almost five centuries, until an article in *National Geographic* inspired retired United Airlines pilot Charles Dent to begin fundraising for the horse's belated bronze embodiment (based on drawings that had been found in Madrid in 1965). His improbable quest yielded Japanese-American sculptor Nina Akamu's *Il Cavallo,* which was presented as a gift to the people of Italy at San Siro on September 30, 1999, five hundred years, to the day, after French archers used Leonardo's original model for target practice. ⊠ *Via Piccolomini, between the racetrack and the soccer stadium, San Siro* ⊕ *www.leonardoshorse.org.*

FANTASY WORLD MINITALIA – Between Milan and Bergamo, this theme park has a relief model of Italy, with about 200 models of the country's most important monuments. ⊠ *A4 autostrada toward Bergamo, Capriate San Gervasio, 35 km (22 mi) east of Milan* ☎ *02/9090169* ⊕ *www.fantasyworld.it* ⊠ *€16* ⊙ *Mar.–Oct., daily 9:30–dusk.*

Where to Eat

$$$$ ✕ **Aimo e Nadia.** It's a bit out of the way, but well worth the pursuit of gastronomic excellence. The freshest ingredients (gathered from every corner of the country), a welcoming contemporary environment, and a world-class sommelier all contribute to Aimo e Nadia's high acclaim. Specialties include *risotto al tartufo* (risotto with truffles) and *tagliolini con totani peperoni dolci e delizie dell'orto* (tagliolini pasta with calamari, sweet peppers, and garden delights). ⊠ *Via Montecuccoli 6, West Milan* ☎ *02/416886* ⚶ *Reservations essential* 🏛 *Jacket and tie* ▤ *AE, DC, MC, V* ⊙ *Closed Sun. and Aug. No lunch Sat.* Ⓜ *Primaticcio.*

★ $$$$ ✕ **Don Carlos.** This restaurant near La Scala is nothing like its indecisive operatic namesake (whose betrothed was stolen by his father). Flavors are bold, their presentation precise and full of flair: broiled red mullet floats on a lacy layer of crispy leek. Walls are saturated with sketches of the theater, and the aria recordings are every bit as well chosen as the wine list, setting the perfect stage for discreet commerce or, better yet, refined romance. ✉ *Grand Hotel et de Milan, Via Manzoni 29, Duomo* ☎ *02/723141* ☎ *Reservations essential.* ▭ *AE, DC, MC, V* ☉ *Closed Mon., Aug., Dec. 15–Jan. 7. No lunch.*

$$$$ ✕ **Giannino.** This century-old institution is a beautiful place to have a meal, with an open kitchen and a winter garden among its aesthetic attractions. The risotto is outstanding, and you would be hard-pressed to find a better version of the classic *cotoletta alla milanese* (breaded veal cutlet) anywhere in the city. ✉ *Via Amatore Sciesa 8, East Central* ☎ *02/55195582* ☎ *Reservations essential* ▭ *AE, DC, MC, V* ☉ *Closed Sun. No lunch Mon.*

★ $$$$ ✕ **L'Antica Osteria del Ponte.** Rich, imaginative seasonal cuisine, composed according to the inspired whims of chef Ezio Santin, is reason enough to make your way 20 km (12 mi) southwest of Milan to one of Italy's finest restaurants. The setting is a traditional country inn, where a wood fire warms the rustic interior in winter. The menu changes regularly; in fall, wild porcini mushrooms are among the favored ingredients. ✉ *Cassinetta di Lugagnano, 3 km (2 mi) north of Abbiategrasso* ☎ *02/9420034* ☎ *Reservations essential* ▭ *AE, DC, MC, V* ☉ *Closed Sun., Mon., Dec. 25–Jan. 15, and Aug.*

$$$$ ✕ **Nobu.** From a minimalist corner of the Armani minimall, Milan's Nobu serves the same delicious Japanese-Peruvian fusion as its siblings in the world's other culinary capitals. Cocktails, appetizers, and beautiful people can be found at the ground-floor bar, well worth a visit even if not dining upstairs. ✉ *Via Pisoni, 1, corner of Via Manzoni 31, Quadrilatero* ☎ *02/72318645* ☎ *Reservations essential* ▭ *AE, DC, MC, V* ☉ *Closed Sun.* Ⓜ *Montenapoleone.*

$$$$ ✕ **Savini.** Classic, classy Savini, in the east wing of Galleria Vittorio Emanuele, is a Milanese institution, with red carpets and cut-glass chandeliers characteristic of its late-19th-century roots. Stick with the standards: the Milanese specialty *risotto al salto* (cooked as a pancake, grilled in the pan) is excellent here, as are the *cotoletta di vitello* (veal cutlet) and osso buco. ✉ *Galleria Vittorio Emanuele, Duomo* ☎ *02/72003433* ▭ *AE, DC, MC, V* ☉ *Closed Sun. and 3 wks mid-Aug.* Ⓜ *Duomo.*

$$$ ✕ **Boeucc.** Milan's oldest restaurant, opened in 1696, is on the same suggestive square as novelist Alessandro Manzoni's house, not far from La Scala. With fluted columns, chandeliers, thick carpets, and a garden, it has come a long way from its basement origins (*boeucc,* pronounced "birch," is old Milanese for *buco,* or hole). You'll savor such dishes as penne *al branzino e zucchini* (with sea bass and zucchini) and *gelato di castagne con zabaglione caldo* (chestnut ice cream with hot zabaglione). ✉ *Piazza Belgioioso 2, Scala* ☎ *02/76020224* ☎ *Reservations essential* ▭ *AE* ☉ *Closed Sat., Aug., Dec. 24–Jan. 2. No lunch Sun.* Ⓜ *Montenapoleone, Duomo.*

$$$ ✕ **Joia.** At this haute-cuisine vegetarian restaurant near Piazza della Repubblica, delicious dishes are artistically prepared by chef Pietro Leemann. The ever-changing menu offers dishes such as ravioli with basil, potatoes, pine nuts, and crisp green beans. A fish menu is also available. ✉ *Via Panfilo Castaldi 18, Porta Venezia* ☎ *02/29522124* ▭ *AE, DC, MC, V* ☉ *Closed weekends, Aug., and Dec. 24–Jan. 8* Ⓜ *Repubblica.*

$$$ ✕ **La Terrazza.** An office building at the edge of the fashion district is home to this stylish eatery, where contemporary design dominates both food and decor. Well-dressed businessmen seem to under-appreciate the inventive "Mediterannean sushi," which might use sunflower seeds, pesto, blood oranges, or olive tapenade. Orzo, even barley, are used instead of rice; a nine-piece sampler is about €20. In warmer weather, the namesake terrace provides a calm view over the Giardini Publici. ✉ *Via*

Palestro 2, Quadrilatero ☎ 02/76002277 ▤ *AE, DC, MC, V* ⊘ *Closed weekends* Ⓜ *Turati.*

$$–$$$ ✕ **Antica Trattoria della Pesa.** Fin de siècle furnishings, dark-wood paneling, and old-fashioned lamps still look much as they must have when this eatery opened 100 years ago. It's authentic Old Milan, and the menu is right in line, offering risotto, minestrone, and osso buco. ⊠ *Viale Pasubio 10, Porta Volta* ☎ 02/6555741 ▤ *AE, DC, MC, V* ⊘ *Closed Sun., Aug., and Dec. 24–Jan. 6* Ⓜ *Porta Garibaldi.*

$$–$$$ ✕ **Nabucco.** This smart, tasteful restaurant in the Brera offers a delightful risotto *alla milanese,* excellent salads, and homemade pastries and desserts. Tables outside accommodate open-air dining in warmer months. ⊠ *Via Fiori Chiari 10, Brera* ☎ 02/860663 ▤ *AE, DC, MC, V* Ⓜ *Lanza.*

$$ ✕ **Hostaria Borromei.** With just a handful of candlelit tables curling around a delightful hidden courtyard, Borromei seems to have forgotten about the bustling financial district outside. Expect authentic, flavorful local cuisine. ⊠ *Via Borromei 4, Duomo* ☎ 02/86453760 ▤ *AE, MC, V* ⊘ *Closed Sun. and Aug.*

$–$$ ✕ **Al Cantinone.** Between La Scala and the Duomo, Cantinone's trattoria is a relaxing place to sip a glass of wine. The surroundings are classic Milanese, the service is fast, and the food is homey and reliable. Try the *cotoletta al Cantinone* (veal cutlets with mushrooms, olives, and a tomato cream sauce) accompanied by one of the some 300 wines the proprietor stocks. ⊠ *Via Agnello 19, entrance on Via Ragazzi del 99, Duomo* ☎ 02/86461338 ▤ *AE, MC, V* ⊘ *Closed Sun., Aug., and Dec. 23–Jan. 3. No lunch Sat.* Ⓜ *Duomo.*

$–$$ ✕ **La Libera.** Although this establishment in the heart of Brera calls itself a *birreria con cucina* (beer cellar with kitchen), its young clientele comes here for the excellent food and relaxed surroundings. A soft current of jazz and sylvan decor soothe the ripple of conversation. The creative cooking varies with the season but could include *insalata esotica* (avocado, chicken, rice, and papaya salad) or *rognone di vitello con broccoletti e ginepro* (veal kidneys with broccoli and juniper berries). ⊠ *Via Palermo 21, Brera* ☎ 02/8053603 ▤ *AE, DC, MC, V* ⊘ *No lunch* Ⓜ *Moscova.*

$–$$ ✕ **Trattoria Milanese.** Between the Duomo and the Basilica of Sant'Ambrogio, this small, popular trattoria has been run by the same family in the same location since 1933. It's invariably crowded, especially at dinner, when the regulars love to linger. Food is classic regional in approach; good choices include risotto and cotoletta alla Milanese. ⊠ *Via Santa Marta 11, Duomo* ☎ 02/86451991 ▤ *AE, DC, MC, V* ⊘ *Closed Tues., Aug., and Dec. 24–Jan. 6* Ⓜ *Duomo, Cordusio, Missori.*

★ $ ✕ **Da Abele.** The superb risotto dishes at this neighborhood trattoria change with the season, and there may be just two or three on the menu at any one time—order them all. The setting is relaxed, the service informal, the prices simply unjust. Outside the touristy center of town, but quite convenient by subway, this trattoria is invariably packed with locals. ⊠ *Via Temperanza 5,* ☎ 02/2613855 ▤ *AE, DC, MC, V* ⊘ *Closed Mon., Aug., and Dec. 15–Jan. 7. No lunch* Ⓜ *Pasteur.*

$ ✕ **La Bruschetta.** This tiny bustling first-class pizzeria near the Duomo serves specialties from Tuscany and other parts of Italy. The wood oven is in full view, so you can see your pizza cooking in front of you, although there are plenty of nonpizza dishes available, too, such as spaghetti *alle cozze e vongole* (with clam and mussel sauce), and grilled and skewered meats. ⊠ *Piazza Beccaria 12, Duomo* ☎ 02/8692494 ▤ *AE, MC, V* ⊘ *Closed Mon., 3 wks in Aug., and late Dec.–early Jan.* Ⓜ *Duomo.*

$ ✕ **La Capanna.** Signora cooks and her husband pours wine at this popular trattoria near the Piola Metro stop (and the university). The food is predominantly Tuscan—Tuscan salami, pappardelle, fish, and steak—but some Milanese specialties are also on the menu. It's possible to dine on the restaurant's veranda year-round. ⊠ *Via Donatello 9, University District* ☎ 02/29400884 ⊟ *AE, DC, MC, V* ⊗ *Closed Sat. and Aug.* Ⓜ *Piola.*

¢–$ ✕ **Al Tempio d'Oro.** It may be noisy, it may have the ambience of an Italian pub, but the food is very good, filling, and—for Milan—surprisingly cheap. This comfort food spot is also near the train station, which makes it a great place to eat before embarking on a journey or, indeed, before beginning your visit to Milan. The menu is hardly haute cuisine, but you'll find an excellent selection of Mediterranean dishes, ranging from a plain pasta to a more exotic Maghrebin couscous. The paella is delicious. ⊠ *Via delle Leghe 23, Stazione Centrale* ☎ 02/26145709 ⊟ *DC, MC, V* ⊗ *Closed Sun. and 2 wks in Aug.* Ⓜ *Pasteur.*

¢ ✕ **Pizza Ok.** Pizza is almost the only item on the menu at this popular spot near Corso Buenos Aires, but it's very good and the dining experience will be easy on your pocketbook. Possibilities for toppings seem endless. ⊠ *Via Lambro 15, Porta Venezia* ☎ 02/29401272 ⊟ *No credit cards* ⊗ *Closed Mon., Aug., and Dec. 24–Jan. 7* Ⓜ *Porta Venezia.*

¢ ✕ **Taverna Morigi.** This dusky, wood-paneled wine bar near the stock exchange is the perfect spot to enjoy a glass of wine with cheese and cold cuts. At lunch, pasta dishes and select entrées are available, although pasta is the only hot dish served in the evening. You can drop in any time for a bite, but if you're coming for a meal, a reservation is a good idea. ⊠ *Via Morigi 8, Sant'Ambrogio* ☎ 02/86450880 ⊟ *MC, V* ⊗ *Closed Sun. and Aug. No lunch Sat.* Ⓜ *Cordusio, Missori.*

Where to Stay

Milan may seem to have fewer tourists than other large Italian cities, but trade fairs and business bookings generate constant competition for rooms. Reservations are recommended year-round and essential in spring and summer.

$$$$ 🏨 **Four Seasons.** The elegant restoration of a 15th-century monastery in the middle of Milan's most exclusive shopping district has produced a precious gem—for which you'll pay dearly. The hotel blends European sophistication with American comfort. Individually decorated rooms have opulent marble bathrooms; most rooms face a quiet courtyard. ⊠ *Via Gesù 8, Quadrilatero, 20121* ☎ 02/77088 🖨 02/77085000 ⊕ *www.fourseasons.com* ⏏ *93 rooms, 25 suites* ♨ *2 restaurants, room service, minibars, cable TV, health club, bar, laundry service, business services, meeting rooms, parking (fee), no-smoking rooms* ⊟ *AE, DC, MC, V.*

$$$$ 🏨 **Grand Hotel Duomo.** This elegant, modern hotel is comfortable, spacious, and so central that if you look out of a front-facing window, you'll find a Duomo gargoyle staring back at you. The rooms and duplex suites are done in swatches of golds, creams, and browns. ⊠ *Via San Raffaele 1, Duomo, 20121* ☎ 02/8833 🖨 02/86462027 ⊕ *www.grandhotelduomo.com* ⏏ *162 rooms* ♨ *3 restaurants, room service, minibars, cable TV, bar, laundry service, business services, meeting rooms, parking (fee), no-smoking rooms* ⊟ *AE, DC, MC, V.*

$$$$ 🏨 **Grand Hotel et de Milan.** This elegant hotel near La Scala opened its doors in 1863 and has served as the theater's unofficial residential annex ever since. Giuseppe Verdi commandeered a suite as his city residence for 20 years; he appeared from his balcony in "the Milan" to accept public adulation following his triumphant return with *Othello,* and medical bulletins were posted in the lobby in his final days (and straw laid down on Via Manzoni to ensure a peaceful passing). Rooms are decorated with beautiful antiques, and the staff is helpful and profes-

sional. ✉ *Via Manzoni 29, Scala, 20100* ☎ *02/723141* 🖷 *02/86460868* ⊕ *www.grandhoteletdemilan.it* ⬗ *87 rooms, 8 suites* ⚭ *2 restaurants, bar, room service, minibars, cable TV, laundry service, parking (fee)* ⊟ *AE, DC, MC, V.*

$$$$ 🏨 **Pierre Milano.** No expense was spared to furnish each room of this intimate luxury hotel in a different style, with color-coordinated fabrics and both modern and antique furniture. Everything is electronic: you can open the curtains, turn off the lights, get personal messages on your TV screen—all at the touch of a button. It's on the inner beltway, near the medieval church of Sant'Ambrogio. ✉ *Via de Amicis 32, Sant'Ambrogio, 20123* ☎ *02/72000581* 🖷 *02/8052157* ⊕ *www. hotelpierremilano.it* ⬗ *51 rooms* ⚭ *Restaurant, room service, in-room safes, minibars, cable TV, bar, laundry service, parking (fee)* ⊟ *AE, DC, MC, V.*

★ $$$$ 🏨 **Principe di Savoia.** Here are all the trappings of an exquisite hotel: public spaces are 19th-century Lombard, with lavish mirrors, drapes, and carpets, and the gracious bedrooms have eclectic fin de siècle furnishings. Newer rooms, added when the Principe took over the neighboring Duca di Milan, are done in an English style, with floral wallpaper. The presidential suite comes with a marbled pool. ✉ *Piazza della Repubblica 17, Porta Nuova, 20124* ☎ *02/62301* 🖷 *02/6595838* ⊕ *www. luxurycollection.com* ⬗ *399 rooms, 5 suites* ⚭ *3 restaurants, room service, minibars, cable TV, health club, bar, laundry service, business services, convention center, meeting room, no-smoking rooms* ⊟ *AE, DC, MC, V.*

$$$$ 🏨 **Westin Palace.** This is Milan's premier hotel for business, offering unequaled comfort (including Westin's incomparable Heavenly Beds®) and connectivity (with high-speed Internet in every room). Don't be fooled by the functional 1950s-era exterior: rooms are decorated with precious Empire-style antiques, and bathrooms are lined with Issoire green and Portugal pink marble. ✉ *Piazza della Repubblica 20, Porta Nuova, 20124* ☎ *02/63361* 🖷 *02/654485* ⊕ *www.westin.com* ⬗ *244 rooms* ⚭ *2 restaurants, room service, in-room data ports, in-room safes, minibars, cable TV, bar, laundry service, Internet, business services, meeting rooms, parking (fee)* ⊟ *AE, DC, MC, V.*

$$–$$$ 🏨 **Hotel Auriga.** Colorful patterned fabrics make for lively decor in this hotel. Comfortable, convenient, and steps from Stazione Centrale, Auriga caters mostly to business travelers. ✉ *Via Pirelli 7, Stazione Centrale, 20124* ☎ *02/66985851* 🖷 *02/0266980698* ⬗ *52 rooms* ⚭ *In-room data ports, minibars, cable TV, bar, meeting rooms* ⊟ *AE, DC, MC, V* ☉ *Closed Aug.*

$$–$$$ 🏨 **Hotel Spadari al Duomo.** This intimate boutique hotel near the Duomo and the Pinacoteca Ambrosiana has its own private art collection. Rooms are elegantly furnished; junior suites on the seventh floor have views of the cathedral. Simple fare is served in the bar. ✉ *Via Spadari 11, Duomo, 20123* ☎ *02/72002371* 🖷 *02/861184* ⊕ *www.spadarihotel.com* ⬗ *40 rooms, 3 suites* ⚭ *Minibars, cable TV, bar* ⊟ *AE, DC, MC, V.*

$$ 🏨 **Antica Locanda Leonardo.** Convenient to *The Last Supper,* and close to the city center, this small hotel looks out onto a peaceful inner courtyard. The friendly staff is happy to provide information about getting tickets to the opera, soccer games, and other Milan events. Many rooms look out onto the courtyard. ✉ *Corso Magenta 78, Sant'Ambrogio, 20123* ☎ *02/463317* 🖷 *02/48019012* ⊕ *www.leoloc.com* ⬗ *20 rooms* ⚭ *Bar* ⊟ *AE, DC, MC, V* ☉ *Closed Dec. 27–Jan. 5, and 3 wks in Aug.*

$$ 🏨 **Ariston.** This hotel near the Duomo was built according to bio-architectural principles, using natural materials, and ionized air circulates throughout. As you might expect from such a progressively minded place, the attitude and ambience are warm and informal. The buffet breakfast

includes organic foods, free Internet access is available in the lobby, and bicycles are available in summer. ⊠ *Largo Carrobbio 2, Duomo, 20123* ☎ *02/72000556* 🖷 *02/72000914* ⊕ *www.brerahotels.com* 📞 *46 rooms* 🛆 *Minibars, cable TV, bicycles, bar, laundry service, Internet, no-smoking rooms, parking (fee)* 🖃 *AE, DC, MC, V* ⊗ *Closed Aug.*

\$\$ 🔲 **Canada.** This friendly, small hotel is close to Piazza del Duomo on the edge of a district full of shops and restaurants. It offers good value, with rooms that are furnished in a nondescript fashion but have the usual modern trappings. ⊠ *Via Santa Sofia 16, Duomo, 20122* ☎ *02/58304844* 🖷 *02/58300282* ⊕ *www.canadahotel.it* 📞 *35 rooms* 🛆 *Cable TV, bar, parking (fee)* 🖃 *AE, DC, MC, V.*

\$\$ 🔲 **Gritti.** The Gritti is a bright, cheerful hotel, with adequate rooms and good views (from the inside upper floor) of tiled roofs and the gold Madonnina statue on top of the Duomo, a few hundred yards away. ⊠ *Piazza Santa Maria Beltrade 4, north end of Via Torino, Duomo, 20123* ☎ *02/801056* 🖷 *02/89010999* ⊕ *www.hotelgritti.com* 📞 *48 rooms* 🛆 *Minibars, cable TV, bar, laundry service, meeting room, some pets allowed, parking (fee)* 🖃 *AE, DC, MC, V.*

\$\$ 🔲 **Hotel Gran Duca di York.** This 1890s Liberty-style building once housed priests but is rather less austere these days, with a welcoming lobby and open public spaces. Peaceful, muted rooms open onto a small elevated courtyard. With an ideal location a few steps west of the Duomo, it offers better value than most. Call ahead to reserve a private terrace at no extra cost. ⊠ *Via Moneta 1/a, Duomo, 20103* ☎ *02/874863* 🖷 *02/8690344* 📞 *33 rooms* 🛆 *Minibars, cable TV, bar, meeting rooms, laundry service, parking (fee)* 🖃 *AE, MC, V* ⊗ *Closed Aug.*

\$\$ 🔲 **Hotel Vittoria.** This family-owned hotel is on a quiet residential street minutes from the Galleria Vittorio Emanuele and the Duomo. The guest rooms are tiny but in pristine condition, and the courteous staff is eager to ensure your comfort. In summer, breakfast is served in the small garden at the back. ⊠ *Via Pietro Calvi 32, East Central, 20129* ☎ *02/5456520* 🖷 *02/55190246* 📞 *20 rooms* 🛆 *In-room safes, minibars, cable TV, no-smoking rooms* 🖃 *AE, DC, MC, V.*

★ \$\$ 🔲 **London.** On a quiet side street of Via Dante, the London's polite, efficient staff hosts its many Anglophone patrons in clean, well-appointed rooms. It's a comfortable choice, with good value and convenient access to Milan's main sights. ⊠ *Via Rovello 3, Castello, 20121* ☎ *02/72020166* 🖷 *02/8057037* ⊕ *www.hotellondonmilano.com* 📞 *29 rooms* 🛆 *Cable TV, bar* 🖃 *MC, V* ⊗ *Closed Aug. and Dec. 23–Jan. 3.*

\$ 🔲 **San Francisco.** In a residential area between the central station and the university, this medium-size hotel is handy to Metro stations on two lines (Loreto or Piola stop). The management is friendly, the rooms are bright and clean, and there's a charming garden. ⊠ *Viale Lombardia 55, University District, 20131* ☎ *02/2361009* 🖷 *02/26680377* ⊕ *www.hotel-sanfrancisco.it* 📞 *31 rooms* 🛆 *Cable TV, bar, Internet, meeting room* 🖃 *AE, DC, MC, V.*

Nightlife & the Arts

The Arts

For listings, consult the monthly *Milano Mese*, free at APT (tourist board) offices, or the weekly *Vivi Milano* (sold with the Wednesday edition of *Corriere della Sera*).

MUSIC   The **Conservatorio** (⊠ Via del Conservatorio 12, Duomo ☎ 02/7621101) is the best place in the city for classical concerts and is a popular venue for the well-heeled all year long. The modern **Auditorium di Milano** (⊠ Corso San Gottardo, corner with Via Torricelli, Conchetta ☎ 02/83389201) houses the **Orchestra Verdi** during its concert season.

OPERA Milan's hallowed **Teatro alla Scala** is closed for restoration, but opera buffs can still see the excellent company perform at **Teatro degli Arcimboldi** (✉ Viale dell' Inovazione and Via Piero Calidrola, Bicocca) from December 7 (St. Ambrose Day) through May. You can find out information about performances and purchase tickets at the La Scala Web site (🌐 www.teatroallascala.org) or by using the automated phone reservation system (📞 02/860775).

THEATER Milan's **Piccolo Teatro** (📞 02/723331) is made up of three separate venues, each of which is noted for its excellent productions. Intimate **Teatro Paolo Grassi** (✉ Via Rovello 2, Castello) is the historical headquarters of the theater, named after its founder. The spacious, modern **Teatro Giorgio Strehler** (✉ Largo Greppi 1, east of the Piazzo Castello, Brera) takes its name from a famous Italian theater director and holds dance and musical performances as well as plays The horseshoe-shape **Teatro Studio** (✉ Via Rivoli 6, Castello) is a popular venue for experimental theater and music concerts.

Nightlife

BARS Milan has a bar somewhere to suit any style; those in the nicer hotels are respectably chic. **El Brellin** (✉ Vicolo Lavandai at Alzaia Naviglio Grande, Navigli 📞 02/58101351) is one of the many bars in this arty district. It also serves Sunday brunch, fast becoming a Milanese tradition; it's closed Sunday evening. In the Brera quarter, check out the **Orient Express** (✉ Via Fiori Chiari 8, Brera 📞 02/8056227), an old-fashioned spot where it's also possible to get a bite to eat and listen to live music. Tony piano bar **Sayonara** (✉ Via Nievo 1, Porta Sempione 📞 02/436635) makes drinking a ritual of indulgence with Japanese-colonial flair. For a break from the traditional, try trendy **SHU** (✉ Via Molina delle Armi, Ticinese 📞 02/58315720), whose gleaming interior looks like a cross between *Star Trek* and Cocteau's *Sleeping Beauty*.

NIGHTCLUBS For an evening of jazz, head to perennial favorite **Le Scimmie** (✉ Via Ascanio Sforza 49, Navigli 📞 02/89402874). **Capolinea** (✉ Via Ludovico Il Moro 119, Navigli 📞 02/89122024) is open every night of the week and presents eclectic jazz performers, from Dixieland to the ultramodern New Beat style. **Hollywood** (✉ Corso Como 15/c, Centro Direzionale 📞 02/6598996) continues to be one of the most popular places for the sunglasses set.

La Banque (✉ Via Bassano Porrone 6, Duomo 📞 02/86996565), near Piazza La Scala, is an exclusive and expensive bar, dance club, and restaurant popular for anything from an *aperitivo* to a night on the town. **Magazzini Generali** (✉ Via Pietrasanta 14, Porta Vigentina 📞 02/55211313), in what was an old warehouse, is a fun, futuristic venue for dancing and concerts. It's closed on Sunday. **Propaganda** (✉ Via Castelbarco 11, Porta Romana 📞 02/58310682), near the Bocconi University, has a spacious dance floor. Music varies but includes Latin American and revival nights. The hip **Café l'Atlantique** (✉ Viale Umbria 42, Porta Romana 📞 02/55193906) is a popular place for dancing the night away and enjoying a generous buffet brunch on a lazy Sunday afternoon; it's closed Monday.

Sports

Car Racing

Lombardy Formula I fans are passionate, living and dying with the fortunes of their beloved team Ferrari. All converge on the second Sunday in September for the **Italian Grand Prix,** held 15 km (9 mi) northeast of Milan in Monza. The track was built in 1922 in the Parco di Monza, where there are also a hippodrome, a golf course, and other facilities.

Soccer

AC Milan and Inter Milan, two of the oldest and most successful teams in Europe, vie for the heart of soccer-mad Lombardy. For residents, the city is *Milano* but the teams are *Milan,* a vestige of their common founding as the Milan Cricket and Football Club in 1899. When an Italian-led faction broke off in 1908, the new club was dubbed Internazionale (or "Inter"), to distinguish it from the bastion of English exclusivity that would become AC Milan (or simply "Milan"). Since then, the picture has become more clouded: while Milan prides itself as the true team of the city and of its working class, and Inter can more persuasively claim pan-Italian support, there is little of the social tension that defines—and enflames—other often-violent intracity rivalries, like the one between Rome's two soccer powers. Milan is too busy, and too sensible for all that.

AC Milan and Inter Milan share the use of **San Siro Stadium (Stadio Meazza)** (⊠ Via Piccolomini) during their August–May season. With more than 60,000 of the 85,000 seats appropriated by season ticket holders, and another couple of thousand allocated to visiting fans, tickets to the Sunday games can be difficult to come by, especially for high-profile matches. You can purchase advance AC Milan tickets at **Cariplo** bank branches, including one at Via Verdi 8, or at the club's Web site (⊕ www. acmilan.com). Inter tickets are available at **Banca Popolare di Milano** branches, including one at Piazza Meda 4, or on-line (⊕ www.inter.it). To reach San Siro, take subway Line 1 (red) toward Molino Dorino, exit at the Lotto station, and board a bus for the stadium. Alcohol—save tasty little bottles of Borghetti coffee liqueur—is not sold inside, but beer poured into plastic cups by vendors outside is allowed past the gates. If you're a soccer fan but can't get in to see a game, you might settle for a **stadium tour** (☏ 02/4042432), which includes a visit to the Milan-Inter museum. Tours run Monday–Saturday on the hour from 10 AM to 5 PM at Gate 4; they cost €10.

Shopping

Milan's *fortissimo* occurs twice a year, at the end of February and October (for women) and June and January (for men), when the world's fashion elite descend on the city for the famous ready-to-wear designer shows that invariably set next season's international styles. Bargain-hunting seasons are in mid-January and again in mid-July, when everything, steeply discounted, flies off the shelves.

Department Stores

La Rinascente (⊠ Piazza del Duomo ☏ 02/88521) is one of the bigger department stores in Milan. Stylish shoppers head to **Coin** (⊠ Piazza Cinque Giornate Porta Vittoria ☏ 02/55192083).

Markets

Food and innumerable other items, new and old, are available in open-air stalls all over Milan. In many markets, bargaining is no longer the custom. You can try to haggle, but if you fear getting ripped off, go to the stalls where prices are clearly marked. Bargains can be found at the huge **Mercato Papiniano** (⊠ Viale Papiniano, and the Fiera di Senigallia, on Via Calatafimi, Porta Genova) on Saturday and Tuesday mornings. If you collect coins, stamps, or telephone cards (collected in Italy like baseball cards in the United States), go on Sunday morning to the market at **Via Armorari** (⊠ Near Piazza Cordusio, Duomo). Milan's most comprehensive antiques market is probably the **Mercatone dell'Antiquario,** held on the last Sunday of each month along the Naviglio Grande. On the third Saturday of each month there are antiques as well as flea-market finds at **Via Fiori Chiari,** near Via Brera.

Shopping Districts

Via Manzoni, at the northern end of Piazza della Scala, leads into the **quadrilatero,** Milan's most luxurious shopping district, perhaps the most luxurious in Italy. In a few small streets laid out like a game of hopscotch— Via Monte Napoleone, Via Sant'Andrea, Via della Spiga—are the shops of the great Italian designers, such as Armani, Versace, and Gianfranco Ferré. Don't come here looking for affordable fashion—that has been relegated to the other side of the Duomo. Shops are usually open 9–1 (except Monday morning) and 4–7:30; many are closed in August. A good locator map of the best boutiques in the area is mounted on a pole at the corner of Via della Spiga and Via Borgospesso.

Wander around the **Brera** to find stores with personality. The densest concentration of wares is along Via Brera, Via Solferino, Corso Garibaldi, and Via Paolo Sarpi. **Corso Buenos Aires,** which runs northeast from the Giardini Pubblici, is a wide boulevard dense with shops catering to locals, and as such often having better prices than those in the city center. **Corso Vittorio Emanuele** has clothing, leather goods, and shoe shops, some with goods at reasonable prices. **Via Monte Napoleone** has several top-notch jewelers and a profusion of antiques stores and designer fashion boutiques.

Specialty Stores

CLOTHING   For the constant redefinition of red-carpet style, **Giorgio Armani** (⊠ Via Sant'Andrea 9, Duomo ☎ 02/76003234) is the fashion temple. The flashy Armani megastore **Armani/Via Manzoni 31** encompasses a number of shops and restaurants, including **Emporio Armani** (⊠ Via Manzoni 31, Brera ☎ 02/72318600). **Cerruti 1881** (⊠ Via della Spiga 20, Duomo ☎ 02/76009777) has elegant styles with an edge for men and women. Head to **Prada** (⊠ Via della Spiga 1, Duomo ☎ 02/76002019) for Miuccia's bewitching minimalist designs (favored by celebrities), smart leather goods, and the famous series of fin de siècle murals. **Gucci** (⊠ Via Monte Napoleone 5, Duomo ☎ 02/771271) reveals designer Tom Ford's take on fashion, including leather goods. **Gianfranco Ferré** (⊠ Via Sant'Andrea 15, Duomo ☎ 02/794864) concentrates on swank, ready-to-wear apparel, with great ties. Daring design is the fashion at **Versace** (⊠ Via Monte Napoleone 11, Duomo ☎ 02/76008528). **Moschino** (⊠ Via Sant'Andrea 12, Duomo ☎ 02/76000832) endlessly challenges convention. **Roberto Cavalli** (⊠ Via della Spiga 42, Duomo ☎ 02/76020900) is the place for zebra stripes and sexy prints. **Fendi** (⊠ Via Sant'Andrea 16, Duomo ☎ 02/76110328) is known for smart purses, fur, and leather. Designer duo **Dolce & Gabbana** (⊠ Via della Spiga 2, Duomo ☎ 02/76001155) favor shrink-wrap lines and strappy shoes. If you want the look without designer prices, **Salvagente** (⊠ Via F. Bronzetti 16, Porta Vittoria ☎ 02/76110328) has brand names at about a third of retail.

HOUSEWARES   **L'Utile e il Dilettevole** (⊠ Via della Spiga, Duomo) sells enchanting Italian country-style items for the home. **Alessi** (⊠ Corso Matteotti 9, Duomo) specializes in kitchenware by famous Italian and international designers. **High-Tech** (⊠ Piazza XXV Aprile 12, Centro Direzionale) has everything you can think of for the house, from kitchen utensils to televisions to imported ottomans.

SHOES &   For top-quality, classic women's shoes, choose **Ferragamo** (⊠ Via Monte
LEATHER   Napoleone 3, Duomo ☎ 02/76000054 ⊠ Men's shoes ⊠ Via Monte
ACCESSORIES   Napoleone 20/5, Duomo ☎ 02/76006660). For a mix of style and tradition, try **Fratelli Rossetti** (⊠ Via Monte Napoleone 1, Duomo ☎ 02/76021650). Shoe addicts will want a gorgeous pair from **Lario 1898** (⊠ Via

CloseUp

CLOTHES MAKE THE CITY

WHEN MARIUCCIA MANDELLI decided in 1954 to stamp her collection with the name "Krizia," she anticipated fashion-mad Milan with an uncanny foresight. The name adopted by the former teacher is derived from a character in one of Plato's dialogues who spends all of his money on clothes and jewelry for fatuous and vain women. Several billion dollars of revenue are earned each year in Milan's Golden Triangle, the approximately 1-km (½-mi) area spanning Via della Spiga, Via Monte Napoleone, and Via Sant'Andrea that's home to most of Italy's high-fashion houses. Milan's designers, Mandelli among them, are known for a subversive attitude. Legends abound: Missoni's famous 1967 show, in which the black silk dresses of bra-less models became transparent on the catwalk; Moschino's

1980s-era anti-fashion Minnie Mouse dresses and fried-egg buttons; the late Gianni Versace's rock-and-roll aesthetic that put chains and leather on the catwalk. One notable exception is Armani, who favors fluid, elegant designs.

It's all but impossible to get in to see the shows, held at the start of January (men's spring–summer), at the end of February (women's spring-summer), at the beginning of October (women's fall–winter), and the end of June (men's fall–winter). Houses hold lavish, celebrity-studded presentations, and admission is by invitation only. The national trade organization, Camera Nazionale della Moda Italiana, suggests giving it a go anyway. If you contact houses directly before the shows, you may be able to wheedle your way in among the glitterati.

Monte Napoleone 21, Duomo ☎ 02/76002641) to add to their collection. Comfortable but stylish shoes are found at **Casadei** (✉ Via Sant'Andrea 17, Duomo ☎ 02/76318293). Python shoes are a trademark of **Sergio Rossi** (✉ Via Monte Napoleone 9, Duomo ☎ 02/76006140).

PAVIA, CREMONA & MANTUA

Once proud medieval fortress towns rivaling Milan in power, these centers of industry and commerce on the Po plain still play a key role in Italy's wealthiest, most populous region. Pavia is celebrated for its extravagant Carthusian monastery, Cremona for its incomparable violin-making tradition. A diminutive utopian Renaissance city, Sabbioneta was the fruit of one man's obsession, and Mantua—the most picturesque of them all—was the home of the fantastically wealthy Gonzaga dynasty for almost 300 years.

Pavia

⑰ *41 km (25 mi) south of Milan.*

Pavia was once Milan's chief regional rival. The city dates from at least the Roman era and was the capital of the Lombard kings for two centuries (572–774). It was once known as "the city of a hundred towers," but only a handful have survived the passing of time. Its prestigious university was founded in 1361 on the site of a 10th-century law school but has roots dating from antiquity.

The 14th-century **Castello Visconteo** now houses the local **Museo Civico** (Municipal Museum), with an archaeological collection and a picture gallery featuring works by Correggio. ⊠ *Viale 11 Febbraio, near Piazza Castello* ☎ *0382/33853* ☑ *€6* ⊙ *Mar.–June and Sept.–Nov., Tues.–Fri. 9–1:30, weekends 10–7; Dec.–Feb. and July and Aug., Tues.–Fri. 9–1:30, Sat. 9–1.*

In the Romanesque church of **San Pietro in Ciel d'Oro,** you can visit the tomb of Christianity's most celebrated convert, St. Augustine, housed in a Gothic marble ark on the high altar. ⊠ *Via Matteotti* ⊙ *Mon.–Sat. 9–noon and 3–5, Sun. mass.*

The main draw in Pavia is the **Certosa** (the Carthusian monastery), 8 km (5 mi) north of the city center. Its elaborate facade shows the same relish for ornamentation as the Duomo in Milan. The Certosa's extravagant grandeur was due, in part, to the plan to have it house the tombs of the family of the first duke of Milan, Galeazzo Visconti III (who died during a plague, at age 49, in 1402). And extravagant it was—almost unimaginable—in an age before modern transport. The very best marble was used, taken undoubtedly by barge from the quarries of Carrara, roughly 240 km (150 mi) away. Though the floor plan may be Gothic—a cruciform divided into a series of squares—the gorgeous fabric that rises above it is triumphantly Renaissance. On the facade, in the lower frieze, are medallions of Roman emperors and Eastern monarchs; above them are low reliefs of the life of Christ and scenes from the career of Galeazzo Visconti III.

The first duke was the only Visconti to be interred here, and then only some 75 years after his death, in a tomb designed by Gian Cristoforo Romano. Look for it in the right transept. In the left transept is a more appealing tomb—that of a rather stern middle-aged man and a beautiful young woman. The man is Ludovico il Moro Sforza (1452–1508), seventh duke of Milan, who commissioned Leonardo to paint *The Last Supper.* The woman is Ludovico's wife, Beatrice d'Este (1475–97), one of the most celebrated women of her day, the embodiment of brains, culture, birth, and beauty. Married when he was 40 and she was 16, they had enjoyed six years together when she died while giving birth to a stillborn child. Ludovico commissioned the sculptor Cristoforo Solari to design a joint tomb for the high altar of Santa Maria delle Grazie in Milan. Originally much larger, the tomb for some years occupied the honored place in Santa Maria delle Grazie as planned. Then, for reasons that are still mysterious, the Dominican monks, who seemed to care no more for their former patron than they did for their faded Leonardo fresco, sold the tomb to their Carthusian brothers to the south. Sadly, part of the tomb and its remains were lost. ⊠ *Certosa, 8 km (5 mi) north of Pavia* ☎ *0382/925613* ⊕ *www.comune.pv.it/certosadipavia* ☑ *Free, donation requested* ⊙ *Open Tues.–Sun. 9–11:30 and 2:30–5.*

Where to Eat

$$$–$$$$ ✕ **Locanda Vecchia Pavia al Mulino.** At this sophisticated, art nouveau restaurant 150 yds from the Certosa, you'll find creative versions of traditional regional cuisine, including *rane* (frogs), the local specialty, in risotto or cooked on a spit. *Casoncelli* (stuffed pasta), *petto d'anatra* (duck breast), and veal cutlet alla milanese are done with style, as are more imaginative seafood dishes. For dessert, consider the hot chocolate pudding with white chocolate sauce. ⊠ *Via al Monumento 5, Certosa* ☎ *0382/ 925894* ♨ *Reservations essential* ⊟ *AE, DC, MC, V* ⊙ *Closed Mon., 2 wks in Aug., and 3 wks in Jan. No lunch Wed.*

Nightlife & the Arts

During the first half of September, Pavia's **Settembre Pavese** festival presents street processions, displays, and concerts.

Cremona

⑱ *104 km (65 mi) east of Pavia, 106 km (66 mi) southeast of Milan.*

Cremona is the world's premier place to buy a violin—as true today as when Andrea Amati (1510–80) invented the modern instrument here in the 16th century. Though cognoscenti continue to revere the Amati name, it was an apprentice of Amati's nephew for whom the fates had reserved wide and lasting fame. In a career that spanned an incredible 68 years, Antonio Stradivari (1644–1737) made more than 1,200 instruments—including violas, cellos, harps, guitars, and mandolins, in addition to his fabled violins. Labeled simply with a small printed slip reading *ANTONIUS STRADIVARIUS CREMONENSIS. FACIEBAT ANNO . . .*—the date inserted in a neat italic hand—they remain the most coveted, most expensive stringed instruments in the world.

Strolling about this quiet, medium-sized city, you will notice that violin-making continues to flourish. There are, in fact, more than 50 *liutai,* many of them graduates of the *Scuola Internazionale di Liuteria* (International School of Violin Making), who continue to work by traditional methods in shops scattered throughout Cremona. You are usually welcome to these ateliers, especially if contemplating the acquisition of your own instrument; the tourist office has addresses.

Cremona's other claim to fame is its native *torrone* (nougat), which is said to have been invented here on the evening of October 25, 1441, in honor of the marriage of Bianca Maria Visconti and Francesco Sforza. Visconti's dowry included not only the usual jewels and riches, but also the city of Cremona itself. A new confection, originally prepared by heating almonds, egg whites and honey over low heat and shaped and named after the city's tower, was created in symbolic celebration. The annual Festa del Torrone is held in the main piazza on the third Sunday in October

The **Piazza del Comune,** surrounded by the Duomo, tower, baptistery, and city hall, is distinctive and harmonious: the combination of old brick, rose- and cream-color marble, terra-cotta, and old copper roofs brings Romanesque, Gothic, and Renaissance together with unusual success. Dominating Piazza del Comune is the **Torrazzo** (Big Tower), the city's symbol and perhaps the tallest campanile in Italy, visible for a considerable distance across the Po plain. It's open to visitors, but in winter hours fluctuate depending on the weather. The tower's astronomical clock is the 1583 original. ☒ *Piazza del Comune* 🔁 €6 ⊙ *Daily 9–6.*

Cremona's Romanesque **Duomo** was consecrated in 1190. Here you'll find the beautiful *Story of the Virgin Mary and the Passion of Christ,* the central fresco of an extraordinary cycle commissioned in 1514 and featuring the work of local artists, including Boccacio Boccancino, Giovan Francesco Bembo, and Altobello Melone. ☒ *Piazza del Comune* ⊙ *Daily 7:30–noon and 3:30–7.*

Legendary violin maker Antonio Stradivari lived, worked, and died near the verdant square at No. 1 **Piazza Roma.** According to local lore, Stradivari kept each instrument in his bedroom for a month before varnishing, imparting part of his soul before sealing and sending it out into the world. In the center of the park is **Stradivari's grave,** marked by a simple tombstone.

The **Museo Stradivariano** (Stradivarius Museum) in Palazzo Affaitati houses the city's collection of stringed treasures: a viola and five violins, including the golden orange "Il Cremonese 1715" Stradivarius. Informative exhibits display Stradivari's paper patterns, wooden models, and various tools. ⊠ *Via Ugolani Dati, 4* ☎ *0372/407770* 🖾 *€7* ⊘ *Tues.–Sat. 9–6, Sun. 10–6.*

Where to Stay & Eat

$$ ✕ **La Sosta.** This traditional Cremonese restaurant looks to the 16th century for culinary inspiration, following a time-tested recipe for a favored first course, gnocchi *Vecchia Cremona*. The homemade salamis are also excellent. To finish off the evening, try the *semifreddo al torroncino* and a dessert wine. ⊠ *Via Sicardo, 9* ☎ *0372/456656* ⊟ *AE, DC, MC, V* ⊘ *Closed Mon. and 3 wks in Aug. No dinner Sun.*

★ $ ✕ **Centrale.** Close to the cathedral, this old-style trattoria is a favorite among locals for traditional Cremonese fare, such as succulent *cotechino* (pork sausage) and *tortelli di zucca* (a small stuffed pasta with pumpkin filling), at moderate prices. ⊠ *Vicolo Pertusio 4* ☎ *0372/28701* ⊟ *AE, DC, MC, V* ⊘ *Closed Thurs. and July.*

$$ 🏨 **Hotel Continental.** This comfortable, modern hotel is well-equipped to satisfy its international business clientele. At the end of the road to the autostrade, on the periphery of the historic center, it makes a convenient base for those wisely disinclined to navigate old Cremona by car. ⊠ *Piazza Libertà 26, 26100* ☎ *0372/434141* 🖷 *0372/454873* ⊕ *www.hotelcontinentalcremona.it* ⤴ *57 rooms* ⚐ *Minibars, cable TV, bar, meeting rooms, parking (fee)* ⊟ *AE, DC, MC, V.*

$ 🏨 **Hotel Astoria.** A central, nondescript three-star hotel two blocks up Via Solferino from the Piazza Del Comune, Astoria has clean rooms and a friendly staff. ⊠ *Via Bordigallo 19, 26100* ☎ *0372/461616* 🖷 *0372/461810* ⤴ *53 rooms* ⊟ *MC, V.*

Nightlife & the Arts

At the end of May and the beginning of June, Cremona hosts an annual festival in honor of native composer Claudio Monteverdi, the great baroque pioneer of modern opera. Contact the **Teatro Ponchiellii** (☎ *0372/407275* ⊕ www.rccr.cremona.it/doc_comu/tea) for details.

Shopping

For sweet tooth-crunching nougat, visit the storied **Sperlari** store (⊠ Via Solferino 26 ☎ 0372/22346 ⊕ www.sperlari.it) Cremona's best nougat and *mostarda* (a soft sweet made from preserved fruit) have been sold from this handsome shop since 1836; Sperlari has since grown into a confection empire. Look for the historical product display, in the back.

Sabbioneta

⑲ *45 km (28 mi) southeast of Cremona, 34 km (21 mi) southwest of Mantua.*

Sleepy Sabbioneta is an unremarkable agricultural town, where nothing of note happened before—or since—an explosion of planning and building in the 16th century. It was conceived, designed, and built by Vespasiano Gonzaga (1531–91), whose glorious attainments in public service were exceeded in fame only by his ignominious treatment of his three wives. Upon retiring from military life at 47, he resolved to turn an old castle and a few squalid cottages into the perfect city—a tiny, urbane metropolis where the most gifted artists and greatest writers would live in perfect harmony with a perfect patron. After some five years of planning and another five of work, the village was transformed into an elegant, star-shape, walled fortress, dubbed Little Athens, with a rational grid of streets, two palaces, two squares, two churches, an exquisite theater (said to be the first in Europe with a roof) designed by Vincenzo Scamozzi (1552–1616), and a noble gallery of antiquities (a forerunner of today's art galleries). Gonzaga died four years later; with him Sabbioneta's aspirations to greatness faded, turning this earliest of planned cities into a surreal ghost-utopia.

The **Ufficio Turistico del Comune di Sabbioneta** (✉ Piazza d'Armi 1 ☎ 0375/221044 ◷ Apr.–Sept., Tues.–Sun., 9:30–12.30 and 2:30–5; Oct.–Mar., Tues.–Sun., 9:30–12.30 and 2:30–4) leads tours to the Palazzo Ducale, the Teatro Olimpico, and the Palazzo del Giardino. Tours begin whenever enough people have assembled. The **tourist promotion office** (APT; ✉ Via Vespasiano Gonzaga 27 ☎ 0375/52039) leads tours to religious sites, including the city's synagogue. The **synagogue,** now a shuttered and derelict building, is the sole trace of Sabbioneta's prosperous 16th-century Jewish community. You'll have to ask someone to point it out.

In the majestic **Palazzo Ducale** (Ducal Palace) are four fine equestrian figures of Vespasiano Gonzaga and his forebears. The **Teatro Olimpico** (an adaptation of Palladio's theater at Vicenza, by the man who helped him build it) has been restored, and its frescoes, once whitewashed, have been uncovered. The **Palazzo del Giardino** has a dusty but impressive gallery of antique sculptures.

Where to Stay & Eat

$ ✕🏠 **Al Duca.** In Sabbioneta's historical center, Al Duca serves local specialties like risotto *alla mantovana* (with sausage), *stracotto di asino con polenta* (donkey roast with polenta), and tortelli di zucca. It also has comfortable, reasonably priced guest rooms. ✉ *Via della Stamperia 18, 46018* ☎ *0375/52474220021* 🛏 *10 rooms* ▭ *MC, V* ☘ *Restaurant* ◷ *Restaurant closed Mon.*

Mantua

⓴ *34 km (21 mi) northeast of Sabbioneta, 192 km (119 mi) southeast of Milan.*

Mantua stands tallest among the ancient walled cities of the Po plain. Its fortifications are surrounded on three sides by the passing Mincio River, which long provided Mantua with protection, fish, and a steady stream of river tolls as it meandered from Lake Garda to join the Po. It may not be flashy or dramatic, but Mantua's beauty is subtle and deep, hiding a rich trove of artistic, architectural, and cultural gems beneath its slightly sombre facade. Winters are foggy and summers are soggy; you'll get the most out of the city in the delightful fall or spring.

Although Mantua first came to prominence in Roman times as the home of Virgil, its grand monuments date to the glory years of the Gonzaga dynasty. From 1328 until the Austrian Habsburgs sacked the city in 1708, the dukes and marquesses of the Gonzaga clan reigned over a wealthy independent *commune,* and the arts thrived under the relative peace of that period. Andrea Mantegna (1431–1506), who served as court painter for 50 years, was only the best known of a succession of artists and architects who served Mantua through the years, and some of his best work, including his only surviving fresco cycle, can be seen here. Leon Battista Alberti (1404–72), who designed two impressive churches in Mantua, was widely emulated later in the Renaissance.

The 500-room **Palazzo Ducale** gives the impression that it took centuries to build. From a distance, the group of buildings dominates the skyline, and the effect is fascinating. The **Appartamento del Paradiso** is praised for its view, but its greatest interest may be its decorator and first resident, Isabella d'Este (1474–1539). Not only was she married at 16, like her younger sister Beatrice (of the tomb in the Certosa at Pavia), she was apparently also Ludovico il Moro Sforza's first choice for a wife—until he learned she was already affianced to a Gonzaga rival. Isabella was one of the great patrons of the Renaissance. She survived her sister by more than 40 years, and the archives of her correspondence, totaling more than 2,000 letters, are considered some of the most valuable records of the era.

The high point of all 500 rooms is the **Camera degli Sposi**—literally, "Chamber of the Wedded Couple," where Duke Ludovico and his wife held court. Mantegna painted it over a nine-year period at the height of his power, finishing at age 44. He made a startling advance in painting by organizing the picture plane in a way that systematically mimics the experience of human vision. Even now, more than five centuries later, you can almost sense the excitement of a mature artist, fully aware of the great importance of his painting, expressing his vision with a masterly, joyous confidence. Don't miss the celebrated trompe l'oeil (overhead), the image of Mantegna himself (in purple, on the right side of the western fresco), or the dwarf peering out from behind the dress of Ludovico's wife (in the northern fresco). Dwarf-collecting was one of the more bizarre pastimes of Renaissance princes—according to historians, the dwarfs were considered to be something between celebrity comics and members of the ducal family.

The interiors of Mantua's Palazzo Ducale may be seen today only on a fast-paced guided tour, conducted in Italian. Signs in each room provide explanations in English; alternatively, call the **tourist office** (☎ 0376/328253) for English-language tours. ✉ *Piazza Sordello* ☎ *0376/382150* ✇ *€6.50* ⊙ *Tues.–Sun. 8:45–6:30.*

Serious Mantegna aficionados will want to visit the **Casa di Andrea Mantegna,** designed by the artist himself and built around an intriguing circular courtyard, which is usually open to view. The interior can be seen only by appointment or during occasional art exhibitions. ✉ *Via Acerbi 47* ☎ *0376/360506* ✇ *€2* ⊙ *Tues.–Sun. 10–12:30; also open 3–6 during exhibitions.*

Mantegna's tomb is in the first chapel to the left in the basilica of **Sant'Andrea** (1472, some sections earlier or later). The current structure, a masterwork by the architect Alberti, is the third built on this spot to house the relic of the Precious Blood. The crypt contains two reliquaries containing earth believed to be soaked in the blood of Christ, brought to Mantua by Longinus, the soldier who pierced his side. They are displayed only on Good Friday. ✉ *Piazza delle Erbe* ⊙ *Daily 8–12:30 and 3–6.*

need a break? **CARAVATTI –** (✉ Portico Broletto 16 on Piazza delle Erbe ☎ 0376/321653) is Mantua's oldest café, serving aperitivi since 1865. As its name suggests, **Bar Sociale** (✉ Piazza Cavallotta 16 ☎ 0376/322122) is a favored meeting place for Mantovani.

Palazzo Te is one of the greatest of all Renaissance palaces, built between 1525 and 1535 by Isabella d'Este's son, Federigo II Gonzaga (1500–40), for his mistress. It is the singular mannerist creation of artist-architect Giulio Romano, decorated with extravagant mythological paintings not to every critic's taste. Nevertheless, as the magnificently frescoed **Sala dei Giganti** (Room of Giants) proves, the palace does not skimp on pictorial drama. This depiction of Jupiter's rage against the Titans, whom he cast down from Mount Olympus, may have served as a warning to ambitious aristocrats contemplating a less-celestial coup. ✉ *Viale Te, south of the town walls* ☎ *0376/323266* ⊕ *www.centropalazzote.it* ✇ *€8* ⊙ *Mon. 1:30–5:30, Tues.–Sun. 9–5:30.*

Where to Stay & Eat

★ **$$$$** ✕ **Al Bersagliere.** One of Lombardy's best restaurants is this rustic four-room tavern in the tiny riverside hamlet of Goito, 16 km (10 mi) north of Mantua on Route 236. It has been run by a single family for more than 150 years. The fish in particular is excellent, as is a Mantuan classic, frog soup. ⊠ *Via Goitese 260, Goito* ☎ *0376/60007* ⚖ *Reservations essential* ▭ *AE, DC, MC, V* ☉ *Closed Tues., 3 wks in Aug. No lunch Mon.*

★ **$$$$** ✕ **Ambasciata.** Heralded by food critics the world over as one of Italy's finest restaurants, Ambasciata (Italian for "Embassy") takes elegance and service to extremes rarely, if ever, achieved outside Europe. Chef Romano Tamani makes frequent appearances abroad (New York's Le Cirque 2000, for one) but is at home in tiny Quistello, 20 km (12 mi) southeast of Mantua, where he offers to those willing to make the trek (and pay the bill) an ever-changing array of superlative creations such as *timballo di lasagne verdi con petto di piccione sauté alla crème de Cassis* (green lasagna, breast of pigeon, and red currant). ⊠ *Via Martiri di Belfiore 33, Quistello* ☎ *0376/619169* ⚖ *Reservations essential* ▭ *AE, DC, MC, V* ☉ *Closed Mon., Jan. 1–20, and Aug. 5–25. No dinner Sun.*

$$$ ✕ **L'Aquila Nigra.** Down a small side street opposite the Palazzo Ducale, this popular restaurant is set in a former medieval convent, where frescoes grace the walls. Diners choose from such local dishes as *medaglione di anguilla all'aceto balsamico* (medallion of eel with balsamic vinegar), *saltarelli e frittata di zucchine* (lightly fried freshwater shrimp and zucchini), and *petto di faraona in pane grattinata con rosmarino* (breaded guinea fowl with rosemary). Reservations are recommended. ⊠ *Vicolo Bonacolsi 4* ☎ *0376/327180* ▭ *AE, DC, MC, V* ☉ *Closed 3 wks in Aug., Sun. (except for Sun. lunch Apr.–May and Sept.–Oct.), and Mon.*

$$ ✕ **Ristorante Pavesi.** Locals have been coming to this central restaurant since 1918 for delicious food at reasonable prices. The menu changes every two months; homemade pasta is always a good bet. In warmer months, you can dine on Mantua's handsome main square. ⊠ *Piazza Erbe 13* ☎ *0376/323627* ▭ *AE, DC, MC, V* ☉ *Closed Feb.*

$$ ✕ **Trattoria dei Martini–Il Cigno.** Set in a romantic 16th-century palazzo with period frescoes, this restaurant scores well for atmosphere. The menu has such local specialties as tortelli di zucca, *insalata di cappone* (capon salad), *luccio in salsa di verdura all'aceto* (pike with vegetable and vinegar sauce), and variations on the Lombard favorite, risotto. Reservations are recommended. ⊠ *Piazza Carlo d'Arco 1* ☎ *0376/327101* ▭ *AE, DC, MC, V* ☉ *Closed Mon., Tues., 1 wk in Jan., and Aug.*

$ ✕ **Trattoria Due Cavallini.** This friendly family-owned restaurant a bit outside the center of town is the spot for Mantuan specialties such as tortelli di zucca. Prices are affordable and portions abundant. ⊠ *Via Salnitro 5* ☎ *0376/322084* ▭ *AE* ☉ *Closed Tues. and mid-July–mid-Aug.*

$$$ ▥ **San Lorenzo.** As if spacious, comfortable rooms, authentic early 19th-century furnishings, and a prime location weren't enough, many rooms here have wonderful views overlooking Piazza Concordia, and some have private terraces. In summer, breakfast is served on the rooftop. ⊠ *Piazza Concordia 14, 46100* ☎ *0376/220500* ▤ *0376/327194* ⊕ *www.hotelsanlorenzo.it* ⇨ *32 rooms* ⚬ *Minibars, cable TV, bar, meeting rooms, free parking* ▭ *AE, DC, MC, V.*

$$ ▥ **Hotel Broletto.** This is the place for comfortable, clean digs in a perfect location. The furniture was new in the '60s and has stuck around long enough to come back in style. ⊠ *Via Accademia 1, 46100* ☎ *0376/6326784* ▤ *0376/221297* ⊕ *http://space.tin.it/viaggi/fsmirnov* ⇨ *16 rooms* ⚬ *Minibars, cable TV* ▭ *AE, DC, MC, V.*

Nightlife & the Arts

Each year on the **Feast of the Assumption** (August 15), a contest is held in Mantua to determine who is the best *madonnaro* (street artist). Some of the painters can re-create masterpieces in a matter of minutes.

Free concerts are held on Sunday afternoons at the opulent **Teatro Bibiena** (⊠ Via Academia 47 ☎ 0376/327653); a 13-year-old Mozart performed at the 1770 inaugural concert.

LAKE GARDA, BRESCIA, BERGAMO

Lake Garda has had a perennial attraction for travelers and writers alike; even essayist Michel de Montaigne (1533–92), whose 15 months of travel journals contain not a single other reference to nature, paused to admire the view down the lake from Torbole, which he called "boundless."

Lake Garda is 50 km (31 mi) long, ranges roughly 1 km–16 km (½ mi–10 mi) wide, and is as much as 1,135 ft deep. The terrain is flat at the lake's southern base and mountainous at its northern tip. As a consequence, its character varies from stormy inland sea to crystalline Nordic-style fjord. It's the biggest lake in the region and by most accounts the cleanest. Drivers should take care on the hazardous, twisting hairpin turns on the lake road.

Bardolino

㉑ *24 km (15 mi) northeast of Sirmione, 157 km (97 mi) east of Milan.*

Bardolino, which makes unremarkable but famous red wine, is one of the biggest summer resorts on the lake. It stands on the eastern shore at the wider end of the lake. Here there are two handsome Romanesque churches: **San Severo,** from the 11th century, and **San Zeno,** from the 9th. Both are in the center of the small town. Bardolino has the lake's most active nightlife. Of its several festivals, the best one is the **Cura dell'Uva** (Grape Cure Festival) in late September–early October. It's a great excuse to indulge in the local vino, which is light, dry, and often slightly sparkling. (Bring aspirin, just in case the cure turns out to be worse than the disease.)

Punta di San Vigilio

㉒ *6 km (4 mi) north of Bardolino, 163 km (101 mi) east of Milan.*

Just about everyone agrees that this is the prettiest spot on Garda's eastern shore. Punta di San Vigilio is full of cypresses from the gardens of the 15th-century **Villa Guarienti di Brenzone** (⊠ Frazione Punta San Vigilio 1); the villa itself is closed to the public.

Malcesine

㉓ *28 km (17 mi) north of Punta di San Vigilio, 190 km (118 mi) east of Milan.*

One of the loveliest areas along the upper eastern shore of Lake Garda, Malcesine is principally known as a summer resort with sailing and windsurfing schools. Its 13 campsites and tourist villages tend to make the town crowded in season, but there are nice walks from the town toward the mountains. Six ski lifts and more than 11 km (7 mi) of runs of varying degrees of difficulty serve skiers. Dominating the town is the 12th-century **Castello Scaligero,** built by the Della Scalas.

The futuristic *funivia* (cable-car) zipping visitors to the top of **Monte Baldo** (5,791 ft) is unique in the world: it rotates. After a 10-minute ride, you're high in the Veneto, where you can stroll while enjoying spectacular views of the lake. You can ride the cable car down, or bring along a mountain bike (or hang glider) for the descent. ⊠ *Piazza Marconi 1* ☎ *0457/ 7400206* 🖃 *€14 round-trip* 🕙 *Daily 8–6.*

Riva del Garda

㉔ *18 km (11 mi) north of Malcesine, 180 km (112 mi) east of Milan.*

Set against a dramatic backdrop of jagged cliffs and miles of lakefront beaches, Riva del Garda is the quintessential Lake Garda resort town. The old city, set around a pretty harbor, was built up during the 15th century, when it was a strategic outpost of the Venetian Republic.

The heart of Riva del Garda, the lakeside **Piazza 3 Novembre,** is surrounded by medieval *palazzi.* Standing in the piazza and looking out onto the lake, you can understand why Riva del Garda has become a windsurfing mecca: mountain air currents ensure good breezes on even the sultriest midsummer days.

The **Torre Apponale,** predating the Venetian period by three centuries, looms above the medieval residences of the main square; its crenellations recall its defensive purpose. The fortress of **La Rocca,** formerly a residence of the Scaligeri princes of Verona, is now a small museum. Inside, you'll find work of varying quality by local artists (visit only if you have time on your hands). ☎ *0464/573869* 🖃 *€2.10* 🕙 *Tues.–Sun. 9:30–5:30.*

off the beaten path

CASCATA DEL VARONE – This waterfall, some 295 ft high, is 4 km (2½ mi) north of Riva del Garda on the road to Tenno. You can walk up to an observation platform and look up at the water plummeting down the cavity it has carved over time; bring a waterproof jacket.

CASTEL TOBLINO – A lovely stop for a lakeside drink or a romantic dinner, this castle is right on a lake in Sarche, about 20 km (12 mi) north of Riva toward Trento. The compound is fabled to have been a prehistoric, then Roman, village and was later associated with the Church of Trento. Bernardo Clesio had it rebuilt in the 16th century in the Renaissance style. It's now a sanctuary of fine food ($$$), serving such dishes as *garganelli alla salsa di carciofi* (grooved tubular-shape pasta with artichoke sauce) and *faraone ripieno alla castagna con salsa al timo* (guinea fowl stuffed with chestnuts in thyme sauce). Lake fish are also among the specialties. ⊠ *Via Caffaro 1, Sarche* ☎ *0461/864036* ▭ *MC, V* 🕙 *Closed Tues., mid-Nov.–Feb. No dinner some Mon.*

Where to Stay

$$$$ 🏨 **Hotel du Lac et du Parc.** Riva's most splendid hotel has elegance befitting its cosmopolitan name, with personalized service rarely found on Lake Garda since its aristocratic heyday. The airy public spaces include a dining room, bar, and a beautifully manicured private garden leading to the public beach. The rooms are well appointed and comfortable; be sure to ask for air-conditioning. ⊠ *Viale Rovereto 44, 38066* ☎ *0464/ 551500* 🖷 *0464/555200* ⊕ *www.hoteldulac-riva.it* 🛏 *170 rooms, 5 suites* ♨ *2 restaurants, minibars, cable TV, 2 tennis courts, indoor pool, gym, hair salon, sauna, Turkish baths, beach, bar, free parking; no a/c in some rooms* ▭ *AE, DC, MC, V* 🕙 *Closed Nov.–Mar.*

$$$ ⊞ **Hotel Sole.** Within a lakeside 15th-century palazzo in the center of town, this lovely understated hotel offers comfortable, affordable rooms. The terraced front rooms open to breathtaking views of the lake, and a secluded rooftop terrace is a perfect retreat from crowded beaches in summer. ⊠ *Piazza 3 Novembre 35, 38066* ☎ *0464/552686* 🖶 *0464/ 552811* ⊕ *www.hotelsole.net* ↜ *52 rooms* ♢ *Restaurant, room service, in-room safes, refrigerators, cable TV, sauna, bicycles, bar, free parking* ⊟ *AE, DC, MC, V.*

$$ ⊞ **Luise.** This cozy, reasonably priced hotel has great amenities, including a big garden and a large swimming pool. Luise's restaurant, La Limonaia, is recommended for its Trentino specialties. ⊠ *Viale Rovereto 9, 38066* ☎ *0464/550858* 🖶 *0464/554250* ⊕ *www.hotelluise.com* ↜ *70 rooms* ♢ *Restaurant, tennis court, pool* ⊟ *AE, DC, MC, V* ◷ *Closed Dec. 26–Jan. 7.*

Sports
Contact **Circolo Surf Torbole** (⊠ Colonia Pavese ☎ 0464/505385) for news on windsurfing in the area.

> **en route**   After passing the town of Limone—where it is said the first lemon trees in Europe were planted—take the fork to the right about 5 km (3 mi) north of Gargnano and head to Tignale. The view from the Madonna di Monte Castello church, some 2,000 ft above the lake, is spectacular. Adventurous travelers will want to follow this pretty inland mountain road to Tremosine; be warned that the road winds its way up the mountain through hairpin turns and blind corners that can test even the most experienced drivers.

Gargnano

㉕   *30 km (19 mi) south of Riva del Garda, 144 km (89 mi) east of Milan.*

This small port town was an important Franciscan center in the 13th century and now comes alive in the summer months when German tourists, many of whom have villas here, crowd the small pebble beach. An Austrian flotilla bombarded the town in 1866, and some of the houses still bear signs of cannon fire. Mussolini owned two houses in Gargnano: one is now a language school and the other, **Villa Feltrinelli** (⊠ Via Rimembranze 40 ☎ 0365/798000 ⊕ www.villafeltrinelli.com), has been restored and reopened as a luxury hotel.

Where to Stay & Eat

$$$$ ✕ **La Tortuga.** This rustic trattoria is more sophisticated than it first appears, with an extensive wine cellar and nouvelle-style twists on local dishes. Specialties include *agnello con rosmarino e timo* (lamb with rosemary and thyme), *persico con rosmarino* (perch with rosemary), and *carpaccio d'anatra all'aceto balsamico* (goose carpaccio with balsamic vinegar). ⊠ *Via XXIV Maggio* ☎ *0365/71251* ⊟ *AE, DC, MC, V* ◷ *Closed Tues. and mid-Jan.–Feb. No dinner Mon. except in summer.*

¢   ⊞ **Hotel Bartabel.** This cozy hotel on the main street offers comfortable accommodations at a rock-bottom price. The restaurant has an elegant terrace overlooking the lake. ⊠ *Via Roma 39, 25084* ☎ *0365/71330* 🖶 *0365/790009* ↜ *10 rooms* ♢ *Restaurant* ⊟ *AE, DC, MC, V* ◷ *Closed mid–late Nov. Restaurant closed Mon.*

Sports & the Outdoors
The **Upper Brescian Garda Park** stretches over nine municipalities on the western side of the lake, from Salò to Limone (the northernmost town in the park), covering 38,000 hectares (147 square mi). The **Limone Hotel Owners Association** (⊠ Via Quattro Novembre 2/C ☎ 0365/954720)

can provide trail and bicycle-rental information. From June to September, the **Gruppo Alpini Limone** leads free treks every Sunday.

Gardone Riviera

㉖ *12 km (7 mi) south of Gargnano, 139 km (86 mi) east of Milan.*

Gardone Riviera, a once-fashionable 19th-century resort now delightfully faded, is the former home of the flamboyant Gabriele d'Annunzio (1863–1938), one of Italy's greatest modern poets. D'Annunzio's estate, **Il Vittoriale**, perched on the hills above the town, is an elaborate memorial to himself, filled with the trappings of conquests in art, love, and war (of which the largest is a ship's prow in the garden), and complete with an imposing mausoleum. ✉ *Gardone Riviera* ☎ *0365/296511* ⊕ *www.vittoriale.it* 💶 *€16 tour of house and museum, €11 for either house or museum, €6 for grounds alone* ⊙ *Grounds Apr.–Sept., daily 8:30–8; Oct.–Mar., daily 9–5. House and museum Apr.–Sept., Tues.–Sun. 9:30–7; Oct.–Mar., Tues.–Sun. 9–1 and 2–5.*

More than 2,000 Alpine, subtropical, and Mediterranean species thrive at the **Giardino Botanico Hruska**. ✉ *Via Roma* ☎ *0365/20347* 💶 *€7* ⊙ *Mar. –Oct., daily 9–7.*

> off the beaten path

SALÒ MARKET – Four kilometers (2½ mi) south of Gardone Riviera is the enchanting lakeside town of Salò, which history buffs may recognize as the capital of the ill-fated Social Republic set up in 1943 by the Germans after they liberated Mussolini from the Gran Sasso. Every Saturday morning in the Piazza dei Martiri della Libertà, an enormous market is held, with great bargains on everything from household items to clothing to foodstuffs. In August or September, a lone vendor often sells locally unearthed *tartufi neri* (black truffles) at affordable prices.

Where to Stay & Eat

★ **$$$$** ✕▢ **Villa Fiordaliso.** The pink-and-white lakeside Villa Fiordaliso—once home to Claretta Petacci, given to her by Benito Mussolini—is a high-quality restaurant, but it also has seven tastefully furnished rooms, some overlooking the lake. The Claretta Suite is where Mussolini and Petacci were said to have carried on their affair. The art nouveau restaurant features seasonal ingredients such as zucchini flowers and porcini mushrooms, paramount in salads and soups. ✉ *Via Zanardelli 150* ☎ *0365/20158* 🖷 *0365/290011* ⊕ *www.villafiordaliso.it* 💤 *6 rooms, 1 suite* ⚭ *Restaurant, cable TV, free parking* ▤ *AE, DC, MC, V* ⊙ *Closed mid-Nov.–mid-Feb. Restaurant closed Mon. No lunch Tues.*

★ **$$$$** ▢ **Villa del Sogno.** A small winding road takes you from town to this imposing villa, which surveys the valley and the lake below it. The large hotel terrace and the quiet surrounding grounds create a sense of escape. You may think twice about a busy sightseeing itinerary once you've settled into position in the sun, cool drink in hand. ✉ *Via Zanardelli 107* ☎ *0365/290181* 🖷 *0365/290230* 💤 *28 rooms, 5 suites* ⚭ *Restaurant, tennis court, pool, gym* ▤ *AE, DC, MC, V* ⊙ *Closed Oct. 20–Mar.*

$$$–$$$$ ▢ **Grand Hotel Fasano.** A former 19th-century hunting lodge between Gardone and Maderno, the Fasano has matured into a seasonal hotel of a high standard. To one side you face the deep waters of Lake Garda; on the others you're surrounded by a 12,000-square-mi private park where the original Austrian owners no doubt spent their days chasing game. Besides myriad activities on the water, there are two golf courses in the vicinity. Rooms with a view—and a balcony—are worth the extra cost. ✉ *Corso Zanardelli 190* ☎ *0365/290220* 🖷 *0365/290221* ⊕ *www.grand-*

hotel-fasano.it ⟲ *68 rooms* ⚐ *Restaurant, minibars, cable TV, tennis court, pool, beach, waterskiing, free parking* ⊟ *No credit cards* ⊘ *Closed Oct.–mid-May.*

¢–$ ▦ **Villa Maria Elisabetta.** Many of the rooms in this charming hotel, run by a group of hospitable nuns, have views of Lago di Garda. You can sit in the hotel's garden or take one of the ground's trails down for a dip in the lake or a bask in the sun. ✉ *Viale Zanardelli 180* ▣▣ *0365/ 20206* ⟲ *45 rooms* ⚐ *Restaurant, bar* ⊟ *No credit cards* ⊘ *Closed Oct. 15–Nov.* ⏏ *CP, FAP, MAP.*

Nightlife & the Arts

Gardone's tranquillity is its greatest attraction, but that doesn't inhibit conviviality. Visitors and locals alike relish a *passeggiata* along the lakefront, stopping perhaps to enjoy an ice cream or aperitif. **Winnie's Bar** (✉ Corso Zanardelli 190 ☎ 0365/290220) in the Grand Hotel Fasano, is particularly elegant. It's named after Winston Churchill, who reputedly enjoyed more than a few brandies in the belle epoque surroundings.

Il Vittoriale (☎ 0365/296506) holds a series of concerts and other performing arts in its outdoor theater in July and August.

Sirmione

★ ㉗ *32 km (20 mi) south of Sirmione, 138 km (86 mi) east of Milan.*

Dramatically rising out of Lake Garda is the enchanting town of Sirmione. *Paene insularum, Sirmio, insularumque ocelle*—sang Catullus in a homecoming poem—"it is the jewel of peninsulas and islands, both." The forbidding Castello Scaligera stands guard behind the small bridge connecting Sirmione to the mainland; beyond, cobbled streets wind their way through medieval arches past lush gardens, stunning lake views, and gawking crowds. Originally a Roman resort town, Sirmione served under the dukes of Verona and later Venice as Garda's main point of defense. It has now reclaimed its original function, bustling with visitors in the summer. Cars aren't allowed into town; parking is available by the tourist office at the entrance.

Locals will almost certainly tell you that the so-called **Grotte di Catullo** (Grottoes of Catullus) were once the site of the villa of Catullus (87–54 BC), one of the greatest pleasure-seeking poets of all time. Present archaeological wisdom, however, does not concur, and there is some consensus that this was the site of two villas of slightly different periods, dating from about the 1st century AD. But never mind—the view through the cypresses and olive trees is lovely, and even if Catullus didn't have a villa here, he is closely associated with the area and undoubtedly did have a villa nearby. The ruins are at the top of the isthmus and are poorly signposted: walk through the historic center and past the various villas to the top of the spit; the entrance is on the right. A small museum offers a brief overview of the ruins (on the far wall); for guided tours in English, call 329/8634805. ✉ *Grotte di Catullo* ☎ *030/916157* 🎟 *€4.13* ⊘ *Mar.–mid-Oct., Tues.–Sun. 8:30–7; mid-Oct.–Feb., Tues.–Sun. 8:30–5.*

The **Castello Scaligero** was built, along with almost all the other castles on the lake, by the Della Scala family. As hereditary rulers of Verona for more than a century before control of the city was seized by the Visconti in 1402, they counted Garda among their possessions. You can go inside to take in the nice view of the lake from the tower, and you can swim at the nearby beach. ✉ *Piazza Castello, Sirmione* ☎ *030/916468* 🎟 *€4* ⊘ *Apr.–Sept., Tues.–Sun. 9–7; Oct.–Mar., Tues.–Sun., 8:30–4:30.*

off the
beaten
path

GARDALAND AMUSEMENT PARK – This park has more than 40 different rides and water slides, making it Italy's largest amusement park. It's 16 km (10 mi) east of Sirmione. ⊠ *Castelnuovo del Garda* ☎ *045/6449777* ⊕ *www.gardaland.it/en/home.html* ⊠ *€20.50* ☺ ☉ *July–Aug., daily 9 AM–midnight; Apr.–June and Sept., daily 10–6; Oct., weekends 10–6.*

Where to Stay & Eat

$$$$ ✕ **La Rucola.** Next to Sirmione's castle, this elegant intimate restaurant has a creative menu, with seafood and meat dishes accompanied by a good choice of wines. Three fixed-price menus are available. ⊠ *Via Strentelle 3* ☎ *030/916326* ⊟ *AE, DC, MC, V* ☉ *Closed Thurs. and Jan.–mid-Feb. No lunch Fri.*

★ **$–$$** ✕ **Vecchia Lugana.** At the base of the peninsula and outside the town, this restaurant is often touted as among Italy's best. Fish from the lake, grilled trout, and fillet of perch with artichokes are especially good. There's also an elegant garden. ⊠ *Piazzale Vecchia Lugana 1, Lugana di Sirmione* ☎ *030/919012* ⊟ *AE, DC, MC, V* ☉ *Closed Tues. and Jan.–mid-Feb. No dinner Mon.*

$ ✕ **Ristorante Al Pescatore.** Lake fish is the specialty at this simple, popular restaurant in Sirmione's historical center. Try grilled trout with a bottle of local white wine and settle your meal with a walk in the nearby public park. ⊠ *Via Piana 20* ☎ *030/916216* ⊟ *AE, DC, MC, V* ☉ *Closed Wed. and 1 wk in Nov.*

★ **$$$$** ▦ **Villa Cortine.** This former private villa in a secluded park risks being just plain ostentatious, but it's saved by the sheer luxury of its setting and the extraordinary professionalism of its staff. The hotel dominates a low hill, and the grounds—a colorful mixture of lawns, trees, statues, and fountains—go down to the lake. The villa itself dates from the early part of the 19th century, although a wing was added in 1952: the trade-off is between the more charming old-world decor in the older rooms and the better lake views from the newer ones. In summer, a three-night minimum stay and half board are required. ⊠ *Via Grotte 6* ☎ *030/9905890* ▤ *030/916390* ⊕ *www.hotelvillacortine.com* ⚑ *48 rooms, 6 suites* ♨ *Restaurant, minibars, cable TV, tennis court, pool, beach, bar, meeting rooms, free parking* ⊟ *AE, DC, MC, V* ☉ *Closed late Oct.–mid-Apr.*

$$$–$$$$ ▦ **Hotel Sirmione.** Just inside the city walls, near the Castello, this hotel and spa sits amid lakeside gardens and terraces. Rooms are furnished with comfortable Scandinavian slat beds, matching floral draperies and wall coverings, and built-in white furniture. Many guests have been returning for years, due largely to the homespun feel and the attentiveness of the staff. ⊠ *Piazza Castello 19* ☎ *030/916331* ▤ *030/916558* ⊕ *www.termedisirmione.com* ⚑ *101 rooms* ♨ *Restaurant, minibars, cable TV, pool, spa, 2 bars, parking (fee)* ⊟ *AE, DC, MC, V* ⊙ *FAP, MAP.*

Brescia

❷❽ *40 km (25 mi) west of Sirmione, 100 km (62 mi) east of Milan.*

Modern, industrial, and thoroughly nondescript, Lombardy's second-largest city is a fine place to do business. Hard-core art hunters may find the few remnants from its storied past a rewarding counterbalance to Brescia's current fascist-era design; otherwise you should skip the town.

The ruins of the **Capitolino,** a temple built by the Emperor Vespasian in AD 73, testify to Brescia's Roman origin. The adjoining Museo Romano is closed indefinitely for restoration, but its outstanding exhibits—including the famed 1st-century bronze *Winged Victory*—can be viewed in the **Santa Giulia Museo della Città** down the street. ⊠ *Via dei Musei 81/b* ☎ *030/2977834* 🎟 *€6* 🕔 *June–Sept., Tues.–Sun. 10–6; Oct.–Mar., Tues.–Sun. 9:30–5:30.*

Works by Raphael (1483–1520), Tintoretto (1518–94), Tiepolo (1727–1804), and Jean Clouet (1485–1540) hang in the **Pinacoteca Civica Tosio Martinengo.** ⊠ *Piazza Moretto, 4* ☎ *030/3774999* 🎟 *€2.50* 🕔 *June–Sept., Tues.–Sun. 10–5; Oct.–May, Tues.–Sun. 9:30–1 and 2:30–5.*

Palladio (1508–80) and Sansovino (1486–1570) contributed to the splendid **Palazzo della Loggia,** the Lombard-Venetian palace of marble overlooking the Piazza della Loggia.

Where to Stay & Eat

★ **$$$$** ✕ **Gualtiero Marchesi.** Never afraid to try something new, owner-chef Gualtiero Marchesi is celebrated as one of the first practitioners of *la cucina nuova* (nouvelle cuisine). Tiny lake fish are served in paper, folded in origami fashion; soups are garnished with caviar; and ravioli are served *aperto* (unsealed at the edges) or *fazzoletto* (folded handkerchief-style). The desserts—and prices—are stellar. ⊠ *Albereta Hotel, Via Vittorio Emanuele 11, Erbusco, 15 mi (24 km) west of Brescia* ☎ *030/7760562* 🍴 *Reservations essential* 👔 *Jacket and tie* 🖃 *AE, DC, MC, V* 🕔 *Closed Jan.*

$$$$ 🏨 **Vittoria.** Centrally located among 16th-century buildings, Vittoria is done in the Venetian style, with a hint of Byzantium and the Spice Routes in its pointed arches and windows. Many of the rooms are adorned with antiques, and the service is on a high level. ⊠ *Via delle X Giornate 20, 25121* ☎ *030/280061* 🖨 *030/280065* ⊕ *www.hotelvittoria.com* 🛏 *66 rooms* 🍴 *Restaurant, bar, meeting room* 🖃 *AE, DC, MC, V.*

$$ 🏨 **Relais I Due Roccoli.** This small, charming hotel overlooking the lake is a reasonably priced choice on the mainland. May is a particularly beautiful time to stay, when the 6,000 rosebushes on the hotel's grounds come into bloom. The high-quality restaurant attracts outside guests. ⊠ *Via Silvio Bonomelli, road for Polavena, Iseo, 25049* ☎ *030/9822977* 🖨 *030/9822980* ⊕ *www.idueroccoli.com* 🛏 *13 rooms* 🍴 *Restaurant, in-room safes, minibars, pool, tennis court* 🖃 *AE, DC, MC, V.*

Bergamo

29 *55 km (34 mi) west of Brescia, 52 km (32 mi) east of Milan.*

From behind a set of battered Venetian walls high on an Alpine hilltop, medieval Bergamo majestically surveys the countryside. Behind are snowcapped Bergamese Alps, and two funiculars connect the ancient **Bergamo Alta** (Upper Bergamo) to the modern **Bergamo Bassa** (Lower Bergamo) below. A worthwhile destination in its own right, Bergamo Bassa's long arteries and ornate piazzas speak to its centuries of prosperity, but it's nonetheless overshadowed by Bergamo Alta's magnificence. The massive **Torre Civica** offers a great view of the two cities. ⊠ *Piazza Vecchia* ☎ *035/224700* 🎟 *€1* 🕔 *Mar.–Apr., Tues.–Sat. 10–12:30 and 2–6, Sun. 10–6; May–Sept., weekends 10–8; Oct., weekends 10–6; Nov.–Feb., weekends 10:30–4.*

Bergamo's **Duomo** and **Battistero** are the most substantial buildings in Piazza Duomo. But the most impressive is the **Cappella Colleoni,** with stunning marble decoration. ⊠ *Piazza Duomo* ☎ *035/217317* 🕔 *Cappella Colleoni weekdays 8–noon and 3–6:30.*

In the **Accademia Carrara** you will find one of Italy's most important art collections. Many of the Venetian masters are represented—Mantegna, Bellini, Carpaccio (circa 1460–1525/26), Tiepolo, Francesco Guardi (1712–93), Canaletto (1697–1768)—as well as Botticelli (1445–1510). ⊠ *Bergamo Bassa, Piazza Carrara* ☎ *035/247149* ⊕ *www. accademiacarrara.it* ⊠ *€2.60, free Sun.* ☉ *Apr.–Sept., Tues.–Sun. 10–1 and 3–6:45; Oct.–Mar., Tues.–Sun. 9:30–1 and 2:30–5:45.*

Where to Stay & Eat

★ **$$$** ✕ **Taverna Colleoni dell'Angelo.** Angelo Cornaro is the name behind the Taverna del Colleoni, on the Piazza Vecchia, right behind the Duomo. He serves imaginative fish and meat dishes, both regional and international, all expertly prepared. ⊠ *Piazza Vecchia 7* ☎ *035/232596* ▭ *AE, DC, MC, V* ☉ *Closed Mon., 1 wk in Jan., and 2 wks in Aug.*

$$ ✕ **Da Ornella.** On the main street in the upper town, the vaulted ceilings of this popular trattoria are marked with ancient graffiti, created by (patiently) holding candles to the stone overhead. Ornella herself is in the kitchen, turning out *casoncelli* (stuffed pasta) in butter and sage and platters of assorted roast meats. Three prix-fixe menus are available during the week, two on the weekend. Reservations are recommended. ⊠ *Via Gombito 15* ☎ *035/232736* ▭ *AE, DC, MC, V* ☉ *Closed Thurs.*

$$ ✕ **La Trattoria del Teatro.** Traditional regional food tops the bill at this good-value restaurant in the upper town. The polenta is a silky delight, and game is recommended in season. Fettuccine *con funghi* (with mushrooms) is deceptively simple but a rich and memorable specialty. ⊠ *Piazza Mascheroni 3* ☎ *035/238862* ▭ *No credit cards* ☉ *Closed Mon. and 2 wks mid-July.*

$ ✕ **Al Donizetti.** Find a table in the back of this central, cheerful *enoteca*
FodorsChoice (wine bar) before choosing local hams and cheeses to accompany your
★ wine (more than 800 bottles available, with many offerings by the glass). Heartier meals are also available, such as eggplant stuffed with cheese and salami, but save room for the desserts, which are well-paired with dessert wines. ⊠ *Via Gombito 17/a* ☎ *035/242661* ▭ *AE, MC, V* ☉ *Closed Tues.*

$$ ✕▭ **Agnello d'Oro.** A 17th-century tavern on the main street in Upper Bergamo, with wooden booths and walls hung with copper utensils and ceramic plates, Agnello d'Oro is a good place to imbibe the atmosphere as well as the good local wine. Specialties are typical Bergamese risotto and varieties of polenta served with game and mushrooms. The same establishment also has 20 modestly priced rooms. ⊠ *Via Gombito 22,* ☎ *035/ 249883* ▭ *035/235612* ▭ *20 rooms* ⚐ *Restaurant* ▭ *AE, DC, MC, V* ☉ *Restaurant closed Mon. and Jan. 7–Feb. 5. No dinner Sun.*

$ ✕▭ **Sole.** To reach your room in this traditional inn, just steps away from Piazza Vecchia, you walk through the ground-floor restaurant, usually packed with guests and locals enjoying first-rate pizzas. Upstairs, the guest rooms are functional and comfortable. Be sure to ask about late-night entry, as the procedure is less than obvious. ⊠ *Via Colleoni 1,* ☎ *035/218238* ▭ *035/240011* ▭ *20 rooms* ⚐ *Restaurant, minibars* ▭ *AE, DC, MC, V* ☉ *Restaurant closed Thurs.*

$$$$ ▭ **Excelsior San Marco.** The most comfortable hotel in Lower Bergamo, the Excelsior San Marco is only a short walk from the walls of the upper town. The rooms are surprisingly quiet, considering the central location. You can breakfast on the rooftop terrace. ⊠ *Piazza della Repubblica 6, 24122* ☎ *035/366111* ▭ *035/223201* ▭ *155 rooms* ⚐ *Restaurant, in-room safes, minibars, cable TV, bar, laundry service, free parking* ▭ *AE, DC, MC, V.*

Nightlife & the Arts

The annual summer **Festival Internazionale del Pianoforte** (International Piano Festival) is held in Bergamo's Teatro Donizetti (⊠ Piazza Cavour 15 ☎ 035/4160602 ⊕ http://teatro.gaetano-donizetti.com). Call the theater for information about drama, opera, and ballet events throughout the year.

| en route | The Chiesa della Madonna del Ghisallo (Church of the Patroness of Bicyclists), open daily from March through November, is not far from the shores of Lake Como and affords a fine view. You will often see cyclists parked outside taking a breather after their uphill struggle, but many come simply in homage to this unique Madonna. It's located 48 km (30 mi) northwest of Bergamo, on the road to Bellagio. |

LAKE COMO

For those whose idea of heaven is palatial villas, rose-laden belvederes, hanging wisteria and bougainvillea, lanterns casting a glow over lakeshore restaurants, and majestic Alpine vistas, heaven is Lake Como. In his *Charterhouse of Parma,* Stendhal described it as an "enchanting spot, unequaled on earth in its loveliness." Virgil called it simply "our greatest" lake. Though summer crowds do their best to vanquish the lake's dreamy mystery and slightly faded old-money gentility, they fail. Como remains a consummate pairing of natural and man-made beauty. The villa gardens, like so many in Italy, are a union of two landscape traditions: that of Renaissance Italy, which values order, and of Victorian England, which strives to create the illusion of natural wildness. Such gardens are often framed by vast areas of picturesque farmland—fruit trees, olive groves, and vineyards.

Lake Como is some 47 km (30 mi) long north to south and is Europe's deepest lake (almost 1,350 ft). If not driving, you arrive at the lake by pulling into the railway station at Como, a leading textile center famous for its silks. Many travelers hasten to the vaporetti waiting to take them to Bellagio and the *centro di lago,* the center region of the lake's three branches, and its most beautiful section. From Bellagio, vaporetti and car ferries traverse the lake, making it easy for travelers to get to the other main towns, Cernobbio, Tremezzo, and Varenna.

Bellagio

FodorsChoice
★

30 km (19 mi) northeast of Como, 56 km (35 mi) northwest of Bergamo.

Sometimes called the prettiest town in Europe, Bellagio always seems to be flag bedecked, with geraniums ablaze in every window and bougainvillea veiling the staircases, or *montées,* that thread through the town. At dusk, Bellagio's nightspots—including the wharf, where an orchestra serenades dancers under the stars—beckon you to come and make merry. It's an impossibly enchanting location, one that inspired Gabriel Faure to call Bellagio "a diamond contrasting brilliantly with the sapphires of the three lakes in which it is set."

Boats ply the lake to Tremezzo, where Napoléon's worst Italian enemy, Count Sommariva, resided at Villa Carlotta; and a bit farther south of Tremezzo, to Villa Balbianello. Check with the **Bellagio tourist office** (⊠ Piazza della Chiesa 14 ☎ 031/950204) for the hours of the launch to Tremezzo.

★ **Villa Serbelloni,** a property of the Rockefeller Foundation, has celebrated gardens on the site of Pliny the Elder's villa overlooking Bellagio. There are only two guided visits per day, restricted to 30 people each, and in May these tend to be commandeered by group bookings. ⊠ *Near Palazza della Chiesa* ☎ *031/950204* 🎟 *€5* 🕐 *Guided visits Apr.–Oct., Tues.–Sun. at 11 and 4; tours gather 15 mins before start.*

The famous gardens of the **Villa Melzi** were once a favorite picnic spot for Franz Lizst, who advised author Louis de Ronchaud in 1837: "When you write the story of two happy lovers, place them on the shores of Lake Como. I do not know of any land so conspicuously blessed by heaven." The gardens are open to the public, and though you can't get into the 19th-century villa, don't miss the lavish Empire-style family chapel. The Melzi were Napoléon's greatest allies in Italy (the family has passed down the name of Josephine to the present). ⊠ *3 km (2 mi) outside Bellagio* ☎ *031/951281* 🎟 *€5* 🕐 *Apr.–Sept., daily 9–6:30; Mar. and Oct., 9–12:30 and 2–4:30.*

Where to Stay & Eat

$ ✕🏠 **La Pergola.** Try to reserve a table on the terrace at this popular lakeside restaurant ($–$$) about 1 km (½ mi) from Bellagio, on the other side of the peninsula. The best dining option is the freshly caught fish. You can also stay in one of the inn's 11 rooms, all of which have baths. ⊠ *Pescallo* ☎ *031/950263* 🖷 *031/950253* ⊕ *www.lapergolabellagio. it* ⏴ *11 rooms* ⚫ *Restaurant* ⊟ *AE, MC, V* 🕐 *Closed Tues.*

$ ✕🏠 **Silvio.** At the edge of town, this family-owned trattoria with a lakeshore terrace specializes in fresh fish. Served cooked or marinated, with risotto or as a ravioli stuffing, the fish is caught by Silvio's family—it's local cooking at its best. Many of the modestly priced guest rooms have balconies and lake views. ⊠ *Lòppia di Bellagio, Via Carcano 10* ☎ *031/950322* 🖷 *031/950912* ⊕ *www.bellagiosilvio.com* ⏴ *21 rooms* ⚫ *Restaurant* ⊟ *MC, V* 🕐 *Closed Jan.–Feb.*

★ $$$$ 🏠 **Grand Hotel Villa Serbelloni.** Designed to cradle nobility in high style, this hotel is a refined haven for the discreetly wealthy, set within a pretty park down the road from the punta di Bellagio. The sense of 19th-century luxury has not so much faded as mellowed: the rooms are immaculate and plush; public areas are gilt and marble, with thick, colorful carpets. Staff is unobtrusive and very knowledgeable about lake transportation. Churchill's and Kennedy's former rooms face the Tremezzina, a group of towns across the lake. ⊠ *Via Roma 1, 22021* ☎ *031/950216* 🖷 *031/951529* ⊕ *www.villaserbelloni.it* ⏴ *83 rooms* ⚫ *2 restaurants, room service, minibars, cable TV, tennis court, 2 pools, hair salon, health club, sauna, Turkish bath, laundry service, free parking* ⊟ *AE, DC, MC, V* 🕐 *Closed mid-Nov.–early Apr.*

$$$ 🏠 **Belvedere.** In Italian, Belvedere means "beautiful view," an apt description of this enchanting spot. The hotel has been in the Martinelli-Manoni family since 1880, and the unbroken tradition of service makes it one of the best places to stay in town. Antique chairs and eye-catching rugs complement the modern, understated rooms. The bathrooms are expertly designed for maximum comfort. Outstanding terraced gardens have replaced the vineyards that once surrounded the house. The restaurant is very good. ⊠ *Via Valassina 31, 22021* ☎ *031/950410* 🖷 *031/950102* ⊕ *www.belvederebellagio.com* ⏴ *70 rooms* ⚫ *Restaurant, cable TV, pool, bar, meeting rooms, no-smoking rooms, free parking* ⊟ *AE, DC, MC, V* 🕐 *Closed Nov.–Mar.*

$$$ 🏠 **Du Lac.** In the center of Bellagio, by the landing dock, this comfortable, medium-size hotel owned by an Anglo-Italian family has a relaxed and congenial feel. Most rooms have views of the lake and mountains,

and there's a rooftop terrace garden for drinks or dozing. ⊠ *Piazza Mazzini 32, 22021* ☎ *031/950320* 📠 *031/951624* ⊕ *www.bellagiohoteldulac. com* 🛏 *48 rooms* ⚒ *Restaurant, minibars, cable TV, bar, free parking* 🖃 *MC, V* ⊘ *Closed Nov.–Mar.*

$$$ 🏨 **Hotel Florence.** This villa dating from the 1880s has an impressive lobby with its vaulted ceiling and imposing Florentine fireplace. Most of the rooms, furnished with interesting antiques, are large and comfortable and have splendid views of the lake. The restaurant and bar draw locals and visitors; there's live music on weekends. ⊠ *Piazza Mazzini 45, 22021* ☎ *031/950342* 📠 *031/951722* 🛏 *36 rooms* ⚒ *Restaurant, cable TV, bar* 🖃 *AE, DC, MC, V* 🍴 *FAP, MAP* ⊘ *Closed Nov.–Mar.*

$$ 🏨 **Excelsior-Splendide.** Chances are you'll be lulled to sleep at night here by the lilting sounds of an orchestra directly under your window—this hotel is opposite Bellagio's enchanting quay, where live music fills summer nights. It's in the town center, handy to restaurants, and a five-minute walk from the stunning gardens of Villa Melzi. ⊠ *Lungo Lario Manzoni, 22021* ☎ *031/950225* 📠 *031/951224* ⊕ *http://splendide.interfree. it* 🛏 *47 rooms* ⚒ *Restaurant, pool* 🖃 *AE, DC, MC, V* ⊘ *Closed Nov.–mid-Mar.*

Varenna

㉛ *6 km (4 mi) northeast of Bellagio, 56 km (35 mi) northwest of Bergamo.*

You can reach Varenna by ferry from Bellagio. The principal sight here is the spellbinding garden of the **Villa Monastero**, which, as its name suggests, was originally a monastery. Now it's an international science and convention center. ⊠ *Varenna* ☎ *0341/295459* 🎟 *€2* ⊘ *Apr.–Oct., daily 9–7.*

Tremezzo

㉜ *34 km (21 mi) north of Cernobbio, 78 km (48 mi) north of Milan.*

If you're lucky enough to visit the small lakeside town of Tremezzo in late spring or very early summer, you will find the magnificent **Villa Carlotta** a riot of color, with more than 14 acres of azaleas and dozens of varieties of rhododendrons in full bloom. The villa was built between 1690 and 1743 for the luxury-loving Marquis Giorgio Clerici. The garden's collection is remarkable, particularly considering the difficulties of transporting delicate plants before the age of aircraft. Palms, banana trees, cacti, eucalyptus, a sequoia, orchids, and camellias are counted among the more than 500 species.

According to local lore, one reason for the Villa Carlotta's magnificence was a competition between the marquis's son-in-law, who inherited the estate, and the son-in-law's archrival, who built *his* summer palace directly across the lake (Villa Melzi, in Bellagio). Whenever either added to his villa and garden, it was tantamount to taunting the other in public. Eventually the son-in-law's insatiable taste for self-aggrandizement prevailed. The villa's last (and final) owners were Prussian royalty (including the "Carlotta" of the villa's name); the property was confiscated during World War I.

The villa's interior is worth a visit, particularly if you have a taste for the romantic sculptures of Antonio Canova (1757–1822). The best known is his *Cupid and Psyche,* which depicts the lovers locked in an odd but graceful embrace, with the young god above and behind, his wings extended, while Psyche awaits a kiss that will never come. The villa can be reached by boats from Bellagio. ☎ 0344/40405 ⊕ *www. villacarlotta.it* 🎫 €6.50 ⊙ *Apr.–Sept., daily 9–6; Mar. and Oct., daily 9–11:30 and 2–4:30.*

off the beaten path

VILLA BALBIANELLO – This may be the most magical house in all of Italy. It sits on its own little promontory, Il Dosso d'Avedo—separating the bays of Venus and Diana—around the bend from the tiny fishing village of Ossuccio. Relentlessly picturesque, the villa is composed of loggias, terraces, and *palazzini* (tiny palaces), all spilling down verdant slopes to the lakeshore, where you'll find an old Franciscan church, a magnificent stone staircase, and statue of San Carlo Borromeo blessing the waters. Don't be surprised if the lakeside location looks as familiar as it does cinematic: the intergalactic romance of *Star Wars: Episode II* was shot here. The villa is most frequently reached by launch, arriving from Como and Bellagio. Check with the **Como tourist office** (☎ 031/269712) for hours. Visits are usually restricted to the gardens, but if you plan in advance, it's also possible to tour the villa itself. You pay €30 for a guide—regardless of how many are in your party—and an additional €3 entrance fee. Send a fax to reserve an **English-speaking guide** (🖷 0344/55575). ⊠ *Il Dosso d'Avedo* ☎ 0344/56110 🎫 *Gardens* €4 ⊙ *Apr.–Oct., Tues. and Thurs.–Sun. 10–12:30 and 3:30–6:30.*

Where to Stay

$$$$ 🏨 **Grand Hotel Tremezzo.** One hundred windows of this turn-of-the-20th-century building face the lake. The hotel, in the middle of a private park stretching over 12½ acres, has many creature comforts, from a heated swimming pool and private landing on the lake to a hillside for jogging. All rooms have a view of the lake or the park. The 18-hole Menaggio & Cadenabbia golf course is about five minutes away by car. ⊠ *Via Regina 8, 22019* ☎ 0344/42491 🖷 0344/40201 ⊕ *www.grandhoteltremezzo. com* 🛏 *98 rooms, 2 suites* ♨ *3 restaurants, room service, minibars, cable TV, tennis court, 2 pools, gym, hair salon, sauna, billiards, Ping-Pong, 3 bars, meeting room, helipad, free parking* ⊟ *AE, DC, MC, V* ⊙ *Closed Nov.–Feb.*

$ 🏨 **Rusall.** Situated on the hillside above Tremezzo in the midst of a large garden, this small and reasonably priced hotel offers quiet and privacy. You can lie out on the terrace and enjoy a nice view. Rooms are simple and comfortable. ⊠ *Via S. Martino, 2, Frazione Rogaro, 22019* ☎ 0344/ 40408 🖷 0344/40447 ⊕ *www.rusallhotel.com* 🛏 *19 rooms* ♨ *Restaurant, tennis court, bar* ⊟ *AE, DC, MC, V.*

Cernobbio

㉝ *5 km (3 mi) north of Como, 53 km (34 mi) north of Milan.*

The legendary resort of Villa d'Este is perhaps the only reason to visit Cernobbio (which is otherwise overrun with private villas)—but it's a reason enough. If you're planning to say "budget be damned" in only one place, this could be it. Built over the course of roughly 45 years for fisherman-turned-cardinal Tolomeo Gallio, the **Villa d'Este** has had a colorful and somewhat checkered history since its completion in 1615, swinging wildly between extremes of grandeur and dereliction. Its tenants have included the Jesuits, two generals, a ballerina, Caroline of Brunswick—the disgraced and estranged wife of the future king of England, George IV—a family of ordinary Italian nobles, and, finally, a czarina of Russia. Its life as a private summer residence ended in 1873, when it was turned into the fashionable hotel it has remained ever since.

Where to Stay & Eat

$$ ✕ **Il Gatto Nero.** This restaurant in the hills above Cernobbio has a splendid view of the lake. Specialties include risotto *ai funghi porcini* (with porcini mushrooms), *pappardelle al ragù di selvaggini* (pasta with wild game sauce), wild game, and lake fish. ✉ *Via Monte Santo 69, Rovenna* ☎ *031/512042* ▭ *AE, DC, MC, V* ✆ *Closed Mon. No lunch Tues.*

$$$$ 🏨 **Villa d'Este.** One of the grandest hotels in Italy, the 17th-century Villa
Fodor'sChoice d'Este has long welcomed Europe's rich and famous, from Napoléon
★ to the Duchess of Windsor. The chandeliers in the vast lobby illuminate marble staircases leading to guest rooms furnished in the Empire style: walnut paneling, sofas in striped silk, and gorgeous antiques. A broad veranda sweeps out to the lakefront, where a swimming pool extends above the water. The fanciful pavilions, temples, miniature forts, and mock ruins make for an afternoon's walk of quietly whimsical surprises. ✉ *Via Regina 40, 22012* ☎ *031/3481* 🖷 *031/348844* ⊕ *www.villadeste. it* 🛏 *148 rooms, 13 suites* ♿ *3 restaurants, room service, minibars, cable TV, 8 tennis courts, indoor pool, sauna, squash, bar, nightclub, laundry service, free parking, no-smoking rooms* ▭ *AE, DC, MC, V* ✆ *Closed mid-Nov.–Feb.*

Como

③④ *5 km (3 mi) south of Cernobbio, 30 km (19 mi) southwest of Bellagio, 49 km (30 mi) north of Milan.*

Como, on the south shore of the lake, is only part elegant resort, where cobbled pedestrian streets wind their way past parks and bustling cafés. The other part is an industrial town, renowned for its silk production. If you're traveling by car, leave it outside the town center, as traffic can be mayhem, and streets are often closed.

The splendid 15th-century Renaissance-Gothic **Duomo** was begun in 1396, the facade was added in 1455, and the transepts were completed in the mid-18th century. The dome was designed in 1744 by Filippo Juvara (1678–1736), chief architect of many of the sumptuous palaces of the royal house of Savoy. The facade has statues of two of Como's most famous sons, Pliny the Elder and Pliny the Younger, whose chronicles are some of the most important documents of antiquity. Inside, the works of art include Luini's *Holy Conversation,* a fresco cycle by Morazzone, and the *Marriage of the Virgin Mary* by Ferrari. ✉ *Piazza del Duomo* ✆ *Daily 7–noon and 3–7.*

> **need a break?** Directly across from the Duomo, **Bar Argentino** (✉ Via Pretorio 1 ☎ 031/304455) offers a cool setting, good English-speaking help, and an extensive list of grappas.

At the heart of Como's medieval quarter, the city's first cathedral, **San Fedele,** is worth a peek, if only because it is one of the oldest churches in the region. ✉ *Piazza San Fedele* ✆ *Daily 7–noon and 3–7.*

If you brave Como's industrial quarter, you will find the beautiful church of **Sant'Abbondio,** a gem of Romanesque architecture begun by Benedictine monks in 1013 and consecrated by Pope Urban II in 1095. Inside, the five aisles of the church converge on a presbytery with a semicircular apse decorated with a cycle of 14th-century frescoes—now restored to their original magnificence—by Lombard artists heavily influenced by the Sienese school. In the nave, the cubical capitals supporting the pillars are the earliest example of this style in Italy. ✉ *Via Sant'Abbondio* ✆ *Daily 7–6.*

Exhibiting the path of production from silkworm litters to *moiré*-finishing machinery, the **Museo Didattico della Seta** (Silk Museum) is small but complete. Within the compound of the Como *Setificio* (textile school), the museum preserves the history of a manufacturing region that continues to supply almost three-fourths of Europe's silk. The friendly staff will give you an overview of the museum; they are also happy to provide brochures and information about local retail shops. The museum is poorly marked: follow the textile school's driveway around to the low-rise concrete building on the left, and follow the shallow ramp down to the entrance. ⊠ *Via Velleggio 3* ☎ *031/303180* ⊕ *www.museosetacomo.com* ⊠ *€8* ⊙ *Tues.–Fri. 9–noon and 3–6.*

| off the beaten path | **CASTIGLIONE OLONA** – This Gothic *collegiata* (collegiate church) and baptistery with superlative-frescoes by Giotto's pupil Masolino da Panicale is 18 km (11 mi) west of Como. ☎ *0331/858903* ⊠ *€2.60* ⊙ *Apr.–Sept., Tues.–Sat. 9:30–noon and 3–6:30; Oct.–Mar., Tues.–Sat. 10–noon and 2:30–5:30. Open by appointment Sun.* |

Where to Stay & Eat

$$$$ ✕ **La Locanda dell'Isola.** Isola Comacina, Lake Como's only island and five minutes by boat from Sala Comacina, is rustic and restful but at times crowded. The same could be said for the Locanda. Forget any notions of choosing from a menu, because here the deal is a set price for a set meal, with drinks included. The good news is that the food is delicious, the service is friendly, and the setting is magnificent. You'll have to pace yourself through a mixed antipasto, salmon, trout, chicken, salad, cheese, coffee, and dessert. ⊠ *Isola Comacina, Sala Comacina* ☎ *0344/55083* ▭ *No credit cards* ⊙ *Closed Nov.–Feb. and Tues. mid-Sept.–mid-May.*

$$ ✕ **Raimondi** This elegant restaurant in the Hotel Villa Flori (2 km toward Cernobbio) offers good value and a superb location, with a large terrace poised over the lake. The local freshwater fish is your best option, but a wide range of Italian dishes are capably prepared. The restaurant's season is longer than most, owing to its popularity with local residents. ⊠ *Via Cernobbio 12* ☎ *031/338233* ▭ *AE, DC, MC, V* ⊙ *Closed Mon. and Dec.–Feb. 14. No lunch Sat.*

$$$$ ▭ **Barchetta Excelsior.** Though it has a rather unprepossessing exterior, this central, modern hotel is comfortable, with many rooms looking directly across Piazza Cavour to Lake Como. The rooms are airy and spacious, with those on the upper floors commanding the best views. Ask for a lake view, though the noise of the piazza can be a distraction. The Barchetta is run by the same group that owns Villa d'Este. ⊠ *Piazza Cavour 1, 22100* ☎ *031/3221* 🖷 *031/302622* ⊕ *www.hotelbarchetta.com* ⤶ *84 rooms* ⚒ *2 restaurants, minibars, bar, no-smoking rooms* ▭ *AE, DC, MC, V.*

$$$–$$$$ ▭ **Villa Flori.** Italian patriot Garibaldi spent his wedding night here, in a suite that now bears his name. The hotel enjoys a panoramic view and has a highly acclaimed restaurant, Raimondi. ⊠ *Via Cernobbio 12, 22100* ☎ *0315/73105* 🖷 *031/33820* ⊕ *www.hotelvillaflori.com* ⤶ *45 rooms* ⚒ *Restaurant, meeting room* ▭ *AE, DC, MC, V.*

★ $$$ ▭ **Terminus.** Commanding a panoramic view over Lake Como, this early 20th-century, art nouveau building is perhaps the city's finest hotel. The marbled public spaces have an understated elegance, and the guest rooms are done in floral patterns and furnished with large, walnut wardrobes and silk-covered sofas. In summer, the garden terrace is perfect for relaxing over a drink. ⊠ *Lungo Lario Trieste 14, 22100* ☎ *031/329111* 🖷 *031/302550* ⊕ *www.albergoterminus.com* ⤶ *38 rooms* ⚒ *Restaurant, in-room data ports, in-room safes, minibars, cable TV,* *massage, sauna, meeting room, free parking, no-smoking rooms* ☐ *AE, DC, MC, V.*

$$–$$$ ☐ **Tre Re.** This clean, spacious, welcoming hotel is a few steps west of the cathedral and convenient to the lake. Although the exterior gives away the age of this 16th-century former convent, the rooms are airy, comfortable, and modern. The moderately priced restaurant shares an ample terrace with the hotel. ✉ *Via Boldoni 20, 22100* ☎ *031/265374* 🖷 *031/241349* ⊕ *www.hoteltrere.com* ⤴ *40 rooms* ⚘ *Restaurant, bar, free parking* ☐ *MC, V* ⊙ *Closed Dec. 15–Jan. 10.*

Sports

Various facilities for waterskiing and all water sports can be found on the lake; contact the **Provincial Tourist Board** in Como (✉ Piazza Cavour 17 ☎ 031/269712).

Shopping

While in Como, seize the opportunity to shop for fine European silk directly from its source. One of the biggest names is **Mantero** (✉ Via San Abbondio 8 ☎ 031/321510), which supplies major design houses like Yves Saint Laurent, Nina Ricci and Trussardi. Not far from the lake, good deals on ties, scarves, and shirts can be found at the factory store of **Binda** (✉ Viale Geno 6 ☎ 031/303440). **Frey** (✉ Via Garibaldi 10 ☎ 031/267012) has a factory outlet on the western edge of the old town. Every Saturday (except the first Saturday of every month), Piazza San Fedele holds a **local crafts market** from 9 to 7.

LAKE MAGGIORE & LAKE ORTA

Magnificently scenic, Lake Maggiore has its mountainous western shore in Piedmont, its lower eastern shore in Lombardy, and its northern tip in Switzerland. The lake stretches nearly 50 km (30 mi), and is up to 5 km (3 mi) wide. The better-known resorts are on the western shore, particularly Stresa, a tourist town that provided a setting for Hemingway's *A Farewell to Arms.* A mountainous strip of land separates Lake Maggiore from Lake Orta, its smaller neighbor to the west, in Piedmont. Orta attracts fewer visitors than the three larger lakes, and can be a pleasant alternative in the summer.

Orta San Giulio

㉟ *76 km (47 mi) northwest of Milan.*

At the end of a small peninsula jutting out into Lake Orta, this charming town is full of 18th-century buildings adorned with wrought-iron balustrades and balconies. The shady main square looks out across the lake to the small island of San Giulio. There is nothing more relaxing than sitting at one of the piazza cafés and watching the languid waters, where sailboats catch mountain breezes.

Rising up behind Orta, **Sacro Monte** (Sacred Mountain) is an interesting hike. Pass the Church of the Assumption at the edge of the old town, and just ahead is a gateway marked Sacro Monte. This leads to a comfortable climb that takes about 40 minutes round-trip. As you approach the top, you pass no fewer than 20 17th-century chapels, all devoted to St. Francis of Assisi. Within them, frescoes and striking, life-size terracotta statue groups (a total of almost 400 figures) illustrate incidents from the saint's life. The campanile of the last chapel provides a view over the lake and the town, about 350 ft below.

The island of **San Giulio** is accessible by hired boat for about €6 round-trip per boatload of up to four people. The island takes its name from the 4th-century St. Julius, who—like St. Patrick in Ireland—is said to have banished snakes from the island. Julius is also said to have founded the **Basilica** in AD 390, although the present building shows more signs of its renovations in the 10th and 15th centuries. Inside, there's a black-marble pulpit (12th century) with elaborate carvings, and a crypt containing relics of the saint. In the sacristy of the church is a large bone, said to be from one of the beasts destroyed by the saint, but it actually resembles a whalebone.

Much of the area is occupied by private villas; it takes only a few minutes to walk around the parts of the island open to the public. The view to Orta, with Sacro Monte behind it, is memorable, particularly in the late afternoon, when the light picks up the glint of the wrought-iron traceries. Signs laud the virtues of silence and contemplation, and the island's quiet is broken only by the pealing of the basilica's bells.

Where to Stay & Eat

$$$$ ✕⊡ **Hotel San Rocco.** Half the rooms in this converted 17th-century lakeside convent on the edge of town have views of the water, garden, and surrounding mountains; many also have balconies. The restaurant ($$$) serves international cuisine and has beautiful views of the lake. ⊠ *Via Gippini 11, 28016* ☎ *0322/911977* 🖷 *0322/911964* ⊕ *www.hotelsanrocco.it* ⇄ *80 rooms* ♿ *Restaurant, pool, bar, parking (fee)* ⊟ *AE, DC, MC, V.*

en route Follow the shore drive from Orta San Giulio north to Omegna, at the head of Lake Orta. A mile or so west of Omegna, in the village of Quarna Sotto, there's a musical-instrument factory that's worth a stop. The shore drive continues around the rest of the lake, and at the southern end you can pick up S229, which will take you back to the A4 autostrada.

If you're going to Stresa from Orta San Giulio, you'll first pass through the town of Armeno, where in late summer and early fall, you're likely to see whole families out in the woods, crouched down in their hunt for wild mushrooms, or—if they're lucky—truffles. Oaks blend into evergreens as you climb "La Borromea," a 9-km (5½-mi) twisting, panoramic mountain road toward Mottarone (at 4,900 ft, the tallest peak between the lakes). The road to continues through Gignese, which offers a last dramatic view of Maggiore before descending to Stresa on its western shore.

Stresa

36 *16 km (10 mi) east of Orta San Giulio, 80 km (50 mi) northwest of Milan.*

Stresa, which has capitalized on its central lakeside position and its good connections to the Isole Borromee (Borromean Islands) in Lake Maggiore, has to some extent become a victim of its own success. The luxurious elegance that distinguished its heyday has faded; the grand hotels are still grand, but traffic now encroaches upon their parks and gardens. Even the undeniable loveliness of the lakeshore drive has been threatened by the roar of diesel trucks and BMW traffic. One way to escape is to head for the Isole Borromee.

As you wander around the palms and semitropical shrubs of **Villa Pallavicino,** don't be surprised if you're followed by a peacock or even an ostrich: they're part of the zoological garden and are allowed to roam almost at will. From the top of the hill on which the villa stands, you can see the gentle hills of the Lombardy shore of Lake Maggiore and, nearer and to the left, the jewel-like Borromean Islands. In addition to a bar and restaurant, the grounds also have picnic spots. ⊠ *Via Sempione Sund 8* ☎ *0323/31533* ☐ *€6.70* ☉ *Early Mar.–Oct., daily 9–6.*

Boats to the **Isole Borromee** leave every 15–30 minutes from the dock at Stresa's Piazza Marconi. Although you can hire a private boatman, it's cheaper and just as convenient to use the regular service. Make sure you buy a ticket allowing you to visit all the islands—Bella, Dei Pescatori, and Madre. The islands take their name from the Borromeo family, which has owned them since the 12th century.

Isola Bella (Beautiful Island) is the most famous of the three, and the first that you'll visit. It is named after Isabella, whose husband, Carlo III Borromeo (1538–84), built the palace and terraced gardens for her as a wedding present. Wander up the 10 terraces of the gardens, where peacocks roam among the scented shrubs, statues, and fountains, for a splendid view of the lake. Before Count Carlo began his project, the island was rocky and almost devoid of vegetation; the soil for the garden had to be transported from the mainland. Visit the palazzo to see the rooms where famous guests—including Napoléon and Mussolini—stayed in 18th-century splendor. ☎ *0323/30556* ☐ *Garden and palazzo €8.50* ☉ *Late Mar.–Sept., daily 9–5:30; Oct., daily 9–5.*

Stop for a while at the tiny **Isola dei Pescatori** (Island of the Fishermen), less than 100 yds wide and only about ½ km (¼ mi) long. Of the three islands, this one has remained closest to the way it was before the Borromeos began building. The island's little lanes, strung with fishing nets and dotted with shrines to the Madonna, are the definition of picturesque; little wonder that in high season the village is crowded with postcard stands.

Isola Madre (Mother Island) is the largest of the three and, like Isola Bella, has a large botanical garden. Even dedicated nongardeners should take time to see the profusion of exotic trees and shrubs running down to the shore in every direction. Two special times to visit are April (for the camellias) and May (when azaleas and rhododendrons are in bloom). Also on the island is a 16th-century palazzo, where an antique puppet theater is on display, complete with string puppets, prompt books, and elaborate scenery designed by Alessandro Sanquirico, who was a scenographer at La Scala in Milan. ☎ *0323/31261* ☐ *€8* ☉ *Late Mar.–Sept., daily 9–5:30; Oct., daily 9–5.*

For more information about the islands and how to get there, contact the **Stresa tourist office** (⊠ Via Canonica 8 ☎ 0323/30150) or ask at the landing stages (look for Navigazione Lago Maggiore signs).

Where to Stay & Eat

$$ ✕ **Ristorante del Barcaiolo.** Stop here on a lakeside drive for thoughtfully prepared lake fish and other specialties. The soft rustic feel of the dining room compensates for the occasionally surly service. ⊠ *Piazza del Popolo 23, in Arona, 6 km (4 mi) south of Stresa* ☎ *0322/243388* ☐ *AE, DC, MC, V* ☉ *Closed Wed., 2 wks in Feb., and 3 wks in Aug.*

$$$$ ☐ **Grand Hotel des Iles Borromées.** This palatial establishment has catered to a demanding European clientele since 1863. And though it still has the spacious salons and lavish furnishings of the turn of the 20th century, it has been discreetly modernized. The bathrooms are luxurious. ⊠ *Lungolago Umberto I 67, 28838* ☎ *0323/938938* 🖶 *0323/32405* ⊕ *www.borromees.it* ➥ *161 rooms, 11 suites* ⚷ *Restaurant, room service, minibars, cable TV, tennis court, indoor pool, spa, bar, laundry service, convention center, helipad, free parking* ☐ *AE, DC, MC, V.*

$ ⊠ **Primavera.** A few blocks up from the lake, Primavera has compact, simply furnished rooms in a 1950s building hung with flower boxes. Most rooms have balconies overlooking the streets of Stresa's old center. ⊠ *Via Cavour 39, 28838* ☎ *0323/31286* 🖷 *0323/33458* 🛏 *32 rooms* ⚭ *Bar, meeting rooms, parking (fee)* ▤ *AE, DC, MC, V* ⊘ *Closed Dec.–Feb.*

Verbania

🏵 *16 km (10 mi) north of Stresa, 95 km (59 mi) northwest of Milan.*

Verbania, across the Gulf of Pallanza from Stresa, is known for the **Villa Taranto**, which has magnificent botanical gardens containing some 20,000 species. Created by the enthusiastic Scotsman captain Neil McEachern, these gardens rank among Europe's finest. ⊠ *Verbania* ☎ *0323/556667* 🎫 *€7* ⊘ *Apr.–Oct., daily 8:30–7:30; last admission 1 hr before closing.*

Regular ferry service (every half-hour during peak times) connects Verbania with Laverno; contact **Navigazione Lago Maggiore** (☎ *0322/46651*).

off the beaten path

SANTA CATERINA DEL SASSO BALLARO – Near the town of Laveno, this beautiful lakeside hermitage was constructed in the 12th century by a local merchant to express his gratitude for being saved from the wrath of a storm. About 20 km (12 mi) farther north on the eastern side of the lake, you will find comfortable and charming Liberty-style lodgings at the family-run **Camin Hotel Luino** ($$). ⊠ *Via Dante 35, 21016 Luino* ☎ *0332/530118* 🖷 *0332/537226* ⊕ *www. caminhotelluino.com* ▤ *AE, DC, MC, V.*

Where to Stay & Eat

$$$$ ✕ **Il Sole di Ranco.** The same family has run this lakeside inn for more than 150 years. The present chefs, the infectiously cheerful Carlo Brovelli and son Davide, do the family proud. Lake trout and perch find their way onto the menu, as do artichoke dishes in spring and eggplant in summer. ⊠ *Piazza Venezia 5, Ranco, near Angera* ☎ *0331/976507* ⚭ *Reservations essential* ▤ *AE, DC, MC, V* ⊘ *Closed Tues., and Dec.–mid-Feb. No lunch Mon.*

$ ✕ **Da Cesare.** Off Piazza Cadorna and close to the embarcadero, this hotel restaurant serves tasty risotto *con filetti di persico* (with perch fillets) and typical Piedmontese meat dishes, such as beef braised in Barolo wine. ⊠ *Da Cesare, Via Mazzini 14* ☎ *0323/31386* ▤ *AE, DC, MC, V* ⊘ *Closed Tues. and mid-Dec.–late Feb.*

$ ⊠ **Il Chiostro.** Originally a 17th-century convent, this hotel expanded into the adjoining 19th-century textile factory, adding some conference facilities. Rooms are clean and functional. ⊠ *Via Fratelli Cervi 14, 28921* ☎ *0323/404077* 🖷 *0323/401231* ⊕ *www.chiostrovb.it* 🛏 *100 rooms* ⚭ *Restaurant, meeting rooms* ▤ *AE, DC, MC, V.*

MILAN, LOMBARDY & THE LAKES A TO Z

To research prices, get advice from other travelers, and book travel arrangements, visit *www.fodors.com.*

AIRPORTS & TRANSFERS

Aeroporto Malpensa (MXP), 50 km (31 mi) northwest of Milan, services all intercontinental flights, as well as many European and domestic flights. Aeroporto Milano Linate (LIN), 10 km (6 mi) east of Milan, handles the remainder of European and domestic traffic. Malpensa Shuttle Buses (€8) run every 90 minutes between the two airports.

The Malpensa Express Train connects Malpensa airport with the Cadorna train station near downtown Milan. The 40-minute train ride costs €9 (€12 round-trip), leaving Cadorna every half hour (5:50 AM–8:20 PM) and leaving Malpensa every half hour, (6:45 AM–9:45 PM). Malpensa Express Buses run on the same route outside of these hours. In addition, Malpensa Shuttle Buses (€5) go to and from Milan's central train station (*stazione centrale*). STAR FLY buses (€4) run between Milano Linate and the central train station every half hour, and municipal Bus 73 (€1) runs to Piazza San Babila.

Driving from Malpensa to Milan takes about an hour; take Route S336 east to the A8 autostrada southeast. From Milano Linate, follow the signage west into the central downtown area.

Taxis wait directly outside the arrival building doors at Malpensa, and will take you downtown for about €70. The fare from Milano Linate is about €20.

Airport Information **Aeroporto Malpensa** ☎ 02/74852200 ⊕ www.sea-aeroportimilano.it. **Aeroporto Milano Linate** ☎ 02/74852200.

Taxis & Shuttles **Malpensa Express Train** ☎ 02/27763 automated system; 02/20222 desk. **Malpensa Shuttle Buses** ☎ 02/58583158. **STAR FLY** ☎ 02/717106.

BOAT & FERRY TRAVEL

There's frequent daily ferry and hydrofoil service among towns on the lakes and a range of round-trip excursions with dining service (optional) aboard.

FARES & SCHEDULES Boat & Ferry Information **Navigazione Laghi** ✉ Via Ariosto 21, Milan ☎ 02/4676101 ⊕ www.navigazionelaghi.it. **Navigazione Lago di Como** ✉ Via Per Cernobbio 18, Tavernola, near Como ☎ 031/579211. **Navigazione Lago di Garda** ✉ Piazza Matteotti 2, Desenzano ☎ 030/9149511. **Navigazione Lago Maggiore** ✉ Viale Baracca 1, Arona ☎ 0322/46651.

BUS TRAVEL

Italian bus service is best avoided on intercity routes, since it is neither faster, cheaper, nor more convenient than the railways; trains are generally better than buses for getting around the cities of the plain. If you are determined to travel by bus, Autostradale serves several destinations from its hub at Autostazione Garibaldi, north of Milan's city center.

There's regular bus service between the small towns on the lakes, and it tends to be a cheaper way of getting around than ferry or hydrofoil service. The bus service around Lake Garda serves mostly towns on the western shore. Call SIA for information.

Bus Information **Autostradale** ☎ 02/637901. **SIA** ☎ 030/3774237.

CAR RENTAL

International car rental companies serve Milan's airports and city locations throughout Lombady. The city of Brescia rents electric cars for €3 per hour, €15 per day—pick one up at the station and float silently through the city.

Local Agencies **Avis** ✉ Piazza Diaz, Milan ☎ 02/89010645 ✉ Aeroporto Milano Linate, Milan ☎ 02/715123 ✉ Aeroporto Malpensa, Milan ☎ 02/5858481. **Europcar** ✉ Via Galbani 12, Milan ☎ 02/66710491 ✉ Aeroporto Milano Linate, Milan ☎ 02/76110258 ✉ Aeroporto Malpensa, Milan ☎ 02/5858621. **Hertz** ✉ Aeroporto Milano Linate, Milan ☎ 02/70200256 ✉ Aeroporto Malpensa, Milan ☎ 02/58581137

Municipal Services **Brescia electric car rental** ☎ 030/3882803.

CAR TRAVEL

Although trains are often more convenient for intercity travel, renting a car is the best way to appreciate Lombardy's varied landscape—and the only way to explore its winding lake roads. Several major autostrada routes cross at Milan, all connected by the circular *tangenziale,* which surrounds the city. The A4 runs west to Turin and east to Venice; A1 leads south to Bologna, Florence, and Rome; A7 angles southwest down to Genoa. To reach the lakes, take A8 northwest to Lago Maggiore, or A9 north, which runs past Lago Como, over Saint Gotthard Pass into Switzerland.

Although these major highways will allow you to make good time among the cities of the plain, you'll have to follow secondary roads—often of great beauty—around the lakes. S572 follows the southern and western shores of Lake Garda, S45b edges the northernmost section of the western shore, and S249 runs along the eastern shore. Around Lake Como, follow S340 along the western shore, S36 on the eastern shore, and S583 on the lower arms. S33 and S34 trace the western shore of Lake Maggiore.

EMERGENCY SERVICES ACI, the Italian auto club, offers 24-hour roadside assistance (free to members, for a fee to nonmembers). Regularly spaced roadside service phones are available on the autostrade.
🚗 **ACI dispatchers** ☎ 803/116.

EMBASSIES & CONSULATES

🏴 Australia **Australian Consulate** ✉ Via Borgogna 2, Milan ☎ 02/777041.
🏴 Canada **Canadian Consulate** ✉ Via Vittor Pisani 19, Milan ☎ 02/67581.
🏴 New Zealand **New Zealand Consulate** ✉ Via Guido d'Arezzo 6, Milan ☎ 02/48012544.
🏴 United Kingdom **U.K. Consulate** ✉ Via San Paolo 7, Milan ☎ 02/723001.
🏴 United States **U.S. Consulate** ✉ Via Principe Amedeo 2, Milan ☎ 02/290351.

EMERGENCIES

English-speaking officers with the carabinieri (the national police) are available 24 hours a day. You can dial the nationwide ambulance number wherever you are, and it will connect you to the nearest local emergency service. For first aid, ask for *pronto soccorso,* and be prepared to give your address.

There are a number of pharmacies open 24 hours a day, including one on the upper level of Stazione Centrale in Milan. Others take turns staying open late and on weekends; to find the nearest one, check the roster outside any pharmacy or the list published in the *Corriere della Sera* newspaper.
🏥 **Ambulance** ☎ 118. **Carabinieri** ☎ 112. **Police** ☎ 62261.
🏥 24-Hour Pharmacies **Stazione Centrale** ✉ Piazza Duca D'Aosta, Milan ☎ 02/6690735.

ENGLISH-LANGUAGE MEDIA

BOOKS **American Bookshop** (✉ Largo Cairoli at Via Camperio, Castello, Milan ☎ 02/878920). **English Bookshop** (✉ Via Ariosto at Mascheroni, Porta Magenta, Milan ☎ 02/4694468). **Feltrinelli Bookstore** (✉ Piazza del Duomo, Milan ☎ 02/86996897). **FNAC** (✉ Via Torino, corner of Via della Palla, Duomo, Milan ☎ 02/869541). **Hoepli** (✉ Via Hoepli 5, Duomo, Milan ☎ 02/864871).

MAIL & SHIPPING

📦 Overnight Services **DHL** ✉ Via Agnello 15, Duomo, Milan ☎ 199199345. **United Parcel Service** ✉ Via Albricci 10, Missori, Milan ☎ 800/877877.
💻 Internet Access **Internet Enjoy** ✉ Via Medici 6, Sant'Ambrogio, Milan ☎ 02/866800 ✉ Piazza 24 Maggio, Naviglio, Milan ☎ 02/8357225. **Virgin** ✉ Piazza Duomo 8, Milan ☎ 02/88001200.
📮 Post Offices **Milan** ✉ Via Cordusio 4, Duomo, Milan ☎ 02/8690460.

SAFETY

Milan is a fairly safe city, but it always pays to keep a close eye on your purse or wallet.

TAXIS

Taxi fares in Milan are expensive compared with those in American cities, but drivers are honest. A short downtown hop averages €10. Taxis wait at stands or can be called; they are difficult (but not impossible) to flag down off the street.

Taxi Companies Autoradiotaxi ☎ 02/8585. **Cooperative Esperia** ☎ 02/8383. **Pronto Taxi** ☎ 02/3100. **Radiotaxi** ☎ 02/5353.

TOURS

For tours in Milan, contact the tourist office, which organizes three-hour walking tours of the city Monday mornings at 10 (€15) as well as guided tours to city museums (many of which do not have their own guides). In the lakes, private launches can often be arranged through your hotel.

TRAIN TRAVEL

Although Milan has a bewildering number of railway stations, only one is of concern, Milano Centrale, unless you travel on local routes at peculiar hours—in which case service can begin or terminate in suburban stations (most notably Milano Lambrate for Bergamo, and Stazione Nord for Como). From Milano Centrale, there's frequent direct service to Como, Bergamo, Brescia, Sirmione, Pavia, Cremona, and Mantua. Premium international (EC) service and premium (IC) domestic service connect Milan with major European cities. For general information on trains and schedules, contact the FS–Trenitalia (it is easier to use the Web site). Metro Line 3 (yellow) links Milano Centrale with Piazza Duomo.

Train Information FS–Trenitalia ☎ 848/888088 ⊕ www.trenitalia.com. **Milano Centrale** ✉ About 3 km [2 mi] northwest of the Duomo ☎ 848/888088 toll-free information; 02/72524370 APT office.

TRANSPORTATION AROUND MILAN

Milan has an excellent system of public transport, consisting of three subway lines and 120 tram and bus routes. Tickets are valid for one trip on the Metropolitana (subway) or 75 minutes on buses and trams, and must be purchased before you board and then stamped at station entrances or poles inside trolleys and buses. Standard tickets cost €1 and can be purchased from news vendors, tobacconists, and—at larger stops—machines (some of which require exact change). All-inclusive subway, bus, and tram tickets cost €3 for 24 hours or €5.50 for 48 hours; they're available at Duomo Metro and Stazione Centrale Metro stations. Trains run from 6 AM to 12:30 AM every five minutes; for more information, call the ATM or visit the information office in the Duomo stop.

There's no free street parking unless you have a special resident's permit, but there are garages and parking meters. Parking in the city center is possible 7 AM–8 PM for a fee. For car service with a driver, call Autonoleggio Pini.

ATM (Azienda Trasporti Milanesi) ☎ 800/016857 ⊕ www.atm-mi.it. **Autonoleggio Pini** ☎ 02/29400555 🖷 02/2047843 ⊕ www.pini.it.

TRAVEL AGENCIES

Local Agent Referrals Compagnia Italiana Turismo CIT ✉ Galleria Vittorio Emanuele, Duomo, Milan ☎ 02/863701. **American Express Travel Agency** ✉ Via Brera 3, Brera, Milan ☎ 02/72003693.

VISITOR INFORMATION

🚶 Tourist Information **Bellagio** ✉ Piazza della Chiesa 14 ☎🖷 031/950204. **Bergamo** ✉ Vicolo Aquila Nera at Piazza Vecchia, Upper Bergamo ☎ 035/242226 🖷 035/242994 ✉ Viale Vittorio Emanuele 20, Bergamo Bassa ☎ 035/213185 🖷 035/230184 ⊕ www.apt.bergamo.it. **Brescia** ✉ Corso Zanardelli 34 ☎ 030/43418 🖷 030/3756450 ⊕ www.bresciaholiday.com. **Cernobbio** ✉ Via Regina 33/b ☎🖷 031/510198. **Como** ✉ Piazza Cavour 17 ☎ 031/269712 🖷 031/240111 ⊕ www.lakecomo.org. **Cremona** ✉ Piazza del Comune 5 ☎ 0372/23233 🖷 0372/534080 ⊕ www.aptcremona.it. **Malcesine** ✉ Via Capitanato del Porto 6 ☎ 045/7400044 🖷 045/7401633. **Mantua** ✉ Piazza A. Mantegna 6 ☎ 0376/328253 🖷 0376/363292 ⊕ www.aptmantova.it. **Milan** ✉ Via Marconi 1 (Piazza Duomo) ☎ 02/72524300 🖷 02/72524350 ✉ Stazione Centrale ☎ 02/72524370 ⊕ www.milanoinfotourist.it. **Pavia** ✉ Via Fabio Filzi 2 ☎ 0382/22156 🖷 0382/32221 ⊕ www.apt.pv.it. **Riva del Garda** ✉ Giardini di Porta Orientale 8 ☎ 0464/554444 🖷 0464/520308 ⊕ www.gardaqui.com. **Sabbioneta** ✉ Via Vespasiano Gonzaga 27 ☎🖷 0375/52039 ✉ Piazza D'Armi 1 ☎ 0375/221044 🖷 0375/222119. **Sirmione** ✉ Viale Marconi 2 ☎ 030/916114 🖷 030/916222. **Stresa** ✉ Via Canonica 3 ☎ 0323/30150 🖷 0323/32561 ⊕ www.stresaonline.com. **Tremezzo** ✉ Piazzale Trieste ☎ 0344/40493.

PIEDMONT/ VALLE D'AOSTA
TURIN, THE COLLINE, THE ALPS, THE PO PLAIN

5

FODOR'S CHOICE

Gener Neuv, restaurant, Asti

Museo Egizio, Turin

Villa Novecento, hotel, Courmayeur

HIGHLY RECOMMENDED

RESTAURANTS   Al Garamond, Turin

Balbo, Turin

Cadran Solaire, Courmayeur

Del Cambio, Turin

Maison de Filippo, Courmayeur

Nuovo Batezar—da Renato, St. Vincent

HOTELS   Asplenia, Bardonecchia

Hermitage, Breuil-Cervinia

La Meridiana, Alba

Les Neiges d'Antan, Breuil-Cervinia

Milleluci, Aosta

Palace Bron, Courmayeur

Victoria, Turin

SIGHTS   Castello Fénis

Courmayeur/Monte Bianco

Mole Antonelliana, Turin

Museo dell'Automobile, Turin

Sacra di San Michele

Updated by
Peter Blackman

FROM ALPINE VALLEYS hemming the highest mountains in Europe to the mist-shrouded lowlands skirting the Po River; from pulsating industrial centers turning out the best of Italian design to tiny stone villages isolated above the clouds; from hearty peasant cooking in farmhouse kitchens to French-accented delicacies accompanied by some of Italy's finest wines—the Piedmont and the spectacular Valle d'Aosta regions, tucked away in the country's northwest corner, are delightful surprises even in a land famed for its natural beauty.

Valle d'Aosta's Italian Alps afford excellent skiing and climbing at renowned resort towns such as Courmayeur and Breuil-Cervinia. In the Piedmontese lowlands, Turin, the regional capital, is a historical center that today also serves as the heart of Italy's auto industry. Don't be put off by Turin's industrial reputation—it also has elegant piazzas, high fashion, fine chocolate, and worthwhile museums. (Currently the city is busy highlighting its attractions in preparation to host the Winter Olympics of 2006.) Near Turin are Alba, home of fragrant Italian white truffles, seasonal delicacies that sell for more than $1,000 per pound; Asti, Barolo, and Barbaresco, the famous wine centers; and the modern business hubs Ivrea, Novara, and Alessandria.

Napoléon's regime controlled both regions in the 19th century, and French influence remains evident in everything from traditional recipes redolent of mountain cheeses, truffles, and cream to Versailles-style gardens and wide, tree-lined boulevards. Well-dressed women in the refined cafés of Turin are addressed more often as *madama* than *signora,* and French is often used in the more remote mountain hamlets.

Piedmont (Piemonte in Italian, meaning "foot of the mountains") was originally inhabited by Celtic tribes who were absorbed by the conquering Romans. As allies of Rome, the Celts held off Hannibal when he came down through the Alpine passes with his elephants, but they were eventually defeated, and their capital—Taurasia, the present Turin—was destroyed. The Romans rebuilt the city, giving its streets the grid pattern that survives today. (Roman ruins can be found throughout both regions and are particularly conspicuous in the town of Aosta.) With the fall of the Roman Empire, Piedmont suffered the fate of the rest of Italy and was successively occupied and ravaged by barbarians from the east and the north. In the 11th century, the feudal French Savoy family ruled Turin briefly; toward the end of the 13th century it returned to the area, where it would remain, almost continuously, for 500 years. In 1798 the French Republican armies invaded Italy, but when Napoléon's empire fell, the house of Savoy returned to power.

Beginning in 1848, Piedmont was one of the principal centers of the Risorgimento, the movement for Italian unity. In 1861 the Chamber of Deputies of Turin declared Italy a united kingdom. Rome became the capital in 1870, marking the end of Piedmont's importance in the political sphere. Nevertheless, the architectural splendors of Turin, together with some unheralded but excellent museums, continue to draw visitors.

Piedmont became one of the first industrialized regions in Italy, and the automotive giant FIAT—the Fabbrica Italiana Automobili Torino—was established here in 1899. Today the region is the center of Italy's automobile, metalworking, chemical, and candy industries, having attracted thousands of workers from Italy's south. The FIAT dynasty, led by the Agnelli family—Italy's equivalent of the Kennedys—has been perhaps the most important player in the region's rise to power and affluence.

5

Numbers in the text correspond to numbers in the margin and on the Piedmont/Valle d'Aosta and Turin maps.

If you have 3 days

If you have limited time, you should concentrate first on ⊞ **Turin** ❶–❶ ⌐, including the **Duomo di San Giovanni** ❶, where the famous shroud is housed; the 17th-century **Palazzo Reale** ❷, former residence of the Savoy royal family; and the churches of **San Carlo** ❺ and **Santa Cristina** ❻, which flank the impressive **Piazza San Carlo** ❼, considered by some to be Italy's finest square. Take time to enjoy one or more of the city's authentic old-world cafés and walk by the striking **Mole Antonelliana** ❿, an odd structure that was once the world's tallest building and now houses an extensive cinema museum. On the second day, head northeast along the A5 motorway to ⊞ **Aosta** ❷⑧ to see its large and well-preserved Roman ruins and enjoy some regional French-influenced cooking. If you have a couple of hours to spare on your way to Aosta, see **Castello Fénis** ❷⑦, well worth the detour. On the third day, continue on to ⊞ **Courmayeur** ❷⑨ for magnificent views of Monte Bianco; if time allows, visit **Breuil-Cervinia** ❷⑥ for a look at another Alpine wonder, Monte Cervino. Alternatively, you can catch a glimpse of one or the other and then double back through Aosta to **Cogne and the Parco Nazionale del Gran Paradiso** ❸⓪. Another alternative is to return to Turin and head southeast into the vineyard-blanketed hills around medieval ⊞ **Asti** ❸①.

If you have 5 days

For your first three days, follow the plan outlined above. On the fourth day double back to Turin and make an excursion to **Saluzzo** ❷①, an old town steeped in 15th-century atmosphere—or, if the Alps are your primary interest, spend the fourth day in the mountains, at the **Parco Nazionale del Gran Paradiso** ❸⓪. On the fifth day travel to ⊞ **Asti** ❸① and the surrounding hills, where great wine and and good food attract gastronomic adventurers.

If you have 7 days

Make ⊞ **Turin** ❶–❶ ⌐ your base for three days, exploring the city and making one or two day trips, to **Saluzzo** ❷①, with its picturesque hilltop center and castles; the castle at **Rivoli** ❶⑦ and the medieval abbeys of **Abbazia di Sant'Antonio di Ranverso** ❶⑧ and **Sacra di San Michele** ❷⓪ (Umberto Eco's inspiration); or the resorts of **Sestriere** ❷② and **Bardonecchia** ❷③, in Piedmont's mountains close to the French border. On the third day head for the mountains of Valle d'Aosta; visit the **Castello Fénis** ❷⑦ on the way to ⊞ **Aosta** ❷⑧, a good base for excursions into the mountains that will keep you moving on the fourth and fifth days to **Courmayeur** ❷⑨, **Breuil-Cervinia** ❷⑥, and **Cogne and the Parco Nazionale del Gran Paradiso** ❸⓪; devote the better part of a day to the stunning national park. Head south on the sixth day, doubling back past Turin and continuing southeast to ⊞ **Asti** ❸①. Follow the provincial roads through the vineyards of the hilly Monferrato and Langhe districts of south-central Piedmont, delving into their culinary and enological delights. On the seventh day head east across the fertile Po plain toward the rice-growing capital of **Vercelli** ❸③, making sure you see the Duomo, the final resting place of several Savoy rulers. The easternmost city of Piedmont is **Novara** ❸④, of little intrinsic interest but a rest stop on the way to Milan, only 50 km (30 mi) away.

SWITZERLAND

Monte Cervino
(Matterhorn)

Monte Bianco
(Mont Blanc)

Breuil-
Cervinia 26

Monte Rosa

Great St. Bernard
Pass

Courmayeur 29

S406

Valtournenche

S26

Gressoney-
la-Trinité

Dora

S26

Aosta 28

Nus Châtillon

St. Vincent 25

Little St. Bernard
Pass

Baltea

VALLE

S26

Castello Fénis 27

Verrès

D'

AOSTA

VALLE
D'AOSTA

Cogne 30

Bard 24

Pont St. Martin

Parco Nazionale
del Gran Paradiso

S20

Ceresole Reale

S460

Ivrea

FRANCE

Forno Alpi Gràie

Orco

Cuorgnè

A5

Balme

Céres

Chivasso

S460

S26

S25

A4

Bardonecchia 23

S24

Susa

Sacra di San Michele 20 19

Abbazia di Sant'Antonio
di Ranverso

A4

Avigliana 18 17

Rivoli

Turin

Sestriere
22 TO
CLAVIERE

S23

Stupinigi 16

1 - 15
see detail
map

S10

A21

S589

ITALY

S23

Carignano

S20

A6

S29

Pinerolo

0   10 miles

0   15 km

Saluzzo 21

TO
BRÀ

Alb

32

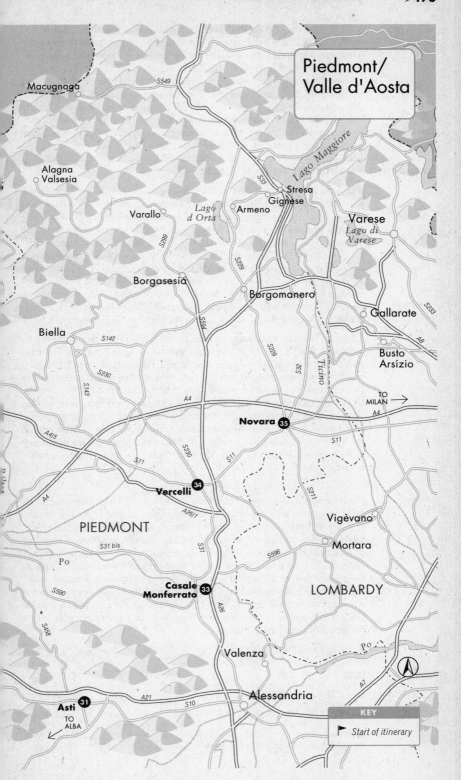

Valle d'Aosta to the north is famous for its Alpine beauty and fortified castles. It was settled in the 3rd millennium BC by people from the Mediterranean and later by a Celtic tribe known as the Salassi, who eventually fell to the Romans. By the 12th century the Savoy family had established itself, and the region's feudal nobles moved into the countryside, building the massive castles that you still see there today. Valle d'Aosta enjoyed relative autonomy as part of the Savoy kingdom and was briefly ruled by the French four separate times. The region is still officially bilingual; though Italian is the mother tongue of most locals, you're likely to encounter French as well.

Exploring Piedmont/Valle d'Aosta

The vast Po plain, which stretches eastward in a wide belt across the top of the Italian peninsula, begins in Piedmont, where the Po River has its source in the Coolidge Glacier on 11,000-ft-high Monviso. But Piedmont is primarily a mountainous region. The Maritime Alps lie to the south of Turin, and the rolling hills of the Monferrato and Langhe districts make up the landscape to the city's southeast. High Alpine crests of Valle d'Aosta rise to the north and west of the plain. As you wind your way northeast into Valle d'Aosta, you are in the Italian Loire, where solid, imposing castles sit in the shadow of Europe's most impressive peaks, Monte Bianco and Monte Cervino. Nature has endowed Piedmont and Valle d'Aosta with some of the most striking scenery in Italy.

Like any rugged, mountainous region, the Italian Alps can be tricky to navigate. Roads that look like superhighways on the map can be narrow and twisting, with steep slopes and cliff-side drops. Generally, roads are well maintained, but the sheer distance covered by all of those curves tends to take longer than you might expect, and so it's best to figure in extra time for getting around. This is especially true in winter, when weather conditions can cause slow traffic and road closings. Be sure to check with local tourist offices and police before venturing off the beaten path, and find out whether you may need tire chains for snowy and icy roads. Train routes, on the other hand, are more or less reliable in the region.

About the Restaurants & Hotels

High standards and opulence are characteristic of Turin's better hotels, and the same is true, translated into the Alpine idiom, at the top mountain resort hotels. Less-expensive hotels in cities and towns are generally geared to business travelers. You can usually count on a measure of charm and comfort at even the more modest resort hotels. Summer vacationers and winter skiers keep occupancy rates and prices high at the resorts during these peak seasons. Many mountain resort hotels accept half- or full-board guests only, occasionally for stays of at least a week; some have off-season rates that can reduce the cost by a full price category. If you're a skier, ask about package deals that can give you a break on the price of lift tickets.

WHAT IT COSTS In euros				
	$$$$	**$$$**	**$$**	**$**	**¢**
RESTAURANTS	over €22	€17–€22	€12–€17	€7–€12	under €7
HOTELS	over €210	€160–€210	€110–€160	€60–€110	under €60

Restaurant prices are for a second course (secondo piatto). Hotel prices are for two people in a standard double room in high season, including tax and service.

ON THE MENU

THESE TWO REGIONS OFFER *rustic specialties from farmhouse hearths, fine cuisine with a French accent— and everything in between. The area's best-known dish is probably polenta, a creamy cornmeal concoction often served with carbonada (veal stew), local sausages, melted cheese, or wild mushrooms. The favorite form of pasta is agnolotti dal plin, made by closing the pasta around a meat filling using a characteristic pinch with the fingers (the "plin"). These are often served with the pan juices of roast veal or with melted butter and shaved truffles. Another regional specialty is fonduta, a local version of fondue, made with melted fontina (a cheese from Valle d'Aosta), eggs, and sometimes grated truffles. Fontina and ham also often deck out the ubiquitous, French-style crepes alla valdostana, served piping hot and casserole style. Alba is the home of tartufi bianchi (white truffles), much rarer and more expensive than black ones and considered the tastiest by connoisseurs. Another local dish is bagna cauda (literally, "hot bath"), a heated sauce made from butter, oil, anchovies, and shredded garlic; it is traditionally served with cardi (edible thistles related to artichokes) and other raw vegetables for dipping.*

Unlike in most other regions of Italy, cheese plates appear frequently on menus as precursors to, if not substitutes for,

dessert—another indication of French influence. From the soft and mild toma to the strong and redolent Castelmagno, a huge variety of cheese types is available. Throughout the region as well, though especially in Turin, you will find that most meals are accompanied by grissini (bread sticks). Invented in Turin in the 17th century to ease the digestive problems of little Prince Vittorio Amedeo II (1675–1730), these, when freshly made and hand-rolled, are a far cry from the thin and dry, plastic-wrapped versions available elsewhere. Napoléon called them petits batons and was, it seems, addicted to them.

Although as a rule desserts here are less sweet than in some other Italian regions, treats like panna cotta (a cooked milk custard), torta di nocciole (hazelnut torte), and bonet (a pudding made with coffee, hazelnut, cocoa, and macaroons) still delight. Turin is renowned for its delicate pastries and fine chocolates, especially for the hazelnut gianduiotti.

Piedmont is one of Italy's most important wine-producing regions. Most of the wines are full-bodied reds, such as Barolo, Barbaresco, Freisa, Barbera, and the lighter Dolcetto. Asti Spumante, a sweet sparkling wine, comes from the region, as does vermouth, which was developed in Piedmont by A. B. Carpano in 1786. Valle d'Aosta is famous for schnappslike brandies made from fruits or herbs.

Timing

Unless you are dead set on skiing, the region can be visited in either summer or winter (and for that matter, there's summer skiing at Monte Cervino). In winter, road conditions can be treacherous, especially higher up in the mountains, requiring the use of snow tires or chains. The ski resorts of Valle d'Aosta are popular with Italians and non-Italians alike, so book your accommodations in advance. Snow conditions for skiing vary drastically year to year—there is nothing approaching the consistency of, say, the Colorado and Utah Rockies—so keep apprised of weather conditions. If you are visiting in summer, try to avoid coming in August, the holiday month for the vast majority of Italians, many of whom will head to the mountains for a vacation of walking, hiking, and relaxing.

TURIN

Turin—Torino, in Italian—is roughly in the center of Piedmont/Valle d'Aosta and 128 km (80 mi) west of Milan; it's on the Po River, on the edge of the Po plain, which stretches eastward all the way to the Adriatic. Turin's flatness and wide, angular, tree-lined boulevards are a far cry from Italian *metropoli* to the south; the region's decidedly northern European bent is quite evident in its nerve center. Apart from its role as northwest Italy's major industrial, cultural, intellectual, and administrative hub, Turin also has a reputation as Italy's capital of black magic and the supernatural. This distinction is enhanced by the presence of Turin's most famous, and controversial, relic, the Sacra Sindone (Holy Shroud), still believed by many Catholics to be the cloth in which Christ's body was wrapped when he was taken down from the cross.

Downtown Turin

Many of Turin's major sights are clustered around Piazza Castello, and others are on or just off the porticoed Via Roma, one of the city's main thoroughfares, which leads 1 km (½ mi) from Piazza Castello south to Piazza Carlo Felice, a landscaped park in front of the train station. First opened in 1615, Via Roma was largely rebuilt in the 1930s, during the Mussolini era.

a good walk

Start on Piazza San Giovanni at the **Duomo di San Giovanni** ❶ ►, the hushed and shadowy repository of the city's famed relic. Head left from the Duomo, walk two blocks, and then turn left into Piazza Castello. To the left is the Piazzetta Reale and the imposing **Palazzo Reale** ❷, where you can visit the sumptuous rococo interiors and, in a separate wing to the east, the Armeria Reale. The massive building occupying an entire block at the center of Piazza Castello is **Palazzo Madama** ❸, parts of which are open to the public. In the northwest corner of the same square, take time to observe Guarini's lively architectural vision in the church of **San Lorenzo** ❹. Go southwest on Via Roma, a street rebuilt with arcades in the 1930s. Continuing a few blocks, you come to the twin churches of **San Carlo** ❺ and **Santa Cristina** ❻ on the **Piazza San Carlo** ❼. Just off the northeast end of Piazza San Carlo is the imposing **Palazzo dell'Accademia delle Scienze** ❽, where you may devote an hour or two to the collections in the Museo Egizio and Galleria Sabauda. To the east, across the street, is the graceful **Palazzo Carignano** ❾, an important building in Italian history and a good example of Piedmontese baroque. The east facade of the palace faces Piazza Carlo Alberto, from where you head north for one block to reach Via Po. Turn right and then continue east to Via Montebello, where you turn left to reach the **Mole Antonelliana** ❿, Turin's oddest and most conspicuous building and the site of a cinema museum.

TIMING This walk takes the better part of a day if you plan to linger in the museums. It includes the most important of Turin's sights, so it's a suitable plan to follow if you're trying to "do" the town in one day.

What to See

► ❶ **Duomo di San Giovanni.** The most impressive part of Turin's 15th-century cathedral is the shadowy, black marble–walled **Cappella della Sacra Sindone** (Chapel of the Holy Shroud), where the famous relic was housed before a fire in 1997. The chapel was designed by the priest and architect Guarino Guarini (1604–83), a genius of the baroque style who was official engineer and mathematician to the court of Duke

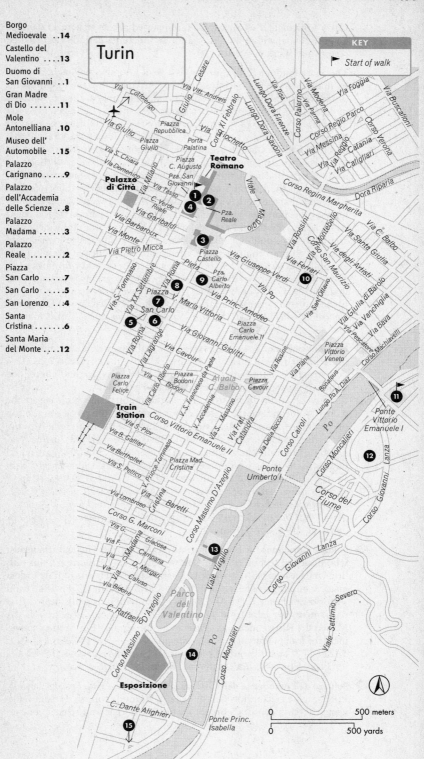

Turin

Carlo Emanuele II of Savoy. The fire caused severe structural damage and the chapel will remain closed for an indefinite period of time while restoration work proceeds.

The Sacra Sindone (Holy Shroud) is a 4-yd-long sheet of linen, thought by millions to be the burial shroud of Christ, bearing the light imprint of his crucified body. The shroud first made an appearance around the middle of the 15th century, when it was presented to Ludovico of Savoy in Chambéry. In 1578 it was brought to Turin by another member of the Savoy royal family, Duke Emanuele Filiberto. It was only in the 1990s that the Catholic Church began allowing rigorous scientific study of the shroud. Not surprisingly, results have bolstered both sides of the argument. On the one hand, three separate university teams—in Switzerland, Britain, and the United States—have concluded, as a result of carbon 14 dating, that the cloth is a forgery dating from between 1260 and 1390. On the other hand, they are unable to explain how medieval forgers could have created the shroud's image, which is like a photographic negative, and how they could have had the knowledge or means to incorporate traces of Roman coins covering the eyelids and endemic Middle Eastern pollen woven into the cloth. Either way, the shroud continues to be revered as a holy relic, displayed on very rare occasions—perhaps once in a decade. For those who miss the real thing, a photocopy is on permanent display near the altar of the Duomo. ⊠ *Piazza San Giovanni, Centro* ☎ *011/4361540* ⊗ *Mon.–Sat. 6:30–noon and 3–7, Sun. 8–noon and 3–7.*

★ ❿ **Mole Antonelliana.** You can't miss the unusual square dome and thin, elaborate spire tower of this Turin landmark above the city's rooftops. This odd structure, built between 1863 and 1889, was originally intended to be a synagogue, but costs escalated and eventually it was bought by the city of Turin. In its time it was the tallest brick building in the world. You can take the crystal elevator to reach the terrace at the top of the dome for an excellent view of the city, the plain, and the Alps beyond. Also worth a visit is the Mole's **Museo Nazionale del Cinema** (National Cinema Museum), which extends more than 34,000 square ft and houses many items of film memorabilia as well as a film library with some 7,000 titles. ⊠ *Via Montebello 20, Centro* ☎ *011/8125658* ⊕ *www.museonazionaledelcinema.it* ✉ *Museum €5.20, elevator €3.62, combination ticket €6.80* ⊗ *Museum Tues.–Fri. and Sun. 9–8, Sat. 9 AM–11 PM; ticket sales end 75 mins before closing; elevator Tues.–Fri. and Sun. 10–8, Sat. 10 AM–11 PM.*

❾ **Palazzo Carignano.** A baroque triumph of Guarino Guarini (the priest who designed several of Turin's most noteworthy structures), this red-brick palace was built between 1679 and 1685 and is one of Italy's most historic buildings. The kings of Savoy Carlo Alberto (1798–1849) and Vittorio Emanuele II (1820–78) were born within its walls. Italy's first parliament met here from 1860 to 1865. The palace now houses the **Museo del Risorgimento**, a museum honoring the 19th-century movement for Italian unity. ⊠ *Via Accademia delle Scienze 5, Centro* ☎ *011/ 5621147* ⊕ *www.regione.piemonte.it/cultura/risorgimento* ✉ *€5* ⊗ *Tues.–Sun. 9–7; ticket sales end 60 minutes before closing.*

❽ **Palazzo dell'Accademia delle Scienze** (Palace of the Academy of Sciences). Priest-architect Guarino Guarini's large baroque tour de force, prefiguring the 18th century's preoccupation with logic and science, houses two of Turin's most famous museums, the Museo Egizio and the Galleria Sabauda. The **Museo Egizio** (Egyptian Museum) is one of the finest of its kind outside Cairo. Its superb collection includes statues of pharaohs and mummies, and entire frescoes taken from royal tombs. Look for the 13th-century BC statue of Ramses II, which still glistens in its original colors. ⊠ *Via Accademia delle Scienze 6, Centro* ☎ *011/ 5617776* ⊕ *www.museoegizio.it* ✉ *€6.50, €8 combined ticket includes Galleria Sabauda* ⊙ *Tues.–Sun. 8:30–7:30; last ticket 1 hr before closing.*

The **Galleria Sabauda** houses the collections of the house of Savoy. It's particularly rich in 16th- and 17th-century Dutch and Flemish paintings: note the *St. Francis with Stigmata* by Jan Van Eyck (1395–1441), in which the saint receives the marks of Christ's wounds while a companion cringes beside him. Other Dutch masterpieces include paintings by Anthony Van Dyck (1599–1641) and Rembrandt (1606–69). *Tobias and the Angel* by Piero del Pollaiuolo (circa 1443–96) is showcased, and other featured Italian artists include Fra Angelico (circa 1400–55), Andrea Mantegna (1431–1506), and Paolo Veronese (1528–88). ⊠ *Via Accademia delle Scienze 6, Centro* ☎ *011/547440* ✉ *€4.50, €8 combined ticket includes Museo Egizio* ⊙ *Tues.–Fri. and Sun. 8:30–7:30, Sat. 8:30 AM–11 PM.*

❸ **Palazzo Madama.** In the center of Piazza Castello, this castle was named for the French queen Maria Cristina, who made it her home in the 17th century. The building incorporates the remains of a Roman gate with later medieval and Renaissance additions. Filippo Juvarra (1678–1736) designed the castle's monumental baroque facade. Open to the public are the atrium; the large central room known as Il Voltone, where a glass floor reveals the castle's Roman foundations; Juvarra's splendid baroque staircase; and the Salone del Senato, where you'll find temporary exhibitions. ⊠ *Piazza Castello, Centro* ✉ *Free, exhibitions €3.50* ⊙ *Tues.–Fri. and Sun. 10–8, Sat. 10 AM–11 PM.*

❷ **Palazzo Reale.** This 17th-century palace, the former Savoy royal residence, is an imposing work of brick, stone, and marble that stands on the site of one of Turin's ancient Roman city gates. In contrast to its sober exterior, the palace's interior is swathed in luxurious, mostly rococo trappings, including tapestries, gilt ceilings, and sumptuous 17th- to 19th-century furniture. Behind the palace, you can relax in the royal gardens. ⊠ *Piazza Castello, Centro* ☎ *011/4361455* ✉ *Palace €5.50, gardens free* ⊙ *Palace, Tues.–Sun. 8:30–6:15; accompanied visits leave every 40 mins; gardens, 9–1 hr before sunset.*

The **Armeria Reale** (Royal Armory), in a wing of the Royal Palace, holds one of Europe's most extensive collections of arms and armor. It's a must-see for connoisseurs. ⊠ *Entrance at Piazza Castello 191, Centro* ☎ *011/ 543889* ✉ *€2.07* ⊙ *Tues.–Sun. 10:30–7:30.*

❼ **Piazza San Carlo.** Surrounded by shops, arcades, fashionable cafés, and elegant baroque palaces, this is one of the most beautiful squares in Turin. In the center stands a **statue of Duke Emanuele Filiberto of Savoy**, victor at the battle of San Quintino in 1557. The melee heralded the peaceful resurgence of Turin under the Savoy, after years of bloody dynastic fighting. The fine bronze statue, erected in the 19th century, is one of Turin's symbols.

need a
break?

A chocolate lover's pilgrimage to Turin inevitably leads to **Al Bicerin** (⊠ Piazza della Consolata 5, Centro ☎ 011/4369325 ☉ Closed Wed.), which first opened its doors in 1763. Cavour, Nietzsche, Puccini, and Dumas have all sipped here, and if you order the house specialty, the *bicerin* (a hot drink with layers of chocolate, coffee, and cream), you'll understand why. Don't be surprised if the friendly and energetic owner, Marité Costa, also tries to tempt you with one of her flavored *zabajoni* (warm eggnogs). For tasteful gifts, you'll find chocolate goodies, including chocolate-flavored pasta, on sale in the café store. The historic **Caffè San Carlo** (⊠ Piazza San Carlo 156, Centro ☎ 011/532586) is usually lively with locals, gathered at the marble-top tables under the huge crystal chandelier. **Caffè Torino** (⊠ Piazza San Carlo 204, Centro ☎ 011/545118) is a long-established coffeehouse worth a stop for its sumptuous decor.

❺ San Carlo. The ornate baroque facade of this 17th-century church was enhanced in the latter part of the 19th century to harmonize with the facade of the neighboring Santa Cristina. ⊠ *Piazza San Carlo, south end of square, right corner Centro* ☉ *Daily 8–noon and 4–6:30, Sat. 8–noon and 4–6, Sun. 9–12:45 and 4–6.*

❹ San Lorenzo. Architect Guarino Guarini was in his mid-60s when he began this church in 1668. The masterful use of geometric forms and theatrical control of light show him working at his mature and confident best. Stand in the center of the church and look up into the cupola to enjoy the full effect. ⊠ *Piazza Castello, Centro* ☉ *Daily 8:30–noon and 4–7.*

need a
break?

Baratti e Milano (⊠ Piazza Castello 27, Centro ☎ 011/5613060), in the glass-roofed Galleria Subalpina near Via Po, is one of Turin's charming old cafés. It's famous for its chocolates—indulge your sweet tooth or buy some *gianduiotti* (hazelnut chocolates) or candied chestnuts to take home to friends.

❻ Santa Cristina. Built in the mid-17th century, this church received a baroque-style face-lift by Juvarra in 1715. ⊠ *Piazza San Carlo, south end of square, left corner Centro* ☉ *Daily 7–noon and 3–7.*

Along the Po

The Po River is narrow and unprepossessing here in Turin, only a hint of the broad waterway that it becomes as it flows eastward toward the Adriatic. It's flanked, however, by formidable edifices, a park, and a lovely pedestrian path.

a good
tour

Start at the east end of Piazza Vittorio Veneto, at the end of Via Po. Cross the river on Ponte Vittorio Emanuele I, the bridge leading to the church of **Gran Madre di Dio** ⑪ ↑, a replica of Rome's Pantheon. To reach the church of **Santa Maria del Monte** ⑫, follow Corso Moncalieri south and then wend your way upward to the top of the hill. Return to Corso Moncalieri and cross the next bridge downstream, Ponte Umberto I, to the Parco del Valentino, opened in 1856. One of the city's many pretty pedestrian paths, Viale Virgilio runs parallel to the river and leads to the **Castello del Valentino** ⑬, reminiscent of castles on the Loire. Go south on Viale Virgilio to the **Borgo Medioevale** ⑭, a replica of a medieval hamlet and castle. From the park, catch a bus or taxi or just keep on walking south on Corso Massimo d'Azeglio for about 25 minutes to the **Museo dell'Automobile** ⑮, a low, modern building filled with the sleek, glamorous cars of yesteryear.

TIMING   Three hours should be enough to allow you to cover the ground with ease, but if you are an automobile buff, allow well over an hour for the Museo dell'Automobile.

What to See

⑭ Borgo Medioevale. This complex was built for a General Exhibition held in Torino in 1884 for the purpose of raising public interest in the past. It's a faithful reproduction of a medieval Piedmont village, with crafts shops, houses, churches, and stores clustering along narrow streets and lanes. In the center of the village sits the **Rocca Medioevale,** a medieval castle and the town's main attraction. ✉ *Southern end of Parco del Valentino, San Salvario* ☎ *011/4431701* 🎟 *Village free, Rocca Medioevale €3* ⊙ *Village Apr.–Oct., daily 9–8; Nov.–Mar., daily 9–7; Rocca Medioevale Tues.–Sun. 9–7; groups of no more than 25 enter the castle every ½ hr; ticket counter closes at 6:15.*

⑬ Castello del Valentino. Originally a simple hunting lodge, the castle owes its present appearance to the restorations ordered by Madama Maria Cristina of France, who received the building as a wedding present when she married Vittorio Amedeo I of Savoy. With memories of 16th-century French châteaux clearly in mind, work was begun in 1620 and completed 40 years later. The building is now the home of Turin's Polytechnical University's Faculty of Architecture and is surrounded by the **Parco del Valentino,** a pleasant riverside park with botanical gardens. ✉ *Parco del Valentino, San Salvario* ☎ *011/5646377 castle; 011/6707446 botanical gardens* 🎟 *Castle free, botanical gardens €3* ⊙ *Castle by appointment only, botanical gardens Apr.–Sept., weekends 9–1 and 3–7.*

▶ ⑪ Gran Madre di Dio. On the east bank of the Po, this neoclassical church is modeled after the Pantheon in Rome. It was built between 1827 and 1831 to commemorate the return of the house of Savoy to Turin after the fall of Napoléon's empire. ✉ *Piazza Gran Madre di Dio, Borgo Po* ⊙ *Mon.–Sat. 7:30–noon and 3:30–7, Sun. 7:30–1 and 3:30–7.*

★ ⑮ Museo dell'Automobile. No visit to car-manufacturing Turin would be complete without a pilgrimage to see perfectly conserved Bugattis, Ferraris, and Isotta Fraschinis. Here you'll get an idea of the importance of FIAT—and automobiles in general—to Turin's economy. There's a collection of antique cars from as early as 1896, and displays show how the city has changed over the years as a result of its premier industry. ✉ *Corso Unità d'Italia 40, Millefonti* ☎ *011/677666* ⊕ *www.museoauto. org* 🎟 *€6* ⊙ *Tues.–Sat. 10–6:30, Sun. 10–8:30.*

⑫ Santa Maria del Monte. The church and convent standing on top of 150-ft Monte dei Cappuccini date from 1583. Don't be surprised if you find yourself in the middle of a wedding party: local couples often come here to have their pictures taken. ✉ *Monte dei Cappuccini, above Corso Moncalieri, Borgo Po* ⊙ *Daily 9–noon and 2:30–6.*

Where to Stay & Eat

★ $$$$ ✕ **Balbo.** This elegant establishment in the center of town is considered by many the best restaurant in Turin. Some of the more creative takes on traditional recipes include *sottopaletta di vitello brasata al barbaresco* (shoulder of veal braised in Barbaresco wine), *astice con verdurine e salsa di crostacei* (crawfish and vegetables in a seafood sauce), and *sformato caldo al gianduja con salsa menta* (hot hazelnut and chocolate pudding with mint sauce). Balbo has a nice array of seafood, and fixed-price menus are available. ✉ *Via Andrea Doria 11, Centro* ☎ *011/8395775* 🍴 *Reservations essential* ▭ *AE, DC, MC, V* ⊙ *Closed Mon. and Aug.*

★ **$$$** ✕ **Del Cambio.** Set in a palace dating from 1757, this is one of Europe's most beautiful and historic restaurants, with decorative moldings, mirrors, and hanging lamps that look just as they did when Italian national hero Cavour dined here more than a century ago. The cuisine draws heavily on Piedmontese tradition and is paired with fine wines of the region. Agnolotti with *sugo d'arrosto* (roast veal sauce) is a recommended first course. ✉ *Piazza Carignano 2, Centro* ☎ *011/546690* 🏛 *Jacket and tie* ⌕ *Reservations essential* ▭ *AE, DC, MC, V* ⊙ *Closed Sun., Jan. 1–6, and 3 wks in Aug.*

$$$ ✕ **Vintage 1997.** The first floor of a town house in the center of Turin makes a fittingly elegant site of this sophisticated restaurant. You might try such specialties as *vitello tonnato alla nostra maniera* (roast veal with a light tuna sauce) or *code di scampi ai fagioli* (prawn tails with beans). The range of meat and seafood dishes is complemented by an excellent wine list. ✉ *Piazza Solferino 16/h, Centro* ☎ *011/535948* ▭ *AE, DC, MC, V* ⊙ *Closed Sun. and 3 wks in Aug. No lunch Sat.*

★ **$$–$$$** ✕ **Al Garamond.** The ocher-colored walls and the ancient brick vaulting set the stage in this small and brightly decorated restaurant. Traditional and innovative dishes of both meat and seafood are prepared with creative flair; you might try the tantalizing *rombo in crosta di patate al barbera* (turbot wrapped in sliced potatoes and baked with Barbera wine). For dessert, the *mousse di liquirizia e salsa di cioccolato bianco* (licorice mousse with white chocolate sauce) is a must, even if you don't usually like licorice. The level of service here is high, even by demanding Turin standards. ✉ *Via G. Pomba 14, Centro* ☎ *011/8122781* ▭ *AE, MC, V* ⊙ *Closed Sun., Jan. 1–6, and 3 wks in Aug. No lunch Sat.*

$$–$$$ ✕ **Hosteria La Vallée.** Small and romantic, with elegant tableware and linens, select pieces of antique furniture and carefully designed lighting, this restaurant, tucked away in a quiet section of central Turin, has developed a devoted clientele. Recommended are *agnello scottato all'aglio e rosmarino* (lamb grilled with garlic and rosemary), followed by *sformato di cacao con cuore di fondente* (warm chocolate pudding). ✉ *Via Provana 3b, Centro* ☎ *011/8121788* ▭ *AE, MC, V* ⊙ *Closed Sun., Jan. 1–7, and Aug. No lunch.*

$$–$$$ ✕ **L'Agrifoglio.** This intimate local favorite has just 10 tables. Specialties change with the seasons, but you might find such delicacies as risotto *al Barbaresco* (with Barbaresco wine) and agnolotti dal plin al sugo d'arrosto on the menu. L'Agrifoglio stays open late for the after-theater and after-cinema crowd. ✉ *Via Accademia Albertina 38, Centro* ☎ *011/837064* ▭ *AE, DC, MC, V* ⊙ *Closed Sun.–Mon. No lunch.*

$–$$ ✕ **Savoia.** The enthusiasm of chef and owner Mario Ferrero permeates three small rooms decorated with a few choice pictures and antique furniture. His kitchen turns out creative takes on Piedmontese specialties that change with the seasons. The bread and pasta are homemade and the wine cellar is tended with equal care. ✉ *Via Corta d'Appello 13, Centro* ☎ *011/4362288* ▭ *AE, DC, MC, V* ⊙ *Closed Sun. No lunch Sat.*

$ ✕ **Porto di Savona.** Look for this centuries-old tavern under the arcades of vast Piazza Vittorio Veneto, where it once served as a terminal for the Turin–Savona stagecoach line. The small street-level and upstairs dining rooms have a decidedly old-fashioned air; the marble stairs are well worn, and the walls are decked with photos of Old Turin. Customers sit at long wooden tables to eat home-style Piedmontese cooking, including gnocchi with Gorgonzola and *bollito misto* (mixed boiled meats, appropriately served only in winter). The Barbera house wine is good. ✉ *Piazza Vittorio Veneto 2, Centro* ☎ *011/8173500* ▭ *MC, V* ⊙ *Closed Mon., 1st 2 wks in Jan., and last 2 wks in Aug. No lunch Tues.*

¢–$ ✕ **Da Mauro.** Tuscan and Piedmontese dishes are served at this lively, family-run trattoria. Specialties include cannelloni *alla Mirella* (baked with mozzarella, prosciutto, and tomato), *involtini al Gorgonzola* (veal roulades with Gorgonzola and a sauce of peppers and olives), and famous grilled Florentine beef. ⊠ *Via Maria Vittoria 21, Centro* ☎ *011/8170604* ⊟ *No credit cards* ⊘ *Closed Mon. and July.*

$$$$ 🏨 **Jolly Hotel Principi di Piemonte.** The centrally located Principi is one of the top hotels in Turin and often caters to a famous clientele. The rooms, with 1930s furnishings, are spacious and light, with high ceilings. Common areas are elegantly decorated and the service is both courteous and efficient. ⊠ *Via Gobetti 15, Centro, 10123* ☎ *011/5577111* 🖷 *011/5620270* ⊕ *www.jollyhotels.it* ⇆ *97 rooms, 8 suites* ♨ *Restaurant, minibars, bar, meeting rooms, Internet, parking (fee), some pets allowed (fee), no-smoking rooms* ⊟ *AE, DC, MC, V.*

$$$ 🏨 **Turin Palace.** You're right across from the train station at this grand, century-old building in the center of town. Quiet, spacious, well-furnished rooms have high ceilings and feature either leather-and-wood classic modern style or imperial Louis XV furnishings. ⊠ *Via Sacchi 8, Centro, 10128* ☎ *011/5625511* 🖷 *011/5612187* ⊕ *www.thi.it* ⇆ *120 rooms, 1 suite* ♨ *Restaurant, minibars, room TVs with movies, bar, meeting rooms, parking (fee), some pets allowed* ⊟ *AE, DC, MC, V.*

★ $$ 🏨 **Victoria.** Rare style, attention to detail, and comfort are the hallmarks of this boutique hotel, furnished and managed to create the feeling of a refined town house. The newer wing has a grand marble staircase and individually decorated guest rooms. The same attention to detail is found in the older rooms, and the sitting room and breakfast room are particularly attractive. ⊠ *Via Nino Costa 4, Centro, 10123* ☎ *011/5611909* 🖷 *011/5611806* ⊕ *www.hotelvictoria-torino.com* ⇆ *94 rooms, 6 suites* ♨ *Pool, bicycles, bar, parking (fee), no-smoking rooms; no a/c in some rooms* ⊟ *AE, DC, MC, V.*

$–$$ 🏨 **Liberty.** *Liberty* is a term used by Italians to refer to the art nouveau style, and this small, conveniently located hotel is true to its name, with period-style furnishings and an ambience to match. It's a favorite of academics, artists, and others who appreciate its solid, old-fashioned comfort, enhanced by the Anfossi family's attentive courtesy. You must reserve ahead for the restaurant. ⊠ *Via Pietro Micca 15, Centro, 10121* ☎ *011/5628801* 🖷 *011/5628163* ⇆ *35 rooms* ♨ *Restaurant, bar* ⊟ *AE, DC, MC, V.*

Nightlife & the Arts

The Arts

MUSIC Classical music concerts are held in the famous **Conservatorio Giuseppe Verdi** (⊠ Via Mazzini 11, Centro ☎011/8121268 ⊠ Piazza Bodoni, Centro ☎ 011/888470) throughout the year but primarily in winter. The **Settembre Musica Festival** (☎011/4424703), held for three weeks in September, highlights classical music; call for specifics. Sacred music and some modern religious pieces are performed in the **Duomo** (⊠ Via Montebello 20, Centro ☎ 011/8154230) on Sunday evening; performances are usually advertised in the vestibule or in the local edition of Turin's nationally distributed newspaper *La Stampa*. The Thursday edition comes with a supplement on music and other entertainment possibilities.

OPERA The **Teatro Regio** (⊠ Piazza Castello 215, Centro, ☎ 011/88151 🖷 011/8815214 ⊕ www.teatroregio.torino.it), one of Italy's leading opera houses, has its season from October to June. You can buy tickets for most performances (premieres sell well in advance) at the box office or on the Web site, where discounts are offered on the day of the show. It's also possible to book tickets via mail or fax. Payment for reservations must be made by credit card, international postal order, or eurocheque within 20 days of confirmation.

Nightlife

Along the Po, south of Piazza Vittorio Veneto, is **Alcatraz** (⊠ Murazzi del Po 37/41, Centro ☎ 011/812570), a very popular disco with a mixed crowd open seven days a week in summer months and from Thursday to Sunday in fall and spring. A popular meeting place in the piazza at the end of Via Po is the wine bar **Caffè Elena** (⊠ Piazza Vittorio Veneto 5, Centro ☎ 011/8123341), open until 2 in the morning every night except Wednesday. A plush after-hours venue for Turin's smart set, **Hennessy** (⊠ Via Mongreno 23, Pino Torinese ☎ 011/8998522) is a large disco in an upscale residential district on the eastern side of the Po; it's open Friday and Saturday nights until late. **Pick Up** (⊠ Via Barge 8, Centro ☎ 011/4472204) is a bar and dance club catering to a mixed crowd of young Turinese, university students, and visitors, open 11–4, Wednesday to Sunday. Hot Latin music, often live, is dished up with gusto at **Sabor Latino** (⊠ Via Stradella 10, Borgata Vittoria ☎ 011/852327) every night except Monday. On the west bank of the Po is **Zoo-bar** (⊠ Corso Casale 127, Madonna del Pilone ☎ 011/8194347), where you can listen to live music, get a drink, or dance to music spun by DJs. It's open Tuesday and Thursday 10:30–3, Friday and Saturday 10:30–4.

Sports

Soccer

Turin's two professional soccer clubs, Juventus and Torino, play their games in the **Stadio delle Alpi** (⊠ 6 km [4 mi] northwest of city, Venaria). Juventus is one of Italy's most successful and most popular teams. There is fierce rivalry between its supporters and those of visiting clubs, especially Inter Milan and AC Milan. Home matches are usually played on Sunday afternoon during the season, which runs from late August to mid-May. It's possible to purchase tickets for Juventus and Torino games in any *tabaccheria* (tobacco shop) with a sign bearing a capital "T."

Shopping

Chocolate

The tradition of making chocolate began in Turin in the early 17th century. It was originally an aristocratic drink, until the 19th-century Piedmontese invention of a machine to further refine cocoa made it possible to create solid bars and candies. The most famous of all Turin chocolates is the *gianduiotto* (with cocoa, sugar, and hazelnuts), first concocted in 1867. The tradition of making these delicious treats has been continued at the small, family-run **Peyrano** (⊠ Corso Moncalieri 47, Centro ☎ 011/6602202 ⊕ www.peyrano.it ☉ Closed Wed. afternoon and Sun.), where more than 80 types of chocolate confections are made and sold. **Stratta** (⊠ Piazza San Carlo 191, Centro ☎ 011/547920), one of Turin's most famous chocolate shops, has been around since 1836 and sells confections of all kinds—not just the chocolates in the lavish window displays but also fancy cookies, rum-laced fudges, and magnificent cakes.

Markets

Go to the famous **Balon Flea Market** (⊠ Piazza Repubblica, Centro) on Saturday morning for excellent bargains on secondhand books and clothing and good browsing among stalls selling local specialties such as gianduiotti. (Be aware, however, that the market is also famous for its pickpockets.) The second Sunday of every month, a special antiques market, appropriately called the **Gran Balon,** sets up shop in Piazza Repubblica.

Specialty Stores

Most people know that Turin produces more than 75% of Italy's cars, but they are often unaware that it's also a clothing manufacturing city. Top-quality boutiques stocking local, national, and international lines are clustered along Via Roma and Via Garibaldi. Piazza San Carlo, Via Po, and Via Maria Vittoria are lined with antiques shops, some—but not all—specializing in 18th-century furniture and domestic items.

Specialty food stores and delicatessens abound in central Turin. For a truly spectacular array of cheeses and other delicacies, try Turin's famous **Borgiattino** (⊠ Via Accademia Albertina 38/a, Centro ☎ 011/8394686 ⊘ Closed Mon.). For hand-rolled grissini—some as long as 4 ft—the bakery **Bersano** (⊠ Via Barbaroux 5, Centro ☎ 011/5627579 ⊘ Closed Wed. afternoon) is the best in town.

THE COLLINE & SAVOY PALACES

As you head west from Turin into the Colline ("little hills"), castles and medieval fortifications begin to pepper the former dominion of the house of Savoy, and the Alps come into better and better view. In the region lie the storybook medieval towns of Avigliana, Rivoli, and Saluzzo; 12th-century abbeys; and, farther west in the mountains, the ski resorts of Bardonecchia and Sestriere, two of the venues chosen for the 2006 Winter Olympics.

Stupinigi

⑯ *8 km (5 mi) southwest of Turin.*

The **Palazzina di Caccia,** in the town of Stupinigi, was built by Juvarra in 1729 as a hunting lodge for the house of Savoy. More like a sumptuous royal villa, its many wings, landscaped gardens, and surrounding forests give a clear idea of the level of style to which the Savoy were accustomed. This regal aspect was not lost on Paolina Buonaparte, who briefly held court here during her brother Napoléon's reign of Italy. Today the Palazzina houses the **Museo d'Arte e Ammobiliamento** (Museum of Art and Furnishings), a vast collection of paintings and furniture gathered from numerous Savoy palaces in the Turin area. You can get there taking Bus 41 from Turin's Stazione Porta Nuova. ⊠ *Via Principe Amedeo 7* ☎ *011/3581220* 🎫 *€5.16* ⊘ *Apr.–Oct., Tues.–Sun. 10–7:30, last entrance at 6; Nov.–Mar., Tues.–Sun. 9:30–5, last entrance at 4.*

Rivoli

⑰ *16 km (10 mi) northwest of Stupinigi, 13 km (8 mi) west of Turin.*

The Savoy court was based in Rivoli in the Middle Ages. The 14th- to 15th-century **Casa del Conte Verde** (House of the Green Count) sits right in the center of town, and the richness of decorations hints at the wealth and importance of the owner (and of Rivoli) during the period. Inside, a small gallery hosts temporary exhibitions. ⊠ *Via Fratelli Piol 8* ☎ *011/9563020* 🎫 *Changes with exhibits* ⊘ *Changes with exhibits.*

The castle of Rivoli now houses the **Museo d'Arte Contemporaneo** (Museum of Contemporary Art). The skeleton of this building, begun in the 17th century and then redesigned but never finished by Juvarra in the 18th century, was given vibrant new life in the late 20th century by minimalist Turin architect Andrea Bruno. On display are changing international exhibitions and a permanent collection of 20th-century Italian art. To get to Rivoli from downtown Turin, take Tram 1 and then Bus 36.

⊠ *Piazzale Mafalda di Savoia* ☎ *011/9565222* ⊕ *www.castellodirivoli. org* 🎫 *€6.20* ⊙ *Tues.–Fri. 10–5, weekends 10–7; 1st and 3rd Sat. of month 10–10.*

Abbazia di Sant'Antonio di Ranverso

🔞 *6 km (3½ mi) west of Rivoli, 23 km (14 mi) west of Turin.*

The abbey was originally an abbey hospital, founded in the 12th century by the Hospitalers of St. Anthony to care for victims of St. Anthony's Fire, a crippling disease contracted by eating contaminated grains. Pilgrims came here over the centuries for cures or, sometimes, to offer thanks for a miraculous recovery. The 15th-century frescoes, with their lifelike depictions of pilgrims and saints, retain their original colors. ⊠ *Buttigliera Alta west of Rivoli, off the S25* ☎ *011/9367450* 🎫 *€3* ⊙ *Sept.–May, Tues.–Sun. 9–noon and 2–4:30; June–Aug., Tues.–Sun. 9–noon and 2–5:30.*

Avigliana

🔞 *6 km (4 mi) west of the Abbazia di Sant'Antonio di Ranverso, 29 km (18 mi) west of Turin.*

Perhaps because of its attractive setting, Avigliana was a favorite of the Savoys up until the mid-15th century. Medieval houses still line the narrow, twisting streets. **Casa della Porta Ferrata,** on the street of the same name, is a well-preserved example of Piedmontese 14th-century domestic architecture. The richly decorated Gothic windows are typical of the period, and the facade was used as a model for similar buildings in the Borgo Medioevale in Turin.

Sacra di San Michele

★ ⑳ *14 km (8½ mi) west of Avigliana, 43 km (27 mi) west of Turin.*

Unless you plan a 14-km (9-mi) hike from Avigliana, a car is essential for an excursion to the Abbey of St. Michael, perhaps best known as inspiration for the setting of Umberto Eco's *The Name of the Rose.* San Michele was built on Monte Pirchiriano in the 11th century to stand out: it occupies the most prominent location for miles around, hanging over a 3,280-ft bluff. When monks came to enlarge the abbey, they had to build part of the structure on supports more than 90 ft high—an engineering feat that was famous in medieval Europe and is still impressive today. By the 12th century, this important abbey controlled 176 churches in Italy, France, and Spain; one of the abbeys under its influence was Mont-Saint-Michel in France. Because of its strategic position, it came under numerous attacks over the next five centuries and was eventually abandoned in 1622. It was restored in the late 19th and early 20th centuries.

From **Porta dello Zodiaco,** a splendid Romanesque doorway decorated with the signs of the zodiac, you climb 150 steps, past 12th-century sculptures, to reach the church. On the left side of the interior are 16th-century frescoes representing New Testament themes; on the right are depictions of the founding of the church. Go down to the crypt to see the 9th- to 12th-century chapels. ⊕ *www.sacradisanmichele.com* 🎫 *€2.50* ⊙ *Mar. 16–Oct. 15, Tues.–Sat. 9:30–12:30 and 3–6, Sun. 9:30–noon and 2:40–6; Oct. 16–Mar. 15, Tues.–Sat. 9:30–12:30 and 3–5, Sun. 9:30–noon and 2:40–5; mandatory accompanied visits leave every 30 mins.*

Saluzzo

㉑ *58 km (36 mi) southwest of Turin.*

The russet-brick town of Saluzzo—once a flourishing medieval center and later seat of a Renaissance ducal court—is a well-preserved gem, with narrow, winding streets, frescoed houses, Gothic churches, and elegant Renaissance palaces. A map with instructions for a **walking tour** of the town's sights is available from the local tourist information office (✉ Via Griselda 6 ☎ 0175/46710 ⊕ www.comune.saluzzo.cn.it). The older and more interesting part of the town hugs a hilltop in the Po Valley and is crowned by **La Castiglia**, a 13th-century castle that has served as a prison since the early 18th century.

The exterior of the **Castello di Manta**, 4 km (2½ mi) south of Saluzzo, is austere, but inside are frescoes and other decorations of the period. Knights and damsels from an allegorical poem written by Marquis Tommaso III of Saluzzo, humanist lord of the castle, parade in full costume in the 15th-century frescoes of the **Sala del Barone.** The castle sometimes hosts exhibits, at which time higher admission is charged. ✉ *Via al Castello 14, Manta* ☎ *0175/87822* 🎟 *€4.15* ⊙ *Mar.–mid-Dec., Tues.–Sun. 10–1 and 2–6.*

Sestriere

㉒ *32 km (20 mi) east of Briançon, 93 km (58 mi) west of Turin.*

In the early 1930s, before skiing became a sport for commoners, the patriarch of the FIAT automobile dynasty had this resort built, with two distinctive tower hotels and ski facilities that have been developed into some of the best in the Alps. The resort lacks the charm of other, older Alpine centers; overdevelopment added some eyesores, and the mountains don't have the striking beauty of those in Valle d'Aosta. But skiers have an excellent choice of trails, some of them crossing the border into France.

Where to Stay

$$$$ 🏨 **Principi di Piemonte.** Large and elegant, this luxurious hotel sits on the slopes above the town, near the lifts and the town's golf course. Its secluded location heightens the sense of exclusivity, a quality appreciated by a very stylish clientele. The restaurant and a cozy bar invite après-ski relaxation. ✉ *Via Sauze, 10058* ☎ *0122/7941* 🖶 *0122/755411* ⊕ *www.framon-hotels.com* 🛏 *96 rooms, 4 suites* 🍴 *Restaurant, indoor pool, hot tub, sauna, Turkish baths, bar, meeting rooms, some pets allowed* 🗂 *AE, DC, MC, V* ⊙ *Closed early Apr.–June and Sept.–Nov.*

$$ 🏨 **Miramonti.** Nearly every room has a terrace at this pleasant, central, modern chalet. The ample comfortable rooms are done in traditional mountain style, featuring lots of wood paneling and coordinated floral-print fabrics. ✉ *Via Cesana 3, 10058* ☎ *0122/755333* 🖶 *0122/ 755375* 📧 *h.miramonti@tiscalinet.it* 🛏 *30 rooms* 🍴 *Restaurant, minibars, exercise equipment, bar, meeting rooms, some pets allowed* 🗂 *AE, DC, MC, V.*

Sports & the Outdoors

SKIING   At 6,670 ft, the **Sestiere ski resort** (☎ 0122/799411 for conditions) was built in the late 1920s under the auspices of Turin's Agnelli family. The slopes get good snow some years from November through May, other years from February through May. The tourist office in Sestriere (☎ 0175/ 46710 ⊕ www.comune.sestriere.to.it) provides complete information about lift tickets, ski-runs, mountain guides, and equipment rentals, here and in neighboring towns such as Bardonecchia and Claviere. Its excellent Web site is also available in English. A quaint village with slate-roof houses, **Claviere** (⊠ 17 km [11 mi] west of Sestriere) is one of Italy's oldest ski resorts. Its slopes overlap with those of the French resort of Montgenèvre.

Bardonecchia

㉓ *36 km (22 mi) northwest of Sestriere, 89 km (55 mi) west of Turin.*

This sunny town is one of Italy's oldest winter ski resorts, attracting hardy sports enthusiasts from Turin since the 1920s. It's near the entrance to the Fréjus train and automobile tunnels.

Where to Stay

$$ 🏨 **Des Geneys-Splendid.** One of the best hotels in the area sits in a pine-filled private park near the town center. The 1930s style is evident in the arched windows on the ground floor, the stucco walls, and the long wrought-iron balconies. The public rooms are spacious and comfortable, and there's a playroom for children. ⊠ *Via Einaudi 21, 10052* ☎ *0122/99001* 🖷 *0122/999295* ⊕ *www.desgeneys.com* 🛏 *53 rooms, 4 suites* ⟁ *Restaurant, gym, piano bar, meeting rooms* ⊟ *AE, DC, MC, V* ⊘ *Closed mid-Apr.–mid-June and mid-Sept.–Nov.*

★ $ 🏨 **Asplenia.** Skiers love this small modern version of a mountain chalet, near the town center and the ski lifts. The ample rooms are comfortably furnished, with a small entryway and a balcony affording beautiful views. ⊠ *Viale della Vittoria 31, 10052* ☎ *0122/999870* 🖷 *0122/901968* 🛏 *17 rooms, 4 suites* ⟁ *Restaurant, some pets allowed* ⊟ *AE, DC, MC, V.*

$ 🏨 **Bucaneve.** Just a short walk from the ski lift, this small family-owned hotel is popular with the ski crowd. A cozy reading room and restaurant add to the allure of these affordable lodgings. ⊠ *Viale della Vecchia 2, 10052* ☎ *0122/999332* 🖷 *0122/999980* ⊕ *www.hotelbucanevebardonecchia.it* 🛏 *20 rooms, 4 suites* ⟁ *Restaurant, bar, Internet, some pets allowed; no a/c* ⊟ *AE, MC, V* ⊘ *Closed Oct.–Nov.*

VALLE D'AOSTA

The unspoiled beauty of the highest peaks in the Alps, the Matterhorn and Monte Bianco, competes with the magnificent scenery of Italy's oldest national park in Valle d'Aosta, a semiautonomous, bilingual region tucked away at the border with France and Switzerland. Luckily, you don't have to choose—the region is small, so you can fit ski, après-ski, and wild ibex into one memorable trip. The main Aosta Valley, largely on an east–west axis, is hemmed in by high mountains where glaciers have gouged out 14 tributary valleys, six to the north and eight to the south. A car is very helpful here, but take care: distances are relatively short as the crow flies, but steep slopes and winding roads add to your mileage and travel time.

Coming up from Turin, beyond Ivrea, the road takes you through countryside that becomes hillier and hillier, passing through steep ravines guarded by brooding, romantic castles. Pont St. Martin, about 18 km (11 mi) north of Ivrea, is the beginning of bilingual (Italian and French) territory.

Bard

㉔ *65 km (40 mi) north of Turin.*

A few minutes beyond the French-speaking village of Pont St. Martin, you pass through the narrow Gorge de Bard and reach the **Forte di Bard** (closed to the public), a 19th-century reconstruction of a fort that stood for eight centuries, serving the Savoys for six of them. In 1800 Napoléon entered Italy through this valley and used the cover of darkness to get his artillery units past the castle unnoticed. Ten years later he remembered this inconvenience and had the fortress destroyed.

St. Vincent

㉕ *28 km (17 mi) north of Bard, 93 km (58 mi) north of Turin.*

The town of St. Vincent has been a popular spa resort since the late 18th century. Its main draw these days is the **Casinò de la Vallée**, one of Europe's largest gambling casinos. If you're planning a stop here, remember to pack your black tie—and plenty of cash.

Where to Stay & Eat

★ **$$$** ✕ **Nuovo Batezar—da Renato.** This tiny restaurant of only eight tables ranks among the best in all of Italy. The ambience is rustic yet elegant, with arches and beamed ceilings enhanced by local antiques and fine crystal. The menu, which changes with the seasons, is Valdostana and Piemontese, with creative variations. Mushrooms, fish, fresh game, and truffles often play prominent roles. As a starter, try the homemade pasta or the *pazzarella* (a small pizza with porcini mushrooms, mozzarella, and truffles). ✉ *Via Marconi 1, steps from casino* ☎ *0166/513164* ⌂ *Reservations essential* ⊟ *AE, DC, MC, V* ✆ *Closed Wed., 3 wks in June, and Nov. 15–30. No lunch weekdays.*

$$$$ ⌂ **Billia.** A luxury Belle Epoque hotel with faux-Gothic touches, the Billia is in a park in the middle of town and connects directly to the casino by a passageway. Half the rooms are done in modern and half in period decor, replete with all creature comforts. The hotel has extensive facilities, including a conference center and a health club. ✉ *Viale Piemonte 72, 11027* ☎ *0166/5231* 🖷 *0166/523799* ✎ *grand.hotel.billia@galactica. it* ⇥ *233 rooms, 7 suites* ⌂ *Restaurant, tennis court, pool, health club, sauna, bar, convention center* ⊟ *AE, DC, MC, V.*

$ ⌂ **Elena.** The central location is the selling point of this hotel near the casino. The spacious rooms, some with balconies and/or king-size beds, are decorated with color-coordinated fabrics in a comfortable modern style. ✉ *Via Biavaz 2 (Piazza Zerbion), 11027* ☎ *0166/512140* 🖷 *0166/ 537459* ✎ *hotel.elena@libero.it* ⇥ *46 rooms, 2 suites* ⌂ *Restaurant, minibars, bar, meeting rooms, gym, sauna, Turkish bath, no-smoking rooms, parking (fee); no a/c in some rooms* ⊟ *AE, DC, MC, V.*

Nightlife

A top nighttime entertainment attraction is the **Casinò de la Vallée**, one of only four casinos in Italy, and one of the largest in Europe. You must present identification and be at least 18 years old to enter. Dress is elegant, with jacket and tie requested at the French gaming tables. ✉ *Via Italo Mus 1* ☎ *0166/5221* ⊕ *www.casinodelavallee.it* ⌑ *Sun.–Fri. €5, Sat. €10* ✆ *Mon.–Thurs. 2 PM–2:30 AM, Fri. 2 PM–3 AM, Sat. 2 PM–3:30 AM, Sun. 10:30 AM–2:30 AM.*

Breuil-Cervinia/The Matterhorn

㉖ *30 km (18 mi) north of St. Vincent, 116 km (72 mi) north of Turin.*

Breuil-Cervinia is a village at the base of the **Matterhorn** (Monte Cervino in Italian; Mont Cervin in French). Like the village, the famous peak straddles the border between Italy and Switzerland, and all sightseeing and skiing facilities are operated jointly. Splendid views of the peak can be seen from **Plateau Rosa** and the **Cresta del Furggen,** both of which can be reached by cable car from the center of Breuil-Cervinia. Although many locals complain that the tourist facilities and the condominiums in the village have changed the face of their beloved Breuil, most would agree that the cable car has given them access to climbing and off-trail skiing in ridges that were once inaccessible.

Where to Stay & Eat

★ **$$$$** ✕🏠 **Les Neiges d'Antan.** In a pine wood at Perrères, just outside Cervinia, this small, rustic, family-run inn is quiet and cozy, with three big fireplaces and a nice view of the Matterhorn. An excellent restaurant ($$$–$$$$) serves French dishes and local specialties, such as *zuppa Valpellinentze* (a hearty soup of bread, cabbage, and Fontina cheese), and an opulent antipasto (local salami, country pâté, tomino cheese, and much more). ⊠ *Località Perrères, 3½ km (2 mi) outside Cervinia, 11021* ☎ *0166/948775* 🖷 *0166/948852* ⊕ *www.lesneigesdantan.it* ⤺ *21 rooms, 3 suites* ⚒ *Restaurant, bar, room TVs with movies, sauna; no a/c* ⊟ *MC, V* ⊙ *Closed May–June, and mid Sept.–Nov.*

$–$$ ✕🏠 **Cime Bianche.** This calm, quiet mountain-lodge restaurant is one of the few dining spots in town to offer regional Valdostana cuisine, serving fonduta, polenta, and wild game, as well as pasta, in a rustic setting. The wood beams and tables are typical of a ski resort, but meals are produced with greater care than your average après-ski affairs. The commanding view covers the Matterhorn and Grandes Murailles. Reservations are highly recommended. There are also 15 guest rooms, all with private bathrooms, TVs, and balconies. ⊠ *Località La Vieille 44, toward the ski area, near the base lift* ☎ *0166/949046* 🖷 *0166/948061* ✎ *le.cime.bianche@galactica.it* ⤺ *15 rooms* ⚒ *Restaurant, bar; no a/c* ⊟ *MC, V* ⊙ *Closed Mon. and May–June.*

★ **$$$$** 🏠 **Hermitage.** A marble relief of St. Theodolus at the entrance reminds you that this was the site of a hermitage, but asceticism has given way to comfort and elegance at what is now one of the most exclusive hotels in the region. It has the look of a relaxed but posh family chalet, with rustic antiques, petit-point upholstery, a fire always glowing in the enormous hearth, and a candlelit dining room. The bright bedrooms have balconies; suites have antique fireplaces and 18th-century furnishings. While here you can make use of the extensive health and beauty facilities and play golf (for half price) at the Cervinia Golf Club. ⊠ *Via Piolet 1, Località Chapellette, 11021* ☎ *0166/948998* 🖷 *0166/949032* ⊕ *www.hotelhermitage.com* ⤺ *30 rooms, 6 suites* ⚒ *Restaurant, golf privileges, indoor pool, health club, massage, sauna, bar, Internet, meeting rooms* ⊟ *AE, DC, MC, V* ⊙ *Closed May–June and Sept.–Oct.*

$$$ 🏠 **Bucaneve.** This small central hotel, catering to longer stays, is decorated in typical mountain style, with lots of wood paneling, cheery floral upholstery in spacious lounges, and terraces dripping with geraniums. Après-ski, there's a restaurant (half board is required) and a cozy bar with a big fireplace and pianist in the evening. ⊠ *Piazza Jumeaux 10, 11021* ☎ *0166/949119* 🖷 *0166/948308* ⊕ *www.hotel-bucaneve.it* ⤺ *20 rooms, 6 suites* ⚒ *Restaurant, gym, hot tub, sauna, piano bar, meeting rooms* ⊟ *AE, MC, V* ⊙ *Closed May–late June and Sept.–Nov., depending on weather* ⊙l *MAP.*

$$$ 🏠 **Chalet Valdotain.** About 2 km (1 mi) outside of town on the road from Châtillon, this Alpine chalet has wooden balconies and snug rooms with terrific views of the Matterhorn. It's known for good food and a friendly atmosphere. ⊠ *Località Lago Bleu 2, 11021* ☎ *0166/949428* 🖷 *0166/948874* ⊕ *www.chaletvaldotain.it* ⤺ *35 rooms* ⚒ *Restaurant, pool, gym, sauna, Turkish baths, bar* ⊟ *AE, DC, MC, V* ⊙ *Closed May–mid-June and mid-Sept.–early Dec.*

Sports & the Outdoors

CLIMBING   Serious climbers can make the ascent of the **Matterhorn** from Breuil-Cervinia after registering with the local mountaineering officials at the **tourist office** (⊠ Via Carrel 29 ☎ 0166/949136). This climb is for skilled and experienced climbers only. Less demanding hikes follow the lower slopes of the valley of the River Marmore, to the south of town.

SKIING   Because its slopes border the Cervino glacier, this resort at the foot of the Matterhorn offers year-round skiing. Sixty lifts and a total of almost 200 mi of ski runs, ranging from beginner to expert, make the area one of the best and most popular in Italy. Contact the **Breuil-Cervinia tourist office** (☎ 0166/949136) for information.

Castello Fénis

★ ㉗   *11 km (7 mi) west of St. Vincent, 104 km (65 mi) north of Turin.*

The best-preserved medieval fortress in Valle d'Aosta, the many-turreted Castello Fénis was built in the mid-14th century by Aimone di Challant, a member of a prolific family related to the Savoys. The castle, which used a double ring of walls for its defense, is the sort imagined by schoolchildren, with pointed towers, portcullises, and spiral staircases. The 15th-century courtyard, surrounded by wooden balconies, is elegantly decorated with well-preserved frescoes. Inside you can see the kitchen, with an enormous fireplace that provided central heat in winter, the armory, and the spacious, well-lit rooms used by the lord and lady of the manor. If you have time to visit only one castle in Valle d'Aosta, this should be it. ☎ *0165/764263* ▣ *€5* ۞ *Mar.–June, daily 9–6:30; July–Aug., daily 9–7:30; Sept., daily 9–6:30; Oct.–Feb., Wed.–Mon. 10–5; maximum of 25 people allowed to enter every ½ hr.*

en route   The highway continues climbing through Valle d'Aosta to the town of **Aosta** itself. The road at this point is heading almost due west, with rivulets from the wilderness reserve Parco Nazionale del Gran Paradiso streaming down from the left to join the Dora Baltea River, one of the major tributaries of the Po and an increasingly popular spot for rafting. Be careful driving here in late spring, when melting snow can turn some of these streams into torrents.

Aosta

㉘   *12 km (7 mi) west of Castello Fénis, 113 km (70 mi) north of Turin.*

Aosta stands at the junction of two of the important trade routes that connect France and Italy—the valleys of the Rhône and the Isère. Its significance as a trading post was recognized by the Romans, who built a garrison here in the 1st century BC. At the eastern entrance to town, in the Piazza Arco d'Augusto and commanding a fine view over Aosta and the mountains, is the **Arco di Augusto** (Arch of Augustus), built in 25 BC to mark Rome's victory over the Celtic Salassi tribe. (The sloping roof was added in 1716 in an attempt to keep rain from seeping between the stones.) The present-day layout of streets in this small city, tucked away in the Alps more than 644 km (400 mi) from Rome, is the clearest example of Roman street planning in Italy. Well-preserved Roman walls form a perfect rectangle around the center of Aosta, and the regular pattern of streets reflects its role as a military stronghold. St. Anselm, born in Aosta, later became archbishop of Canterbury in England.

The **Collegiata di Sant'Orso** is the sort of church that has layers of history in its architecture. Originally there was a 6th-century chapel on this site, founded by the Archdeacon Orso, a local saint. Most of this structure was destroyed or hidden when an 11th-century church was erected over it. This church, in turn, was encrusted with Gothic, and later baroque, features, resulting in a jigsaw puzzle of styles, but, surprisingly, not a chaotic jumble. The 11th-century features are almost untouched in the crypt, and if you go up the stairs on the left from the main church you can see the 11th-century frescoes (ask the sacristan for entrance). These restored frescoes depict the life of Christ and the Apostles: although only the tops are visible, you can see the expressions on the faces of the disciples. Take the outside doorway to the right of the main entrance to see the church's crowning glory, its 12th-century **cloister**. Next to the church, it's enclosed by some 40 stone columns with masterfully carved capitals depicting scenes from the Old and New Testaments and the life of St. Orso. The turrets and spires of Aosta peek out above. ⊠ *Via Sant'Orso* ☎ *0165/40614* ☉ *Apr.–Sept., daily 9–5; Oct.–Mar., daily 10–5.*

The huge **Roman Porta Pretoria,** regally guarding the city, is a remarkable relic from the Roman era. The area between the massive inner and outer gates was used as a small parade ground for the changing of the guard. ⊠ *West end of Via Sant'Anselmo.*

The 72-ft-high ruin of the facade of the **Teatro Romano** guards the remains of the 1st-century BC amphitheater, which once held 20,000 spectators. Only a bit of the outside wall and seven of the amphitheater's original 60 arches remain, and these are built into the facade of the adjacent convent of the sisters of San Giuseppe. The convent will usually allow you in to see these arches (ask at the entrance). ⊠ *Via Anfiteatro 4.*

Aosta's **Duomo** dates from the 10th century, but all that remains from that period are the bell towers. The decoration inside is primarily Gothic, but the main attraction of the cathedral predates that era by 1,000 years: a carved ivory diptych showing the Roman Emperor Honorius and dating from AD 406 is among the many ornate objects housed in the treasury. ⊠ *Via Monsignor de Sales* ☎ *0165/40251* ☉ *Treasury Apr.–Sept., Tues.–Sun. 9–11:30 and 3–5:30; Oct.–Mar., Sun. 3–5:30.*

Where to Stay & Eat

$$$ ✕ **Vecchio Ristoro.** At this centrally located converted mill, furnished with antiques and a large ceramic stove, the chef-proprietor takes pride in creative versions of regional favorites. Among them may be *marbrè di bollito misto con bagnet verde* (terrine of mixed boiled meats with a parsley and anchovy sauce) and *carrè d'agnello gratinato alle erbe* (grilled loin of lamb in a pastry and herb crust). ⊠ *Via Tourneuve 4.* ☎*0165/33238* ▭*AE, DC, MC, V* ☉ *Closed Sun., June, and 1 wk in Nov. No lunch Mon.*

$$–$$$ ✕ **Taverna Nando.** A wine cellar with wooden floors and vaulted ceilings, this family-run tavern is in the center of Aosta, and it has a terrace for outdoor dining. Try regional specialties such as fonduta, carbonada, and *cervo* (venison) with mushrooms. Reservations are recommended. ⊠ *Via de Tillier 41* ☎ *0165/44455* ▭ *AE, DC, MC, V* ☉ *Closed Mon. and June 20–July 10.*

$–$$ ✕ **La Brasserie du Commerce.** Small, lively, and informal, this place is in the heart of Aosta, near central Piazza E. Chanoux. On a sunny summer day try to get a table on the terrace. Typical valley dishes, such as fonduta, are on the menu, as well as many vegetable dishes and salads. ⊠ *Via de Tillier 10* ☎ *0165/35613* ⌖ *Reservations not accepted* ▭ *AE, DC, MC, V* ☉ *Closed Sun.*

$ ✕ **Praetoria.** Just outside the Porta Pretoria, this simple and unpretentious restaurant serves hearty local food. The pasta is homemade, and all of the menu offerings, such as *crespelle alla valdostana* (crepes with cheese and ham), are strictly traditional. ✉ *Via S. Anselmo 9* ☎ *0165/44356* ▭ *AE, DC, MC, V* ◷ *Closed Thurs.*

$$–$$$ ▦ **Holiday Inn Aosta.** This modern, comfortable hotel has the advantages of a central location and rooms with the chain's predictable amenities. There's local color, however, in the attractive Provençal fabrics and the views of the mountains. Rooms are available equipped for people with disabilities. ✉ *Corso Battaglione Aosta 30, 11100* ☎ *0165/236356* 🖷 *0165/236837* ⊕ *www.sixcontinentshotels.com* ⥂ *45 rooms, 5 suites* ♨ *Restaurant, room TVs with movies, bar, business services, some pets allowed (fee), no-smoking rooms* ▭ *AE, DC, MC, V.*

★ $$ ▦ **Milleluci.** This small and inviting family-run hotel sits on a hillside overlooking Aosta, 1 km (½ mi) north of town. A huge brick hearth and rustic wooden beams highlight the lounge. Bedrooms, some with balconies, are bright and pleasantly decorated and have good views of the city and mountains. Ten rooms are reserved for nonsmokers and some rooms are equipped for people with disabilities. The hotel provides breakfast only. ✉ *Località Porossan Roppoz 15, 11100* ☎ *0165/235278* 🖷 *0165/235284* ⊕ *www.hotelmilleluci.com* ⥂ *26 rooms, 5 suites* ♨ *Tennis court, pool, sauna, bar, Internet, no-smoking rooms; no a/c* ▭ *AE, DC, MC, V.*

$ ▦ **Casa Ospitaliera del Gran San Bernardo.** In a castle given as a gift to the Order of St. Bernard by Amedeo of Savoy in 1137, this simple pension 15 km (8 mi) north of Aosta, still part of a monastery and run by monks, is a good base for cross-country skiing or hiking. The no-frills accommodation, the hearty food included in the full meal plan, and the chance to sleep in a 12th-century castle at bargain prices all add to the charm of this place from another time. ✉ *Rue de Flassin 3, 11010 Saint-Oyen (Aosta)* ☎ *0165/78247* ⥂ *15 rooms* ♨ *No a/c, no room phones, no room TVs* ▭ *No credit cards* ◷ *Closed May* ⑩ *FAP.*

Nightlife & the Arts

Each summer a series of **concerts** is held in different venues around the city. Organ recitals in July and August attract performers of world renown. Call the **tourist board** (✉ Piazza E. Chanoux 8 ☎ 0165/236627) for information.

Shopping

Aosta and the surrounding countryside are famous for wood carvings and wrought iron. There's a permanent **crafts exhibition** in the arcades of Piazza E. Chanoux, in the heart of Aosta; it's a good place to pick up a bargain. Each year, in the last two days of January, all of Aosta turns out for the **Sant'Orso Fair,** where all sorts of crafts are on sale, including handmade lace from nearby Cogne, carved wood and stonework, and brightly colored woolens.

Courmayeur/Monte Bianco

★ ㉙ *35 km (21 mi) northwest of Aosta, 150 km (93 mi) northwest of Turin.*

The main attraction of Courmayeur is a knock-'em-dead view of Europe's tallest peak, **Monte Bianco** (Mont Blanc). Jet-set celebrities flock here, following a tradition that dates from the late 17th century, when Courmayeur's natural springs first began to draw visitors. The spectacle of the Alps gradually surpassed the springs as the biggest draw (the Alpine letters of the English poet Shelley were almost advertisements for the region), but the biggest change came in 1965, with the opening of the Mont Blanc tunnel. Since then, ever increasing numbers of travelers have passed through the area.

Luckily, planners have managed to keep some restrictions on wholesale development within the town, and its angled rooftops and immaculate cobblestone streets maintain a cozy (if prepackaged) feeling. There is no train directly into Courmayeur, so if you don't have a car, you'll need to bus it from nearby Pré-Saint-Didier, which is accessible by train from Aosta.

From La Palud, a small town 4 km (3½ mi) north of Courmayeur, you can catch the cable car up to the top of Monte Bianco. In summer, if you get the inclination, once up top you can switch cable cars and descend into Chamonix, in France. In winter you can ski parts of the route off-piste. The Funivie La Palud whisks you up first to the Pavillon du Mont Fréty—a starting point for many beautiful hikes—and then to the Rifugio di Torino, before arriving at the viewing platform at **Punta (Pointe) Helbronner** (more than 11,000 ft), which is also the border post with France. Monte Bianco's attraction is not so much its shape (much less distinctive than that of the Matterhorn) as its expanse and the vistas from the top.

The next stage up—only in summer—is on the **Télépherique de L'Aiguille du Midi**, as you pass into French territory. The trip is particularly impressive: you dangle over a huge glacial snowfield (more than 2,000 ft below) and make your way slowly to the viewing station above Chamonix. It's one of the most dramatic rides in Europe. From this point you're looking down into France, and if you change cable cars at the Aiguille du Midi station you can make your way down to Chamonix itself. The return trip covers the same route. Schedules are unpredictable, depending on weather conditions and demand; you can get information by sending an e-mail to **cable car operators** (info@montebianco.com) or calling the **Courmayeur tourist office** (☎ 0165/842060). ⊠ *Fraz. La Palud 22* ☎ *0165/89925 Italian side (La Palud); 00/33450536210 French side (Aiguille du Midi)* ⊕ *www.montebianco.com* ✉ *€11 round-trip to Pavillon du Mont Fréty, €32 round-trip to Helbronner, €48 round-trip to Aiguille du Midi, €75 round-trip to Chamonix* ⊙ *Call for hrs* ⊙ *Closed mid-Oct.–mid-Dec., depending on demand and weather.*

Where to Stay & Eat

★ **$$–$$$$** ╳ **Cadran Solaire.** This warm and inviting restaurant is in the town center, in what was the oldest tavern in Courmayeur. It's been renovated by the Garin family, in such a way as to highlight the 17th-century stone vault, the old wooden floor, and the huge fireplace. The menu offers seasonal specialties and innovative interpretations of regional dishes and the restaurant's bar is a cozy and popular place for a before-dinner drink. ⊠ *Via Roma 122* ☎ *0165/844609* ╳ *Reservations essential* ⊟ *AE, MC, V* ⊙ *Closed Tues., May, and Oct.*

★ **$$** ╳ **Maison de Filippo.** Here you'll find country-style home cooking in a mountain house with lots of atmosphere, furnished with antiques, farm tools, and bric-a-brac of all kinds. There's a set menu only, which includes an abundance of antipasti, a tempting choice of local soups and pasta dishes, followed by a wide range of second courses. Cheese, dessert, and fresh fruit complete the meal. Reserve in advance, for it's one of the most popular restaurants in Valle d'Aosta. ⊠ *Entrèves* ☎ *0165/869797* ╳ *Reservations essential* ⊟ *MC, V* ⊙ *Closed Tues., mid-May–June, and Oct.–Nov.*

$$$$ ╳▦ **Royal e Golf.** A grand Courmayeur landmark in the town center, the Royal rises high above the surrounding town. Decorated with terraces, flowers, and wood paneling, it is the most elegant, upscale spot in town, with modern rooms and an evening piano bar. The hotel caters to longer stays with half- or full-board service. The main restaurant, Grill Royal e Golf, is a sight in itself, locally renowned for such culinary creations as frogs' legs in a basil fish broth. Reservations (and jacket and tie) are required at the Grill, which is open for dinner only and is closed Monday. ⊠ *Via Roma 87, 11013* ☎ *0165/831611* 🖷 *0165/842093* 🖉 *hotel-royalgolf@ventaglio.com* 🖘 *80 rooms, 6 suites* ⚑ *2 restaurants, minibars, pool, health club, sauna, Turkish bath, bar, piano bar, Internet, meeting rooms, no smoking rooms, some pets allowed; no a/c* 🚬 *AE, DC, MC, V* ⊗ *Closed wk after Easter–mid-June and mid-Sept.–Nov.* ⍩⃝ *MAP.*

$$$$ 🏨 **Pavillon.** Here you'll find an elegant modern version of rustic chalet architecture, complete with warm golden-toned wood paneling, stylish furnishings, and a clubby bar. Some stunning contemporary stained glass decorates the public areas and the well-equipped health center. ⊠ *Strada Regionale 62, 11013* ☎ *0165/846120* 🖷 *0165/846122* ⊕ *www.pavillon.it* 🖘 *40 rooms, 10 suites* ⚑ *Restaurant, indoor pool, health club, hot tub, massage, sauna, steam room, bar, meeting room, some pets allowed* 🚬 *AE, DC, MC, V* ⊗ *Closed end Apr.–June 15, Oct.–Nov.* ⍩⃝ *FAP.*

$$$ 🏨 **Auberge de la Maison.** All the rooms at this cozy and modern hotel have views of Monte Bianco. A massage here can be the perfect ending to a day of hiking or skiing. ⊠ *Via Passerin d'Entrèves, 11013* ☎ *0165/869811* 🖷 *0165/869759* 🖉 *aubergemaison@courmayer.net* 🖘 *30 rooms, 3 suites* ⚑ *Gym, hot tub, massage, sauna* 🚬 *AE, DC, MC, V* ⊗ *Closed May.*

★ **$$$** 🏨 **Palace Bron.** In a lovely stand of pines above the town, this elegant and tranquil hotel is an ideal spot to relax. Guest rooms are bright and pretty, furnished with antiques and local designs. The sitting room has picture windows with magnificent views of Monte Bianco, and for chilly nights the high-quality restaurant offers a cozy fireplace. In winter there's a free shuttle between the hotel, the town center, and ski lifts. ⊠ *Via Plan Gorret 41, 11013* ☎ *0165/846742* 🖷 *0165/844015* ⊕ *www.palacebron.it* 🖘 *26 rooms, 1 suite* ⚑ *Restaurant, minibars, bar, piano bar, meeting room, some pets allowed (fee); no a/c* 🚬 *AE, DC, MC, V* ⊗ *Closed Apr.–mid June and mid Sept.–Nov.*

$$$ 🏨 **Villa Novecento.** Run with the friendly charm and efficiency of Franco
Fodor'sChoice Cavaliere and his son Stefano, the Novecento is a peaceful haven near
★ Courmayeur's busy center. In keeping with the style of a comfortable mountain lodge, colors throughout are warm and muted. The lounge, with deeply cushioned chairs, is lit by a fire in winter, and the guest rooms are soothingly furnished with traditional fabrics, wooden fixtures, and early-19th-century prints. The hotel restaurant, with only a few extra tables for nonguests, serves creative adaptations of traditional cuisine; it's a good choice for a relaxed evening meal. ⊠ *Viale Monte Bianco 64, 11013* ☎ *0165/843000* 🖷 *0165/844030* ⊕ *www.villanovecento.it* 🖘 *24 rooms, 2 suites* ⚑ *Restaurant, bar, gym, sauna, Turkish bath, meeting rooms, some pets allowed; no a/c* 🚬 *AE, DC, MC, V* ⊗ *Closed May–June and mid-Sept.–Dec. 7.*

$$ 🏨 **Croux.** This bright comfortable hotel is near the town center on the road leading to Monte Bianco. Friendly management makes it feel like a more intimate place than you'd expect for its size. Half the rooms have balconies, the other half great views of Monte Bianco. ⊠ *Via Circonvallazione 94, 11013* ☎ *0165/846735* 🖷 *0165/845180* ⊕ *www.hotelcroux.it* 🖘 *33 rooms* ⚑ *Bar* 🚬 *AE, DC, MC, V* ⊗ *Closed mid-Apr.–mid-June and mid-Sept.–mid-Dec.*

Sports & the Outdoors

SKIING Courmayeur pales in comparison to its French neighbor, Chamonix, in both number (it has only 24) and quality of trails. Nevertheless, especially with good natural snow cover, the trails and Alpine vistas are spectacular. A huge gondola leads from the center of Courmayeur to Plan Checrouit, where gondolas and lifts lead to the actual ski slopes. The skiing around Monte Bianco is particularly good, and the off-piste options are among the best in Europe. The off-piste routes from Cresta d'Arp (the local peak) to Dolonne, and from the La Palud area into France, should be done with a guide. Contact the **Funivie Courmayeur/Mont Blanc** (☎ 0165/846658) for complete information about lift tickets, ski runs, and weather conditions. For Alpine guide services contact the **Società delle Guide Alpine** (✉ Strada Villair 2 ☎ 0165/842064 ⊕ www.guidecourmayeur.com) in Courmayeur.

SPORTS CENTER   The **Courmayeur Sports Center** presents you with numerous athletic alternatives to skiing. There are courts for squash, tennis, basketball, and volleyball, as well as a rock-climbing wall, a skating rink, a five-to-a-side soccer field, and an indoor golf course. ✉ *Via dello Stadio 2* ☎ *0165/844096* ⊕ *www.sportcourmayeur.com* ☉ *Daily 10 AM–11 PM.*

Cogne & the Parco Nazionale del Gran Paradiso

30 *52 km (32 mi) southeast of Courmayeur, 134 km (83 mi) northwest of Turin.*

Cogne is the gateway to the Parco Nazionale del Gran Paradiso. This huge park, once the domain of King Vittorio Emanuele II (1820–78) and bequeathed to the nation after World War I, is one of Europe's most rugged and unspoiled wilderness areas, with wildlife and many plant species protected by law. Try to visit in May, when spring flowers are in bloom and most of the meadows are clear of snow. This is one of the few places in Europe where you can see the ibex (a mountain goat with horns up to 3 ft long) or the chamois (a small antelope).

Sports & the Outdoors

HIKING   There's wonderful hiking to be done here, both on daylong excursions and longer journeys with overnight stops in the park's mountain refuges. The **Cogne tourist office** (✉ Piazza E. Chanoux 36 ☎ 0165/74040 ⊕ www.cogne.org) has a wealth of information and trail maps to help.

FORTIFIED CITIES OF THE PO PLAIN

Southeast of Turin, in the hilly wooded area around Asti known as the Monferrato and farther south in a similar area around Alba known as the Langhe, the rolling landscape is a patchwork of vineyards and dark woods dotted with hill towns and castles. This is wine country, producing some of Italy's most famous reds and sparkling whites. And hidden away in the woods are the secret places where hunters and their dogs unearth the precious, aromatic truffles worth their weight in gold at Alba's truffle fair. To the north of these hills, across the Po, are the cities of the plain. Beyond them lies Lago Maggiore, and eastward, across the Ticino River, is Milan.

Asti

31 *60 km (37 mi) southeast of Turin.*

Asti is best known outside of Italy for its wines—excellent reds as well as the famous sparkling white Spumante—but its strategic position on trade routes between Turin, Milan, and Genoa has given it a broad economic base. In the 12th century, Asti began to develop as a republic, at a time when other Italian cities were also flexing their economic and military muscles. It flourished in the following century, when the inhabitants began erecting lofty **towers** for its defense, giving rise to the medieval nickname "city of 100 towers." In the center of Asti, some of

SKIING MONTE BIANCO ON A BUDGET

Skiing is the major sport in both Piedmont and Valle d'Aosta. Resorts with excellent facilities abound near the highest mountains in Europe—Monte Bianco (Mont Blanc), Monte Rosa, Monte Cervino (the Matterhorn), and the Gran Paradiso. Lift tickets, running around €32 for a day's pass, are significantly less expensive than at major U.S. resorts, though often for fewer trails.

When skiing Monte Bianco, you can save money by taking advantage of Settimane Bianche (White Weeks)—promotional packages offered in conjunction with hotels and agriturismi throughout the valley. Prices depend on location and the number of mints you want on your pillow: a week in Courmayeur starts around €250 for six nights with breakfast, while a similar package in Cogne begins at €200. A six day ski-pass will cost an additional €150. Prices vary considerably during the season; contact the Aosta tourist office or visit its Web site for complete details.

these remain, among them the 13th-century **Torre Comentina** and the well-preserved **Torre Troyana**, a tall, slender tower attached to the **Palazzo Troya**. The 18th-century church of **Santa Caterina** (⊠ West end of Corso Vittorio Alfieri) has incorporated one of Asti's medieval towers, the **Torre Romana** (itself built on an ancient Roman base), as its bell tower. Corso Vittorio Alfieri is Asti's main thoroughfare, running west–east across the city. This road, known in medieval times as Contrada Maestra, was built by the Romans.

The **Duomo** in Asti is an object lesson in the evolution of the Gothic architectural style. Built in the early 14th century, it's decorated so as to emphasize geometry and verticality: pointed arches and narrow vaults are counterbalanced by the earlier, Romanesque attention to balance and symmetry. The porch, on the south side of the cathedral facing the square, was built in 1470 and represents Gothic at its most florid and excessive. ⊠ *Piazza Cattedrale* ☎ *0141/592924* ⊙ *Daily 8:30–noon and 3:30–5:30.*

The Gothic church of **San Secondo** is dedicated to Asti's patron saint, reputedly decapitated on the spot where the church now stands. Secondo is also the patron of the city's favorite folklore and sporting event, the annual **Palio**, the colorful medieval-style horse race (similar to Siena's), held each year on the third Sunday of September in the vast Campo del Palio to the south of the church. ⊠ *Piazza San Secondo, south of Corso Vittorio Alfieri* ☎ *0141/530066* ⊙ *Mon.–Sat. 10:45–noon and 3:30–5:30, Sun. 3:30–5:30.*

Where to Stay & Eat

$$$
Fodor's Choice
★

✕ **Gener Neuv.** The family-run Gener Neuv is one of Italy's best restaurants. The setting on the bank of the Tanaro River is splendid, and the menu of regional specialties is served with rustic elegance. Your choices may include agnolotti *ai tre stufati* (with a filling of ground rabbit, veal, and pork), and to finish, *composta di prugne e uva* (prune and grape compote). Fixed-price menus are available with or without the wine included. As you might expect, the wine list is first rate. ⊠ *Lungo Tanaro 4* ☎ *0141/557270* 📠 *0141/436723* ▭ *AE, DC, MC, V* ⊙ *Closed Aug.; Jan–July, Sun.–Mon.; Sept.–Dec., Mon. No dinner Sun.*

$$

✕ **L'Angolo del Beato.** Regional specialties such as bagna cauda and tagliolini *al ragu di anatra* (with a duck sauce) are the main attraction here. This central Asti restaurant, housed in a building that dates back to the

12th century, also has a good wine list. ✉ *Via Guttuari 12* ☎ *0141/531668* ▭ *AE, DC, MC, V* ⊙ *Closed Sun., last wk of Dec., 1st wk of Jan., and 3 wks in Aug.*

$$ **Reale.** This hotel, in a 19th-century building, is conveniently located on Asti's main square. Rooms are spacious though somewhat eclectically decorated. Modern conveniences include satellite TV. ✉ *Piazza Alfieri 6, 14100* ☎ *0141/530240* 🖷 *0141/34357* 🌐 *www.hotel-reale.com* *25 rooms, 2 suites* *Some pets allowed, parking (fee); no a/c* ▭ *AE, DC, MC, V.*

$ **Rainero.** An older hotel near the train station, Rainero has been under the same family management for three generations. It's fitted with cheerful modern furnishings but has no restaurant. Ask for one of the "green rooms," done out in a green-and-white decor. ✉ *Via Cavour 85, 14100* ☎ *0141/353866* 🖷 *0141/594985* 🌐 *www.hotelrainero.com* *53 rooms, 2 suites* *Bar, meeting rooms, parking (fee), some pets allowed* ▭ *AE, DC, MC, V* ⊙ *Closed Jan. 1–15.*

Nightlife & the Arts

September is a month of fairs and celebrations in this famous wine city, and the **Palio di Asti,** a horse race run through the streets of town, highlights the festivities. First mentioned in 1275, this annual event has been going strong ever since. After an elaborate procession in period costumes, nine horses and jockeys, representing different sections of town, vie for the honor of claiming the *palio,* a symbolic flag of victory. Call the tourist office in Asti (☎ 0141/530357 🌐 www.atasti.it) for the schedule of events. For 10 days in early September, Asti is host to the **Douja d'Or National Wine Festival**—an opportunity to see Asti and celebrate the product that made it famous. During the course of the festival, a competition is held to award "Oscars" to the best wine producers, and stands for wine tastings allow visitors to judge the winners for themselves. Musical events and other activities accompany the festival. A complete program is available from the Asti tourist information office.

Shopping

The **Enoteca** on Piazza Alfieri, a square adjacent to Campo del Palio, is a wine center and shop, open Monday–Saturday 9–4:30, where you can try a range of Asti vintages, buy a bottle, and have a light snack. Be aware, though, that prices for Spumante in Asti are not necessarily lower than those elsewhere.

The **McArthur Glen designer outlet** (✉ Serravalle, 30 km [19 mi] south of Alessandria ☎ 0143/609000 🌐 www.mcarthurglen.com) is a bit of a detour from Asti but may be worth it for fans of designer labels. Discounts are about 50% at more than 60 shops, including Armani, Burberry, Ralph Lauren, Versace, Levi's, and Marina Yachting. Directions can be found on the Web site.

Alba

32 *30 km (18 mi) southwest of Asti.*

This small town has a gracious atmosphere and a compact core studded with medieval towers and Gothic buildings. In addition to being a wine center of the region, Alba is known as the "City of the White Truffle" for the dirty little tubers that command a higher price per ounce than diamonds. For picking out your truffle and having a few wisps shaved on top of your food, you shell out an extra €16—which is well worth it. Visit in October for the Fiera del Tartufo (National Truffle Fair), Cento Torri Joust (a medieval jousting festival), and the Palio degli Asini (donkey races), held the first Sunday of the month.

off the beaten path

BAROLO – Some of Italy's finest wines are made within a radius of about 15 km (10 mi) of Alba. Barbaresco is produced to the east, and to the southwest the small town of Barolo lends its name to the "king of Italian wines." The zone is dotted with castles, and every town has an *enoteca* (wine shop) where you can sample the local *vino*. In the town of Barolo, the **Castello di Barolo** houses a wine shop and a museum of wine-making. ☎ *0173/56277* ⊗ *Fri.–Wed. 10–12:30 and 3–6:30* ⊗ *Closed Jan.*

Where to Stay

★ $ ⌧ **La Meridiana.** If Alba strikes your fancy, consider a night at this reasonably priced belle epoque–style bed-and-breakfast, on a hill overlooking the historic center in the midst of Dolcetto and Nebbiolo grapevines. ✉ *Località Altavilla 9* ☎☎ *0173/440112* ⌦ *7 rooms, 2 apartments* ♨ *pool, gym; no a/c, no room phones* ▭ *No credit cards.*

en route

From Alba, double back to Asti to pick up the A21 autostrada. The **road east from Asti to Alessandria** is straight, skirting the southern edge of the Po plain, but for the first half of the drive you see to the south green hillsides covered with vineyards. If you find yourself driving along this road during a thunderstorm (quite common on late summer afternoons), don't be surprised by the sound of explosions. Wine growers will often let off cannons loaded with blanks to persuade heavy clouds to rain rather than build up and develop destructive hailstones.

Casale Monferrato

33 *42 km (26 mi) northeast of Asti, 75 km (46 mi) southwest of Milan.*

Casale Monferrato, strategically situated on the southern bank of the Po, was held by the Gonzagas, rulers of Mantua, before falling into the hands of the Savoys. The 16th-century **Torre Civica**, marking the heart of town in Piazza Mazzini, commands extensive views up and down the Po. It's open the second Saturday and Sunday of every month for free guided visits. In the second half of March, the **Festa di San Giuseppe** brings artisans, musicians, and vendors of traditional sweets to the central Piazza del Castello.

Casale's most enlightening sight is the **Museo Israelitico** (Jewish Museum) in the women's section of its synagogue. Inside is a collection of documents and sacred art of a community that was vital to the prosperity of this mercantile city. The synagogue dates from the late 16th century, and neighboring buildings on the same street formed the Jewish ghetto of that period. ✉ *Vicolo Olper 44, south of Torre Civica* ☎ *0142/71807* ⊗ *Mar.–Dec., Sun. 10–noon and 3:30–5:30; at other times by appointment.*

Vercelli

34 *23 km (14 mi) north of Casale Monferrato, 80 km (50 mi) northeast of Turin.*

Vercelli is the rice capital of Italy and of Europe. Northern Italy's mainstay, risotto, owes its existence to the crop that was introduced to this fertile area in the late Middle Ages. **Piazza Cavour** is the heart of the medieval city and former market square. It was to this small square that merchants across northern Italy came in the 15th century to buy bags of rice, then a novelty grain from the East. Rising above the low rooftops around Piazza Cavour is the **Torre dell'Angelo** (not open to the public), whose forbidding military appearance reflects its origins as a watchtower.

The Vercelli **Duomo,** a mainly late-16th-century construction on the site of what was a 5th-century church, contains tombs of several Savoy rulers in an octagonal chapel along the south (right) wall. The cathedral's **Biblioteca** (chapter library; for entrance, see cathedral office) contains the *Gospel of St. Eusebius,* a 4th-century manuscript, and the *Codex Vercellensis,* an 11th-century collection of Anglo-Saxon poetry. ⊠ *Piazza Sant'Eusebio* ☎ *0161/255205* ☉ *Daily 8–12:30 and 3–6:30, except during mass on Sun.*

The **Basilica di Sant'Andrea,** a Cistercian abbey church built in the early 13th century with funds from another Abbey of St. Andrew (in England), witnessed the growing influence of northern Europe on Italy. Sant'Andrea is one of Italy's earliest examples of Gothic architecture, a style that came from the north but adapted to suit local Italian traditions and tastes. The church interior is a soaring flight of Gothic imagination, with slender columns rising up to the ribbed vaults of the high ceiling. The gardens on the north side of the basilica hold the remains of the abbey itself and some of its secondary buildings. It's only here that the Gothic style is interrupted. The buildings surround a cloister in which you can see pointed Gothic arches resting on severe and more solid 12th-century Romanesque bases. ⊠ *Piazza G. Bicheri* ☎ *0161/255513* ☉ *Daily 8–noon and 3–6:30.*

The **Città Vecchia** is a collection of narrow streets and alleys that includes the Basilica di Sant'Andrea. Many of the houses are five centuries old, and you can see partly hidden gardens and courtyards beyond the wrought-iron gates.

On Tuesday and Friday mornings you can take an unusual guided tour of the **Borsa Merci** (⊠ Via Zumaglini 4 ☎ 0161/5981), the commodities market where rice has been traded for centuries. Vercelli's is the largest rice market in Europe. Contact the **Vercelli tourist office** (⊠ Viale Garibaldi 90, 13100 ☎ 0161/257888) for more information.

Novara

㉟ *23 km (14 mi) northeast of Vercelli, 95 km (59 mi) northeast of Turin.*

Novara is the easternmost city in Piedmont, only about 10 km (6 mi) west of the Ticino River, which forms the border with Lombardy, and 32 km (20 mi) from Milan. Much of the present city dates from the late 19th and early 20th centuries, but there are interesting buildings from earlier periods scattered about, most notably the tall, slender cupola of **San Gaudenzio.** The church itself, built between 1577 and 1690, is wholly baroque in design, with twisted columns and sumptuous statues. The main attraction, though, is its **cupola,** built from 1840 to 1888 and soaring to a height of just under 400 ft. This spire is visible everywhere in the city and in the surrounding countryside and has become as much a symbol of Novara as the Mole Antonelliana is of Turin—not a complete coincidence, since Alessandro Antonelli (1798–1888) designed this cupola and spire as well. ☎ *0321/629894* ☉ *Daily 8–noon and 3–7.*

The **Duomo** in Novara is medieval in origin but was reconstructed in neoclassical style by Alessandro Antonelli between 1863 and 1869. The **Battistero** (Baptistery), outside the entrance to the cathedral, shows its age more clearly. The rotunda-shape building dates from the 5th century, although it was substantially enlarged in the 10th and 11th centuries. Restoration work has uncovered 10th-century frescoes on the interior walls;

apocalyptic scenes are made all the more frightening by the use of vivid colors and a flat, two-dimensional Byzantine style. Also neighboring the cathedral is the **Broletto,** a cluster of well-preserved late-medieval buildings. ⊠ *Piazza Martiri della Libertà* ☎ *0321/35634* ☉ *Daily 8–noon.*

Where to Stay

$$ 🏨 **Italia.** Modern, functional rooms and the location, just a short walk from the Duomo and the central business and shopping areas of Novara, are the main attractions here. Some of the rooms have good views of the town, and the hotel's restaurant is one of Novara's best. ⊠ *Via Solaroli 8, 28100* ☎ *0321/399316* 🖷 *0321/399310* ⊕ *www.panciolihotels.it* ↙ *59 rooms, 4 suites* ♿ *Restaurant, minibars, bar, meeting rooms* 🚭 *AE, DC, MC, V.*

PIEDMONT/VALLE D'AOSTA A TO Z

To research prices, get advice from other travelers, and book travel arrangements, visit www.fodors.com.

AIRPORTS

The region's only international airport, Aeroporto Torino Caselle, is 18 km (11 mi) north of Turin. It's notoriously foggy in winter, and many flights are diverted to Genoa, on the coast, with bus connections provided for the two-hour drive to Turin. From Aeroporto Caselle, local buses to Turin arrive at the bus station on Corso Inghilterra in the city center.

🚹 Airport Information **Aeroporto Torino Caselle** ☎ 011/5676361.

BUS TRAVEL

Turin's main bus station is on the corner of Corso Inghilterra and Corso Vittorio Emanuele. Urban buses and trams are operated by the agency ATM. The Turin-based SADEM line services the autostrada network to Milan and other destinations in Italy. Turin-based SAPAV services the same area—both specialize in bus transportation in Piedmont and Valle d'Aosta. SAVDA specializes in mountain service, providing frequent links between Aosta, Turin, and Courmayeur as well as Milan. SITA buses, part of the nationwide system, also connect Turin with the rest of Italy. There's also a major bus station at Aosta, across the street from the train station. General bus information is available at the numbers below.

🚹 Bus Information **ATM** ⊠ Corso Turati 19/6, 10128 Turin ☎ 800/019152. **SADEM** ⊠ Via della Repubblica 14, 10095 Grugliasco, Turin ☎ 011/3000611. **SAPAV** ⊠ Corso Torino 396, 10064 Pinerolo, Turin ☎ 0121/322032. **SAVDA** ⊠ Strada Ponte Suaz 6, 11100 Aosta ☎ 0165/361244.

CAR RENTAL

🚹 Local Agencies **Avis** ⊠ Porto Nuova, Turin ☎ 011/6699800 ⊠ Corso Turati 37, Turin ☎ 011/500852 ⊠ Aeroporto Torino Caselle, Turin ☎ 011/4701528 **Hertz** ⊠ Via Magellano 12, Turin ☎ 011/502080 ⊠ Aeroporto Torino Caselle, Turin ☎ 011/5678166 ⊠ Via Ascoli 39, Turin ☎ 011/4378175.

CAR TRAVEL

Italy's autostrada network links the region with the rest of Italy and neighboring France. Aosta, Turin, and Alessandria all have autostrada connections, with the A4 heading east to Milan and the A6 heading south to the Ligurian coast and Genoa. Turin is the hub of all the transportation systems in Piedmont, with autostrada connections to the north, south, and east.

For travel across the French, Swiss, and Italian borders in Piedmont–Valle d'Aosta, only a few routes are practicable year-round: the 12-km (7-mi) Mont Blanc tunnel connecting Chamonix with Courmayeur, the Colle del Gran San Bernardo–Col du Grand St. Bernard (connecting Martigny with Aosta on Swiss Highway E27 and Italian Highway S27, with 6-km [4-mi] tunnel), and the Traforo del Fréjus (between Modane and Susa, with 13 km [8 mi] of tunnel). There are other passes, but they become increasingly unreliable between November and April.

EMERGENCY SERVICES — If you have a breakdown on the road, you can walk to one of the roadside stations marked SOS and push the button. You'll be connected to the Automobile Club of Italy (ACI), which will come and assist you, for free if you have a membership card for the automobile club in your home country. (Otherwise, you must pay a fee.) For emergency road assistance, ACI can also be reached at the phone number below.
🚗 ACI ☎ 803/116.

ROAD CONDITIONS — Well-paved secondary roads (*superstrade*) run through the region, following the course of mountain valleys in many places. Sudden winter storms can close off some of the mountain stretches; contact local tourist offices for up-to-date road information before you set out. Bear in mind that this is very rough country, so no matter what time of year and what route you choose, you are always advised to check with the tourist office or, in a pinch, with the police, to make sure roads are passable and safe.

EMBASSIES & CONSULATES
🏛 United Kingdom **U.K. Consulate** ✉ Via Saluzzo 60, Turin ☎ 011/6509202, open Monday and Thursday 9–noon.

EMERGENCIES
Pharmacies throughout the region take turns staying open late and on Sunday. Dial 192 for the latest information (in Italian) on which are open. The Farmacia Boniscontro in Turin takes a lunch break between 12:30 and 3 but is open all night.
🚑 **Emergencies** ☎ 113. **Police** ☎ 112. **Ambulance service** ☎ 118. **Farmacia Boniscontro** ✉ Corso Vittorio Emanuele II, 66, Turin ☎ 011/538271.

MAIL & SHIPPING
📮 Post Offices **Turin** ✉ Via Alfieri 10 ☎ 011/5060040.

OVERNIGHT SERVICES — 📦 Major Services **DHL** ✉ Via Bertolla all'Abbadia Stura, 176, Turin ☎ 800/345345.

PASSPORTS & VISAS
You should have your passport with you when day-tripping into France, even though it's unlikely you'll be asked to show it.

TOURS
Turin's group and personally guided tours are organized by the city's tourist office. Here you can also get information about the Touristibus, a two-hour guided bus trip that leaves from Piazza Castello, at the corner of Via Po, every day but Tuesday at 2:30. Touristibus goes through the historic center of Turin, including Via Roma and Porta Nuova, and then out to view such locations as the Palazzina di Caccia in Stupinigi and the Parco Valentino.

PRIVATE GUIDES — Alpine guides are not only recommended, but essential if you're planning to traverse some of the dramatic ranges outside St. Vincent, Courmayeur, or Breuil-Cervinia. Before embarking on an excursion (however short) into the mountains in these areas, contact the representative of the CAI (Club Alpino Italiano) for information about hikes and the risks.

Guides from the Alpine Guides Association can accompany you on treks and also lead skiing, canyoning, and ice-climbing excursions.

Alpine Guides Association ✉ Strada Villair 2, Courmayeur ☎ 0165/842064. **CAI** ✉ Piazza E. Chanoux 8, Aosta ☎ 0165/40194.

TRAIN TRAVEL

Turin is on the main Paris–Rome TGV express line and is also connected with Milan, only 90 minutes away on the fast train. The fastest (Eurostar) trains cover the 667-km (400-mi) trip to Rome in about six hours, but most trains take about nine hours.

Services to the larger cities east of Turin are part of the extensive and reliable train network serving the Lombard Plain. West of the region's capital, however, the train services soon peter out in the steep mountain valleys. Continuing connections by bus serve these valleys, and information about train-bus mountain services can be obtained from train stations and tourist information offices, or contact the Ferrovie dello Stato (FS); the Italian national train service.

Train Information **FS-Trenitalia** ☎ 848/888088 ⊕ www.trenitalia.com.

VISITOR INFORMATION

Tourist Information **Alba** ✉ Piazza Medford 3, 12051 ☎ 0173/35833 ⊕ www.langheroero.it. **Aosta** ✉ Piazza E. Chanoux 8, 11100 ☎ 0165/236627 ⊕ www.regione.vda.it/turismo. **Asti** ✉ Piazza Alfieri 29, 14100 ☎ 0141/530357 ⊕ www.atasti.it. **Bardonecchia** ✉ Viale Vittoria 44, 10052 ☎ 0122/99032 ⊕ www.comune.bardonecchia.to.it. **Breuil-Cervinia** ✉ Via Carrel 29, 11021 ☎ 0166/949136 ⊕ www.cervinia.it. **Cogne** ✉ Piazza E. Chanoux 36, 11012 ☎ 0165/74040 ⊕ www.cogne.org. **Courmayeur** ✉ Piazzale Monte Bianco 13, 11013 ☎ 0165/842060 ⊕ www.courmayeur.net. **Novara** ✉ Baluardo Quintino Sella 40, 28100 ☎ 0321/394059. **Saluzzo** ✉ Via Griselda 6, 12037 ☎ 0175/46710 ⊕ www.comune.saluzzo.cn.it. **Sestriere** ✉ Via Pinerolo 14, 10058 ☎ 0122/755444 ⊕ www.comune.sestriere.to.it. **Turin** ✉ Piazza Castello 161, 10122 ☎ 011/535181 ✉ Stazione Porta Nuova, 10121 ☎ 011/531327 ⊕ www.turismotorino.org. **Vercelli** ✉ Viale Garibaldi 90, 13100 ☎ 0161/58002 ⊕ www.turismovalsesiavercelli.it.

THE ITALIAN RIVIERA

GENOA, CINQUE TERRE, PORTOFINO, SAN REMO

6

FODOR'S CHOICE

Candidollo, restaurant, near Imperia

La Riserva, hotel, near Ventimiglia

Palazzo Reale, Genoa

Sagra del Pesce, festival, Camogli

HIGHLY RECOMMENDED

RESTAURANTS

Il Pirata, Monterosso al Mare

La Stalla, Santa Margherita Ligure

Miki, Monterosso al Mare

Nuovo Piccolo Mondo, San Remo

HOTELS

Cenobio dei Dogi, Camogli

Grand Hotel Miramare, Santa Margherita Ligure

Nuovo Piccolo Mondo, San Remo

Romantik Hotel Villa Pagoda, Nervi

Royal Sporting, Portovenere

SIGHTS

Camogli

Cinque Terre

Giardini Botanici Hanbury

Portovenere

San Remo

Via Garibaldi, Genoa

Updated by
Peter Blackman

LIKE THE FAMILY JEWELS that bedeck its habitual visitors, the Italian Riviera is glamorous, but in the old-fashioned way. The resort towns and coastal villages that stake intermittent claims on the rocky shores of the Ligurian Sea are the long-lost cousins of newer, overbuilt seaside paradises. Here the grandest palazzi share space with frescoed, angular, late-19th-century apartment buildings, and high-rise glitz seems as foreign as the Maine lobster that some of the region's tiniest restaurants incongruously fly in for dinner. The rustic and elegant, the provincial and chic, the cosmopolitan and the small-town are blended together here in a sun-drenched pastiche that makes up this, the "other" Riviera.

The serpentine arc of Liguria's coastline, sweeping serenely from La Spezia to Ventimiglia, is the defining mark of the region's identity. Although the province technically extends inland to the tops of the Ligurian Alps, Liguria is Italy's seaside region, and its greatest charms are those of the sea (the "Mare Ligure," never the "Mediterraneo"). For centuries, the region has inspired poets and artists. This is where a captivated Percy Shelley praised the "soft blue Spezian bay" and the daredevil Lord Byron swam from Portovenere to Lerici. Today, travelers escaping the conceits of civilization still head to the Italian Riviera for a cure. Mellowed by the balmy breezes blowing off the sea, they bask in the sun and explore the tiny coastal towns whose greatest treasures—peace, quiet, and dramatic natural beauty—remain for the most part undiscovered.

Liguria's narrow strip of mountain-protected coastline varies considerably between the two Rivieras. The western Riviera di Ponente (Riviera of the Setting Sun), which reaches from the French border to Genoa, has protected bays and wide sandy beaches and is generally more developed and commercialized than its counterpart to the east, the Riviera di Levante (Riviera of the Rising Sun). Beginning at the French border, the Ponente includes the fanciful seaside resorts of Bordighera and San Remo, similar to their glittery French cousins to the west in their unabashed dedication to the pursuit of pleasure. Much of the eastward sweep of the Ponente coastline has been developed for the packs of sun worshipers who descend upon it in the summer. The minuscule bays and inlets spanning the Levante coastline from Genoa to Portovenere become steeper, sculpted by nature into rocky cliffs.

If this coast is a necklace hung with jewels, the most dazzling pendant is the Portofino promontory. This must be the most photographed village in the world, and one look is enough to tell you why. Smooth-faced, brightly painted houses frame the port in a burst of color that becomes sheer enchantment at sunset, when the houses are reflected in the dancing waters of the harbor. And the people you encounter are attractions in themselves—it was, after all, Bogart and Bacall and Taylor and Burton who put the place on the map.

Farther east is a second peninsula; here the road weaves inland, leaving you to hike or take a train or boat to explore the Cinque Terre, a collective community of five fishing villages perched on bluffs above the sea. Here are some of Liguria's least-crowded beaches, its sweetest white wine, its most picturesque village squares, and certainly its best views. From the hiking trails that link the Cinque Terre, the tiny villages seem like colorful blooms of flowers clinging to hulking black cliffs that plunge into the sea. Though this is still the Italian Riviera at its unbuttoned best, Vernazza's growing trinket-shop trade and Monterosso's ever-booked hotels are certain signs that even the Cinque Terre have been "discovered."

Set in the heart of the region is Genoa, Italy's largest commercial port, where magnificent Renaissance palaces wearing the dusty patina of time attest to the wealth of the city's seafaring past, intermixed with layers of loud urbanity. Every schoolchild knows Genoa as the birthplace of Christopher Columbus, and many would become wide-eyed upon learning it's also the home of Europe's largest aquarium. Despite the curiously seamy city's considerable charm, most visitors to Liguria are more interested in the less historic waters found up or down the coast—not surprising, given the relaxed, easy lifestyle found along their shores.

Exploring the Italian Riviera

Getting around the Riviera is an expedient affair, though the pace here is leisurely. Public transportation in the region is excellent: trains connect all sights along the coast, and buses snake inland. It takes two hours for a fast train to cover the entire coast (though local trains make innumerable stops and take upward of five hours). With the freedom of a car, you could drive from one end of the Riviera to the other on the autostrada in less than three hours. The A10 and A12 on either side of Genoa, engineering wonders with literally hundreds of long tunnels and towering viaducts, skirt the coast, avoiding local traffic on the beautiful Via Aurelia, which was laid out by the ancient Romans. The Via Aurelia, now known as national highway S1, connects practically all the towns along the coast.

If urban artistic and historic treasures are your passion but you also want some seaside relief, stay in Genoa and make it your base for exploring the rest of the region on day trips. For a more relaxed approach, sea views, and recreation, settle into a resort and take a day trip into Genoa. Be forewarned: driving in Genoa is harrowing and should be avoided whenever possible—if you want to see the city on a day trip, go by train; if you're staying in the city, park in a garage or by valet and traverse the city by foot and taxi throughout your stay.

About the Restaurants & Hotels

Most good hotels in Genoa are set in modern buildings, not the grand old restored villas you might hope for. When choosing a hotel in Genoa, you should know that in its center it is one of Italy's noisiest cities; make sure your windows are double-glazed (*doppi vetri*). Lodging in Genoa and Liguria, as in much of the north, is somewhat expensive, especially in summer. If visiting in the fall, winter, or spring, ask for a *sconto bassa stagione* (low-season discount rate). The best bargains and the warmest welcomes can be found in the less-visited inland areas; there aren't a great number of hotels in this part of Liguria, but many of them are family-run and special because of it. Reserve ahead year-round for Genoa, and during peak Easter and summer seasons for resorts. Beware also of conferences and conventions for which lodging fills up far in advance. Note that many hotels and resorts in the area close for a number of weeks each year, usually late fall and early winter, and some in summer; it's best to call ahead.

WHAT IT COSTS In euros				
$$$$	$$$	$$	$	¢
RESTAURANTS over €22	€17–€22	€12–€17	€7–€12	under €7
HOTELS over €210	€160–€210	€110–€160	€60–€110	under €60

Restaurant prices are for a second course (secondo piatto). Hotel prices are for two people in a standard double room in high season, including tax and service.

Numbers in the text correspond to numbers in the margin and on the Italian Riviera and Genoa maps.

If you have 3 days

With tour time limited, you should rent a car and concentrate on select towns. On your first day begin on the eastern Riviera di Levante. Stop at the fishing villages of Vernazza in the **Cinque Terre** ④ ▶ and **Camogli** ⑩. Check into a hotel in ⊞ **Santa Margherita Ligure** ⑧, then take a short afternoon jaunt to **Portofino** ⑨. On the second day see ⊞ **Genoa** ⑪–㉟, exploring the historic center and old harbor. The western Riviera should be the focus of the third day; head for ⊞ **San Remo** ㊻, allowing about a half day along the way to visit the medieval centers of **Albenga** ㊷ and **Cervo** ㊸.

If you have 5 days

Make Genoa your base and alternate excursions along the coast and into the interior with city sightseeing. On your first day explore ⊞ **Genoa** ⑪–㉟ ▶. If the day is a clear one, take the **Zecca-Righi funicular** ⑭ to the top for an aerial view of the city. On the second day head west, making a detour to Spotorno, and proceed to Noli, one of the best-preserved medieval towns on the entire Riviera. Then see the medieval delights of **Cervo** ㊸ before going on to sophisticated ⊞ **San Remo** ㊻ or palm-studded ⊞ **Bordighera** ㊼, where you can bask in the sun on day three. On the fourth and fifth days explore the eastern Riviera, starting with stately **Nervi** ㊱. Among the many allurements on the Portofino promontory, explore the fishing village of **Camogli** ⑩ and chichi **Portofino** ⑨; don't miss the hamlets of San Rocco, San Niccolò, and Punta Chiappa, accessible on foot from Camogli. Overnight in ⊞ **Santa Margherita Ligure** ⑧ or the similarly stylish ⊞ **Rapallo** ⑦. On the fifth day, take an excursion by train or boat to the five rock-perched coastal villages of the ⊞ **Cinque Terre** ④, with Vernazza the first priority.

If you have 7 days

Begin your visit in ⊞ **Genoa** ⑪–㉟ ▶, spending two days there. Budget time for an excursion to **Nervi** ㊱. On the third day head west, going directly to **Ventimiglia** ㊽ and working your way back toward Genoa. See the extraordinary cactus collection in the **Giardini Botanici Hanbury** ㊾, then turn inland to medieval Dolceacqua, only 10 km (6 mi) away. Stop for tea in genteel ⊞ **Bordighera** ㊼ before continuing on to the much busier and more commercial resort of ⊞ **San Remo** ㊻; San Remo or Bordighera is a good choice for an overnight stay. On the fourth day, discover Noli (bus transport to Noli is via Spotorno). With the exception of **Albisola Marina** ㊴ and **Pegli** ㊲, you can skip the industrialized coast between **Savona** ㊵ and Genoa.

On the fifth day, see the offhand charm of **Camogli** ⑩. Take the turnoff for ⊞ **Rapallo** ⑦ and ⊞ **Santa Margherita Ligure** ⑧ and, if the traffic isn't heavy, head for **Portofino** ⑨. (At the height of the season, opt for an excursion boat to Portofino from Camogli, Santa Margherita Ligure, or Rapallo). On the sixth night, stay in the ⊞ **Cinque Terre** ④ and experience its magical nocturnal calm. Hike the paths in Cinque Terre, and then, on your seventh day, head east to **La Spezia** ③ and look for signs to **Portovenere** ②. Doubling back to La Spezia, take the coast road to charming **Lerici** ①. La Spezia turnoff on the A12 and S1 highways is only about 15 km (9 mi) from the Tuscany border.

Timing

Perhaps more than anywhere else in Italy, season is crucial on the Italian Riviera. Though shops, cafés, clubs, and restaurants stay open late in resorts during high season (at Easter and in summer), during the rest of the year they close early, if they're open at all. Liguria is one of the most seasonal places in the world, and everything from the yacht-dotted playground of Portofino to the rows of seaside restaurants and bars that line the Riviera's quieter shores shuts down from October to February (with the occasional exception of the week around Christmas), leaving little more than starkly barren coasts, boarded-up cafés, and crashing waves. April, May, and September are the best times to visit, with flowers in bloom, pleasant weather, and moderate levels of activity. October and November often bring torrential rains, floods, and landslides to the region, making such excursions as the Cinque Terre walk temporarily impossible. Avoid driving through Ventimiglia on Friday, the busy market day.

RIVIERA DI LEVANTE

Of the two Ligurian Rivieras, the Riviera di Levante, east of Genoa, is overall the wilder and more rugged, yet here you will also find towns like Portofino and Rapallo, world famous for their classic, elegant style. Around every turn of this area's twisting roads, the hills plummet sharply to the sea, forming deep, hidden bays and inlets. Beaches on this coast are rocky, backed by spectacular sheer cliffs. The Portofino promontory has one sandy beach, on the east side, at Paraggi. From Chiavari to Cavi di Lavagna, the coast becomes a bit gentler, with a few sandy areas. Sailing conditions along the rugged coast from Sestri Levante down to Portovenere are good. Waterskiing, tennis, and golf are also popular. You may want to choose a base and take short day trips or explore the area by boat from the larger towns. You can anchor your boat in the relatively calm waters of small *ciazze* (coves) found all along the coast.

Lerici

❶ *11 km (7 mi) east of La Spezia, 65 km (40 mi) west of Lucca.*

Near Liguria's border with Tuscany, this town is set on a magnificent coastline of gray cliffs and pine forests. Shelley was one of Lerici's best-known visitors and spent some of the happiest months of his life in the lovely white village of San Terenzo, 2 km (1 mi) away. After his death in 1822, the bay was renamed the Golfo dei Poeti, in his and Byron's honor.

Lerici once belonged to Tuscan Pisa, and the 13th-century Pisan **Castello di Lerici** standing above the splendid bay has attracted lovers of nature for centuries. The castle now houses a museum of paleontology. ✉ *Piazza S. Giorgio 1* ☎ *0187/969042* ⊕ *www.museocastello.lerici.sp.it* 🎟 *€4.60* ☉ *Mar. 16–June and Sept.–Oct. 19, Tues.–Sun. 10:30–1 and 2:30–6; July–Sept., daily 10:30–12:30 and 6:30–midnight; Oct. 20–Dec. 9 and Dec. 27–Mar. 15, Tues.–Fri 10:30–12:30, Sat.–Sun. 10:30–12:30 and 2:30–5:30.*

Where to Stay & Eat

$$ ✕🏨 **Miranda.** Perched amid the clustered old houses in the seaside hamlet of Tellaro, 4 km (2½ mi) southeast of Lerici, this small family-run inn has become a pricey gourmets' destination ($$$$) because of chef Angelo Cabani's imaginative way with Ligurian cooking. His unusual seafood menu changes daily but might include *insalata di gamberoni e*

6

Boating

With so much coastline—350 km (217 mi)—and so many pretty little harbors, it's no wonder that the Riviera attracts pleasure craft of all shapes and sizes, from rowboats to mega-yachts. San Remo, Rapallo, Santa Margherita Ligure, Chiavari, Finale Ligure, and Sestri Levante have large, well-equipped marinas, and nearly every town has a harbor and at least one marine shop. Kayaking is also popular along Ligurian shores on calmer days. Every October, Genoa hosts a mammoth international boat show.

Hiking & Walking

Liguria's hilly terrain makes walking strenuous but rewarding, with stunning views of the sea and castles and little villages dotting the coast. Portofino invites walking, whether you opt for the popular and relatively easy walk from Portofino to the Abbazia di San Fruttuoso or the more challenging hike from Ruta to the top of Monte Portofino. One of the best treks is between the Cinque Terre fishing towns—rigorous walks rewarded with beautiful views. Everywhere in Liguria roads, mule paths, or footpaths lead into the hills, where you can discover the region at its unspoiled best.

---

aragosta con finocchio (shrimp and lobster salad with fennel) and risotto *mantecato con asparagi e gamberi* (with butter, asparagus, and shrimp). If you stay in one of the seven comfortable rooms with bath, you have the option of half board at €225 for two people. ✉ *Via Fiascherino 92, Tellaro* ☎ *0187/968130* 🖷 *0187/964032* ✍ *locandamiranda@libero. it* 🛏 *5 rooms, 2 suites* ⟷ *Restaurant; no a/c* ⟷ *Reservations essential* 🖃 *AE, DC, MC, V* ⊗ *Restaurant closed Mon. Hotel and restaurant closed Jan.*

$$ 🏨 **Florida.** This seafront, family-run establishment is not the most beautiful from the outside, but it has bright rooms with all the extras you would expect in a higher category, including soundproofing and a balcony with a sea view. For an even better view, loll in one of the deck chairs on the roof terrace. The Florida overlooks a small beach area and is close to tennis courts and a golf course; a solarium is also on the premises. ✉ *Lungomare Biaggini 35, 19032* ☎ *0187/967332* 🖷 *0187/967344* 🌐 *www.hotelflorida.it* 🛏 *37 rooms* ⟷ *Minibars, beach, bar* 🖃 *AE, DC, MC, V* ⊗ *Closed Jan. 6–mid-Mar.*

Portovenere

★ ❷   *12 km (7 mi) south of La Spezia, 114 km (70 mi) southeast of Genoa.*

Portovenere's small colorful houses, some dating from the 12th century, were once all connected to the 12th- to 16th-century citadel, so that in times of attack the villagers could reach the safety of the battlements. The town commands a strategic position at the end of a peninsula that extends southeast from the Cinque Terre and forms the western border of the Gulf of La Spezia. Lord Byron (1788–1824) is said to have written *Childe Harold's Pilgrimage* in Portovenere. Near the entrance to the huge, strange **Grotto Arpaia**, at the base of the sea-swept cliff, is a plaque recounting the poet's strength and courage as he swam across the gulf to the village of San Terenzo, near Lerici, to visit his friend Shelley (1792–1822); the feat is commemorated as well by the name of the stretch of water, Golfo dei Poeti (Poets' Gulf). **San Pietro,** a 13th-century Gothic church open daily 7–6, is built on the site of an ancient pagan shrine, on a formidable solid mass of rock above the Grotto Arpaia. With its black-and-white-stripe exterior, it is a landmark recognizable from far out at sea.

Where to Stay & Eat

$$–$$$ ✕ **Da Iseo.** Try to get one of the tables outside at this waterfront restaurant with bistro accents and paintings of Portovenere. Seafood is the only choice, but it's fresh and plentiful. Pasta courses are inventive; try spaghetti *alla Giuseppe* (with shellfish and fresh tomato) or *alla Iseo* (with a seafood curry sauce). ⊠ *Waterfront* ☎ *0187/790610* ▭ *AE, DC, MC, V* ⊙ *Closed Wed. and Jan. 2–Feb. 15.*

¢–$ ✕ **Antica Osteria del Carrugio.** Near the castle built to defend the coast from Pisan incursions is this 100-year-old tavern with maritime decor. The menu, which varies from day to day, emphasizes seafood. Specialties include *mesc-ciùa* (soup of beans, chickpeas, and wheat), *polpo in insalata* (octopus salad), and *cozze ripiene* (mussels stuffed with garlic, anchovies, oregano, salami, and cheese). ⊠ *Via Cappellini 66* ☎ *0187/790617* ⌨ *Reservations not accepted* ▭ *No credit cards* ⊙ *Closed Thurs. and Nov.*

★ **$$$** ▭ **Royal Sporting.** Appearances are deceptive at this modern hotel on the beach about a 10-minute walk from the village. From the outside, the stone construction seems austere, but the courtyards and interior—with fresh flowers, potted plants, and cool, airy rooms—are colorful and vibrant. The sports facilities are among the best in the area. ⊠ *Via dell'Olivo 345, 19025* ☎ *0187/790326* ⌨ *0187/777707* ⊕ *www.royalsporting.com* ⇜ *56 rooms, 4 suites* ⌂ *Restaurant, minibars, tennis court, saltwater pool, beach, bar, Internet, meeting rooms, parking (fee), some pets allowed (fee)* ▭ *AE, DC, MC, V* ⊙ *Closed Nov.–mid-Mar.*

La Spezia

❸ *103 km (64 mi) southeast of Genoa.*

La Spezia is a large, industrialized naval port on routes to the Cinque Terre and to Portovenere. It lacks the quiet charm of the smaller towns. However, its decaying palm-lined Morin promenade, fertile citrus parks, and lively, balcony-lined streets make parts of La Spezia surprisingly beautiful. The remains of the massive 13th-century **Castel San Giorgio** (⊠ Via XX Settembre) are noteworthy.

Cinque Terre

★ ▶ **❹** *Monterosso al Mare 93 km (58 mi) southeast of Genoa, Riomaggiore 14 km (9 mi) west of La Spezia.*

The aura of isolation that has surrounded five coastal villages known as the Cinque Terre, together with their dramatic coastal scenery, has made them one of the eastern Riviera's most stunning attractions. With the status of National Park, the Cinque Terre have turned into a standard, if not requisite, stop on Italy's tourist trail, in spite of their relative inaccessibility. Clinging haphazardly to steep cliffs, these five enchanting villages are linked by ocean-side footpaths, by train, and by narrow, unpaved, and rather tortuous roads. The local train on the Genoa–La Spezia line stops at each of the villages. The easiest to reach by car is Riomaggiore, the easternmost and closest to La Spezia and the A12 autostrada.

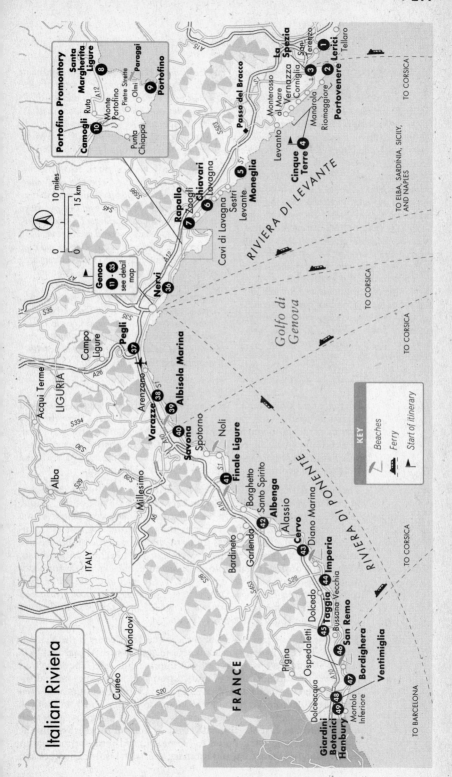

ON THE MENU

LIGURIA'S COOKING might surprise you. It employs all sorts of seafood—especially anchovies, sea bass, squid, and octopus—but it makes even wider use of vegetables and the aromatic herbs that grow wild on the hillsides, together with liberal amounts of olive oil and garlic. Basil- and garlic-rich pesto is Liguria's classic pasta sauce. You will also find pansoti (round pockets of pasta filled with a cheese mixture) and trofie (doughy, short pasta twists sometimes made with chestnut flour) with salsa di noci, an intense sauce of garlic, walnuts, and cream that, as with pesto, ideally is pounded with a mortar and pestle. Spaghetti allo scoglio is mixed with a tomato-based seafood sauce containing an assortment of local frutti di mare. Seafood is the best bet for second courses—the classic preparation is a whole grilled or baked whitefish (branzino, sea bass, and orata, dorado, are good choices) with olives, potatoes, Ligurian spices, and a drizzle of olive oil. A popular meat is cima alla Genovese, breast of veal stuffed with a mixture of eggs and vegetables and rolled, served as a cold cut. You should also try the succulent agnello (lamb), coniglio (rabbit), and fresh wild mushrooms foraged from the hills.

When not snacking on pizza sold by the slice or by weight, the Genovese and other Ligurians eat torta pasqualina (vegetable pie) or focaccia, the salty and oily pizzalike bread with various toppings. Focaccia alla Genovese is usually served plain, and focaccia di Recco, also called focaccia al formaggio, is topped with melted cheese. Local vineyards produce mostly light and refreshing whites such as Pigato, Vermentino, and Cinque Terre. Rossese di Dolceacqua, from near the French border, is the best red wine the region has to offer, but for a more robust accompaniment to meats, opt for the fuller-bodied reds of the neighboring Piedmont region.

All five of the tiny Cinque Terre enclaves are linked by well-established hiking footpaths—for much of their history, these paths were the only way to get from town to town on land. Although today the train and, to a certain extent, the road have replaced the footpaths, they still provide breathtaking ocean views as well as access to the rugged, secluded beaches and grottoes that will never have a train station.

The towns of the Cinque Terre and the pathways that link them are part of the **Parco Nazionale delle Cinque Terre** (National Park of the Cinque Terre) for which an entrance fee is charged. Tickets for the use of the trails as well as tickets that combine the use of the trails with an unlimited use of the second-class trains or the boats that connect the five towns of the Cinque Terre are available at the Levanto, Monterosso, Vernazza, Corniglia, Manarolo, Riomaggiore, and La Spezia train stations. ✉ 1-day pass for footpaths €3, 1-day pass with unlimited 2nd-class train travel Levanto–La Spezia €5.20, 1-day pass with train and boat service between the Cinque Terre €13, 3-day pass with train €12.40, 7-day pass with train €19.60.

The most famous and easiest of the Cinque Terre trails is the **Via dell'Amore** (Lover's Lane), which links Riomaggiore with Manarola (2 km [1 mi], 30 minutes) by a flat path cut into the cliff side. The same trail continues to Corniglia (3 km [2 mi], 1 hour), then becomes more difficult between Corniglia and Vernazza (3 km [2 mi], 1½ hours) and even more difficult from Vernazza to Monterosso (2 km [1 mi], 1½ hours). Still, because of the relative elevations, walking east to west is easier than walking west to east. Additionally, trails lead from Monterosso up the mountainside and back down to Vernazza, and into the mountains from Corniglia, Manarola, and Riomaggiore, with historic churches and great views along the way. Be sure to wear sturdy shoes (hiking boots are best) and a hat, and bring a water bottle, as there is little shade. Also check weather reports before hiking; especially in fall and winter, frequent thunderstorms flying in off the coast can send townspeople running for cover and make the shelterless trails slippery and dangerous. Also be aware that, depending on the year, rainfall in October and November can cause landslides and close the hiking paths for periods in fall and winter. Consult the comprehensive Web site www.5terre.com for updated information.

Try to see the Cinque Terre in early fall or spring, when the weather is good but the waves of tourists aren't so substantial and the towns can be seen in a somewhat more natural state. Advance room reservations are essential if you plan to spend the night here in summer. But, if you do find yourself without a prebooked room, a reasonable and economic solution might be found at one of the area's numerous *affittacamere* (rooms for rent in private homes)—often only indicated by a simple handwritten sign on a front door. These rooms vary considerably in comfort, amenities, and cost. Before deciding, it's advisable to consult the list of officially licensed affittacamere provided by the tourist offices in **Riomaggiore** (✉ Stazione Ferroviaria ☎ 0187/920633) and **Monterosso** (✉ Via Fegina 38, 19016 ☎ 0187/817506). A booking service is provided by the latter.

Riomaggiore
116 km (72 mi) east of Genoa.

In Riomaggiore you'll find the same sorts of flowery little squares that bedeck the town's four siblings, interspersed with modern stucco houses and a sense that the population is less isolated here. This may be because Riomaggiore is comparatively convenient to La Spezia; you can get here by car by following signs from La Spezia's port.

WHERE TO
STAY & EAT
$–$$

✕ **Ripa del Sole.** In summer you can eat on the terrace of this seafood restaurant. Try some of the great local wine with one of the house specialties: *calamari con gran farro* (steamed squid with lemon sauce and barley), *tagliatelle fresche con scampi e tartufo bianco* (fresh pasta with scampi and white truffles), or *filetto di branzino al piatto rovente* (sea bass cooked on the griddle with herbs and garlic). ✉ *Via de' Gaspari 282* ☎ *0187/920143* ☶ *No credit cards* ☉ *Closed mid-Jan.–mid-Feb. and Mon. Nov.–Mar.*

$

▦ **Due Gemelli.** Set above the sea, this small hotel has fabulous views of the turquoise water. The rooms, all with balconies, are simple but clean, bright, and airy. ✉ *Via Litoranea 1, 19017* ☎ *0187/920111* 🖷 *0187/920678* ⊕ *www.duegemelli.it* ⬧ *14 rooms* ⌂ *Restaurant, bar; no a/c* ☰ *AE, DC, MC, V.*

Manarola
1½ km (1 mi) west of Riomaggiore.

In photogenic Manarola, multicolor houses spill down a dark hillside to town squares that hang over the port like balconies overlooking the tiny turquoise harbor. Manarola is the center of Cinque Terre wine-making, and you can taste the fruits of local labor in a number of wineries, as well as the **Cooperativa Agricoltura di Riomaggiore, Manarola, Corniglia, Vernazza e Monterosso** (☎ 0187/920435), just outside town.

WHERE TO STAY
$

▦ **Ca' d'Andrean.** If you want to stay in one of the less crowded of the Cinque Terre, this tiny simple hotel is one of your best options. In summer, breakfast is served in a flower garden. ✉ *Via Discovolo 101, 19010* ☎ *0187/*

920040 🖶 0187/920452 ⊕ www.cadandrean.it ⇐ 10 rooms ♿ Bar; no a/c, no room TVs ⊟ No credit cards ⊙ Closed mid-Nov.–mid-Dec.

Corniglia

3 km (2 mi) west of Manarola.

Tiny, isolated Corniglia, strung back from a hilltop overlooking the sea, is unquestionably the most difficult of the Cinque Terre to visit. It has no port and no (usable) access road for automobiles, so you will have to arrive by local train or on foot, along the difficult trail from Vernazza or the easy one from Manarola. In Corniglia you'll find pretty pastel squares and the 14th-century church of **San Pietro** (☎ 349/3235582 ⊙ Wed. 4–6, Sun. 10–noon). The rose window of marble imported from Carrara is impressive, particularly considering the work required to transport it here.

WHERE TO
STAY & EAT
¢–$

✕▦ **Cecio.** On the winding road between Corniglia and Vernazza, this little, family-run restaurant rents spotless, if small, rooms upstairs, many of which have spectacular views of Corniglia clinging to the cliffs above the bay. That same memorable vista can be taken in while dining alfresco ($) on well-made, inexpensive local seafood dishes. ⊠ *Via Serra 58, 19010* ☎ *0187/812043* 🖶 *0187/812138* ⇐ *12 rooms* ♿ *Restaurant; no a/c, no room phones, no TV in some rooms* ⊟ *DC, MC, V.*

Vernazza

3 km (2 mi) west of Corniglia.

Lovely Vernazza has the largest and best-equipped port of the Cinque Terre towns. Its pink, slate-roofed houses and picturesque squares contrast with the remains of a medieval fort and castle. The castle's tower was struck by lightning in 1896; it's been rebuilt and today offers some of the best views in Cinque Terre. Summertime in Vernazza brings smart-set Italians to the town's cafés and restaurants. Stay in town and delve right in, escape on one of the many footpaths leading up through the hillsides' terraced vineyards, or head to one of the other towns on a relaxing boat ride from the port.

WHERE TO
STAY & EAT
$$–$$$

✕ **Gambero Rosso.** On Vernazza's main square, looking out at the church, this fine trattoria serves such delectable dishes as shrimp salad, vegetable torte, and squid-ink risotto. The creamy pesto, served atop spaghetti, is some of the best in the area. End your meal with Cinque Terre's own *schiacchetrà*, a dessert wine served with semisweet *biscotti* (hard cookies). Don't drink it out of the glass—dip the biscotti in the wine instead. ⊠ *Piazza Marconi 7* ☎ *0187/812265* ⊟ *AE, DC, MC, V* ⊙ *Closed Mon. in Jan.–Feb.*

¢–$

✕▦ **Trattoria Gianni Franzi.** The restaurant here ($$–$$$) is the place to order your pesto with *fagiolini* (green beans), a Ligurian specialty that somehow tastes better when you're eating it outside in a beautiful *piazzetta* (small square) with a view of the port, as you can here. Above the restaurant, a number of simply furnished and economically priced rooms are available. Your choice here is between the smaller, older rooms without private bathrooms but with tiny balconies and great views of the port, or those in the newer section, with en-suite bathrooms but no view. ⊠ *Via G. Marconi 1* ☎ *0187/821003* 🖶 *0187/812228* ⇐ *20 rooms, 12 with bath* ♿ *Restaurant, bar* ⊟ *AE, DC, MC, V* ⊙ *Mar. 9–mid-July and mid-Sept.–Jan. 7, restaurant closed Wed; hotel and restaurant closed Jan. 8–Mar. 8.*

Monterosso al Mare

3½ km (2 mi) west of Vernazza, 12 km (7 mi) east of Levanto.

Monterosso is the largest, most developed, and least pretty of the five fishing towns, with the Cinque Terre's biggest beach, its only sizable hotels, and most of its restaurants. The narrow alleys and colorful houses of the historic center are clustered on a hilltop above the port and its seaside promenade. Stone stairways link the two areas of town, affording lovely views of the mountains that tumble down onto a wide, sandy beach below, which is mobbed in summer. In Monterosso's historic center, the 12th-century **church** (⊠ Piazza Garibaldi) is striped black and white in the Ligurian Gothic fashion. On Thursday morning the town comes alive with its weekly **market,** where you can pick up local anchovies and lemons, among other delicacies. The **Pro Loco tourist office** (⊠ Via Fegina 38, below train station ☎ 0187/817506) can help with trail maps, boat schedules, and also provides a booking service for the many *affittacemere* (rooms for rent) in the area.

WHERE TO
STAY & EAT

$$$ ✕ **Il Gigante.** A good introduction to Ligurian seafood is the *zuppa di pesce* (fish soup) served at this traditional trattoria. It's usually offered as a first course but is filling enough to be an entrée. Daily specials might include risotto *ai frutti di mare* and spaghetti with an octopus sauce. Reservations are essential on weekends and in summer. ⊠ *Monterosso al Mare* ☎ *0187/817401* ⊟ *AE, DC, MC, V* ⊘ *Closed Mon.*

★ **$$–$$$** ✕ **Il Pirata.** Bright and rustic, this trattoria near the port should be the first stop for lunchtime visitors, especially if you make it in time to grab a seat at the long tables on the front porch outside. Specialties are those of the region, with a few surprising gourmet touches, like the French wines lining the shelves and Maine lobster. Reservations are essential on weekends and in summer. ⊠ *Via Molinelli 6/8* ☎ *0187/817536* ⊟ *MC, V* ⊘ *Closed Wed. and mid-Jan.–mid.-Feb.*

★ **$$–$$$** ✕ **Miki.** Specialties here are anything involving seafood. The *insalata di mare* (squid and fish salad) is more than tasty; so are the grilled fish and any pasta with seafood. If you're in the mood for a pizza, you can order that here as well. Miki has a beautiful little garden in the back, perfect for lunch on a sunny day. ⊠ *Via Fegina 104* ☎ *0187/817608* ⊟ *AE, DC, MC, V* ⊘ *Closed Nov.–Dec. and Tues. in Sept.–July.*

¢ ✕ **Il Frantoio.** Some of the best focaccia on the coast is available here. It's a good place for a light lunch or a snack before heading out on the walk to Vernazza. ⊠ *Via Gioberti 1* ☎ *0187/818333* ⊟ *No credit cards.*

$$$–$$$$ ⌷ **Porto Roca.** In a panoramic position above the sea, Porto Roca is set slightly apart, blessedly removed from the crowds. It has the look of a well-kept villa; its interiors have authentic antiques, and there are ample terraces, excellent for breakfast with a view. The rooms with views of the sea are bright and airy, but the back rooms, which are dark, dank, and without a view, should be avoided. ⊠ *Via Corone 1, 19016* ☎ *0187/817502* 🖷 *0187/817692* ⊕ *www.portoroca.it* ⇒ *43 rooms* ⌂ *Restaurant, bar, some pets allowed* ⊟ *AE, MC, V* ⊘ *Closed Nov. 4–Mar. 18.*

en route From the Cinque Terre, small highways connect back out through the edge of La Spezia to state highway S1, which heads inland to the spectacular Passo del Bracco and then turns back out to the sea at Sestri Levante. After Sestri, S1 (which becomes Via Aurelia) hugs the coast, affording dazzling seaside scenery all the way to Genoa, the Riviera Ponente, and the French border.

Moneglia

❺ *12 km (7 mi) southeast of Sestri Levante, 58 km (36 mi) northwest of La Spezia.*

The town of Moneglia, sheltered by the wooded hills of a nature preserve, faces a little bay guarded by ruined castles. An out-of-the-way alternative to fussier resorts, it's a quiet base for walks and excursions by boat, car, or train to Portofino and the Cinque Terre towns. A classical guitar festival is held here in September.

Where to Stay

$$ 🏨 **Villa Edera.** Ingeniously merging an older building on a verdant hillside with a smart contemporary stone-and-glass wing, this hotel is owned by a family committed to personal attention. Terraces, a garden, luminous bedrooms, and lounges with stylish wicker armchairs are among the comforts. Mamma Ida's cooking is special, too. ⊠ *Via Venino 12, 16030* ☎ *0185/49291* 📠 *0185/49470* ⊕ *www.villaedera.com* 📞 *27 rooms* ♦ *Restaurant, pool, gym, sauna, bar, Internet, no-smoking rooms; no a/c in some rooms* 🖃 *AE, MC, V* ☉ *Closed Nov. 8–Feb.*

Chiavari

❻   *22 km (13 mi) east of Portofino, 38 km (23 mi) southeast of Genoa.*

Chiavari is a fishing town (rather than village) of considerable character, with narrow, twisting streets and a good harbor. Chiavari's citizens were intrepid explorers, and many emigrated to South America in the 19th century. The town boomed, thanks to the wealth of the returning voyagers, but Chiavari retains many medieval traces in its buildings.

In the town center, the **Museo Archeologico** (Archaeological Museum) displays objects from an 8th-century BC necropolis, or ancient cemetery, excavated nearby. ⊠ *Palazzo Costaguta, Via Costaguta 4, Piazza Matteotti* ☎ *0185/320829* 🎟 *Free* ☉ *Tues.–Thurs. 9–1, Fri.–Sun. 2–7* ☉ *Closed 1st and 3rd Sun. of month.*

Shopping

The traditional, light—they weigh only 3 pounds—*campane* chairs made of olive wood or walnut are still produced by a few Chiavari craftsmen. Macramé lace can also be found here.

Rapallo

❼   *12 km (7 mi) east of Camogli, 28 km (17 mi) east of Genoa.*

Rapallo was once one of Europe's most fashionable resorts, but it passed its heyday before World War II and has suffered from the building boom brought on by tourism. Ezra Pound and D. H. Lawrence lived here, and many other writers, poets, and artists have been drawn to it. Today, the town's harbor is filled with yachts. A single-span bridge on the eastern side of the bay is named after Hannibal, who is said to have passed through the area after crossing the Alps.

The highlight of the town center, the cathedral of **Santi Gervasio e Protasio** (☎ 0185/52375) at the western end of Via Mazzini, was founded in the 6th century. It's open daily 6:30–noon and 3–6:30.

The **Museo del Pizzo a Tombolo,** in a 19th-century mansion, has a collection of antique lace for which Rapallo was renowned. ⊠ *Villa Tigullio* ☎ *0185/63305* 🎟 *Free* ☉ *Oct.–Aug., Tues.–Wed. and Fri.–Sat. 3–6, Thurs. 10–11:30.*

Where to Stay & Eat

$$–$$$ ✕ **Da Mario.** Simply decorated and brightly lighted, this small and lively trattoria serves some of the best seafood in Rapallo. Don't miss the spaghetti *alla Mario* (with seafood and tomatoes) or the *fritto misto* (lightly fried mixed fish). A small terrace offers outdoor seating in summer. ⊠ *Piazza Garibaldi 23* ☎ *0185/51736* ♦ *Reservations essential* 🖃 *AE, DC, MC, V* ☉ *Closed Tues. and Oct.–Nov.*

$$–$$$ ✕ **Roccabruna.** In a splendid villa outside Rapallo, seafood specialties adorn an abundant menu that changes regularly. Take the Casello–Savagna highway from Rapallo; Savagna is only about 2 km (1 mi) away. ⊠ *Via Sotto la Croce 6, Savagna* ☎ *0185/261400* ▤ *MC, V* ☉ *Closed Mon. and late Nov.–early Dec. No lunch, except Sun. Oct.–June.*

$$$$ ▥ **Grand Hotel Bristol.** This Victorian showcase is in an elevated position overlooking road and sea outside Rapallo and is set in lush gardens with a huge seawater pool. Spacious rooms, many with balcony and sea view, are decorated in soft colors in a smart, contemporary style and have extra-large beds. You can choose between a Rapallo view and a Portofino view. In summer, dinner is served on the roof terrace. ⊠ *Via Aurelia Orientale 369, 16035* ☎ *0185/273313* ▤ *0185/55800* ⊕ *www. tigullio.net/bristol* ↪ *85 rooms, 6 suites* ⊘ *2 restaurants, minibars, saltwater pool, hot tub, sauna, horseback riding, bar, meeting rooms, parking (fee), some pets allowed* ▤ *AE, MC, V* ☉ *Closed Dec.–Feb.*

$$ ▥ **Giulio Cesare.** Only a block from the sea, this old town house was transformed into a hotel that offers rooms with modern furnishings and sea views. Fifteen rooms are reserved for nonsmokers and some rooms are equipped for people with disabilities. Many rooms have balconies, but noise may be a problem because the hotel is on a main street. ⊠ *Corso Colombo 52, 16035* ☎ *0185/50685* ▤ *0185/60896* ⊕ *www. hotel-giulio-cesare.it* ↪ *33 rooms* ⊘ *Restaurant, in-room safes, bar, meeting rooms, some pets allowed, parking (fee), no-smoking rooms* ▤ *AE, DC, MC, V* ☉ *Closed Nov.*

Shopping

The attractive coastal village of **Zoagli** (⊠ On S1, 4 km [2½ mi] east of Rapallo) has been famous for silk, velvet, and damask since the Middle Ages.

Santa Margherita Ligure

❽ *3 km (2 mi) south of Rapallo, 31 km (19 mi) southeast of Genoa.*

A beautiful old resort town favored by well-to-do Italians, Santa Margherita Ligure has everything a Riviera playground should have—plenty of palm trees and attractive hotels, cafés, and a marina packed with yachts. Some of the older buildings here are still decorated on the outside with the trompe-l'oeil frescoes typical of this part of the Riviera. This is a pleasant and convenient base for excursions by land and by sea and, for many visitors, represents the perfect balance in the Italian Riviera—bigger and less Americanized than the Cinque Terre; less glitzy than San Remo; more relaxing than Genoa and environs; and perfectly situated for a day trip to Portofino.

Where to Stay & Eat

★ $$$$ ✕ **La Stalla.** Set in an old hilltop palazzo, this restaurant is worth the harrowing 3-km (2-mi) drive from Santa Margherita's port. While enjoying breathtaking views of Santa Margherita from the restaurant's terrace, you might be tempted to sample homemade fettuccine *ai frutti di mare* (with a seafood sauce) followed by *pescato del giorno alla moda ligure* (catch of the day baked Ligurian style, with potatoes, olives, and pine nuts). ⊠ *Via G. Pino 27, Nozarego* ☎ *0185/289447* ▤ *AE, DC, MC, V* ☉ *Closed Mon. and Nov.*

$$$–$$$$ ✕ **La Paranza.** As befits a spot just off Santa Margherita's port, the specialty here is fresh seafood in every shape and form, from the piles of tiny *bianchetti* (whitebait) in oil and lemon in the antipasto *di mare* (of the sea) to a simple, perfectly grilled whole sole. In between you'll find mussels, clams, octopus, salmon, and whatever else is fresh that day. Lo-

cals say this is the town's best restaurant, but if you're looking for a stylish evening out, look elsewhere—La Paranza is about food, not fashion. ⊠ *Via Jacopo Ruffini 46* ☎ *0185/283686* ⟁ *Reservations essential* ▭ *AE, DC, MC, V* ⊘ *Closed Mon. and Nov.*

$$ ✕ **Trattoria Cesarina.** This typical trattoria offers classic local fare—and that means seafood. The white interior is refreshingly free of bric-a-brac, allowing you to focus on your meal. Don't expect a menu; instead, allow the friendly staff to tell you what to eat. Among other treats, you will likely encounter a delectable antipasto of local *frutti di mare,* a seafood-theme pasta dish, and the catch of the day delicately grilled or baked in that laissez-faire Ligurian style. ⊠ *Via Mameli 2/C* ☎ *0185/286059* ▭ *MC, V* ⊘ *Closed Tues. and Dec.–Jan.*

¢–$ ✕ **La Piadineria.** For a light evening snack, this small establishment makes a huge variety of *piadine* (flatbread sandwiches) and crepes, served with cocktails or Ligurian wines sold by the glass. ⊠ *Via Giunchetto 5* ☎ *0185/* ▭ *No credit cards* ⊘ *Closed for lunch.*

★ $$$$ 🏨 **Grand Hotel Miramare.** You'll get a taste of classic Riviera elegance at this palatial hotel overlooking the bay south of the town center. It has a lush garden, swimming pool, and private swimming area on the sea. The bright and airy rooms have antique furniture and marble bathrooms. ⊠ *Via Milite Ignoto 30, 16038* ☎ *0185/287013* 🖶 *0185/ 284651* ⊕ *www.grandhotelmiramare.it* ⟲ *75 rooms, 9 suites* ⚭ *2 restaurants, in-room safes, minibars, pool, beach, waterskiing, 2 bars, Internet, meeting rooms, some pets allowed* ▭ *AE, DC, MC, V.*

$$$$ 🏨 **Imperiale Palace.** Via Pagana climbs north out of Santa Margherita Ligure on its way toward Rapallo; outside town it passes this traditional luxury hotel, set in an extensive park. Reception rooms with tall windows, plush chairs, and potted plants create a warm welcome. The rooms are furnished with antiques; many overlook the shore drive to the sea. ⊠ *Via Pagana 19, 16038* ☎ *0185/288991* 🖶 *0185/284223* ⊕ *www.hotelimperiale.com* ⟲ *78 rooms, 14 suites* ⚭ *Restaurant, in-room safes, minibars, pool, beach, 2 bars, baby-sitting, meeting rooms* ▭ *AE, DC, MC, V* ⊘ *Closed Nov.–Mar.*

$$$ 🏨 **Continental.** This stately seaside mansion with a columned portico was built in the early 1900s and is in a lush garden shaded by tall palms and pine trees. The decor is a blend of traditional furnishings, mostly in 19th-century style, with some more functional pieces. There's also a modern wing. The hotel's own cabanas and swimming area are at the bottom of the garden. ⊠ *Via Pagana 8, 16038* ☎ *0185/286512* 🖶 *0185/ 284463* ⊕ *www.hotel-continental.it* ⟲ *72 rooms, 4 suites* ⚭ *Restaurant, in-room safes, bar, meeting rooms, some pets allowed* ▭ *AE, DC, MC, V* ⊘ *Closed Nov.–Dec. 23.*

Portofino

❾ *5 km (3 mi) south of Santa Margherita Ligure, 36 km (22 mi) east of Genoa.*

One of the more picturesque villages along the coast, with a decidedly romantic and affluent aura, Portofino is also precious, in the truest sense of the word. Unless you're traveling on a deluxe level and can keep up with the Agnellis and Berlusconis, you will probably want to stay in Rapallo or Santa Margherita Ligure rather than at one of Portofino's few and very expensive hotels. Restaurants and cafés are good but also pricey (don't expect to have a beer here for much under €8). Some of Europe's wealthiest lay anchor in Portofino in summer, but they stay out of sight by day, appearing in the evening after buses and boats have carried off the day-trippers.

Portofino has long been a popular destination for foreigners. Once an ancient Roman colony and taken by the Republic of Genoa in 1229, it has also been ruled by the French, English, Spanish, and Austrians, as well as marauding bands of 16th-century pirates. Elite British tourists first flocked to the lush harbor in the mid-1800s. At first glance, you may wonder what all the fuss is about. There's not actually much to *do* in Portofino, other than stroll around the wee harbor, see the castle, walk to Punta del Capo, look at the pricey boutiques, and sip a coffee while people-watching. However, weaving through picture-perfect cliff-side gardens and gazing at yachts framed by the turquoise Ligurian Sea and the cliffs of Santa Margherita can make for quite a relaxing afternoon. There are also several tame, photo-friendly hikes into the hills from Portofino to nearby villages. Note the meticulous upkeep of streets and public flora in what is surely Italy's cleanest town. Trying to reach Portofino by bus or car on the single narrow road can be a nightmare in summer and on holiday weekends. No trains go directly to Portofino; if traveling by rail, you must stop at Santa Margherita and take the public bus from there (€1). An alternative is to take a boat from Santa Margherita.

From the harbor, follow the signs for the climb to the **Castello di San Giorgio,** the most worthwhile sight in Portofino, with its medieval relics, impeccable gardens, and sweeping views. The castle was founded in the Middle Ages but restored in the 16th through 18th centuries; in true Portofino form, it was owned by Genoa's English consul from 1870 until its opening to the public in 1961. ✉ *€2.50* ⏱ *Apr.–Sept., Wed.–Mon. 10–6; Oct.–Mar., Wed.–Mon. 10–5.*

Sitting on a ridge above the harbor is the small church of **San Giorgio,** rebuilt four times during World War II, which is supposed to contain the relics of its namesake, brought back from the Holy Land by the Crusaders. Portofino enthusiastically celebrates St. George's Day every April 23. ☎ *0185/269337* ⏱ *Daily 7–6.*

Pristine views can be had from the deteriorating lighthouse, or *faro*, at **Punta Portofino,** a 15-minute walk along a marked path from the village. Along the seaside path you can see numerous impressive, sprawling private residences behind high iron gates.

The only sand beach near Portofino is at **Paraggi,** a cove on the road between Santa Margherita and Portofino (the bus will stop there on request).

off the
beaten
path

ABBAZIA DI SAN FRUTTUOSO – On the sea at the foot of Monte Portofino, the medieval Abbey of San Fruttuoso—built by the Benedictines of Monte Cassino—protects a minuscule fishing village that can be reached only on foot or by water (a 20-minute boat ride from Portofino and also reachable from Camogli, Santa Margherita Ligure, and Rapallo). The restored abbey is now the property of a national conservation fund (FAI) and occasionally hosts temporary exhibitions. The church holds the tombs of some illustrious members of the Doria family. The historic abbey and its grounds are a delightful place to spend a few hours, perhaps lunching at one of the modest beach trattorias nearby (open only in summer). But boatloads of visitors can make it very crowded very fast; you might appreciate it most off-season. ☎ *0185/772703* ✉ *€4, €6 when exhibitions are held* ⏱ *Mar.–Apr. and Oct., Tues.–Sun. 10–3:45; May, Tues.–Sun. 10.–5:45; June–Sept., daily 10–5:45; Dec.–Feb., weekends 10–3:45. Call ahead to confirm hrs.*

Where to Stay & Eat

$$$-$$$$ ✕ **Il Pitosforo.** A chic clientele, many with luxury yachts in the harbor, gives this waterfront restaurant a high glamour quotient, augmented by outlandish prices. Spaghetti ai frutti di mare is recommended; adventurous diners might try *lo stocco accomodou* (dried cod in a sauce of tomatoes, raisins, and pine nuts). ⊠ *Molo Umberto I 9* ☎ *0185/269020 or 0335/5615833* ⌘ *Reservations essential* ☰ *AE, DC, MC, V* ◷ *Closed Mon.–Tues. and Jan.–mid-Feb. No lunch.*

$$-$$$ ✕ **Ristorante Puny.** A table at this tiny restaurant is difficult to get in summer, as the manager caters mostly to friends and regulars. If you are lucky enough to get in, however, the food will not disappoint you, nor will the cozy but elegant yellow interior. The unforgettable *pappardelle al portofino* (large, flat noodles) delicately blends two of Liguria's tastes: tomato and pesto. Ligurian seafood specialties include baked fish with laurel, potatoes, and olives as well as the inventive *moscardini al forno* (baked octopus with lemon and rosemary in tomato sauce). ⊠ *P. Martiri dell'Olivetta 4–5, on the harbor* ☎ *0185/269037* ⌘ *Reservations essential* ☰ *No credit cards* ◷ *Closed Thurs. and Jan.–Feb.*

$$$$ ▦ **Splendido.** People resort to superlatives when describing this luxury hotel, built in the 1920s on a hill overlooking the sea. There's a particular attention to color, from the coordinated fabrics and room furnishings to the fresh flowers in the reception rooms and on the large terrace. It's like a Jazz Age film set—you almost expect to see a Bugatti or Daimler roll up the winding drive from Portofino below. Even grander than the hotel are its prices, making this a place for very special occasions indeed. ⊠ *Salita Baratta 16, 16034* ☎ *0185/267801* ⎙ *0185/267806* ⊕ *www.splendido.orient-express.com* ⇝ *34 rooms, 32 suites* ⌔ *Restaurant, tennis court, pool, gym, sauna, 2 bars, meeting rooms, some pets allowed* ☰ *AE, DC, MC, V* ◷ *Closed mid-Nov.–late Mar.*

$$-$$$ ▦ **Eden.** If you must stay in Portofino, this is your only affordable option. Small, unexciting, but comfortable rooms have all the basic amenities, with clean bathrooms, working showers, pinkish walls, and views onto the street but not the bay. Anywhere else, this hotel would be overpriced, but in Portofino it's a good deal. ⊠ *Via Vico Dritto 20, near the harbor, 16034* ☎ *0185/269091* ⎙ *0185/269047* ⊕ *www.hoteledenportofino.com* ⇝ *11 rooms* ⌔ *Restaurant, bar, Internet, some pets allowed* ☰ *AE, DC, MC, V* ◷ *Closed Dec. 1–25.*

Sports & the Outdoors

HIKING   If you have the stamina, you can hike to the Abbazia di San Fruttuoso from Portofino. It's a steep climb at first, and the walk takes about 2½ hours one-way. If you're extremely ambitious and want to make a whole day of it, you can then hike another 2½ hours all the way to Camogli. Much more modest hikes from Portofino include a one-hour uphill walk to Cappella delle Gave, a bit inland in the hills, from where you can continue downhill to Santa Margherita Ligure (another 1½ hours), and a gently undulating paved trail leading to the beach at Paraggi (½ hour). Finally, there's a 2½-hour hike from Portofino that heads farther inland to Ruta, through Olmi and Pietre Strette.

Camogli

★ ⑩   *20 km (12 mi) east of Genoa, 23 km (14 mi) west of Chiavari.*

Camogli, at the edge of the large promontory and nature reserve known as the Portofino peninsula, has always been a town of sailors. By the 19th century it was leasing its ships throughout the continent. Today, multicolor houses, remarkably deceptive trompe-l'oeil frescoes, and a massive 17th-century seawall mark this picturesque harbor community, perhaps as beautiful as Portofino but without the glamour. When exploring on foot, don't miss the boat-filled second harbor, which is reached by ducking under a narrow archway at the end of the first one.

The **Castello Dragone,** built onto the sheer rock face near the harbor, is home to the **Acquario** (Aquarium), which has display tanks of local marine life actually built into the ramparts. 🎫 €3 ☉ *May–Sept., daily 10–noon and 3–7; Oct.–Apr., Fri.–Sun. 10–noon and 2:30–6, Tues.–Thurs. 10–noon.*

off the beaten path

SAN ROCCO, SAN NICCOLÒ, AND PUNTA CHIAPPA – You can reach these hamlets along the western coast of the peninsula on foot or by boat from Camogli. They are more natural and less fashionable than those facing south on the eastern coast. In the small Romanesque church at San Niccolò, sailors who survived dangerous voyages came to offer thanks.

RUTA – The footpaths that leave from Ruta, 4 km (2½ mi) east of Camogli, up to and around Monte Portofino and Camogli thread through rugged terrain, containing a multitude of plant species. Weary hikers will be sustained by stunning views of the Riviera di Levante from the various vantage points along the way.

Where to Stay & Eat

$$–$$$ ✕**Vento Ariel.** This small friendly restaurant serves some of the best seafood in town. In summer months the shaded terrace is a perfect place to dine while watching the bustling activity in the nearby port. Only the freshest of seafood is served; try the spaghetti *alle vongole* (with clams) or the mixed grilled fish. ⊠ *Calata Porto* 🕾 *0185/771080* 🖃 *AE, DC, MC, V* ☉ *Closed Wed. and Jan. 2–15.*

¢–$ ✕**Pizzeria Il Lido.** As the name suggests, this popular spot is right across from Camogli's narrow beach, and the outside tables have great views of the sea. If you don't fancy one of the many varieties of pizza, you can choose from a range of pasta dishes. ⊠ *Via Garibaldi 133* 🕾 *0185/770141* 🖃 *MC, V* ☉ *Closed Tues.*

★ $$$ ▣ **Cenobio dei Dogi.** It's easy to see why this villa once served as the summer home of Genoa's doges. Perched majestically a step above Camogli, overlooking harbor, peninsula, and sea, Cenobio dei Dogi is indisputably the best address in town. Ask for one of the rooms with expansive balconies, which offer the most commanding vistas of Camogli's cozy port. You can relax in the well-kept park affording outstanding views of the Portofino peninsula or enjoy numerous sporting activities. ⊠ *Via Cuneo 34, 16032* 🕾 *0185/7241* 🖷 *0185/772796* ⊕ *www.cenobio.it* ⤶ *102 rooms, 4 suites* ♧ *Restaurant, tennis court, pool, beach, bar, Internet, some pets allowed (fee)* 🖃 *AE, DC, MC, V.*

¢–$ ▣ **Hotel Augusta.** This friendly family-run hotel is an economic and quiet choice in the center of Camogli. Though you won't have a view of the sea, it's just a short walk away. Guest rooms, all with parquet floors and private bathrooms, are bright and modern. ⊠ *Via Schiaffino 100, 16032* 🕾 *0185/770592* 🖷 *0185/770593* ⊕ *www.htlaugusta.com* ⤶ *12 rooms* ♧ *Bar, restaurant; no a/c* 🖃 *AE, DC, MC, V.*

Nightlife & the Arts

During the festival of San Fortunato, held on the second Sunday of May each year, is the **Sagra del Pesce,** a crowded, festive, and free-to-the-public feast of freshly caught fish, cooked outside at the port in a frying pan 12 ft wide.

GENOA

Ligurian beach bums, beware: Genoa (Genova, in Italian) is a busy, sprawling, and cosmopolitan city, apt to break the spell of the coastal towns in a hurry. This isn't necessarily bad news, though; with more than a millennium of history under its belt, magnificent palaces and art, and an elaborate network of ancient hilltop fortresses, Genoa may be just the dose of curious culture you were looking for. The city's faded splendor can be seen through dark shadows and centuries of grime in the narrow alleyways of the historic center—the largest in Europe.

Genoa's winding streets haven't always been so haunted and obscure. This is the birthplace of Columbus, but the city's proud history of trade and navigation predates him by several hundred years. Known as *La Superba* (The Proud), Genoa was from the 13th century a great maritime center rivaling Venice and Pisa in power and splendor. Loud and modern container ships now unload at docks that centuries before served galleons and vessels bound for the spice routes. By the 3rd century BC, when the Romans conquered Liguria, Genoa was already an important trading station. The Middle Ages and the Renaissance saw its rise into a jumping-off place for the Crusaders, a commercial center of tremendous wealth and prestige, and a strategic bone of international contention. A network of fortresses defending the city connected by a wall second only in length to the Great Wall of China was constructed in the hills above, and Genoa's bankers, merchants, and princes adorned the city with palaces, churches, and impressive art collections.

Genoa's downfall began more than 500 years ago as it became eclipsed by other Mediterranean ports and northern Italian powerhouses. By the 17th century, Genoa was no longer a great sea power—but more modern enemies were yet to arrive. Since World War II, the city has fought with—and often lost to—every evil associated with industrialization and urbanity. Crammed into a thin crescent of land between sea and mountains, Genoa has expanded up rather than out, taking on the form of a multilayer wedding cake, with streets, highways, churches, and entire residential neighborhoods built on others' rooftops. Public elevators and funiculars are as common as buses and trains. Traffic-, pollution-, and crime-ridden (by Italian standards), Genoa has lost precious tourist revenue due to its urban-planning follies.

And yet, Europe's biggest boat show, the annual Salone Nautico Internazionale, takes place here. Fine restaurants are abundant, and classical dance and music are richly represented; the Teatro Carlo Felice is the local opera venue, and the internationally renowned annual Niccolò Paganini Violin Contest takes place here. Due to its location and its shipping industry, Genoa is also the most diverse city in Italy; it's one of the only places on the mostly homogeneous boot where you'll find well-established North African, Asian, and South American communities. Just steps away from the port, the darkly shadowed Via del Prè, with its street bazaars and spooky branching alleyways, offers a momentary excursion to a third-world country.

Genoa has been struggling, mostly unsuccessfully, to change its seamy image. A port-side promenade, spider-shape elevator ride with a harbor view, and Europe's largest aquarium were installed for the expensive, much-criticized Columbus Quincentennial celebrations of 1992. Another harbor face-lift took place in preparation for Genoa's designation as one of Europe's "Capitals of Culture" for the year 2004, but it will take more than a flattering label to rescue this once-proud, still fascinating city. But should it be rescued? Perhaps the time to visit is now—before tourists discover Genoa, before the old port is completely overbuilt, and before the city's gritty charm is gone.

Exploring Genoa

The ancient center of Genoa, threaded with tiny streets flanked by 11th-century portals, is roughly the area between the port and Piazza de Ferrari; this maze-like pedestrian zone—no car could fit—is officially called the Caruggi District, but the Genoese, in their matter-of-fact way, simply refer to the area as the place of the *vicoli* (narrow alleys). Between the 12th and 16th centuries, the city expanded—with wider streets— to occupy the area now bounded by Stazione Principe to the west and Stazione Brignole to the east. Divided into *sestieri* (six neighborhoods), this is where the majority of Genoa's most important historical landmarks are found.

Medieval & Renaissance Genoa

a good walk

The best way to begin your exploration of Genoa is to see it from above. From Piazza Acquaverde, behind Stazione Principe, start your walk along Via Balbi, which runs southeast from Stazione Principe toward the medieval town. On Via Balbi you pass Palazzo Balbi Durazzo, also known as **Palazzo Reale** ⑪ ▶, and **Palazzo dell'Università** ⑫. Continue straight past Piazza della Nunziata, stopping at **Santissima Annunziata** ⑬, to Largo di Zecca, from where you can take the **Zecca-Righi Funicular** ⑭ up to a marvelous lookout point on the edge of Genoa's network of fortresses. From Righi you can also walk along the ancient city walls in either direction. After descending, go southeast on Via Cairoli to reach the famed **Via Garibaldi** ⑮, a majestic street where you can pause to see the collections in the museums of **Palazzo Rosso** ⑯ and **Palazzo Bianco** ⑰. Stop in at **Palazzo Tursi** ⑱, Genoa's town hall, and ask the guard at the door if it happens to be open to visitors that day; if it is, you can see one of Paganini's violins. At the end of Via Garibaldi go left and left again to Piazza del Portello, where you can take the **Castelletto** ⑲ elevator for another panoramic view of the city and the port (a fine view is also to be had from the terrace of the **Museo d'Arte Orientale Chiossone** ⑳, located just above Piazza del Portello). Returning to Piazza Fontane Marose at the end of Via Garibaldi, turn southwest, taking Via Luccoli into the medieval Caruggi District. Beyond Piazza Soziglia, detour to the left, taking Via Campetto to Piazza San Matteo, flanked by the well-preserved houses of the Dorias and the church of **San Matteo** ㉑. Follow Salita Arcivescovado and turn right on Via Reggio to the cathedral of **San Lorenzo** ㉒, medieval Genoa's religious heart. North of the cathedral is Vico degli Indoratori, onto which you turn northwest. Follow it to Via degli Orefici, on which you turn left to reach the **Loggia dei Mercanti** ㉓. Head north on Via San Luca, Genoa's best shopping street (hopping on weekend afternoons), to the **Galleria Nazionale** ㉔. At the northern end of Via San Luca is the spooky church of **San Siro** ㉕. From there, if it is daytime and if you're adventurous, you can continue onto Via del Campo back toward Principe until the street becomes Via del Prè, where you'll find Genoa's seamy, multicultural underbelly, in some senses the true center of the ancient port. Prepare yourself for a tour through the human vices; women should not walk alone on Via del Prè.

TIMING Allow a full day for this walk. Note that the Galleria Nazionale is closed on Monday.

What to See

Caruggi District. The winding, picturesque alleys—known as *caruggi*— that make up the popular side of medieval Genoa are the city's heart and soul. Wealthy Genovese built their homes in this quarter in the 16th century, and prosperous guilds, such as the goldsmiths for whom Vico dei Indoratori and Via Orefici were named, set up shop here. In this warren of narrow, cobbled streets, extending north from Piazza Caricamento, you'll find the city's oldest churches punctuating blocks of 500-year-old apartment buildings, and tiny shops selling antique furniture, coffee, rifles, cheese, wine, gilt picture frames, camping gear, even live fish. The apartment buildings along the tiny streets lean in so precariously that penthouse balconies in some cases nearly touch those across the street, blocking what little sunlight would have shone down onto the cobblestones. When exploring these shady passageways, bear in mind that this quarter is the city's most disreputable. Don't come here at night or on holidays, when shops are closed and the alleys deserted, unless you're willing to part with your valuables.

⑲ Castelletto. One of Genoa's handy municipal elevators whisks you skyward from Piazza Portello, at the end of Via Garibaldi, for a good view of the old city. ⊠ *Piazza Portello, Castelletto* 🕾 *€0.50 one-way* ⊙ *Continuous service 6:40 AM–midnight.*

㉔ Galleria Nazionale. This gallery, housed in the richly adorned **Palazzo Spinola** north of Piazza Soziglia, contains masterpieces by Luca Giordano and Guido Reni. The *Ecce Homo*, by Antonello da Messina, is a hauntingly beautiful painting, of historical interest because it was the Sicilian da Messina who first brought Flemish oil paints and techniques to Italy from his sojourns in the Low Countries. ⊠ *Piazza Pellicceria 1, Maddalena* 🕾 *010/2705300* 🕾 *€4, €6 including Palazzo Reale* ⊙ *Tues.–Sat. 9–8, Sun. 2–8.*

Granarolo funicular. Actually a cog railway, this tram takes you up the steeply rising terrain to another part of the city's fortified walls. It takes 15 minutes to hoist you from Stazione Principe, on Piazza Acquaverde, to **Porta Granarolo**, 1,000 ft above, where the sweeping view gives you a sense of Genoa's size. ⊠ *Piazza del Principe, San Teodoro* 🕾 *€0.77 bus tickets valid* ⊙ *Departs every ½ hr, 6 AM–10 PM, and 10:40 PM, 11:20 PM.*

㉓ Loggia dei Mercanti. This merchants' row dating from the 16th century is lined with shops selling local foods and gifts as well as raincoats, rubber boots, and fishing line. ⊠ *Piazza Banchi, Maddalena.*

⑳ Museo d'Arte Orientale Chiossone. In the Villetta di Negro park on the hillside above Piazza Portello, the Chiossone Oriental Art Museum has one of Europe's most noteworthy collections of Japanese, Chinese, and Thai objects. There's a fine view of the city from the museum's terrace. ⊠ *Piazzale Mazzini 1, Piazza Corvetto, Maddalena* 🕾 *010/542285* 🕾 *€3.10, free Sun.* ⊙ *Tues.–Fri. 9–1, weekends 10–7.*

⑰ Palazzo Bianco. Originally white, as its name suggests, this palace—a mainstay of the regal Via Garibaldi—has darkened with age. (A renovation, which will keep it closed until early 2004, includes a cleaning of the facade.) It has a fine art collection, with the Spanish and Flemish schools well represented. ⊠ *Via Garibaldi 11, Maddalena* 🕾 *010/5572013* 🕾 *€3.10, €5.16 combined ticket with Palazzo Rosso, free Sun.* ⊙ *Tues.–Fri. 9–7, weekends 10–7.*

⑫ Palazzo dell'Università. Built in the 1630s as a Jesuit college, this has been Genoa's university since 1803. The exterior is unassuming, but climb the stairway flanked by lions to visit the handsome courtyard, with its portico of double Doric columns. ⊠ *Via Balbi 5, Pré.*

▶ ⑪ Palazzo Reale. In a city where conspicuous consumption was a hobby of high society, this sumptuous 17th-century palace—also known as Palazzo Balbi Durazzo—contains lavish rococo rooms displaying paintings, sculptures, tapestries, and Oriental ceramics. It was built by the Balbi family, enormously wealthy Genovese merchants, and its regal pretensions were not lost on the Savoy, who bought the palace and turned it into a royal residence in the early 19th century. The gallery of mirrors and the ballroom on the upper floor are particularly decadent. You'll also find works by Sir Anthony Van Dyck, who lived in Genoa for six years, beginning in 1621, and painted many portraits of the Genovese nobility. ⊠ *Via Balbi 10, Pré* ☎ *010/2470640* ⊠ *€4, €6 including Galleria Nazionale* ☉ *Sun.–Tues. 9–1:45, Wed.–Sat. 9–7.*

⓰ **Palazzo Rosso.** The 17th-century baroque palace was named for the red stone used in its construction. It now contains, apart from a number of lavishly frescoed suites, works by Titian, Veronese, Reni, and Van Dyck. ⊠ *Via Garibaldi 18, Maddalena* ☎ *010/2476351* ⊠ *€3.10, €5.16 combined ticket with Palazzo Bianco, free Sun.* ☉ *Tues.–Fri. 9–7, weekends 10–7.*

⓲ **Palazzo Tursi.** In the 16th century, wealthy Nicolò Grimaldi had this palace built of pink stone quarried in the region. It's been reincarnated as Genoa's Palazzo Municipale (Municipal Building), and so most of the goings-on inside are the stuff of local politics and quickie weddings. When the rooms aren't in use for Genovese civic proceedings, however, you are welcome to view the richly decorated rooms and the famous Guarnerius violin that belonged to Niccolò Paganini (1782–1840), which is played once a year on Columbus Day (October 12). ⊠ *Via Garibaldi 9, Maddalena* ☎ *010/557111* ⊠ *Free* ☉ *Weekdays 8–noon, call in advance.*

⓶⓶ **San Lorenzo.** This cathedral, at the heart of medieval Genoa, is embellished inside and out with the contrasting black slate and white marble so common in Liguria. It was consecrated in 1118 to St. Lawrence, who passed through the city on his way to Rome in the 3rd century; the last campanile dates from the early 16th century. For hundreds of years the building was used for state and religious purposes such as civic elections. Note the 13th-century Gothic portal, fascinating twisted barbershop columns, and the 15th- to 17th-century frescoes inside. The **Museo del Tesoro di San Lorenzo** (San Lorenzo Treasury Museum) has some stunning pieces from medieval goldsmiths and silversmiths, for which medieval Genoa was renowned. ⊠ *Piazza San Lorenzo, Molo* ☎ *010/2471831 museum* ⊠ *Cathedral free, museum €5* ☉ *Cathedral daily 8–11:45 and 3–6:45; museum, guided visits only, every ½ hr Mon.–Sat. 9–11:30 and 3–5:30.*

⓶⓵ **San Matteo.** This typically Genovese black-and-white-striped church dates from the 12th century; its crypt contains the tomb of Andrea Doria (1466–1560), the Genovese admiral who maintained the independence of his native city. The well-preserved Piazza San Matteo was, for 500 years, the seat of the Doria family, which ruled Genoa and much of Liguria from the 16th to the 18th century. The square is bounded by 13th- to 15th-century houses decorated with portals and loggias. ⊠ *Piazza San Matteo, Maddalena* ☎ *010/2474361* ☉ *Mon.–Sat. 8–noon and 4–7, Sun. 9:30–10:30 and 4–5.*

⓶⓹ **San Siro.** Genoa's oldest church was the city's cathedral from the 4th to the 9th century. Rebuilt in the 16th and 17th centuries, it now feels like a haunted house—imposing frescoes line dank hallways, and chandeliers hold crooked candles flickering in the darkness. ⊠ *Via San Luca, Maddalena* ☎ *010/22461468* ☉ *Daily 7:30–noon and 4–7.*

⓭ **Santissima Annunziata.** The 16th- to 17th-century church has exuberantly frescoed vaults and is an excellent example of Genovese baroque architecture. ⊠ *Piazza della Nunziata, Pré* ☎ *010/297662* ☉ *Daily 9–noon and 3–7.*

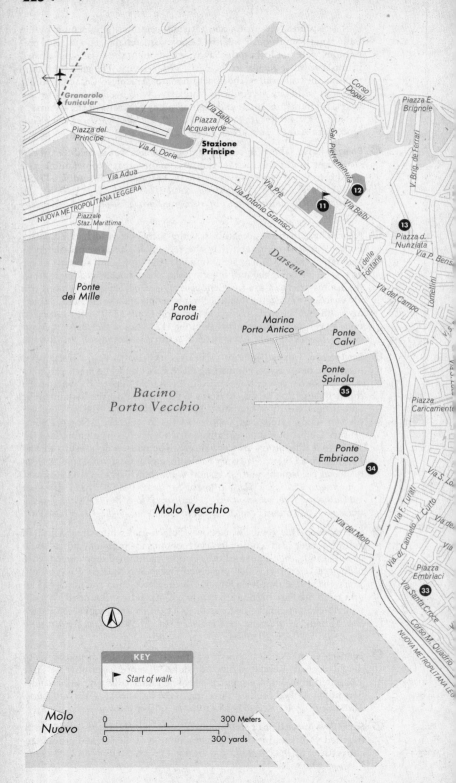

Granarolo funicular

Piazza del Principe

Via A. Doria

Via Adua

NUOVA METROPOLITANA LEGGERA

Piazzale Staz. Marittima

Ponte dei Mille

Ponte Parodi

Bacino Porto Vecchio

Ponte Calvi

Marina Porto Antico

Darsena

Via Balbi

Piazza Acquaverde

Stazione Principe

Via Pre

Via Antonio Gramsci

Corso Dogali

Piazza E. Brignole

V. Brig. de Ferrari

Sal. Pietraminuta

Via Balbi

Piazza d. Nunziata

Via P. Bens

V. delle Fontane

Via del Campo

Lomellini

Ponte Spinola

Piazza Caricamento

Ponte Embriaco

Molo Vecchio

Via del Molo

Via F. Turati

Il Curto

Via S. Lo.

Piazza Embrici

Via Santa Croce

Via dl. Canneto

Corso M. Quadrio

NUOVA METROPOLITANA LE

KEY

► *Start of walk*

Molo Nuovo

0   300 Meters

0   300 yards

Genoa

★ ⑮ **Via Garibaldi.** Thirteen palaces were built along what was once known as the Via Aurea (Golden Street) in just 10 years. Genoa's leading patrician families built their residences here from 1554 onward to escape the cramped conditions of the medieval section. It is one of the most impressive streets in Italy, and the palace-museums house some of the finest art collections in the country. Most of the palaces without museums on Via Garibaldi can be visited only by special application, but many have courtyards open to the public. ⊠ *West from Piazza Fontane Marose, Maddalena.*

⑭ **Zecca-Righi funicular.** This is a seven-stop commuter funicular, beginning at Piazza della Nunziata and ending up at a high lookout on the fortified gates in the 17th-century city walls. Ringed around the circumference of the city are a number of huge fortresses, and this gate was part of the city's system of defenses. From Righi you can undertake scenic all-day hikes from one fortress to the next. ☒ *€0.77, bus tickets valid* ☉ *Departs every ¼ hr 6 AM–11:45 PM.*

Southern Districts & the Aquarium

a good walk

Start downhill from **Porta Soprana** ㉖ ➤ and pay homage to the purported **childhood home of Christopher Columbus** ㉗ on the square. Then follow Via Dante into Piazza de Ferrari to **Teatro Carlo Felice** ㉘ and the **Accademia delle Belle Arti** ㉙. From Piazza de Ferrari, Genoa's unofficial center, you can make a detour and head down and back up Via XX Settembre, Genoa's wide main thoroughfare, with leading-name boutiques, cafés, and bookstores. Back in Piazza de Ferrari, on the west side of the piazza stands the **Palazzo Ducale** ㉚. Follow the palazzo around to its back side, which bears a neoclassic facade on Piazza Matteotti. Leading uphill from Piazza Matteotti, Salita Pollaiuoli takes you to **San Donato** ㉛. On the west side of the church is Stradone Sant'Agostino, which leads to Piazza Negri and **Sant'Agostino** ㉜. At the top of Stradone Sant'Agostino, from the west end of elongated Piazza Sarzano, take Via Santa Croce and turn right and then left onto Via Santa Maria di Castello, climbing up to the church of **Santa Maria di Castello** ㉝ atop the hill. From Piazza Embriaci turn west and follow the little streets downhill to Via Canneto il Curto, turning downhill on Via San Lorenzo to reach Piazza Caricamento and the Old Port, where you can take a ride in the panoramic **Il Bigo** ㉞ elevator, visit the **Acquario di Genova** ㉟, or take a boat tour of the port.

TIMING This walk will take from 2½ to 4 hours, with stops at churches and the museum at Sant'Agostino; add an hour or two if you are stopping at the Acquario di Genova.

What to See

㉙ **Accademia delle Belle Arti.** Founded in 1751, the Academy of Fine Arts, as well as being a school, houses a collection of paintings from the 16th to the 19th century. Genovese artists of the baroque period are particularly well represented. ⊠ *Piazza De Ferrari 5, Portoria* ☎ *010/581957* ☒ *Free* ☉ *Mon.–Sat. 9–1.*

㉟ **Acquario di Genova.** Europe's biggest aquarium, second in the world only to Osaka's in Japan, is the third most-visited museum in Italy and a must for children. Fifty tanks of marine species, including sea turtles, dolphins, seals, eels, penguins, and sharks, share space with educational displays and re-creations of marine ecosystems, including a tank of coral from the Red Sea. If coming in by car just for the aquarium, take the Genova Ovest exit from the autostrada. ⊠ *Ponte Spinola, Porto Vecchio* ☎ *010/2445678* ⊕ *www.acquario.ge.it* ☒ *€12* ☉ *Mar.–June and Sept.–Oct., Mon.–Wed. and Fri. 9:30–7:30, Thurs. 9:30 AM–10 PM, and weekends 9:30–8:30; July–Aug., daily 9:30 AM–11 PM; Nov., Tues.–Wed. and Fri. 9:30–7:30,*

Thurs. 9:30 AM–10 PM and weekends 9:30–8:30; Dec.–Feb., Mon. 10–6, Tues.–Wed. and Fri. 9:30–7:30, and weekends 9:30–8:30. Entrance permitted every ½ hr. Ticket office closes 1½–2 hrs before aquarium.

㉗ Childhood home of Christopher Columbus. The ivy-covered ruins of this fabled medieval house stand strangely all alone in the gardens adjacent to the Porta Soprana. ⊠ *Piazza Dante, Molo.*

Harbor. A boat tour gives you a good perspective on the layout of the harbor, which dates back to Roman times. The Genoa inlet, the largest along the Italian Riviera, was also used by the Phoenicians and Greeks as a harbor and a vantage point from which they could penetrate inland to form settlements and to trade. The port is guarded by the Diga Foranea, a striking wall 5 km (3 mi) long built into the ocean. Boat tours, starting at the acquarium pier, are available for €6 and last approximately one hour. Contact the **Cooperativa Battellieri** (⊠ Stazione Marittima, Ponte dei Mille ☎ 010/265712 ⊕ www.battellierigenova.it) for information. The **Lanterna,** a lighthouse more than 360 ft high, was built in 1544 at the height of Andrea Doria's career; it's one of Italy's oldest lighthouses and a traditional emblem of Genoa. ⊕ *www.portoantico.it.*

㉞ Il Bigo. This bizarre white structure, erected in 1992 to celebrate the Columbus quincentennial, looks like either a radioactive spider or an overgrown potato spore, depending on your point of view. Its most redeeming feature is the **Ascensore Panoramico Bigo** (Bigo Panoramic Elevator), from which you can take in the harbor, city, and sea. Down below, there's ice skating from November or December through March. ⊠ *Ponte Spinola, Porto Vecchio* ☎ 010/23451; 010/2461319 *ice skating* ⊠ €3.30 ☉ *Feb. and Nov., weekends 10–5; June–Aug., Tues.–Wed. and Sun. 10–8, Thurs. and Sat. 10 AM–11 PM; Mar.–May and Sept., Tues.–Sun. 10–6; Oct., Tues.–Sun. 10–5; Dec. 26–Jan 6, daily 10–5.*

㉚ Palazzo Ducale. This palace was built in the 16th century over a medieval hall, and its facade was rebuilt in the late 18th century and later restored. It now houses temporary exhibitions and a restaurant-bar serving fusion cuisine. Guided tours of the palace and its exhibitions are sometimes available, and reservations are necessary to visit the dungeons and tower. Contact the palace for information and schedules. ⊠ *Piazza Matteotti 9 and Piazza de Ferrari, Portoria* ☎ 010/5574004 ⊕ *www.palazzoducale.genova.it* ⊠ *Free, exhibition admission varies* ☉ *Tues.–Sun. 9–9.*

㉖ Porta Soprana. The striking, twin-towered, 12th-century edifice also known as Porta di Sant'Andrea stands at the old gateway to the Roman road that led through Genoa. Uphill from Columbus's boyhood home, Porta Soprana supposedly employed the explorer's father as a gatekeeper. ⊠ *Piazza Dante, Molo.*

㉛ San Donato. Although somewhat marred by 19th- and 20th-century restorations, this 12th-century church with its original portal and octagonal campanile is a fine example of Genovese Romanesque architecture. Inside, you'll find an altarpiece depicting the Adoration of the Magi by the Flemish artist Joos Van Cleve (circa 1485–1540). ⊠ *Piazza San Donato, Portoria* ☎ 010/2468869 ☉ *Mon.–Sat. 8–noon and 3–7, Sun. 9–12:30 and 3–7.*

㉜ Sant'Agostino. This 13th-century Gothic church was damaged during World War II, but it still has a fine campanile and two well-preserved cloisters, which now house an excellent museum. Highlighting the collection are the enigmatic fragments of a tomb sculpture by Giovanni Pisano (circa 1250–circa 1315). ⊠ *Piazza Sarzano 35/r, Molo* ☎ 010/2511263 ⊠ €3.10, free Sun. ☉ *Tues.–Sat. 9–7, Sun. 9–12:30.*

33 **Santa Maria di Castello.** One of Genoa's most significant religious build-ings, an early Christian church, was rebuilt in the 12th century and fi-nally completed in 1513. You can visit the adjacent cloisters and see the fine artwork contained in the museum. Museum hours, which normally match those of the church, may occasionally vary when special religious services are held. ⊠ *Salita di Santa Maria di Castello 15, Molo* ☎ *010/ 2549511* ⊇ *€3* ⊙ *Church daily 9–noon and 3:30–6; museum, call for information.*

28 **Teatro Carlo Felice.** The World War II–ravaged opera house in Genoa's modern center, Piazza de Ferrari, was rebuilt and reopened in 1991 to host the fine Genovese opera company; its massive tower has been the subject of much criticism. ⊠ *Passo Eugenio Montale 4, Piazza De Fer-rari, Portoria* ☎ *010/53811* ⊕ *www.carlofelice.it.*

off the
beaten
path

CIMITERO MONUMENTALE DI STAGLIENO – One of the most famous of Genovese landmarks is this bizarrely beautiful cemetery; its fanciful marble and bronze sculptures sprawl haphazardly across a hillside on the outskirts of town. A **Pantheon** holds indoor tombs and some remarkable works like an 1878 *Eve* by Villa. Don't miss Rovelli's 1896 **Tomba Raggio**, which shoots Gothic spires out of the hillside forest. The cemetery began operation in 1851 and has been lauded by such visitors as Mark Twain and Evelyn Waugh. It covers a good deal of ground; allow at least half a day to explore. It's difficult to locate; the 12, 13, and 14 buses, or a taxi, will take you there. ⊠ *Piazzale Resasco* ☎ *010/870184* ⊇ *Free* ⊙ *Daily 7:30–5. Mass Sun. at 10* AM.

GENOVA-CASELLA RAILROAD – In continuous operation since 1929, the historic Genova-Casella rail line heads from Piazza Manin in Genoa (follow Via Montaldo from the center of town, or take Bus 33 or 34 to Piazza Manin) through the beautiful countryside above the city, finally arriving in the rural hill town of Casella. On the way, the tiny train traverses a series of precarious switchbacks that afford sweeping views of the forested Ligurian hills. In Casella Paese (the last stop), you can hike, eat lunch, or just check out the view and ride back. There are two restaurants and two pizzerias near the Casella station; try local cuisine at **Trattoria Teresin** (☎ 010/9677708) in Località Avosso. From the **Canova** stop, two stops from the end of the line, there are two possible hikes through the hills, one a two-hour trek to a small sanctuary, **Santuario della Vittoria,** and the other a more grueling four-hour hike to the hill town of **Creto** (which requires a return trip of four hours as well, or an additional 2½-hour hike to the *pino* railway station). Another worthwhile stop along the rail line is **Sant'Olcese Tullo,** where you can take a half-hour (one-way) walk, along a river and through the **Sentiero Botanico di Ciaé,** a botanical garden and forest refuge with labeled specimens of Ligurian flora and a tiny medieval castle. For Canova and Sant'Olcese, inform your conductor that you want him to stop. The Casella railroad is a good way to get a sense of the rugged landscape around Genoa, and you'll often have it to yourself, ☎ *010/837321* ⊕ *www.ferroviagenovacasella.it* ⊇ *€3.60 round-trip, €5 Sun.* ⊙ *Train runs about every hr Mon.–Sat. 7:30–7:30, Sun. 9–9.*

Where to Stay & Eat

$$$–$$$$ ✕ **Antica Osteria del Bai.** Set in the historic Quarto dei Mille district, this romantic upscale seaside restaurant is perched on a cliff. One large dark-wood-paneled room offers views straight out over the Ligurian sea.

A seafaring theme pervades the wall decorations and menu, which might include black gnocchi with lobster sauce, and ravioli ai frutti di mare. The restaurant's traditional elegance is reflected in its dress code and its prices. ⊠ *Via Quarto 16, Quarto dei Mille* ☎ *010/387478* 🏛 *Jacket and tie* ⊟ *AE, DC, MC, V* ☉ *Closed Mon., Jan. 10–20, and Aug. 1–20.*

$$$–$$$$ ✕ **Gran Gotto.** Innovative regional dishes are served in this posh, spacious restaurant festooned with contemporary paintings. Try *cappellacci di borragine con vellutata di pinoli* (borage pasta with a pine-nut sauce) followed by *calamaretti brasati con porri e zucchine* (braised baby squid with leeks and zucchini), one of the many excellent second courses. Service is quick and helpful. Gran Gotto is in Piazza della Vittoria, near Stazione Brignole, in the modern part of town. ⊠ *Viale Brigata Bisagno 69/r, Foce* ☎ *010/564344* ♨ *Reservations essential* ⊟ *AE, DC, MC, V* ☉ *Closed Sun. and Aug. 12–31. No lunch Sat.*

$$$–$$$$ ✕ **Zeffirino.** The five Belloni brothers share chef duties at this well-known restaurant full of odd combinations, including decor that ranges from rustic wood to modern metallic. Try the *passutelli* (ravioli stuffed with ricotta cheese, herbs, and fruit) or any of the homemade pasta dishes. With a Zeffirino restaurant in Las Vegas and another in Hong Kong, the enterprising Bellonis have gone international. ⊠ *Via XX Settembre 20, Portoria* ☎ *010/591990* ♨ *Reservations essential* 🏛 *Jacket required* ⊟ *AE, DC, MC, V.*

$$–$$$ ✕ **Enoteca Sola.** Menus are chosen specifically to complement wines at Pino Sola's airy, casually elegant *enoteca* (wine bar) in the heart of the modern town. The short menu emphasizes seafood and varies daily but might include stuffed artichokes or baked stockfish. The real draw, though, is the wine list, which includes some of the best *tre bicchieri* wines in Italy (winners of the coveted three-glass award). Ask the waiters for advice on wine pairings. ⊠ *Via C. Barabino 120/r, Foce* ☎ *010/594513* ⊟ *AE, DC, MC, V* ☉ *Closed Sun. and Aug.*

$–$$ ✕ **Da Genio.** At the top of a pedestrian stairway near Piazza Dante, this is a classic trattoria serving traditional Genovese dishes, including an assortment of fried vegetable appetizers, *trenette al pesto* (pasta with pesto sauce), and minestrone with a dollop of pesto. *Secondi* (main courses) with fish are well prepared. ⊠ *Salita San Leonardo 61/r, Molo* ☎ *010/588463* ⊟ *AE, DC, MC, V* ☉ *Closed Sun. and Aug.*

$ ✕ **Bakari.** Hip styling and ambient lighting hint at the creative, even daring, takes on Ligurian classics offered at this casual centro storico restaurant. Sure bets are the stuffed spinach-and-cheese gnocchi, any of several carpaccios, and the delicate beef dishes. Reserve ahead, requesting a table on the ground floor for a better atmosphere. ⊠ *Vico del Fieno 16/r, northwest of P. San Matteo, Maddalena* ☎ *010/291936* ⊟ *AE, MC, V* ☉ *Closed Sun. No dinner Wed. or Fri.*

$$$$ 🏨 **City.** The location of this hotel can't be beat—it's off Via Roma, the grand shopping street, and one block from Piazza de Ferrari, which divides New Genoa from Old Genoa in the heart of the city. A bland apartment-building exterior gives way to a polished lobby and light, modern rooms that are a bit small but very comfortable. Some have only mediocre views; try for a street-side room on a high floor. ⊠ *Via San Sebastiano 6, Portoria, 16123* ☎ *010/5545* 🖷 *010/586301* ⊕ *www.bestwestern.it/city_ge* ⤴ *63 rooms, 3 suites* ♨ *Restaurant, in-room data ports, in-room safes, bar, parking (fee)* ⊟ *AE, DC, MC, V.*

$$$ 🏨 **Bristol Palace.** This grand hotel in the heart of the shopping district was built in the 19th century and maintains the old-fashioned traditions of courtesy and discretion. The guest rooms are large, with high ceilings; paintings decorate the large reception rooms. ⊠ *Via XX Settembre 35, Portoria, 16121* ☎ *010/592541* 🖷 *010/561756* ⊕ *www.hotelbristolpalace.*

THE ART OF THE PESTO PESTLE

YOU MAY HAVE KNOWN GENOA primarily for its salami or its brash explorer, but the city's most direct effect on your life away from Italy may be through its cultivation of one of the world's best pasta sauces. The sublime blend of basil, extra-virgin olive oil, garlic, pine nuts, and grated pecorino and parmigiano reggiano cheeses that forms pesto alla Genovese is one of Italy's crowning culinary achievements, a concoction that Italian food guru Marcella Hazan has called "the most seductive of all sauces for pasta." Unlike in the United States, where various versions of pesto bedeck everything from pizza to grilled-chicken sandwiches, Ligurian pesto is served only over spaghetti, gnocchi, lasagne, or—most authentically—trenette or trofie (short, doughy pasta twists), and then typically mixed with boiled potatoes and green beans. Pesto is also occasionally used to flavor minestrone. The small-leafed basil grown in the region's sunny seaside hills is considered by many to be the best in the world, and your visit to Liguria will afford you the chance to savor pesto in its original form. Pesto sauce was invented primarily as a showcase for that singular flavor, and the best pesto brings out the fresh basil's alluring aroma and taste rather than masking it with the complementary ingredients. The simplicity and rawness of pesto is one of its virtues, as cooking (or even heating) basil ruins its delicate flavor. In fact, pesto aficionados refuse even to subject the basil leaves to an electric blender; Genovese (and other) foodies insist that true pesto can be made only with mortar and pestle. Although satisfactory versions can surely be prepared less laboriously, the pesto purists' culinary conservatism is supported by etymology: the word pesto is derived from the Italian verb pestare (to pound or grind).

com 🖵 128 rooms, 5 suites ⚒ Restaurant, room TVs with movies, gym, bar, Internet, meeting rooms, parking (fee), some pets allowed ⊟ AE, DC, MC, V.

$ ⊞ **Agnello d'Oro.** In Genoa's centro storico, about 100 yards from Stazione Principe and next to the Palazzo Reale, this hotel has simple and modern rooms, a few with balconies. The friendly owner does double duty as a travel agent and is happy to help you with plane reservations and travel plans. ✉ Vico delle Monachette 6, Pré, 16126 ☎ 010/2462084 🖷 010/2462327 ⊕ www.hotelagnellodoro.it 🖵 25 rooms ⚒ Restaurant, bar, parking (fee), some pets allowed, no-smoking rooms ⊟ AE, DC, MC, V.

$ ⊞ **Cairoli.** This family-run, central hotel is on a historic street near Stazione Principe and the aquarium. It's neatly furnished and has a roof terrace. The rooms have been soundproofed, an important plus in this noisy city. ✉ Via Cairoli 14/4, Maddalena, 16124 ☎ 010/2461454 🖷 010/2467512 ⊕ www.hotelcairoligenova.com 🖵 12 rooms ⚒ Bar ⊟ AE, DC, MC, V.

Nightlife & the Arts

Live Music & Dancing

Especially in summer, the place for nightlife is on the waterfront to the *levante* (southeast) side of the city. From the center, take Corso Italia in the direction of Quarto, Quinto, and Nervi to reach the outdoor nighttime hub. Several beachfront *bagni* (literally, baths) and their accompanying restaurants and bars in the area serve as nighttime summer hangouts. Extraordinarily popular with locals, **Senhor do Bonfim** (✉ Passeggiata Anita Garibaldi, Nervi ☎ 010/3726312), along the water on Nervi's beautiful seaside promenade, offers live music late into the night on weekends, and mellower-than-disco dancing every night. Bigger and better-known discotheques such as the famous **Makò** (⊠ Corso Italia 28/r, Quarto ☎ 010/367652), perched on a cliff about halfway to Nervi, attract most of the nighttime attention from Genovese twenty- and thirtysomethings.

Opera

The opera season (October–May) at **Teatro Carlo Felice** (⊠ Passo Eugenio Montale 4, Piazza De Ferrari, Portoria ☎ 010/53811 ⊕ www.carlofelice.it) attracts lavish productions and occasionally sees the debut of a work. Genoa's opera company, Fondazione Teatro Carlo Felice, is well respected.

Shopping

Liguria is famous for its fine laces, silver and gold filigree work, and ceramics. Look also for bargains in velvet, macramé, olive wood, and marble. Genoa is the best spot to find all these specialties. In the heart of the medieval quarter, **Via Soziglia** is lined with shops selling handicrafts and tempting foods. **Via XX Settembre** is famous for its exclusive shops. You'll find high-end shops lining **Via Luccoli.** The best shopping area for trendy (read: black) but inexpensive Italian clothing is near San Siro, on **Via San Luca.**

Clothing & Leather Goods

At the fancy **Pescetto** (⊠ Via Scurreria 8, Molo ☎ 010/2473433), you'll find designer clothes, perfumes, and gift ideas. **Stefanel** (⊠ Via XX Settembre 36–39, Foce ☎ 010/714755) is the venue of choice for modern Italian women's clothing. Bologna-based **Bruno Magli** (⊠ Via XX Settembre 135, Foce ☎ 010/561890) makes an impeccable line of leather shoes and boots for men and women, handbags, and jackets.

Jewelry

The well-established **Codevilla** (⊠ Via Orefici 53, Maddalena ☎ 010/2472567) is one of the best jewelers on a street full of goldsmiths.

Wines

Vinoteca Sola (⊠ Piazza Colombo 13–15/r, near Stazione Brignole, Foce ☎ 010/561329 ⊕ www.vinotecasola.it), open daily 9:30–12:30 and 3:30–7, stocks a selection of Italian and Ligurian wines. You can even buy futures for advance purchase and have wine shipped overseas.

Side Trip from Genoa

Nervi

36 *11 km (7 mi) east of Genoa, 23 km (14 mi) northwest of Chiavari.*

The identity of this stately late 19th-century resort, famous for its seaside promenade, the Passeggiata Anita Garibaldi (1½ km [1 mi] long), its palm-lined roads, and 300 acres of parks rich in orange trees and exotics, is given away only by the sign on the sleepy train station in the center of town: it's technically part of the city of Genoa. Nervi's secret is an easy one to keep, though: its attractions are peace and quiet, its lush gardens, and the dramatic black cliffs that drop into the sea, as different from Genoa's hustle and bustle as Nervi's clear blue water is from Genoa's crowded port. Despite the contrast, it's easy to visit this remarkable part of the city for a stroll along the water or a day at the beach. Nervi—and the road along the way—also becomes a summer hotbed of nightlife. Frequent trains take 15 minutes from Stazione Principe or Brignole (buy a ticket for Genova–Nervi), or Buses 15 or 17 will take you from Brignole or Piazza de Ferrari to Nervi. Alternatively, a taxi from town center will run about €20 one-way. From the Nervi train station, walk east along the seaside promenade to reach beach stations, a cliff-hanging restaurant, and the 2,000 varieties of roses in the **Parco Villa Grimaldi**, all the while enjoying one of the most breathtaking views on the Riviera.

WHERE TO
STAY & EAT
$–$$

✕ **Marinella.** This restaurant is perched on seaside shoals a few minutes outside Genoa. The impressive wrought-iron chandelier inside takes second billing to the great sea views from windows and terrace. (There's an inexpensive hotel annex, too.) Try the *zuppa di pesce* (fish soup); main dishes change according to the day's catch. ⊠ *Passeggiata Anita Garibaldi 18/r* ☎ *010/3728343* ⊟ *MC, V* ☉ *Closed Mon. and Nov.*

★ $$$

🏨 **Romantik Hotel Villa Pagoda.** This small top-quality hotel in seaside Nervi is a majestic choice that offers the best of both worlds—luxurious peace and quiet with the city's attractions just 15 minutes away. Housed in a 19th-century merchant's mansion modeled after a Chinese pagoda, the hotel has a private park, private access to Nervi's famed cliff-top sea walk, and magnificent sea views. Request a tower room. ⊠ *Via Capolungo 15, 16167* ☎ *010/3726161* 🖷 *010/321218* ⊕ *www. villapagoda.it* ⇆ *13 rooms, 4 suites* ♨ *Restaurant, in-room safes, minibars, tennis court, pool, piano bar, meeting room, some pets allowed* ⊟ *AE, DC, MC, V.*

NIGHTLIFE &
THE ARTS

An **International Ballet Festival** is held every July in the Villa Gropallo park, drawing performers and audiences from all over the world. Contact the **Genoa APT office** (☎ 010/2462633) for ticket and schedule information.

RIVIERA DI PONENTE

The Riviera di Ponente (Riviera of the Setting Sun) stretches from Genoa to Ventimiglia on the French border. For the most part it's an unbroken chain of popular beach resorts sheltered from the north by the Ligurian and Maritime Alps, mountain walls that guarantee mild winters and a long growing season—resulting in its other nickname, the Riviera dei Fiori (Riviera of Flowers). Actually, the name is more evocative than the sight of once-verdant hillsides now swathed in plastic to form massive greenhouses. Many towns on the western Riviera have suffered from an epidemic of overdevelopment, but most have preserved their historic cores, usually their most interesting features. In major resorts, large, modern marinas cater to the pleasure-craft crowd. The Riviera di Ponente has both sandy and pebbly beaches with some quiet bays. Varazze, with a wide, sandy beach and many tall palm trees, is perhaps the last pleasant beach resort on the Riviera di Ponente to resist the encroachment of greater Genoa's industrial influence and the unwelcome effects of the tourist boom.

Pegli

③⑦ *13 km (8 mi) west of Genoa.*

Once a popular summer home for many patrician Genovese families, Pegli has museums, parks, and some regal old villas with well-tended gardens. This residential suburb manages to maintain its dignity despite industrial development and the proximity of airport and port facilities. Two lovely villas make it worth an excursion. Pegli can be reached conveniently by commuter train from Stazione Porta Principe in Genoa.

Villa Doria, near the Pegli train station, has a large park. The villa itself, built in the 16th century by the Doria family, has been converted into a **naval museum.** ✉ *Piazza Bonavino 7* ☎ *010/6969885* 🎟 *Villa €3.10, free on Sun.; park free* ⊘ *Villa Tues.–Fri. 9–1, Sat. 10–1; park daily 9–noon and 2–6.*

Villa Durazzo Pallavicini is set in 19th-century gardens with temples and artificial lakes. The villa has an **archaeological museum.** ✉ *Via Pallavicini 11* ☎ *010/6981048* ⊕ *www.doit.it/pallavicini* 🎟 *€3.10* ⊘ *Tues.–Fri. 9–7, weekends 10–7. Guided tours by reservation.*

Varazze

❸ *23 km (14 mi) southwest of Pegli, 35 km (22 mi) west of Genoa.*

Well-preserved medieval ramparts surround the town, with the remains of a Romanesque church and facade built directly into one of the walls. Varazze is nicknamed *la città delle donne* (the city of women) after an annual festival once held in celebration of women. The name has remained but the festival, last given in 1999, has passed, at least for the moment, from fashion.

Albisola Marina

❸ *11 km (7 mi) southwest of Varazze, 43 km (26 mi) west of Genoa.*

Albisola Marina has a centuries-old tradition of ceramic-making. Numerous shops here sell the distinctive wares, and even a whole sidewalk, **Lungomare degli Artisti,** has been transformed by the colorful ceramic works of well-known artists. It runs along the beachfront. The 18th-century **Villa Faraggiana** has interesting antique ceramics and exhibits on the history of the craft. ✉ *Near the parish church on Via dell'Oratorio* ☎ *019/480622* 🎟 *Free* ⊘ *Apr.–Sept., Wed.–Mon. 3–7.*

Shopping

Ceramiche San Giorgio (✉ Corso Matteotti 5 ☎ 019/482747) has been producing ceramics since the 17th century and is known for both classic and modern designs. **Mazzotti** (✉ Corso Matteotti 25 ☎ 019/481626) has an exclusive ceramics selection and a small museum. In Albisola Superiore, **Ernan** (✉ Corso Mazzini 77 ☎ 019/489916) sells blue-and-white Old Savona patterns typical of the 18th century.

Savona

❹ *4½ km (3 mi) southwest of Albisola Marina, 46 km (29 mi) southwest of Genoa.*

Savona is the fifth-largest seaport in Italy and handles vast oil and coal cargoes, as well as car and truck ferries. Considerably damaged during World War II, much of the town is modern and not very interesting, although a small austere older quarter near the harbor contains some fine homes of the town's merchant class. The large **Palazzo della Rovere** (✉ Via Pia 28), which now houses magistrates' offices and is closed to the public, was designed for Pope Julius II by the Florentine Giuliano da Sangallo in 1495. The city's monuments include the 12th-century **Torre del Brandale,** with its 14th-century annex, the **Palazzo degli Anziani** (✉ Piazza del Brandale 2 ☎ 019/821915 ⊘ By appointment), and two other remaining medieval towers.

Shopping

Watch for shops selling crystallized fruit, a local specialty. In Millesimo, a town 4 km (2½ mi) west and 36 km (18 mi) inland from Savona, little rum chocolates known as *millesimi* are produced. Look for bargains, too, in wrought-iron work, relief work on copperplate, and pieces in local sandstone.

Finale Ligure

❹ *24 km (15 mi) southwest of Savona, 72 km (44 mi) southwest of Genoa.*

Palms, sand strips, *gelaterie* (gelato shops), and good rock-climbing terrain make Finale Ligure a nice break from gaudiness and pastel villages. Finale Ligure is made up of three villages: Finalborgo, Finalmarina, and Finalpia. The latter two have fine sandy beaches and modern resort amenities. The surrounding countryside is pierced by deep narrow valleys and caves; the limestone outcroppings provide the warm pinkish stone found in many buildings in Genoa. Here lurk rare reptiles and exotic flora.

The most attractive of the villages is **Finalborgo,** a hauntingly preserved medieval settlement, planned to a rigid blueprint, with 15th-century walls. The village is crowned by the impressive ruins of the huge **Castel Gavone.** The baroque church of **San Biagio** (⊠ Piazza S. Biagio ☎ 019/695617 ☉ Daily 8–11:30, and 2:30–5) houses many works of art. The 14th- to 15th-century Dominican convent of **Santa Caterina** can be visited to enjoy the shade of the courtyard or to see the museum of local paleontology and natural history. ⊠ *Museo Civico* ☎ *019/690020* 🎫 *€2.60* ☉ *July–Oct., Tues.–Sat. 9–noon and 3–6, Sun. 9–noon; Nov.–June, Tues.–Sat. 9–noon and 2:30–4:30, Sun. 9–noon.*

Where to Stay & Eat

$$$–$$$$ ✕ **Ai Torchi.** You could easily become a homemade-pesto snob at this restaurant in the center of Finalborgo. High prices are justified by excellent inventive seafood and meat dishes. The setting is a restored 5th-century olive-oil refinery. ⊠ *Via dell'Annunziata 12* ☎ *019/690531* 🖃 *AE, DC, MC, V* ☉ *Closed Jan. 7–Feb. 10, and Tues. in Sept.–July.*

¢ 🏨 **Hotel Riviera.** Marzio Alberto is your congenial host at this smartly run hotel in Finale Ligure. Rooms are cheerfully furnished and brightly lit, and some offer views of the sea. There's an additional charge for breakfast if you stay for a brief period of time during high season. ⊠ *Via Ruffini 11, 17024* ☎ *019/692814* 🖷 *019/680013* ⊕ *www.hotelrivierafinale. it* 🛏 *20 rooms* ⚭ *Bar; no a/c in some rooms* 🖃 *AE, DC, MC, V* ☉ *Closed mid-Oct–mid-Dec.*

off the beaten path

NOLI – Just 9 km (5½ mi) northeast of Finale Ligure, picturesque ruins of a castle loom benevolently over the tiny medieval gem of Noli. It's hard to imagine this charming village was—like Genoa, Venice, Pisa, and Amalfi—a prosperous maritime republic in the Middle Ages. If you don't have a car, get a bus for Noli at Spotorno, where local trains stop.

Albenga

❹ *20 km (12 mi) southwest of Finale Ligure, 90 km (55 mi) southwest of Genoa.*

Albenga has a medieval core, with narrow streets laid out by the ancient Romans. A network of alleys is punctuated by centuries-old towers surrounding the 18th-century Romanesque cathedral, with a late 14th-century campanile and baptistery dating back to the 5th century.

off the beaten path

BARDINETO – For a look at some of the Riviera's mountain scenery, make an excursion by car to this attractive village in the middle of an area rich in mushrooms, chestnuts, and raspberries, as well as local cheese. A ruined castle stands above the village. From Borghetto Santo Spirito (between Albenga and Finale Ligure), drive inland 25 km (15 mi).

Where to Stay

$$$$ 🏨 **La Meridiana.** An oasis of Italian hospitality and refinement lies 8 km (5 mi) off the Albenga exit of the A10. The handsome farmhouse compound is spread on a bucolic garden. The interiors are those of a comfortably luxe home, with tasteful, bright prints and colors; fresh flowers; and a mix of traditional and period-style furniture in the common and guest rooms. Il Rosmarino restaurant serves fine wine and seafood dishes. Nearby are the Golf Club Garlenda, a tennis club, and a country club for horseback riding. ⊠ *Via ai Castelli, Garlenda 17033* 🕿 *0182/580271* 🖷 *0182/580150* ⊕ *www.relaischateaux.com/meridiana* ➴ *13 rooms, 15 suites* ♙ *Restaurant, pool, sauna, bicycles, Ping-Pong, bar, Internet, some pets allowed (fee)* ⊟ *AE, DC, MC, V* ♥ *Closed Nov.–Mar.*

Cervo

43 *23 km (14 mi) southwest of Albenga, 106 km (65 mi) southwest of Genoa.*

Cervo is the quintessential sleepy Ligurian coastal village, nicely polished for the tourists who come to explore its narrow byways and street staircases. It's a remarkably well-preserved medieval town, crowned with a big baroque church. In July and August the square in front of the church is the site of chamber music concerts.

Imperia

44 *12 km (7 mi) west of Cervo, 116 km (71 mi) southwest of Genoa.*

Imperia actually consists of two towns: **Porto Maurizio,** a medieval town built on a promontory, and **Oneglia,** now an industrial center for oil refining and pharmaceuticals. Porto Maurizio has a virtually intact medieval center, the Parasio quarter, an intricate spiral of narrow streets and stone portals, and some imposing 17th- and 18th-century palaces. There's little interest in more modern Oneglia, but the 1½ km (1 mi) trip along the seafront from Porto Maurizio into the town is worth taking for a visit to the olive-oil museum.

Imperia is king when it comes to olive oil, and the story of the olive—its cultivation and pressing into oil—is the theme of the small **Museo dell'Olivo** set up by the Fratelli Carli olive-oil company. Displays of the history of the olive tree, farm implements, presses, and utensils show how olive oil has been made in many countries throughout history. ⊠ *Via Garessio 11* 🕿 *0183/720000* ⊕ *www.museodellolivo.com* 🎫 *Free* ♥ *Wed.–Mon. 9–noon and 3–6:30.*

Where to Eat

¢–$ ✕ **Candidollo.** This charming reasonably priced restaurant is worth a detour to the village of Diano Borello, on the valley road a mile or so north of Diano Marina, 6 km (4 mi) east of Imperia. In his rustic country inn, with checkered tablecloths and worn terra-cotta floors, host Bruno Ardissone depends on locally grown ingredients and seasonal traditional recipes. The menu usually includes *coniglio al timo* (rabbit with thyme and other herbs) and *lumache all'agliata* (grilled snails in piquant sauce). ⊠ *Corso Europa 23, Diano Borello* 🕿 *0183/43025* ⊟ *No credit cards* ♥ *Closed Tues. and Nov.–Mar. No lunch Mon.*

FodorsChoice ★

Taggia

㊺ *20 km (12 mi) west of Imperia, 135 km (84 mi) southwest of Genoa.*

The town of Taggia has a medieval core and one of the most imposing medieval bridges in the area. The church of **San Domenico**, south of Taggia, was part of a monastery founded in the 15th century and was a beacon of faith and learning in western Liguria for 300 years. An antiques market is held here on the fourth weekend of the month.

San Remo

★ **㊻** *10 km (6 mi) west of Taggia, 146 km (90 mi) southwest of Genoa.*

The self-styled capital of the Riviera di Ponente, San Remo is also the area's largest resort, lined with polished world-class hotels, exotic gardens, and seaside promenades. Renowned for its royal visitors, famous casino, and romantic setting, San Remo still maintains some of the glamour of its heyday from the late 19th century to World War II. Waterside palm fronds conceal a sizable historic center that, unlike in other Ponente towns, is lively even in the off-season. Restaurants, wine bars, and boutiques are second in Liguria only to Genoa's, and San Remo's cafés bustle with afternoon activity. Consult www.apt.rivieradeifiori.it and www.sanremonet.com for up-to-date information on events in town.

The onion-domed Russian Orthodox church of **San Basilio** stands at one end of the Corso dell'Imperatrice and, like this imposing seafront promenade, is a legacy of Russian empress Maria Alexandrovna, wife of Czar Alexander II, who built a summer house here. San Remo is famous for the **Mercato dei Fiori,** Italy's most important wholesale flower market, held in a market hall between Piazza Colombo and Corso Garibaldi and open to dealers only. More than 20,000 tons of carnations, roses, mimosa flowers, and innumerable other cut flowers are dispatched from here each year.

In the old part of San Remo, **La Pigna** ("the pinecone"), explore the warren of alleyways that climbs upward to Piazza Castello, with a splendid view of the town. The newer parts of San Remo suffer from the same epidemic of overbuilding that changed so many towns on the western Riviera for the worse. And as the center of northern Italy's flower-growing industry, the resort is surrounded by hills where once-verdant terraces are now blanketed with plastic to form immense greenhouses.

The art nouveau **San Remo Casinò** is reminiscent of the turn of the 20th century, with a restaurant, nightclub, and theater that hosts concerts and the annual San Remo Music Festival. ✉ *Corso Inglese* ☎ *0184/5951* 🖾 *Slot machines no cover charge; tables no cover charge Mon.–Thurs.,* €*7.50 Fri.–Sun.* ☉ *Slot machines, Sun.–Fri. 10 AM–2:30 AM, Sat. 10 AM–3:30 AM; tables, Sun.–Fri. 2:30 PM–2:30 AM, Sat. 2:30 PM–3:30 AM.*

off the
beaten
path

BUSSANA VECCHIA – About 8 km (5 mi) east of San Remo, in the hills where flowers are cultivated for export, is Bussana Vecchia, a self-consciously picturesque ghost town largely destroyed by an earthquake in 1877. The inhabitants packed up and left en masse after the quake, and for almost a century the houses, church, and crumbling bell tower were empty shells, overgrown by weeds and wildflowers. Since the 1960s, an artists colony has evolved among the ruins. Painters, sculptors, artisans, and bric-a-brac dealers have restored dwellings for themselves and sell their wares to visitors.

Where to Stay & Eat

★ $ ✕ **Nuovo Piccolo Mondo.** This small central trattoria has plenty of homey charm, found in such details as the old wooden chairs dating from the 1920s, when the place opened. Family-run, it has a faithful clientele, so get there early to grab a table and order Ligurian specialties such as *sciancui* (a roughly cut flat pasta with a mixture of beans, tomatoes, zucchini, and pesto) and *polpo e patate* (stewed octopus with potatoes). ✉ *Via Piave 7* ☎ *0184/509012* 🗏 *No credit cards* ⊘ *Closed Sun.–Mon. and July.*

$$$$ 🏨 **Royal.** It's a toss-up whether this deluxe hotel or the Splendido in Portofino is the most luxurious in Liguria. Only a few paces from the casino and the train station, the Royal is definitely part of San Remo (unlike the Splendido, which is set above Portofino). Rooms here have a mixture of modern amenities and antique furnishings. The heated sea-water swimming pool, open April–September, is in a subtropical garden. On the terrace, candlelight dining and music get under way each night under the stars in season. Keep your eyes open for spectacular off-season discounts. ✉ *Corso Imperatrice 80, 18038* ☎ *0184/5391* 🖷 *0184/661445* ⊕ *www.royalhotelsanremo.com* ➪ *121 rooms, 17 suites* ⚿ *Restaurant, miniature golf, tennis court, saltwater pool, bar, playground* 🗏 *AE, DC, MC, V* ⊘ *Closed Oct. 8–Dec. 20* ◯⦿ *MAP.*

$$ 🏨 **Paradiso.** This small central hotel is adjacent to a lush public park. A quiet palm-fringed garden gives it an air of seclusion, a plus in this sometimes hectic city. Rooms are modern and bright; many have little terraces, and some are reserved for nonsmokers. The hotel restaurant has a good fixed-price menu. ✉ *Via Roccasterone 12, 18038* ☎ *0184/ 571211* 🖷 *0184/578176* ⊕ *www.paradisohotel.it* ➪ *41 rooms* ⚿ *Restaurant, pool, bar, Internet, no-smoking rooms* 🗏 *AE, DC, MC, V.*

Bordighera

㊼ *12 km (7 mi) west of San Remo, 155 km (96 mi) southwest of Genoa.*

Bordighera, on a large, lush promontory, wears its genteel past as a famous winter resort with unstudied ease. A large English colony, attracted by the mild climate, settled here in the second half of the 19th century and is still very much in evidence today; you'll regularly find people taking afternoon tea in the cafés. This garden spot was the first town in Europe to grow date palms, and its citizens still have the exclusive right to provide the Vatican with palm fronds for Easter celebrations. Walk along the **Lungomare Argentina,** a magnificent seafront promenade, 1½ km (1 mi) long, beginning at the western end of the town, for a good view westward to the French Côte d'Azur. Thanks partly to its many year-round English residents, Bordighera does not close down entirely in the off-season like some Riviera resorts but rather serves as a quiet winter haven for elderly people. With plenty of fine hotels and restaurants, Bordighera makes a good base for beachgoing and excursions and is quieter and less commercial than San Remo.

Where to Stay & Eat

$$$–$$$$ ✕ **La Reserve Restaurant.** This traditional informal trattoria, part of the Hotel Parigi a bit out of town toward San Remo, has access to the beach and excellent views of the sea from the dining room. There are even changing rooms for anyone who wants a post-lunch dip. Concentrate on the seafood here: specialties are seafood ravioli *al finocchio selvatico* (with wild fennel) and assorted grilled fish. Reservations are recommended. ✉ *Via Arziglia 20* ☎ *0184/261322* 🗏 *AE, DC, MC, V* ⊘ *Closed Mon., and mid-Nov.–mid-Dec. No dinner Wed.*

$$ ✕ **Le Chaudron.** The charming rustic interior, with ancient Roman arches, has the look of restaurants across the French border in Provence. Ligurian specialties are featured on the predominantly seafood menu of this centrally located restaurant: try the cheese *pansoti con salsa di noci* (ravioli with walnut sauce) and *branzino* (sea bass) with artichokes or mushrooms. A café annex serves a daily lunch special. ⊠ *Piazza Bengasi 2* ☎*0184/263592* ⚑ *Reservations essential* ▭*DC, MC, V* ☉ *Closed Mon., 1st 2 wks in Feb., and 1st 2 wks in July.*

$–$$ ✕ **Piemontese.** Only a block from the seaside and five minutes from the train station, this simple restaurant melds Ligurian cooking and seafood with the cuisine of the neighboring Piedmont region, including *risotto al Barolo* (rice cooked with Barolo wine, sausage, and porcini mushrooms) and the winter specialty *bagna cauda* (raw vegetables with a garlic, oil, and anchovy sauce). ⊠ *Via Roseto 8, off Via Vittorio Veneto* ☎*0184/261651* ▭*AE, MC, V* ☉ *Closed Tues. and mid-Nov.–mid-Dec.*

$$$$ ▥ **Grand Hotel del Mare.** Atop a steep hill rising from the beach, this tasteful hotel lives up to its name, with impeccable service and facilities. The large rooms have panoramic views of the coastline; ask for one facing the water. One floor is filled with antiques. ⊠ *Via Portico della Punta 34, 18012* ☎*0184/262201* ⊜*0184/262394* ⊕*www.grandhoteldelmare. it* ⇝ *75 rooms, 25 suites* ♻ *Restaurant, tennis court, saltwater pool, gym, hair salon, sauna, spa, Turkish bath, beach, piano bar, Internet, some pets allowed (fee)* ▭*AE, DC, MC, V* ☉ *Closed Oct. 12–Dec. 23.*

$$ ▥ **Grand Hotel Capo Ampelio.** This converted villa overlooks the town and the coastline. Traditional architectural details in the reception rooms and staircases are paired with modern features in the rooms, all of which have balconies. The hotel is somewhat outside the town center, so the rooms are quiet. ⊠ *Via Virgilio 5, 18012* ☎ *0184/264333* ⊜ *0184/264244* ⇝ *104 rooms* ♻ *Restaurant, pool, gym, massage, bar, recreation room* ▭*DC, MC, V* ☉ *Closed Nov.–Dec. 22.*

¢ ▥ **Pensione Miki.** Tucked away on a quiet residential street, this small family-run pension offers simply furnished rooms, each with a tiny bathroom and balcony. Full- and half-pension plans are offered, which, because the food is good and the price is right, are worth considering. ⊠ *Via Lagazzi, 18012* ☎ *0184/261844* ⇝ *8 rooms* ♻ *Restaurant, bar; no a/c* ▭ *MC, V.*

Ventimiglia

48 *5 km (3 mi) west of Bordighera, 159 km (98 mi) southwest of Genoa.*

From its past life as a pre-Roman settlement known as Albintimilium, Ventimiglia possesses some important archaeological remains, including a 2nd-century AD amphitheater. A vital trade center for hundreds of years, it declined in prestige as Genoa grew and is now little more than a frontier town that lives on tourism and the cultivation of flowers. (On Friday the large flower market, open to the trade only, creates traffic gridlock; it's best to avoid the town on that day.) Ventimiglia is divided in two by the Roia River. The **Città Vecchia** is a well-preserved medieval old town on the western bank. The 11th-century **Duomo** has a Gothic portal dating from 1222. Walking up Via del Capo, you'll reach the **ancient walls,** which offer fine views of the coast.

off the
beaten
path

DOLCEACQUA – From Ventimiglia, a provincial road swings up the Nervi River valley to this lovely-sounding medieval town (its name translates as Sweetwater) with its ruined castle. Liguria's best-known red wine is the local Rossese di Dolceacqua. Beyond is **Pigna,** another medieval village built in concentric circles on a hilltop.

Where to Stay

$$ **La Riserva.** Just 5 km (3 mi) west of Ventimiglia, but more than 1,100
Fodor'sChoice   ft above sea level, is the village of Castel d'Appio, where you'll find
★   this innlike establishment. Rooms are bright, airy, and simply deco-
rated with contemporary furnishings. The staff is very helpful, pro-
viding, for example, regular lifts into town if you have no car. In
addition to its excellent restaurant, La Riserva offers numerous activities
and a lovely terrace for drinks, sunbathing, or candlelight dinners. Full-
board rates are a good deal. ⊠ *Via Peidago 79, 18039 Castel d'Ap-
pio* ☎ *0184/229533* 🖷 *0184/229712* ⊕ *www.lariserva.it* ⇆ *21
rooms* ⚭ *Restaurant, pool, bicycles, bar* ⊟ *AE, DC, MC, V* ⊘ *Closed
Nov.–Mar.*

Giardini Botanici Hanbury

★ ㊾   *6 km (4 mi) west of Ventimiglia, 165 km (102 mi) southwest of Genoa.*

Mortola Inferiore, only 2 km (1 mi) from the French border, is the site
of the world-famous Giardini Hanbury (Hanbury Gardens), one of the
largest botanical gardens in Italy. Planned and planted in 1867 by a wealthy
English merchant, Sir Thomas Hanbury, and his botanist brother Daniel,
the terraced gardens contain species from five continents, including
many palms and succulents (plants of the cactus group). There are
panoramic views of the sea from the gardens, which descend to the beach.
⊠ *Giardini Hanbury, Loc. Mortola, Ventimiglia* ☎ *0184/229507* 🖷 €6
⊘ *Mar.–June 15, daily 9:30–6; June 16–Sept. 15, daily 9:30–7;
Sept.16–last Sat. in Oct., daily 9:30–6; last Sun. in Oct.–Feb., Tues.–Sun.
10–5. Ticket office closes 1 hr before garden.*

> **off the
> beaten
> path**

BALZI ROSSI – At the French border, 7 km (4½ mi) from Ventimiglia
and 2 km (1 mi) from the Giardino Hanbury, are the Balzi Rossi (Red
Rocks), caves carved in the sheer rock in which prehistoric humans
left traces of their lives and magic rites. You can visit the caves and a
small museum displaying some of the objects found there. ⊠ *Via
Balzi Rosso 9* ☎ *0184/38113* 🖷 €2 ⊘ *Tues.–Sun. 8:30–5:30.*

THE ITALIAN RIVIERA A TO Z

*To research prices, get advice from other travelers, and book travel ar-
rangements, visit www.fodors.com.*

AIR TRAVEL

CARRIERS   There is daily service between Genoa and Zurich (on Crossair), Lon-
don (on British Airways), Paris (on Air France), Munich (on Air Dolomiti),
and Milan and Rome (on Alitalia).

🎝 Airlines & Contacts **Air Dolomiti** ☎ 800/013366. **Air France** ☎ 848/884466. **Ali-
talia** ☎ 848/865641. **British Airways** ☎ 848/812266. **Crossair** ☎ 848/849570.

AIRPORTS

Aeroporto Internazionale Cristoforo Colombo is only 6 km (4 mi) from
the center of Genoa. The nearest airports for direct U.S. flights are
Nice, in France, about 2½ hours west of Genoa (and an easy bus con-
nection from Genoa), and Milan's Linate and Malpensa, about two hours
northeast.

🎝 Airport Information **Aeroporto Internazionale Cristoforo Colombo** ⊠ Sestri Po-
nente ☎ 010/60151.

Volabus services from Cristoforo Colombo Airport connect with Genoa's Stazione Brignole, stopping also at Piazza Acquaverde (Stazione Principe). Tickets cost €2.10 and may be purchased on the bus.

Taxis & Shuttles **Volabus** ☎ 010/5582414.

BOAT & FERRY TRAVEL

Genoa is Italy's largest port and can be reached from the United States as well as other parts of Liguria and Italy (Sardinia, La Spezia, and Savona). Ships berth in the heart of Genoa, including cruise ships of the Genoa-based Costa Cruise Line. Ferries to various ports around the Mediterranean are operated by Tirrenia Navigazione, whose most popular destination is Sardinia (a 13-hour trip), and Grimaldi Lines, which sends cruise ship–like overnight ferries to Barcelona (an 18-hour trip) and Palermo, Sicily (a 20-hour trip). Popular with Genovese escapists, Corsica Ferries runs car ferries from Savona to Bastia and Ile-Rousse in Corsica.

Boat or ferry travel is the most pleasant—and sometimes only—way to get from place to place within Liguria. A busy network of local services connects many of the resorts. For general information about availability of services, contact Servizio Marittimo del Tigullio. Another source is Alimar, or contact Golfo Paradiso, which runs between Camogli, San Fruttuoso (on the Portofino promontory), and Recco. In summer there's also daily service from the port of Genoa and Nervi to Portofino, Cinque Terre, and Portovenere, stopping in Recco and Camogli. Navigazione Golfo dei Poeti runs frequent ferry-shuttle services between Portofino, Portovenere, and Cinque Terre. Cooperativa Battellieri del Porto di Genova runs a tour-boat service in Genoa's old port.

Boat & Ferry Information **Alimar** ✉ Calata Zingari, Genoa ☎ 010/256775. **Cooperativa Battellieri del Porto di Genova** ✉ Stazione Marittima, Ponte dei Mille, Genoa ☎ 010/265712 ⊕ www.battellierigenova.it. **Corsica Ferries** ☎ 019/215511 ⊕ www.corsicaferries.com. **Costa Cruise Line** ✉ Via Gabriele D'Annunzio 2 ☎ 010/54831. **Golfo Paradiso** ✉ Via Scalo 3, Camogli ☎ 0185/772091 ⊕ www.golfoparadiso.it. **Grimaldi Lines** ✉ Stazione Marittima ☎ 010/589331. **Navigazione Golfo dei Poeti** ✉ Viale Mazzini 21, La Spezia ☎ 0187/732987 ⊕ www.navigazionegolfodeipoeti.it. **Servizio Marittimo del Tigullio** ✉ Via Palestro 8/1b, Santa Margherita Ligure ☎ 0185/284670 ⊕ www.traghettiportofino.it. **Tirrenia Navigazione** ✉ Stazione Marittima ☎ 010/2758041 ⊕ www.tirrenia.it.

BUS TRAVEL

The main bus station in Genoa is at Piazza Principe. Local buses, operated by the municipal transport company, AMT, serve the steep valleys that run to some of the towns along the western coast. Tickets may be bought at local bus stations, or at newsstands for local buses. Buy your ticket before you board the bus. AMT also operates the funicular railways and the elevators that service the steeper sections of the city. Tigullio Trasporti provides connections along the Levante coast. Diana Tours operates a bus service between Genoa and the Nice airport in France, but no regular bus service connects Genoa with the towns along the Ponente coast itself.

Bus Information **AMT** ✉ Piazza Acquaverde, Genoa ☎ 010/5582414 ⊕ www.amt.genova.it. **Diana Tours** ✉ Via G Ardoino 151, Diano Marina ☎ 800/651931. **Tigullio Trasporti** ✉ Chiavari ☎ 0185/373233 ✉ Rapallo ☎ 0185/231108 ✉ Santa Margherita Ligure ☎ 0185/288834 ✉ Sestri Levante ☎ 0185/480655.

CAR RENTAL

Local Agencies **Avis** ✉ Via delle Casacce 3, Piazza Acquaverde, Genoa ☎ 010/540906 ✉ Aeroporto Internazionale Cristoforo Colombo, Genoa ☎ 010/6507280 ✉ Via Fratelli Rosselli 74/76, La Spezia ☎ 0187/770270 ✉ Corso Imperatrice 96, San Remo ☎ 0184/

532462; 199/100133 for national inquiries. **Budget** ✉ Aeroporto Internazionale Cristoforo Colombo, Genoa ☎010/6512467. **Hertz** ✉Via Casaregis 76/78, Genoa ☎010/5702625 ✉ Aeroporto Internazionale Cristoforo Colombo, Genoa ☎ 010/6512422 ✉ Via San Bartolomeo 392, La Spezia ☎ 0187/512140 ✉ Via XX Settembre 17, San Remo ☎ 0184/500470.

CAR TRAVEL

Autostrada A12 southeast from Genoa links up with the autostrada network for all northern and southern destinations; Rome is a six-hour drive from Genoa. The 150-km (93-mi) trip north to Milan on A7 takes two hours. Nice is 2½ hours of tunnels west on A10.

Two good roads run parallel to each other along the coast of Liguria. Closer to shore and passing through all the towns and villages is the Via Aurelia, S1, which has excellent views at almost every turn but gets crowded in July and August. More direct and higher up than S1 is the autostrada, A10 west of Genoa and A12 to the east. This route saves a lot of time on weekends, in summer, and on days when festivals slow traffic in some resorts to a standstill. Any time of year, do your best to avoid driving in the center of Genoa.

EMERGENCY
SERVICES
If you break down on the highway, walk along the side of the road until you come to a green emergency telephone. The emergency highway road service will come to your rescue and tow you to the nearest service station—for a hefty fee. On a smaller road, unless you have a cell phone, you'd be better off walking to the nearest town or gas station (usually not too far) and calling ACI Emergency Service (a free call) from any pay phone. In order to describe where you are, be prepared to seek out the help of locals. (*Dove siamo?*—Where are we?)
🚗 **ACI** ☎ 803/116.

EMBASSIES & CONSULATES

🚗 United Kingdom **British Consulate** ✉ Piazza della Vittoria 15/16, 16121 Genoa ☎ 010/416828 🖨 010/416958 ⏰ Mon.-Thurs. 9:30–12:30.

EMERGENCIES

Europa and Ghersi are two late-night pharmacies in Genoa.
🚗**Ambulance** ☎118. **Europa** ✉ Corso Europa 676, Genoa ☎ 010/380239. **Police** ☎112. **Ghersi** ✉ Corso Buenos Aires 18/r, Genoa ☎ 010/541661. **Ospedale Generale Regionale San Martino** ✉Largo Rosanna Benzi 10, Genoa ☎010/5551. **General emergencies** ☎113.

MAIL & SHIPPING

🚗 Post Offices **Genoa** ✉ Via Dante 4A/B, 16121 ☎ 010/5705913. **La Spezia** ✉ Piazza Verdi, 19121 ☎ 0187/735191. **San Remo** ✉ Via Roma 156, 18038 ☎ 0184/523277.

TOURS

BOAT TOURS
Informal harbor cruises or excursion cruises between coastal towns are scheduled and operated by the main ferry lines, but you can have as much fun—if not more—negotiating a price with a boat owner at one of the smaller ports. You're likely to get a boat operator with a rudimentary command of English at best. You can also take a boat tour of Genoa harbor. The tour, which starts from the aquarium pier, costs €6, lasts about an hour, and includes a visit to the breakwater outside the harbor, the Bacino delle Grazie, and the Molo Vecchio (Old Port). For information, contact the Cooperativa Battellieri.
🚗 Fees & Schedules **Cooperativa Battellieri** ✉ Stazione Marittima, Ponte dei Mille, Genoa ☎ 010/265712 ⊕ www.battellierigenova.it.

BUS TOURS
A bus tour of Genoa with an English-speaking guide is a good way to see the city and its panoramic upper reaches. A coach leaves every af-

244 < The Italian Riviera

ternoon at 3 from Piazza Caricamento, by the port, and does the "Giro Giro Tour," a two-hour narrated loop of the city, operated by Genoa's municipal transport company in conjunction with the agency Macrame Viaggi. The cost is €12.90. Call first to check times.

🖅 Fees & Schedules **Macrame Viaggi** ☎ 010/5959779.

TRAIN TRAVEL

Frequent and fast train service connects Liguria with the rest of Italy. Genoa is 1½ hours from Milan and 5½–6 hours from Rome (4½ with the Eurostar). Many services from France (in particular, the French Riviera) pass along the Ligurian Coast on the way to all parts of Italy. Regular service, connecting all parts of Liguria, operates from Genoa's two stations, Stazione Principe and Stazione Brignole. All the coastal resorts are on this line, and many international trains stop along the coast west of Genoa on their way between Paris and Milan or Rome.

🖅 Train Information **Stazione Brignole** points east ✉ Piazza Giuseppe Verdi ☎ 848/888088 ⊕ www.trenitalia.it. **Stazione Principe** points west ✉ Piazza Principe ☎ 848/888088.

VISITOR INFORMATION

🖅 Tourist Information **Genoa** ✉ Palazzina Santa Maria, Old Port ☎ 010/248711 ⊕ www.apt.genova.it ✉ Stazione Principe ☎ 010/2462633 ✉ Aeroporto Internazionale Cristoforo Colombo ☎ 010/6015247 ✉ Via Roma 11 ☎ 010/576791 ✉ Terminale Crociere, Ponte dei Mille ☎ 010/6015247 ⊙ May–Sept. for the arrival of major ferries. **Alassio** ✉ Viale Mazzini 62, 17021 ☎ 0182/647027 ⊕ www.inforiviera.it. **Albenga** ✉ Viale Martiri della Libertà 1, 17031 ☎ 0182/558444 ⊕ www.inforiviera.it. **Bordighera** ✉ Via Roberto 1, 18012 ☎ 0184/262322 ⊕ www.rivieradeifiori.org. **Camogli** ✉ Via XX Settembre 33, 16032 ☎ 0185/771066. **Imperia** ✉ Viale Matteotti 37, 18100 ☎ 0183/660140 ⊕ www.rivieradeifiori.org. **La Spezia** ✉ Via Mazzini 45, 19100 ☎ 0187/770900 ⊕ www.aptcinqueterre.sp.it. **Lerici** ✉ Via Biaggini 6, 19032 ☎ 0187/967346 ⊕ www.aptcinqueterre.sp.it. **Levanto** ✉ Piazza Cavour 12, 19015 ☎ 0187/808125 ⊕ www.aptcinqueterre.sp.it. **Monterosso** ✉ Via Fegina 38, 19016 ☎ 0187/817506 ⊕ www.aptcinqueterre.sp.it. **Portofino** ✉ Via Roma 35, 16034 ☎ 0185/269024 ⊕ www.apttigullio.liguria.it. **Rapallo** ✉ Lungomare V. Veneto 7, 16035 ☎ 0185/230346 ⊕ www.apttigullio.liguria.it. **Riomaggiore** ✉ Stazione Ferroviaria, 19017 ☎ 0187/920633 ⊕ www.aptcinqueterre.sp.it **San Remo** ✉ Palazzo Riviera, Largo Nuvoloni 1, 18038 ☎ 0184/571571 ⊕ www.rivieradeifiori.org. **Santa Margherita Ligure** ✉ Via XXV Aprile 28, 16038 ☎ 0185/2929 ⊕ www.apttigullio.liguria.it. **Varazze** ✉ Viale Nazioni Unite, 17019 ☎ 019/935043 ⊕ www.inforiviera.it. **Ventimiglia** ✉ Via Cavour 61, 18039 ☎ 0184/351183 ⊕ www.rivieradeifiori.org.

EMILIA-ROMAGNA

PARMA, BOLOGNA, FERRARA, RAVENNA, RIMINI

FODOR'S CHOICE

Hotel Ripagrande, Ferrara

Mausoleo di Galla Placidia, Ravenna

Piazza del Duomo, Parma

San Domenico, restaurant, Imola

Santo Stefano, Bologna

HIGHLY RECOMMENDED

RESTAURANTS   Antica Osteria del Teatro, Piacenza

Borso d'Este, Modena

Da Cesari, Bologna

Dallo Zio, Rimini

Enoteca Antica Osteria Fontana, Parma

La Frasca, Castrocaro Terme

La Locanda di San Martino, Rimini

Osteria Al Brindisi, Ferrara

Parma Rotta, Parma

Tamburini, Bologna

Trattoria La Romantica, Ferrara

Victoria, Bologna

HOTELS   Corona d'Oro 1890, Bologna

Grand Hotel, Rimini

Grand Hotel Baglioni, Bologna

SIGHTS   Ferrara

Piazza Maggiore, Bologna

Le Due Torri, Bologna

Galleria Nazionale, Parma

Tempio Malatestiano, Rimini

Updated by
Robin S.
Goldstein

GOURMETS THE WORLD OVER claim that Emilia-Romagna's greatest contribution to humankind has been gastronomic. Birthplace of fettuccine, tortellini, lasagna, prosciutto, and Parmesan cheese, the region has a spectacular culinary tradition. But there are also many cultural riches in the flat, fertile Po plain and its surroundings: Parma's Correggio paintings, Verdi's villa at Sant'Agata, the medieval splendor of Bologna's palazzi and Ferrara's alleyways, and the Byzantine beauty of mosaic-rich Ravenna—glittering as brightly today as it did 1,500 years ago.

Emilia-Romagna owes its beginnings to a road. In 187 BC the Romans laid out the Via Aemelia, a long highway running straight northwest from the Adriatic port of Rimini to the central garrison town of Piacenza, and it was along this central spine that the primary towns of the region developed. Two millennia later, the old Roman road (SS9) is still called Via Emilia, and the autostrada (A1 and A14) runs parallel to it.

Despite the unifying factor of the Via Emilia, the region has had a fragmented history. Its eastern portion, roughly the area from Faenza to the coast, known as Romagna, has looked first to the Byzantine east and then to Rome for art, political power, and, some say, national character. The western portion, Emilia, from Bologna to Piacenza, had a more northern, rather dour sense of self-government and dissent. Italians say that in Romagna a stranger will be offered a glass of wine; in Emilia, a glass of water—if anything at all.

The principal city of the region is Bologna, a busy cultural and culinary capital less trodden but just as exciting to visit as Italy's more famous tourist destinations. It was founded by the Etruscans but eventually came under the influence of the Roman Empire. The Romans established a garrison there, renaming the old Etruscan settlement Bononia, the Bologna of today. It was after the fall of Rome that the region began its fragmentation. Romagna, centered in Ravenna, was ruled from Constantinople. Ravenna eventually became capital of the empire in the West in the 5th century, passing to papal rule in the 8th century. Even today, however, the city is still filled with reminders of two centuries of Byzantine rule.

The other cities of the region, from the Middle Ages on, became the fiefs of important noble families—the Este in Ferrara and Modena, the Pallavicini in Piacenza, the Bentivoglio in Bologna, and the Malatesta in Rimini. Today all these cities bear the marks of their noble patrons. When in the 16th century the papacy managed to exert its power over the entire region, some of these cities were divided among the families of the reigning popes—hence the stamp of the Farnese family on Parma, Piacenza, and Ferrara.

In the years since, Bologna and Emilia-Romagna have established a robust tradition of rebellion and dissent. The Italian socialist movement was born in the region, as was Benito Mussolini (although in keeping with the political atmosphere of his home state he was a firebrand socialist during the early part of his career). Despite being the birthplace of Il Duce, Emilia-Romagna did not take to fascism: it was in this region that the antifascist resistance was born, and during World War II the region suffered terribly at the hands of the Fascists and the Nazis.

Despite a long history of bloodletting, turmoil, and rebellion, the arts—both decorative and culinary—have always flourished in Emilia-Romagna. The great families financed painters, sculptors, and writers (Dante found a haven in Ravenna after being expelled from his native Florence). In modern times, Emilia-Romagna has given to the arts such famous sons as painter Giorgio Morandi, writer Giorgio Bassani (author of *The*

Numbers in the text correspond to numbers in the margin and on the Emilia-Romagna and Bologna maps.

If you have 3 days

Given three days, you should set aside two nights to see 🗺 **Bologna** ⑤–⑭ 🏴 and its environs. The city itself has enough to fill much more than this, but while you are there, make a point of seeing the sights in and around Piazza Maggiore, including **Santo Stefano** ⑩, the **Basilica di San Petronio** ⑤, **Palazzo Comunale** ⑥, and the two towers nearby, and sample the city's legendary cuisine. Where you spend your third day will depend on your route out of Emilia-Romagna. If you're going to Milan or Turin, make a stop about 100 km (62 mi) northwest of Bologna at 🗺 **Parma** ③, where you could cover the major sights in two or three hours. If you're heading toward the Adriatic coast, the calm unspoiled Renaissance city of 🗺 **Ferrara** ⑮ should be your priority stop.

If you have 5 days

Start out in 🗺 **Ravenna** ⑱ 🏴, being sure to see Sant'Apollinare in Classe, outside the city proper but well worth the excursion. (Make a detour to 🗺 **Rimini** ⑲, or begin your trip there, only if it's summer and you're looking for a hard-core resort and disco scene.) On your way to Bologna on day two, drop in on a factory in the ceramic center of **Faenza** ⑰, famed for its *faience* pottery. Stay two nights in 🗺 **Bologna** ⑤–⑭, savoring meals and taking in the sights. From there, take an overnight trip to 🗺 **Ferrara** ⑮, enjoying an amble around its turreted and towered medieval streets. Spend the last night sampling the fine food and wine in 🗺 **Parma** ③, stopping in **Modena** ④, another culinary capital, along the way. Northwest of Parma, make a slight detour from the autostrada or Via Emilia to see the cluster of places associated with the composer Verdi, centered in the village of **Busseto** ②. Still heading northwest, spend your last morning or afternoon in **Piacenza** ①, an elegant and harmonious town in the typical fashion of Emilia-Romagna and a fitting exit or entrance to the region. From here, it's 66 km (41 mi) to Milan.

Garden of the Finzi-Continis), filmmakers Michelangelo Antonioni and Federico Fellini, and tenor Luciano Pavarotti.

Nowadays, the sprawling plants of the industrial food giants of Italy, such as Barilla, Parmalat, and Fini, stand side by side with the fading villas and deteriorating farmhouses that have long punctuated the flat, fertile land of the Po plain. Each fall, the region's trademark low-lying fog rolls in off of the Adriatic and hangs over those Romagnan flatlands for the winter, coloring cities and countryside alike with a spooky, gray glow. As Antonioni once mused: "On the plain in late September, evening comes quickly. The day ends when headlights are turned on unexpectedly. The sunset is not soft, it is mysterious. It is so hard to see what is before my eyes."

Bologna is acknowledged as the leading city of Italian cuisine, and the rest of the region follows—eating is a seminal part of any Emilia-Romagnan experience. The area's history is replete with culinary legends, such as how the original tortellino was modeled on the shape of Venus's navel and the original *tagliolini* (long, thin egg pasta) were served at the wedding banquet of Annibale Bentivoglio and Lucrezia d'Este. Bologna's centuries-old

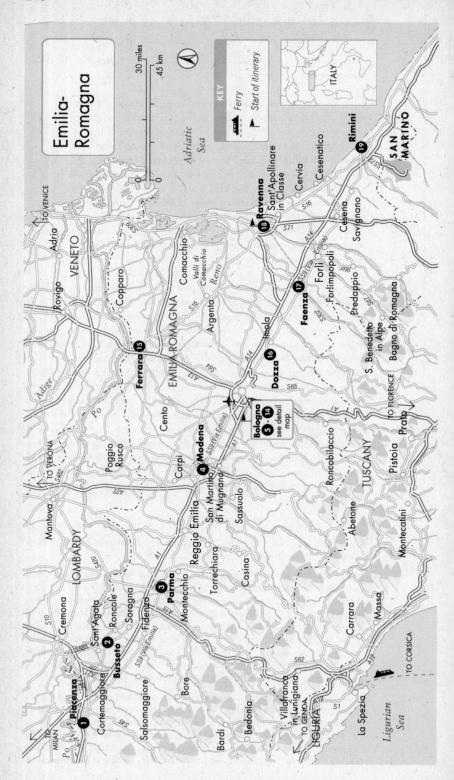

Emilia-Romagna

KEY

--- Ferry

▲ Start of itinerary

ITALY

30 miles

45 km

Adriatic Sea

TO VENICE

VENETO

Adria

Rovigo

S495

Copparo

Comacchio

Valli di
Comacchio

Reno

Ravenna ▲ 18

Sant'Apollinare
in Classe

Cervia

Cesenatico

S16

Rimini 19

SAN
MARINO

Cesena

Savignano

S71

A14

Argenta

Ferrara 15

EMILIA-ROMAGNA

S16

S64

Faenza 17

S9 (Via Emilia)

Forlì

Forlimpopoli

Predappio

S67

S302

S. Benedetto
in Alpe

Bagno di Romagna

Po

Cento

A13

Imola

Dozza 16

S65

A14

TO FLORENCE

S255

TO VERONA

S62

Adige

Poggio
Rusco

Carpi

Modena 4

S9 (Via Emilia)

Bologna

5 · 14

see detail
map

A1

A22

Roncobilaccio

TO FLORENCE

TUSCANY

Prato

Pistoia

Mantova

LOMBARDY

Reggio Emilia

San Martino
di Mugnano

Sassuolo

Casina

Abetone

Montecatini

S10

Cremona

S420

Sant'Agata

Roncole

Soragna

Busseto 2

Fidenza

S9 (Via Emilia)

A15

Montecchio

Parma 3

Torrechiara

Carrara

Massa

S62

Piacenza 1

Cortemaggiore

Salsomaggiore

S45

Bore

Bardi

Bedonia

Villafranca
in Lunigiana

TO GENOA

LIGURIA

La Spezia

S1

TO CORSICA

Ligurian
Sea

A12

TO MILAN

Po

A21

S462

TO VENICE

nickname "the Fat" is anything but pejorative. It's almost impossible to eat badly in Emilia-Romagna, and everything is worth trying—Parma's famed prosciutto and Parmigiano Reggiano cheese, Modena's balsamic vinegar, and the best pasta in the world.

Exploring Emilia-Romagna

Emilia-Romagna has a geographical logic—the Via Emilia (SS9) and its parallel big brother, the Autostrada del Sole (highway A1), bisect through the Po Valley and Romagna plain, making it easy to cover most of the major destinations in the region in order by driving straight through. Alternatively, you could base yourself in the regional capital, Bologna, and make forays from this hub. From Bologna there are three choices of itineraries: head north on A13 to Ferrara and then southeast on S16 to Ravenna, or continue east or west along the Via Emilia (SS9), stopping for short visits at some of the smaller towns en route northwest to Piacenza or southeast to Rimini and the sea.

About the Restaurants & Hotels

Meals here are not light—in Emilia-Romagna, eating light might means leaving half of your tortellini *con noci e panna* (with walnuts and cream) on your plate. Ravioli stuffed with spinach and ricotta cheese, *tortelli* (triangular pasta dumplings) stuffed with squash, and tortellini stuffed with minced pork and beef all have in common one key word—and you'll inevitably be stuffed, too.

Emilia-Romagna has a reputation for an efficiency uncommon in most of the rest of Italy. Even the smallest hotels are well run, with high standards of quality and service. Bologna is very much a businessperson's city, and most hotels there cater to the business traveler, but there are smaller, more intimate hotels as well. Though prices are high, you can expect an experience delightfully free of the condescending attitude and manipulative pricing schemes that sometimes mar Italy's tourist meccas. The one exception to the rule is Rimini, whose business is tourism. Its numerous hotels, unlike those in the rest of Emilia-Romagna, offer tourist-oriented full- and half-board packages. They overflow during July and August but are closed for much of the off-season.

WHAT IT COSTS In euros					
	$$$$	$$$	$$	$	¢
RESTAURANTS	over €22	€17–€22	€12–€17	€7–€12	under €7
HOTELS	over €210	€160–€210	€110–€160	€60–€110	under €60

Restaurant prices are for a second course (secondo piatto). Hotel prices are for two people in a standard double room in high season, including tax and service.

Timing

You would never visit Emilia-Romagna for the weather. In this predominantly flat landscape, the winters are gray and cold, and summers are airless and hot, though sea breezes on the coast offer some respite. If you are here in summer, get up early and do as much as you can in the morning. Ideally, midafternoons in summer should be left unplanned; the hours after five are best for sightseeing and traveling. In winter make sure you are equipped for the frequent rain and damp, penetrating cold. Dense low-lying fog is common throughout the plains in fall and winter and can be starkly beautiful, but it can also be very hazardous on the road. No matter what the season, make sure you reserve ahead for rooms: the cities are often filled with commercial conventions and business conferences. Restaurants and hotels in Rimini are usually closed

ON THE MENU

EMILIA-ROMAGNA'S REPUTATION *as Italy's gourmet haven is well deserved, and maintaining that reputation spurs the region's chefs* on to even greater heights of gastronomic achievement. For you, this means an obligation to eat lots and eat well: a trip through Emilia-Romagna wouldn't be complete without sampling what the region does best.

The specialties are nothing new in name, they're just better here, where they were born—for example, Parma's crumbly Parmigiano Reggiano cheese (not just grated, but also often served by itself as an appetizer or dessert, perhaps drizzled with balsamic vinegar) and world-famous Parma ham. Note that in Parma, as elsewhere in Italy, the product that Americans call prosciutto—raw, cured ham—is called prosciutto crudo (crudo for short), and just plain prosciutto (also called prosciutto cotto or simply cotto) is cooked ham, closer to (but much better than) what Americans would put in a ham sandwich. Look for prosciutto crudo di Parma, the real thing, and its even more prized cousin, culatello. Bologna's pasta (especially tagliatelle) al ragù, a heavenly, slow-cooked mix of onions, carrots, minced pork and beef, and fresh tomatoes, in no way resembles the "Bolognese" sauce served worldwide; likewise the rich, soft, garlicky mortadella that has been reincarnated elsewhere to its detriment as "baloney."

In the smaller trattorie and osterie you might simply be asked whether you'd like your pasta secca (dry, meaning with ragù or butter sauce) or in brodo (in beef or chicken broth, a popular and delectable way of serving tortellini and other stuffed pasta). But look also for the local specialties; although most are served throughout the region, traditionalists will have their zampone (pig's feet stuffed with minced meat) and aceto balsamico (balsamic vinegar) in Modena; their risotto in padella (with fresh herbs and tomatoes) in Piacenza; their brodetto (tangy seafood stew) in Rimini; their ancient Roman piadine (chewy, flat griddle bread) in Romagna; their cappellacci di zucca (squash dumplings) in Ferrara; and everything else in Bologna.

Emilia-Romagna's wines, fittingly, are meant to accompany the region's fine food rather than vie with it for accolades. The best known is Lambrusco, a sparkling red produced on the Po plain that has some admirers and many detractors. It's praised for its tartness and condemned for the same quality. The region's best wines include Sangiovese di Romagna, which can be similar to Chianti, from the Romagnolan hills, and Barbera, from the Colli Piacetini and Apennine foothills. Castelluccio, Bonzara, Zerbina, Leone Conti, and Tre Monti are among the region's top producers—keep your eyes out for their bottles.

up tight during the off-season, but the rest of Emilia-Romagna offers tourists as much during the winter season as in summer.

EMILIA

The Via Emilia runs through Emilia's heart in a straight shot from medieval Piacenza to thoroughly modern Modena. On the way from the past to the present you'll encounter many of Italy's cultural riches—from the culinary and artistic treasures of Parma to the birthplace and home of Giuseppe Verdi. It may be tempting to imitate Modena's Ferraris and zoom over the short (113-km [70-mi]) stretch of highway spanning the region, but if you take time to detour into the countryside, with its decaying farmhouses and 800-year-old abbeys, or stop for a taste of prosciutto, you'll be richly rewarded.

Piacenza

❶ *66 km (41 mi) southeast of Milan, 150 km (94 mi) northwest of Bologna.*

The city of Piacenza has always been associated with industry and commerce. Its position on the Po River has made it an important inland port since the earliest times; the Etruscans, and then the Romans, had thriving settlements on this site. As you approach the city today, you could be forgiven for thinking that it holds little of interest. Piacenza is surrounded by ugly industrial suburbs (with particularly unlovely cement factories and a power station), but forge ahead and you'll discover that they surround a delightfully preserved medieval downtown.

The heart of the city is **Piazza dei Cavalli,** dominated by the massive 13th-century **Palazzo del Comune.** This severely Gothic turreted and crenellated building was the seat of town government before Piacenza fell under the iron fists of the ruling Pallavicini and Farnese families. The flamboyant equestrian statues from which the piazza takes its name are depictions of members of the last and greatest of the Farnese: on the right is Ranuccio Farnese (1569–1622); on the left is his father, Alessandro (1545–92). Alessandro was a beloved ruler, enlightened and fair; Ranuccio, his successor, was less successful. Both statues are the work of Francesco Mochi, a master sculptor of the baroque period.

Attached like a sinister balcony to the bell tower of Piacenza's 12th-century **Duomo** is a *gabbia* (iron cage), where miscreants were incarcerated naked and subjected to the scorn (and missiles) of the crowd in the marketplace below. Inside the cathedral, a less-evocative but equally impressive medieval stonework decorates the pillars and the crypt, and there are extravagant frescoes by Il Guercino (a.k.a. Giovanni Barbieri, 1591–1666) in the dome of the cupola. The Duomo can be reached by following Via XX Settembre from Piazza dei Cavalli. ✉ *Piazza Duomo* ☎ *0523/335154* ⊘ *Mon.–Sat. 7:30–noon and 4–7, Sun. 7:30–1 and 4–7.*

The **Museo Civico,** the city-owned museum of Piacenzan art and antiquities, is housed in the vast **Palazzo Farnese.** The ruling family originally commissioned a monumental palace, but construction, begun in 1558, was never completed. The highlight of the museum's rather eclectic exhibit is the 2nd century BC Etruscan *Fegato di Piacenza,* a bronze tablet in the shape of a *fegato* (liver), with the symbols of the gods of good and ill fortune marked on it. By comparing this master "liver" with one taken from the body of a freshly slaughtered sacrifice, the priests could predict the future. The collection also contains Botticelli's *Madonna with St. John the Baptist,* and a series of Roman bronzes and mosaics. A collection of carriages, arms, and other paraphernalia owned by the Farnese give life to the history of that powerful family. ✉ *Piazza Cittadella* ☎ *0523/326981* ⊕ *www.farnese.net* ✉ *€5.25* ⊘ *Tues.–Thurs. 9:30–1, Fri.–Sun. 9:30–1 and 3–6; guided tours by reservation Tues.–Thurs. 9:30, Fri. 9:30 and 3:30, weekends 9:30–11 and 3–4.*

Where to Eat

★ **$$$$** ✕ **Antica Osteria del Teatro.** Set on a lovely piazza in the center of town, this restaurant is one of the best in all Emilia-Romagna. It's housed in a typical 15th-century building with coffered ceilings and sober furniture, and it effuses elegance, with excellent service and an impeccable wine list. The menu is quite international; try the terrine of duck liver with Williams pears, red pepper, and a pineapple chutney, or the pigeon with wild mushrooms and greens. ✉ *Via Verdi 16* ☎ *0523/323777* ⚄ *Reservations essential* ▭ *AE, DC, MC, V* ⊘ *Closed Sun.–Mon., Aug. 1–25, and Jan. 1–10.*

$ ✕ **Agnello da Renato.** Central (on the corner of Piazza dei Cavalli), simple, small, and cheap, Agnello is an excellent place to plop down for lunch. Try the tortelli *alla Piacentina* (stuffed with ricotta and spinach and bathed in butter and Parmesan) or the *coniglio alla cacciatore* (rabbit in a tomato and white-wine sauce). ✉ *Via Calzolai 9* ☎ *0523/ 320874* ⊟ *No credit cards* ⊘ *Closed Mon.*

en route

If you are driving from Piacenza, take the S10 northeast toward Cremona, but turn off just a couple of miles out of Piacenza and follow the signs for S587 to the town of Cortemaggiore. From Cortemaggiore, turn right onto a smaller rural road (not numbered) and follow the signs for Busseto, some 10 km (6 mi) away.

Busseto

❷ *30 km (19 mi) southeast of Piacenza, 15 km (9 mi) south of Cremona.*

Busseto's main claim to fame is the 15th-century **Villa Pallavicino,** where master composer Giuseppe Verdi (1813–1901) worked and lived with his mistress (and later wife), Giuseppina Strepponi. The small Verdi museum here displays such relics as the maestro's piano, scores, composition books, and walking sticks. If you plan to visit all the area's Verdi sights, invest in an €8 ticket valid for the Villa Pallavicino, Palazzo Orlandi, Teatro Verdi, and Verdi's birthplace (but not Villa Sant'Agata). Call the **Busseto tourist office** (✉ Comune, Piazza Giuseppe Verdi 10 ☎ 0524/92487) for more information. ✉ *Via Provesi 36* ⊕ *www. bussetolive.com* ☎*0524/92239* ☞*€3* ⊘ *Temporarily closed for restoration; call for current status.*

Palazzo Orlandi, owned for the past century by the Orlandi family, was Verdi's home for a few years beginning in 1845. Only a few of its stately rooms are open to the public; it's a good idea to call ahead to confirm that it's open. ✉ *Via Roma 56* ☎ *0524/92308* ☞ *€2.50* ⊘ *By reservation only, Apr.–Sept., Tues.–Sun. 9–noon and 3–7; Oct.–Nov. and Mar., Tues.–Sun. 9:30–noon and 2:30–5.*

In the center of Busseto is the lovely **Teatro Verdi,** dedicated, as one might expect, to the works of the hamlet's famous son. Once inside the well-preserved, ornate 19th century–style theater, use your imagination to get a feel for where he worked. Call the **Busseto tourist office** (✉ Comune, Piazza Giuseppe Verdi 10 ☎ 0524/92487 ⊕ www.bussetolive. com) for the latest on theater performances. Visits are by reservation only. ✉ *Piazza Verdi 10* ☎ *0524/931732 reservations* ☞ *€4* ⊘ *Mar.–Oct., Tues.–Sun. 10–noon and 3:30–6:30; Nov.–Feb., Tues.–Sun. 10–noon and 3–5.*

off the beaten path

VILLA SANT'AGATA – Four kilometers (2½ mi) north of Busseto, Villa Sant'Agata, also known as Villa Verdi, is the grand country home Verdi built for himself in 1849, where some of his greatest works were composed. For Verdi lovers, Sant'Agata is a veritable shrine. Tours are required, and you have to reserve your place a few days in advance, by phone or on the Web. ✉ *Via Verdi 22, Sant'Agata Villanova sull'Arda, 4 km (2½ mi) north of Busseto on S588 toward Cremona* ☎ *0523/830000* ⊕ *www.villaverdi.org* ☞*€6* ⊘ *Apr.–Sept., Tues.–Sun. 9–11:45 and 3–6:45; Jan. 16–Mar. and Oct.–Dec. 15, Tues.–Sun. 9–11:45 and 2:30–5:30; Dec. 16–Jan. 15, Tues.–Sun. by appointment.*

RONCOLE – Giuseppe Verdi was born in a simple farmhouse on the edge of the town of Roncole, 5 km (3 mi) southeast of Busseto. Equally modest is the church in which he took some early steps in his musical career; he was the church organist here when still in his teens. ⊠ *5 km (3 mi) east of Busseto on local road to Soragna (follow signs)* ☞ *Verdi's birthplace €4* ☉ *Apr.–Sept., Tues.–Sun. 9:30–12:30 and 3–7; Oct.–Mar., Tues.–Sun. 9:30–12:30 and 2:30–5:30.*

Parma

❸ *40 km (25 mi) southeast of Busseto, 97 km (61 mi) northwest of Bologna.*

Dignified, delightful Parma stands on the banks of a tributary of the Po River. Much of the lively historic center has been untouched by modern times, despite heavy damage during World War II. Almost every major European power has had a hand in ruling Parma at one time or another. The Romans founded the city—then little more than a garrison on the Via Aemilia—after which a succession of feudal lords held sway. In the 16th century came the ever-avaricious Farnese family (who are still the dukes of Parma) and then, in fast succession, the Spanish, French, and Austrians (after the fall of Napoléon). The French influence is strong. The novelist Stendhal (1783–1842) lived in the city for several years and set his classic *The Charterhouse of Parma* here.

Bursting with gustatory delights, Parma now draws crowds for its sublime cured ham, prosciutto di Parma (known locally simply as prosciutto *crudo*), of which *culatello* is the finest cut; and for the delicate, pale yellow Parmigiano Reggiano cheese, the original—and best—of a class now known around the world as Parmesan. The city's prosperity is due in no small part to the Parmalat dairy empire, which also controls a world-class soccer team, best seen as a dizzying mass of blue and yellow stripes in a celebratory post-goal pile-up.

Thanks to the efforts being made by the city fathers to control traffic, strolling Parma's cobbled streets along with the locals is a charming experience. The draconian traffic regulations, although a boon to pedestrians, are a nightmare for motorists.

Fodor'sChoice
★

The **Piazza del Duomo,** site of the cathedral, the baptistery, the church of San Giovanni, and the palaces of the bishop and other notables, is the heart of the city. This square and its buildings make up one of the most harmonious, tranquil city centers in Italy. The magnificent 12th-century **Duomo** has two vigilant stone lions standing guard beside the main door. The arch of the entrance is decorated with a delicate frieze of figures representing the months of the year, a motif repeated inside the baptistery on the right-hand side of the piazza. Some of the original artwork still exists in the church, notably the simple yet evocative *Descent from the Cross,* a carving in the right transept by Benedetto Antelami (1150–1230), a sculptor and architect whose masterwork is this cathedral's baptistery.

It is odd to turn from this austere work of the 12th century to the exuberant fresco in the dome, the *Assumption of the Virgin,* by Antonio Correggio (1494–1534). The fresco was not well received when it was unveiled in 1530. "A mess of frogs' legs," the bishop of Parma is said to have called it. In contrast to the rather dark, somber interior of the cathedral, though, the beauty and light of the painting in the dome are a welcome relief. Today Correggio is acclaimed as one of the leading masters of Mannerist painting; his many works on view in Parma are some of the city's greatest draws. ⊠ *Piazza del Duomo* ☎ *0521/235886* ⊙ *Daily 9–12:30 and 3–6:45.*

The **Battistero** is a solemn, simple Romanesque on the exterior and uplifting Gothic within. The doors are richly decorated with figures, animals, and flowers, and the interior is adorned with figures carved by Antelami showing the months and seasons. ⊠ *Piazza del Duomo* ☎ *0521/235886* ⊠ *€2.70* ⊙ *Daily 9–12:30 and 3–7.*

Once beyond the elaborate baroque facade of **San Giovanni Evangelista,** the Renaissance interior reveals several works by Correggio; his *St. John the Evangelist* (left transept) is considered the finest of them. Also in this church (in the second and fourth chapels on the left) are works by Girolamo Parmigianino (1503–40)—a contemporary of Correggio's and the spearhead of the Mannerist art movement. Once seen, Parmigianino's swan-necked Madonnas are never forgotten: they pose with all the precious élan of today's fashion models. ⊠ *Piazzale San Giovanni* ☎ *0521/235592* ⊙ *Daily 8–noon and 3:30–6.*

In the adjoining monastery to the church of San Giovanni Evangelista is the **Spezieria di San Giovanni**—once a pharmacy where Benedictine monks mixed medicines and herbals. Although production stopped in 1881, the 16th-century decorations survive. ⊠ *Borgo Pipa 1, off Piazzale San Giovanni* ☎ *0521/233309* ⊠ *€2* ⊙ *Tues.–Sun. 8:30–2.*

★ Works by Parma's own Correggio and Parmigianino as well as Leonardo da Vinci (1452–1519), El Greco (1541–1614), and Bronzino (1503–72) are highlights of the **Galleria Nazionale,** housed in the vast, rather grim-looking **Palazzo della Pilotta,** on the bank of the river. The palace was built in about 1600 and is so big that from the air it is Parma's most recognizable sight—hence the destruction it suffered from Allied bombs in 1944. Much of the building has been restored. The palazzo takes its name from the game *pilotta*, a sort of handball played within the palace precincts in the 17th century.

To enter the Galleria Nazionale, on the ground floor of the palace, you pass through the magnificent baroque **Teatro Farnese,** built in 1628 and based on Palladio's theater in Vicenza. Built entirely of wood, it was burned badly during Allied bombing but has been flawlessly restored. ⊠ *Palazzo della Pilotta, Piazza Pilotta* ☎ *0521/233309* ⊠ *€6, Galleria without Teatro €4* ⊙ *Tues.–Sun. 8:30–2.*

The **Camera di San Paolo** is the former dining room of the abbess of the Convent of St. Paul. It was extensively frescoed by Correggio, and despite the religious character of the building, the decorations aren't Christian, but ravishingly beautiful depictions of mythological scenes—the *Triumphs of the Goddess Diana*, the *Three Graces*, and the *Three Fates*. It's near the Palazzo della Pilotta, off Strada Garibaldi. ⊠ *Via Melloni* ☎ *0521/233309* ⊠ *€2* ⊙ *Tues.–Sun. 8:30–2.*

Near Parma's central Piazza Garibaldi is **Santa Maria della Steccata,** a delightful 16th-century domed church with a wonderful fresco cycle by Parmigianino. The painter took so long to complete it that his patrons imprisoned him briefly for breach of contract. ⊠ *Piazza Steccata 9, off Via Dante* ☎ *0521/234937* ⊕ *www.santuari.it/steccata* ⊙ *Daily 9–noon and 3–6.*

Where to Stay & Eat

$$$–$$$$ ✕ **La Greppia.** The most elegant, most talked-about restaurant in the city is also one of the best. Taste innovative treats like the *anelli con cavolo nero e mostarda della Paola* (local pasta with black cauliflower and caramelized fruits) and the *faraona al tartufo nero di Fragno* (guinea

hen with black truffle and chestnut puree). Service is personal and friendly, thanks to the place's tiny size, and the unpretentious decor keeps all eyes on the food. ⊠ *Via Garibaldi 39/a,* ☎ *0521/233686* ⚐ *Reservations essential* ▭ *AE, DC, MC, V* ⊘ *Closed Mon.–Tues., 1 wk in Jan., 3 wks in July.*

$$$ ✕ **Parizzi.** Named for its exciting young chef, Marco Parizzi, this restaurant rivals La Greppia for the title of Parma's finest. A stylish art nouveau interior complements antipasti such as *culatello di Zibello,* the most highly touted of Parma hams; traditional Parma classics like stuffed tortelli; and sublime risotto di Parmigiano Reggiano with shaved white truffle (in season). The wine list is top-notch. ⊠ *Via Repubblica 71,* ☎ *0521/ 285952* ⚐ *Reservations essential* ▭ *AE, DC, MC, V* ⊘ *Closed Mon. and 3 wks Dec.–Jan.*

$$–$$$ ✕ **Croce di Malta.** The premises of this appealing, old-fashioned restaurant once housed a convent, then an inn. Traditional local fare includes delicate homemade pasta—try the tortelli with squash filling or tagliatelle in any fashion. Second courses include well-prepared, hearty versions of classic veal and cheese dishes. And don't miss a look at the good wine list. ⊠ *Borgo Palmia 8,* ☎ *0521/200272* ⚐ *Reservations essential* ▭ *AE, DC, MC, V* ⊘ *Closed Sun.*

$$ ✕ **Gallo d'Oro.** Warmly lighted, bottle-clad rooms upstairs and a multilevel bodega downstairs each have dozens of tables, which are usually filled. To go along with the atmosphere, the menu features traditional Parma specialties, such as an antipasto of *salumi misti* (local hams) and several varieties of tortelli. Prices are surprisingly low for Parma. ⊠ *Via Borgo della Salina 3* ☎ *0521/208846* ▭ *AE, DC, MC, V* ⊘ *Closed Sun.*

$$ ✕ **Osteria dei Mascalzoni.** This hip, romantic spot just off Via Farini is thoroughly modern in both conception and execution. Mood lighting is carefully placed, and the walls and tables exude expensive design and refined taste, yet the overall feel remains somehow young and casual. The wine list is carefully chosen, though pricey, with a particularly good selection from Sicily. Meat dishes are the menu's strong point; if available, the fillet of beef with a delicate cream of leeks is a good choice. You'll leave satisfied and charmed, if a bit poorer for your wine tab. ⊠ *Vicolo delle Cinque Piaghe 1* ☎ *0521/281809* ▭ *AE, DC, MC, V* ⚐ *Reservations essential* ⊘ *Closed.*

★ $–$$ ✕ **Parma Rotta.** In an old inn about 2 km (1 mi) from downtown, the Parma Rotta is an informal neighborhood trattoria serving hearty dishes like spit-roasted lamb and roast pork, topped off with homemade desserts. Dine outdoors under a pleasant trellis in summer. ⊠ *Via Langhirano 158* ☎ *0521/966738* ⊕ *www.parmarotta.com* ▭ *AE, DC, MC, V* ⊘ *Closed Sun.–Mon. June–Aug. and Mon. Oct.–May.*

★ ¢ ✕ **Enoteca Antica Osteria Fontana.** At lunch and before dinner, gregarious locals flock to this bright blue, old-school *enoteca* (wine bar) serving a star-studded selection of wines at shockingly good prices. You'll have to queue up in anarchic fashion for a table, and service is brusque. But that's all part of the experience the delicious grilled *panini* (sandwiches), filled with Emilia's best *salumi* (deli meats) and other delights, make it worthwhile. (The panini come quartered, so you can share with the table.) If the wait is too long, eat at the bar. Closing time is early (9 PM, sometimes earlier). The enoteca is also the best take-out wine store in town. ⊠ *Strada Farini 24/a, near the Piazza del Duomo* ☎ *0521/ 286037* ▭ *MC, V* ⊘ *Closed Sun.*

$$$ ▦ **Palace Hotel Maria Luigia.** A top-quality hotel convenient to Old Parma and the train station, the Maria Luigia has well-furnished rooms, some with lovely vistas of Parma. Part of the Sina Hotels chain, it's popular with business travelers. ⊠ *Viale Mentana 140, 43100* ☎ *0521/ 281032* 🖷 *0521/231126* ⊕ *www.palacemarialuigia.com* ⇥ *90 rooms,*

11 *suites* ♿ *Restaurant, minibars, bar, meeting room, parking (fee)* 🖃 *AE, DC, MC, V.*

$$$ 🏨 **Park Hotel Stendhal.** The Stendhal, well situated on the edge of the historic center of town, is one of Parma's finest hotels. Rooms are thickly carpeted and spacious, some with chandeliers and antique furniture. Some rooms have views of the Palazzo della Pilotta. Although the hotel is loosely affiliated with Best Western, don't try to reserve through the chain—contact the hotel directly. ⊠ *Via Bodoni 3, 43100* ☎ *0521/208057* 🖨 *0521/285655* ⊕ *www.rsadvnet.it/web/stendhal* ⬩ *67 rooms* ♿ *Restaurant, minibars, bar, meeting room, parking (fee), some pets allowed* 🖃 *AE, DC, MC, V.*

$$ 🏨 **Hotel Torino.** A warm reception and pleasant, relaxed surroundings are the best reasons for staying in this former convent, tucked away in a quiet pedestrian zone in the heart of town. It has modern, smallish rooms with Correggio reproductions on the walls. If traveling by car, fax ahead for a detailed map with driving directions—it's difficult to find. ⊠ *Via Mazza 7, 43100* ☎ *0521/281046* 🖨 *0521/230725* ⊕ *www.hotel-torino.it* ⬩ *33 rooms* ♿ *Bar, free parking, some pets allowed* 🖃 *AE, DC, MC, V.*

Nightlife & the Arts

OPERA &
THEATER
Parma is the region's opera center, with performances held at the landmark **Teatro Regio** (⊠ Via Garibaldi 16 ☎ 0521/218678 ⊕ www.teatroregioparma.org). Opera here is taken just as seriously as in Milan, although tickets are a little easier to come by. Playwright Dario Fo, the 1997 Nobel Prize winner for literature, helped found the **Teatro Due** (⊠ Viale Basetti 12 ☎ 0521/230242), where productions mix comedy and politics—your understanding will be limited without a knowledge of Italian.

Modena

❹ *56 km (35 mi) southeast of Parma, 38 km (23 mi) northwest of Bologna.*

Modena has gained recognition for three very contemporary names: the high-performance cars Maserati and Ferrari come from here, and so does the opera star Luciano Pavarotti. But, with apologies to the Tenor and the Testarossa, Modena's syrupy balsamic vinegar, aged for up to 40 years, is still perhaps its greatest achievement. The modern industrial town that encircles the historic center is extensive, and although the old quarter is small, it is filled with narrow medieval streets, pleasant piazzas, and typical Emilian architecture.

The 12th-century **Duomo,** also known as the Basilica Metropolitana, is one of the finest examples of Romanesque architecture in the country. The exterior is decorated with medieval sculptures depicting scenes from the life of San Geminiano, the patron saint of Modena, and fantastic beasts, as well as a realistic-looking scene of the sacking of a city by barbarian hordes, a reminder to the faithful to be ever vigilant in defense of the church. The bell tower is made of white marble and is known as **La Ghirlandina** (The Little Garland) because of its distinctive weather vane. The somber church interior is divided by an elaborate gallery carved with scenes of the Passion of Christ. The carvings took 50 years to complete and are by an anonymous Modenese master of the 12th century. The tomb of San Geminiano is in the crypt. ⊠ *Piazza Grande* ☎ *059/216078* ⊕ *www.duomodimodena.it* ⊙ *Daily 7–12:30 and 3:30–7.*

Modena's principal museum is housed in the **Palazzo dei Musei,** a short walk from the Duomo. The collection was assembled in the mid-17th

BALSAMIC NECTAR

BEWARE: *the balsamic vinegar you've probably tried—even the pricier Aceto Balsamico di Modena sold at specialty stores and in Italy—may be good on salads, but it bears only a fleeting resemblance to the real thing,* **Aceto Balsamico Tradizionale di Modena.** *The vinegar that passes the strict governmental standards (a winelike D. O.C.—Denominazione di Origine Controllata—regulation) is officially a condiment rather than a vinegar, and it is made with Trebbiano grape must, which is reduced and fermented from 12 to 25 or more years in a series of specially made wooden casks. The result is an intense and syrupy concoction best enjoyed sparingly on meats, strawberries, or Parmigiano Reggiano cheese. The vinegar has such a complexity of flavor that some even drink the stuff as an after-dinner liqueur.*

The **Consorzio Produttori Aceto Balsamico Tradizionale di Modena** *(⊠ Corso Cavour 60 ☎ 059/236981), which can be visited, monitors the quality of the authentic balsamic vinegar, made only by a few licensed restaurants and small producers. The consortium also limits production, keeping prices sky-high (expect to pay €50–€60 for a 100-ml bottle of tradizionale, or €75 and up for the older tradizionale extra vecchio variety). In the United States, though, you'll pay double those prices—if you can even find the product.*

century by Francesco d'Este (1610–58), Duke of Modena, and the **Galleria Estense** is named in his honor. The first room displays his portrait bust, done by Bernini (1598–1680). The duke had many interests, as you can see from the collections—ivories, coins, medals, and bronzes, as well as fine art dating from the Renaissance to the baroque. There are works here by Correggio and masters from other parts of Italy, including Tintoretto (1518–94) and Veronese (1528–88).

The gallery also houses the duke's **Biblioteca Estense,** a huge collection of illuminated books, of which the best known is the beautifully illustrated 15th-century *Bible of Borso d'Este.* A map dated 1501 was one of the first in the world to show Columbus's discovery of America. To get here, follow Via Emilia, the old Roman road that runs through the heart of the town, to Via di Sant'Agostino. ⊠ *Piazza Sant'Agostino 337* ☎ *059/4395711* ⊕ *www.galleriaestense.it* 🖃 *€4* ⊙ *Tues.–Sun. 8:30–7:30.*

Where to Stay & Eat

$$$$ ✕ **Fini.** A Modena institution, fancy, modern Fini is widely held to be the best restaurant in the city. It's Pavarotti's favorite—and you could gain a Pavarotti-esque figure by making a habit of the *gran bollito misto,* a groaning board of boiled meats in a *salsa verde* (vegetable sauce), the excellent local wines, and the homemade desserts. ⊠ *Piazzeta San Francesco* ☎ *059/223314* ⚖ *Reservations essential* 🖃 *AE, DC, MC, V* ⊙ *Closed Mon.–Tues., 3 wks Dec.–Jan., and July 21–Aug. 28.*

★ $$$–$$$$ ✕ **Borso d'Este.** One of the city's most highly regarded restaurants—particularly with the *crema* of the region's monied set—offers some delicious variations on old themes, like ravioli stuffed with game and Parmesan. The space is ultratrendy and modern, despite antiques throughout. In season don't miss the *tartufo* (truffle) specialties: ricotta- and spinach-stuffed tortelloni in a truffle-mushroom sauce, and the mushroom tart with truffles. ⊠ *Piazza Roma 5* ☎ *059/214114* ⚙ *Reservations essential* ⊟ *AE, DC, MC, V* ⊙ *Closed Sun. and Aug. 1–20.*

$$ ✕ **Da Enzo.** This big, cheerful, well-patronized trattoria is in the old town's pedestrian zone, a few steps from Piazza Mazzini. All the classic Modenese specialties are here, including zampone and *cotechino* (animal bladders stuffed with pork). For starters, try the tortelloni *di ricotta e spinaci* (stuffed with ricotta and spinach). Reservations are essential on weekends. ⊠ *Via Coltellini 17* ☎ *059/225177* ⊟ *AE, DC, MC, V* ⊙ *Closed Mon. and Aug. No dinner Sun.*

$$–$$$ 🏨 **Canal Grande.** Once a ducal palace, the Canal Grande offers large, airy, well-appointed rooms. A verdant garden has a fountain in back and a pretty breakfast terrace in summer. The hotel's restaurant, La Secchia Rapita (closed Wednesday and August), gets rave reviews. ⊠ *Corso Canalgrande 6, 41100* ☎ *059/217160* 🖷 *059/221674* ⊕ *www.canalgrandehotel.it* ⇌ *75 rooms, 3 suites* ⚙ *Restaurant, in-room safes, minibars, bar, free parking* ⊟ *AE, DC, MC, V.*

$–$$ 🏨 **La Torre.** Not particularly exciting, La Torre is nonetheless the best hotel choice in this price category, thanks to its location in the town center just off the Via Emilia. The somewhat stuffy rooms are functional, comfortable, and well equipped. ⊠ *Via Cervetta 5, 41100* ☎ *059/222615* 🖷 *059/216316* ⊕ *www.hotelcentrale.com/u_k/latorre.html* ⇌ *26 rooms* ⚙ *Bar, parking (fee)* ⊟ *AE, DC, MC, V.*

BOLOGNA

Centuries of wars, sackings, rebellions, and bombing that left such dramatic evidence in other cities of Emilia-Romagna have not taken their toll on Bologna's old city center. The narrow cobblestone streets remain intact, as do the ancient churches, massive palaces, medieval towers, and arcaded porticoes lining many of the main thoroughfares, shading the walkways to such an extent that you can stroll around town in a rainstorm for hours without feeling a drop.

Through its long history, first as an Etruscan city, then a Roman one, then as an independent city-state in the Middle Ages, Bologna has always played a significant role in the north of Italy. Over the centuries, the city has acquired a number of nicknames: Bologna the Learned, in honor of its venerable university, the oldest in the world; Bologna the Red, for its rosy rooftops and political leanings; Bologna the Turreted, recalling the forest of medieval towers that once rose from the city center (two remarkable examples still exist); and Bologna the Fat, a tribute to its preeminent position in the world of cuisine, the place of origin for mortadella, tortellini, and ragù.

Today one might also be tempted to dub it Bologna the Hip, for its position at the cutting edge of Italian culture. Recent years have brought an explosion of trendy *Newyorkese* bars and lounges with postmodern music and German track lighting, American brunches and California construction cuisine, and pricey boutiques. The result is a jarring juxtaposition of leaning medieval towers and towering modernist fashion billboards. Unfortunately, the influx of people and industry that has accompanied these changes has also brought air and noise pollution, a further distraction from the city's architectural and culinary gems.

While foreign tourists have lately begun to discover Bologna's unique charm and arrive (along with Italians) in increasing numbers, the city's urban vitality still comes in large part from its student population. The university was founded in about the year 1088 and by the 13th century already had more than 10,000 students. It was a center for the teaching of law and theology, and it was ahead of its time in that many of the professors were women. Today the university has one of the most prominent business schools in Italy and the finest faculty of medicine in the country. Guglielmo Marconi, the inventor of the wireless telegraph, first formulated his groundbreaking theories in the physics labs of the university.

Exploring Bologna

Piazza Maggiore and the adjacent Piazza del Nettuno make up the heart of the city. Arranged around these two squares are the imposing Basilica di San Petronio, the massive Palazzo Comunale, the Palazzo del Podestà, the Palazzo di Re Enzo, and the Fontana del Nettuno—one of the most visually harmonious groupings of public buildings in the entire country. From here, sights that aren't on one of the piazzas are but a short walk away, along delightful narrow cobbled streets or under the ubiquitous porticoes that double as municipal umbrellas.

a good walk

Start at the southern end of sprawling Piazza Maggiore at the 14th-century **Basilica di San Petronio** ⑤ ▶, peeking into its museum to see the church's original designs, some never realized. On the west side of Piazza Maggiore is the **Palazzo Comunale** ⑥, especially worthwhile if you like the work of modern artist Giorgio Morandi. Next, it's on to the **Palazzo del Podestà** ⑦ and its Torre dell'Arengo, at the north end of Piazza Maggiore in the adjoining Piazza Nettuno, where stands the Fontana del Nettuno, a.k.a. *Il Gigante*. To the left (west) is **Palazzo Re Enzo** ⑧, with its dark medieval associations. The busy, chic Via Rizzoli runs east from Piazza Nettuno directly into the medieval section of the city to Piazza di Porta Ravegnana, where you can climb the slightly off-kilter Torre degli Asinelli, the taller of **Le Due Torri** ⑨, Bologna's two landmark towers. From Piazza di Porta Ravegnana, you have two choices of routes if you want a shorter walk: head south and southwest to **Santo Stefano** ⑩ and **San Domenico** ⑪, or continue northeast along Via Zamboni for the last three important sights (⑫–⑭). If you want a long walk, explore all five sights. From the piazza, walk five minutes southeast down Via Santo Stefano to the remarkable church of Santo Stefano, actually several churches in one. From there, head west on Via Farini and take a left on Via Garibaldi; a few blocks down take a left to reach Piazza San Domenico and San Domenico, containing the saint's tomb and a minor work by Michelangelo. Retrace your steps back to Piazza di Porta Ravegnana, and walk northeast on Via Zamboni a few blocks to **San Giacomo Maggiore** ⑫, haunt of the Bentivoglio. Continue up Via Zamboni to Via delle Belle Arte and the **Pinacoteca Nazionale** ⑬, with works by Raphael, Giotto, Parmigianino, and Bolognese masters. Stroll north to the **Università di Bologna** ⑭ district for a *caffè* and snack.

TIMING   You'll want at least a full day to explore Bologna; it's compact and lends itself to easy exploration, but there is plenty to see. This walk, allowing a little time to explore each sight, should take at least four hours, not including the hour you should devote to the Pinacoteca Nazionale, a half hour to climb the Torre degli Asinelli, and a lunch break to sample Bologna's culinary bounty.

What to See

▶ ⑤ **Basilica di San Petronio.** Construction on this cathedral began in the 14th century, and work was still in progress on this vast building some 300 years later. It's not finished yet, as you can see: the wings of the transept are missing and the facade is only partially decorated, lacking most of the marble face the architects had intended. The main doorway was carved by the great Sienese master of the Renaissance, Jacopo della Quercia.

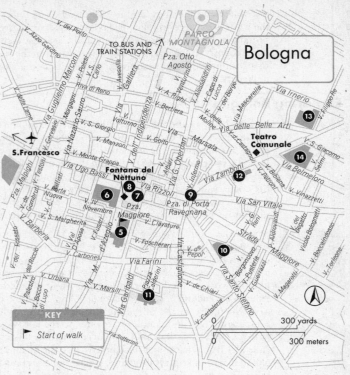

Above the center of the door is a Madonna and Child, flanked by Sts. Ambrose and Petronius, patrons of the city.

The interior of the basilica is huge and echoing, 432 ft long, 185 ft wide, and 144 ft high. It's striking to note that originally the Bolognans had planned an even bigger church—you can still see the columns erected to support the larger church outside the east end—but had to tone down construction when the university seat was established next door in 1561. The **Museo di San Petronio** contains models showing how the church was originally intended to look. The most important artworks in the church are in the left aisle, frescoes by Giovanni di Modena dating from the first years of the 1400s. Also in the left aisle, laid out in the pavement of the church, is a huge sundial, placed there in 1655. ⊠ *Piazza Maggiore* ☎ *051/225442* ✉ *Free* ⊙ *Basilica Apr.–Sept., daily 7:30–1:30 and 2:30–6:30; Oct.–Mar., daily 7:30–1 and 2:30–6. Museo di San Petronio Mon.–Sat. 9:30–12:30, Sun. 2:30–6.*

Fontana del Nettuno. Sculptor Giambologna's elaborate 1566 baroque monument to Neptune occupying Piazza Nettuno has been aptly nicknamed *Il Gigante* (The Giant). Its exuberantly sensual mermaids and undraped God of the Sea drew fire when it was constructed, but not enough, apparently, to dissuade the populace from using the fountain as a public washing stall for centuries. It's also known for another reason: walk behind Neptune and to his right for an infamously lewd angle on the statue. ⊠ *Piazza Nettuno, next to the Palazzo Re Enzo, Piazza Maggiore area.*

★ ❾ **Le Due Torri.** Two landmark towers, the **Torre degli Asinelli** and the **Torre Garisenda**, stand side by side in the in the compact Piazza di Porta Ravegnana. Torre degli Asinelli, at 320 ft the taller of the two, leans an alarming 7½ ft off perpendicular. The Torre Garisenda (closed to visitors), now tilting 10 ft, was shortened to 165 ft for safety in the 1500s. The towers were built at the same time (1488) and are mentioned by Dante in *The Inferno*. They are two of the 60 that remain out of more than 200 that once presided over the city: every family of importance had a tower as a symbol of prestige and power, and as a retreat when that prestige and power were threatened. For a fine view of Bologna's rooftops, climb up the 500 steep stairs of Torre degli Asinelli. ⊠ *Piazza di Porta Ravegnana, east of Piazza Maggiore* ▦ *Torre degli Asinelli* €3 ⊘ *Apr.–Sept., daily 9–6; Oct.–Mar., daily 9–5.*

6 **Palazzo Comunale.** A mélange of building styles and constant modifications characterize this huge palace, dating from the 13th to 15th century. When Bologna was an independent city-state, this was the seat of government, a function it still serves today. Over the door is a statue of Bologna-born Pope Gregory XIII, most famous for reorganizing the calendar. ⊠ *Piazza Maggiore 6* ▦ *051/203111* ⊘ *Free visits of the first-floor Red Room (City Council Hall) on advance request or during some exhibitions.*

Within the palazzo, the **Collezioni Comunali d'Arte** exhibits paintings from the Middle Ages as well as some Renaissance works by Luca Signorelli (circa 1445–1523) and Tintoretto. On the same floor, a separate **Museo Morandi** is dedicated to the 20th-century still-life artist Giorgio Morandi; in addition to his paintings, you'll see a re-creation of his studio and living space. An equally good reason to come is to get a look at the views of the piazza from the upper stories of the palace. ⊠ *Piazza Maggiore 6, west side* ▦ *051/203629* ⊕ *www.museomorandi.it* ▦ *€4 each museum, €6 combined ticket* ⊘ *Collezioni Tues.–Sat. 9–6:30, Sun. 10–6:30; Museo Tues.–Sun. 10–6.*

7 **Palazzo del Podestà.** This classic Renaissance palace facing the Basilica di San Petronio was erected in 1484, and attached to it is the soaring **Torre dell'Arengo.** The bells in the tower have rung since 1453 whenever the city has celebrated, mourned, or called its citizens to arms. ⊠ *Piazza Nettuno, Piazza Maggiore area* ▦ *051/224500* ⊘ *Visits only during exhibitions; call for schedule.*

8 **Palazzo Re Enzo.** King Enzo of Sardinia was imprisoned in this 13th-century medieval palace for 23 years, until his death in 1272. He had waged war on Bologna and was captured after the fierce battle of Fossalta in 1249. The palace has other macabre associations: common criminals received the last rites of the church in the tiny chapel in the courtyard before being executed in Piazza Maggiore. The courtyard is worth looking into, but except during art exhibitions there's nothing to see within the palace, which now houses government offices. ⊠ *Piazza Re Enzo, next to the Palazzo del Podestà, Piazza Maggiore area* ▦ *051/224500.*

13 **Pinacoteca Nazionale.** Bologna's principal art gallery contains many works by the immortals of Italian painting, including Raphael's famous *Ecstasy of St. Cecilia.* There's also a beautiful multipanel painting by Giotto, as well as a Parmigianino *Madonna and Saints.* The centerpieces of the collection, however, are the many rooms devoted to the two most important late-16th-century Bolognese masters, Guido Reni and Annibale Carracci. Some of the most interesting works, from a historical point of view, are by Giuseppe Crespi (circa 1575–1632), a Bolognese painter who avoided grand religious or historical themes, preferring instead to paint scenes of daily life in his native city. These small canvases convey marvelously the boisterous, earthy life of Old Bologna. ⊠ *Via delle Belle*

Arti 56, university district ☎ *051/4211984* ⊕ *www.pinacotecabologna. it* ☒ *€4* ⊙ *Tues.–Sun. 9–7.*

⓫ **San Domenico.** The tomb of St. Dominic, who died here in 1221, is called the **Arca di San Domenico** and is found in this church in the sixth chapel on the right. Many artists participated in its decoration, notably Niccolò di Bari, who was so proud of his contribution that he changed his name to Niccolò dell'Arca to recall this famous work. The young Michelangelo carved the angel on the right. In the right transept of the church is a tablet marking the last resting place of the hapless King Enzo, the Sardinian ruler imprisoned in the Palazzo Re Enzo. In the square in front of San Domenico are two curious tombs raised above the ground on pillars, commemorating two 14th-century lawyers. ☒ *Piazza San Domenico 13, off Via Garibaldi, south of Piazza Maggiore* ☎ *051/ 6400411* ⊙ *Weekdays 7:30–1 and 2:30–8, Sat. 7:30–1 and 2:30–7:30, Sun. 8–1 and 2:30–7:30. Museum open weekdays 9:30–1 and 3–6, Sat. 9:30–1 and 3–5:30, Sun. 3–5:30.*

⓬ **San Giacomo Maggiore.** Inside this church is the burial chamber of the Bentivoglio family, the city's leading family in the Middle Ages. The crypt is connected by underground passage to the Teatro Comunale across the street—a rather odd feature, until you realize that the family palazzo of the Bentivoglio used to stand on that spot. The most notable tomb is that of Antonio Bentivoglio (died 1435), carved by Jacopo della Quercia (circa 1374–1438). You can tell his profession—lecturer in law—from the group of students carved on the base. ☒ *Piazza Rossini, off Via Zamboni, university district* ☎ *051/225970* ⊙ *Daily 6:30–noon and 3:30–6.*

⓾ **Santo Stefano.** This splendid and unusual basilica actually contains between four and seven connected churches (authorities differ). The oldest is **Santi Vitale e Agricola,** which dates from the 8th century and contains a 14th-century nativity scene much loved by Bologna's children, who come at Christmastime to pay their respects to the baby Jesus. The church of **San Sepolcro** (12th century) contains the **Cortile di Pilato** (Courtyard of Pontius Pilate), so named for the basin in its center said to be where Pilate washed his hands after condemning Christ. Also in the building is a **museum** displaying various medieval religious works and with a shop where you can buy sundry items such as honey, shampoo, and jam made by the monks. ☒ *Via Santo Stefano 24, Piazza Santo Stefano, university district* ☎ *051/223256* ☒ *Free* ⊙ *Church and museum open daily 9–noon and 3:30–6.*

• FodorsChoice
★

⓮ **Università di Bologna.** Take a stroll through the streets of the university district, a jumble of buildings, some dating as far back as the 15th century and most to the 17th and 18th. The neighborhood, as befits a college town, is full of bookshops, coffee bars, and cheap restaurants. None of them are particularly distinguished, but they're all characteristic of student life in the city. Try eating at the *mensa universitaria* (cafeteria) if you want to strike up a conversation with local students (most speak English). Political slogans and sentiments are scrawled on walls all around the university and tend to be ferociously leftist. The **University Museums** display scientific instruments and paleontological, botanical, and university-related artifacts. ☒ *Via Zamboni 33, university district* ☎ *051/2049360; 051/2099602 museums* ☒ *Free* ⊙ *Weekdays; museum hrs vary, call for information.*

Where to Stay & Eat

$$–$$$ ✕ **Da Carlo.** Dining on the medieval terrace in summer is a treat in this attractive restaurant, so try to reserve a table outside. The delicate game

dishes, such as braised pigeon with artichokes, are favorites. ☒ *Via March-esana 6, Piazza Maggiore area* ☎ *051/233227* ✍ *Reservations essential* ▭ *AE, DC, MC, V* ☼ *Closed Wed., Jan. 1–22, and Aug. 23–Sept. 3.*

$$–$$$ ✕ **Le Stanze del Tenente.** Looming high above a modern bar, the 17th-century frescoes that line the ceiling of the private chapels of the 1576 Palazzo Bentivoglio provide a spectacular environment for sipping an *aperitivo* or a late-night drink. If you choose to eat at the adjoining avant-garde restaurant, you'll experience modern Italian fusion cooking, with traditional ingredients used in new ways; try the tasting of three soups, including an excellent chickpea ragù and a curried spinach concoction. Or come by just for a drink and to soak up the atmosphere; the bar's open until 1:30 AM (2:30 on Saturday). ☒ *Via del Borgo di S.Pietro 1 university district* ☎ *051/228767* ☼ *Closed July–Aug.* ▭ *DC, MC, V.*

★ **$$** ✕ **Da Cesari.** Well-executed Bologna classics such as tortellini in brodo and veal cutlet Bolognese (with ham and melted cheese) make this one of the best restaurants in Bologna in its price category. But it's the delectable appetizers—such as *coppa di testa con cipolla e aceto bal-samico* (cold, sliced head meat and red onion with balsamic vinegar) and white truffle with celery and shaved Parmesan—that make Da Ce-sari truly memorable. The romantically lighted dining room is warm and welcoming. Accompany the meal with wine made by the owner's fam-ily; Cesari's Sangiovese Riserva is excellent, and the Liano even better. ☒ *Via de' Carbonesi 8, south of Piazza Maggiore* ☎ *051/226769* ✍ *Reservations essential* ▭ *AE, DC, MC, V* ☼ *Closed Sun., Sat. in July, Aug. 1–24, and Jan. 1–6.*

$$ ✕ **Nuovi Notai.** At this spot just off beautiful Piazza Maggiore, the build-ing is 14th century, the decor 19th century, and the food a rich, com-plex blend of classic regional and Tuscan specialties. The *tortino tiepido* (warm tartlet) of porcini mushrooms makes a good starter. ☒ *Via de' Pignattari 1, Piazza Maggiore area* ☎ *051/228694* ✍ *Reservations es-sential* ▭ *AE, DC, MC, V* ☼ *Closed Sun.*

$$ ✕ **Rosteria Luciano.** A changing list of daily specials at this art deco–style restaurant augments what is already one of Bologna's most varied menus. Some of the best offerings are tagliolini *ai fiori di zucca* (with squash flowers), duck breast, and excellent guinea fowl. Among the desserts, the *ricottina al forno* (charcoal-flavored, oven-baked ricotta) is worth the splurge. ☒ *Via Nazario Sauro 19, Piazza Maggiore area* ☎ *051/231249* ✍ *Reservations essential* ▭ *AE, DC, MC, V* ☼ *Closed Wed., Aug., and Sun. in July.*

$–$$ ✕ **Da Bertino.** Happy diners don't seem to mind the close quarters in the large, bustling room here. Maybe it's because popularity hasn't spoiled this traditional neighborhood trattoria and its simple home-style dishes. Highlights are the homemade *paglia e fieno* (yellow and green pasta) with sausage and the choices on the steaming tray of *bollito misto* (boiled meats). ☒ *Via delle Lame 55, Porta San Felice* ☎ *051/522230* ▭ *AE, DC, MC, V* ☼ *Closed Sun.; Mon. Oct.–May; and Aug. 4–31. No dinner Sat. June–July.*

★ **$–$$** ✕ **Victoria.** It's not unusual for this unpretentious and charming trattoria-pizzeria off Via dell'Indipendenza to have lines, so reserve ahead. Al-though locals come for the cheap pizzas, the rest of the menu is not to be overlooked, particularly the tortellini *con noci e speck,* a ridicu-lously rich treatment of Bologna's classic pasta in a sauce of cream, ground walnuts, and cured ham. The back room has a lovely 17th-century painted wooden ceiling. ☒ *Via Augusto Righi 9/c, north of Piazza Mag-giore* ☎ *051/233548* ✍ *Reservations essential* ▭ *AE, DC, MC, V* ☼ *Closed Thurs.*

$ ✕ **Rostaria Antico Brunetti.** Housed next door to a Romanesque tower and steps away from Piazza Maggiore, this large, wood-paneled restaurant was founded in 1873 and is known as Bologna's oldest. Specialties here range from "Mama's tortellini" to veal in a white-wine sauce, but most diners opt for the pizzas or simple pastas with seafood sauces. Dining is on two floors, but even so the restaurant fills quickly. ⊠ *Via Caduti di Cefalonia 5, Piazza Maggiore area* ☎ *051/234441* ⊟ *AE, DC, MC, V* ⊘ *Closed Wed. and Aug. 12–25.*

¢–$ ✕ **La Scuderia.** Representing the modern face of Bologna, this cutting-edge café/wine bar/performance space brings a bit of New York chic to the stunning vaulted ballroom of an old palazzo next door to the university, serving as an informal meeting place for hip students and intellectuals. Salads, desserts, lunches, wines by the glass, and American-style Sunday brunches are offered in the vast hall; though a bit pricey, the light fare is a good break from another pasta dish. You can just as easily sip coffee over a breakfast newspaper or flirt over a martini. Monday nights feature live jazz. ⊠ *Piazza Verdi 2, off Via Zamboni, university district* ☎ *051/6569619* ⊟ *AE, DC, MC, V* ⊘ *Closed Mon.*

¢ ✕ **Cantina Bentivoglio.** This two-floor wine-jazz extravaganza is one of Bologna's classic places to relax by night. The ground floor is a dim, bottle-clad wine cellar; downstairs, live jazz is staged every night (for a €4 cover) in the cavern-like basement. The wine list includes labels from many of Italy's lesser-known regions, and the menu features pastas, meats, and interesting salads and lighter plates, such as crostini with mozzarella, eggplant, tomato, and roasted peppers. Vegetarian offerings are plentiful. Doors stay open until 2 AM, and wine is also available to go. ⊠ *Via Mascarella 4/, university district* ☎ *051/265416* ⊘ *Closed Sun. Oct.–May and Mon.* ⊟ *AE, DC, MC, V.*

★ ¢ ✕ **Tamburini.** This gourmet deli–cum–self-service buffet lunch spot sends the smells of all that is good about Bolognese food wafting through the room and out into the streets. Breads, numerous cheeses, salumi such as Parma and Bologna hams and prosciuttos, roasted peppers, inventive salads, balsamic vinegars, local olive oils, smoked salmon, and fresh pasta are among the delights. Tamburini also vacuum-packs foods for shipping or air travel. ⊠ *Via Drapperie 1, Piazza Maggiore area* ☎ *051/234726* ⊟ *AE, MC, V* ⊘ *Closed Sun., Tues., and Thurs. afternoons in Aug.*

★ $$$$ ▦ **Corona d'Oro 1890.** A medieval printing house in a former life, this hotel has delightful, lyrical art nouveau decor in its public space, an atrium, and enough flowers for a wedding. Guest rooms make opulent use of original 15th- and 16th-century decorations such as painted wood ceilings and Gothic-vault windows. The morning English breakfast buffet is worth getting up for. ⊠ *Via Oberdan 12, north of Piazza Maggiore, 40126* ☎ *051/236456* 🖷 *051/262679* ⊕ *www.bolognahotel.net* ⇗ *35 rooms* ⚐ *In-room safes, minibars, bicycles, bar, meeting room* ⊟ *AE, DC, MC, V* ⊘ *Closed 1st 3 wks in Aug.*

★ $$$$ ▦ **Grand Hotel Baglioni.** Sixteenth-century paintings and frescoes by the Bolognese Carracci brothers are rarely seen outside a museum or church, but in this 15th-century palazzo they provide the stunning backdrop for the public rooms and restaurant of one of Italy's most glamorous hotels. Lady Di slept here, and you'll feel no less royal in a handsome room with antique furniture and brocaded walls. The highly regarded I Carracci restaurant serves top-notch food in regal, formal surroundings. Note that although parking is available, the fee is €27 per day. ⊠ *Via dell'Indipendenza 8, north of Piazza Maggiore, 40121* ☎ *051/225445* 🖷 *051/234840* ⊕ *www.baglionihotels.com* ⇗ *113 rooms, 11 suites* ⚐ *Restaurant, in-room safes, minibars, bar, baby-sitting, meeting room, parking (fee), no-smoking rooms* ⊟ *AE, DC, MC, V.*

$$$ ▦ **Dei Commercianti.** Rooms in this hotel were designed to retain the structural integrity of the 11th-century palace and tower the hotel occupies

and are therefore cozy and unique, with original wood beams built into the walls. Tower rooms and suites have balconies with magnificent views of the church; all rooms are stylishly furnished with, among other things, Carrara marble desks custom-built following a 15th-century design. ⊠ *Via De' Pignattari 11, south of Piazza Maggiore, 40124* ☎ *051/233052* 🖷 *051/224733* ⊕ *www.bolognahotel.net* ⤴ *32 rooms, 2 suites* ♦ *In-room safes, minibars, bicycles, bar* ⊟ *AE, DC, MC, V.*

$$$ 🏨 **Orologio.** Under the same management as the Corona d'Oro and the Dei Commercianti, the Orologio is in a quiet pedestrian zone off Piazza Grande and in an ideal sightseeing location. The hotel occupies a palazzo that was originally a public building, but the interior achieves a contemporary effect. A mid-level lounge and Internet room is a pleasant place to relax, and top-floor rooms have good views of Bologna's skyline. Fax ahead or check the Web site for driving directions. ⊠ *Via IV Novembre 10, Piazza Maggiore area, 40123* ☎ *051/231253* 🖷 *051/260552* ⊕ *www.bolognahotel.net* ⤴ *29 rooms* ♦ *Minibars, bicycles* ⊟ *AE, DC, MC, V.*

$–$$ 🏨 **Accademia.** This small hotel is right in the middle of the university quarter, a comfortable base for exploring the area. The rooms are adequate, the staff friendly. Look for discounts on the Web site. ⊠ *Via delle Belle Arti 6, university district, 40126* ☎ *051/232318* 🖷 *051/263590* ⊕ *www.hotelaccademia.it* ⤴ *28 rooms* ♦ *Bar, parking (fee)* ⊟ *No credit cards.*

$ 🏨 **San Vitale.** Modern furnishings and a garden distinguish this modest hostelry, about 1 km (½ mi) from the center of town. The service is courteous, and rooms are clean and bright. ⊠ *Via San Vitale 94, university district, 40125* ☎ *051/225966* 🖷 *051/239396* ⤴ *17 rooms* ⊟ *No credit cards.*

Nightlife & the Arts

The Arts

BALLET   You can see ballet performances at the historic **Arena del Sole** (⊠ Via Indipendenza 44, north of Piazza Maggiore ☎ 051/2910910 ⊕ www.arenadelsole.it).

FESTIVAL   The **Festa di San Petronio**, held each year during the first weekend in October, features bands, fireworks, and free *mortadella di Bologna* sandwiches in Piazza Maggiore.

MUSIC & OPERA   The city hosts a wide selection of orchestral and chamber-music concerts. The 18th-century **Teatro Comunale** (⊠ Largo Respighi 1, university district ☎ 051/529999 ⊕ www.comunalebologna.it) presents concerts by Italian and international orchestras throughout the year but is dominated by the highly acclaimed opera performances in the winter season. All events sell out quickly, so reserve seats well in advance. Check concert schedules for the **Sala Bossi** (⊠ Piazza Rossini 2, university district ☎ 051/233975). The **Sala Mozart** is the performance venue for the **Accademia Filarmonica** (⊠ Via Guerazzi 13, university district ☎ 051/222997), the city's principal music school. For jazz, check out **Cantina Bentivoglio** (⊠ Via Mascarella 4/b, university district ☎ 051/265416), one of Bologna's most appealing night spots.

THEATER   The winter season at the **Europa Auditorium** (⊠ Piazza Costituzione, Stalingrado ☎ 051/372540) includes shows from comedy to cabaret, with an occasional pop concert thrown in for good measure. Many types of theatrical productions take place throughout the winter at the **Teatro Duse** (⊠ Via Cartoleria 42, south of Piazza Maggiore ☎ 051/231836). There are theater productions at the **Arena del Sole** (⊠ Via Indipendenza 44, north of Piazza Maggiore ☎ 051/2910910).

Nightlife

BARS As a university town, Bologna has long been known for its hopping nightlife. As early as 1300, it was said to have had 150 taverns. Most of the city's current 200-plus pubs and lounges are frequented by Italian students, young adults, and the international study-abroad crowd, with the university district forming the epicenter. In addition to the university area, the pedestrian-only area zone on Via del Pratello, lined with a host of pubs, is also a hopping night scene. For a young, tipsy, boisterous international crowd, head for the Irish pub **The Cluricaune** (✉ Via Zamboni 18/b, university district ☎ 051/263419). If your taste is for an English pub, try **Lord Lister** (✉ Via Zamboni 56, university district ☎ 051/240886), again drawing loads of students and expats.

If you thirst for someplace Italian and low-key, **Contavalli** (✉ Via Belle Arti 2, university district ☎ 051/268395), a wine bar with great ambient lighting and a good draft beer selection, is a good way to go. Across from the picturesque San Francesco church and its pleasant piazza, **Bar de' Marchi** (✉ Piazza San Francesco 4, university district ☎ 051/238945) is the real thing—a local hangout with a raucous mix of old men and students playing cards and drinking the cheapest wine by the glass in town.

Shopping

Books

Capitalizing on the university cleintele, **Feltrinelli** (✉ Piazza Ravegnana 1, east of Piazza Maggiore ☎ 051/266891) is the best bookstore in the region. It's open Monday–Saturday 9–8, Sunday 10–1:30 and 3–7:30. **Feltrinelli International** (✉ Via Zamboni 7/b, east of Piazza Maggiore ☎ 051/268070) stocks innumerable travel guides and maps, and Italy's best selection of English and other foreign-language books. It's open Monday–Saturday 9–7:30, Sun. 10–1 and 3:30–7:30.

Clothing

Galleria Cavour (✉ Piazza Cavour, south of Piazza Maggiore), perhaps the most upscale mall in Italy, houses many of the fashion giants, including Gucci, Versace, and the jeweler and watchmaker Bulgari. A host of small clothing and jewelry shops line **Via d'Azeglio** in the center of town.

Market

The gargantuan **City Market** (✉ Piazza VIII Agosto, off Via dell'Indipendenza north toward the train station), open daily except Sunday during daylight hours, hosts vendors of every imaginable sort hawking wares of variable quality, including clothing, shoes, books, food, and every imaginable household good. Vendors also line the sidewalks of Via dell'Indipendenza on weekends.

Shoes

Bologna-based **Bruno Magli** (✉ Piazza della Mercanzia 1/d, east of Piazza Maggiore ☎ 051/231126) showcases modern Italian fashion design at this, its flagship store. It's open Monday–Wednesday and Friday–Saturday 9–12:30 and 3:30–7:30, Thursday 3:30–7:30.

Wines

Bologna is a good place to buy wine. Several shops offer a bewilderingly large selection—to go straight to the top, ask the owner which wines were awarded *tre bicchieri* (three glasses) the most prestigious honor for an Italian wine, bestowed by Gambero Rosso's wine bible, *Vini d'Italia*. Repeatedly recognized as one of the best wine stores in Italy, **Enoteca Italiana** (✉ Via Marsala 2/b, north of Piazza Maggiore ☎ 051/227132) lives up to its reputation with shelves lined with excellent selections from all over Italy, including many tre bicchieri bottles, all at reasonable prices. The friendly enoteca even has a selection of wines by the glass and excellent panini that make a great light lunch. **Scaramagli** (✉ Strada Maggiore 31/d, university district ☎ 051/227132), is a mid-sized down-to-earth wine store with friendly ownership. The shop is closed in the afternoon from 1 until 5, but reopens from 5 to 8 every evening except Thursday.

ROMAGNA

The Romagna region is dominated by the sophisticated, mist-shrouded city of Ferrara; Ravenna, the site of shimmering Byzantine mosaics; and Rimini, one of Italy's most popular seaside resorts. Ferrara lies just north of Bologna on the A13 autostrada. Heading southeast out of Bologna, Via Emilia (SS9) and the parallel A14 autostrada lead to the towns of Dozza and Faenza. From there, cut north to the Adriatic coast on the S71 to reach Ravenna, or continue on southeast on the A14 to reach Rimini. Alternatively, the slower S16 cuts a northwest-southeast swath through Romagna, directly connecting Ferrara, Ravenna, and Rimini.

Ferrara

★ ⓯ *47 km (29 mi) northeast of Bologna, 74 km (46 mi) northwest of Ravenna.*

When the legendary Ferrarese filmmaker Michelangelo Antonioni called his beloved hometown "a city that you can see only partly, while the rest disappears to be imagined," perhaps he was referring to the low-lying fog that rolls in off the Adriatic each winter and shrouds Ferrara's winding knot of medieval alleyways, turreted pleasure palaces, and ancient wine bars—once inhabited by the likes of Copernicus—in a ghostly mist. But perhaps Antonioni was also suggesting that Ferrara's striking beauty often conceals a dark and tortured past. The picturesque maze of twisting cobblestone streets that forms the old ghetto was also the site of the Jews' dramatic fall from grace as Fascist Italy came under the spell of Nazi Germany. And a majestic, moated castle, which now guards the heart of Ferrara's old town in innocuous splendor, was originally built as a fortress to protect the ruthless Este dukes against their own citizens; deep within the castle's bowels, the Estes kept generations of political dissidents in dank cells barely larger than the human body.

And although the site was first settled before the time of Christ and was once ruled by Ravenna, Ferrara's history really begins with a foreboding event—the arrival of the Estes in 1259. For more than three centuries, the infamous dynasty ruled with an iron fist; brother killed brother, son fought father, husband murdered wife. The greatest of the dukes, Ercole I (1433–1505), attempted to poison a nephew who challenged his power, and when that didn't work, he beheaded him. Yet it is to this pitiless man that Ferrara owes its great beauty. In one of his more empathetic moments, Ercole invited Sephardic Jews exiled from Spain to settle in Ferrara, spawning half a millennium of Jewish history that came to a spectacular end as Italy succumbed to Axis ideology, a tragedy documented in Giorgio Bassani's book and Vittorio De Sica's canonical neo-realist film, *The Garden of the Finzi-Continis.*

In modern times, though, you are likely to be charmed by Ferrara's prosperous air and meticulous cleanliness, its excellent local restaurants and fin de siècle coffeehouses, and its hospitable, youthful spirit, marked by the boisterous mass of wine-drinkers that gathers outside the Duomo on even the foggiest of weekend evenings. Though Ferrara is now a UN-

ESCO world heritage site, the city still draws amazingly few tourists—which only adds to its mysterious appeal.

A museum card, sold at the Palazzo dei Diamanti and at several art museums around town, grants admission to every museum, palace, and castle in Ferrara for €12.40.

Naturally enough, the building that was the seat of Este power dominates the town: it is the massive **Castello Estense,** a perfectly preserved and placed square in the center of the city in Piazza Castello. It is a suitable symbol for the ruling family: cold and menacing on the outside, lavishly decorated within. The public rooms are grand, but deep in the bowels of the fortress are chilling dungeons where enemies of the state were held in wretched conditions—a function these quarters served as recently as 1943, when antifascist prisoners were detained there. In particular, the **Prisons of Don Giulio, Ugo, and Parisina** have some fascinating features, like 15th-century smoke graffiti protesting the imprisonment of the young lovers Ugo and Parisina, who were beheaded in 1425.

The castle was established as a fortress in 1385, but work on its luxurious ducal quarters continued into the 16th century. Representative of Este grandeur are the **Sala dei Giochi** (Game Room), extravagantly painted with pagan athletic scenes, and the **Sala dell'Aurora,** decorated to show the times of the day. From the terraces of the castle and from the hanging garden, reserved for the private use of the duchesses, are fine views of the town and the surrounding countryside. You can cross the castle's moat, traverse its drawbridge, and wander through much of its arched interior at any time, and in the still of a misty night, the experience is haunting. ✉ *Piazza Castello* ☎ *0532/299233* ✆ *€7, Torre dei Leoni €1 extra, art exhibits extra* ☉ *Tues.–Sun. 9:30–6, tower visits Tues.–Sun. 10–4:45.*

The magnificent Gothic **Duomo,** a few steps away from the Castello Estense, has a three-tiered facade of bony arches and beautiful carvings over the central door. It was begun in 1135 and took more than a hundred years to complete. The interior was completely remodeled in the 17th century, and very little of the original decoration remains in place, much of it residing instead in the **Museo del Duomo,** located nearby at the Ex-chiesa e chiostro di San Romano. Displayed here are some of the lifelike carvings taken from the cathedral doors, dating from the 13th century and showing the months of the year. Also in the museum are a statue of the Madonna by the Sienese master Jacopo della Quercia (1374–1438) and two masterpieces by the Ferrarese painter Cosimo Tura, an *Annunciation* and *St. George Slaying the Dragon.* ✉ *Piazza Cattedrale; museum on Via S. Romano 6* ☎ *0532/207449* ⊕ *www.comune. fe.it/musei-aa/schifanoia/catte.html* ✆ *Free, museum €4.20, €6.70 combined ticket with Palazzo Schifanoia and Palazzina Marfisa d'Este* ☉ *Duomo: Mon.–Sat. 7:30–noon and 3–6:30, Sun. 7:30–12:30 and 3:30–7:30. Museum: Tues.–Sun. 9–1 and 3–6.*

The oldest and most characteristic area of Ferrara is to the south of the Duomo, stretching between the Corso Giovecca and the ramparts of the city. Here various members of the Este family built pleasure palaces, the most famous of which is the **Palazzo Schifanoia** (*schifanoia* means "carefree" or, literally, "fleeing boredom"). Begun in the 14th century, the palace was remodeled in 1466 and was the city's first Renaissance palazzo. The interior is lavishly decorated, particularly the **Salone dei Mesi,** with an extravagant series of frescoes showing the months of the year and their mythological attributes. The adjacent **Museo Civico Lap-**

idario has a collection of coins, statuary, and paintings. ⊠ *Via Scandiana 23* ☎ *0532/64178* ⊕ *www.comune.fe.it/musei-aa/schifanoia/skifa. html* ⊠ *€4.20 for both palazzo and museo, free 1st Mon. of month; €6.70 combined ticket with Palazzina Marfisa d'Este and Museo della Cattedrale* ⊙ *Tues.–Sun. 9–6.*

The grand but unfinished courtyard is the most interesting part of the luxurious **Palazzo di Ludovico il Moro,** a magnificent 15th-century palace built for Ludovico Sforza, husband of Beatrice d'Este. The palazzo also houses the region's **Museo Archeologico,** a repository of relics of early man, Etruscans, and Romans found in the country surrounding the city. ⊠ *Via XX Settembre 124, near the Palazzo Schifanoia* ☎ *0532/66299* ⊠ *€4* ⊙ *Tues.–Sun. 9–2.*

The courtyard of the peaceful **Palazzo del Paradiso** contains the tomb of the great writer Ariosto (1474–1533), author of the most popular work of literature of the Renaissance, the poem *Orlando Furioso.* The building now houses the city library, called the **Biblioteca Ariostea.** ⊠ *Via delle Scienze 17* ☎ *0532/418200* ⊠ *Free* ⊙ *Weekdays 9–7:30, Sat. 9–1:30.*

The writer Ariosto spent much of his life in Ferrara under the patronage of the Este. **Casa di Ludovico Ariosto,** one of his homes, has been converted into an office building but is open to the public for free tours of parts of the interior. ⊠ *Via Ariosto 67* ☎ *0532/209988* ⊠ *Free* ⊙ *Tues.–Sat. 10–1 and 3–6, Sun. 10–1.*

One of the best-preserved of the Renaissance palaces along Ferrara's old streets is the charming **Casa Romei.** Downstairs are rooms with 15th-century frescoes and several sculptures collected from destroyed churches. The house lies not far from the Palazzo del Paradiso, in the area behind Ferrara's castle. ⊠ *Via Savonarola 30* ☎ *0532/240341* ⊠ *€2* ⊙ *Tues.–Sun. 8:30–7:30; schedule varies with exhibits.*

On the busy Corso Giovecca is the **Palazzina di Marfisa d'Este,** a grandiose 16th-century home that belonged to a great patron of the arts. The house has painted ceilings, fine 16th-century furniture, and a garden containing a grotto and an outdoor theater. At press time, it was closed for restoration; call for the current status. ⊠ *Corso Giovecca 170* ☎ *0532/209988* ⊕ *www.comune.fe.it/musei-aa/schifanoia/marfi.html* ⊠ *€2, €6.70 combined ticket with Palazzo Schifanoia and Museo della Cattedrale* ⊙ *Tues.–Sun. 9–1 and 3–6.*

The collection of ornate religious objects in the **Museo Ebraico** (Jewish Museum) bears witness to the long history of the city's Jewish community. This history had its high points—1492, for example, when Ercole I invited the Jews to come over from Spain—and its lows, notably 1624, when the papal government closed the **ghetto,** which was reopened only with the advent of a united Italy in 1859. The triangular warren of narrow, cobbled streets that made up the ghetto originally extended as far as Corso Giovecca (originally Corso Giudecca, or Ghetto Street); when it was enclosed, the neighborhood was restricted to the area between Via Scienze, Via Contrari, and Via di San Romano. The museum, in the center of the ghetto, is also the site of Ferrara's **synagogue.** ⊠ *Via Mazzini 95* ☎ *0532/210228* ⊠ *€4* ⊙ *1-hr guided tours Sun.–Thurs. at 10, 11, and noon.*

The **Palazzo dei Diamanti** (Palace of Diamonds) is so called for the 12,600 faceted stone blocks that famously stud the facade. The palace was built in the 15th and 16th centuries and today contains the **Pinacoteca Nazionale,** an extensive art gallery devoted primarily to the

painters of Ferrara. ⊠ *Corso Ercole I d'Este 21* ☎ *0532/205844* 🖃 *€4*
🕐 *Tues.–Wed. and Fri.–Sat. 9–2, Thurs. 9–7, Sun. 9–1.*

Where to Stay & Eat

The **Prenotel hotel reservation hotline** (☎ 0532/462046), run by the city,
allows you to make reservations at any of the accommodations listed
below, among many others.

★ $$–$$$ ✕ **Trattoria La Romantica.** The former stables of a 17th-century mer-
chant's house have been transformed into this casually elegant, welcoming
restaurant, which is a great favorite among well-fed locals. Although
the decor (warm light and wood-beam ceilings, incongruous prints,
and a piano) seems to be in perpetual transition, the haute-rustic food
is fully realized: Ferrarese specialties like *cappellacci di zucca* (squash
dumplings) in a cream-tomato-walnut-Parmesan sauce are served side
by side with French oysters. ⊠ *Via Ripagrande 36* ☎*0532/765975* 🖃*AE,
DC, MC, V* 🕐 *Closed Wed., Jan. 7–17, and July 1–17.*

$$ ✕ **Osteria del Ghetto.** This casually elegant eatery represents the cutting
edge of Ferrarese cooking. Though the Osteria is buried deep in the old
Jewish ghetto, its seasonal menu is anything but old-fashioned. Creative
dishes like basmati rice torte with Colonnata lard and boletus mush-
rooms, eggplant flan with cold Grana cream, and a lukewarm pheas-
ant salad with balsamic vinegar, span the new culinary spectrum of
northern Italy. The interior is modern and relaxing, with wood-beamed
ceilings, a nonsmoking section, and tables on the street in summer. The
wine list is excellent. ⊠ *Via Vittorio 26/28* ☎ *0532/764936* 🖃 *AE, DC,
MC, V* 🕐 *Closed Tues.*

$–$$ ✕ **Guido Ristorante.** Locals in the know populate this restaurant on a cobbled street in the Jewish ghetto. The menu is made up of Ferrarese spe-
cialties, plus some inventive dishes you won't find anywhere else, such
as gnocchi in curry sauce with black olives and zucchini. The cozy dining room has exposed brick and old wooden beams. ⊠ *Via Vignatagliata
61* ☎ *0532/761052* 🖃 *AE, DC, MC, V* 🕐 *Closed Thurs. and July.*

$ ✕ **Hostaria Savonarola.** Into the wee hours, an avant-garde buzz emanates
from this bright, bustling wine bar and informal restaurant, just inches
away from the castle in the very heart of town. Despite the hip scene,
the menu—scrawled on a chalkboard—is simple and traditional, focusing
on a few daily preparations of good local ingredients. Risotto *in crema
di zucca* makes creamy use of Ferrara's trademark squash, while *papardelle
al sugo d'anatra* pairs wide, flat noodles with a duck sauce. Service is
warm, and outdoor tables couldn't be better for castle views. You can
also buy good local salumi to go. ⊠ *Piazza Savonarola 12/16* ☎ *0532/
208681* 🖃 *AE, DC, MC, V.*

★ ¢–$ ✕ **Osteria Al Brindisi.** Ferrara is a city of wine bars, beginning with this,
Europe's oldest, which began pouring in 1435. Al Brindisi is much
more than a historic novelty; it has wine bottles from all over the world
lining its ancient walls, romantic ambient lighting, and a memorable spread
of salumi and local cheeses on offer, along with tasty hot dishes such as
tortellini in brodo. This might just be the most perfect place to drink
wine in Italy—Copernicus, who once lived upstairs, seemed to think so.
Prices are low, and even the music (Otis Redding and the like) somehow feels just right. ⊠ *Via degli Adelardi 11* ☎ *0532/209142* 🖃 *AE,
DC, MC, V* 🕐 *Closed Mon.*

$$$$ 🏨 **Duchessa Isabella.** Live out your Marie-Antoinette fantasies, such as
they are, at this converted 16th-century mansion near Piazza Ariostea.
The splendid dining rooms and entryway are sumptuously decorated in
authentic style; the lacy, satiny rooms, however, teeter between royal and
ridiculous. Some may find the formality wearying and the tone somewhat artificial; others will find a stay here marvelous. A horse and car-

riage are available. ⊠ *Via Palestro 70, 44100* ☎ *0532/202121* 🖷 *0532/ 202638* ⊕ *www.duchessaisabella.it* ⇝ *22 rooms, 5 suites* ⌂ *Restaurant, in-room safes, minibars, bar, meeting room, free parking* ▤ *AE, MC, V.*

$$$
Fodor'sChoice
★
🏨 **Hotel Ripagrande.** The courtyards, vaulted brick lobby, and breakfast room of this 15th-century noble's palazzo retain much of their lordly pre-Renaissance flavor, but rooms are decidedly more down-to-earth. Everything here, from the room service to the showers, is impeccable. Standard doubles and many enormous bi- and tri-level suites have faux-Persian rugs, tapestries, and cozy antique furniture; top-floor rooms and suites with terraces are like a Colorado ski lodge. The suites are a good deal, the location is quiet but prime, and the friendly restaurant is worth a try. ⊠ *Via Ripagrande 21, 44100* ☎ *0532/765250* 🖷 *0532/764377* ⊕*www.ripagrandehotel.it* ⇝*20 rooms, 20 suites* ⌂ *Restaurant, in-room safes, minibars, bar, meeting room* ▤ *AE, DC, MC, V.*

$
🏨 **Hotel San Paolo.** On the edge of the old city, San Paolo is the best inexpensive choice in town. The 10-minute walk from the heart of Ferrara's medieval quarter is pleasant in a town so amenable to strolling, and there are good restaurants in the vicinity. ⊠ *Via Baluardi 9, 44100* ☎*0532/762040* 🖷 *0532/762040* ⊕ *www.hotelsanpaolo.it* ⇝*47 rooms* ⌂ *Bicycles* ▤ *AE, DC, MC, V.*

$
🏨 **Locanda Borgonuovo.** This lovely B&B is set in a 17th-century monastery on a quiet but central pedestrians-only street. It books up months in advance, partly because musicians and actors from the local theater make this their home away from home. Rooms are furnished with antiques, and one has its own kitchen for longer stays. Summer breakfasts are served in the leafy courtyard. ⊠ *Via Cairoli 29, 44100* ☎*0532/211100* 🖷*0532/ 246328* ⊕ *www.borgonuovo.com* ⇝*4 rooms* ⌂ *In-room safes, minibars, bicycles, library, free parking* ▤ *AE, MC, V.*

Nightlife

BARS & CAFÉS
Enoteca Due Gobbi (⊠ Via degli Adelardi 7 ☎ 0532/247690), next door to Osteria Al Brindisi, draws a big crowd of twentysomethings after hours. The dim, stylish **Enobar Estense** (⊠ Piazza Cattedrale 7 ☎ 339/4831510), right next to the cathedral, accompanies wines from all over Italy with endless plates of delightful free Italian tapas and soothing jazz. For live jazz, check out the **Jazz Club Ferrara** (⊠ Torrione San Giovanni ☎ 0532/ 211573), which has a star-studded lineup. The low-key **Leon d'Oro** (⊠ Piazza Cattedrale ☎ 0532/209318) is one of the town's grand old cafés, serving expensive drinks, coffee, and signature Ferrarese cakes in a truly regal environment.

Sports & the Outdoors

BICYCLES
You can pick up a *10 Bicycle Routes in the Province of Ferrara* brochure, available in English, at the tourist office in the castle. For information about guided bike trips around Ferrara for tourists and locals, call **Cicloclub Estense** (☎ 0532/900931). If you want to get around Ferrara the way the locals do, rent a bike at **Pirana e Bagni** (⊠ Piazzale Stazione 2 ☎ 0532/772190), open weekdays 5 AM–8 PM, Saturday 6 AM–6:30 PM.

Dozza

🔟 *31 km (19 mi) southeast of Bologna.*

Dozza is a small village just off the Via Emilia (SS9) where artists from all over flock in September of odd years to take part in a mural competition. As a result, virtually every square foot of the town is covered with colorful scenes, executed with varying degrees of skill. Dozza is crowned with a splendid restored medieval castle, the **Rocca Sforzesca di Dozza.** ☎ *0542/678240* ▦ *€4* ⊙ *Apr.–Sept., Tues.–Sat. 10–1 and*

3–7, Sun. 10–1 and 3–7:30; Oct.–Mar., Tues.–Sat. 10–12:30 and 3–5, Sun. 10–1 and 2:30–6.

Enoteca Regionale, located in Dozza's castle, is the wine "library" for the region. Here, in a cozy stone tavern, you can sample the different vintages from the surrounding countryside, particularly Dozza's own Albana, a white wine that comes dry or sweet. ⊠ *Rocca di Dozza* ☎ *0542/ 678089* ⊕ *www.enotecaemiliaromagna.it* ☾ *Tues.–Fri. 9:30–1 and 2:30–6:30, weekends 10–1 and 3–7. Wine bar open afternoon–evening.*

Where to Eat

$$$$
Fodor'sChoice
★

✕ **San Domenico.** Food critics count San Domenico among Italy's top 10 restaurants, so dedicated gourmands will want to make the trip to the luxe town of Imola, about 15 km (9 mi) east of Dozza. Majestic decor reflects the truly royal prices you'll pay for celebrity chef Valentino Marcattilii's wondrous creations, such as pâté with white truffles; hand-stuffed pasta with rabbit and eggplant in lemon-thyme sauce; and risotto with scampi, black truffle, and artichoke (not to be missed if it's available). The staggering wine list has more than 3,000 choices. Make reservations well in advance. ⊠ *Via G. Sacchi 1, Imola* ☎ *0542/ 29000* ⌂ *Reservations essential* ▭ *AE, DC, MC, V* ☾ *Closed Sun.–Mon. June–Aug., 1st wk in Jan., and 1 wk in Aug. No dinner Sun.–Mon. Sept.–May.*

Faenza

🔟 *23 km (14 mi) southeast of Dozza, 49 km (30 mi) southeast of Bologna.*

The renowned style of pottery called *faience* has been produced in Faenza, on the Via Emilia, since the 12th century. In the central **Piazza del Popolo** are dozens of shops selling the native wares. Faenza, not surprisingly, is home to the **Museo delle Ceramiche,** one of the largest ceramics museums in the world, covering the potter's art in all phases of history the world over. ⊠ *Viale Baccarini 19* ☎ *0546/21240* ⊕ *www. racine.ra.it/micfaenza* ▭ *€6* ☾ *Apr.–Oct., Tues.–Sat. 9–7, Sun. 9:30–1 and 3–7; Nov.–Mar., Tues.–Fri. 9–1, weekends 9–1 and 3–6.*

Where to Eat

★ $$$$

✕ **La Frasca.** This elegant countryside restaurant, by any measure one of the best—and most expensive—in Romagna, and perhaps Italy, features a beautiful outdoor garden for alfresco summer dining. Chef Gianfranco Bolognesi combines fresh Adriatic seafood and Romagnan produce in such unexpected delights as *tortino di gamberi, melanzane e pomodoro* (crayfish, tomato, and eggplant pie with ratatouille and delicately fried basil leaves). A beautiful country drive will bring you to secluded Castrocaro Terme, 11 km (7 mi) from the town of Forlì, and equidistant (40 km/25 mi) from Imola and Ravenna. ⊠ *Viale Mateotti 38, Castrocaro Terme* ☎ *0543/767471* ⌂ *Reservations essential* ▭ *AE, DC, MC, V* ☾ *Closed Tues., Jan. 1–20, and Aug. 15–31.*

en route On SS9 beyond Forlì, you pass through the modern towns of Forlimpopoli, Cesena, and Savignano. At Savignanothere is a reminder that no matter how new the towns might look, you are still traveling in a place of great history. Just outside the town is a small stream, the Rubicone. Cross it and you, too, have crossed the Rubicon, the river made famous by Julius Caesar when, in 49 BC, he defied the Senate of Rome by bringing his army across the river and plunging the country into civil war.

Ravenna

18 *52 km (32 mi) northwest of Rimini, 76 km (47½ mi) east of Bologna.*

Ravenna is a small, quiet city of brick palaces and cobbled streets, whose magnificent monuments are the only indicators of its storied past. The high point in Ravenna's history was 1,500 long years ago, when the city became the capital of the Roman Empire. The honor was short-lived—the city was taken by the barbarian Ostrogoths in the 5th century; in the 6th century it was conquered by the Byzantines, who ruled it from Constantinople.

Because Ravenna spent much of its history looking to the East, its greatest art treasures show much Byzantine influence: above all, Ravenna is a city of mosaics, the finest in Western art. A single ticket, costing €8 from April to September, €6 from October to March (and available at ticket offices of all included sights), will admit you to six of Ravenna's most important monuments: the Tomba di Galla Placidia, the Basilica di San Vitale, the Battistero Neoniano, Sant'Apollinare Nuovo, the church of Spirito Santo, and the Museo Arcivescovile e Cappella Sant'Andrea.

Fodor'sChoice
★
The **Mausoleo di Galla Placidia and the Basilica di San Vitale** are decorated with the best-known, and most elaborate, mosaics in Ravenna. The little tomb and the great church stand side by side, but the tomb predates the church by at least a hundred years. Galla Placidia was the sister of Rome's emperor, Honorius, the man who moved the imperial capital to Ravenna in AD 402. She is said to have been beautiful and strong-willed and to have taken an active part in the governing of the crumbling empire. One of the most active Christians of her day, she endowed churches and supported priests and their congregations throughout the realm. This tomb, constructed in the mid-5th century, is her memorial.

Outside, the tomb is a small, unassuming building of red brick, whose seeming poverty of charm only serves to enhance the richness of the interior mosaics, in deep midnight blue and glittering gold. The tiny, low central dome is decorated with symbols of Christ and the evangelists and striking gold stars. Over the door is a depiction of the Good Shepherd. Eight of the Apostles are represented in groups of two on the four inner walls of the dome; the other four appear singly on the walls of the two transepts. Notice the small doves at their feet, drinking from the water of faith. Also in the tiny transepts are some delightful pairs of deer (representing souls), drinking from the fountain of resurrection. There are three sarcophagi in the tomb, none of which are believed to contain the remains of Galla Placidia. She died in Rome in AD 450, and there is no record of her body having been transported back to the place where she wished to lie.

The octagonal church of San Vitale, next door, was built in AD 547, after the Byzantines conquered the city, and its interior style shows a strong Byzantine influence. In the area behind the altar are the most famous works in the church, accurate portraits of the emperor of the East, Justinian, attended by his court and the bishop of Ravenna, Maximian. Facing him, across the chancel, is the emperor's wife, Theodora, with her entourage, holding a chalice containing the communion wine. The elaborate head-dresses and heavy cloaks of the emperor and empress convey a marvelous sense of the grandeur of the imperial court, and of the mastery of the artisans responsible for the depictions. Presiding over the royal couple from the apse is Christ the King with San Vitale and the founder of the church, Bishop Ecclesio, who holds a model of the building. Notice how the mosaics seamlessly wrap around the columns and curved arches on the upper sides of the altar area. Note that reservations are required in

May and June. ⊠ *Via San Vitale off Via Salara, near Piazza del Popolo* ☎ *0544/217522 reservations; 0544/215193 or 800/303999 information* ⊕ *www.ravennavisitcard.com* ☒ *Combination ticket €8 Apr.–Sept., €6 Nov.–Mar. €2 single-sight ticket available Mar.–May; reservations required Mar. 1–June 15* ⊗ *Jan.–Feb., daily 9–4:30; Mar. and Oct., daily 9–5; Apr.–Sept., daily 9–7.*

The **Museo Nazionale** of Ravenna, next to the Church of San Vitale, contains artifacts of ancient Rome, Byzantine fabrics and carvings, and other pieces of early Christian art. The collection is housed in a former monastery but is well displayed and artfully lighted. ⊠ *Via Fiandrini* ☎ *0544/34424* ☒ *Combination ticket €8 Apr.–Sept., €6 Nov.–Mar.* ⊗ *Tues.–Sat. 8:30–6:30, Sun. 8:30–7:30. Ticket office closes ½ hr before museum.*

Next door to Ravenna's 18th-century cathedral, the **Battistero Neoniano** is one of the town's most important mosaic sights. In keeping with the baptismal purpose of the building, the great mosaic in the dome shows the baptism of Christ, and beneath that scene are the Apostles. The lowest band of mosaics contains Christian symbols, the Throne of God and the Cross. Note the naked figure kneeling next to Christ—he is the personification of the River Jordan. The Battistero building is said to have been a Roman bath dating to the 5th century AD. ⊠ *Via Battistero* ☎ *0544/215201 or 800/303999* ⊕ *www.ravennavisitcard.com* ☒ *Combination ticket €8 Apr.–Sept.; €6 Nov.–Mar.; €2 single-sight ticket available Mar.–May* ⊗ *Jan.–Feb., daily 9–4:30; Mar. and Oct., daily 9–5:30; Apr.–Sept., daily 9–7.*

The **Tomba di Dante** (tomb of Dante) is in a small neoclassical building next door to the large church of St. Francis. Exiled from his native Florence, the author of *The Divine Comedy* died here in 1321. The Florentines have been trying to reclaim their famous son for hundreds of years, but the Ravennans refuse to give him up, arguing that since Florence did not welcome Dante in life it does not deserve him in death. In the church courtyard next door, note the site that served as temporary, less-grand quarters for the poet's distinguished bones: a plaque identifies the mound of earth under which the Franciscan brothers put Dante's remains for safekeeping from March 1944 to December 1945. The small **Museo Dantesco** is also on the site. ⊠ *Tomba Via Dante Alighieri 9, Museo Via Dante Alighieri 4* ☎ *0544/30252* ☒ *Tomb free; museum €2, free Sun.* ⊗ *Tomb Apr.–Sept., daily 9–7; Oct.–Mar., daily 9–noon and 2–5. Museum Apr.–Sept., Tues.–Sun. 9–noon and 3:30–6; Oct.–Mar., Tues.–Sun. 9–noon.*

The mosaics displayed in the church of **Sant'Apollinare Nuovo** date from the early 6th century, making them slightly older than the works in San Vitale. Since the left side of the church was reserved for women, it's only fitting that the mosaic decoration there is a scene of 22 virgins offering crowns to the Virgin Mary. On the right wall are 26 men carrying the crowns of martyrdom. They are approaching Christ, who is surrounded by angels. ⊠ *Via Roma, at intersection with Via Guaccimanni* ☎ *0544/219518 or 800/303999* ⊕ *www.ravennavisitcard.com* ☒ *Combination ticket €8 Apr.–Sept., €6 Nov.–Mar.* ⊗ *Daily 9:30–4:30.*

off the beaten path

SANT'APOLLINARE IN CLASSE – This church, about 5 km (3 mi) southeast of Ravenna, is landlocked now, but when it was built it stood in the center of the busy shipping port of Classis. The arch above and the area around the high altar are rich with mosaics. Those on the arch, older than the ones behind it, are considered superior to the rest. They show Christ in judgment and the 12 lambs of Christianity leaving the cities of Jerusalem and Bethlehem. In the apse is the figure of Sant'Apollinare himself, a bishop of Ravenna, and above him is a magnificent Transfiguration against blazingly green grass, animals in skewed perspective, and flowers. ⊠ *Via Romea Sud, Classe* ☎ *0544/473661* 🎟 *€2 or €6.50 combined ticket with the Ravenna museums and churches, free Sun.* ⏱ *Mon.–Sat. 8:30–7:30, Sun. 1–7.*

Where to Stay & Eat

$$ ✕ **Bella Venezia.** Graceful low archways lead into this attractive restaurant's two small dining rooms. Try the owner's special risotto *Bazzani* (with butter, Parmesan, cured ham, mushrooms, and peas) and, for the second course, *bistecca all'ortolana* (veal in cream sauce with cured ham and zucchini). A good-value tourist menu is available. Reservations are essential on weekends. ⊠ *Via IV Novembre 16* ☎ *0544/212746* ▭ *AE, DC, MC, V* ⏱ *Closed Sun. and 3 wks in Jan.*

$–$$ ✕ **Ca' de Ven.** A vaulted wine cellar in the heart of the old city, the Ca' de Ven is great for a hearty lunch or dinner. You sit at long tables with the other diners and feast on platters of delicious cold cuts, *piadine* (griddle breads), and cold, heady white wine. The *tortelli di radicchio e pecorino* (pasta pillows with radicchio and cheese) are the best first-course bet. ⊠ *Via C. Ricci 24* ☎ *0544/30163* ▭ *AE, DC, MC, V* ⏱ *Closed Mon., 3 wks in Jan.–Feb., and 1st wk of June.*

$$ 🏨 **Hotel Bisanzio.** Just steps from San Vitale and the Tomb of Galla Placidia, this Best Western hotel is the most convenient lodging for mosaic enthusiasts. Rooms are comfortable and modern, and the lobby's Florentine lamps add a touch of style. Ask for a room on the top floor and you may get a view of the basilica. ⊠ *Via Salara 30, 48100* ☎ *0544/217111* 🖷 *0544/32539* ⊕ *www.bisanziohotel.com* 🛏 *38 rooms* ⚐ *In-room safes, minibars, 2 bars, meeting room, parking (fee)* ▭ *AE, DC, MC, V.*

$ 🏨 **Hotel Centrale Byron.** In the heart of Ravenna's old town, this is an old-fashioned, well-managed hotel, its rooms spotless if uninspiring. Because it's in a pedestrian zone, tranquility is assured, though you will have to leave your car in one of the nearby garages. ⊠ *Via IV Novembre 14, 48100* ☎ *0544/212225* 🖷 *0544/34114* ⊕ *www.hotelbyron.com* 🛏 *54 rooms* ⚐ *In-room safes, minibars, bar* ▭ *AE, DC, MC, V.*

¢ 🏨 **Hotel Ravenna.** A functional stopover near the train station but still only a few minutes' walk from the center of town, this modern hotel offers smallish rooms with TVs and telephones. Two rooms are equipped for people with disabilities. ⊠ *Via Maroncelli 12, 48100* ☎ *0544/212204* 🖷 *0544/212077* 🛏 *26 rooms* ⚐ *Bar, parking (fee)* ▭ *MC, V.*

Nightlife & the Arts

The **Ravenna Festival,** a musical extravaganza held every year throughout June and July, brings in orchestras from all over the world to perform in Ravenna's mosaic-clad churches and theaters. Friday evenings in July and August you can experience **Mosaics by Night**—the byzantine masterpieces are lighted. Guided tours are available; consult the **tourist office** (☎ 0544/35404) for information.

en route

There are two routes from Ravenna to Rimini. The coastal road, S16, hugs the shoreline much of the way, passing through Cervia. Although its distance, 52 km (32 mi), is not great, this scenic route is naturally slower (beware of fog in winter). The coast north of Rimini is lined with dozens of small resort towns, only one having any charm—the seaport of Cesenatico; the others are mini-Riminis, and during summer the narrow road is hopelessly clogged with traffic. A faster route is to start on the inland S71 straight out of Ravenna, and then take the A14 back out to the coast, which leads directly into Rimini; the distance is 64 km (39 mi).

Rimini

⑲ *58 km (36 mi) southeast of Faenza, 121 km (76 mi) southeast of Bologna.*

Rimini is the principal summer resort on the Adriatic Coast and one of the most popular holiday destinations in Italy. Every summer, beginning in June and peaking in August, the city is flooded with vacationers, not just from Italy but from France, Austria, Germany, Scandinavia, and Great Britain as well. Be warned: Rimini is given over almost exclusively to tourism, with hundreds of hotels, grand and modest, and with restaurants catering to virtually every palate—you are just as likely to find a Bierkeller or an English tearoom as you are an Italian restaurant. The waterfront is lined with beach clubs that rent deck chairs and umbrellas by the day, week, month, or the entire season. Hotels along the beachfront have staked out their own private turf; swimming without having to pay for the privilege can be done only at one of the public beaches. This is possible, but prepare for sunbathers packed in like sardines. Prepare also for murky seawater; tourists come to Rimini for the company and nightlife, not an idyllic setting. In the off-season (October–March), Rimini is a cold, windy ghost town. Some hotels and restaurants are open, but the majority are closed tight, hibernating until the return of the spendthrift tourists. Summers are so crowded here that it's most unwise to visit without confirmed hotel reservations.

The new town has just about swallowed the old town, but there is evidence here and there of Rimini's long and turbulent history. Rimini stands at the junction of two great Roman consular roads: the Via Emilia and the Via Flaminia. In addition, in Roman times it was an important port, making it a strategic and commercial center.

From the 13th century onward, Rimini was controlled by the Malatesta family, an unpredictable group capable of grand gestures and savage deeds. The famous lovers immortalized in Dante's *Inferno*, Paolo (died 1304) and Francesca (died 1283 or 1284), were Malatestas. Sigismondo Malatesta (1417–68), lord of the city in the middle of the 15th century, banished his first wife, strangled his second, and poisoned his third. He lived with his beautiful mistress, Isotta, until her death, upon which he was so grief-stricken that he raised a magnificent monument ★ in her honor, the **Tempio Malatestiano,** the principal sight in the town. The Renaissance facade by Leon Battista Alberti (1404–72) is in the shape of a Roman triumphal arch and, with its high arcades, deep chapels, and marble balustrades, is considered to be one of Alberti's masterpieces.

The interior is light and spacious and contains the tombs of both the lovers. The dollar-sign-like intertwined *I,* for Isotta, and *S,* for Sigismondo, are everywhere. The carvings of elephants and roses recall the coat of arms of the Malatesta family. To the right of the entrance, in what is now the Tempio's book and gift shop, is a wonderful fresco by Piero della Francesca (1420–92); when the shop is closed, one of the cathedral's staff will unlock the room. Over the main altar of the church is a crucifix attributed to Giotto (1266–1337). ✉ *Via IV Novembre 35* ☎ *0541/51130* ⊕ *www.diocesi.rimini.it* 🎫 *Free* ☽ *Mon.–Sat. 8–12:30 and 3:30–6:30, Sun. 9–1 and 3:30–7.*

Rimini's oldest monument is the **Arco d'Augusto,** now stranded in the middle of a square just inside the city ramparts. It was erected in 27 BC, making it the oldest Roman arch in existence, and it marks the intersection of the Via Emilia and the Via Flaminia. To reach the Arch of Augustus from the Tempio Malatestiano, walk up Via Quattro Novem-

SAN MARINO, A COUNTRY ON A CLIFF

THE WORLD'S SMALLEST and oldest republic," as San Marino dubs itself, is landlocked entirely by Italy. It consists of three ancient castles perched high on cliffs of sheer rock rising implausibly out of the flatlands of Romagna, and a tangled knot of cobblestoned streets below, which are, unfortunately, lined with tourist boutiques, cheesy hotels and restaurants, and gun shops. The 45-minute drive from Rimini is easily justified, however, by the castle-top view of the stunning green countryside far below the tiny country. The 1,000-meter-plus precipices of sheer rock will make jaws drop and acrophobes quiver.

San Marino was founded in the 4th century AD by a stonecutter named Marino who settled with a small community of Christians, escaping persecution by pagan emperor Diocletian. Over the millennia, largely because of the logistical and strategic nightmares associated with attacking a fortified rock, San Marino was more or less left alone by Italy's various conquerors, and continues to this day to operate as a politically independent country (population 26,000) and a member of the United Nations, economically supported almost entirely by its 3-million-visitor-per-year tourist industry.

San Marino's headline attractions are its three castles, which are medieval architectural wonders and, above all, engineering curiosities. The **tre castelli** appear on every coat of arms in the city. Starting in the center of town, you can walk along a paved cliff-top ridge from the 10th-century *Castello della Guaita* (☎ 0549/991369) to the 13th-century *Castello della Cesta* (☎ 0549/991295), which contains a museum of ancient weapons, and finally to the 14th-century *Castello Montale,* the most remote castle (closed to the public). Every step of the way affords spectacular views of Romagna and the Adriatic Sea; it is said that from the castle-top perches, on a clear day, you can see across the sea to Croatia. The walks make for a good day's exercise but are by no means arduous. The longest—and windiest—hike is the one between the second and third castle.

Even if you arrive after castle visiting hours (8–8, shorter hours in winter), the ridge walk from castle to castle is supremely worthwhile.

A must-see while in San Marino is the **Piazza della Libertà,** whose battlemented and clock-topped Palazzo Pubblico is guarded by San Marino's real-life soldiers in their green uniforms. At the **Ferrari Museum** (✉ Maranello Rosso, V. III Settembre 3; park at the border crossing ☎ 0549/900824) you can gaze at the automotive toys of the wealthy. As you'll notice by peering into the shops along the old town's winding streets, the republic is famous for its crossbows—and more: shopping for fireworks, firearms, and other items illegal for sale elsewhere is another popular tourist activity.

Most of the actual 26,000 residents live not in the medieval town above but rather along the more modern and accessible streets below the rock. Visiting San Marino in winter—off-season—increases the appeal of the experience, as tourist establishments shut down and you more or less have the castles to yourself. In August, on the other hand, every inch of walkway on the rock is mobbed with sightseers. To get to San Marino by car, take highway SS72 west from Rimini. From Borgo Maggiore, at the base of the rock, a harrowing but scenic cable car will whisk you up to the castles and town. Alternatively, drive all the way up the winding road; public parking is available in the town itself. Don't worry about changing money, showing passports, learning telephone codes, and the like (although the tourist office will stamp your passport for €1); San Marino is, for all practical purposes, Italy—except, that is, for its majestic perch, its gun laws, and its reported 99% national voter turnout rate.

bre to Piazza Tre Martiri (where, legend says, the mule carrying St. Anthony suddenly stopped and knelt in honor of the Holy Sacrament that was being carried past at the time) and turn left onto Corso d'Augusto. ⊠ *Largo Giulio Cesare.*

Where to Stay & Eat

★ $$ ✕ **Dallo Zio.** Nothing but seafood is served here, and all of it is good and a good value. Two small rooms are unpretentiously furnished, one with antiques. Recommended are the *brodetto dell'Adriatica* (deliciously tangy shellfish broth) and *passatelli al pesce* (pasta twists with mixed fish). ⊠ *Vicolo Santa Chiara 16* ☎ *0541/786747* ♻ *Reservations essential* ⊟ *DC, MC, V* ☉ *Closed Mon. No lunch Tues.–Fri.*

★ $$ ✕ **La Locanda di San Martino.** Some have been known to drive all the way from the Ligurian coast just for the Adriatic delights at this casually elegant restaurant, off the road out of Rimini heading toward Bologna. An outdoor patio in the back is more romantic than the nondescript main dining room. Dishes like *spaghettoni ai frutti di mare* (thick spaghetti with seafood sauce) and *grigliata di pesce mista* (mixed seafood grill) are uniformly fresh and superbly prepared, and the mixed antipasto served with lunch is exquisite. ⊠ *Via Emilia 226* ☎ *0541/680127* ♻ *Reservations recommended* ⊟ *AE, DC, MC, V* ☉ *Closed Mon. in Oct.–May.*

$$ ✕ **Taverna degli Artisti.** The row of stylish glass-and-wood doors that enclose this restaurant give it the air of a French bistro, but once you're inside, the atmosphere is abundantly Italian. A local clientele of resort types and expatriates chats table to table over such specialties as *crudaiola* (spicy spaghetti with tomatoes, basil, tuna, olives, and anchovies) and the Chianina steaks. An enormous wood oven and marble pizza-making counter provide a centerpiece to the sunny dining room. ⊠ *Viale Vespucci 1* ☎ *0541/28519* ⊟ *AE, DC, MC, V.*

¢ ✕ **Piada e Cassoni da Jonny.** This bright, bustling take-out joint in the center of town is the best place for grilled flatbread, one of the traditional specialties of Romagnan cooking. A brisk staff will fill a *piada* (grilled flatbread with cheese, tomato, and meat or vegetables) or *cassoni* (a bigger filled pocket of bread, more like a calzone, but also grilled) to order while you wait, for only a couple of euros—just don't expect to sit down. For when you're feeling lazy, Jonny also delivers. ⊠ *Via Giovanni XXIII 101* ☎ *0541/29675* ⊟ *No credit cards.*

★ $$$$ ▥ **Grand Hotel.** This fin de siècle extravaganza, made famous by Fellini in his *Amarcord,* is grander than ever. The hyperluxe atmosphere set by enormous crystal chandeliers in the lobby, bright pink hallways, and inlaid wood in the rooms seems playful rather than formal; a spotless private beach completes the scene. Entourages and steamer trunks will never be out of place here; neither would it be a surprise to see a greyhound loping through the restaurant on her way to the pool. ⊠ *Via Ramusio, 1, Parco Federico Fellini, 47900* ☎ *0541/56000* ▤ *0541/56866* ⊕ *www.grandhotelrimini.com* ⇆ *98 rooms, 19 suites* ⚘ *2 restaurants, minibars, tennis court, 2 outdoor pools, hair salon, health club, massage, sauna, beach, 2 bars, nightclub, meeting room* ⊟ *AE, DC, MC, V.*

$$–$$$ ▥ **Club House Hotel.** The Club House is a bit of a double-edged sword: for some, the suburban-office-building architecture and commercial-strip location may be off-putting; however, thanks to the design, all rooms have balconies right on the sea. The hotel's rooms and facilities invite less debate: lovely, clean, airy rooms with green-and-white-striped ticking and across-the-street private beach access will spell summer vacation to all. Note that rates go up markedly for two weeks in August. ⊠ *Viale Vespucci 52, 47900* ☎ *0541/391460* ▤ *0541/391442* ⊕ *www.clubhouse.it* ⇆ *28 rooms* ⚘ *Restaurant, minibars, pool, beach, bar* ⊟ *AE, DC, MC, V* ☉ *Closed mid-Dec.–mid-Jan. Restaurant closed Oct.–May.*

¢ 🏠 **Annarita.** Set back on a residential road leading off the main Viale Vespucci, this hotel is small but comfortable, with a loyal clientele (availability may consequently be limited). Facilities are rudimentary, rooms are basic, but the main benefits here are proximity to the beach promenade and a friendly price. Off-season rates are so low that they border on ridiculous. ⊠ *Viale Misurata 24, 47900* 🕾 *0541/391044* ⊕ *www.hotelannarita.it* ⇆ *14 rooms* ⚲ *Restaurant, bar* ⊟ *No credit cards.*

EMILIA-ROMAGNA A TO Z

To research prices, get advice from other travelers, and book travel arrangements, visit www.fodors.com.

AIR TRAVEL

Bologna is an important business and convention center and is therefore well served by European airlines linking it with Italian cities and European capitals, including Rome and Milan (on Alitalia), Paris (on Air France), London (on British Airways and the low-cost carrier easyJet), Barcelona (on Iberia), Amsterdam (on KLM), and Frankfurt (on Lufthansa). There are no direct flights to the United States, however. Those wishing to fly direct often choose instead to fly into and rent a car in Milan Malpensa airport, a 45-minute drive on the A1 autostrada from Piacenza and an easy two hours from Bologna. Parma, Rimini, and Forlì are the smaller hubs in the region. Alitalia operates a daily Rome-Parma flight; the low-cost operator Ryanair runs daily service between London (Stansted) and Forlì; and Air Minerva, which code-shares with Alitalia, connects Rimini with Rome and Milan.

🛄 Airlines & Contacts **Air France** 🕾 848/884466 ⊕ www.airfrance.com. **Alitalia** 🕾 848/865641 ⊕ www.alitalia.com. **British Airways** 🕾 848/81266 ⊕ www.british-airways.com. **easyJet** 🕾 848/887766 ⊕ www.easyjet.com. **Iberia** 🕾 848/870000 ⊕ www.iberia.com. **KLM** 🕾 02/218981 ⊕ www.northwest.com. **Lufthansa** 🕾 0516477730 ⊕ www.lufthansa.com. **Ryanair** 🕾 199/114114 ⊕ www.ryanair.com.

AIRPORTS

The main airport of the region, Guglielmo Marconi, is 10 km (6 mi) northwest of Bologna. Aerobus service (Bus 54, €4.15) connects Guglielmo Marconi with Bologna's central train station as well as a downtown stop. It runs every half hour from 6 AM to 11:30 PM. Parma's small airport is Aeroporto G. Verdi, and Rimini's is called Aeradria; both are connected by bus to their respective cities at arrival and departure times. The airport at Forlì, 6 km (4 mi) from the A14 autostrada is convenient to Ravenna, Rimini, and Bologna (a Bologna-bound bus waits for all Ryanair arrivals).

🛄 Airport Information **Aeradria Rimini Airport** ⊠ Rimini 🕾 0541/715711 ⊕ www.riminiairport.com. **Aeroporto di Forlì** ⊠ Forlì 🕾 0543/474990 ⊕ www.forli-airport.it. **Aeroporto G. Verdi** ⊠ Parma 🕾 0521/982626 ⊕ www.aeroportoparma.it. **Guglielmo Marconi** ⊠ Via Triumvirato 84, Bologna 🕾 051/6479615 ⊕ www.bologna-airport.it.

BUS TRAVEL

Thanks to the autostrada bisecting the region and Emilia-Romagnan efficiency, bus travel in the region is easy—although the train is still easier. Private bus service links all the cities of Emilia-Romagna, with Bologna being the central hub. In Bologna, ATC buses leave from the terminal in Piazza XX Settembre, to the left upon exiting the train station. In Modena, contact ATCM; in Ferrara, ACFT, near the train station; and in Rimini, TRAM, on Via Roma.

For inner-city travel in Bologna, the *autostazione* (bus terminal) is at the top of Via dell'Indipendenza. City-run bus routes connect major towns with smaller villages and hamlets in the district, but routes are round-about, and schedules vary from place to place.

🔢 Bus Information ACFT ☎ 0532/599492. ATC ☎ 051/290290 ⊕ www.atc.bo.it. ATCM ✉ Via Fabriani ☎ 059/218226. **Autostazione** ✉ in Piazza XX Settembre ☎ 051/290290 information ⊕ www.autostazionebo.it. TRAM ☎ 0541/390444.

CAR RENTAL

🔢 Local Agencies **Avis** ✉ Via Triumvirato 84, at the airport, Bologna ☎ 051/6472032 ✉ Via Pietrammellara 27/D, Bologna ☎ 051/255024 ✉ Via Marco Polo 91, Bologna ☎ 051/6341632 ✉ Via Dell'Aeroporto 44/A, at the airport, Parma ☎ 0521/291238 ✉ Viale Trieste 16D, Rimini ☎ 0541/51256. **Europcar** ✉ Via Amendola 12/f, Bologna ☎ 051/247101 ✉ at the airport, Bologna ☎ 051/6472111 ✉ Hotel Baglioni, Viale Piacenza 51/c, Parma ☎ 0521/293035 ✉ at the airport ☎ 0521/293035 ✉ Via Giovanni XXIII 126, Rimini ☎ 0541/54746. **SIXT Autonoleggio** ✉ Viale Mazzini 4/3, Bologna ☎ 051/255546.

CAR TRAVEL

Bologna is on the autostrada network, so driving between cities is a breeze. The Via Emilia (SS9), one of the oldest roads in the world, runs through the heart of the region. It is a straight, low-lying modern road, the length of which can be traveled in a few hours. Ferrara and Ravenna are joined to it by good modern highways. Although less scenic, the A1 ("Autostrada del Sole") and A14 highways, which run parallel to the SS9, will get you where you're going about twice as fast. Note that much of the historic center of Bologna is closed off to cars daily 7 AM–8 PM.

EMERGENCY SERVICES ACI Emergency Service offers 24-hour roadside assistance.
🔢 ACI dispatchers ☎ 803/116.

ROAD CONDITIONS Beware of low-lying fog in fall and winter, especially in Romagna nearer to the Adriatic coast. On some nights the fog can render driving an impossibility.

EMERGENCIES

For first aid, ask for "Pronto Soccorso," and be prepared to give your address. Pharmacies take turns staying open late and on Sunday; for the latest information, consult the current list posted on the front door of each pharmacy or ask at the local tourist office.

🔢 Carabinieri ☎ 112. Police, Ambulance ☎ 113. Doctors and dentists ☎ 113.

MAIL & SHIPPING

🔢 Post Offices **Bologna** ✉ Piazza Minghetti 1, 40124. **Ferrara** ✉ Viale Cavour 27, 44100. **Modena** ✉ Via Emilia Centro 86, 41100. **Parma** ✉ Via Pisacane 1, 43100. **Ravenna** ✉ Piazza Garibaldi 1, 48100. **Rimini** ✉ Largo G. Cesare 1, 47900.

TRAIN TRAVEL

Bologna is an important rail hub for the entire northern part of Italy and has frequent, fast train service to Rome, Milan, Florence, and Venice. The railway follows the Via Emilia (SS9), and all the cities covered can be easily reached by train. Contact Ferrovie dello Stato, the national train operator, for more information.

🔢 Train Information **Ferrovie dello Stato (FS)** ☎ 848/888088 ⊕ www.trenitalia.com.

TRAVEL AGENCIES

🔢 Local Agent Referrals **Marconi Tours** ✉ Via Marconi 47, Bologna ☎ 051/235783. **Viaggi Urbinati** ✉ Viale Vespucci 127, Rimini ☎ 0541/391660.

VISITOR INFORMATION

fl Tourist Information **Bologna** ✉ Aeroporto Guglielmo Marconi ☎ 051/246541 ✉ Stazione Centrale, 40121 ☎ 051/246541 ✉ Piazza Maggiore 1, 40124 ☎ 051/246541 ⊕ www.comune.bologna.it/bolognaturismo. **Busseto** ✉ Comune, Piazza Giuseppe Verdi 10, 43011 ☎ 0524/931732. **Dozza** ✉ Via XX Settembre, 40050 ☎ 0542/678052. **Faenza** ✉ Piazza del Popolo 1, 48018 ☎ 0546/691602. **Ferrara** ✉ Castello Estense, 44022 ☎ 0532/209370 ⊕ www.ferraraterraeacqua.it. **Modena** ✉ Via Scudari 12, 41100 ☎ 059/206660, ✉ Palazzo dei Musei, Via Vittorio Veneto 5 ☎ 059/200125 ⊕ www.comune.modena.it/infoturismo. **Parma** ✉ Via Melloni 1/a, 43100 ☎ 0521/218889 ⊕ turismo.comune.parma.it. **Piacenza** ✉ Piazza Cavalli 7 29100 ☎ 0523/329324 ⊕ www.provincia.pc.it/turismo. **Ravenna** ✉ Via Salara 8, 48100 ☎ 0544/35404 ⊕ www.turismo.ravenna.it. **Rimini** ✉ Piazzale Cesare Battisti, 47037 ☎ 0541/51331 ✉ Piazzale Fellini 3, Marina Centro, 47037 ☎ 0541/56902 ⊕ www.riminiturismo.it. **San Marino** ✉ Contra Omagnano 20 ☎ 0549/882400.

FLORENCE

8

FODOR'S CHOICE
Beacci Tornabuoni, hotel, near Santa Maria Novella
Cibrèo, restaurant, near Santa Croce
Galleria degli Uffizi, near Piazza della Signoria
Residenza Johanna I, hotel, near San Marco
Santa Croce

HIGHLY RECOMMENDED

RESTAURANTS   Beccofino, Lungarno South
Caffètteria Piansa, Santa Croce
La Giostra, Santa Croce
Le Fonticine, San Lorenzo
Osteria de'Benci, Santa Croce
Taverna del Bronzino, San Lorenzo

HOTELS   Bellettini, Santa Maria Novella
Monna Lisa, Santa Croce
Morandi alla Crocetta, Santissima Annunziata

SIGHTS   Bargello
Battistero, Piazza del Duomo
Cappelle Medicee, San Lorenzo
Duomo
Galleria dell'Accademia, San Marco
Palazzo Medici-Riccardi, San Lorenzo
Piazza della Signoria

Updated by
Patricia Rucidlo

YOU CANNOT IMAGINE ANY SITUATION MORE AGREEABLE than Florence," wrote the peripatetic Mary Wortley Montagu in 1740. This "agreeable situation" has captured the hearts and the imaginations of almost everyone who has made his or her way here. Florence (*Firenze* in Italian) casts a spell in the way that few cities can—perhaps because of its sublime art; perhaps because of the views at sunset over the Arno; perhaps because of the way Florentine food and wine delight the palate. Maybe it's because the city has not changed all that much since the 16th century. Though Florence was briefly the capital of a newly united Italy (1865–71), its place in the sun rests squarely on its illustrious, more distant past.

Though Florence can lay claim to a modest antique importance, it did not fully emerge into its own until the 11th century. In the early 1200s, Florence, like most of the rest of Italy, was rent by civic unrest. Two factions, the Guelphs and the Ghibellines, competed for power. The Guelphs supported the papacy, and the Ghibellines supported the Holy Roman Empire. Bloody battles—most notably the famous one at Montaperti in 1260—tore Florence and other Italian cities apart. Sometimes the Guelphs were in power and exiled the Ghibellines; at other times, the reverse was true. By the end of the 13th century the Guelphs ruled securely and Ghibellinism had been vanquished. This didn't end civic strife, however: the Guelphs split into the Whites and the Blacks for reasons still debated by historians. Dante, author of the *Divine Comedy,* was banished from Florence in 1301 because he was a White.

Local merchants had organized themselves into guilds by 1250, and in that year proclaimed themselves the "*primo popolo.*" It was the first attempt at democratic, republican rule. Though the episode lasted only 10 years, it constituted a breakthrough in Western history. Such a daring stance by the merchant class can be attributed to its newfound power, as Florence was emerging as one of the economic powerhouses in 13th-century Europe. Florentines were papal bankers; they instituted the system of international letters of credit; and the gold florin became the international standard of currency. With this economic strength came a building boom. Public and private palaces, churches, and basilicas were built, enlarged, or restructured. Sculptors such as Donatello and Ghiberti were commissioned to decorate them; painters such as Giotto and Botticelli were commissioned to fresco their walls.

Though ostensibly a republic, Florence was blessed (or cursed, depending on point of view) with one very powerful family, the Medici, who came into power in the 1430s and became the de facto rulers of Florence for several hundred years. The Medici originally came from north of Florence, and it was not until the time of Cosimo il Vecchio (1389–1464) that the family's foothold in Florence was securely established. Florence's golden age occurred during the reign of his grandson Lorenzo de' Medici (1449–92). Lorenzo was not only an astute politician, but also a highly educated man and a great patron of the arts. Called "Il Magnifico" (the Magnificent), he gathered around him poets, artists, philosophers, architects, and musicians and organized all manner of cultural events, festivals, and tournaments.

Lorenzo's son, Piero (1471–1503), proved inept at handling the city's affairs. He was run out of town in 1494, and Florence briefly enjoyed its status as a republic while dominated by the demagogic Dominican friar Girolamo Savonarola (1452–98). Savonarola preached against perceived pagan abuses and persuaded his followers to destroy their books, art, women's wigs, and jewelry in public "bonfires of the vanities." Eventually, he so annoyed the pope that he was declared a heretic and hanged.

After a decade of internal unrest, the republic fell and the Medici were recalled to power. But even with the return of the Medici, Florence never regained its former prestige. By the 1530s most of the major artistic talent had left the city—Michelangelo, for one, had settled in Rome. The now ineffectual Medici, eventually attaining the title of grand dukes, remained nominally in power until the line died out in 1737, after which time Florence passed from the Austrians to the French and back again until the unification of Italy (1865–70), when it briefly became the capital under King Vittorio Emanuele II (1820–78).

Florence was "discovered" in the 18th century by upper-class northerners making the grand tour. It became a mecca for travelers, particularly the Romantics, who were inspired by the elegance of its palazzi and its artistic wealth. Today, millions of modern visitors follow in their footsteps. As the sun sets over the Arno and, as Mark Twain described it, "overwhelms Florence with tides of color that make all the sharp lines dim and faint and turn the solid city to a city of dreams," it's hard not to fall under the city's spell.

EXPLORING FLORENCE

Sightseeing in Florence is easy: everything that you'll want to see is concentrated in the relatively small historic center of the city. But there is so much packed into the area that you may find yourself slogging from one mind-boggling sight to another and feeling overwhelmed. If you are not an inveterate museum enthusiast, take it easy. Don't try to absorb every painting or fresco that comes into view. There's second-rate art even in the Galleria degli Uffizi and the Palazzo Pitti (*especially* the Pitti), so find some favorites and enjoy them at your leisure.

Walking through the streets and alleyways in Florence is a discovery in itself, but to save time and energy (especially after a few days in the city), make use of the efficient bus system. Buses also provide the least-fatiguing way to reach Piazzale Michelangelo, San Miniato, and the Forte di Belvedere. It's easy to make excursions to, say, Fiesole or the Medici villas by city bus. Most churches are open from 8 or 9 until noon or 12:30 and from 3 or 4 until about 6. The Duomo has continuous hours.

In between tracking the Renaissance and beyond, stop to breathe in the city, the marvelous synergy between history and modern Florentine life. Firenze is a living, bustling metropolis that has managed to preserve its predominantly medieval street plan and mostly Renaissance infrastructure while successfully adapting to the insistent demands of 21st-century life.

During the 12th and 13th centuries, Florence, like most other Italian towns, was a forest of towers—more than 200 of them, if the smaller three- and four-story towers are included. Today only a handful survive, but if you look closely you'll find them as you explore the centro storico.

Numbers in the text correspond to numbers in the margin and on the Florence map.

Centro Storico: From the Duomo to the Ponte Vecchio

Florence's centro storico, a relatively small area stretching from the Piazza del Duomo south to the Arno, is arguably one of the most beautiful spots in the world. The churches, medieval towers, Renaissance palaces, and world-class museums and galleries are testimony to the artistic and architectural genius of the past millennium; taken together, they

You can see nearly all of Florence's most renowned sights in three days. Plan your day around the opening hours of museums and churches; to gain an edge on the tour groups in high season, go to the most heavily trafficked sights very early in the morning or around closing time. If you can, allow a day to explore each neighborhood.

8

If you have 3 days

Spend Day 1 exploring Florence's centro storico, which will give you an eyeful of such masterpieces as Ghiberti's bronze doors at the Battistero (these are copies; the originals are in the nearby Museo dell'Opera del Duomo), Giotto's Campanile (bell tower), Brunelleschi's cupola majestically poised atop the Duomo, and Botticelli's mystical *Primavera* and *Birth of Venus* at the Galleria degli Uffizi. On Day 2, wander north of the Duomo and take in the superb treasury of works ranging from Michelangelo's *David* at the Galleria dell'Accademia to the lavish frescoes at the Cappella dei Magi and the Museo di San Marco (don't miss San Lorenzo, Michelangelo's Biblioteca Medicea Laurenziana, and the Cappelle Medicee). On this afternoon (or on the afternoon of Day 3) head southeast to Santa Croce or west to Santa Maria Novella. On the third day, cross the Ponte Vecchio to the Arno's southern bank and explore the Oltrarno, being sure not to miss the gargantuan Palazzo Pitti, testament to the power of the Medici, and the Giardino di Boboli, once their own private garden.

If you have 5 days

Break down the tours in the above itinerary into shorter ones, adding a few sights such as Piazzale Michelangelo, halfway up a hill on the Arno's southern bank, and San Miniato—both with expansive views of the city. Climb Giotto's Campanile, which rewards you with sweeping views of the city and hills beyond, or if you're feeling even more adventurous, climb the narrow, twisting stairs to the top of the Duomo. Take Bus 7 from the station or Piazza del Duomo to enchanting Fiesole. Spend more time in the Galleria degli Uffizi and Bargello or at one of the smaller museums such as the Museo dell'Opificio delle Pietre Dure, around the corner from the Galleria dell'Accademia. The little-visited but nevertheless wonderful Museo di Storia della Scienza is worth a trip, as is the Museo di Santa Maria Novella.

If you have 8 days

Add an all-day excursion south to the Tuscan city of Siena or a couple of half-day trips to the Medici villas around Florence. Visit more of Florence's interesting smaller churches; there's a dazzling fresco by Perguino at Santa Maria Maddalena dei Pazzi and a brilliant Pontormo in the Oltrarno's Santa Felicita. On the trail of additional, lesser-known artistic gems, check out Andrea del Castagno's fresco of the *Last Supper* in the former refectory, Cenacolo di Sant'Apollonia, northwest of the Museo di San Marco. It's worth the trip to see Andrea del Sarto's stunning grisaille frescoes in the Chiostro dello Scalzo, north of the Museo di San Marco. The church of Santo Spirito, west of Piazza Pitti, is a fine example of 15th-century architectural rationalism.

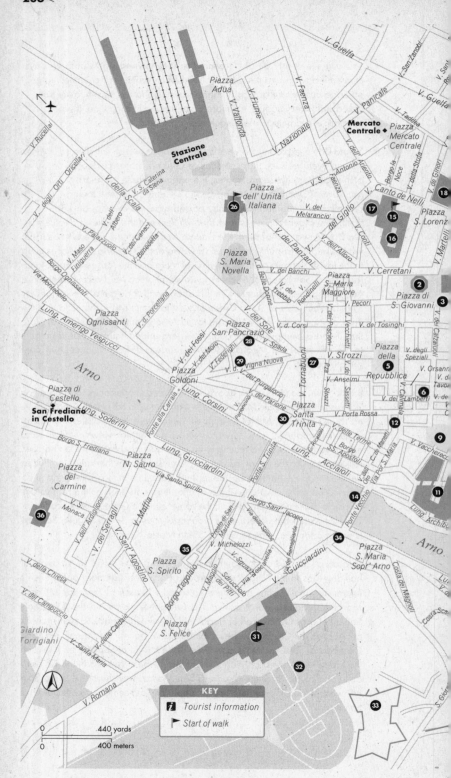

Piazza
Adua

Stazione
Centrale

V. Fiume
V. Vallfonda
V. Faenza
V. Nazionale
V. Panicale
V. Guelfa
V. Guelfa
V. Taddea
V. San Zanobi
V. Sant'...

Mercato
Centrale ◆

Piazza
Mercato
Centrale

V. S. Antonio
V. Faenza
V. dell'Ariento
Borgo la Noce
V. della Stufa
V. de' Ghiri

Piazza
dell' Unità
Italiana

26

Canto de Nelli

17 **15**

16

18

Piazza
S. Lorenzo

V. del Melarancio
V. del Giglio
V. Conti
V. dell'Alloro

V. dei Panzani

V. Martelli

Piazza
S. Maria
Novella

V. di Belle Donne
V. del Trebbio
V. dei Banchi
V. dei Rondinelli

Piazza
S. Maria
Maggiore

V. Cerretani

2

3

Piazza di
S. Giovanni

V. de' Pecori

V. degli Speziali

V. de' Catzanoli

V. de' Tosinghi

Piazza
San Pancrazio

28

V. del Sole
V. d. Corsi
V. dei Pescioni
V. de' Vecchietti

27

V. Strozzi

Piazza
della
Repubblica

5

V. Orsanmichele
V. d. Tavolini

V. Porcellana
V. d. Porcellana

Piazza
Ognissanti

V. dei Fossi
V. del Moro
V. Federighi
V. d. del Purgatorio

29

Vigna Nuova

Piazza
Goldoni

V. Spada

V. Tornabuoni
V. dei Sassetti
Pza. Strozzi
V. degli Anselmi

V. de' Calimala

V. de' Lamberti

6

V. de'...

Borgo Ognissanti

Lung. Amerigo Vespucci

Arno

Piazza di
Cestello

San Frediano
in Cestello

Lung. Soderini

Ponte alla Carraia

Lung. Corsini

30

Piazza
Santa
Trinita

Ponte S. Trinita

V. Parione
V. del Parione

Lung. Acciaioli

V. delle Terme
V. Porta Rossa

12

Borgo
SS. Apostoli
V. de' Mandri

9

V. Vacchereccia

V. Por S. Maria

14

11

Lung. Archibi...

Arno

Borgo S. Frediano

Piazza
N. Sauro

Lung. Guicciardini

Via Santo Spirito

Piazza
del
Carmine

V.S. Monaca
V. dell'Ardiglione
V. dei Serragli
V. Sant'Agostino
V. Maffia

36

35

V. Michelozzi

Piazza
S. Spirito

Borgo Tegolaio
V. Maggio
Sdrucciolo de' Pitti
Presto di San Martino
Via dello Sprone
V. dello Sguazza
Via Mazzetta
Sdrucciolo de' Pitti

Ponte Vecchio

34

Piazza
S. Maria
Sopr' Arno

V. Guicciardini

V. de' Renai
V. de' Bardi

Arno

Costa dei Magnoli

Costa Sca...

V. della Chiesa

V. del Campuccio

Giardino
Torrigiani

V. Santa Maria
V. delle Caldaie

Piazza
S. Felice

Piazza
S. Felice

31

32

33

V. Romana

KEY
ℹ️ *Tourist information*
▶ *Start of walk*

0 ————— 440 yards

0 ————— 400 meters

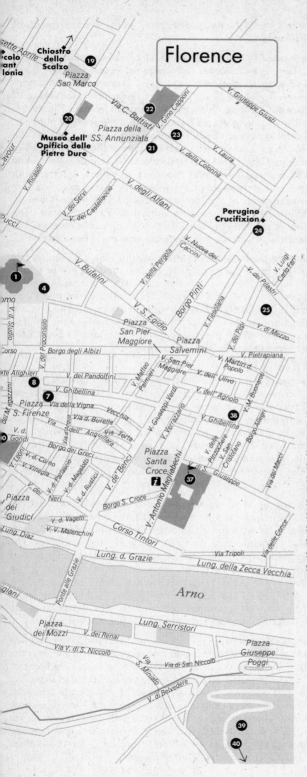

Florence

are a shrine to some of the most outstanding aesthetic achievements of Western history.

Start at the **Duomo** ❶ ⌐ and **Battistero** ❷, climb the **Campanile** ❸ if you wish, and then visit the **Museo dell'Opera del Duomo** ❹, behind the Duomo. Go directly south from the Duomo on Via dei Calzaiuoli, turning right on Via degli Speziali for a detour to **Piazza della Repubblica** ❺ and **Orsanmichele** ❻. Alternatively, go directly south from the Museo dell'Opera del Duomo along Via del Proconsolo to the **Bargello** ❼ museum, opposite the ancient church **Badia Fiorentina** ❽. Head west on Via della Condotta to Via Calzaiuoli, then south to discover the **Piazza della Signoria** ❾, with its Loggia dei Lanzi and **Palazzo Vecchio** ❿. The **Galleria degli Uffizi** ⓫, perhaps Italy's most important art gallery, is at the south side of the piazza. Exit from the piazza's southwest corner along Via Vacchereccia. At the corner of Via Por Santa Maria is the **Mercato Nuovo** ⓬, lined with stores. Follow Via Por Santa Maria to the river; walk east along the north side of the Arno to Piazza dei Giudici to see the **Museo di Storia della Scienza** ⓭. Backtrack west along the Arno to the **Ponte Vecchio** ⓮.

TIMING Though much of the Florence's centro storico is closed to automobile traffic, you still must dodge mopeds, cyclists, and masses of fellow tourists as you walk the narrow streets, especially in the area bounded by the Duomo, Piazza della Signoria, Galleria degli Uffizi, and Ponte Vecchio. It takes about 40 minutes to walk the route, with 45 minutes to 1 hour each for the Museo dell'Opera del Duomo and the Palazzo Vecchio; 1 to 1½ hours for the Bargello; and a minimum of 2 hours for the Uffizi (reserve tickets in advance to avoid long lines).

What to See

❽ **Badia Fiorentina.** This ancient church was rebuilt in 1285; its graceful bell tower, best seen from the interior courtyard, is beautiful for its unusual construction—a hexagonal tower built on a quadrangular base. The interior of the church was halfheartedly remodeled in the baroque style during the 17th century; its best-known work of art is the delicate *Vision of St. Bernard* by Filippino Lippi (circa 1457–1504), on the left as you enter. The painting—one of Lippi's finest—is in superb condition; note the Virgin Mary's beautifully rendered hands. ⊠ *Via Dante Alighieri 4, Bargello* ☎ *055/264402* ☜ *Free* ☾ *Mon. 3–6.*

★ ❼ **Bargello.** During the Renaissance, this building was headquarters for the *podestà*, or chief magistrate. It was also used as a prison, and the exterior served as a "most wanted" billboard: effigies of notorious criminals and Medici enemies were painted on its walls. Today, it houses the **Museo Nazionale,** containing what is probably the finest collection of Renaissance sculpture in Italy. The concentration of masterworks by Michelangelo (1475–1564), Donatello (circa 1386–1466), and Benvenuto Cellini (1500–71) is remarkable; they're distributed among an eclectic array of arms, ceramics, and enamels. For Renaissance art lovers, the Bargello is to sculpture what the Uffizi is to painting.

In 1401 Filippo Brunelleschi (1377–1446) and Lorenzo Ghiberti (circa 1378–1455) vied for the most prestigious commission of the day: the decoration of the north doors of the baptistery in Piazza del Duomo. For the competition, each designed a bronze bas-relief panel depicting the Sacrifice of Isaac; both panels are displayed, together, in the room devoted to the sculpture of Donatello on the upper floor. The judges chose Ghiberti for the commission; see if you agree with their choice. ⊠ *Via del Proconsolo 4, Bargello* ☎ *055/2388606* ⊕ *www.arca.net/db/musei/ bargello.htm* ☜ *€4* ☾ *Daily 8:15–1:50* ☾ *Closed 2nd and 4th Mon. of month and 1st, 3rd, and 5th Sun. of month.*

8

Looking at Art

The abundance of Renaissance art in Florence is staggering—so much so that you may find yourself literally staggering as you try to take it all in. To avoid an art hangover, accept the fact that, no matter how determined you may be, you will not see everything. You're likely to have a more satisfying experience if you pick and choose sights that strike your interest, give yourself the freedom to follow your whims, and ignore any pangs of guilt if you'd rather nap at your hotel than stand in line at the Uffizi. Florence isn't a city that can be "done"; instead, it's a place you can return to again and again, confident that there will always be more treasures to discover.

Shopping

Since the days of the medieval guilds, Florence has been synonymous with fine craftsmanship and good business. Such time-honored Florentine specialties as antiques (and reproductions), bookbinding, jewelry, lace, leather goods, silk, and straw attest to this. Lovely paper products are made here and sold all over town. The leather produced here is of especially good quality. The various shopping areas are a throwback to the Middle Ages, when each district supplied a different product. During the Renaissance, the Oltrarno was the neighborhood where the artisans lived, and if you wander around there now you'll find that little has changed: there are still goldsmiths, leather workers, and furniture restorers, among others, plying their trade.

★ ❷ **Battistero** (Baptistery). The octagonal Baptistery is one of the supreme monuments of the Italian Romanesque style and one of Florence's oldest structures. Local legend has it that it was once a Roman temple of Mars; modern excavations, however, suggest that its foundations date from the 4th to 5th and the 8th to 9th centuries AD, well after the collapse of the Roman Empire. The round-arched Romanesque decoration on the exterior probably dates from the 11th century. The interior dome mosaics from the early 14th century are justly renowned, but—glittering beauties though they are—they could never outshine the building's famed bronze Renaissance doors decorated with panels crafted by Lorenzo Ghiberti. The doors—or at least copies of them—on which Ghiberti spent most of his adult life (1403–52) are on the north and east sides of the Baptistery, and the Gothic panels on the south door were designed by Andrea Pisano (active circa 1290–1348) in 1330. The original Ghiberti doors were removed to protect them from the effects of pollution and acid rain and have been beautifully restored; some of the panels are now on display in the Museo dell'Opera del Duomo.

Ghiberti's north doors depict scenes from the life of Christ; his later east doors (dating 1425–52), facing the Duomo facade, render scenes from the Old Testament. Very different in style, they illustrate the artistic changes that marked the beginning of the Renaissance. Look at the far right panel of the middle row on the earlier (1403–24) north doors (*Jesus Calming the Waters*). Ghiberti captured the chaos of a storm at sea with great skill and economy, but the artistic conventions he used are basically pre-Renaissance: Jesus is the most important figure, so he is the largest; the disciples are next in size, being next in importance; the ship on which they founder looks like a mere toy.

The exquisitely rendered panels on the east doors are larger, more expansive, more sweeping—and more convincing. Look at the middle panel on the left-hand door. It tells the story of Jacob and Esau, and the various episodes—the selling of the birthright, Isaac ordering Esau to go hunting, the blessing of Jacob, and so forth—have been merged into a single beautifully realized street scene. Ghiberti's use of perspective suggests depth: the background architecture looks far more credible than on the north door panels, the figures in the foreground are grouped realistically, and the naturalism and grace of the poses (look at Esau's left leg and the dog next to him) have nothing to do with the sacred message being conveyed. Although the religious content remains, the figures and their place in the natural world are given new prominence and are portrayed with a realism not seen in art since the fall of the Roman Empire more than a thousand years before.

As a footnote to Ghiberti's panels, one small detail of the east doors is worth a special look. Just to the lower left of the Jacob and Esau panel, Ghiberti placed a tiny self-portrait bust. From either side, the portrait is extremely appealing—Ghiberti looks like everyone's favorite uncle— but the bust is carefully placed so that there is a single spot from which you can make direct eye contact with the tiny head. When that contact is made, the impression of intelligent life is astonishing. It is no wonder that these doors received one of the most famous compliments in the history of art from an artist known to be notoriously stingy with praise: Michelangelo himself declared them so beautiful that they could serve as the Gates of Paradise. ⊠ *Piazza del Duomo* ☎ *055/2302885* ⊕ *www. operaduomo.firenze.it* ⊠ *€3* ⊙ *Mon.–Sat. noon–7, Sun. 8:30–2.*

❸ **Campanile.** The Gothic bell tower designed by Giotto (1266–1337) is a soaring structure of multicolored marble originally decorated with reliefs that are now in the Museo dell'Opera del Duomo. A climb of 414 steps rewards you with a close-up of Brunelleschi's cupola on the Duomo next door and a sweeping view of the city. ⊠ *Piazza del Duomo* ☎ *055/ 2302885* ⊕ *www.operaduomo.firenze.it* ⊠ *€6* ⊙ *Daily 8:30–7:30.*

★ ▶ ❶ **Duomo** (Cattedrale di Santa Maria del Fiore). In 1296 Arnolfo di Cambio (circa 1245–circa 1310) was commissioned to build "the loftiest, most sumptuous edifice human invention could devise" in the Romanesque style on the site of the old church of Santa Reparata. The immense Duomo was not completed until 1436, the year when it was consecrated. The imposing facade dates only from the 19th century; it was added in the neo-Gothic style to complement Giotto's genuine Gothic 14th-century campanile. The real glory of the Duomo, however, is Filippo Brunelleschi's dome, presiding over the cathedral with a dignity and grace that few domes to this day can match. ·

Brunelleschi's **cupola** was an ingenious engineering feat. The space to be enclosed by the dome was so large and so high above the ground that traditional methods of dome construction—wooden centering and scaffolding—were of no use whatsoever. So Brunelleschi developed entirely new building methods, which he implemented with equipment of his own design (including a novel scaffolding method). Beginning work in 1420, he built not one dome but two, one inside the other, and connected them with common ribbing that stretched across the intervening empty space, thereby considerably lessening the crushing weight of the structure. He also employed a new method of bricklaying, based on an ancient Roman herringbone pattern, interlocking each new course of bricks with the course below in a way that made the growing structure self-supporting. The result was one of the great engineering breakthroughs of all time: most of Europe's later domes, including St. Peter's in Rome, were built employing Brunelleschi's methods, and today the Duomo has come to symbolize Florence in the same way that the Eiffel Tower symbolizes Paris. The Florentines are justly proud, and to this day the Florentine phrase for "homesick" is *nostalgia del cupolone* (homesick for the dome).

The interior is a fine example of Florentine Gothic. Much of the cathedral's best-known art has been moved to the nearby Museo dell'Opera del Duomo. Notable among the works that remain, however, are two towering equestrian frescoes honoring famous soldiers: *Niccolò da Tolentino,* painted in 1456 by Andrea del Castagno (circa 1419–57), and *Sir John Hawkwood,* painted 20 years earlier by Paolo Uccello (1397–1475); both are on the left-hand wall of the nave. A 10-year restoration, completed in 1995, repaired the dome and cleaned the vast and crowded fresco of the *Last Judgment,* executed by Vasari and Zuccaro, on its interior. Originally Brunelleschi wanted mosaics to cover the interior of the great ribbed cupola, but by the time the Florentines got around to commissioning the decoration, 150 years later, tastes had changed. Too bad: it's a fairly dreadful *Last Judgment* and hardly worth the effort of craning your neck to see it.

You can explore the upper and lower reaches of the cathedral. The remains of a Roman wall and an 11th-century cemetery have been excavated beneath the nave; the way down is near the first pier on the right. The climb to the top of the dome (463 steps) is not for the faint of heart, but the view is superb. ⊠ *Piazza del Duomo* ☎ *055/2302885* ⊕ *www. operaduomo.firenze.it* ☒ *Excavation €3, cupola €6* ☉ *Crypt: weekdays 10–5:40; Sat. 8:30–5:40; 1st Sat. of month 8:30–4. Cupola: weekdays 8:30–7, Sat. 8:30–5:40; 1st Sat. of month 8:30–4. Duomo: weekdays 10–5, Sat., 10–4:45, Sun. 3:30–4:45; 1st Sat. of month 10–3:30.*

⓫ **Galleria degli Uffizi.** The venerable Uffizi Gallery occupies the top floor
★ of the U-shape **Palazzo degli Uffizi** (Uffizi Palace) fronting on the Arno, designed by Giorgio Vasari (1511–74) in 1560 to hold the *uffizi* (administrative offices) of the Medici grand duke Cosimo I (1519–74). Later, the Medici installed their art collections here, creating what was Europe's first modern museum, open to the public (at first only by request) since 1591. Hard-core museum aficionados can pick up a complete guide to the collections at bookshops and newsstands.

Among the highlights are Paolo Uccello's *Battle of San Romano,* its brutal chaos of lances one of the finest visual metaphors for warfare ever captured in paint; the *Madonna and Child with Two Angels,* by Fra Filippo Lippi (1406–69), in which the impudent eye contact established by the angel would have been unthinkable prior to the Renaissance; the *Birth of Venus* and *Primavera* by Sandro Botticelli (1445–1510), the goddess of the former seeming to float on air and the fairy-tale charm of the latter exhibiting the painter's idiosyncratic genius at its zenith; the portraits of the Renaissance duke Federico da Montefeltro and his wife, Battista Sforza, by Piero della Francesca (circa 1420–92); the *Madonna of the Goldfinch,* by Raphael (1483–1520), which, though darkened by time, captures an aching tenderness between mother and child; Michelangelo's *Doni Tondo* (the only panel painting that can be securely attributed to him); a *Self-Portrait as an Old Man* by Rembrandt (1606–69); the *Venus of Urbino* by Titian (circa 1488/90–1576); and the splendid *Bacchus* by Caravaggio (circa 1571/72–1610). In the last two works, the approaches to myth and sexuality are diametrically opposed, to put it mildly. If panic sets in at the prospect of absorbing all this art at one go, visit later in the afternoon when it's less crowded. Advance tickets can be purchased from Consorzio ITA. ⊠ *Piazzale degli Uffizi 6, Pi-*

azza della Signoria ☎ *055/23885* ✉ *Advance tickets* ✉ *Consorzio ITA, Piazza Pitti 1, 50121* ☎ *055/294883* ⊕ *www.uffizi.firenze.it* 🎫 *€8.50, (€1.55 reservation fee)* ☉ *Tues.–Sun. 8:15–6:50.*

need a break?

GustaVino (✉ Via della Condotta 37/r ☎ 055/2399806) calls itself an "enoteca with cucina," which means that you can drink and eat. Its handy location (a minute or two from Piazza Signoria) makes it a perfect spot to recover after a trip to the Uffizi.

⑫ **Mercato Nuovo** (New Market). This open-air loggia was new in 1551. Beyond its slew of souvenir stands, its main attraction is a copy of Pietro Tacca's bronze *Porcellino* (which translates as "little pig" despite the fact that the animal is, in fact, a wild boar) fountain on the south side, dating from around 1612 and copied from an earlier Roman work now in the Uffizi. The Porcellino is Florence's equivalent of the Trevi Fountain: put a coin in his mouth, and if it falls through the grate below (according to one interpretation), it means that one day you'll return to Florence. ✉ *Corner of Via Por Santa Maria and Via Porta Rossa, Piazza della Repubblica* ☉ *Market Tues.–Sat. 8–7, Mon. 1–7.*

❹ **Museo dell'Opera del Duomo** (Cathedral Museum). Ghiberti's original Baptistery door panels and the *cantorie* (choir loft) reliefs by Donatello and Luca della Robbia (1400–82) keep company with Donatello's *Mary Magdalen* and Michelangelo's *Pietà* (not to be confused with his more famous *Pietà* in St. Peter's in Rome). Renaissance sculpture is in part defined by its revolutionary realism, but in its palpable suffering, Donatello's *Magdalen* goes beyond realism. Michelangelo's heart-wrenching *Pietà* was unfinished at his death; the female figure on the left was added by one Tiberio Calcagni (1532–65), and never has the difference between competence and genius been manifested so clearly. ✉ *Piazza del Duomo 9* ☎ *055/2302885* ⊕ *www.operaduomo.firenze.it* 🎫 *€6* ☉ *Mon.–Sat. 9–7:30, Sun. 9–1:40.*

⑬ **Museo di Storia della Scienza** (Museum of the History of Science). Though it tends to be obscured by the glamour of the neighboring Uffizi, this science museum has much to recommend it: Galileo's own instruments, antique armillary spheres—some of them real works of art—and other reminders that the Renaissance made not only artistic but also scientific history. ✉ *Piazza dei Giudici 1, Piazza della Signoria* ☎ *055/265311* ⊕ *www.imss.fi.it* 🎫 *€6.50* ☉ *Oct.–May, Mon. and Wed.–Sat. 9:30–5, Tues. 9:30–1, 2nd Sun. of month 10–1; June–Sept., Mon. and Wed.–Fri. 9:30–5, Tues. and Sat. 9:30–1.*

❻ **Orsanmichele.** This multipurpose structure began as an 8th-century oratory and then in 1290 was turned into an open-air loggia for selling grain. Destroyed by fire in 1304, it was rebuilt as a loggia-market. Between 1367 and 1380 the arcades were closed and two stories added above; finally, at century's end it was turned into a church. Inside is a beautifully detailed 14th-century Gothic tabernacle by Andrea Orcagna (1320–68). The exterior niches contain sculptures dating from the early 1400s to the early 1600s by Donatello and Verrocchio (1435–88), among others, that were paid for by the guilds. Though it is a copy, Verrocchio's *Doubting Thomas* (circa 1470) is particularly deserving of attention. Here you see Christ, like the building's other figures, entirely framed within the niche, and St. Thomas standing on its bottom ledge, with his right foot outside the niche frame. This one detail, the positioning of a single foot, brings the whole composition to life. Most of the sculptures have since been replaced by copies; however, it's possible to see the originals at the **Museo di Orsanmichele** contained within.

✉ *Via dei Calzaiuoli; museum entrance at Via Arte della Lana, Piazza della Repubblica* ☎ *055/284944* 🎟 *Free* 🕐 *Daily 9–noon and 4–6* 🕐 *Closed 1st and last Mon. of month.*

❿ Palazzo Vecchio (Old Palace). Florence's forbidding, fortresslike city hall was begun in 1299, presumably designed by Arnolfo di Cambio, and its massive bulk and towering campanile dominate the Piazza della Signoria. It was built as a meeting place for the heads of the seven major guilds that governed the city at the time; over the centuries it has served lesser purposes, but today it is once again City Hall. The interior courtyard is a good deal less severe, having been remodeled by Michelozzo (1396–1472) in 1453; the copy of Verrocchio's bronze *puttino* (little child), topping the central fountain, softens the space.

Two adjoining rooms on the second floor supply one of the starkest contrasts in Florence. The vast **Sala dei Cinquecento** (Room of the Five Hundred) is named for the 500-member Great Council, the people's assembly established by Savonarola, which met here. The Sala was decorated by Giorgio Vasari, around 1563–65, with huge—almost grotesquely huge—frescoes celebrating Florentine history; depictions of battles with nearby cities predominate. Continuing the martial theme, the Sala also contains Michelangelo's *Victory* group, intended for the never-completed tomb of Pope Julius II (1443–1513), plus other sculptures of lesser quality.

The little **Studiolo** is to the right of the Sala's entrance. The study of Cosimo I's son, the melancholy Francesco I (1541–87), it was designed by Vasari and decorated by Vasari and Bronzino (1503–72). It is intimate, civilized, and filled with complex allegorical art. It makes the vainglorious proclamations next door ring more than a little hollow. ✉ *Piazza della Signoria* ☎ *055/2768465* 🎟 *€5.70* 🕐 *Mon.–Wed. and Fri.–Sat. 9–7, Thurs. 9–2, Sun. 9–7.*

❺ Piazza della Repubblica. This square marks the site of the ancient forum that was the core of the original Roman settlement that was to become Florence. The street plan in the area around the piazza still reflects the carefully plotted grid of the Roman military encampment. The Mercato Vecchio (Old Market), dating from the Middle Ages, was demolished and the current piazza was constructed between 1885 and 1895 as a neoclassical showpiece. The piazza is lined with outdoor cafés affording excellent spots to people-watch.

★ ❾ Piazza della Signoria. This is by far the most striking square in Florence. It was here, in 1497, that the famous "bonfire of the vanities" took place, when the fanatical friar Savonarola induced his followers to hurl their worldly goods into the flames; it was also here, a year later, that he was hanged as a heretic and, ironically, burned. A bronze plaque in the pavement marks the exact spot of his execution.

The statues in the square and in the 14th-century **Loggia dei Lanzi** on the south side vary in quality. Cellini's famous bronze *Perseus* holding the severed head of Medusa is certainly the most important sculpture in the loggia. Other works include *The Rape of the Sabine* and *Hercules and the Centaur,* both late-16th-century works by Giambologna (1529–1608), and, in the back, a row of sober matrons dating from Roman times. (*The Rape of the Sabine* is scheduled to be removed for safe-keeping and to be replaced with a copy.)

In the square, the Neptune Fountain, dating between 1550 and 1575, wins the booby prize. It was created by Bartolomeo Ammannati, who considered it a failure himself. The Florentines call it *Il Biancone*, which may be translated as "the big white one" or "the big white thing." Giambologna's equestrian statue, to the left of the fountain, pays tribute to Grand Duke Cosimo I. Occupying the steps of the Palazzo Vecchio are a copy of Donatello's heraldic lion of Florence, known as the *Marzocco* (the original is in the Bargello); a copy of Donatello's *Judith and Holofernes* (the original is inside the Palazzo Vecchio); a copy of Michelangelo's *David* (the original is now in the Galleria dell'Accademia); and Baccio Bandinelli's insipid *Hercules* (1534).

⓮ Ponte Vecchio (Old Bridge). This charming bridge was built in 1345 to replace an earlier bridge that was swept away by flood, and its shops housed first butchers, then grocers, blacksmiths, and other merchants. But in 1593 the Medici grand duke Ferdinand I (1549–1609), whose private corridor linking the Medici palace (Palazzo Pitti) with the Medici offices (the Uffizi) crossed the bridge atop the shops, decided that all this plebeian commerce under his feet was unseemly. So he threw out the butchers and blacksmiths and installed 41 goldsmiths and eight jewelers. The bridge has been devoted solely to these two trades ever since.

Take a moment to study the **Ponte Santa Trinita**, the next bridge downriver. It was designed by Bartolomeo Ammannati in 1567 (possibly from sketches by Michelangelo), blown up by the retreating Germans during World War II, and painstakingly reconstructed after the war. The view is beautiful from this bridge, which might explain why so many young lovers hang out here.

Michelangelo's Footsteps: From San Lorenzo to the Accademia

Sculptor, painter, architect, and, yes, even poet, native son Michelangelo was a consummate genius. Some of his finest work remains in his hometown. The Biblioteca Medicea Laurenziana is perhaps his most fanciful work of architecture. The key to understanding Michelangelo's genius is in the magnificent Cappelle Medicee, where his sculptural and architectural prowess can be clearly seen. Planned frescoes were never completed, sadly, for they would have shown in one space the artistic triple threat that he certainly was. The towering and beautiful *David,* his most famous work, resides in the Galleria dell'Accademia.

a good walk

Start at the church of **San Lorenzo ⓯ ▶**, visiting the **Biblioteca Medicea Laurenziana ⓰** and its famous anteroom before circling the church to the northwest and making your way through the San Lorenzo outdoor market on Via del Canto de' Nelli to the entrance of the **Cappelle Medicee ⓱**. Retrace your steps through the market and take Via dei Gori east to Via Cavour and the **Palazzo Medici-Riccardi ⓲**, once the home of Florence's most important family throughout the Renaissance. Follow Via Cavour two blocks north to Piazza San Marco and the church of the same name, attached to which is the **Museo di San Marco ⓳**, containing marvelous works by the pious and exceptionally talented painter-friar Fra Angelico. If you have time, go northwest from Piazza San Marco to see Castagno's *Last Supper* at Sant'Apollonia and then north to the Chiostro dello Scalzo. From Piazza San Marco, walk a half block south down Via Ricasoli to the **Galleria dell'Accademia ⓴**. Return to the east side of Piazza San Marco and take Via Cesare Battisti east into Piazza della Santissima Annunziata, one of Florence's prettiest squares, site of the **Spedale degli Innocenti ㉑** and, at the north end of the square, the church of **Santissima Annunziata ㉒**. One block southeast of the entrance to Santissima Annunziata, through the arch and on the left side of Via della Colonna, is the **Museo Archeologico ㉓**. Continue down Via della Colonna to **Santa Maria Maddalena dei Pazzi ㉔**, harboring a superb fresco by Perugino. Return to Via della Colonna and continue heading southeast; take a right on Via Luigi Carlo Farini, where you'll find the **Sinagoga** ㉕ and its Museo Ebraico.

TIMING The walk alone takes about one hour, plus 45 minutes for the Cappelle Medicee, 20 minutes for the Palazzo Medici-Riccardi, 40 minutes for the Museo di San Marco, 30 minutes for the Galleria dell'Accademia (*David*), and 40 minutes for the Museo Archeologico. Note that the Museo di San Marco closes at 1:50 on weekdays. After visiting San Lorenzo, resist the temptation to explore the market that surrounds the church before going to the Palazzo Medici-Riccardi; you can always come back later, when the churches and museums have closed; the market is open until 7 PM.

What to See

⓰ **Biblioteca Medicea Laurenziana** (Laurentian Library). Michelangelo the architect was every bit as original as Michelangelo the sculptor. Unlike Brunelleschi (the architect of San Lorenzo), however, he was not obsessed with proportion and perfect geometry. He was interested in experimentation and invention and in expressing a personal vision at times highly idiosyncratic.

It was never more idiosyncratic than in the Laurentian Library, begun in 1524 and finished in 1568, and its famous **vestibolo.** This strangely shaped anteroom has had scholars scratching their heads for centuries. In a space more than two stories high, why did Michelangelo limit his use of columns and pilasters to the upper two-thirds of the wall? Why didn't he rest them on strong pedestals instead of on huge, decorative curlicue scrolls, which rob them of all visual support? Why did he recess them into the wall, which makes them look weaker still? The architectural elements here do not stand firm and strong and tall, like those inside the church next door; instead, they seem to be pressed into the wall as if into putty, giving the room a soft, rubbery look that is one of the strangest effects ever achieved by classical architecture. It is almost as if Michelangelo purposely set out to defy his predecessors, intentionally flouting the conventions of the High Renaissance in order to see what kind of bizarre, mannered effect might result. His innovations were tremendously influential and produced a period of architectural experimentation, known as Mannerism, that eventually evolved into the baroque. As his contemporary Giorgio Vasari put it, "Artisans have been infinitely and perpetually indebted to him because he broke the bonds and chains of a way of working that had become habitual by common usage."

Nobody has ever complained about the anteroom's staircase (best viewed head-on), which emerges from the library with the visual force of an unstoppable lava flow. In its highly sculptural conception and execution, it's quite simply one of the most original and fluid staircases in the world. ✉ *Piazza San Lorenzo 9, entrance to the left of San Lorenzo* ☎ *055/210760* ⊕ *www.bml.firenze.sbn.it* ✒ *Free, special exhibitions €2.50* ☉ *Daily 8:30–1. Guided tours in English available weekend mornings.*

★ ⓱ **Cappelle Medicee** (Medici Chapels). This magnificent complex includes the **Cappella dei Principi,** the Medici chapel and mausoleum that was begun in 1605 and kept marble workers busy for several hundred years, and the **Sagrestia Nuova** (New Sacristy), designed by Michelangelo and so called to distinguish it from Brunelleschi's Sagrestia Vecchia (Old Sacristy).

Michelangelo received the commission for the New Sacristy in 1520 from Cardinal Giulio de' Medici (1478–1534), who later became Pope Clement VII and who wanted a new burial chapel for his cousins Giuliano

(1478–1534) and Lorenzo (1492–1519). The result was a tour de force of architecture and sculpture. Architecturally, Michelangelo was as original and inventive here as ever, but it is, quite properly, the powerful sculptural compositions of the side-wall tombs that dominate the room. The scheme is allegorical: on the wall tomb to the right are figures representing Day and Night, and on the wall tomb to the left are figures representing Dawn and Dusk; above them are idealized sculptures of the two men, usually interpreted to represent the active life and the contemplative life. But the allegorical meanings are secondary; what is most important is the intense presence of the sculptural figures. Michelangelo's contemporaries were so awed by this force (in his sculpture here and elsewhere) that they invented an entirely new word to describe the phenomenon: *terribilità* (dreadfulness). To this day it's used only when describing his work, and it's in evidence here at the peak of its power. During his stormy relations with the Medici, Michelangelo once hid out in a tiny room that is accessed from the left of the altar. The room contains charcoal sketches—perhaps Michelangelo's? Admission is on the hour (at 9, 10, 11, and noon) is limited to 12 people; tell the ticket seller that you want to see them. Your chances of getting in are better for one of the earlier hours. ⊠ *Piazza di Madonna degli Aldobrandini, San Lorenzo* ☎ *055/294883 reservations* ⊠ *€6* ⊙ *Daily 8:15–5* ⊙ *Closed 1st, 3rd, and 5th Mon. and 2nd and 4th Sun. of month.*

★ ⓴ **Galleria dell'Accademia** (Accademia Gallery). The collection of Florentine paintings, dating from the 13th to the 18th centuries, is largely unremarkable, but the sculptures by Michelangelo are worth the price of admission. The unfinished *Slaves,* fighting their way out of their marble prisons, were meant for the tomb of Michelangelo's overly demanding patron, Pope Julius II (1443–1513). But the focal point is the original *David,* moved here from Piazza della Signoria in 1873. The *David* was commissioned in 1501 by the Opera del Duomo (Cathedral Works Committee), which gave the 26-year-old sculptor a leftover block of marble that had been ruined by another artist. Michelangelo's success with the block was so dramatic that the city showered him with honors, and the Opera del Duomo voted to build him a house and a studio in which to live and work.

Today *David* is beset not by Goliath but by tourists, and seeing the statue at all—much less really studying it—can be a trial, as it is surrounded by a Plexiglas barrier. The statue is not quite what it seems. It is so poised and graceful and alert—so miraculously alive—that it is often considered the definitive embodiment of the ideals of the High Renaissance in sculpture. But its true place in the history of art is a bit more complicated.

As Michelangelo well knew, the Renaissance painting and sculpture that preceded his work were deeply concerned with ideal form. Perfection of proportion was the ever-sought Holy Grail; during the Renaissance, ideal proportion was equated with ideal beauty, and ideal beauty was equated with spiritual perfection. But *David,* despite its supremely calm and dignified pose, departs from these ideals. Michelangelo did not give the statue perfect proportions. The head is slightly too large for the body, the arms are too large for the torso, and the hands are dramatically large for the arms. The work was originally commissioned to adorn the facade of the Duomo and was intended to be seen from a distance and on high. Michelangelo knew exactly what he was doing, calculating that the perspective of the viewer would be such that, in order for the statue to appear proportioned, the upper body, head, and arms would have to

FLORENCE'S TRIAL BY FIRE

One of the most striking figures of
Renaissance Florence was Girolamo
Savonarola, a Dominican monk who, for a
moment, captured the conscience of the city.
In 1491 he became prior of the monastery of
San Marco, where he adopted a life of
austerity and delivered sermons condemning
Florence's excesses and the immorality of his
fellow clergy. Following the death of Lorenzo
di Medici, Savonarola was instrumental in
the formation of the republic of Florence,
ruled by a representative council with Christ
enthroned as monarch. In his most
memorable act, he provoked Florentines to
toss worldly possessions—from frilly dresses
to Botticelli paintings—onto a "bonfire of the
vanities" in Piazza della Signoria.
Savonarola's antagonism toward church
hierarchy led to his undoing: he was
excommunicated in 1497, and the following
year was hanged and burned for prophecy
and sedition. Today at Museo di San Marco
you can visit Savonarola's cell and see his
arresting portrait.

be bigger, as they are farther away from the viewer's line of vision. But
he also did it to express and embody, as powerfully as possible in a single figure, an entire biblical story. David's hands *are* big, but so was Goliath, and these are the hands that slew him. Save yourself a long and
tiresome wait at the museum entrance by reserving your tickets in advance. ⊠ *Via Ricasoli 60, San Marco* ☎ *055/294883 reservations; 055/
2388609 gallery* ⌨ *€8.50, €1.55 reservation fee* ⊙ *Tues.–Sun.
8:15–6:50.*

off the beaten path

MUSEO DELL'OPIFICIO DELLE PIETRE DURE – Ferdinand I established
a workshop in 1588 to train craftsmen in the art of working with
precious and semiprecious stones and marble. Four hundred–plus
years later, the workshop is renowned as a center for the restoration
of mosaics and inlays in semiprecious stones. The little museum is
highly informative and includes some magnificent antique examples
of this highly specialized and beautiful craft. ⊠ *Via degli Alfani 78,
San Marco* ☎ *055/26511* ⌨ *€2* ⊙ *Mon., Wed., and Fri.–Sat.
8:15–2, Thurs. 8:15–7.*

㉓ Museo Archeologico. Of the Etruscan, Egyptian, and Greco-Roman antiquities in this museum, the Etruscan collection is particularly notable—one of the largest in Italy. The famous bronze *Chimera* was
discovered (without the tail, a reconstruction) in the 16th century.
⊠ *Via della Colonna 38, Santissima Annunziata* ☎ *055/23575* ⊕ *www.
comune.fi.it/sogetti/sat* ⌨ *€4* ⊙ *Mon. 2–7, Tues. and Thurs. 8:30–7,
Wed. and Fri.–Sun. 8:30–2.*

⑲ Museo di San Marco. A former Dominican convent adjacent to the church
of San Marco now houses this museum, which contains many stunning
works by Fra Angelico (circa 1400–55), the Dominican friar famous for
his piety as well as for his painting. When the friars' cells were restructured between 1439 and 1444, he decorated many of them with frescoes meant to spur religious contemplation. His paintings are simple and
direct and furnish a compelling contrast to those in the Palazzo Medici-
Riccardi chapel. Whereas Gozzoli's frescoes celebrate the splendors of
the Medici, Fra Angelico's exalt the simple beauties of the contemplative life and quiet reflection. Fra Angelico's works are everywhere, from
the friars' cells to the superb panel paintings on view in the museum.

Don't miss the famous *Annunciation* on the upper floor and the works in the gallery just off the cloister as you enter. Here you can see his beautiful *Last Judgment*; as usual, the tortures of the damned are far more inventive and interesting than the pleasures of the redeemed. ✉ *Piazza San Marco 1* ☎ *055/2388608* 🎫 *€4* ⏱ *Weekdays 8:15–1:50, weekends 8:15–6:50* ⏱ *Closed 1st, 3rd, and 5th Sun., and 2nd and 4th Mon. of month.*

off the beaten path

CENACOLO DI SANT'APOLLONIA – The frescoes of the refectory of a former Benedictine nunnery were painted in sinewy style by Andrea del Castagno, a follower of Masaccio (1401–28). The *Last Supper* is a powerful version of this typical refectory theme. From the entrance, walk around the corner to Via San Gallo 25 and take a peek at the lovely 15th-century cloister that belonged to the same monastery but is now part of the University of Florence. ✉ *Via XXVII Aprile 1, San Marco* ☎ *055/2388607* ⏱ *Daily 8:30–1:30* ⏱ *Closed 1st, 3rd, and 5th Sun., and 2nd and 4th Mon. of month.*

CHIOSTRO DELLO SCALZO – Often overlooked, this small, peaceful 16th-century cloister was frescoed in grisaille by Andrea del Sarto (1486–1530), with scenes from the life of St. John the Baptist, Florence's patron saint. ✉ *Via Cavour 69, San Marco* ☎ *055/ 2388604* ⏱ *Mon., Thurs., and Sat. 8:15–1:50.*

★ ⑱ **Palazzo Medici-Riccardi.** The main attraction of this palace, begun in 1444 by Michelozzo for Cosimo de' Medici, is the interior chapel, the so-called **Cappella dei Magi** on the upper floor. Painted on its walls is Benozzo Gozzoli's famous *Procession of the Magi,* finished in 1460, which celebrates both the birth of Christ and the greatness of the Medici family. Like Ghirlandaio, Gozzoli was not a revolutionary painter and is today considered less interesting than other 15th-century stars such as Masaccio, Botticelli, and Leonardo. Gozzoli's gift, however, was for entrancing the eye, not challenging the mind, and on those terms his success here is beyond question. The paintings are full of activity yet somehow frozen in time in a way that fails utterly as realism but succeeds triumphantly when the demand for realism is set aside. Entering the chapel is like walking into the middle of a magnificently illustrated children's storybook, and this beauty makes it one of the most enjoyable rooms in the entire city. ✉ *Via Cavour 1, San Lorenzo* ☎ *055/2760340* 🎫 *€4* ⏱ *Thurs.–Tues. 9–7.*

▶ ⑮ **San Lorenzo.** The interior of this church, like that of Santo Spirito on the other side of the Arno, was designed by Filippo Brunelleschi in the early 15th century. Both proclaim with ringing clarity the beginning of the Renaissance in architecture (neither was completed by Brunelleschi, and which he worked on last is unknown). Most dramatic is San Lorenzo's floor grid of dark, inlaid marble lines. The grid makes the rigorous geometry of the interior immediately visible and is an illuminating lesson on the laws of perspective. If you stand in the middle of the nave at the church entrance, on the line that stretches to the high altar, every element in the church—the grid, the nave columns, the side aisles, the coffered nave ceiling—seems to march inexorably toward a hypothetical vanishing point beyond the high altar, exactly as in a single-point-perspective painting. Brunelleschi's **Sagrestia Vecchia** (Old Sacristy) has stucco decorations by Donatello; it's at the end of the left transept. The facade of the church was never finished. ✉ *Piazza San Lorenzo* ☎ *055/ 290184* 🎫 *€2.50* ⏱ *Mon.–Sat. 10–5, Sun. 3:30–5.*

off the beaten path

MERCATO CENTRALE – In this huge, two-story market hall, food is everywhere, some of it remarkably exotic. The ground floor contains meat and cheese stalls, as well as some very good bars selling *panini* (sandwiches), and the second floor teems with vegetable stands. If you're looking for dill or mangoes in Florence, this is most likely where you'll find them. ⊠ *Piazza del Mercato Centrale, San Lorenzo* ⏰ *Mon.–Sat. 7–2.*

㉔ Santa Maria Maddalena dei Pazzi. One of Florence's hidden treasures, Perugino's (circa 1445/50–1523) cool and composed *Crucifixion* is in the chapter house of the monastery below this church. Here you can see the Virgin Mary and St. John the Evangelist with Mary Magdalen and Sts. Benedict and Bernard of Clairvaux posed against a simple but haunting landscape. The figure of Christ crucified occupies the center of this brilliantly hued fresco. Perugino's colors radiate—note the juxtaposition of the yellow-green cuff against the orange tones of the Magdalen's robe. ⊠ *Borgo Pinti 58, Santa Croce* ☎ *055/2478420* 💳 *Donation requested* ⏰ *Weekdays 9–noon, 5–5:20, 6:10–7, Sat. 5–6:20, Sun. 9–10:45 and 3–6:50.*

㉒ Santissima Annunziata. Dating from the mid-13th century, this church was restructured in 1447 by Michelozzo, who gave it an uncommon (and lovely) entrance cloister with frescoes by Andrea del Sarto (1486–1530), Pontormo (1494–1556), and Rosso Fiorentino (1494–1540). The interior is a rarity for Florence: a sumptuous example of the baroque. But it's not really a fair example, since it is merely 17th-century baroque decoration applied willy-nilly to an earlier structure—exactly the sort of violent remodeling exercise that has given the baroque a bad name. The **Cappella dell'Annuziata,** immediately inside the entrance to the left, illustrates the point. The lower half, with its stately Corinthian columns and carved frieze bearing the Medici arms, was commissioned by Piero de' Medici in 1447; the upper half, with its erupting curves and impish sculpted cherubs, was added 200 years later. Each is effective in its own way, but together they serve only to prove that dignity is rarely comfortable wearing a party hat. ⊠ *Piazza di Santissima Annunziata* ☎ *055/2398034* ⏰ *Daily 8–12:30 and 4:30–6:30.*

㉕ Sinagoga (Synagogue). Jews were well settled in Florence by 1396, when the first money-lending operations became officially sanctioned. Medici patronage helped Jewish banking houses to flourish, but by 1570 Jews were required to live within the large "ghetto," near today's Piazza della Repubblica, by decree of Pope Pius V (1504–72). Construction of the modern Moorish-style Synagogue, with its lovely garden, began in 1874 as a bequest of David Levi, who wished to endow a synagogue "worthy of the city." Falcini, Micheli, and Treves designed the building on a domed Greek cross plan with galleries in the transept and a roofline bearing three distinctive copper cupolas visible from all over Florence. The exterior has alternating bands of tan travertine and pink granite, reflecting an Islamic style repeated in Giovanni Panti's ornate interior. Of particular interest are the cast-iron gates by Pasquale Franci, the eternal light by Francesco Morini, and the Murano glass mosaics by Giacomo dal Medico. The gilded doors of the Moorish ark, which fronts the pulpit and is flanked by extravagant candelabra, are decorated with symbols of the ancient Temple of Jerusalem and bear bayonet marks from vandals. The synagogue was used as a garage by the Nazis, who failed to inflict much damage in spite of an attempt to blow up the place with dynamite. Only the columns on the left side were destroyed, and, even then, the Women's Balcony above did not collapse. Note the Star of David in black and yellow marble inlaid in the floor. The original capitals can be seen in the garden.

Some of the oldest and most beautiful Jewish ritual artifacts in all of Europe are displayed in the small **Museo Ebraico** upstairs, accessible by stairs or elevator. Exhibits document the Florentine Jewish community and the building of the synagogue. The donated objects all belonged to local families and date from as early as the late 16th century. Take special note of the exquisite needlework and silver items. A small but well-stocked gift shop is downstairs. *Synagogue and museum* ⊠ *Via Farini 4, Santa Croce* ☎ *055/2346654* ✉ *€4* ⊙ *Apr.–Oct., Sun.–Thurs. 10–5, Fri. 10–1; Nov.–Mar., Sun.–Thurs. 10–1 and 3–5, Fri. 10–1. English-guided tours 10:10, 11, 12, 1, 2.*

> **need a break?** Adjacent to Florence's synagogue is **Ruth's** (⊠ Via Farini 2/a, Santa Croce ☎ 055/2480888), the only kosher-vegetarian restaurant in Tuscany. Inexpensive vegetarian and Mediterranean dishes and a large selection of kosher wines highlight the menu. It's closed for Friday dinner and Saturday lunch.

㉑ Spedale degli Innocenti. Built by Brunelleschi in 1419 to serve as a foundling hospital, this takes the historical prize as the very first Renaissance building. Brunelleschi designed its portico with his usual rigor, building it out of the two shapes he considered mathematically (and therefore philosophically and aesthetically) perfect: the square and the circle. Below the level of the arches, the portico encloses a row of perfect cubes; above the level of the arches, the portico encloses a row of intersecting hemispheres. The whole geometric scheme is articulated with Corinthian columns, capitals, and arches borrowed directly from antiquity. At the time he designed the portico, Brunelleschi was also designing the interior of San Lorenzo, using the same basic ideas. But since the portico was finished before San Lorenzo, the Spedale degli Innocenti can claim the honor of ushering in Renaissance architecture. The 10 ceramic medallions depicting swaddled infants that decorate the portico are by Andrea della Robbia (1435–1525/28), done in about 1487. Contained within is a small museum devoted to lesser-known Renaissance works. ⊠ *Piazza di Santissima Annunziata 1* ☎ *055/20371* ✉ *€2.60* ⊙ *Thurs.–Tues. 8:30–2.*

Santa Maria Novella to the Arno

Piazza Santa Maria Novella is near the train station and is marked by a degree of squalor, especially at night. Nevertheless, the streets in and around the piazza have their share of architectural treasures, including some of Florence's most tasteful palazzi.

> **a good walk** Start in Piazza Santa Maria Novella, its north side dominated by the church of **Santa Maria Novella** ㉖ ▶; then take Via delle Belle Donne, which leads from the east side of the piazza to a minuscule square, at the center of which stands a curious shrine known as the Croce al Trebbio. Take Via del Trebbio east and turn right onto Via Tornabuoni, Florence's finest shopping street. At the intersection of Via Tornabuoni and Via Strozzi is the overwhelming **Palazzo Strozzi** ㉗. If you want a dose of contemporary sculpture, follow Via della Spada to the **Museo Marino Marini** ㉘. One block west from Palazzo Strozzi, down Via della Vigna Nuova, is Leon Battista Alberti's groundbreaking **Palazzo Rucellai** ㉙. Follow the narrow street opposite the palazzo (Via del Purgatorio) east almost to its end; then zigzag right and left, turning east on Via Parione to reach Piazza di Santa Trinita, where, in the middle, stands the Colonna della Giustizia (the Column of Justice), a column from Rome's Terme di Caracalla, given to the Medici Grand Duke Cosimo I by Pope Pius IV in 1560. Cosimo placed it here in 1565 to mark the spot where he heard

news that Florentine ducal forces had prevailed over a ragtag army of Florentine republican exiles and their French allies at the 1554 battle of Marciano; the victory made his power in Florence all but absolute. Halfway down the block to the south (toward the Arno) is the church of **Santa Trinita** ㉚, home to Ghirlandaio's glowing frescoes. Then go east on Borgo Santi Apostoli, a typical medieval street flanked by tower houses, and take a right on Via Por Santa Maria to get to the Ponte Vecchio. Alternatively, walk from Piazza Santa Trinita to Ponte Santa Trinita, which leads into the Oltrarno neighborhood.

TIMING   The walk takes about 30 minutes, plus 30 minutes for Santa Maria Novella and 15 minutes for Santa Trinita. A visit to the Museo di Santa Maria Novella and the cloister takes about 30 minutes.

What to See

Croce al Trebbio. A little granite column near Piazza Santa Maria Novella was erected in 1338 by Dominican friars (the Dominican basilica Santa Maria Novella is just down the street) to commemorate a famous local victory: it was here in 1244 that they defeated their avowed enemies, the Patarene heretics, in a bloody street brawl. ⊠ *Via del Trebbio, Santa Maria Novella.*

㉘ **Museo Marino Marini.** One of the few museums in Florence that shows significant art from the last century is this one dedicated to sculptor and painter Marini (1901–80). His 21-ft-tall bronze of horse and rider dominates the main gallery. The museum itself is an eruption of contemporary space in a deconsecrated 9th-century church, designed with a series of open stairways, walkways, and balconies that allow you to peer at Marini's work from all angles. In addition to his Etruscanesque sculpture, the museum houses Marini's paintings, drawings, and engravings. ⊠ *Piazza San Pancrazio, Santa Maria Novella* ☎ *055/219432* 🎫 *€4.10* ⊙ *Oct.–May, Mon. and Wed.–Sat. 10–5, Sun. 10–1; June–Sept., Mon. and Wed.–Sat. 10–5, Thurs. 10–11:30, Sun. 10–1.*

㉙ **Palazzo Rucellai.** Architect Leon Battista Alberti (1404–72) designed perhaps the very first private residence inspired by antique models—going a step further than the Palazzo Strozzi. A comparison between the two is illuminating. Evident on the facade of the Palazzo Rucellai, dating between 1455 and 1470, is the ordered arrangement of windows and rusticated stonework seen on the Palazzo Strozzi, but Alberti's facade is far less forbidding. Alberti devoted a larger proportion of his wall space to windows, which lighten the facade's appearance, and filled in the remainder with rigorously ordered classical elements borrowed from antiquity. The result, though still severe, is less fortresslike, and Alberti strove for this effect purposely (he is on record as saying that only tyrants need fortresses). Ironically, the Palazzo Rucellai was built some 30 years *before* the Palazzo Strozzi. Alberti's civilizing ideas here, it turned out, had little influence on the Florentine palazzi that followed. To Renaissance Florentines, power—in architecture, as in life—was just as impressive as beauty. The palace now serves as apartments for wealthy Florentines. ⊠ *Via della Vigna Nuova, Santa Maria Novella.*

㉗ **Palazzo Strozzi.** The Strozzi family built this imposing palazzo in an attempt to outshine the nearby Palazzo Medici. Based on a model by Giuliano da Sangallo (circa 1452–1516) dating from around 1489 and executed between 1489 and 1504 under Il Cronaca (1457–1508) and Benedetto da Maiaino (1442–97), it was inspired by Michelozzo's earlier Palazzo Medici-Riccardi. The palazzo's exterior is simple, severe, and massive: it's a testament to the wealth of a patrician, 15th-century Florentine family. The interior courtyard is another matter altogether.

It is here that the classical vocabulary—columns, capitals, pilasters, arches, and cornices—is given uninhibited and powerful expression. Blockbuster art shows frequently occur here. ⊠ *Via Tornabuoni, Piazza della Repubblica* ☎ *055/2645155* ⊕ *www.firenzemostre.com* ☾ *Daily 10–7.*

► 26 **Santa Maria Novella.** The facade of this church looks distinctly clumsy by later Renaissance standards, and with good reason: it is an architectural hybrid. The lower half was completed mostly in the 14th century; its pointed-arch niches and decorative marble patterns reflect the Gothic style of the day. About a hundred years later (around 1456), architect Leon Battista Alberti was called in to complete the job. The marble decoration of his upper story clearly defers to the already existing work below, but the architectural motifs he added evince an entirely different style. The central doorway, the four ground-floor half columns with Corinthian capitals, the triangular pediment atop the second story, the inscribed frieze immediately below the pediment—these are borrowings from antiquity, and they reflect the new Renaissance era in architecture, born some 35 years earlier at Florence's Spedale degli Innocenti. Alberti's most important addition, however, the S-curve scrolls that surmount the decorative circles on either side of the upper story, had no precedent in antiquity. The problem was to soften the abrupt transition between wide ground floor and narrow upper story. Alberti's solution turned out to be definitive. Once you start to look for them, you will find scrolls such as these (or sculptural variations of them) on churches all over Italy, and every one of them derives from Alberti's example here.

The architecture of the interior is, like the Duomo, a dignified but somber example of Florentine Gothic. Exploration is essential, however, because the church's store of art treasures is remarkable. Highlights include the 14th-century stained-glass rose window depicting the *Coronation of the Virgin* (above the central entrance); the Cappella Filippo Strozzi (to the right of the altar), containing late-15th-century frescoes and stained glass by Filippino Lippi; the *cappella maggiore* (the area around the high altar), displaying frescoes by Domenico Ghirlandaio (1449–94); and the Cappella Gondi (to the left of the altar), containing Filippo Brunelleschi's famous wood crucifix, carved around 1410 and said to have so stunned the great Donatello when he first saw it that he dropped a basket of eggs.

Of special interest, for its great historical importance and beauty, is Masaccio's *Trinity*, on the left-hand wall, almost halfway down the nave. Painted around 1426–27 (at the same time he was working on his frescoes in Santa Maria del Carmine), it unequivocally announced the arrival of the Renaissance. The realism of the figure of Christ was revolutionary in itself, but what was probably even more startling to contemporary Florentines was the barrel vault in the background. The mathematical rules for employing perspective in painting had just been discovered (probably by Brunelleschi), and this was one of the first works of art to employ them with utterly convincing success. ⊠ *Piazza Santa Maria Novella* ☎ *055/210113* ▦ *€2.60* ☾ *Mon.–Thurs. and Sat. 9:30–5, Fri. and Sun. 1–5.*

In the cloisters of the **Museo di Santa Maria Novella,** to the left of Santa Maria Novella, is a faded fresco cycle by Paolo Uccello depicting tales from Genesis, with a dramatic vision of the Deluge. Earlier and better-preserved frescoes painted between 1348 and 1355 by Andrea da Firenze are in the chapter house, or the Cappellone degli Spagnoli (Spanish Chapel), off the cloister. ⊠ *Piazza Santa Maria Novella 19* ☎ *055/282187* ▦ *€2.60* ☾ *Wed.–Mon. 9–2.*

㉚ Santa Trinita. Started in the 11th century by Vallombrosian monks and originally Romanesque in style, this church underwent a Gothic re-modeling during the 14th century. (Remains of the Romanesque construction are visible on the interior front wall.) Its major work is the cycle of frescoes and the altarpiece in the Cappella Sassetti, the second to the high altar's right, painted by Domenico Ghirlandaio between 1480 and 1485. Ghirlandaio was a wildly popular but conservative painter for his day, and generally his paintings show little interest in the laws of perspective that other Florentine painters had been experimenting with for more than 50 years. But his work here possesses such graceful decorative appeal it hardly seems to matter. The wall frescoes illustrate the life of St. Francis, and the altarpiece, depicting the Adoration of the Shepherds, veritably glows. ⊠ *Piazza Santa Trinita, Santa Maria Novella* ☎ *055/216912* ☉ *Daily 7–noon and 4–7.*

The Oltrarno: Palazzo Pitti, Giardino di Boboli, Santo Spirito

A walk through the Oltrarno takes in two very different aspects of Florence: the splendor of the Medici, manifest in the riches of the mammoth Palazzo Pitti and the gracious Giardino di Boboli; and the charm of the Oltrarno, literally "the other side of the Arno," a slightly gentrified but still fiercely proud working-class neighborhood with artisans' and antiques shops.

a good walk

Starting from Santa Trinita, cross the Arno over Ponte Santa Trinita and continue south down Via Maggio until you reach the crossroads of Sdrucciolo dei Pitti (on the left) and the short Via Michelozzi (on the right). Turn left onto the Sdrucciolo dei Pitti. **Palazzo Pitti ㉛** ➤, Florence's largest palace, lies before you as you emerge onto Piazza Pitti. Behind the palace is the **Giardino di Boboli ㉜**. Find time to walk through the splendidly landscaped gardens. If you have the energy, walk up the hill to the nearby **Forte di Belvedere ㉝**, which commands a wonderful view and sometimes has art exhibits. If you want to take a Mannerist detour to see the Pontormo *Deposition* at **Santa Felicita ㉞**, head northeast from Palazzo Pitti on Via Guicciardini back toward the Ponte Vecchio. Walk down Borgo Sant'Jacopo, cross via Maggio, and take a left at via del Presto di San Martino. Notice the unassuming facade of the church of **Santo Spirito ㉟**. Diagonally across the square from the church entrance, turn right on Via Sant'Agostino to Via dei Serragli. Cross and follow Via Santa Monaca west through the heart of the Oltrarno to Piazza del Carmine and the church of **Santa Maria del Carmine ㊱**, where the famous fresco cycle by Masaccio, Masolino, and Filippino Lippi fills the Cappella Brancacci. Go to the far end of Piazza del Carmine and turn right onto Borgo San Frediano; then follow Via di Santo Spirito and Borgo Sant'Jacopo east to reach the Ponte Vecchio.

TIMING The walk alone takes about 45 minutes; allow one hour to visit the Galleria Palatina in Palazzo Pitti and more if you visit the other galleries. Spend at least 30 minutes to an hour savoring the graceful elegance of the Giardino di Boboli. When you reach the crossroads of the Sdrucciolo dei Pitti and Via Michelozzi, you have a choice. If it's around noon, you may want to postpone the first stop temporarily to see the churches of Santo Spirito, Santa Felicita, and Santa Maria del Carmine before they close for the afternoon. Otherwise, proceed to Palazzo Pitti. The churches can be visited in 15 minutes each.

What to See

㉝ Forte di Belvedere. This impressive structure was built in 1590 to help defend the city against siege. But time has brought about a transformation, and what was once a first-rate fortification is now a first-rate exhibition venue. Farther up the hill is Piazzale Michelangelo, but, as the natives know, the best views of Florence are right here. To the north, all the city's monuments are spread out in a breathtaking panorama. To the south, the nearby hills furnish a complementary rural view, in its way equally memorable. The fortress, occasionally a host of art exhibitions (contact the tourist office for schedule), is adjacent to the top of the Giardino di Boboli. ⊠ *Porta San Giorgio, San Niccolò* 🖾 *Varies with exhibit.*

㉜ Giardino di Boboli (Boboli Garden). The main entrance to this landscaped garden is from the courtyard of Palazzo Pitti. The garden began to take shape in 1549, when the Pitti family sold the palazzo to Eleanora of Toledo, wife of the Medici grand duke Cosimo I. The initial landscaping plans were laid out by Niccolò Tribolo (1500–50). After his death work was continued by Vasari, Ammannati, Giambologna, Bernardo Buontalenti (circa 1536–1608), and Giulio (1571–1635) and Alfonso Parigi (1606–56), among others, resulting in the most spectacular backyard in Florence. The Italian gift for landscaping—less formal than the French but still full of sweeping drama—is displayed here at its best. A copy of the famous *Morgante,* Cosimo I's favorite dwarf astride a particularly unhappy tortoise, is near the exit. Sculpted by Valerio Cioli (circa 1529–99), the work shows a perfectly executed potbelly. ⊠ *Enter through Palazzo Pitti* 🕾 *055/294883* 🖾 *€4, cumulative ticket with Museo delle Porcellane and Museo degli Argenti* ☉ *Apr.–Oct., daily 8:15–5:30; Nov.–Mar., daily 8:15–4:30* ☉ *Closed 1st and last Mon. of month.*

▶ **㉛ Palazzo Pitti.** This palace is one of Florence's largest—if not one of its best—architectural set pieces. The original palazzo, built for the Pitti family around 1460, comprised only the main entrance and the three windows on either side. In 1549 the property was sold to the Medici, and Bartolomeo Ammannati was called in to make substantial additions. Although he apparently operated on the principle that more is better, he succeeded only in proving that more is just that, more.

Today it houses several museums: The **Museo degli Argenti** (🖾 €4, cumulative ticket with Giardino di Boboli ☉ Mon.–Sun. 8:15–1:50) displays a vast collection of Medici household treasures. The **Galleria del Costume** (🖾 €5, cumulative ticket with Galleria d'Arte Moderna ☉ Mon.–Sun., 8:15–1:50) showcases fashions from the past 300 years. The **Galleria d'Arte Moderna** (🖾 €5, cumulative ticket with Galleria del Costume ☉ Mon.–Sun. 8:15–1:50) holds a collection of 19th- and 20th-century paintings, mostly Tuscan. And, most famous of all, the **Galleria Palatina** (🖾 €6.50 ☉ Nov.–Mar., Tues.–Sun. 8:15–6:50; Apr.–Oct., Tues.–Sat. 8:15–10, Sun. 8:15–7), contains a broad collection of paintings from the 15th to 17th centuries. High points include a number of portraits by Titian and an unparalleled collection of paintings by Raphael, notably the double portraits of Angelo Doni and his wife, the sullen Maddalena Strozzi. The rooms of the Galleria Palatina remain much as the Medici left them. Their floor-to-ceiling paintings are considered by some to be Italy's most egregious exercise in conspicuous consumption, aesthetic overkill, and trumpery. The price of admission also allows you to explore the former **Appartamenti Reali,** containing furnishings from a remodeling done in the 19th century. ⊠ *Piazza Pitti* 🕾 *055/210323* ☉ *All but Galleria Palatina closed 2nd and 4th Sun. and 1st, 3rd, and 5th Mon. of month.*

㉞ Santa Felicita. This late baroque church (its facade was remodeled 1736–39) contains the Mannerist Jacopo Pontormo's (1494–1556) tour de force, the *Deposition,* the centerpiece of the Cappella Capponi (executed 1525–28), a masterpiece of 16th-century Florentine art. The remote figures, which transcend the realm of Renaissance classical form, are portrayed in tangled shapes and intense pastel colors (well preserved because of the low lights in the church), in a space and depth that defy reality. Note, too, the exquisitely frescoed *Annunciation,* also by Pontormo, at a right angle to the *Deposition.* The granite column in the piazza was erected in 1381 and marks a Christian cemetery. ✉ *Piazza Santa Felicita, Via Guicciardini, Palazzo Pitti* ⏲ *Mon.–Sat. 9–noon and 3–6, Sun. 9–1.*

㊱ **Santa Maria del Carmine.** The **Cappella Brancacci,** at the end of the right transept of this church, houses a masterpiece of Renaissance painting: a fresco cycle that changed the course of Western art forever. Fire nearly destroyed the church in the 18th century; miraculously, the Brancacci Chapel survived almost intact. The cycle is the work of three artists: Masaccio and Masolino (1383–circa 1440/47), who began it around 1424, and Filippino Lippi, who finished it some 50 years later, after a long interruption during which the sponsoring Brancacci family was exiled. It was Masaccio's work that opened a new frontier for painting, as he was among the first to employ single-point perspective; tragically, he did not live to experience the revolution his innovations caused—he died in 1428 at the age of 27.

Masaccio collaborated with Masolino on several of the frescoes, but by himself he painted the *Tribute Money* on the upper-left wall; *St. Peter Baptizing* on the upper altar wall; the *Distribution of Goods* on the lower altar wall; and, most famous, the *Expulsion of Adam and Eve* on the chapel's upper-left entrance pier. If you look closely at the last painting and compare it with some of the chapel's other works, you will see a pronounced difference. The figures of Adam and Eve possess a startling presence primarily due to the dramatic way in which their bodies seem to reflect light. Masaccio here shaded his figures consistently, so as to suggest a single, strong source of light within the world of the painting but outside its frame. In so doing, he succeeded in imitating with paint the real-world effect of light on mass, and he thereby imparted to his figures a sculptural reality unprecedented in his day.

These matters have to do with technique, but with the *Expulsion of Adam and Eve* his skill went beyond mere technical innovation. In the faces of Adam and Eve, you see more than just finely modeled figures. You see terrible shame and suffering depicted with a humanity rarely achieved in art. ✉ *Piazza del Carmine, Santo Spirito/San Frediano* ☎ *055/2382195* 🎫 *€3.10* ⏲ *Mon. and Wed.–Sat. 10–5, Sun. 1–5.*

㉟ **Santo Spirito.** The plain, unfinished facade gives nothing away, but the interior, although it appears chilly (cold, even) compared with later churches, is one of the most important examples of Renaissance architecture in Italy. The interior is one of a pair designed in Florence by Filippo Brunelleschi in the early 15th century (the other is San Lorenzo). It was here that Brunelleschi supplied definitive solutions to the two main problems of interior Renaissance church design: how to build a cross-shaped interior using architectural elements borrowed from antiquity and how to reflect in that interior the order and regularity that Renaissance scientists (among them Brunelleschi himself) were at the time discovering in the natural world around them.

Brunelleschi's solution to the first problem was brilliantly simple: turn a Greek temple inside out. To see this clearly, look at one of the stately arch-topped arcades that separate the side aisles from the central nave. Whereas ancient Greek temples were walled buildings surrounded by classical colonnades, Brunelleschi's churches were classical arcades within walled buildings. This brilliant architectural idea overthrew the previous era's religious taboo against pagan architecture once and for all, triumphantly reclaiming that architecture for Christian use.

Brunelleschi's solution to the second problem—making the entire interior orderly and regular—was mathematically precise: he designed the ground plan of the church so that all its parts were proportionally related. The transepts and nave have exactly the same width; the side aisles are precisely half as wide as the nave; the little chapels off the side aisles are exactly half as deep as the side aisles; the chancel and transepts are exactly one-eighth the depth of the nave; and so on, with dizzying exactitude. For Brunelleschi, such a design technique would have been a matter of passionate conviction. Like most theoreticians of his day, he believed that mathematical regularity and aesthetic beauty were flip sides of the same coin, that one was not possible without the other. In the refectory of **Santo Spirito** (✉ Piazza Santo Spirito 29, ☎ 055/287043), adjacent to the church, you can see the remains of Andrea Orcagna's fresco of the *Crucifixion*. ✉ *Piazza Santo Spirito, Santo Spirito/San Frediano* ☎ *055/210030* 🎟 *Church free, museum €2.10* 🕙 *Church: Thurs.–Tues., 9–noon and 4–7; Wed. 9–noon. Museum: Tues.–Sat. 9–1:50.*

> **need a break?**
>
> **Cabiria** (✉ Piazza Santo Spirito ☎ 055/215732), just across the piazza from the church of Santo Spirito, draws a funky crowd in search of a cappuccino or quenching ade. When it's warm, sit outside on the terrace.

From Santa Croce to San Miniato al Monte

The Santa Croce quarter, on the southeast fringe of the historic center, was built up in the Middle Ages just outside the second set of city walls. The centerpiece of the neighborhood was the basilica of Santa Croce, which could hold great numbers of worshipers; the vast piazza could accommodate any overflow and also served as a fairground and playing field for traditional, no-holds-barred soccer games. A center of leather working since the Middle Ages, the neighborhood is still packed with leather craftsmen and leather shops.

a good walk

Begin your walk at the church of **Santa Croce** ㊲ ▶; from here you can take a quick jaunt up Via delle Pinzochere to **Casa Buonarroti** ㊳ to see works by Michelangelo. Return to Santa Croce, and at the southwest end of the piazza go south on Via de'Benci and cross the Arno over Ponte alle Grazie. Turn left onto Lungarno Serristori and continue to Piazza Giuseppe Poggi; a series of ramps and stairs climbs to **Piazzale Michelangelo** ㊴, where the city lies before you in all its glory. From Piazzale Michelangelo, climb the stairs behind La Loggia restaurant to the church of San Salvatore al Monte, and go south on the lane leading to the stairs that climb to **San Miniato al Monte** ㊵, cutting through the fortifications hurriedly built by Michelangelo in 1529 when Florence was threatened by troops of the Holy Roman Emperor Charles V (1500–58). You can avoid the long walk by taking Bus 12 or 13 at the west end of Ponte alle Grazie and getting off at Piazzale Michelangelo or at the stop after for San Miniato al Monte; you still have to climb the monumental stairs to and from San Miniato, but you can then take the bus from Piazzale Michelangelo back to the center of town.

TIMING The walk alone takes about 1½ hours one way, plus 30 minutes in Santa Croce, 30 minutes in the Museo di Santa Croce, and 30 minutes in San

Miniato. Depending on the amount of time you have, you can limit your sightseeing to Santa Croce and Casa Buonarroti or continue on to Piazzale Michelangelo. The walk to Piazzale Michelangelo is a long uphill hike, with the prospect of another climb to San Miniato from there. If you decide to take a bus, remember to buy your ticket before you board. Finally, since you go to Piazzale Michelangelo for the view, skip it if it's a hazy day.

What to See

㊳ Casa Buonarroti. Michelangelo Buonarroti the Younger, the grand-nephew of the famed Michelangelo, turned his family house into a shrine honoring the life of his great-uncle. It's full of works executed by Michelangelo, including a marble bas-relief, the *Madonna of the Steps,* carved when Michelangelo was just a teenager, and his wooden model for the facade of San Lorenzo ⊠ *Via Ghibellina 70, Santa Croce* ☎ *055/241752* ⊕ *www.casabuonarroti.it* ⊠ *€6.15* ☉ *Wed.–Mon. 9:30–2.*

㊴ Piazzale Michelangelo. From this lookout, you have a marvelous view of Florence and the hills around it, rivaling the vista from the Forte di Belvedere. It has a copy of Michelangelo's *David* and outdoor cafés packed with tourists during the day and with Florentines in the evening. The **Giardino dell'Iris** (Iris Garden) off the piazza is in full flower in May. The **Giardino delle Rose** (Rose Garden) on the terraces below the piazza is in full bloom in May and June, and only open then.

㊵ San Miniato al Monte. This church, like the Baptistery, is a fine example of Romanesque architecture and one of the oldest churches in Florence, dating from the 11th century. The lively green-and-white marble facade has a 12th-century mosaic topped by a gilt bronze eagle, emblem of San Miniato's sponsors, the Calimala (cloth merchants' guild). Inside are a 13th-century marble floor and apse mosaic. Spinello Aretino (1350–1410) covered the walls of the **Sagrestia** with frescoes on the life of St. Benedict. The adjacent **Cappella del Cardinale del Portogallo** is one of the richest Renaissance works in Florence. Built to hold the tomb of a Portuguese cardinal, Prince James of Lusitania, who died young in Florence in 1459, it has a glorious ceiling by Luca della Robbia, a sculptured tomb by Antonio Rossellino (1427–79), and inlaid pavement in multicolor marble. ⊠ *Viale Galileo Galilei, Piazzale Michelangelo, Lungarno South* ☎ *055/2342731* ☉ *Daily 8–6:15.*

▶ ㊲ Santa Croce. Like the Duomo, this church is Gothic, but, also like the
Duomo, its facade dates from the 19th century. The interior is most famous for its art and its tombs. As a burial place, the church is a Florentine pantheon, probably containing more skeletons of Renaissance celebrities than any other church in Italy. Among others, the tomb of Michelangelo is immediately to the right as you enter; he is said to have chosen this spot so that the first thing he would see on Judgment Day, when the graves of the dead fly open, would be Brunelleschi's dome through Santa Croce's open doors. The tomb of Galileo Galilei (1564–1642), who produced evidence that Earth is not the center of the universe, and was not granted a Christian burial until 100 years after his death because of it, is on the left wall, opposite Michelangelo's. The tomb of Niccolò Machiavelli (1469–1527), the political theoretician whose brutally pragmatic philosophy so influenced the Medici, is halfway down the nave on the right. The grave of Lorenzo Ghiberti, creator of the Baptistery doors, is halfway down the nave on the left. Composer Gioacchino Rossini (1792–1868) is entombed at the end of the nave on the right. The monument to Dante Alighieri (1265–1321), the greatest Italian poet, is a memorial rather than a tomb (he is buried in Ravenna); it's on the right wall near the tomb of Michelangelo.

The collection of art within the church complex is by far the most important of any church in Florence. Historically, the most significant works are probably the Giotto frescoes in the two chapels immediately to the right of the high altar. They illustrate scenes from the lives of St. John the Evangelist and St. John the Baptist (in the right-hand chapel) and scenes from the life of St. Francis (in the left-hand chapel). Time has not been kind to them; over the centuries, wall tombs were introduced into the middle of them, whitewash and plaster covered them, and in the 19th century they were subjected to a clumsy restoration. But the reality that Giotto introduced into painting can still be seen. He did not paint beautifully stylized religious icons, as the Byzantine style that preceded him prescribed; he instead painted drama—St. Francis surrounded by grieving friars at the very moment of his death. This was a radical shift in emphasis, and it changed the course of art. Before him, the role of painting was to symbolize the attributes of God; after him, it was to imitate life. His work is indeed primitive, compared with later painting, but in the proto-Renaissance of the early 14th century it caused a sensation that was not equaled for another 100 years. He was, for his time, the equal of both Masaccio and Michelangelo.

Among the church's other highlights are Donatello's *Annunciation*, one of the most eloquent expressions of surprise ever sculpted (on the right wall two-thirds of the way down the nave); 14th-century frescoes by Taddeo Gaddi (circa 1300–66) illustrating scenes from the life of the Virgin Mary, clearly showing the influence of Giotto (in the chapel at the end of the right transept); and Donatello's *Crucifix*, criticized by Brunelleschi for making Christ look like a peasant (in the chapel at the end of the left transept). Outside the church proper, in the **Museo dell'Opera di Santa Croce** off the cloister, is the 13th-century *Triumphal Cross* by Cimabue (circa 1240–1302), badly damaged by the flood of 1966. A model of architectural geometry, the **Cappella Pazzi**, at the end of the cloister, is the work of Brunelleschi. ⊠ *Piazza Santa Croce 16* ☎ *055/244619* 🖃 *Basilica and museum (cumulative ticket): €3* ☉ *Church: Mar.–Oct., Mon.–Sat. 9:30–5:30, Sun. 3–5:30; Nov.–Feb., Mon.–Sat. 9:30–noon and 3–5:30, Sun. 3–5:30. Cloister and museum: Mar.–Oct., Thurs.–Tues. 10–7; Nov.–Feb., Thurs.–Tues. 10–12:30 and 3–6.*

WHERE TO EAT

Dining hours are earlier here than in Rome, starting at 1 for the midday meal and at 8 for dinner. Many of Florence's restaurants are small, so reservations are a must. You can sample such specialties as creamy *fegatini* (a chicken-liver spread), and *ribollita* (minestrone thickened with bread and beans and swirled with extra-virgin olive oil) in bustling, convivial *trattorie*, where you share long wooden tables set with paper place mats, or in an upscale *ristorante* with linen tablecloths and napkins. Follow Florentines' lead and take a break at an *enoteca* (wineshop or wine bar) during the day and discover some excellent Chiantis and Super Tuscans from small producers who rarely export.

	WHAT IT COSTS In euros				
	$$$$	**$$$**	**$$**	**$**	**¢**
AT DINNER	over €22	€17–€22	€12–€17	€7–€12	under €7

Prices are for a second course (secondo piatto).

Centro Storico

$$ ✕ **Osteria delle Belle Donne.** Down the street from the church of Santa Maria Novella, this gaily decorated spot, festooned with ropes of garlic and other vegetables, has an ever-changing menu and stellar service led by the irrepressible Giacinto. Even the checkered cloth napkins are cheery. The kitchen offers Tuscan standards, but shakes up the menu with alternatives such as *sedani con bacon, verza, e uova* (thick noodles sauced with bacon, cabbage, and egg). If you want to eat outside, request a table when booking. ⊠ *Via delle Belle Donne 16/r, Santa Maria Novella* ☎ *055/238 2609* ▭ *AE, DC, MC, V.*

$–$$ ✕ **Osteria n. 1.** The name "Osteria" is the only pretentious aspect of this romantic restaurant in an old palazzo in the historic center. The place is suffused with a rosy glow from the tablecloths and cream-color walls, lined with painted landscapes and the occasional coat of arms. The food is expertly prepared—try *tagliatelle verdi ai broccoli e salsiccia* (flat noodles with sausage and broccoli) before moving on to any of the grilled meats. ⊠ *Via del Moro 18–20/r, Santa Maria Novella* ☎ *055/284897* ▭ *AE, DC, MC, V* ⊙ *Closed Sun. and 20 days in Aug. No lunch Mon.*

Oltrarno

★ $$–$$$ ✕ **Beccofino.** Forget that the noise level here often reaches the pitch of the Tower of Babel, and ignore the generic urban decor. Concentrate, instead, on the food, which might just be the most creative and best in town. A pale-wood serpentine bar separates the ocher-walled wine bar from the green-walled restaurant. Chef Francesco Berardinelli has paid some dues in the United States, and it shows in the inventiveness of his food (such as his pairing of scallops with bitter greens), which ends up tasting wholly and wonderfully Italian. The wine bar has a less expensive menu. ⊠ *Piazza degli Scarlatti 1/r, Lungarno Guicciardini, Lungarno South* ☎ *055/290076* ⌂ *Reservations essential* ▭ *MC, V* ⊙ *No lunch Mon.–Sat.*

$–$$$ ✕ **Quattro Leoni.** The eclectic staff at this trattoria in a small piazza is an appropriate match for the diverse menu. In winter, you can sample the wares in one of two rooms with high ceilings, and in summer you can sit outside and admire the scenery. Traditional Tuscan favorites, such as *taglierini con porcini* (long, thin, flat pasta with porcini mushrooms), adorn the menu, but so, too, are less typical things like the earthy cabbage salad with avocado, pine nuts, and drops of *olio di tartufo* (truffle oil). Reservations are a good idea. ⊠ *Piazza della Passera, Via dei Vellutini 1/r, Palazzo Pitti* ☎ *055/218562* ▭ *AE, DC, MC, V.*

¢ ✕ **La Casalinga.** *Casalinga* means "housewife," and this place has the nostalgic charm of a 1950s kitchen with Tuscan comfort food to match. If you eat ribollita anywhere in Florence, eat it here—it couldn't be more authentic. Mediocre paintings clutter the semi-paneled walls, tables are set close together, and the place is usually jammed. The menu is long, portions are plentiful, and service is prompt and friendly. ⊠ *Via Michelozzi 9/r, Santo Spirito/San Frediano* ☎ *055/218624* ▭ *AE, DC, MC, V* ⊙ *Closed Sun., 1 wk at Christmas, and 3 wks in Aug.*

¢ ✕ **Osteria Antica Mescita San Niccolò.** It's always crowded, always good, and always cheap. The osteria is next to the church of San Niccolò, and if you sit in the lower part you'll find yourself in what was once a chapel dating from the 11th century. Such subtle but dramatic background plays off nicely with the food, which is simple Tuscan at its best. The *pollo con limone* is tasty pieces of chicken in a lemon-scented broth. In winter, try the *spezzatino di cinghiale con aromi* (wild boar stew with herbs). Reservations are advised. ⊠ *Via San Niccolò 60/r, San Niccolò* ☎ *055/2342836* ▭ *No credit cards* ⊙ *Closed Sun.*

CloseUp

ON THE MENU

A typical Tuscan repast starts with an antipasto of crostini (grilled bread spread with various savory toppings) or cured meats such as prosciutto crudo (cured ham thinly sliced) and finocchiona (salami seasoned with fennel). Primi piatti (first courses) can consist of pasta dishes available throughout Italy. Peculiar to Florence, however, are the vegetable-and-bread soups such as pappa al pomodoro (bread and tomato soup), ribollita, and, in summer, a salad called panzanella (tomatoes, onions, vinegar, oil, basil, and bread). Before they are eaten, these are often christened with a drizzle of the sumptuous local olive oil. Unparalleled among the secondi piatti (second courses) is bistecca alla fiorentina—a thick slab of local Chianina beef, grilled over charcoal, seasoned with olive oil, salt, and pepper, and served rare. Trippa alla fiorentina (tripe stewed with tomato sauce) and arista (roast loin of pork seasoned with rosemary) are also local specialties.

San Lorenzo & Beyond

★ **$$$–$$$$** ✗ **Taverna del Bronzino.** Want to have a sophisticated meal in a 16th-century Renaissance artist's studio? There's nothing outstanding about the decor in the former studio of Santi di Tito, a student of Bronzino's, save for its simple formality, with white tablecloths and place settings. Lots of classic, superb Tuscan food, however, graces the artful menu, and the presentation is often dramatic. A wine list of solid, affordable choices rounds out the menu. The service is outstanding. Reservations are advised, especially for eating at the wine cellar's only table. ✉ *Via delle Ruote 25/r, San Lorenzo* ☎ *055/495220* ▭ *AE, DC, MC, V* ⊙ *Closed Sun. and Aug.*

★ **$–$$$** ✗ **Le Fonticine.** Since owner Silvano Bruci is from Tuscany and his wife, Gianna, is from Emilia-Romagna, their fine-dining oasis near the train station combines the best of two Italian cuisines. Start with the mixed-vegetable antipasto plate and then move on to any of their house-made pastas. The feathery light tortelloni *nostro modo* are stuffed with fresh ricotta and served with a tomato and cream sauce, and should not be missed. The restaurant's interior, filled with the Brucis' painting collection, provides a cheery space for this soul-satisfying food. ✉ *Via Nazionale 79/r, San Lorenzo* ☎ *055/282106* ▭ *AE, DC, MC, V* ⊙ *Closed Sun., Mon., Nov. 24–Jan. 5, and July 25–Aug. 25.*

¢–$ ✗ **Mario.** Florentines flock to this narrow family-run trattoria near San Lorenzo to feast on Tuscan favorites served at simple tables under a wooden ceiling dating from 1536. A distinct cafeteria feel and genuine Florentine hospitality prevail: you'll be seated wherever there's room, which often means with strangers. Yes, there's a bit of extra oil in most dishes, which imparts calories as well as taste, but aren't you on vacation in Italy? Worth the splurge is *riso al ragù* (rice with ground beef and tomatoes). ✉ *Via Rosina 2/r, corner of Piazza del Mercato Centrale, San Lorenzo* ☎ *055/218550* ⊛ *Reservations not accepted* ▭ *No credit cards* ⊙ *Closed Sun. and Aug. No dinner.*

Santa Croce

$$$$ ✗ **Alle Murate.** Creative versions of classic Tuscan dishes are served in this sleek and sophisticated spot. The *involtini di vitella ripieni di melanzane coi fagiolini al dente* (veal rolls stuffed with eggplant garnished with green beans) is remarkably light and flavorful. The main dining room has a rich, uncluttered look, with warm wood floors and paneling and soft lights. In a smaller adjacent room called the *vineria,* you get the same splendid service but substantially reduced prices. There's no middle ground with the wine list—there's only a smattering of inexpensive bottles before it soars to exalted heights. ⊠ *Via Ghibellina 52/r, Santa Croce* ☎ *055/240618* ▭ *AE, DC, MC, V* ⊙ *Closed Mon. No lunch.*

$$$$ ✕ **Cibrèo.** The food at this upscale trattoria is fantastic, from the creamy
Fodor'sChoice crostini *di fegatini* (a savory chicken-liver spread) to the meltingly good
★ desserts. If you thought you'd never try tripe—let alone like it—this is the place to lay any doubts to rest: the *trippa in insalata* (cold tripe salad) with parsley and garlic is an epiphany. Construe chef Fabio Picchi's unsolicited advice as a sign of his enthusiasm for cooking; it's warranted, as the food is among the best and most creative in town. Just around the corner is Cibreino, Cibrèo's budget version, with a shorter menu and a no-reservations policy. ⊠ *Via A. del Verrocchio 8/r, Santa Croce* ☎ *055/2341100* ⚏ *Reservations essential* ▭ *AE, DC, MC, V* ⊙ *Closed Sun. and Mon., July 25–Sept. 5, and Dec. 31–Jan. 7.*

$$$$ ✕ **Enoteca Pinchiorri.** A sumptuous Renaissance palace with high, frescoed ceilings and bouquets in silver vases provides the backdrop for this restaurant, one of the most expensive in Italy. Some consider it one of the best, and others consider it a non-Italian rip-off, as the kitchen is presided over by a Frenchwoman with sophisticated, yet internationalist, leanings. Prices are high and portions are small; the vast holdings of the wine cellar, as well as stellar service, dull the pain, however, when the bill is presented. Interesting pasta combinations like the *ignudi*—ricotta-and-spinach dumplings with a lobster-and-coxcomb fricassee—are always on the menu. ⊠ *Via Ghibellina 87, Santa Croce* ☎ *055/242777* ⚏ *Reservations essential* ▭ *AE, MC, V* ⊙ *Closed Sun., Mon., Aug. No lunch Tues. or Wed.*

$$ ✕ **Cantina Barbagianni** *"Diverso dal solito"* (different from the usual) is the leitmotif here, and this attitude is reflected in the funky furnishings (lots of strategically placed drapery) and avant-garde paintings on the walls. Cristina, the proprietor, presides over it all with great ease. The regularly changing menu strays far from the typical Tuscan path: *l'anatra con mirtillo* (duck with blueberries) is a rare thing in these parts, and the chef is to be commended for his inventiveness. The *risotto al carciofi con scamorza* (artichoke risotto with smoked cheese) is heavenly. ⊠ *Via Sant'Egidio 13, Santa Croce* ☎ *055/248–0508* ▭ *AE, DC, MC, V* ⊙ *Closed Sun.*

★ **$$–$$$** ✕ **La Giostra.** The clubby La Giostra, which means "carousel" in Italian, is owned and run by Prince Dimitri Kunz d'Asburgo Lorena, and his way with mushrooms is as remarkable as his charm. The unusually good pastas may require explanation from Soldano, one of the prince's good-looking twin sons. In perfect English he'll describe a favorite dish, *taglierini con tartufo bianco,* a decadently rich pasta with white truffles. Leave room for dessert: this might be the only show in town with a sublime tiramisu *and* a wonderfully gooey Sacher torte. ⊠ *Borgo Pinti 12/r, Santa Croce* ☎ *055/241341* ▭ *AE, DC, MC, V.*

$–$$$ ✕ **Finisterrae.** Four large, dramatically lighted rooms, dotted with maps detailing various Mediterranean towns, and highly colorful walls and tiles lend an aura of romance to this spot which opened in February 2003. There may not be a prettier restaurant in town. The eminently affordable menu offers a little bit from Lebanon, Spain, France, Morocco and, yes, Italy. The Spanish options are particularly fine, especially the *filetto al cabrales* (beef with Spanish blue cheese and port). The seductive bar, with its expert barmen, is dimly lighted with low-slung seats; they'll even provide tobacco if you want to light up one of the hookahs. ⊠ *Via de' Pepi 3/5r* ☎ *055/2638675* ▭ *MC, V* ⊙ *Closed Mon. Nov.–Mar.*

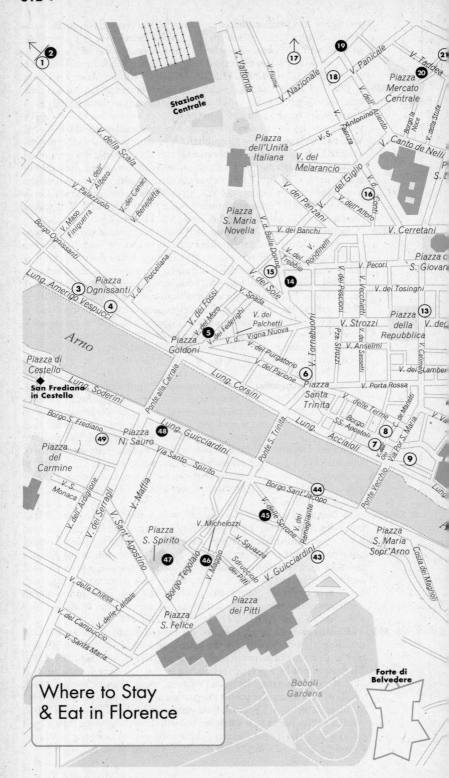

Where to Stay & Eat in Florence

Restaurants ▼

Acquacotta	.30
Alle Murate	.34
Baldovino	.38
Beccofino	.48
Borgo Antico	.47
Cantina Barbagianni	.29
Cibrèo	.32
Coquinarius	.12
da Rocco	.31
Enoteca Baldovino	.39
Enoteca Pinchiorri	.36
Finnisterae	.37
Fuori Porta	.42
La Casalinga	.46
La Giostra	.28
Le Compane	.33
Le Fonticine	.19
Mario	.20
Osteria Antica Mescita San Niccolò	.41
Osteria de'Benci	.40
Osteria delle Belle Donne	.14
Osteria n. 1	.5
Pallottino	.35
Quattro Leoni	.45
Taverna del Bronzino	.23
Zibibbo	.2

Hotels ▼

Albergo Firenze	.10
Albergo la Scaletta	.43
Albergo Losanna	.26
Alessandra	.7
Beacci Tornabuoni	.6
Bellettini	.16
Excelsior	.4
Grand	.3
Hermitage	.9
Hotel Benivieni	.11
Hotel Savoy	.13
J&J	.27
Loggiato dei Serviti	.22
Lungarno	.44
Monna Lisa	.25
Morandi alla Crocetta	.24
Nuova Italia	.18
Palazzo Magnani Feroni	.49
Pensione Ferretti	.15
Porta Faenza	.17
Residenza Johanna I	.21
Torre Guelfa	.8
Villa Azalee	.1

$–$$ ✕ **Acquacotta.** With its closely spaced, red-checked tablecloths, you couldn't get any more "Italian" than this. You almost expect the chef to come out of the kitchen with an accordion and serenade you while you eat. Not to worry: service is offhand (sometimes dismissive), and the chef has better things to do than break into song. The highlight of the menu, with the usual list of grilled meats and pasta starters, is the *acquacotta*, literally cooked water—a favorite from southern Tuscany that rarely appears on Florentine menus. It's a vegetable-based soup with mushrooms and onions that's topped with a poached egg. ⊠ *Via dei Pilastri 51/r, Santa Croce* ☎ *055/242907* ▬ *MC, V* ⊗ *Closed Sun. and Aug.*

★ **$–$$** ✕ **Osteria de' Benci.** Just a few minutes from Santa Croce, this charming osteria serves some of the most eclectic food in Florence. Try the spaghetti *degli eretici* (in tomato sauce with fresh herbs). The grilled meats are justifiably famous; the *carbonata* is a succulent piece of grilled beef served rare. When it's warm, you can dine outside with a view of the 13th-century tower belonging to the prestigious Alberti family. The English-speaking staff shouldn't scare you off: Florentines *do* eat here. ⊠ *Via de'Benci 11-13/r, Santa Croce* ☎ *055/2344923* ▬ *AE, DC, MC, V* ⊗ *Closed Sun.*

$–$$ ✕ **Pallottino.** With its tiled floor, photograph-filled walls, and wooden tables, Pallottino is the quintessential Tuscan trattoria, with hearty, heartwarming classics like pappa al pomodoro and *peposa alla toscana* (a beef stew laced with black pepper). The menu changes frequently to reflect what's seasonal; the staff is friendly, as are the diners who often share a table and, eventually, conversation. ⊠ *Via Isola delle Stinche 1/r, Santa Croce* ☎ *055/289573* ▬ *AE, DC, MC, V* ⊗ *Closed Mon. and 2–3 wks in Aug.*

¢ ✕ **da Rocco.** These are some of the hottest tables (booths, actually) in one of Florence's biggest markets. You can get lunch to go, or cram yourself into one of the booths, swill from the straw-cloaked flask (wine here is *da consumo*—which means they charge you for how much you drink). Food is abundant, Tuscan, and fast. Locals pack it in at lunchtime; the menu changes daily, and the prices are just right. ⊠ *In the Mercato Sant'Ambrogio, Piazza Ghiberti* ☎ *No phone* ▬ *No credit cards.* ⊗ *Closed Sun. No dinner.*

Beyond the City Center

$$–$$$ ✕ **Zibibbo.** Benedetta Vitali, formerly of Florence's famed Cibrèo, has a restaurant of her very own. It's a welcome addition to the sometimes claustrophobic Florentine dining scene—particularly since you have to drive a few minutes out of town to get here. Off a quiet piazza, it has two intimate rooms with rustic, maroon-painted wood floors and a sloped ceiling. The *tagliatelle al sugo d'anatra* (wide pasta ribbons with duck sauce) is aromatic and flavorful, and the *crocchette di fave con salsa di yogurt* (fava bean croquettes with a lively yogurt sauce) are innovative and tasty. ⊠ *Via di Terzollina 3/r, northwest of city center* ☎ *055/433383* ▬ *AE, DC, MC, V* ⊗ *Closed Sun.*

Pizzerias

The *pizzaiuoli* (pizza-makers) successfully merge the Roman (thin) crust with the Neapolitan (thick) crust at **Le Campane** (⊠ Borgo La Croce 85-87/r Santa Croce ☎ 055/2341101). **Baldovino** (⊠ Via San Giuseppe 22/r Santa Croce ☎ 055/241 773) makes pizzas to delight the kids and more sophisticated stuff to satisfy the parents. In the Oltrarno, try **Borgo Antico** (⊠ Piazza S. Spirito 6/r, Santo Spirito/San Frediano ☎ 055/210437), which serves up pizza and other trattoria fare.

Enoteche

Most wine bars also serve light fare, making them yet another option for lunch or dinner. **Enoteca Baldovino** (✉ Via San Giuseppe 18/r, Santa Croce ☎ 055/2347220), closed Monday, has candlelit, tiled tables. Try the *piatti misti* (mixed plate of various specials of the day). It's hard to believe that a wine bar could be so close to the Duomo, but there's tranquil and sophisticated **Coquinarius** (✉ Via delle Oche 15/r, Duomo ☎ 055/2302153), providing a great place to rest one's soul (except on Sunday, when it's closed). **Fuori Porta** (✉ Via Monte alle Croci 10/r, San Niccolò ☎ 055/2342483), one of the oldest and best wine bars in Florence, offers cured meats and cheeses, as well as daily specials such as a sublime spaghetti al curry. It's closed Sunday.

Cafés

Cafés in Italy serve not only coffee concoctions and pastries but also sweets, drinks, and panini, and some have hot pasta and lunch dishes. They are usually open from early in the morning to late at night. **Caffe Giacosa/Roberto Cavalli** (✉ Via della Spada 10 Santa Maria Novella ☎ 055/2776328) is a semi-reincarnation of the old Caffe Giacosa; there's nothing "old" about it now, however, as it's joined at the hip with the Florentine fashion designer's shop. It's open for breakfast, lunch, tea, and cocktails, and it's always crowded. All bars in Italy ought to be like ★ **Caffètteria Piansa** (✉ Borgo Pinti 18/r, Santa Croce ☎ 055/2342362). It's rare that one can pull off a great breakfast and lunch, plus fine drinks at night. Classy **Procacci** (✉ Via Tornabuoni 64/r, Santa Maria Novella ☎ 055/211656) is a Florentine institution dating back to 1885; try one of the panini tartufati and swish it down with a glass of Prosecco. It's closed Sunday and Monday. Perhaps the best spot for people-watching is **Rivoire** (✉ Via Vacchereccia 4/r, Piazza della Signoria ☎ 055/214412). Stellar service, light snacks, and terrific aperitivi are the norm.

Rose's (✉ Via del Parione 26/r, Santa Maria Novella ☎ 055/287090) draws businesspeople at lunch and people sporting multiple body piercings at night. An Italian menu is available at lunchtime, sushi in the evening.

Gelaterie & Pasticcerie

The *pasticceria* (bakery) **Dolci e Dolcezze** (✉ Piazza C. Beccaria 8/r, Sant'Ambrogio ☎ 055/2345458) is somewhat off the beaten path, but if you walk down colorful Borgo La Croce, you'll be rewarded with the prettiest and tastiest cakes, sweets, and tarts in town. It's closed Monday. **Gran Caffè** (✉ Piazza San Marco 11/r, San Marco ☎ 055/215833) is down the street from the Accademia, so it's a perfect stop for a marvelous panino or sweet while raving about the majesty of Michelangelo's *David*. Florentines with serious sweet tooths come to **I Dolci di Patrizio Corsi** (✉ Borgo Albizi 15/r, Santa Croce ☎ 055/2480367), which offers a bewildering array of chocolate- and cream-filled sweets. It's closed on Sunday afternoons. Most people consider **Vivoli** (✉ Via Isola delle Stinche 7/r, Santa Croce ☎ 055/292334) the best gelateria in town. **Vestri** (✉ Borgo Albizi 11/4, Santa Croce ☎ 055/2340374) is devoted to chocolate in all its guises. The small, but sublime selection of chocolate-based gelati includes one with hot peppers.

Salumerie

Salumerie are food shops specializing in fresh meats and cheeses; they're great for picking up a picnic lunch or assembling dinner. Most are closed Monday morning. If you find yourself in the Oltrarno and hungry for lunch or a snack, drop into **Azzarri Delicatesse** (⊠ Borgo S. Jacopo 27b/cr, Santo Spirito/San Frediano ☎ 055/2381714) for a sandwich or fixings. Its impressive list of cheeses include some from France. Looking for some cheddar cheese to pile in your panino? **Pegna** (⊠ Via dello Studio 8, Duomo ☎ 055/282701)—closed Saturday afternoon in July–August, Wednesday afternoon the rest of the year, and Sunday year-round—has been selling both Italian and non-Italian food since 1860. **Perini** (⊠ Mercato Centrale, enter at Via dell'Aretino, San Lorenzo ☎ 055/2398306), closed Sunday, sells everything from prosciutto and mixed meats to sauces for pasta and a wide assortment of antipasti. It's probably the most seductive little food shop in Florence—be prepared to drop some money. At **Salumeria Verdi** (⊠ Via Verdi 36/r, Santa Croce ☎ 055/244517), options include well-prepared sandwiches and everything to assemble a dinner. You can eat in or take out. It's closed Sundays.

WHERE TO STAY

No stranger to visitors, Florence has hotels for all budgets located throughout the city; for instance, you can find both budget and luxury hotels in the centro storico and along the Arno. Whether you are in a five-star hotel or a more modest establishment, you may have one of the greatest pleasures of all: a room with a view. Florence has so many famous landmarks that it's not hard to find lodgings with a panoramic vista. And the equivalent of the genteel pensioni of yesteryear still exists, with the benefit of modern plumbing.

Florence's importance not only as a tourist city but as a convention center and site of the Pitti fashion collections throughout the year means a high demand for rooms. Except in winter, reservations are a must. If you find yourself in Florence with no reservations, go to **Consorzio ITA** (⊠ Stazione Centrale, Santa Maria Novella ☎ 055/282893). You must go there in person to make a booking.

WHAT IT COSTS In euros				
	$$$$	$$$	$$	$	¢
FOR 2 PEOPLE	over € 300	€225–€300	€150–€225	€75–€150	under €75

Prices are for two people in a standard double room in high season.

Centro Storico

$$$$ 🏨 **Hotel Savoy.** From the outside, it looks very much like the turn-of-the-19th-century building that it is. Inside, sleek minimalism and up-to-the-minute amenities prevail. Sitting rooms have a funky edge, their cream-color walls dotted with contemporary prints. Rooms are decorated in muted colors, with streamlined furniture and soaring ceilings; many have views of the Duomo's cupola or the Piazza della Repubblica. The deep marble tubs might be reason enough to stay here—but you'll also appreciate the efficient and courteous staff. ⊠ *Piazza della Repubblica 7 50123* ☎ *055/27351* 🖷 *055/2735888* ⊕ *www.roccofortehotels.com* 🛏 *98 rooms, 9 suites* ♨ *Restaurant, in-room data ports, in-room fax, in-room safes, minibars, cable TV with movies, in-room VCRs, exercise equipment, bar, dry cleaning, laundry service, concierge, Internet, business services, meeting rooms, parking (fee), no-smoking rooms* ▭ *AE, DC, MC, V.*

$$$ 🏨 **Hermitage.** A stone's throw from the Ponte Vecchio, this is a fine little hotel with an enviable location. All rooms are decorated differently with lively wallpaper; some have views of Palazzo Vecchio and others of the Arno. The rooftop terrace, where you can have breakfast or an aperitivo, is decked with flowers. The lobby feels like a friend's living room—its warm yellow walls are welcoming. Double glazing and air-conditioning help keep street noise at bay. (The hotel has an elevator at the top of a short flight of stairs from the street.) ⊠ *Vicolo Marzio 1, Piazza del Pesce, Ponte Vecchio, 50122* ☎ *055/287216* 🖷 *055/212208* ⊕ *www.hermitagehotel.com* ↪ *27 rooms, 1 suite* ⚿ *Cable TV, baby-sitting, laundry service, parking (fee), some pets allowed* ▤ *MC, V.*

$ 🏨 **Alessandra.** The location, a block from the Ponte Vecchio, and the clean, ample rooms make this a good choice. The building, known as the Palazzo Roselli del Turco, was designed in 1507 by Baccio d'Agnolo, a student of Michelangelo's. Though little remains of the original design save for the high wood ceilings, there's still an aura of grandeur. Several of the rooms have views of the Arno, and the sole suite is spacious and a steal for this category. The English-speaking staff is friendly and helpful. ⊠ *Borgo Santi Apostoli 17, Santa Maria Novella 50123* ☎ *055/283438* 🖷 *055/210619* ⊕ *www.hotelalessandra.com* ↪ *26 rooms, 18 with bath, 1 suite, 1 apartment* ⚿ *Cable TV, some minibars, laundry service, Internet, parking (fee), no-smoking rooms* ▤ *AE, MC, V* ☉ *Closed Dec. 10–26.*

$$ 🏨 **Hotel Benivieni.** This quiet, tranquil former 15th-century palace is just one block away from the Duomo. Rooms are spacious with high ceilings, hardwood floors, and sweeping draperies. A winter garden provides a wonderful place to while away some time. The affable Caldana family, wholly fluent in English, ably staffs the front desk. ⊠ *Via delle Oche 5, Duomo 50122* ☎ *055/2382133* 🖷 *055/2398248* ⊕ *www. hotelbenivieni.it* ↪ *15 rooms* ⚿ *In-room safes, cable TV, baby-sitting, dry cleaning, laundry service, Internet, parking (fee), some pets allowed, no-smoking rooms* ▤ *AE, DC, MC, V.*

$$ 🏨 **Torre Guelfa.** Enter this hidden hotel through an immense wooden door on a narrow street, and continue through an iron gate and up a few steps to an elevator that will take you to the third floor. A few more steps and you're in the 13th-century Florentine *torre* (tower). Each guest room is different, some with canopied beds, some with balconies. The Torre Guelfa once protected the fabulously wealthy Acciaiuoli family. Now it's one of the best-located small hotels in Florence, where you can have breakfast or drinks on a rooftop that provides unmatched Florentine panoramas. ⊠ *Borgo Santi Apostoli 8, Santa Maria Novella 50123* ☎ *055/2396338* 🖷 *055/2398577* ↪ *18 rooms, 2 suites* ⚿ *In-room safes, cable TV, baby-sitting, dry cleaning, laundry service, Internet, parking (fee), some pets allowed, no-smoking rooms* ▤ *AE, MC, V.*

$ 🏨 **Albergo Firenze.** A block from the Duomo, this hotel is in one of the oldest piazzas in Florence. Though the reception area and hallways have all the charm of a college dormitory, the similarity ends upon entering the spotlessly clean rooms. For the location, the place is a great bargain; its rooms, often well under 100€, are a great option for travelers on a budget. ⊠ *Piazza Donati 4, Duomo 50122* ☎ *055/214203* 🖷 *055/212370* ⊕ *www.hotelfirenze-fi.it* ↪ *58 rooms* ⚿ *Parking (fee); no a/c* ▤ *No credit cards.*

The Oltrarno

$$$$ 🏨 **Lungarno.** Many rooms and suites here have private terraces that jut out right over the Arno, granting views of the Palazzo Vecchio and Duomo opposite. Four suites in a 13th-century tower preserve details like exposed stone walls and old archways and look out onto a little square with a medieval tower covered in jasmine. The very chic decor approximates a breezily elegant home, with lots of crisp white fabrics with blue trim. A wall of windows and a sea of white couches makes the lobby bar one of the nicest places in the city to stop for a drink. Inquire about the Lungarno Suites, across the river; if you're booking a longer stay, suites include kitchens. ⊠ *Borgo San Jacopo 14, Lungarno South, 50125* ☎ *055/27261* 🖷 *055/268437* ⊕ *www.lungarnohotels.com* ⤴ *60 rooms, 13 suites* ⟳ *Restaurant, cable TV with movies, bar, baby-sitting, dry cleaning, laundry service, concierge, Internet, meeting rooms, parking (fee), some pets allowed, no-smoking rooms* ⊟ *AE, DC, MC, V.*

$$$$ 🏨 **Palazzo Magnani Feroni.** The perfect place to play the part of a Florentine aristocrat is this 16th-century palazzo, which despite its massive halls and sweeping staircases, could almost feel like home. Suites include large sitting rooms and bedrooms, and all are luxuriously decorated in sweeping fabrics, chandeliers, and Renaissance-inspired furniture. The roof-top terrace, complete with bar, offers city-wide views that startle. Though it's only a five-minute walk from the Ponte Vecchio, the street is surprisingly quiet. ⊠ *Borgo San Frediano 5, 50124* ☎ *055/239 9544* 🖷 *055/260 8908* ⊕ *www.florencepalace.com* ⤴ *11 suites* ⟳ *Room service, in-room data ports, in-room safes, cable TV, billiards, exercise equipment, bar, parking (fee), no-smoking rooms* ⊟ *AE, DC, MC, V.*

$ 🏨 **Albergo La Scaletta.** For a tremendous view of the Boboli Garden, look no farther than this exquisite pensione run by a mother and son team. Near the Ponte Vecchio and Palazzo Pitti, it has simply furnished yet rather large rooms and a sunny breakfast room. In warm weather two flower-bedecked terraces are open, one with a stunning 360-degree view of Florence. ⊠ *Via Guicciardini 13, 50125* ☎ *055/283028* 🖷 *055/289562* ⤴ *11 rooms, 10 with bath* ⟳ *Parking (fee), some pets allowed; no TV in some rooms* ⊟ *MC, V.*

Piazza San Marco & Beyond

$$ 🏨 **Loggiato dei Serviti.** Though this hotel was not designed by Brunelleschi, Florence's architectural genius, it might as well have been. A mirror image of the architect's famous Spedale degli Innocenti across the way, the Loggiato is tucked away on one of the city's loveliest squares. Occupying a 16th-century former monastery, the building was originally a refuge for traveling priests. Vaulted ceilings, tasteful furnishings (some antique), canopy beds, and rich fabrics make this spare Renaissance building with modern comforts a find. ⊠ *Piazza Santissima Annunziata 3, 50122* ☎ *055/289592* 🖷 *055/289595* ⊕ *www.loggiatodeiservitihotel. it* ⤴ *29 rooms* ⟳ *In-room safes, minibars, cable TV, bar, baby-sitting, laundry service, parking (fee), some pets allowed* ⊟ *AE, DC, MC, V.*

★ $$ 🏨 **Morandi alla Crocetta.** Near Piazza Santissima Annunziata, this is a charming and distinguished residence in which you're made to feel like privileged friends of the family. The former convent is close to the sights but very quiet and is furnished comfortably in the classic style of a gracious Florentine home. The Morandi is not only an exceptional hotel but also a good value. It's very small, so try to book well in advance. Breakfast is not included in the room rate. ⊠ *Via Laura 50, Santissima Annunziata 50121* ☎ *055/2344747* 🖷 *055/2480954* ⊕ *www. hotelmorandi.it* ⤴ *10 rooms* ⟳ *In-room safes, minibars, cable TV, dry cleaning, laundry service, concierge, Internet, parking (fee), some pets allowed* ⊟ *AE, DC, MC, V.*

¢   **Residenza Johanna I.** Savvy travelers and those on a budget should
Fodor'sChoice look no further, as this "residenza" (residence) offers tremendous value
★   for quality and location. Though it's very much in the *centro storico*,
the place has a homey feel: indeed, you'll be given a large set of keys to
let you into every door, as the staff goes home at 7 pm. Rooms have
high ceilings and are simply decorated in pale pastel floral prints; morning tea and coffee (but no breakfast) is taken in one's room. ⊠ *Via Bonifacio Lupo 14, 50129* ☎ *055/473377* ⊕ *www.johanna.it* ⇱ *11
rooms* ⚒ *Fans, dry cleaning, laundry service, parking (fee), some pets
allowed; no a/c, no room phones, no room TVs* ⊟ *No credit cards.*

San Lorenzo & Beyond

$$ **Porta Faenza.** The 12th-century medieval well discovered during ren-
ovations has now become a focal point in the lobby. Two small pen-
sioni were combined and a ground floor expanded to create this hotel,
which is good value; rooms and bathrooms are spacious and decorated
in Florentine style. Italian Antonio Lelli and his Canadian wife, Rose,
go out of their way to make you feel at home. ⊠ *Via Faenza 77, Santa
Maria Novella 50123* ☎ *055/284119* ⎙ *055/210101* ⊕ *www.
hotelportafaenza.it* ⇱ *25 rooms* ⚒ *In-room data ports, in-room safes,
cable TV, bar, baby-sitting, meeting room, parking (fee), some pets al-
lowed, no-smoking floor* ⊟ *AE, DC, MC, V.*

★ **$**   **Bellettini.** You're in good hands here at this small hotel on three
floors (the top floor has two nice rooms with a view). Sisters Marcia
and Gina Naldini, along with their husbands, run the place and create
a relaxed atmosphere. Attractive public rooms have a smattering of an-
tiques. The low rates include air-conditioning and an ample buffet
breakfast, including tasty homemade cakes. The good-size rooms have
Venetian or Tuscan provincial decor; bathrooms are bright and mod-
ern. ⊠ *Via dei Conti 7, Santa Maria Novella 50123* ☎ *055/213561*
⎙ *055/283551* ⊕ *www.firenze.net/hotelbellettini* ⇱ *28 rooms* ⚒ *In-
room safes, minibars, cable TV, bar, Internet, parking (fee), some pets
allowed* ⊟ *AE, DC, MC, V.*

Santa Croce

$$$–$$$$ **J&J.** On a quiet street within walking distance of the sights, this un-
usual hotel is a converted 16th-century monastery. Its large, suitelike
rooms are ideal for honeymooners, families, and small groups of friends.
Some rooms are on two levels, and all are imaginatively arranged around
a central courtyard. The smaller rooms are more intimate, some open-
ing onto a little shared courtyard. The gracious owners enjoy chatting
in the light and airy lounge; breakfast is served in a glassed-in Renais-
sance loggia or in the central courtyard. ⊠ *Via di Mezzo 20, Santa Croce,
50121* ☎ *055/26312* ⎙ *055/240282* ⊕ *www.jandjhotel.com* ⇱ *19
rooms, 7 suites* ⚒ *Cable TV, bar, dry cleaning, laundry service, Inter-
net, parking (fee)* ⊟ *AE, DC, MC, V.*

★ **$$$–$$$$**   **Monna Lisa.** Housed in a 15th-century palazzo, with parts of the build-
ing dating from the 13th century, this hotel retains some of its original
wood-coffered ceilings from the 1500s, as well as its original marble stair-
case. Though some rooms are small, they are tastefully decorated, each
with different floral wallpaper. The public rooms retain a 19th-century
aura, and the intimate bar, with its red velveteen wallpaper, is a good
place to unwind. ⊠ *Borgo Pinti 27, Santa Croce, 50121* ☎ *055/2479751*
⎙ *055/2479755* ⊕ *www.monnalisa.it* ⇱ *45 rooms* ⚒ *In-room safes,
minibars, cable TV, bar, baby-sitting, dry cleaning, laundry service, con-
cierge, parking (fee), some pets allowed, no-smoking rooms* ⊟ *AE,
DC, MC, V.*

¢   **Albergo Losanna.** Most major sights are within walking distance of this tiny pensione just within the Viale, the edge of the city center. Though dated, the property is impeccably clean and the rooms have high ceilings. Try to get a room facing away from the street; you won't have a view but you will get a quiet night's sleep. ⊠ *Via V. Alfieri 9, Santa Croce, 50121* 🕿 *055/245840* 📑 *8 rooms, 3 with bath* ⚒ *Parking (fee), some pets allowed; no a/c in some rooms, no room phones, no room TVs* ▭ *MC, V.*

Santa Maria Novella to the Arno

$$$$ **Excelsior.** Florentine hotels do not get much more exquisite or expensive than this, which explains why world leaders stay here when they are in Florence. Though they are decorated in Empire style, the rooms still feel up-to-date. High ceilings, dramatic views overlooking the Arno, patterned rugs, tasteful prints—all these provide the rooms with a sense of extravagant well-being. ⊠ *Piazza Ognissanti 3, Lungarno North, 50123* 🕿 *055/264201* 🖷 *055/210278* ⊕ *www.westin.com* 📑 *155 rooms, 16 suites* ⚒ *Restaurant, room service, in-room data ports, in-room safes, minibars, cable TV with movies, bar, baby-sitting, dry cleaning, laundry service, concierge, Internet, business services, meeting rooms, parking (fee), some pets allowed, no-smoking rooms* ▭ *AE, DC, MC, V.*

$$$$ **Grand.** Across the piazza from the Excelsior, this Florentine classic provides all the luxurious amenities of its slightly larger sister. Rooms are decorated in either Renaissance or Empire style; the former have deep, richly hued damask brocades and canopy beds, and the latter a lovely profusion of crisp prints and patterned fabric offsetting white walls. The overall effect is sumptuous, as is the view either of the Arno or overlooking a small rectangular courtyard lined with potted orange trees. The sleek restaurant, with a cutting-edge menu, is a winner. ⊠ *Piazza Ognissanti 1, Lungarno North, 50123* 🕿 *055/288781* 🖷 *055/217400* ⊕ *www.grandhotelflorence.com* 📑 *107 rooms* ⚒ *Restaurant, room service, in-room data ports, in-room safes, minibars, piano bar, baby-sitting, dry cleaning, laundry service, concierge, Internet, business services, meeting rooms, parking (fee), some pets allowed, no-smoking rooms* ▭ *AE, DC, MC, V.*

$$–$$$ **Beacci Tornabuoni.** Florentine pensioni do not come any more classic

FodorsChoice   than this. In a 14th-century palazzo, it has old-fashioned style and just
★   enough modern comfort to keep you happy. The sitting room has a large fireplace, the terrace has a tremendous view of some major Florentine monuments, and the wallpapered rooms are inviting. On Monday, Wednesday, and Friday nights from May through October, the dining room opens, serving Tuscan specialties. ⊠ *Via Tornabuoni 3, Santa Maria Novella 50123* 🕿 *055/212645* 🖷 *055/283594* ⊕ *www.bthotel.it* 📑 *28 rooms* ⚒ *Restaurant, minibars, cable TV, bar, baby-sitting, dry cleaning, laundry service, Internet, parking (fee), some pets allowed* ▭ *AE, DC, MC, V* ⦿ *CP, MAP.*

$$ **Villa Azalee.** Five minutes on foot from the train station and steps from the Fortezza da Basso (site of the Pitti fashion shows), this 19th-century villa deftly recalls its previous incarnation as a private residence. Furniture has quilted, floral-print slipcovers, and the floors are scattered with throw rugs. Many of the rooms have views of the hotel's garden, and some have private terraces. ⊠ *Viale Fratelli Rosselli 44, Santa Maria Novella 50123* 🕿 *055/214242* 🖷 *055/268264* ⊕ *www.villa-azalee.it* 📑 *25 rooms* ⚒ *Minibars, cable TV, bicycles, bar, dry cleaning, laundry service, parking (fee), some pets allowed* ▭ *AE, DC, MC, V.*

$ **Nuova Italia.** Near the train station and within walking distance of the sights, this hotel is run by a genial English-speaking family. Its homey rooms are clean and simply furnished. Air-conditioning and triple-glazed windows ensure restful nights. Some rooms can accommodate extra beds. The low bargain rates include breakfast. ⊠ *Via Faenza 26, Santa Maria Novella, 50123* ☎ *055/268430* ⌨ *055/210941* ⇨ *20 rooms* ⌂ *Cable TV, parking (fee), some pets allowed* ⊟ *AE, MC, V.*

$ ▦ **Pensione Ferretti.** Minutes away from the Piazza Santa Maria Novella, this pensione has views onto a tiny piazza containing the Croce al Trebbio, as well as easy access to the historic center. English-speaking owner Luciano Michel and his South African–born wife, Sue, do just about anything to make you feel at home (including providing 24-hour free Internet access). Ceiling fans make warmer months more bearable. Though it's housed in a 16th-century palazzo, accommodations are simple and no-frills. ⊠ *Via delle Belle Donne 17, Santa Maria Novella, 50123* ☎ *055/2381328* ⌨ *055/219288* ⊕ *www.ferretti.hotelfirenze.it* ⇨ *16 rooms, 6 with bath* ⌂ *Fans, Internet, parking (fee), some pets allowed; no a/c, no room TVs* ⊟ *AE, DC, MC, V.*

NIGHTLIFE & THE ARTS

The Arts

Florence is justifiably famous for its musical offerings, as its annual Maggio Musicale attracts the best international talent; theaters also host visiting American rock stars and cabaret perfomers. Major traveling art exhibitions are mounted at Palazzo Strozzi and Forte Belvedere throughout the year.

Film

You can find movie listings in *La Nazione,* the daily Florentine newspaper. Note that most American films are dubbed into Italian rather than subtitled. The **Odeon** (⊠ Piazza Strozzi, Piazza della Repubblica ☎ 055/214068) shows first-run English-language films on Monday and Tuesday at its magnificent art deco theater. **Festival dei Popoli** (⊠ Borgo Pinti 82/r, Santa Croce ☎ 055/244778) is a weeklong documentary and feature film festival that happens in November or December with screenings at various venues around town.

Music

The **Maggio Musicale Fiorentina,** a series of internationally acclaimed concerts and recitals, is held in the **Teatro Comunale** (⊠ Corso Italia 16, Lungarno North ☎ 055/211158 ⊕ www.maggiofiorentina.com). Tickets can be obtained directly at the **box office:** (⊠ Via Alamanni 39 ☎ 055/210 804) or by dialing (☎ 800 112 211) within Italy from late April through June. Other events—opera, ballet, and additional concerts—occur regularly throughout the year at different venues in town. November to June is the concert season of the **Orchestra della Toscana** (⊠ Via Ghibellina 101, Santa Croce ☎ 055/210804). **Amici della Musica** organizes concerts at the **Teatro della Pergola** (Box office ⊠ Via Alamanni 39, Santissima Annunziata ☎ 055/210804 ⊕ www.pergola.firenze.it).

Opera

Operas are performed in the **Teatro Comunale** (⊠ Corso Italia 12, Lungarno North ☎ 055/211158) from September through December.

Nightlife

Florentines are rather proud of their nightlife options. Most bars have some sort of happy hour, which usually lasts for many hours, often accompanied by substantial snacks. Dance clubs typically don't open until very late in the evening and don't get crowded until 1 or 2 in the morning. Cover charges are steep, but it's fairly easy to find free passes around town.

Bars

For a swanky experience, lubricated with trademark Bellinis and fine martinis, head to **Harry's Bar** (✉ Lungarno Vespucci 22/r, Lungarno North ☎ 055/2396700). **Rex** (✉ Via Fiesolana 23–25/r, Santa Croce ☎ 055/2480331) attracts a trendy, artsy clientele. From June to September, **Via di Fuga** (✉ Via Ghibellina, Santa Croce ☎ No phone) is one of the coolest spots to be; once the courtyard of Le Murate, a former Renaissance convent and 19th-century prison, it hosts big bands, performance art, movies, and more. **Zoe** (✉ Via dei Renai 13/r, San Niccolò ☎ 055/243111) calls itself a "caffetteria" and, although coffee may indeed be served, twentysomething Florentines flock here for the fine (and expensive) cocktails. **Negroni** (✉ Via dei Renai 17/r San Niccolò ☎ 055/243647) teems with well-dressed young Florentines at happy hour. **Capocaccia** (✉ Lungarno Corsini 12-14/r, Lungarno North ☎ 055/210751) is relatively calm at lunch and apertivo time, but at night the crowds flow out of the bar and onto the street **Daria** (✉ Borgo Albizzi 36/r Santa Croce ☎ 055/234 0979) serves hearty panini in the morning, cocktails in the afternoon, and sushi from lunchtime on. **Sant'Ambrogio Caffè** (✉ Piazza Sant'Ambrogio 7–8/r, Santa Croce ☎ 055/241035) has outdoor summer seating with a view of an 11th-century church (Sant'Ambrogio) directly across the street.

Zona 15 (✉ Via del Castellaccia 53-55/r Duomo ☎ 055/211 678) is coolly chic with its pale interior, blond woodwork, and metallic surfaces. Lunch, dinner, cocktails, and live music are on offer for Florentine cognoscenti and others. The oh-so-cool—bordering on pretentious—vibe at **La Dolce Vita** (✉ Piazza del Carmine 6/r, Santo Spirito/San Frediano ☎ 055/284595) attracts Florentines and the occasional visiting American movie star. If you want to have a light lunch, a sparkling aperitivo, or simply check your e-mail, stop in at the **Astor** (✉ Piazza del Duomo 20/r, Duomo ☎ 055/2399000). It's open from early in the morning until late at night.

Nightclubs

Most clubs are closed either Sunday or Monday. **Yab** (✉ Via Sassetti 5/r, Piazza della Repubblica ☎ 055/215160) is one of the largest clubs, with a young clientele. **Space Electronic** (✉ Via Palazzuolo 37, Santa Maria Novella ☎ 055/293082) has two floors, with karaoke downstairs and an enormous disco upstairs. It's full of Italian military types prowling for young foreign women.

Meccanò (✉ Viale degli Olmi 1, in Le Cascine park ☎ 055/331371) provides a multimedia experience with its high-tech club and late-night restaurant. Young, up-to-the-minute Florentines drink and dance 'til the wee hours at **Maramao** (✉ Via dei Macci 79/r, Santa Croce ☎ 055/244341); it opens at 11 PM doesn't really get going until around 2 AM. **Maracaná** (✉ Via Faenza, 4, Santa Maria Novella ☎ 055/210298) is as a restaurant and pizzeria featuring Brazilian specialties; at 11 PM it transforms itself into a cabaret floor show and then opens the floor to dancing. Book a table if you want to eat. If you had a transvestite grandmother, her home would look like **Montecarla** (✉ Via de' Bardi 2, San Niccolò ☎ 055/2340259). On its two crowded floors people sip cocktails against a backdrop of exotic flowers, leopard-print chairs and chintz, and red walls and floors. **BeBop** (✉ Via dei Servi 76/r, Santissima Annunziata) has loud, live music and Beatles nights. **Jazz Club** (✉ Via Nuova de' Caccini 3, corner of Borgo Pinti, Santa Croce ☎ 055/2479700) puts on live music in a smoky basement. The hottest jazz club **Omi Club** (✉ Via Tevere 100 ☎ No phone) is southwest of town. Italy-based jazz artists perform amidst massive photographs of (mostly American) late jazz greats.

When just about everything else has closed, go where the bartenders unwind after their shift: **Loch Ness** (✉ Via de' Benci 19/r, Santa Croce). You can have that last nightcap until 5 AM.

SPORTS

Health Clubs

Palestra Ricciardi (✉ Borgo Pinti 75, Santa Croce ☎ 055/2478444 or 055/2478462), daily €10.40 or weekly €33, has stretching, aerobics, step aerobics, and bodybuilding classes; it also has free weights, stationary bikes, treadmills, and rowing machines.

Running

Don't even think of running on the narrow city streets as tour buses and triple-parked Alfa Romeos leave precious little space for pedestrians. Instead, head for **Le Cascine,** the park along the Arno at the western end of the city. You can run to Le Cascine along the Lungarno (stay on the sidewalk), or take Bus 17 from the Duomo. A cinder track lies on the hillside below **Piazzale Michelangelo,** across the Arno from the city center. A scenic, but not serene, run can be had along the Lungarno, those streets that frame both sides of the Arno.

Soccer

Italians are passionate about *calcio* (soccer), and the Florentines are no exception; indeed, *tifosi* (fans) of Florentia team are fervent supporters. The team plays its home matches at the **Stadio Comunale** (Municipal Stadium ✉ Top of Viale Manfredo Fanti, northeast of the center) in Campo di Marte, usually on Sunday from late August to May. Tickets are sold at the ticket booth **Chiosco degli Sportivi** (✉ Via Anselmi, southwest side of Piazza della Repubblica ☎ 055/292363). A medieval version of soccer, **Calcio Storico** is played around the Festa di San Giovanni on June 24 each year by teams dressed in costumes representing the six Florence neighborhoods. Games take place in Piazza Santa Croce, where they have allegedly been played since the middle of the 16th century.

SHOPPING

Window-shopping in Florence is like visiting an enormous contemporary art gallery, for many of today's greatest Italian artists are fashion designers, and most keep shops in Florence. Shops are generally open 9–1 and 3:30–7:30 and are closed Sunday and Monday morning most of the year. Summer (June–September) hours are usually 9–1 and 4–8, and some shops close Saturday afternoon instead of Monday morning. When looking for addresses of shops, you will see two color-coded numbering systems on each street. The red numbers are commercial addresses and are indicated, for example, as 31/r. The blue or black numbers are residential addresses. Most shops take major credit cards and will ship purchases, but because of possible delays it's wise to take your purchases with you.

Markets

Roam through the stalls under the loggia of the **Mercato Nuovo** (✉ Corner of Via Por Santa Maria and Via Porta Rossa, Piazza della Repubblica) for cheery, inexpensive trinkets. In the streets next to the church of San Lorenzo, the clothing and leather-goods stalls of the **Mercato di San Lorenzo** offer bargains. It's also a great place to take children who

324 < **Florence**

are weary of looking at Renaissance monuments. The **Mercato Centrale**
(⊠ Piazza del Mercato Centrale, San Lorenzo) is a huge indoor food
market that has a staggering selection of things edible. The flea market
on **Piazza dei Ciompi** (⊠ Sant'Ambrogio, Santa Croce) takes place on
the last Sunday of the month. An open-air market is held in **Le Cascine
park** every Tuesday morning.

Shopping Districts

Florence's most fashionable shops are concentrated in the center of
town. The fanciest designer shops are mainly on **Via Tornabuoni** and **Via
della Vigna Nuova**. The city's largest concentrations of antiques shops
are on **Borgo Ognissanti** and the Oltrarno's **Via Maggio**. The **Ponte Vecchio** houses reputable but very expensive jewelry shops, as it has since
the 16th century. The area around **Santa Croce** is the heart of the leather
merchants' district.

Specialty Stores

Antiques

Galleria Luigi Bellini (⊠ Lungarno Soderini 5, Lungarno South ☎ 055/
214031) claims to be Italy's oldest antiques dealer, which may be true,
since father Mario Bellini was responsible for instituting Florence's international antiques biennial. **Giovanni Pratesi** (⊠ Via Maggio 13, Santo
Spirito/San Frediano ☎ 055/2396568) specializes in Italian antiques, in
this case furniture, with some fine paintings, sculpture, and decorative
objects turning up from time to time. Vying with Luigi Bellini as one of
Florence's oldest antiques dealers, **Guido Bartolozzi** (⊠ Via Maggio 18/
r, Santo Spirito/San Frediano ☎ 055/215602) sells predominately period Florentine pieces. **Roberto Innocenti e C. S.N.C.** (⊠ Borgo Pinti
11–13/r and via Matteo Palmieri 29/r, Santa Croce ☎ 055/2478668)
specializes in things more recently antique such as art nouveau and art
deco.

Books & Paper

Pineider (⊠ Piazza della Signoria 13/r and Via Tornabuoni 76/r ☎ 055/
284655 or 055/211605) has shops throughout the world, but the business began in Florence and still does all its printing here. Personalized
stationery and business cards are the mainstay, but the stores also sell
fine leather desk accessories. Since 2002 the store has offered a less stuffy,
more lighthearted line of products. **Centro Di** (⊠ Via dei Renai 20/r, San
Niccolò ☎ 055/2342666) publishes art books and exhibition catalogs
for some of the most important organizations in Europe. One of Florence's oldest paper-goods stores, **Giulio Giannini e Figlio** (⊠ Piazza Pitti
37/r ☎ 055/212621) is *the* place to buy the marbleized stock, which
comes in many shapes and sizes, from flat sheets to boxes and even pencils. Long one of Florence's best art-book shops, **Libreria Salimbeni**
(⊠ Via Matteo Palmieri 14–16/r, Santa Croce ☎ 055/2340905) has an
outstanding selection. **FMR** (⊠ Via delle Belle Donne 41/r, Santa Maria
Novella ☎ 055/283312), the shop of the world-famous art-book editor and tastemaker Franco Maria Ricci, has exquisite art books, handmade papers, and small works on paper. **Alberto Cozzi** (⊠ Via del Parione
35/r, Santa Maria Novella ☎ 055/294968) keeps an extensive line of
Florentine papers and paper products, and the artisans in the shop re-
bind and restore books and works on paper.

Clothing

The usual fashion gurus—such as Prada and Armani—all have shops
in Florence, and nearly all of them populate via Tornabuoni, which more
and more resembles a giant *passarella* (cat walk). If you want to buy

Florentine haute fashion while in Florence, stick to Pucci, Gucci, Ferragamo, and Roberto Cavalli, all of which call Florence home.

Prada (⊠ Via Tornabuoni 67/r, Santa Maria Novella ☎ 055/283439 ⊠ Outlet ⊠ Levanella Spacceo, Estrada Statale 69, Montevarchi ☎ 055/91911), known to mix schoolmarmish sensibility with sexy cuts and funky fabrics, appeals to an exclusive clientele. Cognoscenti will drive or taxi about 45 minutes out of town to the Prada Outlet.

The sleek, classic **Giorgio Armani boutique** (⊠ Via Tornabuoni 48/r, Santa Maria Novella ☎ 055/219041) is a centerpiece of the dazzling high-end shops clustered in this part of town. **Emporio Armani** (⊠ Piazza Strozzi 16/r, Santa Maria Novella ☎ 055/284315) has slightly more affordable, funky, nightclub and office-friendly garb.

The aristocratic Marchese di Barsento, **Emilio Pucci** (⊠ Via Tornabuoni 20-22/r, Santa Maria Novella ☎ 055/2658082), became an international name in the late 1950s when the stretch ski clothes he designed for himself caught on with the dolce vita crowd—his pseudopsychedelic prints and "palazzo pajamas" became all the rage.

Native son **Roberto Cavalli** (⊠ Via Tornabuoni 83/r, Santa Maria Novella ☎ 055/2396226) finally has a place to call his own. His outlandish designs appeal to Hollywood celebrities and those who want to look like a more expensive version of Britney Spears.

Basic (⊠ Via Porta Rossa 109–115/r, Santa Maria Novella ☎ 055/212995) carries a full line of Alberta Ferretti creations, as well as lesser-known Italian and English designers.

Some Florentine boutiques require some straying off the Beaten Fashion Path. **Paola Pardini** (⊠ Borgo Albizzi 70/r ☎ 055/200 1340) has a fine line of body-clinging knitwear in cashmere and other fine wool for women that are decidedly beyond the twentysomething range.

Florentine **Patrizia Pepe** (⊠ Piazza del Duomo ☎ 055/) has body-conscious clothes perfect for all ages, especially for women with a tiny streak of rebelliousness. **L'essentiel** (⊠ Via del Corso 10/r ☎ 055/294 713) has been around since 1990; Michael Calà and Lara Caldieron have spun their club-going years into fashion that works well on the street as well as in the office.

You can take home a custom-made suit or dress from **Giorgio Vannini** (⊠ Via Borgo Santi Apostoli 43/r, Santa Maria Novella ☎ 055/293037), who has a showroom for his pret-a-porter designs. **Bernardo** (⊠ Via Porta Rossa 87/r, Piazza della Repubblica ☎ 055/283333) specializes in men's trousers, cashmere sweaters, and shirts with details like mother-of-pearl buttons. **Gianfranco Ferré** (⊠ Via Tosinghi 52/r, Duomo ☎ 055/292003) captures beauty and luxury in various constructions and fabrics in his couture lines; he has also created a line of sleek jeans.

Embroidery & Linens

Loretta Caponi (⊠ Piazza Antinori 4/r, Santa Maria Novella ☎ 055/213668) is synonymous with Florentine embroidery, and her luxury lace, linens, and lingerie have earned her worldwide renown. **Valmar** (⊠ Via Porta Rossa 53/r, Piazza della Repubblica ☎ 055/284493) is filled with tangled spools of cords, ribbons, and fringes, plus buttons, tassels, sachets, and hand-embroidered cushions. You can also bring in your own fabric, choose the adornments, and they will custom-make your cushion or table runner.

Sant'Jacopo Show (⊠ Borgo Sant'Jacopo 66/r, Santo Spirito/San Frediano ☎ 055/2396912) is an offbeat shop specializing in mannequins, decorations, and shop fittings. Sumptuous silks, beaded fabrics, lace, wool, and tweeds can be purchased at **Valli** (✉ Via Strozzi 4/r, Piazza della Repubblica ☎ 055/282485). It carries fabrics created by Armani, Valentino, and other high-end designers.

Gifts & Housewares

The essence of a Florentine holiday is captured in the sachets of the **Officina Profumo Farmaceutica di Santa Maria Novella** (✉ Via della Scala 16/r, Santa Maria Novella ☎ 055/216276), a turn-of-the-19th century emporium of herbal cosmetics and soaps that are made following centuries-old recipes created by friars. For housewares, nothing beats **Bartolini** (✉ Via dei Servi 30/r, Santissima Annunziata ☎ 055/211895) for well-designed practical items. **Sbigoli Terrecotte** (✉ Via Sant'Egidio 4/r, Santa Croce ☎ 055/2479713) carries traditional Tuscan terra-cotta and ceramic vases, pots, and cups and saucers, made by the mother-daughter team of Antonella Chini and Lorenza Adami, who turn out Florentine-inspired designs based on Antonella's extensive ceramics training in Faenza. **Rampini Ceramiche** (✉ Borgo Ognissanti 32/34, Lungarno North ☎ 055/219720) sells exquisitely crafted ceramics in various patterns, shapes, and sizes.

What to get the person who has everything? Drop into the **Shabby Shop** (✉ Via del Parione 12/r, Santa Maria Novella ☎ 055/294826), which specializes in antique silver—mostly English, dating from George I to George III (1698–1811)—and more recent jewelry from the 1950s. For the record: there's absolutely nothing shabby about this shop.

Jewelry

Cassetti (✉ Ponte Vecchio 54/r, ☎ 055/2396028) combines precious and semiprecious stones and metals in contemporary settings. **Gherardi** (✉ Ponte Vecchio 5/r ☎ 055/211809), Florence's king of coral, has the city's largest selection of finely crafted pieces, as well as cultured pearls, jade, and turquoise. **Carlo Piccini** (✉ Ponte Vecchio 31/r ☎ 055/292030) has sold antique jewelry as well as made pieces to order for several generations; you can also get old jewelry reset. One of Florence's oldest jewelers, **Tiffany** (✉ Via Tornabuoni 25/r, Santa Maria Novella ☎ 055/215506), has supplied Italian (and other) royalty with finely crafted gems for centuries. Its selection of antique-looking classics has been updated with a choice of contemporary silver.

Gatto Bianco (✉ Borgo Santi Apostoli 12/r, Santa Maria Novella ☎ 055/282989) has breathtakingly beautiful jewelry worked in semiprecious and precious stones; the feel is completely contemporary. Affordable necklaces and rings, mostly in silver, can be found at **La Gazza Ladra** (✉ Piazza Salvemini 6, Santa Croce ☎ 055/2466008). **Oreria** (✉ Borgo Pinti, 87/a, Santa Croce ☎ 055/244708), run by two women who create divine designs using silver and semiprecious stones, is the place to direct someone to buy you something significant.

Shoes & Leather Accessories

At peak tourist times, status-conscious shoppers often stand in line outside **Gucci** (✉ Via Tornabuoni 73/r, Santa Maria Novella ☎ 055/264011), ready to buy anything with the famous designer's initials; American Tom Ford has infused freshness into its designs, which, not surprisingly, have a decidedly American flair. Beware, however, of shop assistants with severe attitude problems. Born near Naples, the late Salvatore **Ferragamo** (✉ Via Tornabuoni 2/r, Santa Maria Novella ☎ 055/292123) earned his fortune custom-making shoes for famous feet, especially Hollywood stars. The elegant store, in a 13th-century Renaissance palazzo, displays designer clothing and accessories, but elegant footwear still underlies the Ferragamo success. **Cellerini** (✉ Via del Sole 37/r, Santa Maria Novella ☎ 055/282533) is an institution in a city where it seems that just about everybody is wearing an expensive leather jacket.

For sheer creativity in both color and design, check out the shoes at **Sergio Rossi** (✉ Via Roma 15/r, Duomo ☎ 055/294873) and fantasize about having a life to go with them. **Pollini** (✉ Via Calimala 12/r, Piazza della Repubblica ☎ 055/214738) has beautifully crafted shoes and leather accessories for those willing to pay that little bit extra. **Romano** (✉ Via Speziali 10/r, Piazza della Repubblica ☎ 055/216535) has everything from the staid to the offbeat at very appealing prices. **Beltrami** (✉ Via della Vigna Nuova 70/r, Santa Maria Novella ☎ 055/287779) has long been synonymous with style; classic looks are beautifully updated.

Giotti (✉ Piazza Ognissanti 3–4/r, Lungarno North ☎ 055/294265) has a full line of leather goods and leather clothing. **Leather Guild** (✉ Piazza Santa Croce 20/r ☎ 055/241932) is one of many shops that produce inexpensive, antique-looking leather goods with mass appeal, but here you can see the craftspeople at work. **Il Bisonte** (✉ Via del Parione 31/r, off Via della Vigna Nuova, Santa Maria Novella ☎055/215722) is known for its natural-looking leather goods, all stamped with the store's bison symbol. The ultimate fine leathers are crafted into classic shapes at **Casadei** (✉ Via Tornabuoni 33/r, Santa Maria Novella ☎ 055/287240), winding up as women's shoes and bags. **Madova** (✉ Via Guicciardini 1/r, Palazzo Pitti ☎ 055/2396526) has a rainbow of high-quality leather gloves. **Furla** (✉ Via Calzaiuoli 47/r, Piazza della Repubblica ☎ 055/2382883) makes beautiful leather bags and wallets in up-to-the-minute designs. **Coccinelle** (✉ Via Por Santa Maria 49/r, Piazza della Signoria ☎ 055/2398782) sells leather accessories in bold colors and funky designs.

SIDE TRIPS FROM FLORENCE

FIESOLE & GRACIOUS GARDENS

Fiesole

A half-day excursion to Fiesole, in the hills 8 km (5 mi) above Florence, gives you a pleasant respite from museums and a wonderful view of the city. Fiesole began life as an ancient Etruscan and later Roman village that held some power until it succumbed to barbarian invasions. Eventually it gave up its independence in exchange for Florence's protection. The medieval cathedral, ancient Roman amphitheater, and lovely old villas behind garden walls are clustered on a series of hilltops. The trip from Florence by car or bus takes 20–30 minutes. Take Bus 7 from the Stazione Centrale di Santa Maria Novella, Piazza San Marco, or the Duomo. (You can also get on and off the bus at San Domenico.) There are several possible routes for the two-hour walk from central Florence to Fiesole. One route begins in residential Salviatino (Via Barbacane, near Piazza Edison, on the Bus 7 route), and after a short time, offers peeks over garden walls of beautiful villas, as well as a panorama of Florence in the valley. A walk around Fiesole can take a couple of hours, depending on how far you stroll from the main piazza.

The **Duomo** reveals a stark medieval interior. In the raised presbytery, the **Cappella Salutati** was frescoed by 15th-century artist Cosimo Rosselli, but it was his contemporary sculptor Mino da Fiesole (1430–84) who put the town on the artistic map. The Madonna on the altarpiece and the tomb of Bishop Salutati are fine examples of his work. ✉ *Piazza*

Mino da Fiesole ☎ *055/59400* ⊙ *Nov.–Mar., daily 7:30–noon and 2–5; Apr.–Oct., daily 7:30–noon and 3–6.*

Fiesole's beautifully preserved 2,000-seat **Anfiteatro Romano** (Roman Amphitheater) dates from the 1st century BC and is used for the summer concerts of the **Estate Fiesolana** (✉ Teatro Romano ☎ 055/597 8403), a festival of theater, music, dance, and film that also takes place in the churches of Fiesole. To the right of the amphitheater are the remains of the **Terme Romani** (Roman Baths), where you can see the gymnasium, hot and cold baths, and rectangular chamber where the water was heated. A beautifully designed **Museo Archeologico**, an intricate series of levels connected by elevators, is built amid the ruins and contains objects dating from as early as 2000 BC. The nearby **Museo Bandini** is a small collection with a lot of interesting paintings. It's filled with the private collection of Canon Angelo Maria Bandini (1726–1803); he fancied 13th- to 15th-century Florentine paintings, terra-cotta pieces, and wood sculpture, which he later bequeathed to the Diocese of Fiesole. ✉ *Via San Francesco 3* ☎ *055/59477* ≝ *€6, includes access to the archaeological park and museums* ⊙ *Apr.–Sept., daily 9–7; Oct.–Mar., Wed.–Mon. 9–4:30.*

The hilltop church of **San Francesco** has a good view of Florence and the plain below from its terrace and benches. Halfway up the hill, you'll see sloping steps to the right; they lead to a lovely wooded **park** with trails that loop out and back to the church.

If you really want to stretch your legs, walk 4 km (2½ mi) back toward Florence center along Via Vecchia Fiesolana, a narrow lane in use since Etruscan times, to the church of **San Domenico.** Sheltered in the church is the *Madonna and Child with Saints* by Fra Angelico, who was a Dominican friar here. ✉ *Piazza San Domenico, off Via Giuseppe Mantellini* ☎ *055/59230* ⊙ *Daily 8–noon.*

It's only a five-minute walk northwest from the church of San Domenico to the **Badia Fiesolana,** which was the original cathedral of Fiesole. Parts of it date to the 11th century, but it was substantially enlarged after 1456. ✉ *Via della Badia dei Roccettini* ☎ *055/59155* ⊙ *Weekdays 9–6, Sat. 9:30–12:30.*

Where to Stay & Eat

$-$$$$ ✕ **I' Polpa.** A short distance up the street from Fiesole's main square, this family-owned and -run restaurant has great food and friendly service. Though it's laid out in two oddly shaped rooms, one of which has no windows, the creamy yellow walls and matching table linens impart a sunny feeling. Walls are lined with photos of famous visitors, including Luciano Pavarotti and Sting. The *coniglio in porchetta* (boned rabbit, stuffed and rolled with sausage) is alone worth the trip—has rabbit ever tasted this moist? ✉ *Piazza Mino da Fiesole 21/22* ☎ *055/59485* ⊟ *AE, DC, MC, V* ⊙ *Closed Wed. and Aug.*

$$$$ ▥ **Villa San Michele.** The cypress-lined driveway provides an elegant preamble to this incredibly gorgeous (and incredibly expensive) hotel nestled in the hills of Fiesole. The 16th-century building was originally a Franciscan convent designed by Santi di Tito. Not a single false note is struck in the reception area (formerly the chapel), the dining rooms (a covered cloister and former refectory), or the tasteful antiques and art that decorate the rooms. The open-air loggia, where lunch and dinner are served, provides one of the most stunning views of Florence—a good thing, too, as the food is overpriced and bland. ✉ *Via Doccia 4, 50014* ☎ *055/59451* 🖷 *055/5678250* 🛏 *41 rooms* ⌂ *Restaurant, room service, in-room data ports, in-room safes, in-room VCRs, minibars, cable*

*TV with movies, pool, gym, piano bar, dry cleaning, laundry service,
concierge, Internet, baby-sitting, free parking, some pets allowed, no-
smoking rooms ☰ AE, DC, MC, V ☺ Closed Dec.–Easter.*

¢–$ ▦ **Fattoria di Maiano.** In the foothills between Florence and Fiesole,
these lovely apartments sleep from 4 to 11 people and are rented by the
week. You'll have wood floors, simple and sturdy furniture, and very
modern kitchens. Most apartments have splendid views onto olive tree
groves (olive oil is produced by the Fattoria owners). Here you'll have
all the pleasures of the country, with one significant city (Florence) just
5 km (3 mi) away. ⊠ *Via Benedetto da Maiano 11, 50016* ☎ *055/599600*
🖷 *055/599640* ⊕ *www.fattoriadimaiano.com* ⇗ *8 apartments* ⚲ *Kitch-
nettes, some pets allowed; no a/c in some rooms* ☰ *DC, MC, V.*

Gracious Gardens around Florence

Like any well-heeled Florentine, you too can get away from Florence's
hustle and bustle by heading for the hills. Take a break from city sightseeing to enjoy the gardens and villas set like jewels in the hills around
the city. Villa di Castello and Villa La Petraia, both just northwest of
the center of town in Castello, can be explored in one trip. The Italian
garden at Villa Gamberaia is a quick 8-km (5-mi) jaunt east of the center near Settignano. Plan for a full-day excursion, picnic lunch included,
if visiting all three. Spring and summer are the ideal time to visit, when
flowers are in glorious bloom. For a prime taste of Medici living, venture farther afield to the family's Villa Medicea in Poggio a Caiano, just
south of Prato.

Villa di Castello

A fortified residence in the Middle Ages, Villa di Castello was rebuilt
by the Medici in the 15th century. The Accademia della Crusca, the 400-
year-old institution that is the official arbiter of the Italian language, now
occupies the palace, which is not open to the public. The gardens are
the main attraction. From the villa entrance, walk uphill through the
19th-century park set above part of the formal garden. You'll reach the
terrace, which affords a good view of the geometric layout of the Italian garden below; stairs on either side descend to the parterre.

Though the original garden design has been altered somewhat over the
centuries, the allegorical theme of animals devised by Tribolo in 1537
to the delight of the Medici is still evident. The artificial cave, Grotta
degli Animali (Animal Grotto), displays an imaginative menagerie of
sculpted animals by Giambologna and his assistants. An Ammannati sculpture, a figure of an old man representing *Gennaio* (January), is at the
center of a pond on the terrace overlooking the garden. Two bronze sculptures by Ammannati, centerpieces of fountains studding the Italian garden, can now be seen indoors in Villa La Petraia. Allow about 45
minutes to visit the garden; you can easily visit Villa La Petraia from
here, making for a four-hour trip in total.

To get to Villa di Castello by car, head northwest from Florence on Via
Reginaldo Giuliani (also known as Via Sestese) to Castello, about 6 km
(4 mi) northwest of the city center in the direction of Sesto Fiorentino;
follow signs to Villa di Castello. Or take Bus 28 from the city center
and tell the driver you want to get off at Villa di Castello; from the stop,
walk north about ½ km (¼ mi) up the tree-lined allée from the main
road. ⊠ *Via di Castello 47, Castello* ☎ *055/454791* 🖾 *€2.05, includes entrance to Villa La Petraia* ☺ *Garden Nov.–Feb., daily 8:15–4:30,
Mar.–Oct., daily 9–7. Closed 2nd and 3rd Mon. of month* ☞ *Palace
closed to public.*

Villa La Petraia

The splendidly planted gardens of Villa La Petraia sit high above the Arno plain with a sweeping view of Florence. The villa was built around a medieval tower and reconstructed after it was purchased by the Medici sometime after 1530. Virtually the only trace of the Medici having lived here is the 17th-century courtyard frescoes depicting glorious episodes from the clan's history. In the 1800s the villa served as a hunting lodge of King Vittorio Emanuele II (1820–78), who kept his mistress here while Florence was the temporary capital of the newly united country of Italy.

An Italian-speaking guide will take you through the 19th-century–style salons. The garden—also altered in the 1800s—and the vast park behind the palace suggest a splendid contrast between formal and natural landscapes. Allow 60 to 90 minutes to explore the park and gardens, plus 30 minutes for the guided tour of the villa interior. This property is best visited after the Villa di Castello.

To reach Villa La Petraia by car, travel as though you're going to Villa di Castello (head northwest from Florence on Via Reginaldo Giuliani), but take the right off Via Reginaldo Giuliani, following the sign for Villa La Petraia. You can walk from Villa di Castello to Villa La Petraia in about 15 minutes; turn left beyond the gate of Villa di Castello and continue straight along Via di Castello and the imposing Villa Corsini; take Via della Petraia uphill to the entrance. ⊠ *Via della Petraia 40, Località Castello* ☎ *055/451208* ☞ *€2.05, includes entrance to Villa di Castello* ☉ *Oct.–Mar., garden daily 8:15–4:30, villa tours daily at 9:15, 10, 10:45, 11:30, 12:10, 1:30, 2:20, 3, and 3:40; Apr, May, and Sept., garden daily 9–5, villa tours daily at 9:15, 10, 10:45, 11:30, 12:10, 1:30, 2:20, 3, 3:40, and 4:45; June–Aug., garden daily 9–7, villa tours daily at 9:15, 10, 10:45, 11:30, 12:10, 1:30, 2:20, 3, 3:40, 4:45, 5:35, and 6:35* ☉ *Closed 2nd and 3rd Mon. of month.*

Villa Gamberaia

Villa Gamberaia, near the village of Settignano on the eastern outskirts of Florence, was the rather modest 15th-century country home of Matteo di Domenico Gamberelli, the father of noted Renaissance sculptors Bernardo, Antonio, and Matteo Rossellino. In the early 1600s the villa passed into the hands of the wealthy Capponi family. They spared no expense in rebuilding it and, more importantly, creating its garden, one of the finest near Florence. Studded with statues and fountains, the garden suffered damage during World War II but has been restored according to the original 17th-century design. This excursion takes about 1½ hours, allowing 45 minutes to visit the garden.

To get here by car, go to Piazza Beccaria and turn onto via Gioberti. This eventually becomes Via Aretina; follow the sign to the turnoff to the north to Villa Gamberaia, about 8 km (5 mi) from the center. To arrive by bus, take Bus 10 to Settignano. From Settignano's main Piazza Tommaseo, walk east on Via di San Romano; the second lane on the right is Via del Rossellino, which leads southeast to the entrance of Villa Gamberaia. The walk from the piazza takes about 10 minutes. ⊠ *Via del Rossellino 72, near Settignano* ☎ *055/697205* ☞ *€8* ☉ *Garden Mon.–Sat. 8–6, Sun. 8–noon* ☞ *Parts of villa open by appointment.*

FLORENCE A TO Z

To research prices, get advice from other travelers, and book travel arrangements, visit www.fodors.com.

AIRPORTS & TRANSFERS

Florence's Aeroporto A. Vespucci, called Peretola, receives flights from Milan, Rome, London, and Paris. To get into Florence by car, take the autostrada A11. Tickets for the local bus service into Florence are sold at the airport's second-floor bar. Take Bus 62, which goes directly to the train station at Santa Maria Novella; the airport's bus shelter is beyond the parking lot.

Pisa's Aeroporto Galileo Galilei is the closest landing point with significant international service the SS67 leads directly to Florence. For flight information, call the airport or Florence Air Terminal (an office at Santa Maria Novella, Florence's main train station). A train service connects Pisa's airport station with Santa Maria Novella, roughly a one-hour trip. Trains start running about 7 AM from the airport, 6 AM from Florence, and continue service every hour until about 11:30 PM from the airport, 8 PM from Florence. You can check in for departing flights at the Florence Air Terminal, which is just around the corner from train tracks 1 and 2.

🚩 Airport Information **Aeroporto Galileo Galilei** ✉ 12 km [7 mi] south of Pisa and 80 km [50 mi] west of Florence ☎ 050/500707 ⊕ www.pisa-airport.com. **Florence Air Terminal** ✉ Stazione Centrale di Santa Maria Novella ☎ 055/216073. **Peretola** ✉ 10 km [6 mi] northwest of Florence ☎ 055/373498 ⊕ www.safnet.it.

BIKE & MOPED TRAVEL

Brave souls (cycling in Florence is difficult, at best) may rent bicycles at easy-to-spot locations at Fortezza da Basso, the Stazione Centrale di Santa Maria Novella, and Piazza Pitti. Otherwise try Alinari. You'll be up against dodging hordes of tourists and those pesky *motorini* (mopeds). The Cascine, a former Medici hunting ground turned into a large public park with paved pathways, admits no cars. The historic center can be circumnavigated via bike paths lining the Viali, a road that runs along the center's circumference. If you want to go native and rent a noisy Vespa (Italian for "wasp") or other make of motorcycle or *motorino* (moped), you may do so at Maxirent. Massimo also rents mopeds. However unfashionable, helmets must be rented at either place, and by law are mandatory, much to the chagrin of many Italians.

🚩 Rentals **Alinari** ✉ Via Guelfa 85/r, San Marco ☎ 055/280500. **Massimo** ✉ Via Cairoli 8 ☎ 055/573689. **Maxirent** ✉ Borgo Ognissanti 155/r, Santa Maria Novella ☎ 055/265420.

BUS TRAVEL TO & FROM FLORENCE

Long-distance buses provide inexpensive if somewhat claustrophobic service between Florence and other cities in Italy and Europe.

🚩 Bus Information **Lazzi Eurolines** ✉ Via Mercadante 2, Santa Maria Novella ☎ 055/363041 ⊕ www.lazzi.it. **SITA** ✉ Via Santa Caterina da Siena 17/r, Santa Maria Novella ☎ 055/214721 ⊕ www.sita-on-line.it.

BUS TRAVEL WITHIN FLORENCE

Maps and timetables are available for a small fee at the ATAF (Trasporti Area Fiorentina) booth, or for free at visitor information offices. Tickets must be bought in advance at tobacco stores, newsstands, from automatic ticket machines near main stops, or at ATAF booths. The ticket must be canceled in the small validation machine immediately upon boarding. Small electric buses make the rounds of the centro storico and provide an easy alternative to footing it around town. Use the same ticket as for the regular bus.

FARES & SCHEDULES Two types of tickets are available, both valid for one or more rides on all lines. One costs €1 and is valid for one hour from the time it is first canceled. A multiple ticket—four tickets, each valid for 60 minutes—costs €3.87. A 24-hour tourist ticket costs €3.10. Monthly passes are also available.

🛈 Bus Information **ATAF** ✉ Next to train station; Piazza del Duomo 57/r, Santa Maria Novella ☎ 800/019794 toll free.

CAR RENTAL

🛈 Local Agencies **Avis** ✉ Via Borgo Ognissanti, 128/r, Santa Maria Novella ☎ 055/2398826. **Hertz Italiana** ✉ Via Finiguerra 33/r, Santa Maria Novella ☎ 055/317543. **Maggiore-Budget Autonoleggio** ✉ Via Termine 1, Santa Maria Novella ☎ 055/311256.

CAR TRAVEL

Florence is connected to the north and south of Italy by the Autostrada del Sole (A1). It takes about one hour of driving on scenic roads to get to Bologna (although heavy truck traffic over the Apennines often makes for slower going), about 3 hours to Rome, and 3 to 3½ hours to Milan. The Tyrrhenian Coast is an hour west on A11. In the city, abandon all hope of using a car, since most of the downtown area is accessible only to locals with properly marked vehicles. For assistance or information, call the ACI (Automobile Club Firenze).

🛈 **ACI** ☎ 055/2486246.

EMBASSIES & CONSULATES

🛈 United Kingdom **U.K. Consulate** ✉ Lungarno Corsini 2, Lungarno North ☎ 055/284133 ⊕ www.britain.it.

🛈 United States **U.S. Consulate** ✉ Lungarno Vespucci 38, Lungarno North ☎ 055/266951 ⊕ www.usembassy.it.

EMERGENCIES

You can get a list of English-speaking doctors and dentists at the U.S. Consulate, or contact the Tourist Medical Service. If you need hospital treatment and an interpreter, you can call AVO, a group of volunteer interpreters; it's open Monday, Wednesday, and Friday 4–6 PM and Tuesday and Thursday 10–noon. Comunale No. 13, a local pharmacy, is open 24 hours a day, seven days a week. For a complete listing of other pharmacies that have late-night hours on a rotating basis, dial 192.

🛈 **AVO** ☎ 055/2344567. **Tourist Medical Service** ✉ Via Lorenzo il Magnifico, 59 ☎ 055/475411.

🛈 Emergency Services **Ambulance** ☎ 118. **Emergencies** ☎ 113. **Misericordia** (Red Cross) ✉ Piazza del Duomo 20 ☎ 055/212222. **Police** ✉ Via Zara 2, near Piazza della Libertà ☎ 055/49771.

🛈 24-Hour Pharmacies **Comunale No. 13** ✉ Stazione Centrale di Santa Maria Novella ☎ 055/289435.

ENGLISH-LANGUAGE MEDIA

BOOKS Edison has three sprawling floors teeming with books (the English language section is on the top floor) and a small café.

🛈 **BM Bookshop** ✉ Borgo Ognissanti 4/r, Santa Maria Novella ☎ 055/294575. **Paperback Exchange** ✉ Via Fiesolana 31/r, Santa Croce ☎ 055/2478154. **Edison** ✉ Piazza della Repubblica 27/r ☎ 055/213110.

WHERE TO STAY

VILLA RENTALS 🛈 Local Agents **The Best in Italy** ✉ Via Ugo Foscolo 72, 50124 Florence ☎ 055/223064 🖷 055/2298912 ⊕ www.thebestinitaly.com. **Florence**

and Abroad ✉ Via San Zanobi 58, 50129 San Marco Florence ☎ 055/470603 ⊕ www.florenceandabroad.com. **Custom Travel and Special Events** ✉ Via dell'Ardiglione 19, Santo Spirito/San Frediano, 50124 ☎ 055/2645526 ⊕ www.customitaly.com.

MAIL & SHIPPING

🔢 Post Offices **Florence** ✉ Via Pellicceria 3, Piazza della Repubblica ☎ 055/211147. **Florence** ✉ Via Pietrapiana 53/55, Santa Croce ☎ 055/214600.

OVERNIGHT SERVICES

🔢 Major Services **DHL** ✉ Via della Cupola 234/5 ☎ 800/123800 toll free. **Federal Express** ✉ Via Gioberti 3 ☎ 055/8974001; 800/123800 toll free.

SAFETY

LOCAL SCAMS

Florence is subject to the same types of petty thievery that are practiced in Italy's other large, heavily touristed cities. Pickpockets are known to frequent crowded places, particularly buses. Purse-snatchers sometimes operate on mopeds, making them quick and potentially dangerous. Groups of gypsy children have a number of ruses to part you from your property. Although the odds are against you falling prey to such crimes, it's always wise to keep your valuables well guarded, to be alert to your surroundings, and to err on the side of caution if you find yourself in suspicious circumstances.

TAXIS

Taxis usually wait at stands throughout the city (in front of the train station and in Piazza della Repubblica, for example), or you can call for one. The meter starts at €2.30, with a €3.60 minimum and extra charges at night, on Sunday, or for radio dispatch. A tip of about 10% will be much appreciated.

🔢 Taxi Companies **Taxis** ☎ 055/4390 or 055/4798.

TOURS

BIKE TOURS

Florence by Bike sets off several times a day for one- to three-hour tours of major monuments or for tours with specific themes such as Renaissance Florence or 13th-century Florence. I Bike Italy has one-day tours around Fiesole and Chianti, as well as a two-day tour around Siena. The International Kitchen can arrange biking and walking tours of Florence and Tuscany that also involve cooking and eating; tours should be arranged in advance through the U.S. office.

🔢 Companies **Florence by Bike** ✉ Via San Zanobi 120-122/r, San Lorenzo ☎ 055/488992 ⊕ www.florencebybike.it. **I Bike Italy** ✉ Borgo degli Albizi 11, Santa Croce ☎☎ 055/2342371 ⊕ www.ibikeitaly.com. **International Kitchen** ✉ 55 E. Monroe St., Suite 2840, Chicago, IL 60603 ☎ 800/945-8606 ⊕ www.theinternationalkitchen.com.

BUS TOURS

The major bus operators have half-day itineraries, all of which use comfortable buses staffed with English-speaking guides. Morning tours begin at 9, when buses pick visitors up at the main hotels. Stops include the cathedral complex, the Galleria dell'Accademia, Piazzale Michelangelo, and the Palazzo Pitti (or, on Monday, the Museo dell'Opera del Duomo). Afternoon tours stop at the large hotels at 2 PM and take in Piazza della Signoria, the Galleria degli Uffizi (or the Palazzo Vecchio on Monday, when the Uffizi is closed), nearby Fiesole, and, on the return, the church of Santa Croce. A half-day tour costs about €24.75, including museum admissions.

🔢 Fees & Schedules **Lazzi Eurolines** ✉ Via Mercadante 2, Santa Maria Novella ☎ 055/363041 ⊕ www.lazzi.it. **SITA** ✉ Via Santa Caterina da Siena 17/r, Santa Maria Novella ☎ 055/214721.

WALKING TOURS

🔢 Companies **Custom Travel and Special Events** ✉ Via dell'Ardiglione 19, Santo Spirito/San Frediano, 50124 ☎ 055/2645526 ⊕ www.customitaly.com.

Florence Art Lectures ✉ Palazzo Antellesi Piazza Santa Croce 21–22, Santa Croce ☎ 310/854–3989 in U.S. ⊕ www.florenceart.org.

TRAIN TRAVEL

Florence is on the principal Italian train route between most European capitals and Rome, and within Italy it is served frequently from Milan, Venice, and Rome by Intercity (IC) and nonstop Eurostar trains. Stazione Centrale di Santa Maria Novella is the main station and is in the center of town. Be sure to avoid trains that stop only at the Campo di Marte or Rifredi stations, which are not convenient to the center.

🚆 Train Information **Stazione Centrale di Santa Maria Novella** ☎ 8488/888088.

TRAVEL AGENCIES

🚆 Local Agent Referrals **American Express** ✉ Via Dante Alighieri 22/r, Duomo ☎ 055/50981. **CIT Italia** ✉ Piazza Stazione 51/r, Santa Maria Novella ☎ 055/284145 or 055/212606. **Micos Travel Box** ✉ Via dell'Oriuolo 50–52/r, Santa Croce ☎ 055/2340228. **Thomas Cook** ✉ Lungarno Acciaiuoli 7/r, Lungarno North ☎ 055/289781.

VISITOR INFORMATION

The main Florence tourist office, APT, has offices next to the Palazzo Medici-Riccardi, in the main train station, and around the corner from the Basilica di Santa Croce. Its Web site is in Italian only. Fiesole's office is on the main piazza.

🚆 Tourist Information **Fiesole** ✉ Piazza Mino da Fiesole 37, 50014 ☎ 055/598720 ⊕ www.comune.fiesole.fi.it. **Florence** Agenzia Promozione Turistica (APT) ✉ Via Cavour 1/r, next to Palazzo Medici-Riccardi, San Lorenzo 50100 ☎ 055/290832 ✉ Stazione Centrale di Santa Maria Novella, 50100 ☎ 055/212245 ✉ Borgo Santa Croce 29/r ☎ 055/2340444 ⊕ www.comune.firenze.it.

TUSCANY
LUCCA, PISA, SIENA, CHIANTI, THE HILL TOWNS

9

FODOR'S CHOICE

Basilica di San Francesco, Arezzo
Bucadisantantonio, restaurant, Lucca
Calcione Country and Castle, hotel, near Arezzo
Piazza del Campo, Siena

HIGHLY RECOMMENDED

RESTAURANTS Da Delfina, near Prato
Enoteca I Terzi, Siena
La Grotta, Montepulciano
La Mescita, Pisa
Ristorante Arnolfo, Colle Val d'Elsa
Ristoro di Lamole, near Greve in Chianti

HOTELS Hermitage, Elba
Il Falconiere, Cortona
La Foce, Pienza
La Suvera, Colle Val d'Elsa
Palazzo Alexander, Lucca
Palazzo Ravizza, Siena
Relais Fattoria Vignale, Radda in Chianti

SIGHTS Abbazia di San Galgano
Abbazia di Sant'Antimo
Collegiata, San Gimignano
Duomo, Lucca
Leaning Tower, Pisa
Passeggiata delle Mura, Lucca
Radda in Chianti

Updated by
Patricia Rucidlo

HILLSIDES BLANKETED WITH VINEYARDS and silver-green olive groves and capped by enchanting towns are the essence of Tuscany, one of the most beautiful places in the world. Much seems unchanged since the Renaissance; Siena's square continues to be captivating, while Chianti's narrow roads wind their way through cypress-strewn countryside. A visit here is magic and food for the soul.

Midway down the Italian peninsula, Tuscany, with its hills, snowcapped mountains, dramatic cypress trees, and miles of coastline on the Tyrrhenian Sea, provides breathtaking views everywhere you look. The Arno, its most famous river, stretches clear across the region from Florence before making its way to the sea just beyond Pisa. The beauty of its landscape proves a perfect foil for the abundance of superlative art and architecture typical of the region. It also produces some of Italy's finest wines and olive oils. The combination of unforgettable art, sumptuous views, and eminently drinkable wines that pair beautifully with its simple food makes a trip to Tuscany something beyond special.

Tuscany (Toscana in Italian) was populated, at least by the 7th century BC, by the Etruscans, a mysterious lot who chose to live on hills—the better to see the approaching enemy—in such places as present-day Arezzo, Chiusi, Cortona, Fiesole, and Volterra. Some 500 years later, the Romans came, saw, and conquered; by 241 BC they had built the Aurelia, a road from Rome to Pisa that is still in use today. The crumbling of the Roman Empire and subsequent invasions by marauding Lombards, Byzantines, and Holy Roman Emperors meant centuries of turmoil. By the 12th century, the formation of city-states was occurring throughout Tuscany in part, perhaps, because it was unclear exactly who was in charge.

The two groups vying for power were the Guelphs and the Ghibellines, champions of the pope and the Holy Roman Emperor, respectively. They jostled for control of individual cities and of the region as a whole. Florence was more or less Guelph, and Siena more often than not Ghibelline. This led to bloody battles, most notably the 1260 battle of Montaperti, in which the Ghibellines roundly defeated the Guelphs.

Eventually—by the 14th century—the Guelphs became the dominant force. But this did not mean that the warring Tuscan cities settled down to a period of relative peace and tranquillity. The age in which Dante wrote his *Divine Comedy* and Giotto and Piero della Francesca created their incomparable frescoes was one of internecine strife. Florence was the power to be reckoned with; it coveted Siena, which it conquered, lost, and reconquered during the 15th and 16th centuries. Finally, in 1555, following in the footsteps of Volterra, Pisa, Prato, and Arezzo, Siena fell for good. They were all united under Florence to form the grand duchy of Tuscany. The only city to escape Florence's dominion was Lucca, which remained fiercely independent until the arrival of Napoléon. Eventually, however, even Florence's influence waned, and the 17th and 18th centuries saw the decline of the entire region as various armies swept across it.

Some contend that the purest form of the Italian language is spoken in Tuscany. Tuscans—and Florentines in particular—proudly claim Dante as a native son, and his *Divine Comedy* certainly did much to put the Tuscan vernacular on the map. Boccaccio followed suit with his bawdy *Decameron*, written in the 1350s. However, it was the Aretine Petrarch (1304–74), one of the earliest of the humanists of the Italian Renaissance, whose use of the vernacular in his poetry was most widely imitated.

Numbers in the text correspond to numbers in the margin and on the Tuscany, Lucca, Pisa, and Siena maps.

If you have 3 days

Florence is a practical starting point. See **Lucca** ④ – ⑩ ⚑ and the **Leaning Tower** ⑪ in **Pisa** ⑪ – ⑯, then head for ▦ **San Gimignano** ⑲ to overnight. The next day, explore the medieval alleyways of **Siena** ㉕ – ㉜ for a few hours; then move on to ▦ **Montepulciano** ㊱ for the night. The following day, detour south to the thermal waters of **Saturnia** ㊸ and stroll through the medieval town of **Pitigliano** ㊹; then go north to **Arezzo** ㉝ and head back to Florence via the A1 or, if you have time, along the twisting roads of Chianti (SS69, SS408, SS429, and SS222).

If you have 5 days

From Florence, head for industrial **Prato** ① ⚑ to see its striking *centro storico* (old city); **Pistoia** ②, site of bitter Guelph-Ghibelline feuding; and, if you enjoy resorts, **Montecatini Terme** ③, one of Europe's most famous spas. Stay over in ▦ **Lucca** ④ – ⑩ and spend part of the next day exploring. Head for **Pisa** ⑪ – ⑯, then move on to the enchanting hilltop town of **San Miniato** ⑰ and either ▦ **Volterra** ⑱ or ▦ **San Gimignano** ⑲, the archetypal Tuscan town and a good place to spend your second night. On the third day, head through Chianti to ▦ **Siena** ㉕ – ㉜, perhaps Italy's loveliest medieval city. Next visit the **Abbazia di Monte Oliveto Maggiore** ㉟, **Montalcino** ㊳, and the **Abbazia di Sant'Antimo** ㊴, overnighting in or around ▦ **Montepulciano** ㊱. On the morning of your fifth day drive to **Saturnia** ㊸ and enjoy a thermal bath, then make quick visits to **Pitigliano** ㊹ and **Pienza** ㊲. Move on to handsome and heavily trafficked **Cortona** ㉞, where you can see works by Fra Angelico in the Museo Diocesano; in **Arezzo** ㉝ stop at the church of San Francesco to look at Piero della Francesca's glorious frescoes.

If you have 7 days

As you approach **Prato** ① ⚑, you'll have time to visit the modern collection at the Centro per l'Arte Contemporanea L. Pecci. If you opt to see the resort town of **Montecatini Terme** ③, take the waters at one of the local *terme* (spas) or ride the funicular up to older Montecatini Alto. Extend your ▦ **Pisa** ⑪ – ⑯ exploration beyond the Piazza del Duomo to include the **Museo Nazionale di San Matteo** ⑯, and then stay the night. From Pisa, head to the wine country. Take the SS67 east toward Florence, and before entering the city turn south to pick up the meandering SS222, the Strada Chiantigiana that runs through the heart of Chianti by way of **Panzano** ㉒, where you can sample local wine at one of the many *enoteche* (wine bars). Carry on to ▦ **Castellina in Chianti** ㉔ and plan to stay two nights there or in nearby ▦ **Radda in Chianti** ㉓, dedicating a day to vineyard-hopping. Next, settle into a ▦ **Siena** ㉕ – ㉜ hotel and take a day to see the city. From Siena head south to discover **Montepulciano** ㊱, **Pienza** ㊲, and ▦ **Montalcino** ㊳ for a night. For a moving sight, detour to the **Abbazia di San Galgano** ㊶. East of Siena and well worth the side trip and last overnight are ▦ **Cortona** ㉞ and ▦ **Arezzo** ㉝. For a taste of a more rugged landscape on the way back to Florence, detour through the Casentino, a mountainous region blanketed with a vast forest that is a far cry from the pastoral images associated with Tuscany. You'll take the winding SS70, called the Consuma, a splendidly scenic road with hairpin turns and blind corners.

9

To many, Tuscan art is synonymous with the art of Florence, and that bias can be attributed in part to another Aretine named Giorgio Vasari (1511–74), who, in his *Lives of the Artists*, created an inescapably Florentine canon. Florentine art is indeed dazzling, but the rest of Tuscany should not be overlooked. Nicola Pisano (circa 1215/20–1278/84) carved a groundbreaking pulpit in Pisa, then worked with his son Giovanni on another in Siena. Giovanni carried the tradition to Pistoia. Ambrogio Lorenzetti (documented 1319–48) produced wonderful scenes representing *Good and Bad Government* in the Palazzo Pubblico in Siena. The frescoes of the *Legend of the True Cross* by Piero della Francesca (circa 1420–92) in Arezzo are among the 15th century's most stunning fresco cycles. Siena-born Aeneas Silvius Piccolomini (1405–64), later Pope Pius II, carried out his vision of an ideal Renaissance city in Pienza. Renaissance art was by no means exclusively Florentine.

Many of Tuscany's cities and towns have retained the same fundamental character over the past 500 years. Civic rivalries that led to bloody battles so many centuries ago have given way to soccer rivalries. Renaissance pomp lives on in the celebration of local feast days and centuries-old traditions such as the Palio in Siena or the Giostra del Saraceno (Joust of the Saracen) in Arezzo. Often present-day Tuscans look as though they might have served as models for paintings produced hundreds of years ago. In many ways, the Renaissance still lives in Tuscany.

Exploring Tuscany

Although Tuscany is relatively small—no important destination is more than a few hours' drive from Florence—the desire to linger is strong: can you really get enough of sitting on a *terrazza* (terrace) with a good *caffè* (espresso) or a full-bodied Chianti, watching the evening settle over a landscape of soft-edged hills, proud medieval towns, quiet villages, and cypress-ringed villas?

It's best to have a car when traveling in Tuscany to enjoy fully the region's riches—it's the only way to get to many small towns and vineyards. The cities west of Florence are easily reached by the A11, which heads from Florence to Lucca and then to the sea; the A1 heads south from Florence toward Arezzo. Florence and Siena are connected by a superstrada and also the panoramic SS222, which threads through Chianti wine country. The hill towns north and west of Siena lie along superstradas and winding local roads—all are well marked, but you should arm yourself with a good map.

About the Restaurants & Hotels

Savvy travelers, and those on a budget, might want to consider keeping dining costs down by eating a big lunch instead of a big dinner: many restaurants offer lunch specials. Consider drinking the house wine instead of ordering a bottle: you are, after all, in Tuscany; even house wines are generally more than simply drinkable. And if a sandwich is all you're hankering for, drop in to any *alimentari* (delicatessen) and ask the man or woman behind the counter to make you a *panino*: select from any of the ingredients before you in the glass case, and they'll do so.

Staying in Tuscany is not inexpensive, especially in highly visited cities such as Siena, Lucca, San Gimignano, and Arezzo. But wonderful properties abound, including medieval and Renaissance palazzi evoking the spirit of Lorenzo de' Medici. To keep costs down, overnight in less-frequented towns. You might want to consider staying at an *agriturismo*, a farm that has opened its rooms or apartments to guests; choices range from rustic to stately (note that some require a minimum stay of sev-

Hiking & Biking

Serious hikers and trekkers come to Tuscany for its network of trails and incredible views. the Apennine's Parco dell' Orecchiella in the Garfagnana has extensive forests with trails for hiking and biking, as well as horseback riding and cross-country skiing in winter.

9

In the spring, summer, and fall, bicyclists are as much a part of the landscape as the cypress trees. A drive on any steep Chianti road takes you past groups of bikers peddling up and down endless hills. Many are on weeklong organized tours, but it's also possible to rent bikes for jaunts in the countryside or to join afternoon or day minitours. Most Tuscan roads are in excellent condition, though often narrow, winding, and steep. That said, be cautious—especially as some of the drivers on these narrow, twisting roads may have just stopped at a vineyard for a tasting.

Thermal Baths

Southern Tuscany is shadowed with smoky clouds of steam billowing from natural geysers in the earth. There are also several outdoor naturally heated pools that smell of sulfur but are reputed to be therapeutic. Saturnia is the most famous; others are Venturina, near Piombino; Galleraie, near Montieri; Bagno Vignoni, near San Quirico d'Orcia; and Chianciano Terme, near Chiusi and not far from Lago Trasimeno in neighboring Umbria. But be aware that the baths can be crowded in summer.

Vineyards

Those picturesque vineyards on the Chianti hillsides are not cinematic backdrops; they are working farms, and when fall comes and their grapes are harvested and processed, they produce that world-famous *vino rosso* (red wine) that has been complementing Tuscan food for ages. Chianti's heritage dates back thousands of years, but the borders that define Chianti Classico weren't officially drawn until 1932. The Chianti region is actually surprisingly large, stretching from Pistoia, north of Florence, to Montalcino, south of Siena. (It includes all the areas where various types of Chianti grapes are grown.)

Chianti Classico is at the heart of the Chianti region. Its *gallo nero* (black rooster) logo dates from the 12th century, when the rooster was the symbol of the Chianti League, a military alliance that defended the Florentine border against Siena. Now that rooster signifies some of the highest-quality wines in the entire Chianti region.

Wine tasting lures travelers who want to give their eyes a rest after looking at all those halos in the churches and museums of Florence and Siena. Most of the vineyards have figured this out and offer direct sales and samplings of their products. Some have roadside stands, and others have elaborate sampling rooms in which snacks are served. Tourist-information offices in most Chianti towns have maps to guide you through an itinerary of vineyard hopping.

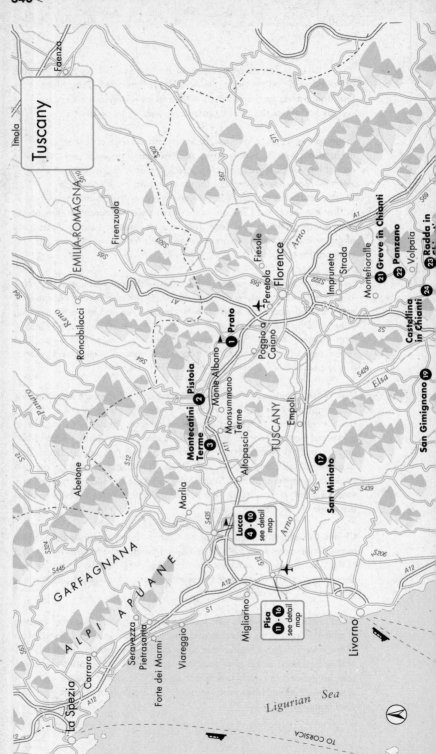

Tuscany

eral days). Villa rental can also be an economical and enjoyable option for groups and families.

	$$$$	$$$	$$	$	¢
WHAT IT COSTS In euros					
RESTAURANTS	over €22	€17–€22	€12–€17	€7–€12	under €7
HOTELS	over €210	€160–€210	€110–€160	€60–€110	under €60

Restaurant prices are for a second course (secondo piatto). Hotel prices are for two people in a standard double room in high season, including tax and service.

Timing

Spring and fall are the best times to come to Tuscany, when the weather is warm but the volume of tourists is relatively low. In summer, try to arrive in towns early in the morning to avoid crowds and the often oppressive heat. Rising early is not hard, as Tuscany is not about late nights; most bars and restaurants close their shutters well before midnight. If you plan to visit the frescoes in the Palazzo Pubblico in Siena at midday, be prepared to wait in line and, once inside, to be shuffled along by iron-willed attendants eager to see you in and out as quickly as possible. If you want to photograph the towers of San Gimignano from a distance, do it in early morning, when the light is good and lines of neon-color tour buses snaking up the hill will not ruin a perfect picture.

WESTERN TUSCANY

In the shadows of the rugged coastal Alpi Apuane, where Michelangelo quarried his marble, this area isn't as lush as southern Tuscany—the hills flatten out, and there are hints of industry. It's well worth the effort to visit these spots, however—there's wonderful art, and some very fine restaurants with prices slightly lower than what you'll find in Florence.

Prato

▶ ❶ *17 km (11 mi) northwest of Florence, 60 km (37 mi) east of Lucca.*

The wool industry in this city, one of the world's largest manufacturers of cloth, was known throughout Europe as early as the 13th century. It was further stimulated in the 14th century by a local cloth merchant, Francesco di Marco Datini, who built his business, according to one of his ledgers, "in the name of God and of profit."

Prato's **Centro per l'Arte Contemporanea L. Pecci** (L. Pecci Center of Contemporary Art) has acquired a burgeoning collection of works by Italian and other artists. ⊠ *Viale della Repubblica 277* ☎ *0574/5317* ⊕ *www.comune.prato.it/pecci* ⊠ €6.20 ☾ *Wed.–Mon. 10–7.*

Prato's Romanesque **Duomo** is famous for its **Pergamo del Sacro Cingolo** (Chapel of the Holy Girdle), to the left of the entrance, which enshrines the girdle of the Virgin Mary. It is said that the Virgin presented it to the apostle Thomas in a miraculous appearance after her Assumption. The Duomo also contains 15th-century frescoes by Prato's most famous son, Fra Filippo Lippi (1406–69), who executed scenes from the life of St. Stephen on the left wall and scenes from the life of John the Baptist on the right in the **Cappella Maggiore** (Main Chapel). As of this writing, the frescoes were undergoing restoration; to find out about guided visits on the scaffolding, call 0574/24112. ⊠ *Piazza del Duomo* ☎ *0574/26234* ☾ *Oct.–June, Mon.–Sat. 7–12:30 and 3–6:30, Sun. 7–12:30 and 3–8; July–Sept., daily 7:30–12:30 and 4–7:30.*

Sculptures by Donatello (circa 1386–1466) that originally adorned the Duomo's exterior pulpit are now on display in the **Museo dell'Opera del Duomo** (Cathedral Museum). ⊠ *Piazza del Duomo 49* ☎ *0574/29339* 🖃 *€5, includes Museo di Pittura Murale* ☉ *Mon. and Wed.–Sat. 9:30–12:30 and 3–6:30, Sun. 9:30–12:30.*

Installed in the **Museo di Pittura Murale** (Museum of Mural Painting) is a collection of paintings by Fra Filippo Lippi and other works from the 13th–15th centuries in a special exhibit called Treasures of the City, on view through 2004. The permanent collection contains frescoes removed from sites in Prato and environs. ⊠ *Piazza San Domenico 8* ☎ *0574/440501* 🖃 *€5, includes Museo dell'Opera del Duomo* ☉ *Mon. and Wed.–Sat. 10–6, Sun. 10–1.*

The church of **Santa Maria delle Carceri** was built by Giuliano Sangallo in the 1490s and is a landmark of Renaissance architecture. ⊠ *Piazza Santa Maria delle Carceri, off Via Cairoli and southeast of the cathedral* ☎ *0574/27933* ☉ *Daily 7–noon and 4–7:30.*

Though in ruins, the formidable **Castello** (Castle) built for Frederick II Hohenstaufen, adjacent to Santa Maria delle Carceri, is an impressive sight, the only castle of its type outside southern Italy. ⊠ *Piazza Santa Maria delle Carceri* ☎ *0574/38207* ☉ *Nov.–Feb., Mon. and Wed.–Fri. 10–1, weekends 9–1 and 3–5; Mar.–Oct., Wed.–Mon. 10–7.*

off the beaten path

POGGIO A CAIANO – For a look at gracious country living Renaissance style, detour south of Prato to the Villa Medicea in Poggio a Caiano. Lorenzo "il Magnifico" (1449–92) commissioned Giuliano da Sangallo (circa 1445–1516) to redo the villa, which was lavished with frescoes by important Renaissance painters such as Andrea del Sarto (1486–1530) and Pontormo (1494–1557). You can take a walk around the austerely ornamented grounds while waiting for entry. ⊠ *Poggio a Caiano, 7 km (4½ mi) south of Prato, follow signs* ☎ *055/877012* 🖃 *€2.05* ☉ *Garden: Mar., Apr., Sept.–Oct., Mon.–Sat. 9–5:30; Nov.–Feb., Mon.–Sat. 9–4:30; May–Aug., 9–6:30, Sun. 9–12:30. Villa: Mon.–Sat. 9–1:30, Sun. 9–noon. Guided visits only, hourly on the ½ hr, 9:30–1 hr before closing* ☉ *Closed 2nd and 3rd Mon. of month.*

Where to Eat

★ **$$–$$$** ✕ **Da Delfina.** Delfina began cooking many years ago for hungry hunters, and now she has four comfortably rustic dining rooms in a farmhouse nestled amid vineyards and olive trees past Poggio a Caiano in Artimino. Here you can enjoy dishes that make the most of pure ingredients, including seasonal vegetables and savory meats accented with herbs. The *secondi* (second courses) such as *coniglio con olive e pignoli* (rabbit sautéed with olives and pine nuts) are a real treat. ⊠ *Via della Chiesa 1, Artimino* ☎ *055/8718074* ♣ *Reservations essential* 🖃 *No credit cards* ☉ *Closed Mon. and 2 wks in Aug. No lunch Tues. No dinner Sun.*

¢–$ ✕ **La Vecchia Cucina di Soldano.** Local Pratesi specialties, including the odd but tasty *sedani ripieni* (stuffed celery), are served here in a completely unpretentious place. You could be sitting in your Italian grandmother's kitchen; tablecloths are red-and-white checked, the service friendly and casual. The place teems with locals enjoying the superb *tagliolini sui fagioli* (thin noodles with beans). Clearly they, too, like the rock-bottom prices. ⊠ *Via Pomeria 23* ☎ *0574/34665* 🖃 *No credit cards.* ☉ *Closed Sun.*

CloseUp

ON THE MENU

JUST AS THE ANCIENT ETRUSCANS introduced cypress trees to the Tuscan landscape, their influence on regional food—in the use of fresh herbs—still lingers after more than three millennia. Simple and earthy, Tuscan food celebrates the seasons with a host of fresh vegetable dishes, wonderful bread-based soups, and savory meats and game perfumed with sage, rosemary, and thyme. Saltless Tuscan bread is grilled and drizzled with olive oil (crostino), or spread with chicken liver (crostino di fegatini), or rubbed with garlic and topped with tomatoes (bruschetta or fettunta). For their love of beans—particularly cannellini (white beans) simmered in olive oil and herbs until creamy—Tuscans have been disparagingly nicknamed mangiafagioli (bean eaters) by Italians from other regions. Pecorino, a cheese made from sheep's milk, is particularly good in these parts—try it when it's young and in a soft,

practically spreadable state, as well as when it's stagionato, or aged. When it's good, it's the equal of the finest Parmesan. Relatively new to Tuscan cuisine is the reintroduction of dishes featuring cinta senese, a once nearly extinct pig.

Grapes have been cultivated here since Etruscan times, and Chianti still dominates. The robust red wine is a staple on most tables; however, the discerning can select from a multitude of other varieties, including such reds as Brunello di Montalcino and Vino Nobile di Montepulciano and such whites as Valdinievole and Vernaccia. Super Tuscans, a fanciful name given to a group of wines by American journalists, now command attention as some of the best wines produced in Italy; they have great depth and complexity. The dessert wine vin santo is produced throughout the region and is often sipped with biscotti (twice-baked cookies), perfect for dunking.

Shopping

Prato's biscotti (twice-cooked cookies) have an extra-dense texture, lending themselves to submersion in caffè or vin santo. The best in town are at **Antonio Mattei** (⊠ Via Ricasoli 20/22 ☎ 0574/25756).

The centuries-old tradition of selling fine textiles crafted into fine clothing continues in Prato. **Enrico Pecci di A. Pecci & C.** (⊠ Via del Pantano 16/e ☎ 055/89890) sells fabric by the meter.

Pistoia

❷ *18 km (11 mi) northwest of Prato, 36 km (22 mi) northwest of Florence.*

Pistoia can claim a Roman past, as well as a bloody history during the Middle Ages when the town was rent by civil strife. Its historic center is a jewel and little visited, which makes coming here all the more worthwhile. The **Cattedrale di San Zeno** in the main piazza houses the *Dossale di San Jacopo*, a magnificent silver altar. The two half-figures on the left were executed by Filippo Brunelleschi (1377–1446). ⊠ *Piazza del Duomo* ☎ *0573/25095* ▧ *Illumination of altarpiece €2.60* ☉ *Church daily 9–noon and 4–7; altar daily 10–noon and 4–5:45.*

The **Palazzo del Comune**, begun around 1295, houses the **Museo Civico**, with works by local artists from the 14th to 20th centuries. ⊠ *Museo Civico, Piazza del Duomo 1* ☎ *0573/371296* ▧ *€2.60, free Sat. 3–7* ☉ *Tues.–Sat. 10–7, Sun. 9–12:30.*

Founded in the 13th century, the **Spedale del Ceppo** (literally, Hospital of the Tree Stump) has a glorious early 16th-century exterior terra-cotta frieze begun by Giovanni della Robbia (1469–1529) and completed by the workshop of Santi and Benedetto Buglioni in 1526–28. ⊠ *Piazza Ospedale, a short way down Via Pacini from Piazza del Duomo.*

An architectural gem in green-and-white marble, the medieval church of **San Giovanni Fuorcivitas** contains a *Visitation* by Luca della Robbia (1400–82), a painting attributed to Taddeo Gaddi, and a holy-water font that may have been executed by Fra Guglielmo around 1270. ⊠ *Via Cavour* ☎ *0573/24784* ⊙ *Daily 8–noon and 4–6:30.*

Although it's not as grand as the silver altar in Pistoia's cathedral, Giovanni Pisano's powerfully sculpted pulpit, executed between 1298 and 1301 in the church of **Sant'Andrea,** is considered by many the town's greatest art treasure. ⊠ *Via Sant'Andrea* ☎ *0573/21912* ⊙ *Nov.–Mar., daily 8–1 and 4–6:30; Apr.–Oct., daily 8–12:30 and 3:30–7.*

⟳ The **Giardino Zoologico,** a small zoo especially laid out to accommodate the wiles of both animals and children, is a 20-minute drive out of town. Take Bus 29 from the train station. ⊠ *Via Pieve a Celle 160/a* ☎ *0573/ 911219* ⊠ *€8.30* ⊙ *Apr.–Sept., daily 9–7; Oct.–Mar., daily 9–5.*

Where to Eat

$$–$$$ ✕ **S. Jacopo.** Bruno Lottini, a gracious host who speaks perfect English, has a charming restaurant, minutes away from the Piazza del Duomo. It's got country-house charm with its white walls and tile floors; tasteful prints and photographs on the walls play nicely off the rustic blue linens that dress the tables. The menu has mostly regional favorites, such as the *maccheroni S. Jacopo,* wide ribbons of house-made pasta with a duck *ragù* (sauce), but the chef can turn out perfectly grilled squid as well. Save room for dessert, especially the apple strudel. ⊠ *Via Crispi 15* ☎ *0573/27786* ⊟ *AE, DC, MC, V* ⊙ *Closed Mon. No lunch Tues.*

¢–$ ✕ **La BotteGaia.** Just off Piazza del Duomo, this popular wine bar has rustic tables in a couple of rooms with exposed brick-and-stone walls (when it's warm, there's outdoor seating); jazz plays softly in the background. Typical wine-bar fare such as plates of *salami e formaggi* (cured ham and cheeses) shares the menu with a surprisingly sophisticated list of daily specials that can include *insalatina con foie gras condita con vinaigrette* (foie gras with dressed greens). Dine al fresco with a view of the splendid Piazza del Duomo in summer. ⊠ *Via del Lastrone 4* ☎ *0573/365602* ⟲ *Reservations essential* ⊟ *AE, DC, MC, V* ⊙ *Closed Mon. and 15 days in Aug. No lunch Sun.*

¢–$ ✕ **Trattoria dell'Abbondanza.** Entering from a quiet side street, you walk into a small place with clean cream-color walls that's busy but not noisy, its staff friendly but never pushy. Traditional dishes include, for first courses, a *minestra di farro* (a hearty soup made with farro, a local, barley-like grain) and *maccheroni sull'anatra* (in a duck sauce). For seconds, there's *baccalà alla Livornese* (salt cod in a tomato sauce), roast rabbit, and tripe. The *torta rustica,* a cake made of cornmeal and cream, makes a fine dessert. ⊠ *Via dell'Abbondanza 10, off via degli Orafi* ☎ *0573/368037* ⊟ *No credit cards* ⊙ *Closed Wed. No lunch Thurs.*

Montecatini Terme

❸ *16 km (10 mi) west of Pistoia, 49 km (30 mi) west of Florence.*

Immortalized in Fellini's 8½, Montecatini Terme has Italy's premier thermal waters, known for their curative powers and, at least once upon a time, for their great popularity among the wealthy. The town's abundance of art nouveau buildings went up during its heyday at the beginning of the 20th century. Like most other well-heeled resort towns, Montecatini attracts the leisured traveler; aside from taking the waters and people-watching in Piazza del Popolo, there's not a whole lot to do here. The mineral springs flow from five sources and are used to treat liver and skin disorders. Those "taking the cure" report each morning to one of the town's *stabilimenti termali* (thermal establishments; ⊠ Via Verdi 73 ☎ 0572/778509 information) to drink their prescribed cupful of water, whose curative effects became known in the 1800s.

Of Montecatini Terme's art nouveau structures, the most attractive is the **Terme Tettuccio** (⊠ Viale Verdi 41 ☎ 0572/778501), a neoclassical edifice with colonnades. Here Montecatini's healthful tonic spouts from fountains set up on marble counters, the walls are decorated with bucolic scenes on painted ceramic tiles, and in the morning an orchestra plays under a frescoed dome.

LUCCA

In this fortress town, Caesar, Pompey, and Crassus agreed to rule Rome as a triumvirate in 56 BC; it was later the first town in Tuscany to accept Christianity. Lucca still has a mind of its own, and when most of Tuscany was voting Communist as a matter of course, its citizens rarely followed suit. Within the city's 16th- to 17th-century ramparts, the composer Giacomo Puccini (1858–1924) was born. He is celebrated, along with his peers, during the summer Opera Theater of Lucca Festival.

Exploring Lucca

The historic center of Lucca is walled, and motorized traffic is restricted. Walking or biking is the most efficient and most enjoyable way to get around. You can rent bicycles, and the center is quite flat, so biking is easy without the threat of traffic.

a good walk

Start at the **Museo Nazionale di Palazzo Mansi** ④ ▶ on Via Galli Tassi, just within the walls. Walk down Via del Toro to Piazza del Palazzo Dipinto, and follow Via di Poggio to **San Michele in Foro** ⑤. From Piazza San Michele, walk around to the back of the church and follow Via Beccheria south through Piazza Napoleone. Make a left through the smaller Piazza San Giovanni, which leads directly to the **Duomo** ⑥. Check out the charming facade before going into the church and looking at the Volto Santo crucifix and the tomb of Ilaria del Carretto. Walk down Via dell'Arcivescovado, which is behind the Duomo; the street name changes to Via Guinigi just after crossing Via Santa Croce. Climb the tower of the **Palazzo Guinigi** ⑦ and admire the view. Make a right heading out of Palazzo Guinigi and proceed down via Sant'Andrea; make a right onto via Fillungo. At Via Fontana, take a left and follow it to Via Cesare Battisti. Make a right and head toward the church of **San Frediano** ⑧, with its strangely mummified Santa Zita, the patron saint of domestic workers. From the church, walk along Via San Frediano back toward the Fillungo; make a right and then a left, and head into the **Piazza del Anfiteatro Romano** ⑨, where the Roman amphitheater once stood. Relax and have an aperitivo at one of the many cafés lining the piazza. Exit the piazza through the doorway to the left where you entered. Veer toward the right following the curve of the buildings. Make a quick left onto Via del Portico and bear right. You will pass the church and piazza of San Pietro Somaldi on your left; just after the piazza make a left onto Via della Fratta. Continue straight; just after passing the church of San Francesco, you will find yourself at the **Museo Nazionale di Villa Guinigi** ⑩.

TIMING   The walk will take about three hours; add a half hour for lingering in each of the museums.

What to See

★ ❻ **Duomo.** The round-arched facade of the cathedral is an example of the rigorously ordered Pisan Romanesque style, in this case happily enlivened by a varied collection of small carved columns. Take a closer look at the decoration of the facade and of the portico below, which make for one of the most entertaining church exteriors in Tuscany. The Gothic interior contains a moving wood crucifix (called the *Volto Santo,* or Holy Face) brought here, as legend has it, in the 8th century (though it probably dates from between the 11th and early 13th centuries). The marble tomb of Ilaria del Carretto (1408) is the masterpiece of the Sienese sculptor Jacopo della Quercia (1371/74–1438). ⊠ *Piazza del Duomo* ☏ *0583/490530* 🎟 *€2* ⊙ *Duomo: weekdays 7–5:30, Sat. 9:30–6:45, Sun. 11:30–11:50 and 1–5:30. Tomb: Nov.–Mar., weekdays 9:30–4:45, Sat. 9:30–6:45, Sun. 11:30–11:50 and 1–4:45; Apr.–Oct., weekdays 9:30–5:45, Sat. 9–6:45, Sun. 9–10, 11:30–noon, and 1–5:45.*

▶ ❹ **Museo Nazionale di Palazzo Mansi.** Highlights here are the brightly colored *Portrait of a Youth* by Pontormo and portraits of the Medici painted by Bronzino (1503–72) and others. ⊠ *Palazzo Mansi, Via Galli Tassi 43, San Donato* ☏ *0583/55570* 🎟 *€4, combination ticket with Museo Nazionale di Villa Guinigi €6.50* ⊙ *Tues.–Sat. 8:30–7:30, Sun. 8:30–1:30.*

❿ **Museo Nazionale di Villa Guinigi.** On the east end of the historic center, the museum houses an extensive collection of local Romanesque and Renaissance art. ⊠ *Villa Guinigi, Via della Quarquonia, Lucca East* ☏ *0583/496033* 🎟 *€4, combination ticket with Museo Nazionale di Palazzo Mansi €6.50* ⊙ *Tues.–Sat. 8:30–6:30, Sun. 8:30–1.*

❼ **Palazzo Guinigi.** The tower of the medieval palace contains one of the city's most curious sights: six ilex trees have established themselves at the top, and their roots have grown into the room below. From the tower there's a magnificent view of the city and the surrounding countryside. ⊠ *Palazzo Guinigi, Via Sant'Andrea 42, Amfiteatro* ☏ *0583/496033* 🎟 *€3.50* ⊙ *Oct.–May, Tues.–Sat. 9–7, Sun. 9–2; June–Sept., daily 9–12:30 AM.*

★ **Passeggiata delle Mura** (the Ramparts). Any time of day when the weather is agreeable, you can find the citizens of Lucca cycling, jogging, strolling, or playing ball in this large, unusual park, atop the ring of ramparts that surrounds the centro storico. Sunlight streams through two rows of tall plane trees to dapple the *passeggiata delle mura* (walk on the walls), a loop almost 5 km (3 mi) in total length. Ten bulwarks are topped with lawns, many with picnic tables, some with play equipment for children. One caution: there are no railings along the ramparts' edge, and the drop to the ground is a precipitous 40 ft.

❾ **Piazza del Anfiteatro Romano.** A Roman amphitheater once stood on this spot; the medieval buildings built over the amphitheater retain its original oval shape and brick arches. It's a popular gathering place, with numerous cafés and some eclectic shops. ⊠ *Off Via Fillungo.*

❽ **San Frediano.** The church contains works by Jacopo della Quercia and, bizarrely, the lace-clad mummy of the patron saint of domestic servants, St. Zita. ⊠ *Piazza San Frediano* ⊙ *Mon.–Sat. 8:30–noon and 3–5, Sun. 10:30–5.*

❺ **San Michele in Foro.** The facade of this church, slightly west of the centro storico, is even more fanciful than the Duomo's. Check out the superb panel painting of Sts. Girolamo, Sebastian, Rocco, and Helen in the right transept by Filippino Lippi (1457/58–1504). ⊠ *Piazza San Michele* ⊙ *Daily 7:40–noon and 3–6.*

Lucca

KEY

▲ Start of walk

Duomo **6**	Palazzo Guinigi **7**
Museo Nazionale di Palazzo Mansi **4**	Piazza del Anfiteatro Romano **9**
Museo Nazionale di Villa Guinigi **10**	San Frediano **8**
	San Michele in Foro . . . **5**

200 yards

200 meters

0

0

off the beaten path

FORTE DEI MARMI – Tuscany's most exclusive summer beach resort is a favorite of moneyed Tuscans and Milanese, whose villas are neatly laid out in a vast pine woods. In summer, a beachcomber's bonanza takes place on Wednesday morning, when everything from faux designer sunglasses to plastic sandals and terry-cloth towels goes on sale. It's 35 km (22 mi) northwest of Lucca and 65 km (40 mi) northwest of Florence—also near the marble-producing towns of Carrara (where Michelangelo quarried his stone), Seravezza, and Pietrasanta.

VILLA REALE – Eight kilometers (5 mi) north of Lucca in Marlia, this villa was once the home of Napoléon's sister, Princess Elisa. Restored by the Counts Pecci-Blunt, the estate is celebrated for its spectacular gardens, originally laid out in the 16th century and redone in the middle of the 17th century. Gardening buffs adore the legendary *teatro di verdura*, a theater carved out of hedges and topiaries; concerts are occasionally held here. Contact the **Lucca tourist office** (✉ Piazza Santa Maria 125 ☎ 0583/919931) for details. ✉ *Villa Reale* ☎ *0583/30108* 🎟 *€6* ⊙ *Mar.–Nov., guided visits Tues.–Sun. at 10, 11, noon, 3, 4, 5, and 6; Dec.–Feb., by appointment.*

Where to Stay & Eat

$$
Fodor'sChoice
★

✕ **Bucadisantantonio.** It's been around since 1782, and you can understand why. The staying power of the place is the result of its superlative Tuscan food, brought to the table by wait staff that doesn't miss a beat. A white-walled interior, hung with copper pots and brass musical instruments, provides a classy, comfortable setting for enjoying the menu, which ranges from the simple but blissful *tortelli lucchesi al sugo* (meat-stuffed pasta with a tomato and meat sauce) to such daring dishes as roast *capretto* (kid) with herbs. ✉ *Via della Cervia 3, San Michele* ☎ *0583/55881* ⌕ *Reservations essential* ▭ *AE, DC, MC, V* ⊙ *Closed Mon., 2 wks in Jan., and 2 wks in July. No dinner Sun.*

$$
✕ **La Mora.** Detour to this former stagecoach station, now a gracious, rustic country inn 9 km (5½ mi) outside Lucca, for local specialties—from *minestra di farro* (soup made with emmer, a wheat that resembles barley) with beans to homemade *tacconi* (a thin, short, wide pasta) with rabbit sauce to lamb raised in the nearby Garfagnana hills. You might be tempted by the varied crostini and delicious desserts. ✉ *Via Sesto di Ponte a Moriano 1748* ☎ *0583/406402* ▭ *AE, DC, MC, V* ⊙ *Closed Wed. and 3 wks in Jan.*

$–$$
✕ **Il Giglio.** Just off Piazza Napoleone, this restaurant has quiet, late 19th-century charm and classic cuisine. It's a place for all seasons, with a big fireplace and an outdoor terrace in summer. Among the local specialties are *farro garfagnino* (a thick soup made with grain and beans) and *coniglio con olive* (rabbit stew with olives). ✉ *Piazza del Giglio 2, Duomo* ☎ *0583/494058* ▭ *AE, DC, MC, V* ⊙ *Closed Wed. and 15 days in Feb. No dinner Tues.*

$
✕ **Osteria del Neni.** Tucked away on a side street a block from San Michele, this delightful little place offers up tasty treats in a cozy space with paper place mats, wooden tables, and walls sponged in two different hues of warm orange. All the pasta is made in house, and if you're lucky enough to find ravioli *spinaci ed anatra in salsa di noci* (stuffed with duck and spinach, with a creamy but light walnut sauce), by all means order it. The menu changes regularly; in summer this splendid food can be enjoyed alfresco. ✉ *Via Pescheria 3, San Michele* ☎ *0583/ 492681* ⌕ *Reservations essential* ▭ *MC, V* ⊙ *Closed Sun. and Jan.*

¢–$ ✕ **Da Giulio in Pelleria.** If Lucchesi businesspeople had a lunchtime cafe-teria, it would be here. This loud, cavernous, atmosphere-free trattoria serves tasty, traditional Tuscan favorites, as well as such local special-ties as *farinata* (vegetable soup thickened to stewlike consistency by the generous addition of cornmeal) to hordes of visitors and locals alike. Don't be surprised to see the affable waitstaff expertly balancing in one hand five plates brimming with food. ✉ *Via delle Conce 45, San Donato* ☎ *0583/55948* ▭ *AE, DC, MC, V* ⊘ *Closed Mon. and 1st, 2nd, and 4th Sun. of month.*

$$$$ ✕▥ **Locanda l'Elisa.** A stay here could evoke home—that is, if home is a neoclassical villa with a lush garden a short ride from the city. Most rooms are suites, with fresh flowers, antiques, and fine fabrics, and you're served by a caring staff. The innovative restaurant, a former Victorian conservatory, has sophisticated twists on Tuscan favorites using such local ingredients as farro and chestnuts. ✉ *Via Nuova per Pisa 1951, 55050* ☎ *0583/379737* ▤ *0583/379019* ⊕ *www.lunet.it/aziende/locandaelisa* ➫ *3 rooms, 8 suites* ♧ *Restaurant, in-room safes, minibars, pool, baby-sitting, dry cleaning, laundry service, some pets allowed* ▭ *AE, DC, MC, V* ⊘ *Closed Jan. 7–Feb. 7.*

$$$–$$$$ ▥ **Hotel Ilaria.** The former stables of the Villa Bottini have been trans-formed into this modern hotel within the historic center. Rooms are done in warm wood veneer, and the second-floor terrace overlooking the villa makes a comfortable place to relax. The availability of free bikes is a great bonus in this bike-friendly city. ✉ *Via del Fosso, 26, Lucca East, 55100* ☎ *0583/469200* ▤ *0583/991961* ⊕ *www.hotelilaria.com* ➫ *30 rooms* ♧ *In-room safes, minibars, bicycles, bar, baby-sitting, dry clean-ing, laundry service, concierge, meeting room, free parking, some pets allowed (fee), no-smoking rooms* ▭ *AE, DC, MC, V.*

★ $$$ ▥ **Palazzo Alexander.** This small, elegantly appointed boutique hotel tucked into a quiet side street is a stone's throw from San Michele in Foro. The building, dating from the 12th century, has been restructured to create the ease common to Lucchesi nobility: timbered ceilings, warm yellow walls, and brocaded chairs adorn the public rooms, and the motif is carried into the guest rooms, all of which have high ceilings and that same glorious damask. Top-floor suites have sweeping views of the town. ✉ *Via S. Giustina 48, San Michele, 55100* ☎ *0583/583571* ▤ *0583/583610* ⊕ *www.palazzo-alexander.com* ➫ *9 rooms, 3 suites, 1 apartment* ♧ *In-room data ports, in-room safes, minibars, cable TV, bicycles, wine bar, baby-sitting, dry cleaning, laundry service, concierge, Internet, parking (fee), no-smoking rooms* ▭ *AE, DC, MC, V.*

$ ▥ **La Luna.** On a quiet airy courtyard close to historic Piazza del Mer-cato, this family-run hotel occupies two renovated wings of an old building. The bathrooms are modern, but some of the rooms still recall Old Lucca. A parking lot is a bonus, as is the friendly and helpful staff; this is a good place to stay if you're traveling with children. ✉ *Corte Compagni 12, at Via Fillungo, Amfiteatro, 55100* ☎ *0583/493634* ▤ *0583/490021* ⊕ *www.hotellaluna.it* ➫ *30 rooms* ♧ *Minibars, cable TV, baby-sitting, parking (fee)* ▭ *AE, DC, MC, V* ⊘ *Closed Jan. 7–31* ▯⊙▮ *EP.*

$ ▥ **Piccolo Hotel Puccini.** Steps away from the busy square and church of San Michele, this little hotel is quiet, calm, and handsomely decorated. It also has parking (which must be reserved in advance) at a reasonable fee, a great advantage. ✉ *Via di Poggio 9, San Michele, 55100* ☎ *0583/55421* ▤ *0583/53487* ⊕ *www.hotelpuccini.com* ➫ *14 rooms* ♧ *Fans, in-room safes, cable TV, bar, baby-sitting, dry cleaning, laundry service, Internet, parking (fee), some pets allowed, no-smoking rooms; no a/c* ▭ *AE, DC, MC, V* ▯⊙▮ *EP.*

Nightlife & the Arts

The **Estate Musicale Lucchese,** one of many Tuscan music festivals, runs throughout the summer in Lucca. Contact the **Lucca tourist office** (✉ Piazza Santa Maria 125, Lucca East ☎ 0583/919931) for details. The **Opera Theater of Lucca Festival,** sponsored by the Opera Theater of Lucca and the school of music of the University of Cincinnati, runs from mid-June to mid-July; performances are staged in open-air venues. Call the Lucca tourist office for information.

Sports & the Outdoors

The centro storico is flat and easily navigated because automobile traffic is severely limited. A splendid bike ride may be had by circling the entire historic center along the top of the bastions—affording something of a bird's-eye view. You can rent bikes at **Barbetti Cicli** (✉ Via Amfiteatro 23, Amfiteatro ☎ 0583/954444). Bikes are available for rental at **Poli Antonio Biciclette** (✉ Piazza Santa Maria 42, Lucca East ☎ 0583/493787).

Shopping

Lucca's justly famed olive oil, available throughout the city, is exported around the world. Look for those made by Fattoria di Fubbiano and Fattoria Fabbri—two of the best. A particularly delicious version of *buccellato*, a sweet, anise-flavored bread with raisins that is a specialty of Lucca, is baked at **Pasticceria Taddeucci** (✉ Piazza San Michele 34 ☎ 0583/494933). Chocoholics can get their fix at **Caniparoli** (✉ Via S. Paolino 96, San Donato ☎ 0583/53456); so serious are they about their sweets that they do not make them from June through August because of the heat. On the second Sunday of the month, there's a **flea market** in Piazza San Martino.

PISA

Pisa may have been inhabited as early as the Bronze Age. It was certainly populated by the Etruscans and, in turn, became part of the Roman Empire. In the early Middle Ages it flourished as an economic powerhouse—along with Amalfi, Genoa, and Venice, it was one of the maritime republics. The city's economic and political power ebbed in the early 15th century as it fell under the domination of Florence, though it enjoyed a brief resurgence under Cosimo I in the mid-16th century. Pisa endured heavy Allied bombing—miraculously, the Duomo and Leaning Tower were spared along with some other grand Romanesque structures. Beyond the kitsch that the Leaning Tower has spawned, Pisa has much to offer. Its treasures are more subtle than Florence's, to which it is inevitably compared; the city's cathedral-baptistery-campanile complex on Piazza del Duomo is among the most dramatic in Italy.

Exploring Pisa

Pisa, like many other Italian cities, is best seen on foot, and most of what's worth seeing is within walking distance. The views along the Arno are particularly grand and shouldn't be missed—there's a sense of spaciousness that doesn't exist along the Arno in Florence. You should weigh the different options for combination tickets to sights on the Piazza del Duomo when you begin your visit. (The combination tickets are sold at the sights.)

a good
walk

Start in the Campo dei Miracoli, exploring the piazza complex containing the **Leaning Tower** ⑪, **Duomo** ⑫, **Battistero** ⑬, **Camposanto** ⑭, and **Museo dell'Opera del Duomo** ⑮. After a coffee or gelato, walk down Via Santa Maria—the Campanile will be behind you. At Piazza Felice Cavallotti, go left onto Via dei Mille and continue through Piazza dei Cavalieri to Via Dini, and make a right onto Borgo Stretto, a major thoroughfare lined with cafés. On the left, before the river, is the church of San Michele in Borgo. With its ornate 14th-century Pisan Romanesque facade and columns, it's vaguely reminiscent of a wedding cake. Walk up to Piazza Garibaldi and turn left along the Lungarno Mediceo. Practically at the Ponte alla Fortezza, on the left, is the **Museo Nazionale di San Matteo** ⑯.

TIMING   The walk takes about an hour and a half without stops—but there's lots to see along the way; stops could take a few hours, depending upon how long you stay in the Museo Nazionale di San Matteo.

What to See

⑬ **Battistero.** The Gothic Baptistery, which stands across from the Duomo's facade, is best known for the pulpit carved by Nicola Pisano in 1260. Ask one of the ticket takers if he'll sing for you inside the baptistery. The acoustics are remarkable; a tip of €3 is appropriate. ⊠ *Piazza del Duomo, Campo dei Miracoli* ☎ *050/561820* ⊕ *www.duomo.pisa.it* 💴 *€5* ⊙ *June 22–Sept. 21, daily 8–7:40; Mar. 22–June 21 and Sept. 22–Dec. 21, daily 9–5:40; Dec. 22–Mar. 21, daily 9–4:40.*

⑭ **Camposanto.** According to legend, the cemetery, a walled structure on the western side of the Campo dei Miracoli, is filled with earth from the Holy Land brought back by returning Crusaders. Contained within are numerous frescoes, notably the *Drunkenness of Noah* by Renaissance artist Benozzo Gozzoli and the disturbing *Triumph of Death* (14th century), whose authorship is disputed but whose subject matter shows what was on people's minds in a century that saw the ravages of the Black Death. ⊠ *Camposanto, Campo dei Miracoli* ☎ *050/561820* ⊕ *www.duomo. pisa.it* 💴 *€5* ⊙ *June 22–Sept. 21, daily 8–7:40; Mar. 22–June 21 and Sept. 22–Dec. 21, daily 9–5:40, Dec. 22–Mar. 21, daily 9–4:40.*

⑫ **Duomo.** Pisa's cathedral was the first building to use the horizontal marble stripe motif (borrowed from Moorish architecture in the 11th century) common with Tuscan cathedrals. It's famous for the Romanesque panels depicting the life of Christ on the transept door facing the tower and for its expertly carved 14th-century pulpit by Giovanni Pisano. ⊠ *Piazza del Duomo, Campo dei Miracoli* ☎ *050/561820* ⊕ *www.duomo. pisa.it* 💴 *€2, free Oct.–Mar.* ⊙ *June 22–Sept. 21, Mon.–Sat. 10–7:40, Sun. 1–7:40; Mar. 22–June 21 and Sept. 22–Dec. 21, Mon.–Sat., 10–7:40, Sun. 1–7:40; Dec. 22–Mar. 21, Mon.–Sat. 10–12:45, Sun. 3–4:45.*

★ ⑪ **Leaning Tower.** The Leaning Tower (Torre Pendente) provided the final grace note for the complex comprising the Duomo, Baptistery, and the Camposanto. Construction started in 1174, and the lopsided settling was evident by the time work began on the third story. The tower's architects attempted to compensate by making the remaining floors slightly taller on the leaning side, but the extra weight only made the problem worse. The settling continued, to a point that by the end of the 20th century many feared it would simply topple over, despite all efforts to prop the structure up. Now it has been firmly anchored to the earth. In early 2000, the final step of restoring the tower to its original tilt of 300 years ago was executed, and it appears to have been successful. After years of being closed, it is once again open to the public for climbing. Legend holds that Galileo conducted an experiment on the nature of

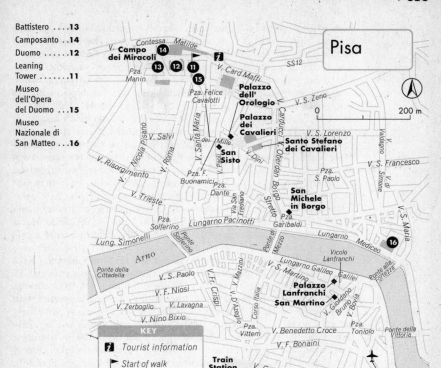

gravity by dropping metal balls from the top of the 187-ft-high tower; historians say this legend has no basis in fact (which is not quite to say that it is false). ✉ *Campo dei Miracoli* ☎ *050/560547* ⊕ *torre.duomo. pisa.it* ✑ *€15, reservations 050/835013 or www.duomo.pisa.it (€17 on line)* ☉ *Nov.–Mar., daily 9–5:50; Apr.–Oct., daily 8–8.*

⑮ Museo dell'Opera del Duomo. At the southeast corner of the sprawling Campo dei Miracoli, the museum holds a wealth of medieval sculptures and the ancient Roman sarcophagi that inspired the figures of Nicola Pisano (circa 1220–84). ✉ *Via Arcivescovado, Campo dei Miracoli* ☎ *050/560547* ⊕ *www.duomo.pisa.it* ✑ *€5* ☉ *June 22–Sept. 21, daily 8–7:20; Mar. 22–June 21 and Sept. 22–Dec. 21, daily 9–5:20; Dec. 22–Mar. 21, daily 9–4:20.*

⑯ Museo Nazionale di San Matteo. On the north bank of the Arno, this museum contains wonderful early Renaissance sculpture and a stunning reliquary by Donatello (circa 1386–1466). ✉ *Lungarno Mediceo, Lungarni* ☎ *050/541865* ✑ *€4.10* ☉ *Tues.–Sat. 9–7, Sun. 9–2.*

Where to Stay & Eat

★ **$$** ✕ **La Mescita.** This cheerful trattoria has high, vaulted brick ceilings and stenciled walls lined with colorful contemporary prints. What better place for the tasty and inventive food on offer: the *tagliolini con ragù bianco di anatra* (house-made thin noodles with minced duck in a delicate white wine sauce) is extraordinary. ✉ *Via Cavalca 2, Santa Maria* ☎ *050/544294* ▤ *AE, DC, MC, V* ☉ *Closed 3 wks in Jan., last 3 wks in Aug., and Mon. No lunch weekdays.*

$–$$ ✕ **Osteria dei Cavalieri.** This charming white-walled *osteria* a few steps from Piazza dei Cavalieri is reason enough to come to Pisa. The chef does it all—serves up grilled fish, pleases vegetarians, and prepares *tagliata* (thin slivers of rare beef) for meat lovers. There are three set menus, from the sea, garden, and earth, or you can order à la carte—which can be agonizing, because everything sounds so good. Finish your meal with a lemon sorbet bathed in Prosecco (dry sparkling wine), and walk away feeling you've eaten like a king at plebeian prices. ⊠ *Via San Frediano 16, Santa Maria* ☎ *050/580858* ⊟ *AE, DC, MC, V* ☉ *Closed Sun., July 25–Aug. 25, Dec. 29–Jan. 7. No lunch Sat.*

¢ ✕ **Vineria alla Piazza.** Translated, the name means, "wine store on the square," and the food here is as straightforward as the name: a simple blackboard lists two or three *primi* (first courses) as well as *secondi* (second courses). When the kitchen runs out, the offering is erased from the board and a new one added—a guarantee the food is made-that-moment fresh. The primi are particularly good, especially the light-as-a-feather *polenta gratinata al gorgonzola* (cornmeal mixed with gorgonzola and run briefly under the broiler). ⊠ *Piazza Vetto Vaglie, Santa Maria* ☎ *No phone* ⚐ *Reservations not accepted* ⊟ *No credit cards* ☉ *Closed Sun.*

$$ ▥ **Fattoria di Migliarino.** Martino Salviati and his wife Giovanna have turned their working *fattoria,* or farm (soy, corn, and sugar beets) 15 minutes northwest of Pisa into a working inn. It now has 10 charming, spacious apartments (accommodating from two to eight people) with rustic furnishings, each complete with kitchen and many with fireplaces. The pool is framed by fields, and the only sound you're likely to hear is the clucking of the hens they keep for eggs. The surrounding woods can be explored on horseback or with a mountain bike. During high season, there is a one-week minimum stay. ⊠ *Viale dei Pini 289, 56010 Migliarino* ☎ *050/803046* 🖷 *050/803170* ⬩ *10 apartments* ⚐ *Kitchenettes, pool, Ping-Pong, Internet; no room TVs* ⊟ *MC, V.*

$–$$ ▥ **Royal Victoria.** In a pleasant palazzo facing the Arno, a 10-minute walk from the Campo dei Miracoli, this hotel has been in the same family since 1837, and such continuity probably explains why Charles Dickens and Charles Lindberg, among others, have enjoyed staying here. It's comfortably furnished, with antiques and reproductions in the lobby and in some rooms, whose style ranges from the 1800s, complete with frescoes, to the 1920s. ⊠ *Lungarno Pacinotti 12, Lungarni, 56126* ☎ *050/940111* 🖷 *050/940180* ⊕ *www.royalvictoria.it* ⬩ *48 rooms, 40 with bath* ⚐ *Room service, cable TV, bar, baby-sitting, dry cleaning, laundry service, concierge, Internet, parking (fee), some pets allowed; no a/c in some rooms* ⊟ *AE, DC, MC, V.*

Nightlife & the Arts

The **Luminaria** feast day on June 16 honors San Ranieri, the patron saint of the city. Palaces along the Arno are lit with white lights, and there are plenty of fireworks; this is the city at its most beautiful.

HILL TOWNS SOUTHWEST OF FLORENCE

Submit to the draw of the enchanting fortified cities, many dating to the Etruscan period, crowning the hills west of Siena. San Gimignano, known as the "medieval Manhattan" because of its sprouting towers built by rival families, is perhaps the most heavily visited; but visitors are old hat to this Roman outpost, and with its tilted cobble streets and stout medieval buildings, the days of the Guelph-Ghibelline conflicts can seem palpable. Rising from a series of bleak gullied hills and valleys, Volterra has always been popular for its minerals and stones, particularly alabaster, which was used by the Etruscans for many implements, some now displayed in the exceptional and unwieldy Museo Etrusco Guarnacci. Blissfully off the tour-bus circuit, San Miniato is a peaceful hill town with a pleasant local museum and a convent where you can spend the night.

San Miniato

⓱ *42 km (26 mi) southeast of Pisa, 43 km (27 mi) southwest of Florence.*

Dating from Etruscan and Roman times, San Miniato was so named when the Lombards erected a church here in the 8th century and consecrated it to the saint. The Holy Roman Empire had very strong ties to San Miniato. Today the pristine, tiny hill town's narrow, cobbled streets are lined with austere facades dating from the 13th to 17th centuries. Its artistic treasures are on a par with some of the similar-size towns in the area, but the real reason for a trip is simply that the place is so pretty. St. Francis founded the 1211 **Convento e Chiesa di San Francesco** (Convent and Church of St. Francis), containing two cloisters and an ornate wooden choir. For a dose of monastic living, you can stay overnight. ✉ *Piazza San Francesco* ☎ *0571/43051* ⊙ *Daily 9–noon and 3–7; or ring bell.*

Although the **Museo Diocesano** is small, the collection has a number of subtle and pleasant works of art. Note the rather odd Fra Filippo Lippi *Crucifixion, Il Redentore* by Verrocchio (1435–88), and the small but sublime *Education of the Virgin,* by Tiepolo (1696–1770). ✉ *Piazza del Castello* ☎ *0571/418071* 🎫 *€1* ⊙ *Nov.–Mar., weekends 9–noon and 2:30–5; Apr.–Oct., Tues.–Sun. 9–noon and 2:30–5.*

Where to Stay

¢ 🏨 **Convento di San Francesco.** For a complete change of pace, stay in this 13th-century convent in the company of five Franciscan friars. Rooms are simple, bordering on spartan, but clean and quiet. You are given keys, so you're not expected back by any certain time. You can partake in some spiritual activities or skip them altogether. All rooms have baths, and there are five rooms that groups can rent. It's a 10-minute walk from the town center. ✉ *Piazza San Francesco, 56020* ☎ *0571/43051* 🖷 *0571/ 43398* 🛏 *30 rooms* ⚒ No a/c, no room phones, no room TVs, no kids under 12 ⊟ No credit cards.

Volterra

⓲ *50 km (31 mi) west of Siena, 27 km (17 mi) southwest of San Gimignano.*

Unlike other Tuscan hill towns that rise above sprawling vineyards and rolling fields of green, Volterra—described by D. H. Lawrence in his *Etruscan Places* as standing "somber and chilly alone on her rock"—is surrounded by desolate terrain marred with industry and mining equipment. The fortress, walls, and gates still stand mightily over Le Balze, a stunning series of gullied hills and valleys to the west that were formed by irregular erosion. The town has long been known for its alabaster, which has been mined since Etruscan times; today the Volterrans use it to make ornaments and souvenirs sold all over town. A €7 combined ticket allows entry to the Museo Etrusco Guarnacci, the Pinacoteca e Museo Civico, and the Museo di Arte Sacra.

Volterra has some of Italy's best small museums. The extraordinarily large and unique collection of the **Museo Etrusco Guarnacci** is an enigma in a region from which many of the Etruscan artifacts have landed in state museums and at the Vatican. If only a curator had thought to cull the best of the 700 funerary urns rather than to display every last one of them. ✉ *Via Don Minzoni 15* ☎ *0588/86347* 🎫 *Combined ticket €7* ⊙ *Mar. 16–Nov. 3, daily 9–7; Nov. 4–Mar. 15, daily 9–2.*

The **Pinacoteca e Museo Civico** houses a highly acclaimed collection of religious art, including a *Madonna and Child with Saints* by Luca Signorelli (1445/50–1523) and a *Deposition* by Rosso Fiorentino (1494–1541) that is reason enough to visit Volterra. ✉ *Via dei Sarti 1* ☎ *0588/87580* ⊕ *www.comune.volterra.pi.it* 🎫 *Combined ticket €7* ⊙ *Mar. 16–Nov. 3, daily 9–7; Nov. 4–Mar. 15, daily 9–2.*

The impressive facade of the medieval **Palazzo dei Priori** is adorned with Florentine coats of arms, medallions, and a large five-sided tower. Although you can go in, what's really of interest is the outside. ✉ *Piazza dei Priori* ☎ *0588/87257* 🎫 *€1* ⊙ *Weekdays 10–1, weekends 2–6.*

Next to the altar in the town's unfinished **Duomo** is a magnificent 13th-century carved wood *Deposition*. Note the fresco by Benozzo Gozzoli (1420–97) in the Cappella della Addolorata. Along the left wall of the nave you can see the arrival of the magi. ✉ *Piazza San Giovanni* ☎ *0588/86192* ⊙ *Daily 7–7.*

Original works from the Duomo and adjacent Baptistery are in the **Museo Diocesano di Arte Sacra.** ✉ *Via Roma 1* ☎ *0588/86290* 🎫 *Combined ticket €7* ⊙ *Mar. 16–Nov. 3, daily 9–1 and 3–6; Nov. 4–Mar. 15, daily 9–1.*

Among Volterra's best-preserved ancient remains is the Etruscan **Porta all'Arco,** an arch dating from the 4th century BC now incorporated into the city walls. The ruins of the 1st-century BC **Teatro Romano,** one of the best-preserved Roman theaters in Italy, are worth a visit. Adjacent to the theater are the remains of the **Roman terme** (baths). The theater complex is just outside the walls past Porta Fiorentina. ✉ *Viale Francesco Ferrucci* 🎫 *€2* ⊙ *Mar.–Nov., daily 10–1 and 2–5:45; Dec.–Feb., weekends 10–1 and 2–5* ⊙ *Closed when it rains.*

Where to Stay & Eat

$–$$ ✕ **Il Sacco Fiorentino.** The understated tone of this small, two-room restaurant gives nothing away—its white walls, tile floors, and pink table-cloths are unremarkable. You'll forgive the lack of ambience, however, once the food starts arriving. The *antipasti del Sacco Fiorentino* is a medley of sautéed chicken liver, porcini, and polenta drizzled with balsamic vinegar. It just gets better: the *tagliatelle del Sacco Fiorentino* is a riot of curried spaghetti with chicken and roasted red peppers. ✉ *Piazza XX Settembre 18* ☎ *0588/88537* 🖃 *AE, DC, MC, V* ⊙ *Closed Wed.*

$ 🏨 **San Lino.** This hotel, once a convent, has wood beams and terra-cotta floors paired with modern-day comforts. It's within the town walls and a 10-minute walk from the main piazza. The restaurant, open only for guests and groups of 20 or more, serves regional specialties, including *zuppa alla volteranna*, a thick vegetable soup. ✉ *Via San Lino 26, 56048* ☎ *0588/85250* 🖷 *0588/80620* ⊕ *www.hotelsanlino.com* 🛏 *43 rooms* ⚑ *Restaurant, minibars, pool, dry cleaning, laundry service, concierge, Internet, parking (fee); no a/c in some rooms* 🖃 *AE, DC, MC, V* ⊙ *Closed Nov.–Jan.*

Shopping

A number of shops in Volterra sell boxes, jewelry, and other objects made of alabaster. The **Cooperativa Artieri Alabastro** (✉ Piazza dei Priori 5 ☎ 0588/87590) has two large showrooms of alabaster pieces. In what was once a medieval monastery, the **Galleria Agostiniane** (✉ Piazza XX Settembre 3 ☎ 0588/86868) crafts alabaster objects of all kinds. You can see a free video on how the mineral is quarried and carved. At **Camillo**

Rossi (✉ Via Lungo le Mura del Mandorlo 7 ☎ 0588/86133) you can actually see the craftspeople at work, creating alabaster objects for all tastes and budgets.

San Gimignano

19 *27 km (17 mi) east of Volterra, 57 km (35 mi) southwest of Florence.*

When you're high on a hill surrounded by centuries-old towers silhouetted against the blue sky, it's difficult not to fall under the medieval spell of San Gimignano. Its high walls and narrow streets are typical of Tuscan hill towns, but it is the surviving medieval "skyscrapers" that set the town apart from its neighbors and create its uniquely photogenic silhouette. Today 15 towers remain, but at the height of the Guelph-Ghibelline conflict there was a forest of more than 70, and it was possible to cross the town by rooftop rather than road. The towers were built partly to defend the town—they provided a safe refuge and were useful for pouring boiling oil on attacking enemies—and partly to bolster the egos of their owners, who competed with deadly seriousness to build the highest tower in town. When the Black Death devastated the population in 1348, power and independence faded fast and civic autonomy was ultimately surrendered to Florence.

Today San Gimignano isn't much more than a gentrified walled city, amply prepared for its booming tourist trade but still very much worth exploring. Despite the remarkable profusion of chintzy souvenir shops lining its main drag, there's some serious Renaissance art to be seen here and an equally important local wine (Vernaccia) to be savored. Escape at midday to the uninhabited areas outside the city walls for a hike and a picnic, and return to explore the town in the afternoon and evening, when things quiet down and the long shadows cast by the imposing towers take on fascinating shapes. You can buy two types of combination tickets for the sights; one costs €7.50 and covers just about everything, while the other costs €5.50 and is slightly more limited.

San Gimignano's most important medieval buildings are clustered around the central **Piazza del Duomo.** The imposing **Torre Grossa** is the biggest tower in town, with views that are well worth the climb. ✉ *Piazza del Duomo 1* ☎ *0577/940008* ✍ *€5* ⊙ *Mar.–Oct., daily 9:30–7:20; Nov.–Feb., daily 10–5:50.*

The **Palazzo del Popolo** houses the **Museo Civico,** featuring Taddeo di Bartolo's celebratory scenes from the life of San Gimignano. The town's namesake was a bishop of Modena who achieved sainthood by driving hordes of barbarians out of the city in the 10th century. Dante visited San Gimignano as an ambassador from Florence for only a single day in 1300, but it was long enough to get a room named after him, which now holds a *Maestà* by 14th-century artist Lippo Memmi. A small room contains frescoes by Memmo di Filippuccio (active 1288–1324) depicting a young couple's courtship, shared bath, and wedding. The highly charged eroticism of the frescoes may be explained, in part, by the fact that they were in what were probably the private rooms of the commune's chief magistrate. ✉ *Piazza del Duomo* ☎ *0577/940008* ✍ *Museo Civico €5* ⊙ *Mar.–Oct., daily 9:30–7:20; Nov.–Feb., daily 10–5:50.*

★ The Romanesque **Collegiata** is a treasure trove of frescoes, including Bartolo di Fredi's cycle of scenes from the Old Testament on the left nave wall dating from 1367. Taddeo di Bartolo's otherworldly *Last Judgment,* on the arch just inside the facade, depicts distorted and suffering nudes—avant-garde stuff for the 1390s. The New Testament scenes on the right wall, which may have been executed by Barna da Siena in the 1330s, suggest a more reserved, balanced Renaissance manner. The **Cappella di Santa Fina** contains glorious frescoes depicting the story of this local saint by Domenico Ghirlandaio (1449–94). ✉ *Piazza del Duomo* ☎ *0577/940316* 🎫 *€3.50* ⊙ *Mar.–Oct., weekdays 9:30–7:30, Sat. 9:30–5, Sun. 1–5; Nov.–Jan. 20, Mon.–Sat. 9:30–5, Sun. 1–5.*

The **Museo di Criminologia Medievale** (Museum of Medieval Criminology) displays cutting-edge medieval torture technology, along with operating instructions and a clear description of the intended effect. Though some scholars dispute the historical accuracy of many of the instruments displayed, the final, very contemporary object—an electric chair imported from the United States—does give pause. ✉ *Via del Castello 1–3* ☎ *0577/ 942243* 🎫 *€8* ⊙ *Mar. 16–July 18, daily 10–7; July 19–Sept. 17, daily 10–midnight; Sept. 18–Nov. 1, weekdays 10–7, weekends 10–8; Nov. 2–Mar. 15, Mon.–Sat. 10–6, Sun. 10–7.*

Before leaving San Gimignano, be sure to see its most revered work of art, at the northern end of town, in the church of **Sant'Agostino**: Benozzo Gozzoli's utterly stunning 15th-century fresco cycle depicting scenes from the life of St. Augustine. ✉ *Piazza Sant'Agostino* ☎ *0577/907012* ⊙ *Nov.–Mar., daily 7–noon and 3–6; Apr.–Oct., daily 7–noon and 3–7.*

Where to Stay & Eat

$$ ✕ **La Mangiatoia.** Gaily colored gingham tablecloths provide an interesting juxtaposition with rib-vaulted ceilings dating from the 13th century in this cozy spot. The lighthearted feminine touch might be explained by chef Susi Cuomo, who has been presiding over her kitchen for more than 20 years. The menu is seasonal—in the autumn, don't miss her *filetto d'anatra con tartufo* (truffled duck breast), and in the summer enjoy lighter fare on the intimate, flower-bedecked terrace in the back. ✉ *Via Mainardi 5, off Via San Matteo* ☎ *0577/941528* ☐ *MC, V* ⊙ *Closed Tues., 3 wks in Nov., and 1 wk in Jan.*

¢ ✕ **Enoteca Gustavo.** The ebullient Maristella Becucci reigns supreme in this tiny wine bar (three small tables in the back, two in the bar, two bar stools) serving divine, and ample, crostini. The *crostino con carciofini e pecorino* (toasted bread with artichokes topped with semi-aged pecorino) packs a punch. So, too, does the selection of wines by the glass: the changing list has about 16 reds and whites, mostly local, all good. The cheese plate is a bit more expensive than the other offerings, but it's worth it. ✉ *Via San Matteo 29* ☎ *0577/940057* ⚲ *Reservations not accepted* ☐ *MC, V* ⊙ *Closed Tues.*

$–$$ ✕🏠 **Bel Soggiorno.** One wall of the spacious restaurant here ($$–$$$) is glass, and beyond it is a sweeping view of Tuscan hillside. The dining room is simple and rustic; the food, however, is not: the *petto di faraona con mele condite, salsa al miele e pecorino di fossa* (breast of guinea fowl with apples, honey, and aged pecorino) is a real treat. The restaurant and the hotel attached to it, with simple, airy rooms, have been in the same family since 1886. If you're looking for a place right within the walls of town, look no further. ✉ *Via San Giovanni 91, 53037* ☎ *0577/ 940375* 🖷 *0577/940375* ⊕ *www.hotelbelsoggiorno.it* ⇨ *17 rooms, 4 suites* ⚘ *Restaurant, cable TV, minibar, baby-sitting, dry cleaning, parking (fee)* ☐ *AE, DC, MC, V* ⊙ *Closed Jan. 6–Feb., restaurant closed Wed.*

$–$$ 🏠 **Pescille.** A rambling farmhouse 4 km (2½ mi) outside San Gimignano has been transformed into a handsome hotel with understated contemporary and country classic motifs. From this charming spot you get a splendid view of San Gimignano and its towers. ✉*Località Pescille, Strada Castel San Gimignano, 53037* ☎*0577/940186* 🖷*0577/943165* ⊕*www. pescille.it* ⇨ *38 rooms, 12 suites* ⚘ *Cable TV, bar, tennis court, pool, gym, Internet, free parking; no a/c in some rooms* ☐ *AE, DC, MC, V* ⊙ *Closed Nov.–Mar.*

Colle Val d'Elsa

⓴ *50 km (31 mi) south of Florence, 24 km (15 mi) northwest of Siena.*

On the road from Florence to Siena, Colle Val d'Elsa rises dramatically along a winding road. Its narrow streets strongly evoke the Middle Ages; they are lined with palazzi dating from the 15th and 16th centuries. For art enthusiasts, it's perhaps best known as the birthplace of Arnolfo di Cambio (circa 1245–1310), architect of Florence's Duomo. Once a formidable producer of wool, the town now produces glass and crystal sold in local shops. Colle has two distinct parts: the relatively modern and less interesting Colle Bassa and the older Colle Alta.

The **Museo Archeologico,** in Palazzo Pretoria, has a small collection of Etruscan objects, including some fascinating vases and funerary objects. ⊠ *Piazza del Duomo 42* ☎ *0577/922954* ✎ *€1.55* ⊘ *Apr.–Sept., Tues.–Fri. 10–noon and 4:45–6:45, weekends 10–noon and 4:30–7:30; Oct.–Mar., Tues.–Fri. 3:30–5:30.*

The **Museo d'Arte Sacra,** just down the street from the Museo Archeologico, displays religious relics as well as triptychs from the Sienese and Florentine schools dating to the 14th and 15th centuries. The **Museo Civico,** which shares the building with the Museo d'Arte Sacra, proudly displays the town's tribute to Arnolfo di Cambio, with photos of the buildings he designed for other towns and some models of the town. Down Via del Castello, at No. 63, is the house-tower where Arnolfo was born in 1245. (It's not open to the public.) ⊠ *Via del Castello 33* ☎ *0577/923888* ✎ *€2.60 for both museums* ⊘ *Apr.–Oct., Tues.–Sun. 10–noon and 4–7; Nov.–Mar., weekends 10–noon and 3:30–6:30.*

Where to Stay & Eat

★ **$$$$** ✕ **Ristorante Arnolfo.** Food lovers should not miss Arnolfo, one of Tuscany's most highly regarded restaurants. Chef Gaetano Trovato sets high standards of creativity; his sublime dishes daringly ride the line between innovation and tradition, almost always with spectacular results. The menu changes frequently and has two fixed-price options, but you are always sure to find fish in the summer and lots of fresh vegetables and herbs. The location is a tranquil spot in the center of town. ⊠ *Piazza XX Settembre 52* ☎ *0577/920549* ☰ *AE, DC, MC, V* ⊘ *Closed Tues., mid-Jan.–mid-Feb., and 2 wks in Aug.*

★ **$$$$** ▦ **La Suvera.** Pope Julius II once owned this luxurious estate in the valley of the River Elsa, 28 km (17 mi) west of Siena and 56 km (33 mi) south of Florence. The papal villa and adjacent building have magnificently furnished guest rooms and suites appointed with antiques and modern comforts. La Suvera's first-rate facilities, including drawing rooms, a library, an Italian garden, a park, and the Oliviera restaurant (serving estate wines), make it hard to tear yourself away. ⊠ *Pievescola (Casola d'Elsa), off SS541, 53030* ☎ *0577/960300* 🖷 *0577/960220* ⊕ *www.lasuvera.it* ⇆ *16 rooms, 16 suites* ⚿ *Room service, restaurant, in-room safes, minibars, cable TV, tennis court, pool, exercise equipment, massage, Turkish bath, mountain bikes, bar, library, dry cleaning, laundry service, concierge, Internet, meeting room; no kids under 12* ☰ *AE, DC, MC, V* ⊘ *Closed Nov.–Easter.*

CHIANTI

Directly south of Florence is the Chianti district, one of Italy's most famous wine-producing areas; its hill towns, olive groves, and vineyards are quintessential Tuscany. Many British and northern Europeans have relocated here, drawn by the unhurried life, balmy climate, and charming villages; there are so many Britons, in fact, that the area has been nicknamed Chiantishire. Still, it remains strongly Tuscan in character, and you'll be drawn to the views framing vine-quilted hills and elegantly elongated cypress trees.

The sinuous SS222, known as the Strada Chiantigiana, runs from Florence through the heart of Chianti. Its most scenic section connects Strada in Chianti, 16 km (10 mi) south of Florence, and Greve in Chianti, whose triangular central piazza is surrounded by restaurants and vintners offering *degustazioni* (wine tastings), 11 km (7 mi) farther south.

Greve in Chianti

㉑ *27 km (17 mi) south of Florence, 40 km (25 mi) north of Siena.*

If there is a capital of Chianti, it is Greve, a friendly market town with no shortage of cafés, enoteche, and craft shops lining its main piazza. The sloping, asymmetrical **Piazza Matteotti** is attractively arcaded and has a statue of Giovanni da Verrazano (circa 1480–1528), the explorer who discovered New York harbor, in the center. At one end of the piazza is the **Chiesa di Santa Croce**, with works from the school of Fra Angelico (circa 1400–55). ✉ *Piazza Matteotti* ☉ *Daily 9–1 and 3–7.*

Where to Stay & Eat

★ **$–$$** ✕ **Ristoro di Lamole.** The location is off the beaten path (in this case, the SS222), on a narrow, winding road lined with olive trees and vineyards, but it's worth the effort to find this place: the view from the outdoor terrace is divine, and so is the food. You'll find simple Tuscan cuisine, exquisitely prepared. Start with the bruschetta drizzled with olive oil or the sublime *verdure sott'olio* (vegetables marinated in oil) before moving on to any of the fine secondi. The kitchen has a way with *coniglio* (rabbit); don't pass it up if it's on the menu. ✉ *Lamole in Chianti* ☎ *055/8547050* ▭ *MC, V* ☉ *Closed Jan. 7–Feb.*

$$–$$$$ ▨ **Villa Vignamaggio.** This historic estate has guest rooms and apartments in a villa, as well as two small houses and a cottage on the grounds. The villa, surrounded by manicured classical Italian gardens, dates from the 14th century but was restored in the 16th. It's reputedly the birthplace of Monna Lisa, the woman later made famous by Leonardo da Vinci. The place also does tastings of its very fine wine; inquire at reception to organize a tasting. ✉ *Via Petriolo 5, 50022* ☎ *055/ 854661* 🖷 *055/8544468* ⊕ *www.vignamaggio.com* ⇴ *2 rooms, 15 apartments, 1 cottage, 2 houses* ♿ *Minibars, tennis court, 2 pools, playground, some pets allowed, no-smoking rooms* ▭ *DC, MC, V* ☉ *Closed Dec. 23–Jan. 6* ⍾ *EP.*

$ ▨ **Castello Vicchiomaggio.** Formerly a fortified castle, this building, now a prestigious wine estate with a tasting facility you can visit, dates from 956 and was rebuilt during the Renaissance. Throughout the nine apartments and two farmhouses is wonderful heavy wooden furniture, in keeping with the estate's history. The restaurant serves homemade pastas and specialties such as *stracotto*, beef cooked in the farm's own prize-winning Chianti Classico. ✉ *Via Vicchiomaggio 4, 50022* ☎ *055/854079* 🖷 *055/853911* ⊕ *www.vicchiomaggio.it* ⇴ *8 apartments, 2 farmhouses* ♿ *Restaurant, in-room safes, kitchenettes, refrigerators, cable TV, pool; no a/c* ▭ *MC, V* ⍾ *EP.*

Panzano

㉒ *7 km (4½ mi) south of Greve, 29 km (18 mi) south of Florence.*

With its magnificent views, Panzano is one of the prettiest stops in Chianti. The town centerpiece is the church of **Santa Maria Assunta**, where you can see an *Annunciation* attributed to Michele di Ridolfo del Ghirlandaio (1503–77). ✉ *Panzano Alto* 🕑 *Daily 7–noon and 4–6.*

Ancient even by Chianti standards, the hilltop church of **San Leolino** probably dates from the 10th century, but it was completely rebuilt in the Romanesque style sometime in the 13th century. The 3-km (2-mi) trip south of Panzano is worth it for the church's exterior simplicity and 14th-century cloister. The 16th-century terra-cotta tabernacles are attributed to Giovanni della Robbia, and there's also a remarkable triptych attributed to the Master of Panzano that was executed sometime in the mid-14th century. Check with the **tourist office in Greve** (✉ Viale Giovanni da Verrazano 33 ☎ 055/8546287) for open days and hours. ✉ *Località San Leolino* ☎ *No phone* 🎫 *Free.*

Where to Stay & Eat

$–$$ ✕ **Oltre il Giardino.** An ancient stone house has been converted into a tasteful dining area with a large terrace and spectacular views of the valley. Try to book a table in time to watch the sunset. The menu captures a little more fantasy than typical Tuscan cuisine. Try the *tagliatelle all'anatra* (a flat noodle tossed with a savory duck sauce) or the *peposo* (a beef stew laced with black pepper). On the weekends, reservations are a must. ✉ *Piazza G. Bucciarelli 42* ☎ *055/852828* 🖃 *DC, MC, V* 🕑 *Closed Mon. and Nov.*

$$$$ 🏨 **Villa La Barone.** Formerly the home of the Viviani della Robbia family, this 16th-century villa retains many aspects of a private home. The honor bar allows you either to enjoy an aperitivo in the tile barroom or on the terrace while admiring the view. And there are views here in abundance, from the pool to the rose garden to the back of the villa. Guest rooms have tile floors, white walls, and timber ceilings. The meal plan is mandatory, and the restaurant is open to guests only. ✉ *Via San Leolino 19, 50020 Località di Panzano* ☎ *055/852621* 🖷 *055/852277* 🛏 *30 rooms* 🍴 *Dining room, tennis court, pool, baby-sitting, laundry service, concierge, Internet; no a/c in some rooms* 🖃 *AE, MC, V* 🕑 *Closed Nov.–Easter* 🍽 *MAP.*

Radda in Chianti

★ ㉓ *33 km (20 mi) south of Greve, 52 km (32 mi) south of Florence.*

Radda in Chianti sits on a hill separating Val di Pesa from Val d'Arbia. It's one of many tiny Chianti villages that invite you to stroll through its steep streets and follow the signs that point you toward the *camminamento*, a covered medieval passageway circling part of the city inside the walls. In Piazza Ferrucci, you'll find the **Palazzo del Podestà**, or Palazzo Comunale, the city hall that has served the people of Radda for more than four centuries. It has 51 coats of arms embedded in its facade. ✉ *Piazza Ferrucci.*

off the beaten path

VOLPAIA – Perched atop a hill 10 km (6 mi) north of Radda is this fairy-tale hamlet, a military outpost from the 10th to 16th centuries and once a shelter for religious pilgrims. Every July, for the Festa di San Lorenzo, people come to Volpaia to watch for falling stars and a traditional fireworks display put on by the family that owns the adjacent wine estate and agriturismo lodging, **Castello di Volpaia** (✉ Piazza della Cisterna 1, 53017 ☎ 0577/738066).

Where to Stay & Eat

¢ ✕ **Osteria Le Panzanelle.** Nada Michelassi and Silvia Bonechi combined their accumulated wisdom in the hotel and restaurant worlds to create this hospitable place a few minutes outside Radda. Its small but care-

BACCHUS IN TUSCANY

TUSCANY IS ITALY'S CLASSIC wine country. In addition to the world-famous Chianti, one of Italy's top wine exports, Tuscan winemakers produce other renowned wines. Many of these are recognizable by the DOCG (Denominazione di Origine Controllata e Garantita) or DOC (Denominazione di Origine Controllata) on their labels, notations that identify the wine within not only as coming from the officially delineated wine regions but also as adhering to rigorous standards of production. Don't be afraid to sample something that doesn't bear this label, however; Tuscans have been making wine for 25 centuries, and DOC or not, most of the winemakers here seem to know what they're doing.

Vino Nobile di Montepulciano, the "Noble Wine," lays claim to its aristocratic title by virtue of royal patronage and ancient history: the Etruscans were making wine here before Rome had even been founded. Much later, in 1669, England's William III sent a delegation to Montepulciano in order to procure this splendid wine. It was an appropriate choice: according to poet Francesco Redi, "Montepulciano d'ogni vino è il re" ("of all wine, Montepulciano is the king"). The less noble but no less popular **Rosso di Montepulciano,** a light, fruity DOC red, is also produced in the area.

With its velvety black berries and structured tannins, **Brunello di Montalcino** is just as sophisticated as Vino Nobile. The strain of the Sangiovese grape variety used to make it was developed in 1870 by a local winemaker in need of vines that would be better able to cope with windy weather. The wine became popular quickly and remained so—it had such success that in 1988 Italy's then-president Francesco Cossiga presided over the centennial of its first vintage. Brunello has a younger sibling, the DOC **Rosso di Montalcino.**

Not all of Tuscany's great wines are reds; in fact, many give the region's highest honors to a white wine, **Vernaccia di San Gimignano.** This golden wine is made from grapes native to Liguria, and it's thought that its name is a corruption of Vernazza, a village that's part of the Ligurian coast's Cinque Terre. Pope Martin IV (1281–85) used to like his with eel; you might try it with rabbit, sausage, or prosciutto and other cured meats.

To the foreigner, **Chianti** evokes Tuscany as readily as gondolas evoke Venice, but if you think Chianti is about straw-covered jugs and deadly headaches, think again. This firm, full-bodied, and powerful wine pressed from mostly Sangiovese grapes is the region's most popular, and it's easy to taste why. More difficult to understand is the difference between the many kinds of Chianti: this DOCG region has seven subregions, including Chianti Classico, the oldest wine-growing area of the region, whose wines can be identified by a gallo nero (black rooster) on the label. Each of these (Chianti Classico, Colli Fiorentini, Colli Senesi, Colli Aretini, Colline Pisane, Montalbano, and Rufina) has its own particularities, but the most noticeable—and costly—difference to keep in mind is that between regular Chianti and the riserva (reserve) stock, aged for at least four years.

Some Italian winemakers, chafing at the strict limitations imposed upon them when making Chianti, sought to break free of the chains by mixing wines the way they wanted, paying little heed to the well-defined recipe. Thus was born the so-called **Super Tuscan,** a largely fanciful title dreamed up by North American journalists. But there's nothing fanciful (or inexpensive) about these French oak–aged wines, which are the toast of Tuscany—and most of the rest of Italy.

fully crafted menu has typical tastes of Tuscany (such as the exquisite *trippa alla fiorentina*). Then there are unexpected treats such as the *crostone con salsiccia fresca* (toasted bread with fresh sausage). Two small, simple rooms and tables outdoors provide the setting to the tasty fare. The wine list, equally well-thought out, is particularly strong on the local product—in this case, Chianti Classico and Super Tuscans. ⊠ *Località Lucarellia 29* ☎ *0577/733 511* ⊟ *MC, V* ⊗ *Closed Mon.*

★ $$$–$$$$ ✕⛺ **Relais Fattoria Vignale.** On the outside, it's an unadorned manor house with an annex across the street. Inside, it's refined country-house comfortable, with terra-cotta floors, sitting rooms, and nice stone- and woodwork. White rooms with exposed brick and wood beams contain simple wooden bed frames and furniture, charming rugs and prints, and modern white-tile bathrooms. The grounds, lined with vineyards and olive trees, are equally inviting, with lawns, terraces, and a pool. The sophisticated Ristorante Vignale ($$$) serves excellent wines and Tuscan specialties; the in-house enoteca ($$$), simpler Tuscan fare. ⊠ *Via Pianigiani 9, 53017* ☎ *Hotel 0577/738300; restaurant 0577/738094; enoteca 0577/738701* 🖷 *0577/738592* ⊕ *www.vignale.it* ➭ *35 rooms, 5 suites* ⅙ *2 restaurants, in-room safes, minibars, cable TV, pool, bar, wine shop, baby-sitting, laundry service, library, concierge, Internet, meeting room, free parking, no-smoking rooms* ⊟ *AE, DC, MC, V* ⊗ *Closed 3 wks in Jan., restaurant closed Thurs., enoteca closed Wed.*

$$$ ⛺ **Palazzo Leopoldo.** A former 15th-century palazzo has been turned into an invitingly intimate small hotel on Radda's main street. Rooms have high ceilings, and a contemporary interpretation of neoclassicism predominates. Chandeliers, in some of the suites and in public rooms, are 19th century, hand-crafted reproductions of Venetian Renaissance originals. The staff speaks English, the tasty breads at breakfast are made locally, and when it's warm, there's an inviting terrace. A spa has beauty treatments, and the restaurant serves mostly Tuscan food. ⊠ *Via Roma 33, 53017* ☎ *0577/735605* 🖷 *0577/738031* ⊕ *www.palazzoleopoldo. it* ➭ *8 rooms, 9 suites* ⅙ *Restaurant, room service, in-room data ports, in-room safes, kitchenettes in some rooms, minibars, refrigerators, cable TV, massage, hot tub, sauna, spa, bar, baby-sitting, dry cleaning, laundry service, concierge, Internet, meeting room, free parking, some pets allowed, no-smoking rooms* ⊟ *AE, DC, MC, V* ⊗ *Closed Jan.–Feb.* ⓉⓄⓁ *BP, MAP, FAP.*

¢   ⛺ **La Bottega di Giovannino.** The name is actually that of the *alimentari* (grocery store) run by Giovannino Bernardoni, who also rents rooms in his house just next door. This is a fantastic place for the budget-conscious traveler, as rooms are immaculate and beds comfortable. Most of the rooms have a stunning view of the surrounding hills. All rooms have their own bath, though most of them necessitate taking a short trip outside one's room. ⊠ *Via Roma 6–8, 53017* ☎ *0577/738056* ➭ *10 rooms* ⅙ *Bar; no A/C, no room phones, no room TVs* ⊟ *No credit cards* ⓉⓄⓁ *EP.*

Castellina in Chianti

㉔   *14 km (8 mi) west of Radda, 21 km (13 mi) north of Siena.*

Castellina in Chianti, or simply Castellina, is on a ridge above the Val di Pesa, Val d'Arbia, and Val d'Elsa, and the panorama is bucolic in most every direction you look. The imposing 15th-century tower hints at the history of this village, which was an outpost during the continuing wars between Florence and Siena.

Where to Stay

$$ ⛺ **Palazzo Squarcialupi.** A refurbished 15th-century palace on the main street in town offers a pleasant, restful place to stay. Rooms have high

ceilings, white walls, and tile floors; bathrooms are tiled in local stone. Many of the rooms have a view of the valley below. Common areas are elegant but comfortable, and the breakfast buffet is ample. The multilingual staff goes out of its way to be helpful. Though there's no restaurant, the hotel will arrange for a light lunch during the warmer months. ✉ *Via Ferruccio 22, 53011* ☎ *0577/741186* 🖷 *0577/740386* ⊕ *www. chiantiandrelax.com* 🛏 *9 rooms, 8 suites* ♢ *Cable TV, pool, bar, babysitting, dry cleaning, laundry service, Internet, free parking, some pets allowed* ▤ *AE, DC, MC, V* ☾ *Closed Nov.–Mar.*

$–$$ 🏠 **Collelungo.** One of the loveliest *agriturismi* in the area, Collelungo consists of a series of abandoned farmhouses that have been carefully remodeled. Set amid a notable vineyard (it produces internationally recognized Chianti Classico), the apartments—all with cooking facilities and dining areas—have exposed stone walls and that typical Tuscan tile floor. The *salone* (lounge), which dates possibly to the 14th century, has satellite TV; adjacent to it is an honor bar. In high season, a minimum one-week stay is required. ✉ *Podere Collungo 53011* ☎🖷 *0577/ 740489* ⊕ *www.collelungo.it* 🛏 *12 apartments* ♢ *Pool, bar, laundry service, free parking; no a/c, no room phones, no room TVs, no kids under 8* ▤ *AE, DC, MC, V* ☾ *Closed Nov.–Mar.*

SIENA

One of Italy's most enchanting medieval cities, Siena is the one city you should visit in Tuscany if you visit no other. Florence's great historical rival was in all likelihood founded by the Etruscans. During the late Middle Ages, it was both wealthy and powerful, for it saw the birth of the world's oldest bank, the Monte dei Paschi, still very much in business. It was bitterly envied by Florence, which in 1254 sent forces that besieged the city for more than a year, reducing its population by half and laying waste to the countryside. The city was finally absorbed by the grand duchy of Tuscany, ruled by Florence, in 1559.

Sienese identity is still defined by its 17 medieval *contrade* (neighborhoods), each with its own church, museum, and symbol. Look for streetlights painted in the contrada's colors, plaques displaying its symbol, and statues embodying the spirit of the neighborhood. The various contrade uphold ancient rivalries during the centuries-old Palio, a twice-yearly horse race (held in July and August) around the main piazza.

Exploring Siena

Practically unchanged since medieval times, Siena stretches over the slopes of three steep hills, but you will find the most interesting sights in a fairly compact area. Be sure to leave some time to wander off the main streets. Most sights are concentrated in the pedestrian-only centro storico, so you will end up walking up and down a lot of steep streets. If you only have one day in Siena, see the Piazza del Campo, the Duomo and its Museo dell'Opera Metropolitana, and the Palazzo Pubblico. If you are seeing more sights, it will probably be worthwhile to buy a cumulative ticket (valid for three days, €7.50), good for entrance to the Duomo's Biblioteca Piccolomini, Battistero, and the Museo dell'Opera Metropolitana. If you can overnight here, by all means do so: the city is filled with day-trippers and tour buses, and in the late afternoon and evening it empties out. Siena's medieval charm and narrow streets are thrown into high relief, and Piazza il Campo positively glows.

From Florence, there are two basic routes to Siena. The speedy modern SS2 is good if you're making a day trip from Florence, as it's a four-lane divided highway. For a jaunt through Chianti, take the narrower and more meandering SS222, known as the Strada Chiantigiana. It's a gorgeous ride on only two lanes—patience is a necessity.

a good walk

Begin at the **Piazza del Campo** ㉕ ☞, one of Italy's finest squares, and visit the **Palazzo Pubblico** ㉖ and climb its adjacent tower, the Torre del Mangia. Cross the piazza and exit on the stairs to the left to Via di Città, one of Siena's main shopping streets. Up on the left is the enchanting Palazzo Chigi-Saracini, where concerts are often held. Step in to admire the especially well-preserved courtyard and cistern. Continue up the hill and take the second right, Via del Capitano, which leads to Piazza del Duomo. The **Duomo** ㉗ is a must-see, along with its **Battistero** ㉘ and **Museo dell'Opera Metropolitana** ㉙. Opposite the front of the Duomo is the **Spedale di Santa Maria della Scala** ㉚. Chief among Siena's other gems is the **Pinacoteca Nazionale** ㉛, a short walk straight back down Via del Capitano (which becomes Via San Pietro). The church of **San Domenico** ㉜ lies in the other direction; you could take Via della Galluzza to Via della Sapienza.

TIMING

This walk should last a full day, taken at a leisurely pace and allowing some time to relax in the Piazza del Campo. Allow two days to really explore Siena. The *passeggiata* (evening stroll) along the main shopping streets should not be missed. Keep in mind that most shops are closed on Sunday and museums have variable hours.

What to See

㉘ **Battistero.** The Duomo's 14th-century Gothic Baptistery was built to prop up one side of the Duomo. There are frescoes throughout, but the highlight is a large bronze 15th-century baptismal font designed by Jacopo della Quercia and adorned with bas-reliefs by various artists, including two by Renaissance masters: the *Baptism of Christ* by Lorenzo Ghiberti (1378–1455) and the *Feast of Herod* by Donatello. ☒ *Piazza San Giovanni, Duomo* ⊕ *www.operaduomo.it* ☒ *€2.50, combined ticket € 7.50 ☉ Nov.–Mar. 14, Mon.–Sat. 10–1 and 2–5, Sun. 2–5; Mar. 15–Oct., Mon.–Sat. 9–7:30, Sun. 2–7:30.*

㉗ **Duomo.** A few minutes' walk west of Piazza del Campo, Siena's Duomo is beyond question one of the finest Gothic cathedrals in Italy. The facade, with its multicolor marbles and painted decoration, is typical of the Italian approach to Gothic architecture, lighter and much less austere than the French. The cathedral as it now stands was completed in the 14th century, but at the time the Sienese had even bigger plans. They had decided to enlarge the building by using the existing church as a transept for a new church, with a new nave running toward the southeast. But in 1348 the Black Death decimated Siena's population, the city fell into decline, funds dried up, and the plans were never carried out. The beginnings of the new nave can be seen from the steps outside the Duomo's right transept.

The Duomo's interior, with its coffered and gilded dome, is striking. It's most famous for its magnificent inlaid marble floors, which took almost 200 years to complete (beginning around 1370); more than 40 artists contributed to the work, made up of 56 separate compositions depicting biblical scenes, allegories, religious symbols, and civic emblems. They are covered for most of the year for conservation purposes but are unveiled every September for the entire month. The Duomo's pulpit, also much appreciated, was carved by Nicola Pisano between 1266 and 1268; the life of Christ is depicted on the rostrum frieze. In the **Biblioteca Piccolomini**, a room painted by Pinturicchio (circa 1454–1513) between 1502 and 1509, frescoes show scenes from the life of native son

Aeneas Sylvius Piccolomini (1405–64), who became Pope Pius II in 1458. They are in excellent condition and reveal a freshness rarely seen in Renaissance frescoes. ⊠ *Piazza del Duomo* ☎ *0577/283048* ⊕ *www. operaduomo.it* 🎫 *Biblioteca Piccolomini €1.50, combined ticket €7.50* ⊙ *Duomo Nov.–mid-Mar., Mon.–Sat. 7:30–5, Sun. 2–5; mid-Mar.–Oct., Mon.–Sat. 7:30–7:30, Sun. 2–7:30. Biblioteca Piccolomini Nov.–mid-Mar., Mon.–Sat. 10–1 and 2–5, Sun. 2–5; mid-Mar.–Oct., Mon.–Sat. 9–7:30, Sun. 2–7:30.*

**need a
break?**

Not far from the Duomo and the Pinacoteca, Siena's **Orto Botanico** (Botanical Gardens; ⊠ Via Pier Andrea Mattioli 4, Città ☎ 0577/ 232874) is a great place to relax and enjoy views of the countryside. It's open weekdays 8–12:30 and 2:30–5:30, Sat. 8–noon.

㉙ Museo dell'Opera Metropolitana. Built into part of the unfinished new cathedral's nave, the museum contains a small but important collection of Sienese art and the cathedral treasury. Its masterpiece is unquestionably the *Maestà* by Duccio (circa 1255–1318), painted around 1310 and magnificently displayed in a room devoted entirely to the artist's work. The tower inside the museum offers a splendid view. ⊠ *Piazza del Duomo, next to the Duomo* ☎ *0577/283048* ⊕ *www.operaduomo.it* 🎫 *€5.50, combined ticket €7.50* ⊙ *Nov.–mid-Mar., daily 9–1:30; mid-Mar.–Sept., daily 9–7:30; Oct., daily 9–6.*

㉖ Palazzo Pubblico. The focal point of the Piazza del Campo, the Gothic Palazzo Pubblico has served as Siena's town hall since the 1300s. It now also contains the **Museo Civico**, its walls covered with early Renaissance frescoes. The nine governors of Siena once met in the Sala della Pace, famous for Ambrogio Lorenzetti's frescoes called *Allegories of Good* *and Bad Government,* painted in the late 1330s to demonstrate the dangers of tyranny. The good government side depicts a utopia, showing first the virtuous ruling council surrounded by angels and then scenes of a perfectly running city and countryside. Conversely, the bad government fresco tells a tale straight out of Dante. The evil ruler and his advisers have horns and fondle strange animals, while the town scene depicts the seven mortal sins in action. Interestingly, the bad government fresco is severely damaged, and the good government fresco is in terrific condition. The **Torre del Mangia,** the palazzo's famous bell tower, is named after one of its first bell ringers, Giovanni di Duccio (called Mangiaguadagni, or earnings eater). The climb up to the top is long and steep, but the view makes it worth every step. ⊠ *Piazza del Campo 1* ☎ *0577/292226* ⬚ *Torre di Mangia €5.50, Museo Civico €6.50, combined ticket for Torre and Museo €9.50* ⊙ *Torre del Mangia Nov.–Mar. 15, daily 10–4; Mar. 16–Oct., daily 10–7. Museo Civico Nov. –Mar. 15, daily 10–6:30; Mar. 16–Oct., daily 10–7.*

㉕ **Piazza del Campo.** Known simply as Il Campo (The Field), this fan-shaped piazza is one of the finest in Italy. Constructed toward the end of the 12th century on a market area unclaimed by any contrada, it's still the heart of town. The bricks of the Campo are patterned in nine different sections—representing each member of the medieval Government of Nine. At the top of the Campo is a copy of the **Fonte Gaia,** decorated in the early 15th century by Siena's greatest sculptor, Jacopo della Quercia, with 13 sculpted reliefs of biblical events and virtues. Those lining the rectangular fountain are 19th-century copies; the originals are in the Spedale di Santa Maria della Scala. On Palio days (July 2 and August 16), the Campo and all its surrounding buildings are packed with cheering, frenzied locals and tourists craning their necks to take it all in.

㉛ **Pinacoteca Nazionale.** The national picture gallery contains an excellent collection of Sienese art, including works by native sons Ambrogio Lorenzetti (active 1319–48), Duccio, and Domenico Beccafumi (1486–1551). ⊠ *Via San Pietro 29, Città* ☎ *0577/281161* ⬚ *€4* ⊙ *Mon. 8:30–1:30, Tues.–Sat. 8:15–7:15, Sun. 8:15–1:15.*

㉜ **San Domenico.** In the church of San Domenico is the **Cappella di Santa Caterina,** with frescoes by Sodoma portraying scenes from the life of St. Catherine. Catherine was a much-respected diplomat, noted for ending the Great Schism by convincing the pope to return to Rome from Avignon. The saint's preserved head and finger are on display in the chapel. ⊠ *Costa di Sant'Antonio, Camollìa* ☎ *0577/280893* ⊙ *Nov.–mid-Mar., daily 9–1 and 3–6; mid-Mar.–Oct., daily 7–1 and 2:30–6:30.*

㉚ **Spedale di Santa Maria della Scala.** A former hospital, built beginning in the late 9th century, is now an exhibition space for contemporary art shows as well as some of the Fonte Gaia sculpted reliefs by Jacopo della Quercia (1371/74–1438). ⊠ *Piazza del Duomo, opposite the front of the Duomo* ☎ *0577/224811* ⬚ *€5.20* ⊙ *Mar. 17–Oct., daily 10–6; Nov.–Dec. 23, daily 10:30–4:30; Dec. 24–Jan. 6, daily 10–6; Jan. 7–Mar. 16, daily 10:30–4:30.*

Where to Stay & Eat

$$$$ ✕ **Antica Trattoria Botteganova.** Just outside the city walls, along the road that leads north to Chianti, the Botteganova is arguably the best restaurant in Siena. Chef Michele Sorrentino's cooking is all about clean flavors, balanced combinations, and inviting presentation. Look for inspiring dishes such as spaghetti *alla chitarra in salsa di astice piccante* (spaghetti with a spicy lobster sauce). The interior, with high

vaulting, is relaxed yet classy, and the service is first rate. There's a small room for nonsmokers. ✉ *Strada per Montevarchi (SS408) 29, 2 km (1 mi) north of Siena* ☎ *0577/284230* ▤ *AE, DC, MC, V* ✆ *Closed Mon.*

$$–$$$ ✕ **Le Logge.** Near Piazza del Campo, this classic Sienese trattoria has rustic dining rooms on two levels and tables outdoors from June to October. Tuscan dishes are the draw, such as *malfatti all'osteria* (ricotta and spinach dumplings in a cream sauce) and *anatra al finocchio* (roast duck with fennel). Reservations are advised. ✉ *Via del Porrione 33, San Martino* ☎ *0577/48013* ▤ *AE, DC, MC, V* ✆ *Closed Sun. and 3 wks in Jan.–Feb.*

★ $–$$ ✕ **Enoteca I Terzi.** Owner Michele Incarnato happily calls his place "anarchic" because it offers a little bit of everything—leisurely or quick business lunches for the locals, lavish dinners, and significant snacks in between. The wine bar, on the ground floor of a 12th-century tower, is hard to beat for a good glass of wine from a lengthy and carefully chosen list. Pasta specials change daily; you'll be blessed if *pici all'anatra e funghi* (thick spaghetti with a duck and mushroom sauce) is on the menu. ✉ *Via dei Termini 7, Camollia* ☎ *0577/44329* ▤ *AE, DC, MC, V* ✆ *Closed Sun.*

$–$$ ✕ **La Taverna di San Giuseppe.** Though it's not too far from il Campo, you would have to know about this place in order to find it, as it's on a residential street with very few tourist attractions. It's one long, cavernous room, filled mostly with people speaking Italian. The menu teems with Tuscan favorites with Sienese twists, including prosciutto *di cinta senese* (prosciutto made from local, once-nearly extinct, porcines). Here they make their version of *fegatini* (chicken livers) with spleen; it's aromatic and flavorful. ✉ *Via G. Duprè 132, San Martino* ☎ *0577/42286* ▤ *AE, DC, MC, V* ✆ *Closed Sun.*

$ ✕ **Osteria Castelvecchio.** In a stall in the oldest part of town, this little restaurant with high ribbed vaults mixes past and present on its menu, which changes daily. You're likely to find such Sienese standards as spaghetti *saporiti con gli aromi* (with tomatoes and herbs) as well as offbeat selections such as *sformatino del pastore con soia e cardi al vino* (a ricotta and greens concoction with cardoons and tofu). Owners Mauro Lombardini and Simone Romi are committed to *piatti di verdura* (vegetarian dishes), and they've got a great wine list. ✉ *Via Castelvecchio 65, Città* ☎ *0577/49586* ▤ *AE, DC, MC, V* ✆ *Closed Tues.*

$$$$ ▥ **Certosa di Maggiano.** A former 14th-century monastery converted into an exquisite country hotel, this haven of gracious living is about 1½ km (1 mi) from the center of Siena. Rooms have the style and comfort of an aristocratic villa, with classic prints and bold colors such as a happy daffodil yellow. Common rooms are luxurious, with fine woods and leather. In warm weather, breakfast is served on the patio next to the garden ablaze with flowers. Half-board is required in high season. ✉ *Via Certosa 82, take the Siena Sud exit off superstrada, 53100* ☎ *0577/288180* ☎ *0577/288189* ⊕ *www.certosadimaggiano.it* ➘ *6 rooms, 11 suites* ♣ *Restaurant, minibars, cable TV, tennis court, pool, exercise equipment, dry cleaning, laundry service, concierge, helipad, no-smoking rooms; no kids under 12* ▤ *AE, MC, V* ❢❂❒ *MAP.*

$$$$ ▥ **Park.** It began life in the 16th century as a home for the prosperous Gori family, and now it's an elegant hotel a short ride from the centro storico. Many of the rooms, with plush carpeting, large bathrooms, and flowered drapery, face a courtyard complete with well and a stunning view of olive trees and Siena beyond. Public rooms have sweeping ceilings, highly polished terra-cotta floors, and comfortable couches. The Olivo restaurant serves regional cuisine, and the breakfast buffet includes splendid scrambled eggs. The staff is extraordinarily helpful and polite. ✉ *Via Marciano 18, 53100* ☎ *0577/44803* 🖷 *0577/49020* ⊕ *www.*

parkhotelsiena.it ⇔ *64 rooms, 1 suite* ⚭ *Restaurant, room service, in-room fax, cable TV, minibar, 6-hole golf course, tennis court, pool, bar, baby-sitting, dry cleaning, laundry service, concierge, business services, meeting rooms, some pets allowed, no-smoking rooms* ⊟ *AE, DC, MC, V* ⦿| *BP.*

★ **$$$** ▦ **Palazzo Ravizza.** There might not be a more romantic and pretty place in the center of Siena than this quietly charming pensione, just outside Porta San Marco and a 10-minute walk to the Duomo. Rooms have high ceilings, antique furniture, big windows, and bathrooms decorated with hand-painted tiles. The attached restaurant serves tasty Tuscan classics, which can be eaten outdoors when it's warm. ⊠ *Pian dei Mantellini, 34, Città, 53100* ☎ *0577/280462* ⎙ *0577/221597* ⊕ *www. palazzoravizza.it* ⇔ *40 rooms, 4 suites* ⚭ *Restaurant, in-room safes, minibars in some rooms, cable TV, bar, laundry service, concierge, free parking, some pets allowed* ⊟ *AE, DC, MC, V.*

$$ ▦ **Duomo.** Occupying the top floor of a 17th-century building near Piazza del Campo, this quiet hotel is furnished in a neat contemporary style, with traces of the past showing in the artfully exposed brickwork in the breakfast room. Many bedrooms have views of the city's towers and the hilly countryside. Two rooms have balconies, and there's a rooftop terrace, often with blooming flowers, which offers a splendid view. Free parking is available a short distance from the hotel. ⊠ *Via Stalloreggi 38, Città, 53100* ☎ *0577/289088* ⎙ *0577/43043* ⊕ *www. hotelduomo.it* ⇔ *23 rooms* ⚭ *Laundry service, Internet, free parking, some pets allowed* ⊟ *AE, DC, MC, V.*

$ ▦ **Antica Torre.** A restored 16th-century tower within the town walls in the southeast corner of Siena, Antica Torre is a 10-minute walk from Piazza del Campo. It's the work of a cordial couple who have carefully evoked a private home, with only eight simply but tastefully furnished guest rooms. The old stone staircase, wooden beams, and original brick vaults here and there are reminders of the building's great age. ⊠ *Via Fieravecchia 7, San Martino, 53100* ☎⎙ *0577/222255* ⇔ *8 rooms* ⚭ *Minibars, cable TV, Internet; no a/c, no TV in some rooms* ⊟ *AE, DC, MC, V.*

¢ ▦ **Alma Domus.** If you're after a contemplative, utilitarian experience, this might be the place for you. Run by seven Dominican nuns, it's just around the corner from the church of San Domenico. Rooms are spartan and very clean. Many have a view of the Duomo and the rest of Siena, which might make the 11:30 curfew liveable. ⊠ *via Camporeggio 37, Camolia 53100* ☎ *0577/44177* ⎙ *0577/47601* ⇔ *31 rooms* ⊟ *No credit cards.*

Nightlife & the Arts

Music

In the last week of July, Siena hosts the **Settimane Musicali Senesi,** a series of concerts held in churches and courtyards with performances of local and other music. Contact **Accademia Musicale Chigiana** (⊠ Via di Città 89, Duomo ☎ 0577/22091 ⊕ www.chigiana.it) for information.

Sports

Siena's **Palio** horse race takes place every year on July 2 and August 16, but its spirit lives all year long. Three laps around a makeshift track in Piazza del Campo by representatives from the city's contrade earn participants the respect or scorn of the city. The event is so important to the Sienese that bribery, brutality, and kidnapping of the jockeys are commonplace—sabotaging a horse's reins is the only thing that remains taboo. A horse doesn't even need its rider to be considered a valid winner. Festivities kick off three days prior to the main event, with trial races, banquets lining the streets, and late-night celebrations. As the Palio approaches, residents don scarves with their contrada's colors and march through city streets in medieval costumes. Tickets are usually sold out months in advance; call the **tourist office** (⊠ Piazza del Campo 56 ☎ 0577/280551) for information. It's possible you might luck out and get an unclaimed seat or two; if not, the center of the piazza is free to all on a first-come, first-served basis, until just moments before the start.

Shopping

Siena is known for its cakes and cookies, their recipes of medieval origin—look for *cavallucci* (sweet spice biscuits), *panforte* (Christmas fruitcake with honey, hazelnuts, almonds, and spices), and *ricciarelli* (almond-paste cookies). The best place in town to find Sienese baked goods, as well as to grab a cappuccino, is **Nannini** (⊠ Banchi di Sopra 24, Camollìa ☎ 0577/239009).

Siena has excellent specialty food and wine shops. For the finest wines and other local foodstuffs such as panforte, try **L'Antica Fattoria** (⊠ Via di Città 51, Duomo ☎ 0577/4225). **La Bottega dei Sapori Antichi** (⊠ Via delle Terme 41, Camollìa ☎ 0577/285501) is a good option for local specialties. Italy's only state-sponsored enoteca, **Enoteca Italiana** (⊠ Fortezza Medicea, Camollìa ☎ 0577/288497) sells wines from all over Italy. **Enoteca I Terzi** (⊠ Via dei Termini 7, Camollìa ☎ 0577/44329) has a comprehensive selection of wines.

Siena Ricama (⊠ Via di Città 61, Duomo ☎ 0577/288339) has embroidered linens and other housewares. If you've always wanted a 14th- or 15th-century Sienese painting to hang on your wall but bemoaned the high cost of an original, you can purchase superb copies by Chiara Perinetti Casoni at **Bottega dell'Arte** (⊠ Via Stalloreggi 47, Città ☎ 0577/40755). Her work in tempera and gold leaf on panel is of the highest quality—you might even be able to pass it off as the real thing.

AREZZO & CORTONA

The hill towns of Arezzo and Cortona carry on age-old local traditions—in June and September, for example, Arezzo's Romanesque and Gothic churches are enlivened by the Giostra del Saracino, a costumed medieval joust. Arezzo has been home to important artists since ancient times when Etruscan potters produced their fiery-red vessels. Fine examples of the work of Luca Signorelli are preserved in Cortona, his hometown.

Arezzo

③ *81 km (50 mi) southeast of Florence, 74 km (46 mi) northwest of Perugia.*

Arezzo was the birthplace of the poet Petrarch and the Renaissance artist and art historian Giorgio Vasari. Guido d'Arezzo, the inventor of musical notation, was also born here. Today Arezzo is best known for the

Fodor'sChoice
★

magnificent frescoes by Piero della Francesca (circa 1420–92) in the **Basilica di San Francesco**. Painted between 1452 and 1466, they depict scenes from the *Legend of the True Cross* on three walls of the *cappella maggiore,* or altar choir. What Sir Kenneth Clark called "the most perfect morning light in all Renaissance painting" may be seen in the lowest section of the right wall, where the troops of the emperor Maxentius flee before the sign of the cross. Unveiled in 2000 after a painstaking

15-year restoration, they may now be seen in all their glory. ✉ *Piazza San Francesco* ☎ *0575/900404* ⊕ *www.pierodellafrancesca.it* 🎫 *€5.03* ⏱ *Nov.–Mar., weekdays 9–5:30, Sat. 9–5, Sun. 1–5; Apr.–Oct., weekdays 9–6:30, Sat. 9–5:30, Sun. 1–5:30. Admission limited to 25 people every ½ hr. Reservations required.*

Some historians maintain that Arezzo's oddly shaped, sloping **Piazza Grande** was once the site of an ancient Roman forum. Now it plays host to a first-Sunday-of-the-month antiques fair as well as the **Giostra del Saracino** (Joust of the Saracen), featuring medieval costumes and competition, held here in the middle of June and on the first Sunday of September. Check out the 16th-century loggia, designed by native son Giorgio Vasari, on the northeast side of the piazza.

The curving, tiered apse on Piazza Grande belongs to **Santa Maria della Pieve,** one of Tuscany's finest Romanesque churches, built in the 12th century. Don't miss the *portale maggiore* (great door) with its polychromed figures representing the months; restored in 2002, they are remarkably vibrant. ✉ *Corso Italia* ☎ *0575/377678* ⏱ *Daily 8–12:30 and 3–6:30.*

Arezzo's medieval **Duomo** (at the top of the hill) contains a fresco of a somber *Magdalen* by Piero della Francesca; look for it next to the large marble tomb near the organ. ✉ *Piazza del Duomo 1* ☎ *0575/23991* ⏱ *Daily 7–12:30 and 3–6:30.*

The **Casa di Giorgio Vasari** (Giorgio Vasari House) was designed and decorated by the region's leading art historian and architect around 1540 as his private home. ✉ *Via XX Settembre 55* ☎ *0575/409040* 🎫 *Free* ⏱ *Mon. and Wed.–Sat. 9–6:30, Sun. 9–1.*

Where to Stay & Eat

$–$$ ✕ **Buca di San Francesco.** A frescoed cellar restaurant in a centuries-old building next to the church of San Francesco, this *buca* (literally "hole," figuratively "cellar") doesn't seem to have changed much from the Middle Ages. You can choose from several straightforward local specialties, including *ribollita* (minestrone thickened with beans and bread). The lean Chianina beef and the *saporita di Bonconte* (a selection of several meats) are succulent treats. ✉ *Via San Francesco 1* ☎☎ *0575/23271* ▭ *AE, DC, MC, V* ⏱ *Closed Tues. and 2 wks in July. No dinner Mon.*

¢ ✕ **La Torre di Gnicche.** If you're looking for a small, intimate place with Italian home-cooking, grab a light lunch or dinner here. This one-room eatery, seating about 30, is part of a Renaissance palazzo. The short menu includes assorted crostini, sensational *delicatezze sott'olio* (vegetables marinated in oil), cheese plates, and an earthy *polpettone* (meat loaf). The formidable and eminently affordable wine list makes eating ribollita a heightened experience. ✉ *Piaggia San Martino 8* ☎ *0575/352 035* ▭ *MC, V* ⏱ *Closed Wed.*

$$ 🏠 **Calcione Country and Castle.** The elegant Marchesa Olivella Lotteringhi della Stufa has turned her six-century-old family homestead into
Fodor'sChoice a top-notch agriturismo. Think sophisticated rustic; many of the apart-
★ ments have open fireplaces, the houses have a private pool (the rest share the estate pool), and there are private lakes for fishing and windsurfing. Calcione is convenient to Arezzo, Siena, San Gimignano, and the delights of Umbria. From June to mid-September, a minimum one-week stay is mandatory. ✉ *Lucignano, 52046* ☎ *0575/837100* 🖷 *0575/ 837153* ⊕ *www.calcione.com* 🛏 *2 houses, 1 cottage, 6 apartments* ♨ *3 pools, 3 lakes, baby-sitting, Internet, some pets allowed; no a/c, no room phones in some rooms, no room TVs* ▭ *No credit cards* ⏱ *Closed Nov.–Mar.*

$–$$ ⊞ **Castello di Gargonza.** Enchantment reigns at this tiny 13th-century hamlet in the countryside near Monte San Savino, part of the fiefdom of the aristocratic Florentine Guicciardini restored by the modern Count Roberto Guicciardini as a way to rescue a dying village. A castle, church, and cobbled streets set the stage. Stays are for a minimum of three nights. From June through August, cottages and apartments are rented by the week; they have one to six rooms each, sleep two to seven people, and have as many as four baths. La Torre restaurant (closed Tuesday) serves local fare. ⊠ *52048 Monte San Savino* ☎ *0575/847021* 🖷 *0575/ 847054* ⊕ *www.gargonza.it* ⤴ *18 rooms, 11 apartments, 1 suite* △ *Restaurant, pool; no a/c, no room TVs* ▭ *AE, DC, MC, V* ⊘ *Closed 3 wks in Jan. and 3 wks in Nov.*

Shopping

FLEA MARKET On the first Sunday of each month, a colorful flea market with antiques and other, less-precious objects for sale takes place in the **Piazza Grande.**

GOLD Gold production here is on an industrial scale. Uno-A-Erre is the largest of several factories supplying local shops. Big-time baubles can be purchased in the town center. For gold jewelry set with precious or semi-precious stones, try **Il Diamante** (⊠ Via Guido Monaco 69 ☎ 0575/ 353450). **Borghini** (⊠ Corso Italia 126 ☎ 0575/24678) has an impressive collection of fine jewelry. **Prosperi** (⊠ Corso Italia 76 ☎ 0575/ 22632) works wonders in gold, silver, and platinum.

Cortona

❸❹ *29 km (18 mi) south of Arezzo, 117 km (73 mi) southeast of Florence.*

Magnificently situated, with olive trees and vineyards creeping up to its walls, pretty Cortona commands sweeping views over Lake Trasimeno and the plain of the Valdichiana. Its two galleries and churches are rarely visited; its delightful medieval streets are a pleasure to wander for their own sake.

Cortona is considered one of Italy's oldest towns—"Mother of Troy and Grandmother of Rome" is how it's popularly known. Tradition claims that it was founded by Dardanus, also the founder of Troy (and after whom the Dardanelles strait is named). He was fighting a local tribe, so the story goes, when he lost his helmet (*corythos* in Greek) on Cortona's hill. In time a town grew up that took its name (Corito) from the missing headgear. By the 5th century BC the Etruscans had built the first set of town walls, whose cyclopean traces can still be seen in the 3-km (2-mi) sweep of the present fortifications. As a member of the Etruscans' 12-city Dodecapolis, it became one of the federation's leading northern cities. An important consular road, the Via Cassia, which passed by the foot of its hill, assured the town's importance under the Romans. Its fortunes waned in the Middle Ages, however, as the plain below reverted to marsh. After holding out against neighbors like Perugia, Arezzo, and Siena, the *comune* was captured by King Ladislas of Naples in 1409 and sold to the Florentines two years later.

The heart of Cortona is formed by **Piazza della Repubblica** and the adjacent **Piazza Signorelli,** where you'll find pleasant shops to browse through. The **Museo Diocesano** (Diocesan Museum) houses an impressive number of large and splendid paintings by native son Luca Signorelli, as well as a stunning *Annunciation* by Fra Angelico, a delightful surprise in this small town. ⊠ *Piazza del Duomo 1* ☎ *0575/62830* 🏷 *€5* ⊘ *Nov.–Mar., Tues.–Sun. 10–1 and 3–5; Apr.–Sept., Tues.–Sun. 9:30–1 and 3:30–7.*

Where to Stay & Eat

$–$$ ✕ **Osteria del Teatro.** Just up the street from Teatro Signorelli, this small osteria is lined with photographs from theatrical productions spanning many years. The food is deliciously simple—try the *filetto in crema di tartufo* (beef in a creamy truffle sauce); service is warm and friendly. ⊠ *Via Maffei 2* ☎ *0575/630556* ⊟ *AE, DC, MC, V* ⊗ *Closed Wed. and 2 wks in Nov.*

★ **$$$$** ✕⊞ **Il Falconiere.** Run by the husband-wife team of Riccardo and Silvia Baracchi, this heavenly hotel, just minutes outside Cortona, consists of rooms in an 18th-century villa and suites in the *chiesetta* (little church) once belonging to an obscure 19th-century Italian poet and hunter. If you desire a little bit more privacy, you can stay at Le Vigne del Falco at the opposite end of the property, where most of the rooms suites with their own entrances; all of them have a grand view of the plain below. The restaurant's inventive menu is complemented by the wine list, the product of Silvia's extensive sommelier training. By all means sample their own estate-produced olive oil. Gourmands should inquire into the week-long cooking classes offered on site. ⊠ *Località San Martino 370, 52044* ☎ *0575/612679* 🖷 *0575/612927* ⊕ *www.ilfalconiere.com* ⇌ *13 rooms, 6 suites* ⟡ *Restaurant, room service, in-room safes, minibars, cable TV, 2 pools, bar, baby-sitting, dry cleaning, laundry service, concierge, Internet, free parking, some pets allowed (fee), no-smoking rooms* ⊟ *AE, DC, MC, V* ⊗ *Restaurant closed Mon. Nov.–Mar.*

SOUTHERN TUSCANY

Along the roads leading south from Siena, soft green olive groves give way to a blanket of oak, dark-green cypress forests, and reddish-brown earth. Towns are the size of the roads—small—and as old as the hills. The scruffy mountain landscapes of Monte Amiata make up some of the wildest parts of Tuscany, and once you're across the mountains the landscape is still full of cliffs, like the one Pitigliano perches on. Southern Tuscany offers good wine (try Brunello di Montalcino or the exceptional, lesser-known Morellino di Scansano for a true treat), thermal baths at Saturnia, Etruscan ruins, and the strands and fishing villages of Elba.

Abbazia di Monte Oliveto Maggiore

㉟ *37 km (23 mi) southeast of Siena, 104 km (65 mi) south of Florence.*

This Benedictine abbey, Tuscany's most visited, is an oasis of olive and cypress trees amid the harsh landscape of a zone known as the Crete, where erosion has sculpted the hills starkly, laying open gashes of barren rock in lush farmland. Secluded amid thick woodlands in the deep-cut hills south of Siena, it is accessible by car but not easily by bus.

Olivetans, or "White Benedictines," founded the abbey in 1313; this breakaway group sought to return to the simple ideals of the early Benedictine order. The monastery's mellow brick buildings, in one of Tuscany's most striking landscapes, protect a treasure or two. Only the **main cloister** and portions of the **park** are open to the public. The wooden choir in the church, with its intarsia designs, is an understated work of art that dates from 1503 to 1505. In the main cloister, frescoes by Luca Signorelli and Sodoma depict scenes from the life of St. Benedict with earthy realism, a quality that came naturally to Sodoma, described by Vasari as "a merry and licentious man of scant chastity." ⊠ *SS451 south of Asciano* ☎ *0577/707611* ⊗ *Daily 9:15–noon and 3:15–5:45.*

Montepulciano

36 *13 km (8 mi) west of the A1, 119 km (74 mi) south of Florence.*

Perched high on a hilltop, Montepulciano is made up of a pyramid of clustered Renaissance buildings set within a circle of cypress trees. At an altitude of almost 2,000 ft, it's cool in summer and chilled in winter by biting winds that sweep its spiraling streets. Montepulciano has an unusually harmonious look, the result of the work of three architects, Antonio da Sangallo il Vecchio (circa 1455–1534), Giacomo da Vignola (1507–73), and Michelozzo (1396–1472), who endowed it with palaces and churches in an attempt to impose Renaissance architectural ideals on an ancient Tuscan hill town. The pièce de résistance
★ is the **Piazza Grande**, a wide expanse of urban space lined with 15th-century family palazzi and the equally grand, but facadeless, Duomo. On the hillside below the town walls is the church of **San Biagio**, designed by Sangallo, a paragon of Renaissance architectural perfection considered to be his masterpiece. ⊠ *Via di San Biagio* ☎ *0578/7577761* ⊗ *Daily 9–12:30 and 3:30–7:30.*

Where to Stay & Eat

★ **$$$** ✕ **La Grotta.** Just across the street from the Tempio di San Biagio, this place has an innocuous entrance that might lead you to pass right by. Don't, as the food is fantastic. The *tagliolini con carciofi e rigatino* (thin noodles with artichokes and bacon) is heavenly, as is the *tagliatelle di grano saraceno con asparagi e zucchine* (flat noodles with asparagus and zucchini). Follow with any of the wonderful *secondi,* and wash it down with the local wine, which just happens to be one of Italy's finest—Vino Nobile di Montepulciano. ⊠ *Località San Biagio* ☎ *0578/757479* ▭ *AE, MC, V* ⊗ *Closed Wed.*

$$$$ ✕▦ **Locanda dell'Amorosa.** This "inn" occupies the 14th-century stone-and-brick hamlet of Amorosa, in the hills crowning the Valdichiana, just south of Sinalunga. The stunning views are matched by the gorgeous, perfectly restored buildings. A lane lined with cypress trees brings you to the gateway of Amorosa, which still has its tiny little church and a group of farmers' houses for the staff. The bedrooms are handsomely decorated with antiques, and the bathrooms are large. The restaurant ($$–$$$), in the old stables, serves both traditional and contemporary dishes. ⊠ *Località Amorosa, Sinalunga, 10 km (6 mi) from the Valdichiana exit off A1, 53048* ☎ *0577/679497* 🖷 *0577/632001* ⊕ *www.amorosa.it* ⤙ *14 rooms, 6 suites* ⚬ *Restaurant, in-room safes, mountain bikes, wine bar, baby-sitting, dry cleaning, laundry service, concierge, Internet, no-smoking rooms* ▭ *AE, DC, MC, V* ⊗ *Closed Jan.–Feb.*

$ ▦ **Il Marzocco.** A 16th-century building within the town walls, this hotel evokes the 19th century, complete with old-fashioned parlors and a billiard room. Furnished in heavy late 19th-century style or in spindly white wood, many bedrooms have large terraces overlooking the countryside and are big enough to accommodate extra beds. ⊠ *Piazza Savonarola 18, 53045* ☎ *0578/757262* 🖷 *0578/757530* ⤙ *16 rooms, 15 with bath* ⚬ *Restaurant, cable TV, billiards, Internet; no a/c* ▭ *AE, DC, MC, V* ⊗ *Closed Jan. 20–Feb. 10.*

Nightlife & the Arts

The **Cantiere Internazionale d'Arte** (⊠ Piazza Grande 7 ☎ 0578/757089) held in July and August, is a festival of art, music, and theater, ending with a major theatrical production in Piazza Grande.

Pienza

③⑦ *120 km (75 mi) south of Florence.*

Pienza owes its urban design to Pope Pius II, who had grand plans to transform his home village of Corsignano—the town's former name—into a model Renaissance town. The man entrusted with the project was Bernardo Rossellino (1409–64), a protégé of the great Renaissance architectural theorist Leon Battista Alberti (1404–74). His mandate was to create a cathedral, a papal palace, and a town hall (plus miscellaneous other buildings) that adhered to the humanist pope's principles. The result was a project that expressed Renaissance ideals of art, architecture, and civilized good living in a single scheme: it stands as a fine example of the architectural canons that Alberti formulated in the early Renaissance and that were utilized by later architects, including Michelangelo (1475–1564), in designing many of Italy's finest buildings and piazzas. Today the cool nobility of Pienza's center seems almost surreal in this otherwise unpretentious village, known locally for its pecorino. Although the cheese is made all over Italy, here it is a superior gastronomic experience.

The **Palazzo Piccolomini,** the seat of Pius II's papal court, was designed by Rossellino in 1459, using Florence's Palazzo Rucellai by Alberti as a model. You can visit the papal apartments, including a library, as well as the **Sala delle Armi,** with an impressive weapons collection, and the music room, with its extravagant wooden ceiling. ✉ *Piazza Pio II* ☎ *0578/748503* 🎫 *€3* 🕐 *Guided tours Tues.–Sun. 10–noon and 3–5:30. Closed 2nd half of Feb., 1st wk in Mar., Nov. 16–Dec. 7.*

The interior of the **Duomo** is simple but richly decorated with paintings from the Sienese school. Begun in 1459 and finished in a record three years' time, the facade is divided into three parts. Renaissance pilasters on the facade draw attention to the pope's coat of arms encircled by a wreath of fruit, the papal tiara, and keys above it. ✉ *Piazza Pio II* 🕐 *Daily 8:30–1 and 2:30–7.*

Where to Stay & Eat

$–$$ ✕ **La Porta.** Montichiello is a hamlet minutes away from Pienza, and this osteria–wine bar is basically the only show in town. But what a show it is—from start to finish, the food is delicious. The menu changes regularly, but you can always count on top quality cheeses (pecorino di Pienza, among others) and lively pasta dishes such as *tagliolini alla chianina* (thin noodles with a hearty minced beef sauce). Second courses are just as strong; if rabbit's on the menu, don't miss it. Reservations are a good idea, especially in summer. ✉ *Montichiello* ☎ *0578/755163* 🖃 *MC, V* 🕐 *Closed Thurs. and 3 wks in Jan.*

¢–$ ✕ **La Chiocciola.** A no-frills trattoria a few minutes' walk from the historic center, this place offers typical Pienza fare, including homemade *pici* (thick, short spaghetti) with hare or wild boar sauce. Their take on *formaggio in forno* (baked cheese) with assorted accompaniments such as fresh porcini mushrooms is reason enough to come here. ✉ *Via dell'Acero 2* ☎ *0578/748063* 🖃 *MC, V* 🕐 *Closed Wed. and 10 days in Feb.*

★ **$$** 🏨 **La Foce.** The various farmhouses and apartments scattered throughout the former estate of noted Anglo-American historian Iris Origo and her husband, Antonio, have been converted into this agriturismo, furnished in simple, rustic style, with wooden furniture, sponged walls, and extraordinary views. Kitchens are fully equipped, and some of the rooms have working fireplaces. If you're looking for peace and quiet, look no further. From May through October, a minimum one-week stay is obligatory. ✉ *Strada della Vittoria 63, Chianciano Terme, 53042* 📠 *0578/*

69101 ⊕ *www.lafoce.com* ⤳ *9 apartments, 6 farmhouses* ⚹ *Fans, kitchens, refrigerators, cable TV in some rooms, tennis court, 8 pools, playground, laundry facilities, laundry service, free parking; no a/c* ⊟ *MC, V* ⫯⊙⫯ *EP.*

Montalcino

③⑧ *24 km (15 mi) west of Pienza, 41 km (25 mi) south of Siena.*

Another medieval hill town with a special claim to fame, Montalcino is the source for Brunello di Montalcino, one of Italy's most esteemed red wines. You can sample it in wine cellars in town or visit a nearby winery for a free guided tour and tasting; you must call ahead for reservations. One Montalcino winery worth visiting is **Fattoria dei Barbi e del Casato** (⊠ Località Podernuovi ☎ 0577/841200). The 14th-century **La Fortezza** (⊠ Via Panfilo dell'Oca ☎ 0577/849211 ⊠ €3 ☉ Nov.–Mar., daily Tues.–Sun. 9–6; Apr.–Oct., daily 9–8) has an enoteca for tasting wines. In the very heart of the *centro storico* is **Alle Logge** (⊠ Piazza del Popolo ☎ 0577/846186 ☉ Thurs.–Tues. 7 AM–1 AM), a sophisticated wine bar where selections by the glass always include a significant Brunello.

Where to Stay & Eat

$$$$ ✕ **Poggio Antico.** One of Italy's renowned chefs, Roberto Minnetti, abandoned his highly successful restaurant in Rome and moved to the country just outside Montalcino. Now he and his wife, Patrizia, serve Tuscan cuisine masterfully interpreted by Roberto in a relaxed but regal dining room with arches and beamed ceilings. The seasonal menu offers *pappardelle al ragù di agnello* (flat, wide noodles in a lamb sauce) and venison in a sweet-and-sour sauce. ⊠ *Località I Poggi, 4 km (2½ mi) outside Montalcino on road to Grosseto* ☎ 0577/849200 ⊟ MC, V ☉ *Closed Mon. and 20 days in Jan. No dinner Sun.*

¢ ✕⊡ **Fattoria dei Barbi e del Casato.** The rustic taverna ($$) of this family-owned wine estate, which produces excellent Brunello as well as its younger cousin, Rosso di Montalcino, is set among vineyards and has a large stone fireplace. The estate farm produces many of the ingredients used in such traditional specialties as *stracotto nel brunello* (braised beef cooked with beans in Brunello wine). Six comfortable, traditionally furnished agritourist apartments are next to the cantina—a one-week minimum stay is required. ⊠ *Località Podernuovi, 53024* ☎ 0577/ 841200 *taverna; 0577/841111 fattoria* 🖷 0577/841112 ⚹ *Reservations essential* ⤳ *6 apartments* ⚹ *Fans, cable TV, kitchenettes, some pets allowed; no a/c* ⊟ AE, DC, MC, V ☉ *Taverna closed Wed. and mid-Jan.–mid Feb. No dinner Tues. in Nov.–Mar.*

Abbazia di Sant'Antimo

★ **③⑨** *10 km (6 mi) south of Montalcino, 51 km (32 mi) south of Siena.*

It's well worth your while to visit this abbey, a 12th-century Romanesque gem of pale stone in the silvery green of an olive grove. The exterior and interior sculpture is outstanding, particularly the nave capitals, a combination of French, Lombard, and even Spanish influences. According to legend, the **sacristy** (rarely open) forms part of the primitive Carolingian church (founded in AD 781), its entrance flanked by 9th-century pilasters. The small **vaulted crypt** dates from the same period. An unusual element is the ambulatory, whose three radiating chapels (rare in Italian churches) were probably copied from the French model. Throughout the day, the monks fill this magnificent space with Gregorian chant. ⊠ *Castelnuovo dell'Abate* ☎ 0577/835659 ⊕ *www.antimo. it* ☉ *Daily 10–12:30 and 3–6:30.*

Monte Amiata

⑩ *86 km (52 mi) southeast of Siena, 156 km (94 mi) southeast of Florence.*

At 5,702 ft high, the dormant volcano Monte Amiata is one of Tuscany's few ski resorts, but it's no match for the Alps or the Dolomites. Its main attraction is a wide-open view of Tuscany. From here you can meander along panoramic mountaintop roads in your car and visit Castel del Piano, Arcidosso, Santa Flora, and Piancastagnaio, towns dating from the Middle Ages.

Abbazia di San Galgano

★ ㉛ *33 km (20 mi) southwest of Siena, 70 km (43 mi) northwest of Montalcino.*

This Gothic cathedral missing its roof is a hauntingly beautiful sight. The church was built in the late 12th century by Cistercian monks, who designed it after churches built by their order in France. Starting in the 15th century it fell into ruin, declining gradually over the centuries. Grass has grown through the floor, and the roof and windows are gone. What's left of its facade and walls makes a grandiose and desolate picture. Behind it, a short climb up a hill brings you to the charming little **Chiesa di San Galgano,** with frescoes by Ambrogio Lorenzetti (active 1319–48), and a sword in stone. Legend has it that Galgano, a medieval knight, had an epiphany on this spot and gave up fighting. He thrust his sword into stone, where it remains to this day.

Elba

㊷ *Portoferraio: 1 hr by ferry from Piombino.*

The largest island in the Tuscan archipelago, ringed with pristine beaches and pocked with rugged vegetation, Elba is an hour by ferry or a half-hour by hydrofoil from Piombino, or a short hop by air from Pisa. Its main port is Portoferraio, fortified in the 16th century by the Medici grand duke Cosimo I. Be sure to sample the local wines, including Moscato and Aleatico. Lively **Portoferraio** is the best base for exploring the island. Good beaches are Biodola, Procchio, and Marina di Campo.

Victor Hugo spent his boyhood on Elba, and Napoléon was here during his famous exile in 1814–15, which resulted in the building of the **Palazzina dei Mulini.** More interesting is the **Villa San Martino** (✉ Località San Martino ☎ 0565/914688) a couple of miles outside town, whose grandiose neoclassical facade was built by the emperor's nephew. ✉ *Piazzale Napoleone 1, Portoferraio* ☎ *0565/915846* 🎟 *€3 for one site, €5 for both* ☉ *Palazzina: Apr.–Sept., Mon. and Wed.–Sat. 9–7, Sun. 9–1; Oct.–Mar., Mon. and Wed. 9–4, Sun. 9–1. Villa: Apr.–Sept., Tues.–Sat. 9–7, Sun. 9–1; Oct.–Mar., Tues.–Sat. 9–4, Sun. 9–1.*

The **Museo Archeologico** reconstructs the island's ancient history through a display of Etruscan and Roman artifacts recovered from shipwrecks. ✉ *Calata Buccari, Portoferraio* ☎ *0565/944024* 🎟 *€2* ☉ *Sept.–May, Mon.–Sat. 9:30–noon and 3–6; June–July, Mon.–Sat. 9:30–7; Aug., Mon.–Sat. 9–1 and 3–midnight.*

Where to Stay & Eat

$$$–$$$$ ✕ **La Canocchia.** In the center of Rio Marina on the eastern shore of Elba is this airy, 40-seat place across from a public garden. Seafood takes center stage here. Specialties include ravioli *scampi e asparagi o calamari* (stuffed with shrimp or squid, in light asparagus sauce) and various saffron-perfumed catches of the day. The *frittura di paranza* (fried fish) are

crisp and light, and the *involtini di pescespada* (swordfish rolls) also shouldn't be missed. Book ahead in summer, as it can get very crowded. ⊠ *Via Palestro 3, Rio Marina* ☎ *0565/962432* ⊟ *MC, V* ☉ *Closed Mon. and Nov.–mid-Feb.*

$$ ✕ **Trattoria da Lido.** In the historic center of Portoferraio, at the beginning of the road to the old Medici walls, this bustling, casual restaurant serves commendable *gnocchetti di pesce* (bite-size potato-and-fish dumplings) with a white cream sauce and fresh *pesce all'elbana* (whitefish baked with vegetables and potatoes). ⊠ *Salita del Falcone 2, Portoferraio* ☎ *0565/914650* ⊟ *AE, DC, MC, V* ☉ *Closed mid-Dec.–mid-Feb.*

★ $$$$ 🏨 **Hermitage.** This fine hotel on the most exclusive bay on Elba, 8 km (5 mi) from Portoferraio, consists of a central building with guest rooms as well little cottages, each with six to eight rooms and its own separate entrance. You have private access to a white sandy beach, where you'll find the hotel's own bar and restaurant. During the high season, half-board is mandatory. ⊠ *Biodola, 57037* ☎ *0565/936911* 🖷 *0565/969984* ⊕ *www.elba4star.it* ⇥ *110 rooms* ⚲ *2 restaurants, 6-hole golf course, 9 tennis courts, 3 pools, soccer, volleyball, 3 bars, Internet, meeting room, some pets allowed* ⊟ *AE, DC, MC, V* ☉ *Closed Nov.–Apr.*

Saturnia

🔟 *47 km (30 mi) south of Monte Amiata, 129 km (77 mi) south of Siena.*

Etruscan and pre-Etruscan tombs cut into the local rock can be seen in this town, a lively center in pre-Etruscan times. Today it is known for its hot sulphur **thermal baths.** There's a modern spa with a luxury hotel attached to it called **Terme di Saturnia,** or you can soak for free at the tiered natural pools of Cascate del Gorello next to the road to Montemerano.

Where to Stay & Eat

$$$$ ✕ **Da Caino.** At this excellent restaurant in the nearby town of Montemerano (on the road to Scansano), specialties include tomatoes and peppers on crisp phyllo dough, lasagna with pumpkin, and such hearty dishes as *cinghiale lardolato con olive* (wild boar larded with olives). ⊠ *Via della Chiesa 4, Montemerano, 7 km (4½ mi) south of Saturnia* ☎ *0564/602817* ⚲ *Reservations essential* ⊟ *AE, DC, MC, V* ☉ *Closed Wed. and Jan.–Feb. No dinner Thurs.*

$$$ ✕ **I Due Cippi–Da Michele.** Owner Michele Aniello has a terrific restaurant with a lengthy and creative menu; emphasis is placed on Maremman cuisine such as wild boar and duck—though there are other treats as well; try the *tortelli di castagne al seme di finocchio* (chestnut-stuffed tortelli with butter sauce and fennel seeds). In good weather you can enjoy your meal on a terrace overlooking the town's main square. ⊠ *Piazza Veneto 26/a* ☎ *0564/601074* ⚲ *Reservations essential* ⊟ *AE, DC, MC, V* ☉ *Closed Tues. in Oct.–June; Dec. 20–26; and Jan. 10–25.*

$$$$ 🏨 **Terme di Saturnia.** Cure takers looking for a most refined approach can don their bathrobes here at the region's premier resort. The hotel, an elegant stone building, wraps around three tufa-rock pools built over the hot springs' source. Every imaginable type of health and beauty treatment is available, supplemented by decidedly unspalike meals in the restaurant. Half-board prices are a good deal. ⊠ *58050 Saturnia* ☎ *0564/601061* 🖷 *0564/601266* ⊕ *www.termedisaturnia.it* ⇥ *140 rooms, 10 suites* ⚲ *Restaurant, snack bar, in-room safes, minibars, cable TV, in-room VCRs, driving range, 2 tennis courts, 4 pools, hair salon, health club, sauna, spa, steam room, bar, piano bar, shops, dry clean-*

ing, laundry facilities, concierge, Internet, helipad, some pets allowed ⊟ AE, DC, MC, V.

$$ ⊡ **Villa Acquaviva.** Perched on top of a hill off the main road 1 km (½ mi) from Montemerano, this elegant villa painted antique rose appears at the end of a tree-lined driveway. It has spacious views and quintessential Tuscan charm. Tastefully decorated rooms are in both the main villa and in a guest house. The farm that fans out around it produces both wine and olive oil. ⊠ Strada Scansanese, 58050 Montemerano ☎ 0564/602890 🖨 0564/602895 ⊕ www.laltramaremma. it/acquaviva 🔄 24 rooms, 2 suites ♻ Restaurant, in-room safes, minibars, cable TV, tennis court, pool, bar, playground, some pets allowed ⊟ AE, DC, MC, V.

$ ⊡ **Villa Garden.** All the rooms at this small place, charmingly furnished with comfortable beds, floral curtains and bedspreads, and tiled bathrooms floors, are named for flowers. Just a few minutes from the center of town, it's a perfect place to stay if you want to take the waters without breaking the bank. The buffet breakfast is good and filling, the staff courteous and efficient. ⊠ Via Sterpeti 56, 58014 ☎ 0564/601182 🖨 0564/601207 ⊕ www.laltramaremma.it/villa_garden 🔄 10 rooms ♻ Minibars, cable TV, bar, Internet, free parking, some pets allowed ⊟ AE, DC, MC, V.

Pitigliano

④④ 33 km (21 mi) east of Saturnia, 147 km (92 mi) southeast of Siena.

From a distance, the medieval stone houses of Pitigliano look as if they melt into the cliffs of the soft tufa rock on which they are set. Etruscan tombs, which locals use to store wine, are connected by a network of caves and tunnels. In 1293, the Orsini family moved its base from Sovana to the more easily defended Pitigliano. They built up the town's defenses and fortified their home, Palazzo Orsini. Later, in the early 1500s, Antonio da Sangallo the Younger added more to the town's fortresslike aspect, building bastions and towers throughout the town and adding a noteworthy aqueduct below the fortress as well.

Savory local specialties include the famous Pitigliano white wine, olive oil, cured meats, and cheeses; local restaurants serve up good food at modest prices. Wander down the narrow streets of the old **Jewish Ghetto**. Though Jews had settled in Pitigliano as early as the 15th century, they arrived in much greater numbers after a 1569 papal bull of Pope Pius V evicted the Jews from Rome.

TUSCANY A TO Z

To research prices, get advice from other travelers, and book travel arrangements, visit www.fodors.com.

AIRPORTS

The largest airports in the region are Pisa's Aeroporto Galileo Galilei and Florence's Aeroporto A. Vespucci, known as Peretola, which connects to Brussels and Paris.

🛪 Airport Information **Aeroporto Galileo Galilei** ☎ 050/500707 ⊕ www.pisa-airport.com. **Peretola** ⊠ 10 km (6 mi) northwest of Florence ☎ 055/373498 ⊕ www.airport.florence.it.

BIKE TRAVEL

I Bike Italy offers one-day tours of the Florence countryside. Also check out Florence by Bike, which offers routes in and around the city. The

Massachusetts-based Ciclismo Classico offers guided bike tours throughout Italy.

🚲 Bike Rentals **Florence by Bike** ✉ Via San Zanobi 120–122/r ☎ 055/488992. **I Bike Italy** ✉ Borgo degli Albizi 11 ☎☎ 055/2342371. **Ciclismo Classico** ✉ 30 Marathon St. Arlington, MA 02474 ☎ 800/866-7314 ⊕ www.ciclismoclassico.com.

BOAT & FERRY TRAVEL

Boat services link the Tuscan islands with the mainland. Passenger and car ferries leave from Piombino and Livorno for Elba. From Piombino, Moby Lines travels to Porto Azzurro and Portoferraio on Elba. Toremar runs ferries between Capraia and Livorno, Pianosa and Elba's Porto Azzurro, and Giglio and Giannutri and Porto Santo Stefano. Prices can differ drastically, so comparison shop before buying your tickets; check both counters, or call both offices, before booking.

🚢 Boat & Ferry Information **Moby Lines** ✉ Piazzale Premuda, Piombino ☎ 0565/221212 ⊕ www.mobylines.it. **Toremar** ⊕ www.toremar.it ✉ Piazzale Premuda 13/14, Piombino ☎ 0565/31100 ✉ Porto Mediceo, Livorno ☎ 0586/896113; ✉ Piazzale A. Candi, Porto Santo Stefano ☎ 0564/810803.

BUS TRAVEL

Tuscany is crisscrossed by bus lines that connect the smaller towns and cities on the autostrade and superhighways. Buses can be a good mode of transport for touring, though getting information and making arrangements, particularly for a non-Italian speaker, can be a test of patience. To see the hill towns around Siena, such as San Gimignano, you can take a Siena-to-Arezzo Tra-In or Lazzi bus; at either Siena or Arezzo you can connect with the main train line. From Colle Val d'Elsa you can catch a CPT bus to get to Volterra. SENA connects Rome with Siena on several scheduled daily trips.

🚌 Bus Information **CPT (Compagnia Pisana Trasporti)** ✉ Piazzale Ginori Conti 2-3, Volterra ☎☎ 800/012773 toll-free ⊕ www.cpt.pisa. it. **Lazzi Eurolines** ✉ Via Mercante 2, Florence ☎ 055/363041 ⊕ www.lazzi.it. **SENA** ✉ Piazza Gramsci, Siena ☎ 0577/283203 ☎ 0577/40731 **Tra-In** ✉ Statale 73, Levante 23, Due Ponti, Siena ☎ 0577/204111.

CAR RENTAL

Hertz and Avis are the tried and true options. It is usually less expensive to arrange for car rental from the United States; explore options before traveling. If you want an automatic transmission, make that clear when placing your reservation. Also doublecheck to make sure that the drop-off point is open on weekends, which is often not the case other than at airports.

🚗 Local Agencies **Avis** ✉ Piazza della Repubblica 1/a, Arezzo ☎ 0575/354232 ✉ Via Città Gemelli, Lucca ☎ 0583/513614 ✉ Via Simone Martini 36, Siena ☎ 0577/270305. **Hertz** ✉ Aeroporto Galileo Galilei, Pisa ☎ 050/49187 ✉ Via Montegrappa 208, Prato ☎ 0574/527774 ✉ Viale Sardegna 37, Siena ☎ 0577/45085.

CAR TRAVEL

The best way to see Tuscany is by car, making it possible to explore the tiny towns and country restaurants that are so much a part of the region's charm. Drivers should be prepared to navigate through bewildering suburban sprawl around Tuscan cities; to reach the historic centers where most of the sights are, look for the CENTRO STORICO signs. In many small towns you must park outside the city walls.

The Autostrada del Sole (A1) connects Florence with Bologna, 105 km (65 mi) north, and Rome, 277 km (172 mi) south, passing by Arezzo and Chiusi (where you turn off for Montepulciano). The A11 leads west from Florence and meets the coastal A12 between Viareggio and Livorno.

A toll-free superstrada links Florence with Siena. For Chianti wine-country scenery, take the SS222 south of Florence through the undulating hills between Strada in Chianti and Greve in Chianti.

EMERGENCY SERVICES If you have a breakdown on the autostrada, or any toll road, you will find along the side of the road "SOS" boxes placed every couple of kilometers. You push a button on the box, a green light pops on, and help is sent—you don't actually talk to a person. If you are on other roads, call ACI, the Italian Auto Club.

🚗 **ACI** ☎ 803/116.

EMERGENCIES

Pharmacies stay open at off hours on a rotating basis. To find out who's open, check the schedule posted in all pharmacy windows.

🚑 **Ambulance, medical emergency** ☎ 118. **Police, fire** ☎ 113.

MAIL & SHIPPING

📮 Post Offices **Lucca** ✉ Via Vallisneri 2 ☎ 0583/43351. **Pisa** ✉ Piazza Vittoria Emanuele ☎ 050/43352. **Siena** ✉ Via Petrilli Savina ✉ Via Rispini 3 ☎ 0577/50286.

📮 Internet Points **Pisa** ✉ Internet Planet, Piazza Cavallotti 3/4 ☎ 050/830 702. ✉ Odissea, via F. Turati 20 ☎ 050/220 0738. **Radda in Chianti** ✉ Bar Sampoli & Lapis, via XI febbraio 2 ☎ no phone. **San Gimignano** ✉ La Tuscia di Panichi Sandra ☎ 0577/942 087.

TOURS

From Florence, American Express operates one-day excursions to Siena and San Gimignano and can arrange for cars, drivers, and guides for special-interest tours in Tuscany. Another option is the Florence-based, American-owned and operated Custom Travel and Special Events, which runs day trips into Chianti wine country and other selected spots in Tuscany.

🎫 Fees & Schedules **American Express** ✉ Via Dante Alighieri 22/r, Florence ☎ 055/50981. **Custom Travel and Special Events** ✉ Via dell'Ardiglione 19, Florence ☎ 055/2645526.

BOAT TOURS Charters in Tuscany are available through the Centro Nautico Italiano. Depart from either Marciana Marina in Elba or Talamone (on the mainland, south of Follonica) for journeys through the Tuscan archipelago, including the islands of Giglio, Capraia, Gorgona, Pianosa, Montecristo, and Giannutri. You can either skipper your own vessel or hire a crew; fleets can accommodate as few as two people or as many as 12. Exploring the Ligurian coast, or Corsica or Sardinia, is also a possibility.

🎫 Fees & Schedules **Centro Nautico Italiano** ✉ Piazza della Signoria 8, Florence ☎ 055/287419 📠 055/284 690 🌐 www.centronautico.it.

BUS TOURS Bus tours can be arranged through any travel agency. Micos Travel Box, for instance, will tailor bus itineraries to suit your tastes and budget.

🎫 Fees & Schedules **Micos Travel Box** ✉ Via dell'Oriuolo 50-52/r, Florence ☎ 055/2340228.

HOT-AIR BALLOON TOURS Ballooning in Tuscany will arrange for an hour balloon ride over the Crete Senese. Flights depart from just outside Pienza and sail over the hills of Montepulciano, Montalcino, and Pienza. The location of touchdown depends on local weather conditions; two cars follow the balloon and are ready for prompt pickup as well as a champagne breakfast on the flight's completion.

🎈 **Ballooning in Tuscany** ✉ Podere La Fratta, Montisi (Si) ☎ 0577/665310 📠 0577/632973 🌐 www.ballooningintuscany.com.

WALKING TOURS A terrific way to discover Tuscany is by walking it. Two companies offer guided tours that cater to anyone from the novice hiker to the expert. Country Walkers offers weeklong (and longer) walking tours throughout Tuscany in spring and fall. Italian Connection, Walking & Culinary Tours offers walking and culinary itineraries through Tuscan hill towns at various times between April and November.

🖪 Fees & Schedules **Country Walkers** ☍ Box 180, Waterbury, VT, 05676 ☎ 802/244-5661 or 888/742-0770. **Italian Connection, Walking & Culinary Tours** ✉ 11 Fairway Dr., Suite 210, Edmonton, Alberta, Canada ☎ 800/462-7911.

TRAIN TRAVEL

The coastal line from Rome to Genoa passes through Pisa and all the beach resorts. The main line from Rome to Bologna passes through Arezzo, Florence, and Prato. Italy's main rail line, which runs from Milan to Calabria, links Florence and Arezzo in Tuscany and runs past Chiusi and Cortona on its way south. Another main line connects Florence with Pisa. There's also regular, nearly hourly service from Florence to Lucca via Prato, Pistoia, and Montecatini. Call FS, the Italian State Railway, toll-free for information.

🖪 Train Information **FS** ☎ 8848/888088 ⊕ www.trenitalia.it.

TRAVEL AGENCIES

🖪 Local Agent Referrals **American Express** ✉ Via Dante Alighieri 22, Florence ☎ 055/50981. **Artemisia** ✉ Via Ricasoli 29, Montalcino ☎ 0577/846021 🖷 0577/846020 ⊕ www.artemisiaviaggi.it **ATUV** ✉ Piazza Martiri della Libertà 4/6, Volterra ☎ 0588/86333 🖷 0588/81356.**CIT Italia** ✉ Piazza Stazione 51/r, Florence ☎ 055/284145. **Micos Travel Box** ✉ Via dell'Oriuolo 50–52/r, Florence ☎ 055/2340228. **Solimano Viaggi** ✉ Via Don Minzoni 29, Volterra ☎ 0588/81364 🖷 0588/81356.

VISITOR INFORMATION

🖪 Agritourist Information **Terranostra** ✉ Via dei Magazzini 2, Florence, 50122 ☎ 055/280539 ⊕ www.terranostra.it. **Turismo Verde** ✉ Via Verdi 5, Florence ☎ 055/2344925.

🖪 Tourist Information **Arezzo** ✉ Piazza della Repubblica 22 ☎ 0575/377678 ⊕ www.apt.arezzo.it. **Colle Val d'Elsa** ✉ Via F. Campana 43 ☎ 0577/922791. **Cortona** ✉ Via Nazionale 42 ☎ 0575/630352 ⊕ www.cortonaweb.com. **Greve in Chianti** ✉ Viale Giovanni da Verrazzano 33 ☎ 055/8546287. **Lucca** ✉ Piazza Santa Maria 125 ☎ 0583/919931 ⊕ www.lucca.tourist.it. **Montalcino** ✉ Costa del Municipio 1 ☎ 0577/442944 ⊕ www.prolocomontalcino.it. **Montecatini Terme** ✉ Viale Verdi 66 ☎ 0572/772244 ⊕ www.montecatini.it. **Montepulciano** ✉ via di Gracciano nel Corso 59/r ☎ 0578/757341 ⊕ www.prolocomontepulciano.it. **Pienza** ✉ Palazzo Pubblico, Piazza Pio II ☎ 0578/749071 ⊕ www.infinito.it/utenti/ufficio.turistico. **Pisa** ✉ Via Cammeo 2 ☎ 050/560464 ⊕ www.pisa.turismo.toscana.it. **Pistoia** ✉ Palazzo dei Vescovi, Via Roma 1 ☎ 0573/21622 ⊕ www.comune.pistoia.it.**Pitigliano** ✉ via Roma 6 ☎ 0564/614433 **Portoferraio** ✉ Calata Italia 26 ☎ 0565/914671 ⊕ www.aptelba.it. **Prato** ✉ Piazza delle Carceri 15 ☎ 0574/24112 ⊕ www.prato.turismo.toscana.it. **Radda in Chianti** ✉ Piazza Ferrucci 1 ☎ 0577/738494 ⊘ open Mar.–Oct. **San Gimignano** ✉ Piazza del Duomo 1 ☎ 0577/940008 ⊕ www.sangimignano.com. **San Miniato** ✉ Piazza del Popolo 3 ☎ 0571/42745. **Siena** ✉ Piazza del Campo 56 ☎ 0577/280551. **Volterra** ✉ Piazza dei Priori 20 ☎ 0588/87257 ⊕ www.comune.volterra.pi.it.

UMBRIA & THE MARCHES

PERUGIA, ASSISI, SPOLETO, ORVIETO

10

FODOR'S CHOICE

Basilica di San Francesco, Assisi
Castello di Petrata, hotel, near Assisi
La Pallotta, hotel, Assisi
Palazzo Ducale, Urbino
Taverna del Lupo, restaurant, Gubbio

HIGHLY RECOMMENDED

RESTAURANTS   Le Grotte del Funaro, Orvieto
Osteria Piazzetta dell'Erba, Assisi
Ristorante Tornasacco, Ascoli Piceno

HOTELS   Hotel Gattapone, Spoleto
Hotel Umbra, Assisi
Hotel San Luca, Spoleto

SIGHTS   Collegio del Cambio, Perugia
Duomo, Orvieto
Palazzo dei Consoli, Gubbio
Palazzo dei Priori, Perugia
Piazza del Popolo, Ascoli Piceno
Ponte delle Torri, Spoleto
Santuario della Santa Casa, Loreto

Updated by
Peter Blackman

BIRTHPLACE OF SAINTS and home of some of the country's greatest artistic-treasures, central Italy is a collection of misty green valleys and picture-perfect hill towns laden with centuries of history. Umbria and the Marches are the Italian countryside as you've imagined it: verdant farmland, steep hillsides topped with fairy-tale fortresses, winding country roads traveled by horses and Fiat 500s carrying crates of fresh olives. No single town here has the extravagant wealth of art and architecture of Florence, Rome, or Venice, but this works in your favor: small jewels of towns feel knowable, not overwhelming. This is not to suggest that the cultural cupboard is bare—far from it. Orvieto's cathedral and Assisi's basilica are two of the most important sights in Italy, and Perugia, Todi, Spoleto, and Urbino are rich in art and architecture. Virtually every small town in the region has a castle, church, or museum worth a visit—but without them you'd still be compelled to stop for the picturesque streets, panoramic views, and natural beauty.

The earliest inhabitants of Umbria, the Umbri, were thought by the Romans to be the most ancient inhabitants of Italy. Little is known about them; with the coming of Etruscan culture the tribe fled into the mountains in the eastern portion of the region. The Etruscans, who founded some of the great cities of Umbria, were in turn supplanted by the Romans. Unlike Tuscany and other regions of central Italy, Umbria had few powerful medieval families to exert control over the cities in the Middle Ages—its proximity to Rome ensured that it would always be more or less under papal domination.

Located in the center of the country, Umbria has for much of its history been a battlefield where armies from north and south clashed. Hannibal destroyed a Roman army on the shores of Lake Trasimeno, and the bloody course of the interminable Guelph-Ghibelline conflict of the Middle Ages was played out here. Dante considered Umbria the most violent place in Italy. Trophies of war still decorate the Palazzo dei Priori in Perugia, and the little town of Gubbio continues a warlike rivalry begun in the Middle Ages—every year it challenges the Tuscan town of Sansepolcro to a crossbow tournament. Today the bowmen shoot at targets, but neither side has forgotten that 500 years ago its ancestors shot at each other. In spite of—or perhaps because of—this bloodshed, Umbria has produced more than its share of Christian saints. The most famous is St. Francis, the decidedly pacifist saint whose life shaped the Church of his time. His great shrine at Assisi is visited by hundreds of thousands of pilgrims each year. St. Clare, his devoted follower, was Umbria-born, as were St. Benedict, St. Rita of Cascia, and the patron saint of lovers, St. Valentine.

East of Umbria, the Marches (Le Marche to Italians) stretch between the hills of the southern Apennines and the Adriatic sea. It's a region of great turreted castles standing on high peaks defending passes and roads—silent testament to the region's bellicose past. The Marches have passed through numerous hands. First the Romans supplanted the native civilizations; then Charlemagne supplanted the Romans (and gave the region its name—it was divided into "marks," or provinces, under the rule of the Holy Roman Emperor); then began the seemingly never-ending struggle between popes and local lords. Despite all this martial tussling, it was in the lonely mountain town of Urbino that the Renaissance came to its fullest flower; the small town became a haven of culture and learning that rivaled the larger, richer, and more powerful city of Florence, and even Rome itself.

Numbers in the text correspond to numbers in the margin and on the Umbria and the Marches, Perugia, Spoleto, and Assisi maps.

10

If you have 3 days

In 🗺 **Perugia** ❶–❹ ►, your main stops should be the Galleria Nazionale dell'Umbria and the Collegio del Cambio, both housed in the atmospheric **Palazzo dei Priori** ❷; much of the rest of your day can be spent ambling along Corso Vannucci and toiling up and down the steep lanes on either side. Devote your second day to the medieval hill town of 🗺 **Assisi** ❺–❽ and its magnificently restored basilica, taking time for a stroll up through the main piazza. On your third day, get an early start and head south to **Spoleto** ⓬–⓲, where narrow streets abound with evocative views and delightful surprises.

If you have 5 days

Given five days, you will be able to spend a couple of them exploring the unspoiled neighboring region of the Marches. The area is somewhat remote, and your means of transportation will dictate what you can see. In any case, start your tour in 🗺 **Perugia** ❶–❹ ►, and follow the itinerary above for your first two days. If you are traveling by public transportation, spend your third night in 🗺 **Spoleto** ⓬–⓲, where you can jump on a train bound for **Ancona** ㉓; from here you can board a bus or a train for Pésaro and 🗺 **Urbino** ㉒. This hilltop gem retains its proud, self-contained character, almost untouched by modern construction. Plan for at least half a day for reaching Urbino from Spoleto, and it's not much shorter by car, crossing the Marches border from 🗺 **Gubbio** ❾, where you might spend your last day appreciating the views, shops, and choice hotels and restaurants.

If you have 7 days

Reserve four days for Umbria and three for the Marches. With greater flexibility you can choose how many nights you want to spend in Umbria's capital, 🗺 **Perugia** ❶–❹ ►, and how many in the region's smaller centers. More time in Perugia will allow you to explore the city thoroughly, including the archaeological museum, and you might take in the easy excursion to the wine village of **Torgiano** ❿ or the ceramics town of **Deruta** ⓫. 🗺 **Spoleto** ⓬–⓲ and 🗺 **Assisi** ❺–❽ are essential stops farther afield; you might stay for a night in each. 🗺 **Gubbio** ❾ is also worth an overnight. From Spoleto, you can explore the classic hill town of **Todi** ⓴, unspoiled **Narni** ㉑, and the wine mecca **Orvieto** ⓳; they can also be seen on your way to or from Rome, only about 90 minutes away. From Spoleto, drive north to the Marches region for your last three days. 🗺 **Urbino** ㉒ is a must-see in the Marches. Head south for the inland town of 🗺 **Ascoli Piceno** ㉕—there is little in the way of hotels, galleries, or sophisticated shops here, but it's marvelously quaint. On the way—or on the way back—drop in at the sanctuary of **Loreto** ㉔, nestled in the mountains 24 km (15 mi) south of Ancona.

Exploring Umbria & the Marches

The region of Umbria is compact enough that you can have a satisfying tour in relatively limited amount of time. If you have a car, Perugia makes a convenient base for exploring the region; you can see all the major sights in the regional capital in one day, then make easy excursions to the hill towns on your other days without feeling overwhelmed by constant travel. Without a car, plan overnights in towns farther afield. East of Perugia, the Marches invite leisurely exploring, but expect some lengthy rides between the main points of interest.

The steep hills and deep valleys that make Umbria and the Marches so picturesque also make for challenging driving. Choose routes carefully to avoid tortuous mountain roads; major towns are not necessarily linked to each other by train, bus, or highway. A detailed local road map is always helpful.

About the Restaurants & Hotels

Virtually every historic town in Umbria and the Marches has some kind of hotel, no matter how small the place may be. A popular trend in Umbria, particularly around Gubbio, Orvieto, and Todi, is the conversion of old villas, farms, and monasteries into first-class hotels. These tend to be out in the countryside, but the splendor of the settings often outweighs the problem of getting into town—although you'll definitely need a car. Interestingly, hotels in town tend to be simpler than their country cousins, with notable exceptions in Spoleto, Gubbio, and Perugia. Chains are few, and most hotels are small, so it's always worth your while to call ahead and absolutely necessary when traveling in high season to Assisi, Spoleto, Orvieto, or Urbino.

WHAT IT COSTS In euros				
$$$$	**$$$**	**$$**	**$**	**¢**
RESTAURANTS over €22	€17–€22	€12–€17	€7–€12	under €7
HOTELS over €210	€160–€210	€110–€160	€60–€110	under €60

Restaurant prices are for a second course (secondo piatto). Hotel prices are for two people in a standard double room in high season, including tax and service.

Timing

The forested hills of Umbria and the Marches ensure beguiling colors in the fall and an explosion of greenery in spring. Bear in mind that winter is longer and colder here than in nearby Rome, so bring warm clothes to enjoy the outdoors from October to April. The consolation is that winter is the high season for the region's cuisine: January to April is truffle time in Norcia and Spoleto, and October to December brings a bounty of fresh local mushrooms. Book accommodations well in advance if you are planning to visit in June and July, when the Spoleto Festival dei Due Mondi and the Jazz Festival of Perugia take place. Sightseers and pilgrims throng the streets of Assisi year-round, but the religious festivals of Christmas, Easter, the feast of St. Francis (October 4), and the Calendimaggio Festival (May 1) draw even bigger crowds.

PERUGIA

The painter Perugino (the Perugian) filled his work with images of his home: soft hills with sparse trees, wide plains dotted with lakes. Despite the development of undistinguished modern suburbs, this peaceful landscape still exists, and venerable Perugia's medieval hilltop city remains almost completely intact. Perugia is the best-preserved hill town of its size; there are few better examples of the self-contained city-state that so shaped the course of Italian history.

Exploring Perugia

The best approach to the city is by train—the station is in the unlovely suburbs, but there are frequent buses running directly to Piazza d'Italia,

10

Cathedrals
While you'll find churches all over Italy that are architectural masterpieces and repositories of splendid art, Umbria has two of the country's most notable gems. In Orvieto, the facade of the Duomo is alone reason enough to visit the region, while inside, Luca Signorelli's frescoes have an incandescent glow that's thrilling to behold. In Assisi, the Basilica di San Francesco—actually two large churches, one Gothic and one Romanesque, standing side by side—is a major pilgrimage site, where throngs of the faithful have been drawing inspiration from the works of Giotto and Cimabue for more than 700 years.

Hiking
Magnificent scenery makes the heart of Italy excellent hiking and mountaineering country. In Umbria, the rocky area around Spoleto is particularly good, and the tourist office supplies itineraries of walks and climbs to suit all ages and levels of ability.

Shopping
Pottery and wine are the two most celebrated Umbrian exports, and examples of both commodities are excellent and unique to the region. Torgiano, south of Perugia, is one of the best-known centers of wine making, where you can watch the process and buy the product; you can find some of the best ceramics at Gubbio, Perugia, and Orvieto, a wine-making center in its own right. Ceramics with the most flair are found in Deruta, south of Torgiano on S3bis (in this case, "bis" means alternate highway). The red glazes of Gubbio pottery have been renowned since medieval times. The secret of the original glaze died with its inventor some 500 years ago, but some contemporary potters produce a fair facsimile.

---

the heart of the old town. If you are driving, leave your car in one of the parking lots near the station and then take the bus or the escalator, which passes through subterranean excavations of the Roman foundations of the city, from Piazza Partigiani to the Rocca Paolina.

a good walk

Starting in Piazza Italia, stroll down Corso Vannucci and head to the **Duomo** ❶ ▶ in Piazza IV Novembre. Visit the **Palazzo dei Priori** ❷, being sure to explore the Galleria Nazionale dell'Umbria and the **Collegio del Cambio** ❸, with its fine Perugino frescoes. A 10-minute walk south of the center along Corso Cavour leads to the **Museo Archeologico Nazionale** ❹. After perusing the Etruscan relics in the museum, return to Piazza IV Novembre, breaking for lunch or an espresso at a café.

TIMING A walk through Perugia takes about an hour, and if stopping at all sights along this itinerary, you should plan on at least a half day.

What to See

★ ❸ **Collegio del Cambio** (Bankers' Guild Hall). The series of elaborate rooms housed the meeting hall and chapel of the guild of bankers and money changers. The walls were frescoed from 1496 to 1500 by the most important Perugian painter of the Renaissance, Pietro Vannucci, better known as Perugino (circa 1450–1523). The iconography prevalent in the works includes common religious themes, like the Nativity and the Transfiguration (on the end walls), but also figures intended to inspire the businessmen who congregated here. On the left wall are female figures

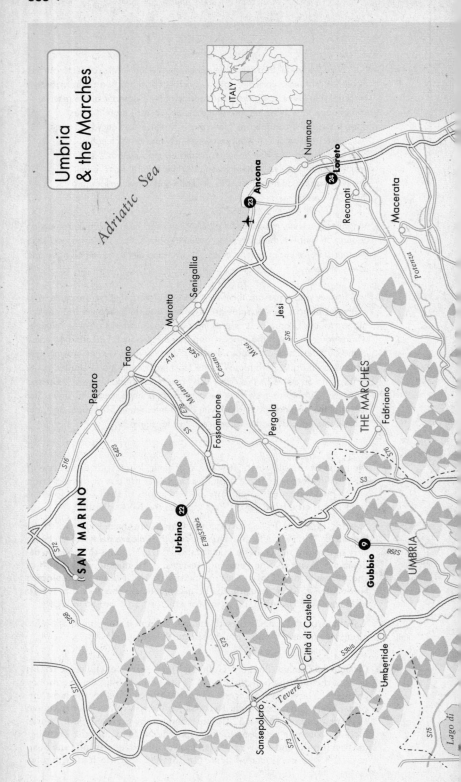

Umbria
& the Marches

ITALY

Adriatic Sea

Numana
Ancona
23
Loreto
24
Recanati
Macerata
Senigallia
Jesi
Marotta
S76
Fano
A14
Pesaro
Metauro
S78
S3
S424
Cesano
Misa
Potenza
Fossombrone
Pergola
THE MARCHES
Fabriano
S16
S16
S423
S3
S72
(SAN MARINO)
Urbino
22
E78/S73bis
Gubbio
9
S298
UMBRIA
E78
S73
Città di Castello
S9bis
S98
S73
Umbertide
S71
Tevere
Sansepolcro
S73
S75
Lago di

ON THE MENU

Central Italy is mountainous, and its food is hearty and straightforward, with a stick-to-the-ribs quality that sees hardworking farmers and artisans through a long day's work and helps them make the steep climb home at night. The region has made several important contributions to Italian cuisine. Particularly prized are winter's tartufi neri (black truffles) from the area around Spoleto and from the hills around the tiny town of Norcia. The local pasta specialties—thick, handmade ciriole

(roughly shaped, fat spaghetti) or stringozzi (long, thin pasta)—are even better prepared al tartufo, enriched with excellent local olive oil and truffles. Norcia's pork products—especially sausages, salami, and arista (roast loin perfumed with rosemary)—are so famous that pork butchers throughout Italy are called norcini, and pork butcher shops are called norcinerie.

representing the Virtues, beneath them the heroes and sages of antiquity. On the right wall are the prophets and sibyls. Perugino's most famous pupil, Raffaello Sanzio, or Raphael (1483–1520), is said to have painted here, his hand, experts say, most apparent in the figure of Fortitude. On one of the pilasters is a remarkably honest self-portrait of Perugino, surmounted by a Latin inscription. The Collegio is on the ground floor of the Palazzo dei Priori, and is entered from Corso Vannucci. ⊠ *Corso Vannucci 25* ☎ *075/5728599* ☎ *€2.60* ☼ *Mar.–Oct., Mon.–Sat. 9–12:30 and 2:30–5:30, Sun. 9–12:30; Nov.–Dec. 19 and Jan. 7–Feb., Tues.–Sat. 8–2, Sun. 9–12:30; Dec. 20–Jan. 6, Tues.–Sat. 9–12:30 and 2:30–5:30, Sun. 9–12:30.*

Corso Vannucci. The heart of the city is the broad stately pedestrian street that runs from Piazza d'Italia to Piazza IV Novembre. As evening falls, Corso Vannucci is filled with Perugians out for their evening *passeggiata*, a pleasant predinner stroll that may include a pause for an *aperitivo* at one of the many cafés that line the street.

▶ ❶ **Duomo.** This church's prize relic is the Virgin Mary's wedding ring, stolen in 1488 from the nearby town of Chiusi. The ring, kept in a chapel on the left aisle, is the size of a large bangle and is kept under lock—15 locks actually—and key year-round except July 30 and the second-to-last Sunday in January. The first date commemorates the day the ring was brought to Perugia, the second Mary's wedding anniversary. The cathedral itself is large and rather plain, dating from the Middle Ages but with many additions from the 15th and 16th centuries. There are some elaborately carved choir stalls, executed by Giovanni Battista Bastone in 1520. Precious objects associated with the cathedral are on display at the **Museo Capitolare,** including vestments, vessels, manuscripts, and gold work. An early masterpiece by Luca Signorelli (circa 1450–1523) is the altarpiece showing the Madonna with St. John the Baptist, St. Onophrio, and St. Lawrence (1484). ⊠ *Piazza IV Novembre* ☎ *075/5723832* ☎ *Duomo free, museum €2.60* ☼ *Duomo, Mon.–Sat. 7–12:30 and 4–6:45, Sun. 8–12:30 and 4–6:45; museum, weekdays 10–1, Sun. 10–1 and 4–6.*

❹ **Museo Archeologico Nazionale.** This museum next to the imposing church of San Domenico contains an excellent collection of Etruscan artifacts from throughout the region. Perugia was a flourishing Etruscan site long before it fell under Roman domination in 310 BC. Other than this col-

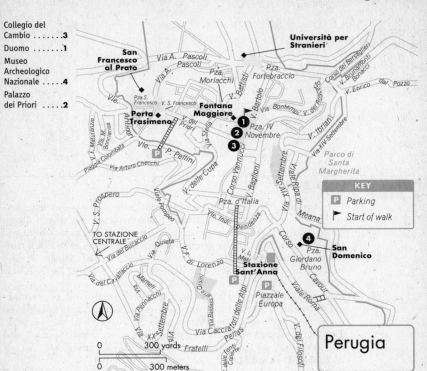

lection, little remains of Perugia's earliest ancestors, although the **Arco di Augusto** (Arch of Augustus), in Piazza Fortebraccio, the northern entrance to the city, is of Etruscan origin. ✉ *Piazza G. Bruno 10* ☎ *075/5727141* ⊕ *www.archeopg.arti.beniculturali.it* 🎫 *€2* ☉ *Mon. 2:30–7:30, Tues.–Sun. 8:30–7:30.*

★ ❷ **Palazzo dei Priori.** The imposing palace, begun in the 13th century, has an unusual staircase that fans out into Piazza IV Novembre. The facade is decorated with symbols of Perugia's former power: the griffin is the city's symbol; the lion denotes Perugia's allegiance to the medieval Guelph (or papal) cause. Both figures support the heavy chains of the gates of Siena, which fell to Perugian forces in 1358. The third floor of the Palazzo dei Priori contains the region's most comprehensive art gallery, the **Galleria Nazionale dell'Umbria.** Enhanced by skillfully lighted displays and well-placed information panels (in Italian and English), the collection includes work by native artists—most notably Pinturicchio (1454–1513) and Perugino—along with others of the Umbrian and Tuscan schools, including Gentile da Fabriano (1370–1427), Duccio (circa 1255–1318), Fra Angelico (1387–1455), Fiorenzo di Lorenzo (1445–1525), and Piero della Francesca (1420–92). The gallery also exhibits frescoes, sculptures, and several superb painted crucifixes from the 13th and 14th centuries; other rooms are dedicated to Perugia itself, illustrating the evolution of the medieval city. ✉ *Corso Vannucci 19, Piazza IV Novembre* ☎ *075/5721009* ⊕ *www.gallerianazionaledellumbria.it* 🎫 *€6.50* ☉ *Sept.16–June 15, daily 8:30–7:30, June 16–Sept. 15, Sun.–Fri. 8:30–7:30, and Sat. 8:30–11 PM; last admission ½ hr before closing* ☉ *Closed 1st Mon. of each month.*

off the
beaten
path

LA CITTÀ DELLA DOMENICA – Umbria's only attraction aimed directly at the younger set is La Città della Domenica, a theme-park–style playground in the town of Montepulito, just west of Perugia on the secondary road that leads to Corciano. The 500 acres of parkland contain buildings based on familiar fairy-tale themes—Snow White's House, the Witches' Wood—as well as a reptile house, aquarium, medieval museum, exhibit of shells from all over the world, game rooms, and a choice of restaurants. ⊠ *Via Col di Tenda 140, Località Montepulito, 8 km (5 mi) west of Perugia* ☎ *075/5054941* ⊠ €9 ⊙ *Easter–mid-Sept., daily 10–7; mid-Sept.–Oct., weekends 10–7; Nov.–Easter, aquarium and reptile house only, Sat. 2–7, Sun. 10–7.*

Where to Stay & Eat

$$ ✕ **La Taverna.** Medieval steps lead to this rustic restaurant on two levels, where wine bottles and artful clutter heighten the tavern atmosphere. The menu features regional specialties; good choices include *ravioli fatti in casa al tartufo nero e pinoli* (homemade ravioli with black truffles and pine nuts), and grilled meat dishes. ⊠ *Via delle Streghe 8, next to the Teatro Pavone, off Corso Vannucci* ☎ *075/5724128* ⋌ *Reservations essential* ⊟ *AE, DC, MC, V* ⊙ *Closed Mon.*

$–$$ ✕ **Il Falchetto.** Here you'll find exceptional food at reasonable prices, making this Perugia's best restaurant bargain. Service is smart but relaxed in the two medieval dining rooms, with the kitchen and chef on view. The house specialty is *falchetti* (homemade gnocchi with spinach and ricotta cheese). ⊠ *Via Bartolo 20* ☎ *075/5731775* ⊟ *AE, DC, MC, V* ⊙ *Closed Mon. and last 2 wks in Jan.*

¢ ✕ **Dal Mi' Cocco.** A great favorite with Perugia's university students, this is a fun, crowded, and truly inexpensive place to enjoy a multicourse, fixed-price meal. You may find yourself seated at a long table with other diners, but some language help from your neighbors could come in handy—the menu is in pure Perugian dialect. Meals change with the seasons, and each day of the week brings some new creation *dal cocco* (from the coconut) of the chef. ⊠ *Corso Garibaldi 7* ☎ *075/5732511* ⋌ *Reservations essential* ⊟ *No credit cards* ⊙ *Closed Mon.*

$$$$ ▥ **Brufani Palace.** A 19th-century palazzo has been turned into an elegant lodging choice. The Brufani's public rooms and first-floor guest rooms have high ceilings and are done in the grand Belle Epoque style. Second-floor rooms are more modern; many on both floors have a marvelous view of the Umbrian countryside or the city. ⊠ *Piazza Italia 12, 06121* ☎ *075/5732541* ☐ *075/5720210* ⊕ *www.brufanipalace.com* ⊠ *63 rooms, 31 suites* ⋋ *Restaurant, pool, gym, bar, meeting room* ⊟ *AE, DC, MC, V.*

$$$ ▥ **Locanda della Posta.** In the center of Perugia's historic district, this hotel is situated in an 18th-century palazzo. Renovation has left the reception and other public areas rather bland, but the rooms, all of which are carpeted, are tastefully and soothingly decorated in muted colors. Bathrooms are spacious and well equipped. Though sound-proofed, rooms at the front of the hotel face the busy Corso Vannucci and should be avoided in favor of those on the upper floors at the back of the building, which also have great views. ⊠ *Corso Vannucci 97, 06121* ☎ *075/5728925* ☐ *075/5732562* ⊠ *38 rooms, 1 suite* ⋋ *Minibars, bar, parking (fee)* ⊟ *AE, DC, MC, V.*

¢–$ ▥ **Rosalba.** Here's a bright and friendly choice on the fringes of Perugia's historic center. Basic rooms are scrupulously clean, and the ones at the back enjoy a view. On the top floor, room 9 has a private terrace and sleeps up to five people, making it perfect for a family or group of friends. Although somewhat out of the way, the hotel is only a matter of minutes from Corso Vannucci by virtue of a nearby public escalator stop. ⊠ *Via del Circo 7, 06100* ☎ *075/5728285* ☎ *075/5720626* ⇱ *11 rooms* ♿ *Free parking; no room TVs* ▭ *No credit cards.*

¢ ▦ **Paola.** This small family-run *pensione* is easily reached by bus from the train station and moments away from the town center by virtue of a nearby public escalator. The beds may be on the soft side, and none of the rooms has a private bathroom, but you can be certain of a warm and friendly welcome from the owner, Signora Paola. If you stay for more than three nights, you're offered access to the kitchen in the evening. ⊠ *Via della Canapina 5, 06121* ☎ *075/5723816* ⇱ *8 rooms with shared bath* ♿ No room phones, no room TVs, no a/c ▭ No credit cards.

Nightlife & the Arts

The monthly *Viva Perugia* (sold at newsstands), with a section in English, is a good source of information about what's going on in town.

Music Festivals

Summer sees two international music festivals in Perugia. The **Umbria Jazz Festival** (☎ 075/5732432 ☎ 075/572256 ⊕ www.umbriajazz.com) is a world-famous concert series lasting for 10 days in July. Call year-round for information about the festival or to buy tickets with a credit card as early as the end of April. The **Sagra Musicale Umbra** (☎ 075/5732800 ⊕ www.umbria.org/eng/eventi), which takes place over 10 days in September, celebrates traditional music of the region.

If you're a music lover, consider trekking to the **Festival delle Nazioni di Musica da Camera** (International Chamber Music Festival; ☎ 075/8521142 ☎ 075/8552461), a two-week event held in late August and early September in Città di Castello, about 80 km (50 mi) north of Perugia on the S3bis. For information, contact the festival office.

Shopping

Chocolate

It's not hard to be tempted by Perugia's famous **Perugina chocolate**, although there's no immediate need to load yourself with presents to bring home, as the brand (a Nestlé company since the early 1990s) is easily found all over Italy. *Cioccolato al latte* (milk chocolate) and *fondente* (dark chocolate), set in tiny jewel-like boxes or in giant gift boxes the size of serving trays, are sold all over town. But the best-known chocolates made by Perugina are the round hazelnut-filled chocolate candies called Baci (literally "kisses"), which come wrapped in silver foil and, like fortune cookies, contain romantic sentiments or sayings in several languages, English included. The third week in October is especially sweet, when Perugia hosts the **Eurochocolate Festival** (⊕ www.eurochocolate.perugia.it), and the streets are filled with stands, sculptures, and—best of all—tastings.

Shopping District

Perugia is a well-to-do town, and judging by the expensive shops on **Corso Vannucci**, the Perugians are not afraid to part with their euros. The main streets are lined with clothing shops selling the best-known Italian designers such as Gucci, Ferragamo, Armani, and Fendi.

ASSISI

The legacy of St. Francis, founder of the Franciscan monastic order, pervades the rosy hills of Assisi, 47 km (30 mi) north of Spoleto and 25 km (16 mi) east of Perugia. Each year, the city hosts several million pilgrims, but not even the massive flow of visitors to this town of only 3,000 residents can spoil the singular beauty of one of Italy's most significant religious centers. The hill on which Assisi sits rises dramatically from the flat plain, and the town is dominated at the top of the mount by a medieval castle; on the lower slope of the hill is the massive Basilica di San Francesco, sitting majestically on graceful arched supports.

Like most other towns in the region, Assisi began as an Umbri settlement in the 7th century BC and was conquered by the Romans 400 years later. The town was Christianized by St. Rufino, its patron saint, in AD 238, but it is the spirit of St. Francis, patron saint of Italy and founder of the Franciscan monastic order, that is felt throughout its narrow medieval streets. The famous 13th-century basilica built in his honor was decorated by the greatest artists of the period. Assisi is pristinely medieval in architecture and appearance, due in large part to relative neglect from the 16th century until 1926, when the celebration of the 700th anniversary of St. Francis's death brought more than 2 million visitors. Since then, Assisi has become one of the most important pilgrimage destinations in the Christian world.

A series of earthquakes in the fall of 1997 devastated Umbria and the Marches, rendering uninhabitable countless homes and causing the partial collapse of the ceiling of Assisi's Upper Basilica, frescoed with some of the great masterpieces of Giotto and Cimabue. It was feared that the frescoes, reduced to rubble, were beyond repair, but a massive effort by art restorers and volunteers is in the process of saving some of them. Although the Upper Basilica has reopened, many of Assisi's medieval stone buildings are still propped up by wooden scaffolding; by and large, however, the town has recovered.

Exploring Assisi

The train station is 4 km (2½ mi) from town, with bus service about every half hour. The walled town is closed to outside traffic, so cars must be left in the parking lots at Porta San Pietro, near Porta Nuova, or beneath Piazza Matteotti. Frequent city minibuses run between the parking lots and the center of town.

a good walk

Much of your time in Assisi will likely be spent visiting churches and walking through the quiet streets. At the top of your list should be the **Basilica di San Francesco** ⑤ ▶, with its miraculously restored upstairs ceiling. Via San Francesco leads back to Piazza del Comune and its Pinacoteca, Museo Civico, and the **Tempio di Minerva** ⑥. From the piazza, Via di San Rufino leads to **San Rufino** ⑦, Assisi's town cathedral. Double back to the piazza and take Corso Mazzini to **Santa Chiara** ⑧. Also of interest outside the city walls are the Eremo delle Carceri, east of the center along Via Santuario delle Carceri, and the church of Santa Maria degli Angeli, near the train station.

TIMING   Devote a half day or more to this walk. After seeing the basilica, stroll the length of town, stopping at churches and shops.

What to See

▶ ⑤   **Basilica di San Francesco.** The basilica is not one church but two, the Gothic upper part built a scant half-century after the Romanesque lower. Work on this two-tiered monolith was begun just a few years after the death of St. Francis. His coffin, unearthed from its secret hiding place after a 52-day search in 1818, is on display in the crypt below the Lower Basilica. Both churches are magnificently decorated artistic treasure houses, covered floor to ceiling with some of Europe's finest frescoes: the Lower Basilica is dim and full of candlelight shadows, while the Upper Basil-

Fodor'sChoice
★

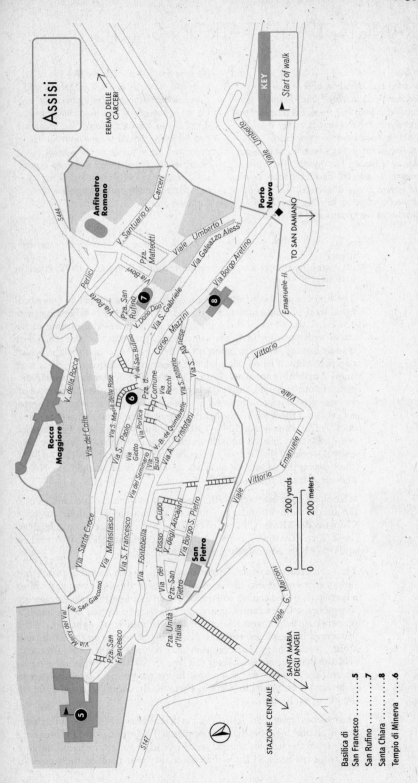

Assisi

KEY

▲ Start of walk

CloseUp

FRANCIS, ITALY'S PATRON SAINT

St. Francis was born in Assisi in 1181, the son of a noblewoman and a well-to-do merchant. His troubled and dissolute youth included a year in prison; he planned on a career in the military, but after a long illness he heard the voice of God, renounced his father's wealth, and began a life of austerity. His mystical embrace of poverty, asceticism, and the beauty of man and nature struck a responsive chord in the medieval mind, and he quickly attracted a vast number of followers.

He was the first saint to receive the stigmata (wounds in his hands, feet, and side corresponding to the torments of Christ on the cross). He died on October 4, 1226, in the Porziuncola, the secluded chapel in the woods where he had first preached the virtue of poverty to his disciples. St. Francis was declared patron saint of Italy in 1939, and today the Franciscans make up the largest of the Catholic orders.

ica, carefully restored after severe earthquake damage in 1997, is bright and airy.

The first chapel to the left of the nave in the **Lower Basilica** was decorated by the Sienese master Simone Martini (1284–1344). Dating from 1322–26, the frescoes show the life of St. Martin—the sharing of his cloak with the poor man, the saint's knighthood, and his death. There is some dispute about the paintings in the third chapel on the right, which depict the life of Mary Magdalen. Experts have argued for years, with many attributing them to Giotto (1266–1337). There is a similar dispute about the works above the high altar, depicting the marriage of St. Francis to poverty, chastity, and obedience—some say they are by Giotto; others claim them for an anonymous pupil. In the right transept are frescoes by Cimabue (circa 1240–1302), including a Madonna and saints, one of them St. Francis himself. In the left transept are some of the best-known works of the Sienese painter Pietro Lorenzetti (circa 1280–1348). They depict the *Madonna with Sts. John and Francis,* the *Crucifixion,* and the *Descent from the Cross.*

It's quite a contrast to climb the steps next to the altar and emerge into the bright sunlight and airy grace of the double-arched Renaissance **Chiostro dei Morti** (Cloister of the Dead). A door to the right leads to the **Tesoro** (Treasury) of the church and contains relics of St. Francis and other holy objects associated with the order.

The reconstruction of the **Upper Basilica** has been hailed as proof that Italian efficiency doesn't have to be an oxymoron. Only two years after a large part of the ceiling collapsed in a series of earthquakes, reducing to rubble the Giotto and Cimabue frescoes that adorned it, the basilica reopened, little the worse for wear. Although the frescoes are still in the process of being pieced together (as the blank spaces on the vaults will attest), there is hope that even they may someday be restored. You can visit the **restoration workshop** (✉ free ⊙ Sat.10–5) behind the basilica and see how the work is going. In the meantime, there's no dearth of intact art treasures to admire, particularly Giotto's famed cycle on the life of St. Francis.

The frescoes show that Giotto, only in his twenties when he painted them, was a pivotal artist in the development of Western painting, breaking away from the stiff, unnatural styles of earlier generations and moving toward a realism and three-dimensionality that reached their peak in the Renaissance. The paintings are meant to be viewed from left to right, starting in the transept. The most beloved of the scenes is probably *St. Francis Preaching to the Birds,* a touching painting that seems to sum up the gentle spirit of the saint. It stands in marked contrast to the scene of the dream of Innocent III (circa 1160–1216). The pope dreams of a humble monk who will steady the church. Sure enough, in the panel next to the sleeping pope, you see a strong Francis supporting a church that seems to be on the verge of tumbling down—a scene that resonates with irony today. ⊠ *Piazza di San Francesco* ☎ *075/819001* ☺ *Lower Basilica, Easter–Oct., daily 6 AM–6:50 PM; Nov.–Easter, daily 6–5:50. Upper Basilica, Easter–Oct., daily 8:30–6:50; Nov.–Easter, daily 8:30–5:50.*

❼ **San Rufino.** St. Francis and St. Clare were among those baptized in Assisi's Duomo, the principal church in town until the 12th century. The baptismal font has since been redecorated, but it is possible to see the **crypt** of San Rufino, the martyred 3rd-century bishop who brought Christianity to Assisi. Admission to the crypt includes a look at the small **Museo Capitolare,** which features detached frescoes and artifacts. ⊠ *Piazza San Rufino* ☎ *075/812283* 🎫 *Duomo free, crypt and museum €2.07* ☺ *Duomo, daily 7–noon and 2–sunset; crypt and museum, Mar. 16–Oct. 15, daily 10–1 and 2–5; Oct. 16–Mar. 15, daily 10:30–1 and 3–6.*

❽ **Santa Chiara.** This striking red-striped 13th-century church is dedicated to St. Clare, one of the earliest and most fervent of St. Francis's followers and the founder of the Order of Poor Clares, in imitation of the Franciscans. The church contains the body of the saint, and in the **Cappella del Crocifisso** is the crucifix that spoke to St. Francis and led him to a life of piety. A heavily veiled member of St. Clare's order is stationed before the cross in perpetual adoration of the image. ⊠ *Piazza Santa Chiara* ☎ *075/812282* ☺ *Daily 7–noon and 2–sunset.*

❻ **Tempio di Minerva.** Pieces of a Roman temple dating from the time of Augustus (63 BC–AD 14) make up this sanctuary dedicated to the goddess of wisdom. The expectations raised by the perfect classical facade are not met by the interior, subjected to a thorough baroque assault in the 17th century, but both are worth a look. ⊠ *Piazza del Comune* ☺ *Daily 7–noon and 2:30–sunset.*

off the beaten path

CANNARA – A pleasant excursion from Assisi leads to this tiny town 16 km (10 mi) away; a half hour's walk then brings you to the fields of Pian d'Arca, the legendary site of St. Francis's sermon to the birds.

EREMO DELLE CARCERI – Just 4 km (2½ mi) east of Assisi is this monastery set in dense woodlands on the side of Monte Subasio. In the caves on the slope of the mountain, Francis and his followers established their first home, to which he returned often during his lifetime to pray and meditate. The church and monastery retain the tranquil, contemplative air St. Francis so prized. From a vantage point within the monastery, there are splendid views of the Umbrian countryside. True to their Franciscan heritage, the friars here are entirely dependent on alms from visitors. ⊠ *Via Santuario delle Carceri* ☎ *075/812301* 🎫 *Donations accepted* ☺ *Nov.–Mar., daily 6:30–5; Apr.–Oct., daily 6:30 AM–7 PM.*

SANTA MARIA DEGLI ANGELI – On the outskirts of town, near the train station, this baroque church was built over the **Porziuncola,** a chapel restored by St. Francis. The shrine is much venerated because it was in the **Cappella del Transito,** then a humble cell, that St. Francis died in 1226. ⊠ *Località Santa Maria degli Angeli* ☺ *Daily 7 AM–sunset.*

Where to Stay & Eat

Advance room reservations are absolutely essential is you are visiting Assisi between Easter and October or over Christmas, especially since hotels in the town itself are the first to fill up; latecomers are often left to choose from those in modern Santa Maria degli Angeli, 8 km (5 mi) out of town. Until the early 1980s, **pilgrim hostels** outnumbered ordinary hotels in Assisi, and they present an interesting and economical alternative to conventional lodgings. These pilgrim hostels are called *ostelli* (hostels) or *conventi* (convents) because they're run by private convents, churches, or other Catholic organizations. Rooms are on the spartan side, but you are virtually assured of a peaceful stay. Check with the Assisi tourist office (⊠ Piazza del Comune 12, 06081 ☎ 075/812534 ⊕ www.comune.assisi.pg.it) for a list.

$–$$ ✕ **Buca di San Francesco.** This central restaurant is Assisi's busiest—it's no wonder, for the setting is lovely no matter what the season. In summer you dine outside in a cool green garden; in winter, under the low brick arches of the restaurant's cozy cellars. The food is first rate: try spaghetti *alla buca,* homemade pasta served with a roasted mushroom sauce. ⊠ *Via Brizi 1* ☎ *075/812204* ▤ *AE, DC, MC, V* ☉ *Closed Mon. and July.*

$ ✕ **La Fortezza.** Parts of the walls of this modern family-run restaurant were built by the Romans. The service is personable and the kitchen reliable. A particular standout is *anatra al finocchio selvatico* (duck with wild fennel). La Fortezza also has seven simple but clean guest rooms available. ⊠ *Vicolo della Fortezza 2/b* ☎ *075/812418* ⌂ *Reservations essential* ▤ *AE, DC, MC, V* ☉ *Closed Thurs. and Feb.*

★ ¢–$ ✕ **Osteria Piazzetta dell'Erba.** A great change of pace in a town with more than its fair share of stodgy tourist eateries, this is an excellent place to come for an informal meal or light snack. There are two different *primi piatti* (first courses) on offer every day, along with various salads and a good selection of toppings to go with the ever-present torta al testo. The "imported" goat cheese is from Sardinia and is a delicious surprise. There are tables outside in the summer. ⊠ *Via San Gabriele dell'Addolorata 15b* ☎ *075/815352* ▤ *AE, DC, MC, V* ☉ *Closed Mon. and 3 wks in Jan.*

¢ ✕ **La Stalla.** Less than a kilometer (½ mi) outside the town, and a good place to stop for lunch on your way to or from the Eremo delle Carceri, this onetime stable has been turned into a simple and rustic restaurant. In summer enjoy lunch or dinner outside under a trellis shaded with vines and flowers. The kitchen turns out hearty country fare; for something light, try the *torte al testo* a crepelike flat bread used to wrap your choice of local cheeses, salami, and grilled meats, and vegetables. ⊠ *Via Santuario delle Carceri 8* ☎ *075/812317* ▤ *No credit cards* ☉ *Closed Mon. in Oct.–June.*

¢ ✕▥ **La Pallotta.** One of the best hotels in its category and a great family-run restaurant are found here under one roof. Upstairs, the beds are firm, and some of the upper floor rooms look out across the rooftops of town. Downstairs, with a separate entrance on the alley around the corner, Vicolo della Volta Pinta ($) is a cozy trattoria with a fireplace and stone walls. Here, a range of tasty local dishes is well prepared and reasonably priced. The *menu di degustazione* (tasting menu) is a good way to sample the house specialities. ⊠ *Via San Ruffino 6, 06081* ☎ *075/812649* ☎▤ *075/812307* ⊕ *www.pallottaassisi.it* ⤴ *8 rooms* △ *Restaurant, bar; no a/c* ▤ *AE, DC, MC, V.*

FodorsChoice ★

$$$ ▥ **Castello di Petrata.** A winding gravel road leads to this peaceful haven in the hills behind Assisi. Built as a fortress in the 14th century, the Petrata dominates its position, with Monte Subasio, Assisi, and the dis-

FodorsChoice ★

tant hills and valleys of Perugia all in view. Every room is different from the next, and all are impeccably furnished. The bathrooms are all well-equipped, but those with tubs are considerably more spacious than those with showers. The hotel's fine restaurant offers a wide range of Umbrian specialities in a particularly elegant setting. ⊠ *Località Petrata 22, Pieve San Nicolò, 6 km (3½ mi) east of Assisi, 06081* ☎ *075/ 815451* 🖶 *075/8043026* ⊕ *www.castellopetrata.com* ⟿ *21 rooms, 2 suites* ⟳ *Restaurant, minibars, pool, bar, Internet, meeting rooms, some pets allowed; no a/c* ⊟ *AE, DC, MC, V* ⊗ *Closed Jan.–Feb.*

$$$ 🖼 **Hotel Subasio.** Close to the Basilica di San Francesco, the Subasio, housed in a converted monastery, has counted Marlene Dietrich and Charlie Chaplin among its guests. Some of the rooms remain a little monastic, but the splendid views, comfortable old-fashioned sitting rooms, flower-decked terraces, and a lovely garden more than balance out a certain austerity in the furnishings. Ask for a room overlooking the valley. ⊠ *Via Frate Elia 2, 06082* ☎ *075/812206* 🖶 *075/816691* ⊕ *www.umbria.org/ hotel/subasio* ⟿ *54 rooms, 8 suites* ⟳ *Restaurant, bar, parking (fee)* ⊟ *AE, DC, MC, V.*

$$ 🖼 **San Francesco.** You can't beat the location—the roof terrace and some of the rooms look out onto the Basilica di San Francesco, which is just opposite the hotel. Rooms and facilities range from simple to homely, but you'll be reminded that looks aren't everything with nice touches like slippers, a good-night piece of chocolate, and soundproofing. Fruit, homemade tarts, and fresh ricotta make for a first-rate breakfast. ⊠ *Via San Francesco 4, 06082* ☎ *075/812281* 🖶 *075/816237* ⊕ *www. hotelsanfrancescoassisi.it* ⟿ *44 rooms* ⟳ *Restaurant, minibars, bar, Internet, some pets allowed* ⊟ *AE, DC, MC, V.*

★ **$** 🖼 **Hotel Umbra.** A 16th-century town house is the locale of this charming hotel in a tranquil part of the city, an area closed to traffic and near Piazza del Comune. The rooms are arranged as small apartments, each with tiny living room and balcony. Ask for an upper room with a view over the Assisi rooftops to the valley below. The restaurant, closed for lunch on Tuesday and Wednesday, has a charming vine-covered terrace leading to a secluded garden. ⊠ *Via degli Archi 6, 06081* ☎ *075/ 812240* 🖶 *075/813653* ⊕ *www.hotelumbra.it* ⟿ *25 rooms* ⟳ *Restaurant, minibars, bar* ⊟ *AE, DC, MC, V* ⊗ *Closed mid-Jan.–mid-Mar.*

NORTHERN UMBRIA

To the north of Perugia, placid, walled Gubbio watches over green countryside, true to its nickname, "City of Silence"—except for its fast and furious festivals in May, as lively today as when they began more than 800 years ago. To the south, along the Tiber River valley, are the towns of Deruta and Torgiano, best known for their hand-painted ceramics and wine—as locals say, go to Deruta to buy a pitcher and to Torgiano to fill it.

Gubbio

❾ *40 km (25 mi) northeast of Perugia, 92 km (57 mi) east of Arezzo.*

There is something otherworldly about this small jewel of a medieval town tucked away in a rugged, mountainous corner of Umbria. Even at the height of summer, the cool serenity of the City of Silence's streets remains intact. The town teeters on the slopes of Monte Ingino, and the streets are dramatically steep. Parking in the central Piazza dei Quaranta Martiri (40 Martyrs Square), named for 40 hostages murdered by the Nazis in 1944, is easy and secure, and it is wise to leave your car there and explore the narrow lanes on foot.

★ The striking Piazza Grande is dominated by the **Palazzo dei Consoli,** the 14th-century meeting place of Gubbio's parliament. The palace is the home of a small museum, famous chiefly for the **Tavole Eugubine** (Gubbio Tablets), seven bronze tablets written in the ancient Umbrian language, employing Etruscan and Latin characters and providing the best key to understanding this obscure tongue. Also in the museum are a captivating miscellany of coins, medieval arms, paintings, and majolica and earthenware pots, not to mention the exhilarating views over Gubbio's roofscape and beyond from the lofty loggia. For a few days at the beginning of May, the palace also displays the famous *ceri,* the ceremonial pillars that are the focus of Gubbio's annual festivities. ⊠ *Piazza Grande* ☎ *075/9274298* ⊕ *www.comune.gubbio.pg.it* ⊠ *€4* ⊘ *Apr.–Oct., daily 10–1 and 3–6; Nov.–Mar., daily 10–1 and 2–5.*

The **Duomo,** on a narrow street on the highest tier of the town, dates from the 12th century, with some baroque additions—in particular, a lavishly decorated bishop's chapel. ⊠ *Via Ducale* ⊘ *Daily 8–12:45 and 3–7:30.*

The **Palazzo Ducale** is a scaled-down copy of the Palazzo Ducale in Urbino (Gubbio was once the possession of that city's ruling family, the Montefeltro). Gubbio's palazzo contains a small museum and a courtyard. There are magnificent views from some of the public rooms. ⊠ *Via Ducale* ☎ *075/9275872* ⊠ *€2.50* ⊘ *Tues.–Sun. 8:30–7:30.*

☾ Just outside Gubbio's walls at the eastern end of town (follow Corso Garibaldi or Via XX Settembre to the end), a **gondola** (⊠ Via S. Girolamo ☎ 075/9273881) provides a bracing panoramic ride to the top of Monte Ingino.Monte Ingino, along with its spectacular views, has the basilica of **Sant'Ubaldo,** repository of Gubbio's famous ceri, three 16-ft poles crowned with statues of Sts. Ubaldo, George, and Anthony. The pillars are transported to the Palazzo dei Consoli on the first Sunday of May, in preparation for the race which takes place during the Festival of the Ceri. ⊠ *Top of Monte Ingino* ⊘ *Daily 9–noon and 4–7.*

Where to Stay & Eat

\$\$–\$\$\$
FodorsChoice
★

✕ **Taverna del Lupo.** This tavern is one of the city's best, and one of the largest—it seats 150 people and can still get a bit hectic during the high season. Lasagna made in the Gubbian fashion, with ham and truffles, is an unusual indulgence. You'll also find excellent desserts and an extensive wine list. ⊠ *Via Ansidei 21* ☎ *075/9274368* ⊟ *AE, DC, MC, V* ⊘ *Closed Mon. in Oct.–Apr.*

\$
✕ **Bosone Garden.** Once the stables of the palace that houses the Hotel Bosone, this is a well-established Gubbio restaurant, with a summer garden that seats 200. Savory treats include a two-mushroom salad with truffles, risotto *alla porcina* (with porcini mushrooms, sausage, and truffles), and leg of pork. ⊠ *Via Mastro Giorgio 2* ☎ *075/9221246* ⊟ *AE, DC, MC, V* ⊘ *Closed Wed. in Oct.–May, and 2 wks in Jan.*

¢
✕🏠 **Grotta dell'Angelo.** A simple hotel and a rustic trattoria in the lower part of the old town, the "Angel's Grotto" is near the main square and tourist information office. Rooms are basic, with modern furnishings, but all have telephones, televisions, and private bathrooms. The restaurant (\$), with a few tables in the hotel's garden, serves simple local specialties, including salami, stringozzi pasta, and lasagna *tartufata* (with truffles). ⊠ *Via Gioia 47, 06024* ☎ *075/9271747* 🖷 *075/9273438* 🛏 *18 rooms* ⟂ *Parking (fee); no a/c* ⊟ *AE, DC, MC, V* ⊘ *Closed 3 wks in Jan.*

\$
🏠 **Hotel Bosone Palace.** This old-style hotel occupies the central Palazzo Raffaelli. Standard rooms vary in size and are comfortably though soberly decorated with heavy wooden furniture. Two enormous suites are furnished with antiques and, like the hotel's small and delightful breakfast room, have elaborately frescoed ceilings. Ask for a room facing the

valley and away from the sometimes noisy street. ⊠ *Via XX Settembre 22, 06024* ☎ *075/9220688* 🖷 *075/9220552* 🛏 *28 rooms, 2 suites* 🖔 *Minibars, bar; no a/c* ⊟ *AE, DC, MC, V* ⊘ *Closed Jan.*

$ 🏨 **Hotel Gattapone.** Right in the town center, this hotel has wonderful views of the sea of rooftops. It's casual and family-run, with good-size, modern, comfortable rooms, some with well-preserved timber-raftered ceilings. ⊠ *Via Ansidei 6, 06024* ☎ *075/9272489* 🖷 *075/9272417* ⊕ *www.mencarelligroup.com* 🛏 *16 rooms, 2 suites* 🖔 *Bar, parking (fee); no a/c* ⊟ *AE, DC, MC, V* ⊘ *Closed Jan. 8–Feb. 8.*

Nightlife & the Arts

🖔 Gubbio explodes with exuberance every May 15 during the **Corsa dei Ceri** (Race of the Poles), held yearly since 1151 in honor of St. Ubaldo, the town's patron saint. Three 16-ft constructions, elaborately decorated and crowned with statues of Sts. Ubaldo, George, and Anthony (representing three medieval guilds), are carried by teams up Mount Ingino. Don't place any bets, though; Ubaldo always wins.

At Christmastime, kitsch is king in Gubbio. From December 7 to January 10, colored lights are strung down the mountainside in a tree pattern as the town stakes its claim as the home of the **world's largest Christmas tree.**

Sports & the Outdoors

🖔 A costumed medieval pageant with its roots in Gubbio's warring past, the **Palio della Balestra** (Crossbow Tournament) takes place on the last Sunday in May; contact the **Gubbio tourist office** (⊠ Piazza Oderisi 6, 06024 ☎ 075/9220693) for details.

Torgiano

⑩ *15 km (9 mi) southeast of Perugia, 18 km (11 mi) southwest of Assisi.*

Wine aficionados are likely to enjoy a visit to Torgiano's **Cantine Lungarotti** winery, best known for Rubesco Lungarotti, San Giorgio, and chardonnay. ⊠ *Via Mario Angeloni 12* ☎ *075/9880348* ⊘ *Tours weekdays 8–1 and 3–6, by appointment only.*

The **Museo del Vino** (Wine Museum) has a large collection of ancient wine vessels, presses, documents, and tools that tell the story of viticulture in Umbria and beyond. Next door at the **Osteria del Museo** (☎🖷 075/9880069), devoted exclusively to the Lungarotti winery, you can taste and buy these highly regarded wines. ⊠ *Corso Vittorio Emanuele 11* ☎ *075/9880200* 🎟 *€2.60* ⊘ *Apr.–Oct., daily 9–1 and 3–7; Nov.–Mar., daily 9–1 and 3–6.*

Deruta

⑪ *7 km (4 mi) south of Torgiano, 20 km (12 mi) southeast of Perugia.*

Deruta has been known for its ceramics since the 16th century. Notable in this medieval hill town are the 14th-century church of San Francesco and the Palazzo Comunale, but Deruta's main attraction is the magnificent ceramics collection in the **Museo Regionale della Ceramica.** ⊠ *Largo San Francesco* ☎ *075/9711000* 🎟 *€2.58* ⊘ *Apr.–June, daily 10:30–1 and 3–6; July–Sept., daily 10–1 and 3:30–7; Oct.–Mar., Wed.–Mon. 10:30–1 and 2:30–5.*

Shopping

CERAMICS Deruta has more than 70 ceramics workshops and boutiques. Start your browsing in the central Piazza dei Consoli, where you'll find a good selection at **Maioliche Cynthia** (⊠ Via Umberto I 1 ☎ 075/9711255), specializing in reproductions of antique designs. **Ceramiche El Frate** (✉ Piazza dei Consoli 29 ☎ 075/9711435) sells unusual tiles and jugs. The workshop at **Fabbrica Maioliche Tradizionali** (✉ Via Tiberina Nord 37 ☎ 075/9711220) is open for visits weekdays 8:30–1 and 2:30–4:30 and also operates one of the largest shops in the area.

SPOLETO

For most of the year, Spoleto is one in a pleasant succession of sleepy hill towns. But for three weeks every summer, it shifts into high gear for its turn in the spotlight: the Festival dei Due Mondi (Festival of Two Worlds), a world-class extravaganza of theater, opera, music, painting, and sculpture, where the world's top artists vie for honors and throngs of art aficionados vie for hotel rooms.

But there is good reason to visit Spoleto any time of the year. Roman and medieval attractions and superb natural surroundings make it one of Umbria's most inviting towns. From the churches set among silvery olive groves on the outskirts of town to the soaring Ponte delle Torri behind it, Spoleto offers sublime views in every direction.

Exploring Spoleto

Spoleto is small, and its sights are clustered in the upper part of town, meaning it's best explored on foot. Several walkways cut down the hill, crossing the Corso Mazzini, which turns up the hill. Parking in Spoleto is always difficult; park outside the walls in Piazza della Vittoria.

a good walk

Begin at Piazza del Duomo, and visit the **Duomo** ⑫ ▶, which stands against a backdrop of hill and sky with La Rocca towering overhead. Cross the piazza and go up the stairs to Via Saffi and the church of **Sant'Eufemia** ⑬ and its museum. If you are short on time, skip Sant'Eufemia and head straight up to **La Rocca** ⑭ and **Ponte delle Torri** ⑮. Retrace your steps back to picturesque Via Fontesecca (Sant'Eufemia), with its shops selling local pottery and other handicrafts; it descends to the **Casa Romana** ⑯. Stop in or continue on to Piazza del Mercato, built on the site of the Roman forum and home to Spoleto's open-air produce market, open Monday–Saturday 8–1:30. At the narrow end of Piazza del Mercato is the **Arco di Druso** ⑰. Turn right on Via Brignone and cross Piazza della Libertà to Via Sant'Agata, which leads to the **Teatro Romano** ⑱ and Museo Archeologico.

TIMING Sightseeing in Spoleto is relaxed; one day will allow you to see the highlights and still have time for a leisurely lunch and a walk across the Ponte delle Torri.

What to See

⑰ **Arco di Druso.** This arch was built in the 1st century AD by the Senate of Spoleto to honor the Roman general Drusus (circa 13 BC–AD 23), son of the emperor Tiberius. It once marked the entrance to the Foro Romano (Roman Forum). ✉ *Piazza del Mercato.*

⑯ **Casa Romana.** Excavated at the end of the 19th century, the house is thought to have belonged to Vespasia Polla, the mother of the Roman Emperor Vespasian. The design is typical for houses of the first century AD and some of the original decoration is still intact, including geometrically patterned marble mosaics and plaster moldings. Admission to the eclectic **Galleria Civica d'Arte Moderna** (✉ Palazzo Collicola, Piazza Collicola ☎ 0743/46434) on the other side of town is included on the same ticket. ✉ *Palazzo del Municipio, Via Visiale 9* ☎ *0743/224656* 🎫 *€4.15* ☉ *Oct. 16–Mar., daily 10–6; Apr.–Oct. 15, daily 10–8.*

KEY

⏴ *Start of walk*

⏴ ⑫ **Duomo.** The church's rather dour 12th-century Romanesque facade is lightened up by a Renaissance loggia, eight rose windows, and an early 13th-century gold mosaic of the Benedictory Christ. The stunning contrast in styles makes this one of the finest church exteriors in the region. Inside, the Duomo holds the most notable art in town, including the immaculately restored frescoes in the apse by Fra Filippo Lippi (1406–69), showing the *Annunciation,* the *Nativity,* and the *Dormition of Mary,* with a marvelous *Coronation of the Virgin* adorning the dome; be ready with a 50-cent euro coin to illuminate the masterpiece. The Florentine artist died shortly after completing the work, and his tomb—designed by his son, Filippino Lippi (1457–1504)—lies in the church's right transept. Another fresco cycle, including work by Pinturicchio, is in the **Cappella Eroli** off the right aisle. ✉ *Piazza Duomo* ☏ *0743/44307* ☼ *Mar.–Oct., daily 8–1 and 3–6:30; Nov.–Feb., daily 8–1 and 3–5:30.*

⑭ **La Rocca.** Built in 1359–63 by the Gubbio-born architect Gattapone, this fortress is the town's dominant structure. Once a high-security prison, it now houses a small museum dedicated to medieval Spoleto. You can admire the formidable exterior from the road that circles around it. ✉ *Via del Ponte* ☏ *0743/223055* 💶 *€4.72* ☼ *Mid-Mar.–June 10 and Sept. 16–Oct., weekdays 10–noon and 3–7, weekends 10–7; June 11–Sept. 15, weekdays 10–7, weekends 10–9; Nov.–mid-Mar., weekdays 10–noon and 3–5, weekends 10–5. Visits are accompanied by a guide and begin on the hr; the last visit begins one hr before closing time.*

★ ⑮ **Ponte delle Torri.** Standing massive and graceful through the gorge that separates Spoleto from Monteluco, this 14th-century bridge is one of Umbria's most-photographed sights, and justifiably so. Built by Gattapone over the foundations of a Roman-era aqueduct, it's 750 ft long and soars

262 ft above the forested gorge at its highest point—higher than the dome of St. Peter's in Rome. Postcard views over the valley and a pleasant sense of vertigo make a walk across the bridge a must, particularly on a starry night. ⊠ *Via del Ponte.*

⑬ Sant'Eufemia. Set in the courtyard of the archbishop's palace, this ancient, austere church dates from the 11th century. Its most interesting feature is the gallery above the nave where female worshipers were required to sit—a holdover from the Eastern Church and one of the few such galleries in this part of Italy. Enter through the Museo Diocesano, attached to the church, which contains paintings including a Madonna by Fra Filippo Lippi. ⊠ *Via Saffi, between Piazza del Duomo and Piazza del Mercato* ☎ 0743/23101 ⊞ €3 ☉ *Oct.–Mar., Wed.–Sat. and Mon. 10–12:30 and 3–6, Sun. 11–5; Apr.–Sept., Wed.–Sat. and Mon. 10–1 and 4–7, Sun. 10:30–1 and 3–6.*

⑱ Teatro Romano. The small but well-preserved Roman theater was the site of a gruesome episode in Spoleto's history. During the medieval struggle between Guelph (papal) and Ghibelline (imperial) factions for control of central and northern Italy, Spoleto took the side of the Holy Roman Emperor. And woe to those who disagreed: 400 Guelph supporters were massacred in the theater, their bodies burned in an enormous pyre. In the end, however, the Guelphs were triumphant, and Spoleto was incorporated into the states of the Church in 1354. Through a door in the west portico, the **Museo Archeologico** displays assorted artifacts and the *Lex Spoletina* (Spoleto Law) tablets dating from 315 BC. This ancient legal document prohibited the destruction of the Bosco Sacro (Sacred Forest), south of town on Monteluco, a pagan prayer site later frequented by St. Francis. The theater is used in summer for Spoleto's arts festival. ⊠ *Piazza della Libertà* ☎ 0743/223277 ⊞ €2 ☉ *Daily 8:30–7:30.*

off the beaten path

SAN SALVATORE – The church and cemetery of San Salvatore seem very much forgotten, ensconced in solitude and cypress trees on a peaceful hillside, with the motorway rumbling below. One of the oldest churches in the world, it was built by eastern monks in the 4th century, largely of Roman-era materials. The highlight is the facade, with three exquisite marble doorways and windows, one of the earliest and best preserved in Umbria. It dates from a restoration in the 9th century and has hardly been touched since. ⊠ *Via della Basilica di San Salvatore, just out of town on the Via Flaminia* ☉ *Nov.–Feb., daily 7–5; Mar.–Apr. and Sept.–Oct., daily 7–6; May–Aug., daily 7–7.*

VALNERINA – This area southeast of Spoleto is the most beautiful of central Italy's many well-kept secrets. The twisting roads that serve the rugged landscape are poor, but the drive is well worth the effort for its forgotten medieval villages and dramatic mountain scenery.

The first stop in the Valnerina area should be the **Cascata delle Marmore,** waterfalls engineered by the Romans in the 3rd century BC. You'll find them a couple of miles east of Terni, on the road to Lake Piediluco and Rieti. The waters are diverted on weekdays to provide hydroelectric power for the town of Terni, so check with the **information office** (☎ 0744/62982) at the falls or the **Terni tourist office** (⊠ Viale Cesare Battisti 7/a, 05100 ☎ 0744/423047)before heading here. On summer evenings, when the falls are in full spate, the cascading water is floodlighted (May, weekends 8–10; June–August, nightly 8–10; mid-March–April and September, weekends 8–9).

TRUFFLE TROUBLE

Umbria is rich with truffles—more are found here than anywhere else in Italy—and those not consumed fresh are processed into pastes or flavored oils. The primary truffle areas are around the tiny town of Norcia, which holds a truffle festival every February, and near Spoleto, where you'll see signs warning against unlicensed truffle hunting posted at the base of the Ponte delle Torri. Although grown locally, the rare delicacy can cost a small fortune, up to $200 for a quarter pound—fortunately, a little goes a long way. At such a price, there's great competition among the nearly 10,000 registered truffle hunters in the province, who use specially trained dogs to sniff them out among the roots of several trees, including oak and ilex. Despite one or two incidences of poisoning truffle-hunting dogs and importing inferior tubers from China, you can be reasonably assured that the truffle shaved onto your pasta has been unearthed locally.

Close to the picturesque town of Ferentillo (northeast of Terni on S209) is the outstanding 8th-century abbey of **San Pietro in Valle,** with fine frescoes in the church nave and a peaceful cloister. One of the abbey outbuildings houses an excellent restaurant with moderate prices.

East of Spoleto in the Valnerina is **Norcia,** the birthplace of St. Benedict but better known for Umbrian pork and truffles. Norcia exports truffles to France and hosts a truffle festival, the Mostra Internazionale del Tartufo Nero di Norcia, every November.

Where to Stay & Eat

$$ ✕ **Il Tartufo.** Spoleto's most famous restaurant has a modern dining room on the second floor and a rustic dining room downstairs—both of them incorporating ruins of a Roman villa. The traditional cooking is spiced up in summer to appeal to the cosmopolitan crowd attending (or performing in) the Festival dei Due Mondi. As its name indicates, the restaurant specializes in dishes prepared with truffles—try the risotto *al tartufo*—but there's a second menu from which you can choose items not perfumed with this expensive delicacy. ⊠ *Piazza Garibaldi 24* ☎ *0743/40236* ⌂ *Reservations essential* ▤ *AE, DC, MC, V* ⊘ *Closed Mon. and last 2 wks in July. No dinner Sun.*

$$ ✕ **Ristorante Panciolle.** In the heart of Spoleto's medieval quarter, this restaurant has one of the most picturesque settings you could wish for. Dining outside in summer is a welcome respite, in a small piazza filled with lemon trees. Specialties change throughout the year and may include pasta dishes served with asparagus or mushrooms, as well as grilled meats. When in season, more expensive dishes prepared with fresh truffles are also available. ⊠ *Vicolo degli Eroli 1* ☎ *0743/45598* ⌂ *Reservations essential* ▤ *AE, DC, MC, V* ⊘ *Closed Wed. and last 2 wks in Nov.*

$–$$ ✕ **Apollinare.** Low wooden ceilings and candlelight make Apollinare one of the more romantic of the restaurants in Spoleto, and definitely the "in" spot in town. The kitchen uses a sophisticated and innovative approach to local cooking, with good-size portions; here the usual stringozzi pasta takes on cherry tomatoes, mint, and a touch of red pepper. Try the *caramella* (light puff pastry roll filled with local cheese, served with a creamy Parmesan sauce). In late spring and summer there's dining under a pergola on the piazza. ⊠ *Via Sant'Agata 14* ☎ *0743/223256* ⊟ *AE, D, MC, V* ⊙ *Closed Tues. Nov.–Mar.*

$–$$ ✕ **Il Pentagramma.** Just off the central Piazza della Libertà, this restaurant housed in a former stable features such local dishes as fresh *tortelli ai carciofi e noci* (artichoke-filled pasta with a hazelnut sauce) and lamb in a truffle sauce. ⊠ *Via Martani 4* ☎ *0743/223141* ⊟ *DC, MC, V* ⊙ *Closed Mon. No dinner Sun.*

$$ ✕⊞ **Hotel dei Duchi.** This well-run hotel is a favorite among performers in the Festival dei Due Mondi. It's in town center, near the Roman theater. Some rooms have fine views of the city. The hotel's restaurant ($$) turns out Umbrian treats laced with mushrooms, truffles, and even juniper berries. ⊠ *Viale G. Matteotti 4, 06049* ☎ *0743/44541* 🖷 *0743/ 44543* ⊕ *www.hoteldeiduchi.com* ↩ *47 rooms, 2 suites* ⚂ *Restaurant, bar, meeting room, free parking, some pets allowed* ⊟ *AE, DC, MC, V.*

$ ✕⊞ **Hotel Clitunno.** A renovated 18th-century building houses this pleasant hotel, a five-minute walk from the town center. Bedrooms and public rooms, some with timbered ceilings, have the sense of a traditional Umbrian home, albeit one with a very good restaurant. ⊠ *Piazza Sordini 6, 06049* ☎ *0743/223340* 🖷 *0743/222663* ↩ *40 rooms* ⚂ *Restaurant, bar, library, meeting room; no a/c* ⊟ *AE, DC, MC, V.*

★ $$$ ⊞ **Hotel Gattapone.** The tiny hotel at the top of the old town, near the Ponte delle Torri, has spectacular views of the bridge and the wooded slopes of Monteluco. Eclectic modern design and picture windows add character to quiet, comfortable rooms. Have breakfast overlooking the gorge on the sunny roof terrace. ⊠ *Via del Ponte 6, 06049* ☎ *0743/ 223447* 🖷 *0743/223448* ⊕ *www.hotelgattapone.it* ↩ *8 rooms, 8 suites* ⚂ *Minibars, bar, meeting room, free parking* ⊟ *AE, DC, MC, V.*

★ $$ ⊞ **Hotel San Luca.** The elegant San Luca is Spoleto's finest hotel, thanks to the commendable attention it pays to details. Spacious rooms (some accessible for people who use wheelchairs) are decorated with hand-painted friezes, firm beds are laid with linen sheets, and the hotel's rose garden provides a sweet-smelling backdrop for your afternoon nap. An ample breakfast buffet, including homemade cakes, is served in a pretty room facing the central courtyard, while afternoon tea can be sipped in oversize armchairs in front of the fireplace. Service is cordial and prices are surprisingly modest. ⊠ *Via Interna delle Mura 21, 06049* ☎ *0743/ 223399* 🖷 *0743/223800* ⊕ *www.hotelsanluca.com* ↩ *33 rooms, 2 suites* ⚂ *Bar, Internet, parking (fee)* ⊟ *AE, DC, MC, V.*

Nightlife & the Arts

The **Festival dei Due Mondi** (Festival of Two Worlds) in Spoleto, held mid-June to mid-July, features accomplished artists in all branches of the arts—particularly music, opera, and theater—and draws thousands of visitors from all over the world. Tickets for all performances should be ordered in advance from the **festival's box office** (⊠ Piazza Duomo 8 ☎ 800/565600 ⊕ www.spoletofestival.it), which has full program information starting in February.

SOUTHERN UMBRIA

Orvieto, built on a tufa mount, produces one of Italy's favorite white wines and has one of the country's greatest cathedrals and most compelling fresco cycles. Nearby Narni and Todi are pleasant medieval hill towns. The former stands over a steep gorge, its Roman pedigree evident in dark alleyways and winding streets; the latter is a fairy-tale village with incomparable views and one of Italy's most perfect piazzas.

Orvieto

⑲ *53 km (32 mi) west of Spoleto, 86 km (53 mi) south of Perugia.*

Carved out of an enormous plateau of volcanic rock high above a green valley, Orvieto has natural defenses that made the high walls seen in many Umbrian towns unnecessary. The Etruscans were the first to settle here, digging a honeycombed network of more than 1,200 wells and storage caves out of the soft stone. The Romans attacked, sacked, and destroyed the city in 283 BC; since then, it has grown up out of the rock into an enchanting maze of alleys and squares. Orvieto was solidly Guelph in the Middle Ages, and for several hundred years popes sought refuge in the city, at times needing protection from their enemies, at times from the summer heat of Rome.

When painting his frescoes inside the Duomo, Luca Signorelli asked that part of his contract be paid in Orvietan wine, and he was neither the first nor the last to appreciate the region's popular white. In past times, the caves carved underneath the town were used to ferment the Trebbiano grapes used in making Orvieto Classico; now local wine production has moved out to more traditional vineyards, but you can still while away the afternoon in tastings at any number of shops in town.

★ Orvieto's **Duomo** may be the most dazzling in all of Italy, a triumph of Romanesque-Gothic architecture. It was built to commemorate a local miracle: a priest in the nearby town of Bolsena suddenly found himself assailed by doubts about the transubstantiation—he could not bring himself to believe that the body of Christ was contained in the consecrated communion host. His doubts were put to rest, however, when a wafer he had just blessed suddenly started to drip blood onto the linen covering the altar. The pope certified the miracle and declared a new religious holiday—the Feast of Corpus Christi. The Duomo was built to celebrate the event and house the stained altar cloth.

The stunning carved-stone facade is the work of some of Italy's finest artists and took 300 years to complete. The bas-reliefs on the lower parts of the pillars by Lorenzo Maitani (circa 1275–1330), one of the Duomo's architects, show scenes from the Old Testament and some scary renderings of the Last Judgment and Hell, as well as a more tranquil Paradise. (See how many scenes you can identify.)

Inside the cathedral, a vast expanse of empty space leads to the major works, at the far end of the church in the transepts. To the left is the **Cappella del Corporale,** where the famous altar cloth is kept in a golden reliquary modeled on the cathedral, inlaid with enamel images of the miracle. The cloth is removed for public viewing on Easter and on Corpus Christi (the ninth Sunday after Easter). A trio of local artists executed frescoes depicting the miracle on the chapel walls. Signorelli's *Stories of the Antichrist,* the artistic jewel of the Duomo, deck the walls of the **Cappella Nuova** (Cappella di San Brizio), in the right transept (buy tickets in the tourist office across the square). In these delightfully gruesome works, the damned fall to hell, and lascivious demons bite off ears, step on heads, and spirit away young girls. Dante would surely have approved; in the chapel, his portrait accompanies *Scenes from Purgatorio.* Signorelli and Fra Angelico, who also worked on the chapel, witness the gory scene. ✉ *Piazza del Duomo* ☎ *0763/342477* 🎫 *Cappella Nuova* €3 🕙 *Nov.–Feb., daily 7:30–12:45 and 2:30–5:15; Mar. and Oct., daily 7:30–12:45 and 2:30–6:15; Apr.–Sept., daily 7:30–12:45 and 2:30–7:15.*

The **Museo Claudio Faina,** across the piazza from the Duomo, holds Etruscan and Roman artifacts; it's designed in a way that makes its Roman coins, bronze pieces, and sarcophagi accessible and interesting. ✉ *Palazzo Faina* ☎ *0763/341511* 🎫 *€4.20, €2.50 with funicular or bus ticket* ⊙ *Oct.–Mar., Tues.–Sun. 10–5; Apr.–Sept., daily 9:30–6.*

On Piazza Cahen, the **Fortezza**, built in the mid-14th century, encloses a public park with benches, shade, and an incredible view. The **Pozzo di San Patrizio** (Well of St. Patrick) was commissioned by Pope Clement VII (1478–1534) in 1527 to ensure a plentiful water supply in case of siege. Descend into the well on a pair of winding mule paths designed to avoid traffic jams. ✉ *Viale Sangallo, off Piazza Cahen* ☎ *0763/343768* 🎫 *€3.10* ⊙ *Oct.–Mar., daily 10–5:45; Apr.–Sept., daily 9:30–6:45.*

Where to Stay & Eat

★ **$–$$** ✕ **Le Grotte del Funaro.** This restaurant has an extraordinary location, deep in a series of caves within the volcanic rock beneath Orvieto. Once you have negotiated the steep steps, typical Umbrian specialties like tagliatelle *al vino rosso* (with red wine sauce) and grilled beef with truffles await. Sample the fine Orvieto wines, either the whites or the lesser-known reds. ✉ *Via Ripa Serancia 41* ☎ *0763/343276* ⚐ *Reservations essential* ⊟ *AE, DC, MC, V* ⊙ *Closed Mon. and 1 wk in July.*

¢ ✕ **Cantina Foresi.** For a light lunch of cheese, salami, bread, and salad, accompanied by a glass of cool white wine, this small *enoteca* (wine bar), is hard to beat. Just opposite the cathedral, the cantina's umbrella-shaded tables offer one of the best views of the church facade in town. ✉ *Piazza del Duomo 2* ☎ *0763/341611* ⊟ *AE, DC, MC, V* ⊙ *Closed Tues. Nov.–Mar.*

$ ✕🛏 **Villa Bellago.** Outside Orvieto, overlooking Lake Corbara, three farmhouses have been completely renovated, resulting in bright, spacious guest rooms and ample facilities. The hotel's fine restaurant specializing in imaginatively prepared Umbrian and Tuscan dishes. Fresh fish is always on the menu. ✉ *Outside the village of Baschi, 7½ km (4½ mi) south of Orvieto on S448, 05018* ☎ *0744/950521* 🖷 *0744/950524* ⊕ *www.argoweb.it/hotel_villabellago* ⇨ *12 rooms, 2 suites* ⚐ *Restaurant, minibars, tennis court, pool, gym, sauna, bar* ⊟ *AE, DC, MC, V* ⊙ *Closed 4 wks in Jan.–Feb. Restaurant closed Tues.*

$$$$ 🛏 **Hotel La Badia.** This is one of the best-known country hotels in Umbria. The 12th-century building, a former monastery, is set in rolling parkland that provides wonderful views of the valley and the town of Orvieto in the distance. Vaulted ceilings and exposed stone walls set a tone of rustic elegance in the guest rooms. ✉ *Località La Badia, 4 km (2½ mi) south of Orvieto, 05018* ☎ *0763/301959* 🖷 *0763/305396* ⊕ *www.labadiahotel.it* ⇨ *21 rooms, 7 suites* ⚐ *Restaurant, 2 tennis courts, pool, bar, meeting room* ⊟ *AE, MC, V* ⊙ *Closed Jan.–Feb.*

$ 🛏 **Grand Hotel Reale.** This hotel is in the center of Orvieto, on a square that hosts a lively market. Facing the impressive Gothic-Romanesque Palazzo del Popolo, rooms are spacious and adequately furnished, with a traditional accent. ✉ *Piazza del Popolo 27, 05018* ☎ *0763/341247* 🖷 *0763/341247* ⇨ *32 rooms* ⚐ *Bar* ⊟ *MC, V.*

Shopping

CHEESE   Like most places in Italy, Orvieto produces a variety of local cheeses. With several small tables, a cheese counter that is second to none, a short menu, and a carefully chosen wine list, you'll find the specialty store **Carraro** (✉ Corso Cavour 101 ☎ 0763/342870) an excellent place for either a *degustazione* (tasting) of Orvietan cheese, or a light lunch.

EMBROIDERY &   Embroidery and lace making flourish in Orvieto. One of the best shops
LACE   for *merletto* (lace) is **Duranti** (✉ Corso Cavour 105 ☎ 0763/342222).

WINE Excellent Orvieto wines are justly prized throughout Italy and the world. The whites pressed from the region's Trebbiano grapes are fruity, with a tart finish. Orvieto also produces its own version of the Tuscan dessert wine *vin santo*. It's darker than its Tuscan cousin and is aged five years before bottling. You can stop for a glass of vino at the **Wine Bar Nazzaretto** (✉ Corso Cavour 40), where there's also a good selection of sandwiches and snacks, and vin santo is on sale.

WOODWORKING Orvieto is a well-known center for woodworking, particularly fine inlay and veneer work. The Corso Cavour has a number of artisan shops specializing in woodwork, the best known being the **Michelangeli family studio** (✉ Via Michelangeli 3, corner of Corso Cavour ☎ 0763/342377), chock-full of imaginatively designed creations ranging in size from a giant *armadio* (wardrobe) to a simple wooden spoon.

Todi

㉚ *30 km (19 mi) east of Orvieto.*

As you stand on **Piazza del Popolo,** it's easy to see why Todi is often described as Umbria's prettiest hill town. The square is a model of spatial harmony, with stunning views over the surrounding countryside. Narrow cobblestone streets go winding around the hill, every so often finishing in a tiny quiet piazza. Todi's 12th-century Romanesque-Gothic **Duomo** is famed for its choir stalls by Antonio Bencivenni da Mercatello and his son Sebastiano, dating from 1530. Its simple square facade is echoed by the solid Palazzo dei Priori across the way. The Renaissance church of **Santa Maria della Consolazione,** with an elegant pale-green dome, offers a pleasant surprise on the outskirts of town.

Where to Stay & Eat

$–$$ ✕ **Ristorante Umbria.** Todi's most popular restaurant for more than four decades, the Umbria is reliable for sturdy country food, plus a wonderful view from the terrace. There's always a hearty soup simmering, as well as homemade pasta with truffles, game, and the specialty of the house, *palombaccio alla ghiotta* (roasted squab). ✉ *Via San Bonaventura 13* ☎ *075/8942737 or 075/8942390* ▤ *AE, DC, MC, V* ⊙ *Closed Tues. and July.*

$$ ▦ **Tenuta di Canonica.** The affable hosts here, Daniele and Maria Fano, have retained the architectural integrity of this brick farmhouse and medieval tower in the Tiber Valley 5 km (3 mi) northwest of Todi. You're bound to marvel at the exposed stone walls, high beamed ceilings, brick floors, and terra-cotta tiles, all in soothing colors. Guest rooms are filled with family furniture and antique pieces. You can hike or ride on horseback through olive groves, orchards, and the forest on the grounds. ✉ *Località La Canonica, 75–76, follow signs to Titignano and Cordigliano, 06059* ☎ *075/8947545* ▤ *075/8947581* ⊕ *www.tenutadicanonica.com* ⊲ *10 rooms, 3 apartments* ♨ *Dining room, bar, pool, library; no a/c, no room TVs* ▤ *MC, V.*

$ ▦ **San Lorenzo Tre.** A narrow alley off Todi's main square and a long flight of stairs lead up to this tiny guest house. More in tune with the 19th than the 21st century, the hotel doesn't pamper you with modern comforts, but, surrounded by antique furniture, paintings, and period knickknacks, you'll get the sense of a time long past. Only three of the six rooms have private bathrooms, but all share a magnificent view, which looks over the valleys and hills to the north of town. ✉ *Via San Lorenzo 3, 06059* ☎ *075/8944555* ⊕ *www.todi.net/lorenzo* ⊲ *6 rooms, 3 with bath* ♨ *No room phones, no room TVs, no a/c* ▤ *No credit cards* ⊙ *Closed Jan.–Feb.*

Narni

㉑ *35 km (22 mi) south of Todi, 84 km (46 mi) southeast of Perugia.*

At the edge of a steep gorge, Narni—like so many other towns in Umbria—is a medieval city of Roman origins. Below its finely paved streets and pretty Romanesque churches, excavations offer glimpses of an intriguing past. The **Lacus,** under Piazza Garibaldi, is an ancient Roman cistern with remnants of a Roman floor that was in use until the late Middle Ages. Two cisterns and assorted Roman fragments are visible in the crypt of the 8th-century church of **Santa Maria Impensole** (⊠ Via Mazzini), open daily 9:30–noon and 4:30–6:30. A macabre note is struck by the symbols and dates on the walls of the rooms under the former church of **San Domenico,** inscribed by prisoners held there during the Inquisition. The best day to visit is Sunday, when the excavated sites are open and tours are given in English. You can take a unique tour of Narni's underground **Roman aqueduct,** the only one open to the public in all of Italy, but it's not for the claustrophobic. Contact Associazione Culturale Subterranea or call the **tourist office** (⊠ Piazza dei Priori 3 ☎ 0744/715362) at least one week ahead to book a visit. ⊠ *Associazione Culturale Subterranea, Giardini di San Bernardo* ☎ *0744/722292* ⊕ *www.narnisotterranea.it* ☉ *Apr.–Oct.*

Where to Eat

$-$$ ✕ **Il Cavallino.** Run by the third generation of the Bussetti family, Il Cavallino is a first-rate trattoria about 3 km (2 mi) outside Narni. There are always several pastas to choose from, but it's the meat that makes this a worthy detour. Rabbit roasted with rosemary and sage and juicy grilled T-bone steaks are house favorites. The wine list features the best of what's local. ⊠ *Via Flaminia Romana 220* ☎ *0744/761020* ▭ *AE, DC, MC, V* ☉ *Closed Tues., July 13–30, and Dec. 20–26.*

THE MARCHES

HIDDEN ITALY

Less touristed than Tuscany or Umbria, the Marches (Le Marche in Italian) have comparably diverse and attractive landscapes; as with its neighbors, the region's patchwork of hills is stitched with grapevines and olive trees producing delicious wine and oil. You're off the beaten path here, so services tend to be less luxurious than in the regions to the west, but with a little luck, you'll have the place to yourself.

Bear in mind that traveling here is not as easy as in Umbria or Tuscany, and a car is recommended. Beyond the narrow coastal plain and away from major towns, the roads are steep and twisting. There's an efficient bus service between the coastal town of Pésaro and Urbino, the principal tourist destinations of the region. Train travel is slow and stops are limited, although you can reach Ascoli Piceno by rail.

Urbino

㉒ *101 km (63 mi) northeast of Perugia, 107 km (66 mi) northeast of Arezzo.*

Majestic Urbino, atop a steep hill with a skyline of towers and domes, is something of a surprise to come upon—it's oddly remote—and it's humbling to reflect that it was once a center of learning and culture almost without rival in western Europe. The town looks much as it did in the glory days of the 15th century, a cluster of warm brick and pale stone buildings, all topped with russet-color tiled roofs. The focal point is the immense and beautiful Palazzo Ducale.

Urbino's tradition of learning continues to this day, and the city takes great pride in its intellectual and humanistic heritage. Its home to the small but distinguished Università di Urbino—one of the oldest in the world—and during school term the streets are filled with students. It is very much a college town, with the usual bookshops, record stores, bars, and coffeehouses. In summer the Italian student population is replaced by foreigners who come to study Italian language and arts at several prestigious private fine-arts academies.

Urbino's fame rests on the reputation of three of its native sons: Duke Federico da Montefeltro (1422–82), the enlightened warrior-patron who built the Palazzo Ducale; Raffaello Sanzio (1483–1520), or Raphael, one of the most influential painters in history and an embodiment of the spirit of the Renaissance; and the architect Donato Bramante (1444–1514), who translated the philosophy of the Renaissance into buildings of grace and beauty. Unfortunately, there's little work by either Bramante or Raphael in the city, but the duke's influence can still be felt strongly, even now, some 500 years after his death.

Fodor's Choice
★
The **Palazzo Ducale** holds the place of honor in the city, and in no other palace of its era are the principles of the Renaissance stated quite so clearly. If the Renaissance was, in ideal form, a celebration of the nobility of man and his works, of the light and purity of the soul, then there is no place in Italy, the birthplace of the Renaissance, where these tenets are better illustrated.

Today the palace houses the **Galleria Nazionale delle Marche** (National Museum of the Marches), with a superb collection of paintings, sculpture, and objets d'art, well arranged and properly lighted. Masterworks in the collection include Paolo Uccello's *Profanation of the Host,* Titian's *Resurrection* and *Last Supper,* and Piero della Francesca's *Madonna of Senigallia.* But the gallery's highlight is Piero's enigmatic work, long known as *The Flagellation of Christ.* Much has been written about this painting, and few experts agree on its meaning. Experts do agree that the work is one of the painter's masterpieces. Piero himself thought so: it's one of the few works he signed (on the lowest step supporting the throne). ⊠ *Piazza Duca Federico* ☎ *0722/2760* ⊕ *www.comune.urbino.ps.it* 🖼 *€4* ☉ *Tues.–Sun. 8:30–7:15 (10 PM Apr.–Oct.), Mon. 8:30–2; ticket office closes 90 mins before Palazzo.*

The **Casa Natale di Raffaello** is where the painter Raphael was born and, under the direction of his artist father, took his first steps in painting. There is debate about the fresco of the Madonna here; some say it is by Raphael, whereas others attribute it to the father—with Raphael's mother and the young painter himself standing in as models for the Madonna and Child. ⊠ *Via Raffaello 57* ☎ *0722/320105* 🖼 *€3* ☉ *Mon.–Sat. 9–2, Sun. 10–1.*

Where to Stay & Eat

$–$$ ✕ **La Vecchia Fornarina.** The two small rooms of this trattoria, just down from Urbino's central Piazza della Repubblica, are often filled to capacity. The specialty is meaty country fare, such as *coniglio* (rabbit) and *vitello alle noci* (veal cooked with walnuts) or *ai porcini* (with mushrooms). There's also a good selection of pasta dishes. ⊠ *Via Mazzini 14* ☎ *0722/ 320007* ✍ *Reservations essential* ▭ *AE, DC, MC, V.*

¢ 🖭 **Hotel San Giovanni.** This hotel in the old town is housed in a renovated medieval building. The rooms are basic, clean, and comfortable—with a wonderful view from Rooms 24 to 30—and there's a handy

restaurant-pizzeria below. ⊠ *Via Barocci 13, 61029* ☎ *0722/2827*
🖩 *0722/329055* 🛏 *31 rooms, 17 with bath* ⏦ *No a/c* ▤ *No credit cards*
🕓 *Closed July and Christmas wk.*

Shopping

Historically, Urbino has been a center for the production of fine majolica ceramic designs, and you'll find both pretty reproductions as well
as contemporary designs at shops throughout. One unique, though
hard-to-carry, gift might be the Stella Ducale (Ducal Star), a complex
three-dimensional decorative wooden star designed out of pyramid
shapes by Renaissance mathematician Luca Pacioli.

Ancona

㉓ *87 km (54 mi) southeast of Urbino, 139 km (87 mi) northeast of Perugia.*

Set on an elbow-shaped bluff (hence its name; *ankon* is Greek for
"elbow") jutting out into the Adriatic, Ancona is one of Italy's most important ports. It's well served by trains, which makes it a good base for
an excursion to Loreto or to Ascoli Piceno, farther south along the Adriatic coast. The city was the target of serious aerial bombing during World
War II, and much was reduced to rubble, only to be rebuilt in a nondescript sprawl of boxy poured concrete. A few blocks from the main
ferry terminal, however, what's left of the city's historic center proves
that Ancona was, and still is in parts, a lovely city. Narrow, cobbled streets
wind steeply up from the waterfront, opening onto wide piazzas edged
with handsome 19th-century brick-and-stucco buildings painted deep
orange, pink, and ochre. The alleys leading downhill from central Piazza del Plebiscito are lined with chic shops offering everything from
handmade linens to herbal cosmetics, and there are cafés and *pasticcerie*
aplenty to stave off hunger before your ferry leaves. There are enough
sights to fill even the longest layover, too.

The 12th-century Romanesque church of **Santa Maria della Piazza** is built
over a church from the 5th century; parts of the foundation and original hand-cut mosaic pavement are visible through handy glass cut-outs
in the floor. The 2nd-century **Arco di Traiano** (Trajan's Arch) out on the
point is worth a look. The **Duomo di San Ciriaco**, built over a Greek temple, was redesigned in the 13th century to make it more visible to ships
coming in to Ancona's port. The **Loggia dei Mercanti**, dating from the
15th century, was Ancona's bazaar, where merchants and traders dealt
in all manner of goods from the Far East.

Where to Stay & Eat

$–$$ ✕ **La Moretta.** This family-run trattoria is on the central Piazza del
Plebiscito, and in summer there's dining outside in the square. Among
the specialties here are *stoccafisso all'Anconetana* (cod baked with capers, anchovies, potatoes, and tomatoes) and the famous *brodetto* fish
stew. ⊠ *Piazza del Plebiscito 52* ☎ *071/202317* ▤ *AE, DC, MC, V*
🕓 *Closed Sun., Jan. 1–10, and Aug. 13–18.*

$$$ 🏨 **Grand Hotel Palace.** This old-fashioned port hotel is widely held to
be the best in town. Rooms are on the small side but beautifully fur-
nished with French beds dressed in yellow damask, and half have a view
directly over the port. Extras like slippers, bath salts, and shaving kits
make for a pleasant stay. Public rooms are grand and elegant, and the
breakfast room is on the top floor with a panoramic view. ⊠ *Lungo-
mare Vanvitelli 24, 60100* ☎ *071/201813* 🖩 *071/2074832* ⊘ *palace.
ancona@libero.it* 🛏 *39 rooms, 1 suite* ⏦ *Gym, bar, meeting rooms, In-
ternet, parking (fee)* ▤ *AE, DC, MC, V* 🕓 *Closed Dec. 23–Jan. 1.*

Loreto

㉔ *31 km (19 mi) south of Ancona, 118 km (73 mi) southeast of Urbino.*

Thousands of pilgrims come to Loreto every year to visit one of the world's best-loved shrines, the **Santuario della Santa Casa** (House of the Virgin Mary), within the **Basilica.** According to legend, angels moved the house from Nazareth to this hilltop in 1295, when Nazareth fell into the hands of Muslim invaders. Excavations made at the behest of the Church have shown that the house did once stand elsewhere and was brought to the hilltop—by either crusaders or a family named Angeli—around the time the angels (*angeli*) are said to have done the job.

Easter week and the Feast of the Holy House on December 10 are marked by processions, prayers, and a deluge of pilgrims; the rest of the year, the shrine is relatively quiet. The house itself consists of three rough stone walls contained within an elaborate marble tabernacle; built around this centerpiece is the giant basilica of the Holy House, which dominates the town. The basilica was begun in Gothic style in 1468 and continued in Renaissance style through the late Renaissance with the help of some of the period's greatest architects: Bramante, Antonio da Sangallo (the Younger, 1483–1546), Giuliano da Sangallo (circa 1445–1516), and Sansovino (1467–1529).

Fearful flyers may take comfort from the fact that the Holy Virgin of Loreto is the patroness of air travelers. You can pick up Pope John Paul II's prayer for a safe flight in the church, where it's available in a dozen languages. ⊠ *Piazza della Madonna* ☎ *071/970104* ⊕ *www. santuarioloreto.it* ☉ *June–Sept., daily 6:45 AM–8 PM; Oct.–May, daily 6:45 AM–7 PM. Santuario della Santa Casa closed daily 12:30–2:30.*

Ascoli Piceno

㉕ *105 km (65 mi) south of Ancona, 175 km (109 mi) southeast of Perugia.*

Ascoli Piceno is not a hill town; rather, it sits in a valley ringed by steep hills and cut by the fast-racing Tronto River. The town is almost unique in Italy in that it seems to have its traffic problems—in the historic center, at any rate—pretty much under control; you can drive *around* the picturesque part of the city, but driving *through* it is most difficult. This feature makes Ascoli Piceno one of the most pleasant large towns in the country for exploring on foot. There is traffic, but without the jams, noise, and exhaust fumes of other Italian cities.

★ The heart of Ascoli Piceno is the majestic **Piazza del Popolo,** dominated by the Gothic church of **San Francesco** and the **Palazzo dei Capitani del Popolo,** a 13th-century town hall that contains a graceful Renaissance courtyard. The square functions as the city's living room: at dusk each evening the piazza fills with people strolling and exchanging news and gossip. Ascoli Piceno's **Giostra della Quintana** (Joust of the Quintana) is held on the first Sunday in August. Children love this medieval-style joust and the processions of richly caparisoned horses that wind through the streets of the old town. Contact the **Ascoli tourist office** (⊠ Piazza del Popolo 1 ☎ 0736/253045) for details.

Where to Stay & Eat

★ **$–$$** ✕ **Ristorante Tornasacco.** At one of Ascoli Piceno's oldest restaurants, you won't find nouvelle cuisine: the owners pride themselves on meaty local specialties such as *olive ascolane* (olives stuffed with minced meat, breaded and deep-fried), *maccheroncini alla contadina* (homemade short pasta in a lamb, pork, and veal sauce), and *bistecca di toro* (bull

steak). ⊠ *Piazza del Popolo 36* ☎ *0736/254151* ▤ *AE, DC, MC, V*
⊘ *Closed Fri., July 15–31, and Dec. 23–28.*

$ ▦ **Il Pennile.** Set in a quiet grove of olive trees, this small, family-run
hotel is just outside the old city center and a short walk from the train
station. Rooms are soberly decorated and functional but offer good views
of the city. ⊠ *Via G. Spalvieri, 63100* ☎ *0736/41645* 🖶 *0736/342755*
⊕ *www.hotelpennile.com* ⇆ *33 rooms* ⚭ *Minibars, gym, bar, Internet, free parking* ▤ *DC, MC, V* ⑩ *CP.*

UMBRIA & THE MARCHES A TO Z

*To research prices, get advice from other travelers, and book travel ar-
rangements, visit www.fodors.com.*

AIRPORTS
Central Italy's closest major airports are in Rome, Pisa, and Florence.
Perugia's tiny Aeroporto Sant'Egidio has flights to and from Milan, Rome
Ciampino, and Palermo.

🛈 Airport Information **Aeroporto Sant'Egidio** ☎ 075/592141 ⊕ www.airport.umbria.
it. **Florence** Peretola ☎ 055/3061700. **Pisa** Galileo Galilei ☎ 050/500707. **Rome** Fiumicino ☎ 06/65954420.

BUS TRAVEL
Perugia is served by the Sulga Line, with daily departures from Rome's
Stazione Tiburtina and from Piazza Adua in Florence. Connections between Rome, Spoleto, and the Marches are provided by the associated
bus companies Bucci and Soget.

There is good local bus service between all the major and minor towns
of Umbria. Some of the routes in rural areas, especially in the Marches,
are designed to serve as many destinations as possible and are, therefore, quite roundabout and slow. Schedules often change, so consult with
local tourist offices before setting out.

🛈 Bus Information **Bucci–Soget** ⊠ Strada delle Marche 56, Pesaro ☎ 0721/32401
⊕ www.mediaworks.it/bucci.htm. **Sulga Line** ☎ 075/5009641 ⊕ www.sulga.it.

CAR RENTAL
🛈 Local Agencies **Avis** ⊠ Sant'Egidio airport, Perugia ☎ 075/6929796 ⊠ Stazione
Ferroviaria Fontivegge, Perugia ☎ 075/5000395 ⊠ Località S. Chiodo 164, Spoleto
☎ 0743/46272 ⊠ Via XX Settembre 80/d, Terni ☎ 0744/287170. **Hertz** ⊠ Via 7 Martiri 32/f, Orvieto ☎ 0763/301303 ⊠ Piazza Vittorio Veneto 4, Perugia ☎ 075/5002439
⊠ Sant'Egidio airport, Perugia ☎ 075/5002439 ⊠ Via Cerquiglia 144, Spoleto ☎ 0743/
46703.

CAR TRAVEL
On the western edge of the region is the Umbrian section of the Autostrada
del Sole (A1), the principal north–south highway in Italy. It links Florence and Rome with Orvieto and passes near Todi and Terni. The S3
intersects with A1 and leads on to Assisi and Urbino. The Adriatica su-
perhighway (A14) runs north–south along the coast, linking the Marches
to Bologna and Venice.

Umbria has an excellent, modern road network. Central Umbria is
served by a major highway, S75bis, which passes along the shore of Lake
Trasimeno and ends in Perugia. Assisi is served by the modern highway
S75; S75 connects to S3 and S3bis, which cover the heart of the region.
Major inland routes connect coastal A14 to large towns in the Marches,
including Urbino, Jesi, Macerata, and Ascoli Piceno, but inland secondary
roads in mountain areas can be tortuous and narrow.

EMERGENCY
SERVICES

When you're on the road, always carry a good road map, a flashlight, and, if possible, a cellular phone so that in case of a breakdown you can call ACI for towing and repairs—ask and you will be transferred to an English-speaking operator. Be prepared to tell the operator which road you're on, the direction you're going (e.g., "*verso* [in the direction of] Perugia") and the *targa* (license plate number) of your car. The great majority of Italians carry cellular phones, so if you don't have one, flag down someone who does for help.

ACI ☎ 803/116.

EMERGENCIES

Emergency numbers are accessible from every phone, including cellular phones, all over Italy. If you have ongoing medical concerns, it's a good idea to make sure someone is on duty all night where you're staying—not a given in Umbria, less so in the Marches. As elsewhere in Italy, every pharmacy in Umbria and the Marches bears a sign at the door listing area pharmacies open in off-hours. Perugia, Spoleto, Assisi, Gubbio, and Urbino all have at least one so-called "night" pharmacy, but out in the countryside you may need a car to get to one. Try to bring extras with you of all medications you take regularly.

Emergencies ☎ 113. **Ambulance** ☎ 118. **Carabinieri** (Military Police) ☎ 112. **Fire** ☎ 115.

MAIL & SHIPPING

Post Offices Assisi ✉ P. del Comune 23 ☎ 075/812355. **Perugia** ✉ P. Matteotti 1 ☎ 075/5720395. **Spoleto** ✉ P. della Libertà 12 ☎ 0743/223198.

TRAIN TRAVEL

Intercity trains connect Florence and Rome with Perugia and Assisi several times a day. Local service, requiring a change of trains in either Terontola (to and from Florence), or Foligno (to and from Rome), is also available. The main Rome–Ancona line passes through Narni, Terni, Spoleto, and Foligno, and intercity trains on the Rome–Florence line make stops at Orvieto. Branch lines link Ancona with the inland towns of Fabriano and Ascoli Piceno. In Umbria, a small, privately owned railway operated by Ferrovia Centrale Umbra (FCU) runs from Città di Castello in the north to Terni in the south via Perugia.

Train Information Ferrovia Centrale Umbra (FCU) ☎ 075/5729121 ⊕ www.fcu.it. **Ferrovie dello Stato (State Railways)** ☎ 848/888088 ⊕ www.trenitalia.it.

VISITOR INFORMATION

Agritourist Information Turismo Verde ✉ Via Maria Angeloni 1, 06124 Perugia ☎ 075/5002953 🖨 075/5002956 ⊕ www.turismoverde.it.

Tourist Information Ancona ✉ Via Thaon de Revel 4, 60100 ☎ 071/358991 ⊕ www.comune.ancona.it. **Ascoli Piceno** ✉ Piazza del Popolo 1, 63100 ☎ 0736/253045 ⊕ www.ascolipiceno.com. **Assisi** ✉ Piazza del Comune 12, 06081 ☎ 075/812534 ⊕ www.comune.assisi.pg.it. **Gubbio** ✉ Via Ansidei 32, 06024 ☎ 075/9220790 ⊕ www.comune.gubbio.pg.it. **Loreto** ✉ Via Solari 3, 60025 ☎ 071/970276 ⊕ www.turismo.marche.it. **Narni** ✉ Piazza dei Priori 3, 05035 ☎ 0744/715362 ⊕ www.comune.narni.tr.it. **Orvieto** ✉ Piazza Duomo 24, 05018 ☎ 0763/341772 ⊕ www.comune.orvieto.tr.it. **Perugia** ✉ Piazza IV Novembre 3, 06123 ☎ 075/5723327 ⊕ www.umbria2000.it. **Spoleto** ✉ Piazza della Libertà 7, 06049 ☎ 0743/49890 ⊕ www.spoleto1.com. **Terni** ✉ Viale Cesare Battisti 7/a, 05100 ☎ 0744/423047. **Todi** ✉ Piazza Umberto I 6, 06059 ☎ 075/8943395. **Urbino** ✉ Piazza Duca Federico 35, 61029 ☎ 0722/2613.

ROME

11

FODOR'S CHOICE

Britannia, hotel

Colle Palatino

Ditirambo, restaurant

La Pergola, restaurant

Museo e Galleria Borghese

Musei Vaticani

Pantheon

HIGHLY RECOMMENDED

SIGHTS Basilica di San Pietro

Campidoglio

Campo de' Fiori

Colosseo

Fontana di Trevi

Foro Romano

Musei Capitolini

Museo Nazionale Etrusco di Villa Giulia

Piazza di Santa Maria in Trastevere

Piazza Navona

San Clemente

Spanish Steps

Via Appia Antica

Villa Farnesina

Rome has many exceptional hotels and restaurants. For other favorites, look for the black stars as you read this chapter.

Updated by
Megan
Williams,
Valerie
Hamilton, and
Giovanna
Dunmall

ROME'S 2,700 YEARS OF HISTORY are on display everywhere you look. The ancient rubs shoulders with the medieval, the modern runs into the Renaissance, and the result is like nothing so much as an open-air museum. Julius Caesar and Nero, the Vandals and the Borgias, Raphael and Caravaggio, Napoléon and Mussolini—they and countless other political, cultural, and spiritual luminaries have left their mark on the city. More than Florence, more than Venice, Rome is Italy's treasure trove, packed with masterpieces from more than two millennia of artistic achievement. This is where a metropolis once bustled around the carved marble monuments of the Roman Forum, where centuries later Michelangelo Buonarroti painted Christian history in the Sistine Chapel, where Gian Lorenzo Bernini's nymphs and naiads dance in their fountains, and where an empire of gold was worked into the crowns of centuries of rulers.

Today Rome's formidable legacy is upheld by its people, their history knit into the fabric of their everyday lives. Students walk dogs in the park that was once the mausoleum of the family of the emperor Augustus; Raphaelesque madonnas line up for buses on busy corners; a priest in flowing robes walks through a medieval piazza talking on a cell phone. Modern Rome has one foot in the past, one in the present—a delightful stance that allows you to have an espresso in a square designed by Bernini, then take the metro back to your hotel room in a renovated Renaissance palace. "When you first come here you assume that you must burrow about in ruins and prowl in museums to get back to the days of Numa Pompilius or Mark Antony," Maud Howe observes in her book *Roma Beata*. "It is not necessary; you only have to live, and the common happenings of daily life—yes, even the trolley car and your bicycle—carry you back in turn to the Dark Ages, to the early Christians, even to prehistoric Rome."

EXPLORING ROME

Updated by
Megan
Williams

Visitors to Rome often face a conundrum: the more you see of the city, the more you'll realize how little you have seen. Take heart; Rome wasn't built in a day. The Italian author Silvio Negro said it best: "*Roma, non basta una vita*" (Rome, a lifetime is not enough). It's wise to start out knowing this and to have a focused but flexible itinerary. A ramble through a picturesque quarter of Old Rome can be just as enchanting as the quiet contemplation of a chapel or a trek through marbled museum corridors.

Though spread out, Rome invites walking, and taxis are rarely far off for the weary. Plan your day taking into account the varying opening hours of the sights you want to visit, which usually means mixing the ancient, classical, and baroque, museums and parks, the center and the environs. Most churches are usually open from 8 or 9 until noon or 12:30 and from 3 or 4 until about 6:30 or 7.

A combination ticket for the Colosseum, Palatine, and the various branches of the Museo Nazionale Romano (including Palazzo Altemps, Crypta Balbi, Terme di Diocleziano, and Palazzo Massimo alle Terme), valid for five consecutive days, is available at each participant's ticket office for €15.50—a good deal for ancient-history buffs.

Numbers in the text correspond to numbers in the margin and on the Rome and Old Rome maps.

Ancient Rome: Glories of the Caesars

A walk through the very core of Roman antiquity, through what was once the capital of the Western world, the Roman Forum, is an impressive introduction to the glories of the ancient city. Although the millennia have reduced this grand complex to fields of picturesque ruins, it is nonetheless awe inspiring to consider that this square was the birthplace of Western civilization. Roman law and powerful armies were created here, banishing the barbarian world for a millennium. Here all Rome shouted as one, "Caesar has been murdered," and crowded to hear Mark Antony's eulogy for the fallen leader. Legend has it that St. Paul traversed the Forum en route to his audience with Nero. Up on the Campidoglio, the harmony of Michelangelo's Renaissance piazza is appropriate testament to the seat of the ancient governments based here 2,000 years before. In the heyday of the Empire, the Forum below occasionally became an enormous banquet hall, where all imperial Rome could be entertained in one place (as our times have observed thanks to such Hollywood epics as *Quo Vadis, Ben-Hur,* and *Cleopatra*). It's fitting that, in the aftermath of centuries of such pageantry, Shelley and Gibbon reflected here on the meaning of *sic transit gloria mundi* (so passes away the glory of the world).

a good walk

Begin your walk on the **Campidoglio** ❶ ▶—the site of Michelangelo's spectacular piazza and Rome's city hall, Palazzo Senatorio, which was built over the Tabularium, the ancient hall of records. Flanking the palazzo are both halves of Rome's most noteworthy museum complex, the **Musei Capitolini** ❷, made up of the Museo Capitolino, the Palazzo dei Conservatori, the Pinacoteca Capitolina, the Taburlarium, and Palazzo Caffarelli. They contain works of art gathered by Pope Sixtus IV, one of the Renaissance papal patrons of the arts. Off to the side of the Campidoglio, at the head of its formidable flight of steps, stands the ancient redbrick church of **Santa Maria d'Aracoeli** ❸. Walk down the road to the left of Palazzo Senatorio, behind the piazza, and look out over the remains of the Roman Forum. From here, steps descend to the gloomy **Carcere Mamertino** ❹, the Mamertine Prison. The road leads out past the Forum of Caesar to Via dei Fori Imperiali. Across the street are the Forum of Trajan and the **Colonna di Traiano** ❺. Continue along the Via dei Fori Imperiali, passing the fora built by Augustus and Nerva, and cross back over the road to the entrance of the **Foro Romano** ❻. At the side of the ancient Via Sacra inside the Forum is the entrance to the **Colle Palatino** ❼, site of Rome's earliest settlement, which dates back to the late Bronze Age. Take the ramp that leads from the Forum–Palatine Hill area to the **Arco di Costantino** ❽ and, beyond it, the **Colosseo** ❾, one of antiquity's most famous monuments. Don't forget to check out the view from the park laid out over the ruins of Nero's **Domus Aurea** ❿, his sumptuous palace, behind the Colosseum.

TIMING   It takes about an hour to walk the route, plus two hours to visit the Musei Capitolini, from two to three hours to explore the Roman Forum and Palatine Hill. The Colosseum takes about a half hour to visit, plus 20 minutes waiting in line.

What to See

❽ **Arco di Costantino.** This imposing arch was erected in AD 315 to celebrate the victory of the emperor Constantine (280–337) over Maxentius (died 312). The largest (69 ft high, 85 ft long, 23 ft wide) and best-preserved of Rome's triumphal arches, it's one of the last great monuments of ancient Rome.

11

If you have
3 days

Begin your first day at Piazza Venezia and survey Rome from atop the Campidoglio. Next, explore the Roman Forum and see the Palatine Hill and the Colosseum. In the afternoon, combine sightseeing with shopping and make your way through the neighborhood around the Spanish Steps and the Trevi Fountain. The following day, visit the Vatican Museums and Sistine Chapel, then St. Peter's, breaking between the two for lunch. Take it easy on your third morning: explore a museum or sight of interest and then relax at a café and watch the passing parade. Spend your final afternoon and evening exploring the Ghetto and Trastevere neighborhoods.

If you have
5 days

On the morning of the fourth day wander through Villa Borghese and see the Canova and Bernini sculptures in the Galleria Borghese (make reservations ahead of time). On the fifth day, take an early-morning excursion along Via Appia Antica. After lunch back in town, see some of Rome's most historic churches, with Michelangelo's *Moses* in San Pietro in Vincoli a highlight.

If you have
7 days

Devote your remaining time to further exploration of the historic center city, with cappuccino stops along the way. Make sure you pass by the Pantheon, an architectural jewel of ancient Rome, and linger in Piazza Navona to see Bernini's fabulous fountains. Finally, return to the neighborhood you've liked best in your week here and don't be shy about poking into its courtyards and churches.

★ ➤ ❶ **Campidoglio** (Capitoline Hill). Though most of the buildings on Michelangelo's piazza date from the Renaissance, this hill was once the nerve center of the Roman Empire, the place where the city's first and holiest temples stood, including its most sacred, the Tempio di Giove (Temple of Jupiter). The city's archives were kept in the Tabularium (hall of records), the tall tufa structure that forms the foundation of today's city hall, the **Palazzo Senatorio.** By the Middle Ages, Monte Caprino (Goat Hill), as the hill was already called, had fallen into ruin. In 1536, Pope Paul III (1468–1549) decided to restore its grandeur for the triumphal entry into the city of Charles V (1500–58), the Holy Roman Emperor, and called upon Michelangelo to create the staircase ramp; the buildings and facades on three sides of Capitol Hill; the slightly convex pavement and its decoration; and the pedestal for the bronze equestrian statue of Marcus Aurelius. A work from the 2nd century AD, the statue stood here from the 16th century until 1981. The only celebrated equestrian bronze statue to survive unburied from classical antiquity, it was mistakenly believed to represent the Christian emperor Constantine rather than the pagan Marcus Aurelius, hence its endurance through the centuries. A legend foretells that some day the statue's original gold patina will return, heralding the end of the world. The city's authorities had it restored and placed in the courtyard of the Museo Capitolino, saving not only what was left of the gold but also the statue's bronze, which had been seriously damaged by air pollution. A copy was placed on the original pedestal in 1997. As Michelangelo's preeminent urban set piece, the piazza sums up all the majesty of High Renaissance Rome.

❹ **Carcere Mamertino** (Mamertine Prison). This series of gloomy cells under a 17th-century church is where Rome's vanquished enemies were finished off. Some historians believe that St. Peter was held prisoner here, and legend has it that he miraculously brought forth a spring of water with which to baptize his jailers. ⊠ *Via del Tulliano, Piazza Venezia* 🎫 *Donation requested* ⊘ *Daily 9–noon and 2:30–5.*

Circo Massimo (Circus Maximus). In the giant arena laid out between Palatine and Aventine hills, more than 300,000 spectators watched chariot races while the emperor surveyed the scene from his palace on the Palatine Hill.

❺ Colonna di Traiano. The ashes of Trajan (AD 53–117) were buried inside the base of this column, built to commemorate the emperor and his military campaigns in Dacia (Romania). It stands in what was once the **Foro di Traiano,** near the huge semicircular **Mercati di Traiano** (Trajan's Market), and the ruins of the **Foro di Augusto.** ⊠ *Entrance: Via dei Fori Imperiali and Via IV Novembre 6, Colosseo* 🕾 *06/692050630* 🎫 *€2* ⊘ *Tues.–Sun. 9–2 hrs before sunset.*

★ ❾ Colosseo. The massive and majestic Colosseum, ancient Rome's most famous monument, was begun by the Flavian emperor Vespasian (AD 7–79) in AD 72 and inaugurated eight years later with a program of games and shows lasting 100 days. More than 70,000 spectators could sit within the arena's 573-yd circumference, which had marble facing, hundreds of statues for decoration, and a velarium—an ingenious system of saillike awnings rigged on ropes manned by imperial sailors—to protect the audience from the sun and rain. Before the imperial box, gladiators would salute the emperor and cry, "*Ave, imperator, morituri te salutant*" (Hail, emperor, men soon to die salute thee); it is said that when one day they heard the emperor Claudius respond "Or maybe not," they were so offended that they called a strike.

Originally known as the Flavian Amphitheater, it took the name the Colosseum after a truly colossal gilt bronze statue of Nero that stood nearby. Gladiator combat and staged animal hunts ended by the 6th century. The arena later served as a quarry from which materials were looted to build Renaissance churches and palaces. Finally, it was declared sacred by the Vatican in memory of the many Christians believed martyred here. (Scholars now maintain that Christians met their death elsewhere.) During the 19th century, romantic poets lauded the glories of the ruins when viewed by moonlight. Now its arches glow at night with mellow golden spotlights—less romantic, perhaps, but still impressive. ⊠ *Piazza del Colosseo* 🕾 *06/7005469; 06/39967700 reservations* 🎫 *€8, includes Palatine Hill admission; €20, multisight ticket; reservation fee €1.50* ⊘ *Tues.–Sun. 9–4:30.*

❿ Domus Aurea. Nero's "Golden House" gives a good sense of the excesses of Imperial Rome. After fire destroyed much of the city in AD 64, Nero took advantage of the resulting open space to construct a lavish palace so large that contemporary accounts complained, "All Rome has become a villa." In this sort of Roman White House, one wing was given over to public functions, and the other was the emperor's private residence, which included a revolving dining room. Today the palace remains impressive in scale, although it requires a bit of imagination to envision its former grandeur (a mediocre audio guide is some help). One wing caved in early 2000 and remains closed at least through 2005. The site is kept cool and damp, so you should dress accordingly. Reservations are strongly recommended. ⊠ *Via della Domus Aurea, Colosseo* 🕾 *06/39967700 reservations* ⊕ *www.pierreci.it* 🎫 *€5; €10 with tour; audio guide €2* ⊘ *Wed.–Mon. 9–7:45.*

Foro di Cesare. Caesar built this forum, including a temple dedicated to himself and the goddess Minerva, to expand the then-crowded original

Opera Alfresco

Roman nightlife moves outdoors in summertime, and that goes not only for pubs and discos but for higher culture as well. Open-air opera is one venerable Italian tradition that has staged a comeback. Competing opera companies commandeer church courtyards, ancient villas, and soccer stadiums for performances that range from student-run mom-and-poperas to full-scale extravaganzas. The quality of performances is generally quite high, even if small productions often resort to school-play scenery and folding chairs to cut costs. Tickets run from about €15 to €40. Look for old-fashioned posters, plastered all over the city, advertising classics like *Tosca* and *La Traviata*, or contact the companies directly to find out what's on.

Shopping

The city's most famous shopping district is conveniently compact, fanning out at the foot of the Spanish Steps in a galaxy of boutiques offering gorgeous wares with glamorous labels. Here you can ricochet from Gucci to Prada to Valentino to Versace with less effort than it takes to pull out your platinum credit card. If your budget is designed for lower altitudes, you also can find great clothes and accessories at less extravagant prices. But buying is not necessarily the point. Taking in window displays that are works of art or imagining you or yours in a little red dress by Valentino or a lean Armani suit can be satisfactions in themselves.

Sidewalk Cafés

Café-sitting is the most popular leisure-time activity in Rome, practiced by all and involving nothing more strenuous than gesturing to catch the waiter's eye. Cafés are meant for relaxing, chatting with a companion, and watching the passing parade, possibly within view of one of the city's spectacular fountains or churches. Part of the pleasure is resting your tired feet; you will never be rushed, even when the cafés are most crowded, just before lunch and dinner.

Roman Forum, which had been built up over the preceding 500 years. In doing so, Caesar set a trend that several emperors followed, building what are now called the Imperial Fora.

★ ❻ **Foro Romano.** Built in what was once a marshy valley between the Capitoline and Palatine hills, the Forum was the civic heart of Republican Rome, the austere enclave that preceded the hedonistic society that grew up under the emperors in the 1st to 4th centuries AD. The area once was filled with stately and magnificent buildings—temples, palaces, shops—and crowded with people from all corners of the world. Today this series of ruins and marble fragments interspersed with crumbling columns is impressive, but it's not easy to envision the grandeur that once was. It may help to bear in mind that what you see today are the ruins not of one period but of almost 900 years, from about 500 BC to AD 400.

Rome's timeless landscape is suggestive enough that you will probably be content to wander, letting your imagination dwell on Cicero (106 BC–43 BC), Julius Caesar (100 BC–44 BC), and Mark Antony (circa 81 BC–30 BC), who delivered the funeral address in Caesar's honor from the rostrum just left of the **Arco di Settimio Severo.** This arch, one of the

Rome

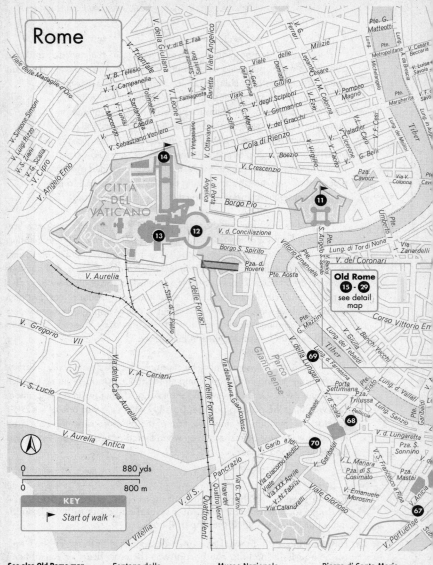

CITTÀ DEL VATICANO

14

13 **12**

11

V. della Giuliana
V. di B. E. Faà
V. Trionfale
V. B. Telesio
V. T. Campanella
V. Santamaria
V. Tolmaide
V. Tunisi
V. Mocenigo
V. Leone IV
V. Famagosta
V. Sebastiano Veniero

V. G. Ferrari
Viale delle Milizie
Viale Giulio Cesare
V. Gen. Della Chiesa
V. degli Scipioni
V. Germanico
V. C. Mario
V. dei Gracchi
V. Cola di Rienzo
V. Boezio
V. Crescenzio
V. Silla

V. Pompeo Magno
V. Virginio Orsini
V. Cicerone
V. Tacito
G. Belli

Pte. G. Matteotti
Lung. Mellini
Pte. Metropolitana
Pte. Cavour
Lung. Marzio
Lung. Prati
Lung. Tor di Nona

Pza. Cavour
Borgo Pio
V. d. Conciliazione
Borgo S. Spirito
Pza. d. Rovere
Pte. Aosta

V. Aurelia
V. Staz. di S. Pietro
V. delle Fornaci

V. Gregorio VII
V. A. Ceriani
V. della Cava Aurelia
V. delle Mura Gianicolensi

V. S. Lucio
V. Aurelia Antica

Parco Gianicolense

69
68
70
67

Old Rome
15 - **29**
see detail map

Corso Vittorio Em

Lung. dei Tebaldi
Lung. Sangallo
V. Giulia
V. dei Farnesina
Porta Settimiana
Pza. Trilussa
V. d. Scala
V. L. Manara
V. di S. Cosimato
Pza. S. Francesco a Ripa
V. Emanuele Morosini
V. d. Lungaretta
Pza. S. Sonnino
Pza. Mastai

Via Giacomo Medici
Viale XXX Aprile
Viale del N. Fabrizi
Via Calandrelli
V. Garib. a Idi.

Viale Glorioso

V. Portuense

V. Pancrazio
V. di S. Quattro Venti
V. G. Carini
V. Vitellia

0   880 yds
0   800 m

KEY

▶ Start of walk

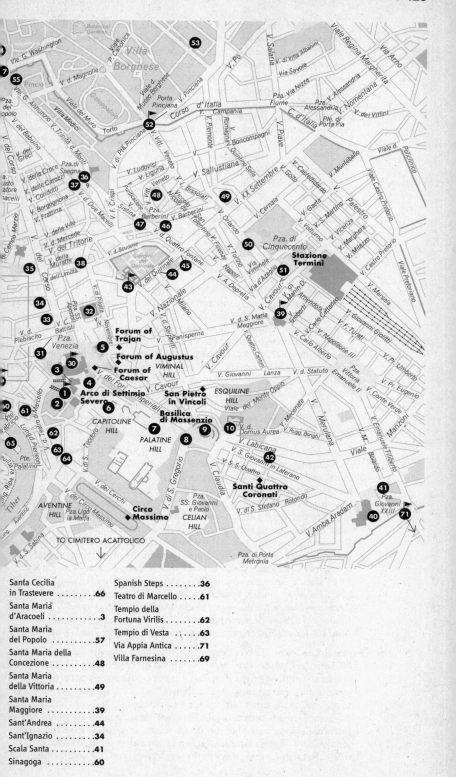

grandest of all antiquity, was built in AD 203 to celebrate the victory of the emperor Severus (AD 146–211) over the Parthians, and was topped by a bronze equestrian statuary group with six horses. Most visitors also explore the reconstruction of the large brick senate hall, the **Curia**; the three Corinthian columns (a favorite of 19th-century poets), all that remains of the **Tempio di Vespasiano** (Temple of Vespasian); the circular **Tempio di Vesta**, where the highly privileged vestal virgins kept the sacred flame alive; and the **Arco di Tito**, which stands in a slightly elevated position on a spur of the Palatine Hill. The view of the Colosseum from the arch is superb and reminds us that it was the Emperor Titus (AD 39–81) who helped finish the vast amphitheater begun by his father, Vespasian. Now cleaned and restored, the arch was erected in AD 81 to celebrate the sack of Jerusalem 10 years earlier, after the great Jewish revolt. A famous relief shows the captured contents of Herod's Temple—including its huge seven-branched menorah—being carried in triumph down Rome's Via Sacra. Audio guides are available at the bookshop–ticket office at the Via dei Fori Imperiali entrance. ⊠ *Entrances at Via dei Fori Imperiali and Piazza del Colosseo* ☎ *06/39967700* ⊕ *www.pierreci.it* ✆ *Free, guided tour €3.50, audio guide €4* ⊙ *Daily 9–4:30.*

❼ Colle Palatino (Palatine Hill). A lane known as the Clivus Palatinus, whose worn paving stones were once trod by emperors and their slaves, climbs from the Forum area to a site that historians identify with Rome's earliest settlement. From 1878 to 1889, illustrious archaeologist Rodolfo Lanciani excavated a site on the Palatine Hill and found evidence of Romulus's presence, thereby contradicting early critics who deemed Romulus a mythical figure. The story goes that the twins Romulus and Remus were abandoned as infants but were nursed by a she-wolf on the banks of the Tiber and adopted by a shepherd. Encouraged by the gods to build a city, the twins chose a site in 735 BC, fortifying it with a wall that Lanciani identified by digging on the Palatine Hill. During the building of the city, the brothers quarreled, and in a fit of anger Romulus killed Remus.

Fodor'sChoice ★

In ancient times, despite the location overlooking the Forum with its traffic, congestion, and attendant noise, the Palatine Hill was Rome's most coveted address. More than a few of the 12 Caesars called the Palatine Hill home—including Caligula, who met his premature end in the Cryptoporticus tunnel, which today still stands (and remains unnerving). The palace of Tiberius was the first to be built here; others followed, most notably the gigantic extravaganza constructed for Emperor Domitian. Views from the ruins of the imperial palaces extend over the Circus Maximus. Today the Palatine is one of the most tranquil places in town, its Renaissance gardens a welcome respite, especially on a hot day. The Palatine Antiquarium holds relics found during excavations on the hill, as well as models of late Bronze Age villages. ⊠ *Entrances at the Arch of Titus in the Roman Forum and Via S. Gregorio 30, Colosseo* ☎ *06/39967700* ⊕ *www.pierreci.it* ✆ *€8, includes Colosseo admission; €20, multisight ticket; reservation fee €1.50* ⊙ *Tues.–Sun. 9–4:30.*

★ ❷ **Musei Capitolini.** The collections in the twin Museo Capitolino and Palazzo dei Conservatori were assembled by Pope Sixtus IV (1414–84), one of the earliest of the Renaissance popes. Although parts of the collection may excite only archaeologists and art historians, others contain some of the most famous pieces of classical sculpture, such as the poignant *Dying Gaul,* the regal *Capitoline Venus,* and the *Exquiline Venus* (identified as another Mediterranean beauty, Cleopatra herself). The delicate *Marble Faun* inspired Nathaniel Hawthorne's novel of the same name. Remember that many of the works here and in Rome's other mu-

AN EMPEROR CHEAT SHEET

OCTAVIAN, later known as **CAESAR AUGUSTUS,** was Rome's first emperor (27 BC–AD 14), and his rule began a 200-year period of peace known as the Pax Romana.

The name of **NERO** (AD 54–68) lives in infamy as a violent persecutor of Christians, and as the murderer of his wife, his mother, and countless others; while it's not certain whether he actually played music as Rome burned in AD 64, he was well known as a singer and a composer of music.

TRAJAN (AD 98–117), the first Roman emperor to be born outside Italy (in southern Spain), enlarged the Empire's boundaries to include modern-day Romania, Armenia, and Upper Mesopotamia.

HADRIAN (AD 117–138), Trajan's younger cousin once removed, expanded the empire in Asia and the Middle East. Best known in Rome for having designed and rebuilt the Pantheon, his majestic villa at Tivoli, and for myriad other constructions across the Empire, he was also the author of the famed wall across Britain.

MARCUS AURELIUS (AD 161–180) is remembered as a humanitarian emperor, a Stoic philosopher whose Meditations are still read today. Nonetheless, he was devoted to expansion and an aggressive leader of the empire.

CONSTANTINE I (AD 306–337) was the first emperor to legalize Christianity. His policy towards Christianity changed the course of history, legitimizing the once-banned religion and paving the way for the papacy in Rome.

seums were copied from Greek originals. For hundreds of years, craftsmen of ancient Rome prospered by producing exact replicas of Greek statues using a process called "pointing."

Portraiture, however, was one area in which the Romans outdid the Greeks. The hundreds of Roman busts of emperors in the Sala degli Imperatori and of philosophers in the Sala dei Filosofi of the **Museo Capitolino** constitute a Who's Who of the ancient world. Within these serried ranks are 48 Roman emperors, ranging from Augustus to Theodosius (AD 346–395). On one console, you'll see the handsomely austere Augustus, who "found Rome a city of brick and left it one of marble." On another rests Claudius "the stutterer," an indefatigable builder brought vividly to life in the novel *I, Claudius* by Robert Graves (1895–1985). Also in this company is Nero, one of the most notorious emperors— though by no means the worst—who built for himself the fabled Domus Aurea. And, of course, there are the baddies: cruel Caligula (AD 12–41) and Caracalla (AD 186–217), and the dissolute, eerily modern boy-emperor, Heliogabalus (AD 203–222).

Unlike the Greeks, whose portraits are idealized, the Romans preferred the "warts and all" school of representation. Many of the busts that have come down to us, notably that of Commodus (AD 161–192), the emperor-gladiator (found in a gallery on the upper level of the museum), are almost brutally realistic. As you leave the museum, be sure to stop in the courtyard. To the right is the original equestrian statue of Marcus Aurelius that once stood in the piazza outside, restored and safely kept behind glass. At the center of the courtyard is the gigantic, reclining figure of Oceanus, found in the Roman Forum and later dubbed *Marforio,* one of Rome's famous "talking statues" to which citizens from the 1500s to the 1900s affixed anonymous satirical verses and notes of political protest. (Another talking statue still in use today sits at Piazza Pasquino, near Piazza Navona.)

The **Palazzo dei Conservatori** is a trove of ancient and baroque treasures. Lining the courtyard are the colossal fragments of a head, leg, foot, and hand—all that remains of the famous statue of the emperor Constantine the Great, who believed that Rome's future lay with Christianity. These immense effigies were much in vogue in the later days of the Roman Empire. The resplendent Salone dei Orazi e Curiazi on the first floor is a ceremonial hall with a magnificent gilt ceiling, carved wooden doors, and 16th-century frescoes. At either end of the hall reign statues of the baroque era's most charismatic popes, a marble Urban VIII (1568–1644) by Bernini (1598–1680) and a bronze Innocent X (1574–1655) by Bernini's rival Algardi (1595–1654). The renowned symbol of Rome, the *Capitoline Wolf,* a 6th-century BC Etruscan bronze, holds a place of honor in the museum; the suckling twins were added during the Renaissance to adapt the statue to the legend of Romulus and Remus. The museum's Pinacoteca, or painting gallery, holds some of baroque painting's great masterpieces, including Caravaggio's *La Buona Ventura* (1595) and *San Giovanni Battista* (1602), Peter Paul Rubens's (1577–1640) *Romulus and Remus* (1614), and Pietro da Cortona's (1627) sumptuous portrait of Pope Urban VIII. The museum complex includes the adjacent **Palazzo Caffarelli** where temporary exhibitions take place and where you can enjoy the view and refreshments on a large open terrace. Admission to the Pinacoteca is included in your ticket. ✉ *Piazza del Campidoglio, Piazza Venezia* ☎ *06/39967800* ⊕ *www.pierreci.it* 🖃 *€6.20, free last Sun. of month* ⊙ *Tues.–Sun. 9–8.*

❸ **Santa Maria d'Aracoeli.** This stark redbrick church was one of the first Christian churches in Rome. According to legend, on this spot the Sibyl predicted to Augustus the coming of a redeemer. The emperor is believed to have responded by erecting the Ara Coeli, the Altar of Heaven. The church is best known for its seemingly endless, steep stairs from Piazza Venezia and for the 15th-century frescoes by Pinturicchio (1454–1513) in the first chapel on the right. ✉ *Piazza d'Aracoeli, Piazza Venezia* ⊙ *Oct.–May, daily 7–noon and 4–6; June–Sept., daily 7–noon and 4–6:30.*

The Vatican: Rome of the Popes

This tiny walled city-state, capital of the Catholic Church, draws millions of visitors every year to its wealth of treasures and spiritual monuments. You might go to the Vatican for its exceptional art holdings—Michelangelo's frescoes, rare archaeological marbles, and Bernini's statues—or to immerse yourself in the unique and grandiose architecture of St. Peter's square. Or you may go in pilgrimage, spiritual or otherwise, to the most overwhelming architectural achievement of the Renaissance and the seat of world Catholicism, St. Peter's Basilica. In between the sacred and the profane lie sights for every taste and inclination: magnificent rooms decorated by Raphael, sculptures such as the *Apollo Belvedere* and the *Laocoön,* frescoes by Fra Angelico, paintings by Giotto and Leonardo, and the celebrated ceiling of the Sistine Chapel. The power that emerged as the Rome of the emperors declined—the Church—gave impetus to a profusion of artistic expression and shaped the destiny of the city for a thousand years. Note that there is a strict dress code for all interior Vatican sights.

a good
walk

Start your walk at the **Castel Sant'Angelo** ⑪ ☞, the fortress that once served as the pope's refuge, and take in the stage-set beauty of the Ponte Sant'Angelo before turning right onto Via della Conciliazione (or taking the more intimate route west along Borgo Pio) to the Vatican. Once inside **Piazza San Pietro** ⑫, rich architectural detail awaits at **Basilica di San Pietro** ⑬, the magnificent seat of the Catholic Church. Below the basilica, visit the Vatican Grottoes, the last repose of many of the popes, and, if you have time, arrange a tour of the excavations below the church and the Vatican Gardens.

TIMING   Allow an hour for a visit to Castel Sant'Angelo. You'll also need an hour to see St. Peter's, plus 30 minutes for the Museo Storico, 15 minutes for the Vatican Grottoes, and an hour to climb to the top of the dome. Note that free one-hour English-language tours of the basilica are offered Monday–Saturday at 10 and 3, Sunday at 2:30 (sign up at the little desk under the portico).

Sights to See

★ ⑬   **Basilica di San Pietro.** The physical proportions of the sublime St. Peter's Basílica are staggering: it covers about 18,100 square yds, extends 212 yds in length, and carries a dome that rises 435 ft and measures 138 ft across its base. Its history is equally impressive: no fewer than five of Italy's greatest artists—Donato Bramante (1444–1514), Raphael (1483–1520), Baldassare Peruzzi (1481–1536), Antonio Sangallo the Younger (1483–1546), and Michelangelo (1475–1564)—died while working on the construction of this new St. Peter's. The history of the original St. Peter's goes back to the year AD 319, when the emperor Constantine built a basilica over the site of the tomb of St. Peter (died AD 64). This early church stood for more than 1,000 years, undergoing a number of restorations, until it was on the verge of collapse. Reconstruction began in 1452 but was abandoned for lack of funds. In 1506 Pope Julius II (1443–1513) instructed the architect Bramante to raze the existing structure and build a new and greater basilica. In 1546 Pope Paul III persuaded the aging Michelangelo to take on the job of completing the building. Revising Bramante's plan, Michelangelo designed the dome to cover the crossing, but his plans, too, were modified after his death. The cupola, one of the most beautiful in the world, was completed by Giacomo della Porta (circa 1537–1602) and Domenico Fontana (1543–1607). The new church wasn't completed and dedicated until 1626—by that time the ground plan had shifted from a Greek cross to a Latin one, creating a longer nave but obscuring the view of the dome from the piazza. Under the portico, 15th-century bronze doors by Filarete (circa 1400–1469), salvaged from the old basilica, fill the central portal. Off the entry portico, Bernini's famous *Scala Regia*, the ceremonial entryway to the Vatican Palace and one of the most magnificent staircases in the world, is graced with Bernini's dramatic statue of Constantine the Great.

The cherubs over the holy-water fonts will give you a sense of the grand scale of St. Peter's: the sole of each cherub's foot is as long as the distance from your fingertips to your elbow. It is because the proportions of this giant building are in such perfect harmony that its vastness may escape you at first. But in its megascale—inspired by the size of the ancient Roman ruins—it reflects Roman *grandiosità* in all its majesty.

Over an altar in a side chapel near the entrance is Michelangelo's *Pietà*. Legend has it that the artist, only 22 at the time the work was completed, overheard passersby expressing skepticism that such a young man could have executed such a sophisticated and moving piece. Offended at the implication, he crept back that night and signed the piece—in big letters, on a ribbon falling from the Virgin's left shoulder across her breast, where no one could possibly miss it. His name is there today.

Four massive piers support the dome at the crossing, where the mighty Bernini **baldacchino** (canopy) rises high above the papal altar. "What the barbarians didn't do, the Barberini did," 17th-century wags quipped when Barberini Pope Urban VIII had the bronze stripped from the Pantheon's portico and melted down to make the baldacchino (using what was left over for cannonballs). The pope celebrates mass here, over the grottoes holding the tombs of many of his predecessors. Deep in the excavations under the foundations of the original basilica is what is believed to be the tomb of St. Peter. The bronze throne behind the main altar in the apse, the Cathedra Petri (Chair of St. Peter), is Bernini's work (1656), and it covers a wooden and ivory chair that St. Peter himself is said to have used. However, scholars contend that this throne probably dates only from the Middle Ages. See how the adoration of a million lips has completely worn down the bronze on the right foot of the statue of St. Peter in front of the near right pillar in the transept. Note: ushers at the entrance of St. Peter's Church and the Vatican Museums will not allow entry to persons with inappropriate clothing— which means no bare knees or shoulders. ⊕ *www.vatican.va* ⊙ *Apr.–Sept., daily 7–7; Oct.–Mar., daily 7–6. Closed during ceremonies in the piazza.*

The entrance to the **Grotte Vaticane** (Vatican Grottoes), which hold the tombs of many popes, is at the crossing. The only exit from the grottoes leads outside St. Peter's, to the courtyard that holds the entrance to the dome. ⊙ *Apr.–Sept., daily 7–6; Oct.–Mar., daily 7–5.*

A small but rich collection of Vatican treasures is housed in the **Museo Storico** in the Sacristy, among them precious antique chalices and the massive 15th-century sculptured bronze tomb of Pope Sixtus V (1520–90) by Antonio del Pollaiuolo (1431–98). ▦ €9 ⊙ *Daily 8–5.*

The **roof** of the church, reached by elevator or stairs, is a landscape of domes and towers. A short interior staircase leads to the base of the dome for a dove's-eye view of the interior of St. Peter's. Then, only if you are stout of heart and sound of lung should you attempt the taxing and claustrophobic climb up the narrow stairs—there's no turning back!—to the balcony of the lantern, where the view embraces the Vatican Gardens and all of Rome. ☎ *06/69883462* ▦ *Elevator €5, stairs €4* ⊙ *Daily 8–5. Closed during ceremonies in the piazza.*

off the beaten path **VATICAN NECROPOLIS –** Visit the pre-Constantine necropolis under St. Peter's for a fascinating glimpse of the underpinnings of the great basilica, which was built over the cemetery where archaeologists believe they have found St. Peter's tomb. Apply in advance by sending a fax or e-mail (scavi@fsp.va) with the name of each visitor, language spoken, possible days for the visit, and a local phone number. Reservations will be confirmed a few days in advance. No children under 15 are admitted. Tickets are sometimes available for same-day tours; apply in person at the Ufficio Scavi (Excavations Office), on the right beyond the Arco delle Campane (Arch of the Bells) entrance to the Vatican, which is left of the basilica. Tell the Swiss Guard you want the Ufficio Scavi, and he will let you by. ☎ *06/69885318* ▦ *06/69885518* ⊕ *www.vatican.va* ▦ €9 ⊙ *Ufficio Scavi Mon.–Sat. 8–5.*

☺ ▶ ⓫ **Castel Sant'Angelo.** For hundreds of years, this fortress guarded the Vatican, to which it is linked by the Passetto, an arcaded passageway. Ac-

MEET THE POPE

*The pope holds audiences in a large, modern hall (or in St. Peter's Square in summer) on Wednesday morning at 10. You must get tickets; apply in writing at least 10 days in advance to the **Papal Prefecture** (Prefettura della Casa Pontificia; ✆ 00120 Vatican City ☎ 06/69883273 📠 06/69885863), indicating the date you prefer, the language you speak, and the hotel where you will be staying. Or go to the prefecture, through the Porta di Bronzo, the bronze door at the end of the colonnade on the right side of the piazza; the office is open Monday–Saturday 9–1, and last-minute tickets may be available. You can also arrange to pick up free tickets on Tuesday from 5 to 6:45 at the **Santa Susanna American Church** (⊠ Via XX Settembre 15, Termini ☎ 06/42014554); call first. For a fee, travel agencies make arrangements that include transportation.*

cording to legend, Castel Sant'Angelo got its name during the plague of 590, when Pope Gregory the Great (circa 540–604), passing by in a religious procession, had a vision of an angel sheathing its sword atop the stone ramparts. Though it may look like a stronghold, Castel Sant'Angelo was in fact built as a tomb for the emperor Hadrian (76–138) in AD 135. By the 6th century, it had been transformed into a fortress, and it remained a refuge for the popes for almost 1,000 years. It has dungeons, battlements, cannon and cannonballs, and a collection of antique weaponry and armor. The lower levels formed the base of Hadrian's mausoleum; ancient ramps and narrow staircases climb through the castle's core to courtyards and frescoed halls, where temporary exhibits are held. Off the loggia is a café.

The upper terrace, with the massive angel statue commemorating Gregory's vision, evokes memories of Tosca, Puccini's poignant heroine in the opera of the same name, who threw herself off these ramparts with the cry, "*Scarpia, avanti a Dio!*" (Scarpia, we meet before God). On summer evenings a book fair with musical events and food stalls surrounds the castle. One of Rome's most beautiful pedestrian bridges, **Ponte Sant'Angelo** spans the Tiber in front of the fortress and is studded with graceful angels designed by Bernini. ⊠ *Lungotevere Castello 50, San Pietro* ☎ *06/39967700* ⊕ *www.pierreci.it* 🎟 *€5* 🕐 *Tues.–Sun. 9–8.*

Giardini Vaticani. A tour provides a two-hour jaunt through the Vatican Gardens, half by bus and half on foot, with a guide. A second option is a combined gardens tour and guided visit to the Sistine Chapel. Tickets are available at the **Guided Visit to Vatican Museums Office** (⊠ Piazza San Pietro ☎ 06/69884466), open Monday–Saturday 8:30–7. Make reservations two or three days in advance. ⊕*www.vatican.va* 🎟*€9 for the Gardens tour, €19 for Gardens and Sistine Chapel* 🕐 *Mon.–Sat.*

⑫ Piazza San Pietro. As you enter St. Peter's Square, you are officially entering Vatican territory. The piazza is one of Bernini's most spectacular masterpieces. Completed in 1667 after 11 years' work—a relatively short time in those days, considering the vastness of the task—the piazza can hold 400,000 people. It's surrounded by a curving pair of quadruple colonnades, which are topped by a balustrade and statues of 140 saints. Look for the two disks set into the pavement on either side of the obelisk at the center of the piazza. When you stand on either disk, a trick of perspective makes the colonnades seem to consist of a single row of columns. Bernini had an even grander visual effect in mind when he designed the square. By opening up this immense, bright, airy space in a neighborhood of narrow, shadowy streets, he created a contrast that would surprise and impress anyone who emerged from the darkness into the light, in a characteristically baroque metaphor. But in the 1930s, Mussolini spoiled the effect. To celebrate the "conciliation" between the Vatican and the Italian government under the Lateran Pact of 1929, he conceived of the Via della Conciliazione, the broad, rather soulless avenue that now forms the main approach to St. Peter's and gives the eye time to adjust to the enormous dimensions of the square and church. Remember to take a look at the Swiss Guards in their 16th century–style uniforms; they stand at the Vatican City entrances to the right and left of St. Peter's.

Vatican Museums: The Sistine Chapel & Beyond

The Vatican Palace has been the papal residence since 1377. Actually, it represents a collection of buildings that covers more than 13 acres, containing an estimated (no one has bothered to count them) 1,400 rooms, chapels, and galleries. Other than the pope and his court, the occupants are some of art's greatest masterpieces. The main entrance to the museums, on Viale Vaticano, is a long walk from Piazza San Pietro. Some city buses stop near the museums' main entrance on Viale Vaticano: Bus 49 from Piazza Cavour stops right in front; Buses 81 and 492 and Tram 19 stop at Piazza Risorgimento, halfway between St. Peter's and the museums. The Ottaviano–S. Pietro and the Cipro-Musei Vaticani on Metro A also are in the vicinity.

a good tour

There are many sections of the **Musei Vaticani** 🄔 besides the Sistine Chapel that are not to be overlooked: the Museo Egizio; the Chiaramonti and Museo Pio Clementino, which are given over to classical sculptures (among them some of the best-known statues in the world—the *Laocoön,* the *Belvedere Torso,* and the *Apollo Belvedere*—which with their vibrant humanism had a tremendous impact on Renaissance art); and the Museo Etrusco. Finally, you should make sure to visit the Stanze di Raffaello and see Raphael's paintings in the Pinacoteca.

TIMING   Plan on about two hours if you just want to see highlights; an in-depth visit will take at least a full morning. To minimize time spent in line, it's usually a good idea to get here just before opening time.

Sights to See

🄔   **Musei Vaticani** (Vatican Museums). The immense collections housed

Fodor'sChoice here are so rich that unless you are an art history buff, you will proba-
★ bly just want to skim the surface, concentrating on pieces that strike your fancy. The Sistine Chapel is a must, of course, and that's why you may have to wait in line to see it; after all, every tourist in Rome has the same idea. Pick up a leaflet at the main entrance to the museums to see the overall layout. The Sistine Chapel is at the far end of the complex, and the leaflet charts two abbreviated itineraries through other collections to reach it. You can rent a taped commentary (€4, about 90 minutes) in English for the Sistine Chapel, the Stanze di Raffaello, and the other main attractions. Or, you can book a guided tour with the **Guided Visit to Vatican Museums Office** (☎ 06/69884466). Phone at least a day in advance. Cost, including entrance, is €16.50.

The **Stanze di Raffaello** (Raphael Rooms) are second only to the Sistine Chapel in artistic interest—and draw crowds comparable to the Sistine's as well. In 1508, Pope Julius II employed Raphael, on the recommendation of Bramante, to decorate the rooms with biblical scenes. The result was a Renaissance tour de force. Of the four rooms, the second and third were decorated mainly by Raphael. The others were decorated by Giulio Romano (circa 1499–1546) and other assistants of Raphael; the first room is known as the Stanza dell'Incendio, with frescoes of the fire (*incendio*) in the Borgo by Romano.

The frescoed **Stanza della Segnatura** (Room of the Signature), where papal bulls were signed, is one of Raphael's finest works; indeed, they are thought by many to be some of the finest paintings in the history of Western art. This was Julius's private library, and the room's use is reflected in the frescoes' themes, philosophy and enlightenment. A paradigm of High Renaissance painting, the works here demonstrate the revolutionary ideals of the time: naturalism (Raphael's figures lack the awkwardness of those painted only a few years earlier); humanism (the idea that human beings are the noblest and most admirable of God's creations); and a profound interest in the ancient world, the result of the 15th-century rediscovery of classical antiquity. Theology triumphs in the fresco known as the *Disputa,* or *Debate on the Holy Sacrament.* The *School of Athens* glorifies some of philosophy's greats, including Plato and Aristotle at the fresco's center. The pensive figure on the stairs is thought to be modeled after Michelangelo, who was painting the Sistine ceiling at the same time Raphael was working here. Michelangelo does not appear in preparatory drawings, so Raphael may have added his fellow artist's portrait after admiring his work.

The tiny **Cappella di Nicholas V** (Chapel of Nicholas V) is aglow with frescoes by Fra Angelico (1387–1455), the Florentine monk whose sensitive paintings were guiding lights for the Renaissance. The **Appartamento Borgia** (Borgia Apartment) is worth seeing for the elaborately painted ceilings, designed and partially executed by Pinturicchio. Among the frescoes, look for the Borgia's family emblem, the bull, and for the blond Lucrezia, the Borgia Pope's daughter, posing piously as St. Catherine.

In 1508, while Raphael was put to work on his series of rooms, the redoubtable Pope Julius II commissioned Michelangelo to paint single-handedly the more than 10,000-square-ft ceiling of the **Cappella Sistina** (Sistine Chapel). The task cost the artist four years of mental and physical anguish. It's said that for years afterward Michelangelo couldn't read anything without holding it up over his head. The result, however, was the masterpiece that you now see, its colors cool and brilliant after restoration. Bring a pair of binoculars to get a better look at this incredible work (unfortunately, you're not allowed to lie down on the floor to study the frescoes above, the viewing position of choice in decades past; by the time you leave the chapel, your neck may feel like Michelangelo's, so you may also want to study it—to take a cue from 19th-century visitors—with the aid of a pocket mirror).

The ceiling is in essence a painted Bible: Michelangelo's subject was the story of humanity before the coming of Christ. Although some of the frescoed panels are veritable stews of figures, others—especially the depiction of God's outstretched hand giving Adam the spark of life in the *Creation of Adam*—are forcefully simple, revealing how much Michelangelo brought to painting from the discipline of sculpture. In 1541, some 30 years after completing the ceiling, Michelangelo was commissioned to paint the *Last Judgment* on the chapel's altar wall. If the artist's ceiling may be taken as an expression of the optimism of the High Renaissance, the *Last Judgment,* by contrast, is a virtual guided tour through hell. The aged and embittered Michelangelo painted his own face on the wrinkled human skin in the hand of St. Bartholomew, below and to the right of the figure of Christ, which he clearly modeled on the *Apollo Belvedere* (now on exhibit in the Vatican galleries). This is not surprising, since in the intervening years Rome had been sacked and pillaged by mercenary troops of Charles V in 1527, who used the Sistine Chapel as a stable.

In only a few years, the grim Counter-Reformation began, and suddenly the nudity in Michelangelo's *Last Judgment* was so repugnant to the papal court that the artist Daniele da Volterra (1509–66)—forever after known as *il braghettone* (the breeches-maker)—was ordered to paint loincloths over the offending parts. Like the ceiling, the *Last Judgment* has been cleaned; the restoration was unveiled in April 1994, surprising viewers with its clarity and color. Was Michelangelo truly a master of vibrant color? Or is the "new" Sistine a travesty of the artist's intentions? Opinions remain divided, but most art historians believe the restoration is true to Michelangelo's original vision.

The exhibition halls of the **Biblioteca Vaticana** (Vatican Library) are bright with frescoes and contain a sampling of the library's rich collections of precious manuscripts. Room X, the Room of the Aldobrandini Marriage, holds a beautiful Roman fresco of a nuptial rite. More classical statues are on view in the new wing. At the Quattro Cancelli, a cafeteria offers a well-earned break. The **Pinacoteca** (Picture Gallery) displays works by such artists as Giotto (circa 1266–1337), Fra Angelico, and Filippo Lippi (circa 1406–69), and Raphael's exceptional *Transfiguration, Coronation,* and *Foligno Madonna.* In all, the Vatican Museums offer a staggering foray into the realms of art and history—so much that it's foolhardy to try to see all the collections in one day. ☒ *Viale Vaticano, San Pietro* ☏ *06/69883041* ⊕ *www.vatican.va* ☒ *€10* ☼ *Mid-Mar.–Oct., weekdays 8:45–4:45, no admission after 3:45, Sat. and last Sun. of month 8:45–1:45, no admission after 12:20; Nov.–mid-Mar., Mon.–Sat. and last Sun. of month 8:45–1:45, no admission after 12:20* ☞ *Note: ushers at the entrance of St. Peter's and the Vatican Museums will not allow entry to persons with bare knees or bare shoulders.*

need a break? There are neighborhood trattorias far better and far less popular with tourists than those opposite the Vatican Museums entrance. Among them is the **Hostaria Dino e Toni** (☒ Via Leone IV 60, San Pietro), where you can dine on typical Roman fare at moderate, even inexpensive prices. **La Caravella** (☒ Via degli Scipioni 32, at Via Vespasiano, off Piazza Risorgimento, San Pietro) serves Roman specialties, including pizza at lunch, every day but Thursday, when it's closed.

Old Rome: Gold & Grandeur

The neighborhood between the Corso and the Tiber bend is one of Rome's most beautiful districts, filled with narrow streets bearing curious names, airy baroque piazzas, and picturesque courtyards. It has been an integral part of the city since ancient times, and its position between the Vatican and the Lateran palaces, both seats of papal rule, put it in the mainstream of Rome's development from the Middle Ages onward. It includes such world-famous sights as the Pantheon, but it is mainly an excursion into the 16th and 17th centuries, when baroque art triumphed. Some of Rome's most coveted residential addresses are here.

The most important clue to the Romans is their baroque art—not its artistic technicalities but its spirit. When you understand this, you will no longer be a stranger in Rome. Flagrantly emotional, heavily expressive, and sensuously visual, the 17th-century artistic movement known as the baroque was born in Rome, the creation of three geniuses, the sculptor and architect Gianlorenzo Bernini, the painter and architect Pietro da Cortona (1596–1669), and the architect and sculptor Francesco Borromini (1599–1667). From the drama found in the artists' paintings to the jewel-laden, gold-on-gold detail of 17th-century Roman palaces, baroque style was intended both to shock and delight by upsetting the placid, "correct" rules of the Renaissance. The style's appeal to the emotions made it a powerful weapon in the hands of the Counter-Reformation.

a good walk

Start on Via del Plebiscito, near Piazza Venezia, at the huge church of **Il Gesù** 15 ▶, the grandmother of all baroque churches. Walk west along Via Celso to Via della Botteghe Oscure and **Crypta Balbi** 16, then head north past **Largo di Torre Argentina** 17, the site where Caesar was slain by Brutus, to Piazza della Minerva and the church of **Santa Maria sopra Minerva** 18. Turn down Via della Minerva to reach the **Pantheon** 19. From Piazza della Rotonda, in front of the Pantheon, take Via Giustiniani onto Via della Dogana Vecchia to the church of **San Luigi dei Francesi** 20, a pilgrimage spot for art lovers everywhere. Just north is the church of **Sant'Agostino in Campo Marzio** 21, in the piazza of the same name. Visit historic **Palazzo Altemps** 22, off Piazza Sant'Apollinare, before arriving at **Piazza Navona** 23, one of Rome's showpiece piazzas, home to Bernini's Fontana dei Quattro Fiumi and the church of Sant'Agnese in Agone, the quintessence of baroque architecture. Leave the piazza at the south end and cross one of Rome's great thoroughfares, Corso Vittorio Emanuele II, to the **Campo de' Fiori** 24. Flowing naturally out of the campo is a short promenade that will take you to **Palazzo Farnese** 25, perhaps the most beautiful Renaissance palace in Rome. Then proceed south to inspect **Palazzo Spada** 26 and its picture gallery. Take Via Baullari to one of the outstanding architectural monuments of Renaissance Rome, the **Palazzo Massimo alle Colonne** 27, and, two blocks east along the bustling street, the huge, 17th-century church of **Sant'Andrea della Valle** 28. Finally, head down Corso del Rinascimento to No. 40, the church of **Sant'Ivo alla Sapienza** 29, with a golden lantern atop the dome in the shape of a spiral.

TIMING Allow about four hours for this walk, including time to linger at Crypta Balbi, Palazzo Altemps, and Palazzo Spada.

What to See

★ 24 **Campo de' Fiori.** This bustling square is home to a famed morning market, a must-see dose of local culture for any Roman holiday. Each morning, vendors fill temporary stalls with all manner of local produce, nuts, cheese, spices, flowers, and seafood; by early afternoon, it's all gone, to resurface in the city's homes and restaurants at dinnertime. If you don't want to join the fray, step back and take a break at one of the many pleasant cafés that edge the market. The view has certainly improved since the Middle Ages, when the square was the scene of public executions, including that of philosopher-monk Giordano Bruno (1548–1600). His statue still broods in the center of the square.

need a break?

Some of Rome's best pizza comes out of the ovens of the **Antico Forno** (☎ 06/68806662) on Campo de' Fiori. Choose pizza *bianca* (topped with olive oil) or *rossa* (with tomato sauce), or any of a half dozen baked goodies on hand. The benches at the foot of Palazzo Farnese in the adjacent piazza make a good place to enjoy your snack.

16 **Crypta Balbi** (Crypt of Balbus). After 20 years of excavation and restoration, these fascinating remains of a porticoed courtyard and theater built in 13 BC, now part of the Museo Nazionale Romano, afford a unique

look at Roman history. Rather than focus on one era, the museum peels back the layers of the site, following the latest techniques in conservation. The well-explained exhibits (with text in English and Italian) give you a tangible sense of the sweeping changes that this spot—and Rome—underwent from antiquity to the 20th century. A partially restored wall provides an example of what marble and tufa constructions looked like before weather took its toll and medieval builders stripped the marble off for reuse. Copies of documents and reconstructed coins and other everyday objects found in drains, rubbish dumps, and tombs are a window into the world of the people who lived and worked here over the ages. ⊠ *Via Delle Botteghe Oscure 31, Piazza Venezia* ☎ *06/39967700* 🖃 *€4* 🕓 *Tues.–Sun. 9–7:45.*

▶ ⑮ **Il Gesù.** Grandmother of all baroque churches, this huge structure was designed by the architect Vignola (1507–73) to be the tangible symbol of Jesuits, a major force in the Counter-Reformation in Europe. It remained unadorned for about 100 years, but when it finally was decorated, no expense was spared. Its interior drips with gold and lapis lazuli, gold and precious marbles, gold and more gold—all covered by a fantastically painted ceiling by Baciccia (1639–1709) that seems to merge with the painted stucco figures at its base. St. Ignatius's apartments, reached from the side entrance of the church, are also worth a visit (afternoons only) for the trompe l'oeil frescoes and relics of the saint. ⊠ *Piazza del Gesù, Piazza Venezia* ☎ *06/697001* 🕓 *Daily 6:30–12:30 and 4–7.*

⑰ **Largo di Torre Argentina.** In the middle of this busy piazza lies Rome's largest fully excavated Republican-era ruins. The site was discovered in 1885 and then further dug up from 1926 to 1929. What came to light was the *Area Sacra* (the sacred area), with columns, altars, and foundations from four temples facing east dating as far back as the 1st century BC. On the west side of the square lies the Curia Pompeia, the site where Caesar was slain in 44 BC. The frescoes on the taller brickwork are from the 12th century church of San Nicola de' Cesarini, which was built into one of the temples. While here it's hard to miss the many cats lounging around the site: the ruins serve as a cat sanctuary for hundreds of the city's strays. In the southwest corner, take the staircase down to visit the cats and the *gattare* (cat ladies) who look after them. You may even get a free tour of the site as a reward for your interest. ☎ *06/6872133* 🌐 *www.romancats.com.*

㉒ **Palazzo Altemps.** If you're interested in ancient sculpture, you should not miss one of Rome's greatest collections of classical antiquities, housed in this 16th-century building. It displays the collections of ancient Roman and Egyptian sculpture of the **Museo Nazionale Romano.** Look for two works in the famed Ludovisi collection: the large, intricately carved *Ludovisi Sarcophagus,* and *Galata,* a poignant work portraying a barbarian warrior who chooses death for himself and his wife rather than humiliation by the enemy. The palace's stunning courtyard and gorgeously frescoed ceilings and loggia make an impressive setting for the sculptures. ⊠ *Piazza Sant'Apollinare 46, Piazza Navona* ☎ *06/39967700* 🖃 *€5* 🕓 *Tues.–Sun. 9–7:45.*

㉕ **Palazzo Farnese.** The Farnese family rose to great power during the Renaissance, in part due to the favor Pope Alexander VI showed to the beautiful Giulia Farnese. The large palace was begun when, with Alexander's aid, Giulia's brother became Cardinal; it was further enlarged on his election as Pope Paul III in 1534. The uppermost frieze decorations and main window overlooking the piazza are the work of Michelangelo, who also designed part of the courtyard, as well as the graceful arch over Via Giulia at the back. The facade on Piazza Far-

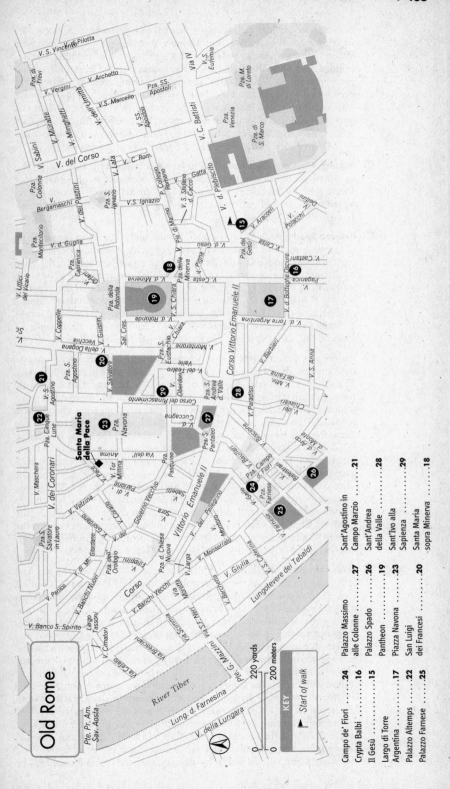

Old Rome

KEY

▲ *Start of walk*

0 220 yards
0 200 meters

nese has been recently cleaned, further revealing geometrical brick configurations that have long been thought to hold some occult meaning. When looking up at the palace catch a glimpse of the splendid frescoed ceilings, including the **Galleria Carracci** vault painted by Annibale Carracci between 1597 and 1604—the second-greatest ceiling in Rome. For permission to view it from the inside, write to the French Embassy, which now occupies the palace. Specify the number in your party, when you wish to visit, and a local phone number, for confirmation a few days before the visit. ⊠ *Servizio Culturale, French Embassy, Piazza Farnese 67, 00186 Rome* ☎ *06/686011* ☐ *Free* ☉ *By appointment only.*

㉗ Palazzo Massimo alle Colonne. A graceful columned portico marks this inconspicuous but seminal architectural monument of Renaissance Rome, built by Baldassare Peruzzi in 1527. Via del Paradiso, across Corso Vittorio Emanuele II, affords a better view. ⊠ *Corso Vittorio Emanuele II 141, Piazza Navona.*

㉖ Palazzo Spada. A dazzling stuccoed facade tucked away in Piazza Capo di Ferro, west of Piazza Farnese, fronts an equally magnificent inner courtyard. On the southeast side of the inner courtyard, the gallery, designed by Borromini, creates an elaborate optical illusion, appearing to be much longer than it really is. (Ask the janitor for admittance to the *giardino segreto.*) On the first floor there are paintings and sculptures that belonged to Cardinale Bernardino Spada, an art connoisseur who collected works by Italian and Flemish masters. ⊠ *Piazza Capo di Ferro 13, Campo de' Fiori* ☎ *06/32810* ⊕ *www.galleriaborghese.it* ☐ *€5* ☉ *Tues.–Sun. 9–7.*

⑲ Pantheon. One of Rome's most impressive and best-preserved ancient monuments, the Pantheon is particularly close to the heart of Romans. The emperor Hadrian designed it around AD 120 and had it built on the site of an earlier temple that had been damaged by fire. The most striking thing about the Pantheon is not its size, immense though it is (until 1960 the dome was the largest ever built); rather, it is the remarkable harmony of the building. Notice that the height of the dome is equal to the diameter of the circular interior. The oculus, or opening in the ceiling, is meant to symbolize the all-seeing eye of heaven; in practice, it illuminates the building and lightens the heavy stone ceiling. Note the original bronze doors, which have survived more than 1,800 years, centuries longer than the interior's rich gold ornamentation, which was plundered by popes and emperors. Art lovers can pay homage to the tomb of Raphael, who is buried in an ancient sarcophagus under the alter of Madonna del Sasso. ⊠ *Piazza della Rotonda, Pantheon* ☎ *06/ 68300230* ☉ *Mon.–Sat. 8:30–7:30, Sun. 9–6, holidays 9–1.*

★ ☕ **㉓ Piazza Navona.** This famed 17th-century piazza, built over the site and following the form of the 1st-century Stadium of Domitian, is one of Rome's showpiece attractions. It still has the carefree air of the days when it was the scene of Roman circus games, medieval jousts, and 17th-century carnivals. Today, it often attracts fashion photographers and Romans out for their evening *passeggiata* (promenade). The Christmas fair held from early December through January 6 fills the piazza with games, nativity scenes (some well crafted, many not so), and multiple versions of the Befana, the ugly but good witch who brings candy and toys to Italian children on the Epiphany. (Her name is a corruption of the Italian word *Epifania.*) Bernini's splashing **Fontana dei Quattro Fiumi** (Fountain of the Four Rivers), with an enormous rock squared off by statues representing the four corners of the world, makes a fitting centerpiece. Behind the fountain is the church of **Sant'Agnese in Agone,** an outstanding example of baroque architecture built by the Pamphili Pope Innocent X and still owned by his descendants, the Doria Pamphili. The

Fodor'sChoice ★

facade—a wonderfully rich mélange of bell towers, concave spaces, and dovetailed stone and marble—is by Carlo Rainaldi (1611–91) and Francesco Borromini (1599–1667), a contemporary and sometime rival of Bernini. One story has it that the Bernini statue nearest the church, which represents the River Plate, has its hand up before his eye because it can't bear the sight of the Borromini facade. Though often repeated, the story is a fiction: the facade wasn't built until after the fountain was installed.

⓴ San Luigi dei Francesi. The clergy of San Luigi considered Caravaggio's roistering and unruly lifestyle scandalous enough, but his realistic treatment of sacred subjects—seen in three paintings in the last chapel—was too much for them. They rejected outright his first version of the altarpiece, and they weren't especially happy with the other two works. Thanks to the intercession of Caravaggio's patron, the influential Cardinal Francesco del Monte, they were persuaded to keep them—a lucky thing, since they are now thought to be among the artist's finest paintings. Have a few one-euro coins handy for the light machine. ⊠ *Piazza San Luigi dei Francesi, Piazza Navona* 🕾 *06/688271* ☉ *Fri.–Wed. 7:30–12:30 and 3:30–7, Thurs. 7:30–12:30.*

㉑ Sant'Agostino in Campo Marzio. Caravaggio's celebrated *Madonna of the Pilgrims*—which scandalized all Rome because it pictured pilgrims with dirt on the soles of their feet—can be found in this small church, over the first altar on the left. Also of interest are Raphael's *Prophet,* on the first pilaster on the left, and the dozens of heart-shape ex votos to Madonna del Parto (Mary of Childbirth) at the entrance. ⊠ *Piazza di Sant'Agostino, Piazza Navona* 🕾 *06/68801962* ☉ *Mon.–Sat. 7:45–noon and 4–7:30, Sun. 4–6.*

㉘ Sant'Andrea della Valle. This huge 17th-century church looms mightily over a busy intersection. Aficionados of Puccini, who set the first act of his *Tosca* here, have been known to hire a horse-drawn carriage at night for an evocative journey that traces the course of the opera (from Sant'Andrea up Via Giulia to Palazzo Farnese—Scarpia's headquarters—to the locale of the opera's climax, Castel Sant'Angelo). Inside, above the apse are striking frescoes depicting scenes from St. Andrew's life by the Bolognese painter Domenichino (1581–1641). ⊠ *Corso Vittorio Emanuele II, Campo de' Fiori* 🕾 *06/6861339* ☉ *Daily 7–noon and 4:30–7:30.*

㉙ Sant'Ivo alla Sapienza. Borromini's eccentric church has what must surely be Rome's most unusual dome—topped by a golden spiral said to have been inspired by a bee's stinger. ⊠ *Corso Rinascimento 40, Piazza Navona* ☉ *Sun. 10–noon.*

⓲ Santa Maria sopra Minerva. In practically the only Gothic-style church in Rome, the attractions are Michelangelo's *Risen Christ* and the tomb of the gentle 15th-century artist Fra Angelico. Have some coins handy to light up the **Carafa Chapel** in the right transept, where exquisite 15th-century frescoes by Filippino Lippi (circa 1457–1504) are well worth the small investment. (Lippi's most famous student was Botticelli.) In front of the church, Bernini's charming elephant bearing an Egyptian obelisk has an inscription on the base stating something to the effect that it takes a strong mind to sustain solid wisdom. ⊠ *Piazza della Minerva, Pantheon* 🕾 *06/6793926* ☉ *Daily 7:30–7.*

Via Giulia. Named after Pope Julius II and having functioned for more than four centuries as the "salon of Rome," this street is still the address of choice for Roman aristocrats. Built with funds garnered by taxing prostitutes, the street is lined with elegant palaces, including the Palazzo

Falconieri, and old churches (one, San Eligio, reputedly designed by Raphael himself). The area around Via Giulia is a wonderful place to wander in to get the feeling of daily life as carried on in a centuries-old setting—an experience enhanced by the dozens of antiques shops in the neighborhood.

Vistas & Views: Piazza Venezia to the Spanish Steps

Though it has a bustling commercial air, this part of the city also holds great visual allure, from the gaudy marble confection that is the monument to Vittorio Emanuele II to the theatrical Piazza di Sant'Ignazio. Among the things to look for are stately palaces, baroque ballrooms, and the greatest example of portraiture in Rome, Velázquez's incomparable *Innocent X* at the Galleria Doria Pamphilj. Those with a taste for the sumptuous theatricality of Roman ecclesiastical architecture—illusionistic ceiling painting in particular—will find this a rewarding stop. The highlights are the Trevi Fountain and the Spanish Steps, 18th-century Rome's most famous example of city planning.

a good walk

Start at the flamboyant **Monumento a Vittorio Emanuele II** 30 ▷ in Piazza Venezia, a mass of marble studded with statuary that has the city's best view from its top. As you look up Via del Corso, to your left is **Palazzo Venezia** 31, an art-filled Renaissance palace from whose balcony Mussolini once addressed the crowds. On Saturday, you can visit the picture gallery, known as the Galleria Colonna, in the **Palazzo Colonna** 32, east of Piazza Venezia. From Piazza Venezia head north on Via del Corso, one of the city's busiest shopping streets, to the **Palazzo Doria Pamphilj** 33, home to an important painting gallery. A quick detour west will bring you to the sumptuous 17th-century church of **Sant'Ignazio** 34. As you continue north on Via del Corso you will reach Piazza Colonna and the ancient **Colonna di Marco Aurelio** 35. Continue north on Via del Corso and take a right onto chic Via Condotti, which gives you a head-on view of the **Spanish Steps** 36 and Piazza di Spagna; to the right of the steps, at No. 26, is the **Keats-Shelley Memorial House** 37, where the English Romantic poet Keats died. A great view across Rome's skyline awaits at the top of the Spanish Steps. From the narrow (southern) end of Piazza di Spagna, take Via Propaganda to Sant'Andrea delle Fratte, take a left onto Via del Nazareno, and then cross busy Via del Tritone to Via della Stamperia. This street leads to the **Fontana di Trevi** 38, one of Rome's most famous landmarks.

TIMING   The walk takes approximately three hours.

What to See

35 **Colonna di Marco Aurelio.** This ancient column—like the one Trajan erected—is an extraordinary stone history book. Its detailed reliefs spiraling up to the top illustrate the victorious campaigns of emperor Marcus Aurelius (AD 121–80) against the barbarians. ✉ *Piazza Colonna, Piazza di Spagna.*

★ 38 **Fontana di Trevi** (Trevi Fountain). Tucked away on a small piazza off Via del Tritone, this huge fountain, designed by Nicola Salvi (1697–1751), is a spectacular fantasy of mythical sea creatures amid cascades of splashing water. It was featured in the 1954 film *Three Coins in the Fountain* and, of course, was the scene of Anita Ekberg's aquatic frolic in Fellini's *La Dolce Vita.* The fountain is the world's most spectacular wishing well: legend has it that you can ensure your return to Rome by tossing a coin into the fountain. By day, it's one of the most busy sites in town; at night, the spotlit piazza takes on the festive air of a crowded outdoor party. ✉ *Piazza Fontana di Trevi.*

off the beaten path **TIME ELEVATOR ROMA** – If you're in need of a basic primer on Roman history, or you're traveling with kids and want to rouse their enthusiasm for the monuments and galleries they'll be traipsing though, try this fun, educational 45-minute joyride back in time. After participating in a group quiz-show on Roman history, you sit in a small movie theater with moving chairs (equipped with seat belts) and watch a movie on the history of Rome. The chairs jostle and slide to create the effect that you are within the film. It's not cheap, but for the Disney generation, it may succeed in arousing enthusiasm about the past. Groups are let in every half hour. ⊠ *Via dei S.S. Apostoli 20, Piazza di Trevi* ☎ *06/69953* ⊠ *€11* ⊙ *Daily 9:30 AM–midnight.*

㊲ Keats-Shelley Memorial House. English Romantic poet John Keats (1795–1821) lived in what is now a museum dedicated to him and his great contemporary and friend Percy Bysshe Shelley (1792–1822). You can visit his tiny rooms, preserved as they were when he died here in 1821. ⊠ *Piazza di Spagna 26, next to the Spanish Steps* ☎ *06/6784235* ⊕ *www.keats-shelley-house.org* ⊠ *€3* ⊙ *Weekdays 9–1 and 3–6, Sat. 11–2 and 3–6.*

off the beaten path **CIMITERO ACATTOLICO AND PIRAMIDE DI CAIO CESTIO** – Behind the Piramide, a stone pyramid built in 12 BC at the order of the Roman *praetor* (senior magistrate) who was buried here, is a cemetery reminiscent of a country churchyard. It was intended for non-Catholics, and here you'll find Keats's tomb and the place where Shelley's heart was buried, as well the tombs of Italian communist Antonio Gramsci and beat poet Gregory Corso. It's about a 20-minute walk south from the Arch of Constantine along Via San Gregorio and Viale Aventino. On the site of the pyramid is a cat colony run by the famous Roman *gattare* (cat ladies). They look after and try to find homes for some 300 of Rome's thousands of stray cats. They also give free tours of the graveyard, the pyramid, and their cat shelter on Saturday afternoon. ⊠ *Via Caio Cestio 6, Piramide* ☎ *06/5741141 ring bell for cemetery custodian* ⊠ *Donation of €1 appreciated* ⊙ *Tues.–Sun. 9–4:30.*

㉚ Monumento a Vittorio Emanuele II. The huge bronze sculpture group atop this vast marble monument is visible from many parts of the city, making this modern Rome's most flamboyant landmark. It was erected in the late 19th century to honor Italy's first king, Vittorio Emanuele II (1820–78), and the unification of Italy. Sometimes said to resemble a wedding cake or a typewriter in the Victorian style, it also houses the **Tomb of the Unknown Soldier** with its eternal flame. A side entrance to the monument will take you to **Museo del Risorgimento,** which charts Italy's struggle for nationhood. The red shirt and boots of revolutionary hero Giuseppe Garibaldi (1807–82) are among the mementos. The views from the top of the "Vittoriano" are unforgettable. Opposite the monument, note the enclosed wooden veranda fronting the palace on the corner of Via del Plebiscito and Via Corso. For the many years that she lived in Rome, Napoléon's mother had a fine view from here of the local goings-on. ⊠ *Entrance at Piazza Ara Coeli, next to Piazza Venezia* ☎ *06/6991718* ⊕ *www.ambienterm.arti.beniculturali.it/vittoriano/index.html* ⊠ *Museum €5* ⊙ *Daily 9:30–4:30.*

㉜ Palazzo Colonna. This fabulous private palace is open to the public once a week. The entrance to the picture gallery, the **Galleria Colonna,** is a secondary one, behind a plain, inconspicuous door. The old masters are lackluster, but the gallery should be on your must-see list because the **Sala Grande** is truly the grandest 17th-century room in Rome. More than 300 ft long, with bedazzling chandeliers, colored marble, and enormous paintings, it's best known today as the site where Audrey Hepburn met the press in *Roman Holiday.* ✉ *Via della Pilotta 17, Piazza di Trevi* ☎ *06/ 6784350* ⊕ *web.tin.it/galleriacolonna* ⊠ *€7* ☉ *Sept.–July, Sat. 9–1; free guided tour in English with reservation.*

㉝ Palazzo Doria Pamphilj. The 18th-century facade of this palazzo on Via del Corso is only a small part of a bona fide patrician palace, still home to a princely family that rents out many of its 1,000 rooms. Visit the remarkably well preserved **Galleria Doria Pamphilj,** a picture gallery that gives you a sense of the sumptuous surroundings of a Roman noble family and how art was once put on display: numbered paintings (the museum catalog, available from the book shop, comes in handy) are packed onto every available wall space. Pride of place is given to the famous (and pitiless) portrait of the 17th-century Pamphilj pope Innocent X by Diego Velázquez (1599–1660), but don't overlook Caravaggio's poignant *Rest on the Flight into Egypt.* The audio guide is by the current Doria Pamphilj prince himself and gives a fascinating personal history of the palace. ✉ *Piazza del Collegio Romano 2, Piazza Venezia* ☎ *06/6797323* ⊕ *www.doriapamphilj.it* ⊠ *Galleria Doria Pamphilj €7.30, includes audio guide* ☉ *Fri.–Wed. 10–5.*

㉛ Palazzo Venezia. A blend of medieval solidity and genuine Renaissance grace, this building houses temporary exhibits and a haphazard collection of mostly early Renaissance weapons, ivories, and paintings in its grand salons, some of which Mussolini used as his offices. Notice the balcony over the main portal, from which Il Duce addressed huge crowds in Piazza Venezia below. The palace hosts major touring art exhibits, so check to see what's currently showing. ✉ *Piazza San Marco 49, Piazza Venezia* ☎ *06/69994319* ⊠ *€4* ☉ *Tues.–Sat. 8:30–7:30.*

㉞ Sant'Ignazio. The false interior dome in this sumptuous 17th-century church is a trompe-l'oeil oddity among the lavishly frescoed domes of the Eternal City. To get the full effect of the illusionistic ceiling painted by Andrea del Pozzo (1642–1709), stand on the small disk set into the floor of the nave to view his *Glory of St. Ignatius Loyola.* The church contains some of Rome's most splendorous, jewel-encrusted altars. If you're lucky, you might be able to catch an evening concert performed here. The church is the focus of Filippo Raguzzini's 18th-century rococo piazza, where the buildings are arranged almost as in a stage set, reminding us that theatricality was a key element of almost all the best baroque and rococo art. ✉ *Piazza Sant'Ignazio, Pantheon* ☎ *06/ 6794406* ☉ *Daily 7:30–12:30 and 4–7:30.*

★ **㊱ Spanish Steps.** Both the steps and the Piazza di Spagna get their names from the Spanish Embassy to the Vatican on the piazza, opposite the American Express office, though the staircase was built with French funds in 1723. In an allusion to the church of Trinità dei Monti at the top of the hill, the staircase is divided by three landings (beautifully banked with azaleas from mid-April to mid-May). This area has always welcomed tourists: 18th-century dukes and duchesses on their Grand Tour, 19th-century artists and writers in search of inspiration—among them Stendhal, Balzac, Thackeray, and Byron—and today's enthusiastic hordes. The **Fontana della Barcaccia** (Fountain of the Old Boat) at the base of the steps is by Pietro Bernini, father of the famous Gian Lorenzo. ✉ *Piazza di Spagna.*

Historic Churches: Heavenly Monuments of Faith

Rome's history can be told through its churches. In both their historical import and artistic mastery, the ubiquitous and incredibly varied buildings bear witness to the centuries they have withstood; they have something for every visitor, regardless of faith. The churches that highlight this walk date to the early centuries of Christianity.

a good walk

Begin your walk at **Santa Maria Maggiore** ㉟ ► off Via Cavour. From here go south on Via Merulana, which leads straight to **San Giovanni in Laterano** ㊵. The adjoining Palazzo Laterano houses the Museo Storico Lateranense; across the street, a small building houses the **Scala Santa** ㊶, or Sacred Stairs, supposedly from Pilate's Jerusalem palace. Circle Palazzo Laterano to see the 4th-century octagonal Battistero di San Giovanni, forerunner of many such buildings throughout Italy. Follow Via San Giovanni in Laterano to **San Clemente** ㊷, and explore the ancient church buried underground.

TIMING The walk alone takes approximately 90 minutes, plus 15–20 minutes in each of the churches. Allow at least an hour to explore San Clemente. A visit to the Museo Storico Lateranense will take you about 30 minutes.

What to See

★ ㊷ **San Clemente.** This church is one of the most extraordinary archaeological sites in Rome. San Clemente is a 12th-century church built on top of a 4th-century church, which in turn was built over a 2nd-century pagan temple to the god Mythras. Little of the temple remains, but the 4th-century church is largely intact, perhaps because it wasn't unearthed until the 19th century. (It was discovered by Irish Dominican monks; members of the order still live in the adjacent monastery.) The upper church, which you enter from street level, holds a beautiful early 12th-century mosaic showing a cross on a gold background, surrounded by swirling green acanthus leaves, teeming with little scenes of everyday life. The marble choir screens, salvaged from the 4th-century church, are decorated with early Christian symbols: doves, vines, and fish. In the left nave is the Castiglioni chapel, holding frescos painted around 1400 by the Florentine artist Masolino da Panicale (1383–1440), a key figure in the introduction of realism and one-point perspective into Renaissance painting. Note the large Crucifixion and scenes from the lives of Sts. Catherine, Ambrose and Christopher, plus an Annunciation (over the entrance). Before you leave the upper church, take a look at the pretty cloister—evening concerts are held here in summer.

From the right nave, stairs lead down to the remains of the 4th-century church, which was active until 1084, when it was damaged beyond repair during a siege of the neighborhood by the Norman prince Robert Guiscard. The vestibule is decorated with marble fragments found during the excavations (which are still under way); and in the nave are colorful 11th-century frescoes depicting stories from the life of St. Clement. Another level down is Mythraeum, a shrine dedicated to the god Mithras, whose cult spread from Persia and gained a hold in Rome during the 2nd and 3rd centuries. ⊠ *Via San Giovanni in Laterano 108, Colosseo* ☎ *06/70451018* ⚍ *€3* ⊙ *Mon.–Sat. 9–noon and 3–6, Sun. 10–12:30 and 3–6.*

㊵ **San Giovanni in Laterano.** Many are surprised when they discover that the cathedral of Rome is not St. Peter's but this church. (St. Peter's is in Vatican City, technically not a part of Rome.) Dominating the piazza whose name it shares, this immense building is where the present pope officiates in his capacity as bishop of Rome. The towering facade and Borromini's cool baroque interior emphasize the majesty of its proportions. The **cloister** is one of the city's finest, with beautifully carved columns surrounding a peaceful garden.

The adjoining **Palazzo Laterano** (Lateran Palace) was the official papal residence until the 13th century and is still technically part of the Vatican. It houses the offices of the Rome Diocese and the rather bland **Museo Storico Laterano** (Lateren Historical Museum). Behind the palace is the 4th-century octagonal **Battistero di San Giovanni** (St. John's Baptistery), forerunner of many similar buildings throughout Italy, and Rome's oldest and tallest obelisk, brought from Thebes and dating from the 15th century BC. ✉ *Piazza San Giovanni in Laterano, Colosseo* ☎ *06/ 69886433* 🖩 *Cloister €2.50, museum €3.50* ☉ *Church Apr.–Sept., daily 7–7; Oct.–Mar., daily 7–6. Cloister 9–½ hr before church closing. Museum Sat. guided tours at 9:15, 10:30, and noon. 1st Sun. of each month 8:45–1. Baptistery daily 9–1 and 5–1 hr before sunset.*

> **off the beaten path**

SAN PIETRO IN VINCOLI – The church takes its name from the *vincoli* (chains) that once held St. Peter (in the case under the altar), but the throngs of tourists come to see Michelangelo's *Moses,* a powerful statue almost as famed as his frescoes in the Sistine Chapel. The *Moses* was destined for the tomb of Julius II, designed to be the largest in St. Peter's Basilica. But Julius's successors had Michelangelo work on other projects, and the tomb was never finished. ✉ *Piazza San Pietro in Vincoli, Colosseo* ☎ *06/4882865* ☉ *Daily 7–12:30 and 3:30–6.*

SANTI QUATTRO CORONATI – The 12th-century Four Crowned Saints church, part of a fortified abbey that provided refuge to early popes and emperors, is in an unusual corner of Rome, a quiet island that has resisted the tide of time and traffic flowing beneath its ramparts. Few places in Rome are so reminiscent of the Middle Ages. Don't miss the cloister with its well-tended gardens and 12th-century fountain. The entrance is the door in the left nave; ring if it's not open. You can also ring at the adjacent convent for the key to the Oratorio di San Silvestro (Oratory of St. Sylvester), with 13th-century frescoes. ✉ *Largo Santi Quattro Coronati, Colosseo* ☎ *06/ 70475427* ☉ *Easter–Christmas, daily 9:30–12:30 and 3:30–6; Christmas–Easter, daily 9:30–12:30.*

▶ ㊴ **Santa Maria Maggiore.** One of Rome's four great pilgrimage churches was built on the spot where a 3rd-century pope witnessed a miraculous midsummer snowfall (which is re-enacted every August 15th). The gleaming mosaics on the arch in front of the main altar date from the 5th century. The apse mosaic dates from the 13th century, and the opulently carved wood ceiling is believed to have been gilded with the first gold brought from the New World. To view the elaborate 14th-century facade mosaics, inquire at the souvenir shop. ✉ *Piazza Santa Maria Maggiore, off Via Cavour, Termini* ☎ *06/4881094* ☉ *Daily 7–7.*

㊶ **Scala Santa** (Sacred Stairs). A small building opposite the Lateran Palace houses what is claimed to be the staircase from Pilate's palace in Jerusalem. The faithful climb it on their knees. ✉ *Piazza San Giovanni in Laterano, Colosseo* ☉ *Daily 6:15–noon and 3:30–6:30.*

Il Quirinale to Piazza della Repubblica:
Palaces & Fountains

You'll see ancient Roman sculptures and early Christian churches, but concentrate on the 16th and 17th centuries, when Rome was conquered by the baroque—and by Bernini.

a good walk

Begin on **Il Quirinale** 43 ▶, the highest of Rome's seven hills. Here you'll find the Palazzo Quirinale, official residence of the president of Italy and once home of the popes. See what's on at Le Scuderie Papale al Quirinale (the Quirinale Stables), which houses top-flight touring art exhibits. Along Via del Quirinale (which becomes Via XX Settembre) is the church of **Sant'Andrea** 44, considered by many to be Bernini's finest work, and, at the Quattro Fontane (Four Fountains) crossroads, the church of **San Carlino alle Quattro Fontane** 45, designed by Bernini's rival Borromini. Take a left on Via delle Quattro Fontane to reach the imposing **Palazzo Barberini** 46, where the Galleria Nazionale d'Arte Antica houses masterpieces by Raphael and Caravaggio. Down the hill is Piazza Barberini and the **Fontana del Tritone** 47 by Bernini. Cross the piazza and begin your gradual climb up Via Vittorio Veneto, which bends past **Santa Maria della Concezione** 48 and the U.S. Embassy, and turn off onto Via Bissolati. On the corner of Piazza San Bernardo is the church of **Santa Maria della Vittoria** 49, known for Bernini's baroque decoration. It's not far down Via Orlando to **Piazza della Repubblica** 50. On one side of the square is an ancient Roman brick facade that marks the church of Santa Maria degli Angeli. Beyond, on the near corner of Piazza del Cinquecento, the vast square in front of Stazione Termini, is the last stop. **Palazzo Massimo alle Terme** 51 houses part of the Museo Nazionale Romano's collections, highlighting examples of the fine mosaics and masterful paintings that decorated ancient Rome's villas and palaces.

TIMING The walk takes approximately 90 minutes, plus 10 to 15 minutes for each church visited, and 1½ hours each for visits to the Galleria Nazionale in Palazzo Barberini and Palazzo Massimo alle Terme.

What to See

47 **Fontana del Tritone** (Triton Fountain). The centerpiece of Piazza Barberini is Bernini's graceful fountain, designed in 1637 for the sculptor's patron, Pope Urban VIII, whose Barberini coat of arms, featuring bees, is at the base of the large shell. Close by is the **Fontana delle Api** (Fountain of the Bees), the last fountain designed by Bernini. ✉ *Piazza Barberini, Via Veneto.*

▶ 43 **Il Quirinale.** The highest of ancient Rome's seven hills, this is where ancient Romans, and later popes, built their residences in order to escape the deadly miasmas and the malaria of the low-lying area around the Forum. The fountain in the square has ancient statues of Castor and Pollux reining in their unruly steeds and a basin salvaged from the Roman Forum. **Palazzo del Quirinale** passed from the popes to Italy's kings in the 19th century; it's now the official residence of the nation's president. Every day at 4 PM, the ceremony of the changing of the guard at the portal includes a miniparade, complete with band.

Directly opposite the main entrance of the Palazzo del Quirinale sits **Le Scuderie Papale al Quirinale** (the Quirinal Stables), which once housed more than 120 horses for the exclusive use of the pope and his guests. The low-lying building was designed by Alessandro Specchi (1668–1729) in 1722 and was among the major achievements of baroque Rome. The stables were remodeled in the late 1990s by eminent architect Gae

Aulenti and now serve as a premier venue for touring art exhibits. ✉ *Piazza del Quirinale Piazza di Trevi* ☎ *06/39967700* 🎫 *€1.95* ⏲ *Sun.–Thurs. 10–8, Fri. and Sat. 10 AM–11 PM.*

㊻ **Palazzo Barberini.** Along with architect Carlo Maderno (1556–1629), Borromini helped make the splendid 17th-century Palazzo Barberini a residence worthy of Rome's leading art patron, Pope Urban VIII, who began the palace for his family in 1625. Inside, the **Galleria Nazionale d'Arte Antica** offers some fine works by Raphael (the *Fornarina*) and Caravaggio. Rome's biggest ballroom is here; its ceiling, painted by Pietro da Cortona (1596–1669), depicts Immortality bestowing a crown upon Divine Providence escorted by a "bomber squadron"—to quote Sir Michael Levey—of mutant bees. (Bees featured prominently in the heraldic device of the Barberini.) ✉ *Via Barberini 18, Via Veneto* ☎ *06/32810* 🌐 *www.galleriaborghese.it* 🎫 *€5* ⏲ *Tues.–Sun. 9–7.*

(51) **Palazzo Massimo alle Terme.** This 19th-century palace in neobaroque style holds part of the collections of antiquities belonging to the Museo Nazionale Romano (also exhibited in the Palazzo Altemps). Here you can see extraordinary examples of the fine mosaics and masterful paintings that decorated ancient Rome's palaces and villas. Don't miss the fresco—depicting a lush garden in bloom—that came from the villa that Livia, wife of Emperor Augustus, owned outside Rome. ✉ *Largo Villa Peretti 2, Termini* ☎ *06/48903501* 🎫 *€6* ⏲ *Tues.–Sun. 9–7.*

㊿ **Piazza della Repubblica.** This piazza has a typical 19th-century layout, but the curving porticoes echo the immense **Terme di Diocleziano** (Baths of Diocletian). Built in the 4th century AD, they were the largest and most impressive of the baths of ancient Rome, with vast halls, pools, and gardens that could accommodate 3,000 people at a time. Also part of the great baths was an **Aula Ottagonale** (Octagonal Hall), which now holds a sampling of the ancient sculptures found there, including two beautiful bronzes. ✉ *Via Romita 8, Termini* ☎ *06/4870690* 🎫 *Free* ⏲ *Tues.–Sat. 9–2, Sun. 9–1.*

The racy **Fontana delle Naiadi** (Fountain of the Naiads), an 1870 addition to the piazza, depicts voluptuous bronze ladies wrestling happily with marine monsters. The curving ancient Roman brick facade on one side of the piazza marks the church of **Santa Maria degli Angeli,** adapted by Michelangelo from the vast central chamber of the colossal baths. Look for the sundial carved on the floor.

㊺ **San Carlino alle Quattro Fontane.** Borromini's church at the Four Fountains crossroads is an architectural gem. In a space no larger than the base of one of the piers of St. Peter's, Borromini attained geometric perfection. Characteristically, he chose a subdued white stucco for the interior decoration, so as not to distract from the form. Don't miss the cloister, which you reach through the door to the right of the alter. The exterior of the church is Borromini at his bizarre best, all curves and rippling movement. Outside, four charming fountains frame views in four directions. ✉ *Via del Quirinale 23, Piazza di Trevi* ☎ *06/4883261* ⏲ *Daily 10-1 and 3–5.*

㊽ **Santa Maria della Concezione.** In the crypt under the main Capuchin church, the bones of some 4,000 dead Capuchin monks are arranged in odd decorative designs around the shriveled and decayed skeletons of their kinsmen, a macabre reminder of the impermanence of earthly life. Signs declare, WHAT YOU ARE, WE ONCE WERE. WHAT WE ARE, YOU SOMEDAY WILL BE. Although not for the easily spooked, the crypt is touching and oddly beautiful. ✉ *Via Veneto 27, Via Veneto* ☎ *06/4871185* 🎫 *Donation expected* ⏲ *Fri.–Wed. 9–noon and 3–6.*

49 Santa Maria della Vittoria. The most famous feature here is Bernini's baroque decoration of the **Cappella Cornaro,** an exceptional fusion of architecture, painting, and sculpture, in which the *Ecstasy of St. Teresa* is the focal point. Bernini's audacious conceit was to model the chapel as a theater: members of the Cornaro family—sculpted in white marble—watch from theater boxes as, center stage, St. Teresa, in the throes of mystical rapture, is pierced by a gilded arrow held by an angel. To quote one 18th-century observer, President de Brosses: "If this is divine love, I know it well." ⊠ *Via XX Settembre 17, Termini* ☎ 06/42740571 ⊙ *Daily 8:30–noon and 3:30–6.*

44 Sant'Andrea. This small but imposing baroque church was designed and decorated by Bernini, who considered it one of his finest works. ⊠ *Via del Quirinale, Piazza di Trevi* ☎ 06/48903187 ⊙ *Mon. and Wed.–Sat. 8–noon and 4–6, Sun. 4–6.*

off the beaten path

GALLERIA COMUNALE DI ARTE MODERNA E CONTEMPORANEA – Located in the former Peroni beer factory, the City Gallery of Modern and Contemporary Art is an example of some of the most interesting industrial design of the early 20th century. The factory, devised by Gustavo Giovannoni and located in a former warehouse district of Rome, now houses touring avant-garde art exhibits that provide a refreshing change from Rome's baroque. ⊠ *Via Reggio Emilia 54, Porta Pia* ☎ 06/8844930 ⊠ € 3 ⊙ *Tues.–Sat. 10–9, Sun. 9–2.*

Amid Sylvan Glades: From the Villa Borghese to the Ara Pacis

Touring Rome's artistic masterpieces while staying clear of its hustle and bustle can be, quite literally, a walk in the park. Some of the city's finest sights are tucked away in or next to green lawns and pedestrian piazzas, offering a breath of fresh air for weary sightseers. Villa Borghese, one of Rome's largest parks, can alleviate gallery gout by offering an oasis in which to cool off under the ilex trees. If you feel like a picnic, have an *alimentare* (food shop) make you some *panini* (sandwiches) before you go, as you'll find only over-priced fast-food carts within the park itself.

a good walk

Start at **Porta Pinciana** 52 ▶, one of the entrances to Villa Borghese. Follow Viale del Museo Borghese to the **Museo e Galleria Borghese** 53 and its fabulous art collection in an extraordinary setting (make sure to reserve a ticket for your visit in advance). Head west inside the park past the zoo and exit the park gates at Viale delle Belle Arti. A five-minute walk downhill will take you to the **Museo Nazionale Etrusco di Villa Giulia** 54, perhaps the best collection in the world of Etruscan artifacts. From Villa Giulia, take the wide flight of steps at Piazzale M. Cervantes back into Villa Borghese. Head to the southwest corner of the park to enjoy the view of Rome from the **Pincio** 55 belvedere before descending the ramps to all-pedestrian **Piazza del Popolo** 56. At the north end of the piazza, next to the 400-year-old city gate, the Porta del Popolo, is the church of **Santa Maria del Popolo** 57, with one of the richest art collections of any church in the city. If you're not out of steam, stroll south along Via di Ripetta to glance at Mausoleo di Augusto, built by Caesar Augustus; next to it is the **Ara Pacis Augustae** 58, built in 13 BC. Both are closed for restoration.

TIMING The walk takes approximately two hours; allow an additional 1½ hours for the Galleria Borghese, 1½ hours for Villa Giulia, and 45 minutes for the stroll past the Mausoleo di Augusto and then the Ara Pacis.

Sights to See

58 Ara Pacis Augustae (Altar of Augustan Peace). This altar on the northwest corner of Piazza Augusto Imperatore was erected in 13 BC to celebrate the era of peace ushered in by Augustus's military victories. Next to it is the imposing bulk of the marble-clad **Mausoleo di Augusto** (Mausoleum of Augustus; ⊠ P. Augusto Imperatore, Piazza di Spagna), built by the emperor for himself and his family. The Ara Pacis is closed for restoration while a new museum to house it is being built. ⊠ *Via Ripetta, Piazza di Spagna* ⊘ *Closed for restoration.*

Explora: Il Museo dei Bambini di Roma. One of the very few sites in the city geared specifically to kids, Explora, the Museum for the Children of Rome, provides two floors of open space filled with hands-on activities and games for toddlers to 12-year-olds, as well a child-friendly restaurant. Just steps from the car-free Piazza del Popolo and a short hike downhill from the playground in Villa Borghese, the museum is well suited to a child-oriented day in the neighborhood. ⊠ *Via Flaminia 82, Villa Borghese* ☎ *06/3613776* ⊠ *€ 6 for children 3 and up, €5 for adults* ⊘ *Weekdays 9:30–7, weekends 10–5, entrance every 2 hrs.*

53 Museo e Galleria Borghese (Borghese Museum and Gallery). The palace,
Fodor'sChoice completed in 1613 for Cardinal Scipione Borghese (1576–1633) to
★ flaunt hisfabulous antiquities collection and hold elegant fetes, is today a monument to 18th-century Roman interior decoration at its most luxurious, dripping with porphyry and alabaster. Throughout the grand salons are ancient Roman mosaic pavements and statues of various deities, including one officially known as *Venus Victrix*. There has never been any doubt, however, as to the statue's real subject: Pauline Bonaparte, Napoléon's sister, who married Prince Camillo Borghese in one of the storied matches of the 19th century. Sculpted by Canova (1757–1822), the princess reclines on a chaise longue, bare-bosomed, her hips swathed in classical drapery, the very model of haughty detachment and sly come-hither. Pauline is known to have been shocked that her husband took pleasure in showing off the work to his guests. This coyness seems curious given the reply she is supposed to have made to a lady who asked her how she could have posed for the work: "Oh, but the studio was heated." Other rooms hold important sculptures by Bernini, including *David* and *Apollo and Daphne*. The renowned picture collection has splendid works by Titian, Caravaggio, and Raphael, among others. Be sure to reserve admission at least a day ahead of time. ⊠ *Piazza Scipione Borghese 5, off Via Pinciana, Villa Borghese* ☎ *06/8548577 information; 06/328102 reservations* ⊕ *www.galleriaborghese.it (information), www.ticketeria.it (reservations)* ⊠ *€8.50, plus €2 reservation fee; audio guide €5* ⊘ *Tues.–Sun. 9–7; reservations required, entrance every 2 hrs.*

★ 54 Museo Nazionale Etrusco di Villa Giulia (National Etruscan Museum at Villa Giulia). This Renaissance papal palace, built by Julius III between 1550 and 1555, sits in the Villa Borghese Gardens and holds a well laid-out collection of art and artifacts of the Etruscans, who predated the Romans. Known for their sophisticated art and design, the Etruscans left a legacy of sarcophagi, bronze sculptures, terra-cotta vases, and stunning jewelry. (Unlike the Greeks, Etruscan women sat at the banquet tables with men and enjoyed displaying their wealth on their body.) Acclaimed pieces of statuary in the gallery include *Dea con Bambino* (goddess with baby) and *Sarcophagus degli Sposi* (Sarcophagus of the Spouses). In the villa's courtyard visit the atmospheric underground Ninfeo, the remains of the Virgin's Aqueduct from the Augustan period. ⊠ *Piazzale Villa Giulia 9, Villa Borghese* ☎ *06/32810* ⊠ *€4* ⊘ *Tues.–Sun. 8:30–7:30.*

need a break? Caffè delle Arti (⊠ Viale delle Belle Arti 131, Villa Borghese ☎ 06/32651236), an exquisite, light-flooded space with towering ceilings and bronze statues, is located inside the Galleria Nazionale d'Arte Moderna, across the street from Villa Giulia. The menu includes tea with a variety of homemade pastries, as well as Roman and Neapolitan dishes. In warm weather sit out on the huge terrace and take in the splendor of the surrounding Villa Borghese.

56 Piazza del Popolo. Designed by neoclassical architect Giuseppe Valadier (1762–1839) in the early 1800s, this piazza is one of the largest in Rome, and it has a 3,000-year-old obelisk in the middle. Always a favorite spot for café-sitting and people-watching, the piazza is closed to automotive traffic, creating a pedestrian oasis. The bookend baroque churches **Santa Maria dei Miracoli** and **Santa Maria in Montesanto** are not, first appearances to the contrary, twins. On the plaza's eastern side, stairs lead uphill to the Pincio. To the north, at the end of the square is the 400-year-old **Porta del Popolo,** Rome's northern city gate. It was designed by Bernini to welcome the Catholic convert Queen Christina of Sweden to Rome in 1605.

55 Pincio. At the southwestern corner of Villa Borghese, the Pincio belvedere and gardens were laid out by architect Giuseppe Valadier as part of his overall plan for Piazza del Popolo. Nineteenth-century counts and countesses liked to take their evening passeggiata here in the hope of meeting Pius IX (1792–1878), the last pope to go about Rome on foot. Nowadays you're more likely to see runners and in-line skaters, as well as throngs of Romans out for a stroll. It's a good place to take in the summer concerts and New Year's fire works that take place in Piazza del Popolo below.

52 Porta Pinciana. One of the historic city gates in the Aurelian Walls surrounding Rome, Porta Pinciana. was built in the 6th century AD, about three centuries after the walls were built to keep out the barbarians. These days it's one of the entrances to Villa Borghese.

57 Santa Maria del Popolo. This church next to the Porta del Popolo goes almost unnoticed, but it has one of the richest art collections of any church in Rome. Here you'll find Raphael's High Renaissance masterpiece the **Cappella Chigi,** as well as two stunning Caravaggios in the **Cappella Cerasi.** Each December, an exhibit of Christmas nativity scenes is held in the adjacent building. ⊠ *Piazza del Popolo, Piazza di Spagna* ☎ *06/3610836* ☉ *Mon.–Sat. 7–noon and 4–7, Sun. 7:30–1:30 and 4:30–7:30.*

Across the Tiber: The Ghetto, Tiberina Island & Trastevere

This walk takes you through separate communities, each staunchly resisting the tides of change, including the old Jewish Ghetto. In picturesque Trastevere you will find a resident colony of foreigners coexisting with "the Romans of Rome." Despite rampant gentrification, Trastevere remains about the most tightly knit community in the city, its natives proudly proclaiming their descent from the ancient Romans.

a good walk Beginning at Largo Argentina, take Via Paganica to Piazza Mattei, where one of Rome's loveliest fountains, the 16th-century **Fontana delle Tartarughe** 59 ☞, is tucked away. Take Via della Reginella into Via Portico d'Ottavia, heart of the Jewish Ghetto. On the Tiber is the **Sinagoga** 60. The **Teatro di Marcello** 61, behind the Portico d'Ottavia, was originally a theater designed to hold 20,000 people. Follow Via di Teatro di Marcello south, passing the ruins of two small temples: the **Tempio della Fortuna Virilis** 62 and the circular **Tempio di Vesta** 63. Across **Piazza Bocca della**

Verità (64) is the 12th-century church of Santa Maria in Cosmedin, with the marble Bocca della Verità. Retracing your steps, walk upstream along the Tiber, cross Ponte Fabricio over **Isola Tiberina** (65), and then head into Trastevere.

Begin your exploration of Trastevere at Piazza in Piscinula (you will need a good map to make your way around this intricate maze of winding side streets), take Via dell'Arco dei Tolomei, cross Via dei Salumi, and turn left onto Via dei Genovesi and then right to the piazza in front of **Santa Cecilia in Trastevere** (66). Baroque enthusiasts will want to walk several blocks southwest down Via Anicia to **San Francesco a Ripa** (67) to see a famous Bernini sculpture. Follow Via San Francesco a Ripa to the very heart of Trastevere, to **Piazza di Santa Maria in Trastevere** (68), site of the lovely 12th-century church of the same name. With a detailed map, find your way through the narrow byways to Piazza Sant'Egidio and Via della Scala, continuing on to Via della Lungara and **Villa Farnesina** (69), where you can see frescoes by Raphael. From Trastevere, climb Via Garibaldi to the Janiculum Hill, which offers views spanning the whole city, and where you'll find the church of **San Pietro in Montorio** (70), built in 1481.

TIMING The walk takes approximately four hours, plus 10 to 15 minutes for each church visited, and about an hour for a visit to Villa Farnesina.

What to See

(59) **Fontana delle Tartarughe.** The 16th-century Fountain of the Turtles in Piazza Mattei is one of Rome's loveliest. Designed by Giacomo della Porta (1539–1602) in 1581 and sculpted by Taddeo Landini (1550–96), the piece revolves around four bronze boys, each clutching a dolphin that jets water into marble shells. Several bronze tortoises, thought to have been added by Bernini, are held in each of the boys' hands and drink from the fountain's upper basin. The piazza is named for the Mattei family, which built **Palazzo Mattei** on Via Caetani (worth a peek for its sculpture-rich courtyard and staircase) and sits at the border of the old Jewish Ghetto. ✉ *Piazza Mattei, Ghetto.*

(65) **Isola Tiberina.** Ancient Ponte Fabricio and Ponte Cestio link the old Jewish Ghetto and the neighborhood of Trastevere to this island, where a city hospital stands on a site that has been dedicated to healing ever since a temple to Aesculapius was erected here in 291 BC. If you have time, and if the river's not too high, walk down the stairs for a different perspective on the island and the Tiber.

Jewish Ghetto. Rome has had a Jewish community since the 1st century BC, and from that time until the present its living conditions have varied widely according to its relations with the city's rulers. In 1555 Pope Paul II established Rome's Jewish "ghetto" in the neighborhood marked off by the Portico d'Ottavia, the Tiber, and Via Arenula. The area quickly became Rome's most squalid and densely populated. At one point, Jews—who had engaged in many businesses and professions in Trastevere—were limited to the sale of used iron and clothing as a trade. The laws were rescinded around the time of the Risorgimento in the 1870s, and not much remains of the ghetto as it was, but some of Rome's 15,000 Jews still live in the area, and a few families still run clothing shops on the Via di Portico d'Ottavia. German troops occupied Rome during World War II, and on October 16, 1943, many of Rome's Jews were rounded up and deported to Nazi concentration camps. In 1982 the synagogue here was attacked with grenades and machine guns by Palestinian terrorists, and in 1986, as a gesture of reconciliation, Pope John Paul II paid a visit to Rabbi Elio Toaff, becoming the first pope ever to pray in a Jewish synagogue. Today, the ghetto is home to Rome's few Judaica shops and kosher groceries, bakeries, and restaurants, as well as linen and shoe stores and the trendy cafés and bars that have moved in with gentrification. Quiet, winding alleys are a shady respite from the center's hustle and are well worth a half hour's stroll.

Palazzo Corsini. This elegant palace holds the 16th- and 17th-century painting collection of the **Galleria Nazionale d'Arte Antica;** even if you're not interested in the paintings, stop in to climb the extraordinary 17th-century stone staircase, itself a drama of architectural shadows and sculptural voids. The adjacent Corsini gardens, now Rome's **Giardino Botanico,** offer a welcome break with native and exotic plants and a stunning view at the top. ⊠ *Via della Lungara 10, Trastevere* ☎ *06/68802323* ⊕ *www.galleriaborghese.it* 🎟 *€4* ☾ *Tues.–Sat. 8:30–2, Sun. 8:30–5.*

64 **Piazza Bocca della Verità.** On the site of the Forum Boarium, ancient Rome's cattle market, this square was later used for public executions. Its name is derived from the marble **Bocca della Verità** (Mouth of Truth) set into the entry portico of the 12th-century church of **Santa Maria in Cosmedin.** In the Middle Ages, legend had it that any person who told a lie with his hand in the mouth of the ancient drain hole cover would have it chomped off. Today, tour groups line up in this noisy, traffic-jammed piazza to give this ancient lie detector a try.

off the beaten path

COLLE AVENTINO – One of the seven hills of ancient Rome, the Aventine is now a quiet residential neighborhood that most tourists don't see. It's home to some of the city's oldest and least-visited churches and some unusual views. Peek through the keyhole in the gate to the **garden of the Knights of Malta** (⊠ Piazza Cavalieri di Malta, Aventino) for a surprise view of the dome of St. Peter's. The city panorama from the walled park next to the church of Santa Sabina, off Via Santa Sabina, is wider, if more conventional.

TERME DI CARACALLA – The scale of the towering ruins of ancient Rome's most beautiful and luxurious public baths, the Baths of Caracalla, hints at their past splendor. Inaugurated by Caracalla in 217, the baths were used until the 6th century. An ancient version of a swank athletic club, the baths were open to all, though men and women used them separately; citizens could bathe, socialize, and exercise in huge pools and richly decorated halls. ⊠ *Via delle Terme di Caracalla 52 Aventino* ☎ *06/39967700* ⊕ *www.pierreci.it* 🎟 *€5* ☾ *Tues.–Sun. 9–4, Mon. 9–2.*

★ **68** **Piazza di Santa Maria in Trastevere.** This piazza is a popular spot for afternoon coffees and evening cocktails at its outdoor cafés, but the showpiece of the square is the 12th-century church of **Santa Maria in Trastevere.** The 13th-century mosaics on the church's facade—which add light and color to the piazza, especially at night when they are in spotlight—are believed to represent the Wise and Foolish Virgins. Inside, the enormous golden mosaic in the apse is the city's finest, a shining burst of Byzantine color and light set off by of giant columns. In August, processions honoring the Virgin Mary gather at the church as part of Trastevere's traditional feast, called *Festa de Noantri* (Our Own Feast). ⊠ *Trastevere* ☎ *06/5814802* ☾ *Daily 7:30–9:30.*

67 **San Francesco a Ripa.** This church in Piazza San Francesco d'Assisi is a must for fans of the baroque. It holds one of Bernini's most dramatic sculptures, of the Blessed Ludovica Albertoni, ecstatic at the prospect of entering heaven as she expires on her deathbed. ⊠ *Piazza San Francesco d'Assisi, Trastevere* ☎ *06/5819020* ⊙ *Daily 7–noon and 4–7.*

70 San Pietro in Montorio. One of Rome's key Renaissance buildings stands in the cloister of this church, built by order of Ferdinand and Isabella of Spain in 1481. Bramante built the **Tempietto** over the spot where St. Peter was thought to have been crucified. It's an architectural gem and was one of his earliest and most successful attempts to design a building in an entirely classical style. ⊠ *Via Garibaldi, Gianicolo, Trastevere* ☎ *06/5813940* ⊙ *Daily 9–noon and 4–6; the Tempietto, Oct.–Mar., daily 9:30–12:30 and 2–4; Apr.–Sept., daily 4–6.*

66 Santa Cecilia in Trastevere. Mothers and children love to dally in the delightful little garden in front of this church in Piazza Santa Cecilia. Duck inside for a look at the 9th-century mosaics and the languid statue of St. Cecilia under the altar. Fragments of a *Last Judgment* fresco cycle by Cavallini, dating from the late 13th century, remain one of his most important works. Though the Byzantine-influenced fragments are obscured by the structure, what's left reveals a rich luminosity in the seated apostles' drapery and a remarkable depth in their expressions. A pretty cloister and remains of Roman houses are visible under the church. Ask to see them at the booth to the left of the main nave. ⊠ *Piazza Santa Cecilia, Trastevere* ☎ *06/5899289* ⊠ *Frescoes €2* ⊙ *Daily 8–12:30 and 2:30–7; frescoes Tues. and Thurs. 10–11:30, Sun. 11:30–noon.*

60 Sinagoga. The large, bronze-roofed synagogue on the Tiber is a Roman landmark. The **Museo Ebraico** documents the history of the Jewish community in Rome. Most of the decorative crowns, prayer books, holy chairs, and tapestries, dating from the 17th century, were donated by prominent Jewish families whose ancestors once lived in the Ghetto. The collection offers a refreshing change from the predominantly Christian art found elsewhere in Rome. ⊠ *Lungotevere Cenci 15, Ghetto* ☎ *06/ 68400661* ⊠ *€6* ⊙ *Mon.–Thurs. 9–4:30, Fri. 9–1:30, Sun. 9–noon.*

61 Teatro di Marcello. The Teatro, hardly recognizable as a theater today, was originally designed to hold 20,000 spectators. It was begun by Julius Caesar; today, the 16th-century apartment building that sprouted out of its remains has become one of Rome's most prestigious residential addresses. The area south of the theater makes a grand stage for chamber music concerts in summer. ⊠ *Via del Teatro di Marcello, Ghetto* ⊙ *Open during concerts only.*

62 Tempio della Fortuna Virilis. This rectangular temple devoted to "manly fortune" dates from the 2nd century BC and is built in the Greek style, as was the norm in the early years of Rome. For its age, it is remarkably well preserved, in part due to its subsequent consecration as a Christian church. ⊠ *Piazza Bocca della Verità, Piazza Venezia.*

63 Tempio di Vesta. All but one of the 20 original Corinthian columns in Rome's most evocative small ruin remain intact. It was built in the 2nd century BC. Researchers now believe the temple was devoted to Hercules by a successful olive merchant. ⊠ *Piazza Bocca dell Verità, Piazza Venezia.*

Trastevere. This area consists of a maze of narrow streets that is still, despite evident gentrification, one of the city's most authentically Roman neighborhoods. Literally translated, its name means "across the Tiber," and indeed Trastevere and the Trasteverini—the neighborhood's natives— are a breed apart. The area is hardly undiscovered, but among its self-consciously picturesque trattorias and trendy tearooms you'll also find old shops and dusty artisans' workshops in alleys festooned with laundry hung out to dry. One of the least affected parts of Trastevere centers on Piazza in Piscinula, where San Benedetto, the smallest medieval church in the city, is opposite the restored medieval Casa dei Mattei. Stroll along Via dell'Arco dei Tolomei and Via dei Salumi, shadowy streets showing the patina of the ages.

Via del Portico d'Ottavia. Along this street in the heart of the Jewish Ghetto are buildings where medieval inscriptions, ancient friezes, and half-buried classical monuments attest to the venerable history of the neighborhood. The old **Chiesa di Sant'Angelo in Pescheria** was built right into the ruins of the Portico d'Ottavia, which was a monumental area enclosing a temple, library, and other buildings within colonnaded porticoes.

★ ⑥⑨ **Villa Farnesina.** Money was no object to extravagant host Agostino Chigi, a Sienese banker who financed many a papal project. His munificence is evident in his elegant villa, built about 1511. When Raphael could steal some precious time from his work on the Vatican Stanze and from his wooing of the Fornarina, he executed some of the frescoes, notably a luminous *Galatea*. Chigi delighted in impressing guests by having his servants clear the table by casting precious dinnerware into the Tiber. Naturally, the guests did not know of the nets he had stretched under the waterline to catch everything. ✉ *Via della Lungara 230, Trastevere* ☎ *06/68027268* ⊕ *www.lincei.it* 🎫 *€4.50* ◷ *Mon.–Sat. 9–1.*

The Catacombs & the Via Appia Antica

The Early Christian sites on the ancient Appian Way are some of the religion's oldest. Catacombs, where early Christians (whose religion prohibited cremation) buried their dead and gathered to worship in secret, lie below the very road where tradition says Christ appeared to St. Peter. The Via Appia Antica, built 400 years before, offers a quiet, green place to walk and ponder the ancient world. The Rome APT office provides an informative free pamphlet for this itinerary.

a good tour

Resist any temptation to undertake the 1½-km (1-mi) walk between Porta San Sebastiano and the catacombs; it's a dull and tiring hike on a heavily trafficked cobblestone road, with stone walls the only scenery. Instead, hop on Bus 660 from the Colli Albani metro stop on Line A to the **Via Appia Antica** ⑦① ▶. (Bus 218 from San Giovanni in Laterano also passes near the catacombs, but you have to walk about ½ km [¼ mi] east from Via Ardeatina to Via Appia Antica.) A slightly more expensive but hassle-free option is to take Bus 110 from Piazza Venezia; it's air-conditioned and allows you to hop on and off as you please.

TIMING Allow one hour for this tour, plus one hour for the catacombs.

Sights to See

★ ▶ ⑦① **Via Appia Antica.** This Queen of Roads, "Regina Viarium," was the most important of the extensive network of roads that traversed the Roman Empire, a masterful feat of engineering that made possible Roman control of a vast area, by allowing efficient transport of armies and commercial goods. Completed in 312 BC by Appius Claudius, the road was ancient Europe's first highway, connecting Rome with Brindisi, 584 km (365 mi) away on the Adriatic coast. Today, part of the route still exists (as Via Appia, SS7), but most of it is a paved, modern highway. The stretch indicated here is the opposite: closed to traffic, the ancient roadway passes through grassy fields and shady groves and by the villas of movie stars (Marcello Mastroianni and Gina Lollobrigida had homes here) and other VIPs. This part is still paved with the ancient *basoli* (basalt stones) over which the Romans drove their carriages. Taverns, houses, temples, and tombs flanked the ancient road, and the occasional lone statue, crumbling wall, or column is still visible, draped in ivy or alone in a patch of wildflowers. Pick a sunny day for your visit, wear comfortable shoes, and bring plenty of water. **San Callisto** is one of the best-preserved of the underground catacombs. A friar will guide you through its crypts and galleries. ⊠ *Via Appia Antica 110* ☎ *06/51301580* ☒ *€5* ⊘ *Feb.–Dec., Mon.–Sat. 8:30–noon and 2:30–5:30.*

The 4th-century **San Sebastiano** catacomb, named for the saint who was buried here, burrows underground on four levels. The only one of the catacombs to remain accessible during the Middle Ages, it's the origin of the term "catacomb," for it was in a spot where the road dips into a hollow, a place the Romans called *catacumbas* ("near the hollow"). Eventually, the Christian cemetery that had existed here since the 2nd century came to be known by the same name, which was applied to all underground cemeteries discovered in Rome in later centuries. ⊠ *Via Appia Antica 136* ☎ *06/7850350* ☒ *€5* ⊘ *Mar.–Jan., Mon.–Sat. 8:30–noon and 2:30–5.*

On the east side of Via Appia Antica are the ruins of the **Circo di Massenzio**, where the obelisk now in Piazza Navona once stood. ⊠ *Via Appia Antica 153* ☎ *06/7801324* ☒ *€3* ⊘ *Oct.–Mar., Tues.–Sun. 9–4:30; Apr.–Sept., Tues.–Sun. 9–7.*

The circular **Tomba di Cecilia Metella** (Tomb of Cecilia Metella), the mausoleum of a Roman noblewoman who lived at the time of Julius Caesar, was transformed into a fortress in the 14th century. The tomb houses a small museum with sculptures from the Via Appia Antica and an interesting reconstruction of the area's geological and historical past. ⊠ *Via Appia Antica 161* ☎ *06/7802465* ☒ *€2* ⊘ *Weekdays 9–1 hr before sunset, weekends 9–1.*

WHERE TO EAT

Updated by
Valerie
Hamilton

Rome is distinguished more by its good attitude toward eating out than by a multitude of world-class restaurants. Don't look for star chefs here, or the latest trends—with a few notable exceptions, the city's food scene is a bit like its historical sights, well worn but still standing. But food lovers nonetheless have much to look forward to. Romans have been known since ancient times for great feasts and banquets, and though the days of the triclinium and the saturnalia are long past, dining out is still Rome's favorite pastime. Many of the city's restaurants cater to a clientele of regulars, and atmosphere and attitude are usually friendly and informal. The flip side is that in Rome, the customer is not always right—the chef and waiters are in charge, and no one will beg forgiveness if you wanted *skim* milk in that cappuccino. Be flexible, and you're sure to *mangiar bene* (eat well). Lunch is served from 12:30 to 2:30 and dinner from 8 until 10:30 or 11, but some restaurants stay open later, especially in summer, when patrons linger at sidewalk tables to enjoy the *ponentino* (evening breeze).

	$$$$	$$$	$$	$	¢
WHAT IT COSTS In euros					
AT DINNER	over €22	€17–€22	€12–€17	€7–€12	under €7

Prices are for a second course (secondo piatto).

Campo de' Fiori

$$ ✕ **Albistrò.** Just a hop, skip, and a jump from Piazza Farnese, this small, surprisingly affordable restaurant turns out both classic Italian dishes and more varied, modern offerings. The small menu changes often, but you will always find interesting risottos, such as pumpkin with bits of almond cookies, and tasty second courses such as guinea fowl with chestnuts. One of the owners is from Switzerland, so be on the lookout for such regional specialties as *pavé*, a semolina pudding with fresh strawberries. ✉ *Via dei Banchi Vecchi 140/a, Campo de' Fiori* ☎ *06/6865274* 🚪 *AE, DC, MC, V* ☻ *Closed Wed. and 3 wks in July–Aug. No lunch Mon.–Sat.*

$ ✕ **Ditirambo.** Don't let the country-kitchen ambience fool you; at this

Fodor'sChoice little spot off Campo de' Fiori, the constantly changing selection of off-

★ beat takes on Italian classics is a step beyond ordinary Roman fare. Simple antipasti consist of vegetables and cured meats, and pastas range from *cacio e pepe* (spaghetti with black pepper and pecorino) to gnocchi with Montasio cheese and radicchio. Grilled sea bass and veal chops with herbs baked in foil are favorite main courses. The homemade ricotta and sour cherry cake is a treat. ✉ *Piazza della Cancelleria 74, Campo de' Fiori* ☎ *06/6871626* 🚪 *AE, MC, V* ☻ *Closed Aug. No lunch Mon.*

Piazza di Spagna

★ **$$$$** ✕ **El Toulà.** Rome's prestigious El Toulà has the warm, welcoming comforts of a 19th-century country house, with white walls, antique furniture in dark wood, heavy silver serving dishes, and spectacular fruit and flower arrangements. There's a cozy bar off the entrance, where you can sip a Prosecco, the Venetian sparkling wine best paired with the chef's Venetian specialties that are always on offer, along with contemporary interpretations of Italian classics. Jacket and tie are required November through February. ✉ *Via della Lupa 29/b, Piazza di Spagna* ☎ *06/6873750* 🍴 *Reservations essential* 🚪 *AE, DC, MC, V* ☻ *Closed Sun. and Aug. No lunch Mon. and Sat.*

$$$–$$$$ ✕ **Reef.** This seafood restaurant is all about ultramodern design, with sand beneath a Plexiglas floor, rusted-iron accents, huge fish-photo blowups, and a full wall of windows that look onto Ara Pacis. Chef Antonello Colonna produces classic Roman fare with a modern twist: try the spigola in *crosta di arachidi* (with a peanut crust). There's a sushi bar at the entrance, where you can sit and view the full workings of the kitchen through a glass wall. ✉ *Piazza Augusto Imperatore 42–48, Piazza di Spagna* ☎ *06/68301430* 🚪 *AE, DC, MC, V* ☻ *Closed Mon. No lunch Tues.*

$$–$$$ ✕ **Dal Bolognese.** This classic restaurant on Piazza del Popolo is a trendy choice for a leisurely lunch between sightseeing and shopping. Contemporary paintings decorate the dining room, but the real attraction is the expansive pedestrian piazza—prime people-watching real estate. As the name promises, the cooking here adheres to the hearty tradition of Bologna, with delicious homemade tortellini *in brodo* (in broth), fresh pastas in creamy sauces, and steaming trays of boiled meats. Among the desserts, try the *dolce della mamma* (a concoction of gelato, zabaglione, and chocolate sauce) and the fruit-shape gelato. ✉ *Piazza del Popolo 1, Piazza di Spagna* ☎ *06/3611426* 🚪 *AE, DC, MC, V* ☻ *Closed Mon. and Aug.*

$$ ✕ **'Gusto.** There's an urban-loft feel to this trendy two-story space—unusual for Rome. The ground floor includes a pizzeria (which also serves salads and light fare at lunch) and a wine bar; the upstairs offers dishes with a mix of Italian and international influences, such as eggplant-and-

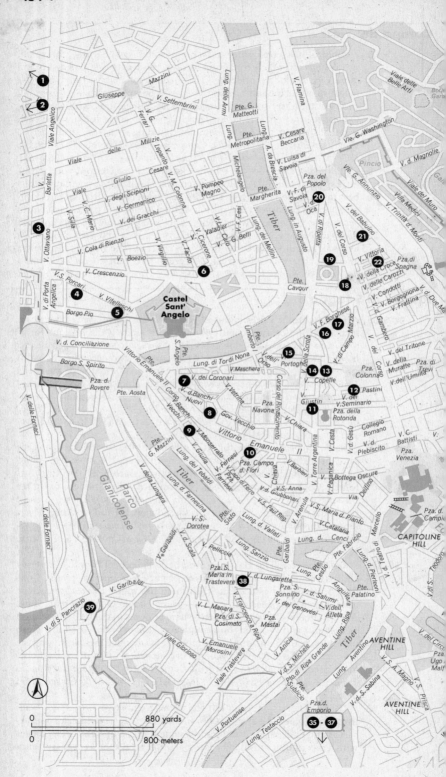

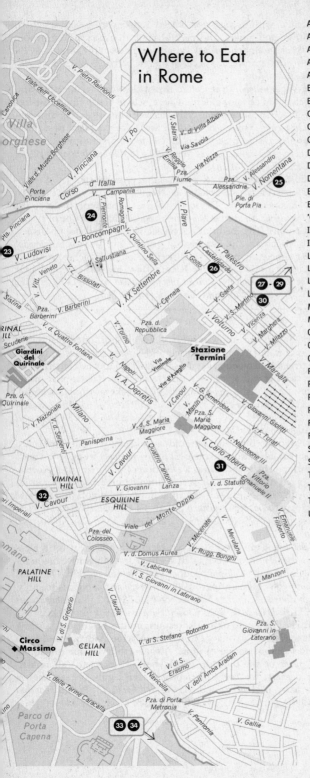

Where to Eat in Rome

chickpea strudel with sesame–goat cheese sauce, wok-tossed spaghetti with vegetables and ginger, and rack of lamb in a porcini mushroom crust. The weekday lunch buffet is good and reasonably priced. ⊠ *Piazza Augusto Imperatore 9, Piazza di Spagna* ☎ *06/3226273* ▤ *AE, MC, V* ☺ *Closed Mon.*

$–$$ ✕ **Margutta Vegetariano.** That Italian rarity, the vegetarian restaurant, takes on a chic and cosmopolitan air here, where you'll find meat-free versions of classic Mediterranean dishes as well as more daring tofu concoctions. Changing displays of modern art make the place fit right in on its gallery-lined street. Service is efficient and professional, and the lunch buffet is a great value. ⊠ *Via Margutta 118, Piazza di Spagna* ☎ *06/ 32650577* ▤ *AE, DC, MC, V.*

$ ✕ **Otello alla Concordia.** The clientele at this popular spot off a shopping street near Piazza di Spagna is about evenly divided between tourists and businesspeople. The former like to sit outdoors in the courtyard in any weather; the latter have their regular tables in one of the inside dining rooms. The menu offers classic Roman and Italian dishes, competently prepared and reasonably priced, and service is friendly and efficient. Since the regulars won't relinquish their niches, you may have to wait for a table; go early. Reservations are not accepted after 8:30. ⊠ *Via della Croce 81, Piazza di Spagna* ☎ *06/6791178* ▤ *AE, DC, MC, V* ☺ *Closed Sun. and 2 wks in Jan. or Feb.*

Piazza Navona

★ $$$–$$$$ ✕ **Sangallo.** Small and intimate, this is an old-fashioned restaurant where the owner buys the fish himself and dinner is meant to last all night. The traditional menu has some sophisticated touches, such as oysters tartare, snapper with foie gras, and a truffle-themed fixed-price menu. There are few tables in the tiny dining room, so make sure to book ahead. ⊠ *Vicolo della Vaccarella 11/a, Piazza Navona* ☎ *06/6865549* ⌔ *Reservations essential* ▤ *AE, DC, MC, V* ☺ *Closed Sun., 1 wk in Jan., and 2 wks in Aug. No lunch Mon.*

$$–$$$ ✕ **Myosotis.** Myosotis does things the old-fashioned way: with hand-rolled pastas, fresh-baked bread, and olive oil brought direct from the owner's farm in Umbria. The vast menu is a selection of updated takes on classic dishes, such as *vellutata di ceci e funghi porcini* (chickpea-and-porcini mushroom soup), and the time-honored spigola filleted and served in *crosta di patate* (a potato crust). ⊠ *Via della Vaccarella 3/5, Piazza Navona* ☎ *06/6865554* ▤ *AE, DC, MC, V* ☺ *Closed Sun. No lunch Mon.*

$$ ✕ **Osteria dell'Ingegno.** This casual but trendy spot is great for a glass of wine or a meal in the city center. The simple but innovative menu focuses on regional and seasonal produce and changes weekly. The walls are hung with colorful paintings by local artists, and service is friendly. ⊠ *Piazza di Pietra 45, Piazza Navona* ☎ *06/6780662* ⌔ *Reservations essential* ▤ *AE, DC, MC, V* ☺ *Closed Sun. and 2 wks in Aug.*

$–$$ ✕ **Orso 80.** The good kind of tourist restaurant, this bright and bustling trattoria near Piazza Navona is known for its wide assortment of fresh seafood and fabulous antipasto table. Also worth trying are the homemade egg pasta or the *bucatini* (thick, hollow spaghetti) all'amatriciana. For dessert, the *torta di ricotta* (sheep's-milk cheesecake), a Roman specialty, is always good. ⊠ *Via dell'Orso 33, Piazza Navona* ☎ *06/6864904* ▤ *AE, DC, MC, V* ☺ *Closed Mon. and Aug.*

San Pietro

$$$$ ✕**La Pergola.** High atop Monte Mario, the Cavalieri Hilton's rooftop
Fodor'sChoice La Pergola restaurant offers a commanding view onto the city below.
★ Trompe-l'oeil ceilings and handsome wood paneling combine with low
lighting to create an intimate atmosphere. Celebrated Wunder-chef
Heinz Beck brings Rome its finest example of Mediterranean *alta cucina*
(haute cuisine); dishes are balanced and light, and presentation is striking. For a window table, reserve a month in advance; otherwise, two
weeks. ⊠ *Cavalieri Hilton, Via Cadlolo 101, Monte Mario* ☎ *06/
3509221* ✍ *Reservations essential* 🍴 *Jacket and tie* ☰ *AE, DC, MC,
V* ✆ *Closed Sun. and Mon. and 2 wks in Dec. No lunch.*

$–$$ ✕**Dal Toscano.** An open wood-fired grill and classic dishes such as *ri-
bollita* (a thick bread and vegetable soup) and *pici* (fresh, thick pasta
with wild hare sauce) are the draw at this great family-run Tuscan trattoria near the Vatican. The cuts of beef visible at the entrance tell you
right away that the house special is the prized bistecca alla fiorentina.
Wash it all down with a strong Chianti or the Tuscan house wine.
Desserts such as apple strudel and *castagnaccio* (a chestnut and pine-
nut treat served in wintertime) are homemade. ⊠ *Via Germanico 58,
San Pietro* ☎ *06/39725717* ☰ *DC, MC, V* ✆ *Closed Mon., Aug., and
2 wks in Dec.*

★ **$$–$$$** ✕**Siciliainbocca.** Finally, Rome has a straight-up, no-nonsense Sicilian
restaurant. The owners, both Sicily natives, decided to open up Siciliainbocca after years of frustration at not finding a decent pasta *alla norma*
(with eggplant, tomato sauce, and aged ricotta cheese) in the capital.
Try specialties such as caponata, risotto *ai profumi di Sicilia* (with
lemon, orange, mozzarella, and zucchini), and delicious grilled swordfish, shrimp, and squid. Even in the dead of winter, Siciliainbocca's yellow walls and brightly colored ceramic plates warm you up. There's
outdoor seating in summer. ⊠ *Via E. Faà di Bruno 26, San Pietro*
☎ *06/37358400* ☰ *AE, DC, MC, V* ✆ *Closed Sun.*

$$ ✕**Alfredo e Ada.** There's no place like home, and you'll feel like you're
back there from the moment you squeeze into a table at this hole in the
wall just across the river from Castel Sant'Angelo. There's no menu, just
plate after plate of whatever Ada thinks you should try, from hearty, clas-
sic pastas to *involtini di vitello* (savory veal rolls with tomato) and home-
made sausage. Sit back, relax, and enjoy—it's all good. By the time you
leave, you may have made some new friends, too. ⊠ *Via dei Banchi Nuovi
14, San Pietro* ☎ *06/6878842* ☰ *No credit cards* ✆ *Closed weekends.*

$$ ✕**Taverna Angelica.** The area surrounding St. Peter's Basilica isn't known
for culinary excellence, but Taverna Angelica is an exception. Its tiny
size (just 20 seats) allows the chef to concentrate on each individual dish,
and the results are impressive. The menu is creative without being pretentious; such dishes as chickpeas with a fondue of pecorino cheese, lentil
soup with pigeon breast, and breast of duck in balsamic vinegar are
exquisitely executed. The candlelit dining room, tasteful decor, and excellent service are icing on the cake. ⊠ *Piazza A. Capponi 6, San Pietro*
☎ *06/6874514* ✍ *Reservations essential* ☰ *AE, V.*

¢–$ ✕**Tre Pupazzi.** The "three puppets," after which the trattoria is named,
are the worn stone figures on a fragment of an ancient sarcophagus that
embellishes a building on this byway near the Vatican. Little has changed
here since the place was built in 1625, and the restaurant upholds a tradition of good food, courteous service, and reasonable prices. The menu
offers classic Roman and Abruzzese trattoria fare, including fettuccine

and abbacchio, plus pizzas at lunchtime, a rarity in Rome. The restaurant opens early, at noon for lunch and 7 for dinner. ⊠ *Borgo Pio 183 at Via dei Tre Pupazzi, San Pietro* ☎ *06/68803220* ▤ *AE, DC, MC, V* ☉ *Closed Sun. and Aug.*

Termini

$$$–$$$$ ✕ **Agata e Romeo.** The husband-and-wife team of Agata Parisella and Romeo Caraccio runs one of Rome's top restaurants. Agata puts an inspired twist on Roman cuisine with dishes such as crepes with chestnut flour and ewe's-milk ricotta, and breaded lamp chops. Romeo acts as maître d' and expert sommelier. A tasting menu, complete with wine, changes monthly to reflect seasonal dishes and allows you to try a range of specialties. Desserts are scrumptious and the wine list excellent. ⊠ *Via Carlo Alberto 45, Termini* ☎ *06/4466115* ▤ *AE, DC, MC, V* ☉ *Closed weekends, 2 wks in July and 2 wks in Aug.*

★ **$$**   ✕ **Uno e Bino.** Giampaolo Gravina's restaurant in an artsy corner of the San Lorenzo neighborhood is popular with Romans from all over town. He works the dining room, offering suggestions from an impressive wine list, and his sister Gloria is in the kitchen turning out inventive cuisine inspired by the family's Umbrian-Sicilian roots. Dishes such as octopus salad with asparagus and carrots, and spaghetti with swordfish, tomatoes, and capers are specialties. ⊠ *Via degli Equi 58, San Lorenzo* ☎ *06/4460702* ▤ *AE, D, MC, V* ☉ *Closed Mon. and Aug. No lunch.*

★ **$**   ✕ **Arancia Blu.** Owner and chef Fabio Passan has a mission—to prove that "vegetarian cuisine" isn't an oxymoron. He succeeds, with flavorful, creative dishes that have won him a devoted clientele of vegetarians and omnivores alike. Start with a leek-and-almond quiche or lemon-ricotta ravioli with squash and sage, and move on to *polpettine vegetali* (meatless meatballs) with a tomato–coriander seed sauce. Gourmet palates will be tickled by the selections of coffee and olive oil, and by the chocolate tasting, 14 chocolate wafers of every flavor and origin. Vegan and wheat-free dishes are available on request. ⊠ *Via dei Latini 65, San Lorenzo* ☎ *06/4454105* ▤ *No credit cards* ☉ *No lunch.*

¢–$ ✕ **Pommidoro.** Mamma's in the kitchen and the rest of the family greets, serves, and keeps you happy and well fed at this trattoria popular with artists, filmmakers, and actors. It's near Rome's main university in the counterculture San Lorenzo neighborhood, a short cab ride east of Stazione Termini. The menu offers especially good grilled meats and game birds as well as classic home-style cucina. You can dine outside in warm weather. ⊠ *Piazza dei Sanniti 44, San Lorenzo* ☎ *06/4452692* ▤ *AE, DC, MC, V* ☉ *Closed Sun. and Aug.*

Trastevere/Testaccio

$$–$$$ ✕ **Paris.** On a small square just off Piazza Santa Maria in Trastevere, Paris (named after a former owner) has a reassuring, understated ambience, without the hokey flamboyance of many eateries in this neighborhood. The menu features the best of classic Roman cuisine: homemade fettuccine, delicate fritto misto, and, of course, baccalà. There's a good wine list. In fair weather opt for tables on the piazza. ⊠ *Piazza San Calisto 7/a, Trastevere* ☎ *06/5815378* ▤ *AE, DC, MC, V* ☉ *Closed Mon. and 3 wks in Aug. No dinner Sun.*

★ **$$$**   ✕ **Antico Arco.** Founded by three friends with a passion for wine and fine food, Antico Arco has won the hearts of foodies from Rome and beyond with its culinary inventiveness and high style. The menu changes with the season, but you may find such delights as *flan di taleggio con salsa di funghi* (taleggio flan with mushrooms), or a *carré d'agnello* (rack

ON THE MENU

ROMAN COOKING IS SIMPLE. *Dishes rarely have more than a few ingredients. Meat and fish are most often roasted, baked, or grilled. Seasonal vegetables are also usually on offer, although they may not be listed on the menu.*

The typical Roman fresh pasta is fettuccine, golden egg noodles at their best when laced with ragù, a rich tomato and meat sauce. Spaghetti alla carbonara is tossed with a sauce of egg yolk, chunks of guanciale (cured pork cheek) or pancetta (salt-cured bacon), pecorino Romano cheese, and lots of freshly ground black pepper. Pasta all'amatriciana has a sauce of tomato, guanciale, and onion. Potato gnocchi, served with a tomato sauce and a dusting of Parmesan or pecorino, are a Roman favorite for Thursday dinner. The best meat on the menu is often abbacchio, milk-fed lamb. Legs of lamb are usually roasted with rosemary and potatoes, and the chops are grilled alla scottadito (literally "burn your finger," for small chops eaten with your fingers hot off the grill). Most Mediterranean fish are light yet flavorful, among them spigola (sea bass), orata (bream), and rombo (turbot or flounder). Romans swoon for batter-fried baccalà (cod), at its best light, flaky, and hot.

Local cheeses are made from sheep's milk; the best-known is the aged, sharp pecorino Romano. Fresh ricotta is a treat all on its own, and finds its way into a number of dishes, including desserts. Cicoria and spinaci ripassati (fried chicory and spinach) are favorite side dishes among Romans and should satisfy your daily quota of greens. Many restaurants make a specialty of the fritto misto (literally "mixed fried") with whatever vegetables are in season. Rome is famous for carciofi (artichokes)—the season runs from November to April—traditionally prepared alla romana (stuffed with garlic and mint and braised in oil) or alla giudia (fried whole, making each petal crisp). A special springtime treat is vignarola, a mixture of tender peas, fava beans, and artichokes, cooked with bits of guanciale.

Typical wines of Rome are from the Castelli Romani, the towns in the hills to the southeast: Frascati, Colli Albani, Marino, and Velletri. Though water in Rome is good to drink, restaurants usually have you choose between bottled waters, either gassata (sparkling) or liscia (not).

---

of lamb) with foie gras sauce and pears in port wine. Don't miss dessert, especially the chocolate soufflé with melted chocolate center: it's justly famous among chocoholics all over the city. ⊠ *Piazzale Aurelio 7, Trastevere* ☎ *06/5815274* ⌦ *Reservations essential* ▭ *AE, DC, MC, V* ⊗ *Closed Sun. and 2 wks in Aug. No lunch.*

$$–$$$ ✕ **Checchino dal 1887.** Literally carved from a hillside composed of potsherds from Roman times, Checchino serves traditional Roman cuisine, carefully prepared and presented without fanfare or decoration. Though the slaughterhouses of Rome's Testaccio quarter—a short cab ride from the city center—are long gone, their memory lives on in the restaurant's Roman soul food: *trippa* (tripe), *testina* (head cheese), *pajata* (intestine), *zampa* (trotter), and *coratella* (sweetbreads and heart of beef). For the less adventuresome, house specialties include *coda alla vaccinara* (stewed oxtail), a popular Roman dish, and *abbacchio alla cacciatora* (braised milk-fed lamb) with seasonal vegetables. ⊠ *Via di Monte Testaccio 30, Testaccio* ☎ *06/5746318* ⊟ *AE, DC, MC, V* ☉ *Closed Sun., Mon., and Aug.*

$ ✕ **Perilli.** A bastion of authentic Roman cooking since 1911 (the decor has changed very little), this trattoria is the place to go to try rigatoni *con pajata* (with calves' intestines)—if you're into this sort of thing. Pasta all'amatriciana and carbonara are also classics. The house wine is a golden nectar from the Castelli Romani. ⊠ *Via Marmorata 39, Testaccio* ☎ *06/ 5742415* ⊟ *AE, DC, MC, V* ☉ *Closed Wed.*

Via Appia Antica

$–$$ ✕ **L'Archeologia.** In this farmhouse just beyond the catacombs, you dine indoors beside the fireplace in cool weather or in the garden under age-old vines in summer. The atmosphere is friendly and intimate. Specialties include fettuccine *al finocchio salvatico* (with wild fennel), abbacchio alla scottadito, and fresh seafood. ⊠ *Via Appia Antica 139* ☎ *06/ 7880494* ⊟ *AE, MC, V* ☉ *Closed Tues.*

$–$$ ✕ **Cecilia Metella.** From the entrance on Via Appia Antica, almost opposite the catacombs, you walk uphill to a low-lying but sprawling construction designed for wedding feasts and banquets. There's a large terrace shaded by vines for outdoor dining. Although obviously geared to larger groups, Cecilia Metella also gives individuals and small groups good service and traditional Roman cuisine. The specialties are the *scrigno alla Cecilia* (baked green noodles) and *pollo al Nerone* (chicken à la Nero—flambéed, of course). ⊠ *Via Appia Antica 125, Via Appia Antica* ☎ *06/ 5136743* ⊟ *AE, DC, MC, V* ☉ *Closed Mon. and last 2 wks in Aug.*

Via Veneto

$$$$ ✕ **La Terrazza dell'Eden.** The Hotel Eden's La Terrazza restaurant has an unparalleled view of Rome's seven hills and food as spectacular as the view. Chef Enrico Derfligher, formerly of Buckingham Palace, refreshes the menu every six months with superb culinary creations that are high on flavor and low on butter. If you're a wine enthusiast, ask the maître d' to view the restaurant's showcase cellar. ⊠ *Hotel Eden, Via Ludovisi 49, Via Veneto* ☎ *06/47812752* ♣ *Reservations essential* 🏛 *Jacket and tie* ⊟ *AE, DC, MC, V.*

★ $$$–$$$$ ✕ **Papá Baccus.** Italo Cipriani takes his meat as seriously as any Tuscan. He uses real Chianina beef, the prized breed traditionally used for the house-specialty *bistecca alla fiorentina,* a thick grilled steak left rare in the middle. Cipriani brings many ingredients from his hometown on the border of Emilia-Romagna and Tuscany. Try the sweet and delicate prosciutto from Pratomagno or the *fagioli zolfini* (tender white beans). The welcome is warm, the service excellent. ⊠ *Via Toscana 36, Via Veneto* ☎ *06/42742808* ⊟ *AE, DC, MC, V* ☉ *Closed Sun. and 2 wks in Aug. No lunch Sat.*

Pizzerias

Pizza may have been invented somewhere else, but in Rome it's hard to walk a block without encountering it in one form or another. Pizza from a bakery is usually made without cheese—pizza *bianca* (with olive oil and salt) or pizza *rossa* (with tomato sauce). Many small shops specialize in pizza *al taglio* (by the slice), priced by the *etto* (100 grams, about a ¼ pound), according to the kind of topping. Both types make a great snack any time of day. Some good places to find the real thing on the go: **Il Forno di Campo de' Fiori** (⊠ Campo de' Fiori), closed Sunday, makes hot pizza bianca and rossa and is crowded all day. **Antico Forno Roscioli** (⊠ Via dei Chiavari 34, Campo de' Fiori) is a truly excellent kosher bakery and pizzeria, closed weekends. **Zí Fenizia** (✉ Via Santa Maria del Pianto 64, Ghetto) makes kosher pizza in the old Jewish Ghetto; it closes Friday at sundown and remains closed Saturday.

But don't leave Rome without sitting down to a classic, wafer-thin, crispy Roman pizza in a lively, no-frills pizzeria. Most are open only for dinner, usually from 8 PM to midnight. Look for a place with a *forno a legna* (wood-burning oven), a must for a good thin crust on your plate-size Roman pizza. Standard models are the *margherita* (tomato, mozzarella, and basil) and the *capricciosa* (a little bit of everything, depending upon the "caprices" of the pizza chef: tomato, mozzarella, sausage, olives, artichoke hearts, prosciutto, even egg), but most pizzerias have a long list of additional options, including tasty mozzarella *di bufala* (made from buffalo milk).

★ ¢–$ ✕ **Remo.** Expect a wait at this perennial favorite in Testaccio frequented by students and neighborhood locals. You won't find tablecloths or other nonessentials, just classic Roman pizza and boisterous conversation. ✉ *Piazza Santa Maria Liberatrice 44, Testaccio* ☎ 06/5746270 ⌨ *Reservations not accepted* ▤ No credit cards ⊘ *Closed Sun., Aug., and Christmas wk.* No lunch.

¢–$ ✕ **La Soffitta.** You pay more, but hey, it's imported. This is Rome's hottest spot for classic Neapolitan pizza (thick, though crunchy on the bottom, rather than paper thin and crispy like the Roman kind) and one of the few *pizzerie* in town certified by the True Neapolitan Pizza Association. Desserts are brought in daily from Naples. ✉ *Via dei Villini 1/e, Termini* ☎ 06/4404642 ⌨ *Reservations not accepted* ▤ AE, DC, MC, V ⊘ *Closed Aug. 10–31.* No lunch.

¢ ✕ **Baffetto.** Down a cobblestone street not far from Piazza Navona, this is Rome's best-known pizzeria and a summer favorite for street-side dining. The plain interior is mostly given over to the ovens, but there's another room with more paper-covered tables. Turnover is fast; this is not the place to linger. ✉ *Via del Governo Vecchio 114, Piazza Navona* ☎ 06/6861617 ▤ No credit cards ⊘ *Closed Aug.* No lunch.

¢ ✕ **Il Leoncino.** Lines out the door on weekends attest to the popularity of this fluorescent-lit pizzeria in the otherwise big-ticket neighborhood around Piazza di Spagna. This is one of the few pizzerias open for lunch as well as dinner. ✉ *Via del Leoncino 28, Piazza di Spagna* ☎ 06/6876306 ⌨ *Reservations not accepted* ▤ No credit cards ⊘ *Closed Sun. and Aug.*

Enoteche

It was not so long ago that wine in Rome (and other towns) was strictly local; you didn't have to walk far to find an *osteria*, a tavernlike establishment where you could buy wine straight from the barrel or sit down to drink and nibble a bit, chat, or play cards. The tradition continues today, as many Roman wineshops are also open as *enoteche* (wine bars). They've done away with the folding chairs and rickety tables— now it's designer interiors and chic ambience. Shelves are lined with hundreds of bottles from all over the country, representing the best in Italian wine making, and many selections are available by the glass. Behind the bar you'll find a serious wine enthusiast, maybe even a sommelier.

$$$–$$$$ ✕ **Il Simposio di Costantini.** At the classiest wine bar in town, done out in wrought-iron vines, wood paneling, and velvet, you can choose from about 30 wines. Food is appropriately fancy: marinated and smoked fish, composed salads, top-quality salami and other cured meats (classical and wild), terrines and pâtés, and several gussied-up hot vegetable and meat dishes. It has 80 assorted cheeses, grouped according to origin or type

(French, Italian, goat, hard, herb-crusted). ✉ *Piazza Cavour 16, San Pietro* ☎ *06/3211502* 🖃 *AE, DC, MC, V* ⊙ *Closed Sun. and last 2 wks of Aug. No lunch Sat.*

$$$ ✕ **Bistro.** The atmosphere here is both airy and intimate; high, pale yellow arched ceilings, immense guilt mirrors, rich oak paneling, and an original wrought-iron bar counter are all true to the art nouveau style. Chef Emanuele Vizzini serves up fusion dishes such as *fettuccine al Cabernet con scampi* (red-wine fettuccine with scampi and vegetables) and Nasdaq taglionini with lobster (the dollar-green pasta is made with curaçao liqueur). The sommelier has selected 300 labels (12 available by the glass) of lesser-known, high-quality wines. ✉ *Via Palestro 40, Termini* ☎ *06/44702868* 🖃 *AE, DC, MC, V* ⊙ *No lunch Sun.*

$–$$ ✕ **Trimani Il Winebar.** This is a handy address for diners in a town where most restaurants don't open before 8 PM. Trimani operates nonstop from 11 AM to 12:30 AM and serves hot food at lunch and dinner. Decor is minimalist, and the second floor provides a subdued, candlelit space to sip wine. There's always a choice of a soup and pasta plates, as well as second courses and *torte salate* (savory tarts). Around the corner is a wineshop, one of the oldest in Rome, of the same name. Call about wine tastings and classes (in Italian). ✉ *Via Cernaia 37/b, Termini* ☎ *06/4469630* 🖃 *AE, DC, MC, V* ⊙ *Closed Sun. and 2 wks in Aug.*

★ ¢–$ ✕ **Cavour 313.** Wine bars are popping up all over the city, but Cavour 313 has been around much longer than most. Open for lunch and dinner, it serves an excellent variety of cured meats, cheeses, and salads. Choose from about 25 wines by the glass or uncork a bottle (there are more than 1,200) and stay a while. ✉ *Via Cavour 313, Colosseo* ☎ *06/6785496* 🖃 *AE, DC, MC, V* ⊙ *Closed Aug. No lunch weekends. No dinner Sun. June 15–Sept.*

¢–$ ✕ **Enoteca Spiriti.** Located near the Pantheon, this modern wine bar makes a good stop for a light meal after seeing the sights in the historical center. At lunch there's always a pasta and soup selection, as well as fish and meat specials of the day. Dinner is lighter, focusing on cured meats and cheeses. ✉ *Via Sant'Eustachio 5, Pantheon* ☎ *06/6833691* 🖃 *MC, V* ⊙ *Closed Sun. and Aug. No lunch Sat.*

Cafés

As elsewhere in Italy, there's a *bar* (coffee bar) on nearly every corner in Rome where you can get coffee drinks, fruit juices, pastries, sandwiches, liquor, and beer. Locals usually stop in for a quick caffeine hit at the counter. If you want to sit at a table, beware: prices can be up to four times higher. Don't be shy to ask what the extra cost is before sitting. Pricey **Antico Caffè Greco** (✉ Via Condotti 86, Piazza di Spagna ☎ 06/6791700) is a national landmark popular with tourists; its red-velvet chairs and marble tables have hosted the likes of Byron, Shelley, Keats, Goethe, and Casanova. **Caffè Sant'Eustachio** (✉ Piazza Sant'Eustachio 82, Pantheon ☎ 06/6861309) makes one of the smoothest cappuccinos anywhere. Its secret? *Crema di caffè* (coffee cream)—a rich, homemade addition slipped into each cup. If you want your *caffè* (espresso) without sugar Sant'Eustachio, ask for it *amaro*. **Tazza d'Oro** (✉ Via degli Orfani 84, Pantheon ☎ 06/6789792) serves some of the best coffee in the city, as well as decadent *granita di caffè* (iced coffee) with a thick wallop of whipped cream mixed in. **Rosati** (✉ Piazza del Popolo 5, Piazza di Spagna ☎ 06/3225859) is Piazza del Popolo's premier people-watching spot. Tables on the car-free piazza fill up quickly on weekends, when it seems the whole city is here. **Antico Caffè della Pace** (✉ Via della Pace 3, Piazza Navona ☎ 06/6861216), has an ornate, old-fashioned atmosphere. **Ciampini** (✉ Piazza San Lorenzo in Lucina 29, Piazza di Spagna ☎ 06/6876606), off the Corso in a jewel of a piazza, is a prime spot for a predinner aperativo. Be sure to ask for the free *assaggini* (nibbles).

Gelaterie & Pasticcerie

For Italians, gelato is more a snack than a serious dessert. **Il Gelato di San Crispino** (✉ Via della Panetteria 42, Piazza di Trevi ☎ 06/6793924), closed Tuesday, is perhaps the most celebrated gelato in all of Italy, made without artificial colors or flavors. It's worth crossing town for. **Fiocco di Neve** (✉ Via del Pantheon 51, Pantheon ☎ 06/6786025) is renowned for its zabaglione and *riso biano* (rice) ice cream. **Fonte della Salute** (✉ Via Cardinal Marmaggi 2, Trastevere ☎ 06/5897471), literally, "fountain of health," serves frozen yogurt as well as traditional gelato. It's closed Tuesday in winter. For decades **Muse** (✉ Via Eleanora Duse 1E, Parioli ☎ 06/8079300), popularly known as *da Giovanni* (after the owner), has been a mecca for Romans in the know. Winter flavors include chestnut and almond. It's closed Sunday. **Giolitti** (✉ Via Uffici del Vicario 40, Pantheon ☎ 06/6991243), just off Via Campo Marzio, has a quaint tearoom.

Romans are not known for their sweet tooths, and there are few *pasticcerie* (pastry shops) in town that distinguish themselves with particularly good examples of the few regional desserts. One exception is the **Forno del Ghetto** (✉ Via del Portico d'Ottavia 1, Ghetto ☎ 06/6878637), closed Friday at sundown, Saturday, and Jewish holidays. This hole in the wall—no sign, no tables, just a take-away counter—is an institution, preserving a tradition of Italian-Jewish sweets that cannot be found anywhere else. The ricotta cake (with sour-cherry jam or chocolate) is unforgettable. For a change of pace, try the Austrian cakes and American pies at **Dolceroma** (✉ Via del Portico d'Ottavia 20/b, Ghetto ☎ 06/6892196); the apple strudel and Sacher torte may not be Italian, but Romans come here in droves just the same. It's closed Sunday afternoon and Monday and four weeks July–August.

Salumerie

There are several hundred *salumerie* (gourmet food shops) in town, but a few stand out for a particularly ample selection and items of rare, superior quality. Foodies should head straight for **Franchi** (✉ Via Cola di Rienzo 200, San Pietro ☎ 06/6864576), closed Sunday, with the city's best take-out treats, including salmon mousse, roast beef, vegetable fritters, and an endless selection of sliced meats and cheeses that you can have vacuum-packed for safe transport home. **Castroni** (✉ Via Cola di Rienzo 196, San Pietro ☎ 06/6864383), closed Sunday, is a fine general food shop with lots of imported items. It's right next door to the Franchi shop. **Volpetti** (✉ Via Marmorata 47, Testaccio ☎ 06/5742352), closed Tuesday afternoon and Sunday, has the highest-quality meats and specializes in aged cheeses from small producers.

WHERE TO STAY

Updated by
Valerie
Hamilton

Rome has the range of accommodations you would expect of any great city, from the squalid little hotels around the railway station to the grand monuments to luxury and elegance on and around Via Veneto. Appearances can be misleading: crumbling stucco facades may promise little from the outside, but they often hide interiors of considerable elegance. By the same token, elaborate reception areas may lead to surprisingly plain rooms. Generally, rooms tend to be small by U.S. standards. Many of the lower-priced hotels are actually old-fashioned *pensioni* set on one or several floors of a large building. One disadvantage of staying in central hotels in lower categories is noise; you can ask for an inside room if you are a light sleeper, but you may end up looking out on a dark courtyard.

Rome is a year-round tourist destination, so you should always try to make reservations, even if only a few days in advance. Always inquire about special low rates, often available in both winter and summer if occupancy is low. If you arrive in Rome without reservations, try **Hotel Reservation Service** (☎ 06/6991000), with an English-speaking operator available daily 7 AM–10 PM, and with desks at Aeroporto Fiumicino and Stazione Termini. A list of all the hotels in Rome, with prices and facilities, is available from the main **EPT information office** (✉ Via Parigi 5, Termini ☎ 06/36004399).

WHAT IT COSTS In euros					
	$$$$	**$$$**	**$$**	**$**	**¢**
FOR 2 PEOPLE	over € 300	€225–€300	€150–€225	€75–€150	under €75

Prices are for two people in a standard double room in high season.

Campo de' Fiori

$$$ ⊞ **Cardinal.** Staying at this hotel is like stepping inside a Renaissance painting—it was built by Bramante and is set on magnificent Via Giulia, whose vistas have scarcely changed since the 15th century. The lobby is a riot of cardinal red, while the rooms are serene and subdued, many with antique engravings and Olympian-high ceilings. And Via Giulia—lined with beautiful palazzi and opulent antiques stores—is right outside your doorstep. ✉ *Via Giulia 62, Campo de' Fiori 00186* ☎ *06/68802719* 🖷 *06/6786376* ⋗ *71 rooms* ⌂ *Bar* ☰ *AE, DC, MC, V* ⧉ *EP.*

$$ ⊞ **Casa di Santa Brigida.** You need to book well in advance at one of the best and best known of the convents that take paying guests. It has an enviable location off Piazza Farnese in the heart of Old Rome. The address is that of the church of Santa Brigida, but the guest-house entrance is around the corner at Via Monserrato 54. There are comfortable lounges and a roof terrace. Rooms have small private baths. The Brigidine sisters are known for their gentle manner; they wear a distinctive habit and veil with a caplike headband. ✉ *Piazza Farnese 96, Campo de' Fiori 00186* ☎ *06/ 68892497* 🖷 *06/68891573* ⋗ *24 rooms* ☰ *AE, DC, MC, V.*

$$ ⊞ **Teatro di Pompeo.** Where else can you breakfast under the ancient stone vaults of Pompey's Theater, historic site of Julius Caesar's assassination? At this intimate and refined little hotel in the heart of Old Rome you are part of that history; at night, you sleep under restored beamed ceilings that date from the days of Michelangelo. The tastefully furnished rooms offer comfort as well as charm. Book well in advance. ✉ *Largo del Pallaro 8, Campo de' Fiori 00186* ☎ *06/68300170* 🖷 *06/68805531* ⋗ *13 rooms* ⌂ *In-room safes, minibars, cable TV, bar, laundry service* ☰ *AE, DC, MC, V.*

$ ⊞ **Campo de' Fiori.** Frescoes, exposed brickwork, and picturesque effects throughout this little hotel could well be the work of a set designer. There's an aura of romanticism in the decoration, with the layout making the most of limited space. Though a few rooms are so compact they're almost claustrophobic, the decor reminds you that you're in the heart of Rome. There's no elevator, but the climb to the roof terrace rewards you with a marvelous view. ✉ *Via del Biscione 6, Campo de' Fiori 00186* ☎ *06/68806865* 🖷 *06/6876003* ⊕ *www.hotelcampodefiori.com* ⋗ *27 rooms, 14 with bath* ☰ *MC, V.*

Colosseo

$$ 🏨 **Duca d'Alba.** This elegant hotel has made a stylish contribution to the ongoing gentrification of the Suburra neighborhood, near the Colosseum and the Roman Forum. The tasteful neoclassical decor includes custom-designed furnishings and marble bathrooms. All rooms are entirely sound-proof and offer satellite TV and modem ports. Breakfast consists of an ample buffet. With its attentive staff and reasonable rates, Duca d'Alba is an exceptional value. ⊠ *Via Leonina 14, Colosseo 00184* ☎ *06/484471* 🖨 *06/4884840* ⊕ *www.hotelducadalba.com* ➥ *27 rooms, 1 suite* ⚿ *In-room safes, some kitchenettes, minibars, bar* ⊟ *AE, DC, MC, V.*

Ghetto

$ 🏨 **Arenula.** This hotel—with a luminous and cheerful all-white interior—is a good bargain by Rome standards. Rooms have pale-wood furnishings and gleaming bathrooms, as well as double-glazed windows and air-conditioning (in summer only; ask when you reserve). Two of the rooms accommodate four beds. The catch at the four-story Arenula is that the graceful oval staircase of white marble and wrought iron is the only way up—there is no elevator. The hotel stands on an age-worn byway off central Via Arenula, on the edge of the quaint Ghetto neighborhood and just across the Tiber from Trastevere. ⊠ *Via Santa Maria dei Calderari 47, off Via Arenula, Ghetto 00186* ☎ *06/6879454* 🖨 *06/6896188* ➥ *50 rooms* ⚿ *Cable TV; no a/c in some rooms* ⊟ *AE, DC, MC, V.*

Piazza di Spagna

$$$$ 🏨 **D'Inghilterra.** Legendary names like Liszt, Mendelssohn, Hans Christian Andersen, Mark Twain, and Hemingway litter the guest book here. With a residential feel and a staff that is as warm as the surroundings are velvety, this hotel near the Spanish Steps was once the guest house of the fabulously rich Prince Torlonia. Rooms are so full of carpets, gilt-framed mirrors, and cozy bergères, you'll hardly notice the snug dimensions. Its chic, ochre restaurant with vaulted ceilings, Café Romano, has tables on via Borgogna and serves eclectic cuisine nonstop from noon to midnight. ⊠ *Via Bocca di Leone 14, Piazza di Spagna 00187* ☎ *06/699811* 🖨 *06/69922243* ⊕ *www.hoteldinghilterraroma.it* ➥ *90 rooms, 8 suites* ⚿ *Restaurant, in-room safes, minibars, cable TV, bar, laundry service, parking (fee), no-smoking rooms* ⊟ *AE, DC, MC, V.*

★ $$$$ 🏨 **Hassler.** At the top of the Spanish Steps, the Hassler has sweeping views of Rome from its front rooms and rooftop restaurant; other rooms overlook the gardens of the Villa Medici. The public rooms have an extravagant 1950s elegance—especially the clubby winter bar, the summer garden bar, and the glass-roof lounge, with gold marble walls and a hand-painted tile floor. Comfortable guest rooms are decorated in a variety of classic styles, some with frescoed walls. The penthouse suite, resplendent with antiques, has a huge terrace. ⊠ *Piazza Trinità dei Monti 6, Piazza di Spagna 00187* ☎ *06/699340* 🖨 *06/6789991* ⊕ *www.lhw.com* ➥ *85 rooms, 15 suites* ⚿ *Restaurant, in-room safes, minibars, cable TV, gym, hair salon, bar, laundry service, concierge, parking (fee), no-smoking rooms* ⊟ *AE, DC, MC, V* ⏀ *EP.*

$$$$ 🏨 **Hotel de Russie.** In the 19th century, this historic hotel counted Russian princes among its guests. Later Picasso and Cocteau leaned out the windows to pick oranges from the trees in the terraced garden, a lush oasis just a few steps from Piazza del Popolo. Famed hotelier Sir Rocco Forte has restored the de Russie to a superlative standard of accommodations and service. Rooms are in chic Italian contemporary style, with Roman mosaic motifs in bathrooms. Many have garden views, and sev-

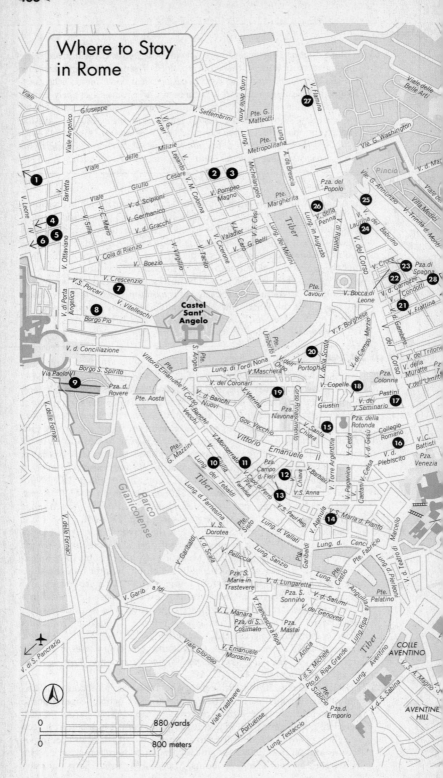

Where to Stay in Rome

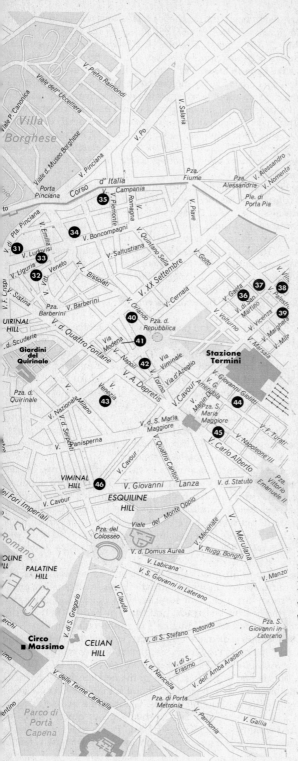

eral suites have panoramic terraces. The spa is luxurious. ⊠ *Via del Babuino 9, Piazza di Spagna 00187* ☎ *06/328881* 🖷 *06/32888888* ⊕ *www.rfhotels.com* ⇆ *130 rooms, 27 suites* ♨ *Restaurant, in-room safes, minibars, cable TV, health club, hair salon, spa, bar* ⊟ *AE, DC, MC, V.*

$$$$ 🖼 **The Inn at the Spanish Steps.** The name of this small, exclusive hotel tells it all. Staying here is like having your own little place on fabled Via Condotti, the elegant shopping street crowned by the Spanish Steps. The hotel occupies the upper floors of a centuries-old palazzo it shares with historic Caffè Greco. Rooms, all junior suites, are handsomely decorated with damask fabrics and antiques. ⊠ *Via Condotti 85, Piazza di Spagna 00187* ☎ *06/69925657* 🖷 *06/6786470* ⊕ *www.atspanishsteps.com* ⇆ *22 rooms* ♨ *In-room safes, minibars, cable TV, airport shuttle, no-smoking rooms* ⊟ *AE, DC, MC, V.*

$$$–$$$$ 🖼 **Scalinata di Spagna.** An old-fashioned pensione that has hosted generations of romantics, this tiny hotel is booked solid for months—even years—ahead. Its location at the top of the Spanish Steps, inconspicuous little entrance, and quiet, sunny terrace where you breakfast add up to the feeling of your own pied-à-terre in the city's most glamorous neighborhood. Thoughtful amenities—from in-room Internet access to a breakfast service until noon—help make you feel at home. ⊠ *Piazza Trinità dei Monti 17, Piazza di Spagna 00187* ☎ *06/6793006* 🖷 *06/69940598* ⊕ *www.hotelscalinata.com* ⇆ *16 rooms* ♨ *In-room safes, minibars, laundry service, Internet, parking (fee), no-smoking rooms.* ⊟ *AE, D, MC, V.*

★ **$$–$$$** 🖼 **Locarno.** Art aficionados and people in the cinema have long appreciated this hotel's preserved fin de siècle charm, intimate feel, and central location off Piazza del Popolo. Wallpaper and fabric prints are coordinated in the rooms, and some rooms have antiques. Everything is lovingly supervised by the owners, a mother-daughter duo. The buffet breakfast is ample, there's bar service on the panoramic roof garden, and complimentary bicycles are available if you feel like braving the traffic. ⊠ *Via della Penna 22, Piazza di Spagna 00186* ☎ *06/3610841* 🖷 *06/3215249* ⇆ *64 rooms, 2 suites* ♨ *In-room data ports, in-room safes, minibars, cable TV, bar, laundry service, no-smoking rooms* ⊟ *AE, DC, MC, V* ⊕ *www.hotellocarno.com.*

$$ 🖼 **Carriage.** The Carriage's location is its main appeal: it's two blocks from the Spanish Steps, in the heart of Rome. The decor of subdued baroque accents, richly colored wallpaper, and antique reproductions lends a touch of elegance. Some furniture has seen better days, and rooms can be pint-sized, but several have small terraces. A roof garden adds to the appeal. ⊠ *Via delle Carrozze 36, Piazza di Spagna 00187* ☎ *06/6990124* 🖷 *06/6788279* ⊕ *www.hotelcarriage.net* ⇆ *24 rooms, 3 suites* ⊟ *AE, DC, MC, V.*

$ 🖼 **Margutta.** For location, good value, and friendly owner-managers, the Margutta is outstanding. The lobby and halls in this small hotel are unassuming, but rooms are a pleasant surprise, with a clean and airy look, attractive wrought-iron bedsteads, and modern baths. Three of the rooms have private terraces. Though it's in an old building, there's an elevator. The location is on a quiet side street between the Spanish Steps and Piazza del Popolo. ⊠ *Via Laurina 34, Piazza di Spagna 00187* ☎ *06/3223674* 🖷 *06/3200395* ⇆ *24 rooms* ♨ *No a/c* ⊟ *AE, DC, MC, V.*

$ 🖼 **Panda.** This is one of the best deals in the neighborhood, particularly remarkable given that the neighborhood is Via della Croce, one of Piazza di Spagna's chic shopping streets. Guest rooms are outfitted in terra-cotta and wrought iron; they're smallish, but quiet, thanks to double-glazed windows, and spotlessly clean. Pay even less by sharing a bath—in low season, you may have it to yourself anyway. ⊠ *Via della*

Croce 35, Piazza di Spagna, 00187 ☎ *06/6780179* 📠 *69942151* 🛏 *20, 14 with bath* ⚘ *No a/c in some rooms* ▤ *MC, V.*

Piazza Navona

$$$$ 🏨 **Raphaël.** This may be Rome's most fascinating hotel. The location is perfect—tucked away behind Piazza Navona—and the vine-covered facade creates a feeling of cozy mystery. The extensive lobby features an array of sculpture, genuine antiques, and original Picasso ceramics. Each room is uniquely decorated with its own treasures, and bathrooms are finished with travertine marble or hand-painted tiles. The two-level Bramante Terrace, where guests can arrange to have meals, has great city views. Some suites have private terraces. ⊠ *Largo Febo 2, Piazza Navona 00186* ☎ *06/682831* 📠 *06/6878993* ⊕ *www.raphaelhotel. com* 🛏 *51 rooms, 7 suites, 10 apartments* ⚘ *Restaurant, gym, sauna, bar, parking (fee)* ▤ *AE, DC, MC, V* ⑩ *EP.*

★ **$$** 🏨 **Cesàri.** The exterior of this intimate hotel on a traffic-free street is as it was when Stendhal stayed here in the 1800s. Inside, the cream-color walls are embellished with old prints of Rome and soft-green drapes and bedspreads, creating an air of comfort and serenity. Bathrooms are done in smart two-tone blue marble. ⊠ *Via di Pietra 89a, Pantheon 00186* ☎ *06/6749701* 📠 *06/67497030* 🛏 *47 rooms* ⚘ *Parking (fee)* ▤ *AE, DC, MC, V.*

★ **$$** 🏨 **Santa Chiara.** Three historic buildings form this gracious hotel behind the Pantheon. It has been in the same family for 200 years, and the personal attention shows in meticulously decorated and maintained lounges and rooms. Each room has built-in oak headboards, a marble-top desk, and an elegant travertine bath. Double-glazed windows look out over the Piazza della Minerva. There are three apartments, for two to five people, with full kitchens. ⊠ *Via Santa Chiara 21, Pantheon 00186* ☎ *06/ 6872979* 📠 *06/6873144* ⊕ *www.albergosantachiara.com* 🛏 *100 rooms, 4 suites, 3 apartments* ⚘ *Some kitchenettes, bar* ▤ *AE, DC, MC, V* ⑩ *CP.*

$ 🏨 **Coronet.** This small hotel occupies part of a floor in one wing of the vast Palazzo Doria Pamphilj; seven interior rooms overlook the family's lovely private garden court. Don't expect palatial ambience, but antique-style molding in the carpeted halls and beam ceilings in several rooms do lend a historic air. The good-size rooms have oldish baths, some very small. Several rooms can accommodate three or four beds. ⊠ *Piazza Grazioli 5, Piazza Venezia 00186* ☎ *06/6792341* 📠 *06/69922705* ⊕ *www.hotelcoronet.com* 🛏 *13 rooms, 10 with bath* ▤ *AE, MC, V.*

$ 🏨 **Abruzzi.** Rarely do magnificent views of world-famous ancient monuments come so cheap. From the windows of this old-fashioned little establishment, the Pantheon is literally in your face. Unfortunately the facilities also recall a Rome of yesteryear: sink in the room, bathroom down the hall (some higher-priced rooms have a private bath). But the rooms are clean and the beds comfortable. To make your reservation, you have to send a signed traveler's check with the name of the hotel also on it. ⊠ *Piazza della Rotonda 69, Piazza Navona 00186* ☎ *06/ 6792021* 📠 *06/69788076* ⊕ *www.hotelabruzzi.it* 🛏 *26 rooms, 15 with bath* ⚘ *In-room safes, minibars, cable TV* ▤ *AE, MC, V.*

¢ 🏨 **Fraterna Domus.** Located on a byway near Piazza Navona, this guest house is run by nuns who do not wear religious habits. Rooms are spartan but have the essentials, including small private bathrooms. Meals are hearty and inexpensive, and the curfew is 11 PM. ⊠ *Vicolo del Leonetto 16, Piazza Navona 00186* ☎ *06/68802727* 📠 *06/6832691* 🛏 *20 rooms* ⚘ *No a/c in some rooms* ▤ *No credit cards.*

San Pietro

$$$-$$$$ ⊞ **Atlante Star.** The lush rooftop-terrace garden café and the restaurant of this comfortable hotel near St. Peter's have a knockout view of the basilica and the rest of Rome. In a distinguished 19th-century building, the rooms are attractively decorated with striped silks and prints for an old-world atmosphere; many bathrooms have hot tubs. The friendly family management is attentive to guests' needs and takes pride in offering extra-virgin olive oil from its own trees in the country. A sister hotel, the **Atlante Garden,** just around the corner, has larger rooms at slightly lower rates. ⊠ *Via Vitelleschi 34, San Pietro 00193* ☎ *06/6873233* 🖷 *06/6872300* ⊕ *www.atlantehotels.com* ↬ *65 rooms, 10 suites* ⟲ *Restaurant, in-room safes, minibars, cable TV, bar, laundry service, concierge, parking (fee), no-smoking rooms.* ▤ *AE, DC, MC, V.*

$$$-$$$$ ⊞ **Giulio Cesare.** An aristocratic town house with a garden in the residential but central Prati district, the Giulio Cesare is a 10-minute walk across the Tiber from Piazza del Popolo. It's beautifully run, with a friendly staff and a quietly luxurious air. The rooms are elegantly furnished, with chandeliers, thick rugs, floor-length drapes, and rich damasks in soft colors. Public rooms have Oriental carpets, old prints and paintings, marble fireplaces, and a grand piano. The buffet breakfast is a veritable banquet. ⊠ *Via degli Scipioni 287, San Pietro 00192* ☎ *06/3210751* 🖷 *06/3211736* ↬ *90 rooms* ⟲ *Bar* ▤ *AE, DC, MC, V.*

★ $$$ ⊞ **Farnese.** A late-19th-century mansion, the Farnese is near the metro and within walking distance of St. Peter's. Furnished with great attention to detail in belle epoque style, it has an intimate atmosphere, dazzling modern baths, lively fresco decorations, and a roof garden. ⊠ *Via Alessandro Farnese 30, San Pietro 00192* ☎ *06/3212553* 🖷 *06/3215129* ↬ *23 rooms* ⟲ *Minibars, cable TV, bar, laundry service, concierge, free parking* ▤ *AE, DC, MC, V* ⦿ *EP.*

$$-$$$ ⊞ **Residenza Paolo VI.** Inside the Vatican walls, the Paolo VI (pronounced Paolo Sesto, Italian for Pope Paul VI) is a convenient base for seeing St. Peter's and the Vatican sights. Rooms in this former monastery are a little sterile, with simple furniture and marble floors, but they're balanced out by a wonderful roof terrace with a view of the basilica. Breakfast is an American-style buffet. ⊠ *Via Paolo VI 29, 00193* ☎ *06/68134108* 🖷 *06/6867428* ⊕ *www.residenzapaolovi.com* ↬ *29 rooms* ⟲ *In-room safes, minibars, cable TV, bar, laundry service, parking (fee), no-smoking rooms.* ▤ *AE, D, MC, V.*

$$ ⊞ **Amalia.** Handy to St. Peter's, the Vatican, and the Cola di Rienzo shopping district, this small hotel is owned and operated by Amalia Consoli and her brothers. On several floors of a 19th-century building, it has large rooms with functional furnishings, pictures of angels on the walls, and gleaming marble bathrooms (hair dryers included). The Ottaviano stop of Metro A is a block away. ⊠ *Via Germanico 66, San Pietro 00192* ☎ *06/39723356* 🖷 *06/39723365* ⊕ *www.hotelamalia.com* ↬ *30 rooms, 25 with bath* ⟲ *In-room safes, minibars, cable TV, laundry service, parking (fee), no-smoking rooms* ▤ *AE, MC, V.*

$$ ⊞ **Sant'Anna.** An example of the gentrification of the picturesque old Borgo neighborhood in the shadow of St. Peter's, this fashionable small hotel has ample bedrooms done in art deco style. The frescoes in the breakfast room and fountain in the courtyard are typical Roman touches. The spacious attic rooms have tiny terraces. ⊠ *Borgo Pio 134, San Pietro 00193* ☎ *06/68801602* 🖷 *06/68308717* ⊕ *www.hotelsantanna.com* ↬ *20 rooms* ⟲ *Minibars, cable TV, parking (fee)* ▤ *AE, DC, MC, V.*

$-$$ ⊞ **Alimandi.** On a side street a block from the Vatican Museums, this family-operated hotel offers excellent value in a neighborhood with moderately priced shops and restaurants. A spiffy lobby and ample lounges, a tavern, terraces, and roof gardens are some of the perks. Rooms are spacious and well furnished; many can accommodate extra beds. ⊠ *Via Tunisi 8, San Pietro 00192* ☎ *06/39723948* 🖷 *06/39723943* ⊕ *www. alimandi.org* ➷ *35 rooms* ⚲ *In-room safes, cable TV, gym, bar, free parking, no-smoking rooms* ▭ *AE, DC, MC, V* ⟡ *EP.*

¢ 🏨 **San Giuseppe della Montagna.** This convent is just outside the Vatican walls, near the entrance to the Vatican Museums. Some of the guest rooms have three beds and all have private bathrooms. There's no curfew; guests are given keys. ⊠ *Viale Vaticano 87, San Pietro 00165* ☎ *06/ 39723807* 🖷 *06/39721048* ➷ *15 rooms* ⚲ *No a/c* ▭ *No credit cards.*

Termini

$$$–$$$$ 🏨 **Mascagni.** Outside is one of Rome's busiest, most central streets, but not a sound filters into the interior of this elegant establishment. It has a cheerful staff and the particular charm of the small hotel. Decorated in early 1920s style, it has handsome mahogany furnishings and coordinated fabrics. The intimate lounges and pleasant bar follow the same decorating scheme, as does the breakfast room, where a lavish buffet is laid in the morning. Discounted rates can be a good deal, so be sure to ask. ⊠ *Via Vittorio Emanuele Orlando 90, Termini 00185* ☎ *06/ 48904040* 🖷 *06/4817487* ⊕ *www.hotelmascagni.com* ➷ *40 rooms* ⚲ *In-room safes, minibars, cable TV, bar, laundry service, concierge, business services, parking (fee), no-smoking rooms* ▭ *AE, DC, MC, V.*

$$–$$$ 🏨 **Britannia.** You'll find here a very special small hotel. The attention to detail of owner Pier Paolo Biorgi is evident in every corner, from the **Fodor's**Choice frescoed halls to the breakfast room. Each guest room has a unique lay-★ out and is furnished with luxury fabrics and original artwork, as well as sybaritic marble bathrooms. The caring management provides such amenities as English-language dailies and local weather reports delivered to your room each morning. The light-filled rooftop suite opens onto a private terrace. ⊠ *Via Napoli 64, Termini 00184* ☎ *06/4883153* 🖷 *06/4882343* ⊕ *www.hotelbritannia.it* ➷ *32 rooms, 1 suite* ⚲ *In-room safes, minibars, cable TV, bar, laundry service, free parking* ▭ *AE, DC, MC, V.*

$$ 🏨 **Montreal.** On a central avenue across the square from Santa Maria Maggiore, only three blocks from Stazione Termini, the compact Montreal occupies three floors of an older building. It's been totally renovated and offers fresh-looking, though small, rooms. The owner-managers are pleasant and helpful, and the neighborhood has plenty of reasonably priced restaurants. ⊠ *Via Carlo Alberto 4, Termini 00185* ☎ *06/ 4457797* 🖷 *06/4465522* ⊕ *www.hotelmontrealroma.com* ➷ *27 rooms* ⚲ *In-room safes, minibars, cable TV, parking (fee)* ▭ *AE, DC, MC, V.*

$$ 🏨 **Romae.** In the better part of the Termini Station neighborhood, the Romae has the advantages of a strategic location—it's within walking distance of many sights, and handy to bus and subway lines. The pictures of Rome in the small lobby and breakfast room, the luminous white walls and light-wood furniture in the rooms, and the bright little baths all have a fresh look. Amenities such as satellite TV, in-room safe, and hair dryer are unusual for a hotel of this price. There are special rates and services for families. ⊠ *Via Palestro 49, Termini 00185* ☎ *06/ 4463554* 🖷 *06/4463914* ⊕ *www.hotelromae.com* ➷ *32 rooms* ⚲ *Restaurant, in-room safes, minibars, cable TV, bar, parking (fee), no-smoking rooms; no a/c in some rooms* ▭ *AE, DC, MC, V.*

$$ 🏨 **Siviglia.** You are transported back to a more opulent era in this 19th-century mansion in the quieter residential fringe of the Stazione Termini area. Like the several embassies in the neighborhood, it has bright flags flying at the entrance. Inside, Venetian glass chandeliers and antique re-

production furniture give the lounges considerable character; rooms are simpler, with a light, airy touch. ✉ *Via Gaeta 12, Termini 00185* ☎ *06/4441197* 🖷 *06/4441195* 🖅 *42 rooms* ♨ *Bar* ⊟ *AE, MC, V.*

$–$$ ▦ **Morgana.** Step into the richly marbled lobby and comfortable lounges (smoking and no-smoking) with antique accents, and experience elegance at its most cordial. Rooms are decorated with fine fabrics and plush carpeting. The location is convenient to the Stazione Termini. ✉ *Via Filippo Turati 33, Termini 00185* ☎ *06/4467230* 🖷 *06/4469142* 🌐 *www.hotelmorgana.com* 🖅 *103 rooms, 2 suites* ♨ *In-room safes, minibars, cable TV, bar, laundry service, concierge, no-smoking rooms.* ⊟ *AE, DC, MC, V.*

$ ▦ **Adler.** This tiny pensione run by the same family for more than three decades provides a comfortable stay on a quiet street near the station for a very good price. Ideal for families, Adler has six spacious rooms that sleep three, four, or five, as well as a single and a double. Rooms are basic, but impeccably clean (owner Serena Biancalana sees to that). Worn but cozy chairs line the lobby, and in summer breakfast can be taken on the leafy courtyard balcony. ✉ *Via Modena 5, Termini 00184* ☎ *06/484466* 🖷 *06/4880940* 🖅 *8 rooms* ♨ *Bar* ⊟ *AE, DC, MC, V.*

★ $ ▦ **Des Artistes.** The three personable Riccioni brothers have transformed their hotel into one of the best in the Termini Station neighborhood in its price range, lavishing it with paintings, handsome furnishings in mahogany, attractive fabrics, and marble baths. There's a floor with 10 simpler rooms for travelers on a budget. ✉ *Via Villafranca 20, Termini 00185* ☎ *06/4454365* 🖷 *06/4462368* 🌐 *www.hoteldesartistes.com* 🖅 *40 rooms, 27 with bath* ♨ *In-room data ports, in-room safes, minibars, cable TV, bar, concierge, parking (fee); no smoking* ⊟ *AE, DC, MC, V.*

$ ▦ **Hotel Venezia.** It's unusual to find a low-priced hotel in Rome that's this *pretty*—16th-century wood tables and sideboards are set off by cozy matching armchairs and tapestries give the public areas the feel of an elegant country house (in miniature). Guest rooms are somewhat simpler but still a cut above other hotels in this price range. It's a few blocks from Termini, making it convenient to public transportation. ✉ *Via Varese 18, 00185* ☎ *06/4457101* 🖷 *06/4957687* 🌐 *www.hotelvenezia.com* 🖅 *60 rooms* ♨ *In-room safes, minibars, cable TV; no a/c in some rooms* ⊟ *AE, D, MC, V.*

$ ▦ **Italia.** Off Via Nazionale, this friendly, family-run hotel offers rooms with big windows, desks, parquet floors, and baths with faux-marble tiles. Satellite TV and a generous buffet breakfast help to make it a good value. Three rooms are triples. An eight-room annex across the street has high ceilings, double-glazed windows, and a slightly more upscale look. Ask for low August and winter rates. ✉ *Via Venezia 18, Termini 00184* ☎ *06/4828355* 🖷 *06/4745550* 🌐 *www.hotelitaliaroma.com* 🖅 *31 rooms* ♨ *Cable TV, parking (fee)* ⊟ *AE, DC, MC, V.*

Via Veneto

★ $$$$ ▦ **Eden.** A superlative hotel that combines dashing elegance and stunning vistas of Rome with the warmth of Italian hospitality, the Eden was once the preferred haunt of Hemingway, Ingrid Bergman, and Fellini. Antiques, sumptuous Italian fabrics, linen sheets, and marble baths are the essence of good taste. Views from the rooftop bar and terrace will take your breath away, and the hotel's top-floor restaurant, La Terrazza dell'Eden, merits raves, too. ✉ *Via Ludovisi 49, Via Veneto 00187* ☎ *06/478121* 🖷 *06/4821584* 🌐 *www.hotel-eden.it* 🖅 *112 rooms, 14 suites* ♨ *Restaurant, in-room safes, minibars, cable TV, gym, bar, laundry service, concierge, parking (fee), no-smoking rooms* ⊟ *AE, DC, MC, V* �🍽 *EP.*

$$$$ ▣ **Majestic.** In the 19th-century tradition of grand hotels, this establishment on Via Veneto·offers luxurious furnishings, spacious, light-filled rooms, and up-to-date accessories and white marble bathrooms. There are authentic antiques in the public rooms, and the excellent restaurant looks like a Victorian conservatory. The Ninfa grill-café on street level is an intimate spot for light meals and drinks. Many suites have whirlpool baths. ✉ *Via Veneto 50, 00187* ☎ *06/421441* 🖷 *06/4880984* ⊕ *www. hotelmajestic.com* ⇨ *100 rooms, 18 suites* ⟁ *2 restaurants, in-room safes, minibars, cable TV, bar, laundry service, concierge, parking (fee), no-smoking rooms* ⊟ *AE, DC, MC, V.*

$$$$ ▣ **Westin Excelsior.** Next-door to the American Embassy, the Excelsior is the hotel of choice for visiting diplomats, celebrities—and American business conferences. It's of the breed of old-fashioned hotels that really put the luxe in deluxe: every corner is lavished with mirrors, moldings, Oriental rugs, crystal chandeliers, and huge, baroque floral arrangements. Guest rooms have elegant drapery, marble baths, top-quality linens, and big, firm beds. ✉ *Via Veneto 125, 00187* ☎ *06/47081* 🖷 *06/4826205* ⊕ *www.westin.com/excelsiorrome* ⇨ *286 rooms, 35 suites* ⟁ *Restaurant, in-room safes, minibars, cable TV, indoor pool, gym, bar, laundry service, concierge, no-smoking rooms* ⊟ *AE, DC, MC, V* ⊙∣ *EP.*

$$$ ▣ **Victoria.** A 1950s-style luxury, reasonable rates, and impeccable management are the main features of this hotel near Via Veneto. Oriental rugs, oil paintings, and fresh flowers are scattered throughout the lobbies, and rooms are well furnished with armchairs and other amenities. American businesspeople, who prize the hotel's personalized service and restful atmosphere, are frequent guests. Some upper rooms and the roof terrace overlook the majestic pines of the Villa Borghese. ✉ *Via Campania 41, Via Veneto 00187* ☎ *06/473931* 🖷 *06/4871890* ⊕ *www. hotelvictoriaroma.com* ⇨ *110 rooms* ⟁ *Restaurant, in-room safes, minibars, cable TV, bar, meeting rooms* ⊟ *AE, DC, MC, V.*

★ **$$**   ▣ **La Residenza.** Mainly Americans frequent this cozy hotel in a converted town house near Via Veneto. Rooms are basic and comfortable (although single rooms are windowless), but the real charm of the hotel is found in its bar, terrace, and lounges (smoking and no-smoking) adorned with warm wallpaper and love seats. Rates include a generous American-style buffet breakfast and an in-house movie every night. ✉ *Via Emilia 22, Via Veneto 00187* ☎ *06/4880789* 🖷 *06/485721* ⊕ *www.thegiannettihotelsgroup.com* ⇨ *28 rooms* ⟁ *In-room safes, minibars, cable TV, bar, laundry service* ⊟ *AE, MC, V.*

Beyond the City Center

$$$$ ▣ **Cavalieri Hilton.** Though the Cavalieri is outside the city center, distance has its advantages, one of them being the magnificent view from the hotel's hilltop position (ask for a room facing the city). This hotel is an oasis of quiet good taste with a distinctive Italian flair. If you can tear yourself away from the gardens and pools, a courtesy shuttle bus to downtown Rome leaves every hour. Don't miss the acclaimed rooftop restaurant, La Pergola. ✉ *Via Cadlolo 101, Monte Mario 00136* ☎ *06/ 35091* 🖷 *06/35092241* ⊕ *www.cavalieri-hilton.com* ⇨ *357 rooms, 17 suites* ⟁ *2 restaurants, tennis court, 2 pools (1 indoor), health club, hair salon, spa, bar* ⊟ *AE, DC, MC, V.*

★ **$$$$**   ▣ **Castello della Castelluccia.** Just 10 miles from the hustle and bustle of Rome's city center, this beautifully renovated 12th-century castle is an oasis of calm set in a small wooded park. The original structure has been preserved intact, complete with crumbling watchtower (now a three-level suite); all that's missing is a medieval knight clinking down the echoing stone halls. Guest rooms are luxuriously appointed, with inlaid-wood antiques and four-poster beds; a few have marble fireplaces, and two have giant, tiled hot-tub alcoves. There's shuttle bus service to central Rome. ⊠ *Via Carlo Cavino, Località La Castelluccia, 00123* ☎ *06/ 30207041* 🖷 *06/30207110* 🌐 *www.lacastelluccia.com* 📼 *18 rooms, 6 suites* ☼ *Restaurant, room service, in-room data ports, minibars, cable TV, pool, spa, horseback riding, bar, laundry service, meeting room, free parking, some pets allowed* ▭ *AE, D, MC, V.*

NIGHTLIFE & THE ARTS

The Arts

Updated by
Giovanna
Dunmall

Rome has a varied and vibrant cultural life, with music, dance, theater, film, and socializing opportunities for every taste. Trends and performance offerings change constantly, so the best way to take stock of the leisure activities at hand is to consult one of the many local publications devoted to the subject. You'll find comprehensive listings in English, along with handy bus and metro information, in the back of the weekly *roma c'è* booklet. A new issue is on sale at newsstands every Wednesday. The monthly *Time Out Roma* gives comprehensive event schedules as well as editors' picks; listings are mainly in Italian (with a small summary in English) but are easy to decipher. Schedules of events are also published in daily newspapers; pick up *Trovaroma,* the weekly entertainment guide published in Italian every Thursday as a supplement to the daily newspaper *La Repubblica.* The monthly *Where* magazine is distributed free at hotels and restaurants. An English-language biweekly, *Wanted in Rome,* is sold at central newsstands and has good listings of events.

Dance

The **Rome Opera Ballet** performs at the **Teatro dell'Opera** (⊠ Piazza Beniamino Gigli 8, Termini ☎06/481601; 06/48160255 tickets), often with leading international guest stars. Rome is regularly visited by classical and modern ballet companies from Russia, the United States, and Europe; performances are at the Teatro dell'Opera, **Teatro Olimpico** (⊠ Piazza Gentile da Fabriano 17, Stadio Olimpico ☎ 06/3265991), or one of the open-air venues in summer. Small dance companies from Italy and abroad perform in various places; check concert listings for details.

Film

A few theaters in the center reserve one night a week for original-language movies: check listings in *roma c'è.* Tickets range in price from €4.50 for matinees and some weekdays up to €8 for weekend evenings. The three-screen **Pasquino** (⊠ Piazza Sant'Egidio 10, Trastevere ☎ 06/ 5815208) shows exclusively original-language films, mainly in English. The **Metropolitan** (⊠ Via del Corso 7, Piazza del Popolo ☎ 06/32600500) has four screens, with one dedicated to English-language films from September to June; its location just off Piazza del Popolo makes it convenient for a post-shopping rest. The five-screen **Warner Village Moderno** (⊠Piazza della Repubblica 45–46, Termini ☎06/47779202) is convenient to the train station.

Music

CLASSICAL There's a wide variety of classical music concerts held at numerous venues large and small throughout Rome, including churches. Christmastime, in particular, is a busy concert season in Rome. Depending on the venue, tickets run from about €8 to €30. Rome's brand new state-of-the-art **Auditorium-Parco della Musica** (⊠ Via de Coubertin 15, Flaminio ☎ 06/ 80241350), a 10-minute tram-ride from Piazza del Popolo, has three halls with perfect acoustics and a large courtyard used for concerts and other events. Of the larger classical music companies, one principal concert series is organized year-round by the **Accademia di Santa Cecilia** (concert hall and box office ⊠ Via della Conciliazione 4, San Pietro ☎ 06/68801044). In summer the Accademia moves into one of the most spectacular and enchanting outdoor stages in the world, the ancient **Terme di Caracalla** (⊠ Via delle Terme di Caracalla 52). The **Accademia Filarmonica Romana** (⊠ Via Flaminia 118, Stadio Olimpico ☎ 06/3201752; 06/3265991 tickets) has concerts at the Teatro Olimpico. **Istituzione Universitaria dei Concerti** (⊠ Aula Magna, Piazzale Aldo Moro 5, San Lorenzo ☎ 06/3610051) offers small concerts with music ranging from swing to Bach. The internationally respected **Oratorio del Gonfalone** (⊠ Via del Gonfalone 32/a, Campo de' Fiori ☎ 06/6875952) series focuses on baroque music. **Il Tempietto** (☎ 06/87131590 ⊕ www.tempietto.it) organizes classical music concerts indoors in winter and in the atmospheric settings of Teatro Marcello and Villa Torlonia in summer.

Many small concert groups perform in cultural centers and churches, and many such concerts are free, including all performed in Catholic churches, where a special ruling permits only religious music. Look for posters outside churches announcing concerts, particularly at the church of **Sant'Ignazio** (⊠ Piazza Sant'Ignazio, Pantheon ☎ 06/6794560), which often hosts concerts in a spectacularly frescoed setting.

ROCK, POP & JAZZ Pop, jazz, and world music concerts are frequent, especially in summer, although even performances by big-name stars may not be well advertised. Many of the bigger-name acts perform outside the center, so it's worth asking about transportation *before* you buy your tickets. Tickets for major events are usually handled by **Orbis** (⊠ Piazza Esquilino 37, Santa Maria Maggiore ☎ 06/4744776). **Box Office** (⊠ Viale Giulio Cesare 88, San Pietro ☎ 06/37500375) sells concert tickets from Monday to Saturday. **Hello Ticket** (⊠ Termini station ☎ 06/47825710), sells tickets to concerts as well as theater and other cultural events.

Opera

Rome's opera season runs from November or December to May, and performances are staged in the **Teatro dell'Opera** (⊠ Piazza Beniamino Gigli 8, Termini ☎ 06/481601; 06/48160255 tickets). Prices range from about €16 to €120 for regular performances; they can go much higher for an opening night or an appearance by an internationally acclaimed guest singer. Standards may not always measure up to those set by Milan's fabled La Scala, but, despite strikes and shortages of funds, most performances are respectable. In summer the Teatro dell'Opera stages performances in various outdoor venues, such as Piazza del Popolo. Small, private companies hold sporadic performances of the classics in venues ranging from school auditoriums to church courtyards. **New Mendelflor Music** (☎ 06/21707618) usually has something in production. The church of **San Paolo entro le Mura** (⊠ Via Nazionale, corner Via Napoli, Termini ☎ 06/4826926) hosts operas and concerts.

Nightlife

La Dolce Vita notwithstanding, Rome's nightlife is not the world's most exciting, though discos, live-music spots, and quiet late-night bars are easy to find. In keeping with the changing times, the "flavor of the month" factor is at work here, too, and many places fade into oblivion after their 15 minutes of fame. The best sources for an up-to-date list of late-night spots are *roma c'è* and *Where,* but if you'd prefer to see where the night takes you, head to Trastevere or the area around Piazza Navona, both filled with bars, restaurants, and people after dark. In summer, all discos and many bars and music clubs close to beat the heat (although some simply relocate to the beach, where many Romans spend their summer nights). The city-sponsored Estate Romana (Rome Summer) festival takes over, lighting up hot city nights with concerts, bars, and discos, all in the open air. Pick up the Roma Estate event guide at newsstands.

Bars

English- and Irish-style pubs have long been a prominent part of the bar scene in Rome, among Italians and foreigners alike. **Trinity College** (⊠ Via del Collegio Romano 6, Piazza Venezia ☎ 06/6786472) is one of the most cosmopolitan bars in town. It has two floors of university-style pub trappings (and Italian snacks all day), with an old-school look and convivial music and drinking 'til 3 AM. The granddaddy of Rome's authentic Hibernian-style pubs, **Fiddler's Elbow** (⊠ Via dell'Olmata 43, Termini ☎ 06/4872110) encourages singing and good *craic* (lively chat).

So where do you go for a cocktail? **Bar della Pace** (⊠ Via della Pace 5, Piazza Navona ☎ 06/6861216) has been the ultratrendy people-watching cocktail bar of choice since time immemorial. **Bar del Fico** (⊠ Piazza del Fico 26, Piazza Navona ☎ 06/6865205) is a down-to-earth, authentically Roman alternative to Bar della Pace around the corner, but expect huge crowds on weekend and summer nights. For a trendy, sophisticated scene, try **BarBar** (⊠ Via Crescenzio 18, San Pietro ☎ 06/68308435), a lounge with ambient music and a cigar room. If you can squeeze in, **Taverna del Campo** (⊠ Campo de' Fiori 16 ☎ 06/6874402) is the place to go for wine and tasty hors d'oeuvres. For that essential predinner aperitivo, head for the buzzing **Friends** (⊠ Piazza Trilussa 34, Trastevere ☎ 06/5816111) across the Tiber from the historic center.

Music Clubs

Jazz, folk, pop, and Latin music clubs are flourishing in Rome, particularly in Trastevere and Testaccio. Jazz clubs are especially popular, and talented local groups may be joined by visiting musicians from other countries. As admission, many clubs require that you buy a membership card, often valid a month, at a cost of €6 and up. On weekend nights it's a good idea to reserve a table in advance no matter where you're going.

Just behind the Vatican Museums, **Alexanderplatz** (⊠ Via Ostia 9, San Pietro ☎ 06/39742171), Rome's most famous jazz club, has a bar and a restaurant and features live jazz and blues played nightly by both local and internationally known musicians. **La Palma** (⊠ Via Giuseppe Mirri 35, Tiburtino ☎ 06/43599029) is the venue favored by experimental jazz musicians. It's near the Tiburtina metro stop. **Big Mama** (⊠ Vicolo San Francesco a Ripa 18, Trastevere ☎ 06/5812551) presents live blues, R&B, African, jazz, and rock. Latin rhythms are the specialty at **No Stress Brasil** (⊠ Via degli Stradivari 35, Trastevere ☎ 06/5813249), where there's a Brazilian orchestra from Tuesday to Saturday. Monday is karaoke night.

In trendy Testaccio, **Caffè Latino** (⊠ Via Monte Testaccio 96, Testaccio ☎ 06/57288556) is a vibrant Roman locale that has live music (mainly Latin) almost every night, followed by recorded soul, funk, and '70s and '80s revival; it's closed Monday. **Il Locale** (⊠ Vicolo del Fico 3, Piazza Navona ☎ 06/6879075), closed Monday, pulls in a lively crowd for Italian rock. **The Place** (⊠ Via Alberico II 27–29, San Pietro ☎ 06/68307137) offers a mixture of live funk, latin, and jazz sounds, accompanied by excellent fusion cuisine.

Nightclubs

Most clubs open about 10:30 PM and charge an entrance fee of about €20, which may include the first drink; subsequent drinks cost about

€10. Most clubs are closed Monday, and all those listed here close in summer, some opening instead at the beaches of Ostia or Fregene. The most lively areas for clubs with a younger clientele are the more gritty working-class districts of Testaccio and Ostiense. **Gilda** (✉ Via Mario de' Fiori 97, Piazza di Spagna ☎ 06/6784838) is a longtime favorite with the slightly older rich and (sometimes) famous set for dinner and disco dancing. Jackets are required for men. **Bella Blu** (✉ Via Luciani 21, Parioli ☎ 06/3230490) is an exclusive club that caters to Rome's thirtysomething elite.

One of Rome's first discos, **Piper** (✉ Via Tagliamento 9, Piazza Fiume ☎06/8414459) is still a magnet for young movers and shakers who favor disco and house beats and spectacular light effects. It's open Saturday and Sunday nights only. A young crowd frequents the row of discos on Via di Monte Testaccio. Among them, **Caruso** (✉ Via di Monte Testaccio 36, Testaccio ☎ 06/5745019) is a club that has proven its staying power; it's a Latin alternative to the many rock clubs that line the strip. **Alibi** (✉ Via di Monte Testaccio 39, Testaccio ☎ 06/5743448) is a multilevel complex that caters to a mixed gay and straight crowd. **Goa** (✉Via Libetta 13, Testaccio ☎06/5748277) is among Rome's most trendy clubs. You can listen to hip-hop, tribal, and house played by some of Europe's most touted DJs. Decor takes its inspiration from Southeast Asia, with incense, exotic artifacts, and slide projections. **Suite** (✉ Via degli Orti di Trastevere 1, Trastevere ☎ 06/5861888) is an inspired reproduction of a luxurious, futuristic hotel suite. On Wednesday, Studio 54 night has a frivolous '70s and '80s theme, drawing a crowd that tends to be in the early thirties. The **Ex Magazzini** (✉ Via dei Magazzini Generali 8 bis, Ostiense ☎ 06/5758040) is a happening disco bar that offers a mix of live and DJ sets and hosts a vintage market on Sunday. The under-25 crowd lets loose to indie rock and weekend live shows at postindustrial **Black Out** (✉ Via Saturnia 18, San Giovanni ☎ 06/70496791). **La Maison** (✉ Vicolo dei Granari 4, Piazza Navona ☎ 06/6833312), provides three distinct dance environments, all very of-the-moment.

SPORTS & THE OUTDOORS

Basketball

Updated by Giovanna Dunmall

Professional basketball is played, usually on Sunday, from October through March at the **Palazzetto dello Sport** (✉ Viale Tiziano, Flaminio ☎ 06/36856552).

Biking

You can rent a bike at **Collalti** (✉ Via del Pellegrino 82, Campo de' Fiori ☎ 06/68801084), closed Monday, which is also a reliable bike-repair shop. **St. Peter Moto** (✉ Via di Porta Castello 43, San Pietro ☎ 06/6875714) is a good place to rent scooters as well as bikes.

Golf

Nonmembers are welcome in these clubs, all with 18-hole courses, so long as they can show membership cards of their home golf or country clubs. The oldest golf club in Italy, dating from 1903, is **Circolo del Golf di Roma** (✉ Via Appia Nuova 716/a, Appia ☎ 06/7803407), known popularly as Acquasanta for its mineral-water fountains; it's closed Saturday–Monday. The most conveniently located golf club in the Rome area (it's a 10-minute drive from the airport) is the **Golf Club Parco de' Medici** (✉ Viale Parco de' Medici 165, Magliana ☎ 06/6553477); it's closed Tuesday. **Country Club Castelgandolfo** (✉ Via di Santo Spirito 13, Castelgandolfo ☎ 06/9312301) is picturesque and hilly. The **Circolo Golf di**

Fioranello (⌧ Via della Falcognana 61, Appia Nuova ☎ 06/7138213), closed Wednesday, is at Santa Maria delle Mole, off Via Appia Nuova. **Olgiata Golf Club** (⌧ Largo dell'Olgiata 15, Cassia-Olgiata ☎ 06/30889141), closed Monday, is one of Rome's largest and most prestigious clubs.

Health Clubs

Day passes at all of the facilities here cost between €26 and €35. The **Cavalieri Hilton** (⌧ Via Cadlolo 101, Monte Mario ☎ 06/35091) has a running path on its grounds as well as outdoor and indoor pools, two clay tennis courts, and a luxurious spa, fitness center, and hair salon, all open to nonguests. The **Sheraton Roma** (⌧ Viale del Pattinaggio 100, EUR ☎ 06/54531) has a heated outdoor pool, a tennis court, two squash courts, a sauna, and a fitness center. The **Sheraton Golf** (⌧ Viale Parco de' Medici 167, Magliana ☎ 06/658588) has a fitness center and 27 holes of golf. Four tennis courts, an outdoor swimming pool, sauna, steam room, and a gym are available at the **Crowne Plaza Rome St. Peter's** (⌧ Via Aurelia Antica 415, Aurelia Antica ☎ 06/66420). The **Roman Sport Center** (⌧ Via del Galoppatoio 33, Via Veneto ☎ 06/3201667) is a vast full-fledged health club next to the underground parking lot in Villa Borghese; it has two swimming pools, a gym, aerobic workout areas, squash courts, and saunas. **Roman Sport Center 2** (⌧ Largo Somalia 60, Parioli ☎ 06/86212411) is an offshoot with fewer facilities.

Horseback Riding

There are numerous riding clubs in Rome. The most central is the **Centro Ippico Villa Borghese** (⌧ Via del Galoppatoio 23, Via Veneto ☎ 06/3200487). **Società Ippica Romana** (⌧ Via Monti della Farnesina 18, Stadio Olimpico ☎ 06/3240592) was the first riding club to open in Rome and has large outdoor facilities and excellent instructors. The **Circolo Ippico Olgiata** (⌧ Largo dell'Olgiata 15, Cassia-Olgiata ☎ 06/30888043) is outside the city on residential Via Cassia.

The **International Riding Show,** held in May, draws a stylish crowd to the amphitheater of Piazza di Siena in Villa Borghese. The competition is stiff, and the program features a cavalry charge staged by the dashing mounted corps of the *carabinieri* (military police). Check with the **tourist office** (⌧ Via Parigi 5, Termini ☎ 06/36004399) for details.

Running

The best bet for running in central Rome is the **Villa Borghese,** with an approximately ⅔-km (½-mi) circuit of the Pincio, among the marble statuary. A longer run in the park itself might include a loop around Piazza di Siena, a grass riding arena. Although most traffic is barred from Villa Borghese, government and police cars sometimes speed through. Be careful to stick to the side of the roads. For a long run away from all traffic, try the hilly and majestic **Villa Ada** in northern Rome in the upscale Parioli neighborhood. **Villa Doria Pamphilj** on the Janiculum is a beautiful spot for a run south of the city. History-loving runners should do as the chariot horses did and run at the old **Circus Maximus.** A standard oval track open to runners is in the park flanked by the **Via delle Terme di Caracalla.**

Soccer

Italy's favorite spectator sport stirs passionate enthusiasm among partisans. Games are usually held on Sunday afternoons throughout the fall-to-spring season. The two home teams—Roma and Lazio—which are both in *Serie A* (the top division), play their home games in the **Stadio Olimpico** (⌧ Viale dello Stadio Olimpico ☎ 06/3237333), part of the Foro Italico complex built by Mussolini on the banks of the Tiber.

There's a chance of soccer tickets being on sale at the box office at game time, but it's a better idea to buy them in advance from **Lazio Point** (✉ Via Farini 34, Termini ☎ 06/4826688) to see the Lazio team play. Go to **Orbis** (✉ Piazza Esquilino 37, Termini ☎ 06/4744776) for tickets to see the Roma soccer team.

Swimming

The outdoor pool of the **Cavalieri Hilton** (✉ Via Cadlolo 101, Monte Mario ☎ 06/35091) is a summertime oasis open to nonguests for a fee of €40 on weekdays, €55 on weekends. A reasonably priced swimming option (€10 per day, €8 after 2 PM) is the **Piscina delle Rose** (✉ Viale America 20, EUR ☎ 06/5926717), a pleasant outdoor pool in leafy the EUR sub-urb and only a five-minute walk from EUR-Laurentina metro stop. The **Roman Sport Center** (✉ Via del Galoppatoio 33, Via Veneto ☎ 06/3201667) has two swimming pools. The entrance fee is €26 per day for nonmembers.

SHOPPING

Updated by
Giovanna
Dunmall

They say when in Rome to do as the Romans do—and the Romans love to shop. Shops are generally open from 9 or 9:30 to 1 and from 3:30 or 4 to 7 or 7:30. There's a tendency for shops in central districts to stay open all day, and hours are becoming more flexible throughout the city. Remember that many stores are closed Sunday, though this is changing, too, especially in the city center. With the exception of food stores, most stores also close on Monday morning from September to mid-June and Saturday afternoon from mid-June through August. You can save some money taking advantage of the Tax-Free for Tourists VAT tax refunds, available at most large stores for purchases over €155. Or hit Rome in late January and early February or in late July, when stores clean house with the justly famous biannual sales.

Bargains

You can often find good buys in knitwear and silk scarves at stands on the fringes of outdoor food markets. Bargaining is still an art at the **Porta Portese** flea market and is routine when purchasing anything from a street vendor. On **Via Cola di Rienzo** there are stands selling everything from CDs to handicrafts. The market at **Via Sannio** (San Giovanni in Laterano) features job lots of designer shoes and stalls selling new and used clothing at bargain prices; it's a great place to hunt for used leather jackets. Hours are weekdays 8–2, Saturday 8–5. The morning market in **Piazza Testaccio,** in the heart of the neighborhood of the same name, is known for stands selling last season's designer shoes at a third of the original price or less.

Department Stores & Malls

Italian department stores have virtually nothing in common with their American and English cousins; most of them are much smaller and do not carry the same variety merchandise. Still, they're worth a stop if you're looking for something in a hurry. **Rinascente** (✉ Via del Corso 189, near Piazza Colonna Trevi ☎ 06/6797691 ✉ Piazza Fiume, Salario ☎ 06/8841231) sells clothing and accessories only in its main store. Its Piazza Fiume branch has the same stock, plus furniture and housewares. Both stores are open Monday–Saturday 9–9, Sunday 10:30–8. **Coin** (✉ Piazzale Appio 7, near San Giovanni in Laterano, Colosseo ☎ 06/7080020 ✉ Via Mantova 1/b Salario ☎ 06/8416279) carries a large and attractive collection of housewares as well as fashions for men and women, and

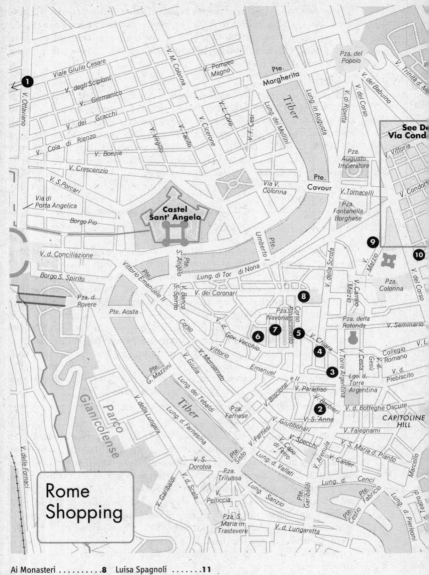

Rome Shopping

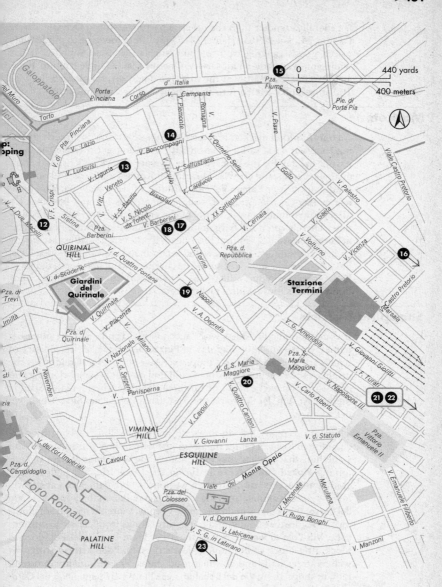

440 yards

400 meters

is generally trendier than the other department stores. **Oviesse** (⊠ Via Candia 74, San Pietro ☎ 06/39743518) offers low-end to moderately priced goods ranging from bathing suits to first-aid supplies; it has while-you-wait shoe-repair service. **Cinecittà Due** (⊠ Viale Palmiro Togliatti 2 ☎ 06/7220910) was the first of Rome's several megamalls, with 100 stores; take Metro A to the Subaugusta or Cinecittà stops.

Markets

All outdoor food markets are open Monday–Saturday from early morning to about 1 PM (a bit later on Saturday), but get there in the early part of the day for the best selection. Beware of pickpockets, and don't go if you can't stand crowds. Downtown Rome's most colorful outdoor food market is at **Campo de' Fiori**, south of Piazza Navona. The **Trionfale market** (⊠ Via Andrea Doria, San Pietro) is big and bustling; it's about a five-minute walk north of the entrance to the Vatican Museums. There's room for bargaining at the Sunday-morning flea market at **Porta Portese** (⊠ Via Ippolito Nievo, Trastevere); it offers seemingly endless rows of dealers in new and secondhand clothing, bootleg CDs, old furniture, car stereos of suspicious origin, and all manner of old junk. Keep an eye on your wallet—the crowds and money changing hands draw Rome's most skillful pickpockets.

Shopping Districts

If your shopping list starts with Gucci, Prada, Fendi, and the other big names, start your shopping day at **Piazza di Spagna,** in the vicinity of which are most of fashion's more exclusive shops. **Via Condotti** is the neighborhood's central axis, but you'll find elegant designer clothing and accessories on every block of this area, bordered by Piazza di Spagna on the east, Via del Corso on the west, from Piazza San Silvestro to Via della Croce.

There are so many hole-in-the-wall boutiques selling top-quality merchandise in Rome's center that even just wandering, you're sure to find something that catches your eye. Shops along **Via Campo Marzio** and adjoining **Piazza San Lorenzo in Lucina** stock eclectic and high-quality clothes and accessories, although without the big names and at slightly lower prices. Running from Piazza Venezia to Piazza del Popolo lies **Via del Corso,** the center's main shopping avenue, more than a mile of clothing, shoes, leather goods, and home furnishings from classic to cutting-edge. **Via Cola di Rienzo,** across the Tiber from Piazza del Popolo, has block after block of boutiques, shoe stores, and department stores, as well as street stalls and gourmet food shops. For top-quality antiques, look in shops along **Via del Babuino,** near Piazza di Spagna. **Via dei Coronari,** across the Tiber from Castel Sant'Angelo, has quirkier antiques and home boutiques. Via Giulia and surrounding streets are good bets for decorative arts. Should your gift list include religious souvenirs, look for everything from rosaries to Vatican golf balls at the shops between Piazza San Pietro and **Borgo Pio.** Liturgical vestments and statues of saints make for good window-shopping on **Via dei Cestari** near the Pantheon. **Via Nazionale** is a good bet for affordable fashions, including shoes, bags, and gloves. Since its refurbishment for the Jubilee in the year 2000, **Termini** station has become a good one-stop place for most shopping needs. Its 60-plus underground shops are open 'til 10 PM and include clothing, cosmetics, eyewear, and food stores as well as an Upim department store on ground level.

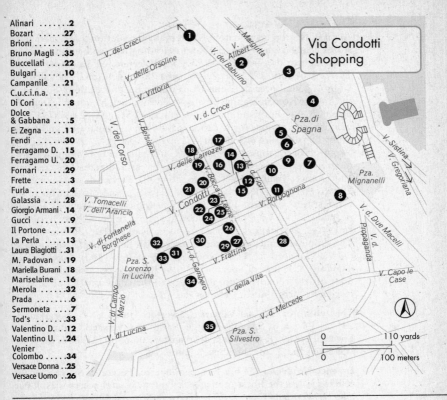

Specialty Stores

Antiques & Prints

For old prints and antiques, **Tanca** (⊠ Salita dei Crescenzi 12, Pantheon ☎ 06/6875272) is a good hunting ground. Early photographs of Rome and views of Italy from the archives at **Alinari** (⊠ Via Alibert 16/a, Piazza di Spagna ☎ 06/6792923) make memorable souvenirs. **Nardecchia** (⊠ Piazza Navona 25 ☎ 06/6869318) is reliable for prints. Stands in **Piazza della Fontanella Borghese** sell prints and old books.

Crafts & Gifts

For fine pottery, handwoven textiles, and other handicrafts, **Myricae** (⊠ Piazza del Parlamento 38, Pantheon ☎ 06/6873742) has a good selection. A bottle of liqueur, jar of marmalade, or bar of chocolate handmade by Cistercian monks in several monasteries in Italy makes an unusual, tasty gift to take home; pick from among these and other goodies at **Ai Monasteri** (⊠ Corso Rinascimento 72, Piazza Navona ☎ 06/68802783). Herbal and floral soaps, lotions, perfumes, and potpourri are easily carried gifts for yourself or a friend and can be found at the Rome branch of Florence's historic apothecary, the **Officina Farmaceutica di Santa Maria Novella** (⊠ Corso Rinascimento 47, Piazza Navona ☎ 06/6872446). Pricey **C.u.c.i.n.a.** (⊠ Via Mario de' Fiori 65, Piazza di Spagna ☎06/6791275) is one of the best kitchen-supply stores in town. At **Spazio Sette** (⊠ Via dei Barbieri 7, Campo de' Fiori ☎ 06/68804261) you'll find objects and furniture for the kitchen, living room, and bathroom from the biggest names in Italian and international design, for sale in a striking frescoed 17th-century palazzo.

Designer Clothing

All of Italy's top fashion houses and many international designers have stores near Piazza di Spagna. Rome's leading Roman couturier, recognized the world over by the "V" logo, is **Valentino** (⊠ **Valentino Donna** ⊠ Via Condotti 13, Piazza di Spagna ☎ 06/6795862 ⊠ **Valentino Uomo** ⊠ Via Bocca di Leone 15, Piazza di Spagna ☎ 06/6783656). If the king of Roman high fashion is Valentino, then its queen is **Laura Biagiotti** (⊠ Via Borgognona 43–44, Piazza di Spagna ☎ 06/6791205), who is justly famous for luxurious knitwear, silk separates, and loose-fitting dresses. **Dolce & Gabbana** (⊠ Piazza di Spagna 82 ☎ 06/6792294), a spin-off of the top-of-the-line D&G store on Via Borgognona, shows the trendiest designer fashions in casual wear and accessories for men and women. **Fendi** (⊠ Via Borgognona 40, Piazza di Spagna ☎ 06/696661) has several stores in Rome; all stock a wide assortment of the Fendi sisters' signature furs and print fashions. Sleek, vaguely futuristic **Prada** (⊠ Via Condotti 92, Piazza di Spagna ☎ 06/6790897) has two entrances, the one for the men's boutique is to the left of the women's. The shop is as understated and elegant as the designs at **Giorgio Armani** (⊠ Via Condotti 77, Piazza di Spagna ☎ 06/6991460). **Gucci** (⊠ Via Condotti 8, Piazza di Spagna ☎ 06/6790405) often has lines out the door of its two-story shop, testament to the continuing popularity of its rich leathers and edgy clothes designs.

The two stores of **Gianni Versace** (⊠ **Versace Uomo** ⊠ Via Borgognona 24–25, Piazza di Spagna ☎ 06/6795037 ⊠ **Versace Donna** ⊠ Via Bocca di Leone 26–27, Piazza di Spagna ☎ 06/6780521) offer the rock-star styles that made the house's name.

MEN'S CLOTHING **Ermenegildo Zegna** (⊠ Via Borgognona 7/e, Piazza di Spagna ☎ 06/6789143) has the finest in men's elegant styles and accessories. **Il Portone** (⊠ Via delle Carrozze 71, Piazza di Spagna ☎ 06/6793355) embodies a tradition in custom shirt-making. For decades a man was a fashion flop without Portone's classic cuts and signature stripes in his closet. **Brioni** (⊠ Via Barberini 79, Piazza di Trevi ☎ 06/484517 ⊠ Via Condotti 21, Piazza di Spagna ☎ 06/6783428) has a well-deserved reputation as one of Italy's top tailors. In addition to impeccable custom-made apparel, you can suit up in ready-to-wear garments.

WOMEN'S CLOTHING **Galassia** (⊠ Via Frattina 21, Piazza di Spagna ☎ 06/6797896) has expensive, extreme, and extravagant women's styles by Gaultier, Westwood, and Yamamoto—this is the place for feather boas and hats with ostrich plumes. **Mariselaine** (⊠ Via Condotti 70, Piazza di Spagna ☎ 06/6795817) is a top-quality women's fashion boutique. The garments at **Luisa Spagnoli** (⊠ Via del Tritone 30, Piazza di Trevi ☎ 06/69202220) are elegant but contemporary, and they go to large sizes. **Mariella Burani** (⊠ Via Bocca di Leone 28, Piazza di Spagna ☎ 06/6790630) mixes classy chic with judicious high-fashion overtones. **Arsenale** (⊠ Via del Governo Vecchio 64, Piazza Navona ☎ 06/6861380) is the boutique of designer Patrizia Pieroni, who creates funky—sometimes outrageous—clothes using from luxurious fabrics. If you're in the market for luxurious lingerie, **La Perla** (⊠ Via Condotti 79, Piazza di Spagna ☎ 06/69941934) has what you're looking for. **Marisa Padovan** (⊠ Via delle Carrozze 81, Piazza di Spagna ☎ 06/6793946) shows exclusive and expensive lingerie.

Embroidery & Linens

Frette (⊠ Piazza di Spagna 11 ☎ 06/6790673) is a Roman institution for luxurious linens. **Venier Colombo** (⊠ Via Frattina 79, Piazza di Spagna

☎ 06/6787705) has a selection of exquisite lace goods, including lingerie and linens. **Lavori Artigianali Femminili** (✉ Via Capo le Case 6, Piazza di Spagna ☎ 06/6781100) offers delicately embroidered household linens, infants' and children's clothing, and blouses.

Jewelry & Silver Objects

What Cartier is to Paris, **Bulgari** (✉ Via Condotti 10, Piazza di Spagna ☎ 06/6793876) is to Rome; the shop's elegant display windows hint at what's beyond the guard at the door. **Buccellati** (✉ Via Condotti 31, Piazza di Spagna ☎ 06/6790329) is a tradition-rich Florentine jewelry house renowned for its silver work; it ranks with Bulgari for quality and reliability. You'll find a tempting selection of small silver objects at **Fornari & Fornari** (✉ Via Frattina 133, Piazza di Spagna ☎ 06/6780105). **Bozart** (✉ Via Bocca di Leone 4, Piazza di Spagna ☎ 06/6781026) features dazzling costume jewelry in keeping with the latest fashions.

Shoes & Leather Accessories

For the latest styles in handbags and a selection of scarves and costume jewelry (all Italian made) at reasonable prices, go to **Furla** (✉ Piazza di Spagna 22 ☎ 06/69200363), which has a number of downtown stores. **Ferragamo Donna** (✉ Via Condotti 73, Piazza di Spagna ☎ 06/6791565) has the ultimate in women's high-fashion shoes, handbags, and scarves. **Ferragamo Umo** (✉ Via Condotti 65 ☎ 06/6781130) sells classic shoes for men. For a vast selection of affordable, high-quality Italian-made bags and accessories sold in a stylish setting, head for **Regal** (✉ Via Nazionale 254, Termini ☎ 06/4884893). Eccentric, handmade leather briefcases and handbags are available at **Claudio Sanò** (✉ Largo degli Osci 67/a, San Lorenzo ☎ 06/4469284), a shop well worth the detour to the vibrant San Lorenzo quarter east of Termini. **Volterra Vague** (✉ Via Barberini 102, Piazza di Trevi ☎ 06/4819315) is well stocked and offers a wide selection of handbags at moderate prices. For gloves as pretty as Holly Golightly's, head to **Sermoneta** (✉ Piazza di Spagna 61 ☎ 06/6791960). **Di Cori** (✉ Piazza di Spagna 53 ☎ 06/6784439) has gloves in every color of the spectrum. **Merola** (✉ Via del Corso 143, Piazza di Spagna ☎ 06/6791961) carries a line of expensive, top-quality gloves and scarves. **Calzature Fausto Santini** (✉ Via Santa Maria Maggiore 165, Santa Maria Maggiore ☎ 06/4880934) is the place for colorful, offbeat, and ever-fashionable Santini shoes at half price. (The flagship store is on upmarket Via Frattina.) **Bruno Magli** (✉ Via del Gambero 1, Piazza di Spagna ☎ 06/6793802 ✉ Via Veneto 70 ☎ 06/42011671) is known for well-made shoes and matching handbags at both moderate and high prices. **Campanile** (✉ Via Condotti 58, Piazza di Spagna ☎ 06/6790731) has two floors of shoes in the latest, as well as classic, styles; they also sell other leather goods. **Tod's** (✉ Via Borgognona 45, Piazza di Spagna ☎ 06/6786828) might sound British, but the signature button-soled moccasins are strictly Italian made. This exclusive Tod's location carries every model and style as well as its line of handmade bags.

Silks & Fabrics

Fratelli Bassetti (✉ Corso Vittorio Emanuele II 73, Campo de' Fiori ☎ 06/6892326) has a vast selection of world-famous Italian silks and fashion fabrics in a rambling palazzo. **Aston** (✉ Via Boncompagni 27, Via Veneto ☎ 06/42871227) stocks couture-level fabrics for men and women. You can find some real bargains when *scampoli* (remnants) are on sale.

ROME A TO Z

To research prices, get advice from other travelers, and book travel arrangements, visit www.fodors.com.

AIRPORTS & TRANSFERS

Most international flights and all domestic flights arrive at Aeroporto Leonardo da Vinci, also known as Fiumicino, 30 km (19 mi) southwest of Rome. Some international and charter flights land at Ciampino, a civil and military airport 15 km (9 mi) southeast of Rome. To get to the city from Fiumicino by car, follow the signs for Rome on the expressway from the airport, which links with the GRA, the beltway around Rome. The direction you take on the GRA depends on where your hotel is, so get directions from the car-rental people at the airport. A taxi from Fiumicino to the center of town costs about €50, including *supplementi* (extra charges) for airport service and luggage, and the ride takes 30–40 minutes, depending on traffic. Private limousines can be hired at booths in the arrivals hall; they charge a little more than taxis but can take more passengers. Ignore gypsy drivers who approach you inside the terminal; stick to the licensed cabs, yellow or white, that wait by the curb. A booth inside the arrivals hall provides taxi information.

You have a choice of two trains to get to downtown Rome from Fiumicino Airport. Ask at the airport (at APT or train information counters) which train takes you closer to your hotel. The nonstop Airport-Termini express takes you directly to Track 22 at Stazione Termini, Rome's main train station, which is well served by taxis and is the hub of metro and bus lines. The ride to Termini takes 30 minutes; departures are every half hour beginning at 6:37 AM from the airport, with a final departure at 11:37 PM. From Termini to the airport, trains leave at 21 and 51 minutes past the hour. Tickets cost €8.80. FM1, the other airport train, runs from the airport to Rome and beyond, terminating in Monterotondo, a suburban town to the east. The main stops in Rome are at Trastevere, Ostiense, and Tiburtina stations; at each you can find taxis and bus and/or metro connections to other parts of Rome. This train runs from Fiumicino from 6:35 AM to 12:15 AM, with departures every 20 minutes, a little less frequently in off-hours. The ride to Tiburtina takes 40 minutes. Tickets cost €2.27. For either train buy your ticket at automatic vending machines. There are ticket counters at some stations (at Termini/Track 22, Trastevere, Tiburtina). Date-stamp the ticket at the gate before you board.

Airport Information Aeroporto Leonardo da Vinci ☎ 06/65951; English-language flight information 06/65953640 ⊕ www.adr.it. Ciampino ⊠ Via Appia Nuova ☎ 06/794941.

BUS TRAVEL TO & FROM ROME

There's no central bus terminal in Rome. COTRAL is the suburban bus company that connects Rome with outlying areas and other cities in the Lazio region. Long-distance and suburban buses terminate either near Tiburtina Station or near outlying metro stops such as Rebbibia and Anagnina. For COTRAL bus information, call weekdays 8 AM–6 PM.

FARES & SCHEDULES   **Bus Information** COTRAL ☎ 800/431784 toll free.

BUS TRAVEL WITHIN ROME

ATAC city buses and tram lines run from about 6 AM to midnight, with night buses (indicated N) on some lines. A 75-minute ticket costs €0.75 and a day pass €3.10. The compact electric buses of Lines 117 and 119 take routes through the center of Rome that can save lots of walking.

◪ Bus Information **ATAC** ☎ 800/431784 toll free.

CAR RENTAL
◪ Local Agencies **Avis** ✉ Via Sardenia 38 ☎ 06/42824728; Fiumicino Airport 06/650011531. **Europcar** ✉ Via Lombardia 7 ☎ 06/4871274; Fiumicino Airport 06/65010879. **Hertz** ✉ Via del Gallopatoio 33 ☎ 06/3216831; Fiumicino Airport 06/65011553. **Maggiore** ✉ Termini Station ☎ 06/4880049; Fiumicino Airport 06/65010678. **Thrifty** ✉ Termini Station ☎ 06/4747825; Fiumicino Airport 06/65010347.

CAR TRAVEL
The main access routes from the north are A1 (Autostrada del Sole) from Milan and Florence and the A12–E80 highway from Genoa. The principal route to or from points south, including Naples, is the A2. All highways connect with the Grande Raccordo Anulare (GRA), which channels traffic into the city center. Markings on the GRA are confusing: take time to study the route you need.

EMBASSIES & CONSULATES
◪ Australia **Australian Consulate** ✉ Via Alessandria 215, Piazza Fiume ☎ 06/852721.
◪ Canada **Canadian Consulate** ✉ Via Zara 30, Piazza Fiume ☎ 06/445981.
◪ New Zealand **New Zealand Consulate** ✉ Via Zara 28, Piazza Fiume ☎ 06/4417171.
◪ United Kingdom **U.K. Consulate** ✉ Via Venti Settembre 80/a, Via Veneto ☎ 06/14200001.
◪ United States **U.S. Consulate** ✉ Via Veneto 121, Via Veneto ☎ 06/46741.

EMERGENCIES
Farmacia Internazionale Capranica, Farmacia Internazionale Barberini, and Farmacia Cola di Rienzo are pharmacies that have some English-speaking staff. Most pharmacies are open 8:30–1 and 4–8; some are open all night. A schedule posted outside each pharmacy indicates the nearest pharmacy open during off-hours (afternoons, through the night, and Sunday). Dial ☎ 1100 for an automated list of three open pharmacies closest to the telephone from which you call. The hospitals listed below have English-speaking doctors. Rome American Hospital is about 30 minutes by cab from the center of town.
◪ Emergency Services **Ambulance** ☎ 118. **Police** ☎ 113. **Red Cross** ☎ 06/5510.
◪ Hospitals **Rome American Hospital** ✉ Via Emilio Longoni 69, Via Prenestina ☎ 06/22551 ⊕ www.rah.it. **Salvator Mundi International Hospital** ✉ Viale delle Mura Gianicolensi 66, Trastevere ☎ 06/588961 ⊕ www.smih.pcn.net.
◪ Pharmacies **Farmacia Cola di Rienzo** ✉ Via Cola di Rienzo 213, San Pietro ☎ 06/3243130. **Farmacia Internazionale Barberini** ✉ Piazza Barberini 49, Via Veneto ☎ 06/4825456. **Farmacia Internazionale Capranica** ✉ Piazza Capranica 96, Pantheon ☎ 06/6794680.

ENGLISH-LANGUAGE MEDIA
BOOKS English-language books in Rome are expensive; most are imported from England, so prices in Rome reflect the strong pound and shipping costs. The Anglo-American Bookstore and the Economy Book and Video Center have the widest selection of genres. The English Bookshop has a smaller selection but better prices. Trastevere's Corner Bookstore carries lots of offbeat new fiction and has a vast history section. For used books at lower prices, try the Open Door. At Feltrinelli International you can pick up novels and guide books in English as well.
◪ **Anglo-American Bookstore** ✉ Via della Vite 102, Piazza di Spagna ☎ 06/6795222 ⊕ www.aab.it. **Corner Bookstore** ✉ Via del Moro 45, Trastevere ☎ 06/5836942. **Economy Book and Video Center** ✉ Via Torino 136, Termini ☎ 06/4746877 ⊕ www.booksitaly.com. **The English Bookshop** ✉ Via di Ripetta 24B, Piazza di Spagna ☎ 06/3203301. **Feltrinelli International** ✉ Via Vittorio Emanuale Orlando 78/81, Termini ☎ 06/

4870171. **Lion Bookshop** ✉ Via dei Greci 33/36, Piazza di Spagna ☎ 06/32654007. **Open Door** ✉ Via della Lungaretta 23, Trastevere ☎ 06/5896478.

NEWSPAPERS &
MAGAZINES

The ubiquitous *International Herald Tribune* is published in Italy with a four-page *Italy Daily* insert, an English-language summary of main Italian news stories and local cultural events. Major English and American news magazines and a few daily papers are available at some newsstands, including those on Via Veneto, Via del Corso (at Via del Tritone), and Campo de' Fiori.

LODGING

APARTMENT &
VILLA RENTALS

For stays of a week or more, especially for families or groups of friends, an apartment or villa rental may be more convenient than a hotel. Always insist on photos, a map with indication of location, and a detailed description of the property. Homes International offers short- and long-term accommodations in Rome. Property International handles monthly and weekly rentals in Rome and Tuscany. The English-language biweekly *Wanted in Rome* lists private-party rentals.

▪ **Local Agents Homes International** ✉ Via Bissolati 20, Via Veneto 00187 ☎ 06/4881800 🖨 06/4881808. **Property International** ✉ Viale Aventino 79, Aventino 00153 ☎ 06/5743170 🖨 06/5743182.

▪ **Rental Listings Wanted in Rome** ⊕ www.wantedinrome.com.

MAIL & SHIPPING

▪ **Post Offices Main post office** ✉ Piazza San Silvestro 19, Piazza di Spagna ☎ 06/6798495.

OVERNIGHT
SERVICES

While DHL and UPS offices are far out of the city center, FedEx has walk-in service on Via Barberini; all three companies will pick up packages from anywhere in Rome.

▪ **Major Services DHL** (800/345345). **Federal Express** ✉ Via Barberini 115, Via Veneto ☎ 800/123800. **UPS** ☎ 800/877877.

MOPED TRAVEL

Zipping and careening through traffic on a *motorino* (moped) in downtown Rome is an attractive way to visit the city for some, but if you're risk averse, pass on it. If your impulses—and reflexes—are fast, you can join the craziness of Roman traffic by renting a moped and the mandatory helmet at numerous rental spots throughout the city. Be extremely careful of pedestrians when riding: Romans are casual jay-walkers and pop out frequently from between parked cars.

▪ **Moped Rentals Enjoy Rome** ✉ Via Marghera 8A, 00185 Termini Rome ☎ 06/4451843 ⊕ www.enjoyrome.com. **Happy Rent** ✉ Via Farini 3, Termini ☎ 06/4818185 ⊕ www.happyrent.it. **Scoot-a-Long** ✉ Via Cavour 302, Termini ☎ 06/6780206. **St. Peter's Motor Rent** ✉ Via di Porta Castello 43, San Pietro ☎ 06/6875714.

SAFETY

LOCAL SCAMS

A word of caution: "gypsy" children, who hang around sights popular with tourists throughout Europe, are rife in Rome and are adept pickpockets. Keep a close eye on your belongings when boarding the bus and subway, particularly at Termini Station. One modus operandi is to approach a tourist and proffer a piece of cardboard with writing on it. While the unsuspecting victim attempts to read the message *on* it, the children's hands are busy *under* it, trying to make off with purses or valuables. If you see such a group (recognizable by their unkempt appearance), do not even allow them near you—they are quick and know more tricks than you do. Also be aware of persons, usually young men, who ride by on motorbikes, grab the shoulder strap of your bag or camera, and step on the gas. Wear or carry your bag on the side away from the street edge of the sidewalk, or, best of all, wear a concealed money belt. Don't carry more money than you need, and don't carry your passport unless you need it to exchange money. A useful expression to ward off pesky panhandlers or vendors is "*Vai via!*" (Go away!).

WOMEN IN ROME   Foreign women can expect to attract extra attention from Italian men, but this is usually harmless flirtation, and rarely will become a safety issue. Do be careful of gropers on subways and buses, particularly on the metro and on buses 64 (Termini–Vatican) and 218 and 660 (Catacombs). They're known to take advantage of the cramped space to press up against women. React like the locals: forcefully and loudly.

SUBWAY TRAVEL
The metro (subway) is the easiest and fastest way to get around and there are stops near most of the main tourist attractions. Service begins at 5:30 AM, and the last trains leave the most distant station at 11:30 PM (on Saturday night, trains run until 12:30 AM). There are two lines—A and B—which intersect at Stazione Termini. The fare is €0.75.

TAXIS
Taxis in Rome do not cruise, but if empty (look for an illuminated TAXI sign on the roof) they will stop if you flag them down. Taxis wait at stands and can also be called by phone, in which case you're charged a bit more. The meter starts at €2.33 from 7 AM to 10 PM, at €3.36 on Sunday and holidays, and at €4.91 after 10 PM. Each piece of baggage will add an extra €2.03 to your fare. Use only licensed, metered yellow or white cabs, identified by a numbered shield on the side, an illuminated taxi sign on the roof, and a plaque next to the license plate reading SERVIZIO PUBBLICO. Avoid unmarked, unauthorized, unmetered gypsy cabs (numerous at airports and train stations), whose renegade drivers actively solicit your trade and may demand astronomical fares. Some taxis accept some credit cards, but you must specify when calling that you will pay that way.

🚖 Taxi Companies **Taxi** ☎ 06/5551, 06/3570, 06/4994, or 06/88177.

TOURS
BIKE TOURS   Enjoy Rome organizes all-day bike tours of Rome for small groups covering major sights and some hidden ones. Remember, Rome is famous for its seven hills; be prepared for a workout.

🚖 Fees & Schedules **Enjoy Rome** ⊠ Via Marghera 8A, 00185 Termini Rome ☎ 06/4451843 ⊕ www.enjoyrome.com.

BUS TOURS   American Express and CIT offer general orientation tours of the city, as well as specialized tours of particular areas such as the Vatican or Ancient Rome. *Stop-'n'-go City Tours* has English-speaking guides and the option of getting off and on at 14 key sites in the city. A day pass costs €12.

🚖 Fees & Schedules **American Express** ☎ 06/67641. **Appian Line** ☎ 06/487861. **ATAC** ☎ 800/431784. **CIT** ⊠ Piazza della Repubblica 64, Termini ☎ 06/4620311 ⊕ www.citonline. it. **Stop-'n'-go City Tours** ☎ 06/48905729

WALKING TOURS   All About Rome, American Express, Enjoy Rome, Scala Reale, Through Eternity, and Walks of Rome offer walking tours of the city and its sites.

🚖 Fees & Schedules **All About Rome** ☎ 06/7100823 ⊕ www.allaboutromewalks. netfirms.com. **American Express** ☎ 06/67641. **Enjoy Rome** ⊠ Via Marghera 8A, Termini 00185 ☎ 06/4451843 ⊕ www.enjoyrome.com. **Scala Reale** ⊠ Via dell'Olmata 30, Termini 00184 ☎ 06/4745673 or 800/732-2863 Ext. 4052 ⊕ www.scalareale.org. **Through Eternity** ☎ 06/7009336 ⊕ www.througheternity.com **Walks of Rome** ⊠ Via Urbana 38 Quirinale 00184 ☎ 06/484853

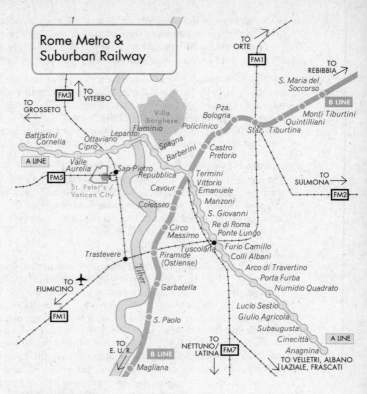

Rome Metro & Suburban Railway

TRAIN TRAVEL

Stazione Termini is Rome's main train terminal; the Tiburtina and Ostiense stations serve some long-distance trains, many commuter trains, and the FM1 line to Fiumicino Airport. Some trains for Pisa and Genoa leave Rome from, or pass through, the Trastevere Station. You can find English-speaking staff at the information office at Stazione Termini, or ask for information at travel agencies. You can purchase tickets up to two months in advance at the main stations or at most travel agencies. Lines at station ticket windows may be very long: you can save time by using the electronic ticket machines, which have instructions in English, or by buying your ticket at a travel agency. You can reserve a seat up to one day in advance at a travel agency or up to an hour in advance at a train station. Tickets for train rides within a radius of 100 km (62 mi) of Rome can be purchased at tobacco shops and at some newsstands, as well as at ticket machines on the main concourse. All train tickets must be date-stamped before you board, at the machine near the track, or you will be fined.

🚆 Train Information **Trenitalia** ☎ 166/105050; 892021 from outside Rome (a small service charge applies) 🌐 www.trenitalia.it.

TRANSPORTATION AROUND ROME

Although most of Rome's sights are in a relatively circumscribed area, the city is too large to be seen solely on foot. Take the metro (subway), a bus, or a taxi to the area you plan to visit, and expect to do a lot of walking once you're there. Wear a pair of comfortable, sturdy shoes to cushion the impact of the *sanpietrini* (cobblestones). Get away from the noise and polluted air of heavily trafficked streets by taking parallel streets whenever possible. You can get free city and transportation-route maps at municipal information booths; the transportation maps are probably more up-to-date than those you can buy at newsstands.

Rome's integrated public transportation system includes buses and trams (ATAC), metro and suburban trains and buses (COTRAL), and some other suburban trains (Trenitalia) run by the state railways. Try to avoid the rush hours (8–9, 1–2:30, 7–8), and beware of pickpockets and gropers. When purchasing tickets for excursions outside Rome on COTRAL buses or trains, buy a return ticket, too, to save time at the other end.

FARES & SCHEDULES A ticket valid for 75 minutes on any combination of buses and trams and one entrance to the metro costs €0.75. You are expected to date-stamp your ticket when you board the first vehicle, stamping it again when boarding for the last time within 75 minutes (the important thing is to stamp it the first time). Tickets for the public transit system are sold at tobacconists, newsstands, some coffee bars, ATMs positioned in metro stations and some bus stops, and at ATAC and COTRAL ticket booths (in some metro stations, on the lower concourse at Stazione Termini, and at a few main bus terminals). A BIG tourist ticket, valid for one day on all public transport, costs €3.10. A weekly ticket (Settimanale, also known as CIS) costs €12.40 and can be purchased only at ATAC booths.

TRAVEL AGENCIES
Local Agent Referrals **American Express** ☎ 06/67641. **Appian Line** ☎ 06/487861. **Carrani Tours** ✉ Via Vittorio Emanuele Orlando 95, Termini ☎ 06/4880510. **CIT** ✉ Piazza della Repubblica 64, Termini ☎ 06/4620311 ⊕ www.citonline.it.

VISITOR INFORMATION
Tourist Information **Tourist office** (Azienda di Promozione Turistica di Roma/APT) ✉ Via Parigi 5, Termini ☎ 06/48899255 ✆ Open Monday to Saturday 9–7 ✉ Aeroporto Leonardo da Vinci ☎ 06/65951 ✆ Open daily 8:15–7

LAZIO, ABRUZZO, AND MOLISE

OSTIA ANTICA, TIVOLI, PARCO NAZIONALE D'ABRUZZO

12

FODOR'S CHOICE

Cantina Palazzo dei Mercanti, restaurant, Viterbo

Locanda di Mirandolina, hotel, Tuscania

Ostia Antica

HIGHLY RECOMMENDED

RESTAURANTS   Enoteca La Torre, Viterbo

Elodia, L'Aquila

Il Grappolo, Tarquinia

La Torre di Lavello, Tuscania

Tre Re, Viterbo

SIGHTS   Castello, L'Aquila

Parco Nazionale d'Abruzzo

Tuscania

Villa Adriana, Tivoli

Villa d'Este, Tivoli

Updated by
Robin S.
Goldstein

PLAYGROUND OF THE ETRUSCANS, united under the Romans, and embellished by renaissance popes, Lazio towers culturally over its Apennine neighbors to the east. But all three regions in this imposing swathe across central Italy contain sites of undiluted charm. The dreamlike landscapes of Abruzzo and Molise are dotted with medieval castles and quaint villages, with many more remote areas begging for discovery. Fine cuisine and hospitality at highly affordable prices add to the appeal of these three lesser-known regions of central Italy.

For the better part of 2,000 years, the grandeur and the glory of Rome have obscured the constellation of attractions in the region around it. Yet exploring Lazio (Latium to the ancient Romans) can immeasurably broaden one's understanding of the Roman empire and its legacy. You can explore selected sights of Lazio on day trips from Rome; the result is a more superficial experience of the region's pleasures, but nonetheless it can be worthwhile. One of the easiest excursions from the capital takes you west 25 km (15 mi) to the sea, where tall pines stand among the well-preserved ruins of Ostia Antica, the main port of ancient Rome and an archaeological site that rivals Pompeii. A visit to Ostia Antica tells you more about the way the ancient Romans lived than the Roman Forum does.

The rolling landscape of Lazio along the coast northwest of Rome was once Etruscan territory, and at Cerveteri and Tarquinia it holds some intriguing reminders of a people who taught the ancient Romans a thing or two about religion, art, and a pleasurable way of life. The Etruscan sites here give you a very concrete impression of the people whose skilled artwork and artifacts are displayed at local museums. Deep in the countryside north of Rome, larger Viterbo has an intact medieval core and historic traces of its days as a papal stronghold interspersed with modern industry.

East of Rome lie some of the region's star sites, along a route that loops through the hills where ancient Romans built their summer resorts. At Tivoli, Hadrian's Villa shows you the scale of individual imperial Roman egos, while Villa d'Este demonstrates that Renaissance egos were no smaller. Eastward at Palestrina lies a vast sanctuary from ancient times. At Subiaco, St. Benedict founded the hermitage that gave rise to Western monasticism. Southeast of Rome are three romantic sites little known outside Italy: a castle at Sermoneta that once belonged to Cesare Borgia, a fairytale garden at Ninfa, and the seaside citadel of Sperlonga.

Still lands of shepherds and wolves, the mountainous regions of Abruzzo and Molise preserve much of their local traditions and culture. Craggy peaks, ruined castles, hill towns, and peasant life unchanged since the Middle Ages abound in both regions. Abruzzo's real treasure is its natural beauty, preserved pristinely in the Parco Nazionale d'Abruzzo. With its hiking trails, immense beech forests and wildlife, it's a must-see for nature lovers. Neighboring Molise, one of the smallest of the Italian regions and blissfully unravaged by tourist development, has astounding archaeological sites set against an impressive Apennine backdrop.

Exploring Lazio, Abruzzo & Molise

Most of Lazio's attractions are within striking distance of Rome and can be covered in day trips from the capital, but there's much to be said for staying overnight and appreciating the area after the day-trippers have moved on. If you intend to combine more than two sights in one day, then a car will be a necessity. For outlying Abruzzo and Molise the best months are May and June, when there's a profusion of spring flowers, though September and October also offer optimal traveling, hiking, and sightseeing conditions. L'Aquila lies in a frost pocket close to the Gran Sasso, the Apennines' highest peak, making traveling conditions sometimes treacherous in winter months. Whether bound for ski slopes or just driving through, you should always check road conditions and weather reports before setting out.

About the Restaurants & Hotels

Meal prices are generally a little lower in the rest of Lazio than in Rome, and good restaurants tend to attract large numbers from the capital on weekends. In Abruzzo and Molise, simplicity is the rule: the most satisfying meals are to be had at modest restaurants where often as not you won't find a menu, just daily specials prepared according to age-old traditions.

With relatively few exceptions (hotels at spas and beach and hill resorts such as Viterbo), accommodations in the region cater more to commercial travelers than to tourists. Public rooms and guest rooms tend to be functional and short on character, though adequate for an overnight. Peak periods, especially in mountain resorts, are the New Year, Easter, and the first three weeks of August, when almost all accommodations have been booked up months in advance.

WHAT IT COSTS In euros				
	$$$$	$$$	$$	$	¢
RESTAURANTS	over €22	€17–€22	€12–€17	€7–€12	under €7
HOTELS	over €210	€160–€210	€110–€160	€60–€110	under €60

Restaurant prices are for a second course (secondo piatto). Hotel prices are for two people in a standard double room in high season, including tax and service.

OSTIA ANTICA

Founded around the 4th century BC, Ostia served as Rome's port city for several centuries until the Tiber changed course, leaving the town high and dry. What has been excavated here is a remarkably intact Roman town in a pretty, parklike setting. Fair weather and good walking shoes are essential. On hot days, be here when the gates open or go late in the afternoon. A visit to the excavations takes two to three hours, including 20 minutes for the museum.

FodorsChoice **Ostia Antica** was inhabited by a cosmopolitan population of rich businessmen, wily merchants, sailors, slaves, and their respective families. The great *horrea* (warehouses) were built in the 2nd century AD to handle huge shipments of grain from Africa; the *insulae* (forerunners of the modern apartment building) provided housing for the growing population. Under the combined assaults of the barbarians and the *Anopheles* mosquito, and after the Tiber changed course, the port was eventually abandoned. Tidal mud and windblown sand covered the city, which lay buried until the beginning of the 20th century. Now the **Scavi di Ostia Antica** (Ostia Antica excavations) have been extensively excavated and are well maintained. ⊠ *Via dei Romagnoli* ☎ *06/56358099* ⊕ *www. itnw.roma.it/ostia/scavi* 🖾 *€4, includes admission to Museo Ostiense* ☉ *Tues.–Sun. 8:30–1 hr before sunset.*

▶ ❶ Before exploring Ostia Antica's ruins, it's worthwhile to take a tour through the **Castello della Rovere,** in the medieval *borgo* (town). This is the distinctive castle, easily spotted as you come off the footbridge from the train station, built by Pope Julius II when he was the Cardi-

Numbers in the text correspond to numbers in the margin and on the Lazio, Abruzzo, and Molise and the Ostia Antica maps.

If you have 2 days

Only 20 minutes from Rome, **Ostia Antica** ❶–❶⑧ ▶ is an obvious destination for the first day. Traveling by car, stop for a look at the ancient Etruscan center of **Tarquinia** ⑳ before continuing to the hill town of 🖼 **Tuscania** ㉑ for your first night. On the second day, take in the gardens of the Villa Lante in **Bagnaia** ㉓ and round the day off with a trip to 🖼 **Tivoli** ㉖ and the Villa D'Este. Spend the night in Tivoli or head back to Rome. If dependent on public transport, choose two of these areas and cover them more thoroughly.

If you have 4 days

With four days, you can focus on Lazio or head into the hills of Abruzzo. If you want to stick to Lazio, after seeing **Ostia Antica** ❶–❶⑧ ▶ on the first day, stop at the necropolis of **Cerveteri** ⑲ and continue on to medieval 🖼 **Tarquinia** ⑳, where you'll spend the night. In the morning, drive inland, stopping at 🖼 **Tuscania** ㉑ on your way to 🖼 **Viterbo** ㉒, with its papal palaces and medieval quarter. Make either Tuscania or Viterbo home for your second night. The next morning, stop in **Bagnaia** ㉓ and **Tivoli** ㉖, seeing the Villa Adriana and Villa d'Este, then continue on to the ancient Roman religious site of 🖼 **Palestrina** ㉗, a good place to overnight. On day four, check out the monasteries of **Subiaco** ㉘. If it's summer, head to the coast and spend an afternoon at the beach in 🖼 **Sperlonga** ㉛ and stay the night there; otherwise, stretch Tivoli, Palestrina, and Subiaco out over two days. Alternatively: if you'd rather see some of Abruzzo, follow the above itinerary until Tivoli, then head through the mountains on the A24 autostrada, forking off toward Pescara and winding up in the valley town of 🖼 **Sulmona** ㉟, an excellent choice for your third night. Come morning, head into the 🖼 **Parco Nazionale d'Abruzzo** ㊱ and spend the last day in the heart of the Apennines.

If you have 7 days

Follow the Lazio itinerary above up through Subiaco on the third day; on day four, take the A25 highway through the mountains to 🖼 **Sulmona** ㉟, where you'll spend your fourth night. From there, head into the 🖼 **Parco Nazionale d'Abruzzo** ㊱, explore all day, and spend the night in Civitella Alfedena. Next comes a choice: if you're a city type and prefer more of Abruzzo, travel northwest, stopping at mysterious **Castel del Monte** ㉝ and **Santo Stefano di Sessanio** ㉞ before heading to the regional capital of 🖼 **L'Aquila** ㉜, whose fine castle and churches make a good backdrop for your sixth night and seventh day. Alternatively, if the weather holds and you like antiquities, go east after the Parco Nazionale to see the Hellenistic theater in the hills of **Pietrabbondante** ㊳ and the medieval town of 🖼 **Agnone** ㊴, spending the sixth night either there or in the Molise regional capital of **Isernia** ㊲. An ambitious seventh day would include the ancient Roman town of **Sepino** ㊵ to the east before heading back west . . . or continuing southeast into Puglia.

12

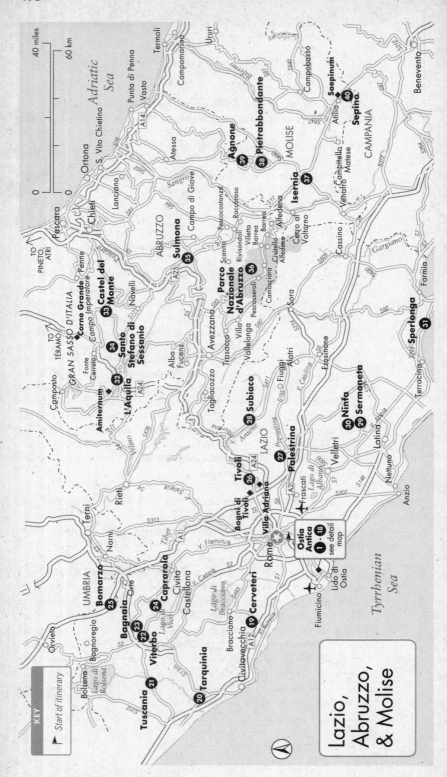

Lazio, Abruzzo, & Molise

KEY
▲ Start of itinerary

Adriatic Sea

Tyrrhenian Sea

40 miles
60 km
0

TO PINETO, ATRI
TO TERAMO

GRAN SASSO D'ITALIA
Corno Grande ◆
Campo Imperatore

Amiternum ◆
L'Aquila
32
Santo Stefano di Sessanio
34
Castel del Monte
33
Novelli
Penne
Fonte
Cerreto
Camposto

UMBRIA
Orvieto
Bagnoregio
Bomarzo
25
Bagnaia
23
22 Viterbo
Caprarola
24
Civita Castellana
Orte
Lago di Vico
Lago di Bracciano
Bracciano

Tuscania
21
Tarquinia
20
Civitavecchia

ABRUZZO
Sulmona
35
Campo di Giove
Scanno
Parco Nazionale d'Abruzzo
36
Pescasseroli
Villa
Vallelonga
Villetta Barrea
Barrea
Scanno
Peschasseroli
Camósciara
Cività Alfedena
Cerro al Volturno
Cassino

Rome
Ostia Antica
1 - 18
see detail map
Lido di Ostia
Fiumicino

Villa Adriana
Bagni di Tivoli
Tivoli
26
Subiaco
28
Palestrina
27
Frascati
Lago di Albano
Velletri
Nettuno
Anzio
Latina

Ninfa
30
Sermoneta
29
Fiuggi
Alatri
Frosinone
Terracina
Sperlonga
31

Isernia
37
Agnone
39
Pietrabbondante
38
MOLISE
Campobasso
Benevento
Saepinum
40
Sepino
CAMPANIA

Pescara
Chieti
Ortona
Lanciano
Atessa
Vasto
Termoli
Campomarino
Ururi
S. Vito Chietino
Punta di Penna

Cerveteri
19

Downhill Skiing

Abruzzo is the main skiing area in central Italy, though snow conditions tend to be more erratic than in the Alps, and trails are likely to be shorter and less varied. Winter weekends see a heavy influx of Romans and Neapolitans on the slopes, so to avoid long waits at the ski lifts, opt for midweek skiing if conditions are right.

Mountain Hikes

Many of the upland areas in the three regions are crisscrossed by scenic trails. The Parco Nazionale d'Abruzzo is open year-round, although it's best appreciated at off-peak times. Avoid public holidays, especially Easter Monday, and the first three weeks of August: the crowds scare the animals away, and popular hiking routes are accessible by reservation only in an attempt to limit congestion. Higher trails may be snowbound from November to April. As in all mountain environments, the weather is prone to sudden changes even in midsummer, so you should take all the standard equipment, particularly sunscreen and raingear.

12

Parks & Gardens

Dating back to antiquity, Lazio has been dotted with the retreats of wealthy Romans, places where they could escape the city to relax in expansive surroundings and indulge their grand and sometimes eccentric gardening tastes. Today one of the primary pleasures of the region is visiting these estates: Hadrian's Villa and Villa d'Este are must-see destinations, but you can also be richly rewarded by visits to lesser-known spots, such as Villa Lante and Palazzo Farnese, where Renaissance cardinals took a break from the papal court; Bomarzo, where a 16th-century prince created a bizarre theme park; and Ninfa, where a modern oasis has developed among medieval ruins.

---

nal Bishop of Ostia in 1483. Its triangular form is unusual for military architecture. Inside are (badly faded) frescoes by Michelangelo's pupil Baldassare Peruzzi.

2 The **Porta Romana,** one of the city's three gates, is where you'll enter the Ostia Antica excavations. It opens onto the Decumanus Maximus, the main thoroughfare crossing the city from end to end. To your right, a staircase leads up to a platform—the remains of the upper floor of the **3** **Terme di Nettuno** (Baths of Neptune)—from which you get a good view of the black-and-white mosaic pavements representing a marine scene with Neptune and Amphitrite. Directly behind the baths is the barracks of the fire department, which played an important role in a town with warehouses full of valuable goods and foodstuffs.

4 On the north side of the Decumanus Maximus is the beautiful **Teatro** (Theater), built by Agrippa, remodeled by Septimius Severus in the 2nd century AD, and finally restored by the Rome City Council in the 20th century. In the vast Piazzale delle Corporazioni, where trade organiza-**5** tions similar to guilds had their offices, is the **Tempio di Cerere** (Temple of Ceres), which is only appropriate for a town dealing in grain imports—Ceres, who gave her name to cereal, was the goddess of agri-**6** culture. You can visit the **Domus di Apuleio** (House of Apuleius), built in Pompeian style, lower to the ground and with fewer windows than **7** was characteristic of Ostia. Next door, the **Mithraeum** has balconies and

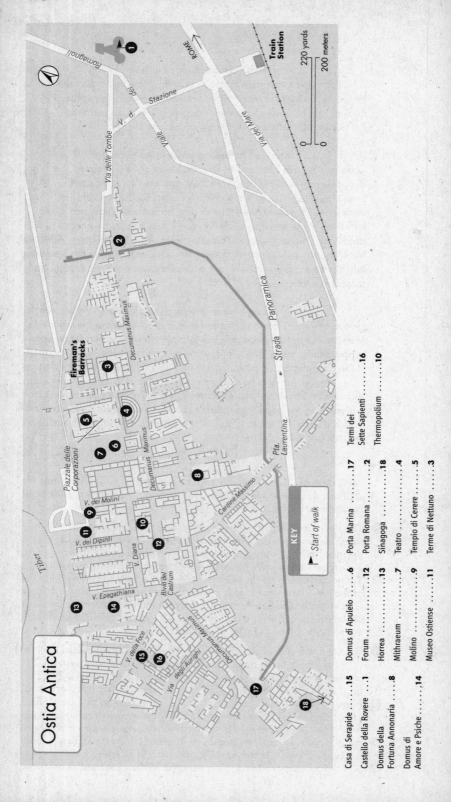

Ostia Antica

KEY

▲ *Start of walk*

Train
Station

ROME

220 yards

200 meters

a hall decorated with symbols of the cult of Mithras. This male-only religion, imported from Persia, was especially popular with legionnaires.

⑧ On Via Semita dei Cippi, just off Via dei Molini, the **Domus della Fortuna Annonaria** (House of Fortuna Annonaria) is the richly decorated residence of a wealthy Ostian, which displays the skill of the mosaic artists of the period. One of the rooms opens onto a secluded garden.

⑨ On Via dei Molini you can see a **molino** (mill), where grain for the warehouses next door was ground with stones that are still here. Along Via
⑩ di Diana you come upon a **thermopolium** (bar) with a marble counter and a fresco depicting the fruit and foodstuffs that were sold here. At
⑪ the end of Via dei Dipinti is the **Museo Ostiense** (Ostia Museum), open the same hours as the Scavi (but leave at least ½ hr before closing to enter the museum), which displays sarcophagi, massive marble columns, and statuary too large to be shown anywhere else, including a beautiful statue of Mithras slaying the bull that was taken from the underground Mithraeum.

⑫ The **Forum,** on the south side of Decumanus Maximus, holds the monumental remains of the city's most important temple, dedicated to Jupiter, Juno, and Minerva; other ruins of baths; a basilica (which in Roman times as a secular hall of justice); and smaller temples.

⑬ Via Epagathiana leads toward the Tiber, where there are large **horrea** (warehouses), erected during the 2nd century AD to receive the enormous amounts of grain imported into Rome during that period, the height of the Empire.

⑭ West of Via Epagathiana, the **Domus di Amore e Psiche** (House of Cupid and Psyche), a residence, was named for a statue found there (now on display in the museum); you can see what remains of a large pool in an enclosed garden decorated with marble and mosaic motifs. Even in ancient times a premium was placed on water views: the house faces the shore, which would have been only about ⅓ km (⅕ mi) away. The
⑮ **Casa di Serapide** (House of Serapis) on Via della Foce is a 2nd-century multilevel dwelling; another apartment building stands one street over
⑯ on Via degli Aurighi. Nearby, the **Termi dei Sette Sapienti** (Baths of the Seven Wise Men) are named for a group of bawdy frescoes found there.

⑰ The **Porta Marina** leads to what used to be the seashore. About 300 me-
⑱ ters (1,000 ft) to the south are the ruins of the **sinagoga** (synagogue), one of the oldest in the Western world.

Where to Eat

$$–$$$ ✕ **Cipriani.** Handily located in the little medieval borgo near the excavations, this elegant trattoria serves Roman specialties and seafood and has an exquisite wine list. The more businesslike mood at lunchtime contrasts with an upgrade in menu, style, and price in the evening. ⊠ *Via del Forno 11* ☎ *06/56359560* ▤ *AE, DC, MC, V* ⊗ *Closed Wed.*

CERVETERI, TARQUINIA, TUSCANIA

Northwest of Rome lie Etruscan sites on coastal hills dominating approaches from all directions. The Etruscans held sway over a vast territory mainly north of Rome from the 8th to the 4th century BC before the Roman Republic's gradual expansion northward. According to the literary sources—mainly written by their Greek and Roman adversaries—Etruscans lived a fairly decadent life and had an unsurpassed reputation in fields as diverse as bronze-working and soothsaying. Though there are few remains of their settlements, they reserved some

ON THE MENU

With a tradition of sumptuous banquets that stretches back millennia, there's no lack of good places to eat in the Lazio region. Each town has its own culinary specialties, including local cheese and wine. The bread that predominates—a dark, crusty country loaf—makes the ultimate bruschetta (toasted bread doused with extra virgin olive oil and topped with vine-ripe tomatoes). Restaurants on the coast, naturally, specialize in seafood.

The diets in Abruzzo and Molise—except along the coastal Adriatic strip—tend toward heartier, meat-based dishes. Homemade maccheroni alla chitarra (spaghetti with a square profile, usually eaten with tomato or mushrooms) is found in most areas, though specialties may vary from one town to the next. You'll also come across Alpine favorites such as polenta in Molise, as well as sheep's- and cow's-milk cheeses.

of their finest construction skills for assuring comfort and style in the afterlife: The Etruscan necropolis, or "city of the dead," was an agglomeration of tombs that most likely aimed to reproduce the homes and lifestyles of the living.

As you make the trip north beyond Rome's city limits, you will traverse green countryside with pastures and endless fields of artichokes, a premium crop in these parts. You catch glimpses of the sea to the west, where the coast is dotted with suburban developments. Because the beaches in this area are popular with Romans, highways (especially the coastal Via Aurelia) and public transportation can be crowded on weekends from spring to fall. Exploring the Etruscan sites requires some agility in climbing up and down uneven stairs, and you need shoes suitable for walking on rough dirt paths.

Cerveteri is the principal Etruscan site closest to Rome and features the Necropoli della Banditaccia, a sylvan setting among mossy stones and variously shaped monuments that are memorials to revered ancestors. Tarquinia is farther north and has impressive painted tombs, as well as an excellent museum full of objects recovered from tombs throughout the region. On the way, you'll pass Civitavecchia, Rome's principal port. From the highway or train you can see the port installations, which include a fort designed by Michelangelo. Northeast of Tarquinia is Tuscania, a finely preserved town brimming with cultural heritage and medieval atmosphere.

Cerveteri

⑲ *42 km (26 mi) northwest of Rome.*

The nucleus of Cerveteri, in the shadow of a medieval castle, stands on a spur of tufa rock that was the site of the Etruscan city of Caere, a thriving commercial center in the 6th century BC. The necropolis is about 2 km (1 mi) from Cerveteri's main piazza, a trip you can make on foot or by taxi.

In the **Necropoli della Banditaccia** (Banditaccia Necropolis), the Etruscan residents of Caere left a heritage of great historical significance. In this monumental complex of tombs—spanning over 500 years from the 7th to the 1st century BC—they laid their relatives to rest, some in simple graves, others in burial chambers that are replicas of Etruscan dwellings. The round tumulus tombs are prototypes of Rome's tombs of Augustus and Hadrian (in the Mausoleo di Augusto and Castel Sant'Angelo) and the Tomb of Cecilia Metella on the Via Appia. Look especially for the **Tomba dei Capitelli,** with carved capitals; the **Tomba dei Rilievi,** its walls decorated with stucco reliefs of household objects; and the similar **Tombe degli Scudi e delle Sedie.** The **Tomba Moretti** has a little vestibule with columns. Some tombs have several chambers. ⊠ *Necropoli della Banditaccia* ☎ *06/9940001* 🎫 *€4* ⊙ *Tues.–Sun. 9–1 hr before sunset.*

Where to Eat

$$ ✕ **Tuchulcha.** About ½ km (⅓ mi) from the entrance to the Banditaccia necropolis, on the road leading to the site, this country trattoria offers simple and satisfying home-style food; two specialties are handmade fettuccine and locally grown artichokes served in various ways. You can dine outside in good weather. ⊠ *Via della Necropoli Etrusca* ☎ *06/9914075* 🍴 *No credit cards* ⊙ *Closed Mon.*

Tarquinia

㉑ *About 90 km (55 mi) northwest of Rome, 50 km (30 mi) northwest of Cerveteri, 20 km (12 mi) north of Civitavecchia.*

Fortified Tarquinia sprawls on a hill overlooking the sea. Once a powerful Etruscan city, it was also a major center in the Middle Ages. Though it lacks the harmony of better-preserved medieval towns, Tarquinia offers unexpected pleasures, among them views of narrow medieval streets opening onto quaint squares dominated by palaces and churches, and the sight of the majestic 12th-century church of Santa Maria di Castello encircled by medieval walls and towers. Be sure to walk to the medieval wall at the inland edge of town for towering views over Etruscan countryside. To focus on Tarquinia's Etruscan heritage, visit the museum in Palazzo Vitelleschi, and then see the frescoed underground tombs in the fields east of the city, a 20-minute walk from Piazza Matteotti, the town's main square. Alternatively, there is infrequent bus service from Piazza Cavour to the necropolis, with only a couple of morning and afternoon departures.

The **Museo Nazionale Tarquiniense** (National Museum of Tarquinia) is housed in Palazzo Vitelleschi, a splendid 15th-century building that contains a wealth of Etruscan treasures. Even if pottery and endless ranks of stone sarcophagi leave you cold, a visit here is memorable for the horses. A relief plaque of two marvelous terra-cotta winged horses gleams against the gray-stone wall on which it has been mounted in the main hall. The horses once decorated an Etruscan temple, and are vibrant proof of the degree of artistry attained by the Etruscans in the 4th century BC. The museum and its stately courtyard are crammed with sarcophagi from the tombs found beneath the meadows surrounding the town. The figures of the deceased recline on their stone couches, mouths curved in enigmatic smiles. Upstairs are vases and other Etruscan artifacts, together with some of the more precious frescoes from the tombs, removed to keep them from deteriorating. ⊠ *Piazza Cavour 1* ☎ *0766/856036* 🎫 *€4, €6.50 including necropolis* ⊙ *Tues.–Sun. 8:30–7:30.*

The entrance to the **Necropoli,** the Etruscan city of the dead, is about 1 km (½ mi) outside the town walls. The tombs date from the 6th to the 2nd century BC, and they were painted with lively scenes of Etruscan life. The colors are amazingly fresh in some tombs, and the scenes show the vitality and highly civilized lifestyle of this ancient people. Of the thousands of tombs that exist throughout the territory of Etruria (there are 40,000 in the vicinity of Tarquinia alone), only a small percentage have been excavated scientifically. Many more have been plundered by "experts" called *tombaroli,* who dig illegally, usually at night. The tombs in the Tarquinia necropolis are bare; the only evidence of their original function is the stone platforms on which the sarcophagi rested. But the wall paintings are intriguing and in many cases quite beautiful. The visit takes about 90 minutes, and good explanations in English are posted outside each tomb. ⊠ *Monterozzi, on the Strada Provinciale 1/ b, Tarquinia–Viterbo* ☎ *0766/856308; 06/9941098 English-language tours* ✆ *€4, €6.50 including Museo Nazionale Tarquiniense* ☉ *Tues.–Sun. 9–1 hr before sunset.*

Where to Stay & Eat

★ ¢–$ ✕ **Il Grappolo.** This central wine bar might just be your much-needed antidote to another pasta meal—a great place for a snack, a drink, or a light meal built around wine and good company. It's cold food only, but the menu includes such fresh creations as *insalata di pera, speck, e grana* (salad with pear, speck, and flakes of grana cheese), perhaps accompanied by Paterno wine, a local Sangiovese thoroughbred, considered Lazio's rival to fine Tuscan reds. The atmosphere is modern, youthful, and welcoming. ⊠ *Via Alberata Dante Alighieri 3* ☎ *0766/ 857321* ▭ *AE, DC, MC, V* ☉ *Closed Mon. and Jan. 7–31. No lunch Nov.–Mar.*

$ ✕▦ **San Marco.** It would be impossible to find a better location for exploring the old center of Tarquinia than this ancient monastery, a huge, complex structure on the town's main square that's been operating as an inn since 1876. Rooms are simple, clean, and inviting, and the bar hops with locals on weekend nights. Lodging is merely the latest chapter in the San Marco's storied history; in the 1500s, these hallowed halls housed the mysterious order of the Frati Neri (Black Monks)—an Augustinian sect whose cloisters remain intact in the hotel's courtyard. The menu at the excellent restaurant (¢–$$) even offers recipes reconstructed from the brothers' 16th-century cookbooks—or pizza, for the less daring. ⊠ *Piazza Cavour 18, 01016* ☎ *0766/842234* ▤ *0766/842306* ⊕ *www.san-marco.com* ⇌ *26 rooms* ⚲ *Restaurant, bar, dance club* ▭ *AE, DC, MC, V.*

Tuscania

★ ㉑ *24 km (15 mi) northeast of Tarquinia, 25 km (16 mi) west of Viterbo.*

Given its small size—a population of only 7,000—compared with neighboring Tarquinia and Viterbo, Tuscania seems to overflow with sites from a number of historical periods. The medieval city walls were tastefully restored after a devastating earthquake in 1971, and the interior abutting the walls has been pleasingly landscaped with lawns and gardens. The long-abandoned ancient nucleus of the town, which includes the two outstanding Romanesque churches of Santa Maria Maggiore and San Pietro, lies a 20-minute walk outside the city walls to the southeast. Exploration back in the walled town also pays dividends: narrow cobblestone streets dotted with medieval towers make for great walks. Piazza Basile in front of the Palazzo Comunale sports a parapet with the sculpted lids of nine Etruscan sarcophagi, while below is the Fontana di Sette Cannelle, the restored city fountain dating from Etrusco-Roman times. North of the city walls is the archaeological museum, housed in the convent of the adjacent 15th century church, Santa Maria del Riposo.

The **Museo Archeologico Tuscanese** displays the necropolis material from two main Etruscan families, the Curunas and Vipinanas, dating from

the 4th to 2nd century BC. The family members are depicted on the sarcophagi in typical banqueting position, looking far from undernour-
ished. Also displayed are the grave goods, which would have been buried
with them, as well as some helpful photographs showing what the tombs
looked like when first excavated. The rooms above have some more
recent finds stretching back to the 8th century BC along with some information panels in English. ⊠ *Via del Riposo 36* ☎ *0761/436209*
🎫 *Free* ☉ *Tues.–Sun. 8:30–7:30.*

Where to Stay & Eat

★ **$–$$** ✕ **La Torre di Lavello.** Opposite the town's medieval tower, this tratto-
ria-cum-pizzeria combines efficient service and stylish presentation at
very reasonable prices. The menu is varied and imaginative. Highly recommended is the *fettucine al ragù bianco* (a pasta dish with beans), as
well as the ricotta cheese *con miele* (with honey) for dessert. To be assured of a seat, arrive early or make a reservation. ⊠ *Via Torre di
Lavello 27* ☎ *0761/434258* 🖃 *DC, MC, V* ☉ *Closed Wed.*

$ 🏠 **Locanda di Mirandolina.** This courteously run guest house in Tusca-
FodorśChoice nia's old town makes a perfect base for visiting ancient Etruria. Rooms
★ are distinguished by door color rather than number, and are fairly small
(dominated by the bed) but cozily furnished and immaculately kept. The
intimate restaurant ($–$$) is an excellent place to sample local recipes.
Book well in advance as this is popular choice, especially with northern Europeans. ⊠ *Via del Pozzo Bianco 40/42* ☎☎ *0761/436595* 🛏 *5
rooms, 2 apartments* 🖃 *MC, V* ☉ *Closed Jan. 6–Feb. 20. Restaurant
closed Tues.*

TUSCIA

The Viterbo region, north of the capital, is rich in history embodied in
cameo scenes of dark medieval stone, dappled light on wooded paths,
a prelate's palace worthy of Rome itself, and another prelate's pleasure
garden, where splashing fountains were aquatic jokes played on unsuspecting guests. From Viterbo and Bagnaia to Caprarola and Villa Lante,
this region has a concentration of first-rate attractions—with the surprising Renaissance theme park at Bomarzo thrown in for good measure. The city of Viterbo, which overshadowed Rome as a center of papal
power for a time during the Middle Ages, lies in the heart of Tuscia, the
modern name for the Etruscan domain of Etruria, a landscape of dramatic beauty punctuated by thickly forested hills and deep, rocky gorges.
The farmland east of Viterbo conceals small quarries of the dark, volcanic *peperino* stone that shows up in the walls of so many buildings
here, as well as in portals and monumental fireplaces. Lake Bolsena is
an extinct volcano, and the sulfur springs still bubbling up in Viterbo's
spas were used by the ancient Romans.

Bagnaia is the site of Villa Lante, where there are Italian gardens and a
vast park; at Caprarola are the huge Renaissance palace and gardens
designed for the Farnese family. Both sites were the work of the virtuoso architect Giacomo Barozzi (circa 1535–1584), known as Vignola,
who later worked with Michelangelo on St. Peter's. He rearranged the
little town of Caprarola, too, to enhance the palazzo's setting.

The ideal way to explore this region is by car, making Bomarzo your
first stop. By train, you can start at Viterbo and get to Bagnaia by local
bus. If you're traveling by train or bus, you will have to check schedules carefully, and you may have to allow for an overnight if you want
to see all four attractions.

Viterbo

22   *104 km (64 mi) north of Rome.*

Viterbo's moment of glory was in the 13th century, when it became the seat of the papal court. The medieval core of the city still sits within 12th-century walls. Its old buildings, with windows bright with geraniums, are made of dark peperino, the local stone that colors the medieval part of Viterbo a dark gray, contrasted here and there with the golden tufa rock of walls and towers. Peperino is also used in the characteristic and typically medieval exterior staircases that you see throughout the old town. More recently, Viterbo has blossomed into a regional commercial center, and much of the modern city is loud and industrial. However, Viterbo's San Pellegrino district is a place to get the feel of the Middle Ages, seeing how daily life is carried on in a setting that has remained practically unchanged over the centuries. The Palazzo Papale and the cathedral enhance the effect. The city has also remained a renowned spa center for its natural hot springs just outside of town, frequented by popes—and the laity—since medieval times.

The Gothic **Palazzo Papale** (Papal Palace) was built in the 13th century as a residence for popes looking to get away from the city. At that time Rome was a notoriously unhealthy place, ridden with malaria and plague and rampaging factions of rival barons. In 1271 the palace was the scene of a novel type of rebellion. A conclave held here to elect a new pope had dragged on for months, apparently making no progress. The people of Viterbo were exasperated by the delay, especially as custom decreed that they had to provide for the cardinals' board and lodging for the duration of the conclave. So they tore the roof off the great hall where the cardinals were meeting, and put them on bread and water. Sure enough, a new pope—Gregory X—was elected in short order. The interior is not always open, but you can climb the stairs to what was once the loggia. ⊠ *Piazza San Lorenzo* ☏ *0761/341124.*

The facade and interior of Viterbo's duomo, **Chiesa di San Lorenzo**, date from the Middle Ages. On the ancient columns inside the cathedral you can see the chips that an exploding bomb took out of the stone during World War II. There's a small adjoining museum. ⊠ *Piazza San Lorenzo* ☏ *0761/309623* ◷ *8–12:30 and 3:30–7.*

The medieval district of **San Pellegrino** is one of the best preserved in Italy. It has charming vistas of arches, vaults, towers, exterior staircases, worn wooden doors on great iron hinges, and tiny hanging gardens. You pass many antiques shops as you explore the little squares and byways. The **Fontana Grande** in the piazza of the same name is the largest and most extravagant of Viterbo's authentic Gothic fountains. ⊠ *Via San Pellegrino.*

☖ Viterbo has been a spa town for centuries, and the **Terme dei Papi** continues the tradition. This excellent spa offers the usual rundown of health and beauty treatments with an Etruscan twist: try a facial with local volcanic mud, or a steam bath in an ancient cave, where scalding hot mineral water direct from the Bullicam spring splashes down a waterfall to a pool under your feet. The Terme dei Papi's main draw, however, is the *terme* (baths) themselves: a 100,000-square-ft outdoor limestone pool of Viterbo's famous hot water, which pours in on the shallow end (which is much hotter) at 59°C (138°F) and intoxicates with its sulphurous odor. Floats and deck chairs are for rent, but bring your own bathrobe and towel unless you're staying at the hotel. ⊠ *Strada Bagni 12, Viterbo* ☏ *0761/3501* ⊕ *www.termedeipapi.it* ▭ *€15* ◷ *Pool, daily 9–5:30; spa, daily 9–6.*

Where to Stay & Eat

★ **$$$$** ✕ **Enoteca La Torre.** One of the best wine cellars in Italy takes center stage at the elegant Enoteca La Torre. It's also a temple to good eating: in addition to an ever-changing menu, there are lists for cheeses, mineral waters, oils, and vinegars. Chestnut fritters and rabbit stew are unusual delicacies, but whatever you choose will be local, traditional, and of the highest quality. ⊠ *Via della Torre 5* ☎ *0761/226467* ⊟ *AE, DC, MC, V* ⊘ *Closed Sun.*

★ **¢—$$** ✕ **Tre Re.** Viterbo's oldest restaurant—and one of the most ancient in Italy—has been operating in (predictably) the city's historic center since 1622, and it still focuses on nothing but traditional local cooking and open, friendly service. A gregarious buzz of Viterbese businessmen and families fills the small, wood-paneled and white-walled room to overflowing at lunchtime, as diners enjoy the truest versions of such Lazio specialties as *acquacotta viterbese* (literally "cooked water," a hearty vegetable and hot-pepper soup that was the ancient sustenance of shepherds and stockmen). ⊠ *Via Macel Gattesco 3* ☎ *0761/304619* ⊟ *AE, MC, V* ⊘ *Closed Thurs.*

¢–$ ✕ **Cantina Palazzo dei Mercanti.** The casual Cantina, which shares a
Fodor'sChoice kitchen and wine list with the elegant Enoteca La Torre, offers the best
★ lunch value in town, with impeccably executed classics served up for pocket change. Try whatever is offered as the daily rotating special, such as *papardelle* with a tomato and meat sauce, or just select a glass or bottle from the Enoteca's epic wine list, which includes a complex matrix of ratings from Italy's foremost wine reviewers. ⊠ *Via della Torre 1* ☎ *0761/226467* ⊟ *AE, DC, MC, V* ⊘ *Closed Sun.*

$$–$$$ ⊡ **Hotel Niccolò V.** This upscale, airy hotel is connected to Viterbo's mineral baths and spa at Terme dei Papi. While the Niccolò, 5 [km] from the center of town, is certainly the most convenient lodging to the baths, the complex is also a surreal mix of doctors in scrubs, half-naked bathers, and lost hotel guests wandering through an enormous mazelike lobby. In the guest rooms, though, marble baths and wooden floors give an air of country-house elegance. Breakfast, a sumptuous buffet is taken in a wood-beamed gallery overlooking a small garden. Hotel guests are allowed free use of the outdoor and indoor pools. ⊠ *Strada Bagni 12, 01100* ☎ *0761/350555* 🖷 *0761/350273* ⊕ *www.termedeipapi. it* 🛏 *20 rooms, 3 suites* ⚐ *Restaurant, in-room safes, minibars, pool, bar, meeting rooms* ⊟ *AE, DC, MC, V.*

Bagnaia

㉓ *5 km (3 mi) east of Viterbo.*

The village of Bagnaia is the site of 16th-century cardinal Alessandro Montalto's summer retreat. Small twin residences are but an excuse for the hillside garden and park that surround them, designed by Vignola for a member of the papal court.

Villa Lante is a terraced extravaganza. On the lowest terrace a delightful Italian garden has a centerpiece fountain fed by water channeled down the hillside. On another, higher terrace a stream of water runs through a groove carved in a long stone table where the cardinal entertained his friends alfresco, chilling wine in the running water. That's only one of the most evident and innocent of the whimsical water games that were devised for the cardinal. The symmetry of the formal gardens contrasts with the wild, untamed park adjacent to it, reflecting the paradoxes of nature and artifice that are the theme of this pleasure garden. ⊠ *Via G. Baroni 71* ☎ *0761/288008* 🎟 *Park free, gardens and residences €2* ⊘ *Tues.–Sun. 9–1 hr before sunset.*

Caprarola

㉔ *19 km (12 mi) south of Viterbo.*

The wealthy and powerful Farnese family took over this sleepy village in the 1500s and endowed it with a palace that rivals the great residences of Rome.

The massive, magnificent, 400-year-old **Palazzo Farnese**, built on an unusual pentagonal plan, has an ingenious system of ramps and terraces designed by Vignola that leads right up to the main portal. This nicety allowed carriages and mounts to arrive directly in front of the door. Though the salons are unfurnished, the palace's grandeur is still evident. An artificial grotto decorates one wall, the ceilings are covered with frescoes glorifying the splendors of the Farnese family, and an entire room is frescoed with maps of the world as it was known to 16th-century cartographers. From the windows you can glimpse the garden, which can be visited only by appointment. ⊠ *Via Nicolai* ☎ *0761/646052* ✉ *€3* ☉ *Tues.–Sun. 9–1 hr before sunset.*

Bomarzo

㉕ *15 km (9 mi) east of Viterbo.*

♻ The eerie 16th-century **Parco dei Mostri** (Monster Park) is populated by weird and fantastic sculptures of mythical creatures and eccentric architecture. It was created by Prince Vicino Orsini for his wife, Giulia Farnese, who is said to have taken one look at the park and died of heart failure. No one really knows why the prince had the sculptures carved in outcroppings of stone in a dusky wood on his estate, but it probably has something to do with the artifices that were an artistic conceit of his time. Children love it, and there are photo ops galore. However, be advised that the park's staff can be brusque. ⊠ *1½ km (1 mi) west of town* ☎ *0761/924029* ✉ *€8* ☉ *Daily 8:30–1 hr before sunset.*

TIVOLI, PALESTRINA & SUBIACO

East of Rome are two of Lazio's star attractions—the Villa Adriana and the Villa d'Este in Tivoli—and, off the beaten path in the mountains beyond them, the lesser-known and wonderfully peaceful Palestrina and Subiaco. The road from Rome to Tivoli passes through uninspiring industrial areas and burgeoning suburbs that used to be lush countryside. You'll know you're close to Tivoli when you see vast quarries of travertine marble and smell the sulfurous vapors of the little spa, Bagni di Tivoli. Both sites in Tivoli are outdoors and entail walking.

With a car, you can continue your loop through the mountains east of Rome, taking in two very different sights that are both focused on religion. The ancient pagan sanctuary at Palestrina is set on the slopes of Mt. Ginestro, from which it commands a sweeping view of the green plain and distant mountains. Subiaco, the cradle of Western monasticism, is tucked away in the mountains above Tivoli and Palestrina. Unless you start out very early and have lots of energy, plan an overnight stop along the way if you want to take in all three.

Tivoli

㉖ *36 km (22 mi) east of Rome.*

★ **Villa Adriana** (Hadrian's Villa), 6 km (4 mi) south of Tivoli, was an emperor's theme park, an exclusive retreat where the marvels of the classical world were reproduced for a ruler's pleasure. Hadrian, who succeeded Trajan as emperor in AD 117, was a man of genius and intellectual curiosity. Fascinated by the accomplishments of the Hellenistic world, he decided to re-create it for his own enjoyment by building this villa over a vast tract of land below the ancient settlement of Tibur. From AD 118 to 130, architects, laborers, and artists worked on the villa, periodically spurred on by the emperor himself when he returned from another voyage full of ideas for even more daring constructions. After his death in AD 138, the fortunes of his villa declined. It was sacked by barbarians and Romans alike; many of his statues and decorations ended up in the Musei Vaticani, but the expansive ruins are nonetheless compelling.

It's not the single elements but the peaceful and harmonious effect of the whole that makes Hadrian's Villa such a treat. Oleanders, pines, and cypresses growing among the ruins heighten the visual impact. To help you get your bearings, maps are issued free with the audio guides (€4) at the ticket office. A visit here should take about two hours, more if you like to savor antiquity slowly. After sunset on Fridays, a special one-hour tour under spotlights is available for €4.65. In summer there's a sound-and-light show at night; check with your hotel concierge or call the ticket office for the schedule. Otherwise, in summer the park should be visited early, to take advantage of cool mornings. ⊠ *Bivio di Villa Adriana, off Via Tiburtina, 6 km (4 mi) southwest of Tivoli* ☎ *0774/ 530203* ⌨ *€6.50* ☉ *Daily 9–1 hr before sunset.*

★ **Villa d'Este,** a late-Renaissance estate, is a playground of artistic whimsy, manifested in the 80-some fountains of all shapes and sizes that tumble down the vast, steep hillside garden. Cardinal Ippolito d'Este (1509–72), an active figure in the political intrigues of mid-16th-century Italy, set about proving his dominance over man and nature by commissioning this monument to architectural excess. His builders tore down part of a Franciscan monastery to clear the site, then diverted the Aniene River to water the garden and feed the fountains. History shows it was worth the effort—the Villa d'Este is still considered one of Italy's most beautiful spots. Tiny drinking fountains, massive reflecting pools, a fountain that once played music through organ pipes, and one that's a scale model of the great monuments of Rome show their years but are still a sight to see, and the green of the peaceful gardens is a pleasant break in summer. Allow an hour for this visit, and bear in mind that you'll be climbing a lot of stairs. ⊠ *Piazza Trento 1* ☎ *0774/312070* ⌨ *€6.50* ☉ *Tues.–Sun. 9–1 hr before sunset.*

Where to Stay & Eat

$$ ✕ **Del Falcone.** A central location—on Tivoli's main street leading off Largo Garibaldi—means that this restaurant is popular and often crowded. In the ample and rustic dining rooms, you can try homemade *crespella* (a rolled pancake), flavored with nuts or ricotta cheese and spinach. Country-style grilled meats are excellent. ⊠ *Via Del Trevio 34* ☎ *0774/312358* ═ *AE, DC, MC, V.*

$-$$ ✕▦ **Adriano.** At the entrance to Hadrian's Villa, this restaurant-inn is a handy place to have lunch before heading up the hill to Villa d'Este. It's also a good base for the night before or after exploring. The restaurant ($$–$$$) is Italian with a sophisticated touch, as in risotto *ai fiori di zucchine* (with zucchini flowers). The atmosphere is relaxing, especially at outdoor tables in summer. The green surroundings also provide a restful backdrop for the Adriano's 10 rooms, which are casually elegant and immaculately kept. ⊠ *Via di Villa Adriana 194* ☎ *0774/ 382235* 🖨 *0774 535122* ⇴ *10 rooms* ♻ *Tennis courts, bar; no smoking.* ═ *AE, DC, MC, V* ☉ *No dinner Sun.*

Palestrina

㉗ *27 km (17 mi) south of Tivoli on S636, 37 km (23 mi) east of Rome along Via Prenestina.*

Palestrina is surprisingly little known outside Italy, except to students of ancient history and music lovers. Its most famous native son, Giovanni Pierluigi da Palestrina, born here in 1525, was the renowned composer of 105 masses, as well as madrigals, magnificats, and motets. But the town was celebrated long before the composer's lifetime.

Ancient Praeneste (modern Palestrina) flourished much earlier than Rome. It was the site of the Temple of Fortuna Primigenia, which dates from the 2nd century BC. This was one of the largest, richest, most frequented temple complexes in all antiquity—people came from far and wide to consult its famous oracle. In modern times, no one had any idea of the extent of the complex until World War II bombings exposed ancient foundations occupying huge artificial terraces stretching from the upper part of the town as far downhill as its central *duomo*.

Large arches and terraces scale the hillside up to the imposing **Palazzo Barberini,** built in the 17th century along the semicircular lines of the original temple. It's now a museum containing material found on the site, dating from throughout the classical period. This well-labeled collection of Etruscan bronzes, pottery, and terra-cotta statuary as well as Roman artifacts takes second place to the chief attraction, a 1st-century BC mosaic representing the Nile in flood. This delightful work—a large-scale composition in which form, color, and innumerable details captivate the eye—is alone worth the trip to Palestrina. But there's more: a model of the temple as it was in ancient times, which will help you appreciate the immensity of the original construction. ✉ *Museo Nazionale Archeologico, Palazzo Barberini* ☎ *06/9538100* 💶 *€3* 🕐 *Daily 9–8; archaeological zone of the temple: daily 9–1 hr before sunset.*

Where to Stay & Eat

¢–$ ✕▦ **Hotel Stella.** In the restaurant ($–$$) of this small central hotel in Palestrina's public garden, you'll receive a cordial welcome, and find on the menu local dishes such as light and freshly made fettuccine served with a choice of sauces, as well as unusual items such as *pasta e fagioli con frutti di mare* (pasta and bean soup with shellfish). Decor tends toward the bright and fanciful. The guest rooms are frilly and a bit worn, but clean and comfortable. ✉ *Piazzale Liberazione, 3 00036* ☎ *06/9538172* 🖷 *06/9573360* 🌐 *www.hotelstella.it* 🛏 *30 rooms* ⚇ *Restaurant, bar* ▭ *AE, DC, MC, V.*

Subiaco

㉘ *54 km (33 mi) east of Rome.*

Tucked in among wooded mountains in the deep and narrow valley of the Aniene River, which empties into the Tiber in Rome, Subiaco is a modern town built over World War II rubble. It is chiefly known (aside from being the birthplace of Gina Lollobrigida, whose family name is common in these parts) as the site of the monastery where St. Benedict devised his rule of communal religious life in the 6th century, founding the order that was so important in transmitting learning through the ages. Even earlier, the place was a refuge of Nero, who built a villa here, said to have rivaled that of Hadrian at Tivoli, damming the river to create three lakes and a series of waterfalls. The road to the monastery passes the ruins of the emperor's villa.

The 6th-century **Monastero di San Benedetto** is a landmark of Western monasticism. It was built over the grotto where the saint lived and meditated. Clinging to the cliff on nine great arches, it has resisted assaults for almost 900 years. Over the little wooden veranda at the entrance, a Latin inscription wishes PEACE TO THOSE WHO ENTER. The upper church is covered with frescoes by Umbrian and Sienese artists of the 14th century. In front of the main altar, a stairway leads to the lower church, carved out of the rock, with another stairway leading down to the grotto where Benedict lived as a hermit for three years. The frescoes here are even earlier than those above; look for the portrait of St. Francis of Assisi, painted from life in 1210, in the **Cappella di San Gregorio** (Chapel of St. Gregory), and for the oldest fresco in the monastery, in the **Grotta dei Pastori** (Shepherds' Grotto). ⊠ *Subiaco* ☎ *0774/85039* 🎫 *Free* ⊗ *Daily 9–12:30 and 3–6.*

Where to Stay & Eat

$–$$ ✕ **Mariuccia.** This modern barnlike restaurant close to the monasteries caters to wedding parties and other groups on weekends but is calm enough on weekdays. There's a large garden and a good view from the picture windows. House specialties are homemade fettuccine with porcini mushrooms and *scaloppe al tartufo* (truffled veal scallops). In summer you can dine outdoors under bright umbrellas. ⊠ *Via Sublacense km 19* ☎ *0774/84851* ▭ *AE, DC, MC, V* ⊗ *Closed Mon. Closed weekdays Nov.–Mar.*

¢–$ ✕🏨 **Miramonti.** This small hotel and its restaurant, La Botte di Bacco ($–$$), are on the road between Subiaco and the monasteries. The restaurant is homey and cordial; specialties include the inviting gnocchi *al radicchio e tartufo* (with radicchio and black truffles) and *bistecca di cinghiale* (wild boar steak). Adequate for an overnight, the rooms are simply furnished but comfortable. ⊠ *Viale Giovanni XXIII 4* ☎☎ *0774/ 83243* 🛏 *11 rooms, 2 suites* ⚐ *Restaurant, bar* ▭ *AE, DC, MC, V* ⊗ *Restaurant closed Tues.*

SERMONETA, NINFA & SPERLONGA

A trio of romantic places south of Rome, set in a landscape defined by low mountains and a broad coastal plain, lure you into a past that seems centuries away from the city's bustle. Sermoneta is a castle town. Ninfa, nearby, is a noble family's fairy-tale garden that is open to the public only at limited times. Both are on the eastern fringe of the Pontine Plain, once a malaria-infested marshland that was ultimately reclaimed for agriculture by one of the most successful projects of Mussolini's regime. Several new towns were built here in the 1930s, among them Latina and Pontinia. Sperlonga is a medieval fishing village perched above the sea near one of emperor Tiberius's most fabulous villas. You need a car to see them all in a day or so, and to get to Ninfa. But Sermoneta and Sperlonga are accessible by public transit.

Sermoneta

❷❾ *80 km (50 mi) southeast of Rome.*

In Sermoneta, the town and castle are one. Within concentric rings of walls, in medieval times, townspeople lived and farmers came to take shelter from marauders. The lords—in this case the Caetani family— held a last line of defense in the tall tower, where if necessary they could cut themselves off by pulling up the drawbridge.

The **Castello Caetani** dates from the 1200s. In the 15th century, having won the castle by ruse from the Caetanis, Borgia Pope Alexander VI transformed it into a formidable fortress and handed it over to his son Cesare. The chiaroscuro of dark and light stone, the quiet of the narrow streets, and the bastions that hint at siege and battle take you back in time. ⊠ *Via della Fortezza* ☎ *0773/695404* 🎟 *€3* 🕝 *Guided tours only* 🕙 *Apr.–Oct., Fri.–Wed. 10–11, 3–4, and 5–6; Nov.–Mar., Fri.–Wed. 10–11:30, 2–3, and 4–5.*

Ninfa

㉚ *5 km (3 mi) north of Sermoneta.*

In the Middle Ages **Ninfa** was a thriving village, part of the Caetani family's vast landholdings around Sermoneta. It was abandoned when malaria-carrying mosquitoes infested the plain, and it fell into ruin. Now it's a place of rare beauty, a dream garden of romantic ruins and rushing waters, of exotic species and fragrant blooms. Ninfa is an oasis of the Worldwide Fund for Nature(WWF), managed in collaboration with the Caetani heirs. Generations of the Caetani family, including English and American spouses and gardening buffs, created the garden over the course of the 20th century. ⊠ *Via Ninfina, Doganella di Ninfa* ☎ *0773/ 632231; 0773/695404 APT Latina-Provincial Tourist Office* 🎟 *€8* 🕝 *Guided tours only* 🕙 *Apr.–Oct: usually weekends 9:30–12 and 2:30–6, but call for designated days and reservations.*

Sperlonga

㉛ *127 km (79 mi) southeast of Rome.*

Sperlonga is a labyrinth of whitewashed alleys, arches, and little houses, like a casbah wrapped around a hilltop overlooking the sea, with broad, sandy beaches on either side. Long a favorite haunt of artists and artisans in flight from Rome's quick pace, the town has ancient origins. The medieval town gates, twisting alleys, and watchtower were vital to its defense when pirate ships came into sight. Now they simply make this former fishing town even more picturesque.

Under a cliff on the shore only 1 km (½ mi) south of Sperlonga are the ruins of a grandiose villa built for Roman emperor Tiberius and known as the **Grotta di Tiberio.** The villa incorporated several natural grottoes, in one of which Tiberius dined with guests on an artificial island. The various courses were served on little boats that floated across the shallow seawater pool to the emperor's table. Showpieces of the villa were the colossal sculpture groups embellishing the grotto. The **Museo Nazionale** (National Museum) was built on the site especially to hold the fragments of these sculptures, discovered by chance by an amateur archaeologist. The huge statues had been smashed to pieces centuries earlier by Byzantine monks unsympathetic to pagan images. For decades the subject and appearance of the originals remained a mystery, and the museum was a work in progress as scholars there tried to put together the 7,000 pieces of this giant puzzle. Their achievement, the immense Scylla group, largest of the sculptures, is on view here. ⊠ *Via Flacca (SS 213, km 16.5)* ☎ *0771/548028* 🎟 *€2* 🕙 *Daily 9–7.*

Where to Eat

$$–$$$ ✕ **Gli Archi.** Tucked into a landing of Old Sperlonga's myriad stairways, this attractive restaurant has brick-arch interiors and tables on a cute piazza for fair-weather dining. A touch of refinement puts it a cut above the establishments closer to the beach, and its owners take pride in serving high-quality ingredients with culinary simplicity. Seafood, including a house favorite *pennette alla seppiolina* (pasta with cuttlefish ink),

predominates, but there are a few meat platters, too. ✉ *Via Ottaviano 17* ☎ *0771/548300* ⊟ *AE, DC, MC, V* ⊘ *Closed Wed. and Jan.*

$$–$$$ ✗ **La Bisaccia.** A favorite with locals, La Bisaccia is popular with seasonal residents, too. It's near the beach in the newer part of town, and you can walk to it in about 10–15 minutes from the center of Old Sperlonga. Book a table for lunch on weekends and in summer. Seafood comes just about any way you want it, from pasta with scampi to fried, baked, or grilled fish. The menu also has some basic meat dishes and a local specialty, creamy buffalo-milk mozzarella. ✉ *Via Romita 19* ☎ *0771/548576* ⊟ *AE, DC, MC, V* ⊘ *Closed Tues.*

ABRUZZO

Central Italy isn't all tranquil hills dotted with picturesque hill towns and vineyards. East of Lazio, the terrain of the often-overlooked Abruzzo region turns rugged, with isolated mountain villages and some of the country's best-preserved wildlife sanctuaries. In Abruzzo, you can enjoy nature in the rough, and there's no better place than the Parco Nazionale d'Abruzzo for hiking and horseback riding. L'Aquila, a walkable town well worth an afternoon stroll, is a good base for exploring the central part of the region. Abruzzese cooking is mountain-style—hearty, simple, local foods. You are likely to find plenty of lamb, mutton, and pork, pecorino cheese and ricotta, and wild mushrooms and lentils on restaurant menus, along with dishes spiced with saffron, which is grown near L'Aquila. The local wines tend toward the robust and the spicy; white Trebbiano and red Montepulciano d'Abruzzo are the best-known types.

L'Aquila

32 *58 km (36 mi) southeast of Rieti, 125 km (78 mi) northeast of Rome.*

The regional capital of L'Aquila was founded when Emperor Frederick II (1482–1556) united the 99 surrounding kingdoms under one flag (which bore an eagle, or *l'aquila*). The town's most famous fountain, **Fontana Delle 99 Canelle,** commemorates the event with 99 spouts, and the church bells in the Duomo ring 99 times each night. A good place to begin a walk is Piazza Battaglione Alpini, which serves as a bus terminal. L'Aquila's austere **Castello** (fortress) looms over the city, offering sweeping vistas of the nearby Gran Sasso mountain range. Built by the Spanish rulers in the 16th century to discourage popular revolt, the Castello also served as a prison. The formidable defense works—which were never put to the test—include a warren of underground passages around the bastions, which are now open to the public.

The castle is the site of temporary art exhibitions and the **Museo Nazionale dell'Abruzzo,** which has a good collection drawn from the region's earthquake-ravaged churches and a gallery of modern art on the top floor. The highlight of the visit is the reconstructed skeleton of a million-year-old mammoth discovered nearby in 1954. ✉ *Viale delle Medaglie d'Oro* ☎ *0862/633200* 🎟 *€4* ⊘ *Mon.–Sat. 9–2, Sun. 9–1. Free guided tours around castle: weekends 10:30, noon, 3, 4, and 5:30.*

The main road from Piazza Battaglione Alpini leads to the center of town. Up on the right is the small Piazza Santa Maria Paganica; a little farther ahead is Via di San Bernardino, which climbs to the left to the Renaissance church of **San Bernardino.** It was built in honor of St. Bernardine of Siena and has a lovely facade featuring the classical orders of columns. The mausoleum that holds the saint's remains was built by a pupil of Donatello (circa 1386–1466), and the altarpiece is by Andrea della

Robbia (1435–1525). The rest of the interior was given a baroque makeover in the early 18th century. ⊠ *Via di San Bernardino* ⊘ *Daily 8–noon and 4–6.*

A 15-minute walk from the church of San Bernardino along Via Fortebraccio brings you outside the city walls, to **Santa Maria di Collemaggio**, probably the most famous church in Abruzzo. It was built at the end of the 13th century by the hermit Peter of Morrone, who was later elected Pope Celestine V, and its fame stems from Peter's. He was so attached to the church that he insisted on being crowned and buried here rather than in Rome; his remains rest in the mausoleum to the right of the altar. The church's simple Romanesque facade is strikingly laced with a geometric pattern of white and pink marble. Gothic elements include the rose windows and decorative portals. The interior is rather bare—it was stripped of its baroque embellishments in the 1970s—although the floor has decorative patterns, and several fine 15th-century frescoes adorn the nave walls. ⊠ *Piazzale Collemaggio 1* ☎ *0862/26744* ⊘ *Daily 9–6:30.*

Where to Stay & Eat

★ **$$** ✕ **Elodia.** A simple local favorite for classic Abruzzese cooking, Elodia specializes in hard-to-find traditional dishes such as *crespelle di ricotta alla montanara* (thin ricotta pancakes), rustic flavors such as chickpea-and-chestnut soup (in winter), and foodie touches such as an olive oil list and wine-tasting menus. Delicious homemade desserts such as apple-chocolate cake and pears baked in Montepulciano d'Abruzzo wine should not be missed. After dinner, ask for a tour of the wine cellar. ⊠ *Frazione Camarda, S17bis del Gran Sasso* ☎ *0862/606219* ▤ *AE, DC, MC, V* ⊘ *Closed Mon. and 1st 2 wks in July. No dinner Sun.*

¢–$ ✕ **Trattoria del Giaguaro.** In the most evocative square in town, this trattoria will welcome you with its homemade pasta dishes, including *maccheroni a chitarra al sugo* (pasta with a tomato and basil sauce) and ravioli filled with first-rate fresh sheep's-milk ricotta. A selection of grilled meat or the popular *ossobuco agli ortaggi* (veal shank in a tomato sauce, served with mixed vegetables) will fill you up, but you should try to save room for homemade crème brûlée. ⊠ *Piazza Santa Maria Paganica 4* ☎ *0862/28249* ▤ *MC, V* ⊘ *Closed Tues., 2 wks July–Aug.*

$ ▥ **Duomo.** The quiet Duomo, housed in 18th-century quarters, is as central as it can be. Many rooms have a view of the lovely square below, and the decor is a nice blend of traditional touches and modern comforts: expect terra-cotta floors and wrought-iron beds matched with practical wooden furniture. Buffet breakfast includes local honey, cakes, and cookies. ⊠ *Via Dragonetti 10, 67100* ☎ *0862/410893* ▤ *0862/413058* ⊕ *www.worldtelitaly.com/aziende/fiordigigli/duomo.html* ⤴ *28 rooms* ⚹ *Bar* ▤ *AE, DC, MC, V.*

Shopping

There's a good **antiques market** in Piazza Santa Maria della Paganica the second weekend of each month. Piazza del Duomo is the location for the town's **produce market** Monday–Saturday 8–1.

Medieval Abruzzo

The landscape surrounding L'Aquila is studded with old castles, guard towers, and tiny hamlets, some perfectly preserved and still inhabited, others in ruins, haunted by the ghosts of past battles. Castel del Monte and Santo Stefano di Sessanio are two medieval *borghi* (hamlets) east of L'Aquila on the S17bis that make a pleasant half-day excursion.

❸ **Castel del Monte** is an unusual example of a *ricetto,* a type of fortified village without external walls. A single steep access road rises to the center of the town, which is crossed by narrow alleys and dark tunnels leading to the more distant houses. In case of attack, the inhabitants could barricade themselves in their houses, block the narrow streets, and pour hot oil down the main street.

34 **Santo Stefano di Sessanio,** 14 km (9 mi) west of Castel del Monte on the S17bis, was first the property of the powerful Roman Piccolomini family, then passed to the Medici. It has the most sophisticated guard tower in the area, built with rounded instead of squared sides to make an attack more difficult. Climb to the top to enjoy a panoramic view of the Campo Imperatore valley and its striking rock formations.

Skiing

The area around L'Aquila is dominated by the **Apennines,** central Italy's greatest mountains. The Alps they're not, but in winter you can find ample choice for a day's skiing at **Campo Imperatore** (☎ 0862/22146), **Campo Felice** (☎ 0862/917803), and **Ovindoli** (☎ 0863/705087), which have a total of 60 km (40 mi) of runs and 100 km (60 mi) of cross-country trails.

Sulmona

35 *63 km (39 mi) southeast of L'Aquila.*

Sulmona may be best known for producing some of Italy's best *confezioni* (candies), but the little town is also one of the visual gems of Abruzzo, buried in a river valley in the region's mountainous heartland. Its winding pedestrian shopping streets and alleyways reveal the fanciful fonts of centuries-old storefronts, fading shades of orange palazzi, and a jumble of grand mirrored candy shops. While Sulmona has little in the way of well-known sights, its jovial evening *passeggiata* (stroll), down-home cooking, and kinship with Abruzzese tradition are unlike anything you might see in the big city. It's also an excellent base for exploring the national parkland nearby.

Corso Ovidio is Sulmona's main strip, worthy of a long stroll, especially in the before-dinner hours. The 18th-century candy stores along the street are all similar, so take your pick if souvenir-shopping; look for exquisite silver candied almonds or Sulmona's trademark, the tiny, white, spherical *confetti*. The Romanesque **Cattedrale di San Panfilio,** at the end of Corso Ovidio, is piled atop the thousand-year-old ruins of a Greek temple to Apollo. In the wide-open Piazza Garibaldi in the shadow of the mountains at the edge of the old town, the central **Fontana del Vecchio** is the terminus of a 13th-century aqueduct that divides the new and old towns.

Where to Stay & Eat

$ ✕ **Da Gino.** A local crowd flocks to this casual basement trattoria in the *centro storico,* especially at lunchtime, to sample from a careful selection of well-priced Abruzzo classics. A cool yellow room with cathedralesque arches occupies the underground space next to the 15th-century Santa Maria della Tomba. Daily specials (don't even think about asking for a menu) might include tasty *involtini* (veal or chicken rolled with ham, mushrooms, peppers, rosemary, and white wine sauce). Don't miss the assortment of *contorni* (vegetables) such as stuffed pepper and zucchini with egg batter. Wash it down with the local red, Montepulciano d'Abruzzo. ⊠ *Piazza Plebiscito, 12* ☎ *0864/52289* ▭ *No credit cards* ⊘ *Closed Sun. No lunch Mon.*

¢ ▦ **Hotel Italia.** Frozen in time, this no-frills hotel in the very heart of the old town will transport you to Italy's past. Beautiful old furniture, fading mirrors, and winding staircases lead to a maze of skeleton-keyed rooms with little in the way of modern facilities, but an abundance of belle epoque character. If you want to go even more rustic, rooms without bath are half the price. A rickety ladder on the top floor leads to a roof with views over the nearby dome of Sant'Annunziata and a panorama of Abruzzo's surrounding mountain terrain—especially spectacular at sunrise. ⊠ *Piazza Salvatore Tommasi* ☎🖨 *0864/52308* ⬑ *45 rooms, 32 with bath* ♿ *Bar; no a/c* ▭ *No credit cards.*

Parco Nazionale d'Abruzzo

★ ㊱ *Civitella Alfedena 109 km (68 mi) southeast of L'Aquila, 18 km (11 mi) east of Pescasseroli.*

Italy's national park system is for the most part underdeveloped, but the 440-square-km (170-square-mi) Abruzzo National Park (🌐 www. pna.it) is a notable exception. Full of lakes, streams, ruined castles, wildlife, and rugged terrain crossed by hiking trails, the park is home to Apennine wolves, Marsican brown bears, Abruzzan chamois, and an interesting mix of Mediterranean and Alpine birds. The Carta Turistica, on sale at local tobacconists or news agents, is a comprehensive topographical map with nearly 150 trails marked and identified with symbols indicating their relative difficulty and the animals that you're most likely to meet on the way. One of the most popular short walks (2½ hours) begins near Opi (path F2) and crosses the lovely Valle Fondillo, with chamois to be spotted on the higher ground of Monte Amaro in the early morning. (Should you miss them, the Opi entrance has a semi-enclosed chamois preserve.) For a full-day loop in the green, try path I1 to the Val di Rosa forest, and then head up to Passo Cavuto and return to town via Valle Ianna'nghera (path K6).

Helpful information offices at the edges of the park in the towns of **Pescasseroli** (⊠ Via Piave 2 ☎ 0863/910097) and **Civitella Alfedena** (⊠ Museo del Lupo, Via Santa Lucia ☎ 0864/890141) have all the information you will need for a hike through the scenery and can also arrange guided tours in English. The visitor centers, open daily 10–1 and 3–7, each themed toward a different kind of wildlife found inside the park, provide great opportunities for children to learn about animals. There's a wolf reserve and wolf museum with exhibits and films in the quasi-Alpine village of Civitella Alfedena, which is the starting point for several major trails. The more bustling town of Pescasseroli at the valley bottom has a nature reserve for injured animals and a nature museum and ecolab with interactive displays for kids.

Where to Stay

$ 🏨 **Albergo Antico Borgo La Torre.** Close to Civitella's medieval tower, this hotel is a hospitality landmark for hikers and family groups, with owner-manager Antonio dispensing both bonhomie and local knowledge in abundance. If available, ask for one of the refurbished wood-paneled rooms in the newer wing. A small adjoining garden has lounge chairs for warm-weather basking. Most guests prefer to stay on half-board terms, and enjoy hearty *cucina abruzzese* in a cozy dining room at the end of the day. ⊠ *Via Castello 3, 67030 Civitella Alfedena* ☎ *0864/890121* 🖨 *0864/890210* 🌐 *www.albergolatorre.com* ⬑ *19 rooms* ♿ *Restaurant, bar* ▭ *No credit cards.*

MOLISE

Established in 1965 after splitting from Abruzzo to the north, the region of Molise has long lived in the shadow of its more glamorous neighboring regions. This has spared it many of the ravages of development:

its mountains have much of their original woodland and grassland, the hill villages are generally well preserved, the archaeological sites are delightfully undervisited, and the cucina has retained its distinct *molisano* flavor with the best of local ingredients. With the exception of Valle d'Aosta, Molise is Italy's smallest region and lends itself to a few days' exploration from a single base. Of the two provincial centers, Isernia has more history and character than its rather brash counterpart to the east, Campobasso.

Isernia

③⑦ *111 km (70 mi) north of Naples, 176 km (110 mi) southeast of Rome.*

Isernia perches at just under 1,500 ft above sea level on what in the distant past must have been an easily defensible ridge, overlooking river valleys and busy viaducts. The town suffered severe collateral damage during Allied bombing raids in World War II—they were aiming for the bridge down in the valley. The northern part of the town is laid out in the standard grid pattern of Italian postwar development. Previous damage had been wrought by an earthquake in 1837, a notable victim being the **Cattedrale,** rebuilt in rather incongruous neoclassical style shortly afterward. Beneath the campanile to the east of the cathedral are four marble statues (in desperate need of restoration) from the Roman era positioned at the corners of the gateway.

In the heart of the old town is the **Museo Nazionale,** which houses finds from Roman necropoli outside ancient Aesernia. You can view an impressive array of funerary sculptures and the remarkably preserved remains of local fauna (including elephant and rhino species) hunted by *Homo aeserniensis* on a grassy river plain more than 700,000 years ago. Ask to see the helpful video (in good English) contextualizing the finds. ⊠ *Ex-convento Santa Maria delle Monache, Corso Marcelli 48* ☎ *0865/415179* 🖃 *€2* 🕑 *Daily 8:30–7:30.*

> **off the beaten path**
>
> **PESCHE –** Travel 4 km (2 mi) northeast of Isernia to Pesche, a village clinging both to its past and the steep limestone slope beneath it. From here, two paths head up and around the Riserva Naturale di Pesche above the village, mainly through holm-oak and deciduous oak forests. In springtime look for orchids among the bare limestone rocks, and enjoy the woodland concert of blackcaps and finches.

Where to Stay & Eat

$$ ✕ **Taverna Maresca.** Don't be misled by the rustic unassuming air of this family restaurant in the heart of Isernia's old town—it's long been an excellent place for sampling local cucina. Warming dishes in winter include such peasant fare as *ceci e fagioli* (beans and chickpeas; Isernia claims Molise's best), and *involtini di melanzane* (eggplant rolls stuffed with meat and cheese) are thankfully served year-round. Dinner reservations are essential on Saturday. ⊠ *Via Marcelli 186* ☎ *0865/3976* 🖃 *AE, DC, MC, V* 🕑 *Closed Sun., Dec. 24–Jan. 2, and Aug.*

¢ 🏠 **Hotel S. Maria del Bagno.** Though not the last word in traditional *molisano* decor, this quiet well-run hotel lies just outside the picturesque medieval hill village of Pesche and makes a perfect base for local country walks exploring nearby Isernia (3 km [2 mi]) and excursions into the rest of Molise. ⊠ *Viale S. Maria del Bagno 1, 86090 Pesche* ☎ *0865/460129* 🖶 *0865/460136* 🖅 *45 rooms* 🍴 *Restaurant, bar, playground, meeting room; no a/c.* 🖃 *AE, DC, MC, V.*

Pietrabbondante

❸❽ *26 km (17 mi) northeast of Isernia, 25 km (16 mi) south of Agnone.*

Identified by some scholars as Bovianum Vetus, the capital of Samnium in antiquity, the site of Pietrabbondante consists of a theater and temple complex built between the 4th and 1st centuries BC, 3,000 ft up in the wilds of Molise. Though attempts to restore two of the monuments are in questionable taste, seeing a **Hellenistic theater** this high up verges on a supernatural experience. ⊠ *Via Macere* ☎ *0865/76129* ⊠ *€2* ⊘ *May–Sept., daily 9–7; Oct.–Apr., daily 9–1:15.*

Agnone

❸❾ *43 km (27 mi) north of Isernia.*

Known since medieval times for its thriving production of bells, Agnone has a rambling old town that's worth exploring. Make a stop at the **Museo Internazionale della Campana,** which chronicles the history of campanology in the area. ⊠ *C/o Fonderia Marinelli, Via F. D'Onofrio 14* ☎ *0865/78235* ⊠ *€4* ⊘ *Tours daily at 10, noon, 4, and 6, in Italian only.*

Where to Stay

¢–$ 🏨 **Albergo Sammartino.** Strategically located just at the entrance to the old town and with views from most rooms sweeping over the Verrino valley, this hotel has been owned by the Sammartino family for almost 90 years. Rooms are simple and light. It's usually quiet, except for Sunday morning, when church bells start up their concerto around dawn. ⊠ *Largo Pietro Micca 44, 86081* ☎ *0865/77577* 🖷 *0865/78239* 🛏 *22 rooms* ♨ *Restaurant, bar, dance club, meeting room; no a/c* ⊟ *AE, DC, MC, V.*

Sepino

❹⓪ *41 km (26 mi) southeast of Isernia, 25 km (16 mi) south of Campobasso.*

The hill town of Sepino takes its name from the ancient Roman town of **Saepinum,** situated off the main S17 near the village of Altìlia. The site, whose monuments were mainly laid out in the Augustan age (27 BC–AD 14), is like a miniature Pompeii, but refreshingly without the hordes of visitors. Saepinum is best tackled by entering through the Porta Tammaro 300 ft from the main road and working your way round counterclockwise via the theater, the baths (note the original stucco on the walls), the *decumanus* (main street) to the basilica (identified by its peristyle of columns), and then out onto the forum, with its standard complement of civic buildings. Southwest of the forum, just off the *cardo* (main cross street) leading to the southwestern gate of Porta Terravecchia are the administrative offices. and visitor center, where site maps and descriptions (in Italian) can be obtained. ⊠ *Contrada Altìlia* ☎ *0874/790207* ⊠ *Free* ⊘ *Daily 8–8.*

LAZIO, ABRUZZO & MOLISE A TO Z

To research prices, get advice from other travelers, and book travel arrangements, visit www.fodors.com.

AIRPORTS

Central Italy's closest major airports are in Rome, Pescara, and Naples. Pescara is served by Ryanair from London and Frankfurt, and by Air One from Milan.

🛈 Airport Information **Naples** Capodichino ☎ 081/7896259 ⊕ www.gesac.it. **Pescara** Abruzzo ☎ 085/4324200 ⊕ www.abruzzo-airport.it. **Rome** Fiumicino ☎ 06/65953640.

BUS TRAVEL

COTRAL buses leave Rome for Cerveteri from the Lepanto stop of Metro A, with service every 40 minutes or so during the day. The ride takes about 70 minutes. Tuscania has a regular bus connection with Viterbo.

Buses leave Rome for Tivoli every 15 minutes from the terminal at the Ponte Mammolo stop on Metro B, but not all take the route that passes near Hadrian's Villa. Inquire which bus passes closest to the villa and tell the driver to let you off there. The ride takes about one hour. From Rome to Palestrina, take the COTRAL bus from the Anagnina stop on Metro A. From Rome to Subiaco, take the COTRAL bus from the Rebibbia stop on Metro B; buses leave every 40 minutes; the circuitous trip takes one hour and 45 minutes.

COTRAL buses for Viterbo depart from the Saxa Rubra stop of the Ferrovie COTRAL train. The *diretta* (direct) bus takes about 75 minutes. Bagnaia can be reached from Viterbo by local city bus. For Caprarola, COTRAL buses leave from the Saxa Rubra station on the Roma Nord line.

COTRAL buses for Sermoneta leave Rome from the EUR Fermi stop of Metro B. The ride takes about one hour.

For Abruzzo, L'Aquila is served by hourly ARPA buses leaving Stazione Tiburtina in Rome, while for the National Park it's best to take the train to Avezzano and then travel onward on the ARPA bus. Buses for Molise (Molise Trasporti) leave Rome (Stazione Tiburtina) roughly every 2 hours and take about 2½ hours to reach Isernia.

🚌 Bus Information **ARPA** ☎ 0863/26561. **COTRAL** ☎ 800/431784 toll free. **Molise Trasporti** ☎ 0874/493080.

CAR TRAVEL

To get from Rome to Ostia (a 30- to 40-minute trip), follow Via del Mare southwest, which leads directly there. If approaching from Rome's ring road, the *Gran Raccordo Anulare,* look for the Ostiense or Ostia Antica exit.

For Cerveteri, take either the A12 Rome–Civitavecchia toll highway to the Cerveteri-Ladispoli exit, or take the more scenic coastal route with stoplights, the Via Aurelia. The trip takes about 40 minutes on the autostrada, twice that on the slow road. To get to Tarquinia, take the A12 Rome–Civitavecchia highway all the way to the end, where you continue on the Via Aurelia to Tarquinia. The trip takes about one hour. From that point, Tuscania is reached by cutting inland for another ½ hour.

For Tivoli, take the Rome–L'Aquila autostrada (A24). To get to Palestrina directly from Rome, take the Autostrada del Sole (A2) to the San Cesareo exit and follow signs for Palestrina; this trip takes about one hour. From Rome to Subiaco, take S155 east for about 40 km (25 mi) and the S411 for 25 km (15½ mi); the trip takes about 70 minutes.

For Viterbo, Bagnaia, and Bomarzo, head out of Rome on the A1 autostrada, exiting at Attigliano. Bomarzo is only 3 km (2 mi) from the autostrada. The trip takes one hour.

The fastest route to sites south of Rome is the Via Pontina, an expressway. For Sermoneta, turn northeast at Latina. The trip takes about 50 minutes. For out-of-the-way Ninfa, proceed as for Sermoneta, but before reaching Sermoneta, follow the signs for Doganella/Ninfa. The trip takes about one hour. For Sperlonga, take the Via Pontina to Latina, then the Via Appia to Terracina and Sperlonga. The trip takes about 1½ hours.

For Abruzzo and Molise, head east from Rome on the scenic A24 autostrada toward L'Aquila, about an hour's drive from Rome. Before L'Aquila, the A25 splits off toward Pescara. For the Parco Nazionale d'Abruzzo, take the A25 past Avezzano, exit at Pescina, and follow signs to Pescasseroli. Sulmona is further along the A25, just off the *autostrada*, about two hours from Rome. For Molise, take *autostrada* A2 to the Cassino exit, and then follow the main road (SS 6) eastward via Venafro to Isernia, about 2½ hours from Rome.

EMERGENCY
SERVICES

When you're on the road, always carry a good road map, a flashlight, and, if possible, a cellular phone so that in case of a breakdown you can call ACI for towing and repairs—ask and you will be transferred to an English-speaking operator. Be prepared to tell the operator which road you're on, the direction you're going (e.g., "*verso* [in the direction of] Perugia") and the *targa* (license plate number) of your car. The great majority of Italians carry cellular phones, so if you don't have one, flag down someone who does for help.
🚗 ACI ☎ 803/116.

EMERGENCIES
Emergency numbers (listed below) are accessible from every phone, including cellular phones, all over Italy. If you have ongoing medical concerns, it's a good idea to make sure someone is on duty all night where you're staying—not a given in Lazio, less so in Abruzzo and Molise. As elsewhere in Italy, every pharmacy in Lazio, Abruzzo, and Molise bears a sign at the door listing area pharmacies open in off-hours, though in the countryside you may need a car to get to one. Try to bring extras with you of all medications you take regularly.
🚑 **Emergencies** ☎ 113. **Ambulance** ☎ 118. **Carabinieri** (Military Police) ☎ 112. **Fire** ☎ 115.

TOURS
CIT has half-day excursions to Villa d'Este in Tivoli. American Express has tours to Hadrian's Villa. Appian Line has excursions to Hadrian's Villa. Carrani Tours has tours that include Hadrian's Villa. For Viterbo, authorized guides are available through the APT office.
🚌 Fees & Schedules **American Express** ☎ 06/67641. **Appian Line** ☎ 06/487861. **Carrani Tours** ☎06/4742501. **CIT** ☎06/478641. **Viterbo APT** ✉ Piazza San Carluccio ☎0761/304795.

TRAIN TRAVEL
Regular train service links the Ostia Antica station with Rome's Piramide Metro B Line station, near Porta San Paolo. Exit the Metro and go to the station called Ostia Lido adjacent to the Metro station. The ride takes about 35 minutes. Trains depart every half hour throughout the day.

For many destinations in the three regions, you may need to take a combination of train and bus. From stations in Rome, FS and Metropolitana suburban trains take you to the Cerveteri-Ladispoli station, where you can get a bus for Cerveteri. The train takes 30 minutes; the bus ride then takes 15 minutes. To get to Tarquinia, take an FS train (Rome–Genoa line) from Rome or from Cerveteri to the Tarquinia station (this service is sometimes operated by bus between Civitavecchia and Tarquinia), then a local bus from the station up to the hilltop town. The trip takes about 75–90 minutes. There's a fast mainline train service from Rome to Viterbo, which takes an hour and 40 minutes. Tuscania is accessible by bus from Viterbo. Trains also stop at Bagnaia, 10 minutes beyond Viterbo.

FS trains connect Rome's Termini and Tiburtina stations with Tivoli in about 30 minutes; Villa d'Este is about a 20-minute uphill walk from the station at Tivoli. The FS train from Stazione Termini to Palestrina takes about 40 minutes; you can then board a bus from the train station to the center of town.

FS trains on the Rome–Formia–Naples line stop at Latina Scalo, where you can get a local bus to Sermoneta, though service is erratic. Traveling time is about one hour. For Sperlonga, on the same line, get off at the Itri station, from which buses leave for Sperlonga. The trip takes about 1½ hours.

Abruzzo is served by trains to Avezzano (10 trains daily from Roma Termini), from where you can get an ARPA bus direct to Pescasseroli and Civitella Alfedena. Sulmona is directly on the Rome-Tivoli-Pescara train line, 2½ hours from Rome. In Molise, as an alternative to direct bus links from Rome, Isernia and Campobasso are reached by local train from Vairano-Caianello, a junction on the Rome–Caserta railway.

🚆 Train Information **FS–Trenitalia** ☎ 848/888088 ⊕ www.trenitalia.com.

VISITOR INFORMATION

🚆 Tourist Information **Cerveteri** ✉ Piazza Risorgimento 19 ☎ 06/99551971. **Isernia** ✉ Via Farinacci 9 ☎ 0865/3992. **L'Aquila** ✉ Piazza Santa Maria di Paganica 5 ☎ 0862/410808 ⊕ www.abruzzoturismo.it. **Latina** ✉ Piazza del Popolo ☎ 0773/480672. **Palestrina** ✉ Piazza Santa Maria degli Angeli ☎ 06/9573176. **Parco Nazionale d'Abruzzo** ✉ Via Piave 2, Pescasseroli ☎ 0863/910097 ⊕ www.regione.abruzzo.it/turismo/parchi/nazionale/index.html. **Subiaco** ✉ Via Cadorna 59 ☎ 0774/822013. **Sulmona** ✉ Corso Ovidio 208 ☎ 0864/53276. **Tarquinia** ✉ Piazza Cavour 1 ☎ 0766/856384 ⊕ www.comune.tarquinia.vt.it. **Tivoli** ✉ Largo Garibaldi ☎ 0774/334522. **Tuscania** ✉ Via del Comune 1 ☎ 0761/436371. **Viterbo** ✉ Piazza Verdi 4/a ☎ 0761/226666.

NAPLES & CAMPANIA
POMPEII, CAPRI, THE AMALFI COAST

13

FODOR'S CHOICE

Cocumella, hotel, Sorrento

La Stanza del Gusto, restaurant, Naples

Pompeii

Ravello

Villa Eva, hotel, Capri

HIGHLY RECOMMENDED

RESTAURANTS   Cumpà Cosimo, Ravello

Da Gemma, Amalfi

Da Tonino, Capri

Don Alfonso 1890, Sorrento

Il Melograno, Ischia

Parrucchiano, Sorrento

Vadinchenia, Naples

HOTELS   Excelsior Vittoria, Sorrento

Le Sirenuse, Positano

Palazzo Sasso, Ravello

Santa Caterina, Amalfi

Scalinatella, Capri

SIGHTS   Arco di Traiano, Benevento

Caserta

Certosa di San Martino, Naples

Herculaneum

Museo Archeologico Nazionale, Naples

Museo di Capodimonte, Naples

Paestum

Positano

Villa San Michele, Capri

Updated by
Mark Walters

CAMPANIA IS A REGION OF EVOCATIVE NAMES—Capri, Sorrento, Pompeii, Herculaneum—that conjure up visions of cliff-shaded coves, sun-dappled waters, and mighty ruins. The gateway to these treasures is the regional capital of Naples (Napoli in Italian), the most operatic of cities, lording over its fabled bay. Campania stretches south in flat coastal plains and low mountains from Baia Domizia, Capua, and Caserta to Naples and Pompeii on the magnificent bay; past the isles of Capri and Ischia; along the rocky coast to Sorrento, Amalfi, and Salerno; and farther still past the Cilento National Park to Sapri and the Basilicata border. Inland lies the rugged Apennine chain and the rolling countryside around Benevento.

On each side of Naples the earth fumes and grumbles, a reminder that all this beauty was born of cataclysm. Toward Sorrento, Vesuvius smolders sleepily over the ruins of Herculaneum and Pompeii, while west of Naples, beyond Posillipo, the craters of the Solfatara spew steaming gases. And nearby are the dark, deep waters of Lago d'Averno, legendary entrance to Hades. With these reminiscences of death and destruction so close at hand, it's no wonder that the southerner in general, and the Neapolitan in particular, plunges so enthusiastically into the task of living each moment to its fullest.

Lying on Mediterranean trade routes plied by several pre-Hellenic civilizations, Campania was systematically settled by the ancient Greeks from approximately 800 BC onward. Here myth and legend blend confusingly with historical fact: the town of Herculaneum is said—rather improbably—to have been established by Hercules himself, while Naples in ancient times was called Parthenope, the name attributed to one of the Sirens who preyed on hapless sailors in antiquity. Nearby Cumae, thought to be the first Greek settlement on the Italian mainland, was home to the famous Sibyl, who pronounced her oracles from the recesses of a dark vaulted chamber. Thanks to archaeological research, some of the layers of myth have been stripped away to reveal an extensive pattern of occupation and settlement well before Rome became established. Greek civilization flourished for hundreds of years all along this coastline, but there was nothing in the way of centralized government until centuries later, when the Roman Republic, uniting all Italy for the first time, surged southward and absorbed the Greek colonies with little opposition. Generally, the peace of Campania was undisturbed during these centuries of Roman rule.

Naples and Campania, with the rest of Italy, decayed with the Roman Empire and collapsed into the abyss of the Middle Ages. Naples itself regained some importance under the rule of the Angevins in the latter part of the 13th century and continued its progress in the 1440s under Aragonese rule. The nobles who served under the Spanish viceroys in the 16th and 17th centuries, when their harsh rule made all Italy quail, enjoyed their pleasures, and taverns and gaming houses thrived, even as Spain milked the area with its taxes. After a short-lived Austrian occupation, Naples became the capital of the Kingdom of the Two Sicilies, which the Bourbon kings established in 1738. Their rule was generally benevolent, as far as Campania was concerned, and their support of papal authority in Rome was an important factor in the development of the rest of Italy. Their rule was important artistically, too, for not only did it contribute greatly to the architectural beauty of the region, but it attracted great musicians, artists, and writers only too willing to enjoy the easy life at court in such magnificent natural surroundings. Finally, Giuseppe Garibaldi launched his famous expedition, and in 1860 Naples was united with the rest of Italy.

Times were relatively tranquil through the years that followed—with visitors of one nation or another thronging to Capri, to Sorrento, to Amalfi, and, of course, to Naples—until World War II. Allied bombings did considerable damage in Naples and the bay area. At the fall of the fascist government, the sorely tried Neapolitans rose up against Nazi occupation troops and in four days of street fighting drove them out of the city. A monument was raised to the *scugnizzo* (the typical Neapolitan street urchin), celebrating the youngsters who participated in the battle. The war ended. Artists, tourists, writers, and other lovers of beauty began to flow again into the Campania region that one ancient writer called "most blest by the Gods, most beloved by man." As the years have gone by, some parts gained increased attention from knowing visitors, while others lost the cachet they once had. Though years of misgovernment have left an indelible mark, the tide appears to be turning: The region's immense cultural and natural heritage is finally being revalued as local authorities and inhabitants alike appreciate the importance of nurturing the area's largest industry—tourism.

Exploring Campania

Many of Campania's attractions are on the Golfo di Napoli (Bay of Naples)—including the city itself and its satellite islands, Capri and Ischia, and the archaeological sites of Pompeii, Herculaneum, and the Campi Flegrei (Phlegrean Fields) at the northern end of the bay. At the southern end, Sorrento also lies in this charmed circle, within easy distance of Positano and the pleasures of the Amalfi Coast. Farther afield, Paestum offers more classical sights, while inland, Caserta has a Bourbon palace and Benevento more majestic Roman remains.

If art and antiquities are high on your list, consider spending a few days in Naples before retreating to the beauty of Capri, Ischia, or the Amalfi Coast. Few fall in love with Naples at first sight, and many complain about its obvious flaws: urban decay and delinquency. But practically everyone who takes the time and trouble to discover its artistic riches and appreciate its vivacious nature considers it worth the effort. Naples is close to Italy's most fabled classical ruins, and you should dedicate at least a morning or afternoon to Pompeii or Herculaneum.

About the Restaurants & Hotels

Campania restaurants are known for their flexible meal times; in the evening many will continue serving until the wee hours. Following the strong oral tradition of southern Italians, many restaurants in Campania don't have menus, or, if there is a menu, the best dishes may not be on it. Instead you're likely to be told what's on offer by your waiter—creating great opportunities for you to expand your Italian culinary vocabulary.

Most areas have fine accommodations in all price categories, but they get very busy (especially the small establishments), so reserve well in advance. High-season rates apply at all coastal resorts from April or May through September, and Christmas and Easter also draw crowds and command top rates. Whereas coastal resorts elsewhere close up tight from fall to spring, some hotels and restaurants are open in Sorrento and on the Amalfi Coast year-round (many lodgings reopen just for the Christmas and New Year period). It's always a good idea to book far in advance, and it's imperative in high season (July to September). In summer, hotels on the coast that serve meals almost always require that you take half-board. Recent years have seen a boom in "agriturismo" or farmhouse lodgings, especially in the Cilento south of Salerno and the province of Benevento. This is an increasingly attractive option for families, budget travelers, and those wanting to practice their Italian.

Numbers in the text correspond to numbers in the margin and on the Campania, Naples, and Pompeii maps.

If you have 3 days

In 🏛 **Naples** ①–⑯ ⚑, a visit to the **Museo Archeologico Nazionale** ⑮ is an essential preparation (or follow-up) for an expedition to **Herculaneum** ㉑ and **Pompeii** ㉔–㊵, indispensable sights for anyone visiting Campania. The islands of **Ischia** ㊺ and **Capri** ㊻ can also be reached from Naples and make an ideal antidote to the city's noise. It's worth spending at least one night out of Naples, and a good alternative to the islands would be 🏛 **Sorrento** ㊼, an easy hydrofoil ride away and a good base from which to tour the nearby Amalfi Coast, where you could visit small towns—**Positano** ㊽, **Amalfi** ㊾, and **Ravello** ㊿, for instance—on a third day's excursion.

If you have 5 days

In 🏛 **Naples** ①–⑯ ⚑, more time will enable you to take in one of the region's greatest palace-museums, the **Museo di Capodimonte** ⑯, housed in one of the Bourbon royal palaces. Outside of town you could also see more than just one of the classical sights, including a visit to the Greek temples of **Paestum** ㉒, highly recommended for a glimpse at some of Magna Graecia's most stunning relics. You might also venture north to **Caserta** ㊶ to wander around the royal palace and its vast grounds. Back in the Bay of Naples, spend your fourth and fifth days exploring 🏛 **Ischia** ㊺ and 🏛 **Sorrento** ㊼, both undemanding holiday resorts with plenty of natural beauty.

If you have 7 days

A week in Campania will allow you to discover some of the more esoteric pleasures that Naples has to offer. Apart from the sheer vibrancy of its shopping streets and alleys, and the glorious views over the waterfront, 🏛 **Naples** ①–⑯ ⚑ has plenty of diversions within its tight mesh of streets, and you should make time for visiting some of its many famous churches—the **Duomo** ⑬, of course, but also **Santa Chiara** ⑩, the art gallery of the **Girolamini** ⑭, and the **Cappella Sansevero** ⑪, with its 18th-century sculptures. Outside town, head west to the volcanic region of the **Phlegrean Fields** ⑰–⑳, where Roman remains lie within a smoking, smoldering area rich with classical history. Spend three nights on the Amalfi Coast, making sure to visit inland 🏛 **Ravello** ㊿ and pass some time in pretty 🏛 **Positano** ㊽, which requires at least a day. 🏛 **Capri** ㊻, too, deserves a couple of nights to appreciate fully its beauty. You might pass a last day, perhaps en route out of Campania, in **Benevento** ㊸, which holds a well-preserved Roman theater and the renowned Arco di Traiano.

	$$$$	$$$	$$	$	¢
WHAT IT COSTS In euros					
RESTAURANTS	over €22	€17–€22	€12–€17	€7–€12	under €7
HOTELS	over €210	€160–€210	€110–€160	€60–€110	under €60

Restaurant prices are for a second course (secondo piatto). Hotel prices are for two people in a standard double room in high season, including tax and service.

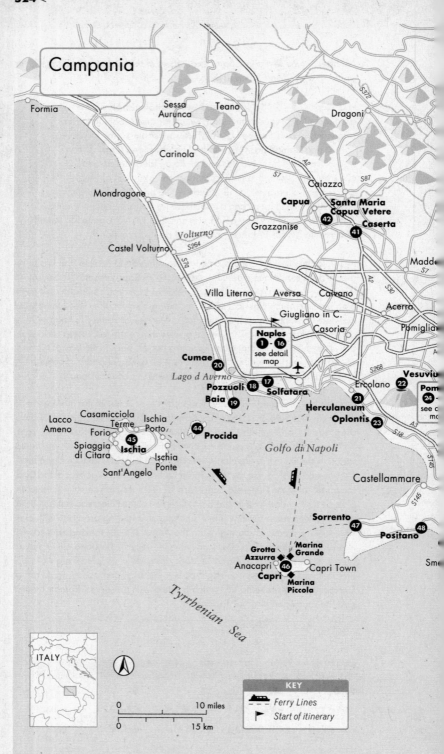

Campania

Formia

Sessa
Aurunca

Teano

Dragoni

S372

Carinola

Caiazzo

Mondragone

Capua

Santa Maria
Capua Vetere

42

Caserta

41

Castel Volturno

Volturno

S264

S7

Grazzanise

Madd

S7

S7a

Villa Literno

Aversa

Caivano

S90

Acerra

Giugliano in C.

Casoria

Pomiglia

Naples
1 – **16**
see detail
map

Cumae

20

Lago d'Averno

Pozzuoli

18

17

Solfatara

Vesuviu

22

Pom

24

see d
ma

Baia

19

Ercolano

21

Herculaneum

Oplontis

23

S18

A3

Lacco
Ameno

Casamicciola
Terme

Ischia
Porto

44

Procida

Golfo di Napoli

Forio

45

Spiaggia
di Citara

Ischia

Ischia
Ponte

Castellammare

Sant'Angelo

S145

S145

Sorrento

47

48

Positano

Grotta
Azzurra

Marina
Grande

Sme

Anacapri

46

Capri Town

Capri

Marina
Piccola

Tyrrhenian Sea

ITALY

0   10 miles

0   15 km

KEY

⛴ *Ferry Lines*

🚩 *Start of itinerary*

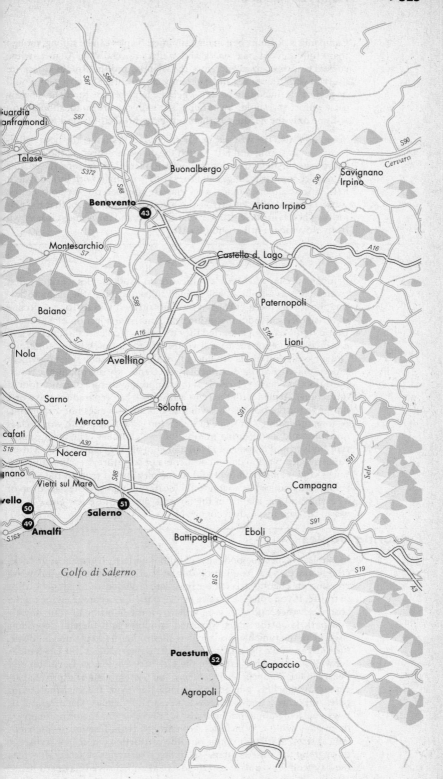

Campania is not at its best in high summer: Naples can be stifling, though thankfully devoid of crowds and traffic especially in August, while coastal resorts such as Sorrento, the islands, and the Amalfi Coast are overrun with tour buses and bad tempers. Any other time of year would be preferable, including winter, when the temperature rarely falls below the comfort threshold. Swimming is possible year-round, though you will see only the hardiest bathers out between October and May.

Summer is also the worst time for ascents to Vesuvius; the best visibility occurs in spring and fall. Watch the clock, however, as the days get shorter; excursions to Vesuvius, Pompeii, Herculaneum, and the islands all require some traveling, and it's easy to get caught with little daylight left. At most archaeological sites you are rounded up one hour before sunset, so the earlier you arrive the better. Remember, too, that the majority of hotels in Sorrento, the Amalfi Coast, and the islands close down from November until around Easter.

NAPLES

Before its decline after Italy's unification in 1860, Naples was a city that rivaled Paris as a brilliant and refined cultural capital, the ultimate destination for northern European travelers on their Grand Tour. A decade of far-sighted city administration and a massive injection of European Union funds has kick-started the city back on course, though it is still a difficult place for the casual visitor to take a quick liking to: Noise and air pollution levels are uncomfortably high, while unemployment protest marches and industrial disputes frequently disrupt public transportation and may even result in the temporary closure of major tourist attractions. Armed with the right attitude—"be prepared for the worst but hope for the best"—you will find that Napoli does not disappoint. Among other things, it's one of Italy's top *città d'arte,* with world-class museums and a staggering number of fine churches. The most important finds from Pompeii and Herculaneum are on display at the Museo Archeologico Nazionale—a cornucopia of sculpture, frescoes, and mosaics—and seeing them will add to the pleasure of trips to the ancient ruins. And Naples has a wonderful location: thanks to the backdrop of Vesuvius and the islands in the bay, it's one of those few cities in the world that are instantly recognizable.

Exploring Naples

In Naples you need a good sense of humor and a firm grip on your pocketbook and camera. You'll probably be doing a lot of walking (take care crossing the chaotic streets), for buses are crowded and taxis get stalled in traffic. If you come to Naples by car, park it in a garage, agree on the cost in advance, and then keep it there for the duration of your stay. (If you park it on the street, smashed windows and theft are constant risks.) Use the funiculars or the new metro (line 1) to get up and down the hills, and take the quick—but erratic—metro line 2 (the city's older subway system) when crossing the city between Piazza Garibaldi and Pozzuoli. For Pompeii, Herculaneum, and Sorrento, take the private Circumvesuviana line, while the Cumana line from Piazza Montesanto takes in Pozzuoli and leads toward Baia and Cumae. The *artecard* allows you to combine public transport and entry to major museums: a three-day card (€25) includes free entry to two museums or archaeological sites, a 50% discount on other attractions, and free transport throughout the museum area—including return trips on fast craft across the bay from Pozzuoli as far afield as Salerno; a seven-day card (€28)

ON THE MENU

CAMPANIA'S SIMPLE CUISINE *relies heavily on the bounty of the region's fertile farmland. Locally grown tomatoes are exported all over the world, but to try them here is another experience completely. Even in winter you can find tomato sauce made with small sun-dried tomatoes plucked from bright red strands that you can see hanging outdoors on kitchen balconies. Pasta is a staple here, and spaghetti al pomodoro (with tomato sauce) and alle vongole (with clam sauce, either white or red) appear on most menus.*

Naples is the homeland of pizza, and you'll encounter it here in two classic forms: alla margherita (with tomato, mozzarella, and basil) and marinara (with tomato, garlic, and oregano). Mozzarella—produced by Campania's thriving buffalo population—is used in many dishes; one of the most gratifying on a hot day is insalata caprese (salad with

mozzarella, tomatoes, and basil). Melanzane (eggplant) and even zucchini are served parmigiana (fried and layered with tomato sauce and mozzarella). Meat may be served alla pizzaiola (cooked in a tomato-and-garlic sauce). Fish and seafood in general can be expensive, though fried calamari and totani (cuttlefish) are usually reasonably priced. Lemons, grown locally, are widely used in cooking and for the sweet and heady liqueur limoncello, especially popular around Sorrento and on the Amalfi Coast. Among the region's grape varieties, Fiano, Greco di Tufo, and Falanghina make fine whites, while the Aglianico grape produces Campania's prestigious red, Taurasi. Wine production here has an impressive pedigree, with Falerno wines (red and white) being mentioned by the Latin poet, Horace, while Lacryma Christi (a blend of grape varieties) is produced from grapes grown around the slopes of Vesuvius.

gives free entry to all sights covered by the program but doesn't include a travel pass. You can purchase the *artecard* and find out more information on the sights covered at the airport stand (outside customs), at the train station at Piazza Garibaldi, and at the Web site ⊕ www.campaniartecard.it.

For standard public transportation, a Giranapoli pass costs €0.77 and is valid for 90 minutes on all public transit within the city boundaries; €2.32 buys a *biglietto giornaliero* (ticket for the whole day). A Fascia 1 ticket (€1.29 for 100 minutes) covers trips between Naples and a radius of about 10 km (6 mi), which includes Pozzuoli and Portici; Fascia 2 (€1.55 for 120 minutes) takes in Ercolano (Herculaneum), Baia, and Cuma; Fascia 3 (€2.01 for 140 minutes) includes Pompeii, Boscoreale, and Castellammare; Fascia 4 (€2.48 for 160 minutes) will take you as far as Vico Equense; and Fascia 5 (€2.84 for 180 minutes) covers trips to Sorrento and beyond.

Royal Naples

a good walk

Start at the **Castel Nuovo** ❶ ▶, facing the harbor on Piazza Municipio, housing a museum of mainly religious art. Pass the **Teatro San Carlo** ❷ on your way to the imposing **Palazzo Reale** ❸, a royal palace rich with the indulgences of Naples's past rulers. Next, turn back to the seafront where, 15 minutes' walk south, is another royal fortress, the **Castel dell'Ovo** ❹, overlooking the Santa Lucia waterfront. Walking along the seafront promenade against the flow of traffic, you might drop into the **Acquario** ❺ set in the extensive grounds of the Villa Comunale before turning inland. Take the quiet Via Bausan to Via Colonna, turn left, and go to the funicular stop at Piazza Amedeo; take a ride up to the **Museo Nazionale della Ceramica Duca di Martina** ❻—though you might be content to take in the extraordinary views from the slopes of the Vomero neighborhood. Also in the Vomero are the **Castel Sant'Elmo** ❼ and the adjacent **Certosa di San Martino** ❽, both commanding magnificent vistas over city and sea to Vesuvius.

TIMING You should start early to fit all these sights into just one day. Allow about two hours for the museum visits, especially the Palazzo Reale and the Certosa di San Martino. The views from the latter over the bay are good at any time, but are especially fine at sunset.

What to See

❺ **Acquario.** Children and art-exhausted adults appreciate the aquarium in the public gardens on Via Caracciolo. Founded by a German naturalist in the late 19th century, it's the oldest in Europe. About 200 species of fish and marine plants thrive in large tanks—unfortunately not always clearly labeled—with one of the highlights being the elegantly patterned moray eels, undoubtedly better off here than in the fairly polluted Bay of Naples, their natural habitat. If you have time you may want to wander in the gardens of the Villa Comunale—where there are a bandstand and play areas for children. On the third and fourth weekends of the month, antiques markets are held here. ⊠ *Stazione Zoologica, Viale A. Dohrn, Chiaia* ☎ *081/5833263 information and library visits* ⊕ *www. szn.it* ⊠ *€1.55* ☉ *Mar.–Oct., Tues.–Sat. 9–6, Sun. 9:30–7:30; Nov.–Feb., Tues.–Sat. 9–5, Sun. 9–2.*

❹ **Castel dell'Ovo.** Dangling over the Porto Santa Lucia on a thin promontory, this 12th-century fortress built over the ruins of an ancient Roman villa commands a view of the whole harbor—proof, if you need it, that the Romans knew a premium location when they saw one. For the same reason, some of the city's top hotels share the site. It's a peaceful spot for strolling and enjoying the views. ⊠ *Santa Lucia waterfront, Via Partenope, Santa Lucia* ☎ *081/2400055* ⊠ *Free* ☉ *Mon.–Sat. 9–5, Sun. 9–1:30.*

▶ ❶ **Castel Nuovo.** Also known as the Maschio Angioino, this massive fortress was built by the Angevins (related to the French monarchy) in the 13th century and completely rebuilt by the Aragonese rulers (descendants of an illegitimate branch of Spain's ruling line) who succeeded them. The decorative marble triumphal arch that forms the entrance was erected during the Renaissance in honor of King Alfonso V of Aragón (1396–1458), and its rich bas-reliefs are credited to Francesco Laurana (circa 1430–1502). Set incongruously into the castle's heavy stone walls, the arch is one of the finest works of its kind. Within the castle, you can see sculptures and frescoes from the 14th and 15th centuries, as well as the city's **Museo Civico,** comprising mainly local artwork from the 15th to 19th century. It's hard to avoid the impression that these last were rejects from the much finer collection at the Museo di Capodimonte, though there are also regular exhibitions worth visiting, and the windows offer views over the piazza and the port below. You can also visit the Palatine Chapel and the octagonal **Sala dei Baroni,** where Ferrante I disposed of a group of rebellious barons in 1485 by inviting them to a mock wedding party and then pouring boiling oil on their heads from the ceiling. The room is still regularly used for city council meetings. In the left corner of the courtyard is the **Sala dell'Armeria,** the Armory, where part of the flooring has been conveniently glassed over to reveal the remains of a Roman villa and a medieval necropolis. ⊠ *Castel Nuovo, Piazza Municipio* ☎ *081/7952003* ⊠ *€5, free Sun.* ☉ *Mon.–Sat. 9–7, ticket office closes at 6; courtyard only Sun. 9–1.*

❼ **Castel Sant'Elmo.** Perched on the Vomero, the castle was built by the Angevins in the 14th century to dominate the port and the old city and remodeled by the Spanish in 1537. The stout fortifications are still in use today by the military, and occasionally there are performances, exhibitions, and fairs. ⊠ *Largo San Martino, Vomero* ☎ *081/5784020* ⊡ *€1* ⊙ *Tues.–Sun. 9–7.*

★ ❽ **Certosa di San Martino.** A Carthusian monastery restored in the 17th century in exuberant Neapolitan baroque style, this structure has now been transformed into a diverse museum complex. The **Museo dell'Opera,** with its impressive galleries around the Chiostro Grande (great cloister), gives a sound introduction to monastic life and a well-signposted history of the Carthusians and San Martino. Room 24 has a helpful 18th-century scale model of the monastic complex, while Room 26 has 19th-century paintings of monastic life. Dalbono's 13 gouaches of Vesuvius in various angry poses are attractively displayed in Room 28; moving back in time, Room 32 contains part of the anonymous Tavola Strozzi depicting the Naples waterfront in the 15th century and the return of the Aragonese fleet from the Battle of Ischia. The *presepi* (Christmas crèches) are a popular exhibit, while the splendidly decorated church and annexes, and the panoramic garden terraces are two other good reasons for coming up here. Take the funicular from Piazza Montesanto to Vomero. ⊠ *Museo Nazionale di San Martino, Vomero* ☎ *081/5781769* ⊡ *€6, includes admission to Castel Sant'Elmo* ⊙ *Tues.–Sun. 8:30–7.*

❻ **Museo Nazionale della Ceramica Duca di Martina.** The lushly shaded park and the view over Naples are two reasons to venture up the Chiaia funicular from Via del Parco Margherita. Set on the slopes of the Vomero hill in a park known as Villa Floridiana, it houses thousands of ceramic pieces from medieval times to the 18th century, including local majolica, a fine collection of European and Asian porcelain, and other objets d'art in a neoclassical residence built in the early 19th century by King Ferdinand I for his wife, Lucia Migliaccio. Their portraits greet you as you enter. Enjoy the view from the terrace behind the museum. ⊠ *Via Cimarosa 77, Vomero* ☎ *081/5788418* ⊡ *€2.50 for museum, park free* ⊙ *Tues.–Sun. 8:30–2. Park 8:30–1 hr before sunset.*

❸ **Palazzo Reale.** Dominating Piazza del Plebiscito, the huge palace—best described as overblown imperial—dates from the early 1600s. It was renovated and redecorated by successive rulers, including Napoléon's sister Caroline and her ill-fated husband, Joachim Murat (1767–1815), who reigned briefly in Naples after the French emperor had sent the Bourbons packing and before they returned to reclaim their kingdom. Don't miss seeing the **royal apartments,** sumptuously furnished and full of precious paintings, tapestries, porcelains, and other objets d'art. The monumental marble staircase gives you an idea of the scale on which Neapolitan rulers lived. ⊠ *Piazza del Plebiscito* ☎ *081/5808111* ⊡ *€4* ⊙ *Thurs.–Tues. 9–7:30.*

need a break?

Besieged by the traffic swirling around the Teatro San Carlo and Piazza Trieste e Trento, the **Caffè Gambrinus** (⊠ Piazza Trieste e Trento, Piazza Plebiscito ☎ 081/417582) is a haven of old-style Naples and the onetime haunt of artists and intellectuals of every persuasion. Gilded and mirrored, this *gran caffè* continues to serve top-quality pastries and gelato alongside savories and the never-ending cappuccinos.

Piazza del Plebiscito. The vast square next to the Palazzo Reale was laid out by order of Murat, whose architect was clearly inspired by the colonnades of St. Peter's in Rome. The large church of **San Francesco di Paola** in the middle of the colonnades was added as an offering of

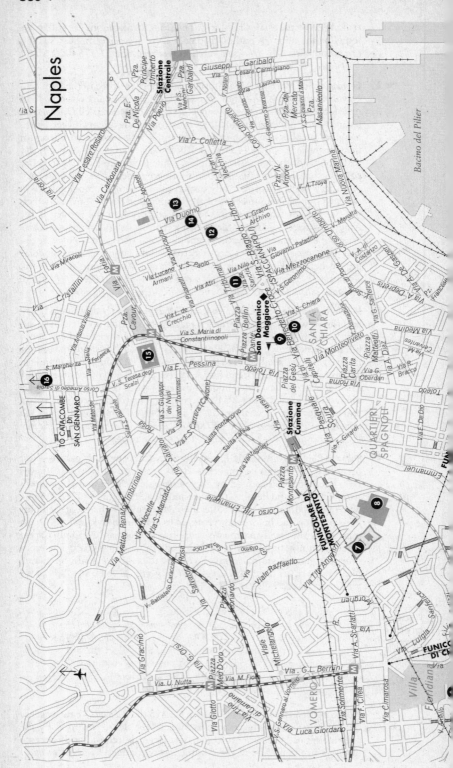

KEY

⊣—⊢ Funicular

M Metro stop

▲ Start of walk

0 ___ 300 yards

0 ___ 300 meters

Stazione **Marittima**

Molo Beverello

Bacino Angioino

Via C.

Galleria Umberto

Via Ro...

Via Nardones

Via C. Console

Via T. Acton

Piazza del Plebiscito

Via Solitaria

Via Chiaia

Via Santa Lucia

Via Gen. Orsini

Santa Lucia

Via N. Sauro

Porto S. Lucia

Via Partenope

SANTA LUCIA

Via Monte di Dio

Via Chiatamone

Pza. dei Martiri

Via Morelli

Piazza Vittoria

CHIAIA

Via del Parco Margherita

Via del Mille

Via Santa Teresa

Via Carlo Poerio

Via Carducci

Via S. Pasquale a Chiaia

Riviera di Chiaia

Via Caracciolo

Villa Comunale

Golfo di Napoli

Via Ascensione

Via G. Bausan

Piazza Amedeo

Via Colon...

Corso Vittorio Emanuele

Via F. Crispi

Via Campanella G. Marco...

V. Campanella...

TO POSILLIPO, MERGELLINA, CITTA DELLA SCIENZA, & PARCO VIRGILIANO

TO EDENLANDIA

thanks for the Bourbon restoration by Ferdinand I, whose titles reflect the somewhat garbled history of the Kingdom of the Two Sicilies, made up of Naples (which included most of the southern Italian mainland) and Sicily. They were united in the Middle Ages, then separated, then unofficially reunited under Spanish domination during the 16th and 17th centuries. In 1816, with Napoléon out of the way on St. Helena, Ferdinand IV (1751–1825) of Naples, who also happened to be Ferdinand III of Sicily, officially merged the two kingdoms, proclaiming himself Ferdinand I of the Kingdom of Two Sicilies. His reactionary and repressive rule earned him a few more colorful titles among his rebellious subjects.

Quartieri Spagnoli. The Spanish garrison was quartered in the now-decaying tenements aligned in a tight-knit grid along incredibly narrow alleys in this neighborhood roughly between Via Toledo (downhill border) and Via Pasquale Scura (western leg of Spaccanapoli). It's a hectic, impoverished (sometimes dangerous) area—chock-full of local color—brooding in the shadow of Vomero, but it's showing signs of improvement. This area is a five-minute walk west of Piazza Municipio, accessible from Via Toledo.

② **Teatro San Carlo.** This large theater was built in 1737, 40 years earlier than Milan's La Scala—though it was destroyed by fire and had to be rebuilt in 1816. You can visit the impressive interior, decorated in the white-and-gilt stucco of the neoclassical era, as part of a prearranged tour, and visitors are sometimes allowed in during morning rehearsals. ✉ *Via San Carlo between Piazza Municipio and Piazza Plebiscito, Piazza Plebiscito* ☎ *081/7972331 or 081/7972412* ⊕ *www.teatrosancarlo. it* 🎫 *€5* ⊙ *Tours by appointment.*

need a break?
Across from the Teatro San Carlo towers the imposing entrance to the glass-roofed neoclassical **Galleria Umberto** (✉ Via San Carlo, Piazza Plebiscito), a shopping arcade where you can sit at one of several cafés and watch the vivacious Neapolitans as they go about their business.

Via Toledo. Sooner or later you'll wind up at one of the busiest commercial arteries, also known as Via Roma, which has thankfully been closed to through traffic—at least along the stretch leading from the Palazzo Réale. Don't avoid dipping into this parade of shops and coffee bars where plump pastries are temptingly arranged.

Vomero. Heart-stopping views of the Bay of Naples are framed by this gentrified neighborhood on a hill served by the Montesanto, Centrale, and Chiaia funiculars. Stops for all three are an easy walk from Piazza Vanvitelli, a good starting point for exploring this thriving district with no shortage of smart bars and trattorias.

Spaccanapoli & Capodimonte

a good walk
Start your walk in Piazza Gesù, built over the old Greco-Roman city, and stroll east along Spaccanapoli (the unofficial name for the long street that cuts a straight line through the heart of Old Naples) taking in the churches of **Gesù Nuovo ⑨** ▶ and **Santa Chiara ⑩** en route. Farther up Spaccanapoli, you need only detour a few steps to see some other art-rich religious monuments: **Cappella Sansevero ⑪**, **San Lorenzo Maggiore ⑫**, the **Duomo ⑬**, and **Quadreria dei Girolamini ⑭**. Continuing north on Via Duomo, take a left onto Via Foria, and you will end up at one of Italy's most important museums, the **Museo Archeologico Nazionale ⑮**, packed with archaeological relics of the classical era and a must before venturing out of town to see Pompeii and Herculaneum. From here, footsore and weary, you deserve a taxi or bus to reach **Museo di Capodimonte ⑯**, the greatest of the Bourbon palaces, where, after ogling

at the artistic masterpieces on display, you can siesta in the Bosco di Capodimonte (park) and admire the wonderful views over the Bay of Naples.

TIMING Allow the better part of a day for this tour. You should aim to arrive at the Museo Archeologico shortly after lunchtime when the crowds have thinned out. Two hours will be just enough to get your bearings, cover the more important collections, and perhaps visit the *Gabinetto Segreto*. The museum in Capodimonte—unlike many of the churches and the archaeological museum—is well lit and can be viewed in fading daylight, so it's best left till last.

What to See

⑪ Cappella Sansevero. Off Spaccanapoli, the Cappella di Santa Maria della Pietà dei Sangro, better known as the Cappella Sansevero, holds the tombs of the noble Sangro di San Severo family. Much of it was designed in the 18th century by Giuseppe Sammartino, including the centerpiece, a striking *Veiled Christ,* carved from a single block of alabaster. If you can stomach it, take a peek in the crypt, where some of the anatomical experiments conducted by Prince Raimondo, a scion of the family and noted 18th-century alchemist, are gruesomely displayed. ⊠ *Via de Sanctis 19, Spaccanapoli* ☎ *081/5518470* ⊠ *€5* ۞ *Oct.–Apr., Mon. and Wed.–Sat. 10–4:40, Sun. 10–1; May–Sept., Mon. and Wed.–Sat. 10–6:40, Sun. 10–1.*

⑬ Duomo. Though the Duomo was established in the 1200s, the building you see was erected a century later and has since undergone radical changes, especially during the baroque age. Inside the cathedral, 110 ancient columns salvaged from pagan buildings are set into the piers that support the 350-year-old wooden ceiling. Off the left aisle, you step down into the 4th-century church of **Santa Restituta**, which was incorporated into the cathedral; though Santa Restituta was redecorated in the late 1600s in the prevalent baroque style, a few very old mosaics remain in the **Battistero** (Baptistery). The chapel also gives access to an archaeological zone, a series of paleochristian rooms dating from the Roman era.

On the right aisle of the cathedral, in the **Cappella di San Gennaro,** are multicolor marbles and frescoes honoring St. Januarius, miracle-working patron saint of Naples, whose altar and relics are encased in silver. Three times a year—on September 19 (his feast day); on the Saturday preceding the first Sunday in May, which commemorates the transference of his relics to Naples; and on December 16—his dried blood, contained in two sealed vials, is believed to liquefy during rites in his honor. On these days large numbers of devout Neapolitans offer up prayers in his memory. ⊠ *Via Duomo 147, Spaccanapoli* ☎ *081/449097* ⊠ *Duomo and Cappella di San Gennaro free, Battistero and archaeological zone €3* ۞ *Duomo and Cappella di San Gennaro daily 8–12:30 and 4:30–7; Battistero and archaeological zone Mon.–Sat. 9–noon and 4:30–6:30, Sun. 9–noon.*

▶ **⑨ Gesù Nuovo.** The oddly faceted stone facade of the church was designed as part of a palace dating from between 1584 and 1601, but plans were changed as construction progressed, and it became the front of an elaborately decorated baroque church. ⊠ *Piazza Gesù Nuovo, Spaccanapoli* ☎ *081/5518613* ۞ *Mon.–Sat. 7–12:30 and 4:15–7:30, Sun. 7–2.*

★ **⑮ Museo Archeologico Nazionale.** The National Archaeological Museum's huge red building, a cavalry barracks in the 16th century, is undergoing a massive restoration program that will fit it out with new galleries and a long-awaited cafeteria; at any given time you may find several rooms

CloseUp

THE GLITTER OF BAROQUE NAPLES

TIME, LIKE A RIVER, has dropped its silt over Naples, leaving in each age its characteristic deposit. Today, however, these deposits are not neatly layered, waiting for a distant spade to uncover, as at Pompeii, but are capricious, unplanned, and disorderly. Naples is a city of dramatic pairings: baroque with medieval, plenty with want, grandeur with muddle. Of the numerous artistic styles that make up this feast, however, none suited the Neapolitan temperament better than the baroque—the style that came to the fore in the 17th century and continued in the 18th century under the Bourbon kings.

In a city of volcanic passions, the flagrantly emotional, floridly luxurious baroque—an art that seems perpetually on the point of bursting its bonds—found immediate favor. The departure of the austere Spanish viceroys in the 17th century gave free rein to the city's natural inclination for this extroverted style, allowing artists such as Caravaggio and the Spaniard Il Ribera, and architects such as Ferdinando Sanfelice and Cosimo Fanzago, to strut their aesthetic stuff.

With untrammeled individualism given full play, the results—most still visible today—were theatrical, dramatic, dynamic, vivid, alive, and sometimes wonderfully showy. Venture into the Gesù Nuovo (mother church of the Padri Gesuiti, or Jesuit Fathers) and note the buoyant swirl of stucco, inlaid marble, and gilt work, a florid tangle that mirrors the chaos of the piazza outside its door. Like the city itself, the decorative scheme is diffuse and disjunctive, with little effort to organize everything into an easily understood scheme. Throughout the city, artists loved using illusionistic trompe l'oeil tricks of ingenious device on church cupolas, as in the Cappella di San Gennaro at the Duomo. Here, as in other churches, you'll see reliquaries studded with semiprecious stones and covered with gold, gold, and more gold. Elsewhere, statues were made hyper-real, either thanks to amazing technique—such as the marble figures in the Cappella Sansevero, where fishing nets and veils were carved from pure

stone—or by being dressed in silk and velvet garments. Thanks to the Counter-Reformation, the Catholic church was then busy making an overt appeal to the congregant, using emotion and motion to get the message across—no more so than in 17th- and 18th-century Naples, a city which, incidentally, had some 20,000 clerics, more than in Rome itself.

The most representative practitioner of Neapolitan baroque was Cosimo Fanzago (1591–1678). A Lombard by birth, he arrived in Naples to study sculpture, so even when he decorated a church, he usually covered it head to toe with colored and inlaid marbles, as in his work at the Church of San Martino in the Certosa (charterhouse) that sits atop the Vomero Hill. Two decades earlier, Caravaggio (1571–1610) had arrived in Naples from Rome and this great painter of chiaroscuro took the city by storm. He was on the point of bringing the baroque style back to earth in Naples—thanks to the unflinching truthfulness and extroverted sensuality in his paintings—but other forces prevailed.

Neapolitan baroque painters were generally a mediocre bunch. Many, in fact, banded together to form a "Facione de' Pittori" headed by the favored painter of the Spanish viceroyalty, Il Ribera. These Dependentii, or disciples, formed more than just a "union": they were a full-fledged gang and led to the persecution that plagued most painters who came to Naples for work, such as the noted Domenichino and Guido Reni, both of whom fled the city and the cabal to save their lives (or nearly so: it was widely believed that Domenichino was mysteriously poisoned shortly after leaving the city). Thanks to the disciples of Spagnoletto (Il Ribera's nickname), pride, pomposity, glitter, and gold conquered all.

closed to the public as the restoration progresses. The museum holds one of the world's great collections of Greek and Roman antiquities, including such extraordinary sculptures as the *Hercules Farnese,* an exquisite Aphrodite attributed to the 4th-century BC Greek sculptor Praxiteles, and an equestrian statue of Roman emperor Nerva. Vividly colored mosaics and countless artistic and household objects from Pompeii and Herculaneum provide insight into the life and art of ancient Rome. For a free guided tour of the limited-access Gabinetto Segreto and its collection of erotic art, ask for information at the ticket office. Invest in an up-to-date printed museum guide or audio-guide, because exhibits tend to be poorly labeled. ⊠ *Piazza Museo 19* ☎ *081/5648941* ⊕ *www.archeona.arti.beniculturali.it* ☜ *€6.50* ☉ *Wed.–Mon. 9–8.*

need a break?

Rescigno (⊠ Via Foria 40, Museo ☎ 081/2110810), close to the Piazza Cavour metro station, is a family bakery that has been in business for more than 200 years. It includes a pastry shop, café, and restaurant (at the far end) serving tasty local snacks.

★ ⑯ **Museo di Capodimonte.** The grandiose 18th-century neoclassical Bourbon royal palace, in the vast Bosco di Capodimonte (Capodimonte Park), which served as the royal hunting preserve and later as the site of the Capodimonte porcelain works, houses an impressive collection of fine and decorative art. Capodimonte's greatest treasure is the excellent collection of paintings well displayed in the **Galleria Nazionale,** on the palace's first and second floors. Besides the art collection, part of the **royal apartments** still has a complement of beautiful antique furniture, most of it on the splashy scale so dear to the Bourbons, and a staggering collection of porcelain and majolica from the various royal residences. The walls of the apartments are hung with numerous portraits, providing a close-up of the unmistakable Bourbon features, a challenge to any court painter. Most rooms have fairly comprehensive, portable information cards in English, while the audio guide is overly selective and somewhat quirky. The main galleries on the first floor are devoted to work from the 13th to 18th century, including many pieces by Dutch and Spanish masters, as well as by the great Italians. On the second floor, look out for stunning paintings by Simone Martini (circa 1284–1344), Titian (1488/90–1576), and Caravaggio (1573–1610). ⊠ *Via Miano 2, Porta Piccola, Via Capodimonte* ☎ *848/800288 information and bookings for special exhibitions* ☜ *€7.50, €6.50 after 2 PM* ☉ *Tues.–Sun. 8:30–7:30, ticket office closes 6:30 PM.*

Piazza Dante. This square, which has a metro station linking up with the Vomero and beyond, is a bibliophile's paradise the Via Port'Alba on the eastern side lined with bargain book stalls.

⑭ **Quadreria dei Girolamini.** Off an improbably quiet cloister enclosing a prolific forest of lemon and loquat trees, the Girolamini art museum is attached to the restored Girolamini church. Its intimate, high-quality collection of 16th- and 17th-century paintings is one of the city's best-kept secrets, well worth a half-hour visit. ⊠ *Via Duomo 142, Spaccanapoli* ☜ *Free* ☉ *Daily 9:30–12:50.*

⑫ **San Lorenzo Maggiore.** It's unusual to find French Gothic style in Naples, but it has survived to great effect in this church. Built in the Middle Ages and decorated with 14th-century frescoes, it's supposed to be where the poet Boccaccio (1313–75) first saw the model for his *Fiammetta.* Outside the 17th-century cloister is the entrance to **excavations** revealing what was once part of the Roman forum, and before that the Greek agora. You can walk among the streets, shops, and workshops of the ancient city and see a model of how the Greek Neapolis might have looked. ✉ *Via Tribunali, 316 Spaccanapoli* ☎ *081/2110860* ⊕ *www.sanlorenzomaggiorenapoli.it* ✉ *Excavations €4* ☉ *Daily 8–noon and 5–7; excavations Mon.–Wed. 9–1 and 3–5:30, Sat. 9–5:30, Sun. 9:30–1:30.*

🔟 **Santa Chiara.** The monastery church is a Neapolitan landmark and the subject of a famous old song. It was built in the 1300s in Provençal Gothic style, and it's best known for the quiet charm of its cloister garden, with columns and benches sheathed in 18th-century ceramic tiles painted with delicate floral motifs and vivid landscapes. An adjoining museum traces the history of the convent; the entrance is off the courtyard at the left of the church. ✉ *Piazza Gesù Nuovo, Spaccanapoli* ☎ *081/5526209* ✉ *Museum and cloister €4* ☉ *Church Apr.–Sept., daily 8:30–noon and 4–7; Oct.–Mar., daily 8:30–noon and 4–6. Museum and cloister Mon.–Sat. 9:30–1 and 2:30–5:30, Sun. 9:30–1.*

need a break? Walking up Via Santa Maria di Costantinopoli, which is lined with shops selling antiques and musical instruments, you'll come upon Piazza Bellini, a leafy square that holds **Intra Moenia** (☎ 081/ 290720), a bookstore and café open every day from 10 AM to 3 AM, serving snacks, salads, and drinks—and selling books, prints, and postcards of Naples. It also stages art exhibitions and neighbors the city's main Internet café.

Spaccanapoli. Nowhere embodies the spirit of backstreet Naples better than the arrow-straight street divided into tracts bearing several names. It runs through the heart of the old city (*spacca* means "split") from west to east, retracing one of the main arteries of the Greek, and later Roman, settlement. **Via Benedetto Croce** was named in honor of the illustrious philosopher born here in 1866, in the building at No. 12. You'll walk past peeling palaces, dark workshops where artisans ply their trades, and many churches and street shrines. Where the street changes to **Via San Biagio dei Librai** and **Via San Gregorio Armeno,** the shops stage special exhibitions of nativity scenes (*presepi*) in the weeks before Christmas. The figures may be carved of wood or made of terra-cotta. ⊹ *Beginning with Via Pasquale Scura, just west of Via Toledo, and ending with Via Vicaria Vecchia east of Via Duomo.*

need a break? While you're exploring the old part of town, take a break at what the Neapolitans call "the best pastry shop in Italy"—**Scaturchio** (✉ Piazza S. Domenico Maggiore 19, Spaccanapoli ☎ 081/ 5516944). The café was founded in 1918 by two brothers, one of whom, Francesco, invented the cakes called *ministeriali* to attract Anna Fouché, a famous actress of the time. You can still buy these cakes today, along with other Neapolitan specialties such as *babà*, *rafiol*, and *pastiera*, which you can eat there with a coffee or have specially gift-wrapped in the room at the back.

off the beaten path **CATACOMBE DI SAN GENNARO** – Many of the catacombs in Naples predate the Christian era by two centuries. These are found behind the imposing bulk of the early 20th-century church (Madre del Buon Consiglio) built over 5th-century foundations and inspired by the design of St. Peter's in Rome. The 45-minute guided tour to the two-level site takes you down a series of vestibules with fine frescoed niche tombs. ✉ *Via Capodimonte 16, Capodimonte* ☎ *081/ 7411071* ✉ *€5.* ☉ *Guided tour (required) daily every 45 mins 9:30 AM–11:45 AM; afternoon tours by appointment, for groups only.*

CITTA DELLA SCIENZA – Occupying a prime bay-side site once dominated by a huge iron-and-steel works, Italy's first science museum is in continuous expansion. Child-friendly, it has exhibitions on astronomy, robotics, and the environment, among others. The best way to get here is by taxi, or take the Cumana railway to Bagnoli. ⊠ *Via Coroglio 104, Bagnoli* ☎ *081/7352260* ⊕ *www.cittadellascienza.it* ⊠ €7 ☉ *Tues.–Sat. 9–5, Sun. 10–7.*

NAPLES UNDERGROUND – Take a revelatory trip exploring the foundations of the city, some of which date back as much as 4,000 years. Forty meters underground, informed guides will show you ancient aqueducts built by the Greeks and Romans, which later served as a bomb shelter during World War II. The commentary is normally in Italian, though with advance notice an interpreter can be hired. ⊠ *Vico S. Anna di Palazzo 52, Piazza Plebiscito* ☎ *081/400256* ⊠ €7 ☉ *Tours Sat. at 10, noon, and 6; Sun. at 10, 11, noon, and 6; Thurs. at 9 PM; or call to arrange other times. Meet at Piazza Trieste e Trento, by Bar Gambrinus.*

PARCO VIRGILIANO – Reopened to the public in 2002 after an extensive restoration, this park, also known to locals as Parco della Rimembranza, straddles the tip of the Posillipo headland and has rapidly become a showpiece for the city. The toddlers' playgrounds are well maintained, cycling paths mercifully well paved, and flower beds landscaped with an imaginative mix of exotic and native plants. The outer panoramic walkway affords memorable views across to the islands and the Phlegrean fields. Confusingly, in Mergellina there is a second Parco Virgiliano containing what's purported to be Virgil's tomb. ⊠ *Viale Virgilio, Posillipo* ⊠ *Free* ☉ *Daily 7 AM–8 PM.*

Where to Stay & Eat

$$$　✕ **La Sacrestia.** Neapolitans flock to this upscale patrician villa for the restaurant's location—on the slopes of the Posillipo hill—and high culinary standards. The seafood and meat specialties range from tasty antipasti to linguine in *salsa di scorfano* (scorpion-fish sauce). ⊠ *Via Orazio 116, Posillipo* ☎ *081/664186* ⊟ *AE, DC, MC, V* ☉ *Closed Sun. July–Aug. and 2 wks mid-Aug. No lunch Mon., no dinner Sun.*

$$　✕ **La Bersagliera.** You'll inevitably be drawn to eating at the Santa Lucia waterfront, in the shadow of the looming medieval Castel dell'Ovo. This spot is big and touristy but fun, with an irresistible combination of spaghetti and mandolins. The menu suggests uncomplicated, timeworn classics, such as spaghetti *alla pescatora* (with seafood sauce) and melanzane alla parmigiana. ⊠ *Borgo Marinaro 10, Santa Lucia* ☎ *081/7646016* ⊟ *AE, DC, MC, V* ☉ *Closed 2 wks Aug. and Tues.*

$$　✕ **La Stanza del Gusto.** The name means "The Room of Taste," and this
Fodor'sChoice　restaurant lives up to the billing. A minute's walk from some of the city's
★　busiest streets, up a flight of stairs opposite the Teatro Sannazzaro on Via Chiaia, it feels removed from the hectic world outside. This is the place to try that great stalwart of Neapolitan winter dishes, *soffritto,* a sauce made from liver, kidney, lung, and other unmentionables, combined to delicious effect. Another old favorite, *arancini* (riceballs), is transformed, stuffed with prawns and served reverently on a bed of fresh local greenery. ⊠ *Vicoletto Sant'Arpino 21, Piazza Plebiscito* ☎ *081/401578* ⊟ *DC, MC, V* ⚏ *Reservations essential* ☉ *Closed Sun., Mon., and Aug. Lunch by appointment only.*

$–$$ ✕ **Mimì alla Ferrovia.** Near the central station, this bustling fish restaurant is as close as you get in Naples to a Parisian brasserie. The service is polite but not obsequious, the atmosphere relaxed, sometimes noisy. Try the *céfalo* (mullet) when it's available, or the lobster. Other sure bets are *peperoni ripieni* (stuffed peppers) and grilled mushrooms. ⊠ *Via Alfonso D'Aragona 21, Piazza Garibaldi* ☎ *081/5538525* ☰ *AE, DC, MC, V* ☾ *Closed last 2 wks Aug. and Sun.*

★ **$–$$** ✕ **Vadinchenia.** Though it identifies itself as a cultural and gastronomic association, Vadinchenia has all the trimmings of a high-class restaurant at surprisingly modest prices. Husband-and-wife team Saverio and Silvana steer their guests through an innovative menu against a backdrop of refreshingly minimalist decor. Adventurous palates will enjoy such bold combinations as *paccheri alle alici e pecorino* (pasta with sardines and sheep's cheese), while meat eaters will delight in the *filletto al vino e sale grosso* (steak cooked in wine and rock salt). In winter round off the meal with the *purée di castagna* made from local chestnuts. ⊠ *Via Pontano 21, Chiaia* ☎ *081/660265* ☰ *AE, DC, MC, V* ☙ *Reservations essential* ☾ *Closed Sun. and Aug. No lunch.*

$–$$ ✕ **Antonio e Antonio.** This ristorante-pizzeria attracts crowds of Neapolitans for its many types of pizza and such typical dishes as spaghetti *alle vongole* (with clams) and homemade*sciallatielli del golfo* (pasta with seafood). On the site of a former nightclub right on the Santa Lucia waterfront, it has modern blue and yellow decor that's easy on the eye. There's another branch at Via Francesco Crispi 89. ⊠ *Via Partenope 24/27, Santa Lucia* ☎ *081/2451987* ☰ *AE, DC, MC, V* ☾ *Closed Mon.*

$ ✕ **L'ebbrezza di Noè.** A safe haven from pizza and seafood, this enoteca has become a popular retreat for wine *appassionati* (enthusiasts). Master of ceremonies Luca dispenses fine wines and advice in abundance, while Mamma's presence in the kitchen ensures a suitable accompaniment for the drink. Try the *zuppa di farro* (spelt soup) if available, or indulge in the cholesterol-boosting three-cheese plate of Gorgonzola, Roquefort, and Stilton. ⊠ *Vico Vetriera a Chiaia 8b/9, Chiaia* ☎ *081/400104* ☰ *AE, DC, MC, V* ☾ *Closed Mon. No lunch.*

$ ✕ **Da Michele.** You have to love a place that has, for more than 130 years, offered only two types of pizza—marinara and Margherita—and a small selection of drinks, and still manages to attract long lines. The prices have something to do with it, but the pizza itself suffers no rivals, and even those waiting in line are good humored; the boisterous, joyous atmosphere wafts out with the smell of yeast and wood smoke onto the street. ⊠ *Via C. Sersale 1/3* ☎ *081/5539204* ☰ *No credit cards* ☾ *Closed Sun. and last 2 wks in Aug.*

¢ ✕ **Sorbillo.** Locals still wait in line for their turn to sit down and devour a basic Neapolitan pizza cooked to perfection—make sure you give your name to one of the serving staff inside if all tables are taken. The third generation of pizza-makers runs this place and knows exactly what is required: rapid service, large pizzas virtually spilling off plates onto the marble table tops, and excellent value. If tiring of pizza margherita, try the pizza al pesto or pizza alla diavola with peppery salami. ⊠ *Via dei Tribunali 32, Spaccanapoli* ☎ *081/446643* ☰ *No credit cards* ☾ *Closed Sun.*

$$$$ ☷ **Grand Hotel Vesuvio.** One of the top Naples hotels, this place on the Santa Lucia waterfront has attracted artists, royalty, and dignitaries to relax in its luxury. Many are lured by its superb facilities, chief among which are its Caruso rooftop restaurant and its comprehensive health club, offering exercise facilities as well as sauna, massage therapies, and beauty treatments. It also has a dedicated children's room with mobiles, a rocking horse, and baby-sitting services. ⊠ *Via Partenope 45, Santa Lucia, 80121* ☎ *081/7640044* ☷ *081/7644483* ⊕ *www.vesuvio.it* ☞ *171* rooms, 16 suites ♻ Restaurant, cable TV, in-room safes, minibars, health club, bar, baby-sitting, meeting room, parking (fee) ⊟ AE, DC, MC, V.

\$\$\$\$ ⊞ **Parker's.** Gracefully old-fashioned, this is a sumptuous home away from home, tucked halfway between the Spanish Quarters and Vomero. Its hillside location affords wonderful views, which can be appreciated from the rooftop restaurant. The lobby and guest rooms reflect the general finery, and you can indulge bookish pursuits in the library filled with rare editions. ⊠ *Corso Vittorio Emanuele 135, Chiaia, 80121* ☎ *081/ 7612474* 🖷 *081/663527* ⊕ *www.grandhotelparkers.it* ⬎ *73 rooms, 10 suites* ♻ *Restaurant, in-room safes, minibars, bar, library, meeting rooms, parking (fee)* ⊟ *AE, DC, MC, V.*

\$\$–\$\$\$ ⊞ **Paradiso.** You can take a taxi or funicular from downtown to the modern, air-conditioned building perched on a hill above the port of Mergellina. Huge window walls in the lobby and front rooms provide gorgeous views. Blue and beige tones make for a restful, attractive setting. Smallish rooms are smart, with built-in furnishings of rosy wood with marble surfaces. A roof terrace invites sitting, dining, and contemplating the entire bay and Vesuvius. ⊠ *Via Catullo 11, Posillipo, 80122* ☎ *081/ 7614161* 🖷 *081/7613449* ⊕ *www.hotelparadisonapoli.it* ⬎ *74 rooms* ♻ *Restaurant, minibars, bar, parking (fee)* ⊟ *AE, DC, MC, V.*

\$\$–\$\$\$ ⊞ **Parteno.** This bed-and-breakfast on the waterfront is in a beautifully restored 18th-century building. The style owes much to the design skills of local sculptor and architect Luigi Mazzella; his presence is felt in the beautiful brass ceiling and door panels and various sculptured lamps, mirrors, and beds, creating the elegance and peace of a patrician house. From the breakfast room there are views to the sea, and all rooms have balconies. ⊠ *Lungomare Partenope 1, Santa Lucia, 80121* ☎🖷 *081/ 2452095* ⊕ *www.parteno.it* ⬎ *6 rooms* ♻ *Room service, minibars, Internet* ⊟ *AE, DC, MC, V.*

\$\$ ⊞ **Hotel Toledo.** A centuries-old palazzo has been tastefully transformed into this boutique hotel, located a two-minute walk up from Via Toledo, near Spaccanapoli and the Royal Palace. Rooms are furnished in a pleasing rustic style, while the leafy rooftop terrace provides a quintessentially Neapolitan backdrop for your breakfast. ⊠ *Via Montecalvario 15, Quartieri Spagnoli, 80134* ☎🖷 *081/406800* ⊕ *www.hoteltoledo.com* ⬎ *18 rooms* ♻ *Minibars, bar* ⊟ *AE, DC, MC, V.*

\$ ⊞ **Donna Regina.** This B&B is in part of the 14th-century monastery of Donna Regina and has been lovingly restored by a family of Neapolitan artists. In the old part of town, it has views of the cloisters and the two churches of Santa Maria Donna Regina. Inside it's filled with antique Neapolitan furniture and family works of art. Donna Gabriella will cook delightful traditional evening meals on request. With only four rooms, it requires that you book well in advance throughout the year. ⊠ *Via Settembrini 80, Spaccanapoli, 80139* ☎🖷 *081/446799* ⬎ *4 rooms* ♻ *Lounge* ⊟ *MC, V.*

\$ ⊞ **Soggiorno Sansevero.** Within the very heart of Spaccanapoli, this pensione is at ground zero of old Naples. It occupies a floor in the former palace of the princes di Sangro di San Severo, and although the palazzo overlooks the opera-set Piazza San Domenico, the tiny Soggiorno is on the palazzo's quiet inner courtyard. Rooms are simply furnished—linoleum floors, modern beds, great-grandmama's boudoir bureau—and may even come with ghosts: Carlo Gesualdo, inventor of the madrigal song, murdered his wife and her lover on the palace's staircase. The staff is very friendly and helpful. ⊠ *Piazza San Domenico 9 (Palazzo Sansevero), 80131* ☎ *081/4201336* 🖷 *081/211698* ⊕ *www.albergosansevero.it* ⬎ *6 rooms, 4 with bath* ⊟ *AE, DC, MC, V.*

¢ ⊞ **Pensione Mancini.** Situated at the heart of the action just off the Piazza Mancini market on the west side of Piazza Garibaldi, this modest, family-run pensione is a safe outpost in the daily carnival of Neapolitan life. Rooms are very plain but clean, some with a balcony, and there are also dormitories. ✉ *Via Mancini 33, Piazza Garibaldi, 80120* ☎ *081/5536731* 🖷 *081/5546675* 🌐 *www.hostelpensionemancini.com* 🛏 *6 rooms, 3 with bath* ⚓ *Bar; no a/c, no room phones* 🚫 *No credit cards.*

Nightlife & the Arts

The Arts

MUSIC　A classical music festival known as **International Music Weeks** takes place throughout May in Naples. Concerts are held at the Teatro San Carlo, the Teatro Mercadante, and in the neoclassical Villa Pignatelli. For information, contact the **Teatro San Carlo box office** (☎ 081/7972331 or 081/7972412).

OPERA　Naples has a full opera season from late fall through early summer. The **Teatro San Carlo** (✉ Via San Carlo, Piazza Plebiscito ☎ 081/7972331 or 081/7972412 🌐 www.teatrosancarlo.it), where the season runs throughout the year apart from July and August, is one of Italy's top opera houses.

Nightlife

NIGHTCLUBS　Nightclubs and bars are found in many areas around Naples. The sophisticated crowd heads to Posillipo and the Vomero, along the seafront (Via Partenope), and the Chiaia area (between Piazza dei Martiri and Via Dei Mille). A more bohemian and literary crowd makes for the *centro storico* and the area around Piazza Bellini. Bear in mind that clubs, and their clientele, may change rapidly, so do some investigating before you hit the town. Following are specific venues to check out.

Around Midnight (✉ Via Bonito 32a, Vomero ☎ 081/5582834) is a focal point for jazz aficionados. The sophisticated **Chez Moi** (✉ Via del Parco Margherita 13, Chiaia ☎ 081/407526) has a dress code—casual is okay, as long as it's style-conscious—and is popular with the fashion jet set. **Tongue** (✉ Via Manzoni 207, Posillipo ☎ 081/7690800) appeals especially to gays and techno-heads.

TRADITIONAL　There are several restaurants where you can eat and then enjoy tradi-
NEAPOLITAN　tional Neapolitan entertainment—singing and dancing in folk costumes.
DANCE　A place worth trying is **'A Canzuncella** (✉ Piazza Santa Maria La Nova 18, Spaccanapoli ☎ 081/5519018). On Saturday evening host and showman Aurelio Fierro lays on a special musical session with banquet and entertainment for a combined price of €55.

Sports & the Outdoors

Bicycling

To rent a bike in town and for information on group excursions, contact **Napoli Bike** (✉ Riviera di Chiaia 201 ☎ 081/411934 🌐 www. napolibike.com), conveniently close to the Villa Comunale.

Boat Tours

Summer evening boat tours take in the waterfront of Naples, from the port at Mergellina to Cape Posillipo, with a view of Castel dell'Ovo on the way back. For bookings contact **Seafront Tours** (✉ Galleria Umberto I 17, Piazza Plebiscito ☎ 081/5519188).

Sailing

Club Nautico (✉ Borgo Marinari, Santa Lucia ☎ 081/7645829) offers courses for sailors or would-be sailors all year round. **Canottieri Savoia** (✉ Borgo Marinari, Santa Lucia ☎ 081/7646162) has courses from October through June.

Thermal Baths

With all the volcanic activity in the area, sulfur baths have been popular here for centuries. There are two ancient Roman-period structures (*sudatoria*) that offer spa facilities, ideal both in summer and winter. **Stufe di Nerone** (⊠ Via Stufe di Nerone 37, Bacoli ☎ 081/8688006) has two pools, one outside where you can sit and sunbathe, another inside with a sauna and various thermal treatments. **Stufe di San Germano** (⊠ Via Agnano Astroni 24, Agnano ☎081/5702122) has thermally heated spring pools and natural steam caves, as well as mud baths and massages with eucalyptus leaves.

Shopping

Leather goods, jewelry, and cameos are some of the best items to buy in Campania. In Naples, you'll generally find good deals on handbags, shoes, and clothing. If you want the real thing, make your purchases in shops, but if you don't mind imitation goods, rummage around at the various street-vendor *bancherelle* (stalls). Most boutiques and department stores are closed till 4:30 on Monday (hours are roughly Monday 4:30–8, Tuesday–Saturday 9:15–1 and 4:30–8). Food shops are open Monday morning, but most close at about 2 PM on Thursday afternoon.

Shopping Districts

The immediate area around **Piazza dei Martiri** has the densest concentration of luxury shopping, with perfume shops, fashion outlets, and antiques on display. Browse **Via Chiaia, Via dei Mille,** and **Via Filangieri.** The small, pedestrian-only **Via Calabritto** is where you'll find high-end retailers such as Prada, Gucci, Versace, Vuitton, Cacharel, Damiani, and Cartier. The **Vomero** district also yields more luxury shops—especially in the **Galleria Scarlatti,** on Via Scarlatti, and the **Galleria Vanvitelli,** off Piazza Vanvitelli. If you're looking for cheaper stores, try **Via Toledo** for the department store La Rinascente and other smaller fashion shops. The *centro storico* area, running down from the Museo Nazionale and Via Duomo, is packed with street markets and also has a fair choice of arts and crafts stores. **Via Santa Maria di Costantinopoli** is the street for antiques shops, and you'll find an antiques market on the third weekend of each month in the gardens of Villa Comunale and a flower market every day in the Castel Nuovo moat.

Specialty Stores

Arte Antica (⊠ Via Domenico Morelli 6, Chiaia ☎ 081/7643704) is famous for Italian antiques, especially flamboyant, richly decorated porcelain. **Monetti** sells elegantly tailored togs. (⊠ Men ⊠ Via Scarlatti 171, Vomero ☎ 081/5780009 ⊠ Women ⊠ Via Merliani 34, Vomero ☎081/5788463) **Gay Odin** (⊠ Via Toledo 214, Piazza Plebiscito ☎081/ 400063) produces handmade chocolates that you can only find in its Naples shops. Buy a delicious chocolate Mount Vesuvius, or try the famous *foresta* (flaked chocolate). You can also visit the **Gay Odin factory** (⊠ Via Vetriera 12, Chiaia ☎ 081/417843). **Mario Raffone** (⊠ Via Santa Maria di Costantinopoli 102, Spaccanapoli ☎☎ 081/459667) is a family printing business where they still use old presses. They sell prints of nativity figures and Vesuvius and have a catalogue of old prints from the 20th century. **Keramos** (⊠ Via Porta Posillipo 40/b, Posillipo ☎ 081/ 7692950), a local artists' studio, is worth visiting if you're interested in modern ceramic work. **Marinella** (⊠ Via Riviera di Chiaia 287/a, Chiaia ☎ 081/2451182) sells made-to-measure ties, supposedly the best in the world.

THE PHLEGREAN FIELDS

The name Campi Flegrei—the fields of fire—was once given to the entire region west of Naples, including the island of Ischia. The whole area floats freely on a mass of molten lava very close to the surface. The fires are still smoldering. Greek and Roman notions of the Underworld were not the blind imaginings of a primitive people; they were the creations of poets and writers who stood on this very ground and wrote down what they saw. Today, it should take about half a day to assess it yourself.

Solfatara

17 *8 km (5 mi) west of Naples.*

Here at the sunken volcanic crater Solfatara you can experience firsthand the volcanic nature of this otherworldly terrain. In fact, the only eruption of this semiextinct volcano was in 1198, though according to one legend, every crater in the Phlegrean Fields is one of the mouths of a hundred-headed dragon named Typhon that Zeus hurled down the crater of Epomeo on the island of Ischia. According to another, the sulfurous springs of the Solfatara are poisonous discharges from the wounds the Titans received in their war with Zeus. The stark, scorched area, slightly marred by the modern apartment blocks peering over the rim, exerts a strange fascination. The area has good visitor facilities, is well-signposted, and is safe for walking if you stick to the path. ☎ 081/5262341 ⊕ *www. solfatara.it* ✉ €5 ⊙ *Daily 8:30–1 hr before sunset.*

Pozzuoli

18 *2 km (1 mi) west of Solfatara, 8 km (5 mi) west of Naples.*

The **Anfiteatro Flavio** here is the third-largest amphitheater in Italy, after the Colosseum and Santa Maria Capua Vetere, and once held 40,000 spectators. Judging from the complex underground network of *carceres* (cells), which definitely merit a visit, entertainment consisted mainly of *venationes* (fights), often involving exotic animals such as lions and tigers brought from far-flung corners of the Roman Empire, through the port of Puteoli (modern Pozzuoli). The *fossa,* the large ditch in the middle of the arena, may well have contained the stage, which could be raised when necessary to provide a scenic backdrop. If visiting between June and September, ask at the ticket office for information about outdoor evening concerts. ☎ 081/5266007 ✉ €4 includes Cuma and the museum and site of Baia ⊙ Daily 9–1 hr before sunset.

You may want to make a short trip to Pozzuoli's **harbor** and imagine St. Paul landing here en route to Rome in AD 61, only 18 years before the eruption of Vesuvius. His own ship had been wrecked off Malta, and he was brought here on the *Castor and Pollux,* a grain ship from Alexandria.

Baia

19 *7 km (4½ mi) south of Pozzuoli, 12 km (7 mi) west of Naples.*

Now largely under the sea, this was once the most opulent and fashionable resort area of the Roman Empire, a place where Sulla, Pompey, Cicero, Julius Caesar, Tiberius, and Nero all built holiday villas. Petronius's *Satyricon* is a satire on the corruption, intrigue, and wonderful licentiousness of Roman life at Baia. (Petronius was hired to arrange parties and entertainments for Nero, so he was in a position to know.) It was here at Baia that Emperor Claudius built a great villa for his wife

Messalina (who spent her nights indulging herself at public brothels); here that Agrippina poisoned her husband and was, in turn, murdered by her son Nero; and here that Cleopatra was staying when Julius Caesar was murdered on the Ides of March in 44 BC. You can visit the excavations of the famous *terme* (baths). ✉ *Via Fusaro 35* ☎ 081/8687592 📷 *€4 includes Cuma, the museum of Baia and the Pozzuoli amphitheater* ⊘ *Tues.–Sun. 9–2 hrs before sunset.*

en route Follow the southern loop around Lago Miseno (a volcanic crater believed by the ancients to be the Styx, across which Charon ferried the souls of the dead) and Lago del Fusaro. You'll take in some fine views of the Golfo di Pozzuoli (Bay of Pozzuoli).

Cumae

⑳ *5 km (3 mi) north of Pozzuoli, 16 km (10 mi) west of Naples.*

Perhaps the oldest Greek colony in Italy, Cumae (Cuma in Italian) overshadowed the Phlegrean Fields, including Naples, in the 7th and 6th centuries BC. The **Antro della Sibilla** (Sibyl's Cave)—one of the most venerated sites in antiquity—is in Cumae. In the 6th or 5th century BC, the Greeks hollowed the cave from the rock beneath the present ruins of Cumae's acropolis. You walk through a dark, massive stone tunnel that opens into a vaulted chamber where the Sibyl uttered her oracles. Standing here, the sense of mystery, of communication with the invisible, is overwhelming. "This is the most romantic classical site in Italy," wrote the English travel writer H. V. Morton (1892–1979). "I would rather come here than to Pompeii."

Virgil (70–19 BC) wrote in his epic *Aeneid* of the Trojan prince Aeneas's descent to the Underworld to speak to his father. To find his way in, he needed the guidance of the Cumaean Sibyl. Virgil did not dream up the Sibyl's cave or the entrance to Hades—he must have stood both in her chamber and along the rim of Lago d'Averno, as you yourself can stand. When he wrote *"Facilis descensus Averno"*—"The way to hell is easy"— it was because he knew the way. In Book VI of the *Aeneid,* Virgil described how Aeneas, arriving at Cumae, sought Apollo's throne (remains of the **Tempio di Apollo** can still be seen) and "the deep hidden abode of the dread Sibyl / An enormous cave. . . ."

Sibyls were not necessarily charlatans; they were mediums, prophets, old women whom the ancients believed could communicate with the Other World. The three most famous Sibyls were at Erythrae, Delphi, and Cumae. Foreign governments consulted the Sibyls before mounting campaigns. Wealthy aristocrats came to commune with their dead relatives. Businessmen came to get their dreams interpreted or to seek favorable omens before entering into financial agreements or setting off on journeys. Farmers came to remove curses on their cows. Love potions were a good source of revenue—women from Baia lined up for potions to slip into the wine of handsome charioteers.

Little of ancient Cumae now stands above ground—the Temple of Apollo has suffered woefully over the millennia—but the underground passages are virtually intact, though not entirely visitable. There are detailed information panels to guide you through the site, with extra information on flora and fauna supplied by the local Worldwide Fund for Nature. As you walk through, you'll soon appreciate what a good choice it was to colonize this site: it was surrounded by fertile land, had relatively easy access to the sea (though no natural harbor), and an acropolis at the top providing an excellent vantage in all directions. Allow at least two hours for this visit to soak up the ambience, study the ruins, and reach the top level overlooking the Acherusia Palus—now Lago Fusaro—to the south and part of the Silva Gallinaria, the thick holm oak ground cover to the north, once an immense forest stretching almost all the way to Rome. ⊠ *Via Acropoli 39* ☎ *081/8543060* 🎟 *€4 includes the Pozzuoli amphitheater and the museum and site of Baia* ⊙ *Daily 9–2 hrs before sunset.*

Lago d'Averno

4 km (2½ mi) south of Cumae, 11 km (7 mi) west of Naples.

Regarded by the ancients as the gateway to Hades, the fabled Lago d'Averno (Lake Avernus) was well known by the time Virgil settled here to write *The Aeneid*. Today the scene has changed a fair amount: in summer, the area pulsates to the sound of disco music, and you would be more likely to come across members of the 21st-century underworld than meet the shades of the dead that Virgil so evocatively describes. As with Lago Lucrino (the Lucrine Lake) less than 1 km (½ mi) to the south, a tarmac road skirts much of the lake. However, some of the spell is restored by the backdrop: Forested hills rise on three sides and the menacing cone of Monte Nuovo looms on the fourth. The smell of sulfur sometimes hangs over the landscape, and blocked-off passages lead into long-abandoned caves into which Virgil might well have ventured.
✣ *Drive west from Pozzuoli on S7 toward Cumae; then turn left (south) on the road to Baia. About 1 km (½ mi) along, turn right; follow signs to Lago Averno.*

HERCULANEUM, VESUVIUS, POMPEII

Volcanic ash and mud preserved the Roman towns of Herculaneum and Pompeii almost exactly as they were on the day Mt. Vesuvius erupted in AD 79, leaving them not just archaeological ruins but museums of daily life in the ancient world. The two buried cities and the volcano responsible can be visited from either Naples or Sorrento, thanks to the Circumvesuviana, the suburban railway that provides fast, frequent, and economical service.

Herculaneum

★ ㉑ *10 km (6 mi) southeast of Naples.*

Lying more than 60 ft below the town of Ercolano, the ruins of Herculaneum are set among the acres of greenhouses that make this area one of Europe's principal flower-growing centers. It had about 5,000 inhabitants when it was destroyed; many of them were fishermen, craftsmen, and artists. In AD 79 the gigantic eruption of Vesuvius (which also destroyed Pompeii) buried the town under a tide of volcanic mud. The semiliquid mass seeped into the crevices and niches of every building, covering household objects and enveloping textiles and wood—sealing all in a compact, airtight tomb.

Casual excavation—and haphazard looting—began in the 18th century, but systematic digs were not initiated until the 1920s. Today less than half of Herculaneum has been excavated; with present-day Ercolano and the unlovely Resina Quarter (famous among bargain hunters as the area's largest secondhand-clothing market) sitting on top of the site, progress is limited. From the ramp leading down to Herculaneum's neatly laid out streets and well-preserved edifices, you get a good overall view of the site, as well as an idea of the amount of volcanic debris that had to be removed to bring it to light.

Though Herculaneum had only one-fourth the population of Pompeii and has only been partially excavated, what has been found is generally better preserved. In some cases, you can even see the original wooden beams, staircases, and furniture. Much excitement is presently focused on one excavation in a corner of the site, the Villa dei Papiri, built by Julius Caesar's father-in-law. The building is named for the 1,800 carbonized papyrus scrolls dug up here in the 18th century, leading scholars to believe that this may have been a study center or library. Given the right funds and political support, it is hoped that the villa can be properly excavated and ultimately opened to the public. Little of the site can be seen aboveground, though visitors to the Getty Villa (formerly the J. Paul Getty Museum) in Malibu, California, can see a modern version, built following 18th-century drawings made by the Swiss archaeologist Carl Weber.

At the entrance to the archaeological park you should pick up a map showing the gridlike layout of the dig. Splurge on an audio-guide (€6 for one, €9 for two; you'll need to leave an I.D. card) and head down the tunnel to start the tour at the old shoreline. Though many of the houses are closed and some are in dire need of restoration, a fair cross section of domestic, commercial, and civic buildings is still accessible. Decorations are especially delicate in the **Casa del Nettuno ed Anfitrite** (House of Neptune and Amphitrite), named for the subjects of a still-bright mosaic on the wall of the nymphaeum (a recessed grotto with a fountain), and in the **Terme Femminili** (Women's Baths), where several delicate black-and-white mosaic pavements embellished the various rooms. Annexed to the former house is a remarkably preserved wineshop, where amphorae still rest on carbonized wooden shelves. On the other side of the house is the **Casa del Bel Cortile** (House of the Beautiful Courtyard). In one of its inner rooms is the temporary display of a cast taken of some skeletons found in the storerooms down at the old seafront, where almost 300 inhabitants sought refuge from the eruption and were ultimately encapsulated for posterity. The palaestra, the sumptuously decorated **Terme Suburbane** (Suburban Baths)—only open mornings—and the **Casa dei Cervi** (House of the Stags), with an elegant garden open to the sea breezes, are all evocative relics of a lively and luxurious way of life. ✉ *Corso Ercolano, a 5-min walk downhill from the Ercolano circumvesuviana station* ☎ *081/8575347* ⊕ *www.pompeiisites.org* 🎫 *€10; €18 including Oplontis, Pompeii, and 2 other sites over 3 days* ⊙ *Apr.–Oct., daily 8:30–7:30, ticket office closes at 6; Nov.–Mar., daily 8:30–5, ticket office closes at 3:30.*

Vesuvius

㉒ *8 km (5 mi) northeast of Herculaneum, 16 km (10 mi) east of Naples.*

The profile of Vesuvius is so inseparable from the Bay of Naples area, and the ferocious power it can unleash so vivid as you tour the sights of the cities that it destroyed, you may be overwhelmed by the urge to explore the crater itself. In summer especially, the prospect of rising above the sticky heat of the city and sights below is a heady one. The view when clear is magnificent, with the curve of the coast and the tiny white houses among the orange and lemon blossoms. If the summit is lost in mist, you'll be lucky to see your hand in front of your face. When you see the summit clearing—it tends to be clearer in the afternoon—head for it. If possible, see Vesuvius after you've toured the ruins of buried Herculaneum to appreciate the magnitude of the volcano's power.

Reaching the crater takes some effort. From the Ercolano stop of the Circumvesuviana, take scheduled buses (trip takes one hour; there are four or five departures a day—check for the latest schedule) or your own car to Quota 1000 (the parking lot and cafeteria area near the top). From here you must climb the soft, slippery cinder track on foot, a 30-minute ascent, and pay €6 for access, which includes compulsory guide service, usually young geologists with a smattering of English. At the bottom, you'll be offered a stout walking stick (a small tip is appreciated on return). The climb can be tiring if you're not used to steep hikes. Wear nonskid shoes (not sandals). ☎ 081/7775720 ⊠ €6 ⊙ *Daily 9* AM*–2 hrs before sunset.*

You can visit **Osservatorio Vesuviano** (the old observatory)—2,000 ft up—and view instruments used to study the volcano, some dating back to the mid-19th century. ☎ 081/7777149 or 081/7777150 ⊕ *www.ov.ingv. it* ⊠ *Free* ⊙ *Weekends 10–2.*

Oplontis

㉓   *20 km (12 mi) southeast of Naples, 5 km (3 mi) west of Pompeii.*

Surrounded by the fairly drab urban landscape of Torre Annunziata, thrown up in the 1960s, Oplontis justifies its reputation as one of the most spectacular archaeological sites to be unearthed during the 20th century. The villa complex has been imaginatively ascribed—based on a mere inscription on an amphora—to Nero's second wife, Poppaea Sabina, whose family was well known among the landed gentry of neighboring Pompeii. As Roman villas go, Poppaea's Villa, or Villa A, as it is called more prosaically by archaeologists, is truly exceptional. Excavation so far has uncovered an area of more than 100 by 75 meters, and because the site is bound by a road to the west and a canal to the south, it may never be possible to gauge its full extent. What's been found includes porticoes, a large peristyle, a *piscina* (pool), baths, and extensive gardens, as well as the standard atria, triclinia, and a warren of *cubicula* (bedrooms). The villa is thought by some to have been a training school for young philosophers and orators. Certainly, for those overwhelmed by the throngs at Pompeii, a modern-day visit to the site of Oplontis offers a chance for contemplation and intellectual refreshment.

Access is easiest from the Circumvesuviana station of Torre Annunziata, about 200 m (650 ft) away. Outside the station turn left and then right downhill, and the site is just after the crossroads down on the left. If coming by car, take the Torre Annunziata turnoff from the Naples–Salerno autostrada, turn right, and then look for signs on the left for Oplontis at the first major crossroads. The main entrance to the site is from the north—you basically go into the villa through the gardens, with the atrium on the southern side lying under about 3 m (10 ft) of pumice and pyroclastic material from Vesuvius. This is a good time to have a close look at the stratigraphy of the volcanic deposits: note the thin layers of the lighter surge-flow deposit near the base of the profile. Pumice fallout presented few problems for local inhabitants during the eruption, but the surge cloud proved lethal, leading rapidly to asphyxiation.

Oplontis offers the full gamut of Roman wall paintings, with its occupants showing a particular penchant for the illusionist motifs of the so-called Second Pompeian Style. There are some good examples in the west wing of the villa, especially in the triclinium (Room 14—look for the room numbers above the doors) giving onto the small portico (Room 13), which abuts the west end of the site and the road above. Although the stucco work in the thermae, or baths, is less impressive than in Pompeii and Herculaneum, the calidarium (Room 8) has a delightful miniature landscape scene surmounted by a peacock in a niche at its eastern end (binoculars are useful). Nearby, in the tepidarium (Room 18), there's an interesting glimpse into the structural design of Roman baths; here the floor is raised by *suspensurae*, small brick supporting pilasters, enabling warm air to pass beneath.

Such opulence is found throughout the site, although there are exceptions to the rule—for example, the relatively small cubicula are conspicuous in their simplicity. In the eastern wing, a warren of rooms gives way to much larger spaces, featuring long corridors, peristyles fit for large gaggles of stoics, and a large piscina, with its complement of porticoes and terraces, at the eastern end. ✉ *Via Sepolcri 1, Torre Annunziata* ☎ *081/ 8575347* ⊕ *www.pompeiisites.org* 💳 *€5 including Boscoreale and Stabiae in 1 day; €18 including Herculaneum, Pompeii, and the 2 other sites over 3 days* ⊙ *Apr.–Oct., daily 8:30–7:30, ticket office closes at 6; Nov.–Mar., daily 8:30–5, ticket office closes at 3:30.*

Pompeii

FodorsChoice
★

11 km (7 mi) southeast of Herculaneum, 24 km (15 mi) southeast of Naples.

Ancient Pompeii was much larger than Herculaneum; a busy commercial center with a population of 10,000–20,000, it covered about 160 acres on the seaward end of the fertile Sarno Plain. In 80 BC the Roman general Sulla turned Pompeii into a Roman settlement, colonized by the standard complement of army veterans. The town was laid out in a grid pattern, with two main intersecting streets. The wealthiest took a whole block for themselves; those less fortunate built a house and rented out the front rooms, facing the street, as shops. The facades of these houses were relatively plain and seldom hinted at the care and attention lavished on the private rooms within. When visitors arrived, they passed the shops and entered an open atrium. In the back was a receiving room. Behind was another open area, called the peristyle, with rows of columns and perhaps a garden with a fountain. Only good friends ever saw this private part of the house, which was surrounded by bedrooms and the dining area.

Pompeian houses were designed around an inner garden, so that families could turn their backs on the world outside. Not that public life was so intolerable. There were good numbers of *tabernae* (taverns), *thermopolia* (hot-food shops) on almost every corner, and frequent shows at the amphitheater. The public fountains and toilets were fed by huge cisterns connected by lead pipes beneath the sidewalks. Since garbage and rainwater collected in the streets of Pompeii, the sidewalks were raised, and huge stepping stones were placed at crossings so pedestrians could keep their feet dry. Herculaneum had better drainage, with an underground sewer that led to the sea.

All households would have had slaves, though in varying numbers depending on financial resources. A small, prosperous family had as many as eight employed in tasks ranging from estate management to education to cooking. Judging from archaeological finds and depictions on wall frescoes, the Pompeians enjoyed a balanced diet, including meat, seafood, walnuts, eggs, bread (made from wheat and barley), grapes, pears, and figs—all washed down with wine made of grapes grown on the slopes of Vesuvius.

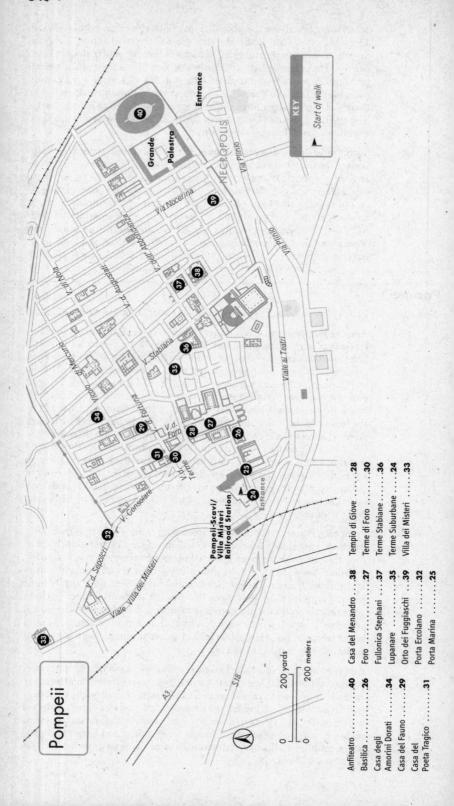

Pompeii

KEY

▲ Start of walk

NECROPOLIS

Entrance

Grande Palestra

Via Nocerina

V. dell' Abbondanza

V. d. Augustali

V. di Nola

Vicolo di Mercurio

V. Stabiana

V. di Fortuna

V. d. Foro

V. d. Terme

V. Consolare

V. d. Sepolcri

Viale Villa dei Misteri

Via Plinio

Viale ai Teatri

Pompeii-Scavi/
Villa Misteri
Railroad Station

Entrance

A3

S18

200 yards
200 meters

Anfiteatro **40**
Basilica **26**
Casa degli
Amorini Dorati . . . **34**
Casa del Fauno **29**
Casa del
Poeta Tragico **31**

Casa del Menandro . . .**38**
Foro **27**
Fullonica Stephani . . .**37**
Lupanare **35**
Orto dei Fuggiaschi . . **39**
Porta Ercolano **32**

Tempio di Giove **28**
Terme di Foro **30**
Terme Stabiane **36**
Terme Suburbane **24**
Villa dei Misteri **33**
Porta Marina **25**

Thanks to those deep layers of pyroclastic deposits from Vesuvius that protected the site from natural wear and tear over the centuries, Pompeii provides unique insights into the sort of things that the locals found important 2,000 years ago. Some 15,000 graffiti have been found in Pompeii and Herculaneum. Many were political announcements—one person recommending another for office, for example, and spelling out his qualifications. Some were announcements of upcoming events—a play at the theater, a gladiatorial show at the amphitheater. Others were public notices—that wine was on sale, that an apartment would be vacant on the Ides of March. A good many were personal and lend a human dimension to the disaster that not even the sights can equal. Here are a couple:

At the baths: "What is the use of having a Venus if she's made of marble?"

At the entrance to the front lavatory at a private house: "May I always and everywhere be as potent with women as I was here."

To get the most out of Pompeii, rent an audio guide (€6 for one, €9 for two; you'll need to leave an I.D. card) and allow at least three or four hours. Come armed with bottled water and a snack—there are some shady underused picnic tables outside the Porta di Nola to the northeast of the site. Two buildings within the site—Terme Suburbane (daily 10–2) and Casa del Menandro (weekends 2–4)—are open for restricted viewing on a first-come, first-served basis. Ask for a free coupon when you purchase your ticket. Pompeii has its own stop (Pompei–Villa dei Misteri) on the Naples–Sorrento Circumvesuviana line, close to the main entrance at the Porta Marina (there's another entrance to the excavations at the far end of the site, near the amphitheater).

24 The first buildings to the left after you've gone through the ticket turnstiles are the ▶ **Terme Suburbane** (Suburban Baths), built—by all accounts without planning permission—right up against the city walls. Opened to public viewing in 2002 partly to compensate for the closure of other sites for restoration, the baths have eyebrow-raising frescoes in the *apodyterium* (changing room) that strongly suggest more than just bathing and massaging went on here.

25 Enter the remains of the old city walls through **Porta Marina,** so called because it faces the sea. You'll note the two entrances here, the smaller one on the left being only used by pedestrians in antiquity. Past the Tem-
26 ple of Venus is the **Basilica,** the law court and the economic center of the city. These oblong buildings ending in a semicircular projection (apse) were the model for early Christian churches, which had a nave (central aisle) and two side aisles separated by rows of columns. Standing in the Basilica, you can recognize the continuity between Roman and Christian architecture.

27 The Basilica opens onto the **Foro** (Forum), the public meeting place, surrounded by temples and public buildings. It was here that elections were held and speeches and official announcements made. At the far (north-
28 ern) end of the forum is the **Tempio di Giove** (Temple of Jupiter). The
29 renowned **Casa del Fauno** (House of the Faun) displayed wonderful mosaics, which can now be viewed in the Museo Archeologico Nazionale in Naples.

30 The **Terme di Foro** (Forum Baths) on Via delle Terme is smaller than
31 the Terme Stabiane, but with more delicate decoration. The **Casa del Poeta Tragico** (House of the Tragic Poet) is a typical middle-class house from the last days of Pompeii. On the floor is a mosaic of a chained dog and the inscription CAVE CANEM ("Beware of the dog").

③② The beautiful **Porta Ercolano** (Herculaneum Gate) was a main gate that led to Herculaneum and Naples, one of seven gates in the ancient city
③③ walls. The **Villa dei Misteri** (Villa of the Mysteries), outside Pompeii's walls, contains what some consider the greatest surviving group of paintings from the ancient world, telling the story of a young bride (Ariadne) being initiated into the mysteries of the cult of Dionysus. Bacchus (Dionysus), the god of wine, was popular in a town so devoted to the pleasures of the flesh. But he also represented the triumph of the irrational—of all those mysterious forces that no official state religion could fully suppress. The cult of Dionysus, like the cult of the Cumaean Sibyl, gave people a sense of control over fate and, in its focus on the Other World, helped pave the way for Christianity.

③④ The **Casa degli Amorini Dorati** (House of the Gilded Cupids) is an elegant, well-preserved home with original marble decorations in the gar-
③⑤ den. On the walls of **Lupanare** (brothel) are scenes of erotic games in
③⑥ which clients could engage. The **Terme Stabiane** (Stabian Baths) had underground furnaces, the heat from which circulated beneath the floor, rose through flues in the walls, and escaped through chimneys. The water temperature could be set for cold, lukewarm, or hot. Bathers took a lukewarm bath to prepare themselves for the hot room. A tepid bath came next, and then a plunge into cold water to tone up the skin. A vigorous massage with oil was followed by rest, reading, horseplay, and conversation.

③⑦ Togas were washed at **Fullonica Stephani**. The cloth was dunked in a tub full of water and chalk and stomped on like so many grapes. Once clean, the material was stretched across a wicker cage and exposed to sulfur fumes. The fuller (cleaner) carded it with a long brush, then placed it under a press. The harder the pressing, the whiter and brighter
③⑧ it became. Many paintings and mosaics were executed at **Casa del Menandro,** a patrician's villa named for a fresco of the Greek playwright
③⑨ Menander. The **Orto dei Fuggiaschi** (Garden of the Fugitives) contains poignant plaster casts of those overwhelmed by the eruption in AD79.

④⓪ The **Anfiteatro** (Amphitheater) was the ultimate in entertainment for local Pompeians and offered a gamut of experiences, but essentially this was for gladiators rather than wild animals. Unlike the amphitheater at Pozzuoli, there are no underground *cellae* for the penning of animals and, besides, *venationes* (combats with wild animals) only really became popular from well into the 1st century AD onward. With the large palaestra close by and the gladiatorial barracks near the theater area, there were extensive facilities to train gladiators in many types of combat. Teams worked for impresarios, who hired them out to wealthy citizens, many of whom were running for office and hoping that the gory entertainment would buy them some votes. Most gladiators were slaves or prisoners, but a few were those from the far-flung reaches of the empire who enjoyed fighting.

By Roman standards, Pompeii's Amphitheater was quite small (seating capacity: 20,000). Built in about 80 BC, it was oval and divided into three seating areas, like a theater. There were two main entrances—at the north and south ends—and a narrow passage on the west, called the *Porta Libitinensis,* through which the dead were most probably dragged out. A wall painting found in a house near the theater (now in the Naples Museum) depicts the riot in the Amphitheater in AD 59 when several citizens from the nearby town of Nucera were killed. After Nucerian appeals to Nero, shows in the Amphitheater were suspended for 10 years. ✉ *Pompei Scavi* ☎ *081/8575347* ⊕ *www.pompeiisites.org* ✒ *€10;*

€18 including Oplontis, Herculaneum, and 2 other sites over 3 days ⊙ Apr.–Oct., daily 8:30–7:30, ticket office closes at 6; Nov.–Mar., daily 8:30–5, ticket office closes at 3:30.

Many visitors to ancient Pompeii are unaware of the modern pilgrimage that many Italians make to visit the **Santuario**, consecrated in 1891, which dominates the central square in modern Pompei. Its main altar contains a painting, *The Virgin of the Rosary with Child*, which has been worshiped all over the world since it was claimed to have healing powers in 1876. The bell tower stands more than 250 ft high and has great views over the Lattari Mountains, Mount Vesuvius, the Sorrento coast, the ruins of Pompeii, and modern Pompeii. ⊠ *Piazza Bartolo Longo* ☎ *081/8577111* ⊠ *Bell tower elevator €0.50* ⊙ *Church daily 6:30–2 and 3–7:30; bell tower May–Sept., Sat.–Thurs. 9–1 and 3–6; Oct.–Apr. 9–1 and 3–5.*

Where to Stay & Eat

$$$ ✕ **President.** A classic restaurant in the heart of contemporary Pompei, President is run by a father and son who have drawn on traditional recipes to create modern dishes made from local produce. Fish is a specialty—try *cicinielli alla brace in foglia di limone* (small fish served in lemon leaves). There's also a good selection of local wines. ⊠ *Piazza Schettini 12, 80045* ☎ *081/8507245* ⊟ *AE, DC, MC, V* ⊙ *Closed Mon. and mid-Aug.*

$–$$ ✕ **Ristorante Pizzeria Carlo Alberto.** This small, efficiently run restaurant with an impressive repertory is comfortably out of the reach of large tour groups. If you're a vegetarian, try *pizza con mozzarella, rucola, e mais* (pizza with mozzarella, arugula, and corn) or just have a plain *focaccetta* instead of bread to accompany your meal. Reservations are essential on the weekends. ⊠ *Via Carlo Alberto 15* ☎ *081/8633231* ⊟ *DC, MC, V.*

$$ ☷ **Amleto.** This elegant hotel offers excellent accommodation near the archaeological site (there aren't many bona fide hotels in the area). The hotel's pillars, mosaics, and murals evoke ancient Pompeii, and bedrooms are in either Venetian or Neapolitan style. From the roof garden you can enjoy views over the ancient and modern towns. There's no restaurant, but a generous buffet breakfast is served. ⊠ *Via Bartolo Longo 10, 80045* ☎ *081/8631004* ⊟ *081/8635585* ⊕ *www.hotelamleto.it* ⬐ *24 rooms, 2 suites* ⚘ *Bar, meeting room* ⊟ *AE, DC, MC, V.*

¢ ☷ **Casa del Pellegrino.** A safe, convenient base for cash-strapped travelers, this former convent was pleasingly converted into a hostel in 2001. It's a 10-minute walk from the amphitheater entrance and close to the action in Pompei's main square, yet seemingly miles away from the tourist throngs. Fairly spartan accommodations consist of dormitories as well as private rooms sleeping up to four. ⊠ *Via Duca D'Aosta 4, 80045* ☎ *081/8508644* ⊕ *www.hostels-aig.org* ⬐ *12 rooms* ⚘ *No a/c, no room phones, no room TVs* ⊟ *No credit cards.*

CASERTA & BENEVENTO

From Caserta, the Italian answer to Versailles, if you proceed to Benevento you'll view an almost perfectly preserved Roman arch. Benevento was badly damaged by World War II bombings, but among the modern structures there are some medieval and even older relics still standing in the Old Town. If you go by car, make a brief detour to the medieval hamlet of Caserta Vecchia on the hillside, where there are one or two good restaurants and a very old cathedral.

Caserta

★ ④ *11 km (7 mi) northeast of Herculaneum, 25 km (16 mi) northeast of Naples.*

The palace known as the **Reggia** shows how Bourbon royals lived in the mid-18th century. Architect Luigi Vanvitelli devoted 20 years to its construction under Bourbon ruler Charles III, whose son, Ferdinand IV (1751–1825), moved in when it was completed in 1774. Both king and architect were inspired by Versailles, and the rectangular palace was conceived on a massive scale, with four interconnecting courtyards, 1,200 rooms, and a vast park. Though the palace is not as well maintained as its French counterpart, the main staircase puts the one at Versailles to shame, and the **royal apartments** are sumptuous. It was here, in what Eisenhower called "a castle near Naples," that the Allied High Command had its headquarters in World War II, and here German forces in Italy surrendered in April 1945. There's also a museum showing items relating to the palace and the Caserta area. Most enjoyable are the gardens and parks, particularly the Cascades, adorned by the classical goddess Diana and her maidens. ⊠ *Piazza Carlo III* ☎ *0823/448084* ⌨ *Royal apartments, Museo dell'Opera, park, and English garden €6; park only €2; minibus €1* ⊙ *Royal apartments Tues.–Sun. 8:30–7:30. Park Mar., Tues.–Sun. 8:30–5; Apr., Tues.–Sun. 8:30–6; May and Aug., Tues.–Sun. 8:30–6:30; June and July, Tues.–Sun. 8:30–7; Sept. and Oct., Tues.–Sun. 8:30–5:30; Nov.–Feb., Tues.–Sun. 8:30–3:30; ticket office closes 1 hr before closing.*

Santa Maria Capua Vetere

④ *8 km (5 mi) west of Caserta, 30 km (18 mi) north of Naples.*

A short hop from Caserta—through somewhat unlovely development—is a cluster of fascinating sites dating back to the Roman period and beyond. The **Anfiteatro Campano,** was modeled on the Colosseum and built under the emperor Hadrian (AD 117–138). It's been stripped of much of its superstructure, but some of the surviving sculptural decorations are on display at the small adjoining Museo dei Gladiatori. The museum's highlight is the helpful reconstruction of one of the amphitheater's original 76 *vomitoria* (entrances), together with then-and-now scale models of the amphitheater. All the information panels are in Italian only. ⊠ *Piazza I Ottobre* ☎ *0823/844206* ⌨ *€2.50* ⊙ *Tues.–Sun. 9–6:30.*

Benevento

④ *35 km (22 mi) east of Caserta, 60 km (37 mi) northeast of Naples.*

Benevento owes its importance to its establishment as the capital of the Lombards, a northern tribe that invaded and settled what is now Lombardy when they were forced to move south by Charlemagne's conquests in the 8th century. Tough and resourceful, the Lombards moved south and set up a new duchy in Benevento, later moving its seat to Salerno, where they saw the potential of the natural harbor. Under papal rule in the 13th century, Benevento built a fine cathedral and outfitted it with bronze doors that were a pinnacle of Romanesque art. The cathedral, doors, and a large part of the town, were blasted by World War II bombs. The **Duomo** has been rebuilt, with the remaining panels of the original bronze doors in the chapter library. Fortunately, the majestic 2nd-century AD **Arco di Traiano** (Trajan's Arch) were unscathed by the World War II bombing that hit Benevento. Roman emperor Trajan, who sorted out Rome's finances, brought parts of the Middle East into the empire, and extended the Appian Way through Benevento to the Adriatic. The ruins

★

of the **Teatro Romano,** which had a seating capacity of 20,000, have been extensively restored and host a summer music and theater season. ⊠ *Take Via Carlo from the Duomo* 🖭 *€2* ☉ *Daily 9–1 hr before sunset.*

PROCIDA, ISCHIA & CAPRI

History's hedonists have long luxuriated on Campania's famous islands. The Roman emperor Tiberius built a dozen villas on Capri in which to indulge his sexual whims. Later residents have included dancer Rudolf Nureyev and droves of artists and writers. These days, day-trippers make up the majority of visitors, diminishing the islands' social cachet. Ischia, less pretty and less chic than Capri, is still a popular destination on account of its spas, beaches, and hot springs. Procida, for long the poor relation of the three, and the closest to Naples, is starting to capitalize on its chief natural asset, the unspoiled isle of Vivara. The pastel colors of Procida's main harbor may be familiar to anyone who has seen the widely acclaimed film *Il Postino,* scenes of which were shot here.

Procida

44 *35 mins by hydrofoil, 1 hr by car ferry from Naples.*

Lying barely 3 km (2 mi) from the mainland and 10 km (6 mi) from the nearest port of Pozzuoli, Procida is an island of enormous contrasts. It is the most densely populated island in Europe—almost 11,000 people crammed into less than 3½ square km (2 square mi)—and yet there are oases such as Marina Corricella and Vivara that seem to have been bypassed by modern civilization. It's no surprise that picturesque Procida has strong artistic traditions and is widely considered a painters' island par excellence.

Singled out for the waterfront scenes in the Oscar-winning film *Il Postino,* **Corricella** has been relatively immune to life in the limelight, and apart from the opening of an extra restaurant and bar, there have been few changes in this sleepy fishermen's village. This is the type of place where even those with failing grades in art class feel like reaching for a paintbrush to record the delicate pinks and yellows of the waterfront buildings.

Where to Stay & Eat

$–$$ ✕ **La Gorgonia.** This atmospheric restaurant sits right on the waterfront down at Corricella. The specialties here are combinations of seafood and locally grown vegetables, such as pasta *con fagioli e cozze* (with beans and mussels). ⊠ *Marina Corricella 50* ☎ *081/8101060* 🖭 *AE, DC, MC, V* ☉ *Closed Mon. and Nov.–Jan.*

$ 🏠 **Casa Gentile.** Spacious rooms overlook Corricella at this quiet hotel, designed to blend in tastefully with the local Mediterranean architecture. If interested in fishing, ask the owner, Vincenzo, if you can join him on his nighttime travels around the Bay of Naples. The hotel offers a water-taxi service to and from port. ⊠ *Marina Corricella 88, Procida 80079* ☎ *081/8967799* 🖷 *081/8969011* ⊕ *www.casagentile.it* 🛏 *10 rooms* ⚒ *Minibars; no a/c* 🖭 *MC, V* ☉ *Closed Nov.–mid-Mar.*

Ischia

45 *45 mins by hydrofoil, 90 mins by car ferry from Naples, 60 mins by ferry from Pozzuoli.*

While Capri wows you with its charm and beauty, Ischia takes time to cast its spell. In fact, an overnight stay is probably not long enough for the island to get into your blood. It does have its share of vine-growing villages beneath the lush volcanic slopes of Monte Epomeo, and unlike Capri, it enjoys a life of its own that survives when the tourists head home. But there are few signs of antiquity here, the architecture is un-remarkable, the traffic can be overwhelming, and hoteliers have yet to achieve a balanced mix of clientele—most are either German (off-season) or Italian (in-season). But should you want to plunk down in the sun for a few days and tune out the world, this is an ideal place to go; just don't expect Ischia to be an unspoiled, undiscovered Capri. When Augustus gave the Neapolitans Ischia for Capri, he knew what he was doing.

Ischia is volcanic in origin. From its hidden reservoir of seething molten matter come the thermal springs said to cure whatever ails you. As early as 1580, a doctor named Lasolino published a book about the mineral wells at Ischia. "If your eyebrows fall off," he wrote, "go and try the baths at Piaggia Romano. If you know anyone who is getting bald, any-one who suffers from elephantiasis, or another whose wife yearns for a child, take the three of them immediately to the Bagno di Vitara; they will bless you." Today the island is covered with thermal baths, often surrounded by tropical gardens.

A good 35-km (22-mi) road makes a circuit of the island; the ride takes most of a day at a leisurely pace, if you're stopping along the way to enjoy the views and perhaps have lunch. You can book a **boat tour** around the island at the booths in various ports along the coast; there's a one-hour stop at Sant'Angelo. The information office is at the harbor. You may drive on Ischia year-round. There's also fairly good bus service, and you'll find plenty of taxis.

Ischia Porto is the largest town on the island and the usual point of de-barkation. It's no workaday port, however, but a lively resort with plenty of hotels, Ischia's best shopping area, and low, flat-roof houses on terraced hillsides above the water. Its narrow streets often become flights of steps that scale the hill, and its villas and gardens are framed by pines.

Most of the hotels are along the beach in the part of town called **Ischia Ponte,** which gets its name from the *ponte* (bridge) built by Alfonso of Aragón in 1438 to link the picturesque castle on a small islet offshore with the town and port. For a while, the castle was the home of Vitto-ria Colonna, poetess, granddaughter of Renaissance Duke Federico da Montefeltro (1422–82), and platonic soul mate of Michelangelo, with whom she carried on a lengthy correspondence. You'll find a typical re-sort atmosphere: countless cafés, shops, and restaurants, and a 1-km (½-mi) stretch of fine-sand beach. **Casamicciola,** a popular beach resort, is 5 km (3 mi) west of Ischia Porto. Chic and upscale **Lacco Ameno,** next to Casamicciola, is distinguished by a mushroom-shape rock offshore and some of the island's best hotels. Here, too, you can enjoy the ben-efits of Ischia's therapeutic waters.

The far western and southern coasts of Ischia are more rugged and at-tractive. **Forio,** at the extreme west, has a waterfront church and is a good spot for lunch or dinner. The sybaritic hot pools of the **Giardini Posei-don Terme** (Poseidon Gardens) spa establishment are on the Citara beach, south of Forio. You can sit like a Roman senator on a stone chair re-cessed in the rock and let the hot water cascade over you—all very campy, and fun. **Sant'Angelo,** on the southern coast, is a charming village; the road doesn't reach all the way into town, so it's free of traffic, and it's a five-minute boat ride from the beach of Maronti, at the foot of cliffs.

The inland town of Fontana is the base for excursions to the top of **Monte Epomeo,** the long-dormant volcano that dominates the island landscape. You can reach its 2,585-ft peak in less than 1½ hours of relatively easy walking.

Where to Stay & Eat

★ $$$ ✕ **Il Melograno.** In a tranquil setting a 10-minute walk south of the center of Forio, this restaurant amply deserves its ranking as one of Campania's finest. With antipasti such as *calamaretti con pera* and many tempting pasta dishes, you could be forgiven for skipping the main course. Try the very reasonably priced local wines (both white and red) from the Pietratorcia winery up the road. Dessert, appropriately called *dulcis in fundo* (the best for last), also merits firsthand attention. ✉ *Via G. Mazzella 110, Forio* ☎ *081/998450* ⬧ *Reservations essential* ▤ *AE, DC, MC, V* ☉ *Closed Mon. Tues. in Nov.–Dec.; and Jan. 7–Mar. 15.*

$$ ✕ **Gennaro.** This small family restaurant on the seafront in Ischia Porto serves excellent fish in a convivial atmosphere. Specialties include spaghetti alle vongole and linguine *all'aragosta* (with lobster). ✉ *Via Porto 66, Ischia Porto* ☎ *081/992917* ▤ *AE, DC, MC, V* ☉ *Closed Nov.–mid-Mar.*

$$$$ ⬚ **Grand Hotel Punta Molino.** Set in its own pinewood grounds on Ischia's northeastern coastline yet within walking distance of the island's shopping boulevards, this pleasingly modern hotel provides privacy, relaxation, and low-key evening entertainment. Rooms are decorated in gentle Mediterranean hues—some of the best are in the villa annex. A crescent-shaped swimming pool wraps round part of the main building, and the gardens have walkways and shady pergolas. Rates include a buffet lunch or candlelight dinner. ✉ *Lungomare C. Colombo 23, 80077* ☎ *081/991544* 🖷 *081/9991562* ⬤ *www.puntamolino.it* ⬈ *90 rooms* ⬧ *2 restaurants, 3 pools, health club, spa, beach, piano bar, meeting rooms* ▤ *AE, DC, MC, V* ☉ *Closed Oct.–Mar.* ⦿ *MAP.*

$$$$ ⬚ **Hotel San Montano.** Modern San Montano is perched commandingly 300 ft up on Monte Vico. Nautical motifs and materials are used in much of the hotel, with portholes in the lobby, brass finishings to the room furniture, and tiller-shaped headboards. With the full gamut of spa treatments available, you could be forgiven for not venturing down to sea level. Note that half-board is required in high season. ✉ *Via Montevico 20, 80076, Lacco Ameno* ☎ *081/994033* 🖷 *081/980242* ⬤ *www.sanmontano.com* ⬈ *65 rooms, 12 suites* ⬧ *Restaurant, minibars, tennis court, 2 pools, spa* ▤ *AE, DC, MC, V* ☉ *Closed Nov.–Mar.* ⦿ *MAP.*

$$$ ⬚ **Villarosa.** A highlight at this gracious family-run hotel—a villa with bright and airy rooms—is the thermally heated pool in the villa garden. In high season, half-board is required, and you must reserve well in advance. It's in the heart of Ischia Porto and only a short walk from the beach. ✉ *Via Giacinto Gigante 5, 80077 Ischia Porto* ☎ *081/991316* 🖷 *081/992425* ⬤ *www.lavillarosa.it* ⬈ *37 rooms* ⬧ *Restaurant, pool* ▤ *AE, DC, MC, V* ☉ *Closed Nov.–Mar.* ⦿ *MAP.*

$ ⬚ **La Pergola.** Here you'll find one of the few opportunities to stay on a working farm on Ischia. La Pergola is a whitewashed villa perched attractively on the slopes of Monte Epomeo and surrounded by vineyards and olive and fruit trees, with sweeping views westward over Citara Beach. Its dynamic young owners also operate a thriving restaurant serving local specialties including the fabled rabbit dish *coniglio all'ischitana.* ✉ *Via San Giuseppe 8, 80075 Forio* ☎ *081/909483* ✎ *giosocol@tin.it* ⬈ *7 rooms* ⬧ *Restaurant; no a/c, no room phones, no room TVs* ▤ *No credit cards.*

Capri

46 *75 mins by boat, 40 mins by hydrofoil from Naples.*

Erstwhile pleasure dome to Roman emperors, and now Italy's most glamorous seaside getaway, Capri (pronounced with an accent on the first syllable) is a craggy island at the southern approach to the Bay of Naples. The summer scene on Capri calls to mind the stampeding of bulls through the narrow streets of Pamplona: if you can visit in spring or fall, do so. Yet even the crowds are not enough to destroy Capri's very special charm. The town is a Moorish opera set of shiny white houses, tiny squares, and narrow medieval alleyways hung with flowers. You can take a bus or the funicular to reach the town, which rests on top of rugged limestone cliffs, hundreds of feet above the sea, and on which herds of *capre* (goats) once used to roam (giving the name to the island). Unlike the other islands in the Bay of Naples, Capri is not of volcanic origin; it may be a continuation of the limestone Sorrentine peninsula.

Limestone caves on Capri have yielded rich prehistoric and neolithic finds. The island is thought to have been systematically settled by Greeks from Cumae in the 6th century BC and later by other Greeks from Neapolis, but it was the Romans in the early imperial period who really left their mark. Emperor Augustus vacationed here; Tiberius built 12 villas scattered over the island, and, in later years, he refused to return to Rome, even when he was near death. Capri was one of the strongholds of the 16th-century pirate Barbarossa, who first sacked it and then made it a fortress. In 1806 the British wanted to turn the island into another Gibraltar and were beginning to build fortifications when the French took it away from them in 1808. Over the next century, from the opening of its first hotel in 1826, Capri saw an influx of visitors that reads like a *Who's Who* of literature and politics, especially in the early decades of the 20th century.

Like much else about Capri, the island's rare and delicious white wine is sensuous and intoxicating. Note that most of the wine passed off as "local" on Capri comes from the much more extensive vineyards of Ischia.

On arrival at the port, pick up the excellent map of the island at the tourist office (€1). You may have to wait in line for the cog railway (€2.60 round-trip) to **Capri Town,** perched some 450 ft above the harbor. If it's not operating, there's a bus and taxi service, as well as a network of steps leading all the way up. From the upper station, walk out into Piazza Umberto I, much better known as the Piazzetta, the island's social hub. You can window-shop in expensive boutiques and browse in souvenir shops along Via Vittorio Emanuele, which leads south toward the many-domed **Certosa di San Giacomo.** You can visit the church and cloister of this much-restored monastery and also pause long enough to enjoy the breathtaking view of Punta Tragara and the Faraglioni, three towering crags, from the viewpoint at the edge of the cliff. ⊠ *Via Certosa* ☎ *081/8376218* ⊘ *Tues.–Sun. 9–2.*

Only when the **Grotta Azzurra** was "discovered" in 1826 by the Polish poet August Kopisch and his Swiss friend, the artist Ernest Fries, did Capri become a tourist haven. The watery cave's blue beauty became a symbol of the return to nature and revolt from reason that marked the Romantic era, and it soon became a required stop on the Grand Tour. In fact, the grotto had long been an island landmark. During the Roman era—as testified by the extensive remains, primarily below sea level, and several large statues, now at the Certosa di San Giacomo—it had been the elegant, mosaic-decorated nymphaeum of the adjoining villa of Gradola. Historians can't quite agree if it was simply a lovely little pavilion where rich patricians would cool themselves or if it was truly a religious site where sacred mysteries were practiced. The extraordinary sapphire color is caused by a hidden opening beneath the surface of the walls that refracts light through the blue water. At highest illumination, the very air inside looks tinted blue.

The Grotta Azzurra can be reached from Marina Grande or from the small embarkation point below Anacapri on the northwest side of the island, accessible by bus from Anacapri. If you're pressed for time, however, skip this sometimes frustrating and disappointing excursion. You board one boat to get to the grotto, then transfer to another smaller boat to take you inside the grotto. If there's a backup of boats waiting to get in, you'll be given precious little time to enjoy the gorgeous color of the water and its silvery reflections. ⊠ *Marina Grande* 🖾 *About €11–€13, depending on boat company, including €4 admission to grotto* ⊙ *Apr.–Sept., daily 9:30–2 hrs before sunset; Oct.–Mar., daily 10–noon.*

From the terraces of **Giardini di Augusto** (Gardens of Augustus), a beautifully planted public garden with excellent views, you can see the village of Marina Piccola below—restaurants, cabanas, and swimming platforms huddle among the shoals—and admire the steep and winding Via Krupp, actually a staircase cut into the rock, all the way down. Friedrich Krupp, the German arms manufacturer, loved Capri and became one of the island's most generous benefactors. The staircase has been closed for years but you can reach the beach by taking a bus from the Via Roma terminus down to Marina Piccola. ⊠ *Via Matteotti, beyond the monastery of San Giacomo* ⊙ *Daily dawn–dusk.*

A tortuous road leads up to **Anacapri,** the island's "second city," about 3 km (2 mi) from Capri Town. To get there, you can take a bus either from Via Roma in Capri Town or from Marina Grande (both €1.30), or a taxi (about €15 one-way; agree on the fare before starting out). Crowds are thick down Via Capodimonte leading to Villa San Michele and around the square, Piazza Vittoria, which is the starting point of the chairlift to the top of Monte Solaro. Elsewhere, Anacapri is quietly appealing. It's a good starting point for walks, such as the 80-minute round-trip journey to the **Migliara Belvedere,** on the island's southern coast.

An impressive limestone formation and the highest point on Capri (1,932 ft), **Monte Solaro** affords gasp-inducing views toward both bays of Naples and Salerno. A 12-minute chairlift ride will take you right to the top (refreshments available at bar), which is a starting point for a number of scenic trails on the western side of the island. Picnickers should note that even in the summer it can get windy at this height, and there are few trees to provide shade or refuge. ⊠ *Piazza Vittoria, Anacapri* ☎ *081/8371428* 🖾 *€4 one-way, €5.50 round-trip* ⊙ *Daily 9–5:30.*

In the heart of Anacapri, the octagonal baroque church of **San Michele,** finished in 1719, is best known for its exquisite majolica pavement, designed by Solimena and executed by the *mastro-riggiolaro* (master tiler) Chiaiese from Abruzzo. A walkway skirts the rich ceramic carpet depicting Adam and a duly contrite Eve being expelled from the Garden of Eden, but you can get a breathtaking overview from the organ loft, reached by a winding staircase near the ticket booth (a privileged perch you have to pay for). Outside the church is the Via Finestrale, which leads to Anacapri's noted **Le Boffe quarter.** This section of town, slightly lower on the hillside, is centered on the Piazza Ficacciate and the Church of Santa Sofia and owes its name to the distinctive domestic architecture prevalent here, which uses vaults and sculpted groins instead of cross beams. ⊠ *Piazza Nicola, Anacapri* ☎ *081/8372396* ▣ €1.05 ⊘ *Nov.–Mar., daily 9:30–5; Apr.–Oct., daily 9–7.*

One of the best excursions from Anacapri is to the ruins of the Roman **Villa di Damecuta.** Sited strategically on a ridge with views sweeping across the Bay of Naples toward Procida and Ischia, the villa would have had its main access point at the landing stage right by the Blue Grotto at Gradola. This was probably one of the villas mentioned by Tacitus in his *Annals* as having been built by Tiberius: "Here on Capreae, in twelve spacious, separately named villas, Tiberius settled." Like Villa Jovis to the east, Villa di Damecuta was extensively plundered over the centuries prior to its proper excavation in 1937. Below the medieval tower (Torre Damecuta) there are two rooms (*domus* and *cubiculum*) that are thought to have been Tiberius's secret summer refuge. Affinities with Villa Jovis may be seen in the *ambulatio* (walkway) complete with seats and a stunning backdrop. To reach Villa Damecuta, get the bus from Anacapri to Grotto Azzurra and ask the driver to let you off at the proper stop. Alternatively, you can walk from the center of Anacapri down the bus route (about 30 minutes, but no sidewalks) or try your luck in the network of virtually traffic-free little alleyways running parallel to the main road. ⊠ *Via A. Maiuri* ▣ *Free* ⊘ *Daily 9–1 hr before sunset.*

★ From Anacapri's Piazza della Vittoria, picturesque Via Capodimonte leads to **Villa San Michele,** the charming former home of Swedish doctor and philanthropist Axel Munthe (1857–1949) that Henry James called "the most fantastic beauty, poetry, and inutility that one had ever seen clustered together." At the ancient entranceway to Anacapri just at the top of the Scala Fenicia and occupying the site of an ancient Roman villa, Villa San Michele was built (beginning in 1896) in accordance with Munthe's instructions. Physician to the Swedish royal family, Munthe practiced in Paris and in Rome, thereby building up a substantial fortune, much of which he plowed into real estate in Anacapri. He was also a philanthropist with a lifelong dedication to the sick and destitute. Munthe's *The Story of San Michele* is an evocative—if not entirely reliable—autobiography.

The villa is set around Roman-style courtyards, marble walkways, and atriums. Rooms display the doctor's varied collections, which range from bric-a-brac to antiquities (once thought so important J. Pierpont Morgan arrived to spend millions on them, but the good doctor knew that most were fakes so refused all offers). Medieval choir stalls, Renaissance lecterns, and gilded statues of saints compose the aesthetic setting, with some rooms preserving the doctor's personal memorabilia. The villa is connected by a spectacular pergola path overlooking the entire Bay of Naples. This leads to the famous Sphinx Parapet, where an ancient Egyptian sphinx looks out toward Sorrento; you cannot see its face—on purpose. It is said that if you touch the sphinx's hindquarters with your left hand while making a wish, it will come true. The parapet is connected to the little Chapel of San Michele, which once stood on the grounds of one of Tiberius's villas.

Besides hosting summer concerts, the Axel Munthe Foundation has an ecomuseum that fittingly reflects Munthe's fondness for animals, where you can learn about various bird species—accompanied by their songs— found on Capri. Munthe bought up the hillside and made it a sanctuary for birds. Today, thanks to the good Dr. Munthe, this little realm is still an Eden. ⊠ *Via Axel Munthe* ☎ *081/837401* ⊕ *www.sanmichele.*

org ☎ €5 ⏱ *May–Sept., daily 9–6; Mar., daily 9:30–4:30; Apr. and Oct., daily 9:30–5; Nov.–Feb., daily 10:30–3:30.*

off the beaten path

BELVEDERE AND ARCO NATURALE – A short walk along Via Tragara leads to a belvedere overlooking the Faraglioni; another takes you out of town on Via Matermània to the so-called Natural Arch, an unusual rock formation near a natural grotto that the Romans transformed into a shrine. The 20-minute walk from the Piazzetta up picturesque Via Madre Serafina and Via Castello to the belvedere at Punta Cannone gives you a panoramic view of the island.

VILLA JOVIS – From Capri Town, the 45-minute hike east to Villa Jovis, the grandest of those built by Tiberius, is strenuous but rewarding. Follow the signs for Villa Jovis, taking Via Le Botteghe from the Piazzetta, then continuing along Via Croce and Via Tiberio. At the end of a lane that climbs the steep hill, with pretty views all the way, you come to the precipice over which the emperor reputedly disposed of the victims of his perverse attentions. From a natural terrace above, near a chapel, are spectacular views of the entire Bay of Naples and, on clear days, part of the Gulf of Salerno. Below are the ruins of Tiberius's palace. Allow 45 minutes each way for the walk alone. ⊠ *Via Tiberio* ☎ *081/8370381* ☎ €2 ⏱ *Daily 9–1 hr before sunset.*

Where to Stay & Eat

$$$–$$$$ ✕ **La Capannina.** One of Capri's finest restaurants, La Capannina is only a few steps from the busy social hub of the Piazzetta. It has a discreet covered veranda—open in summer—for dining by candlelight; most of the regulars avoid the stuffy indoor rooms. The specialties are home-made ravioli and *linguine con lo scorfano* (flat spaghetti with scorpion fish). Look for the authentic Capri wine with the house label. ⊠ *Via Le Botteghe 12 bis and 14, Capri Town* ☎ *081/8370732* ⌂ *Reservations essential* ▤ *AE, DC, MC, V* ⏱ *Closed mid-Jan.–mid-Mar. and Wed. Mar. and Nov.*

$$–$$$ ✕ **La Canzone del Mare.** This is the legendary bathing lido of the Marina Piccola, erstwhile haunt of Grace Fields, Emilio Pucci, Noël Coward, and any number of 1950s and '60s glitterati. The VIPs may have departed for the Bagni di Tiberio beach, but the setting is as magical as ever: Enjoy luncheon (no dinner served) in the thatch-roof pavilion looking out over the sea and I Faraglioni in the distance—this is Capri as picture-perfect as it comes. ⊠ *Via Marina Piccola 93, Capri Town* ☎ *081/8370104* ▤ *AE, DC, MC, V* ⏱ *Closed Nov.–Mar. No dinner.*

$$ ✕ **Al Grottino.** At this small and friendly family-run restaurant near the Piazzetta you'll find arched ceilings and autographed photos of celebrity customers on the walls. House specialties are gnocchi with tomato sauce and mozzarella, and linguine with scampi. ⊠ *Via Longano 27, Capri Town* ☎ *081/8370584* ⌂ *Reservations essential* ▤ *AE, DC, MC, V* ⏱ *Closed Tues. and Nov. 3–Mar. 20.*

★ $$ ✕ **Da Tonino.** It is well worth making the short detour off the beaten track to the Arco Naturale to be pampered by creative chef Tonino. The emphasis here is on land-based dishes; try the *terrina di coniglio* (rabbit terrine) or ask for the pigeon dish with pesto, rosemary, and pine nuts, accompanied by wine from a well-stocked cellar. ⊠ *Via Dentecala 34, Capri Town* ☎ *081/8376718* ▤ *AE, DC, MC, V* ⏱ *Closed Jan. 10–Mar. 15.*

$$ ✕ **I Faraglioni.** With natural shade provided by a 100-year-old wisteria plant, this is a popular, fairly stylish restaurant centrally located and immersed in Mediterranean greenery. Meals here usually kick off with *uovo*

alla Monachina, an egg-shaped dish stuffed with mystery ingredients. For the first course, try the *straccetti con gamberi e pomodorini* (fresh green pasta with shrimp and small tomatoes). ⊠ *Via Camerelle 75, Capri Town* ☎ 081/8370320 ⌁ *Reservations essential* ▤ *AE, DC, MC, V* ⊘ *Closed Nov.–Mar.*

$$ ✕ **Ristorante Pizzeria Aurora.** Though often frequented by celebrities—their photographs adorn the walls—this restaurant offers courtesy and *simpatia* regardless of your fame. Sit outside for maximum visibility or go for extra privacy within. The cognoscenti start off by sharing a pizza *all'acqua,* a thin pizza with mozzarella and a sprinkling of *peperoncino* (chili). If tiring of pasta, try the *sformatino alla Franco* (rice pie in a prawn sauce). Reservations are essential for dinner. ⊠ *Via Fuorlovado 18–20, Capri Town* ☎ 081/8370181 ▤ *AE, DC, MC, V* ⊘ *Closed Jan.–Feb.*

$ ✕ **La Giara.** About a two-minute walk from the bustling Piazza Vittoria in Anacapri, this pizzeria-ristorante has a variety of palatable piatti served briskly and courteously. For a change from seafood, try the *pennette aum aum,* pasta pleasingly garnished with eggplant, mozzarella, cherry tomatoes, and basil. ⊠ *Via Orlandi 67, Anacapri* ☎ 081/8373860 ▤ *AE, DC, MC, V* ⊘ *Closed Dec.–Jan. and Wed.*

$ ✕ **Mamma Giovanna.** This ristorante and pizzeria sits just below Piazza Diaz in the heart of the old town of Anacapri, facing the 16th-century church of Santa Sofia. The no-frills ambience belies the quality of the cuisine: besides *pizze* (served midday and evenings), Mamma Giovanna specializes in *primi piatti,* such as *maccheroncelle al cartoccio* (pasta cooked in the oven with seafood). Reservations are essential for dinner. ⊠ *Via Boffe 3/ 5, Anacapri* ☎ 081/8372057 ▤ *No credit cards* ⊘ *Closed Dec.–Jan.*

$$$$ ✕▨ **Villa Brunella.** This opulent family-run gem is nestled in a garden just below the lane leading to the Faraglioni. Comfortable and tastefully furnished, the hotel has spectacular views and a swimming pool overlooking the sea. The terrace restaurant ($$) also benefits from the superb panorama and is renowned for its seafood and other local dishes. ⊠ *Via Tragara 24, 80073 Capri Town* ☎ 081/8370122 ⎙ 081/8370430 ⊕ *www.villabrunella.it* ⇄ *20 rooms* ⌂ *Restaurant, pool, bar* ▤ *AE, DC, MC, V* ⊘ *Closed Nov.–Mar.*

$$$$ ▨ **Capri Palace.** The feel of a modern resort pervades this large Mediterranean-style hotel set in lovely gardens. The bedrooms are tastefully decorated in bright contemporary style, with white predominating, and have marble bathrooms. The location in Anacapri offers relative seclusion from the summer crowds. Each of four junior suites has a private swimming pool and terrace. ⊠ *Via Capodimonte 2 bis, 80071 Anacapri* ☎ 081/ 8373800 ⎙ 081/8373191 ⊕ *www.capri-palace.com* ⇄ *79 rooms, 4 suites* ⌂ *3 restaurants, pool, spa, billiards, piano bar* ▤ *AE, DC, MC, V* ⊘ *Closed mid-Nov.–Mar.*

$$$$ ▨ **Quisisana.** Catering largely to Americans, this is the most luxurious and traditional hotel in the center of Capri Town. Spacious rooms have some antique accents. Many have arcaded balconies with views of the sea or the charming enclosed garden, surrounding a swimming pool. ⊠ *Via Camerelle 2, 80073 Capri Town* ☎ 081/8370788 ⎙ 081/ 8376080 ⊕ *www.quisi.com* ⇄ *149 rooms* ⌂ *Restaurant, tennis court, pool, sauna, bar, convention center* ▤ *AE, DC, MC, V* ⊘ *Closed Nov.–mid-Mar.*

★ $$$$ ▨ **Scalinatella.** The name means "little stairway," and that's how this charming but modern small hotel is built, on terraces following the slope of the hill, overlooking the gardens, pool, and sea. The bedrooms are intimate, with alcoves and fresh, bright colors; the bathrooms have whirlpool baths. ⊠ *Via Tragara 8, 80073 Capri Town* ☎ 081/8370633 ⎙ 081/8378291 ⊕ *www.scalinatella.com* ⇄ *30 rooms* ⌂ *Restaurant, tennis court, pool, bar* ▤ *AE, DC, MC, V* ⊘ *Closed Nov.–mid-Mar.*

$$–$$$ 🏠 **Villa Sarah.** The whitewashed Mediterranean building here has a homey look and bright, simply furnished rooms. It's close enough to the Piazzetta (a 10-minute walk) to give easy access to the goings-on there, yet far enough away to ensure restful nights. There's a garden and a small bar. ⊠ *Via Tiberio 3/a, 80073 Capri Town* 🕾 *081/8377817* 🖷 *081/8377215* 🌐 *www.villasarah.it*, 🛏 *20 rooms* ♨ *Bar* 🖃 *AE, DC, MC, V* ⊗ *Closed Nov.–Mar.*

$$ 🏠 **Villa Krupp.** Occupying a quiet location overlooking the Gardens of Augustus, this historic hostelry was the onetime home of Maxim Gorky, whose guests included Lenin. Rooms are plain but spacious. ⊠ *Viale Matteotti 12, 80073 Capri Town* 🕾 *081/8370362* 🖷 *081/8376489* 🛏 *12 rooms* ♨ *No a/c in some rooms, no room TVs* 🖃 *MC, V* ⊗ *Closed Nov.–Feb.*

$ 🏠 **Aida.** A 10-minute walk from the town center, on a tiny lane that borders the Gardens of Augustus, the Aida offers a tranquil haven from Capri's bustle and hard sell. The staff is sociable, and the rooms, which look onto a small garden, are spacious, comfortably furnished, and immaculately clean. ⊠ *Via Birago, 80073 Capri Town* 🕾 *081/8370366* 🛏 *4 rooms* ♨ *No a/c* 🖃 *No credit cards* ⊗ *Closed Oct.–Mar.*

FodorsChoice ★ **$** 🏠 **Villa Eva.** Named after its dynamic owner-manager, this is a popular international stopover for young *Wandervögel* (travelers) who have a more laid-back approach to traveling. Accommodations are in small villas set among luxuriant gardens. ⊠ *Via La Fabbrica 8, 80071 Anacapri* 🕾 *081/8371549* 🖷 *081/8372040* 🌐 *www.villaeva.com* 🛏 *24 rooms* ♨ *Pool, bar* 🖃 *AE, DC, MC, V* ⊗ *Closed mid-Nov.–mid-Feb.*

THE AMALFI COAST

As travelers journey down the fabled Amalfi Coast, their route takes them past rocky cliffs plunging into the sea and small boats lying in sandy coves like brightly colored fish. Erosion has contorted the rocks into shapes resembling figures from mythology and hollowed out fairy grottoes where the air is turquoise and the water an icy blue. In winter, nativity scenes of moss and stone are created in the rocks. White villages dripping with flowers nestle in coves or climb like vines up the steep, terraced hills. Lemon trees abound, loaded with blossom or fruit—and netting in winter to protect the fruit. The inhabitants jest that they look after their lemons better than their children. The road must have a thousand turns, each with a different view, on its dizzying 69-km (43-mi) journey from Sorrento to Salerno.

Sorrento

47 *50 km (31 mi) south of Naples, 50 km (31 mi) west of Salerno.*

Sorrento is across the Bay of Naples from Naples itself, on autostrada A3 and S145. The Circumvesuviana railway, which stops at Herculaneum and Pompeii, provides another connection. The coast between Naples and Castellammare, where road and railway turn off onto the Sorrento peninsula, seems at times depressingly overbuilt and industrialized. Yet Vesuvius looms to the left, you can make out the 3,000-ft-high mass of Monte Faito ahead, and on a clear day you can see Capri off the tip of the peninsula. The scenery improves considerably as you near Sorrento, where the coastal plain is carved into russet cliffs rising perpendicularly from the sea. This is the Sorrento (north) side of the peninsula; on the other side is the Amalfi Coast, more dramatically scenic. But Sorrento has at least two advantages over Amalfi: the Circumvesuviana railway terminal and a fairly flat terrain. A stroll around town is a pleasure—you'll encounter narrow alleyways and interesting churches, and the views of the Bay of Naples from the Villa Comunale and the Museo Correale are priceless.

Until the mid-20th century, Sorrento was a small, genteel resort favored by central European princes, English aristocrats, and American literati. During World War I, American soldiers came to recuperate at the Hotel Vittoria. Now the town has grown and spread out along the crest of its famous cliffs, and apartments stand where citrus groves once bloomed. Like most resorts, Sorrento is best off-season, in spring, autumn, or even winter, when Campania's mild climate can make a stay pleasant anywhere along the coast.

A highlight of Sorrento is **Museo Correale di Terranova**, an 18th-century villa with a lovely garden on land given to the patrician Correale family by Queen Joàn of Áragón in 1428. It has an excellent private collection amassed by the count of Terranova and his brother. The building itself is fairly charmless, with few period rooms, but the garden offers an allée of palm trees, citrus groves, floral nurseries, and an esplanade with a panoramic view of the Sorrento coast. The collection itself is one of the finest devoted to Neapolitan paintings, decorative arts, and porcelains, so for connoisseurs of the *seicento* (Italian 17th century), this museum is a must. Magnificent 18th-century inlaid tables by Giuseppe Gargiulo, Capodimonte porcelains, and rococo portrait miniatures are reminders of the age when pleasure and delight were all. Also on view are regional Greek and Roman archaeological finds, medieval marble work, glasswork, old master paintings, 17th-century majolicas—even Tasso's death mask. ⊠ *Via Correale* ☎ *081/8781846* ▣ *Museum and gardens €6* ⊘ *Wed.–Mon. 9–2.*

Worth checking out is the **Museo Bottega della Tarsialignea**, set up by local architects to ensure the continuity of the *intarsia* (wood inlay) tradition. It houses historical collections as well as exhibitions of modern work. There's a shop if you fancy taking home an unusual souvenir. ⊠ *Via San Nicola 28* ☎ *081/8771942* ⊕ *www.alessandrofiorentinocollection. it* ▣ *€8* ⊘ *Museum guided visits (required) every ½ hr Apr.–Oct., Tues.–Sun. 9:30–noon and 5–7; Nov.–Mar., Tues.–Sun. 9:30–noon and 3–5. Shop Tues.–Sun. 9:30–1 and 5–8 (3–6 in winter).*

Via Marina Grande turns into a pedestrian lane, then a stairway leading to Sorrento's only real beach at **Marina Grande,** where fishermen pull up their boats and there are some good seafood restaurants. A frequent bus also plies this route, if you don't fancy the legwork; tickets are sold at the *tabacchi* (tobacconist).

off the beaten path

CAPO DI SORRENTO AND THE BAGNO DELLA REGINA GIOVANNA – Just 2 km (1 mi) west of Sorrento, turn right off Statale 145 toward the sea, and then park and walk a few minutes through citrus and olive groves to get to Capo di Sorrento, the craggy tip of the cape, with the most interesting ancient ruins in the area. They were identified by the Latin poet Publius Papinius Statius as the ancient Roman villa of historian Pollio Felix, patron of the great authors Virgil and Horace. Next to the ruins is Bagno della Regina Giovanna (Queen Joan's Bath). A cleft in the rocks allows the sea to channel through an archway into a clear, natural pool, with the water turning iridescent blue, green, and violet as the sunlight changes angles. The easiest way to see all this is to rent a boat at Sorrento; afterward, sailing westward will bring you to the fishermen's haven of Marina di Puolo, where you can lunch on fresh catch at a modest restaurant.

Where to Stay & Eat

★ **$$$$** ✕ **Don Alfonso 1890.** The most heralded restaurant in Campania is the domain of Alfonso Iaccarino; *haute*-hungry pilgrims come here to feast on culinary rarities, often centuries-old recipes given a unique spin. The braciola of lamb with pine nuts and raisins is a recipe that dates back to the Renaissance, while the cannoli stuffed with foie gras pays homage to the Neapolitan Bourbon court. Nearly everything is home-grown, and the wine cellar is one of the finest in Europe. Those who want to make a night of it can stay in one of five apartments above the restaurant. ✉ *Corso Sant'Agata 13, Sant'Agata sui due Golfi, 7 km south of Sorrento* 🕾 *081/8780026* ▤ *AE, DC, MC, V* ☉ *Closed Mon. and Tues. Oct.–May; Mon. June–Sept.; and Jan. 10–Feb. 25.*

$$$–$$$$ ✕ **Antica Trattoria.** An old-fashioned dining room inside and garden tables in fair weather make this a pleasant place to enjoy the local cooking. The atmosphere is homey and the menu is voluminous; specialties include spaghetti alle vongole and *gamberetti all'Antica Trattoria* (shrimp in tomato sauce). You can also opt for one of the four prix-fixe menus. ✉ *Via Giuliani 33* 🕾 *081/8071082* ▤ *AE, DC, MC, V* ☉ *Closed Mon. and 4 wks in Jan.–Feb.*

$$–$$$ ✕ **Antico Francischiello da Peppino.** Overlooking olive groves seeming to run into the sea, this fourth-generation establishment is situated away from the throng, halfway between Sorrento and Massa Lubrense. Two huge, beamed rooms with sprays of fernery, antique mirrored sideboards, hundreds of mounted plates, brick archways, old chandeliers, fresh flowers, and tangerine-hued tablecloths make for quite a sight. *Tagliolini con zafferano, zucchine e gamberi* (pasta with saffron, zucchini and prawns), ravioli with clams and arugula, and other bountiful country cuisine is *tutta buona.* ✉ *Via Partenope 27,* 🕾 *081/533–9780* ▤ *AE, DC, MC, V* ☉ *Closed Wed. in winter.*

★ **$–$$** ✕ **Parrucchiano.** At one of Sorrento's oldest and best restaurants, you walk up a few steps to glassed-in veranda dining rooms filled, like greenhouses, with vines and plants. The menu offers classic local specialties, among them *panzerotti* (pastry shells filled with tomato and mozzarella) and *scaloppe alla sorrentina* (scallops with tomato and mozzarella). ✉ *Corso Italia 71* 🕾 *081/8781321* ▤ *MC, V* ☉ *Closed Wed. Nov.–Mar.*

$ ✕ **Trattoria da Emilia.** You can sit outside here, right on the Marina Grande, and watch the life of the port go by. This simple, rustic restaurant with wooden tables has been run by Donna Emilia and her offspring since 1947 and provides typical Sorrento home cooking and a family atmosphere. Fried seafood is the specialty. Sofia Loren came to eat here while filming *Pane, amore,* . . . . ✉ *Via Marina Grande 62* 🕾 *081/8072720* ▤ *No credit cards* ☉ *Closed Tues. Oct.–Mar. No dinner Oct.–Mar.*

$$$$ 🏨 **Bellevue Syrene.** This exclusive hotel is set in a cliff-top garden close to the center of Sorrento. It retains its solid, old-fashioned comforts and sumptuous charm, with Victorian nooks and alcoves, antique paintings, and exuberant frescoes. You can find interior-facing rooms at lower prices, if you're willing to forgo the splendid views over the sea. ✉ *Piazza della Vittoria 5, 80067* 🕾 *081/8781024* 🖷 *081/8783963* ⊕ *www.bellevuesyrene. it* ➱ *73 rooms* ⚓ *Restaurant, beach, bar* ▤ *AE, DC, MC, V*

$$$$ 🏨 **Cocumella.** A grand hotel in every sense, the Cocumella seems little
Fodor'sChoice changed since the days when Goethe and the Duke of Wellington stayed
★ here. Set in a cliff-top garden overlooking the Bay of Naples, the hotel occupies a 17th-century monastery complete with frescoed ceilings and antique reliquaries. The amenities are hardly monastic: they include a spectacular pool area, a workout room, summer concerts in the hotel's baroque church, and palatial Empire-style suites with fireplaces. For around €110 per person, you can spend a day cruising in the hotel's 90-ft-long 19th-century yacht. ✉ *Via Cocumella 7, 80065 Sant'Ag-*

nello, Sorrento ☎ 081/8782933 🖷 081/8783712 ⊕ *www.cocumella. com* ⤶ *45 rooms, 15 suites* ⚒ *Restaurant, pool, gym, spa, bar* ▭ *AE, DC, MC, V* ☾ *Closed Nov.–Mar.*

★ **$$$$** 🖫 **Excelsior Vittoria.** Magnificently situated overlooking the Bay of Naples, this is a Belle Epoque dream come true. Gilded salons, stunning gardens, and an impossibly romantic terrace where orchestras lull you twice a week with Neapolitan and modern music: in all, it's a truly intoxicating experience. Caruso stayed here and, more recently, Pavarotti. There's a 15% discount from November to February and a 10% discount in March. ⊠ *Piazza Tasso 34, 80067* ☎ *081/8071044* 🖷 *081/ 8771206* ⊕ *www.exvitt.it* ⤶ *109 rooms, 14 suites* ⚒ *Restaurant, pool, bar, meeting room* ▭ *AE, DC, MC, V.*

$$ 🖫 **Settimo Cielo.** Here's an excellent choice if you want to stay on the water but your budget doesn't extend to one of the luxury hotels. There are gardens and a swimming pool on the grounds, and the beach is a few steps away. The rooms, which all face the sea, are simple and modern. ⊠ *Via Capo 27, 80067* ☎ *081/8781012* 🖷 *081/8073290* ⊕ *www. hotelsettimocielo.com* ⤶ *20 rooms* ⚒ *Restaurant, pool, bar* ▭ *AE, DC, MC, V* ☾ *Closed Nov.–mid-Dec., Jan.–Mar.*

$ 🖫 **Mignon Meublé.** Spacious and simple yet stylish accommodations, a central location, friendly service, and bargain rates: with this combination of characteristics, you'll understand why it's advisable to book well in advance here. Breakfast is served in your room, but there's a small sitting area where you can also relax. ⊠ *Via Sersale 9, 80067* ☎*081/8073824* 🖷 *081/5329001* ⤶ *23 rooms* ⚒ *No room phones* ▭ *AE, DC, MC, V.*

Nightlife & the Arts

BAR At **Circolo dei Forestieri** (⊠ Via de Maio 35 ☎ 081/8773263), you'll get a memorable view of the Bay of Naples from the terrace. Drinks are moderately priced, and there's live music nightly in summer and every weekend the rest of the year. It's closed January and February.

FILM Every October, the **International Cinema Convention** in Sorrento draws an elite collection of producers, directors, and stars. It's less frantic than Cannes; while much of the activity revolves around deal making, a number of previews are screened. For details, contact the Sorrento tourist office (⊠ Via de Maio 35 ☎ 081/80740330).

MUSIC July and August bring the **Summer Music Festival,** held in the 12th-century cloister of St. Francis. There's a wide choice of music to enjoy, from classical and baroque to jazz and folk. Contact the tourist office (⊠ Via de Maio 35 ☎ 081/8074033) for information.

SHOWS **Fauno Notte Club** (⊠ Piazza Tasso 13/a ☎ 081/8781021 ⊕ www. faunonotte.it) puts on Tarantella Shows, which consist of traditional Neapolitan songs and dances performed in typical 17th–19th-century costumes of Sorrento. Shows usually run daily from 9 PM until about 11 PM, with some patrons lingering for slow dances afterward. The admission price (around €21) includes one drink.

Shopping

LOCAL CRAFTS Around **Piazza Tasso** are a number of shops selling embroidered goods and intarsia woodwork, a centuries-old tradition here. Along narrow **Via San Cesareo,** where the air is pungent with the perfumes of fruit and vegetable stands, there are shops selling local and Italian crafts—everything from jewelry boxes to trays and coffee tables with intarsia decoration. **Ferdinando Corcione,** in his shop on Via San Francesco, gives demonstrations of intarsia work, producing decorative plaques with classic or contemporary motifs. You may want to stop in one of the many shops selling the famous lemon liqueur *limoncello.* Piemme and **Villa Massa** are highly recommended brands; the latter is exported to the United States.

Positano

★ *14 km (9 mi) east of Sorrento, 57 km (34 mi) south of Naples.*

When John Steinbeck lived here in 1953, he wrote that it was difficult to consider tourism an industry because "there are not enough *tourists.*" Alas, Positano, a village of white Moorish-style houses clinging to slopes around a small sheltered bay, has since been discovered. The artists came first, and, as happens wherever artists go, the wealthy followed and the artists fled. Another Steinbeck observation still applies, however: "Positano bites deep. It is a dream place that isn't quite real when you are there and becomes beckoningly real after you have gone. Its houses climb a hill so steep it would be a cliff except that stairs are cut in it. I believe that whereas most house foundations are vertical, in Positano they are horizontal. The small curving bay of unbelievably blue and green water laps gently on a beach of small pebbles. There is only one narrow street and it does not come down to the water. Everything else is stairs, some of them as steep as ladders. You do not walk to visit a friend, you either climb or slide."

In the 10th century, Positano was part of Amalfi's Maritime Republic, which rivaled Venice as an important mercantile power. Its heyday was in the 16th and 17th centuries, when its ships traded in the Near and Middle East, carrying spices, silks, and precious woods. The coming of the steamship in the mid-19th century led to the town's decline; some three-fourths of its 8,000 citizens emigrated to America, most to New York.

What had been reduced to a forgotten fishing village is now the number one attraction on the coast. From here you can take hydrofoils to Capri during the summer, escorted bus rides to Ravello, and tours of the Grotta dello Smeraldo. If you're staying in Positano, check whether your hotel has a parking area. If not, you will have to pay for space in a parking lot, which is almost impossible to find during the high season, from Easter to September. The best bet for day-trippers is to arrive by bus—there is a good, regular service—or else get to Positano early enough to find a parking space.

No matter how much time you spend in Positano, make sure you have some comfortable walking shoes (no heels) and that your back and legs are strong enough to negotiate those daunting *scalinatelle* (little stairways). Alternatively, you can ride the municipal bus, which frequently plies along the one-and-only-one-way Via Pasitea, hairpinning from Positano's central Piazza dei Mulini to the mountains and back, making a loop through the town every half hour. Heading down from the Sponda bus stop toward the beach, you pass Le Sirenuse, the hotel where John Steinbeck stayed in 1953. Its stepped terraces offer vistas over the town, so you might splurge on lunch or a drink here on the pool terrace, a favorite gathering place for Modigliani-sleek jet-setters. Continue to Piazza dei Mulini, and make a left turn onto Via dei Mulini.

If you want to catch your breath after a bus ride to Positano, take a quick time-out for an espresso, a slice of Positanese (a delectable chocolate cake), or a fresh-fruit iced *granita* in the lemon-tree garden at **Bar-Pasticceria La Zagara** (⊠ Via Mulini 8 ☎ 089/875964). Past a bevy of resort boutiques, head to Via dei Mulini 23 to view the prettiest garden in Positano—the 18th-century courtyard of the **Palazzo Murat,** named for Joachim Murat, who sensibly chose the palazzo as his summer residence. This was where Murat, designated by his brother-in-law Napoléon as King of Naples in 1808, came to forget the demands of power and lead the simple life. Since Murat was one of Europe's leading style setters, it couldn't be *too* simple, and he wound up building a grand abode (now a hotel) just steps from the main beach.

Beyond the Palazzo Murat is the Chiesa Madre, or parish church of **Santa Maria Assunta,** its green and yellow majolica dome, topped by a perky cupola, visible from just about anywhere in town. Built on the site of the former Benedictine abbey of St. Vito, the 13th-century Romanesque structure was almost completely rebuilt in 1700. The last piece of the ancient mosaic floor can be seen under glass near the apse. Note the carved wooden Christ, a masterpiece of devotional religious art, with its bathetic face and bloodied knees, on view before the altar. At the altar is a Byzantine 13th-century painting on wood of Madonna with Child, known as the Black Virgin, carried to the main beach every August 15 to celebrate the Feast of the Assumption. Legend claims that the painting was once stolen by Saracen pirates, who, fleeing in a raging storm, heard from a voice on high, "*Posa, posa*"—"Put it down, put it down." When they placed the image on the beach near the church, the storm calmed, as did the Saracens. Positano was saved, and the town's name was established (yet again). Embedded over the doorway of the church's bell tower, set across the tiny piazza, is a medieval bas-relief of fishes, a fox, and a Pistrice, the mythical half-dragon, half-dog sea monster. This is one of the sole relics of the medieval abbey of St. Vito. ⊠ *Piazza Flavio Gioia above the main beach* ☎ *089/875067* ⊙ *Daily, 8.30–12 and 4.30–7.*

The walkway from the Piazza Flavio Gioia leads down to the **Spaggia Grande,** or main beach, bordered by an esplanade and some of Positano's best restaurants. Head over to the stone pier to the far right of the beach as you face the water. A staircase leads to the **Via Positanesi d'America,** a lovely seaside walkway. Halfway up the path you'll find the Torre Trasìta, the most distinctive of Positano's three coastline defense towers, which define the edges of Positano in various states of repair. The Trasìta—now a residence occasionally available for summer rental—was one of the defense towers used to warn of pirate raids. Continuing along the Via Positanesi d'America, you pass tiny inlets and emerald coves until the large beach, Spaggia di Fornillo, comes into view.

Where to Stay & Eat

$$–$$$ ✕ **Buca di Bacco.** After an aperitif at the town's most famous and fashionable café downstairs, you dine on a veranda overlooking the beach. The specialties include *zuppa di cozze* (mussel soup), fresh *spigola* (bass), and figs and oranges in caramel. ⊠ *Via Rampa Teglia 8* ☎ *089/ 875699* ▭ *AE, DC, MC, V* ⊙ *Closed Nov.–Mar.*

$$–$$$ ✕ **Donna Rosa.** This minimalist little hideaway in one-street Montepertuso, the hamlet high over Positano, is truly original. Everybody gets into the act: Mamma does the creative cooking, to order; Pappa "makes noise"; and the daughters rule out front. Homemade pasta is the house specialty, along with the delectable desserts, which may include walnut or strawberry mousse and *crostata all'arancio* (orange tart). A wide selection of fine wines is on hand, while live music can be anything from jazz to Australian gospel, with a daughter singing sweetly. Reservations are essential at dinner. ⊠ *Via Montepertuso* ☎ *089/811806* ▭ *AE, DC, MC, V* ⊙ *Closed Mon.*

$$–$$$ ✕ **'O Capurale.** Among the popular restaurants on the beach promenade, this one just around the corner has the best food and lowest prices. Tables are set under vines on a breezy sidewalk in the summer, indoors and upstairs in winter. Spaghetti *con melanzane* (with eggplant) and crepes *al formaggio* (with cheese) are among the specialties. ✉ *Via Regina Giovanna 12* ☎ *089/875374* 🚫 *AE, DC, MC, V* ⊗ *Closed Nov.–mid-Feb.*

$$$$ 🏨 **Casa Albertina.** Clinging to the cliff, this little house is well loved for its Italian charm, its homey restaurant, and its owners, the Cinque family. Rooms have high ceilings, bright fabrics, tile flooring, and sunny terraces or balconies overlooking the sea and coastline. Cars can't drive to the doorway, but porters will ferry your luggage. Note: it's 300 steps down to the main beach. Half- or full board is required in summer (and is reflected in the price category here). ✉ *Via della Tavolozza 3, 84017* ☎ *089/875143* 🖨 *089/811540* 🌐 *www.casalbertina.it* 🛏 *21 rooms* ♿ *Restaurant, minibars, parking (fee)* 🚫 *AE, DC, MC, V* ⊙| *MAP.*

$$$$ 🏨 **Il San Pietro.** A luxurious oasis for the affluent international set, the San Pietro lies a few bends outside the town and is set high above the sea with garden terraces. The hotel has sumptuous Neapolitan baroque decor and masses of flowers in the lounges, elegantly understated rooms (most with terraces), and marvelous views. There's a pool on an upper level, and an elevator whisks you down to the private beach and beach bar. The proprietors organize boating excursions and parties and provide car and minibus service into town. ✉ *Via Laurito 2, 84017* ☎ *089/875455* 🖨 *089/811449* 🌐 *www.ilsanpietro.it* 🛏 *60 rooms* ♿ *Restaurant, tennis court, pool, beach, dock, 2 bars* 🚫 *AE, DC, MC, V* ⊗ *Closed mid-Nov.–mid-Mar.*

★ $$$$ 🏨 **Le Sirenuse.** A handsome 18th-century palazzo in the center of town has been transformed into this luxury hotel, with bright tile floors, precious antiques, and tasteful furnishings. The bedrooms are spacious and comfortable; most have splendid views from balconies and terraces. The top-floor suites have huge bathrooms and whirlpool baths. One side of a large terrace has an inviting swimming pool; on the other is an excellent restaurant. ✉ *Via Cristoforo Colombo 30, 84017* ☎ *089/875066* 🖨 *089/811798* 🌐 *www.sirenuse.it* 🛏 *60 rooms* ♿ *Restaurant, pool, gym, sauna, bar* 🚫 *AE, DC, MC, V.*

$$$$ 🏨 **Palazzo Murat.** The location is perfect—in the heart of town, near the beachside promenade, but set in a quiet, walled garden. The old wing is a historic palazzo with tall windows and wrought-iron balconies; the modern wing is a whitewashed Mediterranean building with arches and terraces. You can relax in antiques-accented lounges or in the charming vine-draped patio, and enjoy gorgeous views from the comfortable bedrooms. ✉ *Via dei Mulini 23, 84017* ☎ *089/875177* 🖨 *089/811419* 🌐 *www.palazzomurat.it* 🛏 *31 rooms* ♿ *Restaurant, bar* 🚫 *AE, DC, MC, V* ⊗ *Closed Jan.–mid-Mar.*

$$ 🏨 **La Fenice.** This tiny, friendly, unpretentious hotel on the peaceful outskirts of town beckons with bougainvillea-laden vistas, castaway cottages, and a turquoise pool (available only in summer), all perched over a private beach. Guest rooms—accented with coved ceilings, whitewashed walls, and native folk art—are simple havens of tranquillity; book the best, those closest to the sea, only if you can handle *very* steep walkways. ✉ *Via G. Marconi 4, 84017* ☎ *089/875513* 🖨 *089/811309* 🛏 *15 rooms* ♿ *Pool; no a/c, no room phones, no room TVs* 🚫 *No credit cards.*

$$ 🏨 **Villa Rosa.** Sharing almost the same views as other hotels with twice the price tag, this family-run hotel has long been a favorite with independent travelers. It's extremely central but slightly set back from the road up the inevitable steps. Ask for a room on the first floor, which is quieter and more panoramic. ✉ *Via C. Colombo 127, 84017* ☎ *089/811955* 🖨 *089/812112* 🌐 *www.villarosapositano.it* 🛏 *18 rooms* 🚫 *AE, DC, MC, V* ⊗ *Closed Nov.–Feb.*

¢ ▦ **La Ginestra.** Set in hikers' paradise at about 2,000 ft over Positano, the farming cooperative La Ginestra dominates the coastline with its converted 18th-century manor house. The peasants' quarters have been transformed into a thriving restaurant, while the guest rooms above are decorated in simple country style. Positano is reached via a network of footpaths—be aware that it's a good hour's slog up from the bottom. If arriving by train, get off the Circumvesuviana train at Vico Equense and take the local orange bus uphill to the village of Santa Maria del Castello, which is about 300 meters from the cooperative. Access by car is also easiest from Vico Equense. ✉ *Via Tessa 2, 80069 Santa Maria Del Castello, Vico Equense* ☏☏ *081/8023211* ⊕ *www.laginestra.org* ↬ *8 rooms* ⚅ *No a/c, no room phones, no room TVs* ▤ *MC, V* ⦿I *MAP.*

Nightlife

L'Africana (✉ Vettica Maggiore, Praiano, 10 km [6 mi] east of Positano on the coast road ☏ 089/874042) is the premier nightclub on the Amalfi Coast, built into a fantastic grotto above the sea.

Grotta dello Smeraldo

13 km (8 mi) east of Positano, 27 km (17 mi) east of Sorrento.

A peculiar green light that casts an eerie emerald glow over impressive formations of stalagmites and stalactites, many of them underwater, inspired the name of the Grotta dello Smeraldo (Emerald Grotto). You can park at the signposts for the grotto along the coast road and take an elevator down, or you can drive on to Amalfi and return to the grotto by the more romantic route—via boat. Boat tours leave from the Amalfi seafront regularly, according to demand; the charge is €6 per person. Call ahead, as hours are subject to change. ▱ *Grotto €5.50* ⊘ *Apr.–Sept., daily 9–5; Oct.–Mar., daily 10–4.*

Amalfi

④⑨ *17 km (11 mi) east of Positano, 35 km (22 mi) east of Sorrento.*

"The sun—the moon—the stars and—Amalfi," Amalfitans used to say. During the Middle Ages, Amalfi was an independent maritime state with a population of 50,000. The ship compass, trivia fans will be interested to know, was invented here in 1302. The republic also brought the art of papermaking to Europe from Arabia. Before World War II there were 13 mills making paper by hand in the Valle Molini, but now only two small ones remain. The town is romantically situated at the mouth of a deep gorge and has some good-quality hotels and restaurants. It's also a convenient base for excursions to Capri and the Grotta dello Smeraldo. The parking problem here is as bad as that in Positano. The small lot in the center of town fills quickly; if you can afford the steep prices, make a luncheon reservation at one of the hotel restaurants and have your car parked for you.

Amalfi's main historical sight is its **Duomo** (also known as Cattedrale di Sant'Andrea), which shows an interesting mix of Moorish and early Gothic influences. You're channeled first into the adjoining **Chiostro del Paradiso** (Paradise Cloister), built around 1266 as a burial ground of Amalfi's elite and one of the architectural treasures of southern Italy. Its flower-and-palm-filled quadrangle has a series of exceptionally delicate, intertwining arches on slender double columns in a combination of Byzantine and Arabian styles. Next stop is the 9th century basilica, a **museum** housing sarcophagi, sculpture, Neapolitan goldsmiths' artwork, and other treasures from the cathedral complex.

Steps from the basilica lead down into the **Cripta di Sant'Andrea** (Crypt of St. Andrew). The cathedral above was built in the 13th century to house the saint's bones, which came from Constantinople and supposedly exuded a miraculous liquid believers call the "manna of St. Andrew." Following the one-way traffic up to the cathedral itself, you finally get to admire the elaborate polychrome marbles and painted, coffered ceilings from its 18th-century restoration; art historians shake their head over this renovation, as the original decoration of the apse must have been one of the wonders of the Middle Ages. ⊠ *Piazza del Duomo* ☎ *089/ 871059* 🖼 *€2.50* ☻ *Daily: Mar.–June and Oct., 9–7; July–Sept., 9–9; Nov.–Feb., 10–1 and 2:30–5:30.*

Valle dei Mulini (Valley of the Mills), uphill from town, was for centuries Amalfi's center for papermaking, an ancient trade learned from the Arabs (who learned it from the Chinese). Beginning in the 12th century, former flour mills in the town were converted to produce paper made from cotton and linen, being among the first in Europe to do so. In 1211 Frederick II of Sicily prohibited this lighter, more readable paper for use in the preparation of official documents, favoring traditional sheepskin parchment, but by 1811 more than a dozen mills here, with more along the coast, were humming. Natural waterpower ensured that the handmade paper was cost-effective, but catastrophic flooding in 1954 closed most of the mills for good, and many of them have now been converted into private housing. The **Museo della Carta** (Museum of Paper) opened in 1971 in a 15th-century mill; paper samples, tools of the trade, old machinery, and the audiovisual presentation are all enlightening. A 20-minute stroll from the Piazza Duomo will take you to the valley via the main thoroughfare of Via Genoa, turning onto Via Capuano at the edge of town. ⊠ *Via delle Cartiere 23* ☎ *089/8304561* ⊕ *www.museodellacarta. it* 🖼 *€3.40* ☻ *Nov.–Mar., Tues.–Sun. 10–3; Apr.–June and Oct., daily 10–6; July–Sept., daily 10–8.*

Where to Stay & Eat

★ **$$$–$$$$** ✕ **Da Gemma.** Amalfi's oldest restaurant, on a side street opposite the Duomo, was established in 1872 by the great-grandmother of the current owner. Here you can dine sublimely on traditional Campanian dishes surrounded by photos of Old Amalfi on the walls. Recommended choices include *zuppa di pesce* (fish soup) and *paccheri del marinaio* (pasta with seafood). ⊠ *Via Fratello Gerardo Sasso 9* ☎ *089/871345* ▤ *AE, DC, MC, V* ☻ *Closed Wed. Sept.–June; mid-Jan.–mid-Feb.*

$$$–$$$$ ✕ **Eolo.** One of the Amalfi Coast's most sophisticated restaurants, Eolo has a tranquil decor—white covered ceilings, Romanesque columns, mounted starfish—and a kitchen that turns out such delights as lobster risotto and sea bass with lemon salt and fennel leaves. Many dishes are fetchingly adorned with blossoms and other visual allures, but nothing compares to the view of Amalfi's harbor from one of the picture-window alcoves; try to get a table there. ⊠ *Via P. Comite 3* ☎ *089/871241* ▤ *AE, DC, MC, V* ☻ *Closed Tues. Sept.–July; Nov.–Mar.*

$$ ✕ **Trattoria di Maria.** At this friendly locals' haunt, presided over by the convivial Enzo (son of Maria), you can dine on delicious pizza cooked in a wood oven, local fish dishes, and lemon profiteroles. Ask for a glass of the limoncello or one of the other homemade liqueurs made from bay leaves, fennel, or bilberries (similar to blueberries). ⊠ *Piazza ad Amalfi* ☎ *089/871880* ▤ *AE, DC, MC, V* ☻ *Closed Mon. and Nov.*

★ **$$$$** ⌖ **Santa Caterina.** A large mansion perched above a terraced and flowered hillside on the coast road just outside Amalfi proper, the Santa Caterina is one of the top hotels on the entire coast. The rooms are tastefully decorated; most have small terraces or balconies with great views. There are lovely lounges, gardens, and terraces for relaxing, and an elevator delivers you to the seaside saltwater pool, bar, and swimming area. On grounds lush with lemon and orange groves, there are two romantic villa annexes. ⊠ *Strada Amalfitana 9, 84011* ☎ *089/871012* 🖶 *089/871351* ⊕ *www. hotelsantacaterina.it* ⇩ *66 rooms* ⚙ *2 restaurants, saltwater pool, gym, beach, 2 bars, meeting room, free parking* ⊟ *AE, DC, MC, V.*

$$ 🏨 **Piccolo Paradiso.** The location in the Amalfi harbor area across from the Arsenale makes this upscale B&B a special choice. A small elevator deposits you in the cozy house, sunny yellow with green shutters, with a casually furnished, sun-bright terrace. A common area has tile flooring; rooms are smallish but comfortable, with wicker seating and wrought-iron headboards. Some rooms have private terraces. ⊠ *Via M. Camera 5, 84011* ☎ *089/873001* ⇩ *5 rooms* ⊟ *No credit cards.*

$–$$ 🏨 **Hotel dei Cavalieri.** This terraced white Mediterranean-style hotel on the main road outside Amalfi has three villa annexes on grounds just across the road that extend all the way to a beach below. Bright rooms are functionally furnished, with splashy majolica tile floors. An ample buffet breakfast is served. ⊠ *Via M. Comite 32, 84011* ☎ *089/831333* 🖶 *089/831354* ⊕ *www.hoteldeicavalieri.it* ⇩ *54 rooms* ⚙ *Restaurant, bar; no a/c in some rooms* ⊟ *AE, DC, MC, V.*

Shopping

Drop in on **Antonio Cavaliere** (⊠ Via Fiume ☎ 089/871954), an elderly resident still making paper by hand, with products for sale. You'll find paper creations, maps, and other souvenirs near the Duomo at **Amalfi nelle Stampe Antiche** (⊠ Piazza Duomo 10 ☎ 089/872368).

Ravello

50
Fodor'sChoice ★

5 km (3 mi) northeast of Amalfi, 40 km (25 mi) east of Sorrento.

Perched on a ridge high above Amalfi and the neighboring town of Atrani, the enchanting village of Ravello has stupendous views, quiet lanes, two important Romanesque churches, and several irresistibly romantic gardens. Set "closer to the sky than the sea," according to André Gide, the town has been the ultimate aerie ever since it was founded as a smart suburb for the richest families of Amalfi's 12th-century maritime republic. Rediscovered by English aristocrats a century ago, the town now hosts one of Italy's most famous music festivals.

In Ravello, pride of place is taken by the **Duomo,** dedicated to patron saint Pantaleone and founded in 1086 by Orso Papiro, the first bishop of Ravello. Rebuilt in the 12th and 17th centuries, it retains traces of medieval frescoes in the transept, an original mullioned window, a marble portal, and a three-story 13th-century bell tower playfully interwoven with mullioned windows and arches. The 12th-century bronze door has 54 embossed panels depicting Christ's life, and saints, prophets, plants, and animals, all narrating biblical lore. It was crafted by Barisano da Trani, who also fashioned the doors of the cathedrals of Trani and Monreale. The nave's three aisles are divided by ancient columns, and treasures include sarcophagi from Roman times and paintings by southern Renaissance artist Andrea da Salerno. Most impressive are the two medieval pulpits: the earlier one (on your left as you face the altar), used for reading the Epistles, is inset with a mosaic scene of Jonah and the whale, symbolizing death and redemption. The more famous one opposite, used for reading the Gospels, was commissioned by Nicola Rufolo in 1272 and created by Niccolò di Bartolomeo da Foggia. It seems almost Tuscan in style, with exquisite Cosmatesque mosaic work and bas-reliefs and six twisting columns sitting on lion pedestals. An eagle grandly tops the the inlaid marble lectern.

A chapel, to the left of the apse, is dedicated to St. Pantaleone, a physician who was beheaded in the 3rd century in Nicomedia. Every July 27 devout believers gather in hope of witnessing a miracle (similar to that of San Gennaro in Naples), in which the saint's blood, collected in a vial and set out on an inlaid marble altar, appears to liquefy and come to a boil; it hasn't happened in recent years. In the crypt is the **Museo del Duomo,** which displays treasures from about the 13th century, during the reign of Frederick II of Sicily. ⊠ *Museo del Duomo, Piazza del Duomo* ☎ *€1.50* ☉ *Church: daily 9–1 and 3–7; museum: Apr.–Oct., daily 9:30–1 and 3–7; Nov.–Mar., weekends 9:30–1 and 3–7.*

Directly off Ravello's main piazza is the **Villa Rufolo,** which—if the master storyteller Boccaccio is to be believed—was built in the 13th century by Landolfo Rufolo, whose immense fortune stemmed from trade with Moors and Saracens. Within is a scene from the earliest days of the Crusades. Norman and Arab architecture mingle in profusion in a welter of color-filled gardens so lush that composer Richard Wagner used them as his inspiration for the home of the Flower Maidens in his opera *Parsifal.* Beyond the Arab-Sicilian cloister and the Norman tower are two flower-bedded terraces that offer a splendid vista of the Bay of Salerno; the lower "Wagner Terrace" is the site for the year-long **Festival Musicale di Ravello** (for information, contact the Ravello Concert Society ☎ 089/858149 🖷 089/858249 ⊕ www.ravelloarts.org). ⊠ *Piazza Duomo, 84010* ☎ *€4* ☉ *Daily 9–sunset.*

From Ravello's main piazza, head west along Via San Francesco and Via Santa Chiara to the **Villa Cimbrone,** a medieval-style fantasy that sits 1,500 ft above the sea. Created in 1905 by England's Lord Grimthorpe and made world-famous when Greta Garbo stayed here in 1937, the Gothic *castello-palazzo* is set in fragrant rose gardens that lead to the **Belvedere dell'Infinità** (Belvedere of Infinity), a grand stone parapet that overlooks the impossibly blue Gulf of Salerno and frames a panorama that Ravello resident Gore Vidal has called "the most beautiful in the world." The villa itself is now a hotel. ⊠ *Via Santa Chiara 26* ☎ *089/ 857459* ☎ *€4.50* ☉ *Daily 9–sunset.*

Where to Stay & Eat

★ $-$$ ✕ **Cumpà Cosimo.** This family-run restaurant a few steps from the cathedral square offers a cordial welcome in two simple but attractive dining rooms. There's no view, but the food is excellent, most of it coming from owner Donna Netta's garden or her butcher shop next door. Among the specialties are cheese crepes, roast lamb, and a dish including seven types of homemade pasta. ⊠ *Via Roma 44* ☎ 089/857156 ▤ *AE, DC, MC, V* ☉ *Closed Mon. Jan.–Mar.*

$-$$ ✕ **Vittoria.** Down the bustling arcade of pottery shops adjacent to the grounds of the Villa Rufolo, this is a good place for a return to reality and an informal bite. Vittoria's thin-crust pizza with loads of fresh toppings is the star attraction, but also consider the pasta, maybe fusilli with tomatoes, zucchini, and mozzarella. Decor is extremely simple, with white walls and a few etchings of Ravello. ⊠ *Via dei Rufolo 3* ☎ 089/857947 ▤ *AE, DC, MC, V* ☉ *Closed Tues. Nov.–Mar.*

$$$$ ▥ **Hotel Palumbo.** Occupying a 12th-century patrician palace outfitted with antiques and modern comforts, this elegant hotel has the feel of a lovely private home. It has beautiful garden terraces, breathtaking views, and a sumptuous upstairs dining room. In summer, you can descend to a villa at sea level and be pampered in the hotel's coastal retreat. Note that half-board is compulsory except in winter, when the restaurant is closed. ⊠ *Palazzo Confalone, Via San Giovanni del Toro 16, 84010*

☎ *089/857244* 📠 *089/858133* ⊕ *www.hotel-palumbo.it* ⇔ *20 rooms* ♨ *Restaurant, bar* ▤ *AE, DC, MC, V* ⦿ *MAP.*

★ **$$$$** ▦ **Palazzo Sasso.** Wagner penned part of his opera *Parsifal* at this 12th-century palace, and among its first guests when it became a hotel was Placido Domingo. The whole experience, from the marble atrium and lofty coastal views to courteous attentive service and finer details of hotel decor, makes the Palazzo Sasso hotel one of the finest in southern Italy. The Rossellini restaurant, open to the public, is also highly recommended. ⊠ *Via San Giovanni del Toro 28, 84010* ☎ *089/818181* 📠 *089/858900* ⊕ *www.palazzosasso.com* ⇔ *38 rooms, 5 suites* ♨ *Restaurant, pool, outdoor hot tub, bar, library* ▤ *AE, DC, MC, V* ⦿ *Closed Nov.–Feb.*

$$$$ ▦ **Villa Cimbrone.** This magical place will take your breath away: suspended over the azure sea and set amid rose-laden gardens, it was once the home of Lord Grimthorpe and the holiday hideaway of Greta Garbo. Now exquisitely transformed into a hotel, the Gothic-style *castello* has guest rooms ranging from palatial to cozy; try for the Peony Room, which has its own terrace. The villa is a strenuous hike from the town center. ⊠ *Via Santa Chiara 26, 84010* ☎ *089/857459* 📠 *089/857777* ⊕ *www. villacimbrone.it* ⇔ *13 rooms* ♨ *Minibars, library* ▤ *AE, DC, MC, V* ⦿ *Closed Nov.–Easter.*

$$ ▦ **Parsifal.** In 1288 this diminutive property was a convent housing an order of Augustinian friars. Today the ancient, ivy-covered stone arches and a tile walkway looking out over the coastline lead to a cozy interior that still feels a bit like a retreat. Sun lounges, a garden, a fountain with reflecting pool, and an alfresco dining area all overlook the sea. Rooms are small (monks' cells, after all), so ask for one with a balcony; Nos. 20, 22, 23, 24, and 26 are best. ⊠ *Viale Gioacchino d'Anna 5, Ravello 84010* ☎ *089/857144* 📠 *089/857972* ⊕ *www.hotelparsifal.com* ⇔ *19 rooms* ♨ *Restaurant, bar* ▤ *AE, DC, MC, V* ⦿ *MAP.*

$ ▦ **Villa Amore.** A 10-minute walk from the Piazza Duomo, this family-run hotel has a garden and an exhilarating view of the sea from most of its bedrooms. If you're looking for tranquillity, you've found it, especially at dusk, when the valley is tinged with a glorious purple light. Rooms are small, with modest, modern furnishings; one of the treats is delicious homemade jam at breakfast. Full board is available, and at least half board is required in summer. Reserve ahead, and specify time of arrival if you need help with luggage from the parking lot or bus stop; you pay €4 per bag. ⊠ *Via Santa Chiara, 84010* ☎📠 *089/857135* ⇔ *12 rooms* ♨ *Restaurant, bar; no a/c, no room TVs* ▤ *DC, MC, V* ⦿ *MAP.*

Salerno

51 *6 km (4 mi) east of Vietri sul Mare, 56 km (35 mi) southeast of Naples.*

Spread out along its bay, Salerno was long a sad testimony to years of neglect and overdevelopment, but the antique port is now reevaluating its artistic heritage. It's a well-connected base for exploring the Cilento area to the south, which has such lovely sea resorts as San Marco di Castellabate and Palinuro, and inland some fine mountain walks and spectacular gorges and caves, such as Castelcivita and Pertosa.

Salerno has an imposing Romanesque **Duomo.** Founded in the mid-9th century and substantially rebuilt by Robert Guiscard from 1076 to 1085, the scene is set by the doorway—see the marble lions at the base—which gives way to a spacious atrium. The Cosmatesque pulpits rival Ravello's for elegance, while ornately carved marbled sarcophagi reinforce the cathedral's stately pedigree. ⊠ *Piazza Duomo* ☎ *089/231387* ⦿ *Daily 10–1:30 and 3–6.*

The **Museo Archeologico Provincale,** in Salerno's medieval Benedictine abbey, has interesting displays of ancient artifacts from the region, with many of the higher quality finds coming from the Greco-Etruscan necropolis in what is now the suburb of Fratte. Some fine Attic and Corinthian vases are on the upper floor, but the show-stealer is the 1st-century BC bronze head of Apollo, fished out of the Gulf of Salerno in 1930. ⊠ *Via San Benedetto 28* ☎ *089/231135* 🎫 *Free* ⊘ *Daily 9–7, Sun 9–1.*

Where to Stay

$ 🏠 **Plaza.** You can easily walk to the harbor, shops, and transportation from these clean no-frills lodgings, right across from the train station and tourist board. The interior is decorated in warm, mellow tones, and guest rooms are spacious, some with air-conditioning and all with TVs. When booking, ask for a room on one of the upper floors, which tend to be quieter, or in the back over the courtyard. ⊠ *Piazza Vittorio Veneto 42, 84123* ☎ *089/224477* 📠 *089/237311* ⊕ *www.plazasalerno. it* 🛏 *42 rooms* ♤ *Minibars, lobby lounge; no a/c in some rooms* 🖃 *AE, DC, MC, V.*

¢   🏠 **Santa Rosa.** This small, family-run pensione-style hotel near the train station offers simple and friendly accommodation on a second floor. Note that breakfast is not provided, and there are no TVs in the rooms. ⊠ *Corso Vittorio Emanuele 14, 84123* ☎☎ *089/225346* ✉ *alb. srosa@tiscalinet.it* 🛏 *12 rooms, 6 with bath* ♤ *No a/c, no room TVs* 🖃 *No credit cards* 🍽 *EP.*

Paestum

★ 52   *42 km (26 mi) southeast of Salerno, 99 km (62 mi) southeast of Naples.*

One of Italy's most majestic sights lies on the edge of a flat coastal plain: the remarkably well preserved **Greek temples** of Paestum. S18 from the north passes the train station (Stazione di Paestum), which is about 800 yards from the ruins, through the perfectly preserved **Porta Sirena** archway. This is the site of the ancient city of Poseidonia, founded by Greek colonists probably in the 6th century BC. When the Romans took over the colony in 273 BC and the name was latinized to Paestum, they changed the layout of the settlement, adding an amphitheater and a forum. Much of the archaeological material found on the site is displayed in the well-labeled **Museo Nazionale,** and several rooms are devoted to the unique tomb paintings discovered in the area, rare examples of Greek and pre-Roman pictorial art.

At the northern end of the site opposite the ticket barrier is the **Tempio di Cerere** (Temple of Ceres). Built in about 500 BC, it's now thought to have been originally dedicated to the goddess Athena. Follow the Roman road southward through the site, past the **Foro Romano** (Roman forum), to the **Tempio di Nettuno** (Temple of Poseidon), a magnificent Doric edifice, with 36 fluted columns and an extraordinarily well preserved entablature (area above the capitals), which rivals the finest temples in Greece. Beyond is the so-called **Basilica,** the earliest of Paestum's standing edifices; it dates from early in the 6th century BC. The name is an 18th-century misnomer, for the structure was in fact a temple sacred to Hera, the wife of Zeus. Try to see the temples in the late afternoon, when the light enhances the deep gold of the limestone and the temples are almost deserted. ☎ *0828/722654* 🎫 *Excavations €4, museum €4, excavations and museum €6.50* ⊘ *Excavations July–Sept., daily 9 AM–10 PM; Oct.–June, daily 9–1 hr before sunset. Museum July–Sept., daily 9 AM–10 PM; Oct.–June, daily 9–6:30; closed 1st and 3rd Mon. of each month.*

Where to Stay & Eat

$ ⨉🏠 **Helios.** Directly across the road from the Porta della Giustizia and a few steps from the temples, the Helios has cottage-type rooms in a garden setting. Seven rooms have whirlpool baths. A pleasant restaurant serves local specialties and seafood. The home-produced ricotta and mozzarella are especially recommended. ⊠ *Via Principe di Piemonte 1, Zona Archeologica, 84063* ☎ *0828/811451* 🖷 *0828/811600* 🖘 *27 rooms* ♿ *Restaurant, pool; no a/c in some rooms, no TV in some rooms* ▭ *AE, DC, MC, V.*

NAPLES & CAMPANIA A TO Z

To research prices, get advice from other travelers, and book travel arrangements, visit www.fodors.com.

AIRPORTS

Aeroporto Capodichino, 8 km (5 mi) north of Naples, serves the Campania region. It handles domestic and international flights, including several daily between Naples and Rome (flight time 45 minutes). Throughout the year there is direct helicopter service with Cab Air between Aeroporto Capodichino and Capri or Ischia. The cost is between €820 and €930.

Taxis are available at the airport for the ride to downtown Naples (€15–20). The transportation company ANM runs the Alibus service, which leaves the airport every 30 minutes with stops at Piazza Garibaldi and Piazza Muncipio (€2). The more frequent but slightly slower Bus 3S also goes to Piazza Garibaldi and to the port (Molo Beverello) beyond. Tickets, bought from the newsstands inside the airport, run €0.77.

🗗 Airport Information **Aeroporto Capodichino** ☎ 081/7896259. **ANM (Azienda Napoletana Mobilità)** ☎ 800/639525. **Cab Air** ☎ 081/5844355 or 081/2587110.

BOAT & FERRY TRAVEL

A variety of fast craft and passenger and car ferries connect the islands of Capri and Ischia with Naples and Pozzuoli year-round. In summer, Capri and Ischia are serviced by boats from the Amalfi Coast. Boats and hydrofoils for these islands and for Sorrento leave from Naples's Molo Beverello. Hydrofoils also leave from Mergellina.

Information on departures is published every day in the local paper, *Il Mattino,* and in local editions of national dailies (*Corriere della Sera* or *La Repubblica*). Alternatively, ask at the tourist office or at the port, or contact the companies—Caremar, Navigazione Libera del Golfo, SNAV, and Alilauro—directly. Always double-check schedules in stormy weather. The Coop Sant'Andrea, a boat company based in Amalfi, organizes trips to many places along the coast, as well as special disco and fireworks cruises.

FARES &   🗗 Boat & Ferry Information **Alilauro** ☎ 081/5522838 ⊕ www.alilauro.it.
SCHEDULES   **Caremar** ☎ 081/5513882 ⊕ www.caremar.it. **Coop Sant'Andrea** ☎ 089/873190 ⊕ www.coopsantandrea.it. **Mergellina** ⊠ About 1½ km [1 mi] to the west of Piazza Municipio. **Molo Beverello** ⊠ Southeast of Piazza Municipio. **Navigazione Libera del Golfo** (NLG) ☎ 081/5527209 ⊕ www.navlib.it. **SNAV** ☎ 081/7612348 ⊕ www.snavali.com.

BUS TRAVEL

Marozzi, a Rome-based line, runs direct, air-conditioned buses from Rome to Pompeii, Salerno, Sorrento, and Amalfi. Buses leave Rome's Stazione Tiburtina weekdays at 3 PM, weekends at 7 AM.

There's an extensive network of local buses in Naples and throughout Campania. ACTP buses connect Naples with Caserta in one hour, leaving every 20 minutes from Piazza Garibaldi in Naples (every 40 minutes on Sunday). Buses to Santa Maria Capua Vetere leave Piazza Garibaldi approximately every 30–40 minutes Monday to Saturday (travel time 45 minutes). There are six buses a day Monday to Saturday from Piazza Garibaldi to Benevento. The trip takes 90 minutes. SITA buses for Salerno leave every 30 minutes Monday to Saturday and every two hours on Sunday from the SITA terminal on Via Pisanelli. SITA buses also serve the Amalfi Coast, connecting Sorrento with Salerno. Curreri operates a service (6 runs daily) between Sorrento and Aeroporto Capodichino.

🔲 Bus Information **ACTP** ☎ 081/7001111. **Curreri** ☎ 081/8015420. **Marozzi** ☎ 06/4076140. **SITA** ✉ Via Pisanelli, near Piazza Municipio ☎ 081/5522176 ⊕ www.sita-on-line.it.

CAR RENTAL
🔲 Local Agencies **Avis** ✉ Stazione FS, Caserta ☎ 0823/443756 ⊕ www.avis.com ✉ Stazione Centrale, Naples ☎ 081/5537171 ✉ Via Piedigrotta 44, Naples ☎ 081/7618354 ✉ Viale Nizza 53, Sorrento ☎ 081/8782459. **Hertz** ✉ Via G. Bosco, Caserta ☎ 0823/356383 ⊕ www.hertz.it ✉ Aeroporto Capodichino, Naples ☎ 081/7802971 ✉ Piazza Garibaldi 91/b, Naples ☎ 081/206228 ✉ Garage Di Leva, Via degli Aranci 9, Sorrento ☎ 081/8071646.

CAR TRAVEL
Italy's main north–south route, the A2 (also known as the Autostrada del Sole), connects Rome with Naples and Campania. In good traffic the drive to Naples takes less than three hours. Autostrada A3, a continuation of the A2, runs south from Naples through Campania and into Calabria. It also connects with the autostrada A16 to Bari, which passes Avellino and is linked with Benevento by expressway. For Herculaneum (Ercolano), Pompeii (Pompei), and Oplontis, take the A3 southeast and turn off at the appropriate exit (for Vesuvius, Ercolano is quickest); for the Sorrento peninsula and the Amalfi Coast, exit at Castellammare di Stabia. To get to Paestum, take A3 to the Battipaglia exit and take the road to Capaccio Scalo–Paestum.

GARAGES In Naples, Garage dei Fiori is near Villa Pignatelli, Grilli is near Stazione Centrale, and Turistico is near the port.
🔲 **Garage dei Fiori** ✉ Via Colonna 21 ☎ 081/414190. **Grilli** ✉ Via Ferraris 40 ☎ 081/264344. **Turistico** ✉ Via de Gasperi 14 ☎ 081/5525442.

ROAD CONDITIONS All roads on the Sorrento peninsula and Amalfi Coast are narrow, serpentine, and tortuous, but they have outstanding views. In high season, from about April through October, only residents' cars are allowed on Ischia and Capri.

EMBASSIES & CONSULATES
🔲 United Kingdom **British Consulate** ✉ Via Dei Mille 40, Naples ☎ 081/4238911 ⊕ www.ukinitalia.it.
🔲 United States **U.S. Consulate** ✉ Piazza della Repubblica 2, Naples ☎ 081/5838111 ⊕ www.usembassy.it.

EMERGENCIES
🔲 **Police** ☎ 112. **Ambulance** in Naples ☎ 081/7520696, 081/7528282, or 081/7520850.
🔲 Pharmacies **Farmacia Helvethia** ✉ Piazza Garibaldi 11, opposite Stazione Centrale ☎ 081/5548894.

ENGLISH-LANGUAGE MEDIA
The monthly *Qui Napoli,* free from tourist offices, has useful information in English on museums, exhibitions, and transportation. For a more comprehensive monthly listing of entertainment and events, buy Le Pagine dell'Ozio, available at most newsstands.

MAIL & SHIPPING

UPS has a location in Casoria, near Naples, but shipping services should be arranged using the toll-free number. Federal Express doesn't have a Naples office but works in conjunction with the service SDA. The main Naples post office is open Monday–Saturday 9 to 7.

🖪 Post Offices **Naples Main Post Office** ⊠ Piazza Matteotti, off Via Toledo ☎ 081/5511456.

🖪 Major Overnight Services **Federal Express** ☎ 02/25088001; 800/123800 toll free. **SDA** ⊠ Via Botteghelle di Portici 203/a, Naples ☎ 081/2583411. **UPS** ⊠ Via Pascoli 8, Casoria ☎ 02/25088001; 800/877877 toll free.

SAFETY

LOCAL SCAMS The main risks in Naples are car break-ins, bag-snatching, pickpocketing, and fraud. As a general rule, give twosomes on scooters a wide berth—it's the one riding pillion that does the snatching—and never make major purchases such as digital cameras from unlicensed dealers. Goods can be artfully switched with worthless packages right under your nose. Be particularly vigilant around the central station area of Piazza Garibaldi in Naples; make sure your valuables are carefully stowed away in an inside pocket.

SUBWAY TRAVEL

Naples's rather old Metropolitana (subway system) provides frequent service and can be the fastest way to get across the traffic-clogged city. Tickets cost €0.77, and trains run from 5 AM until 10.30 PM. The other urban subway system, Metropolitana Collinare, currently links the hill area of the Vomero and beyond with the National Archaeological Museum and Piazza Dante. Construction is under way to extend the route to Piazza Garibaldi by 2005.

🖪 Subway Information **FS** ☎ 848/888088.

TOURS

The Associazione di Donnaregina, run by two Neapolitan artists, organizes small group tours (six to eight people) of Naples and surroundings, offering insights into the culture, traditions, and lesser-known places of the region. Other operators include Carrani Tours, Millevi-aggi, Tourcar, and STS.

🖪 **Associazione di Donnaregina** ⊠ Via Luigi Settembrini 80, Naples ☎ 081/446799 or 338/6401301. **Carrani Tours** ⊠ Via Vittorio Emanuele Orlando 95, Rome ☎ 06/4880510 or 06/4742501. **Millevi-aggi** ⊠ Riviera di Chiaia 252, Naples ☎ 081/7642064. **Tourcar** ⊠ Piazza Matteotti 1, Naples ☎ 081/5521938 ⊕ www.tourcar.it. **STS** ⊠ Via Bernini 90, Naples ☎ 081/5565164.

TRAIN TRAVEL

There are trains every hour between Rome and Naples. Eurostar and Intercity trains make the trip in less than two hours. Trains take either the inland route (through Cassino) or go along the coast (via Formia). Almost all trains to Naples stop at Stazione Centrale.

A network of suburban trains connects Naples with several points of interest. The line used most by visitors is the Circumvesuviana, which runs from Corso Garibaldi Station and stops at Stazione Centrale before continuing to Ercolano (Herculaneum), Pompeii, and Sorrento. Frequent local trains connect Naples with Caserta and Salerno. Travel time between Naples and Sorrento on the Circumvesuviana line is about 75 minutes. Benevento is on the main line between Naples and Foggia. The Circumflegrea runs from Piazza Montesanto Station in Naples toward the archaeological zone of Cumae, with three departures in the morning. The Ferrovia Cumana runs from Piazza Montesanto Station to Pozzuoli and Lucrino. For the archaeological zone of Baia, get the shuttle bus outside Lucrino station.

Train Information **Circumflegrea and Cumana** ☏ 081/5513328 ⊕ www.sepsa.it. **Circumvesuviana** ☏ 081/7722444 ⊕ www.vesuviana.it. **Stazione Centrale** ✉ Piazza Garibaldi ☏ 848/888088 ⊕ www.fs-on-line.it.

VISITOR INFORMATION

The EPT (Ente Provinciale per il Turismo) handles information for the province—which in this case could be the province of Naples or that of Salerno—while information offices run by the local tourist organizations are more ubiquitous, though they cover much the same ground.

Tourist Information **EPT** ✉ Piazza dei Martiri 58, 80121 Naples ☏ 081/405311 ✉ Stazione Centrale, 80142 Naples ☏ 081/268779 ✉ Stazione Mergellina, 80122 Naples ☏ 081/7612102 ⊕ www.ept.napoli.it.

Amalfi ✉ Corso delle Repubbliche 27, 84011 ☏ 089/871107. **Benevento** ✉ Piazza Roma 11, 82100 ☏ 0824/319938 ⊕ www.eptbenevento.it. **Capri** ✉ Marina Grande pier, 80073 ☏ 081/8370634 ✉ Piazza Umberto I, Capri Town, 80073 ☏ 081/8370686 ⊕ www.capritourism.com. **Caserta** ✉ Piazza Dante 35, 81100 ☏ 0823/321137. **Ercolano** ✉ Via 4 Novembre 82, 80056 ☏ 081/7881243. **Naples** ✉ Piazza del Gesù, 80135 ☏ 081/5523328. **Pompeii** ✉ Via Sacra 1, 80045 ☏ 081/8507255. **Porto d'Ischia** ✉ Via Iasolino, Porto Salvo, 80077 ☏ 081/5074231. **Ravello** ✉ Piazza Duomo 1, 84010 ☏ 089/857096. **Salerno** ✉ Piazza Vittorio Veneto, 84100 ☏ 089/231432; 800/213289 toll free ⊕ www.crmpa.it/ept. **Sorrento** ✉ Via de Maio 35, 80067 ☏ 081/8074033 ⊕ www.sorrentotourism.com.

PUGLIA

BARI, GARGANO PROMONTORY, TRULLI DISTRICT, LECCE

FODOR'S CHOICE

Grotta Palazzese, restaurant and hotel, Polignano a Mare

Lecce

Trattoria Casareccia, restaurant, Lecce

HIGHLY RECOMMENDED

RESTAURANTS   La Nuova Mangiatoia, Foggia

Trullo d'Oro, Alberobello

HOTELS   Cicolella, Foggia

Costa Brada, Gallipoli

Hotel Palace, Bari

La Regia, Trani

Pizzomunno, Vieste

SIGHTS   Castel del Monte

Foresta Umbra

Monte Sant'Angelo

Museo Nazionale, Taranto

Updated by
Robin S.
Goldstein

THE HEEL AND SPUR OF ITALY'S BOOT, the ancient land of Puglia has some of the country's most unspoiled scenery, most fascinating artistic and historical sites, and finest beaches. Once merely associated with train or car journeys for Greece-bound travelers, Puglia (known to some English speakers as Apulia, from its Latin name) is slowly gaining recognition as a destination in its own right—but tourists in the region, especially outside the beach towns, are still few and far between.

Beyond the seaside resorts and the few major sights lies sunbaked countryside where expanses of silvery olive trees, *primitivo* vineyards, and giant prickly-pear cacti fight their way through the rocky soil in defiance of the relentless summer heat. Country *trattorie,* oil refineries, buildings eternally under construction, and odd stone *trulli,* curious conical structures dating from the Middle Ages, complete the rural landscape. Meanwhile, the cities and fishing villages do their best to dispel the effects of the sun: whitewashed ports stand coolly over the turquoise Mediterranean, their castles guarding mazes of medieval alleyways dotted with wide-open doorways and grandmothers drying their handmade *orecchiette,* the most Puglian of pastas, in the midday heat.

Puglia has long been inhabited, conquered, and visited. On sea voyages to their colonies and trading posts in the west, the ancient Greeks invariably headed for Puglia first—it was the shortest crossing—before filtering southward into Sicily and westward to the Tyrrhenian coast. In turn, the Romans—often bound in the opposite direction—were quick to recognize the strategic importance of the peninsula. Later centuries were to see a procession of other empires raiding or colonizing Puglia: Byzantines, Saracens, Normans, Swabians, Turks, and Spaniards all swept through, each group leaving its mark. Romanesque churches and the powerful castles built by 13th-century Holy Roman Emperor Frederick II of Swabia (part of present-day Bavaria), king of Sicily and Jerusalem, are among the most impressive of the buildings in the region. Frederick II, dubbed *Stupor Mundi* (Wonder of the World) for his wide-ranging interests in literature, science, mathematics, and nature, was one of the outstanding personalities of the Middle Ages.

The last 50 years have seen a huge economic revival after the centuries of neglect that followed Puglia's golden age under the Normans and Swabians. Having benefited from EU and state incentive programs and subsidies for irrigation, Puglia is now Italy's second-biggest producer of wine, with most of the rest of the land devoted to olives, citrus fruits, and vegetables. The rugged Gargano peninsula has done well as a summer retreat, and the baroque city of Lecce continues to sparkle with vitality. The main ports of Bari, Brindisi, and Taranto are thriving centers, though there remain serious problems of unemployment and poverty. However, the much-publicized arrival of thousands of asylum seekers from Eastern Europe and beyond has not significantly destabilized these cities, as had been feared, and the economic and political refugees have dispersed throughout Italy. Compared with neighboring Albania a mere 70 km (44 mi) away across the Straits of Otranto, Puglia oozes with prosperity—though it can be difficult to find an abundance of lodging facilities outside the business circuit.

Exploring Puglia

Driving is the best—some say only—way to get around the region. The autostrada and superstrada networks connect Bari and Brindisi with the smaller towns. Note that entering the historic centers of many towns requires a small car, folding side-view mirrors, and a bit of nerve; tentative drivers should park outside the center and venture in by foot.

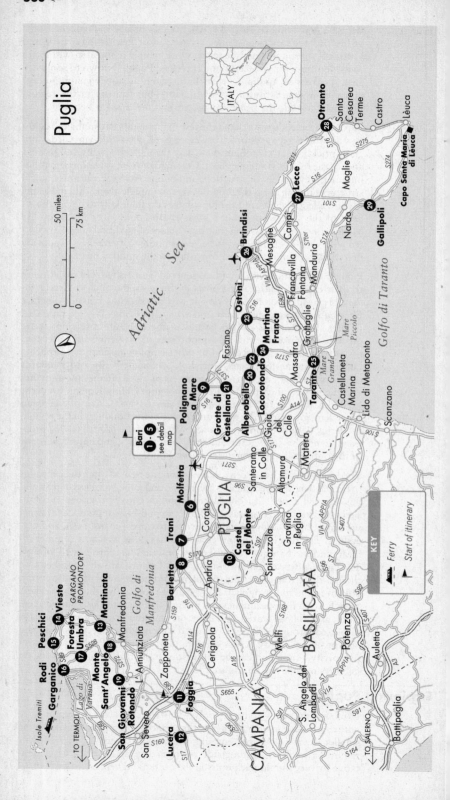

Puglia

Adriatic Sea

50 miles
75 km

ITALY

Isole Tremiti

TO TERMOLI

Rodi
Garganico

Peschici

Vieste

Foresta
Umbra

GARGANO
PROMONTORY

Mattinata

Golfo di
Manfredonia

Manfredonia

L'Annunziata

San Giovanni
Rotondo

Monte
Sant'Angelo

Zapponeta

Foggia

Lucera

San Severo

Cerignola

CAMPANIA

Melfi

S. Angelo dei
Lombardi

TO SALERNO

Potenza

BASILICATA

Auletta

Battipaglia

Molfetta

Trani

Barletta

Andria

Corato

Castel
del Monte

Spinazzola

Gravina in
Puglia

Santeramo
in Colle

Altamura

Matera

PUGLIA

Bari
1 - 5
see detail
map

Polignano
a Mare

Grotte di
Castellana

Alberobello

Locorotondo

Martina
Franca

Massafra

Grottaglie

Mottola

Taranto

Castellaneta
Marina

Lido di Metaponto

Scanzano

Golfo di Taranto

Mare
Piccolo

Mare
Grande

Ostuni

Fasano

Brindisi

Mesagne

Francavilla
Fontana

Manduria

Campi

Lecce

Maglie

Nardo

Gallipoli

Otranto

Santa
Cesarea
Terme

Castro

Capo Santa Maria
di Lèuca

Lèuca

KEY

Ferry

Start of itinerary

14

Puglia and the bordering state of Basilicata, particularly Matera, are well suited to be combined into a single trip, and Calabria can also be easily added to form a pan-*mezzogiorno* itinerary.

Numbers in the text correspond to numbers in the margin and on the Puglia and Bari maps.

If you have 3 days

With three days in Puglia, you should make the southeastern part of the region your priority. If your first landfall is ⊡ **Bari** ❶–❺ ⌖, leave on the Brindisi road and head into the trulli district toward ⊡ **Martina Franca** ㉔ or ⊡ **Alberobello** ⑳, good bases for the first night. Then make your second stop ⊡ **Lecce** ㉗, spending the day in this glorious baroque town. On the third day, keep Lecce as your base, but take the day to explore the Salentine peninsula, visiting the well-preserved historic towns of **Gallipoli** ㉙ and **Otranto** ㉘.

If you have 5 days

If it's summer, spend a day or two exploring the forested **Gargano Promontory** ⑪–⑲ ⌖ and the coastline northwest of **Bari** ❶–❺ along the Adriatic. Take the coast road (S16) from Bari toward **Trani** ❼, a historic port with a famed waterside cathedral. After **Barletta** ❽, the coast road (S159) heads northwest through abandoned salt pans and marshes, now nature preserves of international importance. The seaside fishing villages–cum–resorts of the Gargano Promontory—⊡ **Vieste** ⑭, ⊡ **Peschici** ⑮, and ⊡ **Rodi Garganico** ⑯— offer the best choice of accommodations, although ⊡ **Foggia** ⑪ and nearby ⊡ **Lucera** ⑫ make good bases, too. Aim to spend your third night in ⊡ **Alberobello** ⑳, the capital of trulli country—touristy, but engaging—or in whitewashed ⊡ **Ostuni** ㉓. From Alberobello, it's a short run to **Taranto** ㉕ for a look around the archaeological museum. Break your journey for an hour or two in **Brindisi** ㉖, stopping at the famous column marking the end of the Via Appia, but save your last two nights for the Salentine peninsula and ⊡ **Lecce** ㉗, a treat that will provide some of your most abiding memories of Puglia.

If you have 7 days

For a more in-depth visit to Puglia, choose ⊡ **Bari** ❶–❺ ⌖, with its bustling port and winding medieval old town, as your first base. Stay there two nights, devoting a good part of one day to exploring **Polignano a Mare** ❾, an atmospheric seaside town with good road and rail links to the regional capital. From Bari, venture up to the Gargano Promontory. A car is indispensable since transport connections are tortuous and slow, but be prepared to abandon it for a half-day ramble through the **Foresta Umbra** ⑰ and **Monte Sant'Angelo** ⑱, **San Giovanni Rotondo** ⑲. Proceed down the Adriatic Coast back toward Bari, staying a night in ⊡ **Trani** ❼, perhaps taking in the fine cathedrals of **Barletta** ❽ and **Molfetta** ❻, and making an inland detour to the fascinatingly geometrical **Castel del Monte** ❾. Head southeast toward trulli country, spending a night in ⊡ **Alberobello** ⑳ or ⊡ **Martina Franca** ㉔. At some point take a trip underground at the **Grotte di Castellana** ㉑, a soothing respite from summer heat. The bustling cities of **Taranto** ㉕ and **Brindisi** ㉖ are worth a stop for their archaeological relics. Spend your last three nights in the heel of Italy, with the baroque wonder of ⊡ **Lecce** ㉗ as a base, venturing out to the seaside towns of ⊡ **Otranto** ㉘ or ⊡ **Gallipoli** ㉙ (both also good for overnights in late spring and summer).

If your main interest is spending time at the beach, head to the Gargano Promontory, which has some of Puglia's best coastline but lacks the small-town country character of much of the region. Otherwise, convenient travel bases include Alberobello and Martina Franca in the trulli country; Lecce and Otranto near the tip of the heel; and the small coastal towns of Trani and Polignano, within easy reach of Bari.

Bari and Brindisi are notorious for purse-snatchings, car thefts, and break-ins. If you are driving in these cities, do not leave valuables in the car or trunk, and find a guarded parking space if possible.

About the Restaurants & Hotels

The best—and cheapest—way to eat in Puglia might be to ask around after a rustic family-run trattoria, sometimes referred to as a *casareccia* or *casalinga,* often found in the countryside or outskirts of a city. These bare-bones locales usually don't offer menus—just tastes that rival those of any high-brow restaurant in the region. Assent to the waiter's suggestions with a simple *va bene* and leave yourself in the chef's hands. You'll rarely be disappointed. Note that in many of the region's restaurants, especially the more rural or local ones, you pay one set price for your food, regardless of what you end up ordering.

Outside of the larger cities, hotel accommodations are limited and modest—both in amenities and price—but offer friendly service. Along the miles of sandy beaches on the Gargano spur and elsewhere on the coast, big, white, Mediterranean-style beach hotels have sprung up in profusion. Most are similar in design, price, and quality. In summer many cater only to guests paying full or half board for longer stays. During Easter, rooms in the Alberobello area may be at a premium. Reserve in advance throughout the region. Many establishments, particularly the beach resorts, close during the winter months. And remember that in a region like this—blazing hot in summer and bitter cold in winter—air-conditioning and central heating are important.

Agriturismi (farm stays) in Puglia are an increasingly popular lodging option. Most farms offering accommodation are listed at local tourist offices, and they vary widely in cost, facilities, and English-language competence. But this may be the closest you get to experiencing the Puglian rural lifestyle. It's Puglia at its best.

WHAT IT COSTS In euros				
	$$$$	$$$	$$	$	¢
RESTAURANTS	over €22	€17–€22	€12–€17	€7–€12	under €7
HOTELS	over €210	€160–€210	€110–€160	€60–€110	under €60

Restaurant prices are for a second course (secondo piatto). Hotel prices are for two people in a standard double room in high season, including tax and service.

Timing

Summers are torrid this far south, and even the otherwise perfect villages of the interior are too dazzlingly white for easy comfort from July to early September. So unless you are planning to be thoroughly idle—always an alluring prospect in Puglia—avoid the hot season. Of course, if you're on the Gargano Promontory, which has Puglia's only significant elevation, you'll be able to appreciate the forested interior during these months. And the Gargano and Bari-to-Brindisi coastal regions are strictly summer-holiday zones. Italians vacation in August, and sometimes July, but never June or September.

Beaches Italians and foreign visitors alike return summer after summer to Puglia, drawn by the sea. Though no longer undiscovered, the shores of the Gargano Promontory offer safe swimming and sandy beaches. The whole coastline between Bari and Brindisi is well served with beach facilities. In even the smallest villages you'll find beaches with changing rooms and—essential in the blazing sun—beach umbrellas. If you don't mind venturing farther afield, Gallipoli, on the south coast of the heel, has exceptional strands. From Brindisi south to Leuca on the Adriatic coast, however, the coastline consists of rock, not sand.

14

Festivals In keeping with the provincial nature of Puglia, the arts take on a folk flavor, with processions on religious occasions more prevalent than performing arts in theaters or opera houses. Seeking out festivals and pageants will enrich your experience of life in Italy's deep south. The best newspaper for listings is the daily *Gazzetta del Mezzogiorno* (⊕ www.gdmland.it), which covers the entire region.

Shopping Puglia is rich in folk art, reflecting the influences of the many nations that have passed through the region or ruled it. Look for handmade goods such as pottery, baskets, textiles, carved-wood figures, and painted clay whistles. You won't find boutiques here, but rather modest shops and open-air markets, where some bargaining can enter into the purchase.

Wintertime in Puglia can see heavy rain and wind, often lasting several days at a time. However, the temperatures rarely fall to freezing. In spring, days are usually warm and the skies clear; you can generally find water warm enough for bathing into October. Note that many lodgings can be closed off-season, especially along the coast.

BARI & THE ADRIATIC COAST

The coast has a strong flavor of the Norman presence in the south, embodied in the distinctive Puglian-Romanesque churches, the most atmospheric being in Trani. The busy commercial port of Bari offers architectural nuggets in its compact, labyrinthine Old Quarter abutting the sea, while Polignano a Mare combines accessibility to the major centers with the charm of a medieval town. For a unique excursion, drive inland to the imposing Castel del Monte, an enigmatic 13th-century octagonal fortification.

Bari

260 km (162 mi) southeast of Naples, 450 km (281 mi) southeast of Rome.

Bari is a big rough-and-tumble port and a transit point for travelers catching ferries across the Adriatic to Greece, but also a cosmopolitan city with one of the most interesting historic centers in the region. Most of Bari is set out in a logical 19th-century grid, following the designs of Joachim Murat (1767–1815), Napoléon's brother-in-law and King of the Two Sicilies. The heart of the modern town is **Piazza della Libertà**, but just beyond it, across Corso Vittorio Emanuele, is the *città vecchia* (old town), a maze of narrow streets on the promontory that juts out between Bari's old and new ports, circumscribed by Via Venezia, offering elevated views to the Adriatic in every direction. Stop for an outdoor drink at **Greta** (⊠ Via Venezia 22), for a commanding view of the port and sea. By day, explore the old town's winding alleyways, where Bari's open-door policy offers a glimpse into the daily routine of the mezzogiorno—matrons hand-rolling pasta with their grandchildren home from school for the midday meal, and handymen perched on rickety ladders, patching up centuries-old arches and doorways. Back in the new

❷ town, join the evening *passeggiata* (stroll) on pedestrian-only **Via Sparano**, then stroll among the outdoor bars in Piazza Ferrarese, at the end of Corso Vittorio Emanuele, when night falls.

In the città vecchia, overlooking the sea and just off Via Venezia, is the

❸ **Basilica di San Nicola,** built in the 11th century to house the bones of St. Nicholas, also known as St. Nick, or Santa Claus. His remains, buried in the crypt, are said to have been stolen by Bari sailors from Myra, in what is now Turkey. The basilica, of solid and powerful construction, was the only building to survive the otherwise wholesale destruction of Bari by the Normans in 1152. ⊠ *Piazza San Nicola* ☎ *080/5237247* ◷ *Daily 7–noon and 4–6:30.*

❹ Bari's 12th-century **Cattedrale** is the seat of the local bishop and was the scene of many significant political marriages between important families in the Middle Ages. The cathedral's solid architecture reflects the Romanesque style favored by the Normans of that period. ⊠ *Piazza dell'Odegitria* ☎ *080/5288215* ◷ *Daily 7–1:30 and 4–7.*

❺ Looming over Bari's cathedral is the huge **Castello Svevo.** The current building dates from the time of Holy Roman Emperor Frederick II (1194–1250), who rebuilt an existing Norman-Byzantine castle to his own exacting specifications. Designed more for power than beauty, it looks out beyond the cathedral to the small Porto Vecchio (Old Port). Inside is a haphazard collection of medieval Puglian art and archaeological artifacts, and rotating exhibits of works by local artists. ⊠ *Piazza Federico II di Svevia* ☎ *080/5286219; 0339/1146908 tour reservations* ⊠ *€2* ◷ *Tues.–Sun. 8:30–7:30, ticket office closes at 7 PM. Guided tours Sat. 5:30, Sun. 11 and 5:30.*

Where to Stay & Eat

$$–$$$ ✕ **Trattoria al Pescatore.** This is one of Bari's best fish restaurants, in the old town opposite the castle and just around the corner from the cathedral. Summer cooking is done outside, where you can sit amid a cheerful clamor of quaffing and dining. Try the grilled *céfalo* (mullet) if it is available, accompanied by crisp salad and a carafe of invigorating local wine. Reservations are essential in July and August. ⊠ *Piazza Federico II di Svevia 6* ☎ *080/5237039* ⊟ *AE, DC, MC, V* ◷ *Closed Mon.*

★ $$$ ▥ **Hotel Palace.** This downtown landmark is stationed steps away from Corso Vittorio Emanuele in the new city, but is also extremely convenient to the medieval center. The large, comfortable rooms are furnished lightly and tastefully. For an extra €20, some rooms (ask in advance) whimsically cater to a variety of special tastes, including pet rooms, children's rooms, and a room for music lovers, complete with stereo and classical CD collection. Other amenities include Smart Car rental service (€36 per day) and a buffet breakfast. ⊠ *Via Lombardi 13, 70122* ☎ *080/5216551* 🖷 *080/5211499* ⊕ *www.palacehotelbari. it* ⇄ *189 rooms* ⚬ *Restaurant, bicycles, bar, convention center, meeting room, parking (fee), some pets allowed (fee)* ⊟ *AE, DC, MC, V.*

¢–$ ▥ **Adria.** This lodging's virtues are its convenience to the train station and relative low cost in a city short on inexpensive lodgings. Facilities are undistinguished, but this is primarily a one-night stopover, with guest

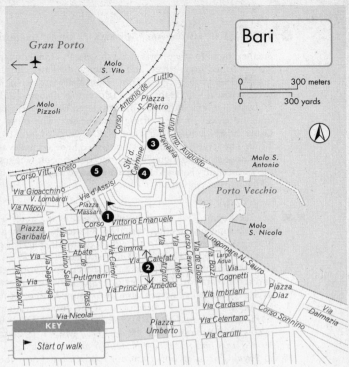

rooms that are basic but fine. Turn right out of the station to find it. ✉ *Via L. Zuppetta 10, 70121* ☎ *080/5246699* 🖷 *080/5213207* 🌐 *http://space.tin.it/viaggi/mlippol* 🛏 *35 rooms, 28 with bath* 🍴 *Restaurant, bar, parking (fee); no a/c* 🖃 *AE, DC, MC, V.*

Nightlife & the Arts

While Bari's famous Teatro Petruzzelli awaits restoration after a fire in 1991, most drama and ballet have been diverted to the **Teatro Piccinni** (✉ Corso Vittorio Emanuele 84 ☎ 080/5210878 🕙 Tickets on sale 10:30–12:30 and 5–8). Ticket prices range from €13 to €27.

By night, **Hakuna Matata** (✉ Corso Vittorio Emanuele 128 ☎ 080/ 5210878) pulls off an African theme with a perfect balance of sophistication and good taste (its name aside), with a large collection of warmly lighted African art and hand-drawn maps setting the stage for the see-and-be-seen crowd. Africanfood is also served.

Sports & the Outdoors

BIKING **G. S. De Benedictis** (✉ Via Nitti 23 ☎ 080/5744345) rents bikes, which are a great way to explore the flat roads of the trulli region.

Molfetta

❻ *25 km (16 mi) northwest of Bari, 108 km (67 mi) east of Foggia.*

The unusual 13th-century **Duomo di San Corrado** of Molfetta, crowning Molfetta's circular old town surrounded on three sides by water, reveals distinct Byzantine features, such as the pyramid-shape covers of the three main domes. If you're in the area around Easter, don't miss Molfetta's colorful Holy Week processions, a hit for young and old alike. ✉*Banchina Seminario* 🕙 *Daily 7–noon and 4–7.*

Trani

❼ *18 km (11 mi) northwest of Molfetta, 43 km (27 mi) northwest of Bari.*

Smaller than the other ports along this coast, Trani has a quaint old town with polished stone streets and buildings, medieval churches, and a harbor filled with fishing boats. Trani is also justly famous for its sweet dessert wine, Moscato di Trani. The 11th-century **Duomo** (⊠ Piazza Duomo ☉ Daily 8–noon and 3:30–7), considered one of the finest in Puglia, is built on a spit of land jutting into the sea. The boxy well-preserved **Castle** (☎ 0883/506603 ☉ Daily 8:30–7:30) was built by Frederick II in 1233. The Jewish community flourished here in medieval times, and on **Via Sinagoga** (Synagogue Street) two of the four synagogues still exist: the 13th-century **Santa Maria Scolanova** and **Santa Anna**, which still bears a Hebrew inscription.

Where to Stay & Eat

★ **$$** ✕ ▥ **La Regia.** This small hotel–restaurant occupies a 17th-century palazzo superbly positioned in front of the Duomo, on a swath of land jutting out into the sea. Don't expect grand or spacious rooms, though they are perfectly adequate. The restaurant ($$–$$$) is a worthwhile stop in its own right, with an antique feel, stonework, vaulted ceilings, and terra-cotta tile floors. Regional specialties are presented imaginatively: try the baked crepes (similar to cannelloni) or grilled fish. Reservations are essential for Sunday lunch and dinner on summer weekends. ⊠ *Piazza Mons. Addazi 2, 70059* ☎ *0883/584444* ▤ *0883/506595* ⤏ *10 rooms* ⌂ *Restaurant, bar* ▭ *AE, DC, MC, V* ☉ *Restaurant closed Mon. Hotel and restaurant closed 15 days in Jan.*

$$ ▥ **Royal.** This is an unpretentious modern hotel near the train station. Rooms are trim and tidy, suited to stopovers rather than extended stays. ⊠ *Via De Robertis 29, 70059* ☎ *0883/588777* ▤ *0883/582224* ⤏ *40 rooms* ⌂ *Restaurant, meeting room* ▭ *AE, DC, MC, V.*

Barletta

❽ *13 km (8 mi) northwest of Trani, 56 km (35 mi) northwest of Bari.*

The **Colossus,** a bronze statue more than 15 ft tall, is thought to be of the Byzantine emperor Valentinian and to date from the 5th century AD. Part of Venice's booty after the sack of Byzantium's capital, Constantinople, in the 1200s, the Colossus was abandoned on the beach near Barletta when the ship carrying it to Venice foundered in a storm. ⊠ *Next to the church of San Sepolcro, Corso Vittorio Emanuele.*

Where to Eat

$ ✕ **La Casaccia.** Near a picturesque castle, this restaurant prides itself on its *zuppa di pesce* (fish soup), made fresh every day, as well as de rigueur local dishes like orecchiette. There's nothing fancy here: the tone is calm and down-home, most tables occupied by discriminating regulars who appreciate the good Puglian cooking and the moderate prices. ⊠ *Corso Cavour 40* ☎ *0883/533719* ▭ *No credit cards.*

Polignano a Mare

❾ *40 km (24 mi) southeast of Bari, 14 km (9 mi) north of Castellana.*

With a well-preserved whitewashed old town perched on limestone cliffs overlooking the Adriatic, Polignano a Mare makes an atmospheric base for exploring the surrounding area and Bari, only a half hour's train ride up the coast. The town is virtually lifeless all winter, but becomes something of a weekend hotspot for city-dwellers in summer.

Where to Stay & Eat

$$ ✕ **Le Antiche Mura.** Built dramatically into the 16th-century stone walls of the old town, this family-run restaurant is popular with locals and visitors alike. Specialties here are mainly—but not exclusively—seafood platters like *cozze a gratin* (mussels filled with bread crumbs) and *seppie al forno* (baked cuttlefish). Reservations are essential on weekends. ⊠ *Via Roma 11* ☎ *080/4242476* ☰ *AE, DC, MC, V* ☯ *Closed Mon.*

$$ ✕▥ **Grotta Palazzese.** Carved out of a cliff opening onto the Adriatic, the Grotta Palazzese inhabits a stunning group of rocks and grottoes that have wowed onlookers from time immemorial. Though all rooms but one have sea views, ask for one of the cave-apartments across the road rather than the more boxlike rooms in the main 1960s block. (Suites 18, 25, and 139 are the most impressive.) The Grotta Palazzese's true tour de force is its summer restaurant ($$$–$$$$), serving impeccably prepared fish (try the assortment of raw Adriatic shellfish) in a dramatic setting that incorporates rock formations; tables actually stand on an implausible bridge inside a jagged cave, while waves cast blue-green shadows on the grotto walls. It's one of the truly romantic settings in all Italy. ⊠ *Via Narciso 59, 70059* ☎ *080/4240677* 🖷 *080/4240767* 🌐 *www. grottapalazzese.it* ⇄ *14 rooms, 14 small apartments* ⚓ *2 restaurants, bar, beach, meeting room, parking (fee)* ☰ *AE, DC, MC, V* ☯ *Outdoor restaurant closed Oct.–Apr.*

Fodor's Choice ★

Castel del Monte

★ ❿ *30 km (19 mi) south of Barletta, 56 km (35 mi) southwest of Bari.*

Built by Frederick II in the first half of the 13th century on an isolated hill, Castel del Monte is a huge, bare, octagonal castle with eight towers. Very little is known about the structure, since virtually no records exist. It has none of the usual defense features associated with medieval castles, so it probably had little military significance. Some theories suggest it might have been built as a hunting lodge or may have served as an astronomical observatory or a stop for pilgrims on their quest for the Holy Grail. ✛ *On signposted minor road 18 km (11 mi) south of Andria* 🎫 *€3* ☎ *0883/569997; 0339/1146908 tour reservations* 🌐 *www. castelli-puglia.org/it/index.html* ☯ *Daily 10–1:30 and 2:30–7:30; June–Sept. also Sat. 9 PM–midnight. Optional guided tours in English and Italian available every 1–2 hrs.*

GARGANO PROMONTORY

Forming the spur of Italy's boot, the Gargano Promontory (Promontorio del Gargano) is a striking contrast to the Adriatic's generally flat, unenthralling coastline. This is a land of whitewashed coastal towns, wide sandy beaches interspersed with secluded coves, and craggy limestone cliffs topped by deep-green pine and lush Mediterranean maquis. Not surprisingly, it pulls in the crowds in July and August, including many Germans and northern Italians; prices are resultingly higher than elsewhere in Puglia. Camping is almost always an option, as plentiful and pretty campgrounds dot the Gargano's curvy mountain cliff–hugging roads. (Driving some of them at night can be harrowing.) For the kids, the beaches and forests of the Gargano National Park are great places to let off steam, and many towns stage puppet shows in public gardens.

Foggia

▶ **⑪**   *95 km (60 mi) west of Bari.*

Foggia, the chief city in Puglia's northernmost province, is not the most inspiring destination, though it makes a useful overnight stop for visitors to the Gargano. The old town is pleasant but fairly modern, having sustained significant war damage. On the main line from Rome and Naples, and easily accessible from the autostrada, Foggia has all the amenities you expect from a major commercial center, hosting numerous fairs and conventions throughout the year. This means that, although it enjoys a decent selection of lodgings and restaurants, you'll need to reserve to ensure accommodations. This is the place to get or exchange cash or rent a car for excursions to the Gargano.

Where to Stay & Eat

★ **$$** ✕ **La Nuova Mangiatoia.** In an old farmhouse, this seafood restaurant looks like a medieval tavern, with arches and wood-beamed ceilings. You can also dine in a large garden, where tables made from wagon wheels surround an old well. The chef will supply recipes for Adriatic dishes, such as spaghetti *ai datteri di mare al cartoccio* (with razor clams). The location is on the main road to Bari, near the Foggia Agricultural Fairgrounds. Reservations are essential on weekends. ⊠ *Via Virgilio 2* ☎ *0881/634457* ▤ *AE, DC, MC, V* ◷ *Closed Mon.*

  $ ✕ **Ambasciata di Orsara.** This hidden pizzeria and restaurant near Foggia's market, also referred to as "Trilussa," is very local, very good, and very small. In the tiny dining room the few tables are surrounded by rows of bottles of the region's best wines, which accompany pizza prepared in an oven that has been in operation since 1526. Local antipasti and primi are also available. ⊠ *Via Tenente Iorio 50, at the corner of Rosati* ☎ *0881/709253* ▤ *No credit cards.* ◷ *Closed Mon.*

★ **$$$** ✕▥ **Cicolella.** This 1920s hotel near the station, one of the best in town, has tasteful rooms with floor-length curtains, regal wallpaper, and restful, discreet lighting. Some have balconies. The suites particularly recommended. The excellent restaurant (closed weekends) specializes in international cuisine, plus well-prepared local dishes. Service is impeccable, and a good regional wine list complements such country classics as puree of fava beans with chicory, drizzled with Puglian olive oil infused with hot peppers. Homemade *cavatelli neri* (dark pasta twists) are paired with a delectable tomato sauce made with pungent *ricotta dura* (hard ricotta) and have salty *grano bruccinto* (grated Parmesan-like cheese) sprinkled on top. ⊠ *Viale Ventiquattro Maggio 60, 71100* ☎ *0881/566111* 🖷 *0881/778984* ⊕ *www.hotelcicolella.isnet.it* ⇆ *91 rooms, 13 suites* ⚒ *Restaurant, meeting room* ▤ *AE, DC, MC, V* ◷ *Restaurant closed weekends and Aug. 1–20.*

Bars

Foggia has a surprisingly active nightlife, with several good wine bars. The **Wine Bar Cairoli** (⊠ Via Mentine), a multiroom cavernlike restaurant and bar, is also a great place to try local food. **Coniglio Mannaro** (⊠ Via Bruno 16 ☎ 0881/740752) is a good local wine bar.

Lucera

⑫   *18 km (12 mi) northwest of Foggia.*

Occupying a commanding position over the Tavoliere, Puglia's flat coastal plains, Lucera flourished during the Roman era, long before Frederick II—in what was considered an enlightened gesture for the 13th

ON THE MENU

ANYONE WHO LIKES TO EAT *will find pleasure in Puglia, where the cuisine has evolved from more than 2,000 years of foreign influences. Southern cuisine is hearty and healthy, based around homemade pastas and cheeses, fresh vegetables, seafood, and local olive oil. Here you will find dishes unavailable elsewhere in Italy, such as 'ncapriata, also called favi e fogghi (a first-course fava-bean puree topped with bitter chicory or other cooked vegetables and drizzled with extra virgin olive oil; mix it all together before eating). The pizza is unremarkable, but focaccia barese (stuffed with fried onions, black olives, anchovies, and ricotta) makes a great snack or lunch.*

Puglia's pasta specialties include orecchiette *(ear-shape pasta) and* strascenate *(rectangles of pasta with one rough side and one smooth side), all served with tomato-based sauces or* cime di rape *(bitter greens).*

Look for handmade fusilli, or any pasta fatto in casa or pasta fatto a mano—rolled out only hours before being served. Don't miss the dairy products, such as ricotta and burrata cheese, actually stuffed with butter.

Puglia produces almost a fifth of Italy's wine, yet little of it is known outside the region. In the last few years, the region has begun to compete on a national scale. The ancient primitivo grape, thought by many to have been brought to California and renamed Zinfandel, yields strong, heady wines. Look for the powerful Primitivo di Manduria, best with food; the robust Salice Salentino, made from Negroamaro grapes; and the sweet red Aleatico di Puglia. Blends like Amativo (a creation from Ca'ntele blending Negroamaro and Primitivo) have recently livened up the Pugliese wine scene. Top winemakers to look for include Conti Zecca, Leone di Castris, Rubino, and Tormaresca.

century—relocated more than 10,000 Sicilian Arabs here in 1224. Though subsequent decades of religious intolerance removed the Arab mosques, Lucera has retained an impressive complement of historical sites and an attentively preserved old town.

After you've explored Lucera's cobblestone streets, head for the 14th-century **Cattedrale,** a curious blend of Romanesque and Gothic architecture, commissioned by Charles II of Anjou to replace an earlier mosque. ⊠ *Piazza Duomo* ☎ *0881/520880* ⊘ *Daily 8–noon and 4–7.*

Lying rather incongruously beyond one of the poorer parts of the modern town is Lucera's partially reconstructed **Anfiteatro Augusteo,** built at the end of the 1st century BC. Although much of the superstructure has been lost, the grandiose entrance gates have been rebuilt, complete with dedication inscriptions. ⊠ *Viale Augusteo* ☎ *0881/522762* ⊘ *Oct.–Apr., Tues.–Sun. 9–2 and 4–8; May–Sept., Tues.–Sun. 9–8.*

The so-called **Fortezza Svevo Angioina,** a 10-minute walk northwest of the old town, is an impressive sight. It was plundered for building material up to modern times, and little but the base remains of Frederick's *palatium,* a palace built in 1233. The castle owes its present form to the Angevins, who transformed it over the next century into a military stronghold, complete with drawbridge, moat, 24 towers, and a wall more than 1 km (½ mi) long. ⊠ *Via Castello* ☎ *0881/522762* ⊘ *Oct.–Apr., Tues.–Sun. 9–2 and 4–8; May–Sept., Tues.–Sun. 9–8.*

In the spirit of cultural enlightenment that pervades Lucera, **guided tours** (☎ 0881/548626 for bookings) are available in Italian and occasionally English, free of charge, at the museum, amphitheater, and castle.

¢–$ 🏨 **La Balconata 2.** This family-run hotel occupies part of a modern con-
dominium and is two minutes' walk from the south gate of Porta Troia
leading to the old town. When booking, ask for the quieter rooms away
from the main road. The restaurant's regional cuisine is also well worth
a try, but you'll need to be immune to cigarette smoke. ⊠ *Viale Ferrovia 15, 71036* ☎ *0881/520998 or 0881/546725* ⊕ *www.labalconata.
it* 🛏 *49 rooms* ⚲ *Restaurant, bar* ▤ *AE, DC, MC, V.*

Mattinata

🔟③ *53 km (32 mi) northeast of Foggia, 138 km (86 mi) northwest of Bari.*

Just inland from a fine sandy beach, where you'll find most of the campsites and hotels, this is a generally quiet village that comes into its own
in the summer season.

Where to Stay & Eat

$$–$$$ ✕ **Trattoria della Nonna.** The waves lapping at the shore just inches out-
side the picture windows of this elegant but unpretentious coastal restaurant, a few km outside of Mattinata, are an indication of how fresh the
fish will be. The memorable assorted raw seafood *antipasto* includes some
shellfish you might not find anywhere else. *Cozze peruse* (an endemic
Puglian clam), hiding inside spiked-hair shells, are briny and buttery;
tiny *noci* shellfish have a wonderful sweetness; and big, rich local oysters are all about texture—it's like kissing the Adriatic. Try sweet grilled
scampi with oil and lemon, and wash it all down with one of the great
white wines on the extensive list. ⊠ *Mattinata Mare* ☎ *0884/559205*
▤ *AE, DC, MC, V* ☯ *Closed Mon. in Oct.–May.*

$$$–$$$$ 🏨 **Baia delle Zagare.** On the shore road around the Gargano Promon-
tory, well north of Mattinata, Baia delle Zagare is a secluded, modern
group of cottages overlooking an inlet. An elevator built into the cliffs
takes you down to a private beach, and the hotel restaurant is good enough
to warrant staying on the premises all day. (You're expected to take half
board in August.) Be careful when approaching on the road, as the gated
entrance is easy to miss. ⊠ *Località Valle dei Mergoli, 17 km (10 mi)
northeast of Mattinata, 71030* ☎ *0884/550155* 🖷 *0884/550884* ⊕ *www.
hotelbaiadellezagare.it* 🛏 *150 rooms* ⚲ *Restaurant, minibars, tennis
court, pool, health club, beach, dance club, theater* ▤ *MC, V* ☯ *Closed
Sept. 15–May* ⊙|¶ *MAP.*

$–$$ 🏨 **Alba del Gargano.** Although it's in the town center, this whitewashed
modern hotel provides a restful atmosphere. Large balconies overlook
a quiet courtyard garden, and a frequent (and free) bus service connects
with a private, rocky beach 2 km (1 mi) away, where you can use the
hotel's beach chairs and umbrellas. Rooms are comfortably furnished,
and there's a good restaurant. Half or full board is mandatory in August. ⊠ *Corso Matino 102, 71030* ☎ *0884/550771* 🖷 *0884/550772*
⊕ *www.albadelgargano.it* 🛏 *40 rooms, 3 suites* ⚲ *Restaurant, beach,
bar* ▤ *MC, V* ⊙|¶ *MAP.*

Vieste

🔟④ *93 km (58 mi) northeast of Foggia, 179 km (111 mi) northwest of Bari.*

This large whitewashed town jutting off the tip of the spur is the
Gargano's main commercial center and an attractive place to wander
around. Though curvy mountain roads render it slightly less accessible
from the autostrada and main-line rail stations than Peschici and Mattinata, the range of accommodations (including camping) makes it a useful base for exploring Gargano. The resort attracts legions of tourists

in summer, some bound for the Isole Tremiti, a tiny archipelago connected to Vieste by regular ferries. While in Vieste, make for the **castle,** its interior not open to the public but offering good views from its high position overlooking the beaches and town.

Where to Stay & Eat

¢ ✕ **Bar Latino.** This local hangout serves draft beer, cocktails, and basic bar food into the wee hours, but bar food rarely tastes this good. The *panino rustico* is an excellent example of southern Italy's strength in simplicity—a grilled sandwich of proscuitto crudo, tomato, mozzarella, and mayonnaise allows the harmonious blend of fresh, delicious ingredients to sing together, and it is bought for pocket change. The two-floor open-air lounge has a strange Viestese version of tropical Caribbean decor. Use your imagination. ⊠ *Near the Punta San Francesco, on the litoranea* ☎ *No phone* ▭ *AE, DC, MC, V* ☯ *Closed Mon.*

★ **$$$$** ▦ **Pizzomunno.** Probably the most luxurious resort on the Gargano, Pizzomunno is right on the beach and surrounded by an extensive park. It is large, white, modern, air-conditioned, and well equipped. The rooms are ample and plush, all with terraces. Here you can unwind, or try your hand at tennis or archery. ⊠ *Spiaggia di Pizzomunno, 71019* ☎ *0884/ 708741* ⬛ *0884/707325* ⇄ *183 rooms* ⌂ *3 restaurants, 3 tennis courts, 2 pools, health club, sauna, archery, cinema, dance club, children's programs* ▭ *AE, DC, MC, V* ☯ *Closed Oct. 11–Apr. 3.*

$ ▦ **Punta San Francesco.** After starting its life as an olive-oil factory, this hotel was tastefully refurbished in the mid-1990s. Thanks to its location near the waterfront in the heart of old Vieste, it is both quiet and close to the action. The owner is a warm, welcoming friend (and ardent promoter of local culture) to all who arrive, and the view from the rooftop is beautiful, especially at dawn. ⊠ *Via San Francesco 2, 71019* ☎ *0884/ 701422* ⬛ *0884/701424* ⇄ *14 rooms* ▭ *MC, V.*

Peschici

⑮ *22 km (14 mi) northwest of Vieste, 199 km (124 mi) northwest of Bari.*

Peschici is a pleasant resort on Gargano's north shore, a cascade of whitewashed houses and streets with a beautiful view over a sweeping cove. Some surrounding areas are particularly popular with campers from northern Europe. Development has not wreaked too much havoc on this whitewashed town, and the mazelike center retains its characteristic low houses topped with little domes.

Rodi Garganico

⑯ *20 km (12 mi) west of Peschici, 40 km (25 mi) west of Vieste.*

This fishing village squeezed between the hills and the sea takes its name from the island of Rhodes, recalling its former Greek population. Ringed by pine woods and citrus groves, Rodi is linked by hydrofoils with the Isole Tremiti, and things can get hectic in summer.

off the
beaten
path

ISOLE TREMITI – A ferry service from Termoli, west of the Gargano (1¾ hours), and hydrofoil service from Vieste, Peschici, and Rodi Garganico (40 minutes to one hour) connect the mainland with these three small islands north of the Gargano. Although somewhat crowded with Italian tourists in summer, they are famed for their sea caves, pine forests, and craggy limestone formations. Interesting medieval churches and fortifications dot the islands.

Where to Eat

$–$$ ✕ **Il Gabbiano.** Admire the view facing the sea in Rodi Garganico at this cheerful restaurant (which also serves as a private beach in summer) while savoring freshly caught seafood. ⊠ *Via Trieste 16* ☎ *0884/965283* ▤ *AE, V* ⊗ *Closed Thurs. in Nov.–Mar.*

Foresta Umbra

★ ⑰   *25 km (16 mi) south of Rodi Garganico, 30 km (19 mi) southwest of Vieste.*

In the middle of the Gargano Promontory is the majestic Foresta Umbra (Shady Forest), a dense growth of beech, maple, sycamore, and oak generally found in more northerly climates, thriving here because of the altitude, 3,200 ft above sea level. Between the trees in this national park are occasional dramatic vistas opening out over the Golfo di Manfredonia. From the north coast, take harrowingly curvy S528 (midway between Peschici and Rodi Garganico) south to head through the interior of the Gargano (do it during the day), or try the gentler ascent between Mattinata and Vieste on S89.

Monte Sant'Angelo

★ ⑱   *16 km (10 mi) north of Manfredonia, 60 km (19 mi) southwest of Vieste.*

Perched amid olive groves on the limestone cliffs overlooking the gulf is the town of Monte Sant'Angelo. Pilgrims have flocked here for nearly 1,500 years—among them, St. Francis of Assisi and crusaders setting off for the Holy Land from the then-flourishing port of Manfredonia. Monte Sant'Angelo is centered on the **Santuario di San Michele** (Sanctuary of San Michele), built over the grotto where the archangel Michael is believed to have appeared before shepherds in the year 490. Walk down a long series of steps to get to the grotto itself; on its walls you can see the hand tracings left by pilgrims.

The **Tomba di Rotari** (Tomb of Rotari), believed to have been a medieval baptistery, has some remarkable 12th-century reliefs. It's reached by steps down and to the left from the Santuario di San Michele. Steep steps lead up to the large, ruined **Castello Normano** (Norman Castle) that dominates the town, with a view of the intricate pattern of the streets and steps winding their way up the side of the valley. Monte Sant'Angelo's medieval quarter, the **Rione Junno,** is a maze of little white houses squeezed into a corner of the narrow valley.

Where to Stay

$ 🏨 **Rotary Hotel.** This simple but welcoming modern hotel is set amid olive and almond groves just outside town. Most rooms have basic decor and terraces with views of the Golfo di Manfredonia. ⊠ *Via (per) Pulsano, Km. 1, 71037* ☎ *0884/562146* 🖷 *0884/562147* ⊕ *www.gargano.it/enti/ proloco/rotar.htm* ⬈ *24 rooms* ⚒ *Restaurant* ▤ *AE, MC, V.*

Shopping

Most food shops in the Junno sell a local specialty called **ostia piena,** a pastry made with candied almonds and wafers of a type similar to communion hosts. The best place to get them—and munch on them—is at the southern end of the Junno, by the Villa Comunale.

San Giovanni Rotondo

⑲   *25 km (16 mi) west of Monte Sant'Angelo, 85 km (52 mi) southwest of Vieste.*

The ancient village of San Giovanni Rotondo, on the winding S272, is a relatively recent center of religious pilgrimage. Devotees flock here to pay their respects to the shrine and **Tomba di Padre Pio** (✉ Chiesa Santa Maria delle Grazie, Piazzale Santa Maria delle Grazie). Pio (1887–1968) was a monk revered for his pious life, his miraculous intercessions, and his having received the stigmata, the signs of Christ's wounds.

| en route | A short ride south on S273, and then east (left) at L'Annunziata, will take you back to Manfredonia, where you can link up with the coastal road to return to Bari. |

THE TRULLI DISTRICT

The inland area to the southeast of Bari is one of Italy's oddest enclaves, mostly flat terrain given over to olive cultivation and interspersed with the idiosyncratic habitations that have lent their names to the district. The origins of the beehive-shaped trulli go back to the 13th century and maybe further. The trulli, found nowhere else in the world, are built of local limestone, without mortar, and with a hole in the top for escaping smoke. Some are painted with mystical or religious symbols; some are isolated, and others are joined together with roofs on various levels. Legends of varying credibility surround the trulli (for example, that they were originally built as they were so that residents could quickly take apart their homes when the tax collectors came by). The center of trulli country is Alberobello, with the greatest concentration of the buildings, though you will spot them all over this region, some in disrepair but always adding a quirky charm to the landscape.

Alberobello

⓴ *59 km (37 mi) southeast of Bari, 45 km (28 mi) north of Taranto.*

Although Alberobello is something of a tourist trap, the amalgamation of more than 1,000 trulli huddled together along steep, narrow streets is nonetheless an unusual sight (as well as a national monument and a UNESCO World Heritage Site). As one of the most popular tourist destinations in Puglia, Alberobello has sprung up some excellent restaurants (and some not-so-excellent trinket shops). Alberobello's largest trullo, the **Trullo Sovrano,** is up the hill through the trulli zone (head up Corso Vittorio Emanuele past the obelisk and the Basilica). Though you can go inside, where you'll find a fairly conventional domestic dwelling, the real interest is the structure itself.

Where to Stay & Eat

$$$$ ✕ **Il Poeta Contadino.** Proprietor Marco Leonardo serves "creative regional cooking" in this upscale country restaurant in the heart of the attractive trulli zone. The room features ancient stone walls, candlelight tables, and a refined, understated ambience. Dishes represent creative uses of local ingredients, and might include *triglie vinaigrette alla menta* (red mullet with a mint vinaigrette) or *coda di rospo con pomodoro candito salsa al basilico* (monkfish in a tomato and basil sauce). In season, try anything with white truffle. The extensive wine list has won awards. ✉ *Via Indipendenza 21* ☎ *080/4321917* ⌚ *Reservations essential* ⊟ *AE, DC, MC, V* ☾ *Closed Mon. and Jan. 7–31.*

★ **$$–$$$** ✕ **Trullo d'Oro.** This welcoming rustic restaurant set in five trulli houses has dark-wood beams, whitewashed walls, and an open hearth. Local country cooking includes dishes using lamb and veal, vegetable and cheese antipasti, pasta dishes with crisp raw vegetables on the side, and almond pastries. Among the specialties are roast lamb with *lampasciuni* (a type of wild onion) and spaghetti *al trullo*, made with tomatoes, *rughetta* (arugula), and four cheeses. ⊠ *Via F. Cavallotti 27* ☎ *080/4323909* ⌂ *Reservations essential* ⊟ *AE, DC, MC, V* ☉ *Closed Mon. (except in June–Aug.) and Jan. 10–31. No dinner Sun.*

$$–$$$ ⊞ **Dei Trulli.** Trulli-style cottages in a pine wood near the trulli zone make this a pleasant hotel. It's decorated with rustic furnishings and folk-art rugs. The modestly priced restaurant serves local specialties. You're expected to take half or full board in high season. ⊠ *Via Cadore 28–32, 70011* ☎ *080/4323555* 🖷 *080/4323560* 🖘 *28 rooms* ⌂ *Restaurant, minibars, pool* ⊟ *AE, MC, V* ⱳ *MAP.*

Grotte di Castellana

㉑ *20 km (12 mi) northwest of Alberobello, 63 km (52 mi) southeast of Bari.*

The Grotte di Castellana is a huge network of caves discovered in 1938. You can take one of the hourly guided tours through the grottoes filled with fantastically shaped stalagmites and stalactites, part of the largest network of caves on the Italian mainland. The two-hour tour takes you on an extra 2-km (1½ mi) hike to another cave (Grotta Bianca). ⊠ *Piazzale Anelli* ☎ *080/4998211* ⊕ *www.grottedicastellana.it* 🖷 *€8 1-hr tour, €13 2-hr tour* ☉ *Apr.–Oct., daily 8:30–7, until 9 in Aug.; Nov.–Mar., daily 9:30–4. Last 2-hr tour leaves 1 hr before closing. English 1-hr tours at 1 and 6:30; English 2-hr tours at 11 and 4.*

Locorotondo

㉒ *9 km (5½ mi) southeast of Alberobello, 40 km (25 mi) north of Taranto.*

Locorotondo is an attractive hilltop town within the trulli district in the Itria Valley (take S172 from Alberobello). The *rotondo* in the town's name refers to the circular pattern of the houses, swirling down from the top. From the top of the town, on the road to Martina Franca, a verdant public garden gives way to lookout points over the entire Valle d'Itria, a landscape dotted with olive groves and trulli. Wander around the cute alleyways of the *centro storico* (historic center) and look for the blazing yellow cathedral in Piazza Fra Giuseppe Andria Rolleo.

$ ✕ **Centro Storico.** The refined ambience and cuisine of this restaurant, set apart from the tourist haunts, make it pricier than its neighbors. But the food and service are worth it: try such regional dishes as *sformato di verdura* (vegetable stew) and *agnello alla castellanese* (local lamb). ⊠ *Via Eroi di Dogali 6* ☎ *080/4315473* ⌂ *Reservations essential* ⊟ *AE, MC, V* ☉ *Closed Wed. and 2 wks in Mar.*

Ostuni

㉓ *50 km (30 mi) west of Brindisi, 40 km (25 mi) northeast of Locorotondo.*

This sun-bleached, picturesque medieval town lies on three hills a short distance from the coast. From a distance, Ostuni is an jumble of blazingly white houses and churches spilling over a hilltop and overlooking the sea—thus earning it the nickname *la città bianca* (the White City). The **old town**, on the highest of the hills, has steep cobbled lanes, wrought-iron lanterns, some good local restaurants, and stupendous views out over the coast and the surrounding plain. **Piazza Libertà**, the city's main square, divides the new town and the old.

Where to Stay & Eat

$$ ✕ **Osteria del Tempo Perso.** Buried in the side streets of the old town, this casual restaurant is decorated with cooking implements of all sorts. An even more atmospheric room (open July–September nightly and October–June Saturday dinner and Sunday lunch) is actually set in an ancient cave. Service is friendly and preparations focus on local cuisine such as delectable stuffed hot peppers and orecchiette with bitter greens and olive oil. ⊠ *Via G. Tanzarella Vitale 47* ☎ *0831/303320* ▭ *AE, DC, MC, V* ☉ *Closed Mon. and Dec. 27–Jan. 15.*

$ ✕ **Vecchia Ostuni.** In the heart of the old town, enjoy regional specialties from this well-established trattoria, whose grills and seafood are renowned among locals. Let yourself go on the antipasti table before settling down to *scallopine al vino bianco e funghi* (veal scallops with white wine and mushrooms) or *costata di maiale alla brace* (pork chop char-grilled). The homemade desserts are worthwhile, and there's a good selection of local wines. ⊠ *Largo Lanza 9* ☎ *0831/303308* ▭ *AE, DC, MC, V* ☉ *Closed Tues. and Jan.*

$ ▥ **Incanto.** At this large, pleasant hotel about a mile outside the old town, you can admire the expansive countryside, sea, and whitewashed hilltop city in the distance from many of its rooms. It makes a convenient overnight base for visiting the area. ⊠ *Via dei Colli, 72017* ☎ *0831/ 301781* ☒ *0831/338302* ⊕ *www.hotelincanto.it* ⤳ *60 rooms, 5 suites* ☖ *2 restaurants, minibars, 2 bars* ▭ *AE, DC, MC, V.*

Nightlife

Especially in summer, Ostuni is livelier by night than you might expect. **Riccardo Cafè** (⊠ Via G. Tanzarello Vitale ☎ 0831/306046) is the hippest spot in town for a drink or a coffee before or after dinner. Grottoes, neon lighting, and postmodern couches transport you to another Ostuni entirely. **Perbaco Jazz Lounge Teatro Café** (⊠ Via Zanardelli 1 ☎ Info 0340/3384040), near the central Piazza Libertà, is a mellow, but still busy, spot with live jazz on weekends.

Martina Franca

㉔ *6 km (4 mi) south of Locorotondo, 36 km (22 mi) north of Taranto.*

Martina Franca is an appealing town with a dazzling mixture of medieval and baroque architecture in the light-color local stone. Ornate balconies hang above the twisting, narrow streets, with little alleys leading off into the hills. Martina Franca was developed as a military stronghold in the 14th century, when a surrounding wall with 24 towers was built, but now all that remains of the wall are the four gates that had been the only entrances to the town. Each July and August, the town holds a music festival.

Where to Stay & Eat

$ ✕ **La Tavernetta.** This small restaurant with a vaulted ceiling in the old town center serves large portions of good home cooking, starting with a pottery bowl full of local olives and excellent house wine. Specialties include favi e fogghi and, in summer, orecchiette with *cocomero* (a vegetable that looks like a miniature watermelon and tastes like a cross between cucumber and honeydew melon). Main courses include a mixed grill of lamb, liver, and spicy local sausage. ⊠ *Via Vittorio Emanuele 30* ☎ *080/4306323* ▭ *MC, V* ☉ *Closed Mon.*

$–$$ ▥ **Park Hotel San Michele.** This garden hotel makes a pleasant base in the warm months, thanks to its pool. The two categories of single rooms have a small price difference; if alone, opt for the higher-priced ones. All rooms are spacious, some embellished with handsome furniture and including complimentary bowls of fruit. ⊠ *Viale Carella 9, 74015*

☎ *080/4807053* 🖷 *080/4808895* ⊕ *www.parkhotelsm.it* ⤳ *85 rooms*
⚒ *Restaurant, pool, bar* ▤ *AE, DC, MC, V.*

ACROSS THE HEEL & SOUTH TO LECCE

This far south, the mountains run out of steam and the land is uniformly flat. The monotonous landscape, besides being agriculturally important, is redeemed by some of the region's best sandy coastline and a handful of small, alluring fishing towns, such as Otranto and Gallipoli. Taranto and Brindisi don't quite fit this description: both are big ports where historical importance is obscured by unsightly heavy industry. Nonetheless, Taranto has its archaeological museum, and Brindisi marks the end of the Via Appia. Farther south, in Salento (the Salentine Peninsula), Lecce is an unexpected oasis of grace and sophistication, and its swirling architecture will melt even the most uncompromising critic of the baroque.

Taranto

㉕ *100 km (62 mi) southeast of Bari, 40 km (25 mi) south of Martina Franca.*

Taranto—the stress is on the first syllable—was an important port even in Roman times. It lies toward the back of the instep of the boot on the broad Mare Grande bay, which is connected to a small internal Mare Piccolo basin by two narrow channels, one artificial and one natural. The old town is a series of old *palazzi* in varying states of decay and narrow cobblestoned streets on an island between the larger and smaller bodies of water, linked by causeways; the modern city stretches inward along the mainland. Circumnavigate the old town and take in a dramatic panorama to the north, revealing Italy's shipping industry at its busiest: steel works, dockyards, a bay dotted with fishing boats, and a fish market teeming with pungent activity along the old town's western edge. Little remains of Taranto's past except the 14th-century church of **San Domenico** (⊠ Via Duomo 33) jutting into the sea at one end of the island, and its famous naval academy.

★ A compendium on the millennia of local history, Taranto's **Museo Nazionale** has a large collection of prehistoric, Greek, and Roman artifacts discovered mainly in the immediate vicinity, including Puglian tombs dating from before 1000 BC. The museum is just over the bridge from the old town on the promontory and is a testament to the importance of this ancient port, which has always taken full advantage of its unique trading position at the end of the Italian peninsula. Telephone ahead before visiting the museum, as hours can be irregular. ⊠ *Corso Umberto 41* ☎ *099/4532112* ▦ *€2* ⊙ *Daily 8:30–7:30.*

Where to Stay

$$ 🏨 **Grand Hotel Delfino.** This big well-equipped hotel downtown caters to business clients. Airy rooms have balconies. The restaurant features regional seafood. ⊠ *Viale Virgilio 66, 74100* ☎ *099/7323232* 🖷 *099/7304654* ⊕ *www.grandhoteldelfino.it* ⤳ *204 rooms* ⚒ *Restaurant, minibars, pool, meeting room* ▤ *AE, DC, MC, V.*

Brindisi

㉖ *114 km (71 mi) southeast of Bari, 72 km (45 mi) east of Taranto.*

Occupying the head of a deep inlet on the eastern Adriatic coast, Brindisi (stress placed on first syllable) has long been one of Italy's most important ports; today most travelers think of it only as a terminus for the ferry crossing that links Italy with Greece, and the seamy area around the port reflects this. Although this impression fails to give credit to the broader importance of the city (which has a population of nearly 100,000) and the assortment of interesting 13th- and 14th-century churches in the atmospheric old town, it is a present-day reminder of the role Brindisi has always played as gateway to the eastern Mediterranean and beyond. Brindisi has seen a constant flow of naval and mercantile traffic over the centuries, and in the Middle Ages it was an important departure point for several crusades to the Holy Land. However, if you're looking for a place to spend the night in conjunction with a ferry departure or arrival, you'd be better served at nearby Lecce or Ostuni rather than here.

The core of Brindisi is at the head of a deep channel, which branches into two harbors with the city between them. Look for the steeple of the cathedral to get your bearings, but go beyond it and down the steps to the water's edge. To the left is a tall **Roman column** and the base of another one next to it. These columns were built in the 2nd century AD and marked the end of the Via Appia (Appian Way), the Imperial Roman road that led from the capital to this important southeastern seaport. ⊠ *Viale Regina Margherita.*

The **Duomo,** a short walk from Brindisi's Roman column, has a mosaic floor in its apse that is worth the stop; the floor dates from the 12th century, although much of the rest of the cathedral was rebuilt in the 18th. ⊠ *Piazza Duomo* ☉ *Daily 7–1 and 4–8.*

The **Castello Svevo,** one of the defense fortifications built by the illustrious Frederick II in the 13th century, guards the larger of Brindisi's two inner harbors. It isn't accessible to the public. ⊠ *Piazza Castello.*

Where to Stay

$ ☒ **Mediterraneo.** Comfort and a central location are the advantages of this modern business-oriented Best Western hotel. Rooms have double-glazed windows and most have balconies, though for the best views it's worth heading up to the restaurant on the seventh floor. ⊠ *Viale Aldo Moro 70, 72100* ☎ *0831/582811* ⎙ *0831/587858* ⊕ *www. hotelmediterraneo.it* ⇆ *65 rooms* ⚐ *Restaurant* ⊟ *AE, DC, MC, V.*

Nightlife & the Arts

The **Festa della Città di Brindisi** (City of Brindisi Festival), July–September, is a citywide display of art and folklore; contact the **tourist office** (⊠ Piazza Dionisi ☎ 0831/523072).

Lecce

㉗ *40 km (25 mi) southeast of Brindisi, 87 km (54 mi) east of Taranto.*

Fodor'sChoice
★

Lecce is the crown jewel of the mezzogiorno. While the city may be affectionately referred to as "the Florence of the South," that sobriquet does an injustice to Lecce's uniqueness in the Italian landscape. Though the city's great shopping, modern bars, and the impossibly intricate baroque architecture conjure up images of the Renaissance masterpieces of the North, Lecce's lively streets, laid-back student cafés, magical evening passeggiata, and openness to visitors are distinctively southern. The city is a cosmopolitan oasis two steps from the idyllic Otranto-Brindisi coastline and a hop from the olive-grove countryside of Puglia. Undiscovered by tourists, Lecce exudes an optimism and youthful joie de vivre unparalleled in any other baroque showcase. There is no Lecce of the North.

Although Lecce was founded before the time of the ancient Greeks, it's almost always associated with the term Lecce baroque, the result of a citywide impulse in the 17th century to redo the town in the baroque fashion. But this was baroque with a difference. Although such architecture is often heavy and monumental, here it took on a lighter, more fanciful air. Just look at the **Chiesa di Santa Croce**, with the **Palazzo della Prefettura** abutting it. Although every column, window, pediment, and balcony is given a curling baroque touch—and then an extra one for good measure—the overall effect is lighthearted. The buildings' scales are unintimidating and the local stone is a glowing honey color: it couldn't look menacing if it tried. ⊠ *Via Umberto I* ☎ *0832/241927* ⊘ *Daily 8–1 and 5–8.*

Lecce's ornate **Duomo,** first built in 1114 but reconstructed in baroque style from 1659 to 1670, is uncharacteristically set in a solitary lateral square off a main street, rather than at a crossroads of pedestrian traffic. To the left of the Duomo, the more austere **bell tower,** reconstructed by Joseph Zimbalo in the 17th century, takes on a surreal golden hue each dusk. The facades of the adjoining 18th-century **Palazzo Vescovile,** farther past the right side of the Duomo, and the **Seminario** on the Piazza's right edge, complement the rich ornamentation of the Duomo to create an effect almost as splendid as that of Santa Croce. The Seminario's tranquil **cloister** is also worth a visit. ⊠ *Piazza Duomo, off Corso V. Emanuele* ☎ *0832/308884* ⊘ *Daily 8–1 and 5–8.*

In the middle of **Piazza Sant'Oronzo,** the city's putative center, surrounded by cafés, pastry shops, and newsstands, is a **Roman column** of the same era and style as the one in Brindisi, but imaginatively surmounted by an 18th-century statue of the city's patron saint, Orontius. Next to the column, the shallow rows of seats in the **Anfiteatro Romano** suggest a small-scale Roman Colosseum or Verona's arena.

Where to Stay & Eat

$ ✕ **Plaza.** Tucked away behind Lecce's castle, this large restaurant has been keeping the city's gourmets happy for 30 years. Regional dishes are given a personal touch. Try the *tubettini alle cozze* (pasta with clams); the antipasti are also worth dipping into. ⊠ *Via 140 Fanteria 10* ☎ *0832/305093* ⊟ *AE, DC, MC, V* ⊘ *Closed Sun. and 3 wks. in Aug.*

$ ✕ **Villa G.C. della Monica.** Set in a gracious 17th-century villa complete with palm trees, courtyard, and fountain, this restaurant comes into its own with summer alfresco dining in the garden. The menu focuses almost entirely on seafood, with the traditional Puglian *antipasto misto,* a generous spread of appetizers, followed by seasonal seafood dishes such as *maccheroni con vongole veraci, cozze tarantine, e fagioli bianchi* (macaroni with small Adriatic clams, mussels, and white beans) and fresh grilled fish. This locale is frequented by, and thus particularly suitable for, families with young children. ⊠ *Via SS. Giacomo e Filippo 40* ☎ *0832/458432* ⊟ *AE, MC, V* ⊘ *Closed Tues.*

¢–$ ✕ **Trattoria Casareccia.** This is an excellent place to try traditional *pugliese* cooking in a warm and casual setting—white walls and loud chatter. Don't expect a menu; choose from the daily specials, which might include homemade whole-wheat pasta served with a delicate sauce of tomato and ricotta forte. The rustic *purè di fave e cicoria* (puree of fava bean with chicory) is topped with local olive oil; mix it all together before eating. Service is informal and welcoming. ⊠ *Via Costadura 19* ☎ *0832/245178* ⊟ *AE, MC, V* ⊘ *Closed Mon., Aug. 27–Sept. 11, 1 wk for Easter, and Dec. 23–Jan. 2. No dinner Sun.*

FodorsChoice
★

$–$$ 🛏 **President.** Rub elbows with visiting dignitaries at this new-school business hotel, well situated three blocks from Piazza Mazzini. The reception is expansive and furnishings are 1980s tasteful, with an emphasis on primary colors and modernist lamps. ⊠ *Via Salandra 6, 73100* ☎ *0832/311881* 🖷 *0832/372283* ⇥ *154 rooms* ᠔ *Restaurant, mini-*

bars, bar, lounge, meeting room, parking (fee) ▬ *AE, DC, MC, V.*

$ ▦ **Risorgimento.** An old-fashioned Liberty-style hotel in a palace in the heart of the old town, the Risorgimento combines historic charm with modern comfort. For undisturbed sleep and summertime siestas during longer stays, ask for rooms overlooking the backstreets or the courtyard. The roof garden has great views. ⊠ *Via Augusto Imperatore 19, Piazza S. Oronzo, 73100* ☎ *0832/242125* 🖷 *0832/245571* ⊕ *www.webshop.it/hotelrisorgimento* ⟿ *57 rooms* ♨ *Restaurant, minibars, lounge, meeting room, parking (fee)* ▬ *AE, DC, MC, V.*

¢ ▦ **Cappello.** This popular hotel is close to the train station but outside the old city walls, about a 10-minute walk from the town center. Space is confined in the walk-up guest rooms, but they are fine for a short stay and an excellent value. Rooms at the back can get noise from the nearby railroad. ⊠ *Via Montegrappa 4, 73100* ☎ *0832/308881* 🖷 *0832/301535* ⊕ *www.webshop.it/hotelcappello* ⟿ *32 rooms* ♨ *Bar, parking (fee)* ▬ *AE, DC, MC, V.*

Shopping

The best place in town to buy gastronomical delights from the Salento region, including olive oil, ricotta forte, hot pepper sauce, and an assortment of local baked goods, is **Golosità del Salento da Valentina** (⊠ Via A. Petronelli 3 ☎ 0832/300549), a few steps from the Piazza del Duomo. The friendly and helpful owner presses his own olive oil, and has infinite patience with—and interest in—visitors from abroad.

Nightlife & the Arts

The most popular hangout for the university crowd is **I Merli** (⊠ Via Federico D'Aragona ☎ 0832/241874), a classy café where scores of locals gather each afternoon and evening for coffee, spirits, and gossip. Hours are 5:30 PM–2 AM (weekends open earlier); closed Monday.

In July, the public gardens are the setting for **drama productions** and, sometimes, opera. A **baroque music festival** is held in churches throughout the city in September. For details on forthcoming events call the **Tourist Information Office** (☎ 0832/248092).

Otranto

🄬 *36 km (22 mi) southeast of Lecce, 188 km (117 mi) southeast of Bari.*

In one of the first great Gothic novels, Horace Walpole's 1764 *The Castle of Otranto*, the English writer immortalized the city and its mysterious medieval fortress in a dark, controversial thriller. Otranto (the accent is on the first syllable) has likewise had more than its share of dark thrills: as the easternmost point in Italy—and therefore closest to the Balkan peninsula—it's often borne the brunt of foreign invasions during its checkered history. A flourishing port from ancient Greek times, Otranto (the Roman *Hydruntum*) has a history like that of most of southern Italy: after the fall of the western Roman Empire, centuries of Byzantine rule interspersed with Saracen incursions, followed by the arrival of the Normans and other dynasties from northern Europe. The town was sacked by Turkish forces in 1480, occupied for a year, and never recovered its former glory. Modern Otranto's dank cobblestoned alleyways alternatively reveal dusty, forgotten doorways and modern Italian fashion chains, and the spooky castle still looms above between city and sea. On a clear day you can see across to Albania.

The centro storico nestles within impressive city walls and bastions, dominated by its famous **Castello** mostly attributed to the Spanish of the 16th century. ⊠ *Piazza Castello* ☎ *0832/930722* ⊙ *Tues.–Sun. 9–1* 🎫 *Free.*

The real jewel in Otranto is the **Cattedrale,** originally begun by the Normans and conserving an extraordinary 12th-century mosaic pavement in the nave and aisles. ⊠ *Piazza Basilica* ☎ *0836/802720* ☉ *Daily 8:30–noon and 5–7:30.*

off the beaten path

COASTLINE SOUTH TO LEUCA – The coastal road between Otranto and Leuca is one of the most beautiful in southern Italy. Sandy beaches are replaced by rocky outcrops and sheer cliffs watched over by scattered castles and seaside pleasure palaces. Along the way, **Santa Cesarea Terme,** with a pleasant Lido and famous fanciful Moorish resort on the water, and **Castro,** with another attractive marina, are worthwhile stops; this is land that few foreign tourists traverse. At the end of the journey, **Capo Santa Maria di Leuca** has a lighthouse at the southeasternmost point in Italy, the end of the Puglian Aqueduct, and the quiet, sparse basilica of **Santa Maria Finibus Terrae** (land's end). The **Marina di Leuca,** below, is a little fishing village with excursion boats and a few summertime hotels and bars. If, after the drive, you're heading back to Lecce or points east, the inland highway is a faster route.

Where to Stay

¢ ▦ **La Fattoria.** This working farm (dairy cows and olives) lies 3 km (2 mi) southwest of Otranto, off the road to Uggiano. It makes an excellent base for visiting Lecce, Gallipoli, and other sights in the Salentine Peninsula. The restaurant specializes in organic food but operates only weekends (and evenings in summer), which means you have to fend for yourself the rest of the time. Bring bath towels and soap! ⊠ *SS Otranto–Uggiano Bivio Casamassetta, 73028* ☎☎ *0836/804651* ⊲ *5 apartments, 5 bungalows* ♨ *Restaurant, playground* ▭ *AE, DC, MC, V.*

Shopping

Otranto's old town has been tastefully gentrified and has an array of shops displaying local products and chain boutiques. **Texum** (⊠ Corso Garibaldi 43) specializes in objets d'art sculpted from *pietra leccese,* the soft local limestone used for much of the baroque architecture in the Salentine Peninsula. If you want to stock up on regional wines and olive oil, stop off at **Il Giardino del Re** (⊠ Corso Garibaldi 64), where wine-tasting sessions are frequently arranged.

Gallipoli

㉙ *37 km (23 mi) south of Lecce, 190 km (118 mi) southeast of Bari.*

The fishing port of Gallipoli, on the Golfo di Taranto, is divided between a new town, on the mainland, and a pleasant fortified town, across a 17th-century bridge, crowded onto its own small island in the gulf. The Greeks called it Kallipolis, the Romans Anxa. Like the famous Turkish town of the same name on the Dardanelles, the Italian Gallipoli occupies a strategic location and thus was repeatedly attacked through the centuries—by the Normans in 1071, the Venetians in 1484, the British in 1809. Today, life in Gallipoli revolves around its fishing trade. Bright fishing boats in primary colors breeze in and out of the bay during the day, and Gallipoli's fish market, below the bridge, throbs with seamy activity all morning.

Gallipoli's historic quarter, a mix of narrow alleys and squares, is guarded by **Castello Aragonese,** a massive fortification that grew out of an earlier Byzantine fortress that you can still see at the southeast corner. After being an operative base for the busy *Guardia di Finanza* (revenue police), it's now being renovated and adapted for future use as a public monument. Gallipoli's **Duomo** (⊠ Via Antonietta De Pace ☎ 0833/261987) open daily 9–12:30 and 5–8, is a notable baroque church. The church of **La Purissima** (⊠ Riviera Nazario Sauro ☎ 0833/261699) has a stuccoed interior as elaborate as a wedding cake, with an especially noteworthy tiled floor. You can visit daily 9–12:30 and 5–7:30.

Where to Stay & Eat

$–$$ ✕ **Marechiaro.** Unless you arrive by boat—as many do—you have to cross a little bridge to reach this simple port-side restaurant, not far from the town's historic center. It's built out onto the sea, replete with wood paneling, flowers, and terraces with panoramic coastal views. Try the renowned *zuppa di pesce alla gallipolina* (fish stew), succulent shellfish, and linguine with seafood. ⊠ *Lungomare Marconi* ☎ *0833/266143* ☐ *AE, DC, MC, V* ☉ *Closed Tues. in Oct.–May.*

★ **$$$$** ☐ **Costa Brada.** The rooms all have terraces with sea views at this modern white beach hotel of classic Mediterranean design. The interiors are uncluttered and tasteful; rooms 110 through 114 are particularly spacious and overlook the beach. The hotel accepts only half- or full-board guests in high season. ⊠ *Baia Verde, Litoranea Santa Maria di Leuca, 73014* ☎ *0833/202551* ☐ *0833/202555* ⊕ *www.grandhotelcostabrada. it* ⟿*78 rooms* ⌂ *2 restaurants, snack bar, 2 pools (1 indoor), gym, sauna, shop* ☐ *AE, DC, MC, V* ⧖ *MAP.*

Sports & the Outdoors

BEACHES   Ample swimming, water sports, and clean, fine sand make Gallipoli's **beaches** a good choice for families. The 5-km (3-mi) expanse of sand sweeping south from town has both public and private beaches, the latter equipped with changing rooms, sun beds, and umbrellas. Water-sports equipment can be bought or hired at the waterfront shops in town.

PUGLIA A TO Z

To research prices, get advice from other travelers, and book travel arrangements, visit www.fodors.com.

AIR TRAVEL

CARRIERS   Several airlines serve the cities of Bari and Brindisi: Alitalia flies regularly between Bari and Brindisi and Rome and Milan; Volare-Air Europe connects Bari with Rome and Milan; Air One serves Bari with flights from Turin, Milan, and Rome, and operates one daily Brindisi-Milan flight; and Air Dolomiti connects Bari with Verona and Turin. Pescara, further up the Adriatic in Abruzzo, but convenient to Puglia, is served by Ryanair from London and Air One from Milan.

🛫 Airlines & Contacts **Air Dolomiti** ☎ 800/013366 ⊕ www.airdolomiti.it. **Air Europe** ☎ 848/848130, Bari 080/5370495 ⊕ www.aireurope.it. **Air One** ☎ 848/848130, Bari 080/5316153 ⊕ www.air-one.it. **Alitalia** ☎ 848/865641 ⊕ www.alitalia.com. **Ryanair** ☎ 199/114114 ⊕ www.ryanair.com.

AIRPORTS

A regular bus service connects the two airports, Bari-Palese (about 10 km [7 mi] northwest of the city center) and Brindisi-Papola (8 km [5 mi] to the north), with their respective cities. Alitalia buses provide service from the cities to arrivals and departures at both airports. Many hotels and taxis within other outlying cities provide service directly to and from the airports, which can be much simpler than public transport—call your hotel for details.

🛫 Airport Information **Bari-Palese** ☎ 080/5835204 ⊕ www.seap-puglia.it. **Brindisi-Papola** ☎ 0831/4117208 ⊕ www.seap-puglia.it

BOAT & FERRY TRAVEL

Ferries ply the waters from Bari and Brindisi to Greece (Corfu, Igoumenitsa, Patras, and Kephalonia), Turkey, Albania, and even Egypt and Croatia. Brindisi's connection to Patras is covered by some rail passes, thus immensely popular with backpackers.

Boat & Ferry Information **Adriatica di Navigazione** to Albania and the Tremiti islands; agents at A. Galli e Figlio ⊠ Corso Manfredi 4, 71043 Manfredonia ☎ 0884/582520 ⊠ Gargano Viaggi Piazza Roma 7, 71019 Vieste ☎ 0884/708501 ⊕ www.adriatica.it. **Blue Star Ferries** only Brindisi to Corfu and Igoumenitsa; agents at Il Globo ⊠ Corso Garibaldi 65, 72100 Brindisi ☎ 0831/527684 ⊕ www.bluestarferries.com.

BUS TRAVEL

Compared to rail, travel times by bus into Puglia from Naples on the far side of the Apennines are substantially shorter. From Rome, contact Autolinee Marozzi, at their Rome office or in Bari. If traveling between Naples and Foggia, contact CLP; Miccolis runs a daily Naples-Lecce service, which takes five hours, about half as long as by train.

Direct, if not always frequent, connections operate between most destinations in Puglia. SITA is the main bus company operating in the region. In many cases bus service is the backup to the train service.

Bus Information **Autolinee Marozzi** ☎ 06/44249519 in Rome; 080/5562446 in Bari. **CLP** ☎ 081/5311706. **Miccolis** ☎ 081/200380. **SITA** ⊠ Piazza Aldo Moro 15/a ☎ 080/5213714.

CAR RENTAL

Local Agencies **Avis** ⊠ Via L. Zuppetta 5/a, Bari ☎ 080/5247154 ⊠ Aeroporto Palese, Bari ☎ 080/5316168 ⊠ Piazza Cairoli 25, Brindisi ☎ 0831/526407 ⊠ Aeroporto Papola, Brindisi ☎ 0831/418826 ⊠ Train station, Foggia ☎ 0881/678912 ⊠ Viale Grassi 158, Lecce ☎ 0832/228585 ⊠ Corso Umberto 61, Taranto ☎ 099/4532278 ⊕ www.avis.com. **Hertz** ⊠ Aeroporto Palese, Bari ☎ 080/5316171 ⊠ Aeroporto Papola, Brindisi ☎ 0831/413060 ⊕ www.hertz.com. **Maggiore-Budget** ⊠ Viale Ventiquattro Maggio 76, Foggia ☎ 0881/773173.

CAR TRAVEL

Driving is the best way to get around Puglia and the only way to see remote sights. Puglia is linked with the Italian autostrada system, making it just a four- or five-hour drive from Rome to the Gargano Promontory or Bari. Roads are good, and major cities are linked by fast autostrade. Secondary roads connect the whole region; more direct—but sometimes less scenic—routes provide a convenient link between Bari, Brindisi, and Lecce. Highways along the coast are usually accompanied by parallel, slower coastal roads with fewer lanes but beautiful vistas. If you're squeamish about getting lost, don't plan on any night driving in the countryside—the roads can become confusing without the aid of landmarks or large towns.

EMERGENCY SERVICES ACI Emergency Service offers 24-hour roadside assistance.

ACI dispatchers ☎ 803/116.

EMERGENCIES

Pharmacies take turns staying open late and on Sunday. A list of hours is posted on each *farmacia* (pharmacy).

General Emergencies ☎ 113.

MAIL & SHIPPING

Post Offices **Bari** ⊠ Via Amendola 116 ☎ 080/5507236. **Brindisi** ⊠ Piazza Vittoria 8 ☎ 0831/525058.

SAFETY

The usual precautions apply here as throughout the south of Italy. Women should pay particular attention in Bari and Brindisi, more so by the port in Brindisi and in Bari's old town at night. Curb-crawlers still abound—local women just ignore them and continue on their way—and evening outings are best done in groups.

TOURS

The Azienda di Promozione Turistica in Bari is the best connection for guided tours in Puglia, otherwise poorly served by tour operators. The office can put you in touch with one of a number of local operators that offer everything from chauffeur-driven cars to a quick regional primer as part of a longer excursion.

 Fees & Schedules **Azienda di Promozione Turistica della Provincia di Bari** ✉ Piazza Moro 32/a, 70122 ☏ 080/5242244 ⊕ www.pugliaturismo.it.

TRAIN TRAVEL

Bari is a transit hub for train connections with northern Italy. Good train service, operated by FS (Italian State Railways), links Bari to Brindisi, Lecce, and Taranto, but smaller destinations can often be reached only by completing the trip on a connecting bus operated by the railroad. The private Ferrovie Sud-Est (FSE) line connects the trulli area and Martina Franca with Bari and Taranto, and the fishing port of Gallipoli with Lecce.

 Train Information **FS** ☏ 848/888088. **Ferrovie Sud-Est (FSE)** ☏ 080/5462111.

TRAVEL AGENCIES

 Local Agent Referrals **Carlson Wagonlit Travel** ✉ Via Cardassi 56, Bari ☏ 080/5540588 ⊕ www.ewt.it. **Crusi Viaggi e Turismo** ✉ Piazza S. Oronzo 21, Lecce 73100 ☏ 0832/305522 🖷 0832/306208. **Utac Viaggi** ✉ Via Santa Lucia 11, Brindisi 72100 ☏ 0831/524921 🖷 0831/529040 ⊕ www.utacviaggi.it.

VISITOR INFORMATION

 Tourist Information **Alberobello** ✉ Piazza Ferdinando IV, 70011 ☏ 080/4325171. **Bari** ✉ Piazza Moro 32/a, 70122 ☏ 080/5242361 ⊕ www.pugliaturismo.it. **Brindisi** ✉ Lungomare R. Margherita, 72100 ☏ 0831/523072. **Foggia** ✉ Via Perrone 17, 71100 ☏ 0881/723141. **Lecce** ✉ Via Vittorio Emanuele 24, 73100 ☏ 0832/248092. **Ostuni** ✉ Corso Mazzini 6, 72017 ☏ 0831/301268. **San Giovanni Rotondo** ✉ Piazza Europa 104, 71013 ☏ 0882/456240. **Taranto** ✉ Corso Umberto 113, 74100 ☏ 099/4532392. **Trani** ✉ Piazza Trieste 10, 70059 ☏ 0883/585530. **Vieste** ✉ Piazza Kennedy, 71019 ☏ 0884/708806 ✉ kiosk in Piazza della Repubblica, summer only ☏ 0883/43295.

BASILICATA & CALABRIA

MATERA, COSENZA, THE TYRRHENIAN COAST

15

FODOR'S CHOICE
Museo Nazionale della Magna Grecia, Reggio di Calabria
Sassi, Matera
Taverna Kerkira, restaurant, Bagnara Calabra

HIGHLY RECOMMENDED
RESTAURANT   Wine Bar DOC, Cosenza

SIGHT   Castello Svevo, Cosenza

Updated by
Robin S.
Goldstein

THE *MEZZOGIORNO*, the informal name for Italy's south, reaches its full apotheosis in the regions of Basilicata and Calabria, often referred to as the instep and toe of Italy's boot. Here, in an area of Italy off most tourist itineraries, the southern sun burns on a quiet, sparsely populated landscape where government neglect and archaic social patterns have prevented the kind of industrialization and rush to modernity experienced in other parts of the country. Half-built structures dot the countryside, road signs are few and far between, and cities become ghost towns for up to five hours at midday. Despite the undeveloped state of large tracts of these two regions, however, Basilicata and Calabria have become increasingly popular among Italians, and hotels and leisure facilities along the coasts are more than adequate, if lacking character. Among the untrammeled scenery here, hardly altered since the city-states of Magna Graecia (Greek colonies) ruled the coasts, you'll find the bizarre cave dwellings of Matera, a shining example of Byzantine church-building at Stilo, country *trattorie* buried in the hills, the tranquil and sun-drenched beaches of Tropea and Scilla—and some of Italy's friendliest people.

Exploring Basilicata & Calabria

The regions of Basilicata and Calabria can be toured as either brief side trips from Campania, Puglia, or Sicily or as a series of select stops en route to these other regions. Basilicata, particularly Matera, makes a natural and convenient accompaniment to any visit to Puglia. The best and fastest way to explore these regions is to stick to the coasts, making inland jaunts from there. West of Taranto, follow the Ionian coast for the classical remains at Metaponto, Locri, and other Greek sights strung along the S106, making brief detours to visit such curiosities as the troglodyte city of Matera and, if time allows, the Norman stronghold of Gerace. South of Salerno, the route along the Tyrrhenian coast takes in a brief stretch of Basilicata—among whose cliffs nestles the smart resort of Maratea—before swooping down into Calabria, where you can divide your time between first-class beaches on the Tropea promontory, or at Scilla, and the high inland ranges of Sila and Aspromonte.

Basilicata and Calabria are well served by transport connections, and drivers and bus and train passengers alike should find no difficulty circulating within these regions. The toll-free A3 autostrada gives a clear run from Salerno all the way down to Reggio di Calabria (although you get what you pay for—it's under eternal construction, so allow extra time), while the much more scenic S18 runs parallel, hugging the Tyrrhenian coast; the S106 traces the Ionian coast from Taranto to Reggio and is often empty of traffic. Trains also follow these coastal routes, with frequent connections on the Naples–Villa San Giovanni line and fewer trains on the Ionian side. Things get much busier, of course, in midsummer, when beaches and resorts burst into activity and hotel rooms can be hard to find.

About the Restaurants & Hotels

Many restaurants in the region, especially the more rural or local ones, don't have prices for individual courses. Instead, they charge you one set price regardless of what you eat (with a separate charge for drinks). If you just order one course, you'll either be charged for a full meal or your waiter will make up a price on the spot.

Hotels are generously distributed throughout this region. They range from grand, if slightly faded, high-class complexes with pools, tennis courts, and copious grounds to family-run places where the famous southern hospitality compensates for a lack of amenities. Note that many hotels close in winter, especially those by the sea, and that hotels in skiing areas will be open in summer and winter but are closed for the rest of the year. Children are welcome everywhere and are usually a prominent presence in the region's hotels. Many families vacation in the numerous campsites along both coasts, most fully equipped and often with bungalows or apartments for rent by the week or less; these can get congested in August. Most campsites are closed in winter.

	$$$$	**$$$**	**$$**	**$**	**¢**
RESTAURANTS	over €22	€17–€22	€12–€17	€7–€12	under €7
HOTELS	over €210	€160–€210	€110–€160	€60–€110	under €60

WHAT IT COSTS In euros

Restaurant prices are for a second course (secondo piatto). Hotel prices are for two people in a standard double room in high season, including tax and service.

Timing

The regions of Basilicata and Calabria suffer from intense heat in summer and, away from the coasts, bitter winter cold. Unless coming for the beach party scene, avoid August, since accommodations can be limited and facilities generally strained; any time on either side, though, would be ideal for touring these regions. Beaches are comparatively empty and the water temperature is comfortable in June, July, and September. Avoid the coastal resorts in winter if you want to find hotels open and anything more than a lonely dog on the streets. The months of January and February see snow inland, which is great if you want to ski but can make driving conditions difficult. Spring and fall see the forests of Basilicata and Calabria at their best.

BASILICATA

Occupying the instep of Italy's boot, Basilicata has long been one of Italy's poorest regions, memorably described by Carlo Levi in his *Christ Stopped at Eboli,* a book that brought home to the majority of the Italians the depths of deprivation to which this forgotten region was subject. (The tale of Levi's internment was poignantly filmed by Francesco Rosi in 1981.) Basilicata was not always so desolate, however. For the ancient Greeks, the area formed part of Magna Graecia, the loose collection of colonies founded along the coasts of southern Italy whose wealth and military prowess rivaled those of the city-states of Greece itself. Metaponto (formerly Metapontion or Metapontum) was one of the most important of these colonies; its remains easily reached along the coastal S106. Farther inland, the city of Matera, the region's true highlight, is built on the side of an impressive ravine that is honeycombed with prehistoric dwellings (sassi), some of them still occupied, forming a separate enclave that contrasts vividly with the attractive baroque town above.

Metaponto

❶ *48 km (30 mi) southwest of Taranto, 182 km (114 mi) south of Bari.*

Greek Metapontion was founded around 700 BC by an Achaean colony from the city-states of Sybaris and Kroton (farther down the coast, in what is now Calabria). The great mathematician and philosopher Pythagoras, banished from Kroton, established a school here in about 510 BC and eventually died in the city. Punished for its support of the Carthaginian general Hannibal (247–183 BC) after his victory over Rome at Cannae (216 BC), Metapontum, as it was known by the Romans, endured long

15

Your itinerary while exploring Basilicata and Calabria will depend on the direction you're traveling. An ideal route is to come from the north either along the Tyrrhenian coast—from Campania on the S18 or the faster A3 highway—or from Puglia on the S106. If you're traveling in Basilicata, you can cross over to the Tyrrhenian coast without any difficulty on the panoramic S653, passing through the Pollino range and enabling you to make a stop at Maratea. Farther south, you can change coasts at Sibari, Catanzaro, Stilo, and Locri. From the Tyrrhenian coast, head inland at Paola to go through the Sila range to Crotone on the Ionian Sea.

Numbers in the text correspond to numbers in the margin and on the Basilicata and Calabria map.

If you have 3 days

If it's summer and you're heading south from Campania, spend a night in the resort of 🔲 **Maratea** ④ ▶, a perfect marriage of cliffs and beaches. On your second day, stop for lunch at **Diamante** ⑤ , then catch a glimpse of **Pizzo** ⑧ and stop for the night at 🔲 **Tropea** ⑨ , close to some of Calabria's best beaches. From here, it's a short trip to the Sicily ferries at Villa San Giovanni. Alternatively, coming from Puglia, make a stop at the archaeological site at **Metaponto** ① before crossing over to Basilicata's west coast for a night at 🔲 **Maratea** ④ ; then continue south as above. With an extra day at your disposal, you might return to the Ionian coast to see the lovely Byzantine La Cattólica church at 🔲 **Stilo** ⑰ . Spend the night here, and then drive the brief distance down the coast to see the classical ruins of **Locri** ⑮ before heading west to the archaeological museum at **Reggio di Calabria** ⑬ then continue on to Sicily or head back up to Stilo for the final night. If traveling in fall or winter, substitute a night in either 🔲 **Cosenza** ⑥ , Calabria's layered hillside metropolis, or the wondrous cave town of 🔲 **Matera** ② , for Maratea and other beach towns.

If you have 5 days

From Puglia, allow two or three hours to explore the classical remains at **Metaponto** ① before heading inland on the fast S407 to 🔲 **Matera** ② ▶, a must for its fascinating *sassi*, prehistoric rock dwellings, and an ideal first overnight stop. Cross over to the Tyrrhenian and spend your second night at 🔲 **Maratea** ④ , and then head south via **Diamante** ⑤ . At Paola, veer east across the coastal chain to get a taste of inland Calabria, spending your third night in 🔲 **Cosenza** ⑥ , the frozen-in-time provincial capital. Explore Cosenza's old town, or take a day trip to hike or ski in neighboring **Camigliatello** ⑦ . (If it's fall or winter, skip Maratea and Diamante and head straight for Cosenza, spending an extra day there.) The next day, make your way south to the attractive seaside town of 🔲 **Pizzo** ⑧ , and later head to beautiful 🔲 **Tropea** ⑨ , either of which makes a good fourth-night stop. If you can pull yourself away, continue down the coast the following day; you might stop at the eclectic museum at **Palmi** ⑩ , lunch by the harbor at **Bagnara Calabra** ⑪ , siesta on the beach at **Scilla** ⑫ , and if archaeology strikes your fancy, pass through **Reggio di Calabria** ⑬ , where the archaeological museum is one of southern Italy's best. If you have time left over, either make an excursion on to the brooding massif of **Aspromonte** ⑭ or skirt south around this range to the Greek site at **Locri** ⑮ and the nearby Norman town of **Gerace** ⑯ . Otherwise, it's just a short hop over the Straits to Messina and Sicily.

years of decline—sacked by the slave-rebel Spartacus (died 71 BC) and subsequently ravaged both by malaria and Saracen raids. Most of what remained was used for building elsewhere in the region, but the *zona archeologica* (archaeological zone), which covers a vast area, retains enough interest to merit a visit. You'll need a car: allow about an hour for the museum, which is best seen before the sight, to view the plans and maps and put it all into context, and then an hour or two for the excavations. When you've finished here, you might take a dip at Lido di Metaponto, where there are sandy well-equipped beaches.

The modern **Museo Archeologico Nazionale** displays 4th- and 5th-century statuary, ceramics, jewelry, and coins on a rotating basis—sadly, representing only a tiny fraction of the total number of finds until work on a new wing is completed.Perhaps most interesting are examples of coins stamped with images of grain, symbolizing the cereal production to which Metapontion owed its prosperity. Also noteworthy is the section showing how the study of fingerprints on shards found in the artisans' quarter has revealed information on the social makeup of the ancient city. Maps and aerial photographs of the site with accounts of the excavations are useful for your visit. The museum lies about 2 km (1 mi) outside Lido di Metaponto (look out for the scanty signs). ⊠ *Borgo Metaponto, Via Aristea* ☎ *0835/745327* 🎟 *€2.50* ☉ *Sept.–May, daily 9–7; June–Aug., daily 9 AM–11 PM.*

Highlights of Metaponto's sprawling **zona archeologica,** accessible to the east of the Museo Archeologico Nazionale, include the **Santuario di Apollo Licio** (Sanctuary of Apollo Lykaios), a 6th-century BC Doric temple which, archaeologists have deduced, once had 32 columns. Only the foundations and a few capitals and shafts are to be seen today. Nearby, encircled by an expanse of grass, lie the remains of a 4th-century BC **Teatro,** much restored. More compelling is the better-preserved Tempio di Hera (Temple of Hera), commonly known as **Tavole Palatine,** found 2–3 km (1–2 mi) north, where the main S106 crosses the Bradano River. With 15 of its fluted Doric columns surviving, it's the most evocative remnant of this once mighty state. ⊠ *Metaponto Borgo* ☎ *0835/745327* 🎟 *Free* ☉ *Daily 9–1 hr before sunset.*

Matera

▶ ❷ *45 km (28 mi) north of Metaponto, 62 km (39 mi) south of Bari.*

Matera is one of southern Italy's most unusual towns. On their own, the elegant baroque churches, palazzi, and broad piazzas—filled to bursting during the evening *passeggiata*, when the locals turn out to stroll the streets—would make Matera stand out in Basilicata's impoverished landscape. But what really sets this town apart is its sassi.

Fodor'sChoice
★
Matera's **sassi** are rock-hewn dwellings piled chaotically atop one other, strewn across the sides of a steep ravine. They date to Paleolithic times, when they were truly cave homes. In the years since, the grottoes were slowly adapted as houses only slightly more modern, with their exterior walls closed off and canals regulating rainwater and sewage. Until relatively recently, these troglodytic abodes presented a Dante-esque vision of squalor and poverty, graphically described in Carlo Levi's *Christ Stopped at Eboli,* but in the 1960s most of them were emptied of their inhabitants, who were largely consigned to the ugly blocks seen on the way into town. Today, however, having been designated a World Heritage Site, the area has been cleaned up and is gradually being populated once again—and even gentrified, as evidenced by the bars and restaurants that have moved in. The wide Strada Panoramica leads you

15

Beaches

The lack of industry in Basilicata and Calabria has one positive result for beach fans—acres of sand and a largely unpolluted sea running almost continuously down both coasts of the peninsula. This is not the place for you if you like your beaches impeccably tended but crowded with regimented lines of sunbathers and ranks of uniform beach umbrellas. Here you can pick and choose strands at whim and spread out. What's more, there's a pronounced difference between the two coasts: the more developed Tyrrhenian littoral, on the western side, has more villages and facilities and is more scenic, with the mountains a constant backdrop; the eastern Ionian shore, on the other hand, is flatter and wilder, has fewer towns and villages, and holds less visual interest. The best Tyrrhenian spots are around Maratea, Praia a Mare, Amantea, Tropea, and Scilla. On the Ionian, head for Lido di Metaponto, Sibari, Capo Rizzuto, and Soverato. Remember that if you don't have your own beach umbrella, the summer sun can be oppressive and even dangerous: borrow or buy one if you can, and arm yourself with plenty of sunscreen. Alternatively, stick to your hotel beach or seek out those few spots where there are lidos and amenities to rent, such as at Metaponto, Soverato, and around Tropea.

Hiking & Skiing

Most vacationers in Basilicata and Calabria think of only swimming and sunbathing as the main pastimes, unaware of the hiking and skiing that can be done in the forested or craggily bare peaks and valleys of the predominantly mountainous landscape. Three zones have been made into nature reserves with cross-country and downhill skiing facilities; the best slopes are at Camigliatello and Gambarie, where you can rent equipment. Farthest north, the Parco Nazionale del Monte Pollino, riddled with lush canyons and marked paths, straddles the boundary between Basilicata and Calabria and is a good place to spot eagles and even wild boars. The villages of Morano Calabro, off the A3 autostrada to the south, and San Severino Lucano, off S653 to the north, are good starting points for these mountains, which reach up to 7,500 ft. Occupying the widest part of the Calabrian peninsula, the Sila Massif (which rises to 6,300 ft) attracts the most visitors, though the thick pine, beech, and chestnut forests are vast enough for you to find your own space. Farthest south, the Aspromonte Massif, with peaks as high as 6,500 ft soaring above Reggio di Calabria, is a welcome retreat from summer temperatures. Access is easiest from the S183 between Melito di Porto Salvo and Gambarie. For further information, including walking and hiking itineraries and the state of the slopes, contact local tourist offices.

---

safely through this desolate region, which still retains its eerie atmosphere and panoramic views.

There are two areas of sassi, the **Sasso Caveoso** and the **Sasso Barisano,** and both can be seen from vantage points in the upper town. Then follow the Strada Panoramica down into the sassi and feel free to ramble among the strange structures, which, in the words of H. V. Morton in his *A Traveller in Southern Italy,* "resemble the work of termites rather than of man." Among them, you will find several *chiese rupestri,* or rock-hewn churches, some of which have medieval frescoes, notably **Santa**

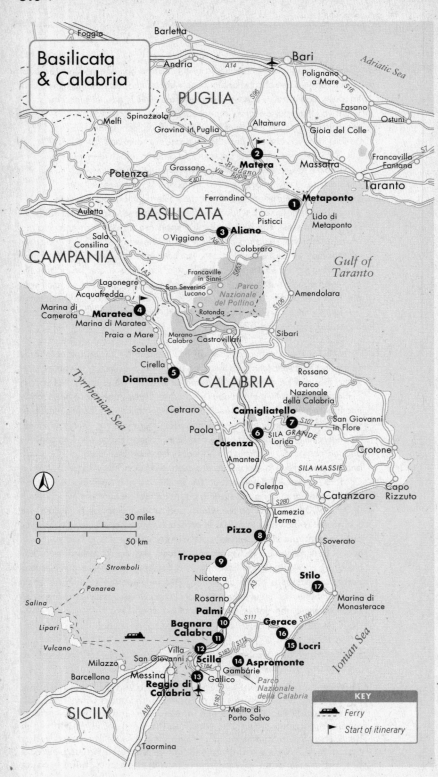

Basilicata
& Calabria

Foggia

Barletta

Andria

A14

Bari

Adriatic Sea

PUGLIA

Polignano
a Mare

S16

Fasano

Ostuni

Spinazzola

Melfi

Gravina in Puglia

Altamura

Gioia del Colle

Francavilla
Fontana

S7

2 Matera

Massafra

Taranto

Potenza

Grassano

Grottole

Via Appia

Bradano

S407

Ferrandina

1 Metaponto

BASILICATA

Pisticci

Lido di
Metaponto

Aulletta

Sala
Consilina

Viggiano

3 Aliano

Colobraro

Gulf of
Taranto

CAMPANIA

Lagonegro

Acquafredda

Francaville
in Sinni

San Severino
Lucano

Parco
Nazionale
del Pollino

Amendolara

Marina di
Camerota

4 Maratea

Marina di Maratea

Rotonda

Praia a Mare

Scalea

Morano
Calabro

Castrovillari

Sibari

Cirella

5 Diamante

CALABRIA

Rossano

Parco
Nazionale
della Calabria

Cetraro

Camigliatello

7 S107

San Giovanni
in Flore

Paola

6

SILA GRANDE

Lorica

Cosenza

Amantea

SILA MASSIF

Crotone

Falerna

Catanzaro

Capo
Rizzuto

S280

Lamezia
Terme

Tyrrhenian Sea

Pizzo

8

Soverato

0   30 miles

0   50 km

Tropea **9**

Stromboli

Nicotera

Panarea

Rosarno

Stilo

17

Salina

Lipari

Vulcano

Palmi

**Bagnara
Calabra** **10**

11

S111

A3

Marina di
Monasterace

Gerace

S106

16

15 Locri

S112

Milazzo

San Giovanni

Barcellona

Messina

**Reggio di
Calabria**

Villa

12

Scilla

S183

14 Aspromonte

Gambarie

S184

13

Gallico

Parco
Nazionale
della Calabria

Ionian Sea

SICILY

A18

Melito di
Porto Salvo

S183

KEY

Ferry

Start of itinerary

Taormina

ON THE MENU

BASILICATA AND CALABRIA *are renowned for both their seafood— calamari, bream, sea bass, and swordfish to name a few—and their produce. Look for various types of funghi (mushrooms), particularly in the fall; intense ricotta forte, antipasti of roasted vegetables soaked in local olive oil; lamb stew; and handmade fusilli (pasta twists). Pork is the region's meat staple, and it takes many delightful forms, including roast suckling pig; salame piccante (Calabrian spicy salami infused with peppercorns, known all over Italy as an integral part of a salumi plate and also a common pizza topping); and savory salsiccia piccante, hot Italian sausage (often sold by street vendors in a roll with peppers, onions, french fries, and mayonnaise). Methods of preparing and even naming mezzogiorno dishes vary widely, providing many opportunities for*

adventurous eating. One taste experience you will find universally available, however, is peperoncini (small dried hot chile peppers), the sweat-inducing seeds of which are often added to pasta dishes, especially pasta prepared simply with a spot of garlic, oil, and fresh pomodorini, (cherry tomatoes) boiled down. But if you're used to spicy food, nothing in the region will ever daunt you.

Maria de Idris, right on the edge of the Sasso Caveoso, near the ravine. A few minutes east of Santa Maria, in the so-called Albanian quarter (settled by refugees in the 15th century), the 10th-century **Santa Lucia alle Malve** has Byzantine-style frescoes dating from 1250. Hours for both churches may vary, as you have to get the custodian to open them up. ⊠ *Sasso Caveoso* 🎫 *Gratuity expected* ⊙ *Daily 9–1 and 3:30–dusk.*

The **Duomo** in Matera was built in the late 13th century and occupies a prominent position between the two areas of sassi. It has a pungent Apulian-Romanesque flavor; inside, some of the columns came from Metaponto, and there's a recovered fresco, probably painted in the 14th century, showing scenes from the *Last Judgment.* On the Duomo's facade, the figures of Sts. Peter and Paul stand on either side of a sculpture of Matera's patron, Madonna della Bruna. ⊠ *Via Duomo* ☎ *0835/ 335201* ⊙ *Daily 8–noon and 3:30–7.*

In town you'll find the 17th-century church of **San Francesco d'Assisi,** which contains eight panels of a polyptych by Bartolomeo Vivarini (circa 1432–99), set above the altar. The church's ornate baroque style was superimposed on two older churches that can be visited through a passage in the third chapel on the left; inside are traces of some 11th-century frescoes. ⊠ *Piazza San Francesco* ⊙ *Daily 8–noon and 3:30–7.*

Matera's excellent **Museo Ridola** is housed in the ex-monastery of Santa Chiara. Illustrating the human and geological history of the area, the museum includes an extensive selection of prehistoric and classical finds, notably Bronze Age weaponry and beautifully decorated Greek plates and amphoras. ⊠ *Via Ridola 24* ☎ *0835/310058* 💶 *€2.60* ⊙ *Daily 9–8, 9 AM–11 PM in summer.*

Where to Stay & Eat

$ ✕ **Trattoria Lucana.** This trattoria is a simple family-run place in the center of town, where you can enjoy local recipes in a friendly, rustic environment—try out the *agnello allo spiedo* (lamb on the spit) or *bocconcini di vitello* (veal). ✉ *Via Lucana 48* ☎ *0835/336117* ⚓ *Reservations essential* ▤ *AE, DC, MC, V* ☾ *Closed Sun. Nov.–Feb. and 1 wk in late Sept.*

¢–$ ✕ **Oi Mari.** Along the main road below the Hotel Sassi, this lively restaurant is an excellent choice within the sassi themselves. Friendly servers cater to a mix of tourists and locals in a network of ancient, cavelike rooms that are painted brightly enough not to be spooky. The sassi ambience accompanies great pizza, salumi, and a good selection of typical local dishes at very reasonable prices. The wine list includes many of Puglia and Basilicata's most up-and-coming reds. ✉ *Vico Fiorentini 66, Rione Sassi* ☎ *0835/346121* ▤ *AE, DC, MC, V* ☾ *Closed Tues. and 1st 2 wks in Oct.*

$ 🛏 **Albergo Italia.** Central and stylish, the Italia is a reliably comfortable accommodation choice, housed in a well-preserved old building steps away from the sassi and Museo Ridola. The best rooms are ornate but unfussy, with pastel color-coordinated curtains and comforters; some have balconies. There's a small, elegant restaurant as well as a modern bar. ✉ *Via Ridola 5, 75100* ☎ *0835/333561* 🖷 *0835/330087* ⊕ *www.basilicata.bancadati.it/albergoitalia.html* ⇒ *46 rooms* ⚐ *Restaurant, bar, minibars* ▤ *AE, DC, MC, V* ☾ *Closed 2 wks in Aug.*

$ 🛏 **Hotel Sassi.** For the full sassi experience, this place can't be beat—it's right in the heart of the Sasso Barisano, directly across from the Duomo. It has a raw, cavelike design, with rough-hewn walls and stairs (and so not advised for anyone with mobility difficulties). Facilities are minimal; rooms are small and plain but clean, comfortable, and air-conditioned. The hotel's position at the bottom of the valley provides supreme views. Two rooms are set aside for hostel-type bunk accommodation at budget rates. Parking is a bit of a hike from the hotel, something to consider if you have heavy baggage. ✉ *Via San Giovanni Vecchio 89, 75100* ☎ *0835/331009* 🖷 *0835/333733* ⇒ *17 rooms, 1 suite* ⚐ *Minibars, bar* ▤ *AE, DC, MC, V.*

The Outdoors

WALKING TOURS The agency **Nuovi Amici dei Sassi** (✉ Piazza Sedile 20, 75100 ☎ 0835/331011) arranges up to four tours of the sassi area a day, charging around €10 per person for a group of four or more. Call ahead to request an English-speaking guide. Independent guides also offer their services on the spot, pricing by length of tour and the number in your party.

Nightlife

BARS Matera's after-dinner scene—of which there is not much—takes place entirely in the sassi. Try the warm, dark, and popular **Bodeguita Latina** (✉ Via dei Fiorentini 1/3, Sasso Barisano ☎ 0835/256373 ☾ Closed Monday), for music including live jazz and blues, drinks, and late-night food.

Aliano

❸ *127 km (79 mi) southwest of Matera, 102 km (63 mi) southeast of Potenza.*

This remote village off S598 in the center of Basilicata's empty interior was the site of Carlo Levi's internment during 1936 and 1937. After the war, Levi (1902–75) published his account of that time in his classic *Christ Stopped at Eboli*, later filmed by Francesco Rosi. Not significantly different from any of the countless villages scattered over the featureless clay gullies and outcrops stretching out on all sides, Aliano (called Gagliano by Levi) has not altered much, and readers can identify the church, the piazza where the Fascist mayor addressed the impassive peasants, and the timeless views. The house in Aliano where Carlo Levi stayed has been preserved as the **Museo Storico Carlo Levi**, displaying some personal items as well as other articles of local interest. It's best to phone first or stop in the Bar Centrale in the center of the village for the custodian, Don Pierino Dilenga. ✉ *Palazzo Caporale* ☎ *0835/568074* 💶 *€1.50* 🕐 *Sept.–May, daily 9–noon and 3–6; June–Aug., daily 9–1 and 4–7.*

Maratea

▶ **4** *103 km (64 mi) southwest of Aliano, 217 km (135 mi) south of Naples.*

When encountering Maratea for the first time, you can be forgiven for thinking you've somehow arrived at the French Riviera. The high, twisty road resembles nothing so much as a corniche, complete with glimpses of a turquoise sea below. Divided by the craggy rocks into various separate localities—Maratea, Maratea Porto, Maratea Marina—the sequence ends above the main inland village, a tumble of cobblestone streets where the ruins of a much older settlement can be seen (Maratea Antica). At the summit of the hill a dramatic, gigantic Christ stands, a floating white ghost in the night sky, reminiscent of the one in Rio de Janeiro. Most of the area's hotels and restaurants lie in the Fiumicello–Santa Venere neighborhood, a short walk from an enticing beach. But there's no shortage of secluded sandy strips in between the rocky headlands, which can get crowded in August. A summer minibus service connects all of the various points once or twice an hour.

Where to Stay & Eat

$$ ✕ **Taverna Rovita.** Housed in a former convent with exposed beams, this restaurant in the heart of the old town offers a menu based on traditional recipes, but the food here is in a different league from that of Maratea's other eateries. The antipasti, for a start, are various and abundant, and the homemade pasta comes with a selection of rich sauces that changes according to the season. Choose a locally caught fish for the main course. Reservations are advised. ✉ *Via Rovita 13* ☎ *0973/876588* 🖃 *AE, DC, MC, V* 🕐 *Closed Nov.–Feb. and Tues. in Oct. and Mar.–May.*

$$$$ 🏨 **Santavenere.** This deluxe hotel is worth a splurge, if only for the grounds and the opulent architectural style of the public rooms. The nonsuite guest rooms are disappointingly ordinary, but most enjoy an incredible panorama of rock and sea. A tennis court, private beach, and round pool complete the picture. The high tab is reduced by up to 50% outside summer. ✉ *Località Fiumicello di Maratea, 85040* ☎ *0973/876910* 📠 *0973/877654* 🌐 *www.santavenerehotel.com* 🛏 *40 rooms* ♿ *2 restaurants, minibars, pool, tennis court, gym, beach, bar* 🖃 *AE, DC, MC, V* 🕐 *Closed Nov.–Mar.*

CALABRIA

Italy's southernmost mainland region has seen more than its fair share of oppression, poverty, and natural disaster, but the region of Magna Graecia, mountains, and *mare* (sea) also has more than its share of fantastic scenery and great beaches. The accent here is on the landscape, the sea, and the constantly changing dialogue between the two. Don't expect much in the way of sophistication in this least trodden of regions, but be open to the simple pleasures to be found—the country food, the friendliness, the disarming hospitality of the people. Aside from coast and culture, there are also some sights worth going out of your way for,

from the vividly colored murals of Diamante to the ruins of Magna Graecia at Locri. The drive on the southbound S13 highway alone is a
breathtaking experience, the more so as you approach Sicily, whose image
grows tantalizingly nearer as the road wraps around the coastline once
challenged by Odysseus. This is the road you should take for the big
picture—but don't forget to stop for a bit to get a closer view of this
fascinating land.

Diamante

❺ *51 km (32 mi) south of Maratea, 225 km (140 mi) south of Naples.*

One of the most fashionable of the string of small resorts lining Calabria's north Tyrrhenian coast, Diamante makes a good stop for its whitewashed maze of narrow alleys, brightly adorned with a startling variety
of large-scale murals. The work of various local artists, the murals, which
range from cartoons to poems to serious portraits, and tasteful to downright ugly, give a sense of wandering through a huge open-air art gallery.
Flanking the broad, palm-lined seaside promenade are sparkling beaches
to the north and south.

Where to Stay & Eat

$$ ✕ **Taverna del Pescatore.** One of a pair of good moderately priced fish
restaurants down by the seafront at Diamante's Spiaggia Piccola (the
other is Lo Scoglio), this is the less formal of the two, and the more wel-
coming, with spartan but bright decor. Naturally, fish predominates—
whatever's hauled in is cooked in a variety of ways. Phone first to secure
a table outside. ✉ *Via Calvario 2* ☎ *0985/81482* 🖃 *MC, V* ☯ *Closed
Tues. in Oct.–May.*

$$$ 🏨 **Grand Hotel San Michele.** A survivor from a vanishing age, the San
Michele occupies a belle epoque–style, cliff-top former hunting lodge
near the village of Cetraro, 20 km (12 mi) south of Diamante on SS18.
Mingling Mediterranean charm with old-style elegance, the hotel is set
within extensive gardens, and an elevator takes you down to the private beach at the base of the cliff. The only downside is its isolation. If
you're inclined to venture out from this palatial retreat, you need a car.
✉ *Località Bosco 8/9, 87022 Cetraro* ☎ *0982/91012* 📠 *0982/91430*
🌐 *www.sanmichele.it* 🛏 *73 rooms* ♿ *Restaurant, 9-hole golf course,
tennis court, beach, bar* 🖃 *AE, DC, MC, V* ☯ *Closed Nov.*

Cosenza

❻ *75 km (48 mi) south of Diamante, 185 km (115 mi) north of Reggio di
Calabria.*

Cosenza, Calabria's biggest city, has a steep, stair-laden centro storico
that truly hails from another age. Wrought-iron balconies overlook
narrow alleyways with old-fashioned storefronts and bars that have barely
been touched by centuries of development. Flung haphazardly—and beautifully—across the top and side of a steep hill ringed by mountains, and
watched over by a great, crumbling medieval castle, Cosenza also provides the best gateway for the Sila, whose steep walls rear up to the town's
eastern side. Though Cosenza's outskirts are largely modern and ugly,
culinary and photographic gems await in the rolling farmland nearby
and the mountains to the east.

★ Crowning the Pancrazio hill above the Old City, with views across to
the Sila mountains, **Castello Svevo** is largely in ruins, having suffered successive earthquakes and a lightning strike that ignited gunpowder stored
within. The castle takes its name from the great Swabian emperor Frederick II (1194–1250), who added two octagonal towers, though it dates

back originally to the Normans, who fortified the hill against their Saracen foes. Occasional exhibitions and concerts are staged here in summer. ⊠ *Porta Piana.* ⌨ *Free* ⊙ *Apr.–Sept., weekdays 9–12:30 and 4–6.*

Cosenza's noblest square, **Piazza XV Marzo** (commonly known as Piazza della Prefettura), houses government buildings as well as the elegant **Teatro Rendano.** From the square, the **Villa Comunale** (public gardens) provides plenty of shady benches for a rest.

need a break?

In the heart of the centro storico, the charming and historic **Gran Caffè Renzelli** (⊠ Corso Telesio 46 ☎ 0984/412538) makes a fine spot for a pause in your perambulations. At tables inside or out (there is a no-smoking room as well as an outside terrace), you can enjoy *varciglia* (a dry almond cake) along with a host of sweet and wonderful coffee-liqueur combinations, each served with cream in a tall glass. Join in the *chiacchiere al caffè* (talks over coffee), echoing the discussions of the literary salon that once met here.

Cosenza's original **Duomo** was probably built in the middle of the 11th century but was destroyed by the earthquake of 1184. A new cathedral was consecrated in the presence of Emperor Frederick II in 1222. After many baroque additions, later alterations have restored some of the Provençal Gothic style. Inside, look for the lovely tomb of Isabella of Aragon, who died after falling from her horse en route to France in 1271. ⊠ *Piazza del Duomo,* ☎ *0984/77864* ⊙ *Daily 7:30–noon and 3:30–7.*

Where to Stay & Eat

$–$$ ✕ **L'Arco Vecchio.** This tavern-restaurant, located right in the middle of the old town, appropriately under the famous Arch of Ciaccio, serves traditional Calabrian dishes in a warm, elegant vaulted room. Try the excellent *orecchiette* (ear-shape pasta) ⊠ *Piazza Archi di Ciaccio 21* ☎ *0984/72564* ☰ *AE, DC, MC, V* ⊙ *Closed Sun.*

★ $ ✕ **Wine Bar DOC.** Representing the contemporary edge of Cosenza, this postmodern feat of interior decorating oozes fusion, whimsically plopping spreads of tempting traditional Calabrian salumi and a superlative collection of wines amid a whirl of glass and exposed stone, all tucked into the cozy arches of an ancient palazzo. All the trendiest locals come out not just for the voluminous wine list, which showcases Calabria's absolute best, but also for the wonderful smoked meats, cheeses, and inventive pasta dishes. Come to eat or just to drink. ⊠ *Vico San Tommaso 13, off Corso Telesio* ☎ *0984/73110* ☰ *AE, DC, MC, V* ⊙ *Closed Mon. No lunch.*

¢–$ ✕ **Da Giocondo.** In the new part of town, but near the centro storico, you can sample simple homemade dishes in a modern yet homey setting. Go for the local freshly picked mushrooms from the Sila as an antipasto, followed by *polpettine* (meatballs), washed down with local Cirò wine. ⊠ *Via Piave 52* ☎ *0984/29810* ☰ *AE, MC, V* ⊙ *Closed Sun. and 2–3 wks in Aug.*

$ ▦ **Royal.** Though lacking much character, this modern hotel in the new part of town is handy for buses departing for the Sila. The public spaces have a classical style with columns and Persian carpets on the marble floor. The restaurant specializes in local Calabrian dishes. ⊠ *Via Molinella 24/e, 87100* ☎ *0984/412165* 🖷 *0984/412461* ⇝ *44 rooms* ⌂ *Restaurant, bar, meeting room* ☰ *AE, DC, MC, V.*

¢ ▦ **Excelsior.** Used for years as an army barracks, this 1900 Liberty-style building has been restored to its former grandeur. The public areas are imposing, retaining their fin-de-siècle feel, while the spacious guest rooms are adequate if uninspiring. It's close to the shops of Cosenza's main drag, Corso Mazzini, and an easy walk across the Busento river from the centro storico. ⊠ *Piazza Matteotti 14, 87100* ☎ *0984/74383* 🖷 *0984/74384* 💤 *40 rooms* ⚒ *Restaurant, bar, meeting room* ▭ *AE, DC, MC, V.*

Camigliatello

❼ *36 km (22 mi) east of Cosenza.*

Lined with chalets, Camigliatello, between Crotone and Cosenza, is one of the Sila Massif's major resort towns. Most of the Sila is not mountainous at all; it is, rather, an extensive, sparsely populated plateau with areas of thick forest. Unfortunately, the region has been exploited by construction and fuel industries, resulting in considerable deforestation. However, since 1968, when the area was designated a national park (Parco Nazionale della Calabria), strict rules have limited the felling of timber, and forests are now regenerating. There are well-marked trails through pine and beech woods, and ample opportunities for horseback riding. Fall and winter see droves of locals hunting mushrooms and gathering chestnuts, while ski slopes near Camigliatello also draw crowds. A couple of miles east of town, Lago Cecita makes a good starting point for exploring **La Fossiata**, a lovely wooded conservation area within the park.

Where to Stay

¢-$ 🏨 **Tasso.** On the edge of Camigliatello, less than 1 km (½ mi) from the ski slopes, this hotel is in a peaceful, picturesque location. Don't be put off by its oddly futuristic 1970s looks—it's well equipped, with plenty of space for evening entertainment, including live music, and relaxation after a day of hiking or skiing. The restaurant has a terrace shaded by a walnut tree, and all rooms have balconies. ⊠ *Via degli Impianti Sportivi, Spezzano della Sila, 87058* ☎☎ *0984/578113* ⊕ *www.hoteltasso.it* 💤 *82 rooms* ⚒ *Restaurant, bar, lounge, nightclub, recreation room, meeting room, free parking* ▭ *AE, DC, MC, V* ⊗ *Closed Mar.–May and Nov.*

Sports & the Outdoors

HIKING & WALKING
One of the best hikes around Camigliatello is the **Strada delle Vette** (Peaks Road), a 13-km (8-mi) route that links the Sila's highest mountains. For maps and itineraries, contact the **Camigliatello tourist office** (⊠ Via Roma 5 ☎ 0984/578243).

HORSEBACK RIDING
With plenty of trails winding through woods and around lakes, horseback riding is one of Sila's year-round attractions. Contact **Maneggio Sila** (⊠ Via Molarotta, 3 km [2 mi] outside Camigliatello ☎ 0360/283252).

SKIING
The slopes in the area are small and get quite crowded. The best place to rent equipment is at the ski lift. Call for rental information and **slope conditions** (☎ 0984/578037).

Pizzo

❽ *148 km (92 mi) south of Diamante, 107 km (66 mi) north of Reggio di Calabria.*

Built up along the slope of a steep promontory overlooking the coast and a fishing port, Pizzo has a good selection of seafood restaurants and a small cliff-top Aragonese castle (built in 1486) near the center of town. Here the French general Joachim Murat (1767–1815) was imprisoned, tried, and shot in October 1815, after a bungled attempt to rouse the people against the Bourbons and reclaim the throne of Naples given him by his brother-in-law Napoléon.

While in Pizzo, sample the renowned gelato di Pizzo, a rich, creamy delight available in many flavors at any of the outdoor bars in the central Piazza della Repubblica.

The **Chiesetta di Piedigrotta**, a little over a mile north of Pizzo's castle, at the bottom of a flight of steps leading down to the beach, is a 17th-century church implausibly hewn out of rock by shipwrecked Neapolitan sailors in thanks for their rescue. They filled it with statues of biblical and historical figures, and the collection today includes a bizarre ensemble showing Fidel Castro kneeling before Pope John XXIII (1881–1963) and President Kennedy (1917–63). ⊠ *Via Nazionale* ⊙ *Daily 9–1 and 3–7:30.*

Where to Stay

$ 🏨 **Hotel Murat.** Here's a good central choice for accommodation if you decide to overnight in Pizzo. Right in the town's main square, a stone's throw from the castle and perched overlooking the water, the Murat has comfortable rooms, of which the ones on the sides are biggest and have the best views (ask for No. 207). ⊠ *Piazza della Repubblica 41, 89812* ☎ *0963/534201* 🖷 *0963/534469* ⏎ *12 rooms* ⌂ *Restaurant, bar* ▭ *AE, DC, MC, V.*

Tropea

❾ *28 km (17 mi) southwest of Pizzo, 107 km (66 mi) north of Reggio di Calabria.*

Ringed by cliffs and wonderful sandy beaches, the Tropea promontory is still undiscovered by the big tour operators. The main town, Tropea, easily wins the contest for prettiest town on Calabria's Tyrrhenian coast, its old palazzi built in simple golden stone on an elevation above the sea. On a clear day, the seaward views from the waterfront promenade extend to embrace Stromboli's cone and at least four of the other Aeolians—the islands can be visited by motorboats that depart daily from Tropea in summer. Accommodations are good, and beach addicts will not be disappointed by the choice of magnificent sandy bays within easy reach of here. Some of the best are south at Capo Vaticano and north at Briatico.

In Tropea's harmonious warren of lanes, seek out the old Norman **Cattedrale**, whose interior displays a couple of unexploded U.S. bombs from World War II, with a grateful prayer to the Madonna attached to each. ⊠ *Piazza Sedile* ⊙ *Daily 7–noon and 4–7.*

From the belvedere at the bottom of the main square, Piazza Ercole, the church and Benedictine monastery of **Santa Maria della Isola** glistens on a rocky promontory above an aquamarine sea. Stroll out to visit the church on a path lined with fishermen's caves. Of Basilian origin, the church was remodeled in the Gothic style, then given another face-lift after an earthquake in 1905. The interior has an 18th-century nativity and some fragments of medieval tombs. ⊠ *Santa Maria della Isola* ⊙ *Daily 7–noon and 4–7.*

Where to Stay & Eat

$$ ✕ **Pimm's.** This underground restaurant in Tropea's historic center has offered the town's top dining experience since its glory days in the 1960s. Seafood is the best choice, with such specialties as pasta with sea urchins, smoked swordfish, and stuffed squid. The splendid sea views are an extra enticement. ⊠ *Corso Vittorio Emanuele 2* ☎ *0963/666105* ▭ *AE, DC, MC, V* ⊙ *Closed Nov.–Jan.; closed Mon. in Oct. and Feb.–May.*

$–$$ ⊞ **Villaggio Torre Ruffa Robinson.** Near the beach 6 km (4 mi) south of Tropea, this whitewashed hotel, part of a huge camping-bungalow-tourist village complex, has everything you need for a quiet sojourn away from the madding crowd. Cane furniture, banana trees, and bright wisteria help to create a luxurious enclave. It also makes a great center for sports enthusiasts, offering weekly packages that include sailing, windsurfing, tennis, aerobics, and diving, with the opportunity to gain PADI certification. Round out the day with an evening cabaret show. Full pension and a minimum of one week's stay are required. Apartments are cheaper and ideal for larger groups. ⊠ *Località Torre Ruffa 1, Capo Vaticano, 89865 Ricadi* ☎ *0963/663185* 🖷 *0963/663934* ⊕ *www. villaggiorobinson.it* 🖙 *40 rooms* ↻ *Restaurant, tennis court, beach, bar* 🖃 *AE, DC, MC, V* ⊘ *Closed Oct.–May* ⅠⓄⅠ *FAC.*

Palmi

⑩ *60 km (37 mi) south of Tropea, 47 km (29 mi) north of Reggio di Calabria.*

The small town of Palmi is worth a stop for its excellent **Casa della Cultura Leonida Repaci** museum complex. Named after a local writer and artist, it includes an archaeological section, displaying pottery and other items dredged up from the seabed; a *pinacoteca* with paintings by old masters, including Tintoretto (circa 1518–94) and Il Guercino (1591–1666); a gallery of modern art, mainly by southern Italian artists such as Renato Guttuso; and Calabria's best collection of folklore items. The museum is above the town, close to the S18. ⊠ *Via San Giorgio, Palmi* ☎ *0966/262250* 🖃 *€1.55* ⊘ *Tues., Wed., and Fri. 8–2, Mon. and Thurs. 8–2 and 3–6.*

Bagnara Calabra

⑪ *11 km (7 mi) south of Palmi, 36 km (22 mi) north of Reggio di Calabria.*

Fishing is in the blood of the local villagers in Bagnara Calabra, particularly when in pursuit of swordfish, for which the town has long enjoyed widespread fame. Casual trattorias make this a great lunch stop.

Where to Eat

$$ ✕ **Taverna Kerkira.** Centrally located on Bagnara's main street, this casual restaurant emphasizes food above all else. The chef's mother hails from Corfu, and dishes thus represent creative Greek spins on Calabrian classics. Antipasti feature fish you'll find in few other places, such as delicately marinated, sashimilike *carpaccio di alalonga* (raw Tyrrhenian tunny with olive oil and soy sauce). *Farfalle* are prepared with Greek yogurt, lemon zest, cucumber, and a hint of mullet—a sublime creation. The chef also excels at *pesce spada* (swordfish)—try it breaded and baked with mint, vinegar, and parmigiano. ⊠ *Corso Vittorio Emanuele 217* ☎ *0966/372260* 🖃 *AE, DC, MC, V* ⊘ *Closed Mon.–Tues., Aug. 15–Sept. 15, and Dec. 21–Jan. 10.*

FodorśChoice
★

Scilla

⑫ *10 km (6 mi) south of Bagnara Calabra, 26 km (16 mi) north of Reggio di Calabria.*

According to Homer's *Odyssey,* ancient Scylla was where one of two monsters resided, dreaded by passing sailors. The other was Charybdis, modern-day Cariddi, on the Messina side of the Straits. Today, nothing in Scilla looks remotely threatening, especially in summer, when the broad, sandy beach is the focus for sunning and swimming by day, and carousing by night. At the northern end of the bay, a castle rises loftily on a rocky spur—a grand vantage point for watching the tall-masted *felucche* swordfish boats patrolling the Straits. Most of these are based in Bagnara Calabra, to the north.

Reggio di Calabria

13 *26 km (16 mi) south of Scilla, 499 km (311 mi) south of Naples.*

Reggio di Calabria, the city on Italy's toe tip, is the jumping-off point for Messina- and Sicily-bound ferries, and was laid low by the same catastrophic earthquake that struck Messina in 1908. This raw city is one of Italy's most active ports, where you'll find every category of container ship and smokestack, but there's also a pleasant lido lined with palm fronds and urban beaches.

Reggio possesses one of southern Italy's most important archaeological museums, the **Museo Nazionale della Magna Grecia.** Prize exhibits here are two statues, known as the **Bronzi di Riace,** happened upon by an amateur deep-sea diver off Calabria's Ionian coast in 1972. Flaunting physiques that gym enthusiasts would die for, the pair are thought to date from the 5th century BC and have been attributed to both Phidias and Polyclites. It's possible that they were destined for the temple at Delphi when the vessel that carried them was shipwrecked. Coins and votive tablets are among the numerous other treasures from Magna Graecia contained in the museum. ⊠ *Piazza de Nava, Corso Garibaldi* ☎ *0965/ 812255* 🔁 *€5* ⊙ *Daily 9–7:30* ⊙ *Closed 1st and 3rd Mon. of month.*

FodorśChoice ★

Where to Stay

$$ 🏨 **Miramare.** On the seafront midway between the port and the station, Miramare has one of the best locations in Reggio. It has been restored to evoke the charm of the early 20th century yet has all modern facilities. ⊠ *Via Fata Morgana 1, 89127* ☎ *0965/812444* 🖷 *0965/812450* ⊕ *www.reggiocalabriahotels.it* 🛏 *96 rooms* ♿ *Restaurant, bar, parking (fee)* ⊟ *AE, DC, MC, V.*

$ 🏨 **Palace Masoanri's.** Right behind the Museo Nazionale, under the same management as the fancier Miramare, this modern hotel sits on a quiet side street with seaward views. Rooms are uninspiring though adequate for a night or two, and many have views over the straits. ⊠ *Via Vittorio Veneto 95, 89121* ☎ *0965/26433* 🖷 *0965/26436* ⊕ *www. reggiocalabriahotels.it* 🛏 *65 rooms* ♿ *Bar, meeting room, parking (fee)* ⊟ *AE, DC, MC, V.*

Aspromonte

14 *Gambarie: 42 km (26 mi) northeast of Reggio di Calabria.*

Rising to the east of Reggio di Calabria, Aspromonte is the name of the sprawling massif that dominates mainland Italy's southern tip. Long the haunt of brigands and still the refuge of modern-day kidnappers—for whom industrialists, not tourists, are the usual targets—this thickly forested range reaches nearly 6,560 ft and is popular with skiers in winter. In summer, it makes a cool respite from the heat of the coast, offering endless opportunities for hiking and shady picnicking. On a clear day, you can see right across to Mt. Etna, 60 km (36 mi) south. To get here going north from Reggio, turn inland off the autostrada or coast road at Gallico, 12 km (7 mi) north of town; driving east from Reggio on S184, turn left onto the S183 at Melito di Porto Salvo. Ask at **Reggio's tourist office** (⊠ *Corso Garibaldi 329* ☎ *0965/892012*) for Aspromonte walking itineraries.

> **en route**
>
> The fast S106 hugs Calabria's Ionian coast, leading south out of Reggio di Calabria and curving around Aspromonte to your left. Having rounded Capo Spartivento, the road proceeds north. If you don't want to continue farther north, turn left onto the S112dir, shortly before Bovalino and 14 km (9 mi) before reaching Locri. This winding mountain road takes you around the rugged northern slopes of Aspromonte, a highly scenic but rigorously winding route.

Locri

⑮ *100 km (62 mi) east of Reggio di Calabria.*

South of the seaside town of Locri, visit the excavations of **Locri Epizefiri,** where one of the most important of Magna Graecia's city-states stood. Founded around the 7th century BC, Locris became a regional power when— apparently assisted by Castor and Pollux—10,000 Locrians defeated an army of 130,000 from Kroton on the banks of the Sagra River, 25 km (16 mi) north. Founding colonies and gathering fame in the spheres of horse-breeding and music, Locris was responsible for the first written code of law in the Hellenic world. The walls of the city, parts of which are still visible, measured some 8 km (5 mi) in circumference. The best-preserved archeological remains are a 5th-century BC Ionic temple, a Roman necropolis, and a Graeco-Roman theater. ☎ *0964/390023* ✉ *Site free, museum €2* ⊙ *Site daily 9–1 hr before sunset; museum daily 9–7:30; museum and archaeological zone closed 1st and 3rd Mon. of month.*

Gerace

⑯ *10 km (6 mi) west of Locri, 110 km (68 mi) east of Reggio di Calabria.*

When the Saracens plundered Locri in the 7th century AD, the survivors fled inland to found Gerace, on an impregnable site that was later occupied and strengthened by the Normans. It's worth the short detour to visit this redoubt, its ruined castle tottering precariously on a jagged outcrop. Gerace's **Duomo** was founded in 1045 by Robert Guiscard (circa 1015–85), enlarged by Frederick II two centuries later, and today is still the biggest church in Calabria. Its simple, well-preserved interior has 20 columns of granite and marble, each different, and the 10th on the right, in verd antique (a green marble), changes tone according to the weather. ⊠ *Piazza Vittorio Emanuele* ☎ *0964/356010* ⊙ *Mar.–June, Aug.–Sept., daily 9:30–1 and 3–7; July, Tues.–Sun. 9–1 and 3–7; Oct.–Feb., daily 9:30–1 and 3–7.*

Stilo

⑰ *50 km (31 mi) north of Locri, 138 km (86 mi) northeast of Reggio di Calabria.*

Grandly positioned on the side of the rugged Monte Consolino, the village of Stilo is known for being the birthplace and home of the philosopher Tommaso Campanella (1568–1639), whose magnum opus was the socialistic *La Città del Sole* (*The City of the Sun*, 1602)—for which he spent 26 years as prisoner of the Spanish Inquisition. A tangible reason to visit the village is the tiny 10th-century Byzantine temple **La Cattólica.** Standing on a ledge above the town, this tiled and three-turreted building is believed to be the best-preserved of its kind. ⊠ *Via Cattólica* ✉ *Free* ⊙ *daily 9–7.*

Where to Stay

¢ 🏨 **San Giorgio.** Tucked away off Stilo's main Via Campanella, this hotel is housed in a 17th-century cardinal's palace, Palazzo Lamberti, and decked out in the style of that period, with elegantly furnished guest rooms. There are exhilarating views seaward from the garden. Half or full board is required—the food is acceptable, and there's nowhere else in town to eat anyway. ✉ *Via Citarelli 8, 89049* ☎☎ *0964/775047* ↪ *10 rooms* ⚴ *Restaurant, pool, bar* ☉ *Closed Oct.–Apr.* ⑩ *MAP.*

en route

From Stilo you can take the S110 inland—a long twisty road that goes through the high Serra region, covered with a thick mantle of chestnut forest. There are terrific views to be enjoyed over the Ionian coast, and you can continue across the peninsula to Calabria's Tyrrhenian littoral, emerging at Pizzo. The total road distance between Stilo and Pizzo is around 80 km (50 mi).

BASILICATA & CALABRIA A TO Z

To research prices, get advice from other travelers, and book travel arrangements, visit www.fodors.com.

AIRPORTS

Twenty-seven kilometers (17 mi) north of Pizzo, Aeroporto di Lamezia caters to international charters and domestic flights, with connections to Milan, Bologna, and Rome; airlines servicing the airport are Alitalia and Air One. Reggio di Calabria's Aeroporto Titto Minniti handles Alitalia domestic flights only, with five departures daily to Rome, two to Milan.

🛈 Airport Information **Aeroporto Titto Minniti** call Alitalia ☎ 8488/65641 ⊕ www.sogas.it. **Aeroporto di Lamezia** ☎ 0968/51766 or 0968/51205 ⊕ www.sacal.it. **Air One** ☎ 800/900966 ⊕ www.air-one.it. **Alitalia** ☎ 8488/65641.

BOAT & FERRY TRAVEL

Hydrofoils, ferries, and fast ferries ply the Straits of Messina once or twice hourly from Reggio di Calabria and from Villa San Giovanni, day and night (reduced service in winter). Crossings take about 20 minutes from Reggio, about 40 minutes from Villa. Hydrofoils also run from Reggio to Sicily's Aeolian Islands. In Reggio contact SNAV and FS; in Villa, FS and Caronte.

🛈 Boat & Ferry Information **Caronte** ☎ 0965/793111 ⊕ www.carontespa.it. **FS** ☎ 0965/863545. **SNAV** ☎ 0965/29568 ⊕ www.snav.it.

BUS TRAVEL

Matera is linked with Bari and Metaponto by frequent buses operated by Ferrovie Appulo-Lucane, and with Taranto by SITA buses. In Calabria, various bus companies make the north–south run with stops along both coasts; Ferrovie della Calabria operates many of the local services. In Reggio di Calabria, contact Lirosi for buses to Rome, leaving three times daily. From Reggio di Calabria, Salzone runs to Scilla, and Federico to Locri and Stilo.

🛈 Bus Information **Federico** ☎ 0965/590212. **Ferrovie Appulo-Lucane** ☎ 0835/332861. **Ferrovie della Calabria** ☎ 0984/36851. **Lirosi** ☎ 0966/575552. **Salzone** ☎ 0965/751586. **SITA** ☎ 0835/835007.

CAR RENTAL

You can rent cars at the Lamezia and Reggio di Calabria airports, at downtown locations in Matera, and at the Cosenza train station.

🛈 Local Agencies **Avis** ✉ Vico XX Settembre 8, Matera ☎ 0835/336632 ✉ Aeroporto Tito Minniti, Reggio di Calabria ☎ 0965/643023 ⊕ www.avisworld.com. **Damasco** ✉ Vico XX Settembre 12, Matera ☎ 0835/334605. **Hertz** ✉ Aeroporto dello Stretto, Reggio di Calabria ☎ 0965/643093 ⊕ www.hertz.it. **Maggiore-National** ✉ Aeroporto dello Stretto, Reggio di Calabria ☎ 0965/643148 ⊕ www.maggiore.it.

CAR TRAVEL

Metaponto is a major road and rail junction for routes along the coast and inland. To get to Metaponto by car from Puglia's Taranto, take the S106 southwest for 45 km (28 mi). From Puglia's Bari, take the S96 south for 44 km (28 mi) to Altamura, then the S99 south 19 km (12 mi) to Matera. The A3 Autostrada del Sole runs between Salerno and Reggio di Calabria, with exits for Crotone (the Sila Massif), Pizzo, Rosarno (for Tropea), Palmi, and Scilla; it takes an inland route as far as Falerna, then tracks the Tyrrhenian coast south (except for the bulge of the Tropea promontory). Take the S18 for coastal destinations—or a better view—on the Tyrrhenian side, likewise S106 (which is uncongested and fast) for the Ionian. To drive from Basilicata's Metaponto to Matera, take the S175 northwest for 45 km (28 mi). You can cross the Strait of Messina from Villa San Giovanni or Reggio.

EMERGENCY SERVICES
ACI Emergency Service offers 24-hour roadside assistance.
🚗 **ACI dispatchers** ☎ 803/116.

EMERGENCIES

In Reggio di Calabria, the pharmacies Curia and Caridi are open at night. Elsewhere, late-night pharmacies are open on a rotating basis; information on current schedules is posted on any pharmacy door.
🚗 **Police, Ambulance, Fire** ☎ 113. **Hospital** ☎ 0965/8501 in Reggio di Calabria; 0835/2431 in Matera. **Curia** ✉ Corso Garibaldi 455 ☎ 0965/332332. **Caridi** ✉ Corso Garibaldi 327 ☎ 0965/24013.

LANGUAGE

The dialects of Basilicata and Calabria, which vary from village to village, are impenetrable to anyone with a knowledge only of textbook Italian. All locals speak Italian, however, and you'll find a considerable number of older people, returned émigrés from the United States or Canada, who are happy to show off their rusty English.

MAIL & SHIPPING

🚗 Post Offices **Cosenza** ✉ Via Vittorio Veneto. **Matera** ✉ Via Vittorio Veneto. **Reggio** ✉ Via Miraglia.

SAFETY

LOCAL SCAMS
The area is not noticeably more crime-ridden than any other Italian region, as far as foreign visitors are concerned. Car crime is probably the biggest threat: don't leave anything visible in your car overnight, and never leave your car unlocked.

WOMEN IN BASILICATA & CALABRIA
The south is more old-fashioned about independent women than other parts of Italy. But things have improved dramatically, and women can expect nothing more menacing than stares from men.

TOURS

Foderaro organizes weekly bus tours of Reggio di Calabria, Scilla, Locri, and Gerace and boat tours to the Aeolian Islands. For English-language tours of Matera's sassi, consult the Matera tourist office for operators.
🚗 Fees & Schedules **Foderaro** ✉ Via Mazzini 185, Catanzaro 88100 ☎ 0961/726006 🌐 www.foderaro.it.

TRAIN TRAVEL

The main north–south FS (Italian State Railways) line has hourly services from Reggio north to Palmi, Pizzo, Diamante, and Maratea, continuing on as far as Salerno, Naples, and Rome. There are nine daily Intercity or Eurostar trains linking Reggio di Calabria with Naples (4–5 hours) and Rome (6–7 hours). All FS trains also stop at Villa San Giovanni (for connections to Sicily), a 20-minute ride from Reggio. Two fast Eurostar trains run daily between Metaponto and Naples (3¾ hours) and Rome (5½–6 hours), and three others connect Metaponto and Salerno (2¾–3½ hours), from where there are frequent connections to Naples and Rome. There are two connections to Milan, fastest time 11½ hours.

Within the region, the main FS line from Taranto stops in Metaponto, from which there are regular departures to Matera on Ferrovie Appulo-Lucane (FAL) trains. The FAL rail line links Matera to Altamura in Apulia (for connections to Bari) and to Ferrandina (for connections to Metaponto or Potenza). South of Metaponto, FS trains run into Calabria, either following the Ionian coast as far as Reggio di Calabria or swerving inland to Cosenza and the Tyrrhenian coast at Paola. Main FS services run along both coasts but can be crowded along the Tyrrhenian. Call for information on times.

🚆 Train Information **Ferrovie Appulo-Lucane** ☎ 0835/332861. **FS** (Italian State Railways) ☎ 147/888088.

TRAVEL AGENCIES
🚆 Local Agent Referrals **Simonetta** ✉ Corso Garibaldi 521, Reggio di Calabria ☎ 0965/331444.

VISITOR INFORMATION
🚆 Tourist Information **Camigliatello** ✉ Via Roma 5, 87052 ☎ 0984/578243. **Cosenza** ✉ Via P. Rossi, 87100 ☎ 0984/390595. **Maratea** ✉ Piazza del Gesù 32, 85046 ☎ 0973/876908. **Matera** ✉ Via de Viti de Marco 9, off Via Roma, 75100 ☎ 0835/331983. **Pizzo** ✉ Piazza della Repubblica, 88026 ☎ 0963/531310. **Reggio di Calabria** ✉ Corso Garibaldi 329, 89100 ☎ 0965/892012. **Tropea** ✉ Piazza Ercole, 88038 ☎ 0963/61475.

SICILY

PALERMO, AGRIGENTO, SIRACUSA, THE AEOLIAN ISLANDS

FODOR'S CHOICE

B & B Belvedere, Siracusa

Duomo, Siracusa

Il Mulinazzo, restaurant, near Palermo

Imperial Roman Villa, Piazza Armerina

San Domenico Palace, hotel, Taormina

Valle dei Templi, Agrigento

HIGHLY RECOMMENDED

RESTAURANTS   Antica Focacceria San Francesco, Palermo

Casa del Brodo, Palermo

Costa Azzurra, Catania

Don Camillo, Siracusa

Il Filippino, Lipari

Il Ristorantino, Palermo

HOTELS   B & B Belvedere, Siracusa

Baia del Capitano, Mazzaforno

La Canna, Filicudi

Les Sables Noires, Vulcano

Massimo Plaza Hotel, Palermo

SIGHTS   Cattedrale, Palermo

Cefalù

Duomo, Monreale

Mt. Etna

Museo Eoliano, Lipari

San Cataldo, Palermo

Teatro Greco, Siracusa

Tempio Greco, Segesta

Updated by
Robin S.
Goldstein

SICILY HAS BECKONED SEAFARING WANDERERS since the trials of Odysseus were first sung in Homer's *Odyssey*—perhaps the world's first travel guide. Strategically poised between Europe and Africa, this mystical land of three corners and a fiery volcano once hosted two of the most enlightened capitals of the West—one Greek, in Siracusa, and one Arab-Norman, in Palermo. The island has been a melting pot of every great civilization on the Mediterranean: Greek and Roman; then Arab and Norman; and finally French, Spanish, and Italian. Today, the ancient ports of call peacefully fuse the remains of sackings past, with graceful Byzantine mosaics rubbing elbows with baroque flights of fancy, piled atop stalwart Greek columns. Amidst the buildings, blond-haired, blue-eyed Norman descendants walk alongside the sultry, dark-eyed Mediterraneans more commonly considered typical of the region. The island shows something of all the cultures that have touched it in its artistic heritage, a rich tapestry of art and architecture that includes massive Romanesque cathedrals, two of the best-preserved Greek temples in the world, Roman amphitheaters, and the delicate wrought-iron balconies of baroque palaces.

In the *Odyssey,* Sicily represented the unknown end of the world, yet the region eventually became a center of it under the Greeks and Normans, who recognized a paradise in its deep blue skies and temperate climate, its lush vegetation and rich marine life. Add to this paradise Sicily's unique cuisine—another harmony of elements, mingling Arab and Greek spices with Spanish and French influences using some of the world's tastiest seafood—along with the island's big, warm, fruity wines, and you can understand why those who arrived here were often reluctant to leave.

In modern times, the traditional graciousness and nobility of the Sicilian people have continued to exist side by side with the destructive influences of the Mafia under Sicily's semi-autonomous government, although increasingly organized law enforcement suggests that the Mafia's grip on the island is slowly being loosened. Alongside some of the most exquisite architecture in the world lie the shabby, half-built products of some of the worst speculation imaginable. In recent years, coastal Sicily, like much of the Mediterranean coast, has experienced a boom in tourism and a surge in condominium development. The chic boutiques purveying lace and linen in jet-set resort towns like Taormina give no clue of the lingering poverty in which their wares are produced. And yet, in Sicily's wind-swept heartland, a region that tourists have barely begun to explore, rolling vineyards, olive groves, and lovingly kept dirt roads leading to family farmhouses still tie Sicilians to land and tradition, forming a connected happiness that economic measures could not possibly describe.

It's not uncommon in small towns for visitors to receive invitations to a local's house for dinner. It doesn't matter if you don't speak Italian or speak only a little: they usually aren't offended if your pronunciation isn't perfect. One of the reasons for this, no doubt, is the fact that many Sicilians or their close relatives have themselves been strangers in foreign lands, and empathy goes a long way.

Exploring Sicily

The rewards of a rental car are great in Sicily: the island is about 180 km (112 mi) north to south and 270 km (168 mi) across, filled with places of interest—sometimes out of the way. With a car at your disposal, though, you can see both the interior and coastline without the headaches of the notoriously spotty public transportation. The Aeolian Islands are connected by hydrofoils and ferries.

About the Hotels & Restaurants

Sicily is Italy's largest region, with some of the most remote countryside. The good-quality hotels tend to be limited to the major cities and resorts of Palermo, Taormina, Siracusa, and Agrigento. There are some other superb establishments, such as converted villas with sea views and well-equipped modern hotels, but it's best not to expect to come across some enchanting oasis in the middle of nowhere. Recently there has been an explosion in the development of *agriturismo* lodgings (rural B&Bs), many of them quite basic, though others providing the same facilities found in hotels.

WHAT IT COSTS In euros					
	$$$$	**$$$**	**$$**	**$**	**¢**
RESTAURANTS	over €22	€17–€22	€12–€17	€7–€12	under €7
HOTELS	over €210	€160–€210	€110–€160	€60–€110	under €60

Restaurant prices are for a second course (secondo piatto). Hotel prices are for two people in a standard double room in high season, including tax and service.

Timing

Sicily comes into its own in spring, but you're not alone in knowing this. Taormina and Erice attract a flood of visitors around Easter, and any visit scheduled for this time should be backed up by solid advance bookings. Many sights, such as inland Segesta, are at their best in the clear spring light and are far enough off the beaten track to ensure a fairly hassle-free time. August is hot and crowded, and beaches are clogged with vacationers. Come in September or October, and you'll find acres of beach space. As with Easter, Christmas and New Year's draw visitors to the island, and reservations should always be made as early as possible. Other festivals, such as Agrigento's almond festival in February and the *Carnevale* in Acireale, can also mean a dearth of vacancies.

PALERMO

Once the intellectual capital of southern Europe, Palermo has always been at the crossroads of civilization. Favorably situated on a crescent-shape bay at the foot of Monte Pellegrino, it has attracted almost every people and culture touching the Mediterranean world. To Palermo's credit, it has absorbed these diverse cultures into a unique personality that is at once Arab and Christian, Byzantine and Roman, Norman and Italian. The city's heritage encompasses all of Sicily's varied ages, but its distinctive aspect is its Arab-Norman identity, an improbable marriage that, mixed in with Byzantine and Jewish elements, created some resplendent works of art. These are most notable in the churches, from small jewels such as San Giovanni degli Eremiti to larger-scale works such as the cathedral. No less noteworthy than the architecture is Palermo's chaotic vitality, on display at some of Italy's most vibrant outdoor markets, public squares, street bazaars, food vendors, and above all, a grand, discordant symphony of motorists, motor bikers, and pedestrians that triumphantly climaxes in the new town center each evening in Italy's most spectacular *passeggiata*.

Palermo was first colonized by Phoenician traders in the 6th century BC, but it was their descendants, the Carthaginians, who built the important fortress here that caught the covetous eye of the Romans. After the First Punic War, the Romans took control of the city in the 3rd century BC. Following several invasions by the Vandals, Sicily was settled by Arabs, who made the country an emirate and established Palermo as a showpiece cap-

Numbers in the text correspond to numbers in the margin and on the Sicily, Palermo, Agrigento, and Siracusa maps.

16

If you have 3 days

A three-day visit to the island shouldn't require a car if you base yourself in 🗺 **Palermo** ① – ⑪ ✈. In this hub of Norman Sicily, the highlights include the **Palazzo Reale** ① and the **Museo Archeologico Regionale** ⑩, as well as a handful of churches. Head out to **Monreale** ⑫ to admire the splendid cathedral, and compare it with the slightly earlier mosaic-laden monument at 🗺 **Cefalù** ⑮. Spend your last day exploring this seaside resort.

If you have 5 days

There are two distinct approaches to a five-day itinerary in Sicily, the first focusing on the island's western half, the second on the east. For the western itinerary, spend your first two nights in 🗺 **Palermo** ① – ⑪ ✈; then head west, dropping in on the half-finished temple of **Segesta** ⑰ and making 🗺 **Erice** ⑱ your next overnight stop. From Erice, follow the island's curve to the cliffside ruins of **Selinunte** ㉒ and leave much of the day for the Greek temple site at 🗺 **Agrigento** ㉓ – ㉙, where you can spend your fourth night. On your last day strike north on the S640 to meet the A19 autostrada near Caltanisetta, which will bring you back up to the Tyrrhenian coast. Get your shut-eye in 🗺 **Cefalù** ⑮ before turning westward back to Palermo. The eastern itinerary starts with one day in 🗺 **Palermo** ① – ⑪; on the second day, head southeast on the A19 through the island's interior, stopping for lunch at **Enna** ㊸ before reaching the Ionian Sea and turning north along the coast on the A18 to 🗺 **Taormina** ㊿②, where you'll spend your second night in the shadow of **Mt. Etna** ㊿. Spend your third day in town or at the volcano before heading south along the Ionian coast to experience 🗺 **Siracusa** ㉚ – ㊷, exploring the town's Greek and Roman amphitheaters and remarkable Duomo. On the fourth day, head southwest on the S115 around the corner of the island to 🗺 **Agrigento** ㉓ – ㉙. On your final day, head back to Palermo.

If you have 9 days

Begin by following the western five-day itinerary above, but at Agrigento make for lofty and mysterious **Enna** ㊸; then spend the afternoon viewing the mosaics of the Roman villa at Casale, near **Piazza Armerina** ㊹. If you have time, stop off to see the Museo della Ceramica at **Caltagirone** ㊺ before continuing on the S124 to 🗺 **Siracusa** ㉚ – ㊷ for a day's exploring and a night's rest. From here, see the cathedral in **Noto** ㊽, then head north up the coast and continue on to the baroque town of **Acireale** ㊿①, perhaps stopping for a fish lunch before landing for two nights at 🗺 **Taormina** ㊿②. From here, it's a brief drive or walk up to the village of **Castelmola** ㊿③, with its memorable views over Taormina and **Mt. Etna** ㊿. An excursion onto the volcano—either a drive round its lower slopes or an expedition to the top—will take the better part of a day. From Taormina, drive up the coast to **Messina** ㊿④, where the Museo Regionale will give you a last blast of Sicilian art before crossing—either from Messina or Milazzo, on the north coast—to the Aeolian archipelago, where 🗺 **Lipari** ㊿⑤ has the biggest selection of accommodations and a superb Museo Archeologico. From here, you can opt to explore the remaining six islands, or else return to the Sicilian mainland for your last night at 🗺 **Cefalù** ⑮.

ital that rivaled both Cordoba and Cairo in the splendor of its architecture. Nestled in the fertile Conca d'Oro (Golden Conch) plain, full of orange, lemon, and carob groves and enclosed by limestone hills, Palermo became a magical world of palaces and mosques, minarets and palm trees.

It was so attractive and sophisticated a city that the Norman ruler Roger de Hauteville (1031–1101) decided to conquer it and make it his capital (1072). The Norman occupation of Sicily resulted in the Golden Age of Palermo (1072–1194), a remarkable period of enlightenment and learning in which the arts flourished. The city of Palermo, which in the 11th century counted more than 300,000 inhabitants, became the center of the Norman court in all Europe and one of the most important ports of trade between East and West. Eventually the Normans were replaced by the Swabian ruler Frederick II (1194–1250), the Holy Roman Emperor, and incorporated into the Kingdom of the Two Sicilies. You will also see plenty of evidence in Palermo of the baroque art and architecture of the long Spanish rule. The Aragonese viceroys also brought the Spanish Inquisition to Palermo, which some historians believe helped foster the protective secret societies that evolved into today's Mafia.

Exploring Palermo

The Sicilian capital is a multilayered, vigorous metropolis; approach it with an open mind, and you'll find it an enriching city, with a strong historical profile. You're likely to encounter some frustrating instances of inefficiency and, depending on the season, stifling heat. If you have a car, park it in a garage as soon as you can, and don't take it out until you are ready to depart.

Palermo is easily explored on foot, though you may choose to spend a morning taking a bus tour to help you get oriented. The Quattro Canti, or Four Corners, is the hub that separates the four sections of the old city: La Kalsa (the old Arab section) to the southeast, Albergheria to the southwest, Capo to the northwest, and Vucciria to the northeast. Each of these is a tumult of activity during the day, though at night the narrow alleys empty out and are best avoided altogether in favor of the more animated avenues of the new city, north of Teatro Massimo. Sights you will want to see by day are scattered along three major streets: Corso Vittorio Emanuele, Via Maqueda, and Via Roma. The tourist information office in Piazza Castelnuovo will give you a map and a valuable handout that lists opening and closing times, which sometimes change with the seasons.

a good tour

Start at the **Palazzo Reale** ❶ ▶, at the far west end of Corso Vittorio Emanuele, to see the mosaics in the Cappella Palatina and the royal apartments. Walk down Via dei Benedettini, following the five pink domes of **San Giovanni degli Eremiti** ❷. Back east on the Corso stands Palermo's **Cattedrale** ❸, a cacophony of Arab, Norman, and Gothic influences. Head east, stopping for a glance at the baroque balconies in Piazza Bologni to your right, and continue until you reach the intersection of Corso Vittorio Emanuele and Via Maqueda, the **Quattro Canti** ❹. Just east off Quattro Canti is Piazza Pretoria, adjacent to which Piazza Bellini holds a trio of eminent churches: the baroque **Santa Caterina** ❺ and, up the stairs, **San Cataldo** ❻ and **La Martorana** ❼, which form a delightful Norman complex. Cross Via Roma into the Arab Kalsa neighborhood and follow Via Santa Anna to Piazza dei Vespri, turning left onto Vicolo dei Corriere to Piazza San Francesco d'Assisi, a great place to stop for a snack at the historic Focacceria San Francesco on Via Paternostro. Head across the piazza, down Via Merlo, and across to Via Alloro. Continuing east to **Palazzo Abatellis** ❽ and its Galleria Regionale, holding a fine collection of medieval and Renaissance art. If you like puppets, take Via Alloro east

Marionette Theater Almost every major city in Sicily has a theater giving performances of the world-famous Sicilian *pupi* (marionettes). Adults as well as children will enjoy the colorful shows, the most popular of which are in Palermo, Acireale, and Taormina. Stories center on heroes from the Norman fables, distressed damsels, and Saracen invaders. Even if you can't understand Italian, the action is fast and furious, so it's easy to figure out what's going on.

16

Ceramics, Crafts & Carts Sicily is one of the leaders in the Italian ceramics industry, with important factories at Caltagirone, in the interior, and Santo Stefano di Camastra, along the northern coast between Messina and Cefalù. Colorful Sicilian folk pottery can still be bought at bargain prices. Place mats, tablecloths, napkins, and clothing decorated with fine petit point are good buys in Cefalù, Taormina, and Erice, but they are nonetheless not cheap. Collectors have been combing Sicily for years for pieces of the colorful *carretti siciliani* (Sicilian carts). Before the automobile, these were the major form of transportation in Sicily, decorated in primary colors and in primitive styles.

and go northwest (left) on Via Butera to the **Museo delle Marionette** ⑨. Then, either take Bus 104 or 105 back along Corso Vittorio Emanuele to transfer to 101 heading north along Via Roma to the **Museo Archeologico Regionale** ⑩. Cut through Via Bara all'Olivella to Piazza Verdi and the **Teatro Massimo** ⑪, and finally, if it's between the hours of 6 PM and 9 PM, head north along Via Ruggero Settimo to take your place in the larger-than-life evening passeggiata and join the teeming mass of humanity in Piazza R. Settimo in front of the Teatro Politeama.

TIMING Allow the better part of a day for this tour, with lunch around the Quattro Canti.

What to See

★ ❸ **Cattedrale** (Cathedral). This church is a lesson in Palermitan eclecticism—originally Norman (1182), then Catalan Gothic (14th–15th centuries), then fitted out with a baroque and neoclassical interior (18th century). Its turrets, towers, dome, and arches come together in the kind of meeting of diverse elements that King Roger II (1095–1154), whose tomb is inside along with that of Frederick II, fostered during his reign. The back of the apse is gracefully decorated with interlacing Arab arches, inlaid with limestone and black volcanic tufa. ✉ *Corso Vittorio Emanuele, Capo* ☎ *091/334376* 🎫 *Crypt €1* ⏱ *Church Mon.–Sat. 7–7, Sun. 8–1:30 and 4–7; crypt Mon.–Sat. 9:30–5:30.*

off the beaten path

CONVENTO DEI CAPPUCCINI – Have you ever looked thousands of dead bodies in the eye, all in a row? The spookiest sight in all of Sicily, this 16th-century catacomb houses over 8,000 corpses of men, women, and young children, many mummified and preserved, hanging on the walls. Many of the fully clothed corpses wear priests' smocks (most of the dead were Capuchin monks). The Capuchins were founders and proprietors of the bizarre establishment from 1559 to 1880. It's memorable and not for the faint of heart; children (and adults) might be frightened or disturbed. ✉ *Piazza Cappuccini North of Palazzo Reale* ☎ *091/212633* 🎫 *€2* ⏱ *Daily 9–noon and 3–5.*

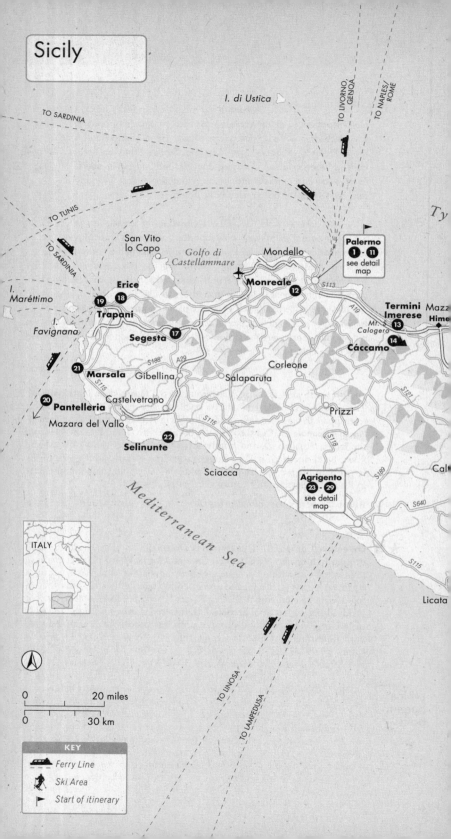

Sicily

I. di Ustica

TO SARDINIA

TO LIVORNO, GENOA

TO NAPLES/ ROME

TO TUNIS

TO SARDINIA

San Vito lo Capo

Golfo di Castellammare

Mondello

Ty

Erice
18

I. Maréttimo

Palermo
1 - **11**
see detail map

Monreale
12

S113

19
Trapani

A19

Termini Imerese
13

Mazz Hime

I. Favignana

Segesta
17

Mt. S Calogero

14

Cáccamo

S121

21

Marsala

Gibellina

S188   A29

Corleone

Salaparuta

S115

20
Pantelleria

Castelvetrano

Prizzi

S118

Mazara del Vallo

22
Selinunte

S115

Sciacca

Agrigento
23 - **29**
see detail map

S189

Cal

S640

Mediterranean Sea

ITALY

Licata

TO LINOSA

TO LAMPEDUSA

N

0   20 miles

0   30 km

KEY

Ferry Line

Ski Area

Start of itinerary

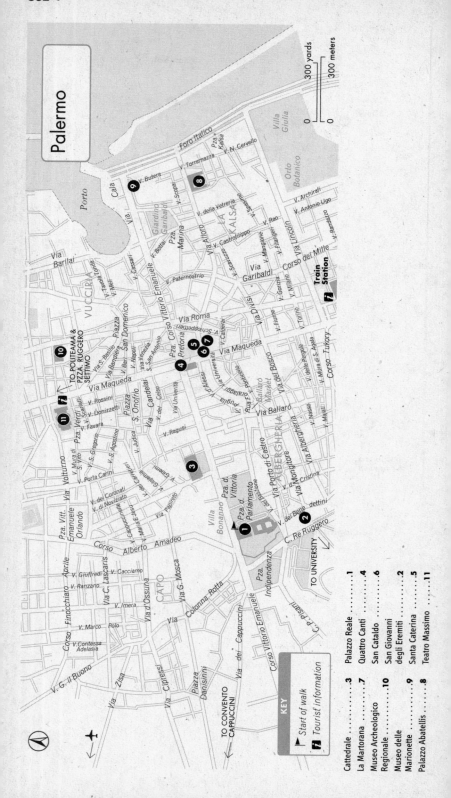

Palermo

Porto

Cala

Foro Italico

Villa Giulia

Orto Botanico

Train Station 🚉

KEY

▲ Start of walk
🚉 Tourist information

Cattedrale	**3**
La Martorana	**7**
Museo Archeologico Regionale	**10**
Museo delle Marionette	**9**
Palazzo Abatellis	**8**
Palazzo Reale	**1**
Quattro Canti	**4**
San Cataldo	**6**
San Giovanni degli Eremiti	**2**
Santa Caterina	**5**
Teatro Massimo	**11**

0   300 yards
0   300 meters

❼ La Martorana. Distinguished by an elegant Norman campanile, this church was erected in 1143 but had its interior altered considerably during the baroque period. High along the western wall, however, is some of the oldest and best preserved mosaic artwork of the Norman period. Near the entrance is an interesting mosaic of King Roger II being crowned by Christ. In it, Roger is dressed in a bejeweled Byzantine stole, reflecting the Norman court's penchant for all things Byzantine. Archangels along the ceiling wear the same stole, wrapped around their shoulders and arms. ✉ *Piazza Bellini 3, Kalsa* ☎ *091/6161692* ⊙ *Mon.–Sat. 8–1 and 3:30–5:30, Sun. 8:30–1.*

❿ Museo Archeologico Regionale (Regional Museum of Archaeology). Especially interesting pieces in this small but excellent collection are the examples of prehistoric cave drawings and a marvelously reconstructed Doric frieze from the Greek Temple at Selinunte. The frieze reveals the high level of artistic culture attained by the Greek colonists in Sicily some 2,500 years ago. ✉ *Piazza Olivella 24, Via Roma* ☎ *091/6116805* 🎫 *€4.15* ⊙ *Weekdays 8:30–6:30, weekends 8:30–1.*

❾ Museo delle Marionette (Museum of Marionettes). The traditional Sicilian *pupi*, with their glittering armor and fierce expressions, have become a symbol of Norman Sicily. Plots center on the chivalric legends of the troubadours, who, before the puppet theater, kept alive tales of Norman heroes in Sicily, such as Orlando Furioso and William the Bad (1120–66). There are weekly performances here. ✉ *Via Butera 1, Kalsa* ☎ *091/328060* ⊕ *www.museomarionettepalermo.it* 🎫 *€3* ⊙ *Weekdays 9–1 and 4–7* ⊙ *Closed Aug. 13–26.*

❽ Palazzo Abatellis. Housed in this late 15th-century Catalan Gothic palace with Renaissance elements is the **Galleria Regionale.** Among its treasures are an *Annunciation* (1474) by Sicily's prominent Renaissance master Antonello da Messina (1430–79) and an arresting fresco by an unknown painter, titled *The Triumph of Death*, a macabre depiction of the plague years. ✉ *Via Alloro 4, Kalsa* ☎ *091/6164317* 🎫 *€4.15* ⊙ *Mon., Wed., Fri., and Sat. 9–1:30, Tues. and Thurs. 9–1:30 and 3–7:30, Sun. 9–1.*

❶ Palazzo Reale (Royal Palace). This historic palace, also called Palazzo dei Normanni (Norman Palace), was for centuries the seat of Sicily's semi-autonomous rulers. Because it now houses the Sicilian Parliament, little is viewable by the public. However, the **Cappella Palatina** (Palatine Chapel) remains open, built by Roger II in 1132 and a dazzling example of the unique harmony of artistic elements produced under the Normans. Here the skill of French and Sicilian masons was brought to bear on the decorative purity of Arab ornamentation and the splendor of 11th-century Greek Byzantine mosaics. The interior is covered with glittering mosaics and capped by a splendid 10th-century Arab honeycomb stalactite wooden ceiling. Biblical stories blend happily with scenes of Arab life—look for one showing a picnic in a harem—and Norman court pageantry.

The building is an interesting mesh of abutting 10th-century Norman and 17th-century Spanish structures. Upstairs are the royal apartments, including the **Sala di Re Ruggero** (King Roger's Hall), decorated with medieval murals of hunting scenes—an earlier (1120) secular counterpoint to the religious themes seen elsewhere. Tour guides escort you around these halls, which once hosted one of the most splendid courts in Europe. French, Latin, and Arabic were spoken here, and Arab astronomers and poets exchanged ideas with Latin and Greek scholars in one of the most interesting marriages of culture in the Western world. ✉ *Piazza*

Indipendenza, Albergheria ☎ 091/7054317 palace; 091/7054732 chapel ⊠ Free ☉ Chapel weekdays 9–11:45 and 3–4:45, Sat. 9–11:45, Sun. 9–9:45 and 11:15–12:45. Apartments temporarily closed, but may be visited by appointment.

Piazza Pretoria. The square's centerpiece, a lavishly decorated fountain originally intended for a Florentine villa, is covered by scaffolding due to extensive renovation (you can see the sculptures by peeking in through the plastic windows). Its abundance of nude figures so shocked some Palermitans when it was unveiled in 1575 that it got the nickname "Fountain of Shame." It's even more of a sight when illuminated at night.

❹ Quattro Canti. The Four Corners is the intersection of Corso Vittorio Emanuele and Via Maqueda. Four rather traffic-blackened baroque palaces from the Spanish rule meet at concave corners, each with its own fountain and representations of a Spanish ruler, patron saint, and one of the four seasons.

★ ❻ San Cataldo. Three orange-red domes mark this church, built in 1154. Its spare but intense stone interior, punctuated by antique Greek columns, retains much of its original medieval simplicity. At press time, the interior could not be visited. ⊠ *Piazza Bellini 3, Albergheria ☉ Interior closed.*

❷ San Giovanni degli Eremiti. Distinguished by its five pink domes, this 12th-century church was built by the Normans on the site of an earlier mosque—one of 200 that once stood in Palermo. The emirs ruled Palermo for almost two centuries and brought to it their passion for lush gardens and fountains. One is reminded of this while sitting in San Giovanni's delightful cloister of twin half-columns, surrounded by palm trees, jasmine, oleander, and citrus trees. ⊠ *Via dei Benedettini, Albergheria ☎ 091/6515019 ⊠ €4.15 ☉ Mon.–Sat. 9–7, Sun. 9–1.*

❺ Santa Caterina. The walls of this splendid baroque church (1596) in Piazza Bellini are covered with decorative 17th-century inlays of precious marble. ⊠ *Piazza Bellini, Kalsa ☎ 091/6162488 ☉ Open by appointment for groups only.*

⓫ Teatro Massimo. Construction of this formidable neoclassic theater was started in 1875 by Giovanni Battista Basile and completed by his son, Ernesto, in 1897. A fire in 1974 rendered the theater inoperable, but it reopened with great fanfare in 1997, and its interior is now as glorious as ever. Claimed to be Italy's largest, the theater was featured in scenes in *The Godfather Part III.* Visits are by 25-minute guided tour only. ⊠ *Piazza Verdi 9, at the top of Via Maqueda ☎ 091/6090831 ⊕ www. teatromassimo.it ⊠ €3 ☉ Tues.–Sat. 10–4, except during rehearsals.*

Vucciria outdoor market. "Vucciria," in dialect, means "voices" or "hubbub," and it's easy to see why. In the maze of side streets around Piazza San Domenico, hawkers everywhere deliver their unceasing chants from behind stands brimming with mounds of olives, blood oranges, wild fennel, and long-stemmed artichokes. One of them goes at the trunk of a swordfish with a cleaver, while across the way another holds up a giant squid or dangles an octopus. It may be Palermo, but this is really the Casbah. Morning is the best time to see the market in full swing. If you're hungry, look for calzoni (deep-fried meat- or cheese-filled pockets of dough) or *panelle* (chickpea-flour fritters). ⊠ *Around Piazza San Domenico, Vucciria ☉ Daily dawn–dusk.*

Where to Stay & Eat

★ $$–$$$ ✕ **Il Ristorantino.** A few miles into suburban Palermo—an easy taxi ride from the center—Pippo Anastasio, one of the true personalities of the

Sicilian cooking, has created one of the most modern restaurants in all of Sicily. Here, pesce spada reaches its loftiest heights, served simply marinated with olive oil, lemon, herb butter, and toast; meanwhile, Pippo's flights of fancy include *astice* (lobster) tortellini with cherry tomatoes, bottarga, and hot pepper. Dark wood contrasts with recessed lighting and stylized wall panels to create a design fusion that echoes the creativity of the menu. ⊠ *Piazzale Alcide De Gasperi 19, Resuttana* ☎ *091/512861* ▭ *AE, DC, MC, V* ☉ *Closed Mon., Jan. 1–9, and Aug.*

$$–$$$ ✕ **Osteria dei Vespri.** This temple to modern Sicilian cuisine is foodie paradise in the *centro storico*. Local fish is simply presented in dishes like tartare of bluefish with vinaigrette, while culinary skill is showcased in *casareccia* (homemade pasta) with tuna ragù. The wine list is one of the best in Palermo; try Planeta's Chardonnay if available. ⊠ *Piazza Croce dei Vespri 6, Kalsa* ☎ *091/6171631* ▭ *AE, DC, MC, V* ☉ *Closed Sun., Nov., and 2 wks in Aug.*

$$ ✕ **Capricci di Sicilia.** It's said that this spot, in the heart of Palermo next to the Teatro Politeama, is the best place in town for cassata siciliana. The atmosphere is a bit impersonal, but you'll find only typical Sicilian specialties here, such as tuna with garlic and mint, sardine *poplette* (minced sardine balls), or spaghetti with a ragù of sausage and fresh ricotta. ⊠ *Via Pignatelli 6, Piazza Luigi Sturzo, Vucciria* ☎ *091/327777* ▭ *AE, DC, MC, V.*

$$ ✕ **Gusto Divino.** Vaulted stone archways, exposed brick, and rows of fine bottles of Sicilian wine set the scene for nouveau Sicilian cuisine served up to a chic business and university crowd. A well-thought-out list of Sicilian and Italian wines accompanies an ever-changing menu with novelties like *linguine con bottarga di tonno* (linguine with cured tuna roe and lemon zest). Pistachio features prominently in dishes. For dessert, don't miss one of Palermo's best versions of the classic *torta sette veli* (seven-layer chocolate cake), made with seven kinds of chocolate. ⊠ *Corso Pisani 30, Alberghiera* ☎ *091/6457001* ▭ *AE, DC, MC, V* ☉ *Closed Sun.*

$$ ✕ **Il Mulinazzo.** Palermitans drive 45 minutes to savor modern and startling combinations in chef Nino Graziano's traditional country house, probably Sicily's best restaurant. Fava bean puree ("macco"), a staple of the rural poor, is playfully paired with scampi, and finished with ricotta, speck, peppercorns, and fried basil leaf. A delicate filet of pork is encrusted with pistachios and served with chocolate sauce, rice fritters, cinnamon applesauce, and swirls of raspberry. The wine list is excellent, and prices are shockingly reasonable—even for the spectacular tasting menu. Coming from Palermo, the restaurant is on the right side of SS121, after 17 km (11 mi). It's after the Villafrati exit and a car dealership; its sign is tiny and easy to miss. ⊠ *SS 121, Località Bolognetta Nord, Villafrati* ☎ *091/8724870* ▭ *AE, DC, MC, V* ☉ *Closed 15 days in Jan., 15 days in July, and Mon. No dinner Sun.*

FodorśChoice ★

$–$$ ✕ **Strascinu.** The specialty in this informal and busy restaurant, on the outskirts of the city center, is pasta *con le sarde* (with sardines), the region's ubiquitous Arab-Sicilian dish. Amphoras, Sicilian ceramics, and even a miniature, electrically operated puppet theater enliven the rustic decor, and there's a large garden with gazebos. ⊠ *Viale Regione Siciliana 2286, Circumvallazione* ☎ *091/401292* ▭ *AE, DC, MC, V* ☉ *Closed 2 wks in mid-Aug.*

★ **$** ✕ **Casa del Brodo.** On the edge of the Vucciria and dating back to 1890, this restaurant—its two small rooms usually crowded with a mix of tourists and locals—is one of Palermo's oldest. You can't go wrong with classics like pasta *alle sarde* or the *carni bollite* (boiled meats); the risotto with mushrooms or asparagus is also a standout. ⊠ *Corso Vittorio*

ON THE MENU

SICILIAN CUISINE IS ONE of the oldest in existence, going back to Siracusan cooking competitions in 600 BC. The Sicilians even have a reasonable claim to the invention of pasta; maccheroni (long, thin pasta tubes) may well be today's purest survivor of the original. Today's cuisine represents Sicily's unique cultural mix, imaginatively combining fish, fruits, vegetables, and nuts with Italian pastas and Arab and North African ingredients such as couscous. Sweet and sour tastes are deftly mingled, and cooks have distinctive touches, such that caponata (an antipasto of eggplant, capers, olives, and, in eastern Sicily, peppers) and pasta con le sarde (an emblematic dish that goes back to the Saracen conquerors, with fresh sardines, olive oil, raisins, pine nuts, and wild fennel) are different at every restaurant.

In Sicily, naturally, you'll enjoy the freshest seafood in all of Italy. Grilled tonno (tuna) and triglie (red mullet) are reliable coastal staples. King, however, is pesce spada (swordfish), best enjoyed marinated (marinato), smoked (affumicato), or as the traditional involtini di pesce spada (swordfish roulades). Delicate ricci (sea urchins), are a specialty of Mondello, near Palermo, and spaghetti alla Norma, with a sauce of tomato, fried eggplant, ricotta, and basil, call Catania home. Also not to be missed are uniformly excellent acciughe (anchovies); unique, salty bottarga (flakes of cured tuna roe); and the arancino, Sicily's most typical snack food, a deep-fried, orange-size ball of creamy rice, sometimes filled with ragù (a meat and tomato stew). Meanwhile, the Sicilian bitter almond (mandorla), prize crop of the Valley of the Temples, is highlighted in everything from the gentle risotto alle mandorle to incomparable almond granita, an absolute must in summer.

Desserts from Sicily are famous, none more than the wonderful cannoli, whose delicate pastry shell and just-sweet-enough ricotta barely resemble their foreign impostors. The traditional Easter cake is the cassata siciliana, a rich sponge cake with candied fruit and marzipan. From behind bakery windows and glass cases beam tiny marzipan sweets, bizarrely fashioned into brightly colored apples, cherries, hamburgers, and even prosciutto. Do as the locals do and dip your summer morning brioche—the best in Italy—into a cup of brilliantly refreshing coffee granita; the world's first ice cream is said to have been made by the Romans from the snow on the slopes of Mount Etna. The dessert wine Marsala is Sicily's most famous; long neglected, Sicilian reds and whites are some of the most up-and-coming in the wine world, but still the bargains of Italy. The earthy nero d'avola grape bolsters many of Sicily's traditionally sunny, expansive reds, but lately it's often cut with Cabernet or Merlot. Meanwhile, the islands of Lipari and Pantelleria offer sweet, golden dessert wines, Malvasia and Passito. The Frappato grape makes for fresh, young wines full of strawberry flavors. It's hard to go wrong with anything from Planeta, a 1995 upstart whose daring experimentation with international grapes like Merlot and Syrah has quickly made it the darling of the Italian wine industry. Planeta's Chardonnay is world-class, as is its Cabernet ("Burdese"). Nor can you go wrong with wines from Tasca d'Almerita (try the Rosso del Conte), Cos, Abbazia Sant'Anastasia (whose Litra is truly spectacular) or Donnafugata (Tancredi and the Ben Ryè Passito di Pantelleria are standouts). Marsala's storied Baglio Hopps makes an excellent red, Incantari. Best of all, it's difficult to spend more than 20 euros on any Sicilian bottle at a wine store.

Emanuele 175, Vucciria ☎ 091/321655 ▭ AE, DC, MC, V ⊘ Closed Tues. Oct.–Easter.

★ ¢ ✕ **Antica Focacceria San Francesco.** This neighborhood bakery with turn-of-the-20th-century wooden cabinets and cast-iron ovens is an institution. It serves the snacks that locals love—and from which you can make an inexpensive meal. The big pan on the counter holds the delicious regional specialty *pani cu' la meusa* (boiled, sliced calf's spleen with Parmesan-like cacciocavallo cheese and salt). The squeamish can opt for the *panelle* (potato croquettes) instead. Sit at marble-topped tables or take to food to-go. ✉ *Via Paternostro 58, Kalsa* ☎ 091/320264 ⌔ *Reservations not accepted* ▭ *No credit cards* ⊘ *Closed Tues.*

¢ ✕ **Pani Ca Meusa.** This supremely local institution right on Palermo's old fishing port has had only one item on the menu—and one manager-cum-sandwichmaker—for over 50 years. Calf's spleen sandwich, the joint's namesake, is sprinkled with a bit of salt and some lemon and served with or without cheese to a buzzing crowd of Palermo's battle-wearied elders. In our book, it beats the Focacceria San Francesco for the title of best in town. ✉ *Via Cala 62, Kalsa* ☎ *No phone* ⌔ *Reservations not accepted* ▭ *No credit cards* ⊘ *Closed Sun. and Mon. and unpredictable other days.*

$$$$ ▦ **Villa Igiea.** A short taxi ride through some rough-looking districts of Palermo takes you to this historic oasis of luxury and comfort in its own tropical garden at the edge of the bay. A meander through the grounds reveals such relics as an ancient Greek temple at the water's edge. Large rooms are furnished individually, the nicest with an Italian art nouveau flavor. Spacious lobbies and public rooms unfold onto a terrace and restaurant. There's hourly shuttle service to the city center. ✉ *Salita Belmonte 43, Acquasanta, 3 km (2 mi) north of Palermo, 90142* ☎ *091/6312111* 🖷 *091/547654* ⊕ *www.villaigiea.thi.it* ⇌ *101 rooms, 12 suites* ⌔ *Restaurant, minibars, tennis court, pool, gym, bar, free parking* ▭ *AE, DC, MC, V.*

$$$ ▦ **Grand Hotel et des Palmes.** This grande dame's fabled charm glows once more. The public rooms suggest the elegant life of Palermo society before World War I, when it was marked by tea dances and balls. Wagner finished writing the opera *Parsifal* during a stay here. Guest rooms are filled with antiques and heavy fabrics. What's new is an American-style cocktail bar as well as a couple of banquet halls. ✉ *Via Roma 398, Vucciria, 90139* ☎ *091/6028111* 🖷 *091/331545* ⊕ *www.despalmes. thi.it* ⇌ *183 rooms, 6 suites* ⌔ *Restaurant, minibars, bar, parking (fee)* ▭ *AE, DC, MC, V.*

$$$ ▦ **Hotel Principe di Villafranca.** Not far from Palermo's glitzy shopping district, this hotel creates the feel of a luxurious private home with fine Sicilian antiques, imperial striped silks, creamy marble floors, and vaulted ceilings. It's easy to get comfortable in the understated surroundings: relax in the library with an aperitif or savor an authentic meal in the rustic adjoining Ristorante Firriato, which drizzles its dishes with a sublime, homemade balsamic vinegar. Rooms are elegant, with fine linens and more antiques. Ask for a room on the street side; back rooms can actually be noisier. ✉ *Via G. Turrisi Colonna 4, Libertà, 90141* ☎ *091/6118523* 🖷 *091/588705* ⊕ *www.principedivillafranca.it* ⇌ *30 rooms, 4 suites* ⌔ *Restaurant, café, gym, library, meeting room, free parking* ▭ *AE, DC, MC, V.*

★ $$$ ▦ **Massimo Plaza Hotel.** This hotel has one of Palermo's best locations—right opposite the renovated Teatro Massimo. It is small and select, its few rooms spacious, comfortably furnished, and well insulated from the noise on Via Maqueda. Service is personal and polite. ✉ *Via Maqueda 437, Vucciria, 90133* ☎ *091/325657* 🖷 *091/325711* ⊕ *www. massimoplazahotel.com* ⇌ *15 rooms* ⌔ *Minibars, bar, parking (fee)* ▭ *AE, DC, MC, V.*

$$–$$$ 🏨 **Mondello Palace.** This is the leading hotel at the Mondello resort, making the best use of its location near the beach just north of Palermo. The private beach has cabins and changing rooms for the use of hotel guests. The rooms are large, with luxury baths, and most have balconies. In summer this is indisputably the place to be. ⊠ *Viale Principe di Scalea, 90139, Mondello Lido* 🕿 *091/450001* 🖷 *091/450657* 🛏 *83 rooms, 9 suites* ♻ *Restaurant, minibars, pool, gym, beach, windsurfing, boating, bar, free parking, pets allowed* ▤ *AE, DC, MC, V.*

$ 🏨 **Hotel Moderno.** This third-floor hotel is a slice of patient old Palermo, right down to the 1930s technology at the reception desk. A slightly shabby, mirrored reception area and bar give way to simple but clean and comfortable rooms, some with balconies overlooking Via Roma. The location couldn't be better. Singles are a particularly good deal, at close to half the double room rate. ⊠ *Via Roma 276, corner of Via Napoli, Vucciria, 90139* 🕿 *091/588683* 🖷 *091/588260* 🛏 *38 rooms* ♻ *Bar, parking (fee).* ▤ *AE, DC, MC, V.*

$ 🏨 **Principe di Belmonte.** This is a tasteful choice among Palermo's cheaper hotels. It's family-run, friendly, and central—a convenient walk both from the port and Piazza Castelnuovo—but is on a relatively quiet street. Rooms are smallish. Advance reservations are advised. ⊠ *Via Principe di Belmonte 25, Libertà, 90139* 🕿 *091/331065* 🖷 *091/6113424* 🛏 *17 rooms, 14 with bath* ♻ *Bar* ▤ *AE, DC, MC, V.*

Nightlife & the Arts

The Arts

CONCERTS & OPERA **Teatro Massimo** (⊠ Piazza Verdi, at the top of Via Maqueda, Vucciria 🕿 091/6053111 ⊕ www.teatromassimo.it), modeled after the Pantheon in Rome, is truly larger than life—it's the biggest theater in Italy. Concerts and operas are presented throughout the year. Live out your Godfather fantasies; an opera at the Massimo is an unforgettable Sicilian experience. The shamelessly grandiose **Teatro Politeama Garibaldi** (⊠ Piazza Ruggero Settimo, Libertà 🕿 091/6053315) stages a winter season of opera and orchestral works.

FESTIVALS The street fair **Festa di Santa Rosalia** is held July 9–15 in honor of the city's patron saint. Fireworks light up the evenings. **Epiphany** (January 6) is celebrated with Byzantine rites and a procession of townspeople in local costume through the streets of Piana degli Albanesi, 24 km (15 mi) south of Palermo. The village is named for the Albanian immigrants who first settled there, bringing with them the Byzantine Catholic rites.

PUPPET SHOWS Children and adults alike will enjoy Palermo's tradition of puppet theater. Street artists often perform outside the Teatro Massimo in summer. Contact the **Opera dei Pupi, Mimmo Cuticchio** (⊠ Via Bara all'Olivella 52, Kalsa 🕿 091/323400) to see what's playing, or check with the tourist office for details.

Nightlife

Each night between 6 and 9 PM, all of Palermo's youth gather to shop, socialize, flirt, and plan the evening's affairs in an epic passeggiata along Via Ruggero Settimo (a northern extension of Via Maqueda) and filling Piazza Ruggero Settimo in front of Teatro Politeama. Some trendy bars also line Via Principe del Belmonte, intersecting with Via Roma and Via Ruggero Settimo.

BARS One of the most fascinating places in town to drink or socialize is **Kursaal Kalhesa** (⊠ Foro Umberto I 21, Kalsa 🕿 091/6161282), down by the port and the Porta Felice. A bursting, eclectic crowd of Palermitan youth take in lively jazz, coffee, and drinks inside an ancient city wall with spectacular 100-ft ceilings and an idyllic courtyard—it's truly representative of the New Palermo. Excellent, if pricey, Sicilian food is served in the adjacent restaurant. The best wine bar (and wineshop) in town is **Enoteca Picone** (✉ Via Marconi 36, Libertà ☎ 091/331300 ☾ Closed Mon.), with a fantastic selection of Sicilian and national wines by the glass and bottle.

A cultural center, wine bar, cafè, language school, and historic-tour operator—what isn't the cutting-edge, intellectual **Parco Letterario Giuseppe Tomasi di Lampedusa** (✉ Vicolo della Neve all'Alloro 25, near the Piazza Marina, Kalsa ☎ 091/6160796 ⊕ www.parcotomasi.it)? Down by the port in the deep heart of the Kalsa, the center, open Tuesday–Sunday 9 AM–1 AM, offers courses in Italian for foreigners, excellent local wines, a student social scene, and art shows; its little library (and just about everything else) focuses not just on Palermitan history but on the life and times of the center's namesake, Lampedusa, author of the canonical *Il Gattopardo* (The Leopard).

NIGHTCLUBS Most nightclubs and discotheques are scattered around the northern, newer end of town. In summer, the nightlife scene shifts to **Mondello**, Palermo's seaside satellite on the other side of Monte Pellegrino. Check out the hip **Mikalsa** (✉ Via Torremuzza 27, Kalsa ☎ 3473023307), a coolly lit nightspot with Sicily's best selection of Belgian beers. **Kandisky** (✉ Discesa Tonnara 4 Arenella suburbs ☎ 091/6375611) is a disco-bar-restaurant strikingly situated in a restored tuna factory.

The Outdoors

At the sandy beach of Mondello, sailing and windsurfing facilities and instruction are available through **Albaria** (✉ Viale Regina Elena 89/a ☎ 091/453595).

Sicily's most important center of scuba diving and other water sports is on the island of **Ustica**, north of Palermo. Its rugged coast is dotted with grottoes that are washed by crystal-clear waters and filled with an incredible variety of interesting marine life. In July, Ustica hosts the International Meeting of Marine Fishing, which attracts sportsmen as well as marine biologists from all over the world.

Shopping

Most shops are open 9–1 and 4 or 4:30–7:30 or 8 and closed Sunday; in addition, most food shops close Wednesday afternoon, while other shops normally close Monday morning. One main shopping area is around the **Politeama** and **Libertà**. A second nerve center for shoppers are the two parallel streets connecting modern Palermo with the train station, **Via Roma** and **Via Maqueda**, where boutiques and shoe shops become increasingly upmarket as you move from the **Quattro Fontane** past Teatro Massimo to **Via Ruggero Settimo.**

North of Piazza Castelnuovo, **Via della Libertà** and the streets around it represent the luxury end of the scale, with some of Palermo's best-known stores. The area behind the Cattedrale, in the midst of the flea market on Via Papireto and spreading to the next street, Corso Amedeo, is the antiques-store neighborhood.

For men's shirts and suits, try the elegant but friendly **Barbisio** (✉ Corso Vitt. Emanuele 284–298, half a block from the Quattro Canti ☎ 091/329992).At **Pasticceria Alba** (✉ Piazza Don Bosco 7/c, Libertà ☎ 091/309016 ☾ Closed Mon.) you'll find all the favorite Sicilian pastries, including the famous *cassata siciliana* (ice cream with sponge cake, candied fruit, and marzipan), cannoli, and *frutta di Martorana* (fruits and other shapes made out of almond paste), as well as original creations. It's at the top of Via della Libertà, near the entrance to La Favorita Park.

Markets

Looking to pick up antique marionettes of the Norman cavaliers or brilliantly colored pieces from the carretti siciliani? Head to the **mercato** (flea market), held daily behind Palermo's Cattedrale, on Via Papireto. Don't miss the raucous outdoor market around Vucciria's **Piazza San Domenico,** every day but Sunday. Between Via Roma and Via Maqueda, **Via Bandiera** is a riot of *bancherelle*—market stalls selling everything from clothes to imitation designer handbags.

MONREALE & THE TYRRHENIAN COAST

Sicily's northern shore, the Tyrrhenian coast, is mostly a succession of small holiday towns interspersed with stretches of sand. It's often difficult to find a calm spot here among the thousands of other tourists and locals in high summer, though the scene quiets down considerably after August. The biggest attraction is the old town of Cefalù, with one of Sicily's most remarkable medieval cathedrals, encrusted with mosaics. The coast on either side is dotted with ancient archaeological remains and Arab-Norman buildings. You need only venture a couple of miles south of Cefalù to explore the Monti Madonie national park, which contains the highest peak in Sicily after Mount Etna—Pizzo Carbonara at 6,500 ft. Piano della Battaglia has a fully equipped ski resort with lifts. The area has a very un-Sicilian aspect, with Swiss-type chalets, hiking paths, and even alpine churches.

From Palermo, it's an easy drive or bus ride to Monreale, whose cathedral provides an instructive comparison to the one at Cefalù, built at around the same time. The glittering mosaics here are among the finest in the whole Mediterranean. Fans of military architecture and great views should make the short drive inland to the castle of Cáccamo, site of a formidable Norman castle midway between Palermo and Cefalù.

Monreale

10 km (6 mi) southwest of Palermo.

★ Monreale's splendid **Duomo** is lavishly executed with mosaics depicting events from the Old and New Testaments. After the Norman conquest of Sicily, the new princes showcased their ambitions through monumental building projects. William II (1154–89) built the church complex with a cloister and palace between 1174 and 1185, employing Byzantine craftsmen. The result was a glorious fusion of Eastern and Western influences, widely regarded as the finest example of Norman architecture in Sicily.

The major attraction is the 68,220 square ft of glittering gold mosaics decorating the cathedral interior. Christ Pantocrator dominates the apse area; the nave contains narratives of Creation; and scenes from the life of Christ adorn the walls of the aisles and the transept. The painted wooden ceiling dates from 1816 to 1837. A small pair of binoculars will make it easier to read the Latin inscriptions. The roof commands a great view (a reward for climbing 172 stairs).

Bonnano Pisano's **bronze doors,** completed in 1186, depict 42 biblical scenes and are considered among the most important of medieval artifacts. Barisano da Trani's 42 panels on the north door, dating from 1179, present saints and evangelists. ✉ *Piazza del Duomo* ☎ *091/6404413* ✒ *Free* ☾ *Daily 8–6.*

The lovely **cloister** of the abbey adjacent to the Duomo was built at the same time as the church but enlarged in the 14th century. The beautiful enclosure is surrounded by 216 double columns, every other one decorated in a unique glass mosaic pattern. Note the intricate carvings on the bases and the capitals of the columns. Afterward, don't forget to walk behind the cloister to the **belvedere**, with stunning panoramic views over the Conca d'Oro (Golden Conch) valley toward Palermo. ✉ *Piazza del Duomo* ☎ *091/6404403* 💶 *€4.15* ⊙ *Mon.–Sat. 9–6:30, Sun. 9–1.*

Where to Eat

$–$$ ✕ **La Botte.** It's worth the short drive or inexpensive taxi fare from Monreale to reach this restaurant, a good value for well-prepared local specialties. Dine alfresco on daily specials such as *pennette agli odori* (little penne with tomato, garlic, parsley, basil, mint, and oregano) or regular favorites including *involtini* (meat or fish roulades). Local wines are a good accompaniment. ✉ *Contrada Lenzitti 20, S186* ☎ *091/414051* 🟰 *AE, DC, MC, V* ⊙ *Closed Mon. and June 20–Sept. 20. No dinner Sun.*

Termini Imerese

⑬ *40 km (25 mi) east of Palermo.*

This port town takes its name from the Greeks who founded it (refugees from nearby Himera), and the natural spa baths, or *terme,* that helped to make it an important Roman city. Plutarch, among others, sung its praises. Termini's upper town, occupying a high promontory above the port, holds the few survivals from the town's classical period—the ruins of an amphitheater and the foundations of a public building, enveloped among the trees of the public gardens. More compelling are the outstanding vistas seen from the belvedere.

> **off the beaten path**

HIMERA – From Termini Imerese, drive or take a taxi to the site of ancient Himera, 15 km (8 mi) east along the coast, site of the original 7th-century BC Chalcidinian (Greek) settlement. All that's left of the city that once stood here is the massive **Tempio della Vittoria** erected to commemorate the Greek victory over a huge Carthaginian army in 480 BC and built by the Carthaginian prisoners themselves. The victory marked the beginning of Greek ascendancy in Sicily, though for Himera the celebrations were short lived: Hamilcar's nephew, Hannibal, wreaked his revenge in 409 BC by razing the city to the ground, forcing the surviving citizens west to what is now Termini Imerese. Little remains of the original Doric monument, but it's still redolent of ancient glory. ✉ *Buonfornello* ☎ *091/8140128* 💶 *€2* ⊙ *Mon.–Sat. 9–5:30, Sun. 9–2; ticket office closes 1 hr earlier.*

Where to Stay

$$ 🏨 **Grand Hotel delle Terme.** Dominating Termini's lower town, this hotel was built at the end of the 19th century over the spring from which Termini's famous spa waters gush forth. You can take full advantage of the curative waters in the classically styled thermal complex in the basement, where treatments include massage and mud therapy. Public rooms are sumptuously furnished, but guest rooms tend to be on the small side. A rooftop pool provides a pleasant lounging area even if you aren't tempted to take a dip. ✉ *Piazza delle Terme, 90018* ☎ *091/8113557* 🖷 *091/8113107* ⊕ *http://web.tin.it/siciliatraveland/terme.htm* 🛏 *56 rooms, 11 suites* 🍴 *Restaurant, minibars, pool, health club, hair salon, massage, spa, bar, dance club* 🟰 *AE, DC, MC, V.*

Cáccamo

⓮ *12 km (8 mi) south of Termini Imerese, 52 km (32 mi) southeast of Palermo.*

The quiet village of Cáccamo rises on an inland spur that the Normans could not resist fortifying, and the mighty **Castello** that they raised here in the 12th century still stands, superbly restored, its sheer white walls a landmark from miles around. It's one of Sicily's largest and most impressive bastions, bristling with turrets and crenellations, and among its 130 rooms is the **Sala della Congiura**, where a baron's plot against William I was hatched in 1160. If the castle's entrance gate isn't open, ring at Corso Umberto 6 (the door nearest the war memorial opposite the main entrance). ✉ *Corso Umberto* ☎ *091/8103248* ✍ *Free, donation requested* ☉ *Daily 9:30–12:30 and 3–6.*

Where to Eat

¢ ✕ **A Castellana.** For a meal by the castle, this medieval-looking pizzeria-restaurant is ideal. Have a simple pizza or pasta con le sarde. ✉ *Piazza Monumento 4* ☎ *091/8148667* ═ *AE, DC, MC, V* ☉ *Closed Mon.*

Cefalù

★ **⓯** *38 km (24 mi) northeast of Termini Imerese, 70 km (42 mi) east of Palermo.*

Cefalù is a classically appealing Sicilian old town built on a spur jutting out into the sea. It's dominated by a massive 12th-century Romanesque **Duomo**, one of the finest Norman cathedrals in Italy. Ruggero II began it in 1131 as an offering of thanks for having been saved here from a shipwreck. Its mosaics rival those of Monreale; while Monreale's Byzantine Pantocratic Christ figure is an austere and powerful image, emphasizing Christ's divinity, the Cefalù Christ is softer, more compassionate, and more human. The traffic going in and out of Cefalù town can be heavy in summer; you may want to take the 50-minute train ride from Palermo instead of driving. At the Duomo you must be suitably attired—no shorts or beachwear are permitted. ✉ *Piazza Duomo* ☎ *0921/421293* ☉ *Daily 8–noon and 3:30–6:30.*

> **off the beaten path**

REGIONAL PARK OF THE MADONIE – This park is a great place to ski or hike; **Piano Battaglia** provides the best base. For maps and more information contact the **Club Alpino Italiano Rifugio Marini** (☎ 0921/649994) or the office of the **Parco Regionale** (✉ Corso Pietro Agliata 16, Petralia Sottana ☎ 0921/684011).

Where to Stay & Eat

$–$$$ ✕ **Gabbiano.** "Seagull" is an appropriate name for a beach-side seafood restaurant with a nautical theme. House specialties are *involtini di pesce spada* (swordfish roulades) and spaghetti marinara. ✉ *Via Lungomare Giardina 17* ☎ *0921/421495* ═ *AE, DC, MC, V* ☉ *Closed mid-Dec.–Jan. and Wed. mid-Sept.–June.*

$–$$ ✕ **La Brace.** This bistro-style restaurant near the cathedral has been serving upscale dishes in a lively setting since 1977. Graceful ceiling vaults and rustic walls give it an informal air. A Dutchman, Dietmar Beckers, and an Indonesian, Thea de Haan, pride themselves on creatively reworking local ingredients. Look for dishes like *vitello in salsa agrodolce al mango ed uva sultanina* (veal cutlet in mango sweet-and-sour sauce with grapes), and save room for one of the parfaits. Prices are quite good given the quality. ✉ *Via XXV Novembre 10* ☎ *0921/423570* ═ *AE, DC, MC, V* ☉ *Closed Mon., and Dec. 15–Jan. 15. No lunch Tues.*

$$–$$$ ⊞ **Kalura.** Caldura, 3 km (2 mi) east along the coast, is the site of this modern hotel on a small promontory that's hard to reach without a car; it's only a few minutes by taxi from Cefalù, though. Sports facilities keep you from getting too sedentary, and the private beach is ideal for swimming. Rooms are bright and cheerful. Half-board is required high season (July and August). ⊠ *Via V. Cavallaro 12, 90015, Località Caldura* ☎ *0921/421354* 🖷 *0921/423122* ⊕ *www.kalura. it* ⇌ *65 rooms* ⚒ *Restaurant, tennis court, pool, beach, bar* ⊟ *AE, DC, MC, V.*

★ **$–$$$** ⊞ **Baia del Capitano.** This whitewashed hotel with large rooms and great amenities is in the peaceful district of Mazzaforno, about 5 km (3 mi) outside town. The ranch-style building is less than 30 years old, but it blends in with the rural surroundings. The colorful gardens, extending to the surrounding olive groves, are an ideal setting for reading or an afternoon siesta in the shade. A good sandy beach is a short walk away. ⊠ *Contrada Mazzaforno, 90015 Mazzaforno* ☎ *0921/420003* 🖷 *0921/420163* ⇌ *46 rooms* ⚒ *Restaurant, tennis court, pool, beach, Ping-Pong, bar, playground* ⊟ *AE, DC, MC, V* ⊠ *MAP.*

Santo Stefano di Camastra

16 *33 km (20 mi) east of Cefalù, 152 km (95 mi) west of Messina.*

When the original village of Santo Stefano di Camastra was destroyed in a landslide in 1682, the local duke, Giuseppe Lanza, rebuilt it on the coast according to strict military principles—a geometric street grid, and artery roads connecting the center with the periphery. Today, Santo Stefano is filled with the vividly colored pottery for which the town has an international reputation. For a comprehensive pottery education, drop in on the **Museo della Ceramica** in the center of town. ⊠ *Via Palazzo* ☎*0921/331110* 🎟*Free* ⊙ *May–Sept., weekdays 9–1 and 4–8; Oct.–Apr., weekdays 9–1 and 3:30–7:30.*

Shopping

The Franco family has a long tradition of creating ceramic objets d'art by borrowing styles from past eras. Thus, Renaissance Madonnas rub shoulders with florid baroque vases, all richly colored and skillfully finished. View them at the two outlets of **Ceramiche Franco** (⊠ Via Nazionale 8 ☎ 0921/337222 ⊠ Via Nazionale 40 ☎ 0921/339925) on Santo Stefano's main street.

WESTERN COAST TO AGRIGENTO

LAND OF TEMPLES

Western Sicily has a remote air, less developed than the eastern coast, and bearing traces of the North African culture that for centuries exerted a strong influence on this end of the island. Influences are most tangible in the coastal towns of Trapani and Marsala, and the outlying island of Pantelleria, nearer to the Tunisian coast than the Sicilian. In contrast, the cobbled streets of the hilltop town of Erice, outside Trapani, retain a strong medieval complexion, giving the town the air of a last outpost gazing out over the Mediterranean. The Greek presence is still strong, however, in the splendidly isolated site of Segesta and the cluster of cliffside ruined temples at Selinunte. The crowning glory of this region is the concentration of Greek temples at Agrigento, occupying a fabulous position on a height between the modern city and the sea.

Segesta

⑰ *30 km (19 mi) east of Trapani, 85 km (53 mi) southwest of Palermo.*

★ Segesta is the site of a **Tempio Greco** (Greek temple) that's one of Sicily's most impressive, constructed on the side of a windswept barren hill overlooking a valley of wild fennel. Virtually intact today, the temple is considered by some to be finer in its proportions and setting than any other Doric temple left standing. The temple was actually started in the 5th century BC by the Elymian people, who some believe were refugees from Troy. At the very least, evidence indicates that they were non-Greeks; for example, they often sided with the Carthaginians. However, the style is in many ways Greek. The temple was never finished; the walls and roof never materialized, and the columns were never fluted. Just over 1 km (½ mi) away, near the top of the hill, are the remains of a fine **amphitheater**, with impressive views, especially at sunset, of nearby Monte Erice and the sea. ☎ *0924/952356* 🎫 *€4.15* ⊙ *Daily 9–1 hr before sunset.*

off the beaten path

GIBELLINAI AND SALAPARUTA – On the night of January 14, 1968, a fierce earthquake devastated the wine-producing district of the Valle del Belice, causing 400 deaths and displacing more than 50,000 mostly poor inhabitants of the area. Two of the towns most affected were Gibellina and Salaparuta, and while most other damaged centers were (eventually) rebuilt, these were left as a memorial to the catastrophe. It's a disturbing, rather grim, though deeply peaceful landscape to visit today, a tangle of destruction in which broken walls protrude from mountains of rubble. Contact the **Fondazione Orestiadi** (⊠ Baglio di Stefano, 91024 Gibellina Nuova ☎ 0924/67844 🖷 0924/67855) for details.

Erice

⑱ *35 km (22 mi) west of Segesta, 112 km (70 mi) west of Palermo.*

Erice is perched 2,450 ft above sea level, an enchanting medieval mountaintop aerie of castles and palaces, fountains, and cobblestone streets. Erice was the ancient Eryx and was dedicated to the fertility goddess whom the Phoenicians called Astarte, the Greeks Aphrodite, and the Romans Venus. When the Normans arrived, they built a castle where today you'll find a public park with benches and belvederes, from which there are striking views of Trapani, the Egadi Islands, and, on a *very* clear day, Cape Bon and the Tunisian coast. Because of Erice's elevation, clouds conceal much of the view for most of the winter.

Fans of Sicilian sweets will make a beeline for **Pasticceria Grammatico** (⊠ Via Vittorio Emanuele 14 ☎ 0923/869390), run by Maria Grammatico, a former nun who gained international fame with *Bitter Almonds,* her life story co-written with Mary Taylor Simeti. Molded into striking shapes, including dolls and animals, her almond-paste creations are works of art. The balcony from the tearoom upstairs has wonderful views. At **Pasticceria del Convento** (⊠ Via Guarnotta 1 ☎ 0923/869777), Maria Grammatico's sister sells the same delectable treats that are found at Pasticceria Grammatico.

Where to Stay & Eat

$–$$ ✕ **Monte San Giuliano.** Hidden within the labyrinth of lanes that makes up Erice, this restaurant near the main piazza has a satisfying traditional feel. Sit out on the tree-lined stone patio and sample spicy Arab-influenced seafood couscous, risotto with *rucola* (arugula) and swordfish, or good grilled tuna. Wash it all down with a good white Donnafugata, from the Rallo vineyards at Marsala. ✉ *Vicolo San Rocco 7* ☎ *0923/869595* ▭ *AE, DC, MC, V* ⊘ *Closed Mon., 2 wks mid-Jan., 1st 2 wks Nov.*

$$ ✕▭ **Moderno.** Local crafts and some antiques decorate the gracious balconied rooms of this intimate, well-run hotel on the cobblestone streets of the medieval town. Some rooms are in the modern annex. The renowned restaurant ($–$$) serves seafood pasta and homemade desserts. In winter, a fire is always blazing. ✉ *Via Vittorio Emanuele 67, 91016* ☎ *0923/869300* ⊟ *0923/869139* ⊕ *www.pippocatalano.it* ⇆ *40 rooms* ⌂ *Restaurant, minibars, bar* ▭ *AE, DC, MC, V.*

$ ▤ **Ermione.** Spectacular views and cool breezes are the rewards of a visit to Erice, and this 1960s hotel overlooking the Tyrrhenian Sea is in a position to offer both. Nearly every room has a good view, although some would say that the terrace bar has the most panoramic vista. The hotel restaurant is popular locally, with fish couscous a standout. ✉ *Via Pineta Comunale 43, 91016* ☎ *0923/869138* ⊟ *0923/869587* ⊕ *www.ermionehotel.com* ⇆ *46 rooms* ⌂ *Restaurant, pool, bar* ▭ *AE, DC, MC, V.*

The Outdoors

Near Erice, Capo San Vito is a sandy beach on a promontory overlooking a bay in the Gulf of Castellammare.

Trapani

⑲ *30 km (18 mi) west of Segesta, 107 km (67 mi) west of Palermo.*

The modern town of Trapani, below Erice, is the departure point for ferries to the Egadi Islands and the island of Pantelleria, near the African coast. This rugged western end of Sicily is reminiscent of the many spaghetti Westerns that were filmed here. If you fancy North African couscous, Trapani is the place to try the Sicilian version, made with fish instead of meat.

The lanes of Trapani near Corso Italia hold a handful of churches worth wandering into. **Santa Maria di Gesù** (✉ Via San Pietro) has Gothic and Renaissance doors and a Madonna by Andrea della Robbia (1435–1525). **Sant'Agostino** (✉ Piazzetta Saturno), behind the town hall, has a 14th-century rose window.

Where to Eat

$–$$ ✕ **P&G.** Opposite the Villa Margherita public gardens near the train station, this small restaurant has a quiet, dignified air and attentive service. The local pasta, *busiate*, is cooked with swordfish and eggplant, while the couscous features fish in summer (Friday only) and meat in winter. A mixed grill of meats in a zesty orange sauce will revive any appetite suffering from fish fatigue. Reservations are a good idea on weekends. ✉ *Via Spalti 1* ☎ *0923/547701* ▭ *MC, V* ⊘ *Closed Sun. and Aug.*

Pantelleria

⑳ *100 km (62 mi) southwest of Sicily, 6 hrs by ferry from Trapani.*

Pantelleria, near the Tunisian coast, is one of Sicily's most evocative islands, although some find its starkness unappealing. If you're travel-weary and need a place to hole up for a few days in blissfully calm surroundings, however, this makes an ideal spot, its few hotels and restaurants catering to your basic needs. Many opt to rent accommodations in the traditional dammuso houses, with stout walls and domes for maximum coolness in the fierce summer heat. The hilly terrain offers plenty to explore, either on foot or astride a rented moped. Its volcanic formations, scant patches of forest, prehistoric tombs, and dramatic seascapes constitute an otherworldly landscape. From its grapes—the *zibibbo*—the locals make an amber-colored dessert wine called *Passito,* with a special process that involves drying the grapes. Daily ferries and, in summer, hydrofoils connect the island with Trapani.

Marsala

㉑ *30 km (18 mi) south of Trapani, 140 km (87 mi) southwest of Palermo.*

The quiet seaside town of Marsala was once the main Carthaginian base in Sicily, from which Carthage fought for supremacy of the island against Greece and Rome. Nowadays, it's more readily associated with the world-famous, rich-colored, sweet wine named after the town. In 1773 a British merchant named John Woodhouse happened upon Marsala and discovered that the wine here was as good as the port the British had long imported from Portugal. Two other wine merchants, Whitaker and Ingram, rushed in, and by 1800 Marsala was exporting its wine all over the British Empire.

A sense of Marsala's past as a Carthaginian stronghold is captured by the well-preserved Punic warship displayed in the town's **Museo Archeologico Baglio Anselmi,** along with some of the amphoras and other artifacts recovered from the wreck. The vessel, which was probably sunk during the great sea battle that ended the First Punic War in 241 BC, was dredged up from the mud near the Egadi Islands in the 1970s and is now installed under a climate-controlled plastic tent. ⊠ *Lungomare Boéo 30* ☎ *0923/952535* 🎫 *€2* ☉ *Mon., Tues., and Thurs. 9–2, Wed. and Fri.–Sun. 9–2 and 4–7.*

One of Sicily's foremost wine producers, the 150-year-old **Donnafugata Winery** is open for tours of their Cantina (reservations required) right in downtown Marsala. It's an interesting look at the winemaking process in Sicily, and it ends with a tasting of several whites and reds, and a chance to buy wine as well; don't miss the famous Ben Ryè Passito di Pantelleria, a sweet dessert wine made from dried grapes, with intense notes of apricot. ⊠ *Via Lipari 18* ☎ *0923/724200* ⊕ *www.donnafugata. it* 🎫 *Free* ☉ *Mon.–Sat. 9–4, by appointment only.*

> **off the beaten path**

MAZARA DEL VALLO – Easily accessible at the end of the A29 highway, Mazara del Vallo is a typical time-frozen Sicilian port town with a beautiful baroque old center and pleasant palm-lined *lungomare* running along the ocean. Virtually unknown to tourists, Mazara buzzes with beachy activity in summer but is fairly sleepy in winter; it's a very relaxing place for a night's stopover or for lunch at one of the many seafood places and pizzerias lining the boardwalk or in the *centro storico.* The old port is a raw, colorful graveyard for rusty tugboats and fishing vessels.

Selinunte

㉒ *88 km (55 mi) southeast of Marsala, 114 km (71 mi) south of Palermo.*

Near the town of Castelvetrano, numerous **Greek temple ruins** perch on a plateau overlooking an expanse of Mediterranean at Selinunte (or Selinus). The city was one of the most superb colonies of ancient Greece. The original complex held seven temples scattered over two sites separated by a harbor. Of the seven, only one—reconstructed in 1958—stands.

Founded in the 7th century BC, Selinunte became the rich and prosperous rival of Segesta, which in 409 BC turned to the Carthaginians for help. The Carthaginians sent an army commanded by Hannibal to destroy the city. The temples were demolished, the city was razed, and 16,000 of Selinunte's inhabitants were slaughtered. The remains of Selinunte are in many ways unchanged from the day of its sacking—burn marks still scar the Greek columns, and much of the site still lies in rubble at its exact position of collapse at the hands of the Carthaginian attack. Selinunte is named after a local variety of wild parsley (*Apium graveolens* or *petroselinum*) that in spring grows in profusion among the ruined columns and overturned capitals. ☎ *0924/46277* ⬚ *€4.13* ⊙ *Daily 9–1 hr before sunset.*

Agrigento

100 km (60 mi) southeast of Selinunte, 126 km (79 mi) south of Palermo.

In Agrigento you will be treated to what many experts consider the world's best-preserved remains of classical Greece. The natural defenses of Akragas, the city's Greek name, depended on its secure, and quite lovely, position between two rivers on a flood plain, a short distance from the sea. Settled in 582 BC, Akragas grew wealthy through trade with Carthage, just across the Mediterranean. Despite attacks from the Carthaginians at the end of the 5th century BC, the city survived through the Roman era, the Middle Ages (when it came under Arab and Norman rule), and into the modern age. Famous sons include the ancient Greek philosopher Empedocles (circa 490–430 BC) and the Italian playwright Luigi Pirandello (1867–1936).

Fodor'sChoice Whether you first come upon the **Valle dei Templi** (Valley of the Temples) in the early morning light, bathed by golden floodlights at night, or at very their best in February, when the valley is awash in the fragrant blossoms of thousands of almond trees, it's easy to see why Agrigento was celebrated by Pindar as "the most beautiful city built by mortal men." One ticket covers all temples, and none of the plaques is particularly helpful. ⊠ *Zona Archeologica, Via dei Templi* ☎ *0922/497221* ⬚ *€4.50, €7 including museum* ⊙ *Daily 8:30–7, later in summer.*

❷❸ The eight pillars of the **Tempio di Ercole** (Temple of Hercules) make up Agrigento's oldest temple complex, dating from the 6th century BC. Partially reconstructed in 1922, it reveals the remains of a large Doric temple that originally had 38 columns. Like all the area temples, it faces east. The Museo Archeologico Nazionale contains some of the marble warrior figures that once decorated its pediment.

❷❹ The beautiful **Tempio della Concordia** (Concord), up the hill from the Temple of Hercules, is perhaps the best-preserved Greek temple in existence. The structure dates from about 430 BC, and owes its exceptional state of preservation to the fact that it was converted into a Christian church in the 6th century and was extensively restored in the 18th. Thirty-two Doric columns surround its large interior. It's a tradition in Agrigento for couples to visit the temple on their wedding day. On the left of the temple is a Paleochristian **necropolis**. Early Christian tombs were both cut into the rock and dug into underground catacombs.

❷❺ The **Tempio di Giunone** (Juno), east on the Via Sacra from the Temple of Concord, commands an exquisite view of the valley, especially at sunset. It's similar to but smaller than the Concordia and dates from about 450 BC. Traces of a fire that probably occurred during the Carthaginian attack in 406 BC, which destroyed the ancient town, can be seen on the

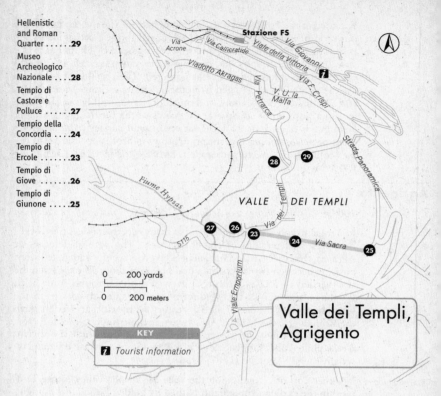

Valle dei Templi,
Agrigento

walls of the cellar. Thirty of the original 34 columns still stand, of which
16 still retain their capitals.

26 Though never completed, the **Tempio di Giove** (Jupiter) was considered
the eighth wonder of the world. The temple was probably built in gratitude for victory over Carthage and was constructed by prisoners captured
in that war. Basically Doric in style, it did not have the usual colonnade
of freestanding columns but rather a series of half-columns attached to a
solid wall. Inside the excavation you can see a cast (not the original) of
one of the 38 colossal Atlas-like figures, or telamones, that supported the
massive roof of the temple. This design is unique among known Doric
temples, and with a length of more than 330 ft the building is the largest
known classical temple. It's first site that you'll encounter in the western archaeological zone of the Valle dei Tempi, across the parking lot from
the Tempio di Ercole. Note that it usually closes at 5.

27 The four columns supporting part of an entablature of the **Tempio di
Castore e Polluce** (Castor and Pollux) have become emblematic of Agrigento, but, in fact, the reconstruction of 1836 haphazardly put together
elements from diverse buildings.

The **Santuario delle Divinità Ctonie** (Sanctuary of the Chthonic Divinities)
has cultic altars and eight small temples dedicated to Demeter, Perse-
phone, and other Underworld deities. It's located to the north of the Temple of Castor and Pallux; in the vicinity are two columns of a temple
dedicated to Hephaestus (Vulcan). ☎ 0922/497221 ⊠ Free ⊙ Daily
8:30–5, later in summer.

28 At the end of Via dei Templi, where it turns left and becomes Via Pe-
trarca, stands the **Museo Archeologico Nazionale.** An impressive col-

lection of antiquities from the site includes vases, votives, everyday objects, weapons, statues, and models of the temples. Visit the museum after you've seen the temples. ☒ *Contrada San Nicola* ☎ *0922/401565* ☒ *€4.50, €7 including temples* ☉ *Mon., Tues., and Sun. 9–1, Wed.–Sat. 9–1 and 2–6.*

29 The **Hellenistic and Roman Quarter,** across the road from the archaeological museum, consists of four parallel streets, running north–south, that have been uncovered, along with the foundations of some houses from the Roman settlement (2nd century BC). Some of these streets still have their original mosaic pavements.

There's little reason to go up the hill from Valle dei Templi to the rather dreary modern city of Agrigento, where stacks of 1960s abominations sit in contrast to the Valley of the Temples below—except to ring the doorbell at the **Convento di Santo Spirito** and try the almond cakes and the *kus-kus* (sweet cake), made of pistachio nuts and chocolate, that the nuns there prepare. There are no regular hours. ☒ *Salita di Santo Spirito, off Via Porcello.*

| off the beaten path |

CASA PIRANDELLO – The plays of distinguished dramatist Luigi Pirandello (1867–1936), such as *Six Characters in Search of an Author,* express the fundamental ambiguity of life. Pirandello's ashes lie under a pine tree behind this house where he was born, in Piazzale Caos, a couple of miles west of town. His house is now a museum of memorabilia and very year, a festival of Pirandello's plays is held in Agrigento from late July to early August. ☒ *Piazzale Caos* ☎ *0922/ 511102* ☒ *€2.10* ☉ *Daily 8 AM–8 PM.*

Where to Stay & Eat

$$ ✕**Trattoria dei Templi.** Near the archaeological area, between olive and almond groves, this simple restaurant can get very busy in the early evening, when it becomes too dark for temple exploring. The menu has all the classic Sicilian dishes, including spaghetti *ai ricci* (with sea urchin) in season, and plenty of grilled fish. The antipasti are exceptional. ☒ *Via Panoramica dei Templi 15* ☎ *0922/403110* ☱ *AE, DC, MC, V* ☉ *Closed Fri. in Sept.–June, Sun. in July and Aug., and Jan. 1–20.*

$ ✕**Kokalos.** On a hillside opposite the temple ridge, 8 km (5 mi) to the southeast—near the Villagio Mosè, this restaurant in an old village house has beautiful views over the temples. As well as serving local specialties, Kokalos includes a pizzeria and *enoteca* (wineshop). ☒ *Via Cavaleri Magazzeni 3, Villagio Mosè* ☎ *0922/606427* ☱ *AE, MC, V.*

$ ✕**Le Caprice.** The high points of this popular restaurant in the temple area are the overflowing trays of antipasti and abundant plates of seafood, including a good swordfish involtini. The wine list is relatively extensive. ☒ *Via Panoramica dei Templi 51* ☎ *0922/26469* ☱ *AE, DC, MC, V* ☉ *Closed Fri. and 1st 2 wks in July.*

$$$$ 🏠**Foresteria Baglio della Luna.** Fiery sunsets and moonlight cast a glow over this hotel in the valley below the temples, a couple of miles from town and easily accessible by taxi. A tower dating from the 8th century is central to the stone farmhouse complex, set around a peaceful geranium- and ivy-filled courtyard and a garden beyond. Standard rooms, some with views of the temples, are cozy but nothing fancy, with mellow walls and wooden furniture. The intimate, rustic restaurant serves Sicilian specialties, including an excellent risotto ai scampi, with good local wines. Note that the dirt road up to the hotel is unmarked. ☒ *Contrada Maddalusa, Valle dei Templi, 92100* ☎ *0922/511061* 🖷 *0922/ 598802* 🌐 *www.venere.com/it/agrigento/bagliodellaluna* ➹ *22 rooms, 3 suites* ♿ *Restaurant, minibars, bar* ☱ *AE, DC, MC, V.*

PRIZZI'S HONOR

BURIED IN THE HEART of Mafia country, Prizzi (population 6,000) is a fairytale aerie, a floating apparition of twisting stone alleyways and brown rooftops gently dusting the peak of a 3,267-ft mountain. Its medieval layout and architecture—surreally frozen in another age—and dreamy views of the surrounding countryside, perhaps best seen at sunset, make it well worth a stop along the way between Palermo and Agrigento. Prizzi was founded by the Greeks in about 480 BC, and was alternately conquered by the Byzantines (8th century AD) and Saracens (9th century AD); the latter of whom built three lofty castles and created a "cult of water" with an elaborate network of drinking troughs. Christian conquest came in the 11th century. Today, aside from when Good takes Evil during the "dance with the devil" festival at Easter, Prizzi offers little in the way of significant art or monuments, and the secrets of the Mafia presence lie out of reach to visitors, buried in inaccessible crevices of local culture. But you can spend hours wandering in and out of the maze of steeply sloped alleyways, with tiny, still-inhabited houses built into the rock, eventually giving way to the remains of the three castles and the mountain's dazzling peak, from which, on a clear day, you can view the sea of Sciacca to one side and the cone of Mt. Etna to the other. Coming from Palermo, follow the signs to Sciacca; both Prizzi and Corleone are on the way.

$$$$ ⊡ **Villa Athena.** There is much demand for this former villa, the only hotel right in the midst of the archaeological zone, so make reservations as early as possible. The price reflects its privileged position, as the hotel itself, although pleasant, is not outstanding. Many rooms have terraces overlooking the large gardens and the swimming pool. The temples are an easy walk away, and there's a convivial atmosphere in the bar, where a multinational crowd swaps stories. The restaurant is also excellent, though pricey, and a destination in itself. ⊠ *Via dei Templi 53, 92100* ☎ *0922/596288* 🖷 *0922/402180* ⊕ *www.athenahotels.com* 📠 *40 rooms* ⚒ *Restaurant, minibars, indoor pool, bar, Internet* ⊟ *AE, DC, MC, V.*

$ ⊡ **Tre Torri.** Stay here if you are sports-minded and bent on exploring the countryside around Agrigento. The owner, a keen cyclist, provides special weekly half-board packages for bikers, hikers, and equestrians. A boat can also be booked for fishing trips, and water sports can be arranged. Public areas are spacious, and the modern rooms simply furnished. The hotel's location, Villagio Mosè, 8 km (5 mi) southeast of town, is on a regular bus route. Book on the Internet for a 10% discount. ⊠ *Villagio Mosè, 92100* ☎ *0922/606733* 🖷 *0922/607839* ⊕ *www.mediatel.it/public/tre-torri* 📠 *118 rooms* ⚒ *Restaurant, indoor pool, health club, sauna, bicycles, bar, nightclub, meeting room* ⊟ *AE, DC, MC, V.*

Nightlife & the Arts

On the first weekend in February, Agrigento hosts a **Festa delle Mandorle,** or Almond Blossom Festival, with international folk dances, a costumed parade, and the sale of marzipan and other sweets made from almonds.

SIRACUSA

Siracusa (also known to English-speakers as Syracuse), old and new, is a wonder to behold. One of the great ancient capitals of Western civilization, the city was founded in 734 BC by Greek colonists from Corinth and soon grew to rival, and even surpass, Athens in splendor and power; Siracusa became the largest, wealthiest city-state in the West and a bulwark of Greek civilization. Although the city lived under tyranny, rulers such as Dionysius filled their courts with Greeks of the highest artistic stature—among them Pindar, Aeschylus, and Archimedes. The Athenians did not welcome the rise of Siracusa and set out to conquer Sicily, but the natives outsmarted them in what was one of the greatest naval battles of ancient history (413 BC). Siracusa continued to prosper until it was conquered two centuries later by the Romans.

Siracusa still has some of the finest examples of baroque art and architecture; dramatic Greek and Roman ruins; and a Duomo that is the stuff of legend, a microcosm of the city's entire history in one edifice. The modern city also offers a wonderful lively baroque old town worthy of extensive exploration, pleasant piazzas, outdoor cafés and bars, and a wide assortment of excellent seafood. There are essentially two areas to explore in Siracusa: the Parco Archeologico, on the mainland; and the island of Ortygia, the ancient city first inhabited by the Greeks, which juts out into the Ionian sea and is connected to the mainland by two small bridges.

Exploring Siracusa

Siracusa's old nucleus of Ortygia is a compact area, a pleasure to amble around without getting unduly tired. In contrast, mainland Siracusa is a grid of wider avenues. At the northern end of Corso Gelone, above Viale Paolo Orsi, the orderly grid gives way to the ancient quarter of Neapolis, where the sprawling Parco Archeologico is accessible from Viale Teracati (an extension of Corso Gelone). East of Viale Teracati, about a 10-minute walk from the Parco Archeologico, the district of Tyche holds the archaeological museum and the church and catacombs of San Giovanni, both off Viale Teocrito (drive or take a taxi or city bus from Ortygia). Coming from the train station, it's a 15-minute trudge to Ortygia along Via Francesco Crispi and Corso Umberto.

Parco Archeologico & Museo Archeologico

a good walk

Start your tour of mainland Siracusa at the **Parco Archeologico** ㉚ ▶ (entrance from Largo Anfiteatro). Before reaching the ticket booth, pause briefly at the meager remains of the Ara di Ierone. Beyond the ticket office, the extensive Latomia del Paradiso stretches out on the right, while the archaeological park's pièce de résistance lies to the left: the awesome expanse of the Teatro Greco. Leave by the same way you entered, making a diversion before the park's exit (you'll need to show your entry ticket) to view the elliptical Anfiteatro Romano. From Largo Anfiteatro, head east along the busy Viale Teocrito, where, after a few minutes, you'll pass the **Museo Archeologico** ㉛. A few steps beyond is the much smaller but still intriguing **Museo del Papiro** ㉜. From here, retrace your steps along Viale Teocrito before turning right up Via San Giovanni to visit the church of San Giovanni and the **Catacombe di San Giovanni** ㉝ beneath. From here, drive or take one of the frequent city buses down Corso Gelone and Corso Umberto for the old city.

TIMING Allow at least a full day for this tour, which can be quite taxing. The Parco Archeologico has little or no shade, so early morning or late afternoon are the best times to visit on hot days.

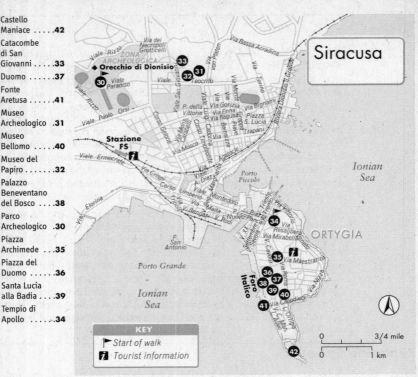

Siracusa

KEY
► *Start of walk*
🏠 *Tourist information*

0 ———— 3/4 mile
0 ———— 1 km

What to See

③③ **Catacombe di San Giovanni.** Not far from the Archaeological Park, off Viale Teocrito, the catacombs below the church of San Giovanni are one of the earliest-known Christian sites in the city. Inside the crypt of San Marciano is an altar where St. Paul preached on his way through Sicily to Rome. The frescoes in this small chapel are still bright and fresh, though some dating from the 4th century AD show their age. ⊠ *Piazza San Giovanni, archeological zone* ☎ *0931/66571* 💶 *€3.10* ⊙ *Tues.–Sun. 9–12:30 and 2:30–5:30; longer hrs in summer.*

③① **Museo Archeologico.** The impressive collection of Siracusa's splendid archaeological museum is organized by region around a central atrium and ranges from neolithic pottery to fine Greek statues and vases. You will want to compare the *Landolina Venus*—a headless, stout goddess of love who rises out of the sea in measured modesty (she is a 1st century AD Roman copy of the Greek original)—with the much earlier (300 BC) elegant Greek statue of Hercules in Section C. Of a completely different style is a marvelous fanged Gorgon, its tongue sticking out, that once adorned the cornice of the temple of Athena to ward off evildoers. One exhibit depicts the Temple of Apollo, the oldest Doric temple in Sicily, on the island of Ortygia. ⊠ *Viale Teocrito, archeological zone* ☎ *0931/ 464022* 💶 *€4.50, €7 including archaeological park, €8 including Museo Bellomo* ⊙ *Mon.–Sat. 9–1 and 3:30–7:30 (6:30 in winter), Sun. 9–1.*

③② **Museo del Papiro.** Close to Siracusa's Museo Archeologico, the Papyrus Museum demonstrates how papyruses are prepared from reeds and then painted—an ancient tradition in the city. Siracusa, it seems, has the only climate outside the Nile Valley in which the papyrus plant—from which the word "paper" comes—thrives. ⊠ *Viale Teocrito 66, archeological zone* ☎ *0931/61616* 💶 *Free* ⊙ *Tues.–Sun. 9–1.*

▶ ㉚ **Parco Archeologico** (Archaeological Park). Siracusa is without a doubt most famous for its dramatic set of Greek and Roman ruins. Though the various ruins can be visited separately, you'll certainly want to see them all, along with the Museo Archeologico. If the park is closed, go up Viale G. Rizzo from Viale Teracati, to the belvedere overlooking the ruins, which are floodlit at night. ✉ *Viale Augusto* ☎ *0931/66206* 🖃 *€4.50 for all sites, €7 including Museo Archeologico* ☉ *Sept.–May, daily 9–4; June–Aug., daily 9–7; last tickets sold 1 hr before closing.*

Before the park's ticket booth is the gigantic **Ara di Ierone** (Altar of Hieron), which was once used by the Greeks for spectacular sacrifices involving hundreds of animals. The first attraction in the park is the **Latomia del Paradiso,** a lush tropical garden full of palm and citrus trees. This series of quarries served as prisons for the defeated Athenians, who were enslaved; the quarries once rang with the sound of their chisels and hammers. At one end is the famous Orecchio di Dionisio, with an ear-shape entrance and unusual acoustics inside, as you'll discover if you clap your hands. The legend is that Dionysius used to listen in at the top of the quarry to hear what the slaves were plotting below.

★ The **Teatro Greco** (Greek Theater) is the chief monument in the Archaeological Park—and indeed one of Sicily's greatest classical sites and the most complete Greek theater surviving from antiquity. Climb to the top of the seating area (which could accommodate 15,000) for a fine view: all the seats converge upon a single point—the stage—which has the natural scenery and the sky as its background. Hewn out of the hillside rock in the 5th century BC, the theater saw the premieres of the plays of Aeschylus. Greek tragedies are still performed here in May and June of even-numbered years. Above and behind the theater runs the Via dei Sepulcri, in which streams of running water flows through a series of Greek sephulcres.

The well-preserved and striking **Anfiteatro Romano** (Roman Amphitheater) reveals much about the differences between the Greek and Roman personalities. Where drama in the Greek theater was a kind of religious ritual, the Roman amphitheater emphasized the spectacle of combative sports and the circus. This arena is one of the largest of its kind and was built around the 2nd century AD. The corridor where gladiators and beasts entered the ring is still intact, and the seats, some of which still bear the occupants' names, were hauled in and constructed on the site from huge slabs of limestone.

need a break? For some great Sicilian cakes and ice cream on your way to the archaeological park, visit the bar-cum-*pasticceria* **Leonardi** (✉ Viale Teocrito 123, archeological zone ☎ 0931/61411). It's popular with the locals, so you may have to queue for your cakes in holiday times. It's closed Wednesday.

Ortygia Island

a good walk The central part of Siracusa is a modern city, with Corso Gelone its main shopping street. At its southern end, Corso Umberto leads to the Ortygia Island bridge, which crosses a harbor lined with fish restaurants. Begin at Piazza Pancali, the square where you arrive after crossing the bridge. Behind the piazza stand the scanty remains of the **Tempio di Apollo** ㉞ ▶. Proceed from here to **Piazza Archimede** ㉟, from which it's a brief walk to **Piazza del Duomo** ㊱, the main square of the old town and site of Siracusa's ancient and splendid **Duomo** ㊲. Other impressive buildings to see in the piazza include the **Palazzo Beneventano del Bosco** ㊳ and the church of **Santa Lucia alla Badia** ㊴; the Palazzo Bellomo, housing the **Museo Bellomo** ㊵, is just around the corner. After you've had your fill of this, stroll onto the waterfront where several bars cluster around the lovely **Fonte Aretusa** ㊶, a perfect spot for a break. Walking along the seafront promenade to the southern tip of Ortygia will bring you to the **Castello Maniace** ㊷. Ortygia's backstreets are largely composed of elegant baroque palazzi whose uniformity is the result of the major reconstruction that took place following an earthquake in 1693, at a time when this style of baroque was de rigueur. Be sure to wander along Via della Maestranza, the main lateral street of the island, or Via Veneto, on the eastern side, where you'll notice the bulbous wrought-iron balconies, said to have been fashioned to accommodate ladies' billowing skirts, and facades embellished with mermaids and gargoyles—and don't miss the stucco decoration on Palazzo Lantieri, on Via Roma (off Piazza Archimede).

TIMING   You'll need the better part of a day to do justice to Ortygia. Obviously, the more detours you make—and there are distractions aplenty here—the longer you'll spend. The Duomo alone can take an hour or so to see properly, while you could easily spend two more hours in the Museo Bellomo. There's no lack of inviting bars and restaurants to break up your tour.

What to See

㊷ **Castello Maniace.** The southern tip of Ortygia island is occupied by a castle built by Frederick II (1194–1250), now an army barracks, from which there are fine views of the sea.

㊲ **Duomo.** Siracusa's Duomo is an archive of island history, beginning with the bottom-most excavations that have unearthed remnants of Sicily's distant past, when the Siculi inhabitants worshiped their deities here. During the 5th century BC (the same time as Agrigento's Temple of Concord was built), the Greeks built a temple to Athena over it, and in the 7th century, Siracusa's first Christian cathedral was built on top of the Greek structure. The massive columns of the original Greek temple were incorporated into the present structure and are clearly visible, embedded in the exterior wall along Via Minerva. The Greek columns were also used to dramatic advantage inside, where on one side they form chapels connected by elegant wrought-iron gates. The baroque facade, added in 1700, displays a harmonious rhythm of concaves and convexes. In front, the piazza is encircled by pink and white oleanders and elegant buildings ornamented with filigree grillwork. ✉ *Piazza del Duomo, Ortygia* ☎ *0931/65328* ✆ *Daily 8–noon and 4–7:30.*

FodorsChoice
★

need a break?   When you're in need of refreshment, the elegant **Antico Caffè Minerva** (✉ Via Minerva 15, Ortygia ☎ 0931/22606), around the corner from the Duomo, will satisfy your cravings. It's closed on Wednesday.

㊶ **Fonte Aretusa.** Just off the promenade along the harbor you'll find the Fountain of Arethusa, a freshwater spring next to the sea. This anomaly is explained by a Greek legend that tells how the nymph Arethusa was changed into a fountain by the goddess Artemis (Diana) when she tried to escape the advances of the river god Alpheus. She fled from Greece, into the sea, with Alpheus in close pursuit, and emerged in Sicily at this spring. It's said if you throw a cup into the Alpheus River in Greece, it will emerge here at this fountain, which is home to a few tired ducks and some dull-colored carp—but no cups. If you want to stand right by the fountain, you need to gain admission through the aquarium; otherwise look down on it from Largo Aretusa.

40 **Museo Bellomo.** Siracusa's principal museum of art is inside Palazzo Bellomo, a lovely Catalan-Gothic building with mullioned windows and an elegant exterior staircase. Among the paintings and sculptures is a *Santa Lucia* by Caravaggio (1573–1610) and a damaged but still brilliant *Annunciation* by Antonello da Messina. There are also exhibitions of Sicilian nativity figures, silver, furniture, ceramics, and religious vestments. ⊠ *Via Capodieci 14, Ortygia* ☎ *0931/69511* 🎫 *€4* ⊙ *Mon.–Sat. 9–5, Sun. 9–2.*

38 **Palazzo Beneventano del Bosco.** On a corner of the Piazza del Duomo, this elegant palazzo, a private residence, has an impressive interior courtyard ending in a grand winding staircase. ⊠ *Piazza del Duomo, Ortygia.*

35 **Piazza Archimede.** This center of this piazza has a baroque fountain, the *Fontana di Diana*, festooned with fainting sea nymphs and dancing jets of water. Look for the Chiaramonte-style **Palazzo Montalto,** an arched-window gem just off the piazza on Via Montalto.

36 **Piazza del Duomo.** In the heart of Ortygia, this ranks as one of Italy's most beautiful piazzas, its elongated space lined with Sicilian baroque gems and outdoor cafés.

39 **Santa Lucia alla Badia.** This baroque church stands at one end of Piazza del Duomo, featuring an engaging wrought-iron balcony and pleasant facade. ⊠ *Piazza del Duomo, Ortygia* ⊙ *Closed for restoration.*

▶ **34** **Tempio di Apollo.** Scattered through the piazza just across the bridge to Ortygia you'll find the ruins of a temple dedicated to Apollo, a model of which is in the Museo Archeologico. In fact, little of this noble Doric temple still remains today, except for some crumbled walls and shattered columns; the window in the south wall belongs to a Norman church that was built much later on the same spot. ⊠ *Piazza Pancali, Ortygia.*

off the
beaten
path

CASTELLO EURIALO – West of the city, on the highlands that overlook the sea, the Euryalus Castle was created by Dionysius between 402 and 397 BC for protection against the Carthaginians. This astonishing boat-shape structure once covered 135,000 square ft. The intricate maze of tunnels is fascinating, and the view from the heights is superb. ⊠ *Belvedere, 8 km (5 mi) northwest of Siracusa* 🎫 *Free* ⊙ *Daily 9–1 hr before sunset.*

Where to Stay & Eat

★ **$$–$$$** ✕ **Don Camillo.** Bursting with locals in the know, this renowned Ortygia restaurant is set in a gracious series of delicately arched rooms lined with wine bottles and sepia-toned images of old Siracusa. Uniformly outstanding local dishes include the sublime *spaghetti delle Sirene*, with delicate *ricci* (sea urchin), shrimp, and butter; and the bolder *pennette alle pesce spada* (pasta tubes with swordfish, raisins, tomato, pine nuts, basil, and Marsala). End with a spicy cheese plate counterbalanced by Sicilian honey and sweet Marsala wine. ⊠ *Via Maestranza 96, Ortygia* ☎ *0931/67133* 🟰 *AE, DC, MC, V* ⊙ *Closed Sun., Nov., 2 wks in July, and 2 wks in Aug.*

$–$$$ ✕ **Fermento.** This hip wine bar–restaurant–Internet café is truly one of Sicily's most enchanting settings in which to dine or drink: warm lighting, dark vaulted stone, candles everywhere, a dim buzz, and Sicilian wines served in huge, beautiful tasting glasses. The menu really revolves around wine, with an excellent (if pricey) selection of local classics. Stick to the pasta dishes and creative salads rather than the meats. ⊠ *Via Crocifisso 44/46, Ortygia* ☎ *0931/60762* 🟰 *AE, DC, MC, V* ⊙ *Closed Tues.*

$–$$ ✕ **Ionico.** Enjoy seaside dining in the coastal Santa Lucia district. The Ionico has a terrace and veranda for alfresco meals, and the interior is plastered with diverse historical relics and has a cheerful open hearth for the winter. Chef-proprietor Roberto Giudice cooks meals to order or will suggest a specialty from a selection of market-fresh ingredients. Try the pasta *con acciughe e il pan grattato* (in an anchovy sauce). ⊠ *Riviera Dionisio il Grande 194, Santa Lucia* ☎ 0931/65540 ▭ *AE, DC, MC, V* ⊘ *Closed Tues.*

$ ✕ **Archimede.** The *antipasto misto* (mixed antipasto) should whet your appetite for the predominantly seafood menu of this small establishment. Risotto di mare and pesce spada are specialties. Sample the *involtini all'Archimede* (roulades stuffed with fish and bread crumbs) or the *tagliatelli all'Archimede* (a fish and pasta dish). ⊠ *Via Gemmellaro 8, Ortygia* ☎ 0931/69701 ▭ *AE, DC, MC, V* ⊘ *Closed Sun. Dec.–Mar.*

¢   ✕ **La Siciliana.** This is an ideal spot for an inexpensive pizza and a cool beer or white wine. There are more than 50 varieties of pizza, from the most exotic to the local fried variety only served in the evening, *Siciliana*, a crusty and flavorful calzone stuffed with *tuma* (fresh, unsalted cheese), anchovies, and black pepper. Other choices on the menu include pasta and fish. ⊠ *Via Savoia 17, Ortygia* ☎ 0931/68944 ▭ *No credit cards.*

$$$ ▥ **Grand Hotel.** An elegant, fantasy-inspired design prevails at this venerable institution, which has enjoyed a prime position overlooking the Porto Grande since 1898. A modern seascape sets a dreamy tone in the lobby, which is decked out in periwinkle leather club chairs, antiques, gilt mirrors, and marble inlaid floors lined with lights. Guest rooms have fine wood floors, modern fixtures, and stained-glass windows. The roof-garden restaurant has superb views over the Grand Harbor and seafront of Ortygia as well as excellent food. A shuttle service is provided to the hotel's nearby private beach. ⊠ *Viale Mazzini 12, Porto Grande, 96100* ☎ 0931/464600 ☐ 0931/464611 ⊕ *www.grandhotelsr.it* ⇌ *39 rooms, 19 suites* ⌂ *Restaurant, minibars, beach, bar, meeting room, free parking* ▭ *AE, DC, MC, V.*

$$$ ▥ **Grand Hotel Villa Politi.** This grand 18th-century villa was frequented by European royalty and various VIPs, including Winston Churchill. Now equipped with modern luxuries, it still retains its charm and elegance. The hotel is located near the archaeological zone but set back from the road in the ancient extensive gardens of the Latomie dei Cappuccini, overlooking a small archaeological site. High-quality service and all the trimmings are the standard. ⊠ *Via M. Politi Laudien 2, archeological zone, 96100* ☎ 0931/412121 ☐ 0931/36061 ⊕ *www.villapoliti.com* ⇌ *97 rooms* ⌂ *2 restaurants, in-room safes, pool, tennis, bar, library, free parking* ▭ *AE, DC, MC, V.*

$$ ▥ **Domus Mariae.** You can see the sea at the end of the corridor as you enter this hotel on Ortygia's eastern shore. In an unusual twist, it's run by nuns of the Ursuline order, who help to make the mood placid and peaceful. Don't expect monastic conditions, however; refined furnishings distinguish the public rooms, and guest rooms—four with sea views and others with great Ortygia street balconies—are bright, modern, and comfortable. The hotel's modest restaurant downstairs also serves truly superlative local food—walnut-radicchio risotto and citrus and seared eggplant salad both shine. ⊠ *Via Vittorio Veneto 76, Ortygia, 96100* ☎☐ 0931/24854 *or* 0931/24858 ⊕ *www.sistemia.it/domusmariae* ⇌ *12 rooms* ⌂ *Restaurant, bar, free parking* ▭ *AE, DC, MC, V.*

$–$$ ▥ **Park Hotel Helios.** This unpretentious hotel is in a quiet part of town north of the archaeological zone. Rooms are spacious and warmly lit, the foyer bedecked with potted palms and Persian rugs. Outside are a barbecue and a play area for children. ⊠ *Via Filisto 80, archeological zone, 96100* ☎ 0931/812366 ☐ 0931/812378 ⇌ *143* rooms ⬧ *Restaurant, pool, playground, meeting room, free parking* ▭ *AE, DC, MC, V.*

$ ⊡ **Il Limoneto.** Awash with orchards and citrus groves, this *agriturismo* 9 km (5½ mi) from Siracusa offers a haven of peace after the rigors of sightseeing in the city (if you're here to see the city, don't come without a car). Expect splendid home cooking; the renowned Adele will let you watch her make pasta and even induct you into the secrets of Mamma's recipes. In the evenings, guests are encouraged to gather and may be regaled with Sicilian poetry. Guest rooms are furnished in a rustic style, and some have mezzanine floors (perfect for children). Because there are only eight rooms available, be sure to book far in advance; you can always come just for a meal. ⊠ *Via del Platano 3, SP 14 Mare–Monti, 96100* ☎☎ *0931/717352* ⇝ *8 rooms* ⬧ *Restaurant, bicycles, bowling, playground* ▭ *DC, MC, V* ⊘ *Closed Nov.*

★ ¢ ⊡ **B & B Belvedere.** In a pretty old palazzo in the heart of Ortygia, this bed-and-breakfast (liberally interpreted—breakfast is included at a nearby bar) caters mostly to backpackers and young people who have the stamina to brave the four-story climb up the stairs. The location is prime; rooms are spotless and spacious, some overlooking the coastline. Service is friendly and hassle-free (you get your own keys to the building), and the price can't be beat. ⊠ *Via Maestranza 111, 96100* ☎☎ *0931/69005* ⊕ *www.bedandbreakfastsicily.com* ⇝ *7 rooms* ⬧ *Lounge* ▭ *No credit cards.*

Nightlife & the Arts

Festivals

The feast of the city's patroness, Santa Lucia (St. Lucy), is held on December 13 at **Santa Lucia alla Badia** (⊠ Piazza del Duomo, Ortygia). A splendid silver statue of the saint is carried through Ortygia from the church on the site of her martyrdom, near the Catacombs of San Giovanni, to the cathedral. A torchlight procession and band music accompany the bearers, while local families watch from their balconies. In May and June of even-numbered years only, Siracusa's **Teatro Greco** (⊠ Parco Archeologico ☎ 0931/465831 ⊕ www.drammantico.it) stages performances of classical drama and comedy.

Bars

On the edge of Ortygia, the **Ulysses Irish Pub** (⊠ Vicolo al Forte Vigliena 3/15 Ortygia ☎ 0931/465615) is a raucous home base for expats, suburbanites, and locals. Popular and full with locals, **Il Bagatto** (⊠ Piazza S. Giuseppe 1 Ortygia ☎ 0931/464076) is in the heart of Ortygia.

Shopping

The specialty of Siracusa is papyrus paper. But beware—most of what you buy is commercially produced, hard, and of inferior quality to the handmade paper, which feels like fabric. One of the best of the few places to buy the genuine article is **Galleria Bellomo** (⊠ Via Capodieci 15, Ortygia ☎ 0931/61340), opposite the Museo Bellomo. It's run by an artist who sells cards and paintings and will also give a demonstration of how to make the paper.

EASTERN SICILY

ON THE ROAD TO TAORMINA

Sicily's interior is for the most part underpopulated and untrammeled, though the Imperial Roman Villa at Casale, outside Piazza Armerina, gives precious evidence from an epoch gone by. Don't miss misty Enna, the navel of Sicily, or Caltagirone, a ceramics center of renown. Halfway up the eastern coast, Catania packs the vivacity of Palermo, if not the artistic wealth; the city makes a good base for exploring lofty Mt. Etna, as does Taormina. Messina's scant attractions include its unparalleled position opposite the mountains of Calabria and one of the island's best museum collections.

Enna

43 *105 km (63 mi) northeast of Agrigento, 136 km (85 mi) southeast of Palermo.*

Deep in Sicily's interior, the fortress city of Enna commands exceptional views of the surrounding rolling plains, and, in the distance, Mt. Etna. Virtually unknown by tourists and relatively untouched by industrialization, this sleepy mountaintop city (altitude 2,844 ft) charms and prospers in a distinctly old-fashioned, provincial, and Sicilian style. Enna makes a good stopover for the night or just for lunch, as it's right along the autostrada between Palermo and Catania (and thus Siracusa). The narrow, winding streets are dominated at one end by the impressive cliffhanging **Castello di Lombardia,** built by Frederick II, easily visible as you approach town.

The mysterious and mystical **Torre di Federico II** (closed for restoration, but still viewable from outside) stands above the lower part of town. This octagonal tower, of unknown purpose, has been celebrated for millennia as marking the exact geometric center of the island—thus the tower's, and city's, nickname, *Umbilicus Siciliae* (navel of Sicily); and indeed, the top of the tower just might be the only vantage point in all Sicily from which all three corners are ever visible.

In town, head straight for Via Roma, which leads to **Piazza Vittorio Emanuele,** the center of Enna's shopping scene and evening passeggiata. The attached **Piazza Crispi,** dominated by the shell of the grand old Hotel Belvedere, affords breathtaking panoramas of the hillside and smoking Etna looming in the distance.

Where to Stay & Eat

$-$$ ✕ **Centrale.** This casual place has served meals since 1889. The bright walls of an old *palazzo* are adorned with Sicilian pottery, and an outdoor terrace soothes diners in summer. The varied menu features local preparations such as *coppole di cacchio* (peppers stuffed with spaghetti, potato, and basil), grilled pork chops, and a good choice of Sicilian wines. ✉ *Piazza VI Dicembre 9* ☎ *0935/500963* ▬ *AE, DC, MC, V* ☯ *Closed Sat. Oct.–May.*

¢ ✕ **Terra Orsa.** While the menu pays homage to tradition—*orrecchiette alla Norma* is a Sicilian classic—cooking is impeccably modern and upscale at this downtown *osteria* and wine bar. A vaulted old room with white walls is the relaxed setting, and an excellent wine list washes the day's troubles away. ✉ *Via Roma 488* ☎ *0935/503134* ▬ *AE, DC, MC, V* ☯ *Closed Sun.*

$ ⊟ **Hotel Sicilia.** Sicily's interior has few decent accommodations, so if overnighting, you'll have little choice but to stay at the Sicilia. Centrally located, the Sicilia is aging, institutional-feeling and monopoly-priced, but it has bright, clean rooms, some with excellent views. Reserve ahead for one with a bathtub and a view over the town and hillside rather than onto the piazza. ✉ *Piazza Napoleone Colajanni 7, 94100* ☎ *0935/500850* 📠 *0935/500488* ➲ *76 rooms* ♨ *Bar* ▬ *AE, DC, MC, V.*

Nightlife

After dark, **Wine Bar Up** (✉ Piazza Garibaldi ☎ 0935/501111), upstairs from Caffè Italia, is a hip place to stop for a drink.

Piazza Armerina

44 *120 km (75 mi) west of Catania.*

A quick look around Piazza Armerina is rewarding—the fanciful town has a feel of provincial warmth, and the crumbling yellow stone architecture with Sicily's trademark bulbous balconies create quite an effect. The greatest draw, however, lies just down the road.

Fodor'sChoice
★
The exceptionally well preserved **Imperial Roman Villa** in Casale, 4 km (2½ mi) from Piazza Armerina, is thought to have been a hunting lodge of the emperor Maximianus Heraclius (4th century AD). The excavations were not begun until 1950, and the wall decorations and vaulting have been lost. However, some of the best mosaics of the Roman world cover more than 12,000 square ft under a shelter that hints at the layout of the original buildings. The mosaics were probably made by North African artisans, because they are similar to those in the Tunis Bardo Museum. The entrance was through a triumphal arch that led into an atrium surrounded by a portico of columns. Through this the *thermae*, or bathhouse, is reached. It's colorfully decorated with mosaic nymphs, a Neptune, and slaves massaging bathers. The peristyle leads to the main villa, where in the Salone del Circo you look down on mosaics illustrating Roman circus sports. Room 38 even reveals a touch of eroticism—surely only scratching the surface of the bacchanalian festivities that Maximilian conjured up. ✉ *Casale* ☎ *0935/680036* 🖃 *€4* ⊙ *Weekdays 9–1:30 and 3–1 hr before sunset, weekends 9–1 hr before sunset.*

Caltagirone

45 *30 km (18 mi) southeast of Piazza Armerina, 60 km (37 mi) southwest of Catania.*

Built over three hills, this charming baroque town is a center of the Sicilian ceramics industry. Here you will find majolica balustrades, tile-decorated windowsills, and a monumental tile staircase of 142 steps—each decorated with a different pattern—leading up to the neglected **Santa Maria del Monte.** On the feast of San Giacomo (July 24), the staircase is illuminated with candles that form a tapestry design over the steps. It is the result of months of work preparing the 4,000 *coppi*, or cylinders of colored paper that hold oil lamps. At 9:30 PM on July 24, a squad of hundreds of boys springs into action to light the lamps, so that the staircase flares up all at once. ⊙ *Daily 7–noon and 4–7.*

Shopping

Of the numerous ceramic shops and workshops in Caltagirone's old center, **Branciforti** (✉ Scala Santa Maria del Monte 3 ☎ 0933/24427), right on Caltagirone's fabled ceramic steps, is one of the best, selling eye-catching work with deep shades of blue and swirling arabesques.

Palazzolo Acreide

46 *60 km (40 mi) southeast of Caltagirone, 40 km (25 mi) west of Siracusa.*

This small inland town is best known for its archaeological zone, the old Greek *Akrai*, founded by the Siracusan in 664 BC. The zone contains the foundations of a temple dedicated to Aphrodite, and a well-preserved theater, while the town itself is unspectacularly baroque.

Ragusa

47 *25 km (15 mi) southwest of Palazzolo Acreide.*

Ragusa and Modica are the two chief cities in Sicily's smallest and sleepiest province, and the centers of a region known as Iblea. The dry, rocky, gentle countryside filled with canyons and grassy knolls is a unique landscape in Sicily. Iblea's trademark squat stone walls divide out swaths of land in a manner reminiscent of the high English countryside—but summers are decidedly Sicilian, with dry heat so intense that life grinds to a standstill for several hours each day. This remote province hums along to its own tune, clinging to local customs, cuisines, and traditions in aloof disregard even for the rest of Sicily.

Ragusa is known for its wonderful Ragusano DOP cheese (a creamy, doughy, flavorful version of *caciocavallo,* made by hand at every step of the way) along with some great local red wines. It's a modern city with a beautiful old town called **Ibla,** which was completely rebuilt after the devastating earthquake of 1693—thus Ibla's architecture is baroque and its structure is medieval. A tumble of buildings perched on a hilltop and suspended between a deep ravine and a sloping valley, Ibla towers in midair, a floating apparition by night.

Noto

48 *30 km (18 mi) east of Ragusa, 34 km (21 mi) southeast of Palazzolo Acreide, 32 km (19 mi) southwest of Siracusa.*

Noto presents a pleasing ensemble of honey-color baroque architecture, strikingly uniform in style but never dull. The dome of the majestic cathedral, Noto's centerpiece (completed in 1776), collapsed during a thunderstorm in 1996, probably due to a previous botched restoration.

Where to Eat

$$ ✕**Trattoria del Carmine.** Simple but ever reliable local dishes are the staples at this affable eatery in the center of town. If you're not tempted by the fish of the day, you can choose between the various land-based dishes on offer, such as ravioli with a pork ragù, *salsiccia al finocchietto* (sausage cooked with fennel), and rabbit with peppers. ⊠ *Via Ducezio 1/a* ☎ *0931/838705* ▭ *AE, MC, V* ☻ *Closed Mon.*

Catania

49 *60 km (37 mi) north of Siracusa, 94 km (59 mi) south of Messina.*

The chief wonder of Catania, Sicily's second city, is that it is there at all. Its successive populations were deported by one Greek tyrant, sold into slavery by another, and driven out by the Carthaginians. Every time the city got back on its feet, it was struck by a new calamity: plague decimated the population in the Middle Ages, a mile-wide stream of lava from Mt. Etna swallowed most of the city in 1669, and 25 years later a disastrous earthquake forced the Catanese to begin again. Today the city needs considerable renovation. Traffic flows in ever-increasing volume and adds to the smog from the industrial zone between Catania and Siracusa, but the views of Mt. Etna from Catania are superb. Many of Catania's buildings are constructed from solidified lava, and the black lava stone has given the city a singular appearance. As a result, Catania is known as the city of lava and oranges (it has orange groves as well).

The pastry shops along Via Etnea are good places to sample cannoli. If you're in need of something more substantial, duck into one of the trattorias along this street and order Catania's (and Sicily's) trademark pasta *alla Norma.*

Catania's greatest native son was the composer Vincenzo Bellini (1801–35), whose operas have thrilled audiences since their premieres in the first half of the 19th century. His home, now the **Museo Bellini- ano,** preserves memorabilia of the man and his work. ⊠ *Piazza San Francesco 3* ☏ *095/7150535* ✉ *Free* ☉ *Sept.–May, Mon.–Sat. 9–1:30, Sun. 9–12:30; June–Aug., daily 9–12:30.*

The **Duomo** is a fine work by Vaccarini (1736), as is the obelisk-balancing elephant—the informal mascot of Catania—carved out of lava stone in the piazza before it. Vincenzo Bellini is buried inside the cathedral. ⊠ *Bottom end of Via Etnea* ☏ *095/320044* ☉ *Daily 8–12:30 and 4–7:30.*

Where to Stay & Eat

★ **$–$$** ✕ **Costa Azzurra.** At this seafood restaurant in the Ognina district, reserve a table on the veranda by the edge of the sea with good views of the harbor. The fritto misto can be ordered as an antipasto or a main course, and the pesce spada steak is a simple classic, served grilled with a large slice of lemon. ⊠ *Via De Cristofaro 4, Ognina, north of the center, on the way to the Taormina road* ☏ *095/497889* 🖃 *AE, DC, MC, V* ☉ *Closed Mon. and last 2 wks in Aug.*

$$$$ 🏨 **Excelsior.** Ask for a room facing Piazza Verga, a neat tree-lined square in this quiet but central district of Catania. The relatively new Excelsior has air-conditioning and sound-insulated windows in all rooms, which are impeccably furnished with a careful balance of old and new motifs. The American Bar should provide solace if you're feeling nostalgic for a Manhattan. ⊠ *Piazza Verga 39, 95129* ☏ *095/7476111* 🖶 *095/ 537015* ⊕ *www.excelsiorcatania.thi.it* ⇆ *158 rooms, 18 suites* ⚅ *Restaurant, gym, steam room, bar, parking (fee)* 🖃 *AE, DC, MC, V.*

$$ 🏨 **Savona.** This is a conveniently located and very modern hotel a stone's throw from Piazza del Duomo. The rooms are spacious, solidly furnished, and well equipped. Reception can help with parking suggestions. ⊠ *Via Vittorio Emanuele 210, 95124* ☏ *095/326982* ⊕ *www. hotelsavona.it* ⇆ *30 rooms* ⚅ *Bar, in-room safes, minibars* 🖃 *MC, V.*

Nightlife & the Arts

The opera season at the **Teatro Bellini** (⊠ Piazza Bellini, Catania ☏ 095/ 7306111), October to mid-June, attracts top singers and productions to the birthplace of the great composer.

Mt. Etna

★ ㊿ *30 km (19 mi) north of Catania, 60 km (37 mi) south of Messina.*

Mt. Etna is one of the world's major active volcanoes and is the largest and highest in Europe—the cone of the crater rises to 10,958 ft above sea level. Plato sailed in just to catch a glimpse in 387 BC; in the 9th century AD, the oldest *gelato* of all was shaved off of its snowy slopes; and in the 21st century, the volcano still claims annual headlines. Etna has erupted 11 times in the past 30 or so years, most spectacularly in 1971, in 1983, 2001, and 2002, when in each case rivers of molten lava destroyed the two highest stations of the cable car that rises from the town of Sapienza. While each eruption is predictably declared a "tragedy" by the media due to the economic losses, Etna almost never threatens human life. Travel in the proximity of the crater depends on Mt. Etna's temperament, but you can walk up and down the enormous lava dunes and wander over its moonlike surface of dead craters. The rings of vegetation change markedly as you rise, with vineyards and pine trees gradually giving way to growths of broom and lichen. Catania and Taormina are the departure points for excursions around—but not always to the top of—Mt. Etna. Buses leave from Catania's train station in early morning. There's **gondola service** (✉ Piazza Vittorio Emanuele 45 ☎ 095/911158 or 095/914209) from the town of Nicolosi, which can take you to an altitude of 8,200 ft; the cost is approximately €40–€50 for the two- to three-hour round-trip, including cable car, jeep, and guide. The gondola closed due to the 2002 eruption; check with the tourist office to see if it's running again. For personalized guided tours, contact Nicolosi's **information office** (✉ Via Garibaldi 63 ☎ 095/911505) or call the **Gruppo Guide Alpine Etna** (☎ 095/7914755). Closer to the ground, an alternative view of the volcano can be had from the **Circumetnea railroad** (✉ Via Caronda 352, Catania ☎ 095/541243 ⊙ Closed Sun.), which runs near the volcano's base. The private railway travels 114 km (71 mi) between Riposto and Catania—30 km (19 mi) apart on the coast—almost circling Mt. Etna. The line is small, slow, and only single-track but offers some dramatic vistas of the volcano and goes through lava fields. The round-trip takes about five hours, there are about 10 departures a day, and tickets cost €5.15 one-way. Service was disrupted by the 2002 eruption, so call ahead.

For a bird's-eye view of Mt. Etna, you may be tempted to try paragliding or hang-gliding; contact **No Limits Etna Center** (✉ Via Milano 6/a, Catania ☎ 095/7213682 ☎ 095/7212447 ⊕ www.etnacenter.net). For nonpilots, there are tandem flights and microlight trips, as well as courses of varying lengths. The company also organizes free climbing, caving, and diving expeditions.

> **off the beaten path**
>
> **BRONTE –** On the slopes of Mt. Etna, Bronte was where Admiral Nelson was given a duchy by the grateful Bourbon monarchy, but it's better known as Italy's center for pistachio cultivation. The pistachio was introduced to Sicily with the Roman and Arab conquests. The bars here offer various pistachio delicacies such as nougat, *colomba*, *panettone* (both cakes), and ice cream.

Acireale

 16 km (10 mi) north of Catania.

Acireale sits amid a clutter of rocky pinnacles and lush lemon groves. The craggy coast is known as the Riviera dei Ciclopi, after the legend narrated in the *Odyssey,* in which the blinded cyclops Polyphemus hurled boulders at the retreating Ulysses, thus creating spires of rock, or *faraglioni.* Tourism has barely taken off here, so it's a good destination if you feel the need to put some distance between yourself and the busloads of tourists in Taormina. And though the beaches are rocky, there's good swimming here, too.

During Carnival celebrations, considered the best in Sicily, streets are jammed with thousands of fancy-dressed revelers and floats dripping with flowers and gaudy papier-mâché models.

Begin your visit to Acireale with a stroll down to the public gardens, **Villa Belvedere,** at the end of the main Corso Umberto, for superb coastal views. There's a good vista from **Belvedere di Santa Caterina,** near the Terme, visited by Lord Byron (1788–1824) during his Italian wanderings.

With its cupola and twin turrets, Acireale's **Duomo** is an extravagant baroque construction dating back to the 17th century. In the chapel to the right of the altar, look for the 17th-century silver statue of Santa Venera, patron saint of Acireale, made by Mario D'Angelo, and the early 18th-century frescoes by Antonio Filocamo. ⊠ *Piazza Duomo* ☎ *095/601797* ☉ *Daily 8–noon and 4–7.*

need a break?

Acireale is renowned in Sicily for its marzipan, made into fruit shapes and delicious biscuits. You'll find the tasty treat in pasticcerias around town. **El Dorado** (⊠ Corso Umberto 5 ☎ 095/601464) serves delicious ice creams, and the *granita di mandorla* (almond granita), available in summer, invites a first-hand acquaintance. **Castorina** (⊠ Piazza del Duomo 25 ☎ 095/601546) serves both marzipan and ice cream.

The sulfur-rich volcanic waters from Mt. Etna found at **Terme di Acireale** were first used by the Greeks. In the 2nd century AD, Acireale's patron saint, Venera, was martyred, after which the waters were accorded miraculous powers. After 1873, when the Santa Venera bathing establishment was created with its park, the baths attracted a stream of celebrated visitors including Wagner. Book in advance to use the baths and have mud treatments and massages (multiday treatment packages are available). Nonpatrons can wander the gardens for free. ⊠ *Via delle Terme 47* ☎ *095/601508* ☎ *095/606468* ⊕ *www.terme-acireale.com* ✉ *Gardens free* ☉ *Treatments by appointment, daily 7–1 and 2–8. Gardens daily 9–8.*

off the beaten path

SANTA MARIA LA SCALA – A half-hour's walk from Acireale's center, this picturesque harbor is the scene of fishermen unloading brightly colored boats. Inexpensive lunches are served in the many restaurants along the harbor. The price of your fresh fish dish depends upon its weight.

Where to Stay & Eat

$$ ✕ **Al Molino.** Right next to the old water mill on the *lungomare* in Santa Maria la Scala, this stylish local haunt is devoted to seafood, from the antipasto and pasta to the main course. Follow local tradition and finish the meal with a lemon sorbet. ⊠ *Via Molino 104, Santa Maria la Scala* ☎ *095/7648116* ▭ *AE, MC, V* ☉ *Closed Wed. and Jan. 23–Feb. 7.*

$ ✕ **La Grotta.** This conventional-looking trattoria is a front for a dining room within a cave with an actual rock-face wall. Try the *insalata di mare* (a selection of delicately steamed fish served with lemon and olive oil) or fish grilled over charcoal. Chef Carmelo Strano's menu is small but immaculate; you will need to book in advance. ⊠ *Via Scalo Grande 46* ☎ *095/7648153* ⌑ *Reservations essential* ▭ *AE, MC, V* ☉ *Closed Tues. and mid-Oct.–early Nov.*

Nightlife & the Arts

Acireale is known for its puppet theater, a Sicilian tradition that has all but died out in other parts of the island, with the exception of Palermo. See shows at **Coop E. Magri** (⊠ Corso Umberto 11 ☎ 095/606272). The **Teatro dell'Opera dei Pupi** (⊠ Via Nazionale 95, Turi Grasso ☎ 095/7648035) has puppet shows and also an exhibition of puppets.

Shopping

At **Bottega d'Arte** (⊠ Via Vittorio Emanuele 86 ☎ 095/606805), you can see a local artist at work, carving wood statues and traditional carts, as his father and grandfather did before him. He also makes brass and wooden puppets.

Taormina

52 *43 km (27 mi) southwest of Messina, 50 km (31 mi) north of Catania.*

The natural beauty of the medieval mountaintop town of Taormina is so great that even its considerable overdevelopment has not spoiled its grandeur. The view of the sea and Mt. Etna from its jagged cactus-covered cliffs is as close to perfection as a panorama can get, especially on clear days when the snowcapped volcano's white puffs of smoke rise against the blue sky. Writers have extolled Taormina's beauty almost since its founding in the 6th century BC by Greeks from Naples; Goethe and D. H. Lawrence were among its more recent enthusiasts. The Greeks put a premium on finding impressive locations to stage their dramas, and Taormina's **Teatro Greco** occupies one of the finest of theater sites. It was built during the 3rd century BC and rebuilt by the Romans during the 2nd century AD. Its acoustics are exceptional: even today a stage whisper can be heard in the last rows. In summer, Taormina hosts an arts festival of music and dance events and a film festival; many performances are held in the Teatro Greco. ⊠ *Via Teatro Greco* ☎ *0942/232220* 🎟 *€4* ☉ *Daily 9–1 hr before sunset.*

Taormina's many 14th- and 15th-century palaces have been carefully preserved. Especially beautiful is the **Palazzo Corvaja** (⊠ Largo Santa Caterina ☎ 0942/23243), with characteristic black-lava and white-limestone inlays. Today it houses the tourist office and the **Museo di Arte e Storia Popolare**, which has a collection of cribs, carts, puppets, and folklore. ⊠ *Palazzo Corvaja* 🎟 *€2.60* ☉ *Tues.–Sun. 9–1 and 4–8.*

You can approach the medieval **Castello Saraceno** (⊠ Monte Tauro), enticingly perched on an adjoining cliff above town by footpath or car, but you cannot continue all the way to the castle itself.

From the main Corso Umberto, stroll down Via Bagnoli Croce to the **Parco Duca di Cesarò**, the public gardens designed by Florence Trevelyan Cacciola, a Scottish lady "invited" to leave England following a romantic liaison with the future Edward VII (1841–1910). Arriving in Taormina in 1889, she married a local professor and devoted herself to the gardens, filling them with Mediterranean plants, ornamental pavilions (known as the beehives), and fountains. Stop by the panoramic bar, which has stunning views.

> **need a break?**
>
> A marzipan devotee should not leave Taormina without trying one of the gooey sweets—maybe in the guise of the ubiquitous *fico d'India* (prickly pear)—at **Bar Mocambo** (⊠ Piazza IX Aprile ☎ 0942/23350).

Where to Stay & Eat

$$$–$$$$ ✕ **La Giara.** Known throughout southern Italy, this is one of Taormina's oldest restaurants, elegant and classical in style, and enhanced by columns of Syracuse stone sculpted by local master stonecutters. The kitchen blends upscale modern techniques with the simple flavors of traditional specialties. Try the *involtini di cernia al finocchietto selvatico* (stuffed grouper with wild fennel). You can extend your evening by taking an after-dinner drink at the popular piano bar. ⊠ *Vico La Floresta 1* ☎ *0942/23360* 🖃 *AE, DC, MC, V* ☉ *Closed Mon. Oct.–June and Sun.–Thurs. Nov. and Feb.–Mar. No lunch.*

$$–$$$ ✕ **Luraleo.** Here you can dine indoors by candlelight or, in summer, in the vine-covered garden. It's touristy, but the food is of a high standard, with the accent on fish—delight in the unusual risotto with salmon and pistachios, a house specialty, or choose a live lobster. There's a rich selection of antipasti. Service can be slow. ⊠ *Via Bagnoli Croce 27*

☎ 0942/24279 ▤ AE, DC, MC, V ☺ Closed Wed. Oct.–June and 3 wks Feb.–Mar.

$$–$$$ ✕ **Granduca.** There's an antiques shop in the entrance of this tastefully decorated restaurant, where cane chairs and luxurious plants jostle for space among the objets d'art. Your attention, however, will be principally occupied by the riveting views from the terrace. In summer, you can eat outside in the floral gardens. Try such well-executed dishes as *fettuccine al Granduca* (wide-ribbon pasta with a creamy vegetable sauce). There's also a wood-fired oven for pizzas. ☒ *Corso Umberto 172* ☎ 0942/24983 ▤ AE, DC, MC, V ☺ Closed Nov., 3 wks Feb.–Mar., and Tues. Dec.–Easter.

$$ ✕ **La Dracena.** Just behind the castle, this place takes its name from the dragon tree in the garden and is ideal for an alfresco meal. The *mezze lune* (half-open ravioli) and dishes with zucchini are very good. ☒ *Via Michele Amari 4* ☎ 0942/23491 ▤ AE, DC, MC, V ☺ Closed Mon. and mid-Jan.–mid-Mar.

$$$$ ▥ **Grand Hotel Timeo.** The deluxe Timeo wears a graceful patina that suggests it's been here—in a princely perch overlooking the town and just below the Teatro Greco—untouched since the dolce vita days. A splash of baroque mixes with the Mediterranean flavor in the lobby, with wooden floors, tile- and brickwork, and vaulting. Wrought-iron and wicker chairs surround marble tables in the bar and on the adjoining palatial patio. The rooms are luxuriously decorated with fine earth-tone linens and drapes, Oriental rugs, gilt-framed prints, and exquisite moldings on butter-color walls. ☒ *Via Teatro Greco 59, 98039* ☎ 0942/23801 ᕟ 0942/628501 ⊕ *www.framon-hotels.com* ⤳ 34 rooms, 22 suites ᗉ *Restaurant, room service, in-room safes, minibars, bar, convention center* ▤ AE, DC, MC, V ⦿ FAP, MAP.

$$$$ ▥ **San Domenico Palace.** Sweeping views from this converted 15th-century convent will linger in your mind long after you're gone. And the gardens—full of red trumpet flowers, bougainvillea, and lemons—have a dramatic vista of the castle, the sea, and Mt. Etna. Luxury and comfort are bywords in this deluxe hotel, which has even managed to incorporate wheelchair access and climate control. The essential Renaissance flavor is preserved, however, with the cloisters and the chapel, now a bar. ☒ *Piazza San Domenico 5, 98039* ☎ 0942/613111 ᕟ 0942/625506 ⊕ *www.sandomenico.thi.it* ⤳ 100 rooms, 15 suites ᗉ 3 *restaurants, minibars, pool, gym, bar, free parking* ▤ AE, DC, MC, V.

$$$$ ▥ **Villa Diodoro.** High on a cliff near the Greek amphitheater, this hotel commands superlative views. One of its most attractive features is the relaxing, sprightly garden, where you can have a drink and watch the play of light over the sea. A regular hotel bus service runs to the beach (€2.60). ☒ *Via Bagnoli Croce 75, 98039* ☎ 0942/23312 ᕟ 0942/23391 ⊕ *www.gaishotels.com* ⤳ 99 rooms ᗉ *Restaurant, minibars, 3 tennis courts, pool, bar* ▤ AE, DC, MC, V.

$$$–$$$$ ▥ **Romantik Villa Ducale.** Formerly the summer residence of a local aristocrat, this stupendously sited villa, a 10–15-minute walk from the center of Taormina, has been converted into a comfortable hotel by his great-grandson. Individually styled rooms furnished with antiques and an intimate wood-paneled library create an atmosphere at once homelike and palatial, while the vast roof terrace, where breakfast is served, takes full advantage of the wide panorama embracing Etna and the bay below. In summer, a free shuttle bus connects the hotel with the area's best beaches. ☒ *Via L. da Vinci 60, 98039* ☎ 0942/28153 ᕟ 0942/28710 ⊕ *www.hotelvilladucale.it* ⤳ 15 rooms, 1 suite ᗉ *Minibars, bar* ▤ AE, DC, MC, V ☺ Closed Nov. 26–Feb. 27.

$$ ▥ **Villa Fiorita.** This converted private home near the Greek amphitheater has excellent northerly coastal views from nearly every room.

Rooms vary in size and furnishings, but most are bright, breezy, and colorful, with large windows and balconies (do ask). Prices are reasonable considering the compact swimming pool and garden. The elevator is at the top of 65 steps. ✉ *Via Pirandello 39, 98039* ☎ *0942/24122* 🖷 *0942/ 625967* ⊕ *www.villafioritahotel.com* ⇋ *24 rooms, 1 suite* ♨ *Pool, bar* ⊟ *AE, MC, V.*

$ 🏨**Arathena Rocks Hotel.** Here's a good choice if you want to stay near the sea. Giardini-Naxos makes a great base, in summer just as lively as Taormina, and the broad, sandy beach is a bonus. The hotel stands at one end of the bay, right on the cape where Greek settlers first landed in Sicily. There's also a splendid pool, around which Sicilian singers and musicians entertain you every other night in summer. A twice-daily free bus service links the hotel to Taormina. ✉ *Via Calcide Eubea 55, 98035 Giardini Naxos* ☎ *0942/51349* 🖷 *0942/51690* ⇋ *49 rooms* ⊕ *www. hotelarathena.com* ♨ *Restaurant, pool, bar* ⊟*AE, DC, MC, V* ⊙ *Closed Nov.–Easter.*

Nightlife & the Arts

FESTIVALS The Greek Theater and the Palazzo dei Congressi, near the entrance to the theater, are the main venues for the summer festival dubbed **Taormina Arte** (☎0942/21142 ⊕www.taormina-arte.com) held each year from May to September and encompassing classical music, ballet, theater, and also the famous **film festival** (⊕ www.taorminafilmfest.it) in June and July.

Sports & the Outdoors

Sant'Alessio and Santa Teresa, north of Taormina, are worth stretching out on (the beaches just below Taormina itself are disappointing). If you feel like braving the ups and downs of Taormina and its surroundings by bike, you can have one delivered by **Rent a Bike** (✉ Via Naxos 39–41 ☎ 0942/56090; 0942/23193 Nov.–Easter)

Castelmola

53 *5 km (3 mi) west of Taormina, 65 km (40 mi) south of Messina.*

If your passion for heights hasn't been quelled, visit Castelmola, the tiny town above Taormina with a spectacular 360-degree panorama. Local bars make their own refreshing almond wine.

> **en route** The 50-km (30-mi) stretch of road between Taormina and Messina is flanked by lush vegetation and seascapes. Inlets are punctuated by gigantic, oddly shaped rocks. It was along this coast, legend says, that the giant one-eyed Cyclops hurled his boulders down on Ulysses and his terrified men as they fled to the sea in Homer's *Odyssey*.

Messina

54 *43 km (27 mi) northeast of Taormina, 94 km (59 mi) northeast of Catania.*

Messina's ancient history lists a series of disasters, but the city nevertheless managed to develop a fine university and a thriving cultural environment. At 5 o'clock in the morning on December 28, 1908, Messina changed from a flourishing metropolis of 120,000 to a heap of rubble, shaken to pieces by an earthquake that turned into a tidal wave and left 80,000 dead and the city almost completely leveled. As you approach the sickle-shape bay, through which ferries connect Sicily to the mainland, you won't notice any outward indication of the disaster, except for the modern countenance of a 3,000-year-old city. The somewhat flat look is a precaution of seismic planning: tall buildings are not permitted.

The reconstruction of Messina's Norman and Romanesque **Duomo,** originally built by the Norman king Roger II in 1197, has retained much of the original plan, including a handsome crown of Norman battlements, an enormous apse, and a splendid wood-beam ceiling. The adjoining **bell tower**—of a much later date—contains one of the largest and most complex mechanical clocks in the world, constructed in 1933 with a host of gilded automatons, including a roaring lion—that spring into action every day at the stroke of noon. ⊠ *Piazza del Duomo* ☎ *090/675175* ⊙ *Daily 8–12:30 and 4–7.*

Where to Stay & Eat

$$ ✕ **Da Piero.** An institution in Messina for decades, this centrally located restaurant (four blocks up from Piazza Cairoli) trades on its well-deserved reputation for classic Sicilian dishes, particularly seafood. In season, try the *involtini di pesce spada* (stuffed swordfish), while the exquisite calamari are good at any time. Marsala sipped with one of the rich homemade desserts makes for a grand finale. ⊠ *Via Ghibellina 121* ☎ *090/718365* ⊟ *AE, DC, MC, V* ⊙ *Closed Sun. and Aug.*

$$$$ ▦ **Grand Hotel Liberty.** Across the piazza from the train station, this hotel—at the top end of Messina's offerings—is a cool haven from the bustle of the surrounding streets. The entrance and public rooms are sumptuously fitted out in a white-marble neoclassical style with a meticulous attention to detail, while bedrooms are plainer but comfortably equipped. ⊠ *Via I Settembre 15, 98123* ☎ *090/6409436* 🖷 *090/6409340* ⊕ *www.framon-hotels.com* ⇗ *51 rooms* ⚹ *Restaurant, minibars, bar, meeting rooms* ⊟ *AE, DC, MC, V.*

THE AEOLIAN ISLANDS

Off Sicily's northeast coast lies an archipelago of seven spectacular islands of volcanic origin. The Isole Eolie (Aeolian Islands), also known as the Isole Lipari (Lipari Islands), were named after Aeolus, the Greek god of the winds, who is said to keep all the earth's winds stuffed in a bag in his cave here. The Aeolians are a world of grottoes and clear-water caves carved by waves through the centuries. Superb snorkeling and scuba-diving abound in the clearest and cleanest of Italy's waters. Of course, the beautiful people of high society discovered the archipelago years ago—here Roberto Rossellini courted his star and future wife Ingrid Bergman in 1950—and you should not expect complete isolation, at least on the main islands. August, in particular, can get unpleasantly overcrowded, and lodging and travel should always be booked as early as possible.

Lipari provides the widest range of accommodations and is a good jumping-off point for day trips to the other islands. Most exclusive are Vulcano and Panarea, the former noted for its black sands and stupendous sunsets (and prices), as well as the acrid smell of its sulfur emissions, while the latter is, according to some, the prettiest. Most remarkable is Stromboli (pronounced with the accent on the first syllable) with its constant eruptions, and remotest are Filicudi and Alicudi, where electricity was only introduced in the 1980s. Access to the islands is via ferry and hydrofoil from Sicily (usually Messina) or Naples. The bars in the Aeolian Islands, and especially those on Lipari, are known for their granitas of fresh strawberries, melon, peaches, and other fruits. Many Sicilians, especially on the Aeolians and in Messina, Taormina, and Catania, begin the hot summer days with a *granita di caffè* (a coffee ice topped with whipped cream), into which they dunk their breakfast rolls. You can get one any time of day.

Lipari

⑤⑤ *37 km (23 mi) north of Milazzo, 2 hrs 10 mins by ferry, 1 hr by hydrofoil; Milazzo: 41 km (25 mi) west of Messina.*

The largest and most developed of the Aeolians, Lipari welcomes you with distinctive pastel-color houses. Fields of spiky agaves dot the northernmost tip of the island, Acquacalda, indented with pumice and obsidian quarries. In the west is San Calogero, where you can explore hot springs and mud baths. From the red lava base of the island rises a plateau crowned with a 16th-century castle and a 17th-century cathedral.

★ The vast, multibuilding **Museo Eoliano** is one of the best archaeological museums in Europe, with an intelligently arranged collection of prehistoric finds—some dating as far back as 4000 BC—from various sites in the archipelago. ⊠ *Via Castello* ☎ *090/9880174* ☒ *€4.50* ⊗ *Daily 9–1 and 4–7.*

Where to Stay & Eat

★ **$$** ✕⌂ **Il Filippino.** The views from the flower-strewn outdoor terrace of this restaurant in the upper town are a fitting complement to the superb fare. Founded in 1910, the restaurant ($–$$$) is rightly rated one of the archipelago's best. Top choice is seafood: the *zuppa di pesce* and the *antipasto* platter of smoked and marinated fish are absolute musts. Leave some room for the local version of cassata, accompanied by sweet Malvasia wine from Salina. The restaurant also runs Residence Albergo Mendolita, a comfortable bed-and-breakfast 300 yards away. ⊠ *Piazza Municipio* ☎ *090/9811002; 090/9812374 Mendolita* 🖷 *090/9814879* ⊕ *www.filippino.it, www.mendolita.it* 🛏 *18 rooms, 1 suite* ▭ *AE, DC, MC, V* ⊗ *Closed Mon. in Oct.–Mar. and Nov. 10–Dec. 20.*

$$–$$$$ ⌂ **Gattopardo Park Hotel.** Bright bougainvillea and fiery hibiscus set the tone in this grand villa, whose restaurant has sweeping views of the sea. Guest quarters are in the 19th-century main villa or in whitewashed bungalows in the surrounding tranquil parkland. Public rooms have wood-beamed ceilings and rustic-style furnishings. A minibus shuttles between the hotel and Spiagge Bianche. There are also trips round the island, boat excursions to Vulcano and Stromboli, and folklore evenings. Halfboard is required in summer; weekly discounts are available. ⊠ *Via Diana, 98055* ☎ *090/9811035* 🖷 *090/9880207* ⊕ *www.netnet.it/hotel/gattopardo* 🛏 *53 rooms* ⟨ *Restaurant, bar* ▭ *MC, V* ⊗ *Closed Nov.–Mar.* ⁋⌀ *MAP.*

$$$ ⌂ **Villa Augustus.** Tucked away off a side street in the center of Lipari's old town, this is a peaceful enclave, where a simple homey spirit prevails, with friendly service and a discreet attention to detail. In addition to a palm-shaded backyard garden, there's a roof-garden offering good sea views. Apartment-style rooms are bright and spacious. You'll have to arrive during daytime hours, as the hotel is managed by only one person. ⊠ *Vico Ausonia 16, 98055* ☎ *090/9811232* 🖷 *090/9812233* ⊕ *www.villaaugustus.it* 🛏 *34 rooms* ⟨ *Piano bar* ▭ *AE, DC, MC, V* ⊗ *Closed Nov.–Feb.*

Vulcano

⑤⑥ *18 km (11 mi) northwest of Lipari, 25 mins by ferry, 10 mins by hydrofoil; 55 km (34 mi) northwest of Milazzo.*

True to its name—and the origin of the term—Vulcano has a profusion of fumaroles sending up jets of hot vapor, but the volcano here has long been dormant. Many come to soak in the strong-smelling sulfur baths, whose odors will greet you, when the wind is in the right direction, long before you disembark. The island has some of the archipelago's best beaches, though the volcanic black sand can be off-putting at first. You can ascend to the crater (1,266 ft above sea level) on muleback for a wonderful view or take boat rides into the grottoes around the base. From Capo Grillo there is a view of all the Aeolians.

Where to Stay

★ $$$$ 🖼 **Les Sables Noires.** Named for the black sands of the beach in front, this luxury hotel is superbly sited on the beautiful Porto di Ponente. The cool modern furnishings and inviting pool (for those unwilling to lounge on the private beach) induce a sybaritic mood, while the white-walled guest rooms are also tasteful and spacious. The restaurant, naturally, looks out over the bay: sunsets are framed by the towering *faraglioni* (pillars of rock rising dramatically out of the sea). Week-long stays are required in high season. ⊠ *Porto di Ponente, 98050* ☎ *090/9850* 📠 *090/9852454* ⊕ *www.framon-hotels.com* ➾ *48 rooms* ⚹ *Restaurant, pool, beach, bar* ☰ *AE, DC, MC, V* ⊗ *Closed mid-Oct.–mid-Apr.*

Salina

57 *15 km (9 mi) north of Lipari, 50 mins by ferry, 20 mins by hydrofoil; 52 km (38 mi) northwest of Milazzo.*

The second largest of the Aeolian Islands, Salina is also the most fertile—which accounts for its excellent Malvasia dessert wine. Excursions go up Mt. Fossa delle Felci, which rises to more than 3,000 ft. Salina is also the highest of the islands, and the vineyards and fishing villages along its slopes add to its allure. Malvasia wine here is locally produced, unlike that found on other islands. Salina has reasonably priced accommodations and restaurants—and fewer crowds than Lipari.

Where to Stay

$–$$$ 🖼 **Bellavista.** This is a quiet hotel in a quiet location, even though it's right next to the port. Rooms are simply furnished and cheerfully decorated with bright materials and ceramic tiles. Almost all have sea views, which can be enjoyed from the balconies. The management provides a list of things to do while on Salina and can organize boat excursions and transport around the island, though you may well opt for the *dolce far niente* (idle life). ⊠ *Via Risorgimento, Santa Marina Salina, 98050* 📠📠 *090/9843009; 090/9281558 in winter* ➾ *13 rooms* ☰ *No credit cards* ⊗ *Closed Nov.–Mar.*

Panarea

58 *18 km (11 mi) north of Lipari, 2 hrs by ferry, 25–50 mins by hydrofoil; 55 km (33 mi) north of Milazzo.*

Panarea has some of the most dramatic scenery of the islands: wild caves carved out of the rock and dazzling flora. The exceptionally clear water and the richness of life on the sea floor make Panarea especially suitable for underwater exploration, though there is little in the way of beaches. The outlying rocks and islets make a gorgeous sight, and you can enjoy the panorama on an easy excursion to the small Bronze Age village at Capo Milazzese.

Where to Stay

$$$$ 🖼 **La Raya.** This discreet, expensive hotel is perfectly in keeping with the elite style of Panarea, most exclusive of the Aeolian islands. Public rooms, including bars, a broad terrace, and an open-air restaurant, are built into a hillside right on the port; the residential area is a 10-minute walk inland, though the rooms still enjoy the serene prospect of the sea and Stromboli from their balconies. The decor is elegant and understated,

with Moorish-type hangings and low divans helping to create a tone of serene luxury. Families with young children are asked to book elsewhere. ⊠ *San Pietro, 98050* 🕿 *090/983103* ⊕ *www.hotelraya.it* 🛏 *30 rooms* ⚇ *Restaurant, minibars, bar, nightclub* ☱ *AE, DC, MC, V* ⊙ *Closed mid-Oct.–mid-Apr.*

Stromboli

❺⓿ *40 km (25 mi) north of Lipari, 3 hrs 45 mins by ferry, 65–90 mins by hydrofoil; 63 km (40 mi) north of Milazzo.*

This northernmost of the Aeolians (also accessible from Naples) consists entirely of the cone of an active volcano. The view from the sea—especially at night, as an endless stream of glowing red-hot lava flows into the water—is unforgettable. Stromboli is in a constant state of mild dissatisfaction, and every now and then its anger flares up, so authorities insist that you climb to the top (about 3,031 ft above sea level) only with a guide. The round-trip—climb, pause, and descent—usually starting at around 6 PM, takes about four hours. Some choose to camp overnight atop the volcano—again, a guide is essential. You will find a small selection of reasonably priced hotels and restaurants in the main town, and a choice of lively clubs and cafés for the younger set. In addition to the island tour, excursions include boat trips around the naturally battlemented isle of Strombolicchio.

Numerous tour operators are available for Stromboli, among them **Società Navigazione Pippo** (🕿 090/986135 or 0338/9857883). Rates are around €20 per person for four hours.

Alicudi

❻⓿ *65 km (40 mi) west of Lipari, 3 hrs 25 mins–3 hrs 50 mins by ferry, 60–95 mins by hydrofoil; 102 km (68 mi) northwest of Milazzo.*

The farthest outpost of the Aeolians remains sparsely inhabited, wild, and at peace. Here and on Filicudi there is a tiny selection of accommodations, but you can rent rooms cheaply. Only the coming and going of hydrofoils disturbs the rhythm of life here, and the only noise is the occasional braying of donkeys.

Filicudi

❻❶ *30 km (16 mi) west of Salina (30–60 mins by hydrofoil); 82 km (54 mi) northwest of Milazzo.*

Just a dot in the sea, Filicudi is famous for its unusual volcanic rock formations and the enchanting **Grotta del Bue Marino** (Grotto of the Sea Ox). The crumbled remains of a prehistoric village are at Capo Graziano. The island, which is spectacular for walking and hiking and is still a truly undiscovered, restful haven, has a handful of hotels and pensions, and some families put up guests. Car ferries are only available in summer.

Where to Stay

★ **$–$$** ⊡ **La Canna.** Set on a height above the tiny port, this *pensione* commands fabulous views of sky and sea from its flower-filled terrace. It's wonderful to wake up to the utter tranquillity that characterizes any stay on this island. Rooms are small but adequate, kept clean and tidy by the friendly family staff, and the cooking is quite good, usually centered around the day's catch (half- or full board required in peak season). Arrange to be collected at the port. ⊠ *Via Rosa 43, 98050* 🕿 *090/9889956* 📠 *090/9889966* ⊕ *www.lacannahotel.it* 🛏 *10 rooms* ⚇ *Restaurant, bar* ☱ *MC, V* ⊚ *FAP, MAP.*

SICILY A TO Z

To research prices, get advice from other travelers, and book travel arrangements, visit www.fodors.com.

AIRPORTS
Sicily can be reached from all major cities via Rome, Milan, or Naples on Alitalia. Meridiana and Air One also connect Catania and Palermo to other cities all over Italy, and Alitalia operates periodic connections to Cagliari, Sardinia. Planes land at Aeroporto Falcone-Borsellino (also known as Aeroporto Punta Raisi), 32 km (19 mi) west of Palermo at Punta Raisi, or Catania's Aeroporto Fontanarossa, 5 km (3 mi) south of city center, the main airport on Sicily's eastern side. There are also direct flights to Sicily from London on Meridiana and Munich on Lufthansa. Note that flights from Sicily to points elsewhere, especially one-way flights, can be bought much cheaper from travel agencies in Italy than internationally or through Web sites.

🛈 Airport Information **Aeroporto Punta Raisi** ☎ 091/591698 ⊕ www.gesap.it. **Aeroporto Fontanarossa** ☎ 095/7239111 ⊕ www.aeroporto.catania.it.

TRANSFERS Prestia & Comandè buses run every half hour between Palermo's Punta Raisi airport and the city center (Piazza Castelnuovo and the central station); tickets cost €4.65. Taxis charge around €35 for the same 45-minute trip. To get directly to the train station, take the hourly train leaving from the airport. There are also less frequent bus connections directly to and from Agrigento and Trapani on Sal and Segesta lines, respectively. Catania's Fontanarossa airport (closed frequently because of volcanic dust from Etna) is served by Alibus, which leaves about every 20 minutes from the airport and the central train station, with a stop at Piazza Stesicoro, on Via Etna. The journey takes around 25 minutes; tickets cost €1. Taxis cost around €20.

🛈 Taxis & Shuttles **Alibus** ☎ 095/7360450. **Prestia & Comandè** ☎ 091/580457.

BOAT & FERRY TRAVEL
Frequent car ferries cross the strait between Villa San Giovanni in Calabria and Messina on the island. The crossing usually takes about half an hour, but during the summer months there can be considerable delays. Overnight car ferries operated by Tirrenia run daily all year between Naples and Palermo. Tirrenia also runs regular service between Palermo and Cagliari, Sardinia, and between Trapani and Tunisia (in winter, frequency can be as low as once per week). SNAV has a daytime service (April–October) by faster catamarans, which also carry vehicles. Passenger-only *aliscafi* (hydrofoils) also cross the strait from Reggio di Calabria to Messina in about 15 minutes. Grimaldi Lines' Grandi Navi Veloci run beautiful cruise-ship–like ferries to Genoa (a 20-hour trip) year-round. The Aeolian Islands are reachable by hydrofoil from Naples, Messina, Palermo, and Milazzo. From Milazzo you can get ferry service to the islands. Call SNAV or Siremar, the other major ferry company serving the Aeolians.

FARES & 🛈 Boat & Ferry Information **Grandi Navi Veloci** ☎ 091/587404 in Palermo
SCHEDULES ⊕ www.gnv.it. **Siremar** ☎ 081/5800340. **SNAV** ☎ 091/6118525 Palermo; 081/7612348 Naples ⊕ www.snavali.com. **Tirrenia** ☎ 081/7201111 Naples; 091/6021111 Palermo ⊕ www.tirrenia.it.

BUS TRAVEL
Air-conditioned coaches connect major and minor cities and are often faster and more convenient than local trains but slightly more expensive. Various companies serve the different routes. SAIS runs frequently

between Palermo and Catania, Messina, and Siracusa, in each case arriving at and departing from near the train stations. Cuffaro runs between Palermo and Agrigento. On the south and east coasts and in the interior, SAIS connects the main centers, including Catania, Agrigento, Enna, Taormina, and Siracusa. Etna Trasporti operates between Catania, Caltagirone, Piazza Armerina, and Taormina. Interbus serves the routes between Messina, Taormina, Catania, and Siracusa.

🚍 Bus Information **Cuffaro** ☎ 091/6161510. **Etna Trasporti** ☎ 095/530396. **Interbus** ☎ 095/532716. **SAIS** ☎ 091/6166028 Palermo; 095/536168; 095/536201 Catania.

CAR RENTAL

Renting a car is the best way to get around Sicily. Trains are unreliable and slow, and buses, though faster and air-conditioned in summer, can be subject to delays and strikes. Cars can be rented at airports and downtown locations in every major city.

🚗 Local Agencies **Avis** ✉ Aeroporto Fontanarossa, Catania ☎ 095/340500 ✉ Piazza S. Calogero 11, Agrigento ☎ 0922/26353 ✉ Aeroporto Punta Raisi, Palermo ☎ 091/591684 ✉ Via F. Crispi 113/115/117, Palermo ☎ 091/586940. **Hertz** ✉ Aeroporto Fontanarossa, Catania ☎ 095/341595 ✉ Via Toselli 16/c, Catania ☎ 095/322560 ✉ Efeso Viaggi, Via Imera 209, Agrigento ☎ 0922/556090 ✉ Aeroporto Punta Raisi, Palermo ☎ 091/213112 ✉ Via Messina 7/e, Palermo ☎ 091/331668. **Maggiore** ✉ Aeroporto Fontanarossa, Catania ☎ 095/340594 ✉ Piazza Verga 48, Catania ☎ 095/536927 ✉ Aeroporto Punta Raisi, Palermo ☎ 091/591681 ✉ Stazione Marittima, Palermo ☎ 091/6810801.

CAR TRAVEL

This is the ideal way to explore Sicily. Modern highways circle and bisect the island, making all main cities easily reachable. A20 (supplemented by S113 at points) connects Messina and Palermo; Messina and Catania are linked by A18; running through the interior, from Catania to west of Cefalù, is A19; threading west from Palermo, A29 runs to Trapani and the airport, with a leg stretching down to Mazara del Vallo. The superstrada S115 runs along the southern coast, and connecting superstrade lace the island.

You will likely hear stories about the dangers of driving in Sicily. Some are true, and others less so. In the big cities—especially Palermo, Catania, and Messina—streets are a honking mess, with lane markings and traffic lights taken as mere suggestions; you can avoid the chaos by leaving your car in a garage. However, once outside the urban areas, autostrade, superstrade, and regional state roads turn into a driving enthusiast's dream—they are winding, sparsely populated, and well paved and maintained, and they usually reveal a new, ripping view around every bend.

RULES OF THE ROAD Sicilians, especially in Palermo, are among the country's most aggressive drivers. Traffic lights are taken with a grain of salt, and many large intersections are just games of chicken—you'll sit all day if you don't lurch out at some point. Do keep your eye out for all-important yield signs, which can be easy to miss but often take the place of stop signs or stop lights. An informal system exists in which people within earshot routinely double park—if you're blocked in, don't worry, just start honking and the owner will come move his car (and then, of course, take your space).

EMBASSIES & CONSULATES

🇬🇧 United Kingdom **U.K. Consulate** ✉ Via Cavour 121, Palermo ☎ 091/326412.

EMERGENCIES

🚑 **Ambulance, Police, Fire** ☎ 113. **Hospital** Palermo ☎ 091/288141 or 095/7591111.

INTERNET
🔲 Internet Shops **Internet Shop** ✉ Via Napoli 32/34, Kalsa Palermo ☎ 091/320697). **Aboriginal Internet Cafe** ✉ Via S. Spinuzza 51, Teatro Massimo area Palermo ☎ 091/6622229.

LANGUAGE
The Sicilian language is still strong on the island and varies enormously from town to town and from village to village. It sounds nothing like standard Italian; however, most Sicilians will speak to strangers (and do business) in standard Italian.

MAIL & SHIPPING
OVERNIGHT SERVICES In Palermo, the local courier used by UPS is Randazzo. The local FedEx courier in Palermo is SDA. To call for pickups or information from either Federal Express or UPS, use their national service numbers.
🔲 Major Services **Federal Express** ☎ 800/123800 or 02/2188444. **Randazzo** ✉ Via Sturzo 260, Zona Industriale, Carini ☎ 091/868-0200. **SDA** ✉ Via Pablo Picasso, Palermo ☎ 800/016027. **UPS** ☎ 02/25088001.
🔲 Post Offices **Palermo** ✉ Via Roma 322, Kalsa ☎ 091/7531111. **Siracusa** ✉ Piazza delle Poste, Ortygia ☎ 0931/489111.

OUTDOORS & SPORTS
There is a surfeit of beaches in Sicily, but many of them are too rocky, too crowded, or too dirty to be enjoyed for long. Tours in the Sicilian national parks re organized by Biosport. Walking expeditions by the day or week, as well as canoeing and biking in the Etna, Nebrodi, Madonie, and Peloritani parks, can all be arranged.
🔲 Tour Operator **Biosport** ✉ Via Garibaldi 110, 98100 Messina ☎ 090/6409800 or 091/545623 🖷 090/6409497.

SAFETY
Don't be paranoid about safety in Sicily, but do be careful. In the cities, particularly Palermo and Catania, it's not recommended to wander around unpopulated streets, especially at night, and you should never flaunt expensive watches, jewelry, and the like. Women traveling alone should keep out of deserted areas at all times. Watch your bags constantly (it's best to securely strap your handbag across your chest), especially at airports. Leaving valuables visible in your car while you go sightseeing is inviting trouble. Take precautions; then enjoy the company of the Sicilians. You will find them friendly and often willing to go out of their way to help you.

TOURS
Tours of Palermo and Monreale are provided by the Italian tour operator CST on Friday afternoon and Saturday morning, with pickups from your hotel or a central location such as outside the Politeama theater. Contact the agency to confirm details. CST also arranges tours of Taormina and Etna, bookable from their office in Taormina, as well as to Piazza Armerina, Agrigento, and western Sicily, or you can join a seven-day tour of all Sicily's major sights in a comfortable air-conditioned coach with an English-speaking guide, with weekly departures from either Palermo or Catania; the cost includes all meals and accommodations in luxury hotels.
🔲 Fees & Schedules **CST** ✉ Via E. Amari 124, Palermo ☎ 091/7439655 ⊕ www.tin.it/cst ✉ Corso Umberto 101, Taormina ☎ 0942/24189.

TRAIN TRAVEL
There are direct express trains from Milan and Rome to Palermo, Catania, and Siracusa. The Rome–Palermo and Rome–Siracusa trips take at

least 10 hours. After Naples, the run is mostly along the coast, so try to book a window seat on the right if you're not on an overnight train. At Villa San Giovanni, in Calabria, the train is separated and loaded onto a ferryboat to cross the strait to Messina.

Main lines connect Messina, Taormina, Siracusa, and Palermo. Secondary lines are generally very slow and unreliable. The Messina–Palermo run, along the northern coast, is especially scenic. Call FS for information.

Train Information FS (Italian State Railways) ☎ 147/888088.

VISITOR INFORMATION

Tourist Information Acireale ✉ Via Oreste Scionti 15, 95024 ☎ 095/892129 ⊕ www. acirealeturismo.it. **Agrigento** ✉ Viale della Vittoria 225, 92100 ☎ 0922/401352 ✉ Via Cesare Battisti 15, 92100 ☎ 0922/20454. **Caltagirone** ✉ Via V. Libertini 3, 95041 ☎ 0933/53809. **Caltanisetta** ✉ Corso Vittorio Emanuele 109, 93100 ☎ 0934/530411 ⊕www.aapit.cl.it. **Catania** ✉Via Cimarosa 10, 95124 ☎095/7306222 ⊕www.apt.catania. it ✉ Stazione Centrale, 95129 ☎ 095/7306255 ✉ Aeroporto Fontanarossa, 95121 ☎ 095/7306266. **Cefalù** ✉ Corso Ruggero 77, 90015 ☎ 0921/421050 ⊕ www.cefalu-tour.pa.it. **Enna** ✉ Via Roma 411, 94100 ☎ 0935/528228 ⊕ www.apt-enna.com. **Erice** ✉ Via Conte Pepoli 56, 91016 ☎ 0923/869388. **Lipari** ✉ Corso Vittorio Emanuele 202, 98055 ☎ 090/9880095 ⊕ www.tau.it/aapitme/isole.html. **Marsala** ✉ Via XI Maggio 100, 91025 ☎ 0923/714097. **Messina** ✉ Piazza della Repubblica, 98122 ☎ 090/672944 ✉ Via Calabria 301bis, 98123 ☎ 090/674236 ⊕ www.azienturismomessina.it. **Monreale** ✉ Piazza Duomo, 90046 ☎ 091/6564570. **Noto** ✉ Piazzale XVI Maggio, 96017 ☎ 0931/836744. **Palermo** ✉ Piazza Castelnuovo 35, 90141 ☎ 091/6165914 ✉ www. aapit.pa.it ✉ Stazione Centrale, Piazza Giulio Cesare, 90141 ☎ 091/583847 ⊕ www. aapit.pa.it ✉ Stazione Centrale, Piazza Giulio Cesare, 90141 ☎ 091/6165914 ✉ Aeroporto Punta Raisi, 90045 ☎091/591698. **Piazza Armerina** ✉Via Cavour 15, 94015 ☎0935/680201. **Siracusa** ✉Via San Sebastiano 43, 96100 ☎0931/481200 ⊕ www.apt-siracusa. it ✉ Via Maestranza 33, 96100 ☎ 0931/464255. **Taormina** ✉ Palazzo Corvaja, Largo Santa Caterina, 98039 ☎ 0942/23243 ⊕ www.gate2taormina.com. **Trapani** ✉ Piazza Saturno, 91100 ☎ 0923/29000 ⊕ www.apt.trapani.it.

SARDINIA

CAGLIARI, SU NURAXI, PORTO CERVO

FODOR'S CHOICE

Festa di Sant'Efisio, Cagliari
Su Gologone, restaurant and hotel, Nuoro
Su Nuraxi

HIGHLY RECOMMENDED

RESTAURANT   Il Faro, Oristano

HOTELS   Is Morus Relais, Pula
Hotel Le Dune, Costa Verde
Villa Las Tronas, Alghero

SIGHTS   Nora, Pula
Porto Cervo

Updated by
Robin S.
Goldstein

AN UNCUT JEWEL OF AN ISLAND, Sardinia remains unique and enigmatic. The mysterious stone *nuraghi* hint at the lifestyles of prehistoric settlers, while summer settlers of a more modern variety sail their yachts to the sparkling beaches of the Costa Smeralda to find modern luxury. But most of Sardinia's rugged land remains shepherd's country, silent and stark. Beautiful in its severity, Sardinia is a true getaway.

Sardinia is the second-largest island in the Mediterranean—it's just smaller than Sicily—and at about 180 km (112 mi) from mainland Italy is very much off the beaten track. A Phoenician stronghold in ancient times and later a Spanish dominion, it doesn't seem typically Italian in its color and flavor. It lies a bit too far from the mainland—from imperial and papal Rome and from the palaces of the Savoy dynasty—to have been transformed by the events that forged a national character. Yet Giuseppe Garibaldi, the charismatic national hero who led his troops in fervid campaigns to unify Italy in the mid-19th century, chose to spend his last years in relative isolation on the small island of Caprera, just off the coast of Sardinia.

Although Sardinia (Sardegna in Italian) is less than an hour by air and only several hours by boat from mainland Italy, it is removed from the mainstream of tourism except in July and August, when Italians take its beautiful coasts and clean waters by storm. But the interior is *never* crowded; Italian tourists in Sardinia come for the sea, less for the rugged and deserted mountain scenery.

In both its landscape and its character, Sardinia closely resembles Corsica, the French island across the 16-km-wide (10-mi-wide) windswept Strait of Bonifacio to the north. A dense bush, or *macchia,* barely penetrable in some districts, covers large areas. The terrain is rough, like the short, sturdy shepherds you see in the highlands—impassive figures engaged in one of the few gainful occupations the stony land allows. Shaggy flocks of sheep and goats, bells around their necks, are familiar features in the Sardinian landscape, just as their meat and pecorino cheese are staples of the island's cuisine.

Aside from the chic opulence of the Costa Smeralda, there's little sophistication in Sardinia, but the cost of living on the island is typically higher than on the mainland. The sprawling cities of Cagliari and Sassari have a distinctly provincial air. Even newer hotels may seem a little old-fashioned, and hotels of any vintage are hard to find inland. There's little traffic on the roads, and trains, buses, and people in general move at a gentle pace. The main highway linking Cagliari with Sassari was begun in 1820 by the Savoy ruler Carlo Felice; designated S131, but still referred to as the Strada Carlo Felice by the islanders, it runs through the fertile Campidano Plain for 216 km (134 mi) between the two cities.

Sardinians are courteous but remote, often favoring their forbidding native dialect over modern Italian. In hamlets. Women swathed in black shawls and long, full skirts look with suspicion upon strangers passing through. Like mainland Italians, the Sardinians are of varied origin. On the northwest coast, fine traceries of ironwork around a balcony underscore the Spanish influence. In the northeast, the inhabitants have Genoese or Pisan ancestry, and the headlands display the ruined fortresses of the ancient Pisan duchy of Malaspina on the Italian mainland. As you explore the southern coast, you'll come upon the physiognomies, customs, dialects, place names, and holy buildings of the Turks, Moors, Phoenicians, Austrians, and mainland Italians. If there are any pure Sardinians—or Sards—left, perhaps they can be found in the south-central

Numbers in the text correspond to numbers in the margin and on the Sardinia and Cagliari maps.

If you have 3 days

Unless you're planning a summer beach getaway, you would do well to confine the first two days of your visit to 🗺 **Cagliari** ①–⑥ ▶. In Sardinia's capital you'll find Italianate architecture, churches of all styles, and the **Museo Archeologico** ①, with the island's best antiquities collection. If you do not have your own transport, you can use taxis or buses to make easy day trips from Cagliari. Make a half a day's excursion on the second day to **Pula** ⑧; here great beaches rim the coast, and just outside is Nora, a Carthaginian and Roman archaeological site. On your third day, stop at **Su Nuraxi** ⑪, the island's most imposing nuraghic monument. Have lunch at **Oristano** ⑬ before continuing on to 🗺 **Alghero** ⑰, an appealing walled town about three hours from Cagliari on the northwest coast. Stay in Alghero for the third night.

17

If you have 5 days

Follow the itinerary above for the first three days. On days four and five, choose between luxury and adventure. For the former, stay in one of the hotels in or near 🗺 **Porto Cervo** ㉒, about three hours from Alghero. For the latter (a more economical option), make 🗺 **Nuoro** ⑮ your base from which to explore the rugged interior of the island. Don't spend much time exploring the provincial capital; instead veer south into the Barbagia region.

If you have 7 days

Spend your first two days exploring 🗺 **Cagliari** ①–⑥ ▶ and the beaches at **Villasimius** ⑦. On your third day, go southwest from Cagliari, taking in the ancient remains outside **Pula** ⑧, and follow along the western coast on the Strada Carlo Felice as far as the village of **Sant'Antioco** ⑨. Here a 20-minute ferry ride takes you to the island of 🗺 **San Pietro** ⑩ for the night. Continue up toward Oristano, making an inland detour to **Su Nuraxi** ⑪, outside the town of Barumini. Wildlife enthusiasts should take another jaunt north of Barumini to the **Giara di Gesturi** ⑫. On your fourth night, stay in 🗺 **Oristano** ⑬, which merits a cursory walk-through and a glimpse of the Carthaginian ruins at **Tharros** ⑭, just outside town. Head northeast for **Nuoro** ⑮ and its museum of folk culture before striking south into the Barbagia region, where tortuous roads wind their way over a wild terrain. If you prefer coastal attractions, spend no more than half a day exploring the region, then head west from Nuoro on road 129 to Bosa, where you turn right and travel through hilly scrub country to 🗺 **Alghero** ⑰, on the northwest coast. Spend your fifth night here. The next day head northeast across a coastline fringed with low cliffs, inlets, and small bays; stop to appreciate the seaside resorts, including **Castelsardo** ⑲. Stay the night at the fishing village of 🗺 **Santa Teresa di Gallura** ⑳, surrounded by fine beaches and well-equipped hotels. Spend your last day on the sun-kissed beaches of one of Europe's premier summer holiday destinations, the Costa Smeralda. Its most exclusive address is 🗺 **Porto Cervo** ㉒, the place for a final splurge before taking a ferry or plane back to the mainland from Olbia.

mountains, south of Nuoro, under the 6,000-ft crests of the Gennargentu Massif, in the rugged country still ironically called Barbagia, "Land of Strangers."

Exploring Sardinia

The island is about 260 km (162 mi) from north to south and takes three to four hours to drive on the main roads; it's roughly 120 km (75 mi) across. By car is the best way to see the island's most interesting sights, though Sardinia's mountainous terrain can make driving rigorous and slow; avoid night driving and beware of mountain fog. Local transportation is not geared to the needs of visitors, so you can cover more ground in less time if you have a car. Make an effort to take smaller roads for better views and a more rural experience. If you don't have a car, establish yourself in one of the larger towns and make excursions to as many attractions as time and schedules allow. There are bus and train connections to most places, except some areas of the Costa Smeralda and Su Nuraxi.

About the Restaurants & Hotels

The island's most luxurious hotels are on the Costa Smeralda. They have magnificent facilities but close from fall to spring; many are too remote to be good touring bases. Other, equally attractive coastal areas have seen a spate of resort hotels and villa colonies sprouting up; they, too, close from October through April, which narrows the choice of hotels considerably in other months. In the cities suggested as touring bases, you can expect to find standards of comfort slightly below those on the mainland. The best accommodations may be available at commercial hotels, which can mean little atmosphere. In smaller towns throughout the island, you'll find modest hotels offering basic accommodations, restrained but genuine hospitality, and low rates.

WHAT IT COSTS In euros					
	$$$$	$$$	$$	$	¢
RESTAURANTS	over €22	€17–€22	€12–€17	€7–€12	under €7
HOTELS	over €210	€160–€210	€110–€160	€60–€110	under €60

Restaurant prices are for a second course (secondo piatto). Hotel prices are for two people in a standard double room in high season, including tax and service.

Timing

If you can help it, avoid Sardinia in steamy August, when the island is swamped not only with tourists from the mainland but the Sards, too, taking their annual break. May and September are much quieter and still temperate. Sudden storms can be a hazard, but these blow over quickly. The sea remains warm enough for swimming well into October. The mountainous interior is probably at its best in spring, when the woods and valleys are alive with color and burgeoning growth. For the gradations of color, fall is also a good time. In winter, rain and clouds are common over high ground—and most of Sardinia is mountainous—and it snows most years in the Barbagia region. In the south, the weather rarely turns cold, but winter is not beach weather. Additionally, many resorts are closed from October to April, limiting lodging possibilities. Try to schedule your visit to Sardinia to coincide with one of the famous annual festivals. They are mega-affairs, with accommodation and restaurant space at a premium, so plan well ahead.

17

Beaches

For their fine sand and lack of crowds, Sardinia's beaches are among the best in the Mediterranean; its waters are among the cleanest, with the exception of those in the immediate vicinity of Cagliari, Arbatax, and Porto Torres. The beach resorts of the Costa Smeralda, on the northeastern tip of the island, are exclusive and expensive, but elsewhere on the island you can find beach areas with a wide range of prices. Many agree that the most beautiful beaches on the island are those of Cala di Luna and Cala Sisine, hidden among the rocky cliffs between Baunei and Dorgali, on the eastern coast; these remote strands can be reached only by boat from Cala Gonone or Arbatax. For more accessible beaches with more amenities, go to Santa Margherita di Pula, near Cagliari, where you'll find several hotels; to Villasimius and the Costa Rei, on the southeastern coast; or to the sandy coves sheltered by wind-carved granite boulders on the northern coast in the Gallura district and the archipelago of La Maddalena.

Festivals

As one of Italy's most remote regions—perhaps *the* most remote—Sardinia is not really a prime spot for sophisticated visual or performing arts. This same remoteness, however, can prove fruitful for sampling the local *feste*, or festivals. Ostensibly, the festivals celebrate a religious occasion, but often they are imbued with an almost pagan feel. The main festivals are at Cagliari (Festa di Sant'Efisio, May 1), Sassari (Ascension Day, the 40th day after Easter; La Cavalcata, penultimate Sunday of May, and I Candelieri, August 14), and Nuoro (penultimate Sunday in August). Some of the best are the smaller festivals in the mountain villages of the interior; in Fonni, in the heart of the Barbagia, locals celebrate the Festa di San Giovanni, held June 24, in traditional costume.

Setting Sail

Sailing enthusiasts tack for Sardinia and its craggy coast full of wildly beautiful inlets accessible only by sea. You can watch the very rich engage in one of their favorite sports—yachting—at the posh resorts of the Costa Smeralda each August, when a number of regattas are held. Berthing and provisions facilities are available on all coasts, though concentrated in the area around the Costa Smeralda and La Maddalena areas in the northeast. Altogether, there are 15 nautical schools, nearly half of these in the northeast. The harbor master, or *capitano di porto*, can issue permits for anchorage. The **Lega Navale Italiana** (☎ 070/303794 ⊕ www.leganavale.it) at Marina Piccola in Cagliari has information on the island's facilities.

Shopping

Sardinia is crafts heaven. Locally produced goods include bright woolen shawls and rugs, hand-carved wooden objects, gold filigree jewelry in traditional designs, coral jewelry, and, above all, handwoven baskets in all shapes and sizes. The best places to go for crafts are the various government-sponsored ISOLA centers in Cagliari, Sassari, Castelsardo, and Nuoro.

CAGLIARI & THE SOUTHERN COAST

Sardinia's southern coast is a stunning succession of wild rocky inlets and pristine beaches. Though blissfully uncommercialized for the most part, the coast does have pockets of development that have sprouted as tourism has found a niche. However, you'll find hotels artfully concealed behind thick swathes of eucalyptus and lush pine groves at Santa Margherita di Pula, one of Sardinia's most luxurious holiday enclaves. The main center in these parts is Pula, an inland town within easy reach of both good beaches and what is Sardinia's most important archaeological site, the Carthaginian and Roman city of Nora. South and west of Santa Margherita, the protected coast has few beaches but jaw-dropping vistas unspoiled by any construction.

North and east of Pula is Sardinia's largest city, Cagliari (pronounced *Cahl*-yah-ree). The island's capital is characterized by its busy commercial center and waterfront with broad avenues, as well as by the typically narrow streets of the old hilltop citadel. This is where you'll find Sardinia's principal art and archaeology museums, as well as its old cathedral and the medieval towers, which have lofty views of the surrounding sea, lagoons, and mountains.

East of Cagliari, the coast is no less scenic, though it's more built up, especially around the resort of Villasimius, which is also within a short distance of some first-class sandy beaches.

Cagliari

268 km (166 mi) south of Olbia.

The island's vertical capital has impressive Italianate architecture and churches in a variety of styles. Medieval Spanish conquerors from Aragon as well as Pisans and Piemontese all left their marks, and grand, decaying castles, floodlighted by night, overlook the old center's winding streets and bustling port from far above.

▶ ❶ Begin your visit at the **Museo Archeologico** within the walls of the castle that the Pisans erected in the early 1300s to ward off attacks by the Aragonese and Catalans, from what is now Spain. Among the intriguing artifacts from Nuraghic, Carthaginian, and Roman times are bronze statuettes from the tombs and dwellings of Sardinia's earliest inhabitants, who remain a prehistoric enigma. These aboriginal people left scant clues to their origins. Ancient writers called them the Nuraghic people, from the name of their stone dwellings, the nuraghi. The structures are unique to Sardinia, just as the Aztec pyramids are to Mexico. Archaeologists date most of the nuraghi from about 1300–1200 BC, a migratory time when the ancient Israelites were establishing themselves in Canaan. During the next 1,000 years, the Nuraghic people gradually withdrew to the island's highland fastnesses to avoid more disciplined and better-armed invaders. The Nuraghic people's only weapons, say the chroniclers, were stones and boulders they hurled down from the hilltops. They eventually succumbed when the Romans, following on the heels of Carthaginian invaders, conquered the island in the 3rd century BC. ⊠ *Cittadella dei Musei, Piazza Arsenale* ☎ *070/655911* 🏷 *€4* ⊙ *Tues.–Fri. and Sun. 9–8, Sat. 9 AM–11 PM.*

❷ The medieval **Torre di San Pancrazio,** part of the imposing Pisan defenses, is just outside Cagliari's archaeological museum. You can climb up the tower for a fabulous panorama of the city and its surroundings. ⊠ *Piazza Indipendenza* ☎ *070/41108* 🏷 *Free* ⊙ *Tues.–Sun. 9–1 and 3:30–7:30.*

Sardinia

CORSICA
(FRANCE)

TO TOULON

TO GENOA

TO LIVORNO

Bonifacio

Santa Teresa
di Gallura

La Maddalena

21

Caprera

20

Palau

TO GENOA,
LIVORNO,
CIVITAVECCHIA

Baia Sardinia

22

Arzachena

Porto Cervo

Isola
Asinara

Golfo dell'
Asinara

Stintino

Castelsardo

19

Porto Rotondo

24

Golfo Aranci

Olbia

23

Porto Torres

Sassari

18

Anghelu
Ruiu

Ozieri

Oschiri

Capo Caccia
Grotta di Nettuno

17

Alghero

Siniscola

TO GENOA

ITALY

Bosa

Macomer

Nuoro

15

Mt. Ortobene

Dorgali

Cala
Gonone

Oliena

Cala di
Luna

Golfo
di
Orosei

Lago
Omodeo

Orgosolo

Fonni

16

Cala Sisine

Mt. Spada

San
Salvatore

Sorgono

Tonara

Baunei

Bruncu Spina

San Giovanni
di Sinis

Cabras

14

Oristano

13

Giara di
Gesturi

12

Aritzo

Monti del
Gennargentu

Arbatax

Tharros

Arborea

Su Nuraxi

11

Barumini

Isili

Lago di
Flumendosa

Guspini

Ingurtosu

Grotta di
San Giovanni

Iglesias

Domusnovas

San Sperate

Cagliari

1 · 6

see detail
map

Carloforte

Portoscuso

Carbonia

Costa
Rei

Capo
Sandalo

Mt. Sirai

San
Pietro

10

Calasetta

9

Sant'Antioco

Pula

8

Nora

Villasimius

7

Capo
Boi

Capo
Carbonara

TO CIVITAVECCHIA

Golfo
di
Cagliari

TO NAPLES

Santa
Margherita
di Pula

Mediterranean
Sea

TO PALERMO

TO TUNIS

TO MALTA

KEY

Ferry Lines

Start of itinerary

0   30 miles
0   45 km

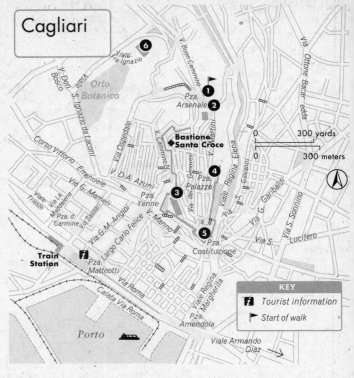

❸ The **Torre dell'Elefante**, twin to the tower of San Pancrazio, is at the seaward end of Cagliari's bastions. ⊠ *Via Università* ☎ *070/659674* ⊙ *Tues.–Sun. 9–1 and 3:30–7:30.*

❹ **Piazza Palazzo,** at the top of Via Martini, is where you'll find the **Duomo,** which has been extensively rebuilt and restored. The tiers of columns on the facade echo those of medieval Romanesque Pisan churches, but only the central portal is an authentic relic of that era. ⊠ *Piazza Palazzo* ☎ *070/663837* ⊙ *Daily 8–noon and 4–8.*

On the narrow streets of the **Castello quarter,** below the Duomo, humble dwellings still open directly onto the sidewalk and the wash is hung out to dry on elaborate wrought-iron balconies.

❺ The Bastion of St. Remy, better known as the **Terrazza Umberto I,** is a monumental neoclassical staircase and arcade. It was added in the 19th century to the bastion built by the Spaniards 400 years earlier. ⊠ *Piazza Costituzione.*

❻ Below the Museo Archeologico are the **Anfiteatro Romano,** some very old churches, and a few good restaurants near the waterfront. The amphitheater, which dates from the 2nd century AD, is a well-preserved arena complete with underground passages and a beasts' pit, evidence of the importance of this Roman outpost. ⊠ *Viale Fra Ignazio* ☎ *070/652956* 🎟 *Free* ⊙ *Daily 10–1 and 3–6; call to confirm seasonal hrs.*

Where to Stay & Eat

$$$ ✕ **Dal Corsaro.** This formal restaurant near the port is one of the island's most recommended eating places, so make reservations. The interior is refined, the welcome cordial. The menu specializes in seafood and meat, with such dishes as seafood antipasto and *porcheddu* (roast suckling pig).

The restaurant opens a branch at the seaside, at Marina Piccola, for a month each August. ✉ *Viale Regina Margherita 28* ☎ *070/664318; 070/ 370295 at Marina Piccola* ⌖ *Reservations essential* ▭ *AE, DC, MC, V* ◷ *Closed Sun., 2 wks in Aug., and Dec. 23–Jan. 6.*

$ ✕ **Il Gatto.** "The Cat," near the train station and the central Piazza del Carmine, is popular with locals; make sure you have reservations, because the place can fill up quickly. It serves some of the best Sardinian seafood, such as risotto with shellfish, but if you want a change of pace, try the zesty *insalata di funghi, rucola, e grana padano* (salad of mushrooms, arugula, and a young Parmesan cheese). ✉ *Viale Trieste 15* ☎ *070/663596* ⌖ *Reservations essential* ▭ *AE, DC, MC, V* ◷ *No lunch weekends.*

$$ ☷ **Panorama.** With its unprepossessing exterior, this hotel in downtown Cagliari is geared to the business class. Rooms are spacious and comfortable with modern, functional furniture. Try to reserve one on the higher of the nine floors and enjoy the view over the harbor and bay. ✉ *Viale Armando Diaz 231, 09126* ☎ *070/307691* 🖷 *070/305413* ⊕ *www.hotelpanorama.it* ➷ *64 rooms, 28 suites* ⌂ *Restaurant, pool, bar, meeting room, parking (fee)* ▭ *AE, DC, MC, V.*

$ ☷ **AeR Bundes Jack.** Despite the unprepossessing entrance under the arcades of Via Roma, this central third-floor (*secondo piano*) pensione (there's an elevator) is cozy, with simple furnishings. The port is directly opposite, though rooms are all inward-facing; the bus and train stations steps away, and Via Roma itself presents an entertaining parade of shops and sit-down bars. You can also expect polite, friendly service. ✉ *Via Roma 75, 09100* ☎ *070/657970* ➷ *14 rooms, 3 without bath* ▭ *No credit cards.*

Nightlife & the Arts

Fodor'sChoice ★ Sardinia's greatest annual festival, the **Festa di Sant'Efisio**, May 1–4, involves thousands of costumed villagers, many of them on horseback, parading through town, and a four-day procession between Cagliari and Pula. It's a good chance to take part in the centuries-old folklore. Cagliari's **university** (✉ Via Università) holds concerts throughout the academic year; contact the tourist office for information.

The coolest nighttime café-bar in all of Sardinia might just be the **Libarium** (✉ Bastioni di Santa Croce ☎ 070/650943), a dim, bohemian haunt tucked into a nook of the medieval castle. The gilded, historic **Antico Caffè** (✉ Piazza Costituzione ☎ 070/650943), an equally good place for a coffee or a cocktail, has sat downtown at the corner of Via Garibaldi and Regina Margherita since 1855.

Sports & the Outdoors

FISHING For information on obtaining a fishing license, contact the **Assessorato Regionale alla Difesa dell'Ambiente** (✉ Via Biasi 7/9, Cagliari, 09100 ☎ 070/6066620).

Shopping

The best place for crafts is **ISOLA** (✉ Via Bacaredda 176 ☎ 070/492756 ✉ Via Santa Croce 34 ☎ 070/651488), a government-sponsored exhibition of artisanal crafts where most of the work is for sale.

off the beaten path

SAN SPERATE – Walls throughout this small town 20 km (12 mi) north of Cagliari have been brightened with *murales* (mural paintings) by local artists and some well-known Italian painters. The murals were begun in 1968 and continue to be expanded upon today, transforming the entire town into an open-air art gallery.

Villasimius

❼ *50 km (31 mi) east of Cagliari, 296 km (184 mi) south of Olbia.*

The eastern route takes you through some dismal industrial suburbs on the road that leads to the scenic coast and beaches of Capo Boi and Capo Carbonara. Villasimius ranks as the chief resort here; the beautiful beaches lie a couple of miles north of town, on the golden sands of the Costa Rei.

Pula

❽ *29 km (18 mi) southwest of Cagliari, 314 km (195 mi) southwest of Olbia.*

Resort villages sprawl along the coast southwest of the capital, which has its share of fine scenery and good beaches. On the marshy shoreline between Cagliari's Aeroporto di Elmas and Pula, huge flocks of flamingos are a common sight. From Cagliari, first follow the S195 toward Teulada, then take the turnoff for Pula at km 27.

★ The narrow promontory called **Nora,** less than 3 km (2 mi) outside the town of Pula, was the site of a Phoenician, then Carthaginian, and later a Roman settlement. Extensive excavations have shed light on life in this ancient city from the 8th century BC onward. An old Roman road passes the moss-covered ruins of temples, an amphitheater, and a small Roman theater. You can make out the channels through which hot air rose to warm the Roman baths; watch for the difference between the simple mosaic pavements laid by the Carthaginians and the more elaborate designs of the Romans. Taking in the views from Nora, you can see why the Phoenicians chose the site for settlement. They scouted for locations with good harbors, cliffs to shelter their craft from the wind, and an elevation such as a promontory, from which they could defend themselves against attack. If the sea is calm, look under the clear waters along the shore for more ruins of the ancient city, submerged by earthquakes, rough seas, and erosion. ☎ 0709/209138 🎟 €3.60, €5 including Museo Archeologico Comunale ⊘ Excavations daily 9–7:30. Guided tours hourly.

The small **Museo Archeologico Comunale** has archaeological finds from the Nora site, including amphoras, anchors, and inscribed stones, mostly dredged up from the sea. ✉ Corso Vittorio Emanuele 67 ☎ 070/9209610 🎟 €3.60, €5, including Nora ⊘ Daily 9–7.

Sant'Efisio, the little Romanesque church at the base of the Nora promontory, plays a part in one of the island's most colorful annual events. Efisio, the patron saint of Sardinia, was a 3rd-century Roman soldier who converted to Christianity. A procession in early May accompanies a statue of the saint all the way from Cagliari and back again. The processional round-trip takes four days, with festive stops along the way, and culminates in a huge parade down Cagliari's main avenue. If you're in Sardinia from May 1 to May 4, don't miss it. ✉ Nora ☎ 070/9208473 ⊘ Apr.–Sept., Sat. 3–6, Sun. 9:30–1 and 3–7:30; Oct.–Mar., Sun. 9:30–noon and 3–5; other times by appointment.

Where to Stay

Lodging and beaches that cater to the summer crowds visiting Pula and Nora are concentrated a little over a mile south, in a conglomeration of hotels that makes up the town of Santa Margherita di Pula. Hotel prices are considerably more reasonable outside of high season, which runs roughly from mid-June to late August.

★ $$$$ **Is Morus Relais.** A luxurious enclave, the Is Morus is on a sandy cove and offers all the amenities of a fine beach resort. Stay in the main villa or in one of a stunning assortment of individual pine-shaded cottages in the complex's private park. There's an option (for guests taking half or full board) of golf at the fine Is Molas course, about 11 km (7 mi) away. ✉ *SS195, km 37.4, Santa Margherita di Pula, 09010* ☎ *070/921171* 🖷 *0709/21596* ⊕ *www.ismorus.it* ☞ *85 rooms* ♿ *Restaurant, mini-bars, golf privileges, miniature golf, tennis court, pool, beach, spa, 2 bars* ▭ *AE, DC, MC, V* ⊙ *Closed Oct. 27–Apr.* ¶◎¶ *MAP.*

$$$$ **Flamingo.** Directly on the beach and in a shady setting, this resort hotel has a main building and six two-story cottages surrounded by eucalyptus trees. Balconied rooms are light and airy, overlooking park or sea, and full sports facilities are offered, including diving and windsurfing. The outdoor pool is open late into the night, a welcome treat in the balmy summer. ✉ *Santa Margherita di Pula, 09010* ☎ *070/9208361* 🖷 *0709/ 208359* ⊕ *www.hotelflamingo.it* ☞ *134 rooms* ♿ *Restaurant, minibars, miniature golf, tennis court, pool, piano bar, dance club, private beach* ▭ *AE* ⊙ *Closed Oct. 18–Apr. 18.*

Sports

GOLF   If you're staying at any of the hotels in Santa Margherita di Pula you can avail yourself of the 18-hole **Is Molas** (☎ 0709/241014), which has won tributes from Tom Watson and Jack Nicklaus.

Sant'Antioco

⑨ *75 km (47 mi) west of Pula, 100 km (62 mi) west of Cagliari.*

Off Sardinia's southwest coast is Sant'Antioco, a popular holiday spot with good beaches. You drive over a causeway to get onto the tiny island, where the most hectic activity seems to be the silent repairing of nets by local fishermen who have already pulled in their daily catch. Before leaving the main town, also called Sant'Antioco, take time to visit the **zona archeologica** at the top of the old section, which has terrific views of the Sardinian mainland. Here you can see a Punic necropolis and a tophet, or burial site, dedicated to the Carthaginian goddess Tanit, scattered with urns that contained the cremated remains of stillborn children. 🎟 *€4.15, including guided tour of site, and ethnographic and archaeological museums* ⊙ *Apr.–Sept., daily 9–1 and 3:30–7; Oct.–Mar., daily 9–1 and 3–6.*

off the beaten path

CARBONIA AND IGLESIAS – If your curiosity prods you to explore more esoteric places, you could go inland from Sant'Antioco to explore the rugged, once booming mining country around Carbonia (14 km [9 mi] northeast of Sant'Antioco), a town built by Mussolini in 1938 to serve as an administrative center for the coal miners and their families. With its time-frozen fascist architecture—ordered rows of houses around a core of monumental public buildings on the broad Piazza Roma—it has been called an urban UFO set down in the Sardinian landscape. In the piazza, look for the "dopolavoro," a fascist institution that organized coal workers' free time for them. Managers lived closest to the center, while laborers lived in the shantytowns on the outskirts. For better or worse, Carbonia's coal industry was short-lived, and the enormous mines are long since abandoned; just outside of town, you can see the wind whistle through their ghostly shells among rows of still-inhabited public housing projects.

CloseUp

ON THE MENU

Sardinian regional cuisine is basically Italian, with interesting local variations. Meat dishes are usually veal, lamb, or porcheddu (roast suckling pig—often available only if ordered a day in advance). On the coast, seafood is king. Langouste or aragosta (lobster) is a specialty of the northern coast and can get pricey. Those with a taste for the unusual will love the signature ricci (sea urchins), which, unlike the Japanese uni, are served atop pasta. Bottarga, another prized Sardinian product, is a dried, cured tuna roe that's best when shaved off a block directly onto pasta. Foreign conquerors left legacies of bouillabaisse (known here as zimino), couscous, and paella, but there are also native pastas: malloreddus (small shells of bran pasta sometimes flavored with saffron) and culurgiones (the Sardinian version of ravioli). Italy's original, and best, pecorino cheese, made from sheep's milk, and thin, crispy bread called carta di musica are typical island fare.

Monte Sirai, near Carbonìa and open daily 9–1 hour before sunset, holds the remains of Sardinia's most important Carthaginian military stronghold, impregnably sited atop a hill that dominates the outlook inland and far out to sea; admission is €2.60. Iglesias, 20 km (12 mi) north of Carbonia, is an authentic Sardinian town with a medieval cathedral; traveling east past Domusnovas on the Cagliari–Iglesias highway, you can detour and drive right through an immense cave, the Grotta di San Giovanni.

San Pietro

⑩ *5 km (3 mi) northwest of Sant'Antioco.*

A ferry at the small northern port of Calasetta connects Sant'Antioco with the smaller island of San Pietro at the main town of Carloforte. This classic little Italian port village and its surrounding coastline are a favorite of wealthy Cagliarians, many of whom have built weekend cottages here. The best views are from Capo Sandalo, on San Pietro's rugged western coast, but head to the island's southern tip for the beaches. The ferry departs every 20 minutes in summer and every 30 in winter—the trip takes 20 minutes.

Where to Stay

$ 🏨 **Hieracon.** This ornate, art nouveau lodging sits on the harbor in Carloforte. Rooms are whitewashed and modern. A small internal garden has a few palm trees and bungalow-style apartments. Try to get a front-facing room, though there may be some traffic noise; rooms at the top have low ceilings and no view. The central location means that you're a short walk from some good restaurants if you don't want to eat at the hotel. ⊠ *Corso Cavour 63, 09014* ☎ *0781/854028* 🖶 *0781/854893* ➷ *17 rooms, 7 suites* ♨ *Restaurant, minibars, bar* ➡ *AE, MC, V.*

SU NURAXI TO THE COSTA SMERALDA

A more traditional—and wild—Sardinia awaits the traveler who ventures into the mountainous inland of the island. The Taviani brothers, noted Italian filmmakers, made the hinterland of the Barbagia region, where traditional Sardinian customs are maintained in remote hilltop villages, the subject of the extraordinary film *Padre Padrone* (1977). Inland Sardinians are hardy souls, used to living in a climate that is as unforgiving in winter as it is intolerable in summer. Old traditions, including the vendetta, are firmly rooted in the social fabric of this mountainous land, which is barren and beautiful. Here, rare species of wildlife share the rocky uplands with sturdy medieval churches and mysterious nuraghi, ancient stone citadels left by prehistoric people. You may want to make your base Oristano, on the west coast and the medieval center of Sardinian nationalism.

As you move northward, the timeless beauty of the landscape begins to show greater signs of 20th-century development. The sunny resort of Alghero, the Spanish-influenced port on the west coast, is one of the island's premier holiday spots. In the 1960s and '70s, the Costa Smeralda, the luxury resort complex developed by the Aga Khan on the northeast corner of Sardinia, was *the* place to summer, along with the Côte d'Azur. Even today, it's as prestigious a summer getaway as any in Italy.

Su Nuraxi

⑪ *60 km (37 mi) north of Cagliari.*

Fodor'sChoice ★

It's worth making a detour to the fascinating **nuraghe** of Su Nuraxi, off the main road outside the quiet little town of Barumini. You could spend hours clambering over this extraordinary structure of concentric rings of stone walls, chambers, passages, wells, a beehive tower, and the small surrounding village with the ruins of homes and streets. The main nuraghe is probably about half its original height, and some of the smaller towers around it have been reduced by pillaging and erosion to mere circles of stones on the ground.

The nuraghi (that's the plural), which were built beginning in the 16th century BC—the middle bronze age—vary from single defensive towers to multitowered complexes sheltering whole communities, prehistoric versions of medieval walled towns and the forts of the American West. The uses of the nuraghi remain mysterious largely because their construction predates written or pictorial history; thus, as a visitor, your amateur guess as to the structures' function might well be as good as an archaeologist's. Though this particular type of construction is unique to Sardinia, similar buildings dating from the same era are found in other parts of the Mediterranean, such as Cyprus and the Balearic islands off Spain. Of the 7,000 nuraghi on Sardinia, Su Nuraxi is the most impressive, with those of Sant'Antine and Losa, both near Macomer, close runners-up. It's a good idea to take a flashlight along. ⌧ *1 km (½ mi) west of Barumini* ☎ *0337/813087* ⌦ *€4* ⊙ *Apr.–Sept., daily 9–7:30; Oct.–Mar., daily 9–5. 20-min guided tour required, starts about every ½ hr.*

Giara di Gesturi

⑫ *8 km (5 mi) north of Barumini, 68 km (42 mi) north of Cagliari.*

On the basalt plateau of Giara di Gesturi roam some of the island's more exotic wildlife, including a species of wild dwarf horse. Another rare species in the Giara is the mouflon, a wild sheep distinguishable from its domesticated counterpart by its long, curving horns and skittishness. Long hunted for their horns, the mouflon are now an endangered species, with only a few surviving on Sardinia and Corsica.

Costa Verde

80 km (50 mi) northwest of Cagliari, 40 km (25 mi) south of Oristano.

If you've come to Sardinia in search of untrammeled wilderness and sweeping sands as far as the eye can see, then this deserted coast is the place to find them. Hidden away in the forgotten northwest corner of Cagliari province, the Costa Verde is accessible only by a bumpy, unpaved track. The effort is worth it. The dune-backed sands shelter rare grasses and bird life, as well as providing magnificent swimming.

You can approach the coast either from the town of Guspini, on the straggling S126, or from a turnoff a couple of miles farther south, which will lead you through the abandoned mining town of **Ingurtosu**. It's a strange, ghostly cluster of chimneys and workers' dwellings, forlorn amid the encroaching scrubland. Drive down the dirt track another 10 km (6 mi) or so, through woods of lentisk and juniper, to reach the sea.

Where to Stay

★ **$$** 🏨 **Hotel Le Dune.** A remote oasis on the beach, this hotel was formerly a deposit for the minerals dug out from the surrounding hills, and you can still see the remains of wagons, rails, and other mining bric-a-brac scattered about, which only add to the desolate allure. Simple guest rooms have a light, spacious feel from the bamboo furnishings; 11 of the rooms have their own sitting rooms. Though facilities are minimal, they include a good cocktail bar where you can contemplate the limitless sands stretching out on either side. For exploring, guides are available on request. ✉ *Via Bau, 09031 Piscinas di Ingurtosu* ☎ *0709/77130* 🖨 *0709/77230* 📫 *32 rooms* ⏚ *Restaurant, minibars, pool, bar; no room TVs* 🖃 *AE, DC, MC, V.*

Oristano

🔞 *25 km (16 mi) north of Giara di Gesturi, 93 km (58 mi) northwest of Cagliari.*

Oristano, on the west coast, shone in the Middle Ages when it was capital of the Giudicato of Arborea, an independent duchy led by Sardinia's own Joan of Arc–type heroine, Eleanora di Arborea (circa 1340–1402). In between valiant struggles with the more powerful Aragonese, Eleanora made a lasting contribution to Sardinia by implementing a code of law that was adopted throughout the island and remained in effect until Sardinia's unification with Italy in 1847. Oristano is now the scene of livestock fairs and a rousing series of horse races, called Sa Sartiglia, marking the end of February's Carnival. Otherwise, the city's beautiful but small colonial center exudes a slow pace of life, and Oristano's evening *passeggiata* has an unambitious friendliness that is uncharacteristic for the guarded island.

off the beaten path

CABRAS – Ten kilometers (6 mi) northwest of Oristano you can see extensive marshlands where fishermen pole round-bottomed rush boats through shallow ponds teeming with eels and crayfish. Cabras is also home to the Torre di San Giovanni di Sinis, a striking 16th-century ruin of a perfectly cylindrical fortified tower atop a hill overlooking the water.

Where to Stay & Eat

★ **$$$** ✕ **Il Faro.** Locals and visiting foodies agree that this elegant seafood restaurant, serving authentic, well-prepared seasonal dishes, is one of the best in the area. There's *capretto allo spiedo* (spit-roasted goat) around Easter, porcheddu in the fall, *agnello* (lamb) in winter, and an aromatic *zuppa di fave* (fava-bean soup) with bacon and fennel in spring. Service is impeccable. ✉ *Via Bellini 25* ☎ *0783/70002* 🖃 *AE, DC, MC, V* 🕔 *Closed Sun. and mid-Dec.–mid-Jan.*

$ ✕ **Da Gino.** Extremely central (off Piazza Roma), this simple trattoria, run by the same family under different names for nearly a century, has authentic local seafood dishes. Try the pâté of dorado or sea bass and the delicious spaghetti *alla bottarga* (with smoked fish roe). The lobster "alla Gino" is a memorable splurge. Service is friendly and attentive. It's a popular spot for locals and an ideal lunch stop. ⊠ *Via Tirso 13* ☎ *0783/ 71428* ▤ *MC, V* ☉ *Closed Sun., 1 wk in Jan., and 3 wks in Aug.*

$$$ 🏨 **Ala Birdi.** Buried within pinewoods fringing the Golfo di Oristano— 4 km (2½ mi) outside Arborea and 15 km (9 mi) south of Oristano— this "vacation center" of three hotels (the Castello, Medar, and Ribot) doubles as the hub of horseback riding on the island. Although the guest rooms are simple and the food generally bland, the nearby sandy beach and pools (a beautiful one in front of the Ribot makes that set of rooms a great choice), daytime excursions, nightly entertainment, and extensive sports facilities ensure a good time. ⊠ *Strada a Mare 24, 09092 Arborea* ☎ *0783/80500* 🖷 *0783/801086* ⊕ *www.alabirdi-arborea.it* ⮔ *385 rooms* ⌂ *3 restaurants, tennis court, 3 pools, gym, horseback riding, 2 bars, recreation room* ▤ *AE, DC, MC, V.*

$ 🏨 **Mistral 2.** Oristano's most comfortable hotel is primarily oriented toward business travelers, with first-class facilities. Modern, yellow, and a bit unappealing from the outside, this seven-story block, well maintained and efficiently run, is on the western outskirts of town (well signposted) and convenient for drivers. ⊠ *Via XX Settembre, 09170* ☎ *0783/ 210389* ⊠ *Mistral* (closer to the center; older facilities but lower rates) ⊠ *Via XX Settembre* ☎ *0783/210389* 🖷 *0783/211000* ⊕ www.shg. it/mistral2 ⮔ 132 rooms ⌂ Restaurant, minibars, pool, bar, meeting rooms, some pets allowed ▤ AE, DC, MC, V.

Nightlife & the Arts

The **Sartiglia** festival, on the last Sunday of February's Carnival season, includes rich costumes and a ritual joust. Each summer, the town holds an **arts-and-crafts exhibition,** with local foods and wines given prominence. Contact the **tourist office** (⊠ Via Cagliari 278 ☎ 0783/74191) for information.

Tharros

🔟 *20 km (12 mi) west of Oristano, 113 km (70 mi) northwest of Cagliari.*

The **ruins** of the Carthaginian and Roman city of Tharros (Cabras in Italian) are along the road marked San Giovanni di Sinis; its position affords a strategic view over scenic Sinis peninsula. Like Nora to the south, the site was chosen because it commanded the best views of the harbor and could provide an easy escape route if inland tribes threatened. Four Corinthian columns still stand, and there are baths and fragments of mosaics from the Roman city. As at Nora, there is much more submerged under water. ⊠*20 km [12 mi] west of Oristano* 🎫 €4 ☉ *Daily 9–1 hr before sunset.*

At the **Museo Civicó di Cabras** you can view many of the better-preserved urns and other items that have been recovered from the Tharros ruins. ⊠ *Via Tharros 121* 🎫 €2.60 ☉ *June–Aug. 9–1 and 4–8, Sept.–May 9–1 and 3–7.*

On your way to Tharros, you'll pass the ghost town of **San Salvatore,** revived briefly in the 1960s as a locale for spaghetti Westerns and since abandoned. The saloon of the movie set still stands. Among the dunes past San Salvatore are large **rush huts** formerly used by fishermen and now much in demand as back-to-nature vacation homes. The 5th-century church of **San Giovanni di Sinis,** on the Sinis peninsula, is the oldest Christian church in Sardinia.

Nuoro

⑮ *89 km (56 mi) northeast of Oristano, 181 km (113 mi) north of Cagliari.*

The somewhat shabby provincial capital of Nuoro is on the edge of a gorge in the harsh mountainous area that culminates in **Gennargentu**, the island's highest massif (6,000 ft). The only things likely to interest you are the views from the park on Sant'Onofrio hill and the exhibits in the **Museo della Vita e delle Tradizioni Popolari Sarde** (Museum of Sardinian Life and Folklore), where you can see some domestic and agricultural implements, traditional jewelry, and local costumes draped on mannequins. ⊠ *Via Mereu 56* ☎ *0784/242900* ☜ *€2.60* ☽ *Mid-June–Sept., daily 9–8; Oct.–mid-June, daily 9–1 and 3–7.*

Make an excursion about 3 km (2 mi) east of Nuoro to **Monte Ortobene** (2,900 ft) for lofty views over the gulch below. Here you can also see up close the imposing statue of Christ the Redeemer overlooking the city. Picnic tables make this a handy spot for an alfresco lunch.

> **off the beaten path**
>
> **ORGOSOLO** – This old center of banditry halfway between Nuoro and Fonni is still a poor and undeveloped village, but the houses have been daubed with *murales* (mural paintings) vividly depicting political and cultural issues. The effect is startling and lively. The forest and grassy plain above the village make fine walking country.

Where to Stay & Eat

$$$
Fodor's Choice
★

✕🏨 **Su Gologone.** Despite attracting tourists in droves, this country inn near Oliena (20 km [12 mi] southeast of Nuoro) still manages to be cozy and quiet, with guest rooms that are impeccably furnished private retreats. The rustic restaurant with its fireplace and wooden furnishings is worth a detour for an authentic Sardinian meal. Island specialties include *maccarones de busa* (thick homemade pasta), culurgiones, porcheddu, and sebadas. Wash it all down with the local Cannonau wine, much of it from grapes grown in the countryside around the inn. The hotel organizes jeep and hiking expeditions and has bikes for your use. ⊠ *Località Su Gologone, Oliena 08025* ☎ *0784/287512* 🖷 *0784/287668* ⊕ *www.sugologone.it* ➷ *60 rooms, 8 suites* ♿ *Restaurant, miniature golf, 2 tennis courts, pool, gym, massage, bicycles, bar, some pets allowed* 🖃 *AE, DC, MC, V* ☽ *Closed mid-Nov.–mid-Dec. and mid-Jan.–mid-Mar.*

Nightlife & the Arts

Nuoro's **Festa del Redentore** (Feast of the Redeemer) is held on the next-to-last Sunday in August. It's the best time to view the various traditional costumes of Sardinia's interior all in one place.

Shopping

Crafted for local festivals, wooden masks are available at local shops and make unusual and festive souvenirs. The local shop of **ISOLA** (⊠ *Via Monsignor Bua 10* ☎ *0784/31507*) is in the middle of the old town.

Fonni

⑯ *30 km (19 mi) south of Nuoro, 137 km (85 mi) south of Olbia.*

In the heart of the Barbagia region, Fonni is the highest town on the island and a good base for excursions by car to all sights of interest, including Monte Spada and the Bruncu Spina refuge on the Gennargentu Massif, in this mountainous district that is Sardinia's most primitive. Life in some villages seems not to have changed much since the Middle Ages. Here a rigidly patriarchal society perpetuates the unrelenting

SARDINIA BY RAIL

If you have the stamina, take the rickety old train on a leg of the journey that runs on a single-gauge track between Cagliari and Arbatax, midway up the east coast (involving a change at Mandas). The line has been operating since 1893; if all goes well, it takes about seven hours to cover the approximately 250 km (155 mi) of track, guaranteeing you a look at a Sardinia few tourists ever see. With daily, early-morning departures, the train rattles up into the Barbagia district through some breathtaking mountain scenery, then eases down into the desert landscape inland from Arbatax, where the trip ends on the dock next to the fishing boats. The train is run by the **Ferrovie Complementari** (☎ 070/7278107), and the ticket costs around €15. In Tortoli, just outside Arbatax, **Dolce Casa** (✉ Via Sarcidano 3 ☎ 0782/624235; 44/07803452748 off season in Britain 🖷 0782/623484) is a modest hotel run by an English-speaking couple. It's open June–September only.

practice of vendetta, and strangers are advised to mind their own business. High mountain roads wind and loop their way through the landscape; towns are small and undistinguished, their social fabric existing in complete isolation. On feast days, elaborate regional costumes are taken out of mothballs and worn as an explicit statement of community identity.

Nightlife & the Arts

You can see one of the most characteristic of the Barbagia's celebrations in local costume in Fonni during the **Festa di San Giovanni**, held June 24.

Shopping

Special candies are made from honey and nougat and sold in hilltop Tonara, southwest of Fonni. In the mountain village of Aritzo, about 45 km (28 mi) south of Fonni, high up in the Barbagia, you'll find hand-crafted wooden utensils and furniture.

en route   From Nuoro, take S129 west about 65 km (40 mi) to coastal Bosa, where you turn right into hilly and arid scrub country, with its abundance of cactus and juniper. Pines and olive trees shelter low buildings from the steady winds that make these parts ideal for sailing. About the only cash crop here is cork from the cork trees dotting the landscape. Yet in the low valleys and along the riverbeds, masses of oleanders bloom in summer, creating avenues of color.

Alghero

17   40 km (25 mi) north of Bosa, 137 km (85 mi) southwest of Olbia.

Among the larger centers on the northwest coast is Alghero, a pretty walled resort town with a distinctly Spanish flavor. It was built and inhabited in the 14th century by the Aragonese and Catalans, who constructed seaside ramparts and sturdy towers encompassing an inviting nucleus of narrow, winding streets with whitewashed *palazzi*. Rich wrought-iron scrollwork decorates balconies and screened windows; a Spanish motif appears in stone portals and in bell towers. The dialect spoken here is a version of Catalan, not Italian, although you'll probably have to attend one of the masses conducted in Algherese to hear it.

Near Alghero are broad sandy beaches and the spectacular heights of **Capo Caccia**, an imposing limestone headland to the west. At the base of the sheer cliff, the pounding sea has carved an entrance to the vast

Grotta di Nettuno, a fantastic cavern that you must visit with a guide. By land, you reach the entrance at the base of the cliff by descending the more than 600 steps of the aptly named *escala del cabirol* (mountain goat's stairway), a dizzying enterprise—and the ascent is just as daunting. The excursion by sea is much less fatiguing but is not possible in winter or when seas are rough. Boats leave the port of Alghero four times daily, or every hour or so in peak season, and the trip takes 2½ hours. *Boat tour* ⊠ *Navisarda* ☎ *079/950603* ▱ *Grotto €8, includes mandatory tour; boat tour €10, excluding ticket for grotto* ☾ *Grotto Apr.–Sept., daily 9–sunset; Oct., daily 10–5; Nov.–Mar., daily 9–2; tours on the hr. Boat tours Apr., May, and Oct., daily 4 per day, 9–4; June–Sept., daily 9–5 on the hr.*

Where to Stay & Eat

$$–$$$ ✕ **Al Tuguri.** The name is dialect for "old abandoned house," but this place has an elegance to its rustic style. Space is limited to one small upstairs room and an attic, but this only enhances the feeling of friendly intimacy—even if this eatery is a bit touristy. Host Benito Carbonella will explain the finer points of Catalan cookery, whose traditional recipes he has "revisited." Seafood is the main ingredient, artfully prepared and presented, for example in the mousse with *ricci* (sea urchins) and seafood paella. ⊠ *Via Maiorca 113* ☎ *079/976772* ▤ *MC, V* ☾ *Closed Sun. and mid-Dec.–mid-Jan.*

$$–$$$ ✕ **La Lepanto.** A covered veranda by the seafront marks out Alghero's top seafood restaurant, an expansive and sunny room usually filled with both locals and tourists. The specialty is *aragosta* (lobster) cooked in a variety of ways, including *alla catalana* (with tomato and onions)—or try it with ricotta foam, parsley, basil, and tomato. For starters, try risotto *nero di seppia* (with cuttlefish ink). ⊠ *Via Carlo Alberto 125* ☎ *079/979116* ▤ *AE, DC, MC, V* ☾ *Closed Mon. Oct.–May.*

$ ✕ **Da Pietro.** On a narrow street in the picturesque old town near Largo San Francesco, this bustling seafood restaurant has vaulted ceilings and a menu that includes *bucatini all'algherese* (pasta with a sauce of clams, capers, tomatoes, and olives) and baked fish with a white-wine sauce. ⊠ *Via Ambrogio Machin 18* ☎ *079/979645* ▤ *AE, DC, MC, V* ☾ *Closed Wed. and 1 wk at Christmas.*

★ $$$$ ▥ **Villa Las Tronas.** The villa is a former royal mansion on a rocky promontory above the sea but still near the center of town. The gardens around a narrow drive that separates the hotel's little island from the road impart a regal sense of seclusion, and there are great views across the water to the old town. The belle epoque interior is complemented by modern comforts and good in-room amenites. It's open year-round, a rarity in these parts. ⊠ *Lungomare Valencia 1, 07041* ☎ *079/981818* 🖷 *079/981044* ⊕ *www.hotelvillalastronas.it* ⤶ *20 rooms, 5 suites* ♨ *Restaurant, pool, gym, beach, free parking* ▤ *AE, DC, MC, V.*

$$$ ▥ **Carlos V.** Opposite the Villa Las Tronas on the shore boulevard, about 1 km (½ mi) from the center of town, this modern hotel (pronounced Carlos Quinto) is endowed with an array of gardens and terraces and a big pool overlooking the sea. All rooms—airy but lacking in character—have a balcony, but don't settle for the slightly cheaper ones facing the back; the pleasure here is all in the magnificent sea view. Low-season rates are a bargain. ⊠ *Lungomare Valencia 24, 07041* ☎ *079/979501* 🖷 *079/980298* ⊕ *www.hotelcarlosv.it* ⤶ *110 rooms* ♨ *Restaurant, miniature golf, 2 tennis courts, 2 pools, playground, meeting rooms, free parking* ▤ *AE, DC, MC, V.*

$ ▥ **San Francesco.** In Alghero's Spanish quarter, this central hotel occupies the convent that was once attached to the church of San Francesco. The rooms are grouped around the 14th-century cloister and, though

somewhat cramped, are modern and quiet. ✉ *Via Machin 2, 07041*
☎ *079/980330* ✆ *hotsfran@tin.it* 🛏 *20 rooms* ⚐ *Bar, meeting
room* ▭ *DC, MC, V* ⊘ *Closed Nov.–mid-Dec.*

Shopping

Coral, still harvested in the bay, and gold jewelry are displayed in many
specialty shops as well as more touristy outlets throughout Alghero's
old quarter.

Cafés

For a glass of local wine or just a coffee, the historic **Caffè Costantino**
(✉ Piazza Civica 30 ☎ 079/976154), open until midnight, is sumptuous and elegant with yellow flowered walls, chandeliers, classical music,
and a warm crowd of distinguished, well-dressed Algherese.

Sassari

⑱ *34 km (21 mi) northeast of Alghero, 212 km (132 mi) north of Cagliari.*

Inland Sassari is an important university town and administrative center, notable for its historic, ornate cathedral, its good archaeological museum, and a history of intellectualism and bohemian student culture.
Sassari is the hub of several highways and secondary roads leading to
various coastal resorts, among them Stintino and Castelsardo.

Shopping

Sassari has Sardinia's main **ISOLA** (✉ Giardini Pubblici ☎ 079/230101),
an exhibition center in the public gardens next to Viale Mancini built
specifically as a showcase for gifts and souvenirs.

Castelsardo

⑲ *32 km (20 mi) northeast of Sassari, 100 km (62 mi) west of Olbia.*

The walled seaside citadel of Castelsardo is a delight for basket lovers.
Roadside stands and shops in the old town sell tons of island crafts: rugs,
wrought iron, and baskets—in myriad shapes and colors. Take the children to see the appropriately shaped **Roccia dell'Elefante** (Elephant Rock)
on the road into Castelsardo; it was hollowed out by primitive man to
become a *domus de janas* (literally, "fairy house," in fact a neolithic burial
chamber).

Shopping

There's an **ISOLA** (✉ Via Roma 104 ☎ 079/471413), where local handicrafts are sold. The local specialty is a brightly colored basket made of
dwarf palms.

Santa Teresa di Gallura

⑳ *68 km (42 mi) northeast of Castelsardo, 65 km (41 mi) northwest of
Olbia.*

At the northern tip of Sardinia, Santa Teresa di Gallura retains the relaxed, carefree air of an authentic fishing village-turned-resort.

Where to Stay & Eat

¢–$ ✕🏨 **Canne al Vento.** This cheerful, family-run hotel and restaurant on
the main road into town is a quiet, tasteful haven. The restaurant ($$)
specializes in authentic island cuisine, for example *zuppa cuata* (bread,
cheese, and tomato soup), porcheddu, or seafood. The hotel has a de-
fiantly rustic feel, despite the bland, modern exterior, with a bamboo-
roofed restaurant and the odd ornamental wagon wheel. Rooms are
sparsely furnished but cool and comfortable. Ask for one of the quieter

ones at the back. ⊠ *Via Nazionale 23, 07028* ☎ *0789/754219* 🖷 *0789/754948* 📞 *22 rooms* ♻ *Restaurant, minibars; no a/c* 🟰 *MC, V* ⊘ *Closed Oct.–Mar.; restaurant closed Mon. Mar.–mid.-Jun.*

$$$–$$$$ 🏨 **Grand Hotel Corallaro.** This hotel offers luxury accommodations in a panoramic spot right by the beach, a brief walk from the town center. Rooms are functional and some have balconies. Public rooms are much grander, furnished with wicker chairs, and there are terraces and lawns where you can sip preprandial drinks. Half- or full board is required in high season; low season discounts are sizeable. ⊠ *Località Rena Bianca, 07028* ☎ *0789/755475* 🖷 *0789/755431* 🌐 *www.hotelcorallaro.it* 📞 *82 rooms* ♻ *Restaurant, indoor pool, gym, Turkish baths* 🟰 *MC, V* ⊘ *Closed mid-Oct.–Easter* 🍴 *MAP.*

La Maddalena

㉑ *30 km (19 mi) east of Santa Teresa di Gallura, 45 km (20 mi) northwest of Olbia.*

From the port of Palau you can visit the archipelago of La Maddalena, seven granite islands embellished with lush green scrub and wind-bent pines. Pilgrims pay homage to **Garibaldi's tomb** (1807–82) on the grounds of his hideaway on Isola Caprera, the island to the east of Isola Maddalena. ☎ *0789/727162* 🎟 *€2* ⊘ *Daily 9–1:30.*

Porto Cervo

★ ㉒ *30 km (19 mi) north of Olbia.*

Sardinia's northeastern coast is fringed with low cliffs, inlets, and small bays. This has become an upscale vacationland, with glossy resorts such as Baia Sardinia and Porto Rotondo, just outside the confines of the famed Costa Smeralda, developed by the Aga Khan (born 1936), who accidentally discovered the coast's charms—and potential—in 1965, when his yacht took shelter here from a storm. The Costa Smeralda is still dominated by his personality; its attractions remain geared to those who can measure themselves by the yardstick of his fabled riches. Italy's most expensive hotels are here, and the world's most magnificent yachts anchor in the waters of Porto Cervo. The trend has been to keep this enclave of the very rich an exclusive haven through the construction of discreet, luxurious villas and golf courses.

All along the coast, carefully tended lush vegetation surrounds vacation villages and elaborate villa colonies that have sprung up over the past decade in a range of spurious architectural styles best described as bogus Mediterranean. Outside the peak season, however, prices plunge and the majesty of the natural surroundings shines through, justifying all the hype and giving grounds for the Emerald Coast's fame as one of the truly romantic corners of the Mediterranean.

Where to Stay

$$$$ 🏨 **Cala di Volpe.** Long a magnet for the beautiful people, this hyperglamorous establishment, now part of the Starwood Luxury Collection, was built to resemble an ancient Sardinian village. The hotel's interior is rustic-elegant, with beamed ceilings, Sardinian arts and crafts, and porticoes overlooking the sea. The presidential suite in the highest tower has a private pool. Prices are truly astronomical—this is one of the most expensive hotels in Europe. ⊠ *Cala di Volpe, 07020* ☎ *0789/976111* 🖷 *0789/976617* 🌐 *www.luxurycollection.com* 📞 *107 rooms, 14 suites* ♻ *Restaurant, 3 tennis courts, pool, gym, beach, waterskiing, bar* 🟰 *AE, DC, MC, V* ⊘ *Closed Nov.–mid-Apr.*

$$$$ Cervo. Low Mediterranean buildings surround a large pool and garden in the heart of the Costa Smeralda's Porto Cervo. This Starwood Hotels complex is next to the marina and *piazzetta* (small piazza), a popular spot to see and be seen. The rooms are large and most have a terrace. In summer, you have access to five good tennis courts that are lighted at night. High-season prices are through the roof, but in winter, prices fall to as low as one-tenth the summer rate. ⊠ *Porto Cervo, 07020* ☎ *0789/931111* 🖨 *0789/931613* ⊕ *www.starwood.com* 🛏 *86 rooms, 6 suites* ⚙ *5 restaurants, 5 tennis courts, 3 pools (1 indoor), gym, beach, squash, 4 bars, piano bar* ⊟ *AE, DC, MC, V.*

$$$–$$$$ Nibaru. Pinkish-red brick buildings with tiled roofs stand in a secluded inlet set in lush gardens—not bad for a hotel that enjoys all the best features of the Costa Smeralda at comparatively low rates. Guest rooms are just a few yards from the sea and some superb swimming spots and also within easy access of the Pevero Golf Club and the tennis courts of Porto Cervo. Even closer is Nibaru's lagoonlike outdoor pool. ⊠ *Località Cala di Volpe, 07020* ☎ *0789/96038* 🖨 *0789/96474* ⊕ *www. hotelnibaru.it* 🛏 *50 rooms, 2 suites* ⚙ *Minibars, pool, bar* ⊟ *AE, DC, MC, V* ⊗ *Closed mid-Oct.–mid-Apr.*

Sports & the Outdoors

GOLF   The world-class, 18-hole **Pevero Golf Course** (☎ 0789/958020), designed by Robert Trent Jones, is on the Bay of Pevero, near Porto Cervo.

SAILING   The **Yacht Club Costa Smeralda** (⊠ Via della Marina ☎ 0789/902200) at Porto Cervo offers use of its pool, restaurant, bar, and guest rooms to those with memberships at other yacht clubs.

Shopping

Contemporary pottery displaying traditional motifs is a hot item, snatched up at whim along the Costa Smeralda. Porto Cervo's Sottopiazza has some big-name boutiques, and there's also an **ISOLA** (⊠ Villaggio Sottopiazza ☎ 0789/94428) outlet here.

Olbia

㉓   *30 km (19 mi) south of Porto Cervo, 106 km (66 mi) north of Nuoro.*

Set amid the resorts of Sardinia's northeastern coast, Olbia is a lively little seaport and port of call for mainland ferries at the head of a long, wide bay. The little basilica of **San Simplicio,** a short walk behind the main Corso Umberto, is worth searching out if you have any spare time in Olbia. The simple granite structure dates from the 11th century, part of the great Pisan church-building program, using pillars and columns recycled from Roman buildings. ⊠ *Via San Simplicio* ⊗ *Daily 6:30–12:30 and 4–7.*

Where to Stay & Eat

$ ✕ Barbagia. This classic local spot in downtown Olbia, with a simple, bright array of tables, is one of the best places to try traditional dishes from Sardinia's wild interior fused with local ingredients. Antipasti include a refreshing salad of sliced tomato and fresh cheese (called *sa t'amata chi sa frughe*). Try *maccarones* (handmade pasta twists) with a wild boar sauce; you might also find roast lamb and suckling pig in season. A good selection of pizza is served for dinner only. ⊠ *Via Galvani 94* ☎ *0789/51640* ⊟ *AE, DC, MC, V* ⊗ *Closed Jan. and Wed. Oct.–June.*

$$ Martini. An eye-catching site on the shore of a lagoon north of town, this hotel is a 20-minute walk or easy taxi ride to the port and center. Plush, modern, and businesslike, the hotel has lounge chairs on the roof with views of the port but is thankfully detached from the early morning and late-night comings and goings of ferries embarking. Most bedrooms benefit from the excellent vista. There's no restaurant, but next door there's the elegant Delle Rose, serving classic Italian fare. ✉ *Via G. D'Annunzio 21, 07026* ☎ *0789/26066* 📠 *0789/26418* *66 rooms* *Bar, meeting room* ▭ *AE, DC, MC, V.*

Golfo Aranci

24 *19 km (12 mi) northeast of Olbia.*

At the mouth of the Gulf of Olbia, Golfo Aranci is a small-scale resort and major arrival point for ferries from the mainland. The craggy headland west of town has been left undeveloped as a nature reserve, and there are some inviting beaches within an easy drive.

SARDINIA A TO Z

To research prices, get advice from other travelers, and book travel arrangements, visit www.fodors.com.

AIR TRAVEL

Flying is by far the fastest and easiest way to get to the island. Sardinia's major airport is in Cagliari, with smaller ones at Alghero and Olbia, the latter providing access to the Costa Smeralda. Alitalia connects Cagliari with Rome and Palermo. Meridiana runs service between Cagliari and Paris, Bologna, Naples, Pisa, Venice, and Verona; between Olbia and Bologna, Milan, Pisa, and Rome; and a Cagliari-Olbia service. Air One, in conjunction with Air Littoral, connects Alghero with Rome, Milan, and Nice; Olbia with Nice; and Cagliari with Milan and Strasbourg, France. RyanAir, the British low-cost carrier, runs a daily flight between London and Alghero. The Rome–Cagliari flight takes about 40 minutes.

Airlines & Contacts **Air One** ☎ 06/488800 in Rome; 848/848880 elsewhere in Italy 🌐 www.air-one.it. **Alitalia** ☎ 800/223-5730 in U.S.; 020/7602-7111 in London; 0990/448-259 in U.K.; 06/65641 in Rome; 848/865641 elsewhere in Italy 🌐 www.alitalia.it. **Meridiana** ☎ 06/6529005 in Rome; 119/111333 elsewhere in Italy 🌐 www.meridiana.it. **RyanAir** ☎ 199/114114 in Italy; 0870/1-569-569 in U.K. 🌐 www.ryanair.com.

AIRPORTS

Cagliari's Aeroporto di Elmas is about 6 km (4 mi) west of town center, and there is regular bus service from the airport to Piazza Matteotti, in front of the train station. Alghero's Aeroporto Fertilia is 13 km (8 mi) from the city. A bus links the airport with the bus station in the center of town. Aeroporto Costa Smeralda is 4 km (2½ mi) southeast of Olbia, linked by local bus to Olbia.

Airport Information **Aeroporto Costa Smeralda** ☎ 0789/52634 🌐 www.geasar.com. **Aeroporto di Elmas** ☎ 070/2128263. **Aeroporto Fertilia** ☎ 079/935282 or 079/935033 🌐 www.algheroaeroporto.it.

BOAT & FERRY TRAVEL

Large modern ferries run by Tirrenia Lines, Moby Lines, and the FS (Italian State Railways) connect Sardinia (ports at Porto Torres, Olbia, Arbatax, and Cagliari) with the mainland. These ferries are a popular mode of transport. Naples-Cagliari is Tirrenia's most popular route, but Tirrenia also connects La Spezia and Genoa with Porto Torres, Olbia, Arbatax, and Cagliari; Civitavecchia with Olbia, Arbatax, and Cagliari; Fiumicino with Golfo Aranci and Arbatax; and Cagliari with Palermo, Trapani, and Tunis. Moby Lines transports passengers and cars between Livorno and Olbia and between Civitavecchia and Olbia. FS ferries carry trains as well as passengers and cars; they sail from Civitavecchia to Golfo Aranci, near Olbia. Grimaldi's Grandi Navi Veloci run very comfortable ferries that resemble cruise ships between Genoa, Porto Torres, and Olbia, and French SNCM ferries also transport passengers to and from Marseilles, France.

FARES & SCHEDULES

The ferry ride on Tirrenia from Naples to Cagliari takes about 17 hours and costs approximately €60–€90 for first-class passage in mid- or high season, with a berth. The Civitavecchia–Olbia/Golfo Aranci run (€27–€60) takes about eight hours and there are overnight sailings, or take a more expensive high-speed ferry (summer only), which takes just four to six hours but costs more and gets booked up weeks ahead during the peak of the season in mid-August. Generally speaking, depending on the time of year, the normal ferry service is scheduled two or three times a week, while high-speed ferries depart one to four times daily in season; reservations are essential in the summer.

🚢 Boat & Ferry Information **FS** ☎ 1478/88088.**Grandi Navi Veloci** ☎ Olbia 0789/200126; Porto Torres 079/51604 ⊕ www.gnv.it. **Moby Lines** ☎ 06/4201 1455; 0586/826824 ⊕ www.mobylines.it. **SNCM** ☎ Italy 02/66117104; France 33/08/91701801 ⊕ www.sncm.fr. **Tirrenia** ☎ 1478/99000; 081/3172999 from cellular phones and abroad ⊕ www.tirrenia.it.

BUS TRAVEL

Cagliari is linked with the other towns of Sardinia by a network of buses. Local destinations are served by ARST. Major cities, excluding Olbia, are served by PANI. The heart of the Sardinian bus system is the Stazione Autolinee, across the square from the main tourist office in Cagliari. City buses in Cagliari and Sassari operate on the same system as those on the mainland: buy your ticket first, at a tobacco shop or machine, and cancel it by punching it in the machine on the bus. Fares are €0.65 per ride.

🚌 Bus Information **ARST** ☎ 070/4098324 or 1678/65042. **PANI** ☎ 070/652326. **Stazione Autolinee** ✉ Piazza Matteotti.

CAR RENTAL

🚗 Local Agencies **Avis** ✉ Aeroporto di Fertilia, Alghero ☎ 079/935064 ✉ Piazza Sulis 9, Alghero ☎ 079/979577 ✉ Via Roma, Cagliari ☎ 070/668128 ✉ Aeroporto di Elmas, Cagliari ☎ 070/240081 ✉ Aeroporto Costa Smeralda, Olbia ☎ 0789/69540 ✉ Via Mazzini 2, Sassari ☎ 079/235547 ⊕ www.avis.com. **Hertz** ✉ Aeroporto di Fertilia, Alghero ☎ 079/935054 ✉ Piazza Matteotti 8, Cagliari ☎ 070/651078 ✉ Aeroporto di Elmas, Cagliari ☎ 070/240037 ✉ Aeroporto Costa Smeralda, Olbia ☎ 0789/66024 ✉ Via Regina Elena 34 Olbia ☎ 0789/66024 ⊕ www.hertz.com. **Maggiore** ✉ Via Sassari 87, Alghero ☎ 079/979375 ✉ Aeroporto di Fertilia, Alghero ☎ 079/935045 ✉ Viale Monastir 116, Cagliari ☎ 070/273692 ✉ Aeroporto di Elmas, Cagliari ☎ 070/240069 ✉ Via D'Annunzio, Olbia ☎ 0789/22131 ✉ Aeroporto Costa Smeralda, Olbia ☎ 0789/69457 ✉ Piazza Santa Maria 6, Sassari ☎ 079/235507 ⊕ www.maggiore.it.

CAR TRAVEL

The best way to get around Sardinia is to drive. Cars may be taken on board most of the ferry lines connecting Sardinia with the mainland. The north–south S131 (Strada Carlo Felice), a major highway but something less than an *autostrada,* connects Cagliari, Oristano, Sassari, and Porto Torres. The S131 Dir and S129 connect the Carlo Felice Highway with Nuoro and the Barbagia. The S597 connects Sassari and Olbia.

EMERGENCY SERVICES

ACI Emergency Service offers 24-hour roadside assistance.
🚗 ACI dispatchers ☎ 803/116.

ROAD CONDITIONS

The roads are generally in good condition, but bear in mind that such roadside conveniences as gas stations and refreshment stands are infrequent on some routes, especially in the east. Try to avoid driving at night, when mountain roads are particularly hazardous and slow; and especially in winter, beware the fog when traversing the mountains at night (or even by day).

RULES OF THE ROAD In general, Sardinia is a much calmer place to negotiate than elsewhere in southern Italy, whether you're driving or trying to cross the road. Cagliari and Sassari can get busy, but elsewhere there's normally less traffic and people are more patient.

EMERGENCIES

Late-night pharmacies are open on a rotating basis; information on current schedules is pinned up on any pharmacy door or can be obtained by calling 192.

🗎 **Ambulance** ✉ Cagliari ☎ 070/4092901. **Hospital** Ospedale Civile San Michele ✉ Via Peretti, Cagliari ☎ 070/543266. **Police** ☎ 112 or 113.

LANGUAGE

Although the Sard dialect is incomprehensible to mainland Italians, let alone to foreigners, most locals can switch from dialect to perfect standard Italian with ease. In the main tourist areas, most people you deal with will have a smattering of English—but often less than elsewhere in Italy.

MAIL & SHIPPING

OVERNIGHT SERVICES The local courier used by Federal Express is SDA, in Fangario, near Cagliari. The local courier used by UPS is La Freccia, in Cagliari. To call for pickups or information from either Federal Express or UPS, use their national service numbers.

🗎 **Major Services Federal Express** ☎ 800/123800 ⊕ www.fedex.com. **La Freccia** ✉ Viale Monastir, Kilometro 7,382, Cagliari ☎ 070/23622310. **SDA** ✉ Viale Elmas, Kilometro 1,5, Fangario ⊕ www.sda.it. **UPS** ☎ 02/25088001.

🗎 **Post Offices Cagliari** ✉ Piazza del Carmine ☎ 070/663356. **Sassari** ✉ Via Brigata Sassari ☎ 079/231609.

TOURS

Guided tours are a good introduction to Sardinia. Travel from the Italian mainland is included, as are travel and accommodations on Sardinia. They must be booked through a travel agent, such as Viaggi Orrù.

🗎 **Fees & Schedules Viaggi Orrù** ✉ Via Roma 95 and Via Napoli 1 ☎ 070/659858 ⊕ www.viaggiorru.it.

BUS TOURS Chiariva offers two group tours of Sardinia by bus with guide. A nine-day tour leaves from Genoa; an eight-day tour departs from Rome. Both operate April–September. Aviatour has a similar eight-day tour leaving from either Milan or Rome. The tour also runs from April to September only. All bus tours can be booked through a travel agent.

🗎 **Fees & Schedules Chiariva** ☎ 0521/288444

HORSEBACK RIDING TOURS The Associazione Nazionale di Turismo Equestre can provide information on renting mounts and joining riding parties with itineraries along the coast or into the heart of the island. The Centro Vacanze Ala Birdi organizes riding vacations.

🗎 **Fees & Schedules Associazione Nazionale di Turismo Equestre** ✉ Via Carso 35/a, Sassari ☎ 079/299889. **Centro Vacanze Ala Birdi** ✉ Arborea, near Oristano ☎ 0783/80500 ⊕ www.alabirdi-arborea.it.

TRAIN TRAVEL

The Stazione Centrale in Cagliari is next to the bus station on Piazza Matteotti. There are fairly good connections between Olbia, Cagliari, Sassari, and Oristano. You can reach Nuoro via Macomer; Alghero is reached via Sassari. Service on the few other local lines is infrequent and slow. The fastest train between Olbia and Cagliari takes more than four hours. Local trains connect Golfo Aranci, the Ferrovie dello Stato (FS) port for the train ferry, with Olbia (20 minutes) and Sassari with Alghero (35 minutes).

🚆 Train Information **FS–Trenitalia** ☎ 848/888088 ⊕ www.trenitalia.com.

TRAVEL AGENCIES

🚆 Local Agent Referrals **Cagliari** Viaggi Orrù ✉ Via Roma 95 ☎ 070/659858 ⊕ www. viaggiorru.it.

VISITOR INFORMATION

🚆 Tourist Information **Alghero** ✉ Piazza Porta Terra 9, 07041 ☎ 079/979054. **Cagliari EPT, regional information** ✉ Piazza Deffenu 9, 09100 ☎ 070/651698; 800/013153 toll free ⊕ www.regione.sardegna.it/turismo/sirt_ept.htm ✉ Aeroporto di Elmas ☎ 070/240200. **Golfo Aranci** ✉ City Hall, 07026 ☎ 0789/21672 June–Aug. **Nuoro** ✉ Piazza Italia 19, 08100 ☎ 0784/30083 ⊕ www.regione.sardegna.it/turismo/sirt_ept.htm. **Olbia** ✉ Via Catello Piro 1, 07026 ☎ 0789/21453 ✉ Aeroporto Costa Smeralda ☎ 0789/21453. **Oristano** ✉ Via Cagliari 278, 09170 ☎ 0783/74191 ⊕ www.regione.sardegna.it/turismo/sirt_ept.htm. **Sassari** ✉ Viale Caprera 36, 07100 ☎ 079/299544 ⊕ www.regione.sardegna.it/turismo/sirt_ept.htm.

UNDERSTANDING
ITALY

THE PALMS OF SICILY

Excerpted from Bella Tuscany: The Sweet Life in Italy *(1999), by Frances Mayes*

'M NOT OFF THE PLANE IN PALERMO five minutes before I have an arancino in my hand, ready to taste the signature dish of Sicily. Ed has gone to find the rental car office and I head to the bar right in the center of the airport. There they are, a line of the deep-fried risotto balls formed into the size and shape of oranges. "What's inside?" I ask.

A man with those amazing black, Sicilian deep-as-wells eyes points to the round ones. "Ragà, signora. And the oval ones—besciamella e prosciutto." His eyes fascinate me as much as the arancini. All through the airport I've seen the same þByzantine, hidden, historical eyes. At the bar, savoring the crisp creamy texture of the rice, I'm watching a parade of these intensely Italian-looking Italians. Women with gobs of dark curls cascading and flowing, slender men who seem to glide instead of walk. Tiny girls with miniature gobs of the same dark curls, and old men formed by stoop labor, carrying their hats in their hands. Crowds surge to meet planes coming in from Rome, which is only an hour away. They're all waving and shouting greetings to deplaning Sicilians who probably have been gone a few days, judging from their carry-on bags. Ed comes back, bearing keys. He, too, polishes off an arancino and orders an espresso. He looks startled when he sees how small it is, barely a spoonful, with rich crema. One taste and he's transported.

The waiter sees his surprise. He's about 5'3". He looks up at Ed, almost a foot taller. "The farther south you go, signore, the smaller and the stronger."

Ed laughs, "È fantastico." He wheels our bag out to the green Fiat and zooms out of the garage.

Along the coastal road to Palermo, we glimpse the sea and cubical north African–style houses in a rocky landscape. The instant we enter Palermo, we're in wild traffic, careening traffic, traffic moving too fast for us to locate where we are going. Lanes disappear, avenue names keep changing, we turn and turn in mazes of one-way streets. "That barista should have said 'smaller, stronger, and faster,' " Ed shouts. At a light, he rolls down the window and calls desperately to a man revving his motorcycle in anticipation of the green, "Per favore, which way to Hotel Villa Igiea?"

"Follow me," he shouts back and he's off, spiraling among cars and glancing back now and then to see if we're behind him. Somehow we are. Ed seems to be in his wake, just going. At highway speeds on city streets, cars are neck-and-neck. On all four sides, we are two inches from other bite-sized cars. If someone braked, we'd be in a hundred-car pile-up. But no one brakes. At an intersection, the motorcyclist points to the left then waves. He swerves right so hard his ear almost touches the ground. We're tossed into a roundabout, spun, and emptied suddenly onto a quiet street. And there's the hotel. We creep into the parking lot and stop.

"Let's don't get in this car again until we leave. That was absolutely the worst."

"Suits me," Ed agrees. He's still gripping the wheel. "Let's take taxis. Everywhere. This is more like the running of the bulls than driving." We grab our bag, lock the Fiat, and don't look at the car again until we check out.

* * *

THE TAXI ARRIVES quickly and we launch into the bumper-car traffic. Yes, it's always like this, the driver tells us. No, there aren't many accidents. Why? He shrugs, everybody is used to it. We sit back, and he's right, we begin to feel the double-time rhythm of driving here. Drivers look alert, as though engaging in a contact sport. He drops us in the center near an esplanade closed to traffic. Out of the street's chaos, we're greeted by the scent of flowers. Vendors are selling freesias in all the Easter colors, purple, yellow, and white. Instead of the puny bouquets I buy at home, these are sold in armfuls, wrapped in a ruff of brazen pink foil and trailing ribbons.

Not wanting to take time for lunch, we sample sfincione, pizza with big bread crumbs on top, then keep going—palms, outdoor tables filled with people, small shops of luxurious bags and shoes, waiters with trays aloft carrying pastries and espresso.

Pastries! Every pasticceria displays an astonishing variety. We're used to drier Tuscan pastries; these are mounded with cream. A woman arranges her shop window with realistic marzipan pineapples, bananas, prickly pears, lemons, cherries, and, for the Easter season, lambs complete with curls. Inside, her cases display almond cakes, wild strawberry tarts, biscotti, and, of course, cannoli, but in all sizes, from thumb-sized to a giant as large as a leg of lamb. Two bakers pause in the kitchen doorway and all the customers step back as they gingerly balance and step. They bring out a three-foot tree made from small cannoli, a stiff pyramid like a French croquembouche at Christmas. Sfince, rice fritters filled with ricotta, cinnamon, candied oranges or strawberries, honor San Giuseppe, whose onomastico, name day, is March 19, when Italians also celebrate Father's Day.

The freezers glow with sorbetti—pistachio, lemon, watermelon, cinnamon, jasmine, almond, as well as the usual fruits. Most children seem to prefer gelato, not in a cup or cone, but stuffed inside a brioche. Just looking at the almond cake is almost enough satisfaction, but we instead split one of the crisp cannoli lined with chocolate and heavenly, creamy ricotta. No harm done; we're planning to walk for the rest of the afternoon.

* * *

O N THE FIRST DAY in a new place, it's good to wander, absorb colors, textures, and scents, see who lives here, and find the rhythm of the day. We'll crank into tourist mode later, making sure we don't miss the great sights. Dazed by actually coming to Palermo, by the flight, the espresso, and the day, we just take the appealing street, turning back if it begins to look dicey. Palms are everywhere. I wish I could take one back to Bramasole to replace the one December's freeze probably killed. Not only do I love palms because they mean tropical air, I love the image Wallace Stevens made: "the palm at the end

of the mind." To imagine the end of the mind and to see not a blank wall or a roadblock or an abyss but a tall swaying palm seems felicitous to me.

We come upon a botanical park, dusty and empty except for cacti, carob, mulberry, agave, and shrubs with primitive, broad leaves. The palm looks native but was brought by Arabs in the ninth century along with their fountains, spices, arabesques, ice cream, mosaics, and domes. Palms and domes—gold, pomegranate, aqua, verdigris—characterize Palermo. How bold to color the five domes of San Giovanni degli Eremiti a burnt red. Inside, aromatic citrus blossoms and jasmine suffuse a cloister garden, a secretive respite from the tortured road outside.

On the map, we see that the Palazzo dei Normanni is nearby and decide to go in the famous Cappella Palatina today. The subjects of the mosaics, the guidebook says, seem to have been chosen with reference to the Holy Spirit and the theology of light. I'm intrigued, since these two concepts seem identical in my mind.

Originally built by those busy Arabs in the ninth century, the palace was expanded by the Normans in the twelfth century and established as the residence for their kings. Later residents and royalty left their bits and pieces, and today the styles have so long overlapped that the architecture simply looks like itself. Byzantine Greeks began the mosaic decoration in the twelfth century. Tessera by tessera, it must have taken them forever; every Bible story I ever heard glitters around this room. The floors, too, are mosaic or inlaid marble in designs like Oriental rugs.

The Holy Spirit and theology of light are only a layer. A lot is going on. It's like Palermo—each square inch occupied with life. I love the word "tesserae." It seems to shower silver and gold on its own. There's the whole Adam and Eve saga, the flood, there's Jacob wrestling with the angel, and in the dome and apse, Christ. In the dome he's surrounded by foreshortened angels, each in intricate clothes. Christ offers a blessing in the apse. In both mosaics, he has long, long fingers. Looking through my opera glasses, I focus for a long time on his right hand, just this one small moment in the entire chapel—the hand held up, the thumb holding down the next-to-last finger, the other three straight, all formed with delicacy and subtle coloration. Late afternoon sun has a weak hold on the walls but still the gold around him sings with burnished amber light.

The rest of the Palazzo is closed. Walking back toward the center of Palermo, we pass rubble-filled lots still unrestored since World War II bombings. We look in open storefronts where hideous junk is sold and step off crowded sidewalks with fry-stations selling chickpea fritters. People are out gathering last minute food for dinner. About their business, the people look contained, silent, often weary. When they meet an acquaintance their faces break into vibrant expression. In the taxi back to the hotel, we hardly notice the near-death encounters.

The first two restaurants Ed selects for dinner are nixed by the hotel desk clerk. Dangerous areas, he tells us, making the motion of someone slicing a throat. He takes a ballpoint and scribbles out whole areas of our map. "What about this one?" Ed asks, pointing in our Italian restaurant guide to the highly regarded, unpronounceable N'grasciata. "And what does that mean?"

"In local dialect that means 'dirty' but don't be alarmed, just a way of speaking."

Speaking of what? I think. Dirty means dirty. "Your highest recommendation?"

"Sì, authentic. They have their own fishing boat. You won't see tourists there. I will call and they will expect you."

We're dropped off at a plain place which is even plainer inside. No tablecloths, a TV somewhere, no decor, no menu, harsh lighting and the buzz of bugs hitting the zapper. The waiter starts bringing out the food. I'm crazy about the panelli, chickpea fritters, and the platter of fried artichokes. Then comes pasta with pomarola, that intense, decocted tomato sauce, and baby octopus. I'm not so sure about this dish. I chew for a long time. The platter comes round again and Ed has more. We're offered another pasta, this one bucatini with sardines, currants, and fennel. The next dish is a grilled orata, which my dictionary translates as "gilthead," surrounded by fried frutta di mare—just various fish. I'm slowing down. I like a little bit of fish, not a lot. Ed loves anything that comes from the sea and is so obviously relishing the food

that the waiter starts to hover, commenting on each morsel. He's pouring wine to the brim of the glass. His dolorous eyes look like Jesus' in the mosaic dome. His long fingers have tufts of black curly hair on each digit, and a matt of hair escapes the collar of his shirt. He has the long, four-inch-wide face I associate with newspaper photos of hijackers.

I revive briefly for the spicy melanzane—here's a touch of the Arabic, eggplant with cinnamon and pine nuts—but balk at the appearance of the stuffed squid (all those suction cups on the arms) and the sea bream sausage. Is he bringing us everything in the kitchen? Next comes a plate of fried potatoes. "Signora," our waiter says. "Signora." He can't believe that I have stopped eating. He pulls up a chair and sits down. "You must."

I smile and shake my head. Impossible. He rolls those dolorous eyes to heaven. "Ho paura," I'm afraid, I try to joke, pointing at the squid. He takes me literally and eats a bite himself to prove there's no cause for alarm. Still, I shake my head no. He takes my fork, gently grabs a handful of my hair and starts to feed me. I am so astonished I open my mouth and eat. I really hate the texture, like tenderized erasers.

As an afterthought, he brings out involtini, veal rolled around a layer of herbs and cheese, but even Ed has stopped by now. He's thanking the waiter. "The best fish in Palermo," he tells him.

"How do you know?" I ask him on the way out. The waiter bares his teeth in a big grin. No, he looks more like a wolf than Jesus.

"It had to be. That was a down-home place."

* * *

WE'RE OUT EARLY. In the Vucciria quarter, the market is stupendous. I've been to markets in France, Spain, Peru, San Francisco, all over Italy. This is the market. For the senses, ecstasy and assault. Because Palm Sunday is this weekend, perhaps it is more of an assault than usual. Lines of lambs, gutted and dripping, eyeballs bulging, hang by their feet. Their little hooves and tails look so sad. Their little guts look so horrifying. The rainbows of shining fish on ice, the mounds of shrimp still wiggling their antennae, painted carts of lemons, jewel-colored candied fruits, bins of olives, nuts, seeds—everything is presided over by dealers who shout, sing, cajole, joke, curse, barter, badger. They're loud and raucous. Could it be true, as I've read, that the Mafia runs the heroin trade out of here? A vendor holds out a basket of eels that look like live sterling silver. He gyrates his hips to emphasize their movement. This feels more like a carnival than the more decorous Tuscan markets we're used to. I wish for a kitchen so I could gather some of the lustrous eggplants and clumps of field greens. My stomach is growling so loud it sounds like a tiny horse neighing. Cooks here are in paradise. I'll never eat lamb again.

Ed refuses to go to the Catacombe dei Cappuccini, where 8,000 desiccated corpses are on exhibit. I have already bought a postcard of a red-haired girl under glass for decades, her delicate nostrils still stuffed with cotton, a ribbon in her hair. We have visited the same sort of place in Guanajuato, Mexico. I was fascinated; he was revolted. We decide on the Museo Archeologico, and we don't come out until it closes. I find this one of the best museums I've ever visited—so much of what interests me is gathered in this old convent. Phoenician anchors and amphoras dredged from the sea lie around the courtyard. Mysterious stelae painted with portraits were found on ancient grave sites in Marsala. Etruscan treasures, some with traces of paint, from the tombs at Chiusi, near us in Tuscany, somehow have ended up in Sicily. Here we get to see the sixth- and fifth-century BC metopes (panels of the temple frieze) removed from the Greek site at Selinunte, one of the most important Greek sites on the island. We find Demeter, the Cretan bull; Perseus, Hercules, and Athena star in various triumphs. Hera marries Zeus, and Actaeon becomes a stag. Seeing the familiar mythic players as they actually were on temples brings the legends closer to my imagination. These images come from the time when they were real to people, not just characters from the history of myth—an astounding telescoping of distance. The enormous scale, too, prepares us for the dimensions of the ruins we'll see.

We can't look at all 12,000 of the votive figures also excavated at Selinunte but we look until we can't look anymore. That only leaves rooms and rooms of Roman sculpture, Greek vases, and more and more. We meander through, stopped by painted fragments from Pompeii, a fantastic third century BC Bronze ram, and a blur of mosaic pavements. Then, out. Onto the plain sidewalk, dazed and dazzled by what we've seen.

* * *

AS THE FREESIAS BEGIN to wilt in our room, we decide to start our tour of the island tomorrow morning. We have a glass of blood orange juice on our balcony. All we can hear is the rattle of palms below us in the breeze and the jingle of rigging on the sailboats in the bay.

"Do you want to come back?" I ask.

"Yes. We haven't seen whole areas of Palermo."

"It's hard to get a sense of the place. So layered, so crude, so complex—a daunting city."

"My core impression is of a chaos everyone here has learned how to survive."

* * *

BUT I SUDDENLY REMEMBER a story a woman I met in Milwaukee told me about someone she knew. "This Midwestern soldier in World War II was on a ship which was bombed by retreating Germans in the harbor of Palermo," I tell Ed. "He survived even though almost everyone else was killed. He swam to shore and was stranded here. I think the Germans were retreating by then. One night he went to the opera—he'd never been before. At the end, he was so moved by the music he started to cry. All the horrors caught up with him. He just stood there during the applause and afterwards, openly crying. The audience started to file out. A man looked at him, paused, and touched him on the head, as though he were bestowing a benediction. As all the people passed him, each one stopped and touched him on the head.

"That's one of the best things I've ever heard. So that's Palermo."

Each succeeding conqueror of Sicily—Greeks, Carthaginians, Romans, Arabs, Normans, and all the rest—must have brought pocketfuls of wildflower seeds. The countryside in primavera is solidly in flower, rivers of yellow, purple cascading around rocks, roadsides lined with tiny blue-eyed blooms, and almond orchards whose long grasses are overtaken by white daisies. We made an easy exit, considering. We were only lost half an hour. Even though Ed was intimidated by traffic in Palermo, once we were out on the open road, I noticed his new skills, learned from the back seat of the taxis. He's relaxing into the concept that lanes do not exist much; the road is an open field for getting where you're going. The white line is the center of an imaginary lane to be used as needed.

Driving along the coast and meandering inland, the Mar Tirreno seven shades of blue out one window, and rampantly flowering hills out the other, it is easy to see why all those conquering hoards wanted this island. The landscape is everywhere various or dramatic. Anytime the perfume of orange and lemon groves wafts in the window, the human body has to feel suffused with a languorous well-being.

Soon we come to the turn-off for Segesta, first of the many Greek temples we hope to see in Sicily—the number rivals Greece itself. The Doric temple rises, just off the highway, where it has loomed on the hillside since the fifth century BC, which is close to forever. Along the climbing path, we see gigantic fennel growing, ten feet, even more. I always wondered how Prometheus took fire back to the Greeks in a fennel stalk. In these you could stash quite a few coals. In the process, maybe he invented grilled fennel.

The guidebook says of Segesta: "It is peripteral and hexastyle with 36 unfluted columns (9 m high, 2 m wide at base) on a stylobate 58 m by 23 m. The high entablature and the pediments are intact. The bosses used for maneuvering the blocks of the stylobate into position remain. Refinements include the curvature of the entablature and the abaci." Well, yes, but it's beautiful.

So is the equally ancient theater a short hike away. Greece was the first country I ever wanted to see. My longing was produced by a total immersion in Lord Byron when I was a senior in high school. In college, my friend Rena and I took a course in Greek drama. We wrote for brochures from Greek freighters and decided to drop out and see the world. We wanted to book passage on Hellenic Destiny, until our parents said absolutely not. I've never yet been to Greece. A few years ago I saw the magnificent temples at Paestum in the south of Italy and the longing was reawakened. "The mountains look on Marathon / and Marathon looks on the sea / and musing there an hour alone, / I dreamed that Greece might still be free." Something like that—it seems to scan into iambic tetrameter.

Like Paestum, Segesta is stripped down to pure silence, its skeletal purity etched against the sky. No one is here, though there were several people in the gift shop. We're alone with history and swallows swooping from their nests.

* * *

'M GLAD I DON'T HAVE TO take a test on Agrigento. For an American used to a comparatively straightforward history, all the Italian past seems hopelessly convoluted. The saga of the Greek ruins multiplies this complexity. Agrigento, since its Greek founding in the sixth century BC has been tossed among Carthaginians, Romans, Swabians, Arabians, Bourbons and Spaniards. Subjected to a name change during Mussolini's zeal to Italianize all things, the old name Akragas became Agrigento. I've seen the same zeal on the plaque outside where John Keats lived in Rome, cut off from his love and dying from tuberculosis. He's called Giovanni Keats, which somehow makes him seem more vulnerable than ever.

Akragas/Agrigento was Luigi Pirandello's birthplace. Traveling in Sicily casts his plays and stories, with their quirky sense of reality, in quite a natural light. The coexistence of the Greek ruins, the contemporary ruins, the tentacles of the Mafia, and the mundane day-to-day would skew my sense of time and place, too. The sun, Pirandello wrote, can break stones. Even in March, we feel the driving force on our heads as we walk in the Valley of the Temples.

All over a valley of almond trees and wildflowers stand a mind-boggling array of remains from an ancient town, from temples to sewer pipes. You could stay for days and not see everything. Unlike other sites, this one is quite populated with visitors. The Temple of Concordia is the best-preserved temple we've seen. Patch up the roof and the populace could commune with Castor and Pollux, to whom it probably was dedicated.

Five days ago I knew almost nothing about these ruins. Now the ancient dust covers my feet through my sandals; I have seen the unlikely survival of these buildings through rolls and rolls of time. These temples, men selling woven palm fronds for Palm Sunday, schoolchildren hiding among the columns, awed travelers like us with dripping gelato—all under the intense Sicilian sky. I'm thrilled. Just as I think that, Ed says, "This is a thrill of a lifetime."

Meandering, we stop at a cypress-guarded cemetery near Modica. Extravagant tombs are elaborately carved miniature houses laid along miniature streets. Here's the exuberance of Modica's art of the Baroque in microcosm. Through the grates or gates, the little chapels open to linen-draped altars with framed portraits of the dead and potted plants or vases of flowers. At thresholds, a few cats sun on the warmed marble. A woman is scrubbing, as she would her own stoop. With a corner of her apron, she polishes the round photo of a World War I soldier. A young girl weeds the hump of earth over a recent grave in the plain old ground. These dead cool off slowly; someone still tends flowers on plots where the inhabitants have lain for fifty years.

Cortona's cemetery, too, reflects the town, although not as grandly. A walled city of the dead situated just below the live city, it glows at night from the votive lights on each grave. Looking down from the Piazza del Duomo, it's hard not to imagine the dead up and about, visiting each other as their relatives still do right up the hill. The dead here probably would want more elaborate theatrical entertainments.

* * *

NEXT ON OUR ROUTE, AVOLA retains some charm. One-room-wide Baroque houses line the streets. Could we take home at least a dozen of the gorgeous children in their white smocks? On the corners men with hand-held scales scoop cockles from a mound on the sidewalk. Open trucks selling vegetables attract crowds of women

with baskets. We keep turning down tiny roads to the sea. We can't find the beaches we expect—the unspoiled littoral dream of the island's limpid waters—only bleak beach towns, closed and depressing out of season.

It's only in Siracusa that I finally fall in love. In my Greek phase in college, I took Greek and Roman History, Greek and Roman Drama, Greek Etymology. At that point, my grandfather who was sending me to college, drew a line. "I am not paying for you to stick your head in the clouds. You should get a certificate for teaching so you have something to fall back on." The message being, if your husband—whom you have gone to college to acquire, and no Yankees, please—dies or runs off. Meanwhile, I was loving Aeschylus, the severe consequences of passion, pure-as-milk marble sculptures, the explorative spirit of the Greeks. Siracusa, therefore, is tremendously exciting to visit. Mighty Siracusa, ancient of ancients. Second to Athens in the classical world. We opt for a super-luxurious hotel on the connecting island of Ortigia, with a room surrounded by views of the water. We're suddenly not tired exactly, but saturated. We spend the afternoon in the huge bed, order coffee sent up, pull back the curtains and watch the fishing boats nosing—isn't that a Greek blue—into the harbor.

After siesta, we find Ortigia in high gear for Easter. Bars display chocolate eggs two feet tall, wrapped in purple cellophane and ribbons. Some are open on one side to reveal a marzipan Christ on the cross. Others have a surprise inside. I'd love to buy marzipan doves, lambs in baskets, chocolate hens. The lambs are like stuffed animals, large, decorated from nose to tail with fanciful marzipan curls. At the Antica Dolceria, they've gone into marzipan frenzy: Noah's ark complete with animals, the Greek temples, olives, pencils. Marzipan—called pasta reale—we realize is a serious folk art form. For me, three bites will suffice; maybe you have to have been born in Sicily to be able to eat more.

Ortigia is fantastic. The vague, intuitive sense of oppression I've felt in Sicily entirely lifts. Is the Mafia not in control here? People seem more lighthearted, playful, and swaggering. They look you in the eye, as people do in the rest of Italy. In the late afternoon, we walk all over the small island. It has its own Greek ruins just lying in a grassy plot at an intersection. An inscription carved into steps identifies the site as a temple to Apollo. Dense ficus trees along a walkway bordering the water are home to thousands of birds singing their evening doxology. Views across the water, Baroque iron balconies, Venetian Gothic windows, boarded up palazzi, and intricate medieval streets—layers and layers of architecture and time. Suddenly the streets intersect and widen at the Piazza del Duomo. The Baroque facade and entrance of the church in no way prepares you for the stunning surprise inside. Along one wall, the building incorporates a row of twelve majestic columns from the fifth-century BC Tempio di Atene. At evening, spikes of sunlight fall across the piazza, lighting the faces of those having an aperitivo at outdoor tables. Ordinary people, with the sun, like the sheen of gold mosaics, transforming their faces.

* * *

WE'RE READY TO PUT IN a full day on foot. In the museum on Ortigia, Caravaggio's painting of the burial of Santa Lucia, a local martyr in 304, who cut out her own eyes when a suitor admired them, occasioned a lecture from the guard worthy of any docent. And where are we from? Ah, he has a cousin in California; we should meet him when we return. Ed loves Annunciation paintings and the peeling one by da Messina enthralls him. Small local museums are my favorite kind. They stay close to the source, usually, and deepen a tourist-level connection with a place.

We walk across the bridge and through a park then through a honeycomb of streets. The Museo Archeologico in Siracusa proper is world class. Intelligently arranged and exhibited, the art and craft of succeeding waves of life in this area are displayed. Beginning with prehistory we trace the history through one stunning room after another. Artifacts, statues, lion faces from the temple in ruins in Ortigia, Greek ex-votos, and an amazing bronze horse—oh, so much.

The amphitheater in Siracusa—what fabulous siting. The stone cup of the hill was chopped out into natural seating, a 300-degree arrangement focusing on a stage. Corridors were carved out for gladiators to enter and exit. In summer, the Greek plays are still performed here. What fun it would be to act in one. The ruins we've seen are the major ones; hundreds of other temples, foundations, baths, and unknown stones cover the island. This must be the ideal time to see them because hardly anyone is around. The solitude of these places sharpens the experience of happening upon them, the sense of discovery that for me lies at the heart of travel.

Frances Mayes is also the author of the best-selling *Under the Tuscan Sun: At Home in Italy* (1996) and *In Tuscany* (2000), with photographs by Bob Krist. Her books are available from Broadway Books and in audio from Bantam, Doubleday, Dell.

THE ARTLESS ART OF ITALIAN COOKING

YOU ARE STAYING WITH FRIENDS in their villa in a windswept olive orchard above Florence. After a day in town—a morning at the Palazzo Pitti, afternoon in the Brancacci Chapel—you have returned to rest. In the garden, you find your hostess lifting heavy tomatoes into a basket, the acrid smell of their skins wafting up in the gentle September heat. You pick basil and tug figs from a tree that warms its back against the 14th-century kitchen wall. Inside, you watch while your hostess rinses the greens in the quarried stone sink. The tomatoes are still sun-warm when she scoops them, chopped, into a blender with the basil and a stream of olive oil; she pours the mixture into a faience bowl over steaming pasta. You eat at the kitchen table, pour wine from a crockery pitcher, and wipe your bowl with torn chunks of flour-flecked bread. Over the greens your hostess drizzles more olive oil and a bit of rock salt pinched from an open bowl. The figs melt in your mouth like chocolate. A scalding syrup of Arabic coffee streams from the *macchinetta*, and you're ready for a midnight survey of the olive groves.

Simple, earthy, at once wholesome and sensual, as sophisticated in its purity as the most complex cuisine, as inspired in its aesthetics as the art and architecture of its culture, Italian cooking strikes a chord that resonates today as it did in the Medici courts. Its enduring appeal can be traced to an ancient principle: respect for the essence of the thing itself—nothing more, nothing less. Like Michelangelo freeing the prisoners that dwelt within the stone—innate, organic—an Italian chef seems intuitively to seek out the crux of the thing he is about to cook and flatter it, subtly, with the purest of complements. To lay a translucent sheet of prosciutto—earthy, gamey, faintly redolent of brine—across the juicy pulchritude of a melon wedge is a stroke of insight into the nature of two ingredients as profound as the imaginings of Galileo.

Considering the pizzas, lasagnas, and red-drenched spaghetti that still pass for Italian food in many places abroad, it's no surprise that visitors to Italy are often struck by the austerity of the true Italian dishes put before them. The pasta is only lightly accented, not drowning in an industrial ladleful of strong, soupy sauce. And while there may have been a parade of vegetable *antipasti,* the salad itself bears no resemblance to the smorgasbord of Anglo-American salad bars—it's a simple mix of greens, a drizzle of oil, a spritz, perhaps, of red-wine vinegar. If you've just come from Germanic countries, you'll notice a lack of Maggi, the bottled brown "flavor enhancer" that singes the tongue with monosodium glutamate, on the table. If you've come from Belgium, you'll miss the sauceboat of Hollandaise. And if you've come from France, you may shrug dismissively at the isolated ingredients you're served, saying as other Frenchmen before you, "But this is not really a true *cuisine. . . ."*

Ah, but it is. Shunning the complexities of heavy French sauces and avoiding the elaborate farce, Italian cuisine—having unloaded the aspirations of *alta cucina* onto its northern neighbors when Catherine de' Medici moved (chefs and all) to Paris—stands alone, proud, purist, unaffected.

The Italians' pride comes in part from a confidence in their raw ingredients, an earthiness that informs the appreciation of every citizen-connoisseur, from the roughest peasant in workers' blue to the vintner in shoulder-tied cashmere: they are in touch with land and sea. In the country, your host can tell you the source of every ingredient on the table, from the neighbor's potted goose to the porcini gathered in the beech grove yesterday. In the city, the market replaces the country network, and aggressive shopping will trace the genealogy of every mushroom, every artichoke, every wooden scoop of olives. And in balconies overhanging the seashore, the squid floating in their rich, blue-black ink were bought from a fisherman on the beach at dawn.

The spectrum of Italian regional cooking is as broadly varied as Italy's terrain, and cuisine and countryside are intimately allied. Emerging into sunlight from the Great St. Bernard pass into the Valle d'Aosta, the Piedmont, the hills of Lombardy, you'll find wood-lined alpine trattorias offering rib-sticking gnocchi and air-dried beef, bubbling pots of *bagna cauda* (hot dipping sauce of olive oil and garlic), slabs of polenta, hearty walnut *torta* (cake). The pearl-spotted rice of Arborio, in the Po Valley, fuels an extraordinary array of risottos in Milan, where chefs shun olive oil in favor of the region's rich butter. Descend to Alba and savor the earthy perfume of truffles, the muscular Barolo wines. Cross over into Liguria and the cuisine changes as abruptly as the landscape: wild herbs, greens, and ground nuts flavor a panoply of sauces (consider the famous pesto, flavored with a "riviera" basil rarely found elsewhere), served as condiments to meat as often as over pasta. The succulent pink pork of a Parma ham, the golden butterfat in a Reggiano cheese were nurtured on the same fertile soil of Emilia-Romagna, both the culinary and agricultural heart of Italy, while the *bistecca* of Tuscany comes from Chianina beef, pampered on local prairie grass and slaughtered at a tender age. Head south for sun-plumped eggplant, and quasi-tropical artichokes—in Rome, fried in delicate batter; in Calabria, stuffed with meat and sharp Pecorino from its hillside sheep herds. The chickpeas in Sicilian dishes remind you you're nearly in North Africa. And, of course, on this slender leg of land you are never far from the sea, and the harvest of its *frutti di mare* graces nearly every region—but none more than the islands and tide-washed shores of the south.

* * *

CAREENING IN YOUR RENTAL CAR down the western coast, clinging to the waterfront through sea-shanty villages that cantilever over the roaring surf, you feel a morning lag: your breakfast of *latte macchiato* and sugary *cornetto* has worn away. A real espresso would hit the spot; you hurtle down a web of switchbacks and pull into a seaside inn. You sip aromatic coffee and watch the waves. An hour passes in reverie—an aperitif, perhaps? Another hour over the Martini rosso, and you give in to the impulse, adjourning to the dining room. The odor of wood smoke drifts from the kitchen. A nutty risotto with a blush of tomato precedes a vast platter— austere, unembellished—of smoke-grilled fish, still sizzling, lightly brushed with oil, and glittering with rock salt. At the table

beside yours, when the platter arrives, the woman rises and fillets the fish dexterously, serving her husband and sons.

There's a wholesomeness in the way Italians eat that is charming and contagious. If American foodies pick and kvetch and French gastronomes worship, Italians plunge into their meal with frank joy, earnest appreciation, and ebullient conversation. Yet they do not overindulge: portions are light, the drinking gentle, late suppers spartan with concern for digestion uppermost. It's as if the voice of Mamma still whispers moderation in their ear. They may, on the other hand, take disproportionate pleasure in watching guests eat, in surrounding them with congenial company, in pouncing on the bill. (This wholesome spirit even carries into the very bars: unlike the dark, louche atmosphere of Anglo lounges and pubs, in Italy you'll drink your *amaro* in a fluorescent-lit coffee bar without a whiff of sin in the air.)

Yet for all their straightforwardness, Italians are utterly at ease with their heritage, steeped from birth in the art and architecture that surrounds them. Without a hint of the grandiose, they'll construct a still life of figs and Bosc pears worthy of Caravaggio; a butcher will drape iridescent pheasants and quail, heads dangling, with the panache of a couturier. Consider the artless beauty of ruby-raw beef on an emerald bed of arugula, named for the preferred colors of the Venetian painter Carpaccio; pure white porcelain on damask; a mosaic of olives and pimientos in blown glass; a flash of folkloric pottery on a polished plank of oak.

In fact, it must be said: a large part of the pleasure of Italian dining is dining in Italy. We have all eaten in Italian restaurants elsewhere. The food can be superb, the ingredients authentic, the pottery and linens imported by hand. Yet who can conjure the blood-red ocher crumbling to gold on a Roman wall, the indigo and pastel hues of fishing boats rocking in a marina, the snow flurry of sugar papers on a café floor? These impart the essence that—as much as the basil on your *bruschetta*—flavors your Italian dining experience.

Inside the great walls of Lucca, you are lunching—slowly, copiously, and at length—in the shade of a vaulted portico. Strips of roasted eggplant and pepper steeped in garlic and oil; tortelloni stuffed with squab in a pool of butter and sage; roasted veal laced with green peppercorns; blackberries in thick cream. The bottle of Brunello di Montalcino, alas, is drained. It has been a perfect morning, walking the ramparts, and you have found the perfect restaurant: a Raphaelesque perspective of arcades and archways, pillars, porches, and loges spreads before you. The shadows and lines are strong in the afternoon sun; you admire from your seat in the cross breeze. It's only slowly that you realize that this Merchant/Ivory moment has a sound track, so organic to the scene you hadn't noticed—but now you feel goose bumps rising on your neck. It is Puccini: a young woman is singing, beautifully, from a groined arcade across the square, accompanied by a portable tape player.

". . . Ma quando vien lo sgelo . . . il primo sole è mio . . ."

Your coffee goes cold, untouched until the song, the moment, are over—and, in all its multifaceted magnificence, your Italian meal as well.

—Nancy Coons

THE PASSIONATE EYE: ITALIAN ART THROUGH THE AGES

ITALIAN ART FLOWS as naturally as its wine, its sunshine, and its amore, and it has been springing from the Italian spirit for nearly as long. Perhaps nowhere else in the world has such a vital creative impulse flourished so bountifully within the noble sweep of the classical tradition. Perhaps no other country's cultural life has been so inextricably interwoven with its history.

And yet, Italy lives comfortably in the midst of all her accumulated treasures. She accepts them casually and affectionately, as she does her children and her flowers. True, some of her precious store has been gathered into world-famous museums, but Italians know best and love most intimately the art that surrounds their daily activity. They go to church among thousand-year-old mosaics, buy their groceries in a shop open since the time of Columbus, picnic on the steps of a temple that was old when Christ was born, and attend the opera in the same theaters where Rossini and Verdi saw their works premiered. Italy wears the raiment of her heritage with a light and touching grace. She must: it is the very fabric of her life. For travelers from other countries, however, Italian art remains unique, extraordinary, worthy of worship. Here we offer a short history, focusing on Italy's greatest artistic achievement, the Renaissance—often called the nursery of Western art. The discoveries of 14th- and 15th-century Italian artists making it possible to render a realistic image of a person or an object determined the course of Western art right up until the late 19th century. Following the essay is a glossary of art and architectural terms that will prove useful in understanding the artistic treasures of Italy.

Art in the Middle Ages

The eastern half of the Roman Empire, based in Constantinople (Byzantium), was powerful long after the fall of Rome in AD 476: Italy remained influenced—and at times ruled—by the Byzantines. The artistic revolution began when artists started to rebel against the Byzantine ethic, which dictated that art be exclusively Christian and that its aim be to arouse a sensation of mystical awe and reverence in the on-looker. This ethic forbade frivolous pagan portraits, bacchanalian orgy scenes, or delicate landscapes with maidens gathering flowers, as painted and sculpted by the Romans. Instead, biblical stories were depicted in richly colored mosaics—rows of figures against a gold background. (You can see some of the finest examples of this art at Ravenna, once the Western capital of the Empire, on the Adriatic coast.) Even altarpieces, painted on wood, followed the same model—stiff figures surrounded by gold, with no attempt made at an illusion of reality.

In the 13th century, the era of St. Francis and of a new humanitarian approach to Christianity, artists in Tuscany began to portray real people in real settings. Cimabue was the first to feel his way in this direction, but it was Giotto who broke decisively with the Byzantine style. Even if his sense of perspective is nowhere near correct and his figures still had typically Byzantine slanting eyes, he painted palpably solid people who, presumably, experienced real emotions.

By the end of the 14th century, the International Gothic Style (which had arrived in Italy from France) had made further progress toward realism, but more with depictions of plants, animals, and clothes than of the human figure. And, as you can see from Gentile da Fabriano's *Adoration of the Magi*, housed in the Galleria degli Uffizi in Florence, it was mainly a decorative art, still very much like a Byzantine mosaic.

Italian architecture during the Middle Ages followed a number of different trends. In the south, the solid Norman Romanesque style was dominant; towns such as Siena and Pisa in central Italy had their own Romanesque style, more graceful than its northern European counterparts. Like northern Romanesque, it was dominated by simple geometric forms, but buildings were covered with decorative toylike patterns done in multicolored marble. In northern Italy, building was in a more solemn red brick.

In Tuscany, the region around Florence, the 13th century was a time of great political and economic growth, and there was a desire to celebrate the new wealth and power in the region's buildings. This is why such civic centers as the Palazzo Vecchio in Florence are so big and fortresslike. Florence's cathedral, the Duomo, was built on a colossal scale mainly in order to outdo the Pisans and the Sienese, Florence's rivals. All these Tuscan cathedrals are in the Italian version of Gothic, a style that originated in France and found its expression there in tall, soaring, light-and-airy verticality, intended to elevate the soul. The spiritual aspect of Gothic never really caught on in Italy, where the top priority for a church (as representative of a city) was to be grander and more imposing than the neighboring cities' churches.

Art in the Renaissance

The Renaissance, or "rebirth," did not evolve simply from a set of newfound artistic skills; the movement represented a revolution in attitudes whereby each individual was thought to play a specific role in the divine scheme of things. By fulfilling this role, it was believed the individual gained a new dignity. It was no coincidence that this revolution took place in Florence, which in the 15th century was an influential, wealthy, highly evolved city-state. Artists here had the leisure, prestige, and self-confidence to develop their talent and produce works that would reflect this new dignity and strength as well as their own prowess.

The sculptor Donatello, for example, wanted to astound, rather than please, the spectator with his defiant warts-and-all likenesses and their intense, heroic gazes. In painting, Masaccio's figures have a similarly assured air.

Art had changed gears in the early Renaissance: the Classical Age was now the model for a noble, moving, and realistic art. Artists studied ancient Roman ruins for what they could learn about proportion and balance. They evolved the new science of perspective and took it to its limits with sometimes bizarre results, as in Uccello's dizzily receding *Deluge* (in Florence's church Santa Maria Novella) or his carousel-like *Battle of San Romano* (in the Uffizi in Florence). One of the most frequently used perspective techniques was that of foreshortening, or making an object seem smaller and more contracted, to create the illusion of distance. From this technique emerged the *sotto in su* effect—literally, "from below upward," meaning that the action in the picture takes place above you, with figures, buildings, and landscapes correspondingly foreshortened. It's a clever visual trick that must have delighted visitors who walked into, for example, Mantegna's Camera degli Sposi in Mantua and saw what appeared to be people curiously looking down at them through a gap in the ceiling.

The concept of the universal man was epitomized by the artist who was at home with an array of disciplines, including the science of perspective, Greek, Latin, anatomy, sculpture, poetry, architecture, philosophy—even engineering, as in the case of Leonardo da Vinci, the universal man par excellence. Not surprisingly, there was a change in attitude toward artists: whereas previously they had been considered merely anonymous workmen trained to carry out commissions, now they were seen as giant personalities, immensely skillful and with highly individual styles.

The new skills and realistic effects of Florentine painting rapidly found a sympathetic response among Venetian painters. Gentile Bellini and Antonio Carpaccio, just two of the many whose work fills the Accademia, took to covering their canvases with crowd scenes, buildings, canals, processions, dogs, ships, parrots, and chimneys. These were generally narrative paintings, telling the story of a saint's life or simply depicting everyday scenes.

It was the emphasis on color, though, that made Venetian art Venetian, and it was the late-15th-century masters of color, preeminently Giovanni Bellini and Giorgione, who began to use it no longer as decoration but as a means to create a particular atmosphere. How different the effect of Giorgione's *Tempest* (in the Accademia) would be with a sunny blue sky instead of the ominous grays and dark greens that fill the background! For the first time, the atmosphere, not the figures, became the central focus of painting.

In architecture the Gothic excesses of the 13th century were toned down in the 14th, while the 15th ushered in a completely new approach. The humanist ideal was expressed through classical Roman design.

In Florence, Brunelleschi used Roman columns for the basilica of San Lorenzo and Roman round arches—as opposed to pointed Gothic ones—for his Spedale degli Innocenti (Foundling Hospital), which is generally considered the first truly classical building of the Renaissance. Leon Battista Alberti's treatise on ideal proportion was even more influential as a manifesto of the Renaissance movement. Suddenly, architects had become erudite scholars and architecture far more earnest.

High Renaissance & Mannerism

Florence in the late 15th century and Rome in the early 16th (following its sacking in 1527) underwent a traumatic political and religious upheaval that naturally came to be reflected in art. Classical proportion and realism no longer seemed enough. The heroic style suddenly looked hollow and outdated. Tuscan artists such as Pontormo and Rosso Fiorentino found expression for their unease in discordant colors, elongated forms, tortured looks in staring eyes. Giambologna carved his *Hercules and the Centaur* (in Florence's Museo del Bargello) at the most agonizing moment of their battle, when Hercules bends the Centaur's back to the point where it is about to snap. This is Mannerism, a style in which optimism and self-confidence are gone. What remains is a self-conscious, stylized show of virtuosity, the effect of which is neither to please (like Gothic) nor to impress (like Renaissance art) but to disquiet. Even Bronzino's portraits are cold, unsmiling, and far removed from the relaxed mood of the Renaissance portrait. By the 1530s an artistic exodus from Florence had taken place, and the city's golden age was over.

Venice, meanwhile, was following its own path. Titian's painting was a more virtuoso version of Bellini's and Giorgione's poetic style, but Titian later shifted the emphasis back to figures, rather than atmosphere, as the central focus of his paintings. Titian's younger contemporaries in Venice—Veronese, Tintoretto, and Bassano—wanted to make names for themselves. They started working on huge canvases—which gave them more freedom of movement—playing all sorts of visual games: juggling with viewpoints and perspective and using dazzlingly bright colors. This visual trickery suggests a natural parallel with the self-conscious artifice of Florentine painting of the same period, but the exuberance of these Venetian painters, and the increasingly emotional quality of their work, remained significantly more vital than the arid and ever more sterile works of central Italy toward the end of the 16th century.

Mannerism found a fairly precise equivalent in architecture. In Florence the rebellious younger generation (Michelangelo, Ammanati, Vasari) used the same architectural vocabulary as the Renaissance architects but distorted it deliberately and bizarrely in a way that would have made Alberti's hair stand on end. Michelangelo's staircase at the Biblioteca Laurenziana in Florence, for example, spills down like a gush of stone water, filling almost the entire floor space of the vestibule. Likewise, the inside walls are treated as if they were facades, though with columns and niches disproportionately large for the size of the room.

Andrea del Palladio, whose theories and elegant palaces were to be immensely influential on architecture elsewhere in Europe and as far north as England, was one of the greatest architects of the period.

The 17th & 18th Centuries

In the second half of the 16th century, Italy was caught up in the Counter-Reformation. This movement was a reaction against the Protestant Reformation of the Christian church that was sweeping through Europe. The Counter-Reformation enlisted art as a weapon, an instrument for the diffusion of the Catholic faith. Artists were discouraged from expressing themselves as freely as they had been before and from creating anything that was not of a religious nature. But within this religious framework they were able to evolve a style that appealed to the senses.

The Baroque—an emotional and heroic style that lasted through most of the 17th century—was propaganda art, designed to overwhelm the masses through its visual illusion, dramatic lighting, strong colors, and violent movement. There was an element of seduction in this propaganda: the repressive religiosity of the Counter-Reformation went hand in hand with a barely disguised eroticism. The best-known example of this ambiguity is Bernini's sculpture of the *Ecstasy of Saint Teresa* in

Rome, in which the saint sinks back in what could be a swoon of either pain or pleasure, while a smiling angel stands over her holding an arrow. Both the painting and architecture of this period make extensive use of sensuous curves.

The cradle of the Baroque was Rome, where Pietro da Cortona and Bernini channeled their genius into spectacular theatrical frescoes, sculptures, palaces, and churches. Rome had become the artistic center of Italy. Florence was artistically dead by this time, and Venice was producing only hack imitations of Titian's and Tintoretto's paintings.

In the 18th century, Venice came back into its own and Rome was practically finished as an artistic center. Venetian artists adopted the soft, overripe version of Baroque—known as rococo—that had originated in France. Free from the spiritual ideals that motivated the Baroque style, rococo celebrated sensuousness (and sensuality) for its own sake. Although Venice was nearing the last stages of its political decline, there was still immense wealth in the city, mostly in the hands of families who wished to make the world know about it—and what better way than through vast, dazzling rococo canvases, reassuringly stylized and removed from reality? The revival began with Sebastiano

Ricci and was expertly elaborated on by Tiepolo. But it could never have taken place had there not been a return to the city's great artistic traditions. Late-16th-century color technique and expertise were drawn on and fused with what had been learned from the Baroque to create the breathtaking, magical, decadent world of the Venetian rococo.

This was the final flowering of Venetian painting. The death of Francesco Guardi in 1793, compounded by the fall of the Republic of Venice in 1797, marked the effective end of the city's artistic life. Neoclassicism found no champion here, except for the sculptor Canova, who, in any case, did his finest work after he left Venice.

Today, the great tradition of Italian art is widely diffused, perhaps diluted, but it is certainly too early to write its obituary. That has been done periodically over the past 20 centuries, inevitably to the chagrin of the mistaken commentator. In the midst of the burgeoning vitality, which charms and occasionally maddens the visitor, the arts are not long to be neglected. Italians live the tradition too deeply.

—Sheila Brownlee

ARTISTICALLY SPEAKING: A GLOSSARY

The eloquence of the world's greatest masterpieces can be deafening, and Italy's treasures—their message made manifest in marble, pigment, and precious metals—instill a spirit of awe. The privilege of enjoying this bounty of the ages can be enhanced by a familiarity with the terms of art-speak. Here is a limited glossary. Many of these Italian words are now part of the basic art-history vocabulary.

Acanthus: Sculptural ornamentation from antiquity; it's based on the foliage of the acanthus plant.

Apse: A semicircular terminus found behind the altar in a church.

Atrium: The courtyard in front of the entrance to an ancient Roman villa or an early church.

Badia: Abbey.

Baldacchino: A canopy—often made of stone—above a church altar, supported by columns.

Baptistery: A separate structure or area in a church where rites of baptism are held.

Baroque: A 17th-century European art movement in which dramatic, elaborate ornamentation was used to stir viewers' emotions. The most famous Italian baroque artists were Carracci and Bernini.

Basilica: A rectangular Roman public building divided into aisles by rows of columns. Many early churches were built on the basilican plan, but the term is also applied to some churches without specific reference to architecture.

Belvedere: Usually a lookout point for vistas; the word means "beautiful view."

Campanile: A bell tower of a church.

Capital: The crowning section of a column, usually decorated with Doric, Ionic, or Corinthian ornament.

Chiaroscuro: Literally "light/dark;" used to describe the distribution of light and shade in a painting, either with a marked contrast or a muted tonal gradation.

Cinquecento: Literally, "five hundred," used in Italian to refer to the 16th century.

Contrapposto: A dramatic pose of a sculpted figure in which the upper portion of the body is placed in opposition to the lower portion.

Cortile: Courtyard.

Cupola: Dome.

Duomo: Cathedral.

Fresco: A wall-painting technique, used in Roman times and again in the early Renaissance, in which pigment was applied to wet plaster.

Gothic: Medieval architectural and ornamental style featuring pointed arches, high interior vaulting, and flying buttresses to emphasize height and, symbolically, an ascension to heaven.

Grotesques: Decorations of fanciful human and animal forms, embellished with flowers; first used in Nero's Golden House and rediscovered during the Renaissance.

Loggia: Roofed balcony or gallery.

Maestà: The Virgin and Child enthroned in majesty often surrounded by angels, saints, or prophets.

Mannerism: Style of the mid-16th century, in which artists—such as Pontormo and Rosso Fiorentino—sought to replace the warm, humanizing ideals of Leonardo and Raphael with super-elegant, emotionally cold forms. Portraits in the Mannerist style feature lively colors and often strangely contorted bodies.

Nave: The central aisle of a church.

Palazzo: A palace, or more generally, any large building.

Perspective: The illusion of three-dimensional space that was obtained in the early 15th century with the discovery that all parallel lines running in one direction meet at a single point on the horizon known as the vanishing point.

Piano nobile: The main floor of a palace (the first floor above ground level).

Pietà: Literally "piety"; refers to an image of the Virgin Mary holding the crucified body of Christ on her lap.

Polyptych: A painting—often an altarpiece—on multiple wooden panels that are joined.

Predella: A series of small paintings found below the main section of an altarpiece.

Putti: Cherubs, cupids, or other images of infant boys in painting.

Quattrocento: Literally "four hundred"; refers to the 15th century.

Renaissance: Major school of Italian art, literature, and philosophy (14th century–16th century) that fused innovations in realism with the rediscovery of the great heritage of classical antiquity. After Giotto introduced a new naturalism into painting in the early 14th century, Florentine artists of the early and mid-15th century, such as Masaccio and Fra Filippo Lippi, paved the way for the later 15th-century realism of Botticelli and Ghirlandaio. The movement particularly flourished in Florence and Venice, but most other Italian cities were participants as well. Some scholars believe that the movement culminated in Rome with the High Renaissance (circa 1490–1520) and the masterpieces of Leonardo, Raphael, and Michelangelo.

Rococo: Light, dainty 18th-century art and architectural style created in reaction to heavy baroque. Tiepolo is the leading painter of the rococo style.

Romanesque: Architectural style of the 11th and 12th centuries that reworked ancient Roman forms, particularly barrel and groin vaults. Stark, severe, and magisterial, Romanesque basilicas are among Italy's most awe-inspiring churches.

Sacra conversazione: A "holy conversation" wherein saints act as intercessor to the Madonna and Child.

Tondo: Circular painting or sculpture.

Triptych: A three-panel painting executed on wood.

Trompe l'oeil: An artistic technique employed to "fool the eye" into believing that the object or scene depicted is actually real.

Veduta: A painting of a city or landscape as viewed from afar, popular in the 18th century.

BOOKS & MOVIES

Books

Italian history, art, and culture have been examined in countless English-language books. Their profusion is a testament both to the wonders of Italy and to the challenge of defining what exactly "Italian" is. *The Italians*, by Luigi Barzini, dates from 1964 but remains a valuable effort toward this end; its lively analysis of the national character is both enlightening and frustrating in ways that make reading it a genuinely Italian experience.

Before, during, and after a visit to Italy, it's a pleasure to compare notes with your fellow travelers. Classics in the travel-essay genre, often mixing firsthand experience and selected history, include James and Jan Morris's *World of Venice*, Mary McCarthy's *Venice Observed* and *The Stones of Florence*, Eleanor Clark's *Rome and a Villa*, and James Lees-Milne's *Roman Mornings* and *Venetian Mornings*. Stepping further back in time, you can sample perceptive musings about Italy in Henry James's *Italian Hours* and Edith Wharton's *Italian Backgrounds* and *Italian Villas and their Gardens*.

Some English-speaking visitors have chosen to settle in Italy long-term, and the resulting expatriate memoirs make up their own literary subgenre. In *A Tuscan Childhood*, Kinta Beevor lovingly recounts growing up in a castle near Carrara between the two world wars. Those with a yen to buy a dilapidated farmhouse and restore it can check out the experience of Frances Mayes in *Under the Tuscan Sun: At Home in Italy*. Matthew Spender's *Within Tuscany: Reflections on a Time and Place* and Lisa St. Aubin de Terán's *A Valley in Italy: The Many Seasons of a Villa in Umbria* are both rewarding reads. Shirley Hazzard deftly chronicles her 1960s friendship with English writer Graham Greene in *Greene on Capri*, and in the process reveals much about the island. Tim Parks's *Italian Neighbors* tells with candor and good humor of the contemporary expatriate life in Verona.

For a general historical and art history framework, Harry Hearder's *Italy, A Short History* cuts right to the chase, with 2,000 years covered in less than 300 pages. For in-depth classical history, there's nothing quite like Edward Gibbon's *Decline and Fall of the Roman Empire*, an 18th-century masterpiece (available in abridged form) that has withstood the test of time. If you're more interested in recent events, consult Paul Ginsborg's *Italy and Its Discontents: 1980–2001* or Peter Robb's *Midnight in Sicily*, the latter a mix of memoir and 20th-century history concerning the beauties and brutalities of the *mezzogiorno*. Ann Cornelisen's *Women of the Shadows* gives another perspective on southern Italy, portraying the lives of peasant women in the years following World War II.

Michael Levey's clear and concise treatments of the Renaissance, *Early Renaissance* and *High Renaissance*, are good introductions to the most vaunted of artistic periods. Two wonderfully written and beautifully illustrated volumes on the subject are John T. Paoletti and Gary M. Radke's *Art in Renaissance Italy* and Evelyn Welch's eloquent *Art and Society in Italy 1350–1500*. *The Civilization of the Renaissance in Italy*, by 19th-century Swiss historian Jacob Burckhardt, is the classic study of the culture and politics of the time.

You can learn about the Renaissance from those who actually lived it in *The Autobiography of Benvenuto Cellini*, Giorgio Vasari's *Lives of the Artists*, and Machiavelli's *The Prince*, and some recent studies of famous Renaissance and baroque figures offer fine opportunities to enter into lives lived centuries ago. Ross King's highly anecdotal *Brunelleschi's Dome* tells in detail about the making of Florence's fabled cupola. R.W.B. Lewis fleshes out the details of perhaps Italy's most famous poet in *Dante*; also worth a look in the Penguin Lives series is Sherwin Nuland's *Leonardo da Vinci*. A more scholarly, but eminently readable, biography is *Leon Battista Alberti: Master Builder of the Italian Renaissance* by Princeton Renaissance historian Anthony Grafton. Though the title is somewhat of a misnomer (as it's more about the father), Dava Sobel's *Galileo's Daughter* artfully brings to life the brilliant astronomer and his devotion to his family, particularly his first-born,

Suor Maria Celeste. Christopher Hibbert's *House of Medici* details the rise and fall of Florence's first family.

For aficionados of Rome's artistic treasures, Georgina Masson's *Companion Guide to Rome* is a must. Eloquent writing and important scholarship are found in the works of such celebrated art historians as Richard Krautheimer, John Pope-Hennessy, John Shearman, Irving Lavin, Charles de Tolnay, and André Chastel. *Inside Rome,* from Phaidon Press, is a picture book that gives you a tantalizing peek into the sumptuous palaces, galleries, private homes, athletic clubs, and even historic coffeehouses of the eternal city. Fodor's *Holy Rome: A Millennium Guide to the Christian Sights* traces Christianity in Rome, as it can be seen today, through gorgeous photography, thematic essays, easy-to-follow itineraries, and biographical sketches. To some observers, the most beautiful book about the most beautiful city in the world is Richard de Combray's *Venice, Frail Barrier.*

Fiction often imparts a greater sense of a place than straight history books: George Eliot reconstructs 15th-century Florentine life in *Romola*; Margaret Forster provides a first-hand account of the life of the Brownings (Robert and Elizabeth Barrett) in Italy as seen through the eyes of a servant in *Lady's Maid.* Umberto Eco's *The Name of the Rose* is a gripping murder mystery that will leave you with tremendous insight into monastic life in Italy. Lovers of detective stories will be highly entertained by the antics of Aurelio Zen, Michael Dibdin's bumbling detective. It's best to read them in order, as he builds on characters and situations; each novel is set in an Italian city. The series commences in Perugia with *Ratking.* Iain Pears writes about Italian art heists in his colorful novels; *Giotto's Hand* is a good place to start.

Susan Sontag's *Volcano Lover,* set in 18th-century Naples, is about Sir William Hamilton, his wife Emma, and Lord Nelson. *The Leopard,* by Giuseppe di Lampedusa, is a compelling portrait of Sicily during the political upheavals of the 1860s. Historical fiction set in pre–World World II includes Giorgio Bassani's quietly moving *Garden of the Finzi-Contini,* which tells of the lives of an upper-class Jewish family from Ferrara. Also worth a read is *History: A Novel,* by Elsa Morante.

If you truly want to understand the Italian psyche, learn about the national passion for *calcio* (soccer). Joe McGinness offers some fine insights on the subject as he tags along with a team from Seria B in *The Miracle of Castel di Sangro.* Tim Parks made his own soccer odyssey with the Verona club and recorded his experiences in *A Season with Verona.*

To catch glimpses of the Tuscan landscape, pick up Harold Acton's *Great Houses of Tuscany: The Tuscan Villas* or Carey More's *Views from a Tuscan Vineyard.* The glories of historic Italian gardens are caught in the ravishing photographs of Judith Chatfield's *Gardens of the Italian Lakes,* Ethne Clark's *Gardens of Tuscany,* and Nicolas Saphiena's *Gardens of Naples.* Fodor's own Escape Guides illuminate two of Italy's special regions in photos and prose. In the pages of *Escape to Tuscany,* stay at the convent where *The English Patient* was filmed and go ballooning over Chianti's vineyards, and in *Escape to the Amalfi Coast,* witness that area's impossible array of blues.

Although every year there are more and more cookbooks on Italian food, Waverley Root's *Food of Italy,* published in 1977, is still a handy (if not infallible) reference. Cooking inspiration may be found in Ada Boni's *The Talisman Italian Cook Book,* the Italian equivalent of the *Joy of Cooking.* Marcella Hazan's *Essentials of Italian Cooking* may be the definitive work in English. And finally, consult Burton Anderson's *Best Italian Wines* to help guide you through wine lists.

Movies

You'll recognize Italy's idyllic scenery in numerous English-language films, including the Academy Award–winning *The English Patient* (1996). *Tea with Mussolini* (1999) is Franco Zeffirelli's love letter to a group of Anglophone women who helped raise a character very much like the director himself in pre–World War II Tuscany. *Dangerous Beauty* (1998) may unintentionally venture into high camp, but it will give you an idea of what the life of a talented Venetian courtesan was like in the 16th century. *The Talented Mr. Ripley* (1999), based on a Patricia Highsmith novel, is set in sumptuous Italy of the 1950s. Indispensable and not at all dated are Merchant/Ivory's *A Room with a View*

(1986) and *Enchanted April* (1991), which depicts the awakening spirits of four English women in Italy. Italian filmmaking has been prolific and often excellent. The acknowledged master is Federico Fellini, creator of the classics *Nights of Cabiria,* *La Strada,* and *La Dolce Vita,* among many others. More recent favorites include *Il Postino* (The Postman, 1995), and *La Vita è Bella* (Life Is Beautiful, 1997), Roberto Benigni's tale of the Holocaust in fascist Italy. Other popular and critically acclaimed Italian films of recent vintage are *Pane e Tulipani* (Bread and Tulips, 2000), *L'Ultimo Bacio* (The Last Kiss, 2001), and *La Stanza del Figlio* (The Son's Room, 2001).

CHRONOLOGY

ca. 800 BC	Rise of Etruscan city-states.
753	Traditional date for the founding of Rome.
750	Greek city-states begin to colonize Sicily and southern Italy.
600	Latin language becomes dominant in Etruscan League; Rome becomes established urban center.
510	Foundation of the Roman republic; expulsion of Etruscans from Roman territory.
410	Rome adopts the 12 Tables of Law, based on Greek models.
343	Roman conquest of Greek colonies in Campania.
312	Completion of Via Appia (Appian Way) to the south of Rome; an extensive Roman road system begins to develop.
264–241	First Punic War (with Carthage): increased naval power helps Rome gain control of southern Italy and then Sicily.
218–200	Second Punic War: Hannibal's attempted conquest of Italy, using elephants, is eventually crushed.
150	Roman Forum begins to take shape as the principal civic center in Italy.
146	Third Punic War: Rome razes city of Carthage and emerges as the dominant Mediterranean force.
133	Rome rules entire Mediterranean Basin except Egypt.
49	Julius Caesar conquers Gaul.
45	Civil War leaves Julius Caesar as sole ruler; Caesar's Forum is established.
44	Julius Caesar is assassinated.
31	The Battle of Actium resolves the power struggle that continued after Caesar's death; Octavian becomes sole ruler.
27	Rome's Imperial Age begins; Octavian (now named Augustus) becomes the first emperor and is later deified. The Augustan Age is celebrated in the works of Virgil (70 BC–AD 19), Ovid (43 BC–AD 17), Livy (59 BC–AD 17), and Horace (65–8 BC).
14 AD	Augustus dies.
29	Jesus is crucified in the Roman colony of Judea.
43	Rome invades Britain.
50	Rome is the largest city in the world, with a population of a million.
65	Emperor Nero begins the persecution of Christians in the empire; Saints Peter and Paul are executed.
70–80	Vespasian builds the Colosseum.
98–117	Trajan's military successes are celebrated with his Baths (98), Forum (110), and Column (113); the Roman Empire reaches its apogee.
ca. 150–200	Christianity gains a foothold within the Empire, with the help of the theological writings of Clement, Tertullian, and Origen.

165   A smallpox epidemic ravages the Empire.

212   Roman citizenship is conferred on all nonslaves in the Empire.

238   The first wave of Germanic invasions penetrates Italy.

293   Diocletian reorganizes the Empire into West and East.

313   The Edict of Milan grants toleration of Christianity within the Empire.

330   Constantine founds a new Imperial capital (Constantinople) in the East.

410   Rome is sacked by Visigoths.

476   The last Roman emperor, Romulus Augustus, is deposed. The Empire of Rome falls.

552   Eastern emperor Justinian (527–565) recovers control of Italy.

570   Lombards gain control of much of Italy, including Rome.

590   Papal power expands under Gregory the Great.

610   Heraldius revives the Eastern Empire, thereafter known as the Byzantine Empire.

774   Frankish ruler Charlemagne (742–814) invades Italy under papal authority and is crowned Holy Roman Emperor by Pope Leo III (800).

ca. 800–900   The breakup of Charlemagne's (Carolingian) realm leads to the rise of Italian city-states.

811   Venice is founded by mainlanders escaping Barbarian invasions.

1054   The Schism develops between Greek (Orthodox) and Latin churches.

ca. 1060   Europe's first university is founded in Bologna.

1077   Pope Gregory VII leads the Holy See into conflict with the Germanic Holy Roman Empire.

1152–90   Frederick I (Barbarossa) is crowned Holy Roman Emperor (1155); punitive expeditions by his forces (Ghibellines) are countered by the Guelphs, supporters of the powerful Papal States in central Italy. Guelph–Ghibelline conflict becomes a feature of medieval life.

1204   Crusaders, led by Venetian doge Dandolo, capture Constantinople.

1257   The first of four wars is declared between Genoa and Venice; at stake is the maritime control of the eastern Mediterranean.

1262   Florentine bankers issue Europe's first bills of exchange.

1264   Charles I of Anjou invades Italy, intervening in the continuing Guelph–Ghibelline conflict.

1275   Marco Polo (1254–1324) reaches the Orient.

1290–1375   Tuscan literary giants Dante Alighieri (1265–1321), Francesco Petrarch (1304–74), and Giovanni Boccaccio (1313–75) give written imprimatur to modern Italian language.

1309   The pope moves to Avignon in France, under the protection of French kings.

1355   Venetian doge Marino Falier is executed for treason.

1376   The pope returns to Rome, but rival Avignonese popes stand in opposition, creating the Great Schism until 1417.

1380   Venice finally disposes of the Genovese threat in the Battle of Chioggia.

1402   The last German intervention into Italy is repulsed by the Lombards.

1443   Brunelleschi's (1377–1446) cupola is completed on Florence's Duomo.

1447   Nicholas V founds the Vatican Library and inaugurates an era of papal enrichment of the arts.

1469–92   Lorenzo "Il Magnifico" (1449–92), the Medici patron of the arts, rules in Florence.

1498   Girolamo Savonarola (1452–98), the fanatical Dominican friar, is executed for heresy after leading Florence into a drive for moral purification, typified by his burning of books and ephemera in the "Bonfire of Vanities."

1499   Leonardo da Vinci's (1452–1519) *Last Supper* is completed in Milan.

1508   Michelangelo (1475–1564) begins work on the Cappella Sistina.

1509   Raphael (1483–1520) begins work on his Stanze in the Vatican.

1513   Machiavelli's (1469–1527) *The Prince* is published.

1521   The Pope excommunicates Martin Luther (1483–1546) of Germany, precipitating the Protestant Reformation.

1545–63   The Council of Trent formulates the Roman Catholic response to the Protestant Reformation.

1546   Andrea Palladio (1508–80), architectural genius, wins his first commission in Vicenza.

1571   The combined navies of Venice, Spain, and the Papacy defeat the Turks in the Battle of Lepanto.

1626   The Basilica di San Pietro is completed in Rome.

1633   Galileo Galilei (1564–1642) faces the Inquisition.

1652   Sant'Agnese in Agone church, Borromini's (1599–1667) Baroque masterpiece, is completed in Rome.

1667   The Piazza di San Pietro, designed by Bernini (1598–1680), is completed.

ca. 1700   Opera develops as an art form in Italy.

1720–90   The Great Age of the Grand Tour: northern Europeans visit Italy and start the vogue for classical studies. Among the famous visitors are Edward Gibbon (1758), Jacques-Louis David (1775), and Johann Wolfgang von Goethe (1786).

1778   Teatro alla Scala is completed in Milan.

1796   Napoléon begins his Italian campaigns, annexing Rome and imprisoning Pope Pius VI four years later.

1815   Austria controls much of Italy after Napoléon's downfall.

1848   Revolutionary troops under Risorgimento (Unification) leaders Giuseppe Mazzini (1805–72) and Giuseppe Garibaldi (1807–82) establish a republic in Rome.

1849   French troops crush rebellion and restore Pope Pius IX.

1860   Garibaldi and his "Thousand" defeat the Bourbon rulers in Sicily and Naples.

1870 Rome is finally captured by Risorgimento troops and is declared capital of Italy by King Vittorio Emanuele II.

1900 King Umberto I is assassinated by an anarchist; he is succeeded by King Vittorio Emanuele III.

1915 Italy enters World War I on the side of the Allies.

1922 Fascist "black shirts" under Benito Mussolini (1883–1945) march on Rome; Mussolini becomes prime minister and later "Il Duce" (literally "leader") of Italy.

1929 The Lateran Treaty: Mussolini recognizes Vatican City as a sovereign state, and the Church recognizes Rome as the capital of Italy.

1940–44 In World War II, Italy fights on the side of the Axis powers until its capitulation (1943), when Mussolini flees Rome. Italian partisans and Allied troops from the landings at Anzio (January 1944) win victory at Cassino (March 1944) and force the eventual withdrawal of German troops from Italy.

1957 The Treaty of Rome is signed, and Italy becomes a founding member of the European Economic Community.

1966 November flood damages many of Florence's artistic treasures.

1968–79 The growth of left-wing activities leads to the formation of the Red Brigades and provokes right-wing reactions. Bombings and kidnappings culminate in the abduction and murder of Prime Minister Aldo Moro (1916–78).

1980 Southern Italy is hit by a severe earthquake.

1991 Waves of refugees from neighboring Albania flood southern ports on the Adriatic. Mt. Etna erupts, spewing forth a lava stream that threatens the Sicilian town of Zafferana.

1992 The Christian Democrat Party, in power throughout the postwar period, loses its hold on a relative majority in Parliament.

1993 Italians vote for sweeping reforms after the Tangentopoli (Bribe City) scandal exposes widespread political corruption, including politicians' collusion with organized crime. A bomb outside the Galleria degli Uffizi in Florence kills five but spares the museum's most precious artwork; authorities blame the Cosa Nostra, flexing its muscles in the face of a crackdown.

1994 A center-right coalition wins in spring elections, and media magnate Silvio Berlusconi becomes premier—only to be deposed within a year. Italian politics seem to be evolving into the equivalent of a two-party system.

1995 Newly appointed Lamberto Dini takes hold of the government's rudder and, as president of the Council of Ministers, institutes major reforms and replaces old-line politicians.

1996 A league of center-left parties wins national elections and puts together a government coalition that sees the Democratic Party of the Left (PDS), the former Communist party, into power for the first time ever in Italy.

1997 Political stability and an austerity program put Italy on track toward the European Monetary Union and adoption of the single euro currency. Though only a copy, the statue of Roman emperor Marcus Aurelius is returned to its pedestal on the Campidoglio as a symbol of Rome's historic grandeur. A series of earthquakes hits the mountainous interior of central Italy, severely damaging villages and some historic towns. In Assisi, portions of the vault of the Basilica di San Francesco crumble, destroying frescoes by Cimabue.

1998   In February a U.S. Navy jet fighter on a low-flying training mission through the Italian Alps cuts a ski gondola cable, killing 20 people. Romano Prodi's center-left government, widely praised for its economic policies and lack of scandals, is brought down by a no-confidence vote in October, after the Reformed-Communist Party (PCI) withdraws its support for Prodi. The center-left regroups and forms a new government under Massimo D'Alema, leader of the former Communist Party, who in large part continues Prodi's policies. The pope visits Cuba. More than a million people see the Shroud of Turin, on display for just a few months.

1999   Italy serves as a principal base for NATO air raids against Serbia. Rome continues preparations for the Jubilee celebrations in 2000 with an array of public works projects. The International Olympic Committee chooses Turin to host the 2006 Winter Olympics.

2000   The Jubilee of the third millennium is proclaimed by Pope John Paul II. Millions of pilgrims flock to Rome.

2001   Media mogul Silvio Berlusconi is elected prime minister for the second time.

2002   The lira is supplanted by the euro as the currency of the land. Padre Pio (1887–1968), a revered Franciscan from Puglia and the first priest in church history to receive the stigmata, is canonized.

ITALIAN VOCABULARY

English	Italian	Pronunciation

Basics

English	Italian	Pronunciation
Yes/no	Sí/No	see/no
Please	Per favore	pear fa-**vo**-ray
Yes, please	Sí grazie	see **grah**-tsee-ay
Thank you	Grazie	**grah**-tsee-ay
You're welcome	Prego	**pray**-go
Excuse me, sorry	Scusi	**skoo**-zee
Sorry!	Mi dispiace!	mee dis-spee-**ah**-chay
Good morning/ afternoon	Buongiorno	bwohn-**jor**-no
Good evening	Buona sera	**bwoh**-na **say**-ra
Good bye	Arrivederci	a-ree-vah-**dare**-chee
Mr. (Sir)	Signore	see-**nyo**-ray
Mrs. (Ma'am)	Signora	see-**nyo**-ra
Miss	Signorina	see-nyo-**ree**-na
Pleased to meet you	Piacere	pee-ah-**chair**-ray
How are you?	Come sta?	**ko**-may **stah**
Very well, thanks	Bene, grazie	**ben**-ay **grah**-tsee-ay
And you?	E lei?	ay **lay**-ee
Hello (phone)	Pronto?	**proan**-to

Numbers

one	uno	**oo**-no
two	due	**doo**-ay
three	tre	tray
four	quattro	**kwah**-tro
five	cinque	**cheen**-kway
six	sei	say
seven	sette	**set**-ay
eight	otto	**oh**-to
nine	nove	**no**-vay
ten	dieci	dee-**eh**-chee
eleven	undici	**oon**-dee-chee
twelve	dodici	**doe**-dee-chee
thirteen	tredici	**tray**-dee-chee
fourteen	quattordici	kwa-**tore**-dee-chee
fifteen	quindici	**kwin**-dee-chee
sixteen	sedici	**say**-dee-chee

seventeen	diciassette	dee-cha-**set**-ay
eighteen	diciotto	dee-**cho**-to
nineteen	diciannove	dee-cha-**no**-vay
twenty	venti	**vain**-tee
twenty-one	ventuno	vain-**too**-no
twenty-two	ventidue	vain-tee-**doo**-ay
thirty	trenta	**train**-ta
forty	quaranta	kwa-**rahn**-ta
fifty	cinquanta	cheen-**kwahn**-ta
sixty	sessanta	seh-**sahn**-ta
seventy	settanta	seh-**tahn**-ta
eighty	ottanta	o-**tahn**-ta
ninety	novanta	no-**vahn**-ta
one hundred	cento	**chen**-to
one thousand	mille	**mee**-lay
ten thousand	diecimila	dee-eh-chee-**mee**-la

Useful Phrases

Do you speak English?	Parla inglese?	**par**-la een-**glay**-zay
I don't speak Italian	Non parlo italiano	non **par**-lo ee-tal-**yah**-no
I don't understand	Non capisco	non ka-**peess**-ko
Can you please repeat?	Può ripetere?	pwo ree-**pet**-ay-ray
Slowly!	Lentamente!	**len**-ta-men-tay
I don't know	Non lo so	non lo **so**
I'm American/ British	Sono americano(a)	**so**-no a-may-ree-**kah**-no(a)
	Sono inglese	**so**-no een-**glay**-zay
What's your name?	Come si chiama?	**ko**-may see kee-**ah**-ma
My name is . . .	Mi chiamo . . .	mee kee-**ah**-mo
What time is it?	Che ore sono?	kay **o**-ray **so**-no
How?	Come?	**ko**-may
When?	Quando?	**kwan**-doe
Yesterday/today/ tomorrow	Ieri/oggi/domani	**yer**-ee/**o**-jee/ do-**mah**-nee
This morning/ ternoon	Stamattina/Oggi pomeriggio	sta-ma-**tee**-na/**o**-jee af-po-mer-**ee**-jo
Tonight	Stasera	sta-**ser**-a
What?	Che cosa?	kay **ko**-za
What is it?	Che cos'è?	kay ko-**zay**
Why?	Perché?	pear-**kay**
Who?	Chi?	kee
Where is . . . the bus stop?	Dov'è . . . la fermata dell'autobus?	doe-**veh** la fer-**mah**-ta del ow-toe-**booss**

the train station?	la stazione?	la sta-tsee-**oh**-nay
the subway station?	la metropolitana?	la may-tro-po-lee-**tah**-na
the terminal?	il terminale?	eel ter-mee-**nah**-lay
the post office?	l'ufficio postale?	loo-**fee**-cho po-**stah**-lay
the bank?	la banca?	la **bahn**-ka
the . . . hotel?	l'hotel . . .?	lo-**tel**
the store?	il negozio?	eel nay-**go**-tsee-o
the cashier?	la cassa?	la **kah**-sa
the . . . museum?	il museo . . .?	eel moo-**zay**-o
the hospital?	l'ospedale?	lo-spay-**dah**-lay
the first aid station?	il pronto soccorso?	eel **pron**-to so-**kor**-so
the elevator?	l'ascensore?	la-shen-**so**-ray
a telephone?	un telefono?	oon tay-**lay**-fo-no
Where are the restrooms?	Dov'è il bagno?	do-**vay** eel **bahn**-yo
Here/there	Qui/là	kwee/la
Left/right	A sinistra/a destra	a see-**neess**-tra/ a **des**-tra
Straight ahead	Avanti dritto	a-**vahn**-tee **dree**-to
Is it near/far?	È vicino/lontano?	ay vee-**chee**-no/ lon-**tah**-no
I'd like . . .	Vorrei . . .	vo-**ray**
a room	una camera	oo-na **kah**-may-ra
the key	la chiave	la kee-**ah**-vay
a newspaper	un giornale	oon jor-**nah**-lay
a stamp	un francobollo	oon frahn-ko-**bo**-lo
I'd like to buy . . .	Vorrei comprare . . .	vo-**ray** kom-**prah**-ray
a cigar	un sigaro	oon see-**gah**-ro
cigarettes	delle sigarette	**day**-lay see-ga-**ret**-ay
some matches	dei fiammiferi	**day**-ee fee-ah-**mee**-fer-ee
some soap	una saponetta	oo-na sa-po-**net**-a
a city plan	una pianta della città	oo-na **pyahn**-ta day-la chee-**tah**
a road map of . . .	una carta stradale di . . .	oo-na **cart**-a stra-**dah**-lay dee
a country map	una carta geografica	oo-na **cart**-a jay-o-**grah**-fee-ka
a magazine	una rivista	oo-na ree-**veess**-ta
envelopes	delle buste	**day**-lay **booss**-tay
writing paper	della carta da lettere	**day**-la **cart**-a da **let**-air-ay
a postcard	una cartolina	oo-na car-toe-**lee**-na
a guidebook	una guida turistica	oo-na **gwee**-da too-**reess**-tee-ka
How much is it?	Quanto costa?	**kwahn**-toe **coast**-a
It's expensive/cheap	È caro/economico	ay **car**-o/ay-ko-no-mee-ko
A little/a lot	Poco/tanto	**po**-ko/**tahn**-to
More/less	Più/meno	pee-**oo**/**may**-no

Enough/too (much)	Abbastanza/troppo	a-bas-**tahn**-sa/**tro**-po
I am sick	Sto male	sto **mah**-lay
Call a doctor	Chiama un dottore	kee-**ah**-mah oon doe-**toe**-ray
Help!	Aiuto!	a-**yoo**-toe
Stop!	Alt!	ahlt
Fire!	Al fuoco!	ahl **fwo**-ko
Caution/Look out!	Attenzione!	a-ten-**syon**-ay

Dining Out

A bottle of . . .	Una bottiglia di . . .	**oo**-na bo-**tee**-lee-ah dee
A cup of . . .	Una tazza di . . .	**oo**-na **tah**-tsa dee
A glass of . . .	Un bicchiere di . . .	oon bee-key-**air**-ay dee
Bill/check	Il conto	eel **cone**-toe
Bread	Il pane	eel **pah**-nay
Breakfast	La prima colazione	la **pree**-ma ko-la-**tsee**-oh-nay
Cocktail/aperitif	L'aperitivo	la-pay-ree-**tee**-vo
Dinner	La cena	la **chen**-a
Fixed-price menu	Menù a prezzo fisso	may-**noo** a **pret**-so **fee**-so
Fork	La forchetta	la for-**ket**-a
I am diabetic	Ho il diabete	o eel dee-a-**bay**-tay
I am vegetarian	Sono vegetariano/a	**so**-no vay-jay-ta-ree-**ah**-no/a
I'd like . . .	Vorrei . . .	vo-**ray**
I'd like to order	Vorrei ordinare	vo-**ay** or-dee-**nah**-ray
Is service included?	Il servizio è incluso?	eel ser-**vee**-tzee-o ay een-**kloo**-zo
It's good/bad	È buono/cattivo	ay **bwo**-no/ka-**tee**-vo
It's hot/cold	È caldo/freddo	ay **kahl**-doe/**fred**-o
Knife	Il coltello	eel kol-**tel**-o
Lunch	Il pranzo	eel **prahnt**-so
Menu	Il menù	eel may-**noo**
Napkin	Il tovagliolo	eel toe-va-lee-**oh**-lo
Please give me . . .	Mi dia . . .	mee **dee**-a
Salt	Il sale	eel **sah**-lay
Spoon	Il cucchiaio	eel koo-kee-**ah**-yo
Sugar	Lo zucchero	lo **tsoo**-ker-o
Waiter/Waitress	Cameriere/cameriera	ka-mare-**yer**-ay/ka-mare-**yer**-a
Wine list	La lista dei vini	la **lee**-sta **day**-ee **vee**-nee

MENU GUIDE

English	Italian
Set menu	Menù a prezzo fisso
Dish of the day	Piatto del giorno
Specialty of the house	Specialità della casa
Local specialties	Specialità locali
Extra charge	Extra . . .
In season	Di stagione
Cover charge/Service charge	Coperto/Servizio

Breakfast

Butter	Burro
Croissant	Cornetto
Eggs	Uova
Honey	Miele
Jam/Marmalade	Marmellata
Roll	Panino
Toast	Pane tostato

Starters

Assorted cold cuts	Affettati misti
Assorted seafood	Antipasto di pesce
Assorted appetizers	Antipasto misto
Toasted rounds of bread, fried or toasted in oil	Crostini/Crostoni
Diced-potato and vegetable salad with mayonnaise	Insalata russa
Eggplant parmigiana	Melanzane alla parmigiana
Fried mozzarella sandwich	Mozzarella in carrozza
Ham and melon	Prosciutto e melone
Cooked sausages and cured meats	Salumi cotti
Filled pastry shells	Vol-au-vents

Soups

"Angel hair," thin noodle soup	Capelli d'angelo
Cream of . . .	Crema di . . .
Pasta-and-bean soup	Pasta e fagioli
Egg-drop and parmesan cheese soup	Stracciatella

Pasta, Rice, and Pizza

Filled pasta	Agnolotti/ravioli/tortellini
Potato dumplings	Gnocchi
Semolina dumplings	Gnocchi alla romana
Pasta	Pasta
with four cheeses	*al quattro formaggi*
with basil/cheese/pine nuts/ garlic sauce	*al pesto*

with tomato-based meat sauce	al ragù
with tomato sauce	al sugo or al pomodoro
with butter	in bianco or al burro
with egg, parmesan cheese, and pepper	alla carbonara
green (spinach-based) pasta	verde
Rice	Riso
Rice dish	Risotto
with mushrooms	ai funghi
with saffron	alla milanese
Noodles	Tagliatelle
Pizza	Pizza
Pizza with seafood, cheese, artichokes, and ham in four different sections	Pizza quattro stagioni
Pizza with tomato and mozzarella	Pizza margherita
Pizza with oil, garlic, and oregano	Pizza marinara

Fish and Seafood

Anchovies	Acciughe
Bass	Persico
Carp	Carpa
Clams	Vongole
Cod	Merluzzo
Crab	Granchio
Eel	Anguilla
Lobster	Aragosta
Mackerel	Sgombro
Mullet	Triglia
Mussels	Cozze
Octopus	Polpo
Oysters	Ostriche
Pike	Luccio
Prawns	Gamberoni
Salmon	Salmone
Shrimp	Scampi
Shrimps	Gamberetti
Sole	Sogliola
Squid	Calamari
Swordfish	Pescespada
Trout	Trota
Tuna	Tonno

Methods of Preparation

Baked	Al forno
Cold, with vinegar sauce	In carpione
Fish stew	Zuppa di pesce
Fried	Fritto
Grilled (usually charcoal)	Alla griglia
Seafood salad	In insalata
Smoked	Affumicato
Stuffed	Ripieno

Meat

Boar	Cinghiale
Brain	Cervella
Braised meat with wine	Brasato
Chop	Costoletta
Duck	Anatra
Lamb	Agnello
Baby lamb	Abbacchio
Liver	Fegato
Pheasant	Fagiano
Pork roast	Arista
Rabbit	Coniglio
Steak	Bistecca
Sliced raw steak with sauce	Carpaccio
Mixed boiled meat	Bollito misto

Methods of Preparation

Battered with eggs and crumbs and fried	. . . alla milanese
Grilled	. . . ai ferri
Grilled (usually charcoal)	. . . alla griglia
Raw, with lemon/egg sauce	. . . alla tartara
Roasted	. . . arrosto
Very rare	. . . al sangue
Well done	. . . ben cotta
With ham and cheese	. . . alla valdostana
With parmesan cheese and tomatoes	. . . alla parmigiana

Vegetables

Artichokes	Carciofi
Asparagus	Asparagi
Beans	Fagioli
Brussels sprouts	Cavolini di Bruxelles
Cabbage	Cavolo
Carrots	Carote
Cauliflower	Cavolfiore
Cucumber	Cetriolo
Eggplants	Melanzane
Green beans	Fagiolini
Leeks	Porri
Lentils	Lenticchie
Lettuce	Lattuga
Mushrooms	Funghi
Onions	Cipolle
Peas	Piselli
Peppers	Peperoni
Potatoes	Patate
Roasted potatoes	*Patate arroste*
Boiled potatoes	*Patate bollite*
Fried potatoes	*Patate fritte*
Small, roasted potatoes	*Patatine novelle*
Mashed potatoes	*Purè di patate*

Radishes	Rapanelli
Salad	Insalata
vegetable	*mista*
green	*verde*
Spinach	Spinaci
Tomatoes	Pomodori
Zucchini	Zucchini

Sauces, Herbs, and Spices

Basil	Basilico
Bay leaf	Lauro
Chervil	Cerfoglio
Dill	Aneto
Garlic	Aglio
Hot dip with anchovies (for vegetables)	Bagna cauda
Marjoram	Maggiorana
Mayonnaise	Maionese
Mustard	Mostarda *or* senape
Oil	Olio
Parsley-based sauce	Salsa verde
Pepper	Pepe
Rosemary	Rosmarino
Tartar sauce	Salsa tartara
Vinegar	Aceto
White sauce	Besciamella

Cheeses

Fresh:	Caprino fresco
	Mascarpone
	Mozzarella
	Ricotta
Mild:	Caciotta
	Caprino
	Fontina
	Grana
	Provola
	Provolone dolce
	Robiola
	Scamorza
Sharp:	Asiago
	Gorgonzola
	Groviera
	Pecorino
	Provolone piccante
	Taleggio
	Toma

Fruits and Nuts

Almonds	Mandorle
Apple	Mela
Apricot	Albicocca
Blackberries	More
Black currant	Ribes nero

Blueberries	Mirtilli
Cherries	Ciliege
Chestnuts	Castagne
Coconut	Noce di cocco
Dates	Datteri
Figs	Fichi
Green grapes	Uva bianca
Black grapes	Uva nera
Grapefruit	Pompelmo
Hazelnuts	Nocciole
Lemon	Limone
Melon	Melone
Nectarine	Nocepesca
Orange	Arancia
Pear	Pera
Peach	Pesca
Pineapple	Ananas
Plum	Prugna/Susina
Prune	Prugna secca
Raisins	Uva passa
Raspberries	Lamponi
Red currant	Ribes
Strawberries	Fragole
Tangerine	Mandarino
Walnuts	Noci
Watermelon	Anguria/Cocomero
Dried fruit	Frutta secca
Fresh fruit	Frutta fresca
Fruit salad	Macedonia di frutta

Desserts

Custard filed pastry, with candied fruit	Cannoli
Ricotta filled pastry shells with sugar glaze	Cannoli alla siciliana
Ice cream with candied fruit	Cassata
Ricotta filed cake with sugar glaze	Cassata siciliana
Chocolate	Cioccolato
Cup of ice cream	Coppa gelato
Caramel custard	Crème caramel
Pie	Crostata
Fruit pie	Crostata di frutta
Ice cream	Gelato
Flaked pastry	Millefoglie
Chestnuts and whipped-cream cake	Montebianco
Whipped cream	Panna montata
Pastries	Paste
Sherbet	Sorbetto
Chocolate-coated ice cream	Tartufo
Fruit tart	Torta di frutta
Apple tart	Torta di mele
Ice-cream cake	Torta gelata

Vanilla	Vaniglia
Egg-based cream with sugar and Marsala wine	Zabaione
Ice-cream filled cake	Zuccotto

Alcoholic Drinks

On the rocks	Con ghiaccio
Straight	Liscio
With soda	Con seltz
Beer	Birra
light/dark	*chiara/scura*
Bitter cordial	Amaro
Brandy	Cognac
Cordial	Liquore
Aniseed cordial	Sambuca
Martini	Cocktail Martini
Port	Porto
Vermouth	Vermut/Martini
Wine	Vino
blush	*rosé*
dry	*secco*
full-bodied	*corposo*
light	*leggero*
red	*rosso*
sparkling	*spumante*
sweet	*dolce*
very dry	*brut*
white	*bianco*
Light wine	Vinello
Bottle	Bottiglia
Carafe	Caraffa
Flask	Fiasco

Nonalcoholic Drinks

Mineral water	Acqua minerale
carbonated	*gassata*
still	*non gassata*
Tap water	Acqua naturale
Tonic water	Acqua tonica
Coffee with steamed milk	Cappuccino
Espresso	Caffè espresso
with milk	*macchiato*
decaffeinated	*decaffeinato*
lighter espresso	*lungo*
with cordial	*corretto*
Fruit juice	Succo di frutta
Lemonade	Limonata
Milk	Latte
Orangeade	Aranciata
Tea	Tè
with milk/lemon	*col latte/col limone*
iced	*freddo*

INDEX

NOTES

FODOR'S KEY TO THE GUIDES

America's guidebook leader publishes guides for every kind of traveler.
Check out our many series and find your perfect match.

FODOR'S GOLD GUIDES
America's favorite travel-guide series offers the most detailed insider reviews of hotels, restaurants, and attractions in all price ranges, plus great background information, smart tips, and useful maps.

COMPASS AMERICAN GUIDES
Stunning guides from top local writers and photographers, with gorgeous photos, literary excerpts, and colorful anecdotes. A must-have for culture mavens, history buffs, and new residents.

FODOR'S CITYPACKS
Concise city coverage in a guide plus a foldout map. The right choice for urban travelers who want everything under one cover.

FODOR'S EXPLORING GUIDES
Hundreds of color photos bring your destination to life. Lively stories lend insight into the culture, history, and people.

FODOR'S TRAVEL HISTORIC AMERICA
For travelers who want to experience history firsthand, this series gives in-depth coverage of historic sights, plus nearby restaurants and hotels. Themes include the Thirteen Colonies, the Old West, and the Lewis and Clark Trail.

FODOR'S POCKET GUIDES
For travelers who need only the essentials. The best of Fodor's in pocket-size packages for just $9.95.

FODOR'S FLASHMAPS
Every resident's map guide, with 60 easy-to-follow maps of public transit, parks, museums, zip codes, and more.

FODOR'S CITYGUIDES
Sourcebooks for living in the city: thousands of in-the-know listings for restaurants, shops, sports, nightlife, and other city resources.

FODOR'S AROUND THE CITY WITH KIDS
Up to 68 great ideas for family days, recommended by resident parents. Perfect for exploring in your own backyard or on the road.

FODOR'S HOW TO GUIDES
Get tips from the pros on planning the perfect trip. Learn how to pack, fly hassle-free, plan a honeymoon or cruise, stay healthy on the road, and travel with your baby.

FODOR'S LANGUAGES FOR TRAVELERS
Practice the local language before you hit the road. Available in phrase books, cassette sets, and CD sets.

KAREN BROWN'S GUIDES
Engaging guides—many with easy-to-follow inn-to-inn itineraries—to the most charming inns and B&Bs in the U.S.A. and Europe.

BAEDEKER'S GUIDES
Comprehensive guides, trusted since 1829, packed with A–Z reviews and star ratings.

OTHER GREAT TITLES FROM FODOR'S
Baseball Vacations, The Complete Guide to the National Parks, Family Vacations, Golf Digest's Places to Play, Great American Drives of the East, Great American Drives of the West, Great American Vacations, Healthy Escapes, National Parks of the West, Skiing USA.